KT-216-347

Latin

Dictionary

Seen JNT Oct '11

W

Hampshire
COUNTY COUNCIL

County Library

WATERLOOVILLE 254626/7

For use in

Library only

C003097916

CL.14a(7/93).

2/95

First published in 1913
by Routledge & Kegan Paul

11 New Fetter Lane
London EC4P 4EE

Reprinted nineteen times
Twentieth impression 1977
Reprinted and first published as a
Paperback in 1982
Reprinted in 1983, 1987 and 1991

Printed in Great Britain by
Cox & Wyman Ltd
Reading, Berks

ISBN 0–415–06605–0

HAMPSHIRE COUNTY LIBRARY

473
21

0415066050

C003097916

PREFACE
TO THE ORIGINAL EDITION

I HAVE adopted for the work here offered to the public the title of *The Englishman's Pocket Latin-English and English-Latin Dictionary*, since my object is to serve not merely the classical scholar, but that wider public which has little or no familiarity with the dead languages.

Many Latin words and phrases derived from classical or medieval times are still current among us. Science pays homage to the humanities by borrowing largely from Latin for her technical terminology, and, where necessary, invents a quasi-classical vocabulary by furnishing modern words with a Latin termination. All forms of Latinity are incorporated in the present volume.

A difficulty present itself in the marking of quantities. Ancient and modern pronunciations are sometimes in violent opposition; for example, the word 'clematis,' which in modern speech has the first syllable short and the second long or short according to the fancy of the speaker, has in classical Latin the first syllable long and the second syllable short. In such cases I have invariably adhered to the ancient values.

A vowel preceding another vowel is left unmarked, because the rules of prosody require that it should be short. Only violations of the law are noted.

A list of geographical and proper names will be found between the Latin-English and the English-Latin sections.

S. C. WOODHOUSE.

LIST OF ABBREVIATIONS

a.	.	.	. adjective.
abl.	.	.	. ablative.
acc.	.	.	. accusative.
ad.	.	.	. adverb.
c.	.	.	. common (masculine or feminine) or conjunction.
dat.	.	.	. dative.
dep.	.	.	. deponent (passive in form, active in meaning).
e.g.	.	.	. *exempli gratia* (for example).
etc.	.	.	. *et cetera.*
f.	.	.	. feminine.
fig.	.	.	. figuratively.
g.c.	.	.	. *generis communis* (of common gender).
gen.	.	.	. genitive.
gr.	.	.	. grammatically.
i.	.	.	. interjection.
indecl.	.	.	. indeclinable.
ir.	.	.	. irregular.
m.	.	.	. masculine.
mil.	.	.	. military.
mod. hort.	.	.	. modern horticultural.
mus.	.	.	. musical.
n.	.	.	. neuter.
p.	.	.	. participle.
p. and a.	.	.	. participle and adjective.
pl.	.	.	. plural.
pn.	.	.	. pronoun.
poet.	.	.	. used only in poetry.
pr.	.	.	. preposition.
s.	.	.	. substantive (noun).
spec.	.	.	. specifically.
v.	.	.	. verb.
v.a.	.	.	. verb active (transitive).
v.n.	.	.	. verb neuter (intransitive).

In the Latin-English section a word followed immediately by its genitive ending is a substantive.

The numerals 1. 2. 3. 4. after verbs refer to their conjugation.

As a help to pronouncing, the sign — over a vowel signifies that the vowel should be made long ; ‿ that the vowel should be pronounced short.

LATIN—ENGLISH

A, ab (abs), pr. of, from; by (of the agent); away; since;—ab initio, from the beginning;—ab origine, from the first appearance;—ab ovo, from the egg;—ab ōvo usque ad mala, from the egg to the apples, from the hors d'œuvre to the dessert;—ab uno disce omnes, learn the character of all from one example;—ab urbe condita, from the foundation of the city;—a fortiori, with all the stronger reason, all the more;—a mensa et toro, from board and bed; formula of divorce;—a priori (argument), from cause to effect; —a posteriori (argument), from effect to cause.

ăbăcus, i, m. counting-board, counter; side-board; square stone on the top of columns.

ăbăliēnātio, ōnis, f. cession by sale or contract.

ăbăliēno, 1. v.a. to estrange; to cede by sale or contract; remove.

ăbăvus, i, m. great-grandfather's or great-grandmother's father, ancestor.

abbās, ātis, abbot.

abbātia, ae, abbey.

abbātissa, ae, abbess.

abdĭcātio, ōnis, f. renunciation; disowning (of a son).

abdĭco, 1. v.a. to resign; to abrogate, to abolish; to disinherit.

abdīco, xi, ctum, 3. v.a. to refuse; to deprive by judicial sentence.

abdĭtē, ad. secretly, privately.

abdo, ĭdi, ĭtum, 3. v.a. to hide, to conceal; to plunge; to remove.

abdōmĕn, ĭnis, n. lower part of the belly, paunch; gluttony.   [carry off.

abdūco, xi, ctum, 3. v.a. to lead away, abductio, ōnis, f. abduction.

ăbeo, ĭvi, (ii), ĭtum, ire, 4. v.n. to go away, to depart; to vanish; to escape; to be changed.

ăberrātio, ōnis, f. wandering, diversion (from).

ăberro, 1. v.n. to go astray, to deviate (from); to differ.

ăbhinc, ad. from this time, since, ago.

ăbhorreo, ui, 2. v.n. to be averse (to), to shudder at; to be inconsistent (with).

ăbiegnus, a. made of fir.

ăbiēs, ĕtis, f. white fir; ship; spear.

ăbigeus, i, cattle stealer.

ăbigo, ēgi, actum, 3. v.a. to drive or send away.   [fig. outlet; end.

ăbĭtus, ūs, m. going away; departure;

abjectē, ad. despondingly; meanly, abjectly.

abjectus, a, um, a. downcast, mean, abject, base.

abjĭcio, jēci, jectum, 3. v.a. to throw away; fig. to slight, to give up; to humble, to debase.

abjūdĭco, 1. v.a. to deny or deprive by judicial sentence.

abjungo, nxi, nctum, 3. v.a. to unyoke, to remove, to separate.

abjūrātio, ōnis, f. false oath.

abjūro, 1. v.a. to deny on oath, to abjure.

ablăqueātio, ōnis, f. baring the roots of a tree.   [trees.

ablăqueo, 1. v.a. to lay bare the root of

ablātīvus, i, m. ablative case.

ablēgātio, ōnis, f. sending away, exile.

ablēgo, 1. v.a. to send away, to remove.

ablĭgūrio, ĭvi, ĭtum, 4. v.a. to consume in riot and excesses.

ablŏco, 1. v.a. to lease, to let.

ablūdo, si, sum, 3. v.n. to differ from, to be unlike.

abluo, ui, ūtum, 3. v.a. to wash away, to blot out, to purify; to quench, to remove.

ablūtio, ōnis, f. washing away, cleansing.

abnĕgo, 1. v.a. to deny, to refuse.

abnormis, e, a. irregular, singular.

abnuo, ui, ūtum, 3. v.a. fig. to deny, to refuse, to reject.   [stroy.

ăbŏleo, ēvi, ĭtum, 2. v.a. to abolish, deăbŏlesco, lēvi, 3. v.n. to decay, to cease, to be extinct.

ăbŏlītio, ōnis, f. abolition, annulment.

ăbolla, ae, f. a thick woollen garment worn by soldiers and philosophers.

ăbōmĭnātio, ōnis, f. detestation, object of hate.   [nate, to detest.

ăbōmĭnor, ātus, āri, 1. v. dep. to abomi-

ăbŏrīgĭnes, um, m. pl. original inhabitants.

ăbŏrior, ortus, orīri, 4. v.n. dep. to miscarry; *fig.* to fail.

ăbortio, ōnis, f. premature delivery, miscarriage.

ăbortīvus, a, um, a. abortive; addled.

ăbortus, ūs, m. miscarriage.

abrăcădabra, a magical collocation of letters arranged in a triangle and worn as a charm.

abrādo, si, sum, 3. v.a. to scratch off, to shave; *fig.* to extort, to rob.

abripio, pui, eptum, s. v.a. to drag away by force; to ravish.

abrōdo, si, sum, 3. v.a. to gnaw off.

abrŏgātio, ōnis, f. repeal of a law.

abrŏgo, 1. v.a. to repeal wholly, to abolish.

abrŏtŏnum, i, n. southernwood.

abrumpo, ūpi, uptum, 3. v.a. to break off, to tear asunder, to cut through.

abrūptē, ad. abruptly, rashly.

abruptio, ōnis, f. breaking off; *fig.* divorce.

abruptus, a, um, a. precipitous, steep; rough; hasty, rash.

abs, pr., v. ab.

abscēdo, cessi, cessum, 3. v.n. to go away, to depart; to desist.

abscessio, ōnis, f., abscessus, ūs, m. going away, absence. [move.

abscīdo, cīdi, cīsum, 3. v.a. to cut off, to abscindo, cīdi, cissum, 3. v.a. to cut off, tear away; to put an end to.

abscīsus, a, um, a. steep, abrupt.

abscondĭtē, ad. secretly, profoundly.

abscondo, condi & dĭdi, condĭtum, 3. v.a. to hide; to leave behind; —, v.n. to

absens, entis, p. & a. absent. [set.

absentia, ae, f. absence.

absīdātus, a, um, a. vaulted.

absīlio, ii & ui, 4. v.n. to leap away.

absīmĭlis, e, a. unlike.

absinthium, i, n. wormwood.

absis *or* apsis, īdis, f. vault.

absisto, stĭti, 3. v.n. to stand off, to go away; to desist from, to leave off.

absŏlūtē, ad. perfectly.

absŏlūtio, ōnis, f. acquittal, perfection.

absŏlūtus, a, um, a. free, complete, unconditional.

absolvo, vi, ūtum, 3. v.a. to absolve (from), to discharge, to dismiss, to release; to finish.

absŏnus, a, um, a. out of tune, discordant, incongruous.

absorbeo, bui & psi, ptum, 2. v.a. to absorb, to suck in; *fig.* to engross.

absque, pr. without, except.

absque me esset, had it not been for me.

abstēmius, a, um, a. sober, temperate; fasting.

abstergeo, rsi, rsum, 2. v.a. to wipe off *or* dry *or* clean; to remove. [away.

absterreo, ui, ĭtum, 2. v.a. to frighten

abstĭnens, entis, p. & a. abstinent, temperate.

abstĭnenter, ad. abstinently.

abstĭnentia, ae, f. abstinence; fasting; moderation. [stain, to forbear.

abstĭneo, ui, tentum, 2. v.a. & n. to ababsto, stĭti, stitum, 1. v.n. to stand aloof *or* off.

abstrăho, xi, ctum, 3. v.a. to drag away from; to separate.

abstrūdo, ūsi, ūsum, 3. v.a. to thrust away, to conceal.

abstrūsus, a, um, a. secret, reserved.

absum, afui, abesse, v.n. ir. to be absent *or* away (from) *or* distant; to be wanting;—absit omen, may no evil attend.

absūmo, mpsi, mptum, 3. v.a. to spend, to waste, to ruin.

absurdē, ad. absurdly.

absurdus, a, um, a. of a harsh sound; absurd, nonsensical.

ăbundanter, ad. abundantly, copiously.

ăbundantia, ae, f. abundance, plenty, riches.

ăbundātio, ōnis, f. inundation.

ăbundē, ad. abundantly. [rich.

ăbundo, 1. v.n. to abound (in), to be

ăbūsus, ūs, m. misuse.

ăbūtilon (mod. hort.), Indian mallow.

ăbūtor, ūsus, 3. v. dep. to use up, to waste; to misuse.

ăbyssus, i, f. abyss, hell.

āc, c. and, and besides; than.

ăcācia, ae, f. acacia.

ăcădēmia, ae, f. academy, university.

ăcădēmĭcus, a, um, a. academic; —, i, m. academician.

ăcălanthis, ĭdis, f. gold-finch.

ăcanthion, i, n. white-thorn.

ăcanthis, ĭdis, f. goldfinch; groundsel.

ăcanthus, i, m. bear's-foot.

accēdo, cessi, cessum, 3. v.n. to go *or* come to, to approach; to attack; to fall to one's share, to be added, to come over to; to be like, to enter upon.

accĕlĕro, 1. v.a. & n. to accelerate, to hasten; to make haste.

accendo, ndi, nsum, 3. v.a. to set on fire, to light, to illuminate; *fig.* to inflame.

accenseo, ui, nsum, 2. v.a. to reckon to *or* among, to add to.

accensus, i, m. supernumerary soldier; attendant, usher.

accentus, ūs, m. accent, tone.

acceptio, ōnis, f. taking, accepting; meaning, sense.

accepto, 1. v.a. to accept, to receive.

acceptor, ōris, m. receiver.

acceptus, a, um, a. welcome.

accessio, ōnis, f. approach; increase, addition; (med.) fit.

accessus, ūs, m. approach, admittance, inlet, accessory.

accidens, entis, n. (in logic) accident as opposed to property. [weaken.

accīdo, cīdi, cīsum, 3. v.a to cut short, to **accīdo, cīdi,** 3. v.n. to fall at or near; to happen.

accieo, 2. v.a. to fetch, to bring.

accingo, nxi, nctum, 3. v.a. to gird on or about; to provide (with), to prepare (for); to set about.

accio, 4. v.a. to send for, to summon.

accipio, cēpi, ceptum, 3. v.a. to accept, to receive; to undertake; to hear, to learn, to find; to get; to sustain; to obey; to treat.

accipiter, tris, m. hawk; fig. shark.

accire mortem, to commit suicide.

accitus, ūs, m. summons, call.

acclāmātio, ōnis, f. acclamation, shout; crying against.

acclāmo, 1. v.n. to shout (at), to huzza, to cry out against.

acclāro, 1. v.a. to make clear, to reveal.

acclīnis, e, a. leaning (on); inclined, disposed (to). [(to).

acclīno, 1. v.a. to lean against, to incline

acclīvis, e, acclīvus, a, um, a. steep.

acclīvitas, ātis, f. acclivity, ascent.

accōla, ae, c. neighbour. [near.

accōlo, cōlui, cultum, 3. v.n. to dwell

accommōdātē, ad. aptly, suitably.

accommōdātio, ōnis, f. adjustment, compliance.

accommōdātus, a, um, a. fit, suitable.

accommōdo, 1. v.a. to adjust, to fit, to suit; to apply.

accommōdus, a. um, a. fit, convenient.

accrēdo, dīdi, dītum, 3. v.a. to believe wholly.

accresco, ēvi, ētum, 3. v.n. to grow on, to increase, to swell, to be annexed to.

accrētio, ōnis, f. increasing, increment.

accūbitio, ōnis, f. a. reclining (at meals).

accūbo, ui, ĭtum, 1. v.n. to lie near or by; to recline at table.

accūdo, ěre, 3. v.a. to coin in addition.

accumbo, cŭbui, cŭbĭtum, 3. v.n. to lie (sit) down at table.

accūmŭlātio, ōnis, f. heaping up.

accūmŭlātor, ōris, m. heaper up. [up.

accūmŭlo, 1. v.a. to accumulate, to heap

accūrātē, ad. accurately, carefully.

accūrātio, ōnis, f. accuracy, carefulness.

accūrātus, a, um, a. accurate, with care, choice, strict.

accūro, 1. v.a. to take care of, attend to.

accurro, curri, cursum, 3. v.n. to run or hasten to.

accursus, ūs, m. concourse.

accūsābĭlis, e, a. blameable.

accūsātio, ōnis, f. accusation.

accūsātivus, i, m. (gr.) accusative.

accūsātor, ōris, m. accuser, plaintiff.

accūsātōriē, ad. after the manner of an accuser; with exaggeration.

accūsātōrius, a, um, a. accusatory.

accūsātrix, īcis, f. female accuser.

accūso, 1. v.a. to accuse, to blame, to reäcer, ěris, n. maple-tree. [primand.

ācer, cris, cre, a. sharp, sour, pungent, piercing; violent; keen, furious, swift, active, ardent, courageous.

ācerbē, ad. sharply, bitterly.

ācerbĭtas, ātis, f. acerbity, sourness; fig. severity, bitterness; anguish, hardäcerbo, 1. v.a. fig. to embitter. [ship.

ācerbus, a, um, a. unripe, sour, bitter; crude; shrill, rough, violent; severe; grievous.

ācernus, a, um, a. of maple.

ācerra, ae, f. censer.

ācersěcōmēs, ae, m. a young man (lit. one having unshorn hair).

ācervātim, ad. in heaps, summarily, without any order.

ācervo, 1. v.a. to heap up, to multiply.

ācervus, i, m. heap; (a logical figure), sorites.

ācesco, acui, 3. v.n. to turn sour.

ācētābŭlum, i, n. vinegar-cruet, saucer; flower-cup.

ācētāria, orum, n. salad. [raillery.

ācētum, i, n. vinegar; fig. wit, shrewdness,

āchātēs, ae, m. agate.

āchillēa, ae, f. (mod. hort.), milfoil.

āchrās, ādis, f. wild pear.

ācĭdĭtas, ātis, f. acidity.

ācĭdŭlus, a, um, a. sourish.

ācĭdus, a, um, a. acid, sour.

ācĭēs, ei, f. edge, point; battle-array; pupil of the eye; quickness of apprehension. [berry; kernel.

ācĭnus, i. m., ācĭnum, i, n. grape, ivyācipenser, ěris, m. sturgeon. ·

āclys, ydis, f. small javelin, arrow.

ācŏlythus, i, m. acolyte.

ācŏnītum, i, n. wolf's-bane, aconite, monk's-hood.

ācŏpum, i, n. a tonic.

ācor, ōris, m. sourness.

acquiesco, ēvi, ētum, 3. v.n. to lie down to rest; to acquiesce (in), to assent.

acquīro, sīvi, sītum, 3. v.a. to acquire, to get, to obtain.

ācrĭcŭlus, a, um, a. somewhat sharp; testy. [briskness.

ācrĭmōnĭa, ae, f. acrimony, sharpness.

ācrĭter, ad. sharply, vehemently; severely, steadfastly.

acroāmā, ătis, n. anything heard with pleasure; actor, entertainer.

acroāsis, is, f. lecture.

acrŏpŏdium, i, n. pedestal.

acrostĭchis, ĭdis, f. acrostic.

acta, ōrum, n. pl. acts, exploits; chronicles, record.

acta, ae, f. sea-shore.

actio, ōnis, f. action; duties; plot (of a play); judicial process.

actĭto, ı. v.n. to act or plead frequently.

actīvus, a, um, a. active. [player, actor.

actor, ōris, m. plaintiff, advocate; agent;

actŭālis, v.a. practical.

actŭārius, a, um, a. swift, nimble, light.

actŭārius, i, m. clerk, book-keeper, secretary.

actŭōsē, ad. actively, vivaciously.

actŭōsus, a, um, a. active, busy.

actus, ūs, m. act, performance, action; delivery; act (of a play)).

actūtum, ad. forthwith, instantly.

ăcŭleātus, a, um, a. prickly; fig. stinging, sharp, subtle. [sarcasm.

ăcŭleus, i, m. sting, prickle, point;

ăcūmĕn, ĭnis, n. sharpened point, sting, sharpness, cunning, fraud.

ăcuo, ui, ūtum, 3. v.a. to whet, to sharpen; to spur on, to provoke.

ăcus, ūs, f. needle, pin, bodkin.

ăcūtē, ad. acutely, sharply, keenly.

ăcūtŭlus, a, um, a. somewhat sharp or subtle.

ăcūtus, a, um, a. sharp, pointed; violent, severe; glaring; acute, sagacious.

ad, pr. to, towards, near by, at, before, up to, until, about; in comparison with, according to, in order, for; in addition to, after, concerning;— ad arbitrium, at will;—ad captandum vulgus, to tickle the populace;—ad extremum, to the very last;—ad hoc for this particular purpose;—ad infinitum, to infinity;—ad interim, for the meanwhile;—ad libitum, as much as one pleases;— argumentum ad misericordiam, an appeal to pity;—ad nauseam, such as to produce disgust; —ad valorem, according to value.

ădactio, ōnis, f. compulsion, force.

ădæquē, ad. equally, so much.

ădæquo, ı. v.a. & n. to equalize, to level, to compare (to); to be equal.

ădæro, ı, v.a. assess, value.

ădăgium, i, n. proverb, adage.

ădămantēus, a, um, a. adamantine.

ădămantĭnus, a, um, a. hard as adamant.

ădămas, antis, m. the hardest iron; diamond.

ădămo, ı. v.a. to love passionately.

ădăpĕrio, ui, ertum, 4. v.a. to throw open, to uncover.

ădăpertĭlis, e, adj. that may be opened.

ădapto, v.a. adjust, fit.

ădăquo, ı. v.a. to water. [water.

ădăquor, atus, ı. v. dep. (mil.) to fetch

ădauctus, ūs, m. increase, growth.

ădaugeo, xi, ctum, 2. v.a. to increase, to aggravate. [to suck in.

adbibo, bĭbi, bĭbĭtum, 3. v.a. to drink,

addĕcet, 2. v. imp. it becomes.

addenso, ı. addenseo, 2. v.a. to press together, to crowd.

addīco, xi, ctum, 3. v.a. be propitious; to adjudge; to confiscate; to knock down to, to award; consecrate; to sacrifice;—addictus, as adj. made over as a bondman.

addictio, ōnis, f. adjudication.

addisco, dĭdĭci, 3. v.a. to learn besides.

addĭtāmentum, i, n. addition.

addo, dĭdi, dĭtum, 3. v.a. to add, to give, to bring to, to say in addition;— addendum, something to be added.

addŭbĭto, ı. v.n. & a. to doubt, to hesitate.

addūco, xi, ctum, 3. v.a. to bring or lead to; fig. to induce, to contract, to tighten. [waste.

ădēdo, ēdi, ēsum, 3. v.a. to eat up, to

Adelphi, s. The Brothers. The Greek title of a play by Terence.

ădemptio, onis, f. taking away.

ădĕo, īvi & ii, ĭtum, 4. v.n. to go to or approach, to address, to accost, to visit; to attack; to undergo, to take a part in; to enter on (an inheritance).

ădeō, ad. so much, to such a degree, so, so far, just, even, much more, much less.

ădeps, ĭpis, c. fat, tallow; corpulence; bombast.

ădeptio, ōnis, f. obtaining, attainment.

ădĕquĭto, ı. v.a. to ride up to.

ădhæreo, hæsi, hæsum, 2. or adhæresco, 3. v.n. to adhere, to stick, to cling to.

ădhæsio, ōnis, f. adhesion.

ădhĭbeo, ui, ĭtum, 2. v.a. to apply, to hold (to), to use; to invite, to admit.

ădhinnio, īvi, ĭtum, 4. v.n. to neigh after; fig. to applaud.

ădhortātĭo, ōnis, f. exhortation.

ădhortātor, ōris, m. encourager.

ădhortor, ātus, ı. v. dep. to exhort, to encourage. [still; besides.

ădhūc, ad. to this point, hitherto; yet,

adiantum, i, n. maidenhair.

ădĭgo, ēgi, actum, 3. v.a. to drive, to bring, to drive in, to bind by oath.

ădĭmo, ēmi, emptum, 3. v.a. to take away, to rescue, to deprive.
adĭpiscor, eptus, 3. v. dep. to reach, to get, to obtain, to arrive (at), to overtake.
adĭtus, ūs, m. access, way, means.
adjăceo, cui, 2. v.n. to lie near, to adjoin.
adjectĭo, ōnis, f. addition, cornice of a pedestal.
adjĭcio, jēci, jectum, 3. v.a. to throw to, to place at (to), to add to; to outbid.
adjūdĭcātio, ōnis, f. award.
adjūdĭco, 1. v.a. to adjudge, to impute.
adjŭgo, 1. v.a. yoke, together, unite.
adjūmentum, i, n. help, assistance.
adjunctĭo, ōnis, f. union, addition.
adjunctum, i, n. quality, characteristic; —a, ōrum, pl. accessory circumstances.
adjungo, nxi, nctum, 3. v.a. to join to, to yoke, to add to, to apply.
adjūrātĭo, ōnis, f. oath. [solemnly.
adjūro, 1. v.a. to adjure, to swear
adjūto, 1. v.a. to help, to succour.
adjūtor, ōris, m. adjutant, assistant, helper.
adjūtōrium, i, n. help, assistance.
adjūtrix, ĭcis, f. female assistant, helper.
adjŭvo, jūvi, jūtum, 1. v.a. to assist, to help, to cherish, to favour. [out to.
admētĭor, mensus, 4. v. dep. to measure
admĭnĭcŭlum, i, n. prop, stay, means, aid, assistance. [agent.
admĭnister, tri, m. servant, assistant,
admĭnistrātĭo, ōnis, f. administration; aid, assistance; execution, management, care of affairs. [ager.
admĭnistrātor, ōris, m. attendant, man-
admĭnistro, 1. v.a. to administer, to manage, to serve. [strange.
admīrābilis, e, a. admirable, wonderful,
admīrābĭlitas, ātis, f. admirableness.
admīrābĭlĭter, ad. admirably, astonishingly. [ing.
admīrātĭo, ōnis, f. admiration, wonder-
admīrātor, ōris, m. admirer. [wonder at.
admīror, atus, 1. v. dep. to admire, to
admisceo, scui, xtum, 2. v.a. to mix, to mingle with; fig. to mix up with, to involve.
admissio, ōnis, f. letting in, admission.
admissum, i, n. trespass, crime.
admitto, mīsi, missum, 3. v. to let in, to admit, to grant, to permit, to commit, to spur on;—admisso equo, with horse at a gallop.
admixtĭo, ōnis, f. (ad)mixture.
admŏdum, ad. quite, very, excessively; just so; certainly.
admŏneo, ui, ĭtum, 2. v.a. to admonish, to warn; to remind; to persuade.
admŏnĭtio, ōnis, f. admonition; chastisement.

admŏnĭtor, ōris, m. admonisher.
admŏnĭtrix, ĭcis, f. female admonisher.
admŏnĭtus, ūs, m. admonition, rebuke.
admordeo, momordi, morsum, 2. v.a. take a bite at.
admŏveo, mōvi, mōtum, 2. v.a. to move or to bring to, to apply, to use, direct; to lay on; —, v.n. to come near.
admurmuro, 1. v.n. murmur in protest or adno, 1. swim to. [approval.
ădŏleo, ui, ultum, 2. v.a. to burn; to honour by burnt offering.
ădŏlesco, ēvi, ultum, 3. v.n. to grow up, to increase.
ădōnis, (mod. hort.), ox-eye. [over.
ădŏpĕrio, ĕrui, ertum, 4. v.a. to cover all
ădop(tā)tĭo, ōnis, f. adoption of a child.
ădoptīvus, a, um, a. adoptive.
ădopto, 1. v.a. to select, to adopt.
ădor, ōris, m. spelt, grain.
ădōrātĭo, ōnis, f. worship.
ădōreus, a, um, a. of grain;—adorea, ae, f. a reward for bravery, hence honour.
ădōrĭor, ortus, 4. v. dep. to attack, to undertake, to try. [pare, to adorn.
ădorno, 1. v.a. to equip, to set off, to pre-
ădōro, 1. v.a. to adore, to worship.
adrādo, si, sum, 3. v.a. to scrape, to shave, to prune.
adrēpo, psi, ptum, 3. creep to.
adsum, adfui, adesse, v.n. ir. to be near, to be present, to arrive, to aid.
ădūlātĭo, ōnis, f. fawning, flattery.
ădūlātor, ōris, m. flatterer.
ădūlātōrius, a, um, a. flattering, adulatory.
ădūlescens, entis, c. young man or girl.
ădūlescentia, ae, f. youth (time of life).
ădūlescentŭla, ae, f. young girl.
ădūlescentŭlus, i, m. young man, lad.
ădūlor, atus, 1. v. dep. to fawn (as a dog); to flatter, to cringe. [adulteress.
ădulter, ĕri, m., adultĕra, ae, f. adulterer,
ădultĕr, a, um, a. adulterous; counterfeit.
ădultĕrīnus, a, um, a. counterfeit, false.
ădultĕrium, ii, n. adultery.
ădultĕro, 1. v.a. & n. to debauch, to commit adultery; (also fig.) to falsify, to corrupt.
ădultus, a, um, a. full grown, adult.
ădumbrātĭo, ōnis, f. sketch.
ădumbro, 1. v.a. to shadow out, to sketch in outline; to represent.
ăduncĭtas, ātis, f. hookedness, curvature.
ăduncus, a, um, a. crooked, hooked.
ădurgeo, ursi, 2. v.a. press hard, pursue.
ădūro, ussi, ustum, 3. v.a. to burn, to scorch; to consume.
ădusque, pr. even to, until, as far as; —, ad. through and through.

ădustio, ōnis, f. burning.
advectīcius, a, um, a. imported, foreign.
advĕho, xi, ctum, 3. v.a. to carry, to bring, to convey (to);—advehor, to ride to.
advĕna, ae, c. foreigner, stranger; —, a. strange, foreign, ignorant, inexperienced. [to arrive at, to fall to.
advĕnio, vēni, ventum, 4. v.a. to come to,
adventīcius, a, um, a. coming from abroad, foreign, unusual.
advento, 1. v.n. to approach, to arrive.
adventor, ōris, m. guest, customer.
adventus, ūs, m. arrival, approach.
adverbium, ii, n. adverb.
adversārius, a, um, a. opposite; —, m. opponent, enemy; —a, ōrum, n. pl. memorandum-book.
adversātor, ōris, m. antagonist.
adversātrix, īcis, f. female antagonist.
adversor, ātus, 1. v. dep. to be against, to oppose, to withstand.
adversum, adversus, ad. opposite to, against; —, pr. towards, before.
adversus, a, um, a. opposite, before; adverse, evil, hostile; unfavourable; —vulnus adversum, a wound in the front;—adverso flumine, against the stream.
adverto, ti, sum, 3. v.a. to turn or direct to, to apply;—ănĭmum adverto, to notice. See ănĭmadverto. [proaches.
advespĕrascit, āvit, 3. v. imp. evening ap-
advĭgilo, 1. v.n. to watch by, to take care.
advŏcātio, ōnis, f. legal support; delay; fig. counsel, the bar.
advocatus diaboli, the devil's advocate, one who pleads an unjust cause.
advŏcātus, i, m. counsellor, advocate.
advŏco, 1. v.a. to call for, to summon, to call in as counsel.
advŏlo, 1. v.n. to fly to, to hasten towards.
advolvo, vi, vŏlūtum, 3. v.a. to roll to or towards;—genibus advolvor, fall at the knees (of anyone). [sanctuary.
ădȳtum, i, n. innermost part of a temple,
ædēs (ædis), is, f. sing. temple; pl. house, room. [closet.
ædīcŭla, ae, f. small house, chapel, niche,
ædĭfĭcātio, ōnis, f. house-building; building.
ædĭfĭcātor, oris, m. builder, architect.
ædĭfĭcium, ii, n. building. [create.
ædĭfĭco, 1. v.a. to build, to make, to
ædīlĭcius, a, um, a. of an aedile.
ædīlis, is, m. aedile, surveyor.
ædīlĭtas, ātis, d. aedileship.
ædĭtĭmus, i, temple-attendant.
ædĭtuus, i, m. church-warden, sacristan.
æger, gra, grum, a. sick, infirm, sad, sorrowful, painful, grievous.

ægis, ĭdis, f. the Aegis (Minerva's shield); fig. shield, defence.
ægŏcĕrōs, ōtis, m. the sign Capricorn.
ægrē, ad. uncomfortably, reluctantly, with difficulty, scarcely.
ægresco, ĕre, 3. v.n. to become sick, to grow worse, to grieve.
ægrĭmōnia, ae, f. sorrow, anxiety.
ægrĭtūdo, ĭnis, f. indisposition, sickness, grief, sorrow.
ægrōtātio, ōnis, f. sickness, disease.
ægrōto, 1. v.n. to be sick, to languish.
ægrōtus, a, um, a. sick, diseased.
æmŭlātio, ōnis, f. emulation, rivalry.
æmŭlātor, ōris, m. imitator, rival.
æmŭlātus, ūs, m. emulation, envy.
æmŭlor, atus, 1. v. dep. to emulate; to be envious, jealous of.
æmŭlus, a, um, a. emulous; envious, grudging, (things) comparable to; —, as subs., rival.
aēneus, āhēneus, a, um, a. brazen.
ænigmă, ātis, n. enigma, riddle.
aēnus, ahēnus, a, um, a. brazen;—aēnum, a. brazen vessel.
æquābĭlis, e, a. equal, alike, uniform.
æquābĭlitas, ātis, f. equality, impartiality, uniformity.
æquābĭlĭter, ad. uniformly, equally.
æquævus, a, um, a. of the same age.
æqualis, e, a. even, equal, of the same age, coeval; —, as subs., contemporary.
æquālĭtas, ātis, f. evenness; equality.
æquālĭter, ad. equally, evenly.
æquănĭmitas, ātis, f. evenness of mind, patience, calmness.
æquātio, ōnis, f. equal distribution.
æquē, ad. equally, in the same manner as.
æqui bonique facere, to take in good part.
æquĭlĭbrium, ii, n. even balance, equili-
æquĭnoctialis, e, a. equinoctial. [brium.
æquĭnoctium, i, n. equinox.
æquĭpăro, 1. v.a. to compare, to liken; —, v.n. to come up to.
æquĭtas, ātis, f. evenness, conformity, symmetry, equity, equanimity.
æquo, 1. v.a. to level; to equal; to compare; —, v.n. to come up to.
æquo animo, with mind untroubled.
æquor, ōris, n. level surface, plain, surface of the sea, sea.
æquŏreus, a, um, a. of the sea, bordering on the sea.
æquus, a, um, a. level, even, equal, like, just, kind, favourable, impartial, patient, contented.
āēr, āĕris, m. air, atmosphere; fig. cloud,
ærārium, ii, n. treasury. [mist.
ærārius, a, um, a. pertaining to copper, brass, etc.; —, as subs., a citizen of the lowest class.

ærātus, a, ι⁴n, a. covered with or made of copper or brass.

ære perennius (monumentum), (a monument) more lasting than brass.

æreus, a, um, made of brass.

æripes, brazen-footed.

āĕrius, aerial, towering, airy.

ærosus, a, um, a. rich in copper.

ærūgĭnōsus, a, um, a. rusty.

ærūgo, ĭnis, f. rust of copper, verdigris; fig. envy, ill-will, avarice.

ærumna, ae, f. toil, hardship, calamity.

ærumnōsus, a, um, a. full of trouble, wretched.

æruscātor, ōris, m. vagrant who gets money by juggling.

æs, æris, n. copper ore, copper; bronze; money, pay, wages, bronze statues, etc.;—alienum, debt.

æscŭlētum, i, n. oak-forest.

æscŭleus, a, um, a. of oak.

æscŭlus, i, f. winter oak, horse-chestnut.

æstas, ātis, f. summer; fig. a year.

æstĭfer, a, um, a. producing heat, sultry.

æstĭmābĭlis, e, a. estimable.

æstĭmātĭo, ōnis, f. valuation, value, price.

æstĭmātor, ōris, m. valuer, appraiser; fig. judge.

æstimo, 1. v.a. to value; to estimate.

æstīva, orum, n. pl. summer-quarters; summer-house; campaign.

æstīvo, 1. v.n. to pass the summer.

æstīvus, a, um, a. summer-like, summer . . . [morass.

æstuārium, ii, n. estuary, frith, marsh,

æstuo, 1. v.n. to boil, to foam, to billow; fig. to rage, to waver, to be undecided.

æstuōsus, a, um, a. hot, sultry, billowy.

æstus, ūs, m. heat, fire, tide, swell of the sea; passion; hesitation, anxiety.

ætas, ātis, f. life-time, age, period (of time); generation;—aurea ætas, the golden age.

ætātŭla, ae, f. the tender age of childhood.

æternĭtas, ātis, f. eternity, immortality.

æterno, 1. v.a. immortalize.

æternus, a, um, a. eternal, everlasting, imperishable;—in æternum, for ever.

æther, ĕris, m. upper air, ether, heaven.

æthĕreus, a, um, a. ethereal, heavenly.

æthra, ae, f. clear sky. [generation.

ævum, i, n. time of life, age, old age,

affābĭlis, e, easy of access, affable.

affātim, ad. sufficiently, enough.

affātus, ūs, m. address, discourse.

affectātĭo, ōnis, f. seeking after; affectation, conceit.

affectātor, ōris, m. one who seeks after.

affectĭo, ōnis, f. feeling disposition, affection, love. [sire, to aspire.

affecto, 1. v.a. to affect, to aim at, to de-

affectus, ūs, m. disposition, state (of body and mind), affection, passion, love.

affĕro, attŭli, allātum, afferre, 3. v.a. to bring to, to bring word, to allege, to produce, to contribute, to cause.

afficio, affēci, affectum, 3. v.a. to affect, to move, to influence.

affīgo, ixi, ixum, 3. v.a. to fasten to, to fix on; to impress on.

affingo, inxi, ictum, 3. v.a. to form, to fashion, to invent, to annex, to counterfeit, to attribute (wrongly).

affinis, e, a. neighbouring, adjacent, related by marriage, privy to.

affīnĭtas, ātis, f. neighbourhood; relationship (by marriage).

affirmātĭo, ōnis, f. affirmation, assertion.

affirmātīvus, a, um, a. affirmative.

affirmo, 1. v.a. to affirm, to assert, to confirm.

afflātus, ūs, m. breathing on, breeze, blast, breath; fig. inspiration.

afflictātĭo, ōnis, f. pain, sorrow. [vex.

afflicto, 1. v.a. to inflict, to damage, to

afflictus, a, um, a. damaged, wretched, desponding, base, vile;—res afflictæ, damaged fortunes.

afflīgo, ixi, ictum, 3. v.a. to afflict, to throw down, to crush, to grieve, to humble, to weaken. [to inspire.

afflo, 1. v.a. & n. to blow or breathe on;

affluenter, ad. abundantly, copiously.

affluentĭa, ae, f. abundance, profusion.

affluo, xi, xum, 3. v.a. to flow on; fig. to flock together, to abound.

affor, fātus sum, āri, 1. v. dep. to speak to, to accost.

affulgeo, ulsi, 2. v.n. to shine on; to smile upon.

affundo, ūdi, ūsum, 3. v.a. to pour upon (into);—affundor, to prostrate oneself.

ăgăpanthus (mod. hort.), African lily.

agaricum, ī, n. mushroom.

ăgāso, ōnis, m. driver, groom.

ăgāve (mod. hort.), aloe.

ăgĕ, ăgĕdum, ad. come! well! all right!

ăgellus, i, m. little field, farm.

ăgĕrātum (mod. hort.), floss-flower.

ăger, gri, m. field, ground, territory, country, farm.

aggemo, 3. v.n. to groan at.

agger, ĕris, m. heap, mound, dam; mudwall; rampart; causeway.

aggĕro, gessi, gestum, 3. v.a. to carry to, to bring, to add.

aggĕro, a. v.a. to heap up, to fill up, to increase.

aggestus, ūs, m. piling up.

agglŏmĕro, 1. v.a. to wind up, to gather into a body.

agglŭtĭno, 1. v.a. to glue to, to fasten to.

aggrăvo, 1. v.a. to aggravate, to bear hard upon.

aggrĕdior, gressus, 3. v. dep. to address (one), to ply, to attack, to undertake.

aggrĕgo, 1. v.a. to attach;—se aggregare, to ally oneself to.

aggressio, ōnis, f. attack, introduction to a speech.

ăgĭlis, e, a. agile, nimble, quick, busy.

ăgĭlĭtas, ātis, f. activity, quickness.   [tion.

ăgĭtātĭo, ōnis, f. agitation, exercise; mo-ăgĭtātor, ōris, m. driver, charioteer.

ăgĭto, 1. v.a. to agitate, to drive or shake or move about, to revolve; to consider, to pursue, to exercise, to manage; to keep, to celebrate.

agmĕn, ĭnis, n. quick motion, herd, flock, troop, swarm, army (on the march);— primum agmen, the van;—novissimum agmen, the rear.

agna, ae, f. ewe lamb.

agnascor, natus, 3. v. dep. to be born after a father has made his will.

agnātĭo, ōnis, f. consanguinity on the father's side.

agnātus, i, m. relation on the father's side; one born after a father has made his will.

agnellus, i, m. lambkin.

agnīna, ae, flesh of a lamb.   [ledge.

agnĭtĭo, ōnis, f. acknowledgment, know-agnōmen, ĭnis, n. surname.

agnosco, nōvi, nĭtum, 3. v.a. to recognize, to allow, to acknowledge.

agnus, i, m. lamb.

ăgo, ēgi, actum, 3. v.a. to drive, to act, to do, to transact, to carry off, to steal, to apply, to rouse, to cause to bring forth, to urge, to deal, to think, to manage, to exercise, to accuse, to deliver (a speech), to play (as an actor), to behave (as), to pass, to spend, to disturb;—gratias agere, to thank; —agenda, business to be done;—actum est de, it is all over with;— agere cum, to plead with.

agrārĭus, a, um, a. agrarian.

agrestis, e, a. rustic, rude, wild, savage; —, as subs., a peasant.   [turist.

agricŏla, ae, m. husbandman, agricul-agrĭcultūra, ae, f. agriculture.

agrimōnĭa (mod. hort.), agrimony.

ah, i. ah! alas! ha! fie! ho! ho!

ăhă, i. aha! ah! haha!

ăhēnus, ăhēneus, v. aēnus.

ai, i. ah! alas!   [to affirm.

āĭo, v. dep. to say, to say yes, to assent,

ajŭga (mod. hort.), bugle.

āla, ae, f. wing; arm-pit, shoulder-blade; an army's wing.

ălăbaster, tri, m. an alabaster casket.

ălăbastrītes, ae, m. alabaster.

ălăcer, cris, e, a. cheerful, brisk, gay, active, courageous, eager, ready.

ălăcrĭtas, ātis, f. cheerfulness, eagerness, briskness.

ălăpa, ae, f. box on the ear.

ālāris, e, ālārĭus, a, um, a. pertaining to an army's wing.

ālātus, a, um, a. winged.

ălauda, ae, f. lark.

albāmentum, i, n. white of egg.

albātus, a, um, a. clothed in white.

albeo, 2. v.n. to be or grow white.

albesco, 3. v.n. to become white.

albĭcēris, e, albĭcērus, a, um, albĭcērātus, a, um, a. cream-coloured.

albĭco, 1. v.n. be white.

albĭdus, a, um, a. whitish.

albūgo, ĭnis, f. disease of the eye.

album, i, n. white (the colour); white tablet, list of names, register.

albūmen, ĭnis, n. white of egg.

albus, a, um, a. white, pale, hoary, bright, clear, favourable, fortunate.

alcēdo, ĭnis, & alcyon, ōnis, f. kingfisher;— alcedonia, n. pl., or dies alcyonii, halcyon days.

alces, is, f. elk.

ālea, ae, f. die, cube, dice-play, gambling, chance, venture, risk.

alea jacta est. The die is cast.

āleātor, ōris, m. dice-player, gamester.

āleātōrĭus, a, um, a. of dice; —ia damna, losses at play.

āleo, ōnis, m. gambler.

āles, ālĭtis, c. bird, fowl; —, a. winged, swift, light.

alga, ae, f. sea-weed; fig. rubbish.

algeo, alsi, 2. v.n. to be cold, to feel chilly.

algesco, alsi, 3. v.n. to catch cold, to be-algor, ōris, m. coldness.   [come cold.

ălĭā, ad. by another way.

ălĭās, ad. at another time, elsewhere, otherwise; a name not one's own.

ălĭbī, ad. elsewhere, in another place; a legal defence whereby the accused pleads he was elsewhere when the wrong was committed.

ălĭca, ae, f. grain, spelt.

ălĭcārĭa, ae, f. prostitute.

ălĭcŭbi, ad. somewhere, anywhere, hereabouts.   [some one.

ălĭcundĕ, ad. from some place, from

ălĭēnātĭo, ōnis, f. transference, aversion, dislike.

ălĭēnĭgĕna, ae, m. stranger, foreigner.

ălĭēno, 1. v.a. to alienate, to transfer by sale, to estrange; ălĭēnor, āri, v. dep. to avoid (with antipathy); to become apostate; to be insane.

äliēnus, a. um, a. another's, foreign; contrary, averse, hostile; unfavourable, insane;—æs alienum, debt.

äliger, a, um, a. winged.

älimentum, i, n. nourishment, food.

älimōnia, ae, f., älimōnium, i, n. support.

äliō, ad. elsewhither. [else.

alioquī(n), ad. in other respects, besides,

äliorsum, ad. in another direction, elsewhere, in a different sense.

älipes, ĕdis, a. wing-footed, swift.

äliptēs, ae, m. superintendent of a school of wrestlers.

äliquā, ad. somehow.

äliquamdiū, ad. for some time.

äliquando, ad. sometimes, at length, formerly, hereafter.

äliquantisper, ad. for some time.

äliquanto, ad. somewhat, a little, in some degree.

äliquantŭlum, ad. a little, somewhat.

äliquantus, a, um, a. somewhat, considerable.

äliquätĕnus, ad. for some distance, in some measure.

äliqui, aliquæ, aliquod, a. some, any.

äliquis, aliquid, pl. aliqui, pn. someone, somewhat, something.

äliquō, ad. to some place or other.

äliquŏt, num. (indecl.) some, a few.

äliquŏties, ad. several times.

älitĕr, ad. otherwise, else.

äliŭbi, ad. elsewhere. [place.

äliundĕ, ad. from another person or

alius . . . alius, one . . . another.

älius, a, ud, a. another, different, changed.

allābor, psus, v. dep. to glide towards, to move forwards.

allăbŏro, I. v.a. to labour or toil at, to add. [proach.

allapsus, ūs, m. gliding to, stealthy ap-

allatro, I. v.a. to bark at; to rail at.

allecto, I. v.a. to allure, to entice.

allēgātio, ōnis, f. despatching, mission, excuse. [to allege; to instigate.

allēgo, I. v.a. to depute, to commission;

allēgo, ēgi, ectum, 3. v.a. to choose, to admit.

allēgŏria, ae, f. allegory.

allēgŏrice, ad. allegorically.

allēgŏricus, a, um, a. allegorical.

allēvo, I. v.a. to lift up, to raise; fig. to alleviate, to diminish, to weaken, to console.

allicio, lexi, lectum, 3. v.a. to draw gently to, to entice.

allido, si, sum, 3. v.a. to dash against; (in pass.) v. dep. to suffer damage.

alligo, I. v.a. to bind to, to entangle; fig. to bind by an obligation.

allino, ēvi, itum, 3. to smear over.

allium, i, n. garlic. [rangue.

allŏcūtio, ōnis, f. address, consolation, ha-

allŏquium, ii, n. address, consolation.

allŏquor, cūtus, 3. v. dep. to speak to, to address.

allūdo, ūsi, ūsum, 3. v.a. & n. to play with, to jest; (of the waves) to dash upon.

alluo, ui, 3. v.a. to wash against, to bathe.

allŭvies, ei, f. alluvial pool.

allŭvio, ōnis, f. flood, alluvial land.

almus, a, um, a. nourishing, kind, propitious;—alma mater, foster - mother, applied to a university.

alnus, i, f. alder; boat.

älo, älui, altum & älitum, 3. v.a. to nourish, to maintain; to promote; to cherish.

äloē, ēs, f. aloe.

älŏpēcia, ae, f. a kind of mange.

alphăbētum, i, n. alphabet.

alpīnus, a, um, a. of the Alps.

alsius, a, um; alsus, a, um, a. cold.

altāre, is, n., altāria, ium, n. pl. altar.

altē, ad. on high, highly, deeply.

altĕr, a, um, a. another, the other, any other, the former, the latter;—alter ego, a second self;—unus et alter, one or two. [debate.

altercātio, ōnis, f. contention, dispute,

altercor, atus, I. v. dep. to bicker, to dispute, to quarrel.

alterno, I. v.a. to do by turns, to vary;— v.n. to alternate, to waver.

alternus, a, um, a. alternate, one after the other, by turns, mutual;—alternis (sc. vicibus), alternately, by turns.

altĕrūter, utra, utrum, a. either, one of two.

althæa, ae, f. hollyhock.

alticinctus, a, um, a. high-girt; fig. active.

altilis, e, a. fattened, rich.

altisŏnus, a, um, a. high-sounding, lofty.

altĭtŏnans, antis, a. thundering from on high.

altĭtūdo, dĭnis, f. height, depth; fig. loftiness, magnanimity, secrecy.

altĭvŏlans, antis, a. high-flying.

altor, ōris, m. nourisher, foster-father.

altrinsĕcus, ad. on or from the other side.

altrix, īcis, f. female nourisher, wet-nurse.

altus, a, um, a. high, deep, shrill, lofty, noble; deeply rooted; far-fetched;— altum, i, n. the deep, the sea; a height.

älūcinātio, ōnis, f. dreaming, reverie.

älūcinor, atus, I. v. dep. to wander in mind, to talk idly, to dream.

älūmen, ĭnis, n. alum.

älumnus, a, um, a. nourished, brought up: —, as subs. nursling, foster-child, disciple.

ălūta, ae, f. alum-dressed leather; shoe; patch (on the face).

alveārium, ii, n. bee-hive.

alveŏlus, i, m. little trough; gaming-board; small river-channel.

alveus, i, m. cavity; tub; tray; hold of a ship, boat; gaming-board; bee-hive; bathing-tub; river-bed.

alvus, i, f. belly, paunch, womb, stomach; bee-hive.

alyssum (mod. hort.), alyssum.

ămābĭlis, e, a. amiable, pleasant. [antly.

ămābĭlĭter, ad. lovingly, amicably, pleas

ămando, I. v.a. to send away, to dismiss.

ămans, antis, g.c. lover, sweetheart, mistress.

ămanter, ad. lovingly, affectionately.

ămănuensis, is, m. secretary.

ămārăcus, i, c., ămārăcum, i, n. marjoram.

ămārantus, i, m., amaranth, love-lies-bleeding.

ămārē, ad. bitterly.

ămārĭtūdo, ĭnis, f. bitterness; fig. sharpness, disagreeableness.

ămārus, a, um, a. bitter, harsh, shrill, sad, calamitous; sarcastic, irritable.

ămāryllis (mod. hort.), belladonna lily.

ămātor, ōris, m. lover, gallant.

ămātōrius, a, um, a. loving, amorous, procuring love.

ămātrix, īcis, f. sweetheart, mistress.

ambāges, is, f., pl. ambăges, um, round-about way, shifting, shuffling, prevarication; tedious story; obscurity, ambiguity.

ambarvālis, e, a., ambarvalis hostia, a victim led round the fields and sacrificed.

ambĕdo, ēdi, esum, 3. to gnaw round the edge, to consume.

ambĭgo, 3. v.n. to wander about; fig. to hesitate, to be in doubt, to argue, to wrangle.

ambĭguē, ad. doubtfully, undecidedly.

ambĭguĭtas, ātis, f. ambiguity, equivocalness.

ambĭguus, a, um, a. changeable, varying, doubtful, dark, ambiguous, wavering, fickle.

ambĭo, īvi & ii, ītum, 4. v.n. & a. to surround, to solicit, to ask, to aspire to; to canvass. [canvassing, flattery.

ambĭtĭo, ōnis, f. ambition; vanity; effort,

ambĭtĭōsē, ad. ambitiously, diligently.

ambĭtĭōsus, a, um, a. ambitious, vain-glorious, gracious, stately, admired.

ambĭtus, ūs, m. circuit; canvass, bribery; circumlocution; ostentation.

ambŏ, bae, bō, a. both (two together).

ambrŏsia, ae, f. food of the gods; unguent of the gods.

ambrŏsius, a, um, a. immortal, divine, lovely. [courtesan.

ambūbaia, ae, f. a Syrian musician and

ambŭlātĭo, ōnis, f. walking about; place for promenading. [walking.

ambŭlātiuncŭla, ae, f. small place for

ambŭlātōrius, a, um, a. movable.

ambŭlo, I. v.n. to go about, to take a walk, to travel.

ambūro, ussi, ustum, 3. v.a. to burn around, to scorch, to burn wholly up; to nip [with cold.

ambustum, i, n. a burn.

āmens, entis, a. mad, frantic.

āmentia, ae, f. madness, stupidity.

āmento, I. v.a. to furnish with a thong.

āmentum, i, n. thong; shoe-latchet.

āmes, ĭtis, m. pole.

ămēthystĭnus, a, um, a. of amethyst.

ămēthystus, i, f. amethyst.

ămia, ae, f. tunny-fish.

ămiantus, i, m. asbestos.

ămīca, ae, f. female friend, concubine.

ămīcē, ad. kindly, amicably.

ămĭcio, īcui & ixi, ictum, 4. v.a. to wrap about; fig. to veil.

ămīcĭtia, ae, f. friendship, alliance, service.

ămictus, ūs, m. upper garment, dress, clothing.

ămīcŭla, ae, f. courtesan, mistress.

ămīcŭlum, i, n. mantle, cloak.

ămīcŭlus, i, m. little friend, dear friend.

ămīcus, i, m. friend, ally, lover, patron; counsellor, courtier; —, a, um, a. friendly, fond of;—amicus curiæ, a friend to the court; one who gives information to a judge, his interests being unaffected by the case.

āmissĭo, ōnis, f. āmissus, ūs, m. loss.

ămita, ae, f. father's sister, aunt.

āmitto, īsi, issum, 3. v.a. to lose, to dismiss, to let fall.

amnĭcus, a, um, a. of a river.

amnis, is, m. stream, river.

āmo, I. v.a. to love, to like, to be fond of, to be wont;—amantium iræ amoris integratio est, lovers' quarrels are the renewing of love.

ămœbæus, a, um, adj. answering;—carmen amœbæum, a song in which two singers perform alternately.

ămœnē, ad. pleasantly, sweetly.

ămœnĭtas, ātis, f. pleasantness, delight, beauty. [beautiful.

ămœnus, a, um, a. pleasant, delightful,

āmōlior, ītus, 4. v. dep. to remove by great effort, to send away; fig. to avert, to refute.

āmōmum, i, n. balsam.

ămor, ōris, m. love; the beloved; Cupid; eager desire. [to steal; to banish.

āmŏveo, mōvi, mōtum, 2. v.a. to remove,

ampĕlopsis (mod. hort.), ampelopsis.
amphĭbŏlia, ae, f. amphibology, double-meaning.
amphisbæna, ae, f. a species of serpent that can move with either end foremost.
amphĭtheātrum, i, n. amphitheatre.
amphŏra, ae, f. two-handled pitcher, firkin.
amplē, ad. abundantly, splendidly.
amplector, exus, 3. v. dep. to embrace, to lay hold of; to surround, to contain; to cherish; to understand.
amplexor, ātus, 1. v. dep. v. amplector; fig. to love, to esteem.
amplexus, ūs, m. embracing, embrace, surrounding. [geration.
amplĭfĭcātio, ōnis, f. enlargement, exag-
amplĭfĭco, 1. v.a. to amplify, to enlarge, to extol. [to adjourn.
amplio, 1. v.a. to make wider, to enlarge;
amplĭter, ad. abundantly, fully.
amplĭtūdo, ĭnis, f. width, breadth, size, bulk; importance; fulness of ex-pression.
amplius, ad. more, further. [glorious.
amplus, a, um, a. ample, large, wide;
ampulla, ae, f. cruet, flagon, pot; fig. flowers of speech.
ampullor, 1. v.n. use turgid language.
ampŭtātio, ōnis, f. pruning, lopping off.
ampŭto, 1. v.a. to lop off, to prune, to shorten, to mutilate.
ămŭlētum, i, n. amulet, charm.
ămurca, ae, f. lees of oil.
ămussis, is, f. carpenter's rule;—ad amussim, according to rule.
ămygdăla, ae, f. almond. [tree.
ămygdălus, i, f., ămygdălum, i, n. almond
ăn, c. whether? or, either.
ănăbăsis, is, f. march up country
ănăbathrum, i, n. pulpit, rostrum.
ănădēma, ătis, n. fillet.
ănăgallis, ĭdis, f. pimpernel.
ănaglypta, ōrum, n. pl. bas-relief.
ănănas (mod. hort.), pineapple.
ănăpæstum, i, n. anapæstic verse.
ănăpæstus, i, m. anapæst, metrical foot, two shorts followed by a long.
ănas, ănătis, f. duck.
ănăthēma, ătis, n. a victim for sacrifice, a curse, cursed thing.
ănătĭcŭla, ae, f. little duck; fig. duckling.
ănătōcismus, i, m. compound interest.
anceps, cĭpĭtis, a. two-headed; danger-ous, doubtful; double, undecided.
anchūsa (mod. hort.), alkanet.
ancīle, is, n. small oval shield.
ancilla, ae, f. maid-servant, female slave.
ancillŭla, ae, f. little serving-maid, young female slave.
ancŏra, ae, f. anchor; fig. refuge, support.

ancŏrāle, is, n. cable. [anchor.
ancŏrārius, a, um, a. belonging to an
andăbăta, ae, m. a gladiator who fought in a helmet without eye-holes and on horseback.
andrŏgўnus, i, m. hermaphrodite.
andrŏsăcē (mod. hort.) rock-jasmine.
ănellus, i, m. little ring.
ănĕmōne, es, f. anemone, wind flower.
ănēthum, i, n. dill, anise.
anfractus, ūs, m. curving, bending, circuit, windings; fig. digression.
angăria, ae, f. service exacted by au-thority.
angelĭca (mod. hort.), Holy Ghost.
angĕlus, i, m. angel.
angĭna, ae, f. quinsy. [row street or alley.
angĭportus, ūs, m., angĭportum, i, n. nar-
ango, xi, ctum, 3. v.a. to press tight, to throttle; to cause pain, to vex, to trouble. [tion.
angor, ōris, m. quinsy; fig. anguish, vexa-
anguicŏmus, a, um, a. with snaky hair.
anguĭfer, a, um, a. snake-bearing.
anguilla, ae, f. eel.
anguĭneus, a, um, a. snaky.
anguĭnus, a, um, a. of a snake, snaky.
anguis, is, c. snake; serpent; (constella-tion) the Dragon;—anguis in herba, a snake in the grass, a lurking peril.
angŭlāris, e, a. angular. [ing-place.
angŭlus, i, m. angle, corner, nook, lurk-
angustē, ad. narrowly, sparingly, briefly, with difficulty.
angustiæ, arum, f. pl. strait, defile, nar-rowness, want, perplexity, trouble.
angusto, 1. v.a. to make narrow, to straiten.
angustus, a, um, a. narrow, strait, scanty, poor, needy, low, mean; narrow-minded;—res angusta domi, poverty at home.
ănhēlĭtus, ūs, m. panting, puffing, breath-ing, breath, exhalation. [breathe out.
ănhēlo, 1. v.n. & a. to pant, to gasp, to
ănhēlus, a, um, a. panting, puffing.
ănĭcŭla, ae, f. little old woman.
ănīlis, e, a. old-womanish. [living being.
ănĭma, ae, f. air, breeze, breath, soul, life,
ănĭmadversio, ōnis, f. observation, atten-tion, reproach, chastisement.
ănĭmadverto, ti, sum, 3. v.a. to observe, to attend to, to remark, to notice, to understand, to perceive, to avenge, to punish, to blame.
ănĭmăl, ālis, n. animal.
ănĭmālis, e, a. made of air, animate.
ănĭmans, antis, p. & a. living; —, as subs., c. being, animal.
ănĭmo, 1. v.a. & n. to animate, to en-courage, give life to.

ănĭmōsē, ad. courageously, ardently, eagerly.

ănĭmōsĭtas, ătis, f. spirit, anger.

ănĭmōsus, a, um, a. gusty, lifelike, courageous, bold, strong, ardent.

ănĭmŭla, ae, f. little soul, life.

ănĭmus, i, m. (rational) soul, mind, will, purpose, desire, character; courage; anger; pride; pleasure, inclination; memory, judgment, consciousness; opinion; vital power, life;—ex animo, from the heart, with sincerity;—bono animo esse, to be of good heart;— aequo animo, with equanimity.

annāles, ĭum, m. pl. annals, year-books.

annālis, e, a. relating to the year, annual.

annāto, 1. v.n. to swim towards.

anne, c. whether or no?   [annex.

annecto, exui, exum, 3. v.a. to tie on, to

annellus, v. anellus.

annĭcŭlus, a, um, a. a year old.

annĭfer, a, um, a. bearing (fruit) all the year.   [upon; fig. to strive.

annītor, nīsus & nixus, 3. v. dep. to lean

annĭversārius, a, um, a. annual, yearly.

anno, 1. v.n. to swim near or towards.

annōna, ae, f. year's produce, provision, victuals, price of grain or other food.

annōsus, a, um, a. aged, old.

annōtātor, oris, m. observer.

annōtĭnus, a, um, a. of last year.

annōto, 1. v.a. note down, remark on.

annŭmĕro, 1. v.a. to count out to, to pay, to reckon among.

annuntio, 1. to announce.

annuo, ui, ūtum, 3. v.n. to nod at or to, to assent, to promise, to grant, to intimate by a nod, to declare.

annus, i, m. year, season, year's produce; age;—anno Domini, in the year of the Lord;—annus mirabilis, a year of marvels.

annuus, a, um, a. yearly, lasting a year.

anquīro, quīsīvi, ītum, 3. v.a. to search diligently after, to inquire into, to examine judicially.

ansa, ae, f. handle, haft; fig. opportunity.

ansātus, a, um, a. having a handle.

anser, ĕris, m. goose.

ansĕrīnus, a, um, of a goose.   [of a door.

antae, ārum, f. pilasters on either side

antĕ, pr. before, since; —, ad. in front, before (of time), forwards, sooner than.

anteā, ad. before this, formerly.

anteambŭlo, ōnis, m. a servant who clears the way for his master.

antĕcănis, is, m. the Lesser Dog-star.

antĕcăpio, cēpi, ceptum, 3. v.a. to take beforehand, to preoccupy, to anticipate.

antĕcēdens, entis, n. antecedent.

antĕcēdo, essi, essum, 3 v.n. to go before, to precede, to excel, to surpass.

antĕcello, 3. v. to surpass, to excel.

antĕcessio, ōnis, f. going before; surpassing; antecedent cause.   [decessor.

antĕcessor, ōris, m. advance guard, pre

antĕcursor, ōris, m. forerunner; —es, pl. advanced guard.

anteeo, īvi & ii, 4. v.n. to go before; to surpass; to anticipate; to prevent.

antĕfĕro, tŭli, lātum, ferre, 3. v.a. to carry before; fig. to prefer.

antĕgrĕdior, essus, 3. v. dep. to go before, to precede.

antehāc, ad. before this time; earlier.

antĕlūcānus, a, um, a. before daybreak.

antĕmĕrīdiānus, a, um, a. before noon.

antĕmitto, 3. v.a. to send before.

antenna, ae, f. sail-yard.

antĕpīlāni, ōrum, m. pl. men who fought in the first or second line.

antĕpōno, sui, situm, 3. v.a. to place before; fig. to prefer.

antĕquam, ad. before that.

antĕrīdes, um, f. pl. buttress.

antĕrĭor, ĭus, a. former; in front (of).

antes, ĭum, m. pl. rows (of plants).

antĕsignānus, i, m. standard-bearer; leader.   [fore; to excel.

antesto or antisto, stĕti, 1. v.n. to stand be

antestor, atus, 1. v. dep. to call to witness.

antĕvĕnio, vēni, ventum, 4. v.n. to come before; to anticipate, to prevent.

antĕverto, ti, sum, 3. v.n. & a. to outstrip; to anticipate; to prefer.

anthĕricum (mod. hort.) St. Bernard's lily.   [lily.

anthrax, ăcis, m. carbuncle.

anticĭpātio, ōnis, f. preconception.

anticĭpo, 1. v.a. & n. to anticipate.

antĭdōtum, i, n. antidōtus, i, f. counterpoison; fig. antidote.

antĭpŏdes, um, m. pl. the Antipodes.

antĭquārĭus, ii, m. antiquarian.

antĭquē, ad. of old, in ancient time.

antĭquĭtas, ātis, f. antiquity; the ancients; virtue of olden time.

antĭquĭtŭs, ad. in former times.

antĭquo, 1. v.a. to reject (a bill).

antĭquus, a, um, a. old, ancient; aged; of the old stamp, simple, honest, venerable.

antirrhīnum, i, n. snap-dragon.

antistes, stĭtis, g.c. high-priest; chief priestess; fig. master (in).

antistĭta, ae, f., v. antistes.

antrum, i, n. cave, cavern.

ānŭlārĭus, i, m. ring-maker, goldsmith.

ānŭlŭs, i, m. ring; signet-ring.

ānus, i, m. seat, fundament.   [aged.

ănus, ūs, f. old woman; sibyl; —, a. old,

anxiē, ad. anxiously.

anxiĕtas, ātis, f. anxiety; carefulness.

anxius, a, um, a. anxious, uneasy; disturbed; concerned; curious.

ăpăgĕ, i, begone! go to!

ăpathīa, ae. f. insensibility to feeling.

ăper, pri, m. wild boar.

ăpĕrio, ĕrui, ertum, 4. v.a. to open; to discover; to show, to explain.

ăpertē, ad. openly, clearly.

ăpertus, a, um, open; public; exposed; wide, extended; cloudless; clear; frank;—**aperto vivere voto,** to live with ideals one is not ashamed to confess.

ăpex, ĭcis, m. point, top, summit; cap, crown; conical cap of a priest; highest honour. [boat.

aphractus, i, f. **aphractum, i,** n. undecked

ăpiārium, i, n. bee-hive.

ăpiastrum, i, n. wild parsley.

ăpis or **apes, is,** f. bee.

ăpiscor, aptus, 3. v. dep. reach, obtain.

ăpium, ii, n. wild celery or parsley.

ăplūda, ae, f. bran, chaff.

ăplustre, is, n. curved stern of a ship.

ăpŏcălypsis, is, f. revelation.

ăpŏcŏlŏcyntōsis, is, f. Pumpkinification. A satire of Seneca's in which the Emperor Claudius is changed into a pumpkin.

ăpŏdōsis, is, f. clause in a conditional sentence.

ăpŏdўtērium, ii, n. undressing-room in a bathing-house.

ăpŏlŏgus, i, m. narrative; fable.

ăpŏphŏrēta, orum, n. pl. gifts received at a banquet and taken home.

ăpŏsiōpēsis, is, f. a breaking off in the middle of a sentence.

ăpostăta, ae, m. apostate.

ăpostŏlus, i, m. apostle.

ăpostrŏphus, i, m. apostrophe. [cellar.

ăpŏthēca, ae, f. shop, storehouse, wine-

ăpŏtheōsis, is, f. deification.

ăpoxŷomenus, i, m. the name of a statue by Lysippus representing a man scraping himself with a strigil after the bath.

appărātē, ad. luxuriously. [splendid.

appărātus, a, um, p. & a. prepared, ready;

appărātus, ūs, m. preparation; provision; equipment; splendour, pomp.

appăreo, ui, ĭtum, 2. v.n. to appear; to be evident; to attend or serve;—**apparet,** it is clear. [servants.

appărĭtio, ōnis, f. service, attendance;

appărĭtor, ōris, m. (public) servant; subaltern; beadle.

appăro, i. v.a. to prepare, to fit out, to provide; to attempt.

appellātio, ōnis, f. accosting; appeal; calling by name; name, title; pronunciation.

appellātor, ōris, m. appellant. [name.

appellĭto, i. v.a. to be accustomed to

appello, i. v.a. to call upon; to address; to dun; to appeal (to); to bring into court; to accuse; to name, to entitle, to pronounce.

appello, pŭli, pulsum, 3. v.a. to drive to; to bring to land; fig. to apply, to devote; —, v.n. to come ashore.

appendix, ĭcis, f. appendage; supplement.

appendo, endi, ensum, 3. v.a. to weigh.

appĕtens, entis, p. & a. eager for; avaricious.

appĕtentia, ae, f. longing after, appetite.

appĕtītio, ōnis, f. strong desire; grasping (at); earnest endeavour (after).

appĕtītus, ūs, m. eager desire, passion.

appĕto, ivi & ii, ītum, 3. v.a. & n. to seek or grasp after; to assail; to strive eagerly after, to long for; —, v.n. to approach. [in writing.

appingo, 3. v.a. to paint upon; to add

applaudo, si, sum, 3. v.a. to strike together; to clap; to applaud. [tion.

applĭcātio, ōnis, f. application, inclina-

applĭcātus, a, um, p. & a. attached to; inclined (to).

applĭco, avi & ui, atum & ītum, i. v.a. to join to, to place near; to apply (to); to devote (to); fig. to connect.

appōno, pŏsui, pŏsitum, 3. v.a. to put or lay to; to apply to; to add to; to serve up. [cause.

apporto, i. v.a. to carry, to bring to; to

appŏsĭtē, ad. appropriately.

appŏsĭtus, a, um, a. contiguous, near; fit, appropriate.

apprĕhendo, di, sum, 3. v.a. to seize, to lay hold of; to allege.

apprĭmē, adv. in particular, especially.

approbātio, ōnis, f. approbation; proof.

approbo, i. v.a. to approve; to prove; to confirm; to justify; to allow; to make good. [hurry.

apprŏpĕro, i. v.a. & n. to hasten, to

apprŏpinquātio, ōnis, f. approach, drawing near. [draw near.

apprŏpinquo, i. v.n. to approach, to

approprio, i. v.a. take to oneself, appropriate. [attack.

appugno, i. v.a. to fight against, to

appulsus, ūs, m. driving to; landing; approach; influence.

aprĭcātio, ōnis, f. a basking in the sun.

aprĭcor, i. v. dep. to sun oneself.

aprĭcus, a, um, a. exposed to the sun; sunny.

aprīlis, is, m. April. [sunny.

aprīnus, a, um, a. of a wild boar.

aptē, ad. closely; fitly, suitably.

apto, 1. v.a. to fit, to apply, to put on; to adjust; to prepare, to furnish.

aptus, a, um, p. & a. attached to; connected, suitable, adapted.

ăpŭd, pr. at the house of, at, by, near, with; among; in; before; in the time of;—apud se esse, to be in one's right mind.

ăqua, ae, f. water; rain; sea; lake; river;—aquæ, pl. springs, baths.

ăquæductus, ūs, m. conduit, aqueduct.

ăquæmānālis, is, m. washhand-basin.

ăquārius, a, um, a. relating to water; —, ii, m. water-carrier; water-bailiff; water-bearer (as a constellation).

ăquātĭcus, a, um, a. aquatic; watery, humid.

ăquātĭlis, e, a. aquatic. [watering-place.

ăquātĭo, ōnis, f. fetching of water;

ăquātor, ōris, m. water-carrier.

ăquĭfŏlium, i, n. holly tree.

ăquĭfŏlius, a, um, a. with pointed leaves.

ăquĭla, ae, f. eagle; standard of a Roman legion.

ăquĭlēgia (mod. hort.), columbine.

ăquĭlex, ĕgis, m. a water-inspector.

ăquĭlifer, ĕri, m. standard-bearer.

ăquĭlīnus, a, um, a. like an eagle, aquiline.

ăquĭlo, ōnis, m. north wind; north.

ăquĭlōnāris, e, a. northerly, northern.

ăquĭlōnius, a, um, a. northern.

ăquor, ātus, 1. v. dep. to fetch water.

ăquōsus, a, um, a. abounding in water, humid, rainy.

ăquŭla, ae, f. a small stream.

āra, ae, f. altar; sanctuary; home; refuge, shelter.

ărăbarches, ae, m. Egyptian tax-gatherer.

ărăbis (mod. hort.), rock-cress.

ărānea, ae, f. spider; cobweb.

ărāneōsus, a, um, a. covered with spiders' webs.

ărāneus, i, m. spider.

ărāneus, a, um, a. of a spider.

ărātĭo, ōnis, f. ploughing; agriculture; tilled ground.

ărātor, ōris, m. ploughman, farmer.

ărātrum, i, n. plough.

araucăria (mod. hort.), monkey-puzzle.

arbĭter, tri, m. hearer, eye-witness; umpire, arbiter, lord, master;—arbiter bibendi, master of the revels.

arbitra, æ, f. female witness.

arbĭtrārius, a, um, a. depending on (someone's) will.

arbĭtrātu..., ūs, m. arbitration; will, pleasure, choice; superintendence.

arbĭtrium, i, n. judgment of an arbitrator; sentence; will, mastery, authority.

arbĭtror, ātus, 1. v. dep. to observe, to perceive, to pass sentence; to believe, to think.

arbor, ōris, f. tree; mast; oar; ship.

arbŏrētum, i, n. plantation of trees.

arbŏreus, a, um, a. pertaining to a tree.

arbor vĭtæ (mod. hort.), thuya, arbor vitæ.

arbuscŭla, ae, f. shrub.

arbustum, i, n. plantation, grove of trees; shrub.

arbūteus, a, um, adj. of the strawberry tree. [strawberry tree.

arbūtum, i, n. wild strawberry; wild

arbūtus, i, wild strawberry tree.

arca, ae, f. chest, strong box, coffer; purse; coffin; prison-cell, ark.

arcāno, ad. secretly.

arcānum, i, secret, mystery.

arcānus, a, um, a. secret, hidden, mysterious.

arceo, cui, 2. v.a. to keep off, to prevent; to save, to protect.

arcĕra, ae, f. litter.

arcesso, īvi, ītum, 3. v.a. to send for, to call; to procure; to summons, accuse.

archĭĕpiscŏpus, i, archbishop.

archĭtectūra, ae, f. architecture.

archĭtectus, i, m. architect; inventor, author.

arcĭtĕnens, entis, a. holding a bow (epithet of Apollo), (constellation) the Archer.

arcte, arcto, arctuş. See arte, arto, artus.

arctos, i, f. the Great Bear or the Little Bear; the north.

arctŏus, a, um, adj. northern.

arctūrus, i, m. brightest star in the constellation Bootes.

arcŭla, ae, f. small box, casket.

arcuo, 1. to bend in the shape of a bow.

arcus, ūs, m. arch; bow; rainbow; anything arched or curved.

ardea, ae, f. heron.

ardĕlio, ōnis, m. busybody.

ardens, entis, p. & a. burning; glowing, fiery; eager, ardent.

ardenter, ad. ardently, eagerly.

ardeo, arsi, arsum, 2. v.n. to burn, to blaze; to flash; to glow, to sparkle; to be inflamed.

ardesco, arsi, 3. v.n. to take fire, to kindle; fig. to be inflamed.

ardor, ōris, m. fire, flame, heat; brightness; ardour, love, rage.

arduus, a, um, a. steep, high; difficult, arduous.

ārea, ae, f. open space; thrashing-floor; granary; courtyard; fig. field for enterprise.

ārĕfăcio, fēci, factum, 3 v.a. to dry up.

ărēna, ae, f. sand; sandy land or desert; seashore; place of contest, amphi-ărēnāria, ae, f. sand-pit. [theatre.

ărēnārius, i. gladiator.

ărēnōsus, a, um, a. sandy.

āreo, 2. v.n. to be dry; to be thirsty.

āresco, 3. v.n. to become dry.

argentāria, ae, f. banking-house; silver-mine.

argentārius, a, um, a. pertaining to silver or money; —, ii, m. money-changer, argentātus, a, um, a. silvered. [banker.

argenteus, a, um, a. of silver; silvery.

argentum, i, n. silver; silver plate; silver money.

argilla, ae, f. white clay, potter's earth.

argillāceus, a, um, a. clayey.

argillōsus, a, um, a. full of clay.

argūmentātio, ōnis, f. argumentation; proof.

argūmentor, atus, 1. v. dep. to prove by argument, to reason.

argūmentum, i, n. argument, proof; sub-ject, plot (of a play);—argumentum ad hominem, an appeal based on the circumstances of a particular in-dividual;—argumentum ad miseri-cordiam, an appeal to pity.

arguo, ui, ūtum, 3. v.a. to prove, to as-sert, to accuse; to censure; to con-vince.

argūtē, ad. acutely; craftily.

argūtiæ, ārum, f. pl. smartness; wit, shrewdness.

argūtus, a, um, a. in motion, bright, lively, active, sharp; melodious; dis-tinct, clear; sagacious, witty; cun-ning, sly.

ārĭdĭtas, ātis, f. dryness.

ārĭdum, i, dry land.

ārĭdus, a, um, a. dry, parched; barren; thirsty; poor; avaricious.

ărĭēs, ĭĕtis, m. ram; battering-ram; the Ram (in the zodiac).

ărĭĕtĭnus, a, um, a. of a ram.

ărĭĕto, 1. v a. & n. to butt like a ram; to strike violently.

ărista, ae, f. awn or beard of an ear of grain. [pipe

aristolochia (mod. hort.), Dutchman's

ărithmētĭca, ōrum, n. pl. arithmetic.

ărithmētĭcus, a, um, a. arithmetical.

arma, ōrum, n. pl. arms, weapons; tools; tackling; shield; soldiers, army; war; battle;—arma virumque cano, I sing of arms and the hero . . . the beginning of Vergil's Æneid;—vi et armis, by force of arms.

armāmenta, ōrum, n. pl. tackle of a ship.

armāmentārium, ii, n. arsenal, armoury.

armārium, ii, n. chest, safe.

armātūra, ae, f. armour, harness; armed armentālis, e, a. of cattle. [soldiers.

armentarius, ii, m. herdsman.

armentum, i, n. herd (of large cattle).

armĕria (mod. hort.), thrift.

armĭfĕr, a, um, armĭgĕr, a, um, a. armed, warlike; —, m. armed person; shield-bearer; adherent.

armilla, ae, f. bracelet.

armillum, i, n. vessel for wine.

armĭpŏtens, entis, a. powerful in arms, valiant, warlike. [arms.

armĭsōnus, a, um, a. resounding with

armo, 1. v.a. to equip; to arm; to kindle; to inflame. [shoulder.

armus, i, m. forequarter (of an animal),

ăro, 1. v.a. to plough, to till; to furrow, to wrinkle; to reap;—lītus arare, to plough the sand, perform a useless work.

ărōma, ătis, n. spice.

arquātus, a, um, a. arched;—arquatus morbus, jaundice. [wards.

arrēpo, psi, ptum, 3. v.n. to creep to-arrha or arra, ae, f., arrhăbō or arrăbō, ōnis, m. earnest-money.

arrĭdeo, rīsi, rīsum, 2. v.n. to smile upon; to be kindly disposed to; to please.

arrĭgo, rexi, rectum, 3. v.a. to set up-right, to raise; to animate, to rouse.

arrĭpio, rĭpui, reptum, 3. v.a. to snatch away; to take hold of; to hurry; to learn quickly; to appropriate; to arrest; to rail at. [nibble at.

arrōdo, rōsi, rōsum, 3. v.a. to gnaw or arrōgans, antis, p. & a. arrogant.

arrōganter, ad. arrogantly.

arrōgantia, ae, f. arrogance, conceit.

arrōgātio, ōnis, f. adoption.

arrōgo, 1. v.a. to ask, to question; to arrogate to one's self, to claim; to confer (upon).

ars, artis, f. skill; art; work of art; pro-fession; theory; manner of acting; cunning, artifice, hypocrisy.

ārsĭs, is, f. raising (of the voice).

artē, ad. closely, tightly, briefly.

artĕmisia, ae, f. southernwood.

artĕria, ae, f. windpipe; artery.

arthrītis, ĭdis, inflammation of the joints.

artĭcŭlātim, ad. piecemeal; distinctly.

artĭcŭlus, i, m. joint, knuckle; fig. mem-ber; moment; part, division; mo-ment of time;—in articulo mortis, at the very point of death.

artĭfex, ĭcis, m. artist, artificer; maker, author; —, a. skilful; artificial.

artĭfĭcĭōsē, ad. skilfully.

artĭfĭcĭōsus, a, um, a. skilful; ingenious; artificial.

artĭfĭcium, ii, n. handicraft, art, trade; skill; theory, system; cunning.

arto, 1. v.a. to compress, to contract; *fig.* to abridge, to limit.

artus, a, um, a. close, thick, narrow; short; strict; scanty, brief.

artŭs, uum, m. pl. joints; limbs.

ărŭla, æ, f. small altar.

arum (mod. hort.), cuckoo-pint.

ărundĭneus, a, um, a. of reeds; reedy.

ărundo, ĭnis, f. reed; angling rod; arrow-shaft; arrow; pen; flute; hobby-

aruspex, v. haruspex. [horse.

arvālis, e, a. of the fields;—Fratres Arvales, priests who made offerings for the fertility of the fields.

arvīna, ae, f. grease, fat.

arvum, i, n. arable field; country; land, shore; stretch of plain.

arvus, a, um, a. arable.

arx, arcis, f. stronghold, citadel; palace, the Capitol, summit at Rome; temple; *fig.* defence, refuge.

as, assis, m. a pound-weight divided into 12 ounces.

ăsărōtum, i, n. tesselated floor.

ascendo, ndi, nsum, 3. v.n. to mount up, to ascend. [an orator.

ascensio, ōnis, f. ascent; *fig.* soaring (of

ascensor, ōris, m. rider, driver.

ascensus, ūs, m. ascending, ascent; degree; approach.

ascia, ae, f. axe, hatchet. [admit.

ascio, 4. v.a. to take to *or* to associate, to

ascisco, ĭvi, ĭtum, 3. v.a. to receive, to admit, to approve, to associate; to appropriate, to adopt.

ascītus, a, um, p. & a. assumed, affected.

ascrībo, psi, ptum, 3. v.a. to add to in a writing; *fig.* to ascribe, to impute; to appoint; to enrol; to reckon, to number;—ascriptus glæbæ, bound to the soil (as a serf). [ized.

ascriptīcius, a, um, a. enrolled, natural-

ăsella, æ, f. she-ass.

ăsellus, i, m. little ass, ass's colt.

ăsīlus, i, m. horse-fly.

ăsīna, ae, f. she-ass.

Ăsināria, ae, f. name of a comedy of Plautus.

ăsĭnārius, a, um, a. of an ass.

ăsĭnīnus, a, um, a. of an ass.

ăsĭnus, i, m. ass; blockhead.

ăsōtus, i, m. debauchee.

aspărăgus, i, m. asparagus.

aspecto, 1. v.a. to look *or* gaze at; *fig.* to observe; (geographically) to look towards.

aspectus, ūs, m. looking at, glance, view; sight; horizon; appearance; aspect, mien.

aspello, 3. to drive away.

aspĕr, a, um, a. rough; uneven; harsh, sour; bitter; rude, violent, unkind, savage; wayward; austere; wild, fierce; critical, adverse.

aspĕrē, ad. roughly; severely, rudely.

aspergo, ersi, ersum, 3. v.a. to besprinkle; *fig.* to defile, to stain.

aspergo, ĭnis, f. besprinkling; spray.

aspĕrĭtas, ātis, f. roughness; severity; harshness; tartness; shrillness; fierceness.

aspernor, atus, 1. v. dep. to despise.

aspĕro, 1. v.a. to make rough; to sharpen; *fig.* to rouse up, to excite.

aspersio, ōnis, f. sprinkling.

asphŏdĕlus, i, m. asphodel.

aspicio, exi, ectum, 3. v.a. to look at, to behold; (geographically) to look towards; to consider, to contemplate.

aspĭdistra (mod. hort.), parlour palm.

aspīrātio, ōnis, f. exhalation; aspiration; sounding an 'h.'

aspiro, 1. v.a. to breathe *or* blow upon; to infuse; —, v.n. to breathe *or* blow upon; *fig.* to be favourable to; to assist; to aspire to.

aspis, ĭdis, f. asp, viper.

asplēnium, i, n. spleenwort.

asportātio, ōnis, f. carrying away.

asporto, 1. v.a. to carry away; to trans-

asprētum, i, n. rough ground. [port.

assa, ae, f. dry-nurse.

assa, ōrum, n. pl. sweat-bath.

assecla, assēcŭla, ae, m. attendant, servant; hanger on, sycophant.

assectātio, ōnis, f. waiting on, attendance.

assectātor, ōris, m. follower; disciple.

assector, atus, 1. v. dep. to accompany, to attend.

assensio, ōnis, f. assent, applause.

assensor, ōris, m. approver.

assensus, ūs, m. assent, approbation.

assentātio, ōnis, f. flattering.

assentātor, ōris, m. flatterer.

assentātrix, īcis, f. female flatterer.

assentĭor, sensus, 4. v. dep. to assent to, to approve. [comply with.

assentor, atus, 1. v. dep. to flatter, to

assēquor, sĕcūtus, 3. v.n. dep. to follow on, to pursue; to overtake; to gain, to attain to; to equal, to rival; to understand.

asser, ĕris, m. pole, post, stake.

assero, ĕrui, ertum, 3. v.a. to assert; to free; to claim; to deliver.

assertor, ōris, m. restorer of liberty; protector, advocate; champion.

asservo, 1. v.a. to keep, to preserve, to watch, to observe.

assessor, ōris, m. assessor, assistant.

asséveranter, ad. earnestly.
assévērātio, ōnis, f. affirmation, asseveration; rigour.
assévēro, 1. v.a. to act with earnestness; to assert strongly.
assídeo, sēdi, sessum, 2. v.n. to sit by; to be an assessor; to besiege; to resemble.
assído, sēdi, 3. v.n. to sit down.
assídué, ad. continually, constantly.
assiduïtas, ātis, f. attendance; assiduity, care; recurrence, repetition.
assiduus, a, um, a. assiduous; continual, unremitting.
assignātio, ōnis, f. assignment.
assigno, 1. v.a. to assign; to impute; to consign.
assílio, sílui, sultum, 4. v.n. to leap upon, to spring upon.
assimilis, e, a. similar, like.
assimŭlo, 1. v.a. & n. to make like; to compare; to counterfeit, to pretend, to feign.
assis, is, m., see as & axis.
assisto, astíti, 3. v.a. to stand at or by, to attend, to be present at.
assóleo, 2. v.n. def. to be accustomed or wont.   [custom.
assuēfăcio, fēci, factum, 3. v.a. to accustom (to); to be wont.
assuesco, ēvi, ētum, 3. v.a. & n. to accustom (to); to be wont.
assuētūdo, ĭnis, f. custom, habit.
assuētus, a, um, a. accustomed, customary, usual.
assŭla, ae, f. chip, splinter.
assŭlātim, ad. in bits, piecemeal.
assulto, 1. v.n. to jump at; to attack.
assultus, ūs, m. attack, assault.
assum, v. adsum.
assūmo, mpsi, mptum, 3. v.a. to take up, to adopt, to receive; to add to; to usurp, to arrogate.   [minor premiss.
assumptio, ōnis, f. adoption; choice;
assuo, 3. v.a. to sew or patch on.
assurgo, surrexi, surrectum, 3. v.n. to rise or stand up; to rise, to swell; to soar.
assus, a, um, a. roasted; dry, simple;—assa, ae, f. dry-nurse;—assa, orum, n. pl. sweat bath.
ast, c., see at.
aster, ĕris, m. aster.
astēriscus, i, m. asterisk.
asterno, 3. v.a. to strew upon, to stretch
asthmăticus, a, um, asthmatic.   [out.
astípŭlor, 1. v. dep. to agree with.
asto, stíti, 1. v.n. to stand at or by; to assist; to stand upright.
astrăgălus, i, m. milk-vetch.   [applaud.
astrēpo, ui, 1. to make a noise at, to
astricte, ad. concisely, briefly.   [stingy.
astrictus, a, um, a. tight, close, brief,

astringo, inxi, ictum, 3. v.a. to tighten, to bind or fasten; to oblige, to contract.
astrōlōgia, ae, f. astronomy, astrology.
astrōlōgus, i, m. astronomer, astrologer.
astrum, i, n. star, constellation; fig. immortality;—tollere, ferre ad astra, to raise to heaven, glorify;—sic itur ad astra, thus is the road to heaven won.
astruo, uxi, uctum, 3. v. to build near or to; fig. to add to; to furnish with.
astu, n. indecl. city (spec. Athens).
astŭpeo, 2. v.n. to be stunned or astonished (at).
astus, ūs, m. craft, cunning.
astūtē, ad. craftily, cunningly.
astūtia, ae, f. dexterity; cunning, slyness.   [cunning.
astūtus, a, um, a. clever, expert; sly,
ăsȳlum, i, n. place of refuge, sanctuary.
ăsyndĕton, i, n. a grammatical term expressing the absence of connecting particles, e.g. abiit, excessit, evasit, erupit.
ăt, ast, c. but, yet; but then; on the contrary; at least.
ătăt, i. oh! ah! alas! lo! wonderful!
ătāvus, i, m. great-great-grandfather's father, ancestor.   [mal, unlucky.
āter, tra, trum, a. black; gloomy, disātheos, i, m. atheist.
āthlēta, ae, m. wrestler, athlete.
athlēticus, a, um, a. athletic.
ătōmus, i, f. atom.
atque, c. and, and also, and even, and too; yet, nevertheless; after words expressing comparison, as, than.
atqui, c. but, yet, notwithstanding, however, rather, but now; and yet; well now.   [blacking.
ātrāmentum, i, n. writing-ink; shoe-
ātrātus, a, um, a. darkened; wearing mourning.
atriensis, is, m. steward.
atriŏlum, i, n. vestibule.
ātrium, ii, n. hall in a Roman house; palace; courtyard of a temple.
atrōcĭtas, ātis, f. fierceness; savageness, cruelty; severity.
atrōcĭter, ad. fiercely, cruelly, severely.
atrŏphia, ae, f. atrophy.
atrox, ōcis, a. savage, cruel, fierce, severe.
attactus, ūs, m. touch.
attăgen, ēnis, m. woodcock.
attămen, ad. but yet, but however, nevertheless.
attendo, endi, entum, 3. v.a. to turn towards; to apply; to mark; to attend to.
attentē, ad. diligently, carefully.
attentio, ōnis, f. attention.

attento, 1. v.a. to try, to attempt; to assail, to attack.

attentus, a, um, attentive; careful; industrious. [fected.

attĕnuātus, a, um, a. weakened; af-

attĕnuo, 1. v.a. to thin, to weaken, to lessen, to diminish.

attĕro, trīvi, trītum, 3. v.a. to rub against; to wear out, to impair.

attestor, 1. v. dep. bear witness to; to confirm.

Attĭcē, ad. in the Attic manner; elegantly. [elegant.

Attĭcus, a, um, a. Attic, Athenian; fine,

attĭneo, tĭnui, tentum, 2. v.a. & n. to hold on *or* fast; to delay; to reach to; to belong (to).

attingo, tĭgi, tactum, 3. v.a. to touch; to arrive at; to border upon; *fig.* to affect; to mention in passing; to undertake, to manage; to relate to.

attollo, 3. v.a. to lift up; to erect, to build; *fig.* to exalt; to extol.

attondeo, tondi, tonsum, 3. v.a. to clip, to prune.

attŏnĭtus, a, um, a. thunder-struck; stupefied, amazed; inspired, frenzied.

attŏno, ui, ĭtum, 1. v.a. to thunder at; to stun.

attorqueo, 2 v.a. to hurl upwards.

attrăho, xi, ctum, 3. v.a. to attract; to drag on.

attrecto, 1. v.a. to touch, to handle; to meddle with.

attrĭbuo, ui, ūtum, 3. v.a. to assign, to associate; to attribute *or* impute to.

attrĭbūtio, ōnis, f. assignment of a debt; predicate, attribute.

attrĭbūtum, i, n. predicate, attribute.

attrītus, a, um, a. worn away, wasted.

au, i, v. hau.

aubrētia (mod. hort.), purple rock-cress.

auceps, cŭpis, m. fowler; bird-seller; *fig.* caviller.

auctio, ōnis, f. public sale, auction.

auctiōnārius, a, um, a. pertaining to an auction. [public sale.

auctiōnor, atus, 1. v. dep. to put up to

auctĭficus, a, um, a. giving increase.

aucto, 1. v.a. to increase.

auctor, ōris, g.c. creator, maker, inventor; father; teacher; leader; founder, author; promoter; adviser; protector; witness; vendor; bail; guardian, champion. [ward.

auctōrāmentum, i, n. wages, pay; re-

auctōrĭtas, ātis, f. authority, power; reputation, credit; opinion, judgment; command; influence, importance; credibility. [to hire oneself.

auctōror, atus, 1. v. dep. to bind oneself,

auctumnālis, e, a. autumnal.

auctumnus, i, m. autumn.

auctus, a, um, p. & a. increased; great, abundant.

auctus, ūs, m. growth, increase.

aucŭpium, ii, n. bird-catching; lying in wait for; *fig.* quibbling.

aucŭpor, atus, 1. v. dep. to go a fowling; to lie in wait for.

audācia, ae, f. boldness; courage, valour; audacity. [ously.

audācĭtĕr, audactĕr, ad. boldly, courage-

audax, ācis, a. bold, courageous, audacious; desperate.

audens, entis, p. & a. daring, bold.

audenter, ad. boldly, courageously.

audentia, ae, f. boldness, courage. [ture.

audeo, ausus, 2. v.a. & n. to dare, to ven-

audiens, entis, m. hearer, auditor.

audientia, ae, f. hearing; audience, attention.

audio, īvi & ii, ītum, 4. v.a. to hear; to listen, to hearken; to regard; to grant; to obey;—**bene audire,** to be well spoken of;—**audi alteram partem,** listen to the other side.

audītio, ōnis, f. hearing; report, hearsay.

auditor, ōris, m. hearer, auditor; disciple.

auditōrium, ii, n. lecture-room.

audītus, ūs, m. hearing, listening; sense of hearing; report.

aufĕro, abstŭli, ablātum, auferre, v.a. to bear away; to snatch away; to carry off; to obtain; to destroy.

aufŭgio, fūgi, 3. v.n. to flee away *or* from.

augeo, auxi, auctum, 2. v.a. to increase, to augment; to extol. [come greater.

augesco, 3. v.n. to begin to grow, to be-

augmen, ĭnis, n. growth, increase.

augur, ŭris, c. augur; soothsayer.

augŭrālis, e, a. pertaining to augurs, relating to soothsaying.

augŭrātio, ōnis, f. divining.

augŭrāto, ad. after taking the auguries.

augŭrātus, ūs, m. office of an augur.

augŭrium, ii, n. profession of an augur, soothsaying.

augŭror, atus, 1. v. dep. to act as augur; to foretell; to conjecture.

Augustālis, e, a. of Augustus, Augustan.

augustē, ad. reverentially.

augustus, a, um, a. sacred, venerable; majestic, august; Augustan, imperial; —, m. August (month).

aula, ae, f. fore-court of a house; hall; palace; royal court; princely power; courtiers.

aulæum, i, n. curtain; canopy; tapestry.

aulĭcus, a, um, a. belonging to the court, princely; —, i, m. courtier.

aulŭla, æ, f. small pot.

Aulŭlāria, ae, f. name of a comedy of Plautus called after the money-pot of a miser.

aura, ae, f. air, gentle breeze; breath; wind; *fig.* gleam, glittering; odour, exhalation;—**superæ auræ,** the air of heaven;—**sub auras ferre,** to bring to the light of day;—**popularis aura,** the breath of popular favour.

aurārius, a, um, a. golden; gold.

aurātus. a, um, p. & a. gilt, golden.

aureŏlus, a, um, golden, splendid.

aureus, a, um, a. golden; gilded; shining rich; beautiful;—**aurea ætas,** the golden age;—**aurea mediocritas,** the golden mean.

aurĭcŏmus, a, um, a. golden-haired.

aurĭcŭla, ae, f. ear-lap.

aurĭfĕr, a, um, a. gold-bearing.

aurĭfex, ĭcis, m. goldsmith.

aurīga, ae, g.c. charioteer; helmsman; (a constellation) the waggoner.

auris, is, f. ear; hearing;—**aurem** *or* **aures præbēre,** to lend ear;—**auribus tenere lupum,** to hold the wolf by the ears, to catch a Tartar. [eared.

aurītus, a, um, a. hearing well; long-aurō a, ae, f. dawn, daybreak.

aurūgo, ĭnis, f. jaundice.

aurum, i, n. gold; gold plate; gold coin; colour of gold;—**auri sacra fames,** the cursed hunger for gold.

ausculto, 1. v.a. & n. to listen to; to overhear; to answer the door; to obey.

auspex, ĭcis, m. diviner by birds; soothsayer; leader; — **Teucro duce et auspice Teucro,** with Teucer for our guide, and Teucer for our leader.

auspĭcāto, ad. after taking the auspices; auspiciously.

auspĭcātus, a, um, p. & a. consecrated by auguries; favourable, auspicious.

auspĭcātus, ūs, m. divining, augury.

auspĭcium, ii, n. auspices; the right of taking auspices; *fig.* sign, omen.

auspĭcor, ātus, 1. v. dep. to take the auspices.

auster, tri, m. south wind; south.

austērē, ad. rigidly, severely.

austērĭtas, ātis, f. harshness; gloominess; severity.

austērus, a, um, a. austere; harsh; sour; sharp; rough, dark, stern.

austrālis, e, a. southern.

austrīnus, a, um, a. southern.

ausum, i, n. daring attempt, enterprise.

aut, c. or; or else, either;—**aut Cæsar aut nullus,** either Cæsar or nobody, the highest position or none.

autem, c. but; however; indeed; on the contrary.

autochthōnes, um, m. pl. original inhabitants of a country.

autogrăphus, a, um, adj. autograph.

autor, etc., v. **auctor,** etc.

autumnalis, etc., *see* **auctumnalis,** etc.

autŭmo, 1. v.n. say yes, affirm; say, **auxĭliāris, e,** a. auxiliary. [mention.

auxĭliārius, a, um, a. helping, auxiliary; —**milites auxiliarii,** auxiliary troops.

auxĭlior, ātus, 1. v. dep. to give aid, to assist. [auxiliary forces.

auxĭlium, ii, n. help, aid, assistance;

ăvārē, ad. greedily.

ăvārĭtia, ae, f. avarice.

ăvārus, a, um, a. avaricious, covetous.

ăvĕho, vexi, vectum, 3. v.a. to carry away;—**avehi,** to ride away.

ăvello, velli & vulsi, vulsum, 3. v.a. to pluck away, to tear off; to separate by force.

ăvēna, ae, f. oats; wild oats; stem stalk, straw; oaten pipe.

ăveo, 2. v.n. to be happy *or* in good health;—**ave,** hail! be of good cheer!

aveo, 2. v.a. to long for. [farewell!

ăverrunco, 1. v.a. to avert (something bad).

ăversor, ātus, 1. v. dep. to turn oneself away; to avoid, to repulse.

ăversor, ōris, m. embezzler.

ăversus, a, um, p. & a. turned away; averse; hostile; disinclined;—**aversus vulnerari,** to be wounded in the back.

ăverto, ti, sum, 3. v.a. to turn away from *or* aside; to steal, to embezzle; to divert, to estrange.

ăvia, æ, f. grandmother.

ăviārium, i, n. haunt of birds; aviary.

ăvidē, ad. eagerly, greedily.

ăvidĭtas, ātis, f. eagerness; avarice.

ăvidus, a, um, a. eager, greedy; avari-**ăvis, is,** f. bird; omen, portent. [cious.

ăvītus, a, um, a. ancestral; very ancient.

ăvius, a, um, a. out of the way; pathless; straying;—**avia,** n. pl. a pathless wilderness.

ăvŏcāmentum, i, n. a distraction.

ăvŏco, 1. v.a. to call off; to remove; to divert the mind.

ăvŏlo, 1. v.n. to fly away; to hasten away. [uncle.

ăvuncŭlus, i, m. (maternal) uncle; great-**ăvus, i,** m. grandfather; ancestor.

axamenta, orum, n. pl. ritual hymns sung by the Salii.

axilla, ae, f. arm-pit.

axis, is, m. axle; chariot; axis (of the earth); north pole; heaven; sky; region, climate; board, plank.

axungia, ae, f. carriage grease.

azālea (mod. hort.), azalea.

Bābæ, ĭ. wonderful!   [pearl.
bāca. bacca, ae, f. berry; olive-berry;
bācātus, a, um, a. strung with pearls.
Baccha *or* **Bacche, ae,** f. a Bacchante.
Bǎcchānālia, um, n. pl. Bacchanalian
   orgies, feast of Bacchus.
Bacchantes, um, f. pl. Bacchantes.
bacchǎr, ǎris, n. foxglove.
Bacchēus, a, um, a. bacchic.
Bacchĭcus, a, um, a. bacchic.
Bacchĭs, ĭdis, f. Bacchante.
Bacchĭus, a, um, a. bacchic.
bacchor, ātus, ɪ. v. dep. to celebrate the
   festival of Bacchus; to revel, to rave;
   to riot.
Bacchus, ĭ, m. the god of wine; *fig.*
   vine; wine.
bācǐfěr, a, um, a. berry-bearing.   [staff.
bǎcillum, ĭ, n. little staff, wand; lictor's
bǎcǔlum, ĭ, n. stick, walking-stick.
bājǔlus, ĭ, m. porter, carrier.
bǎlæna, æ, f. whale.
bǎlǎnus, ĭ, f. acorn; balsam; shell-fish.
bǎlatro, ōnis, m. buffoon.
bālātus, ūs, m. bleating of sheep.
balbus, a, um, a. stammering, stuttering.
balbūtio, 4. v.a. & n. to stammer, to
   stutter.
bal(l)ista, æ, f. large military engine for
   throwing stones and other missiles.
balneæ, ārum, f. pl., v. **balneum.**
balneāria, ōrum, n. pl. bathing-room;
   bath.
balneārius, a, um, a. pertaining to baths.
balneātor, ōris, m. bath-attendant.
balneum, ĭ, n. bath, place for bathing.
bālo, ɪ. v.n. to bleat;—**bālans, antis,** c.
   sheep.
balsǎmum, ĭ, n. balsam-tree, balm.
balteus, ĭ, m. belt; sword-belt; woman's
   girdle.
bambūsa (mod. hort.), bamboo.
baptisma, ătis, n. **baptismus, ĭ,** m.
   baptism.
baptistes, ae, m. baptizer, baptist.
baptistērium, ii, n. baptistery, font.
baptizo, ɪ, v.a. to baptize.
bǎrathrum, ĭ, n. abyss; whirlpool.
barba, ae, f. beard.
barbǎrē, ad. barbarously.
barbǎria, ae, f. foreign country; barbarousness; barbarism (in language);
   savageness.
barbǎrĭcus, a, um, a. outlandish; bar-
barbaries, v. barbaria.   [barous.
barbǎrus, a, um, a. foreign, barbarous;
   rude; cruel, savage; —, ĭ, m. foreigner, barbarian.   [beard.
barbǎtǔlus, a. um, a. having a small
barbātus, a, um, a. bearded; adult; —,
   ĭ, m. ancient Roman, sage.

barbĭtŏn, n., barbĭtŏs, m. & f. (without
   genitive) lyre, lute.
barbǔla, ae, f. little beard.
bardus, ĭ, m. Gallic bard.
bāro, ōnis, m. simpleton, block-head.
barrio, 4. v.n. to trumpet like an elephant.
barrus, ĭ, m. elephant.
bāsiātio, ōnis, f. a kiss.
basĭlica, ae, f. portico.
bāsĭliscus, ĭ, m. basilisk.
bāsio, ɪ. v.a. to kiss.   [wall.
bāsis, is, f. pedestal; base; foundation-
bāsium, ii, n. a kiss.
bătillum, ĭ, fire-shovel; chafing-dish.
Batrǎchŏmyŏmǎchia, ae, f. The battle of
   the frogs and the mice (a poem attri-
   buted to Homer).
beātē, ad. happily.
beātĭtas, ātis, beātĭtūdo, ĭnis, f. happiness, blessedness.
beātus, a, um, happy, blessed; wealthy;
   abundant; splendid;—**beati possidentes,**
   happy those in possession; possession
   is nine points of the law.
běgōnia (mod. hort.), begonia.
bellātor, ōris, m. warrior; —, a. warlike,
   valorous.   [warlike.
bellātrix, īcis, f. female warrior; —, a.
bellē, ad. finely, elegantly, well.
bellĭcōsus, a, um, a. fond of war, warlike.
bellĭcus, a, um a. pertaining to war,
   military; warlike.
bellĭgěr, a, um, a. waging war, martial.
bellĭgěro, ɪ. v.a. to wage or carry on war.
bellĭpŏtens, entis, a. powerful in war.
bellĭs, ĭdis, f. daisy.
bello, ɪ. v.n. (*also* **bellor, ɪ.**) to wage war,
bellua, v. belua.   [to war; to fight.
bellum, ĭ, n. war; combat, fight;—
   belli, at the wars.
bellus, a, um, a. handsome, pretty, neat,
   agreeable, polite.
bēlua, ae, f. beast; monster; *fig.* brute.
bēluōsus, a, um, a. abounding in beasts *or*
   monsters.
běně, ad. well, rightly, beautifully,
   pleasantly; in the nick of time.
běnědīco, xi, ctum, 3. v.n. & a. to speak
   well of; to bless, to consecrate.
běnědictio, ōnis, f. blessing, benediction.
běněfĭcentia, ae, f. beneficence.
běněfĭciārii, ōrum, m. pl. soldiers ex-
   empted from certain military services.
běněfĭcium, ii, n. benefit, kindness;
   favour, help; promotion.
běněfĭcus, a, um, a. beneficent.
běněvŏlē, ad. benevolently.
běněvŏlens, entis, a. benevolent, well-
   wishing, kind-hearted.
běněvŏlentia, ae, f. benevolence, good-
   will, kindness, favour.

bĕnĕvŏlus, a, um, a. well-wishing, kind, friendly, devoted.

bĕnignē, ad. kindly, benevolently; readily, willingly; generously.

bĕnignĭtas, ātis, f. good-heartedness, kindness, mildness; liberality, bounty.

bĕnignus, a, um, a. kind-hearted, mild, affable; liberal, bounteous; fruitful.

beo, 1. v.a. to make happy, to bless.

berbĕris (mod. hort.), barberry.

bēryllus, i, m. beryl.   [(= 8 ounces).

bēs, bessis, m. two-thirds of a thing

bestia, ae, f. beast; wild beast;—ad bestias condemnare, to condemn to fight with beasts in the arena.

bestiārius, i, m. fighter with wild beasts at public shows.

bestiŏla, ae, f. little beast.

bēta, ae, f. beet; beetroot.

bētŏnica, ae, f., v. vettonica.

bētŭla, ae, f. birch-tree.

bibliŏpōla, ae, m. bookseller.

bibliŏthēca, ae, f. library.

bibliŏthēcārius, ii, m. librarian.

bĭbo, bĭbi, bĭbĭtum, 3. v.a. to drink; to imbibe; to absorb, to suck up; fig. to drink in.

bĭbŭlus, a, um, a. fond of drinking, ever thirsty; soaking, spongy.

biceps, cĭpĭtis, a. two-headed; with two summits.

bĭcŏlor, ōris, a. of two colours.

bĭcorniger, i, the two-horned (god); epithet of Bacchus.

bĭcornis, e, a. two-horned; two-pronged.

bĭdens, entis, m. two-pronged fork.

bĭdens, entis, f. sheep.

bĭdental, ālis, n. place or object struck by lightning, and enclosed as sacred.

bĭduum, i, n. period of two days.

biennium, ii, n. period of two years.

bĭfāriam, ad. twice, doubly.

bĭfĕr, a, um, a. bearing fruit twice a year.

bĭfĭdus, a, um, a. cloven, forked.

bĭfŏris, e, a. having folding doors; bĭformis, e, a. two-shaped.   [double.

bĭfrons, ontis, a. with two foreheads or bĭfurcus, a, um, a. two-forked.   [faces.

bīga, ae, or bīgæ, arum, f. pl. two-horsed chariot.

bīgātus, i, m. a piece of money stamped with a representation of the bigae.

bignōnia (mod. hort.), bignonia, trumpet-flower.

bĭjŭgis, e, bĭjŭgus, a, um, a. two-horsed.

bĭlībris, e, a. weighing two pounds.

bĭlinguis, e, a. two-tongued; speaking two languages; double-tongued, hypo-critical.

bīlis, is, f. gall, bile; wrath, anger; madness.

bĭlustris, e, a. lasting two lustres, lasting 10 years.   [seas.

bĭmāris, e, a. situated between two

bĭmembris, e, a. having limbs of two kinds.

bĭmestris, e, a. two months old; lasting two months.   [years.

bīmus, a, um, a. two years old; for two

bīni, ae, a, two by two; two each.

bĭnōmĭnis, e, a. having two names.

bĭpartio, ītum, 4. v.a. to bisect.

bĭpartīto, ad. in two parts or ways.

bĭpātens, entis, a. opening two ways.

bĭpĕdālis, e, a. two feet long, wide or thick.

bĭpennĭfer, a, um, a. wielding a battle-axe.   [edged axe.

bĭpennis, e, a. two-edged; —, is, f. two-bĭpes, ĕdis, a. two-footed.

bĭrēmis, e, a. two-oared; —, is, f. galley with two banks of oars.

bĭs, ad. twice;—bis tantum, twice as much;—bis dat qui cito dat, he gives twice who gives quickly.

bīson, ontis, m. bison.

bĭsulcus, a, um, a. forked; cloven-bĭtūmen, ĭnis, n. bitumen.   [footed.

bĭvius, a, um, a. where two ways meet;—bĭvium, ii, n. a meeting-place of two roads.

blandē, ad. flatteringly, courteously, coaxingly.   [tery, charms.

blandīmentum, i, n. blandishment, flat-blandior, ītus, 4. v. dep. to flatter, to coax; to allure; to please.

blandĭtia, ae, f. flattering, compliment; —ae, pl. flatteries, courtship, dalliance.

blandŭlus, a, um, a. charming.

blandus, a, um, a. smooth; flattering; pleasant, alluring, charming;—notæ blandæ, love-letter.

blasphēmia, ae, f. blasphemy.

blasphēmo, 1. v.a. to blaspheme.

blasphēmus, i, m. blasphemer.

blătĕro, 1. v.a. to talk foolishly, to babble.

blatta, ae, f. cockroach; moth.

boa, ae, f. serpent; small-pox.

boārius, a, um, a. of oxen;—forum boarium, the cattle market.

bōlētus, i, m. mushroom.

bombus, i, m. buzzing.

bombȳcĭnus, a, um, silken.

bombyx, ȳcis, m. silk-worm.

bŏnĭtas, ātis, f. goodness; kindness, bene-volence.

bŏnum, i, n. good; wealth, goods; benefit; advantage; profit; endow-ment, virtue;—pro bono publico, for the public advantage;—cui bono? for whose advantage? who gains by it?—summum bonum, the highest good (philosophical term).

bŏnus, a, um, a. good; kind; beautiful; pleasant; right; useful; considerable; rich; virtuous; promising, happy; favourable; high, honourable;—**bona fide,** in good faith.

boo, I. v.n. to cry aloud, to roar.

bŏrāgo (mod. hort.), borage.

bŏreālis, e, a. northern;—**aurora borealis,** northern lights.

bŏreas, ae, m. north wind.

bŏrēus, a, um, bŏrīus, a, um, a. northern.

bōs, bŏvis, c. ox, bull; cow.

bŏvārius, v. **boarius.**

brācæ, ārum, f. pl. trousers, breeches.

brācātus, a, um, a. breeched; foreign, barbarian; effeminate.

brāchium, ii, n. arm; fore-arm; claw; bough, tendril; earthwork connecting fortified points; (poet.) sail-yard.

bractea, ae, f. gold-leaf.

brassica, ae, f. cabbage.

brĕviārium, ii, n. summary, abridgment.

brĕvĭlŏquentia, ae, f. brevity of speech.

brĕvis, e, a. short, little, brief; small; concise; shadow;—**brevia,** n. pl. shallows;—**brevi,** ad. briefly, in a few words;—**(in) brevi,** soon;—**brevi manu,** summarily.

brĕvitas, ātis, f. shortness; smallness; brevity.

brĕvĭter, ad. shortly, briefly.

briza (mod. hort.), quaking-grass.

brūma, ae, f. winter solstice; winter.

brūmālis, e, a. wintry.

brūtus, a, um, a. heavy, unwieldy; *fig.* dull, stupid;—**brutum fulmen,** a thunderbolt that misses its aim.

būbo, ōnis, m. long-horned owl.

būbulcus, i, m. ox-driver; ploughman.

būbŭlus, a, um, a. of oxen;—**būbŭla, ae,** beef.

bucca, ae, f. cheek.

buccŭla, ae, little cheek; beaver of a helmet.

būcĕrus, a, um, a. ox-horned.

bucina, ae, f. trumpet; war-trumpet; watch-horn.

bucinātor, ōris, m. trumpeter; proclaimer.

Būcōlĭca, ōrum, n. pl. pastoral poems.

būcōlĭcus, a, um, a. pastoral, bucolic.

būcŭla, ae, f. heifer.

būfo, ōnis, m. toad.

bulbus, i, m. bulb; onion.

bulla, ae, f. bubble; boss, knob, stud; an ornament worn by children.

bullātus, a, um, a. wearing a bulla.

būris, is, m. curved beam of the plough.

bustum, i, n. tomb, sepulchre.

būtŷrum, i, n. butter.

buxeus, a, um, a. made of box-wood.

buxĭfer, a, um, a. bearing box-trees.

buxum, i, n. box-wood; top; flute.

buxus, i, f. evergreen box-tree; box-wood; (poet.) flute.

byssĭnus, a, um, a. made of fine flax.

byssus, i, f. fine flax.

Căballus, i, m. jade, nag; pony.

căcăbus, i, m. cooking vessel.

căchinnātĭo, ōnis, f. violent, immoderate laughter.

căchinno, I. v.n. to laugh immoderately.

căchinnus, i, m. immoderate laughter.

căcoēthĕs, is, n. inordinate desire, itch;—**scribendi cacoethes,** the itch for writing.

căcozēlus, i, m. a faulty imitator.

cactus (mod. hort.), cactus.

căcula, ae, m. military servant.

căcūmen, ĭnis, n. tip, end; peak, summit.

căcūmĭno, I. v.a. to point.

cădāver, ĕris, n. dead body, corpse, carcass.

cădo, cĕcĭdi, cāsum 3. v.n. to fall (down, from); to be slain; to abate, to decay; to happen; to end, to close; to fall through, to fail.

cădūceātor, ōris, m. officer sent with a flag of truce.

cădūceum, i, n., **cădūceus, i,** m. herald's staff; wand of Mercury.

cădūcĭfer, a, um, a. bearing a herald's wand.

cădūcus, a, um, a. ready to fall; *fig.* frail, perishable, vain.

cădus, i, m. cask, jar, jug; funeral urn.

cæcĭtas, ātis, f. blindness.

cæco, I. v.a. to blind; *fig.* to obscure.

Cæcŭbum, i, n. Caecuban wine.

cæcus, a, um, a. blind; obscure; hidden, secret; confused; rash; vain, uncertain.

cædes, is, f. felling; slaughter; murder; persons slain.

cædo, cĕcĭdi, cæsum, 3. v.a. to fell, to hew; to cut; to slaughter; to murder.

cæduus, a, um, a. ripe for cutting.

cælātor, ōris, m. engraver.

cælātūra, ae, f. engraving.

cælebs, lĭbis, a. unmarried, single.

cælĕs, ĭtis, a. heavenly; —, m. a god.

cælestis, e, a. heavenly; divine; god-like; —**es,** m. pl. the gods.

cælĭcŏla, ae, c. inhabitant of heaven.

cælo, I. v.a. to engrave, to chase.

cælum, i, n. heaven; sky; climate, weather; height of happiness.

cælum, i, n. graving-tool.

cælus, i, m. (poet.), v. cælum.

cæmentum, i, n. rough stone; mortar, cement.

cæna, etc., v. cena, etc.

cænosus, a, um, a. muddy.

cænum, i, n. mud, filth.

cæpa, ae, f., cæpe, is, n. onion.

cærĕfŏlium, ii, n. chervil.

cærimōnia, ae, f. ritual; reverence, worship; sanctity.

cærŭl(e)us, a, um, a. dark blue; dark-coloured; dark green; azure; dark, sable. [beard.

cæsāries, ēi, f. head of hair; hair of the

cæsim, ad. by cutting; with the edge of the sword; fig. in short clauses.

cæspēs, ĭtis, m. turf, sod, sward; hut, hovel; altar.,

cæstus, ūs, m. boxing-glove.

cæsūra, ae, f. the break or pause in a line of verse.

cæterus, a, um, v. ceterus.

cætra, ae, v. cetra.

calamintha (mod. hort.), calamint.

călămister, tri, m. curling-iron; fig. flourish. [curling-iron.

călămistrātus, a, um, a. curled with the

călămĭtas, ātis, f. damage, loss, misfortune; defeat.

călămītes, æ, m. green frog.

călămĭtōsē, ad. unfortunately, miserably.

călămĭtōsus, a, um, a. calamitous; miserable; hurtful; damaged.

călămus, i, m. reed, cane; reed-pen; reed-pipe; arrow; angling-rod; stalk, stem, blade.

călăthus, i, m. wicker basket, flower basket; wool basket, fruit basket; milk-bowl; wine-cup; cup of a flower.

călātor, oris, m. servant.

calcar, āris, n. spur; fig. stimulus.

calceāmentum, i, n. shoe.

calceo, i. v.a. to put on shoes, to shoe.

calceŏlāria (mod. hort.), calceolaria, slipper-wort.

calceŏlārius, ii, m. shoemaker.

calceŏlus, i, m. half-boot.

calceus, i, m. shoe, half-boot.

calcĭtro, i. v.n. to kick; fig. to be refractory.

calco, i. v.a. to tread under foot; fig. to trample upon, to spurn, to despise.

calcŭlātor, ōris, m. one who counts on pebbles, arithmetician.

calcŭlus, i, m. pebble, stone used for reckoning, reckoning, calculation; chess-man.

caldārium, ii, n. hot-bath.

călĕfăcio, fēci, factum, 3. v.a. to warm, to heat; fig. to anger, to excite.

calĕfīo, ĕri, factus, v. pass. to be heated or warmed.

călendæ, v. kalendæ.

calendŭla (mod. hort.), marigold.

căleo, ui, 2. v.n. to be warm or hot, to glow; to be intent (upon); to be in love; to be excited.

călesco, 3. v.n. to grow warm or hot; to become inflamed.

calida, ae, f. hot water.

călĭdus, a, um, caldus, a, um, a. warm, hot; fig. fiery, eager; fierce.

călīga, ae, f. soldier's boot.

călĭgāris, e, călĭgārius, a, um, a. of a soldier's boot.

călĭgĭnōsus, a, um, a. foggy, dark.

călīgo, ĭnis, f. mist; fig. darkness, gloom; dulness; calamity.

călīgo, i. v.n. to be darkened; to cause darkness; to grope about.

Călĭgŭla, ae, f. little boot (of soldiers); nickname of the emperor who succeeded Tiberius.

călix, ĭcis, m. cup, goblet.

calleo, 2. v.n. to be callous; to be versed in; —, v.a. to know well, to understand. [ningly.

callidē, ad. shrewdly; expertly; cunning-

callĭdĭtas, ātis, f. shrewdness, skilfulness; slyness. [sly.

callĭdus, a, um, a. expert, skilful; crafty,

callis, is, m. narrow footpath, mountain-track.

callōsus, a, um, a. thick-skinned; hard.

callum, i, n. hardened skin; brawn; fig. callousness; lack of feeling.

călo, ōnis, m. soldier's boy; low servant.

călor, ōris, m. warmth, heat; fig. passion, zeal, ardour; love.

caltha, ae, f. marsh marigold.

călumnia, ae, f. sophistry; false accusation.

călumnĭātor, ōris, m. pettifogger.

călumnior, atus, i. v.a. dep. to cavil; to contrive false accusations; to depreciate.

călumnĭōsus, a, um, a. sophistical, false.

calvĭtium, ii, n. baldness.

calvus, a, um, a. bald.

calx, cis, f. heel.

calx, cis, f. chalk, limestone, goal (because the goal-line was marked with chalk).

calyc̣nthus (mod. hort.), all-spice.

călyx, ўcis, m. cup of a flower; egg-shell.

cămella, ae, f. cup.

camellia (mod. hort.), camellia.

cămēlŏpardălis, is, f. cămēlŏpardus, i, m. camelopard, giraffe.

cămēlus, i, m. camel, dromedary.

Cămēna, æ, f. Muse; poetry.

cămĕra, æ, f. vault, arched roof; flat ship with a covering of planks.

camīnus, i, m. smelting furnace, forge; fireplace. [bury bell.

campanula (mod. hort.), harebell, Canter-

campester, tris, tre, a. flat, level, open; of the Campus Martius.

campestre, is, n. wrestling apron.

campus, i, m. plain, field; field of battle; level surface; place for games, exercise, etc.;—Campus Martius, an open space by the side of the Tiber at Rome; fig. field of action.

cămus, a, um, a. crumpled.

cănālis, is, m. channel, conduit, canal.

cancellārius, ii, m. doorkeeper, secretary.

cancelli, ōrum, m. pl. railing, lattice; barrier; fig. boundaries, limits.

cancer, cri, m. crab; a sign of the zodiac; the south; the disease cancer.

candēla, ae, f. candle; waxed cord.

candēlābrum, i, n. candlestick, chandelier.

candens, dazzling, glowing.

candeo, ui, 2. v.n. to be of brilliant whiteness, to shine.

candesco, ui, 3. v.n. to begin to glisten; to begin to glow.

candĭco, I. v.n. to be white.

candĭdātus, i, m. candidate; fig. aspirant.

candĭdus, a, um, a. dazzling white, clear, bright; clean, spotless; candid, frank.

candor, ōris, m. dazzling whiteness, brightness; fairness, beauty; fig. candour, honesty.

cāneo, ui, 2. v.n. to be hoary.

cānesco, 3. v.n. to grow hoary; to grow old. [days.

cănĭcŭla, ae, f. little dog; dog-star, dog-

cănĭcŭlāris, e, a. of the dog-star.

cănīnus, a, um, a. canine; fig. abusive, snarling. [star.

cănis, is, c. dog; hound; parasite; dog-

cănistra, ōrum, n. pl. wicker basket.

cānĭties, ēi, f. hoariness; grey hair; old age.

canna, ae, f. reed, cane; reed-pipe.

cannăbis, is, f. cannăbum, i, n. hemp.

căno, cĕcĭni, cantum, 3. v.n. to sing; to crow; to sound; —, v.a. to sing, to recite; to celebrate in song or poetry; to prophesy; to blow (signals); to sound (for a retreat).

cănōn, ōnis, f. measuring-rod; fig. rule, discipline. The accepted scriptures.

cănŏnĭcus, a, um, a. regular, according to rule.

cănor, ōris, m. song tune.

cănōrus, a, um, a. melodious, harmonious; (as a fault in speaking) droning. [witched.

cantātus, a, um, a. enchanted, be-

canthăris, ĭdis, f. beetle; Spanish fly.

canthărus, i, m. jug, pot, wine-cup.

cant(h)ērius, ii, m. gelding;—in fossa, in a helpless condition.

cantĭcum, i, n. song; solo; ballad.

cantĭlēna, ae, f. old song; fig. gossip.

cantio, ōnis, f. incarnation, spell.

cantĭto, i, v.a. to sing over and over.

canto, I. v.n. to sing; fig. to drawl; —, v.a. to sing, to play, to recite; to praise; to forewarn; to enchant; to bewitch;—cantabit vacuus coram latrone viator, the traveller with nothing to lose can whistle before the highwayman.

cantor, ōris, m. singer; poet; eulogist.

cantrix, ĭcis, f. songstress.

cantus, ūs, m. song, poem; singing; melody; prophecy; incantation.

cānus, a, um. a. hoary, grey; foamy; old, aged;—cāni, orum, grey hairs.

căpācĭtas, ātis, f. capacity, largeness.

căpax, ācis, a. spacious, roomy; fig. capable, capacious.

căpēdo, ĭnis, f. a cup used in sacrifices.

căpella, ae, f. she-goat; kid.

căper, pri, m. he-goat.

căpesso, īvi, ītum, 3. v.a. to seize eagerly; to strive to reach; to manage; to undertake; to pursue with zeal.

căpillāmentum, i, n. false hair, wig.

căpillātus, a, um, a. hairy. [hair.

căpillus, i, m. hair of the head; brush of

căpio, cēpi, captum, 3. v.a. to take, to seize; to capture, to occupy; to get, to obtain; to captivate, to win over; to make choice of; to find out; to understand.

căpis, ĭdis, f. v. capedo.

căpistrum, i, n. halter, muzzle.

căpĭtāl(e), n. capital crime or the punishment due to it.

căpĭtālis, e, a. belonging to the head or life; deadly, mortal; dangerous; excellent, first-rate.

Căpĭtōlium, ii, n. the Capitol (at Rome).

căpĭtŭlātim, ad. by heads, summarily.

căpĭtŭlum, i, n. little head; chapter.

cappăris, is, f. cappări, n. the shrub that bears capers.

capra, ae, f. she-goat.

caprea, ae, f. wild she-goat.

capreŏlus, i, a young roebuck.

capricornus, i, m. Capricorn (a sign of the zodiac).

caprĭfīcus, i, f. wild fig-tree; wild fig.

caprifolium (mod. hort.), honeysuckle.
caprigĕnus, a, um, a. of goats.
caprile, is, n. stall for goats.
caprinus, a, um, a. pertaining to goats.
capripes, pĕdis, a. goat-footed.
capsa, ae, f. chest, case (for books).
capsicum (mod. hort.), cayenne pepper.
capsŭla, ae, f. small box or chest.
captātio, ōnis, f. aiming at; bickering.
captātor, ōris, m. legacy hunter.
captio, ōnis, f. deception, fraud; sophism; disadvantage.
captiōse, ad. captiously. [captious.
captiōsus, a, um, a. fallacious, deceptive,
captīvĭtas, ātis, f. captivity; capture.
captīvus, a, um, a. taken prisoner (in war, as booty); of captives; —, prisoner, captive.
capto, 1. v.a. to snatch, to endeavour to catch; fig. to strive after; to lie in wait for; to hunt legacies; to ensnare;—ad captandum, for the purpose of tripping up an opponent.
captus, ūs, m. power of comprehension, capacity. [sword-hilt.
căpŭlus, i, m. bier, tomb; handle;
căpŭt, ĭtis, n. head; top; end; source; beginning; principal point; mouth (of a river); article, chapter; life; person; civil rights; intelligence; author, leader, chief; capital city; capital as opposed to interest.
carbāseus, a, um, a. made of fine linen.
carbāsus, i, f. fine linen; sail; linen garment.
carbo, ōnis, m. charcoal; glowing coal.
carbuncŭlus, i, m. carbuncle (jewel or a tumour).
carcer, ĕris, m. prison, jail; barrier (in the circus); starting-point; beginning; jail-bird.
carchēsium, ii, drinking-cup.
carcinōma, atis, n. cancer, tumour.
cardamīne (mod. hort.), cuckoo flower.
cardămōmum, i, cardamon.
cardiăcus, a, um, a. of the stomach; suffering in the stomach.
cardĭnālis, e, a. principal, cardinal.
cardo, ĭnis, m. door-hinge; pole, axis; fig. chief point or circumstance.
carduēlis, is, f. goldfinch.
carduus, i, m. thistle.
cārē, ad. dearly, highly.
cărectum, i, n. sedge plot.
căreo, ui, ĭtum, 2. v.n. to be without, to want; to be absent from; to miss, to lose.
cārex, ĭcis, f. sheer-grass; sedge.
cāries, ēi, f. rottenness, decay.
cărīna, ae, f. bottom of a ship, keel;
cărĭōsus, a, um, a. rotten. [ship.

cārĭtas, ātis, f. dearness; dearth; love.
carmen, ĭnis, n. song, strain; poem; (in epic poetry) book, canto; oracle, prophecy; magic formula; formulary.
carnārium, ii, n. meat-safe; larder.
carnĭfex, ĭcis, m. executioner, hangman; murderer; scoundrel.
carnĭfĭcīna, ae, f. place of execution; torture. [pieces.
carnĭfĭco, 1. v.a. to behead; to cut in
carnĭvŏrus, a, um, a. feeding on flesh.
carnōsus, a, um, a. fleshy.
căro, carnis, f. flesh; meat; (in contempt) creature.
carpentum, i, n. two-wheeled carriage.
carpīnus, i, f. hornbeam.
carpo, psi, ptum, 3. v.a. to pick, to pluck (off); to gather; to browse; to tear off; to rob, to plunder; fig. to enjoy, to use; to slander; to weaken; to consume; to harass; to cut to pieces; —carpere viam or iter, to take one's [way.
carptim, ad. in detached parts.
carrāgo, ĭnis, f. barricade.
carrus, i, m. cart, waggon.
carthămus (mod. hort.), safflower.
cartĭlāgo, ĭnis, f. gristle, cartilage.
carum (mod. hort.), parsley.
cārus, a, um, a. dear, costly; precious, carya (mod. hort.), hickory. [loved.
căryātĭdes, um, f. pl. female figures used to support buildings in place of pillars.
căsa, ae, f. hut, cottage; shed.
cascus, a, um, a. old, primitive.
căseus, i, m. cheese.
căsĭa, ae, f. cinnamon.
cassē, ad. in vain.
casses, ium, m. pl. hunting-net, snare; cassĭa, v. casĭa. [cobweb.
cassĭda, ae, cassis, ĭdis, f. helmet.
cassus, a, um, a. empty; wanting, deprived of; vain, fruitless;—lumine cassus, robbed of light, dead;—in cassum, in vain.
castănea, ae, f. chestnut-tree; chestnut.
castē, ad. purely; chastely; piously.
castellāni, ōrum, m. pl. garrison of a fort.
castellum, i, n. castle, citadel; dwelling on a height; fig. shelter, refuge.
castīgātio, ōnis, f. punishment, correction.
castīgātor, ōris, m. corrector, reprover.
castīgo, 1. v.a. to chastise, to punish; to censure; to correct, to mend; to rein in, to restrain.
castĭmōnia, ae, f. chastity, abstinence; purity of morals.
castĭtas, ātis, f. chastity.
castor, ōris, m. beaver.
castŏreum, ei, n. aromatic secretion obtained from the beaver.

castratio, ōnis, f. castration.
castrensis, e, a. pertaining to the camp.
castro, i, v.a. to castrate; *fig.* to impair, to weaken.
castrum, i, n. castle, fortress;—**castra, ōrum,** n. pl. military camp; war-service; day's march;—**ponere castra,** to pitch camp;—**movere castra,** to break camp. [pious; sacred.
castus, a, um, a. pure; spotless; chaste;
cāsus, ūs, m. fall, overthrow; error; accident, chance; occasion; misfortune; death; (gram.) case;—**cāsū,** by chance, by accident;—**casus belli,** a case for war;—**casus fœderis,** a case for alliance.
cătaphractes *or* **ta, ae,** m. coat of mail.
cătaphractus, i, m. soldier armed in mail.
cătăpulta, ae, f. catapult.
cătăr(r)acta, ae, f. waterfall; portcullis.
cătasta, ae, f. platform where slaves were exhibited for sale.
cătē, ad. shrewdly.
cătēgoria, ae, f. in logic, a category, predicable, list of ideas.
cătella, ae, f. little chain.
cătellus, i, m. little dog, puppy, whelp.
cătēna, ae, f. chain; fetter; *fig.* barrier, restraint.
cătēnātus, a, um, a. chained, fettered.
căterva, ae, f. crowd; troop, company; flock. [masses.
cătervātim, ad. in troops; in disordered
căthēdra, ae, f. arm-chair; a professor's chair;—**ex cathedra,** (pronounced) from the chair of authority.
cătillus, i, m. small bowl or dish.
cătīnus, i, m. bowl, large dish, pot.
cătŭlus, i, m. young dog, puppy, whelp.
cătus, a, um, a. knowing, shrewd, wise;
cauda, ae, f. tail. [sly.
caudex, v. codex.
caulæ, ārum, f. pl. passage; sheepfold.
caulis, is, m. stalk; cabbage.
caupo, ōnis, m. huckster; innkeeper.
caupōna, ae, f. inn, tavern.
caupōnius, a, um, a. of an innkeeper.
caurus, v. corus.
causa, caussa, ae, f. cause, reason, motive; occasion; pretence; excuse; matter, subject; affair, business; process, suit; (political) party; blame, fault; connection, friendship; fit (of a sickness); condition, state; —, abl. on account of, for . . . sake;—**indicta causa,** with the case unexplained, without a hearing.
causia, ae, f. broad-brimmed hat.
causidicus, i, m. advocate.
causor, ātus, I. v. dep. to allege as an excuse; to pretend.

causŭla, ae, f. petty lawsuit.
cautē, ad. cautiously; with security.
cautēla, ae, f. precaution.
cautērium, ii, n. branding iron, cautery.
cautēs, is, f. rough pointed rock.
cautio, ōnis, f. caution, heedfulness; bond, security. [curity.
cautor, ōris, m. one who goes bail, se-
cautus, a, um, a. cautious, heedful; made safe, secured. [house.
căvædium, ii, n. quadrangle in a Roman
căvatus, a, um, a. hollowed out, hollow.
căvea, ae, f. enclosure, cage, coop; audience part of a theatre; theatre.
căveo, căvi, cautum, 2. v.n. to be on one's guard, to take care; beware of; to give security; to get security; to order or stipulate (by will, in writing);—**caveat emptor,** the buyer must look out for himself.
căverna, ae, f. cavern, grotto.
căvillātio, ōnis, f. quibbling, shuffling; banter, jeering.
căvillātor, ōris, m. scoffer, caviller.
căvillor, ātus, I. v. dep. to cavil at; to scoff, to jeer, to satirize.
căvo, I. v.a. to hollow out; to pierce through; to round off, to fabricate.
căvum, i, n., **căvus, i,** m. hole, cavity.
căvus, a, um, a. hollow, concave; deep-channelled.
cēdo, cessi, cessum, 3. v.n. to go, to walk; to turn out, to come to pass; fall to, devolve; to yield, to give way; to withdraw; to go off; to succeed;— v.a. to allow, to grant; to give up.
cĕdo, i. give here! pray! let us hear, tell!
cedronella (mod. hort.), balm of Gilead.
cedrus, i, f. cedar; cedar-oil.
cĕlĕber, bris, bre, a. much frequented, populous; renowned, famous.
cĕlĕbrātio, ōnis, f. throng; festival.
cĕlĕbrātus, a, um, a. usual, frequent; solemn, festive; celebrated.
cĕlĕbritas, ātis, f. concourse; solemnity; celebrity.
cĕlĕbro, I. v.a. to frequent; to do frequently; to repeat; to celebrate; to make known.
cĕler, ĕris, e, a. swift, quick; lively; hurried; rash, hasty.
cĕlĕres, um, m. pl. bodyguard of the Roman kings.
cĕlĕritas, ātis, f. swiftness, quickness.
cĕlĕriter, ad. quickly.
cĕlĕro, I. v.a. & n. to quicken, to accelerate; —, v.n. to make haste.
cĕlēs, ētis, m. racehorse; racing-boat.
cella, ae, f. cell; cellar; storehouse; pantry; shrine (in a temple), chapel; servants' room; honeycomb.

cēlo, 1. v.a. to hide, to conceal; to muffle up.

celosia (mod. hort.), cockscomb.

cĕlox, ōcis, f. cutter, yacht.

celsus, a, um, ad. high, lofty; *fig.* great, sublime; haughty.   [dinner.

cena, ae, f. dinner, supper, course for

cēnācŭlum, i, n. dining-room, upperroom, attic.

cēnātio, ōnis, f. dining-room.

cēnito, i, v.n. to dine often.

cēno, i, v.n. to dine, to sup, to dine on.

cēnŏtăphium, ii, n. cenotaph, empty tomb.

censeo, ui, censum, 2. v.a. to count, to reckon; to tax, to assess; to estimate, to value; to think, to be of opinion; to decree; to vote to.   [critic.

censor, ōris, m. censor; *fig.* censurer,

censōrius, a, um, ad. pertaining to the censor; *fig.* rigid, severe.

censūra, ae, f. censorship; judgment, opinion.

census, ūs, m. valuation of every Roman citizen's estate; registering of a man (his age, family, profession, etc.); sum assessed; property; mustering of the people.   [taury.

centaurēa (mod. hort.), cornflower, cen-

centaurēum, i, n. centaury.

centēnārius, a, um, a. consisting of a hundred.

centēni, ae, a, a. a hundred each.

centēsĭma, ae, f. hundredth part.

centēsĭmus, a, um, a. the hundredth.

centĭceps, cĭpĭtis, a. hundred-headed.

centies, ad. a hundred times.

centĭmănus, ūs, a. hundred-handed.

centĭpĕda, ae, f. centipede.

centĭpes, pĕdis, a. hundred-footed.

cento, ōnis, m. patched clothes.

centrum, i, n. centre.

centum, a. indecl. a hundred.

centumvĭri, ōrum, m. pl. a panel of judges chosen annually to decide civil suits.

centuplex, ĭcis, a. hundredfold.

centŭria, ae, f. century, company of 100 men; political century.

centŭriātim, ad. by centuries.

centŭrio, 1. v.a. to divide into centuries; —comitia centuriata, the assembly in which the Romans voted by centuries.

centŭrio, ōnis, m. commander of a century, captain, centurion.

cepa, v cæpa.

cēra, ae, f. wax; wax-covered writingtablet; letter; seal of wax; waxen image.

cĕrastes, ae, *or* is, m. horned serpent.

cĕrăsus, i, f. cherry-tree; cherry.

cerdo, ōnis, m. a. mechanic, artisan.

cĕreālis, e, a. of Ceres, of corn;—Cĕreālia, ium, n. pl. the festival of Ceres.

cĕrĕbellum, i, n. small brain.   [anger.

cĕrĕbrum, i, n. brain; *fig.* understanding,

Cĕrēs, ĕris, f. goddess of agriculture; *fig.* bread, fruit, corn.

cēreus, a, um, a. waxen; wax-coloured; pliant, soft; —, i, m. wax-taper.

cerno, crēvi, crētum, 3. v.a. to sift; *fig.* to discern, to perceive; to foresee; to decide; to determine; to resolve; to enter upon (a legacy).   [wards.

cernuus, a, um, a. prone, stooping for-

cēro, 1. v.a. to wax.   [wrestlers contend.

cērōma, ătis, n. wrestler's oil; place where

cerrītus, a, um, a. frantic, mad.

certāmen, ĭnis, n. contest, struggle; battle, rivalry, combat.

certātim, ad. emulously, earnestly.

certātio, ōnis, f. striving, contest.

certē, ad. certainly, surely; really; yet indeed, at least.

certo, ad. certainly, surely.

certo, 1. v.a. to fight, to contend; to strive, to emulate; to contend at law.

certus, a, um, a. certain; sure, safe; distinct; fixed, agreed upon; steady, resolute; constant, faithful; unerring;—certus eundi, determined to go;—pro certo scire, to know for certain;—certior fieri, to be informed;—certiorem facere, to inform.   [pencil.

cērula, ae, f. little piece of wax; red

cērussa, ae, f. white-lead, ceruse.

cerva, ae, f. hind, doe; deer.

cervĭcal, ālis, n. pillow.

cervīnus, a, um, a. pertaining to a stag.

cervisia, ae, f. beer.

cervix, ĭcis, f. neck, nape.   [de frise.

cervus, i, m. hart, stag;—cervi, chevaux

cespes, v. cæspes.

cessātio, ōnis, f. cessation; idleness.

cessātor, ōris, m. loiterer, idler.

cesso, 1. v.n. to leave off, to delay, to loiter; to cease (from); to idle; to be wanting; *fig.* to go wrong.

cestus, i, m. belt; the girdle of Venus.

cētārium, ii, fish-pond.

cētārius, ii, m. fish-monger.

cētĕrā, ad. as to the rest, otherwise.

cētĕrōqui(n), ad. in other respects, otherwise.

cētĕrum, ad. for the rest; but; besides.

cētĕrus, a, um, a. the other;—ceteri, pl. the others, the rest;—et cetera, n. pl. and so forth;—ceteris paribus, other things being equal.

cetos, v. cetus.

cētra, ae, f. short Spanish leather-shield.

cētrātus, a, um, a. armed with a light shield.

cētus, i, m. whale; shark; dolphin.

ceu, ad. as, just as; as if.   [ore.

chalcītes, ae, m. chalchītis, ĭdis, f. copper

chălybs, ўbis, m. steel.

chălўbēius, a, um, a. of steel.

chămæleon, ōnis or ontis, m. chameleon.

chămæmēlon, i, n. camomile.

Chaos (accus. Chaos, abl. Chao), n. in finite space; pit of the Lower World; confused, shapeless mass, chaos.

chăracter, ēris, m. mark; characteristic; style.

chăristia, ōrum, n. pl. feast of reconciliation and love among kinsfolks.

charta, ae, f. (leaf of) paper; letter; writing; poem; book; plate.

chartula, ae, f. scrap of paper, bill.

cheiranthus (mod. hort.), wallflower, gilliflower.

Chelæ, ārum, f. pl. the claws of Scorpio (astronomical name).

chēlĭdōnia, æ, f. celandine.

chelydrus, i, m. water-snake.

chĕlys (accus. —yn), f. lyre.   [hand.

chīragra, ae, chĕragra, ae, f. gout in the

chīrogrăphum, i, n. autograph; bond, surety.

chīrŏnŏmus, i, m. pantomime actor.

chīrurgia, æ, f. surgery.

Chīum, i, n. Chian wine.   [state mantle.

chlămys, ўdis, f. Grecian military cloak;

chŏraules, ae, m. one who accompanies a dance on the flute.

chorda, ae, f. gut-string, string, lute-

chŏrēa, ae, f. dance.   [string.

chŏrēus, i, m. a long syllable followed by a short.

chŏriambus, i, m. a choreus followed by an iambus, i.e. one long syllable followed by two shorts and a long.

chŏrus, i, m. dance; chorus, choir; crowd, multitude.

chrŏnĭcus, a, um, a. chronic, lingering, as opposed to acute.   [themum.

chrysanthĕmum (mod. hort.), chrysan-

chrўsŏlĭthus, i, c. topaz.

chrўsoprăsus, i, m. chrysoprase (a jewel).

cībāria, ōrum, n. pl. food, victuals, provisions, fodder.

cībārius, a, um, a. ordinary, common; coarse (bread).

cībōrium, ii, n. drinking-cup.

cībus, i, m. food; fare.

cicāda, æ, f. cricket, cicada.

cicătrix, īcis, f. scar, cicatrice.

cicer, ĕris, n. chick-pea.

cichŏrēum, i, n. chicory; endive.

cicindēla, æ, f. glow-worm.

cicōnia, æ, f. stork.

cĭcur, ŭris, a. tame.

cicūta, æ, f. hemlock; shepherd's pipe.

cieo, cīvi, cītum, 2. v.a. to move; to shake; to rouse; to disturb; to provoke; to call on, invoke; to cause, to

cīmex, īcis, m. bug.   [produce.

cincinnātus, a. with curled hair.

cincinnus, i, m. curled hair; fig. rhetorical flourish.

cinctus, ūs, m. girding;—cinctus Gabinus, a way of girding up the toga.

cinctūtus, a, um, a. girded up, ancient.

cingo, xi, nctum, 3. v.a. to gird; to surround; to beleaguer; to crown;—cingor, to make oneself ready.

cingŭlum, i, n. girdle; sword-belt.

cinĭflo, ōnis, m. hair-curler (a slave).

cinis, ĕris, m. ashes; ruins.

cĭnnābăris, is, f. cinnabar.

cinnăm(ōm)um, i, n. cinnamon.

cippus, i, m. pointed stake; palisade; tombstone.

circā, ad. (all) around; everywhere; —, pr. about, near to; concerning.

circenses, m. pl. games and exercises of wrestling, running, fighting, etc., in the circus;—panem et —, food and shows.

circĭno, I. v.a. to round.

circĭnus, i, m. pair of compasses.

circĭter, ad. & pr. about, near; towards.

circuĭtio, ōnis, f. a going round; patrol; fig. circumlocution.

circuĭtus, ūs, m. going round, circuit; way round; circumference; fig. circumlocution.   [groups.

circŭlor, atus, I. v. dep. to form in

circŭlus, i, m. circle; orbit; ring, hoop, chain; company.

circum, ad. (all) around, about; —, pr. around, about, among; at, near.

circumăgo, ēgi, actum, 3. v.a. to drive in a circle, to turn round; to wheel; to pursue.

circumcīdo, cīdi, cīsum, 3. v.a. to cut around, to clip; to circumcise; fig. to abridge, to diminish.

circumcīsio, onis, f. circumcision.

circumclūdo, si, sum, 3. v.a. to enclose on all sides.

circumcŏlo, 3. v.a. to dwell round about.

circumdo, dĕdi, dătum, I. v.a. to put round; to surround; to enclose.

circumdūco, xi, ctum, 3. v.a. to lead or draw around; to lead out of the way; to cheat; to cancel.

circumeo or circuĕo, ivi & ii, circuitum, 4. v.n. & a. to go or march around; to encompass; to go about canvassing; fig. to circumvent.

circumfĕro, tŭli, lātum, ferre, 3. v.a. to carry about or round; to spread about, to divulge; to purify by lustration; to roll (one's eyes).

circumfluo, xi, 3. v.n. & a. to flow round; to overflow with; to be rich in.

circumflŭus, a, um, a. circumfluent, surrounding; surrounded with water.

circumfŏrāneus, a, um, a. all around the market or forum; strolling about from market to market; borrowed from the bankers.

circumfundo, fūdi, fūsum, 3. v.a. to pour around;—**circumfundor,** to flow round, to crowd around, to press upon; to surround. [round, to surround.

circumgrĕdior, gressus, 3. v. dep. to walk

circumjăceo, 2. v.n. to lie round about.

circumjectus, us, m. encompassing, embrace.

circumjĭcio, jēci, jectum, 3. v.a. to cast or place around; to encompass with; —**circumjectus, a, um,** surrounding.

circumlĭgo, 1. v.a. to bind round or to; to encompass.

circumlĭnio, lĭtum, 3. v.a. (**circumlinio,** 4.) to smear all over; fig. to lard (a discourse).

circumlŏcūtio, onis, f. circumlocution.

circumluo, 3. v.a. to wash or flow around. [send around.

circummitto, mīsi, missum, 3. v.a. to

circummūnio, īvi, ītum, 4. v.a. to wall around, to fortify.

circummūnītio, ōnis, f. circumvallation.

circumplector, plexus, 3. v. dep. to embrace, to surround: to circumvallate.

circumplĭco, 1. v.a. to twine around.

circumpōno, sui, sĭtum, 3. v.a. to put or place around.

circumrētio, tĭtum, 4. v.a. to ensnare.

circumrōdo, si, 3. v.a. to gnaw all round; fig. to slander. [to enclose.

circumsæpio, psi, ptum, to fence round,

circumscrībo, psi, ptum, 3. v.a. to draw a line around; fig. to circumscribe; to hem in; to cheat, to entrap; to cancel, to annul. [term).

circumscriptē, ad. in periods (rhetorical

circumscriptio, ōnis, f. encircling; circle; boundary; outline; deceiving; (rhetorical) period.

circumscriptor, ōris, m. cheat; defrauder.

circumsĕco, sectus, 1. v.a. to cut around.

circumsĕdeo, ēdi, essum, 2. v.a. to sit around; to besiege.

circumsĭdo, 3. v.a. to besiege.

circumsisto, stĕti, 3. v.a. to stand round.

circumsŏno, 1. v.n. & a. to resound on every side, to ring again with; to echo round.

circumspectē, ad. cautiously.

circumspectio, onis, f. caution.

circumspecto, 1. v.a. to look about searchingly.

circumspectus, a, um, a. circumspect, cautious; wary.

circumspĭcio, exi, ectum, 3. v.n. & a. to look about; to be on the watch, to take heed; —, v.a. to survey; to seek for. [round; to surround.

circumsto, stĕti, 1. v.n. & a. to stand

circumstrĕpo, pĭtum, 3. v.a. to make a noise around.

circumvādo, si, 3. v.n. to attack, to harass.

circumvăgus, a, um, a. flowing around.

circumvallo, 1. v.a. to circumvallate.

circumvectio, ōnis, f. circuit, revolution.

circumvector, atus, 1. v. dep. to sail round, to traverse, to describe.

circumvĕhor, vectus, 3. v. dep. to ride around; to sail around; to describe in detail.

circumvĕnio, vēni, ventum, 4. v.a. to come round; to surround; to beat; to oppress; fig. to circumvent.

circumvōlĭto, 1. v.n. & a. to flutter around.

circumvŏlo, 1. v.a. to fly around.

circumvolvo, vŏlūtum, 3. v.a. to roll round, to twine around.

circus, i, m. circle; circus (at Rome).

cirrātus, a, um, a. having ringlets.

cirrus, i, m. curl, ringlet.

cis, pr. on this side (of); within.

Cisalpinus, a, um, a. lying on the south side of the Alps.

cĭsium, ii, n. two-wheeled carriage.

cista, ae, f. chest, box.

cistella, ae, f. small chest.

Cistellāria, ae, f. a play of Plautus in which a small chest of jewels plays a part.

cisterna, ae, f. cistern.

cistŏphŏrus, i, m. an Asiatic coin worth about 3s.

cistus (mod. hort.) rock-rose.

cĭtātus, a, um, a. quick, rapid;—**equo citato,** at full gallop.

cĭtĕrior, us, a. on this side, hithermost; nearer. [the guitar.

cĭthăra, ae, f. guitar; art of playing

cĭthărista, ae, m. guitar-player. [guitar.

cĭthărœdus, i, m, one who sings to the

cĭtĭmus, a, um, a. nearest, next.

cĭtŏ, ad. comp. **cĭtius;** sup. **cĭtissime,** soon; quickly;—**serius aut citius,** sooner or later.

cĭto, 1. v.a. to cite; to recite; to summon; to excite; to encourage; to cause.

citrā, pr. & a. on this side; within, short of; without, apart from, except.

citreus, a, um, a. of citron.

citrō, ad. to this side, hither;—**ultro citroque,** to and fro; in and out.

citrus, i, f. citron, orange, lemon-tree.

cĭtus, a, um, a. quick. swift, rapid.

civĭcus, a, um, a. civic, civil; pertaining to the state;—civĭca corona, a crown of oak leaves presented to one who had saved a fellow-countryman in war.

civīlis, e, a. civic, civil; political, public, polite, courteous;—jus civile, law relating to the private rights of a citizen.

civīlĭter, ad. citizen-like; kindly, courteously.   [woman.

civis, is, c. citizen; countryman or civĭtas, ātis, f. citizenship; citizens; city; state; Rome.

clādes, is, f. defeat; destruction; ruin; plague; slaughter.

clam, ad. & pr. secretly; unknown to.

clāmātor, oris, m. declaimer.

clāmĭto, 1. v.n. to bawl out, to vociferate.

clāmo, 1. v.n. to call; to cry, to complain, to call upon.

clāmor, ōris, m. shout, cry, clamour; applause; noise, din.

clancŭlum, ad. & pr. secretly, without the knowledge of.   [destine.

clandestīnus, a, um, secret, hidden, clanclangor, oris, m. clang, noise.

clārē, ad. brightly; clearly; aloud; intelligibly.

clāreo, 2. v.n. to shine; to be illustrious.

clāresco, ui, 3. v.n. to begin to shine; to become audible; to become clear or evident; to become famous.

clāritas, ātis, clārĭtūdo, ĭnis, f. clearness, brightness; distinctness; celebrity; renown.   [illustrious.

clāro, 1. v.a. fig. to brighten, to make clārus, a, um, a. clear, bright; loud, distinct; evident; illustrious, famous.

classiārius, i, m. mariner; sailor, seaman; pl. naval forces.

classĭcum, i, n. sound of a trumpet; signal of battle; trumpet.

classĭcus, a, um, a. belonging to the fleet; belonging to the highest class; classic.

classis, is, f. class of the Roman people; division; army; fleet.

clāthri, orum, m. pl. grating.

claudeo, 2. or claudo, sum, 3. v.n. to limp, to halt; fig. to be weak.

claudĭco, 1. v.n. to limp, to be lame; fig. to waver, to be defective.

claudo, si, sum, 3. v.a. to shut, to close; to conclude; to finish; to enclose; to imprison; to surround; to besiege.

claudo, 3. v.n., v. claudeo.

claudus, a, um, a. limping, lame; fig. defective, wavering, uncertain.

claustra, ōrum, n. pl. enclosure; barrier; door, gate; bulwark; dam.

clausŭla, ae, f. conclusion, end; close of a period.

clausum, i, n. enclosure; confinement.

clāva, ae, f. cudgel, club.   [vine.

clāvicŭla, ae, f. small key; tendril of a clāvĭgĕr, i, m. club-bearer; key-bearer.

clāvis, is, f. key.

clāvus, i, m. nail; tiller of a rudder; rudder;—latus clavus, a broad purple stripe worn on the robes of senators.

clēmātis, ĭdis, f. clematis, virgin's bower.

clēmens, entis, a. merciful, gentle, mild; quiet, peaceable; courteous; moderate.   [calmly; mercifully.

clēmenter, ad. gently, softly, mildly; clēmentĭa, ae, f. clemency, mercy; mildness; calmness; courtesy.

clēpo, psi, ptum, 3. v.a. to steal.

clepsydra, ae, f. water-clock.

cliens, entis, c. client; vassal; dependent.

clienta, ae, f. female client.

clientēla, ae, f. clientship; vassalage; patronage; clients; vassals; alliance.

clīmacter, eris, m. a certain period of time at the close of which the body suffers some great change; a climacteric.

clīmax, ăcis, f. climax (rhetorical term).

clīnĭce, es, f. attendance at a sick-bed, the art of prescribing.

clīnĭcus, i, m. a doctor who attends a patient in bed.

clĭpeātus, a, um, furnished with a shield.

clĭpeus, i, m. round, brazen shield; disk of the sun.

clītellæ, ārum, f. pl. pack-saddle.

clīvōsus, a, um, a. hilly, steep.

clīvus, i, m. declivity; height, hill.

cloāca, æ, f. sewer, drain.

clueo, 2. to be called, to be named, to be reputed.

clūnis, is, c. buttock, haunch.

clyster, eris, m. an injection; syringe.

coăcervātĭo, ōnis, f. heaping together or up.

coăcervo, 1. v.a. to heap together or up.

coăcesco, ăcui, 3. v.n. to become sour, to become corrupt.

coactor, ōris, m. collector; enforcer.

coactum, i, n. coverlet of stout cloth.

coaequo, 1. v.a. to equalize.

coagmentātĭo, ōnis, f. combination, union.

coagmento, 1. v.a. to join, to connect; to conclude.

coagmentum, i, n. joint.

coăgŭlo, 1. v.a. to curdle.

coăgŭlum, i, n. rennet, runnet.

coălesco, ălŭi, ălĭtum, 3. v.n. to grow together; to close; to curdle.   [press.

coangusto, 1. v.a. fig. to limit, to compel.

coarguo, ŭi, 3. v.a. to prove, to convince; to reprove; to refute.

coar(c)to, 1. v.a. to press together, to straiten; *fig.* to abridge.

coaxo, 1. v.n. to croak (like a frog).

coccineus, a, um, coccinus, a, um, a. scarlet-coloured.

coccum, i, n. berry of the scarlet oak; scarlet colour; scarlet cloth.

cochlea, ae, f. snail.

cochlear, āris, n. spoon; spoonful.

cochleāria (mod. hort.), horse-radish.

cocos (mod. hort.), cocoanut palm.

coctilis, e, a. baked (of bricks), built of baked bricks.

cōdex, icis, m. trunk of a tree; piece of wood; (bound) book; account-book.

cōdicillus, i, m. little book; short note *or* writing, billet; little writing-tablet; coelo, v. cælo, etc.   [codicil.

coëmo, ēmi, emptum, 3. v.a. to buy up.

coëmptio, ōnis, f. a pretended purchase (legal term), a marriage ceremony.

coena, v. cena, etc.

coenosus, v. cænosus.

coenum, v. cænum.

coeo, īvi & ii, ĭtum, 4. v.n. to go *or* come together, to meet, to clash; to assemble; to cohabit; to conspire; to agree; to curdle; to heal; to unite.

coepio, coepi, coeptum, 3. v.a. & n. to begin, to undertake.

coepto, 1. v.a. & n. to begin, to attempt.

coeptum, i, n. beginning, undertaking.

coerceo, cui, cĭtum, 2. v.a. to enclose; to limit; to correct, to punish; to bridle; to restrain; to keep in awe.

coercĭtio, ōnis, f. coercion, restraint; chastisement.   [pany.

coetus, ūs, m. meeting, assemblage, com-coffēa (mod. hort.), coffee tree.   [sive.

cōgĭtābundus, a, um, a. thoughtful, pen-cōgĭtātio, ōnis, f.** thinking, meditation; thought; intention; plan; opinion; reasoning power.

cōgĭto, 1. v.a. to consider, to ponder, to think; to meditate; to intend.

cognātio, ōnis, f. relationship by birth; relatives, family; *fig.* resemblance, affinity.

cognātus, a, um, a. related by birth; *fig.* related; similar; —, g.c. kinsman, kinswoman.

cognĭtio, ōnis, f. knowledge; judgment; idea, notion; examination, inquiry.

cognĭtor, ōris, m. attorney; witness; voucher.

cognōmen, ĭnis, n. family name; epithet.

cognōmentum, i, n. surname; name.

cognōminis, e, a. of the same name.

cognōmino, 1. v.a. to give a surname.

cognosco, gnōvi, gnĭtum, 3. v.a. to learn; to inform oneself: to know; to

understand; to investigate; to observe, to perceive; to identify.

cōgo, cōēgi, cōactum, 3. v.a. to drive together; to collect; to bring up; to curdle; to force, to compel; to infer, to conclude.

cohæreo, si, sum, 2. v.n. to adhere (to); to stick together; *fig.* to be consistent.

cohæresco, si, 3. v.n. to cohere.

cohērēs, ēdis, c. co-heir, joint-heir.

cohĭbeo, ui, ĭtum, 2. v.a. to hold together; to restrain; to curb; to hinder; to confine.

cŏhŏnesto, i, v.a. to honour, to grace.

cŏhorresco, ui, 3. v.n. to shudder.

cŏhors, rtis, f. cattle-yard; (mil.) cohort; bodyguard; attendants.

cŏhortātio, onis, f. exhortation, encouragement.

cŏhortor, atus, 1. v. dep. to cheer up, to encourage; to exhort.

coïtio, ōnis, f. meeting; conspiracy, plot.

coïtus, ūs, m. combination; cohabitation.

cŏlăphus, i, m. box on the ear.

colchĭcum (mod. hort.), autumn crocus.

collăbĕfacto, 1. v.a. to overturn.

collăbĕfīo, factus, fieri, v.n. to be made to reel; *fig.* to be brought low.

collābor, lapsus, 3. v. dep. to fall in ruins; to fall in a swoon *or* in death.

collacrĭmo, 1. v.a. & n. to weep, to weep over.

collacteus, i, m. foster-brother;—collactea, ae, f.** foster-sister.

collare, is, n. collar.

collātio, ōnis, f. (pecuniary) contribution; collection; comparison; simile.

collaudātio, ōnis, f. high praise.

collaudo, 1. v.a. to praise very much.

collecta, ae, f. pecuniary contribution.

collectāneus, a, um, a. gathered *or* scraped together.   [tion.

collectio, ōnis, f. collection; recapitula-collēga, æ, m.** colleague.

collēgium, ii, n. college, corporation; brotherhood; partnership.

collĭbet, collŭbet, buit *or* bĭtum est, 2. v. imp. it pleases.

collīdo, si, sum, 3. v.a. to strike, *or* dash together; to bruise; to attack.

collĭgo, ēgi, ectum, 3. v.a. to collect, to assemble; to acquire; to catch (something falling); to infer; to reckon; to sum up; to comprehend; to recollect;—**se colligere, animum colligere,** to recover oneself, to recover one's spirits.

collĭgo, 1. v.a. to bind together, to connect; to fetter; to restrain, to hinder.

collīno, lēvi, lĭtum, 3. v.a. to besmear; **collis, is, m.** hill.   [*fig.* to pollute.

collŏcātio, ōnis, f. placing together; arrangement; betrothal.

collŏco, 1. v.a. to place together, to arrange; to bestow; to employ; to lend; to lay out; to give in marriage.

collŏcūtio, ōnis, f. conversation, conference.

collŏquium, ii, n. conversation, discourse, interview.

collŏquor, lŏcūtus, 3. v. dep. to talk together, to converse.

collūceo, 2. v.n. to shine all round.

collūdo, si, sum, 3. v.n. to play together; to act in collusion.

collum, i, n. neck.

coĭluo, ui, ūtum, 3. v.a. to rinse; fig. to moisten, to quench.

collūsio, ōnis, f. secret understanding.

collūsor, ōris, m. playmate.

collustro, 1. v.a. to lighten up; fig. to survey on all sides.

collŭviēs, ĕi, collŭvio, ōnis, f. wash, filth, offscouring; sink.

collŷbus, i, m. exchange; banking business.

collȳrium, ii, n. liquid eye-salve.

cŏlŏcāsia, ae, f. the Egyptian bean.

cōlo, 1. v.a. to filter, to strain.

cŏlo, ui, cultum, 3. v.a. to cultivate; to take care of; to dwell, to inhabit; fig. to honour, to pay court to, to revere; to worship; to adorn; to make love; to exercise; to practise.

cōlon, i, n. the colon; colic.

cŏlōna, ae, f. country woman.

cŏlōnia, ae, f. colony; colonists; farm.

cŏlōnĭcus, a, um, a. from a colony.

cŏlōnus, i, m. husbandman, farmer.

cŏlor, ōris, m. colour, complexion; beauty, outward show; fig. pretence, excuse; style of writing or speaking.

cŏlōrātus, a, um, p. & a. variegated; sunburnt.

cŏlōro, 1. v.a. to colour, to paint; to dye; to tan; fig. to cloak.

colossēus, a, um, a. like a colossus, huge.

cŏlossus, i, m. gigantic statue.

cŏlostra, ae, f. first milk, biestings.

cŏlŭber, bri, m. serpent, snake, adder.

cŏlŭbra, ae, f. serpent, snake.

cŏlŭbrĭfer, a, um, a. snaky.

cōlum, i, n. strainer, colander.

cŏlumba, ae, f. dove, pigeon.

cŏlumbārium, ii, n. dove-cot, pigeon-house. [dove or pigeon.

cŏlumbīnus, a, um, a. pertaining to a cŏlumbus, i, m. male dove or pigeon.

cŏlŭmella, ae, f. small column, pillar.

cŏlŭmen, ĭnis, n. height, peak; roof, gable; fig. summit, head, chief; support, stay.

cŏlumna, ae, f. column, pillar; fig. support, stay; pillory; bookseller's shop;—Herculis Columnæ, the pillars of Hercules.

cŏlumnārium, ii, n. a pillar-tax, house-tax. [tree.

cŏlurnus, a, um, a. made of the hazel-

cōlus, ūs, f. distaff. [of meat.

cōlȳphia, ōrum, n. pl. choice pieces

cŏma, ae, f. hair of the head, head of hair; wool; fig. foliage.

cŏmans, antis, p. & a. hairy; long-haired; leafy.

cŏmātus, a, um, a. long-haired;—Gallia Comata, Transalpine Gaul.

combĭbo, bĭbi, 3. v.a. to drink up, to absorb. [up; fig. to ruin.

combūro, bussi, bustum, 3. v.a. to burn

cŏmĕdo, ēdi, ēsum, (estum), 3. v.a. to eat up, to consume; fig. to waste, to squander.

cŏmes, ĭtis, c. companion, comrade, partner; tutor, teacher; suite (of officials); attendant.

cŏmētes, ae, m. comet.

cōmĭcē, ad. in the manner of comedy.

cōmĭcus, a, um, a. comic; —, i, m. comedian; writer of comedy.

cōmĭnus, v. comminus. [loving.

cōmis, e, a. courteous, kind, friendly,

cōmissābundus, a, um, a. mafficking, wassailing. [revelling.

cōmissātio, ōnis, f. merry-making, a

cōmissātor, ōris, m. reveller.

cōmissor, atus, 1. v. dep. to carouse, to revel. [friendliness.

cōmĭtas, ātis, f. courteousness, kindness,

cōmĭtātus, ūs, m. escort, train, retinue; imperial retinue; company, troop.

cōmĭter, ad. courteously, kindly, civilly, readily.

comitia, ōrum, v. comitium.

cōmĭtiālis, e, a. pertaining to the comitia.

cōmĭtium, ii, n. a place in the forum, where the comitia were held;— comitia, orum, n. pl. elections, hust-

cōmĭto, v. cōmitor. [ings.

cōmĭtor, atus, 1. v.a. dep. to accompany, to attend.

comma, ătis, n. punctuation mark, comma. [defile.

commācŭlo, 1. v.a. to spot, to pollute,

commeātus, ūs, m. passage; furlough; caravan; transport; provisions.

commĕmĭni, isse, v. def. to recollect thoroughly.

commĕmŏrābĭlis, e, a. memorable.

commĕmŏrātio, ōnis, f. remembrance, a reminding, mention.

commĕmŏro, 1. v.a. to remember; to remind; to mention.

commendābĭlis, e, a. commendable.
commendātio, ōnis, f. recommendation; excellence.
commendo, 1. v.a. to commend to; to recommend, to set off.
commentārĭŏlum, i, n. short treatise.
commentārius, ii, m. commentarium, ii, n. note-book, memorandum; commentary; brief. [comment.
commentātio, ōnis, f. meditation; gloss, commentīcius, a, um, a. feigned, devised; imaginary; forged, false.
commentor, ātus, 1. v. dep. to study; to devise; to feign; to fabricate; to meditate; to imitate.
commentor, oris, m. deviser.
commentum, i, n. invention, fiction; fable; falsehood.
commeo, 1. v.n. to go to and fro; to pass; to travel; to haunt.
commercium, ii, n. commercial intercourse, trade; traffic, communication, correspondence, fellowship. [of.
commēreo, ui, ĭtum, 2. v.a. to be guilty
commētior, mensus, 4. v. dep. to proportion. [enter.
commigro, 1. v.n. to migrate, move, to
commīlĭtium, ii, n. companionship in service. [rade.
commīlĭto, ōnis, m. fellow-soldier; com-
comminātio, ōnis, f. threatening.
commĭniscor, mentus, 3. v. dep. to devise, to invent; to forge; to fabricate. [menace.
comminor, atus, 1. v. dep. to threaten, to
commĭnuo, ui, ūtum, 3. v.a. to crumble, to crush; to diminish; to split; to weaken. [near; instantly.
commĭnus, ad. hand to hand; at hand,
commisceo, scui, xtum (stum), 2. v.a. to mix together, to intermingle.
commĭsĕrātio, ōnis, f. compassion.
commĭsĕror, atus, 1. v. dep. to pity; to excite compassion.
commissio, ōnis, f. a bringing together; a matching one against another; the opening of the games; a prize speech (such as is spoken at the opening of the games).
commissum, i, n. enterprise, trust, secret; transgression, crime. [seam.
commissūra, ae, f. joining together; joint,
committo, mīsi, missum, 3. v.a. to join, to unite; to commit, to intrust; to match (one against another); to compare; to venture; to begin; to.perpetrate; to engage in;—committere praelium, to join battle.
commŏdē, ad. suitably, fitly.
commŏdĭtas, ātis, f. fitness, convenience; advantage; courtesy, kindness.

commŏdo, 1. v.a. to accommodate; to oblige, to lend, to serve.
commŏdum, i, n. opportunity, convenience; profit; wages; privilege; loan; advantage; good.
commŏdum, ad. in good time; just then; in the nick of time.
commŏdus, a, um, a. suitable, convenient, fit; advantageous; lucky; obliging, kind, gentle. [mind, to admonish.
commŏnĕfăcio, fēci, factum, 3. v.a. to re-
commŏneo, ui, ĭtum, 2. v.a. to remind, to warn.
commonstro, 1. v.a. to point out clearly.
commŏrātio, ōnis, f. sojourning; delay; fig. dwelling (upon). [gether.
commŏrior, mortuus, 3. v. dep. to die to-
commŏror, ātus, 1. v.n. dep. to sojourn, to stay; to tarry; to dwell upon.
commōtio, ōnis, f. agitation, commotion.
commōtus, a, um, a. moved; excited; passionate.
commŏveo, mōvi, mōtum, 2. v.a. to move, to stir; to excite; to disturb; to astonish; to affect. [imparting.
commūnĭcātio, ōnis f. communication, an
commūnĭco, 1. v.a. to communicate; to impart; to share with; to receive a share of.
commūnio, īvi (ii), ĭtum, 4. v.a. to fortify, to intrench. [munion.
communio, ōnis, f. fellowship, com-
commūnis, e, a. common, general, ordinary; familiar; affable; equal; public;—in commune, for the common good. [bility.
commūnĭtas, ātis, f. community; affa-
commūnĭter, ad. in common, commonly, generally.
commūtābĭlis, e, a. changeable.
commūtātio, ōnis, f. change.
commūto, 1. v.a. to change, to alter; to exchange, to barter.
cōmo, mpsi mptum, 3. v.n. to arrange, to comb; to dress, to adorn.
cōmoedĭa, ae, f. comedy.
cōmoedus, i, m. comedian, comic actor.
compăciscor, pactus, 3. v. dep. to make an agreement.
compactĭlis, e, a. thick-set, compact.
compactus, a, um, a. compact.
compāges, is, compāgo, ĭnis, f. connection, joint, structure, framework.
compar, ăris, a. like, equal (to); equal, comrade; lover, consort.
compărābĭlis, e, a. comparable.
compărātio, ōnis, f. comparison; proportion; preparation; acquirement.
compărātīvus. a, um, a. comparative.
comparco, parsi, 3. v.a. to scrape together; v.n. to refrain.

compāreo, ui, 2. v.n. to appear, to be visible; *fig.* to be present; to be in existence.

compăro, 1. v.a. to unite; to compare; to prepare; to provide (for); to acquire; to raise (a force); to appoint; to hire.

compasco, to feed together.

compĕdio, īvi, ītum, 4. v.a. to shackle.

compello, pŭli, pulsum, 3. v.a. to drive together *or* along; to collect; to impel; to force.

compello, 1. v.a. to accost, to address; to chide, to rebuke; to abuse.

compendiārius, a, um, a. short, abridged.

compendium, ii, n. abridgment, abstract; a short cut, profit, interest.

compensātio, ōnis, f. requital; compensation.   [pensate.

compenso, 1. v.a. to balance, to com-

compĕrendino, 1. v.a. to adjourn till the 3rd day.

compĕrio, pĕri, pertum, 4. v.a. to find out, to learn, to know for certain.

compes, ĕdis, f. shackle (for the feet); *fig.* fetters.   [to restrain.

compesco, ui, 3. v.a. to confine, to curb,

compĕtītor, ōris,m. rival, competitor.

compĕto, īvi & ii, ītum, 3. v.n. to meet; to happen; to coincide; to suit, to agree; to correspond; to be sound *or* capable.   [tion.

compīlātio, ōnis, f. plundering; collec-

compīlo, 1. v.a. to rob, to plunder.

compingo, pēgi, pactum, 3. v.a. to join; to frame; to compose; to fasten up.

compitālia, ium, n. pl. festival celebrated at cross-roads in honour of the rural

compĭtum, i, n. cross-way.   [gods.

complăceo, ui, & complăcĭtus sum, 2. v.n. to be very pleasing.

complector, xus, 3. v. dep. to clasp around; to encompass, to embrace; to lay hold of; to contain; to comprehend (mentally); to comprise.

complēmentum, i, n. complement.

compleo, ēvi, ētum, 2. v.a. to fill up; to fill; to complete; to fulfil; to perfect; to supply; to recruit; to make good.

complētus, a, um, a. filled full, full; *fig.* complete, perfect.

complexio, ōnis, f. combination, connection; summary; period; conclusion (from premises); dilemma.

complexus, ūs, m. embrace; affection; love; connection.

complico, 1. v.a. to fold up.

complōrātio, ōnis, f., complōrātus, ūs, m. loud complaint, lamentation.

complōro, 1. v.a. to bewail.

complūres, a, a. several, many.

complŭvium, ii, n. an open space in a Roman house where all the rain from the surrounding roofs was collected.

compōno, pōsui, pŏsĭtum, 3. v.a. to put *or* lay together; to arrange; to compose; to adjust; to compare; to match; to construct; to build; to compose (books, etc.); to adorn; to appease, to settle; to bury.

comporto, 1. v.a. to carry together, to collect.

compos, ōtis, a. participating, guilty of; —compos mentis, in full possession of one's faculties;—compos voti, having obtained one's wish.

compŏsĭtē, ad. in good order, regularly.

compŏsĭtio, ōnis, f. composition; disposal, agreement; appointment; matching.

compŏsĭtor, oris, m. dispenser, creator, arranger.

compŏsĭtus, a, um, a. compound; false, feigned; well-arranged; fit, suitable, calm.   [symposium.

compōtātio, ōnis, f. drinking company,

compōtor, ōris, m. drinking-companion.

compransor, ōris, m. boon companion.

comprĕcātio, ōnis, f. a. calling on (a deity) by prayer.   [to implore.

comprĕcor, atus, 1. v. dep. to supplicate,

comprĕhendo, di, sum, 3. v.a. to seize *or* grasp; to comprise; to include; to attack; to embrace; to describe; to express; to arrest *or* lay hold of; to understand.   [telligible.

comprĕhensĭbĭlis, e, a. conceivable, in-

comprĕhensio, ōnis, f. arrest, seizure; comprehension, idea; expression, style; period.

compressē, ad. briefly.   [brief expressing.

compressio, ōnis, f. pressing together; *fig.*

comprimo, pressi, pressum, 3. v.a. to press *or* squeeze together; to keep *or* hold back *or* in; to suppress.

comprŏbātio, ōnis, f. approval.

comprŏbo, 1. v.a. to approve; to attest, to confirm.

comprōmissum, i, n. mutual engagement to abide by an award.

comprōmitto, mīsi, missum, 3. v.a. to engage to abide by an award.

comptus, a, um, a. adorned.

compunctio, ōnis, f. sting (of remorse).

compungo, nxi nctum, 3. v.a. to sting, to prick.   [to cast up.

compŭto, 1. v.a. to sum up, to compute;

cōnāmen, ĭnis, n. attempt; effort, exertion.

cōnātum, i, n. undertaking, venture.

cōnātus, ūs, m. attempt, undertaking; effort; impulse.

concædes, ium, f. pl. barricade.
concălĕfăcio, fēci, factum, 3. v.a. to warm thoroughly. [to burn.
concălesco, ui, 3. v.n. to become hot.
concallesco, ui, 3. v.n. to become hard or callous; *fig.* to become insensible.
concăvo, 1. v.a. to hollow out.
concăvus, a, um, a. hollowed out, concave; arched.
concēdo, cessi, cessum, 3. v.n. to go away, to depart, to withdraw; to yield to, to submit; —, v.a. to allow, to grant; to forgive. [to publish.
concĕlĕbro, 1. v.a. to haunt; to celebrate;
concēnātio, onis, f. a company at supper.
concentus, ūs, m. singing together, harmony, melody; *fig.* concord.
conceptio, ōnis, f. conception; a comprehending.
conceptīvus, a, um, a. fixed specially by the authorities, movable (of festivals).
conceptus, ūs, m. conception.
concerpo, psi, ptum, 3. v.a. to tear in pieces. [troversy.
concertătio, ōnis, f. dispute, con-
concerto, 1. v.a. to dispute, to debate.
concessio, ōnis, f. permission, grant, plea of excuse.
concessus, ūs, m. concession; permission.
concha, ae, f. shell-fish, cockle; pearl; mussel-shell; oyster-shell; Triton's trumpet.
conchÿliātus, a, um, a. of a purple colour.
conchÿlium, ii, n. shell-fish; testacean; oyster; purple.
concĭdo, cĭdi, 3. v.n. to fall down or into decay; to fail; to faint; to be slain; to die.
concīdo, cīdi, cīsum, 3. v.a. to cut to pieces; to break up; to cudgel soundly; to cut down, to kill; *fig.* to weaken; to confute; to destroy.
concieo, ivi, itum, 2. v.a. to move, to stir up; to call together.
conciliābŭlum, i, n. place of assembly, market-place. ' [over; desire.
conciliātio, ōnis, f. union; a winning
conciliātor, ōris, m. author, promoter.
conciliātrix, ĭcis, f. procuress; she who occasions.
conciliātus, a, um, a. beloved.
concilio, 1. v.a. to call together; to unite; to procure; to win over; to obtain; to recommend; to cause, to occasion.
concilium, ii, n. assembly; council; diet.
concinnē, ad. elegantly. [gance.
concinnitas, ātis, f. fitness, neatness, ele-
concinno, 1. v.a. to make fine or fit; to prepare; to dress; to cause; to render.
concinnus, a, um, a. neat, pretty, elegant, pleasing.

concino, cĭnui, 3. v.n. to sing, to play, or to sound in concert; —, v.a. to celebrate; to foretell.
concio, v. concieo.
concio, conciabundus, etc., **v. contio, contiabundus.**
concĭpio, cēpi, ceptum, 3. v.a. to take up; to conceive; to devise; to understand; to compose; to imbibe; to harbour; to commit; to repeat a formula.
concīsus, a, um, a. short, concise.
concĭtātio, ōnis, f. rapid motion; passion; sedition, tumult.
concĭtātē, ad. rapidly; passionately.
concĭtātus, a, um, a. rapid; passionate.
concĭto, 1. v.a. to rouse, to spur, to excite; to disturb; to pursue; to cause. [lamentation.
conclāmātio, ōnis, f. loud shouting;
conclāmo, 1. v.n. to cry (out) together, to shout; to bewail (the dead); to proclaim. [cage.
conclāve, is, n. room, cabinet, closet,
conclūdo, si, sum, 3. v.a. to enclose together; to conclude, to end; to comprise; to infer; to stop; to close.
conclūsio, ōnis, f. conclusion, end; siege; peroration; logical conclusion from premises. [clusion.
conclūsiuncŭla, ae, f. a sophistical con-
concŏlor, ōris, a. of the same colour.
concŏquo, coxi, coctum, 3. v.a. to digest; to mature; to put up with; *fig.* to consider well; to devise.
concordia, ae, f. harmony, concord.
concorditer, ad. harmoniously.
concordo, 1. v.n. to harmonize.
concors, dis, a. agreeing, harmonious.
concrēdo, dĭdi, dĭtum, 3. v.a. to intrust, to commit to.
concrĕmo, 1. v.a. to burn up entirely.
concrĕpo, pui, pĭtum, 1. v.n. to rattle, to clash; to snap (one's fingers); —, v.a. to strike.
concresco, ēvi, ētum, 3. v.n. to grow together; to curdle; to congeal; to clot.
concrētio, ōnis, f. concretion; matter (as opposed to mind).
concrētus, a, um, concreted, stiff, frozen.
concŭbīna, ae, f. concubine.
concŭbīnatus, ūs, m. concubinage.
concŭbĭtus, ūs, m. coition. [first sleep.
concŭbius, a, um, a. —**a nocte,** in the
conculco, 1. v.a. *fig.* to trample upon; to abuse; to despise. [with.
concumbo, cŭbui, cŭbĭtum, 3. v.n. to lie
concŭpisco, ivi & ii, ĭtum, 3. v.a. to long much for, to covet, to strive after.
concurro, curri, cursum, 3. v.n. to run or assemble together; to join battle; to

fall foul of one another; to meet; to happen.

concursātio, ōnis, f. running together; medley; riot; skirmishing.

concursātor, ōris, m. skirmisher.

concursio, ōnis, f. concourse, meeting; repetition.

concurso, 1. v.n. to run hither and thither; to skirmish; —, **v.a.** to frequent.

concursus, ūs, m. concourse, crowd; riot; encounter; attack; concurrence; *fig.* combination.

concussio, onis, f. shaking, concussion.

concŭtio, cussi, cussum, 3. v.a. to shake violently, to brandish; to terrify; to trouble.

condālium, ii, n. a ring worn by slaves.

condemnātio, ōnis, f. condemnation.

condemno, 1. v.a. to condemn, to doom; to convict.

condenso, 1., condenseo, 2., to press together; to condense.

condensus, a, um, a. dense, thick; wedged together.

condĭcio, ōnis, f. condition, situation, rank; stipulation; term, agreement; marriage; married person; (in contempt) paramour;—**condicio sine qua non,** a condition without which agreement is impossible.

condīco, xi, ctum, 3. v.a. to agree (upon), to order, to declare; to promise; to undertake; to engage; to claim.

condignē, ad. worthily.

condignus, a, um, a. worthy.

condīmentum, i, n. spice, seasoning.

condio, īvi & ii, ītum, 4. v.a. to preserve, to pickle; to embalm; to spice; to perfume; to make pleasant; to soften; to temper.

condiscĭpŭlus, i, m. school-fellow.

condisco, dĭdĭci, 3. to learn thoroughly.

conditio, v. condicio. [author, compiler.

condĭtor, ōris, m. builder, founder,

condĭtōrium, ii, n. coffin; tomb.

condītus, a, um, a. seasoned, savoury; polished.

condo, dĭdi, dĭtum, 3. v.a. to build, to found; to compose, to write; to make; to hide; to sheathe; to lay *or* treasure up; to preserve, to pickle; to bury; to thrust (into). [pain.

condōlesco, dŏlui, 3. v.n. to be in great

condōno, 1. v.a. to give as a present; to forgive; to remit; to devote *or* sacri-

condūcĭbilis, e, a. profitable. [fice.

condūco, xi, ctum, 3. v.a. to lead together, to assemble; to hire; to undertake; to contract for; —, **v.n.** to be of use; to profit.

conductio, ōnis, f. hiring, farming.

conductor, ōris, m. tenant; contractor.

condŭplico, 1. to double. [together.

confābŭlor, atus, 1. v. dep. to converse

confarreātio, ōnis, a marriage ceremony, in which meal (**far**) was given as an offering.

confectio, ōnis, f. making up, preparation; completing; mastication.

confector, ōris, m. preparer, finisher.

confercio, fertum, 4. v.a. to stuff together, to press close together.

confĕro, contŭli, collātum, conferre, 3. v.a. to bring *or* carry together, to collect; to contribute, to add; to join; to bestow; to lay out; to apply; to discourse *or* talk together; to match; to compare; to put off; to refer; to transfer; to impute; to compress; to betake.

confertim, ad. in close order, closely.

confervesco, ferbui, 3. v.n. to begin to boil, to grow hot.

confessio, ōnis, f. confession, acknowledgment.

confestim, ad. immediately, speedily;— **confestim a prælio,** immediately after the battle.

confĭcio, fēci, fectum, 3. v.a. to finish; to effect; to arrange; to produce, to cause; to conquer; to kill; to use up; to consume, to weaken; to spend; to prove; to bargain.

confidens, entis, p. & a. bold, daring; impudent.

confidenter, ad. boldly, confidently; impudently. [ness; impudence.

confidentia, ae, f. confidence; bold-

confido, fīsus sum, 3. v.n. to trust to, to confide in.

configo, fixi, fixum, 3. v.a. to fasten together; to pierce through.

confingo, finxi, fictum, 3. v.a. to fashion, to invent, to feign.

confĭnis, e, a. adjoining, contiguous, similar.

confīnium, ii, n. boundary, border; neighbourhood; *fig.* close connection.

confirmātio, ōnis, f. confirmation, assurance. [tain, proved.

confirmātus, a, um, a. courageous; cer-

confirmo, 1. v.a. to confirm; to strengthen; to encourage; to prove; to say boldly.

confisco, 1. v.a. to confiscate, seize for the public purse. [to reveal.

confiteor, fessus, 2. v. dep. to confess;

conflagro, 1. v.n. to be in a blaze.

conflictio, ōnis, f. contest, conflict.

conflicto, 1. v.a. to harass; to trouble; to ruin.

conflictus, ūs, m. concussion.
confligo, xi, ctum, 3. v.a. to contrast;
—, v.n. to be dashed together; to strive;
to fight; to dispute.
conflo, 1. v.a. to blow together, to melt;
to inflame; to raise, to bring about.
confluens, entis, m. confluence.
confluo, xi, 3. v.n. to flow together; *fig.*
to flock together.
confŏdio, fŏdi, fossum, 3. v.a. to dig
round about; to pierce.
conformātio, ōnis, f. shape, form;
arrangement; idea, notion; figure of
speech.
conformo, 1. v.a. to shape, to fashion;
to finish, to complete.
confrăgōsus, a, um, confrăgus, a, um, a.
rough, uneven. [echo.
confrĕmo, ui, 3. v.n. to murmur, to
confrico, 1. v.a. to rub.
confringo, frēgi, fractum, 3. v.a. to break
in pieces; *fig.* to bring to naught; to
consume.
confŭgio, fūgi, 3. v.n. to flee to, to have
recourse to.
confŭgium, ii, n. refuge, shelter.
confundo, fūdi, fūsum, 3. v.a. to pour *or*
mix together; to confound; to violate; to bewilder.
confūsē, ad. confusedly, without order.
confūsio, ōnis, f. mingling; confusion,
disorder, trouble.
confūto, 1. v.a. *fig.* to check, to repress;
to put to silence; to disprove.
congĕlo, 1. v.a. to congeal; to curdle;
—, v.n. to freeze; to grow hard.
congĕmino, 1. v.a. to redouble.
congĕmo, ui, 3. v.a. & n. to sigh loudly,
to bewail.
conger, gri, m. conger-eel.
congĕries, ei, f. heap, pile, mass.
congĕro, gessi, gestum, 3. v.a. to heap
up, to get together; to build; to
compile; *fig.* to impute.
congestīcius, a, um, a. piled up.
congestus, ūs, m. heap, pile, mass.
congiārium, ii, n. largess for soldiers;
gift in corn.
congius, ii. m. a liquid measure, six pints.
conglŏbo, 1. v.a. to make into a ball; to
crowd together.
conglŏmĕro, 1. v.a. to wind up into a
ball. [gether.
conglūtinātio, ōnis, f. *fig.* joining to-
conglūtino, 1. v.a. to glue together.
congrătŭlor, 1. v. dep. to congratulate.
congrĕdior, gressus, 3. v. dep. to meet;
to fight.
congrĕgātio, ōnis, f. society, association.
congrĕgo, 1. v.a. to collect (into a flock);
to unite.

congressio, ōnis, f. meeting, visit, assembly; conflict, attack.
congressus, ūs, m. conference, conversation; encounter, fight.
congruens, entis, a. congruous; consistent; harmonious. [consistently.
congruenter, ad. fitly, harmoniously,
congruo, ui, 3. v.n. to run *or* come together; to agree, to accord; to suit.
congruus, a, um, a. agreeing, concordant.
cōnifer, a, um, a. bearing cone-shaped
fruit. [tion.
conjectio, ōnis, f. conjecture, interpreta-
conjecto, 1. v.a. to conjecture; to interpret; to think *or* imagine.
conjectūra, ae, f. conjecture; inference,
soothsaying.
conjectūrālis, e, a. conjectural.
conjectus, ūs, m. throwing; directing;
shot; glance.
conjĭcio, jēci, jectum, 3. v.a. to throw
together; to cast, to fling; to drive;
to direct; to conjecture; to foretell;
to interpret.
conjŭgālis, e, a. conjugal, matrimonial.
conjŭgātio, ōnis, f. conjugation.
conjŭgiālis, e, a. conjugal, matrimonial.
conjŭgium, ii, n. marriage, wedlock;
wife; husband.
conjŭgo, ātum, 1. v.a. to join together.
conjunctē, ad. conjointly; in a confidential manner.
conjunctim, ad. unitedly, in common.
conjunctio, ōnis, f. union, conjunction;
agreement; mutual love; familiarity;
match; fellowship; (grammatically) a
conjunction.
conjunctus, a, um, a. bordering upon,
near; *fig.* connected with, agreeing
with; married; allied, friendly.
conjunx. See conjux.
conjungo, nxi, nctum, 3. v.a. to yoke together; to connect; to couple; to
ally; to associate.
conjūrātio, ōnis, f. conspiracy, plot;
band of conspirators.
conjūrātus, a, um, a. leagued;—con-
jūrāti, ōrum, a. pl. conspirators.
conjūro, 1. v.n. to swear together; to
conjure, to conspire.
conjux, jŭgis, g.c. spouse, wife; husband; bride.
connecto, xui, xum, 3. v.a. to tie, to
fasten *or* join together, to connect; to
implicate; *fig.* to infer, to conclude.
connītor, nixus & nīsus, 3. v. dep. to endeavour eagerly; to struggle; to
travail.
connīveo, nīvi & nixi, 2. v.n. to close the
eyes; *fig.* to wink at, to overlook.
connūbiālis, e, a. conjugal.

connūbium, ii, n. marriage, wedlock.
cōnōpēum, i, n. gauze curtains.
cōnor, ātus, 1. v. dep. to try, to venture,
to undertake.
conquasso, 1. v.a. to shake violently.
conquĕror, questus, 3. v.a. & n. dep. to
complain of, to bewail.
conquestio, ōnis, f. bewailing, complaint.
conquiesco, quiēvi, quiētum, 3. v.n. to
repose; to rest; to be inactive; to
sleep; *fig.* to find rest.
conquīro, quīsīvi, quīsītum, 3. v.a. to
search for diligently; to rake up; to
procure; (mil.) to levy.
conquīsītio, ōnis, f. (mil.) levy. [costly.
conquīsītus, a, um, a. select, chosen,
consæpio, ptum, 4. v.a. to enclose, to
consæptum, i, n. enclosure. [fence.
consălūtātio, ōnis, f. mutual salutation.
consălūto, 1. v.a. to greet, to hail, to
salute.
consănesco, nui, 3. v.n. to be healed.
consanguĭneus, a, um, a. related by
blood; (poet.) brotherly, sisterly;
—ei, m. pl. relatives. [relationship.
consanguĭnĭtas, ātis, f. consanguinity;
conscĕlĕrātus, a, um, wicked, depraved;
criminal, villain. [grace.
conscĕlĕro, 1. v.a. to dishonour, to dis-
conscendo, di, sum, 3. v.a. & n. to mount,
to ascend; to embark.
conscientia, ae, f. conscience, consciousness; knowledge; remembrance; reflection; feeling; remorse; innocence.
conscindo, scĭdi, scissum, 3. v.a. to rend
to pieces.
conscisco, scīvi, scītum, 3. v.a. to decree;
to adjudge;—mortem sibi consciscere,
to commit suicide.
conscius, a, um, a. conscious; knowing;
guilty;—mens sibi conscia recti, a
conscience void of offence.
conscrībo, psi, ptum, 3. v.a. to enlist *or*
enrol; to compose, to write;—
Patres Conscripti, the title by which
senators were addressed.
conscriptio, ōnis, f. composition; treatise.
consĕco, cui, ctum, 1. v.a. to dismember.
consecrātio, ōnis, f. consecration; deification. [cate; to hallow; to deify.
consecro, 1. v.a. to consecrate; to dedi-
consectārius, a, um, a. (logically) conse-
consectio, ōnis, f. cutting up. [quent.
consector, ātus, 1. v. dep. to pursue
eagerly; to strive after, to imitate;
to emulate; to persecute.
consĕcūtio, ōnis, f. consequence; order,
sequence; logical consequence.
consĕnesco, nui, 3. v.n. to grow old; to
become weak; *fig.* to lose consideration *or* respect; to fall into disuse.

consensio, ōnis, f. agreement, unanimity;
conspiracy.
consensus, ūs, m. unanimity, concord;—
consensu *or* omnium consensu, unanimously.
consentāneus, a, um, a. agreeable;
proper; consistent.
consentio, sensi, sensum, 4. v.n. & a. to
consent; to agree; to decree; to conspire; to be consistent with.
consēpio, v. consæpio.
consĕquens, entis, a. suitable; fit;
reasonable. [quence.
consĕquentia, ae, f. consequence, se-
consĕquor, sĕcūtus, 3. v. dep. to follow
after; to overtake; to get *or* obtain;
to procure, to purchase; to effect; to
imitate; to reach, to come up to, to
befall. [to plant with.
consĕro, sēvi, sĭtum, 3. v.a. to sow over,
consĕro, sĕrui, sertum, 3. v.a. to join;
to link; to engage;—manum con-
serere, to engage in hostilities.
conserva, ae, f. fellow-slave (female).
conservātio, ōnis, f. keeping, preservation.
conservātor, ōris, m. keeper; defender.
conservo, 1. v.a. to keep up, to preserve.
conservus, i, m. fellow-slave.
consessor, ōris, m. assessor. [court.
consessus, ūs, m. assembly; audience;
consīdĕrātē, ad. considerately, deliberately. [flection.
consīdĕrātio, ōnis, f. consideration, re-
consīdĕrātus, a, um, a. considerate,
cautious, deliberate.
consīdĕro, 1. v.a. to inspect; to consider, to contemplate.
consīdo, sēdi, sessum, 3. v.n. to sit down;
to settle; to sink down; (mil.) to encamp; to take up one's residence; to
hold a session; *fig.* to abate; to cease.
consigno, 1. v.a. to seal up; to sign, to
subscribe; to attest.
consĭliārius, ii, m. adviser; interpreter.
consĭlior, ātus, 1. v. dep. to take counsel;
to advise.
consĭlium, ii, n. counsel, advice; reason;
purpose, plan; stratagem; resolution,
will; judgment; prudence;—consĭlio,
on purpose.
consĭmĭlis, e, a. entirely similar.
consisto, stĭti, stĭtum, 3. v.n. to stand
(together *or* fast); to be frozen; to
make a stand; to be steadfast; to be
in existence; to consist (of); to halt;
to cease.
consistōrium, ii, n. place of meeting,
meeting-place of the emperor's ad-
visers.
consĭtor, ōris, m. sower, planter.

consōbrīnus, i, m. —a, f. cousin-german.
consōciātio, ōnis, f. association.
consōcio, 1. v.a. to associate, to unite; to share. [encouragement.
consōlātio, ōnis, f. consolation, comfort;
consōlātor, ōris, m. comforter.
consōlātōrius, a, um, a. consolatory.
consōlor, ātus, 1. v. dep. to console, to encourage, to cheer; to alleviate.
consōnans, antis, f. (in grammar) a consonant.
consōno, ui, 1. v.n. to make a great noise, to resound; to agree; to harmonize.
consōnus, a, um, a. sounding together; harmonious; *fig.* accordant.
consōpio, ītum, 4. v.a. to lull to sleep, to stupefy.
consors, ortis, a. partaking of; brotherly, sisterly; —, c. colleague, partner; fellow.
consortio,· ōnis, f. fellowship; partnership; intercourse.
consortium, ii, n. fellowship, participation.
conspectus, a, um, a. visible; remarkable;—ūs, m. look, sight, view; presence; *fig.* consideration;—e conspectu, out of sight;—in conspectu, in sight.
conspergo, si, sum, 3. v.a. to besprinkle.
conspiciendus, a, um, a. worth seeing, distinguished.
conspicio, spexi, spectum, 3. v.a. & n. to behold, to observe; to descry;—conspicior, to attract attention, to be admired. [sight of, to descry.
conspicor, ātus, 1. v. dep. to get a
conspicuus, a, um, a. in sight, visible; illustrious, remarkable.
conspīrātio, ōnis, f. concord, harmony; unanimity; conspiracy.
conspīro, 1. v.n. to harmonize, to agree; to conspire.
consponsor, ōris, m. joint surety.
conspuo, ui, ūtum, 3. v.a. to spit on; to contemn; to besprinkle.
constans, antis, a. steadfast, firm, immovable, constant; secure; consistent; sure, steady.
constanter, ad. firmly, steadily, etc.
constantia, ae, f. steadfastness, firmness, constancy, perseverance; resolution; agreement; consistency.
consternātio, ōnis, f. confusion, dismay; mutiny; sedition.
consterno, strāvi, strātum, 3. v.a. to bestrew; to throw down; to pave.
consterno, 1. v.a. to terrify, to confuse.
constīpo, 1. v.a. to press *or* crowd closely together.

constītuo, ui, ūtum, 3. v.a. to put, to set *or* place; to constitute, to appoint; to fix *or* establish; to range; to build; to establish; to agree (upon); to manage; to determine; to dispose; to intend; to settle.
constītūtio, ōnis, f. constitution, disposition; point in dispute; ordering; arrangement; ordinance.
constītūtum, i, n. institution, law; agreement, compact.
consto, stīti, stātum, 1. v.n. to stand still; to last; to be settled *or* certain *or* known; to cost; to agree (with); to exist *or* be; to consist (of); not to yield;—constat, it is agreed.
constringo, inxi, ictum, 3. v.a. to bind fast, tight; *fig.* to check; to compress.
constructio, ōnis, f. building, construction. [up; to make, to build.
construo, uxi, uctum, 3. v.a. to heap
constupro, 1. v.a. to ravish. [tom.
consuēfăcio, fēci, factum, 3. v.a. to accus-
consuesco, suēvi, suētum, 3. v.a. & n. to accustom; to become accustomed; to be wont.
consuētūdo, ĭnis, f. custom, habit, use; manner; companionship, familiarity, conversation;—ex consuetudine, according to custom.
consul, ŭlis, m. consul; one of the chief Roman magistrates;—Consule Planco, in the consulship of Plancus.
consŭlāris, e, a. consular; worthy of a consul.
consŭlātus, ūs, m. consulate, consulship.
consŭlo, sŭlui, sultum, 3. v.n. & a. to take counsel; to consider; to consult (one); to consult the interest of; to take care of; to provide for; to take steps;—boni consulere, to take in good part.
consultātio, ōnis, f. consultation.
consultē, consulto, ad. deliberately, on purpose. [counsel.
consulto, 1. v.a. to consult, to take
consultor, ōris, m. adviser; consulter, client.
consultum, i, n. consultation;—Senatus consultum, decree of the Senate.
consultus, a, um, p. & a. well-considered; knowing, experienced;—juris consultus *or* consultus alone, i, m. lawyer.
consummātio, onis, f. consummation; bringing to perfection.
consummo, 1. v.a. to sum up; to accomplish, to consummate.
consūmo, sumpsi, sumptum, 3. v.a. to use up; to eat; *fig.* to consume; to squander, to destroy; to employ.

consumptio, ōnis, f. wasting, consumption. [gether; to plot.

consuo, ui, utum, 3. v.a. to stitch to-

consurgo, surrexi, surrectum, 3. v.n. to rise or stand up in a body; to grow, to arise. [gradually.

contābesco, bui, 3. v.n. to waste away

contăbŭlātio, ōnis, f. flooring, floor, timber-frame. [cover.

contăbŭlo, 1. v.a. to board over; to

contactus, ūs, m. touch, contact; contagion.

contāges, is, f. contact; infection.

contāgio, ōnis, f., contāgium, ii, n. contagion, contact, touch; influence; infection. [stain.

contāmĭno, 1. v.a. to contaminate, to

contĕgo, xi, ctum, 3. v.a. to cover (up); to hide.

contĕmĕro, 1. v.a. to defile, to pollute.

contemno, tempsi, temptum, 3. v.a. to scorn, to contemn.

contemplātio, ōnis, f. view, survey, contemplation; meditation; respect, regard.

contemplātus, us, m. contemplation.

contemplor, ātus, 1. v. dep. to survey, to observe; to contemplate.

contempŏrāneus, a, um, a. contemporary.

contemptim, ad. contemptuously.

contemptio, ōnis, f. contempt, scorn, disdain.

contemptor, ōris, m. contemner, despiser.

contemptrix, īcis, f. despiser.

contemptus, a, um, contemptible, vile;— contemptus, ūs, m. contempt, scorn.

contendo, di, tum, 3. v.a. & n. to stretch, to strain; to hurl; to contend; to fight; to dispute; to strive, to exert; to labour; to request; to urge; to state emphatically; to go or march; to hasten; to steer; to direct; to compare.

contentē, ad. with great exertion.

contentio, ōnis, f. exertion; contest, fight; dispute; comparison; contrast; antithesis.

contentus, a, um, p. & a. tense, tight; eager, intent;—contentus, a, um, a. contented, satisfied.

conterminus, a, um, a. bordering upon; —conterminum, i, n. confine, border.

contĕro, trīvi, trītum, 3. v.a. to grind, to bruise, to crumble; to waste; to spend; to exhaust; to tease.

conterreo, ui, ĭtum, 2. v.a. to frighten.

contestor, ātus, 1. v. dep. to call to witness; to give evidence, to affirm.

contexo, xui, xtum, 3. v.a. to entwine, to twist together; to construct; to contrive.

contextē, ad. in close connection.

contextus, ūs, m. connection, coherence; series. [to cease.

contĭcesco, tĭcui, 3. v.a. to keep silence;

contignātio, ōnis, f. raftering; story, floor.

contignŏ, 1. v.a. to rafter, to floor.

contĭguŏs, a, um, a. adjoining, bordering upon; within reach.

continens, entis, p. & a. contiguous, adjacent; uninterrupted; continent, temperate;—continens, entis, m. continent, mainland.

continenter, ad. without interruption; temperately. [tinence.

continentia, ae, f. abstemiousness, con-

contĭneo, ui, tentum, 2. v.a. & n. to hold together; to bind; to contain; to retain; to comprise; to confine; to keep secret; to hinder, to prevent; to stop.

contingo, tĭgi, tactum, 3. v.a. & n. to touch; to seize; to border upon; to reach; to influence, to affect; to stain; to befall; to come to pass; to be akin; to be connected with.

continuātio, ōnis, f. continuation, succession; period.

continuo, ad. immediately, forthwith.

continuo, 1. v.a. to put in a line; to join; to deal with successively, to prolong.

continuus, a, um, a. continuous; successive. [tion.

contio, ōnis, f. assembly, meeting; ora-

contiōnābundus, a, um, a. haranguing in a public assembly. [assembly.

contiōnālis, e, a. belonging to a public

contiōnātor, ōris, m. haranguer of the people; demagogue.

contiōnor, ātus, 1. v. dep. to deliver an oration to a public assembly.

contiuncŭla, ae, f. short harangue to the people.

contorqueo, torsi, tortum, 2. v.a. to hurl; to brandish; to fling.

contortē, ad. intricately, obscurely.

contortio, ōnis, f. complication.

contortus, a, um, a. vehement; intricate.

contrā, ad. & pr. against; opposite to; contrary to; on the contrary; otherwise; mutually; face to face.

contractio, ōnis, f. contraction; abridgment.

contractus, a, um, p. & a. close; abridged; stinted. [say or contradict.

contrādīco, xi, ctum, 3. v.n. to gain-

contrādictio, ōnis, f. objection, contradiction.

contrăho, xi, ctum, 3. v.a. to draw together; to gather; to tighten; to abridge; to check; to agree; to bargain; to incur; to get; to cause.

contrārīē, ad. in an opposite direction *or* manner.

contrārius, a, um, a. opposite, contrary; inimical; harmful;—ex contrario, on the contrary. [survey.

contrecto, 1. v.a. to touch, to handle; to contrĕmisco, mui, 3. v.n. & a. to tremble all over; to tremble at.

contrībuo, ui, ūtum, 3. v.a. to incorporate; to contribute.

contristo, 1. v.a. to make sad, to afflict; *fig.* to darken; to bring together.

contrōversia, ae, f. civil lawsuit; controversy; dispute.

contrōversiōsus, a, um, a. controverted.

contrōversus, a, um, a. controverted, disputed. [slaughter.

contrūcīdo, 1. v.a. to cut down, to contrudo, si, sum, 3. v.a. to thrust together, to press in.

contŭbernālis, is, g.c. tent-companion; comrade, mate.

contŭbernium, ii, n. companionship in a tent; attendance on a superior; common war tent. [to perceive.

contueor, tuĭtus, 2. v. dep. to look on; contuĭtus, ūs, m. survey, view.

contŭmācia, ae, f. stubbornness, firmness.

contŭmācĭter, ad. obstinately, stubbornly.

contŭmax, ācis, a. stubborn, firm.

contŭmēlia, ae, f. insult, affront, ignominy; damage.

contŭmēliōsē, ad. insolently, reproachfully. [sive.

contŭmēliōsus, a, um, a. insolent, abucontŭmŭlo, 1. v.a. to bury.

contundo, tŭdi, tūsum, 3. v.a. to bray *or* bruise *or* crush; *fig.* to weaken; to tame; to destroy.

conturbātio, ōnis, f. confusion, panic.

conturbātus, a, um, a. disturbed, perplexed.

conturbo, 1. v.a. to perplex; to disquiet; to make bankrupt.

contus, i, m. long pole, staff.

conub... *See* connub...

cōnus, i, m. cone; apex of a helmet.

convălesco, lui, 3. v.n. to recover, to get better.

convallāria (mod. hort.), lily of the valley.

convallis, is, f. a valley (much shut in).

convecto, 1. v.a. convĕho, vexi, vectum, 3. v.a. to carry together, to gather.

convello, velli, vulsum, 3. v.a. to tear, to pull *or* pluck up; to rend; to wrench; to shatter; *fig.* to overthrow, to annul.

convĕna, ae, c. assembly of strangers.

convĕniens, entis, p. & a. fitting; appropriate.

convĕnienter, ad. fitly, suitably.

convĕnientia, ae, f. agreement, harmony; fitness.

convĕnio, vĕni, ventum, 4. v.n. to come together, to assemble; to meet; to agree; to fit, to suit; to be due; —, v.a. to address, to visit, to interview.

conventĭcŭlum, i, n. small assemblage; place of assembly.

conventio, ōnis, f., conventum, i, n. agreement, compact.

conventus, ūs, m. meeting, assembly; provincial court; district.

converro, verri, versum, 3. v.a. to sweep together, to sweep away.

conversātio, ōnis, f. intercourse, conversation.

conversio, ōnis, f. turning round, revolution; periodical return; alteration, change; conclusion of a rhetorical period.

converso, 1. v.a. to turn round frequently;—conversor, to live, to pass one's time, to frequent.

converto, ti, sum, 3. v.a. to turn round; to convert; to change *or* transform; to apply; to translate;—convertere signa, to wheel.

convestio, īvi, ītum, 4. to clothe entirely.

convexus, a, um, a. convex; arched, vaulted; sloping;—convexa, ōrum, n. pl. vault.

convīcior, ātus, 1. v. dep. to revile, to reproach. [ing; reproach, abuse.

convīcium, ii, n. cry, clamour; bawlconvictio, ōnis, f. companionship, intimacy. [friend.

convictor, ōris, m. messmate, familiar convictus, ūs, m. living together, intimacy; banquet, feast.

convinco, vīci, victum, 3. v.a. to convict, to prove clearly.

convinctio, onis, f. a conjunction (grammatical term).

convīva, æ, c. table-companion, guest.

convīvālis, e, a. convivial.

convīvātor, ōris, m. entertainer, host.

convīvium, ii, n. feast, entertainment, banquet.

convīvor, 1. v.n. to feast together.

convŏco, 1. v.a. to call together, to convoke, to assemble.

convŏlo, 1. v.n. to fly together; *fig.* to run together.

convolvo, vi, vŏlŭtum, 3. v.a. to roll together *or* round, to intertwine.

convolvŭlus, i, m. bindweed; a worm that destroys vine-leaves.

coŏpĕrio, rui, rtum, 4. v.a. to cover wholly, to overwhelm.

cooptātio, ōnis, f. election.

coopto, i. v.a. to choose, to elect, to admit. [forth.

coŏrior, ortus, 4. v. dep. to arise; to break

copa, ae, f. hostess of an inn; barmaid.

cŏphĭnus, i, m. basket.

cōpia, ae, f. abundance, plenty; riches; store; provision (of victuals); ability; power; opportunity, means.

copiæ, ārum, f. pl. (military) forces.

cōpiōsē, ad. in great abundance; diffusely. [wealthy; eloquent.

cōpiōsus, a, um, a. plentiful, rich,

cōpo, v. **caupo.**

cōpŭla, ae, f. bond, tie.

cōpŭlātĭo, ōnis, f. connecting, uniting.

cōpŭlo, i. v.a. to couple, to bind or tie together, to connect, to unite.

cŏqua, ae, f. cook.

cŏquīnārius, a, um, culinary.

cŏquo, xi, ctum, 3. v.a. to cook; to boil, to fry, to bake; to burn; to parch; to ripen; to digest; fig. to meditate; to plan; to vex.

cŏquus, i, m. cook.

cŏr, cordis, n. heart; mind, judgment;— **cordi esse,** to be pleasing.

cŏrālium, ii, n. coral.

cŏram, ad. & pr. in the presence of, face to face; personally;—**coram populo,** in public.

corbis, is, c. wicker basket.

corbīta, ae, f. ship of burden, hoy.

cordātus, a, um, a. shrewd, wise.

coreopsis (mod. hort.), coreopsis.

coriandrum, i, n. coriander.

Cŏrinthium æs, composition of gold, silver, and copper.

cŏrium, ii, n. skin, leather, hide.

corneus, a, um, a. of horn, horny.

corneus, a, um, a. of the cornel-tree.

cornĭcen, ĭnis, m. horn-blower.

cornĭcŭla, ae, f. little crow.

cornĭcŭlum, i, n. a little horn.

cornĭgĕr, a, um, a. horn-bearing, horned.

cornĭpēs, ĕdis, a. horn-footed, hoofed.

cornix, ĭcis, f. crow;—**cornĭcor,** i. v. dep. to chatter like a crow.

cornu, ūs, n. horn; hoof; bill of a bird; the horns of the moon; arm of a bay; peak, cone of a helmet; bow; trumpet; wing of an army; lantern; funnel;— **cornu copiæ,** the goat's horn, or horn of plenty, filled with fruit and flowers by the nurse of Zeus: see **Amalthea;**— **cornua sumere,** to exalt one's horns, to gain courage.

cornum, i, n. cornel-cherry.

cornum, i, n., v. **cornu.**

cornus, i, f. cornel-cherry-tree, dogwood.

cornūtus, a, um, a. horned.

cŏrolla, ae, f. small garland.

cŏrollārium, ii, n. gift, present, corollary, inference; overplus.

cŏrōna, ae, f. garland, wreath, crown; circle (of men); line of circumvallation;—**sub corona vendere,** to sell as a slave.

cŏrōnārius, a, um, a. of garlands;—**aurum coronarium,** money subscribed for a victorious general. [surround.

cŏrōno, i. v.a. to crown, to wreathe; to

corpŏreus, a, um, a. corporeal; fleshly.

corpŭlentus, a, um, a. fat.

corpus, ŏris, n. body, substance; flesh; corpse; trunk; frame; system; corporation.

corpuscŭlum, i, n. little body, atom.

corrādo, si, sum, 3. v.a. to scrape together. [tion.

correctĭo, ōnis, f. improvement, correc-

corrector, ōris, m. corrector, improver.

correpo, psi, 3. v.n. to creep.

correptē, ad. shortly.

corrĭgia, ae, f. shoe-latchet.

corrĭgo, rexi, rectum, 3. v.a. to straighten, to set right; fig. to correct;—**corrigenda,** things to be corrected.

corrĭpio, rĭpui, reptum, 3. v.a. to snatch up, to lay hold of; to rebuke; to chastise; to shorten; to hasten; to steal away;—**corripere viam,** to hasten on one's way. [roborate.

corrōbŏro, i. v.a. to strengthen, to cor-

corrōdo, si, sum, 3. v.a. to gnaw (to pieces). [lect.

corrōgo, i. v.a. to get by begging, to col-

corrūgo, i. v.a. to wrinkle.

corrumpo, rūpi, ruptum, 3. v.a. to spoil, to deface; to falsify; to bribe; to corrupt, to seduce. [to the ground.

corruo, ui, 3. v.n. to break down, to fall

corruptē, ad. corruptly, incorrectly.

corruptēla, ae, f. corruption, seduction; bribery; corrupter.

corruptĭo, ōnis, f. corruption; bribery.

corruptor, ōris, m. corrupter, seducer, briber.

corruptrix, ĭcis, f. corrupter (feminine).

cortex, ĭcis, m. (& f.) bark, rind; cork.

cortīna, ae, f. tripod of Apollo; oracle.

cōrus, i, m. north-west wind.

cŏrusco, i. v.a. & n. to brandish, to shake; to flash, to coruscate. [flashing.

cŏruscus, a, um, a. vibrating, tremulous;

corvīnus, a, um, a. of a raven.

corvus, i, m. raven; (mil.) grapnel.

cŏrȳlētum, i, n. copse of hazel-trees.

cŏrȳlus, i, f. hazel-tree. [berries.

cŏrymbĭfer, i, m. bearing clusters of ivy-

cŏrymbus, i, m. cluster of fruit or flowers.

cŏrȳphæus, i, m. leader, chief, head.

cŏrȳtus, i, m. quiver.

cos., coss., abbrevs. for **consul, consules.**
cōs, cōtis, f. flint-stone; whetstone; **cotes,** pl. rocks.
cosmos (mod. hort.), Mexican aster.
costa, ae, f. rib; side, wall.
costum, i, n., costos, i, f. spikenard.
cŏthurnātus, a, um, a. wearing the buskin; in lofty style.
cŏthurnus, i, m. boot worn by Greek tragic actors; elevated style.
cotōneaster (mod. hort.), rose box.
cottidie, v. **quotidie.**
cŏturnix, īcis, f. quail.
cŏtȳlēdon, ŏnis, f. pennywort.
cŏum, i, n. Coan wine.
cŏvīnus, i, m. war-chariot.
coxa, ae. f. hip.
coxendix, īcis, f. hip, hip-bone.
crābro, ŏnis, m. hornet;—**irritare —nes,** to disturb a hornets' nest.
crambē, ēs, f. sea-kale, cabbage; *fig.* — **repetita,** cabbage warmed up again, a stale story. [sickness, headache.
crāpŭla, ae, f. drunkenness; next day's
crās, ad. to-morrow; future.
crassē, ad. grossly, rudely, dimly.
crassitūdo, ĭnis, f. thickness, density.
crassus, a, um, a. thick, dense, fat, gross, **crastinus, a, um,** a. of to-morrow. [rude.
crātægus (mod. hort.), may-tree.
crātēr, ēris, m. crātēra, ae, f. mixingbowl; receptacle for oil, trough, crater of a volcano; Cup (constellation).
crātes, is, f. wicker-work; harrow; framework.
creātio, ōnis, f. election. [father.
creātor, ōris, m. creator, author, founder;
creātrix, creatress, mother.
crēber, bra, brum, a. thick, close, pressed together, frequent, numerous; abundant.
crēbresco, brui, 3. v.n. to become frequent, to increase, to grow strong; to spread abroad.
crēbritas, ātis, f. frequency.
crēbro, ad. repeatedly, frequently.
crēdĭbĭlis, e, a. trustworthy, credible.
crēdĭbĭliter, ad. credibly.
crēdĭtor, ōris, m. lender, creditor.
crēdĭtum, i, n. loan.
crēdo, dĭdi, dĭtum, 3. v.a. to believe; to trust; to entrust; to think *or* to be of opinion; **credat Judæus Apella,** let the Jew Apella believe; no one but a superstitious Jew is likely to believe.
crēdŭlĭtas, ātis, f. credulity. [lous.
crēdŭlus, a, um, a. easy of belief, credu-
crēmātio, onis, f. cremation.
crēmo, i. v.a. to burn, to consume by fire.
crēmor, ōris, m. cream, thick juice (of barley).

creo, i. v.a. to create, to make, to produce; to choose; to elect; to cause; to establish; to ordain.
crĕpĭda, ae, f. slipper, sandal;—**ne sutor supra —m,** let the cobbler stick to his last.
crĕpĭdātus, a, um, a. wearing sandals.
crĕpīdo, ĭnis, f. pedestal; brink, border, pier, bank.
crĕpĭtācŭlum, i, n. rattle. [rustle.
crĕpĭto, i. v.n. to rattle, to clatter, to
crĕpĭtus, ūs, m. rattling, clashing, rustling; (of thunder) crash; (of the teeth) chattering.
crĕpo, ui, ĭtum, i. v.n. to rattle, to rustle, to clatter; to snap the fingers; to jingle; to boast, to prate. [cymbals.
crĕpundia, ōrum, n. pl. child's rattle;
crĕpuscŭlum, i, n. twilight, dusk.
cresco, crēvi, crētum, 3. v.n. to grow; to arise, to spring; to appear; to get advantage; to increase; to attain honour, to be advanced, to be strengthened.
crēta, ae, f. Cretan earth; chalk; clay; paint.
crētātus, a, um, a. marked with chalk.
crētio, ōnis, f. declaration respecting the acceptance of an inheritance. [clay.
crētōsus, a, um, a. abounding in chalk *or*
crētŭla, ae, f. white chalk used for sealing
crībrum, i, n. sieve. [letters.
crīmen, ĭnis, n. crime, offence, fault; scandal; reproach; accusation;— **crim ne ab uno disce omnes,** from one base- act learn the character of the whole nation.
crīmĭnātio, ōnis, f. accusation; calumny.
crīmĭnor, ātus, i, v. dep. to accuse; to charge (with).
crīmĭnōsē, ad. by way of accusation, reproachfully; calumniously.
crīmĭnōsus, a, um, a. accusatory; reproachful, slanderous.
crīnālis, e, a. pertaining to the hair.
crīnis, is, m. hair; tail of a comet.
crīnītus, a, um, a. hairy; having long locks;—**stella —a,** comet.
crīnum (mod. hort.), Cape lily.
crispo, i. v.a. to curl, to crisp; to swing, to brandish. [quivering.
crispus, a, um, a. curled; curly-headed;
crista, ae, f. crest; cock's comb; plume (of a helmet). [plumed.
cristātus, a, um, a. tufted, crested;
crithmum (mod. hort.), samphire.
crĭticus, a, um, a. critical;—**apparatus criticus,** critic's stock-in-trade.
crĭticus, i, m. critic. [coloured; golden.
crŏceus, a, um, a. of saffron; saffron-
crŏcĭnus, a, um, a. of saffron; **crocinum, i, n.** saffron ointment.

crŏcŏdīlus, i, m. crocodile.

crŏcus, i, m. crŏcum, i, n. crocus; saffron; saffron-colour.　　[the castanets.

crŏtălīstria, ae, f. a girl who dances to

crŏtălum, i, n. rattle, castanet.

crŭciābĭlis, e, a. torturing.

crŭciāmentum, i, n. torture, pain.

crŭciātus, ūs, m. torture; execution; *fig.* misery.

crŭcio, i. v.a. & n. to torture; to grieve.

crūdēlis, e, a. rough, bloodthirsty; cruel.

crūdēlĭtas, ātis, f. cruelty, barbarity.

crūdēlĭter, ad. cruelly.　　　　　　[bad.

crūdesco, dŭi, 3. v.n. to become hard *or*

crūdĭtas, ātis, f. overloading of the stomach.

crūdus, a, um, a. raw; bloody; undigested; unripe, sour; fresh; immature; vigorous; harsh; cruel.

cruento, i. v.a. to stain with blood.

crŭentus, a, um, a. gory, bloody; bloodthirsty; blood-red.　　　　　　[money.

crŭmēna, crŭmĭna, ae, f. purse; *fig.*

crŭor, ōris, m. gore, blood; murder.

crūs, ūris, n. leg, shank, shin.

crusta, ae, f. rind, shell, crust, bark; stucco, mosaic.　　　　　　[with mosaic.

crūsto, i. v.a. to incrust; to cover

crustŭlum, i, n. confectionery.

crustum, i, n. pastry.

crux, ŭcis, f. cross *fig.* gallows-bird; *fig.* torture, trouble, misery, destruction; —abi in malam crucem, go to the

crypta, ae, f. cave, pit, vault.　　[deuce!

cryptŏportĭcus, us, f. covered passage; cloister.　　　　　　　　　　[chamber.

cŭbĭcŭlāris, e, a. pertaining to a bed-

cŭbĭcŭlārius, i, m. valet.

cŭbĭcŭlum, i, n. bed-chamber　[*fig.* den.

cŭbīle, is, n. couch, bed; marriage-bed;

cŭbĭtal, is, n. elbow-cush'

cŭbĭtālis, e, a. an ell long

cŭbĭto, i. v.n. to lie down often.

cŭbĭtum, i, n. elbow; ell, cubit.

cŭbo, ŭi, ĭtum, i. v.n. to lie down; to lie asleep; to recline at table; to keep one's bed.

cŭcullus, i, m. hood;—cucullus non facit monachum, the cowl does not make the

cŭcŭlus, i, m. cuckoo.　　　　　　[monk.

cŭcŭmis, ĕris, m. cucumber.

cŭcurbĭta, ae, f. gourd.　　　　[to coin.

cūdo, 3. v.a. to strike; to forge; to knock;

cui bono, v. quis.

cūjas, ātis, pn. of what country *or* town?

cūjus, a, um, pn. whose, whereof.

culcĭta, ae, f. bed, cushion, pillow.

cŭleus, i, m. leather bag, a liquid measure.

cŭlex, ĭcis, m. gnat, midge.

cūlīna, ae, f. kitchen; *fig.* fare, victuals.

culleus, i, v. culeus.

culmen, ĭnis, n. top, summit, dome; gable; *fig.* acme.

culmus, i, m. stalk, stem; thatch.

culpa, ae, f. fault, crime, blame; negligence; unchastity; bane.

culpo, i. v.a. to blame, to find fault with;

cultē, ad. elegantly.　　　　　　[to accuse.

cultellus, i, m. small knife.

culter, tri, m. knife, razor.

cultio, ōnis, f. cultivation; agriculture.

cultor, ōris, m. husbandman; cultivator, inhabitant; *fig.* supporter; tutor, teacher; worshipper.　　[inhabitant.

cultrix, ĭcis, f. female supporter, female

cultūra, ae, f. agriculture; care, culture, cultivation.

cultus, a, um, a. cultivated, polished, elegant, civilized;—culta, orum, n. pl. tilled land.

cultus, ūs, m. worship, reverence; culture; refinement; civilization; luxury; splendour (of dress).

cŭlullus, i, m. cup, bowl.

cum, pr. with; along with; amid; with words expressing strife, contention, etc., against;—cum magno reipublicae periculo, to the great danger of the state;—cum privilegio, (published) under licence.

cum, c. when; since; although; as soon

cumba, v. cymba.　　　　　　　　[as.

cŭmēra, ae, f. corn-vessel, meal-tub.

cŭmĭnum, i, n. cumin.

. . . cumque, ad. . . . . ever, . . . soever.

cŭmŭlātē, ad. amply, copiously.

cŭmŭlātus, a, um, a. complete, perfect.

cŭmŭlo, i. v.a. to heap up; to accumulate; to fill full.

cŭmŭlus, i, m. heap, pile; surplus, increase; summit, crown.

cūnābŭla, ōrum, n. pl. cradle; *fig.* earliest dwelling-place; birth, earliest childhood.

cūnæ, ārum, f. pl. cradle; birth.　[hood.

cunctābundus, a, um, a. lingering, loitering.

cunctans, antis, p. & a. lingering, dilatory.

cunctanter, ad. slowly.

cunctātio, ōnis, f. delay, hesitation, doubt.

cunctātor, ōris, m. loiterer, lingerer.

cunctor, atus, i. v. dep. to tarry, to linger, to hesitate.　　　　　　[all, entire.

cunctus, a, um, a. all together, the whole,

cŭnĕātim, ad. in the form of a wedge.

cŭnĕātus, a, um, a. wedge-shaped.

cŭnĕŏlus, i, m. little wedge.

cŭneus, i, m. wedge; battalion, etc., drawn up in the form of a wedge; rows of seats in a theatre.

cŭnĭcŭlus, i, m. rabbit; underground passage; (mil.) mine; cavity, canal.

cŭnīla, æ, f. wild marjoram.

cunque, v. cumque.

cūpa, æ, f. tub, cask
cūpēd, v. cupped.
cŭpĭdē, ad. eagerly; vehemently.
cŭpĭdĭtas, ātis, f. longing, desire; passion; avarice; party-spirit.
cŭpĭdo, ĭnis, f. desire, greediness; appetite; love; avarice; —, m. the god of love.
cŭpĭdus, a, um, a. longing for, desiring, eager; loving; greedy, passionate.
cŭpiens, entis, p. & a. desirous, longing, eager for. [to desire; to covet.
cŭpio, īvi & ii, ītum, 3. v.a. to long for,
cuppedia, æ, f. love of dainties; dainties.
cuppēdo, ĭnis, f. delicacies;—Forum Cuppedinis, a market at Rome where delicacies were sold.
cuppes, ĕdis, a. fond of delicacies.
cupressētum, i, n. grove of cypress-trees.
cupresseus, a, um, a. of cypress.
cupressĭfer, ĕra, ĕrum, a. cypress-bearing.
cupressus, i, f. cypress; box of cypress-cur, ad. wherefore? why? [wood.
cūra, æ, f. attention, care; administration; office; written work; guardian; sorrow; anxiety, concern; trouble; love; object of love.
curalium, v. coralium.
cūrātē, ad. carefully, diligently.
cūrātio, ōnis, f. administration, management; healing, cure, guardianship.
cūrātor, ōris, m. manager, superintendent; trustee. [good condition.
cūrātus, a, um, a. careful, solicitous; in
curcŭlio, ōnis, m. weevil.
cūria, æ, f. division of the Roman people, court, senate-house, senate.
cūriātus, a, um, a. pertaining to curiae;—comitia curiata, the assembly in which people voted according to curiae.
cūrio, ōnis, m. chief priest of a curia.
cūriōsē, ad. curiously, inquisitively.
cūriōsus, a, um, a. careful, diligent; curious, inquisitive.
cŭris, ītis, f. spear (Sabine word).
cūro, 1. v.a. to take care of, to mind; to value, to respect; to order; to attend to; to heal; to cure.
currĭcŭlum, i, n. race; race-ground; chariot; fig. career.
curro, cŭcurri, cursum, 3. v.n. to run, to hasten;—currente calamo, with running pen; off-hand.
currus, ŭs, m. chariot, car; triumphal car; triumph; horses (in a chariot).
cursim, ad. swiftly, hastily.
cursĭto, 1. curso, 1. v.n. to run hither and thither. [courier.
cursor, ōris, m. runner; chariot-racer;
cursus, ŭs, m. running; course, voyage, journey; race; direction; march; fig. career; manner.

curto, 1. v.a. to shorten; to lessen.
curtus, a, um, a. shortened; fig. incomplete.
cŭrūlis, e, a. pertaining to a chariot;—equi curules, horses provided at state expense for the public games;—sella curulis, a seat of honour used by consuls, praetors, and aediles.
curvāmen, ĭnis, n. bending, bend.
curvātūra, æ, f. bending, bend; rim; vault.
curvo, 1. v.a. to crook, to bend, to curve.
curvus, a, um, a. crooked, bent, curved.
cuspĭdātus, a, um, a. pointed.
cuspis, ĭdis, f. point, spike; spear; trident (of Neptune); scorpion's sting.
custōdia, æ, f. watch, guard, care; watch-house; body-guard; confinement; prison.
custōdio, īvi & ii, ītum, 4. v.a. to watch, to guard; to preserve; to take heed; to retain.
custos, ōdis, c. keeper; guardian; protector; watchman; jailer; spy; receptacle;—custos rotulorum, Keeper of the Rolls.
cŭtĭcŭla, æ, f. skin. [cup.
cŭtis, is, f. skin.
cyāthus, i, m. wine-ladle, wine-measure, cyclamen (mod. hort.), cyclamen.
cy̆clicus, i, m. cyclic poet.
cy̆dōnia, ōrum, n. pl. quince.
cygnēus, a, um, a. of a swan; swan-like.
cygnus, i, m. swan; fig. poet.
cy̆lindrus, dri, m. cylinder; roller (for levelling the ground).
cymba, æ, f. boat, skiff.
cymbălum, i, n. cymbal.
cymbium, ii, n. small drinking vessel.
cymnum, i, v. cuminum.
cynăra (mod. hort.), globe artichoke.
cy̆nicus, i, m. (cyn. philosopher).
cy̆norrhŏdŏı, i, n. dog-rose.
cy̆nosbătos, i, f. dog-rose. [lation).
cy̆nŏsūra, æ, f. the Lesser Bear (constel-cyparissus, i, v. cupressus.
cyprīnum, i, n. cyprus oil.
cyprĭpedium (mod. hort.), lady's slipper.
Cyprius, a, um, a. of copper;—Cyprium, [ii, n. copper.
cy̆tĭsus, i, c. broom.

D = 500.
dacty̆licus, a, um, a. dactylic.
dacty̆lus, i, m. (metre) dactyl, a long foot succeeded by two short.
dædălus, a, um, a. fig. skilful; skilfully made; variegated.
dæmon, ōnis, m. spirit; devil. [devil.
dæmoniacus, a, um, a. possessed of a dahlia (mod. hort.), dahlia.

damma, ae, f. fallow-deer, doe.
damnātio, ōnis, f. condemnation.
damnātōrius, a, um, condemnatory.
damno, 1. v.a. to condemn, to sentence,
to disapprove.
damnōsē, ad. hurtfully; very.
damnōsus, a, um, a. hurtful, injurious,
destructive; prodigal;—damnosa hereditas, a legacy involving the recipient
in loss. [fine.
damnum, i, n. damage, injury, loss; hurt,
dănista, ae, m. money-lender.
daphne (mod. hort.), garland-flower.
daps, dăpis, f. sacrificial feast; banquet.
dapsĭlis, e, a. bountiful, rich.
dardanārius, ii, m. speculator, one who
makes a corner in any commodity.
data, n. pl., v. do.
dătio, ōnis, f. giving, right of alienation.
dător, ōris, m. giver.
dătūra (mod. hort.), thorn apple.
dătīvus, i, m. dative (case).
daucus, i, m. carrot.
davallia (mod. hort.), hare's-foot fern.
dē, pr. down from; from; away from, out
of; about; (made) of, concerning; for;
by reason of; after, according to;—
diem de die, day after day;—de more,
according to custom;—de facto, in
reality;—de jure, legally;—de integro,
de novo, afresh;—de profundis, from
the depths.
dea, ae, f. goddess.
dealbo, 1. v.a. to whitewash.
deambŭlo, 1. v.n. to walk about.
dēbacchor, ātus, 1. v.n. dep. fig. to rage
violently.
dēbellātor, ōris, m. conqueror.
dēbello, 1. v.n. to bring a war to an end;
to vanquish.
dēbeo, ui, ĭtum, 2. v.a. to owe, to be in
debt; fig. to be obliged or bound or
destined.
dēbĭlis, e, a. weak, feeble; crippled.
dēbĭlĭtas, ātis, f. weakness, debility.
dēbĭlĭtātio, ōnis, f. weakening, maiming.
dēbĭlito, 1. v.a. to weaken; to maim; fig.
dēbĭtor, ōris, m. debtor. [to discourage.
dēbĭtum, i, n. debt; duty. [repeat often.
dēcanto, 1. v.a. to sing off, to chant; to
dēcēdo, cessi, cessum, 3. v.n. to go away,
to depart; to retire, to yield; to
cease; to die; to disappear; to decrease;—decedere de, to retire from.
dĕcem, a. num. indecl. ten.
Dĕcember, bris, m. December. [rod.
dĕcempĕda, ae, f. ten-foot measuring
dĕcemplex, ĭcis, a. tenfold. [oars.
dĕcemrēmis, e, a. having ten banks of
dĕcemvirālis, e, a. decemviral.
dĕcemvirātus, ūs, m. decemvirate.

dĕcemvĭri, ōrum, m. pl. commission of ten
(magistrates at Rome).
decennis, e, a. lasting ten years; ten years
old. [fit; handsome, comely.
dĕcens, entis, p. & a. becoming, decent;
dĕcenter, ad. decently.
dēcerno, crēvi, crētum, 3. v.a. & n. to
distinguish; to judge; to decide; to
settle; to contend.
dēcerpo, psi, ptum, 3. v.a. to pluck or pull
off; to destroy; to enjoy.
dēcerto, 1. v.n. to fight out; to dispute.
dēcessio, ōnis, f. going away, departure;
retirement; diminution; abatement.
dēcessor, ōris, m. predecessor.
dēcessus, ūs, m. departure; retirement;
decrease; ebb; death. [it is proper.
dĕcet, cuit, 2. v.n. it beseems or behoves,
dēcĭdo, cĭdi, 3. v.n. to fall down; to pass
away; to die.
dēcīdo, cīdi, cīsum, 3. v.a. to cut off; fig.
to determine, to put an end to.
dēcĭduus, a, um, a. falling off, deciduous.
dĕcĭēs, ad. ten times.
dĕcĭma, ae, f. tenth part; tithe.
dĕcĭmānus, dĕcŭmānus, a, um, a. belonging to the tithes; —, i, m. farmer of
tithes;—porta decumana, the chief
gate of a Roman camp.
dĕcĭmo, 1. v.a. to choose by lot every
tenth man (for punishment).
dĕcĭmus, dĕcŭmus, a, um, a. tenth;—
decimum, ad. for the tenth time.
dēcĭpio, cēpi, ceptum, 3. v.a. to beguile,
to cheat.
dēcĭsio, ōnis, f. settlement, decision.
dēclāmātio, ōnis, f. declamation; bawl-
dēclāmātor, ōris, m. declaimer. [ing.
dēclāmātōrius, a, um, a. declamatory,
rhetorical.
dēclāmĭto, 1. v.n. & a. to declaim; fig.
to bluster;—, v.a. to plead causes (by
way of practice).
dēclāmo, 1. v.n. to declaim; to bawl.
dēclārātio, ōnis, f. statement, declaration.
dēclāro, i. v.a. to declare; to prove; to
explain. [ance; (gr.) inflection.
dēclīnātio, ōnis, f. declination; avoid-
dēclīno, 1. v.a. & n. to turn aside; to
avoid; to deviate.
dēclīvis, e, a. sloping downwards, steep;—
declīve, is, n. slope, declivity.
dēclīvitas, ātis, f. declivity.
dēcoctor, ōris, m. spendthrift; bankrupt.
dēcollo, 1. v.a. to decapitate.
dēcŏlor, ōris, a. discoloured, faded; fig.
degenerate. [to soil.
dēcŏlōro, 1. v.a. to discolour, to deface,
dēcŏquo, xi, ctum, 3. v.a. to boil away;
fig. to waste away; to become bankrupt.

dĕcor, ōris, m. comeliness, grace; charm.

dĕcōrē, ad. decorously; charmingly.

dĕcŏro, 1. v.a. to adorn, to grace; to extol.

dĕcōrus, ă, um, a. decorous; proper; suitable; graceful, handsome; noble.

dĕcrĕpĭtus, a, um, a. very old, decrepit.

dĕcresco, crēvi, crētum, 3. v.n. to decrease; to diminish; to disappear.

dĕcrētum, i, n. decree, decision; principle, decuma, etc., v. decima, etc.   [doctrine.

dēcumbo, cŭbui, 3. v.n. to lie down; to recline at meals; to fall down and die.

dĕcŭria, ae, f. division, class (of ten).

dĕcŭrio, 1. v.a. to divide into companies of ten.

dĕcŭrio, ōnis, m. the head of a decuria.

dēcurro, (cŭ)curri, cursum, 3. v.n. to run down; to sail; to have recourse to; to skirmish; —, v.a. to run through.

dēcursio, ōnis, f. (mil.) charge.

dēcursus, ūs, m. downward course; declivity; (mil.) charge.

dēcurto, 1. v.a. to cut off, to mutilate.

dĕcus, ōris, n. grace, ornament; glory; beauty; virtue; chastity;—decora, um, pl. noble deeds.

dĕcussis, is, m. a coin worth ten asses.

dĕcusso, 1. v.a. to divide cross-wise.

dĕcŭtio, cussi, cussum, 3. v.a. to shake down or off.   [is unseemly.

dēdĕcet, cuit, a. v. imp. it misbecomes, it

dēdĕcor, ōris, a. disgraced.

dēdĕcŏro, 1. v.a. to disgrace.

dēdĕcŏrus, a, um, a. dishonourable.

dēdĕcus, ōris, n. disgrace, infamy; shame; dishonour; unchastity.

dēdĭcātio, ōnis, f. dedication, consecration.

dēdĭco, 1. v.a. to dedicate, to devote.

dēdignor, atus, 1. v. dep. to disdain; to refuse.   [forget.

dēdisco, dĭdĭci, 3. v.a. to unlearn, to

dēdĭtio, ōnis, f. surrender, capitulation.

dēdĭtīcius, surrendered; —, ii, one who has surrendered; prisoner.

dēdĭtus, a, um, devoted to, fond of.

dēdo, dĭdi, dĭtum, 3. v.a. to surrender; to capitulate; to abandon; to yield.

dēdŏceo, 2. v.a. to unteach.

dēdŏleo, ui, 2. v.n. to cease to grieve.

dēdŏlo, 1. v.a. to hew away.

dēdūco, xi, ctum, 3. v.a. to lead or draw down; to bring away or off; to plant (a colony); to launch; to conduct; to escort; to derive; to compose; to withdraw; to subtract.

dēductio, ōnis, f. conveyance; abatement, deduction; colonization; reasoning from the general to the particular.

dēductus, a, um, p. & a. bent inwards;

deero, 1. v.n. to go astray.   [low, weak.

dēfaeco, 1. v.a. to strain; to cleanse; fig. to clear up.

dēfătīgātio, ōnis, f. weariness, fatigue.

dēfătīgo, 1. v.a. to tire, to fatigue.

dēfectio, ōnis, f. failure, deficiency; defection, revolt.

dēfector, ōris, m. apostate, rebel.

dēfectus, ūs, m. failure, lack; disappearance, eclipse.

dēfendo, di, sum, 3. v.a. to defend, to guard; to preserve; to keep off; to affirm, to maintain.

dēfensio, ōnis, f. defence.

dēfensĭto, 1. v.a. to defend often.

dēfenso, 1. v.a. to keep off carefully; to defend.   [protector.

dēfensor, ōris, m. defender, guardian,

dēfĕro, tŭli, lātum, ferre, v.a. ir. to bring or carry down or off; to convey; to bring word; to bestow; to present; to tell; to transfer; to accuse, to indict.

dēfervesco, fervi or ferbui, 3. v.n. fig. to grow calm; to become moderate.

dēfĕtiscor, fessus, 3. v.n. dep. to grow weary or faint.

dēficio, fēci, fectum, 3. v.n. & a. to fail; to cease; to faint; to be discouraged; to sink under; to be wanting or defective; to decay; to break; to die; to desert, to forsake.

dēfigo, xi, xum, 3. v.a. to fix down, to fasten; to thrust into; fig. to astound, to curse, to bewitch;—oculos defigere, to cast down the eyes.

dēfinio, īvi, ītum, 4. v.a. to limit; to define; to determine; to end.

dēfinītē, ad. precisely, definitely.

dēfinītio, ōnis, f. limiting; definition.

dēfinītīvus, a, um, a. definitive, explanatory.

dēfinītus, a, um, p. & a. definite, precise.

dēfio, ĕri, 3. v.n. pass. to lack, to be wanting.   [struction.

dēflagrātio, ōnis, f. conflagration; destruction.

dēflagro, 1. v.n. to be burnt down; to perish; to abate; —, v.a. to burn down; to destroy.

dēflecto, xi, xum, 3. v.a. & n. to bend or turn aside or off; to pervert.   [wail.

dēfleo, ēvi, ētum, 2. v.a. to deplore, to bewail.

dēflōresco, rui, 3. v.n. to fade, to wither.

dēfluo, xi, xum, 3. v.n. to flow down; to glide down; to cease to flow; to fade, to decay; to disappear; to be ended.

dēfŏdio, fōdi, fossum, 3. v.a. to dig; to bury.   [less; odious; base.

dēformis, e, a. ill-formed, ugly; shape-

dēformĭtas, ātis, f. deformity, ugliness, baseness.

dēformo, 1. v.a. to shape, to fashion; to delineate, to describe.

dēformo, 1. v.a. to disfigure; *fig.* to dishonour.

dēfraudo, 1. v.a. to cheat, to defraud.

dēfrēnātus, a, um, a. unbridled.

dēfrĭco, cui, catum & ctum, 1. v.a. to rub hard. 　　　　　[off, *or* to pieces.

dēfringo, frēgi, fractum, 3. v.a. to break

defrŭtum, i, n. new wine boiled down with spices.

dēfŭgio, fūgi, 3. v.a. & n. to avoid, to run away (from), to escape. 　[down *or* out.

dēfundo, fūdi, fūsum, 3. v.a. to pour

dēfungor, functus, 3. v. dep. to discharge, to finish; to have done with; to die.

dēgĕner, is, a. degenerate; low-born; base.

dēgĕnĕro, 1. v.n. & a. to degenerate; to make worse; to dishonour.

dēgo, dēgi, 3. v.a. to spend *or* pass; to live.

dēgrăvo, 1. v.a. to weigh down; to overpower; to incommode.

dēgrĕdior, gressus, 3. v. dep. to march down, to descend; to dismount.

dēgusto, 1. v.a. to taste; *fig.* to try; to test; to touch slightly on.

dēhinc, ad. hereafter; hence; henceforth; next; since then.

dēhisco, hīvi, 3. v.n. to gape, to split asunder. 　　　　　　　[grace.

dēhŏnestāmentum, i, n. blemish, disdēhŏnesto, 1. v.a. to disgrace.

dēhortor, atus, 1. v.a. dep. to dissuade.

dein, v. deinde. 　　　　[and so forth.

deinceps, ad. successively; in a series, deindĕ, ad. from thence; afterward, hereafter; then; next.

dējectĭo, ōnis, f. ejection.

dējectus, a, um, p. & a. low; disheartened; —, ūs, m. throwing down; fall; declivity.

dējero, v. dejuro, to swear.

dējĭcio, jēci, jectum, 3. v.a. to throw down; to dislodge; to fell; to kill; to rob of; to dispossess;—**spe dejici,** to **dējūro**, 1. v. dejero. 　[despair.

dēlābor, lapsus, 3. v. dep. to slip *or* fall down; to descend; to sink.

dēlasso, 1. v.a. to weary *or* tire out.

dēlātĭo, ōnis, f. accusation, denunciation.

dēlātor, ōris, m. accuser, informer.

dēlectābĭlis, e, a. delightful, agreeable.

dēlectāmentum, i, n. delight, amusement.

dēlectātĭo, ōnis, f. delight, pleasure, amusement. 　　　[amuse; to charm.

dēlecto, 1. v.a. to entice; to delight; to **dēlectus, ūs**, m. selection, choice; levy;—**delectum habere,** to hold a levy.

dēlēgātĭo, ōnis, f. transference to another; delegation; assignment (of a debt).

dēlēgo, 1. v.a. to assign; to delegate, to depute; to impute; to transfer.

dēlēnīmentum, i, n. charm, allurement.

dēlēnio, īvi, ītum, 4. v.a. to mitigate, to smooth down; to entice; to cajole.

dēleo, lēvi, lētum, 2. v.a. to efface; to suppress; to destroy; to kill; to annul.

dēlībĕrābundus, a, um, a. weighing well, deliberating. 　　　　　[sideration.

dēlībĕrātĭo, ōnis, f. deliberation, con-dēlībĕro, 1. v.a. to consult, to deliberate; to resolve.

dēlībo, 1. v.a. to taste (of), to touch lightly; to enjoy; *fig.* to diminish, to detract (from). 　　　　　　[to peel.

dēlibro, atum, 1. v.a. to take off the bark, **dēlĭbuo, ui, ūtum**, 3. v.a. to smear, to anoint.

dēlĭcātē, ad. delicately, elegantly.

dēlĭcātus, a, um, a. charming, elegant; delicate, tender; voluptuous; luxurious; effeminate; affected; full of pretensions.

dēlĭciæ, ārum, f. pl. delight, pleasures; dalliance; sports; airs and graces; darling; sweetheart.

dēlĭcium, ii, v. **deliciæ.**

dēlĭco, 1. v.a. to explain.

dēlictum, i, n. fault, offence, crime;—**flagrante delicto,** (to catch) with the crime still hot, (to catch) in the act of commission.

dēlĭgo, lēgi, lectum, 3. v.a. to choose out, to select, to cull.

dēlĭgo, 1. v.a. to bind down, to tie up.

dēlĭneo, 1. v.a. to sketch.

dēlinquo, līqui, lictum, 3. v.a. & n. to fail (in duty); to offend, to do wrong.

dēlĭquesco, licui, 3. v.n. to melt away; to dissolve; to disappear.

dēlĭquo, 1. v.a. to strain.

dēlīrātĭo, ōnis, f. silliness, folly, madness.

dēlīro, 1. v.n. to be crazy *or* silly, to dote.

dēlīrus, a, um, a. silly, doting, crazy.

dēlĭtesco, tui, 3. v.n. to lie hid, to lurk.

dēlĭtīgo, 1. v.n. to rail.

delphinium (mod. hort.), larkspur.

delphīnus, i, delphīn, īnis, m. dolphin.

delta, ae, f. the Greek letter Δ;—**Delta,** indeclin.; the Delta of the Nile, which is shaped like the Greek letter.

deltōton, i, n. Triangle (constellation).

dēlūbrum, i, n. shrine, sanctuary, temple.

dēlūdo, si, sum, 3. v.a. to delude, to deceive; to mock, to disappoint.

dēlumbo, atum, 1. v.a. *fig.* to weaken, to enervate. 　　　　　[all over.

dēmădesco, dui, 3. v.n. to become moist

dēmando, 1. v.a. to give in charge, to intrust, to commend.

dēmens, entis, a. senseless; mad, foolish.

dēmenter, ad. senselessly, madly.

dēmentia, ae, f. madness, folly.

demento, I. v.a. to craze, to rob of wits; —**quem deus vult perdere dementat prius,** whomsoever the god wishes to destroy he robs of his senses first.

dēmĕreo, ui, 2. v.a. to deserve well of; to oblige.

dēmergo, si, sum, 3. v.a. to plunge (into), to dive;—**demergor,** to sink, to be overwhelmed. [out.

dēmētior, mensus, 4. v.a. dep. to measure

dēmĕto, messui, messum, 3. v.a. to mow, to reap, to cut off; to pluck.

dēmigrātio, onis, f. emigration.

dēmigro, I. v.n. to wander away, to emigrate; to move.

dēmīnuo, ui, ūtum, 3. v.a. to lessen, to diminish.

dēmīnūtio, ōnis, f. diminution, decrease; — **capitis,** loss of civil rights.

dēmīror, ātus, I. v. dep. to wonder at, to be amazed.

dēmissē, ad. low; *fig.* humbly; abjectly.

dēmissio, ōnis, f. letting down; *fig.* low spirits, dejection.

dēmissus, a, um, p. & a. low-lying; hanging down; *fig.* downcast; humble; unassuming; (of the voice) low.

dēmitto, mīsi, missum, 3. v.a. to let sink, to lower; to send down; to dismiss; to thrust (into); to plunge; to sink; to submit; to stoop.

dēmo, mpsi, mptum, 3. v.a. to take away; to tear off; to pare; to lessen.

dēmōlior, ītus, 4. v. dep. to pull down, to demolish; to remove, to destroy.

dēmōlītio, ōnis, f. pulling down, demolishing. [clear proof.

dēmonstrātio, ōnis, f. demonstration,

dēmonstrātivus, a, um, a. pointing out; demonstrative.

dēmonstro, I. v.a. to point at; to prove, to demonstrate; to describe; to represent.

dēmŏrior, mortuus, 3. v. dep. to die off.

dēmŏror, ātus, I. v.a. & n. dep. to keep back, to detain; to tarry, to abide.

dēmŏveo, mōvi, mōtum, 2. v.a. to move away, to put away, to remove, to withdraw. [entice.

dēmulceo, mulsi, mulctum, to stroke, to

dēmum, ad. at length, at last;—**tum demum,** then and then only; then at last; indeed.

dēmurmŭro, I. v.a. to mutter over.

dēmūto, I. v.a. & n. to change for the worse, to alter.

dēnārius, a, um, a. containing ten; —, ii, m. Roman coin worth about 10d.

dēnarro, I. v.a. to relate fully.

dēnĕgo, I. v.a. to refuse, to deny.

dēni, ae, a, a. num. ten each, by tens.

dēnĭcālis, e, a. —**es feriæ,** solemn purification of a house, on the tenth day after the death of a person.

dēnĭque, ad. at last, finally, in fact; in short.

dēnōmĭno, I. v.a. to name, to call.

dēnŏto, I. v.a. to specify, to denote, to brand.

dens, dentis, m. tooth; tusk; ivory; fluke (of an anchor); prong.

densē, ad. thickly, closely; frequently.

denseo, ētum, 2. v.a. **denso,** I. v.a. to thicken; to press close together.

densus, a, um, a. thick, dense; thickly planted with; frequent; concise.

dentāle, is, n. the share-beam of a ploughshare.

dentātus, a, um, a. toothed; jagged;— **charta dentata,** paper highly polished (with a tooth).

dentĭcŭlatus, a, um, a. set with small teeth.

dentifrĭcium, ii, tooth powder. [teeth.

dentio, ivi, ītum, 4. v.n. to cut the teeth.

dentītio, onis, f. a cutting of the teeth.

dēnūbo, psi, ptum, 3. v.n. to marry; to marry beneath one's condition.

dēnūdo, I. v.a. to make naked, to uncover; *fig.* to reveal; to plunder.

dēnuntiātio, ōnis, f. denunciation, declaration; threat; prognostic; summons.

dēnuntio, I. v.a. to announce, to declare; to denounce; to foretell; to threaten; to summon (a witness); to order.

dēnuo, ad. anew, afresh, again.

deŏnĕro, I. v.a. to unload.

deorsum, deorsus, ad. downwards, beneath, below;—**sursum deorsum,** up and down.

Deo volente, D.V., God being willing.

dēpăciscor, pactus, 3. v. dep. to bargain for, to covenant, to agree upon.

depango, pactum, 3. v.a. to drive in.

depasco, pāvi, pastum, 3. v.a. to pasture, to browse; to waste, to consume.

dēpecto, xum, 3. v.a. to comb down; (jest.) to cudgel. [of the state.

dēpĕcūlātor, ōris, m. plunderer, robber

dēpĕcūlor, ātus, I. v. dep. to plunder, to embezzle. [dislodge; to dissuade.

dēpello, pŭli, pulsum, 3. v.a. to expel; to

dēpendeo, 2. v.n. to hang down, from *or* on; *fig.* to depend upon.

dēpendo, di, sum, 3. v.a. to pay for, to expend. [to ruin; to lose.

dēperdo, dīdi, dītum, 3. v.a. to destroy,

dēpĕreo, ii, 4. v.n. to perish; to be lost.

dēpilo, I. v.a. to strip of hair.

dēpingo, nxi, pictum, 3. v.a. to paint, to depict; to portray; *fig.* to describe; to imagine.

dēplango, nxi, 3. v.a. to bewail. [imagine.

dēplōro, 1. v.n. & a. to bewail, to deplore; *fig.* to give up for lost.

dēpōno, pŏsui, pŏsĭtum, 3. v.a. to lay down *or* aside; to deposit; to commit; to intrust; to resign; to fix *or* set *or* plant; to stake, to wager; to impose (upon); to quench;—dēpŏsĭtus, all but dead, despaired of.

dēpŏpŭlātĭo, ōnis, f. laying waste, plundering. [dering.

dēpŏpŭlātor, oris, m. plunderer.

dēpŏpŭlo, 1. v.a. dēpŏpŭlor, ātus, 1. v.a. dep. to lay waste, to plunder; to destroy.

dēporto, 1. v.a. to carry away *or* off; to convey; to banish; *fig.* to carry away with one, to gain. [estly, to require.

dēposco, pŏposci, 3. v.a. to ask for earn-

dēpŏsĭtum, i, n. deposit, trust.

dēprāvātĭo, ōnis, f. corruption; misinterpretation. [to corrupt.

dēprāvo, 1. v.a. to distort; to deprave,

dēprĕcātĭo, ōnis, f. deprecation; begging off; intercession; cursing, imprecation.

dēprĕcātor, ōris, m. intercessor; one who begs off.

dēprĕcor, ātus, 1. v.a. dep. to deprecate, to pray against; to beg off; to beg pardon; to avert by prayer; to curse; to urge in excuse.

dēprĕhendo, di, sum, 3. v.a. to catch, to find out; to discern, to perceive; to reach *or* overtake; to catch in the act; to surprise; to embarrass.

dēpressus, a, um, p. & a. lying low.

dēprĭmo, pressi, pressum, 3. v.a. to depress; to keep down; to sink; to plant deep; *fig.* to trample on, to depress.

dēprœlior, 1. v. dep. to make fierce war.

dēprōmo, prompsi, promptum, 3. v.a. to take down, to bring forth.

depso, sui, stum, 3. v.a. to knead.

dēpŭdet, uit, 2. v. imp. to become shameless. [hard.

dēpugno, 1. v.n. & a. to fight out *or*

dēpulsĭo, ōnis, f. driving away; defence.

dēpulsor, oris, m. one who repels.

dēpurgo, 1. v.a. to cleanse. [consider.

dēpŭto, 1. v.a. to prune; to reckon, to

dēque, v. susque.

dērēlictĭo, ōnis, f. desertion, neglect.

dērēlinquo, lĭqui, lictum, 3. v.a. to leave behind, to abandon, to neglect.

dērēpentĕ, ad. suddenly. [to deride.

dērīdeo, risi, rīsum, 2. v.a. to laugh at,

dērīdĭcŭlus, a, um, a. laughable, ridiculous. [lousness.

dērīdĭcŭlum, i, n. laughing-stock, ridicu-

dērīgesco, gui, 3. v.n. to grow stiff *or* rigid; to bristle. [to remove.

dērĭpĭo, rĭpui, reptum, 3. v.a. to tear off,

dērīsor, ōris, m. mocker, scoffer.

dērīsus, ūs, m. mockery, derision.

dērīvātĭo, ōnis, f. turning off (into another channel); (grammatically) etymology.

dērīvo, 1. v.a. to divert, to turn *or* draw off; (grammatically) to derive.

dērŏgo, 1. v.a. to derogate; to repeal partially; to take away, to diminish.

dērōsus, a, um, p. & a. gnawed away, nibbled. [precipitous.

dēruptus, a, um, p. & a. craggy, steep,

dēsævĭo, ii, 4. v.n. to rage, to cease to rage.

dēscendo, di, sum, 3. v.n. to descend; to fall; to alight; to slope; to penetrate; to enter (an arena); to condescend.

dēscensus, ūs, m. climbing down; descent;—**facilis descensus Averno**, easy is the path that leads down to Hell.

dēscisco, ivi & ii, ītum, 3. v.n. to fall off; to desert.

dēscrībo, psi, ptum, 3. v.a. to copy; to assign; to distribute; to describe.

dēscriptĭo, ōnis, f. delineation; description; definition; distribution; arrangement. [ranged.

dēscriptus, a, um, p. & a. properly ar-

dēsĕco, cui, ctum, 1. v.a. to cut off.

dēsĕro, rui, rtum, 3. v.a. to forsake; to desert; to give up; to fail.

dēserta, ōrum, n. pl. wilderness.

dēsertĭo, ōnis, f. *fig.* slighting, neglect.

dēsertor, ōris, m. abandoner; deserter; fugitive. [waste.

dēsertus, a, um, p. & a. desert, lonely,

dēservĭo, 4. v.n. to serve diligently, to be devoted to.

dēsēs, ĭdis, a. slow, sluggish, lazy.

dēsicco, 1. v.a. to dry.

dēsĭdeo, sēdi, 2. v.n. to sit at ease; to loiter.

dēsīdĕrābĭlis, e, a. desirable.

dēsīdĕrĭum, ii, n. desire, wishing, longing for; regret for what is absent; love; want; petition; request.

dēsīdĕro, 1. v.a. to wish for, to desire; to need, to want; to require; to miss;— desideror, to be missed;—desideratum, something required.

dēsĭdĭa, ae, f. idleness, sloth.

dēsĭdĭōsus, a, um, a. indolent, lazy.

dēsīdo, sēdi, 3. v.n. to sink, to fall down.

dēsignātĭo, ōnis, f. appointment, designation.

dēsignātor, ōris, m. undertaker (of funerals); umpire (at the games).

dēsigno, 1. v.a. to delineate, to designate; to denote; to appoint; to choose;— **consul designatus**, consul-elect.

dēsĭlĭo, sĭlui, sultum, 4. v.n. to leap down, to alight. [leave off, to cease, to desist.

dēsĭno, ivi & ii, ĭtum, 3. v.a. & n. to

dēsĭpio, 3. v.n. to act foolishly;—desipere in loco, to unbend at the proper time. [desist from.

dēsisto, stĭti, stĭtum, 3. v.n. to leave off, to

dēsōlo, 1. v.a. to abandon, to desert.

despecto, 1. v.a. to look down upon; to overlook; to despise.

despectus, ūs, m. prospect, panorama; point of vantage, height; contempt.

despēranter, ad. despairingly.

despērātio, ōnis, f. despair. [of.

despērātus, a, um, a. desperate, despaired

despēro, 1. v.n. & a. to despair (of).

despĭcientia, ae, f. contempt.

dēspĭcio, exi, ectum, 3. v.n. & a. to look down upon; to despise.

despŏlio, 1. v.a. to rob, to plunder.

despondeo, spondi, sponsum, 2. v.a. to promise (in marriage);—animum despondere, to despair.

despūmo, 1. v.a. to skim off.

despuo, 3. v.n. & a. to spit (out), to reject.

desquāmo, 1. v.a. to take the scales off, strip off.

destillātio, onis, f. running, catarrh.

destillo, 1. v.a. & n. to trickle down.

destĭnātio, ōnis, f. resolution, determination.

destĭno, 1. v.a. to fix, to determine, to design; to doom; to destine.

destĭtuo, ui, ūtum, 3. v.a. to leave, to desert, to abandon; to give up.

destringo, inxi, ictum, 3. v.a. to strip off; to draw (a sword); to graze (gently); fig. to censure.

destructio, ōnis, f. destruction; refutation. [to destroy, to ruin.

destruo, xi, ctum, 3. v.a. to pull down; fig.

dēsŭbĭto, ad. all of a sudden.

dēsūdo, 1. v.n. fig. to exert oneself.

dēsuēfăcio, fēci, factum, 3. v.a. to disuse, to break off (a habit).

dēsuesco, suēvi, suētum, 3. v.a. & n. to disuse; to break off (a habit); to become unaccustomed.

dēsuētūdo, ĭnis, f. discontinuance, disuse.

dēsultor, ōris, m. vaulter; one who leaps from one horse to another; inconstant person.

dēsultōrius, a, um, a. vaulting, leaping from one point to another; fickle.

dēsum, fui, esse, v.n. to be wanting, to fail. [choose.

dēsūmo, mpsi, 3. v.a. to pick out, to

dēsŭper, ad. from above.

dēsurgo, 3. v.n. to rise up.

dētĕgo, xi, ctum, 3. v.a. to uncover, to lay bare; fig. to reveal; to betray.

dētendo, sum, 3. v.a. to strike (tents).

dētergeo, si, sum, 2. v.a. to wipe off; to remove; to strip off.

dētĕrior, ius, a. comp. inferior; worse,

dētĕrius, ad. worse. [meaner.

dētermĭnātio, ōnis, f. boundary, end.

dētermĭno, 1. v.a. to set bounds to, to limit, to determine.

dētĕro, trīvi, trītum, 3. v.a. to wear away; to weaken.

dēterreo, ui, ĭtum, 2. v.a. to deter; to prevent; to dissuade.

dētestābĭlis, e, a. abominable, detestable.

dētestātio, ōnis, f. cursing, detestation, averting.

dētestor, ātus, 1. v. dep. to execrate, to detest; to deprecate; to avert.

dētexo, xui, xtum, 3. v.a. to finish weaving, to complete.

dētĭneo, tĭnui, tentum, 2. v.a. to hold down or off, to detain; to occupy.

dētondeo, tŏtondi & tondi, tonsum, 2. v.a. to shear off, to strip off. [raging.

dētŏno, ui, 1. v.n. to thunder; fig. to cease

dētorqueo, si, tum, 2. v.a. to turn or twist off; to direct towards; to distort.

dētractio, ōnis, f. withdrawal.

dētractor, ōris, m. detractor, defamer.

dētrăho, xi, ctum, 3. v.a. to draw off; to pluck; to remove; to lessen; to take away; fig. to detract from; to impair.

dētrectātio, ōnis, f. refusal.

dētrecto, 1. v.a. to refuse; to depreciate.

dētrīmentum, i, n. detriment, loss, damage; defeat.

detrītus, a, um, a. worn down.

detrītus, us, m. a rubbing, a wearing away.

dētrūdo, si, sum, 3. v.a. to thrust down or from; to expel; to dispossess; to reduce; to postpone.

dētrunco, 1. v.a. to lop off; to behead.

dēturbo, 1. v.a. to drive down; to dislodge; to pull down; to disturb, to confound.

deunx, uncis, m. eleven-twelfths of the as, eleven-twelfths of any measure.

deūro, ussi, ustum, 3. v.a. to burn down; (of cold) to nip.

deus, i, m. god;—deus ex machina, a god introduced into a play to get over a dramatic impasse;—di meliora, God save us;—quod di prohibeant, God forbid;—di te ament, God bless you;—per deos immortales, by the immortal gods. [flower.

deutzia (mod. hort.), Japanese snow-

dēvasto, atum, 1. v.a. to lay waste.

dēvĕho, xi, ctum, 3. v.a. to carry away, to convey;—devehor, to sail down; to ride down. [down, to tear off.

dēvello, velli, vulsum, 3. v.a. to pull

dēvĕnĕror, 1. v. dep. to worship; to avert by worship.

dēvĕnio, vĕni, 4. v.n. to come down, to arrive at; to fall into.

dēversor, atus, 1. v. dep. to put up at an inn; to lodge.

dēversōrium, ii, n. inn, lodging-house.

dēvertĭcŭlum, i, n. by-road; *fig.* digression; inn; refuge.

dēverto, ti, sum, 3. v.a. & n. to turn aside; to lodge; *fig.* to digress.

dēvexĭtas, ātis, f. slope.

dēvexus, a, um, a. sloping, shelving, steep.

dēvincio, nxi, nctum, 4. v.a. to bind fast, to tie up; *fig.* to oblige.

dēvinco, vīci, victum, 3. v.a. to conquer entirely, to subdue. [attached to.

dēvinctus, a, um, p. & a. devoted, much

dēvīto, 1. v.a. to avoid.

dēvius, a, um, a. out of the way, devious; retired, erroneous.

dēvŏco, 1. v.a. to call off; to invite.

dēvŏlo, 1. v.n. to fly down or away; to hasten down, to hasten away.

dēvolvo, volvi, vŏlūtum, 3. v.a. to roll down; to wind off; to utter.

dēvŏro, 1. v.a. to devour; *fig.* to absorb; to gulp down; to check; *fig.* to drink in; to enjoy. [curse.

dēvōtio, ōnis, f. devoting; vow; spell;

dēvōtus, a, um, p. & a. devoted, faithful; cursed. [devote; to curse; to bewitch.

dēvŏveo, vōvi, vōtum, 2. v.a. to vow, to devote.

dextans, antis, m. five-sixths of any measure.

dextĕr, a, um, tra, trum, a. on the right side, right; *fig.* dexterous, skilful; propitious.

dext(ĕ)ra, ae, f. right hand; right side, pledge.

dext(ĕ)rē, ad. skilfully.

dextĕrĭtas, ātis, f. skilfulness, readiness.

dextrorsum, dextrorsus, ad. to the right.

diăbŏlus, i, m. devil.

diăcŏnus, i, m. deacon.

diădēma, ătis, n. diadem, tiara.

diærĕsis, is, f. (in grammar) a dividing of one syllable into two, as soluisse for solvisse.

diæta, ae, f. diet; apartment; chamber.

diălectica, ae, f. dialectics, logic; —, ōrum, n. pl. logical questions.

diălectĭcē, ad. logically. [logician.

diălectĭcus, a, um, a. dialectical;—, i, m.

Diālis, e, a. pertaining to Jupiter.

diălŏgus, i, m. dialogue.

diămetros, i, f. diameter.

dianthus (mod. hort.), pink.

diăpāsōn, at the interval of a whole octave.

diaphragma, ătis, n. midriff.

diārĭum, ii, n. daily allowance of food or pay, a journal.

dīca, ae, f. lawsuit. [pay, a journal.

dĭcācĭtas, ātis, f. raillery, banter.

dĭcax, ācis, a. witty, smart, sarcastic.

dĭcio, ōnis, f. sway; dominion; authority.

dicis causa or gratia, for form's sake.

dīco, 1. v.a. to dedicate, to consecrate; to set apart; to appoint; to devote (oneself).

dīco, xi, ctum, 3. v.a. to say, to tell; to order; to call; to declare; to express; to harangue; to plead; to promise; to appoint; to mean.

dicrōtum, i, n. a light galley propelled by two banks of oars.

dictamnus, i, f., dictamnum, i, n. dittany.

dictāta, ōrum, n. pl. things dictated, lessons.

dictātŏr, ōris, m. dictator; chief magistrate.

dictātōrius, a, um, a. dictatorial.

dictātūra, ae, f. dictatorship.

dictērium, ii, n. a witticism.

dictio, ōnis, f. saying, delivery; style; speech; oracular response.

dictĭto, 1. v.a. to say often or emphatically; to plead often.

dicto, 1. v.a. to say often; to dictate (for writing); to compose.

dictum, i, n. saying, word; maxim; joke; order; prophecy.

dido, dĭdi, dĭtum, 3. v.a. to distribute, to spread abroad.

dīdūco, xi, ctum, 3. v.a. to draw or lead aside; to separate; to divide; to scatter; to open.

diēcŭla, ae, f. a little while.

diēlȳtra (mod. hort.), bleeding-heart.

diērectus, a, um, a. crucified (used as a term of abuse);—i dierectus, go and hang yourself.

dies, ēi, m. day; daylight; term; birthday; festival; time; life; the heavens; in, —, day by day;—de die in diem, from day to day;—in diem vivere, to live only for the day;—dies non, a day on which no work can be done.

diffāmo, 1. v.a. to defame, to divulge.

differentia, ae, f. difference.

differo, distŭli, dīlātum, differre, ir. v.a. & n. to put off, to delay; to disperse; to spread; to tear to pieces; to tease; to bear; —, v.n. to differ; to disagree.

differtus, a, um, p. & a. filled, crowded.

difficĭlē, ad. with difficulty.

difficĭlis, e, a. difficult; obstinate, morose.

difficĭlĭter, ad. with difficulty.

difficultas, ātis, f. difficulty; trouble; dearth; poverty; moroseness.

difficulter, ad. with difficulty.

diffīdenter, ad. diffidently.

diffīdentia, ae, f. mistrust, distrust.

diffīdo, fīsus sum, 3. v.n. to distrust; to despair.

diffindo, fĭdi, fissum, 3. v.a. to split; to open;—diem diffindere, to put off to the following day.

diffingo, 3. v.a. to remodel.

diffĭteor, 2. v. dep. to disavow, to deny.

difflŭo, 3. v.n. to flow asunder; to melt; to vanish; to be dissolved in.

diffŭgio, fŭgi, 3. v.n. to flee asunder, to disappear.

diffundo, fŭdi, fūsum, 3. v.a. to pour forth; to diffuse, to spread; to cheer.

diffūsē, ad. diffusely.

dĭgĕro, gessi, gestum, 3. v.a. to distribute, to spread over; to arrange, to dispose.

dĭgesta, orum, m. a system of law, digests. [arrangement.

dĭgestio, ōnis, f. orderly distribution,

dĭgĭtālis (mod. hort.), foxglove.

dĭgĭtellum, i, n. house-leek.

dĭgĭtŭlus, i, m. little finger.

dĭgĭtus, i, m. finger; toe; claw;—digitum transversum, a hair's breadth.

dĭglădior, 1. v. dep. to fight for life.

dignātio, ōnis, f. appreciation; dignity,

dignē, ad. worthily; fitly. [honour.

dignĭtas, ātis, f. worthiness, merit; dignity, authority; office; grace; value, excellence.

dignor, ātus, 1. v.a. dep. to deem worthy.

dignosco, 3. v.a. to distinguish, to discern.

dignus, a, um, a. worthy, deserving; deserved; decent; proper.

dĭgrĕdior, gressus, 3. v.n. dep. to depart, to go away; to digress (from the purpose). [gression.

dĭgressio, ōnis, f. going away; fig. di-

dĭgressus, ūs, m. departure; digression.

dijūdĭco, 1. v.a. to decide, to determine; to distinguish.

dijungo, v. disjungo.

dīlābor, lapsus, 3. v.n. dep. to fall asunder or to pieces; to disperse; to melt away; to decay; to disperse.

dīlăcĕro, 1. v.a. to tear to pieces.

dīlănio, 1. v.a. to tear to pieces.

dīlăpĭdo, 1. v.a. to squander.

dīlargior, ītus, 4. v.a. dep. to bestow liberally; to lavish.

dīlātio, ōnis, f. delay, postponement.

dīlāto, 1. v.a. to make wider, to enlarge, to extend, to dilate.

dīlaudo, 1. v.a. to praise exceedingly.

dīlemma, ătis, n. in logic, an argument containing two contrary propositions, each of which is fatal to the cause of its supporter.

dīligens, entis, p. & a. careful, diligent, frugal, thrifty.

dīligenter, ad. diligently, earnestly.

dīligentia, ae, f. diligence; economy, frugality.

dīligo, lexi, lectum, 3. v.a. to esteem highly, to love.

dīlŭceo, 2. v.n. to be clear.

dīlŭcesco, luxi, 3. v.n. to begin to shine, to dawn.

dīlŭcĭdē, ad. brightly, plainly, distinctly.

dīlŭcĭdus, a, um, a. plain, distinct.

dīlŭcŭlum, i, n. daybreak, dawn.

dīlŭdium, ii, n. interval between two plays.

dīluo, ui, ūtum, 3. v.a. to soak, to wash (off); to temper; to dilute; to dissolve; fig. to weaken; to remove; to refute.

dīlŭvies, ēi, f. inundation, flood.

dīlŭvium, ii, n. deluge; fig. destruction.

dīmensio, ōnis, f. measuring. [out.

dīmētior, mensus, 4. v.a. dep. to measure

dīmĭcātio, ōnis, f. fight, combat; struggle.

dīmĭco, avi & cui, ātum, 1. v.n. to fight; to struggle, to strive.

dīmĭdiātus, a, um, a. halved.

dīmĭdium, ii, n. the half.

dīmĭdiŭs, a, um, a. through the middle; half.

dīmĭnuo, 3. to break in pieces.

dīmĭnūtio, v. deminutio.

dīmissio, ōnis, f. sending forth; dismissal.

dīmitto, mīsi, missum, 3. v.a. to send out or forth; to dismiss; to disband; to release; to divorce; to break up; to detach; to let slip; to give up, to renounce. [ate; to put aside; to remove.

dīmŏveo, mōvi, mōtum, 2. v.a. to separ-

dīnosco, v. dignosco.

dīnŭmĕrātio, ōnis, f. enumeration.

dīnŭmĕro, 1. v.a. to count over, to enumerate. [cese.

diœcēsis, is, f. district, government, dio-

diœcētes, ae, m. overseer of the revenue, treasurer.

dioptra, ae, f. an instrument for measuring heights from a distance.

diōta, ae, f. two-handled wine-jar.

diplois, ĭdis, f. a cloak. [tion.

diplōma, ătis, n. letter of recommenda-

dīpondium, v. dupondium.

dipsăcus, i, f. teasel. [causes thirst.

dipsăs, ădis, f. a serpent whose bite

dīrectē, ad. directly.

dīrecto, ad. directly; immediately.

dīrectus, a, um, p. & a. straight, perpendicular; steep; direct, simple.

dīremptus, ūs, m. separation.

dīreptio, ōnis, f. plundering.

dīreptor, ōris, m. plunderer.

dīrĭbeo, ĭtum, 2. v.a. to sort the tablets when taken out of the ballot-boxes.

dīrĭbĭtio, onis, f. sorting of votes.

dīrĭbĭtor, oris, m. sorter of votes.

dīrĭgo, rexi, rectum, 3. v.a. to direct, to guide; to steer; to set in order.

dīrĭmo, ēmi, emptum, 3. v.a. to take asunder; to separate; to interrupt; to destroy; to frustrate; to adjust, to compose.

dīrĭpio, ui, reptum, 3. v.a. to snatch away; to tear to pieces; to rob; to destroy.

dīrĭtas, ātis, f. fierceness, cruelty.

dīrumpo, rūpi, ruptum, 3. v.a. to break off, to shatter, to burst;—dirumpor, fig. to burst with envy.

dīruo, rui, rŭtum, 3. v.a. to demolish, to destroy; to scatter;—dirutus, bankrupt.

dīrus, a, um, a. fearful, awful; horrible.

dis, ditis, a. rich; v. dives.

discēdo, cessi, cessum, 3. v.n. to go asunder; to go off; to march off; to be divided; to cease; to vanish; to die; to depart from; to except;—discedere victor, to come off conqueror.

disceptātio, ōnis, f. discussion, debate.

disceptātor, ōris, m. umpire, arbitrator.

disceptatrix, īcis, f. female arbitrator.

discepto, 1. v.a. to decide; to dispute; to debate. [ate; to discern, to distinguish.

discerno, crēvi, crētum, 3. v.a. to separate; to die.

discerpo, psi, ptum, 3. v.a. to pluck or tear in pieces; to mangle; to disperse.

discessio, ōnis, f. separation; departure; division (in parliamentary language).

discessus, ūs, m. going apart; separation; departure; marching off.

discĭdium, ii, n. separation, divorce, disagreement. [less, dissolute.

discinctus, a, um, p. & a. slovenly, careless; to split; to divide.

discindo, scĭdi, scissum, 3. v.a. to split; to divide.

discingo, nxi, nctum, 3. v.a. to ungird, to deprive of the girdle (as a punishment).

disciplīna, ae, f. instruction; knowledge; science; discipline; system; doctrines, custom; method.

discĭpŭla, ae, f. female disciple.

discĭpulus, i, m. scholar, pupil, disciple.

disclūdo, si, sum, 3. v.a. to separate; to keep apart.

disco, dĭdĭci, 3. v.a. to learn, to study; to become acquainted with;—crimine ab uno disce omnes, from the guilt of one learn the character of all.

discŏbŏlus, i, m. quoit-thrower (a famous statue).

discŏlor, ōris, a. of another colour; of various colours; variegated; different.

disconvĕnio, 4. v.n. to disagree, to be inconsistent.

discordia, ae, f. disagreement, discord.

discordo, 1. v.n. to be at variance, to quarrel; to be different. [different.

discors, cordis, a. discordant, disagreeing;

discrĕpantia, ae, f. discord; dissimilarity.

discrĕpātio, ōnis, f. difference, dispute.

discrĕpo, ui, 1. v.n. to be out of tune; fig. to disagree, to differ. [assign.

discrībo, psi, ptum, 3. v.a. to divide, to

discrīmen, ĭnis, n. distance; separation; division; distinction, difference; crisis, risk.

discrīmĭno, 1. v.a. to divide, to part.

discriptio, onis, f. assignment, division.

discrŭcio, 1. v.a. to torture.

discumbo, cŭbui, cŭbĭtum, 3. v.n. to lie down; to recline at table.

discurro, cŭcurri & curri, cursum, 3. v.n. to run about.

discursus, ūs, m. running about.

discus, i, m. quoit.

discŭtio, cussi, cussum, 3. v.a. to strike asunder; to shatter; to dissipate; fig. to frustrate.

disertē, ad. clearly, expressly, eloquently.

disertus, a, um, a. well-spoken; eloquent.

dīsjĭcio, jēci, jectum, 3. v.a. to scatter; to disperse; to squander; to rout; to destroy; to frustrate;—disjecta membra, severed limbs.

disjunctio, ōnis, f. separation; difference.

disjunctus, a, um, p. & a. separate, distinct; distant. [separate; to disjoin.

disjungo, xi, ctum, 3. v.a. to unyoke; to

dispando, 3. v.a. to spread out.

dispar, ăris, a. unequal, unlike.

dispărilis, e, a. dissimilar; different.

dispăro, 1. v.a. to separate, to divide.

dispello, pŭli, pulsum, 3. v.a. to drive asunder, to disperse.

dispendium, ii, n. expense, cost; loss.

dispensātio, ōnis, f. management; stewardship.

dispensātor, ōris, m. steward; treasurer.

dispenso, 1. v.a. to weigh out; to pay; to manage; to dispense, to distribute; to lay out; to arrange. [to squander.

disperdo, didi, dĭtum, 3. v.a. to destroy;

dispĕreo, ii, 4. v.n. to perish utterly;—dispĕrii, I am undone.

dispergo, si, sum, 3. v.a. to scatter about, to disperse.

dispersē, ad. here and there.

dispersio, onis, f. scattering abroad.

dispertio, īvi & ii, ītum, 4. v.a. to distribute, to divide; to assign.

dispĭcio, spexi, spectum, 3. v.n. & a. to look about; to discover; to espy; to consider.

displĭceo, ui, ĭtum, 2. v.a. to displease.

displōdo, ōsum, 3. v.a. to spread out, to dilate;—displodor, to explode.

dispōno, pŏsui, pŏsitum, 3. v.a. to distribute, to set in order; to appoint; to arrange; to draw up.

dispŏsĭtē, ad. in an orderly manner.

dispŏsĭtio ōnis, f. arrangement.

dispungo, xi, ctum, 3. v.a. to tick off, to balance.

dispŭtātio, ōnis, f. disputation, debate.

dispŭtător, ōris, m. disputant.

dispŭto, 1. v.a. to discuss, to investigate.

disquīro, 3. v.a. to examine; to inquire

disquīsītio, ōnis, f. inquiry. [into.

dissæpio, psi, ptum, 4. v.a. to sunder; to divide. [separate; to dissect.

dissēco, ui, ctum, 1. v.a. to cut up; to

dissēmĭno, 1. v.a. to scatter seed; *fig.* to spread abroad.

dissensio, ōnis, f. dissension, discord.

dissensus, ūs, m. dissension, discord.

dissentāneus, a, um, a. disagreeing, contrary. [disagree; to differ.

dissentio, si, sum, 4. v.n. to dissent, to

dissēpio, v. **dissæpio**.

dissĕrēno, 1. v.n. to be clear (of weather).

dissĕro, rui, rtum, 3. v.a. to discuss, to examine; to speak of.

dissĕro, sēvi, sĭtum, 3. v.a. to sow.

disserto, 1. v.a. to discuss, to dispute.

dissĭdeo, sēdi, sessum, 2. v.n. to be at variance; to disagree; to quarrel; to be unlike; to be separated.

dissĭlio, ui, 4. v.n. to leap *or* burst asunder; to fly in pieces.

dissĭmĭlis, e, a. unlike, dissimilar.

dissĭmĭlĭter, ad. in a different manner.

dissĭmĭlĭtūdo, ĭnis, f. unlikeness, differ-

dissĭmŭlanter, ad. secretly. [ence.

dissĭmŭlātio, ōnis, f. dissimulation, dissembling.

dissĭmŭlātor, ōris, m. dissembler.

dissĭmŭlo, 1. v.a. to dissemble, to disguise; to hide. [ing; annihilation.

dissĭpātio, ōnis, f. squandering; scatter-

dissĭpo, 1. v.a. to disperse; to squander; to destroy; to put to flight; *fig.* to circulate;—**dissĭpatus**, disconnected.

dissŏcĭābĭlis, e, a. sundering; incompatible.

dissŏcĭo, 1. v.a. to disunite; to sunder; to set at variance.

dissŏlūbĭlis, e, a. capable of dissolution, dissoluble.

dissŏlūtē, ad. loosely; carelessly.

dissŏlūtio, ōnis, f. dissolution; destruction; disconnection; dissoluteness; refutation. [ligent; dissolute.

dissŏlūtus, a, um, p. & a. loose; lax; neg-

dissolvo, solvi, sŏlūtum, 3. v.a. to unloose; to dissolve, to destroy; to melt; to pay; to refute; to annul.

dissŏnus, a, um, a. dissonant, discordant; different. [shared.

dissors, rtis, a. of a different fate, un-

dissuādeo, si, sum, 2. v.a. to dissuade.

dissuāsio, ōnis, f. dissuasion.

dissuāsor, ōris, m. dissuader.

dissulto, 1. v.n. to fly *or* burst asunder.

dissuo, ūtum, 3. v.a. to unstitch, to rip open; *fig.* to dissolve.

dissūpo, v. **dissĭpo**.

distantia, ae, f. distance; difference.

distendo, di, tum, 3. v.a. to stretch asunder, to stretch out, to extend; to swell out; to fill; to divide. [dary.

distermĭno, 1. v.a. to divide by a boun-

distĭchon, i, n. a distich, a couplet consisting of a hexameter and pentameter.

distillo, v. **destillo**.

distinctē, ad. distinctly, clearly, finely.

distinctio, ōnis, f. distinction; difference; ornament. [decorated.

distinctus, a, um, a. separate, distinct;

distĭneo, tĭnui, tentum, 2. v.a. to keep asunder; to separate; to prevent, to delay; to occupy; *fig.* to distract;—**distentus**, busy.

distinguo, nxi, nctum, 3. v.a. to divide, to part; to distinguish; to decorate.

disto, 1. v.n. to stand apart, to be distant; to be different. [to distort.

distorqueo, torsi, tortum, 2. v.a. to twist,

distortio, ōnis, f. contortion.

distortus, a, um, p. & a. distorted, deformed; ugly.

distractio, ōnis, f. wrenching; *fig.* dissension, discord.

distrăho, xi, ctum, 3. v.a. to pull *or* draw asunder; to wrench; to separate; to sell in small lots; to distract; to set at variance; to estrange. [distribute.

distrĭbuo, ui, ūtum, 3. v.a. to divide, to

distrĭbūtē, ad. in an orderly manner.

distrĭbūtio, ōnis, f. division, distribution.

districtus, a, um, p. & a. distracted; busy.

distringo, nxi, ctum, 3. v.a. to stretch out; to detain; to occupy; to engage.

disturbātio, ōnis, f. destruction.

disturbo, 1. v.a. to disturb; to demolish; to frustrate.

dītesco, 3. v.n. to grow rich.

dīthўrambus, i, m. dithyramb; a poem in honour of Bacchus.

dītĭo, ōnis, v. **dicio**.

dīto, 1. v.a. to enrich.

dĭu, ad. by day; a long while; long since; — **diutius**, longer; — **diutissime**, very long.

dĭurnus, a, um, a. daily;—**acta diurna**, n. pl. a record of transactions, gazette.

dīus, a, um, godlike.

dĭūtĭnus, a, um, a. lasting, long.

dĭūtĭus, dĭūtissĭmē, v. **diu**.

dĭūturnĭtas, ātis, f. long duration.

dĭūturnus, a, um, lasting long.

dīva, ae, f. goddess.

dīvărĭco, 1. v.a. & n. to spread asunder; to straddle.

dīvello, velli, velsum, 3. v.a. to tear in pieces; to tear away; to estrange.

dīvendo, dĭtum, 3. v.a. to sell in small lots; to retail.

dīverbĕro, 1. v.a. to strike asunder, to divide. [comedy).

dīverbĭum, ĭi, n. the dialogue (of a **dīversē,** ad. hither and thither, differently. [ence.

dīversĭtas, ātis, f. contrariety; differ-

dīversōrĭum, v. **deversorium.**

dīversus, a, um, p. & a. opposite; separate, apart; unlike, different; hostile; contrary; distant; several; distinct.

dīverto, tĭ, sum, 3. v.n., v. **deverto.**

dīves, ĭtis, a. rich; splendid.

dīvexo, 1. v.a. to rend asunder; to vex.

dīvĭdo, vīsi, vīsum, 3. v.a. to separate, to divide; to remove; to distribute; to distinguish; to break up; to assign;— **divide et impera,** rule by playing off your rivals against each other.

dīvĭduus, a, um, a. divisible; divided; half.

dīvīnātĭo, ōnis, f. divination; a preliminary inquiry to consider which of several advocates should conduct a prosecution. [vinely.

dīvīnē, ad. by divine inspiration; di- **dīvīnĭtas, ātis, f.** godhead, divinity; divination; divine quality.

dīvīnĭtus, ad. by divine inspiration; divinely, excellently.

dīvīno, 1. v.a. to divine; to prophesy.

dīvīnus, a, um, a. divine; prophetic; blessed; excellent; —, **i, m.** prophet.

dīvīsĭo, ōnis, f. division; distribution.

dīvīsor, ōris, m. distributor; a candidate's agent hired to distribute bribes.

dīvīsus, ūs, m. division.

dīvĭtĭæ, ārum, f. pl. riches, wealth.

dīvortĭum, ĭi, n. separation; divorce; point of separation; bifurcation; watershed.

dīvulgo, 1. v.a. to publish, to divulge.

dīvum, ĭ, n. sky, open air; —**sub dīvo,** in the open air; —**sub dīvum,** into the light of day.

dīvus, a, um, a. divine; godlike; holy;— **dīvus, ĭ, m.** god.

do, dĕdi, dătum, dăre, 1. v.a. to give; to ascribe; to grant, to permit; to furnish, to offer; to lend; to tell; to cause; to deal;—**do ut des,** I give to you that you may give to me;—**data,** materials at hand (from which to form a judgment). [tell; to show.

dŏceo, cui, ctum, 2. v.a. to teach; to **dŏcĭlis, e,** docile.

dŏcĭlĭtas, ātis, f. docility.

doctē, ad. learnedly, shrewdly.

doctor, ōris, m. teacher, instructor.

doctrīna, ae, f. teaching, instruction; science, learning; system of rules.

doctus, a, um, a. learned, versed, experienced; witty; shrewd.

dŏcŭmentum, ĭ, n. lesson, example; warning; proof; specimen.

dōdrans, antis, m. three-fourths.

dogma, ătis, n. doctrine, dogma, teaching.

dŏlābra, ae, f. pickaxe.

dōlenter, ad. painfully.

dŏleo, ui, ĭtum, 2. v.n. & a. to feel *or* suffer pain; to ache; to deplore; to grieve

dōlĭŏlum, ĭ, n. small cask. [for.

dōlĭum, ĭi, n. wine-cask. [hew; to cudgel.

dŏlo, 1. v.a. to fashion with an axe, to

dŏlor, ōris, m. pain, ache; grief; anguish; sorrow; resentment.

dŏlōrōsus, sorrowful;—**via dolorosa,** the path of sorrow.

dŏlōsus, a, um, a. crafty, deceitful.

dŏlus, ĭ, m. fraud, deceit.

dŏmābĭlis, e, a. tamable.

dŏmestĭcus, a, um, a. domestic, familiar; native; made at home; civil; private, **dŏmi,** ad., v. **domus.** [personal.

dŏmĭcĭlĭum, ĭi, n. dwelling, abode, home.

dŏmĭna, ae, f. mistress of a family; lady; wife; lady-love.

dŏmĭnātĭo, ōnis, f. dominion; despotism.

dŏmĭnātor, ōris, m. ruler, lord.

dŏmĭnātrix, ĭcis, f. female ruler, mistress.

dŏmĭnātus, ūs, m. command; despotism.

dŏmĭnĭcus, a, um, a. of a lord;—**dominica dies,** the Lord's day.

dŏmĭnĭum, ĭi, n. absolute possession; banquet. [to rule.

dŏmĭnor, ātus, 1. v.n. dep. to domineer;

dŏmĭnus, ĭ, m. master of the house; owner; lord, ruler; host; lover.

dŏmĭporta, ae, f. (poet.) snail.

dŏmĭto, 1. v.a. to tame, to break in.

dŏmĭtor, ōris, m. tamer; conqueror.

dŏmĭtrix, ĭcis, f. female tamer. [quer.

dŏmo, ui, ĭtum, 1. v.a. to tame; to con- **dŏmus, ūs & ĭ, f.** house; home; household; family; native country; temple; sect;—**domi,** at home;—**domum,** homewards, to the house;—**domo,** from home; out of the house.

dōnārĭum, ĭi, n. temple, sanctuary, altar, votive offering.

dōnātĭo, ōnis, f. donation.

dōnātīvum, ĭ, n. largess.

dōnĕc, c. as long as, until.

donicum, v. **donec.**

dōno, 1. v.a. to present, to bestow; to forgive; to give up; to sacrifice; to grant.

dōnum, ĭ, n. gift, present; sacrifice.

dorcas, ădis, f. gazelle. [rest.
dormio, īvi & ii, ītum, 4. v.n. to sleep; to
dormīto, 1. v.n. to be sleepy, to fall
asleep; to be dreaming or stupid;—
quandoque bonus dormitat Homerus,
whenever the great Homer nods.
doronicum (mod. hort.), leopard's-bane.
dorsum, i, n. back; slope of a hill, ridge.
dōs, ōtis, f. dowry; fig. talent, quality.
dōtālis, e, a. pertaining to a dowry, gift.
dōto, 1. v.a. to dower, to endow, to portion.
draba (mod. hort.), whitlow-grass.
dracæna (mod. hort.), dragon plant.
drachma, ae, f. drachm (coin), about 10d.
drăco, ōnis, m. dragon, snake.
drāma, ătis, n. drama;—dramatis per-
sonæ, cast of a play.
drŏmas, ădis, m. dromedary.
drosĕra (mod. hort.), sundew. [priests.
Druidæ, arum, Druides, um, m. pl. Gallic
dŭbiē, ad. doubtfully.
dŭbitābilis, e, a. admitting of doubt.
dŭbitanter, ad. doubtingly; hesitatingly.
dŭbitātio, ōnis, f. doubt; hesitation; irresolution.
dŭbito, 1. v.n. & a. to doubt; to be uncertain or irresolute; to hesitate.
dŭbius, a, um, a. doubtful; variable; uncertain; dangerous; critical;—non est
dubium quin . . ., there is no doubt
that. [each; two hundred.
dŭcēni, ae, a, a. num. pl. two hundred
dŭcentēsimus, a, um, a. the two-hun-
dredth.
dŭcenti, ae, a, pl. two hundred; an indefinitely large number.
dŭcenties, ad. two hundred times; ever
so many times.
dūco, xi, ctum, 3. v.a. to lead, to conduct,
to draw, to bring; to run (a wall, etc.);
to derive; to guide; to marry; to persuade; to deceive; to prolong; to
think, to esteem; to reckon; to pass;
to spend.
ductilis, e, a. easily led, malleable.
ducto, 1. v.a. to lead about; fig. to cheat.
ductor, ōris, m. leader, commander.
ductus, ūs, m. conducting; generalship.
dūdum, ad. a little while ago; formerly;
—jam dudum, long ago.
duellum, i, n. war.
dulcĕ, ad. sweetly, pleasantly.
dulcēdo, ĭnis, f. sweetness; charm.
dulcis, e, a. sweet; pleasant, charming;
dear, beloved.
dulciter, ad. sweetly, delightfully.
dum, c. whilst, as long as; until; provided that (as enclitic, with impera-
tives), a moment;—māne dum, stop a
moment.

dūmētum, i, n. thicket.
dummŏdo, c. provided that.
dūmōsus, a, um, a. brambly. [far.
dumtaxat, ad. only, at least, to wit; so
dūmus, i, m. brushwood; bramble.
duntaxat, v. dumtaxat.
duŏ, ae, o, a. num. two.
duŏdĕcies, ad. twelve times.
duŏdĕcim, a. num. twelve;—Duodecim
Tabulæ, The Twelve Tables (containing the laws).
duŏdĕcĭmus, a, um, a. num. the twelfth.
duŏdēni, ae, a, a. num. twelve each, by
twelves.
duŏdēquadrāgēsĭmus, a, um, a. num.
thirty-eighth.
duŏdēquadrāgintā, a. num. thirty-eight.
duŏdēquinquāgēsĭmus, a, um, a. num.
forty-eighth. [eighth.
duŏdēsexāgēsĭmus, a, um, a. num. fifty-
duŏdētrīciēs, ad. twenty-eight times.
duŏdētrīgintā, a. num. twenty-eight.
duŏdēvicēni, ae, a, a. num. eighteen each.
duŏdēvicēsĭmus, a, um, a. num. eigh-
duŏdēvigintī, a. num. eighteen. [teenth.
duplex, ĭcis, a. two-fold, double; divided;
thick, stout; false.
duplicārius, ii, m. soldier who receives
double pay.
dupliciter, ad. doubly.
duplico, 1. v.a. to double; to repeat; to
enlarge; to bend double.
duplus, a, um, a. double, twice as much or
large.
dŭpondium, ii, n., dŭpondius, ii, m. a coin
the value of two asses.
dūrābilis, e, a. lasting, durable. [fruit).
dūrācinus, a, um, a. hard (of berries or
dūrāteus, a, um, a. wooden. [strictly.
dūrē, ad. hardly, harshly; awkwardly;
dūresco, rui, 3. v.n. to harden.
dūritas, ātis, f. hardness, harshness.
dūriter, v. dure.
dūritia, ae, f., dūrities, ei, f. hardness;
austerity; rigour.
dūro, 1. v.a. & n. to make hard; to dry;
to inure; to dull or blunt; —, v.n. to
become hard or stern, etc.; to endure;
to last out; to live.
dūrus, a, um, a. hard; harsh; rude;
hardy, vigorous; stern; unfeeling;
inflexible; toilsome; burdensome;—
dūrā, orum, n. pl. hardships.
duumvir, v. duumviri.
duumvirātus, ūs, m. duumvirate.
duumvirī, ōrum, m. pl. chief magistrates
in municipal town, two in number.
dux, dŭcis, c. leader, guide; commander,
general.
dȳnastēs, ae, m. ruler, prince.
dȳsentĕria, ae, f. dysentery.

E, pr., v. **ex.**

eādem, ad. in the same way.

eātěnus, ad. so far.

ěběnus, i, f. & m. ebon-tree, ebony.

ěbĭbo, bi, bĭtum, 3. v.a. to drink up, to drain; *fig.* to absorb; to squander.

ēblandĭor, ītus, 4. v.a. dep. to obtain by

ēbrĭětas, ātis, f. drunkenness.   [flattery.

ēbriōsus, a, um, a. given to drinking.

ēbrĭus, a, um, a. drunk; *fig.* intoxicated; full.   [of.

ēbullio, 4. v.a. to bubble up; *fig.* to boast

ēbŭlum, i, n. **ěbŭlus, i,** m. dane-wort.

ěbur, ŏris, n. ivory; ivory statue.

ěburneus, ěburnus, a, um, a. of ivory; white as ivory.

ěcastor, i, by Castor (an oath generally used by women).

eccě, i. lo! see! behold! here!

ecclēsia, ae, f. church.

ecdĭcus, i, m. syndic.

ěchidna, ae, f. adder, snake.

ěchīnātus, a, um, a. prickly.

echīnops (mod. hort.), globe thistle.

ěchīnus, i, m. hedgehog; sea-urchin;

ěchō, ūs, f. echo.   [rinsing bowl.

eclŏga, ae, f. a short poem;—**Eclogæ,** the name of Vergil's pastoral poems.

ecquando, ad. ever, at any time.   [any ?

ecquis, ecquæ, ecqua, ecquod, pn. is there

ecquis, ecquid, pn. is there anyone who ?

ěcŭleus, v. **equuleus.**

ědācĭtas, ātis, f. voracity, gluttony.

ědax, ācis, a. voracious, gluttonous; *fig.*

ēdentŭlus, a, um, a. toothless. [devouring.

ěděpōl, i. by Pollux! faith! truly!

ēdīco, xi, ctum, 3. v.a. to publish, to de-clare; to order.

ēdictum, i, n. proclamation, edict.

ēdisco, dĭdĭci, 3. v.a. to learn by heart; to study; to know.

ēdissěro, rui, rtum, 3. v.n., **ēdisserto, i.** v.a. to explain, to relate.

ēdĭtio, ōnis, f. publishing; edition; state-ment;—**editio princeps,** first edition of a book.   [stronger.

ēdĭtus, a, um, a. high, lofty; editior,

ědo, ēdi, ēsum, 3. v.a. to eat; to devour; to squander.

ēdo, dĭdi, dĭtum, 3. v.a. to put forth, to emit; to publish; to relate; to bring forth; to beget; to proclaim; to bring about; to cause.

ēdŏceo, cui, ctum, 2. v.a. to teach thoroughly; to inform.

ēdŏmo, ui, ĭtum, 1. v.a. to tame completely, to conquer.   [away; to sleep off.

ēdormio, īvi & ii, 4. v.n. & a. to sleep

ēdŭcātio, ōnis, f. bringing up; education; rearing.

ēdŭcātor, ōris, m. bringer up, tutor.

ēdŭco, xi, ctum, 3. v.a. to lead *or* draw out; to bring away; to summon; to rear; to educate; to raise, to erect; to produce; to hatch; to pass; to spend.

ēdŭco, i. v.a. to bring up, to rear, to edu-cate; to produce; to maintain.

ědūlis, e, a. eatable.

ēdūro, i. v.n. to last out, to endure.

ēdūrus, a, um, a. very hard.

effarcio, fertum, 4. v.a. to stuff full.

effectio, ōnis, f. performing; practice.

effector, ōris, m. producer, author.

effectus, ūs, m. execution, performance; effect.   [feminate.

effēmĭnātus, a, um, p. & a. womanish, ef-

effēmĭno, i. v.a. to make a woman of; *fig.* to effeminate, to enervate.   [fierce.

effěrātus, a, um, p. & a. wild, savage.

effěritas, ātis, f. wildness, savageness.

effěro, extŭli, ēlātum, efferre, 3. v.a. ir. to bring *or* carry out; to produce; to bury; to exalt; to utter; to raise, to advance; to proclaim;—**se efferre, efferri,** to be haughty.

effěro, i. v.a. to make savage.

effěrus, a, um, a. excessively wild, savage.

effervesco, ferbui, 3. v.n. to effervesce, to glow, to rage.

effervo, 3. v.n. to boil up *or* over.

effētus, a, um, a. *fig.* exhausted, worn out.

efficācĭtas, ātis, f. efficacy, potency.

efficācĭter, ad. efficaciously.

efficax, ācis, a. efficacious, effectual.

efficiens, entis, p. & a. effective, efficient.

efficienter, ad. efficiently.

efficientia, ae, f. efficacy.

efficio, fēci, fectum, 3. v.a. to effect, to execute, to accomplish, to make; to produce; to prove; to build; to make

effigies, ēi, f. portrait, image, effigy.   [up.

effingo, finxi, fictum, 3. v.a. to form; to represent, to portray; to wipe out; to stroke.   [treaty.

efflāgĭtātio, ōnis, f. urgent demand, en-

efflāgĭtātus, ūs, m. earnest *or* urgent re-quest.   [gently.

efflāgĭto, i. v.a. to demand *or* ask ur-

efflo, i. v.a. & n. to blow *or* breathe out; to breathe one's last.   [to bloom.

efflōresco, rui, 3. v.n. to blossom forth;

effluo, xi, 3. v.n. to flow forth; to escape; to vanish; to decay; to be forgotten.

efflŭvium, ii, n. outlet.   [scratch out.

effŏdio, fōdi, fossum, 3. v.a. to dig out; to

effor, ātus, i. v.a. dep. to utter; to mark out (a site) (used of augurs).

effrēnātē, ad. unrestrainedly.

effrēno, ātum, i. v.a. to unbridle, to let loose.   [strained.

effrēnus, a, um, a. unbridled; *fig.* unre-

effringo, frēgi, fractum, 3. v.a. to break open, to break in pieces.

effūgio, fūgi, 3.; v.n. & a. to escape; to flee from, to avoid; to be unnoticed; to be forgotten.

effūgium, ii, n. flight; way of escape.

effulgeo, si, 2. v.n. to shine forth, to glitter.

effultus, a, um, p. & a. propped up, supported.

effundo, fūdi, fūsum, 3. v.a. to pour out, to shed; to send *or* drive out; to shoot in great numbers; to discharge; to resign; to give up; to waste, to squander, to spread abroad; to bring forth abundantly;—**se effundere, effundi,** to stream forth.

effūse, ad. far and wide; lavishly; immoderately.

effūsio, ōnis, f. pouring forth; prodigality; excess.

effūsus, a, um, p. & a. vast, wide; dishevelled; scattered; prodigal; *fig.* immoderate.

effūtio, ītum, 4. v.a. to blab out.

egēlidus, a, um, a. lukewarm.

egens, entis, p. & a. needy, very poor; destitute of.

egēnus, a, um, a. in want of, destitute of.

egeo, ui, 2. v.n. to want; to need; to require; to be without.

ēgero, gessi, gestum, 3. v.a. to carry *or* bear out; to discharge; to utter.

ēgestas, ātis, f. extreme poverty, want.

ego, pn. I; I myself.

egomet, pn. I myself; I for my part.

ēgredior, gressus, 3. v.n. & a. dep. to step, to march *or* come out; to set sail; to land; to go beyond; to ascend; *fig.* to surpass.

ēgregiē, ad. excellently, exceedingly.

ēgregius, a, um, a. excellent, eminent; beautiful; illustrious.

ēgressus, ūs, m. departure; flight; landing; place of egress, mouth (of a river); digression.

ēhem, ah! aha! exclamation of pleasure.

ēheu, 1. alas!

ei, i., v. hei.

eia, i. ho! quick! come!   [throw out.

ējǎcŭlor, ātus, 1. v.a. dep. to hurl *or*

ējectio, ōnis, f. casting out; exile.

ējecto, 1. v.a. to cast out.

ejero, v. ejuro.

ējicio, jēci, jectum, 3. v.a. to throw *or* cast out; to thrust out; to expel; to banish; to vomit; to dislocate; to cast ashore; to reject; to hiss.

ējŭlātus, ūs, m. waiting, lamentation.

ējŭlo, 1. v.n. to wail.

ējuncĭdus, a, um, a. lean.

ējūro, v.a. to abjure; to resign; to reject on oath (a judge); to forswear, to disown.   [to slip away.

ēlābor, lapsus, 3. v.n. & a. dep. to escape;

ēlăbōro, 1. v.a. & n. to work out, to elaborate; to labour, to take pains.

ēlanguesco, gui, 3. v.n. to slacken, to relax.

ēlātē, ad. loftily, proudly.

ēlātio, ōnis, f. *fig.* soaring, sublimity; exaltation.

ēlātus, a, um, p. & a. exalted, lofty, proud.

ēlectio, ōnis, f. choice, selection.

ēlectrum, i, n. amber; mixed metal of gold and silver.   [cellent.

ēlectus, a, um, p. & a. select, choice, ex-

ēlĕgans, antis, a. elegant, fine, handsome; tasteful; dainty, critical; discriminate, polite.   [discriminately, etc.

ēlĕganter, ad. elegantly, finely, tastefully,

ēlĕgantia, ae, f. elegance; niceness; taste; politeness.

ēlĕgi, ōrum, m. pl. elegiac verses, elegy.

ēlĕgīa, ae, ēlĕgēa, ae, *or* **ēlĕgēia, ae,** f. elegy.   [ments; beginnings.

ēlĕmenta, ōrum, n. pl. elements; rudi-

ēlenchus, i, m. pearl; earring.

ēlĕphantiăsis, is, f. leprosy.

ēlĕphās, antis, ēlĕphantus, i, m. elephant; ivory.

ēlĕvo, 1. v.a. to lift up, to raise; to alleviate; to weaken; to lessen; to disparage.   [age.

ēlĭces, um, m. pl. trench, drain.

ēlĭcio, lĭcui & lexi, lĭctum, 3. v.a. to elicit; to call forth; to conjure.

ēlīdo, si, sum, 3. v.a. to strike *or* dash out; to expel; to shatter; to crush out; to strangle; *fig.* to destroy.   [choose.

ēligo, lēgi, lectum, 3. v.a. to pick out, to

ēlimĭno, ātum, 1. v.a. to turn out of doors; *fig.* to blab.

ēlīmo, 1. v.a. to polish; *fig.* to elaborate.

ēlinguis, e, a. tongue-tied; without eloquence.

ēlīsio, ōnis, f. cutting off a letter; elision.

ēlixus, a, um, a. parboiled; sodden.

elleborum, i, v. helleborum.   [of speech.

ellipsis, is, f. ellipsis, leaving out a part

ellychnium, ii, n. lamp-wick.

ēlōco, 1. v.a. to let out, to farm.

ēlŏcūtio, ōnis, f. elocution.

ēlōgĭum, ii, n. sentence, maxim; epitaph; clause in a will.

ēlŏquens, entis, p. & a. eloquent.

ēlōquenter, ad. eloquently.   [quence.

ēlōquentia, ae, f. **ēlōquium, ii,** n. elo-

ēlŏquor, lŏcūtus, 3. v.a. dep. to speak out, to utter.   [show itself; to be manifest.

ēlūceo, xi, 2. v.n. to shine forth; *fig.* to

ēluctor, ātus, 1. v.n. & a. dep. to force a way through; to surmount a difficulty.

ēlūcubro, 1. v.a. ēlūcubror, 1. v. dep. to compose at night; *fig.* to burn the midnight oil over.

elūdo, si, sum, 3. v.n. & a. to elude, to escape; to parry; to baffle; to cheat; to frustrate; to banter *or* mock.

ēlūgeo, xi, 2. v.a. to mourn.

ēlumbis, e, a. emasculated.

ēluo, ui, ūtum, 3. v.a. to rinse out; *fig.* to wash away, to clear oneself (of).

ēlūtus, a, um, p. & a. watery, insipid.

ēlŭvio, ōnis, ēlŭvies, ēi, f. inundation.

ēmancĭpātio, ōnis, f. emancipation, (legal) conveyance.

ēmancĭpo, 1. v.a. to emancipate (a son from his father's authority); to alienate; *fig.* to give up.

ēmāno, 1. v.n. to flow out; to arise, to emanate from; to become known.

ēmātūresco, rui, 3. v.n. *fig.* to ripen, to grow softer.

ēmax, ācis, a. fond of buying.

emblēma, ātis, n. inlaid work, mosaic.

embŏlium, ii, n. interlude, ballet.

ēmendābĭlis, e, a. amendable, corrigible.

ēmendātē, ad. faultlessly, perfectly.

ēmendātio, ōnis, f. correction, emendation.

ēmendātor, ōris, m. corrector, amender.

ēmendo, 1. v.a. to correct, to amend.

ēmentior, ītus, 4. v.a. dep. to feign, to lie; to counterfeit.   [bribe.

ēmercor, ātus, 1. v.a. dep. to buy up, to

ēmĕreo, ui, ĭtum, 2. v.a. ēmĕreor, ĭtus, 2. v. dep. to merit, to earn; (mil.) to serve out one's time.

ēmĕrĭtus, i, m. veteran.

ēmergo, si, sum, 3. v.a. & n. raise *or* to rise (up); *fig.* to extricate; to emerge; to escape; to appear; to arrive.

ēmĕtica, æ, f. an emetic.

ēmētior, mensus, 4. v.a. dep. to measure out; to traverse.

ēmēto, 3. v.a. to mow down.

ēmico, cui, cātum, 1. v.n. to spring forth, to shine forth, to appear suddenly.

ēmigro, 1. v.n. to emigrate, to move.

ēmĭnens, entis, a. lofty; prominent; *fig.* eminent.   [high lights.

ēmĭnentia, ae, f. prominence; (in paint)

ēmĭneo, ui, 2. v.n. to project; to stand out; *fig.* to be eminent; to excel.

ēmĭnus, ad. at a distance.

ēmīror, v.a. dep. to wonder greatly at.

ēmissārium, ii, n. outlet.

ēmissārius, ii, m. emissary, spy.

ēmissio, ōnis, f. sending out; darting forth.

ēmitto, mīsi, missum, 3. v.a. to send out *or* forth; to set free; to fling; to let fall; to utter; to empty; to drain off.

ēmo, ēmi, emptum, 3. v.a. to buy; *fig.* to gain over, to obtain.

ēmŏdĕror, 1. v.a. dep. to moderate.

ēmŏdŭlor, 1. v.a. dep. to sing, to celebrate.

ēmŏlīmentum, i, v. emolumentum.

ēmollio, ii, ītum, 4. v.a. to soften; to ener-

ēmŏlŭmentum, i, n. gain, profit.   [vate.

ēmŏrior, mortuus, 3. v.n. dep. to die off; to die; *fig.* to perish; to cease.

ēmŏveo, mōvi, mōtum, 2. v.a. to remove; to expel.

emphăsis, is, f. stress.   [to expel.

empīrĭcus, i, m. a quack, a dŏctor who is guided only by experience, not by scientific knowledge.

emplastrum, i, n. plaster.   [town.

empŏrium, ii, n. trading-station, market-

emptio, ōnis, f. buying, purchase.

emptor, ōris, m. buyer, purchaser.

ēmungo, nxi, nctum, 3. v.a. to blow the nose; to cheat;—**emunctæ naris,** (a man) of delicate taste.

ēmūnio, īvi & ii, ītum, 4. v.a. to fortify; to make roads through.

ēn, i. lo! behold! see!

ēnarrābĭlis, e, a. that may be related.

ēnarro, 1. v.a. to explain *or* relate in detail.   [arise.

ēnascor, ātus, 3. v.n. dep. to spring up, to

ēnāto, 1. v.n. to escape by swimming; *fig.* to extricate oneself.   [over.

ēnāvĭgo, 1. v.n. & a. to sail out; to sail

encænia, orum, n. pl. festival commemorative of the opening of some new foundation.   [enamel; encaustic.

encaustus, a, um, a. represented in

enchiridion, ii, n. manual.

endrŏmis, ĭdis, f. a woollen cloak worn by athletes when heated by exertion.

ēnĕco, cui, ctum, *or* nĕcātum, 1. v.a. *fig.* to exhaust; to plague to death, to kill.

ēnervis, e, a. enervated.

ēnervo, 1. v.a. to enervate.

enico, v. eneco.

ēnim, c. indeed, for, yes indeed; certainly;—**enim vero,** verily, on my word.

ēnĭteo, tui, 2. v.n. to shine forth.

ēnĭtesco, tui, 3. v.n. to shine forth, to become bright.

ēnītor, nīsus & nīxus, 3. v.n. & a. dep. to force one's way up; to climb; to strive; —, v.a. to bear (young), to as-

ēnīxē, ad. earnestly, zealously.   [cend.

ēnixus, a, um, p. & a. earnest, zealous.

ēno, 1. v.n. to swim out.

ēnōdātē, ad. clearly, plainly.

ēnōdātio, ōnis, f. explanation.

ēnōdĭs, e, a. without knots; smooth; *fig.* clear, plain.   [explain.

ēnōdo, 1. v.a. to free from knots; *fig.* to

ēnormis, e, a. irregular; immense, enormous.

ensĭfer, a, um, a., ensĭger, a, um, a. wear-
ensis, is, m. sword. [ing a sword.
entĕrŏcēle, es, f. hernia.
ēnūbo, psi, 3. v.n. to marry out of one's
rank; to marry and leave the house of
one's father.
ēnucleātē, ad. plainly, unadornedly.
ēnucleātus, a, um, a. pure; plain; unvarnished. [fig. to explain.
ēnucleo, 1. v.a. to take out the kernels;
ēnŭmĕrātio, ōnis, f. enumeration; recapitulation.
ēnŭmĕro, 1. v.a. to enumerate. [tion.
ēnuntiātio, ōnis, f. declaration, proposi-
ēnuntiātum, i, n. saying, proposition.
ēnuntio, 1. v.a. to speak out, to say, to
express, to declare; to disclose.
ēnutrio, īvi & ītum, 4. v.a. to nourish,
to bring up, to rear.
eo, īvi & ii, īre, 4. v.n. ir. to go; to walk,
to march; to flow; to come in; to ride,
to sail; to march against; to pass by;
to happen; to turn out; — i, (imperative) go to!
eō, ad. thither; so far; therefore; so
much (more or less);—eo usque, just so
long.
eōdem, ad. to the same place or purpose.
eōs, (only used in nom.) f. dawn.
ĕŏus, i, day-star.
ĕŏus, a, um, a. eastern.
ĕphēbus, i, m. a youth.
ĕphēmĕris, ĭdis, f. daybook, diary.
ĕphippium, ii, n. horsecloth.
ephŏrus, i, m. an ephor, one of the chief
magistrates at Sparta.
ĕpĭcus, a, um, a. epic.
ĕpigramma, ătis, n. inscription; epigram.
epilobium (mod. hort.), willow herb.
ĕpĭlŏgus, i, m. epilogue, peroration.
ĕpiscōpālis, e, a. of a bishop, episcopal.
ĕpiscōpus, i, m. bishop.
ĕpiscōpor, āri, 1. v.n. to be bishop.
ĕpistŏla, ae, f. letter, epistle.
ĕpĭtāphĭum, ii, n. funeral oration.
ĕpĭtŏma, ae, ĕpĭtŏmē, ēs, f. abridgment,
epitome.
ĕpōdos, i, m. epode, a poem in a lyric
metre in which a long verse is followed
by a shorter.
ĕpops, ŏpis, m. hoopoe.
ĕpos, n. (only in nom. and acc. sing.),
heroic poem.
ĕpōto, avi, pōtum, 1. v.a. to drink off; to
absorb; to quaff; to swallow up.
ĕpŭlæ, ārum, v. epulum.
ĕpŭlāris, e, a. of a banquet.
ĕpŭlo, ōnis, m. a banqueter; a member of
a college of priests who superintended
banquets to the gods.
ĕpŭlor, atus, 1. v.n. & a. dep. to feast.

ĕpŭlum, i, n. banquet, feast.
ĕqua, ae, f. mare.
ĕquĕs, ĭtis, m. horseman, rider; horse-
soldier;—equites, pl. cavalry; order of
knights.
ĕquester, tris, tre, a. equestrian; pertaining to cavalry, or to the order of
knights. [of course.
ĕquĭdem, ad. truly, indeed, at all events;
ĕquīnus, a, um, a. pertaining to horses.
ĕquīria, ōrum, n. pl. annual horse-race in
honour of Mars.
ĕquĭtātus, ūs, m. cavalry.
ĕquĭto, 1. v.n. & a. to ride. [ture).
ĕquŭleus, i, m. colt, foal; rack (for tor-
ĕquŭlus, i, m. young horse; foal.
ĕquus, i, m. horse;—ĕqui, chariot.
ĕra, ae, f. mistress.
ērādīco, 1. v.a. to root out.
ērādo, si, sum, 3. v.a. to scratch out, to
erase; fig. to obliterate.
ercisco, v. hercisco.
ērectus, a, um, upright, erect; loft'; animated; resolute; noble; haughty.
ĕrĕmūrus (mod. hort.), eremurus.
ērēpo, psi, 3. v.n. & a. to creep out.
ēreptor, ōris, m. robber, plunderer.
ergā, pr. opposite to; against, towards.
ergastŭlum, i, n. workhouse; reforma-
tory; in pl., convicts.
ergō, ad. wherefore; therefore; then,
now;—quid — P why then?—as prep.,
on account of.
ĕrīce, es, f. heather.
ērĭcius, ii, m. chevaux-de-frise.
ērĭgĕron (mod. hort.), fleabane.
ērĭgo, rexi, rectum, 3. v.a. to erect; to
raise; to build; fig. to arouse; to cheer
up, to encourage.
ĕrīlis, e, a. of a master or mistress.
ērĭpio, rĭpui, reptum, 3. v.a. to snatch
away, to take by force; to rescue.
ērōdo, sum, 3. v.a. to gnaw away; to consume. [tion.
ērŏgātio, ōnis, f. paying out, distribu-
ērŏgo, 1. v.a. to pay out; to bequeath.
errābundus, a, um, a. wandering.
errātĭcus, a, um, a. roving, erratic; wild.
errātio, ōnis, f. wandering.
errātum, i, n. error, mistake.
errātus, ūs, m. wandering about.
erro, 1. v.n. & a. to wander or stray
about; to go astray; to err, to mistake.
erro, ōnis, m. wanderer; vagrant.
error, ōris, m. straying about; winding;
maze; uncertainty; error; deception;
distraction of the mind. [blush (at).
ērŭbesco, bui, 3. v.n. & a. to redden; to
ērūca, ae, f. caterpillar, rocket (a sort of
colewort). [to exhale.
ēructo, 1. v.a. to belch, to vomit; to emit;

ērŭdio, īvi & ii, ītum, 4. v.a. t⟩ polish, to educate, to instruct, to teach.

ērŭdītē, ad. learnedly, eruditely.

ērŭdītio, ōnis, f. instruction; learning, erudition.

ērŭdītus, a, um, p. & a. learned, skilled, experienced.

ērumpo, rūpi, ruptum, 3. v.a. & n. to break out; to sally forth.

ēruo, ui, ūtum, 3. v.a. to pluck or dig or root up; to overthrow; to destroy; to elicit.   [tion; eruption of a volcano.

ēruptio, ōnis, f. (mil.) sally; skin erup-

ērus, i, m. master; owner.

ervum, i, n. bitter vetch.

ēryngium, ii, n. sea-holly.

erythronium (mod. hort.), dog-tooth violet.

esca, ae, f. food; fig. bait.

ēscendo, di, sum, 3. v.n. & a. to mount up; to land; to ascend; to go up-country.

ēscensio, onis, f. climbing; landing.

eschscholtzia (mod. hort.), Californian

escŭlentus, a, um, a. eatable.   [poppy.

esculus, v. æsculus.

ēsĭto, 1. v.a. & n. to eat.

essēdārius, ii, m. fighter in a war-chariot.

essēdum, i, n., essēda, ae, f. two-wheeled war-chariot.   [desire eagerly.

ēsŭrio, ītum, 4. v.n. & a. to be hungry; to

et, c. and; also; even; moreover; both — and; as well as.

ětenim, for; truly; since; because.

ětēsiæ, ārum, m. pl. Etesian winds.

ēthĭcē, es, f. morals, moral science, ethics.

ethnĭcus, a, um, a. heathen.

ēthōlŏgus, i, m. mimic.

ětiam, c. and also, too, besides; nay even; yes indeed, yes; as yet; — atque —, again and again.

ětiamnum, ětiamnunc, c. even at the present time, yet, still; till then.

ětiamsi, c. even if, although.

ětiamtum, c. even then, till then.

etsi, c. although, even if.

ětȳmŏlŏgia, ae, f. etymology.

eu, i. well done! bravo!

ɔucălyptus (mod. hort.), blue gum.

euchăristia, ae, f. the Lord's Supper, the eugē! i. capital! bravo!   [Eucharist.

Euhān, m. name given to Bacchus.

euhans, antis, a. uttering the name Euhan.

Euhius, ii, a. title given to Bacchus.

euhoe! a cry of joy used by the votaries eunŭchus, i, m. eunuch.   [of Bacchus.

euōnymus, i, f. spindle-tree.

euphorbia (mod. hort.), spurge.

euphrasia (mod. hort.), eye-bright.

eurīpus (os), i, m. narrow channel, strait; eurōus, a, um, eastern.   [aqueduct.

eurus, i, m. east wind; the east.

ēvādo, si, sum, 3. v.n. & a. to go or come out; to escape, to avoid; to fall out, to happen; to mount; to leave behind.

ēvăgor, ātus, 1. v.n. & a. dep. to wander forth; to digress; to spread about; to overstep.

ēvălesco, lui, 3. v.n. to increase in strength; to grow; to be able; to prevail; to come into vogue.   [disappear.

ēvānesco, nui, 3. v.n. to pass away, to

ēvangĕlium, ii, n. the gospel.

ēvangĕlizo, 1. v.n. to preach the gospel.

ēvānidus, a, um, a. vanishing, passing ēvan, v. euhan.   [away.

ēvasto, 1. v.a. to devastate.

ēvĕho, vexi, vectum, 3. v.a. to carry forth, to convey out; to extol; to promote; —evehi, to ride out or up.

ēvello, velli, vulsum, 3. v.a. to pluck or tear out; fig. to root out.

ēvĕnio, vēni, ventum, 4. v.n. to come out; fig. to come to pass; to result.

ēventum, i, n. occurrence, event; result, effect.   [fate.

ēventus, ūs, m. occurrence, event; result;

ēverbĕro, 1. v.a. to flog, to beat.

ēvergo, 3. v.a. to send out or forth.

ēverrĭcŭlum, i, n. drag-net.

ēverro, verri, versum, 3. v.a. to sweep out; fig. to make a clean sweep of; plunder.   [tion.

ēversio, ōnis, f. overthrowing; destruc-

ēversor, ōris, m. subverter, destroyer.

ēverto, ti, sum, 3. v.a. to turn out, to thrust out; to upset; to overthrow; to destroy.

ēvestīgātus, a, um, p. & a. found out.

ēvĭdens, entis, a. apparent, evident.

ēvĭdenter, ad. evidently.

ēvĭdentia, ae, f. clearness.

ēvĭgĭlo, 1. v.n. & a. to be wakeful; to compose by study at night.   [wind round.

ēvincio, nxi, nctum, 4. v.a. to bind up, to

ēvinco, vīci, victum, 3. v.a. to vanquish utterly; fig. to prevail; to prove.

ēviscĕro, ātum, 1. v.a. to disembowel; to ēvitābĭlis, e, a. avoidable.   [lacerate.

ēvīto, 1. v.a. to shun, to avoid.

ēvīto, 1. v.a. to kill.

Evius, v. Euhius.   [to service; reservists.

ēvŏcāti, ōrum, m. pl. veterans again called

ēvŏcātor, ōris, m. one who calls forth.

ēvŏco, 1. v.a. to call out; to summon: to elicit; to challenge.

evoe, i., v. euhoe.

ēvŏlo, 1. v.a. to fly out; to rush forth.

ēvŏlūtio, onis, f. unwinding, turning over (of a book).

ēvolvo, volvi, vŏlūtum, 3. v.a. to unroll, to unfold; to extricate; to peruse; to explain.

ēvŏmo, ui, ĭtum, 3. v.a. to vomit forth.
ēvulgo, 1. v.a. to publish, to divulge.
ex, ē (before consonants), pr. out of, from; down from, off; by; after; on account of; according to;—ex abundanti cautela, from a superfluity of precaution;—ex cathedra, (a pronouncement made) from the chair of authority;—ex hypothesi, according to a principle assumed to be true;—ex officio, by virtue of one's official position; —ex parte, partisan;—ex pede Herculem, to judge of Hercules by his footmark;—ex post facto, from what has occurred afterwards;—ex tempore, off-hand;—ex vi termini, from the very meaning of the term.
exăcerbo, 1. v.a. to exasperate.
exactio, ōnis, f. driving out; exaction; calling in (of debts); tax, tribute.
exactor, ōris, m. expeller; exactor; collector of taxes.
exactus, a, um, p. & a. exact, accurate.
exăcuo, ui, ūtum, 3. v.a. to make sharp or pointed; to stimulate. [against.
exadversum, exadversus, ad. & pr. over
exaedificātio, ōnis, f. building up. [finish.
exaedifico, 1. v.a. to build up; fig. to
exaequātio, ōnis, f. fig. equalizing.
exaequo, 1. v.a. & n. to equalize; fig. to regard as equal; to be equal (to).
exaestuo, 1. v.n. & a. to boil up; to effervesce. [plification.
exaggĕrātio, ōnis, f. fig. elevation, amexaggĕro, 1. v.a. to dam up; to enlarge; fig. to exaggerate.
exăgito, 1. v.a. to drive out; to stir up; to disturb; to tease; to terrify; to censure, to rail at.
exalbesco, bui, 3. v.n. to turn pale.
exāmen, ĭnis, n. swarm (of bees); crowd; tongue of a balance; fig. examination.
exāmino, 1. v.n. & a. to weigh; fig. to consider, to examine. [actly.
exāmussim, ad. according to rule, exexanclo, 1. v.a. fig. to go through, to suffer.
exănĭmātio, ōnis, f. fig. terror, fright.
exănĭmis, e, a. lifeless, dead.
exănĭmo, 1. v.a. to deprive of life; to kill; to alarm greatly.
exănĭmus, a, um, v. exanimis.
exantlo, v. exanclo. [fig. to break out.
exardesco, arsi, arsum, 3. v.n. to take fire;
exāresco, rui, 3. v.n. to dry up; fig. to become exhausted.
exarmo, 1. v.a. to disarm; to weaken.
exāro, 1. v.a. to plough or dig up; to plough; fig. to note down (by scratching the wax on the tablets). [asperate.
exaspero, 1. v.a. to roughen; fig. to ex-

exauctōro, 1. v.a. to dismiss from service.
exaudio, īvi & ii, ītum, 4. v.a. to hear plainly; to hearken; to grant; to obey.
exaugŭratio, ōnis, f. profanation.
exaugŭro, 1. v.a. to profane. [river, etc.).
excaeco, 1. v.a. to blind; to stop up (a
excalceo, 1. v.a. to take off (someone's) shoes, to unshoe;—excalceor, to doff one's shoes.
excalfăcio, factum, 3. v.a. to heat.
excandesco, dui, 3. v.n. to glow.
excanto, 1. v.a. to charm forth, to remove by incantation.
excarnifico, ātum, 1. v.a. to tear the flesh to pieces; fig. to torture.
excăvo, atum, 1. v.a. to hollow out.
excēdo, cessi, cessum, 3. v.n. & a. to go out or away; to withdraw; to digress; to go beyond; to die; to leave; to surpass; to exceed. [excellent.
excellens, entis, p. & a. fig. distinguished, excellenter, ad. excellently.
excellentia, ae, f. superiority, excellence.
excello, cellui, celsum, 3. v.n. to be eminent, to excel.
excelsĭtas, ātis, f. loftiness. [lime.
excelsus, a, um, p. & a. lofty, high; subexceptio, ōnis, f. exception, restriction.
excepto, 1. v.a. to take out, to take up; to inhale. [out, to separate.
excerno, crēvi, crētum, 3. v.a. to sift
excerpo, psi, ptum, 3. v.a. to pick out; fig. to select.
excerptum, i, n. extract from a book.
excessus, ūs, m. departure; death; digression.
excetra, ae, f. snake; fig. trickish woman.
excidium, ii, n. overthrow, destruction.
excido, cĭdi, 3. v.n. to fall out; to escape; to swoon; to forfeit; to perish; to disappear; to be forgotten.
excīdo, cīdi, cīsum, 3. v.a. to cut out or off, to hew down; to raze; to destroy; fig. to banish.
excieo, īvi, ītum, 2. excio, īvi & ii, ītum, 4. v.a. to rouse; to call out, to send for; to summon; to challenge; to frighten.
excipio, cēpi, ceptum, 3. v.a. to exempt; to except; to catch; to receive; to succeed; to relieve; to continue; to listen to.
excipŭla, orum, n. pl. receptacles, basins.
excitātus, a, um, p. & a. lively, vehement, loud.
excito, 1. v.a. to rouse up, to wake up; to raise, to erect; fig. to arouse; to cause.
exclāmātio, ōnis, f. exclamation.
exclāmo, 1. v.n. & a. to call or cry out; to exclaim; to bawl.
exclūdo, si, sum, 3. v.a. to shut out, to exclude; to hatch; to remove; to prevent.

excōgĭtātio, ōnis, f. contriving, invention.
excōgĭto, 1. v.a. to contrive; to think out.
excŏlo, cŏlui, cultum, 3. v.a. *fig.* to improve; to refine; to enrich.
excŏquo, xi, ctum, 3. v.a. to boil; to temper (by heat); to boil away; to melt
excors, cordis, a. silly, stupid.   [out.
excrēmentum, i, n. excrement; spittle, mucus.   [to grow up; *fig.* to grow.
excresco, ēvi, ētum, 3. v.n. to grow forth;
excrŭcio, 1. v.a. to torture; to torment; to pain.   [guard.
excŭbiæ, ārum, f. pl. watching; watch,
excŭbitor, ōris, m. watchman, sentinel.
excŭbo, bui, bĭtum, 1. v.n. to sleep in the open; to keep watch; to be attentive.
excūdo, di, sum, 3. v.a. to strike out; to forge; to make; *fig.* to compose.
exculco, 1. v.a. to stamp down.
excurro, cŭcurri (curri), cursum, 3. v.n. & a. to run out; to make an excursion; to sally; to extend; to project.
excursio, ōnis, f. running forth; sally; invasion; opening of a speech.
excursor, ōris, m. skirmisher; spy.
excursus, ūs, m. running out; excursion; sally; invasion.
excūsābĭlis, e, a. excusable.
excūsātē, ad. blamelessly.
excūsātio, ōnis, f. excuse.
excūso, 1. v.a. to excuse; to plead as an excuse; to absolve; to dispense with.
excŭtio, cussi, cussum, 3. v.a. to shake out *or* off; to cast out; to banish; to shoot off; to search, to examine.
execo, v. exseco.
exĕdo, ēdi, ēsum, 3. v.a. to eat up, to consume; to hollow; to destroy; *fig.* to exhaust.
exedra, ae, f. a courtyard with seats round in which philosophers met and disputed.
exemplar, āris, n. model, pattern, example; copy; image, likeness.
exemplum, i, n. sample; example; precedent; warning; punishment; portrait; copy; kind, mode;—**exempli gratia,** to serve as an example.
exentĕro, 1. v.a. to disembowel.
exeo, ii, ĭtum, 4. v.n. & a. to go out *or* away; to march out; to escape; to end; to die; to perish; to be spread abroad; to rise; to avoid; to exceed; —**exeunt omnes,** all leave (the stage).
exequiæ, exequor, etc., v. **exsequiæ,** etc.
exerceo, ui, ĭtum, 2. v.a. to drill, to exercise; to employ; to practise; to administer; to till, to cultivate; to harass.
exercĭtātio, ōnis, f. exercise, practice.
exercĭtātus, a, um, p. & a. practised, versed; agitated, troubled.

exercĭtium, ii, n. exercise.
exercĭto, 1. v.a. to practise.
exercĭtor, ōris, m. trainer.
exercĭtus, ūs, m. army; swarm, flock.
exero, v. exsero.
exhālātio, ōnis, f. exhalation, vapour.
exhālo, 1. v.a. to breathe out; to evaporate; to steam; to die.
exhaurio, hausi, haustum, 4. v.a. to drain; to empty; to drink up; *fig.* to exhaust; to suffer to the end.
exhērēdo, 1. v.a. to disinherit.
exhēres, ēdis, a. disinherited; —, c. disinherited person.
exhĭbeo, ui, ĭtum, 2. v.a. to present, to deliver, to offer; to furnish; to exhibit; to employ; to procure; to cause.
exhĭlăro, 1. v.a. to gladden, to delight.
exhorresco, rui, 3. v.n. & a. to be terrified; to tremble at.
exhortātio, ōnis, f. exhortation.
exhortor, ātus, 1. v.a. dep. to exhort, to encourage.
exĭgo, ēgi, actum, 3. v.a. to drive out; to banish; to plunge, to thrust; to demand, to exact; to pass, to spend; to finish; to deliberate, to consult; to examine, to weigh.
exĭguē, ad. briefly; narrowly; scantily.
exĭguĭtas, ātis, f. shortness, scarcity.
exĭguus, a, um, a. scanty, small, petty, short, poor.
exīlis, e, a. small, thin; poor.   [ness.
exīlĭtas, ātis, f. thinness, weakness, poor-
exīlĭter, ad. thinly, feebly.
exīlĭum, ii, v. exsilium.
exim, v. exinde.
exĭmie, ad. exceedingly, excellently.
exĭmius, a, um, a. select, extraordinary, excellent, fine.
exĭmo, ēmi, emptum, 3. v.a. to take out, to remove; to free, to release; *fig.* to waste.
exin, ad., v. exinde.
exĭnānio, īvi & ii, ĭtum, 4. v.a. to empty.
exindĕ, ad. thence; after that; then.
exintero, v. exentero.
existĭmātio, ōnis, f. judgment; opinion; reputation; credit.
existĭmātor, ōris, m. judge, critic.
existĭmo, 1., **existŭmo,** 1. v.a. to judge, to esteem, to think.
existo, v. exsisto.
exĭtĭābĭlis, e, exĭtĭālis, e, a. destructive, deadly.
exĭtĭōsus, a, um, a. destructive, pernici-
exĭtĭum, ii, n. ruin, mischief; death.   [ous.
exĭtus, ūs, m. egress, departure; end; outlet; result; death.
exlex, ēgis, a. lawless.
exmoveo, v. emoveo.

exōdium, ii, n. comic interlude, afterpiece. [to grow out of use; to cease.
exōlesco, ēvi, ētum, 3. v.n. to grow up;
exōněro, 1. v.a. to unload, to disburden, to discharge. [for.
exŏpto, 1. v.n. to wish much, to long
exōrābilis, e, a. exorable. [evil spirits.
exorcismus, i, m. exorcism, expulsion of
exorcizo, 1. v.a. to drive out (evil spirits).
exordior, orsus, 4. v.a. dep. to begin, to commence. [preface.
exordium, ii, n. beginning; introduction,
exōrior, ortus, 4. v.n. dep. to arise; to begin; to originate; to spring up.,
exornātio, ōnis, f. ornament; embellishment. [embellish.
exorno, 1. v.a. to furnish, to adorn, to
exōro, 1. v.a. to gain or obtain by entreaty; to appease. [prises.
exorsa, orum, n. pl. beginnings, enter-
exortus, ūs, m. rising (of the sun, etc.).
exoscŭlor, 1. v. dep. to kiss.
exosso, 1. v.a. to bone; to deprive of bones. [exceedingly.
exōsus, a, um, p. & a. hating or hated
exōticus, a, um, a. foreign, exotic.
expallesco, lui, 3. v.n. to turn very pale.
expando, pandi, passum & pansum, 3. v.a. to spread out, to expand; fig. to expound.
expatior, v. exspatior.
expăvesco, pāvi 3. v.a. to fear greatly.
expecto, v. exspec o.
expēdio, īvi & ii,,ītum, 4. v.a. to extricate; to despatch; to make ready; to free; to arrange; to unfold;—expedit, it is profitable or expedient.
expēdītē, ad. promptly, expeditely.
expēdītio, ōnis, f. expedition, campaign.
expēdītus, a, um, p & a. free, easy; ready; ready for action; without baggage; unencumbered.
expello, pŭli, pulsum, 3. v.a. to expel; to banish; to reject.
expendo, di, sum, 3. v.a. to pay; to lay out; fig. to weigh, to judge; to expiate.
expergēfăcio, fēci, factum, 3. v.a. to arouse, to awake.
expergiscor, perrectus, 3. v.n. dep. to awake; fig. to bestir oneself.
expěriens, entis, p. & a. experienced, active, industrious.
expěrientia, ae, f. trial, experiment; experience;—experientia docet, experience teaches.
expěrimentum, i, n. trial, experiment, experience;—fiat experimentum in corpore vili, let a trial be made on a worthless body.
expěrior, pertus, 4. v.a. dep. to try; to experience, to find; to attempt.

expers, tis, a. destitute of, without; having no experience.
expertus, a, um, p. & a. experienced, having tried; skilful;—experto crede, trust the man of experience.
expěto, īvi & ii, ītum, 3. v.a. & n. to covet, to desire; to aspire to; to demand; to happen; to befall.
expiātio, ōnis, f. atonement, expiation.
expīlātio, ōnis, f. plundering.
expīlo, 1. v.a. to plunder.
expingo, nxi, ctum, 3. v.a. to paint.
expio, 1. v.a. to atone for, to expiate.
expiro, v. exspiro. [out, to find out.
expiscor, atus, 1. v.a. dep. fig. to search
explānātio, ōnis, f. explanation.
explānātor, ōris, m. explainer.
explāno, 1. v.a. fig. to explain.
explendesco, v. exsplendesco.
expleo, ēvi, ētum, 2. v.a. to fill out or up, to complete; to finish; to satisfy; to satiate; to fulfil, to perform.
explētus, a, um, p. & a. complete, perfect.
explĭcātio, ōnis, f. unfolding; fig. explanation.
explĭcātor, ōris, m. expounder, explainer.
explĭcātus, ūs, m. expounding.
explĭcātus, a, um, a. clear, regular.
explĭco, āvi & ui, ātum & ītum, 1. v.a. to unfold; to open; to smooth; to display; to deploy; to disentangle; to exhibit; to develop; to explain.
explōdo, si, sum, 3. v.a. to hiss (an actor); to reject.
explōrātē, ad. certainly; securely.
explōrātio, ōnis, f. exploration.
explōrātor, ōris, m. spy, scout.
explōro, 1. v.a. to explore; to reconnoitre; to try, to test.
explōsio, ōnis, f. driving off by noise.
expōlio, īvi & ii, ītum, 4. v.a. to polish; to refine.
expōlītio, ōnis, f. smoothing off; polishing; embellishing.
expōno, pŏsui, pŏsitum, 3. v.a. to set out; to expose; to disembark; to publish; to offer; to exhibit, to explain. [out.
exporrigo, rexi, rectum, 3. v.a. to stretch
exportātio, ōnis, f. exportation.
exporto, 1. v.a. to export.
exposco, poposci, 3. v.a. to ask earnestly; to request; to implore; to demand (for punishment).
expŏsĭtio, ōnis, f. exposition; narration.
expostŭlātio, ōnis, f. remonstrance, complaint.
expostŭlo, 1. v.a. & n. to demand urgently, to require; to find fault, to remonstrate.
expressē, ad. expressly, distinctly.
expressus, a, um, p. & a. clear, express.

exprĭmo, pressi, pressum, 3. v.a. to squeeze out; to copy, to portray; to express; to extort. [braiding.

exprobrātio, ōnis, f. reproaching, upexprobro, 1. v.a. to upbraid, to reproach.

exprōmo, mpsi, mptum, 3. v.a. to bring forth; to show forth, to display; to disclose, to state. [assault.

expugnābĭlis, e, a. expugnable, open to

expugnātio, ōnis, f. taking by storm.

expugnātor, ōris, m. attacker.

expugnax, ācis, a. powerful, efficacious.

expugno, 1. v.a. to take by assault, to storm; to conquer; to accomplish by effort.

expulsio, ōnis, f. expulsion.

expungo, nxi, nctum, 3. v.a. to erase; to discharge; to settle.

expuo, v. exspuo. [to exculpate.

expurgo, 1. v.a. to purge out, to purify;

expŭto, 1. v.a. to examine, to fathom.

exquīro, sīvi, sītum, 3. v. to search out, to inquire.

exquīsĭte, ad. exquisitely, accurately.

exquīsītus, a, um, p. & a. choice, excellent, exquisite. [feeble.

exsanguis, e, a. bloodless; pale, wan; fig.

exsătio, 1. v.a. to satisfy, to satiate.

exsătŭrābĭlis, e, a. that may be satiated.

exsătŭro, 1. v.a. to satiate.

exscendo, v. escendo.

exscensio, ōnis, f. landing.

exscidium, v. excidium. [to destroy.

exscindo, ĭdi, issum, 3. v.a. to extirpate,

exscrībo, psi, ptum, 3. v.a. to write off, to copy.

exsculpo, psi, ptum, 3. v.a. to chisel out, to carve; to erase; fig. to elicit.

exsĕco, cui, ctum, 1. v.a. to cut out or away; to castrate.

exsecrābĭlis, e, a. execrating; execrable.

exsecrātio, ōnis, f. execration; oath; curse. [to execrate; to take an oath.

exsecror, atus, 1. v.a. & n. dep. to curse,

exsectio, ōnis, f. cutting out.

exsĕcūtio, ōnis, f. performance, execution.

exsĕcūtor, ōris, m. performer. [relics.

exsĕquiae, ārum, f. pl. funeral procession;

exsĕquiālis, e, a. funereal.

exsĕquor, cūtus, 3. v.a. dep. to follow (to the grave); to pursue; to accomplish; to relate; to assert; to punish; to avenge.

exsĕro, sĕrui, sertum, 3. v.a. to stretch forth; to thrust out;—exsertus, a, um, protruding; bare.

exserto, 1. v.a. to stretch forth.

exsībilo, 1. v.a. to hiss off (an actor).

exsiccātus, a, um, p. & a. dry, jejune.

exsicco, 1. v.a. to dry up; to empty (a bottle).

exsĭlio, sĭlui, 4. v.n. to spring forth, to leap up.

exsĭlium, ii, n. exile; retreat.

exsisto, stĭti, stĭtum, 3. v.n. to step forth, to appear; to arise; to become; to be; to exist.

exsolvo, solvi, sŏlūtum, 3. v.a. to set free; to pay; to throw off; to release; to [solve.

exsomnis, e, a. sleepless, wakeful. [solve.

exsorbeo, ui, v.a. to suck up; drain

exsors, sortis, a. without share. [deep.

exspătior, atus, 1. v.n. dep. to wander from the course; to digress, to expati-

exspectātio, ōnis, f. expectation. [ate.

exspecto, 1. v.a. to await, to expect; to anticipate; to desire; to fear; to require.

exspergo, spersum, 3. v.a. to sprinkle over.

exspēs, a. hopeless.

exspīrātio, ōnis, f. exhalation.

exspīro, 1. v.a. & n. to breathe out; to exhale; to expire; to die; to cease.

exsplendesco, dui, 3. v.n. to shine forth.

exspōlio, 1. v.a. to plunder.

exspuo, ui, utum, 3. v.a. to spit out; to eject; to shed.

externo, 1. v.a. to terrify, to madden.

exstĭmŭlo, 1. v.a. to goad; to stimulate.

exstinctio, ōnis, f. extinction, annihilation.

exstinctor, ōris, m. extinguisher; destroyer.

exstinguo, nxi, nctum, 3. v.a. to quench, to extinguish; to kill; to destroy.

exstirpo, 1. v.a. to root out, to extirpate.

exsto, 1. v.n. to stand out or forth; to project; to be visible; to exist, to be.

exstructio, ōnis, f. erection.

exstruo, xi, ctum, 3. v.a. to pile up; to build up, to raise.

exsūdo, 1. v.n. & a. to exude; to sweat out; fig. to toil through.

exsūgo, xi, ctum, 3. v.a. to suck out.

exsul, ŭlis, c. exile.

exsŭlo, 1. v.n. to be an exile.

exsultātio, ōnis, f. exultation.

exsulto, 1. v.n. to jump about; to let oneself go; fig. to exult; to boast.

exsŭpĕrābĭlis, e, a. able to be overcome.

exsŭpĕrantia, ae, f. superiority.

exsŭpĕro, 1. v.n. & a. to excel; to overtop; to surpass; to overpower.

exsurdo, 1. v.a. to deafen, to dull, to blunt.

exsurgo, surrexi, 3. v.n. to rise, to stand up; to recover. [to stir up, to excite.

exsuscĭto, 1. v.a. to awaken; to kindle; fig.

exta, ōrum, n. pl. bowels, entrails.

extābesco, bui, 3. v.n. to waste away; to vanish.

extemplo, ad. immediately, forthwith.

extempŏrālis, e, a. extemporary.

extendo, di, tum & sum, 3. v.a. to stretch out, to extend; to enlarge; to prolong; to continue. [extenuation.

extĕnuātio, ōnis, f. thinning, diminution,

extĕnuo, 1. v.a. to make thin; to diminish; to weaken.

exter, extĕrus, tĕra, tĕrum, a. outward, external, foreign;—**exterior, exterius,** outer, exterior;—**extrēmus & extĭmus,** uttermost, utmost, extreme, last.

extergeo, tersi, tersum, 3. v.a. to clean out.

exterior, ius, v. **exter.**

extermino, 1. v.a. to drive out or away, to banish; to remove.

externus, a, um, a. outward, external; foreign, strange. [to crush.

extĕro, trīvi, trītum, 3. v.a. to rub out;

exterreo, ui, ĭtum, 2. v.a. to strike with terror, to frighten.

extĕrus, a, um, v. **exter.**

extimesco, mui, 3. v.n. & a. to be greatly afraid of; to fear much.

extĭmus, a, um, v. **exter.**

extinguo, v. **exstinguo.**

extirpo, v. **exstirpo.**

extispex, ĭcis, m. soothsayer.

exto, v. **exsto.** [extol, to exalt.

extollo, 3. v.a. to raise; to lift up; to

extorqueo, si, tum, 2. v.a. to twist or wrench out; to force (from); to extort.

extorris, e, a. exiled.

extrā, ad. & pr. without; out of, beyond; except;—**extra quam,** unless.

extrăho, xi, ctum, 3. v.a. to draw out or forth; to extricate; to extract; to prolong; to spend or waste.

extrāneus, a, um, a. external, extraneous, foreign; strange.

extraordĭnārius, a, um, a. extraordinary.

extrārius, a, um, a. external.

extrēmĭtas, ātis, f. extremity, end.

extrēmum, ad. at last; for the last time.

extrēmus, a, um, v. **exter.** [cate, to free.

extrico, 1. v.a. to disentangle, to extri-

extrinsĕcus, ad. from without; on the outside. [drive out.

extrūdo, si, sum, 3. v.a. to thrust out; to

extruo, v. **exstruo.**

extundo, tŭdi, tūsum, 3. v.a. to beat or strike out; to invent.

exturbo, 1. v.a. to thrust out; to divorce; to disturb. [abound.

exūbĕro, 1. v.n. to grow luxuriantly; to

exul, v. **exsul.**

exulcĕro, 1. v.a. to ulcerate, to exasperate, to aggravate.

exulo, v. **exsulo.**

exulto, v. **exsulto.** [invoke with cries.

exūlŭlo, 1. v.n. & a. to cry aloud; to

exundo, 1. v.n. to rush forth; to overflow with.

exuo, ui, ūtum, 3. v.a. to put off; to doff; to strip; to shake off; to deprive of; fig. lay aside; to cast off.

exupero, v. **exsupero.**

exurgo, v. **exsurgo.**

exūro, ussi, ustum, 3. v.a. to burn up; to consume; to inflame; to dry up; to destroy.

exustio, ōnis, f. conflagration.

exūviæ, ārum, f. pl. things stripped off; spoils, booty.

Făba, ae, f. bean.

făbālis, e, a. of beans. [short play.

făbella, ae, f. short story; short fable;

făber, bri, m. artisan, workman; smith; carpenter; —, **bra, brum,** a. skilful, ingenious.

făber, ri, m. a. kind of fish, dory.

fabrĭca, ae, f. workshop; art; trade; product; building; fig. trick.

fabrĭcātio, ōnis, f. making, manufacture.

fabrĭcātor, ōris, m. artificer, framer; contriver.

fabrĭco, 1. v.a., **fabrĭcor, ātus,** 1. v.a. dep. to make, to fabricate, to fashion.

fabrīlis, e, a. pertaining to an artificer.

făbŭla, ae, f. story; tale; fable; drama, play;—**fabulæ !** rubbish! [invent.

făbŭlor, ātus, 1. v. dep. to tell stories, to

făbŭlōsus, a, um, a. storied, fabulous.

făcesso, cessi, ītum, 3. v.a. & n. to do; to accomplish; to go away.

făcētē, ad. wittily, humorously.

făcētiæ, ārum, f. pl. witty sayings; humour; sarcasms. [ous; graceful, fine.

făcētus, a, um, a. merry; witty, humor-

făcies, ēi, f. figure; face, look, pretence; appearance. [first.

făcĭlĕ, ad. easily;—**facile princeps,** easily

făcĭlis, e, a. easy; pliable; gentle; courteous; good-natured, affable.

făcĭlĭtas, ātis, f. easiness, facility; readiness; good nature, courteousness, affa-

făcĭnŏrōsus, a, um, a. criminal. [bility.

făcĭnus, ōris, n. exploit; atrocious deed, crime.

făcio, fēci, factum, 3. v.a. & n. to make; to do; to fashion; to cause; to compose; to practise; to commit; to render; (with the genitive) to value; (with dat. or ad acc. or absol.) to be of service.

factĭcius, a, um, a. manufactured; artificial; factitious.

factio, ōnis, f. faction, party.

factiōsus, a, um, a. factious, seditious.

factĭtius, v. **factĭcius.** [to practise.

factĭto, 1. v.a. to make or do frequently;

factum, i, n. deed, exploit.

fäcultas, ätis, f. capability; possibility; means; opportunity; abundance, wealth; stock; estate.

fäcundē, ad. eloquently.

fäcundia, ae, f. eloquence.

fäcundus, a, um, eloquent.

fæcŭla, ae, f. lees of wine (used as a flavouring).

fæcŭlentus, a, um, a. thick, muddy.

fænebris, e, a. pertaining to interest.

fænĕrātio, ōnis, f. usury, money-lending.

fænĕrātor, ōris, m. usurer, money-lender.

fænĕro, I. v.a. **fænĕror,** I. v. dep. to lend on interest.

fænĭcŭlum, i, n. fennel.

fænīlia, um, n. pl. hay-loft.

fænisex, ĕcis, m., **fænisĕca, ae,** m. mower; **fænum, i,** n. hay.   [farm-servant.

fænus, ĕris, n. interest; *fig.* profit; gain.

fæx, fæcis, f. sediment, dregs; *fig.* dregs of the people.

fägeus, a, um, a. beechen.

fägin(e)us, a, um, a. beechen.

fägus, i, f. beech-tree.

fälärica, ae, f. a missile (thrown generally by a catapult).

falcārius, ii, m. scythe-maker.

falcātus, a, um, a. armed with scythes; scythe-shaped, crooked.

falcifĕr, a, um, a. carrying a scythe.

Fälernum, i, n. Falernian wine.

fallācia, ae, f. deceit, trick, stratagem.

fallāciter, ad. deceitfully, fallaciously.

fallax, ācis, a. deceitful, fallacious.

fallo, fĕfelli, falsum, 3. v.a. to cheat, to deceive; to disappoint; to escape notice; to lighten; to help to pass.

falsō, ad. falsely, untruly; unjustly.

falsus, a, um, p. & a. false; deceiving; spurious.   [war-engine.

falx, falcis, f. sickle; scythe; hook-shaped

fāma, ae, f. common talk; rumour; fame; renown; ill-fame.

fämēlicus, a, um, a. famished, starving.

fämēs, is, f. hunger; famine; *fig.* greediness.

fämīlia, ae, f. family; servants *or* slaves belonging to one master; property; household; sect; troop.

fämīliāris, e, a. of the family; familiar; intimate; —, **is,** c. friend.

fämīliārĭtas, ātis, f. familiarity, intimacy, friendship.   [terms.

fämīliāriter, ad. intimately, on friendly

fämōsus, a, um, a. famed, renowned; infamous, notorious; slanderous, libellous.

fämŭla, ae, f. female slave; maid-servant.

fämŭlāris, e, a. of slaves, servile.

fämŭlor, ātus, I. v. dep. n. to act as servant, to attend.

fämŭlus, i, m. slave, servant; attendant; —, **a, um,** a. serviceable, servile.

fänātĭcus, a, um, a. enthusiastic; furious, mad.

fandus, a, um, p. & a. that may be spoken; right.

fänum, i, n. sanctuary, temple.

fär, farris, n. spelt.   [cram.

farcio, farsi, fartum, 4. v.a. to stuff, to

färīna, ae, f. meal, flour. [a hotch-potch.

farrāgo, ĭnis, f mixed fodder; mash; *met.*

fartor, ōris, m. poulterer.

fas, n. indecl. divine law; right; equity; — **est,** it is lawful *or* permitted *or* possible; it is destined.

fascia, ae, f. band, fillet; girth.

fascicŭlus, i, m. small bundle, packet; bunch (of flowers).

fascĭno, I. v.a. to enchant, to fascinate.

fascĭŏla, ae, f. small bandage.

fascis, is, m. bundle, parcel;—**fasces,** pl. bundles of rods, carried before the highest magistrates of Rome, with an axe bound up in the middle of them; (poet.) consulship.

fasti, ōrum, m. pl. list of pleading-days; calendar; annals.

fastīdio, īvi & ii, ītum, 4. v.n. & a. to disdain; to loathe; to be scornful.

fastīdiōsē, ad. squeamishly; scornfully.

fastīdiōsus, a, um, a. squeamish; scornful; loathsome.

fastīdium, ii, n. squeamishness, loathing; scornful contempt; pride.

fastīgātus, a, um, p. & a. sloping.

fastīgium, ii, n. slope, declivity; gable, roof; ridge; extremity; height; depth; *fig.* highest rank, dignity.

fastus, a, um, a. dies —, day on which the courts could sit; lucky day.

fastus, ūs, m. contempt; haughtiness.

fātālis, e, a. destined, fated; fatal.

fātālĭter, ad. fatally.   [acknowledge.

fāteor, fassus, 2. v.a. dep. to confess; to

fātĭcānus, a, um, fātĭcĭnus, a, um, a. prophetic.   [prophet.

fātĭdĭcus, a, um, a. prophetic; —, **i,** m.

fātĭfĕr, a, um, a. deadly; fatal.

fātĭgātio, ōnis, f. weariness, fatigue.

fātĭgo, I. v.a. to weary, to tire, to fatigue; to harass; to importune; to torment; to reprove.

fātisco, 3. v.n., **fātiscor,** 3. v. dep. to gape, to crack; *fig.* to grow weak *or* exhausted.   [death.

fātum, i, n. fate, destiny; doom; ill-fate;

fātuus, a, um, a. foolish, silly; clumsy; —**ignis fatuus,** will-o'-the-wisp.

fauces, ium, f. pl. throat; voracity; narrow entrance; defile; gulf, abyss.

Faunus, i, m. a country deity, faun.

faustus, a, um, a. favourable; auspicious; lucky, prosperous.

fautor, ōris, m. favourer, patron.

fautrix, īcis, f. patroness, protectress; —, a. favourable.

făveo, făvi, fautum, 2. v.n., to favour, to befriend, to protect;—**favēre linguis,** to abstain from words of ill-omen; to be silent.

făvilla, ae, f. glowing ashes, embers.

Făvōnius, ii, m. west wind. [applause.

făvor, ōris, m. favour, good-will; bias,

făvus, i, m. honey-comb.

fax, făcis, f. torch, link; fire-brand; fig. stimulus; love-flame; wedding.

febrĭcŭla, ae, f. slight fever.

febris, is, f. fever, ague.

februa, ōrum, n. pl. Roman festival of purification.

februārius, ii, m. February.

fēcundĭtas, ātis, f. fertility, fecundity.

fēcundus, a, um, a. fruitful, fertile; abundant. [anger, wrath.

fel, fellis, n. gall, bile; poison; fig. (poet.)

fēles, is, f. cat.

fēlīcĭtas, ātis, f. good fortune, felicity.

fēlīcĭter, ad. luckily, happily.

fēlix, īcis, a. fruitful; lucky, happy, fortunate; successful.

felo, ōnis, m. felon;—**felo de se,** one who commits a felony on himself; a suicide.

fēmina, ae, f. female, woman.

fēmĭneus, a, um, a. womanly, feminine, womanish, effeminate. [gender.

fēmĭnīnus, a, um, a. of the feminine

fēmur, ōris, or **ĭnis,** n. (upper) thigh.

fener . . ., v. **fæner . . . :**

fĕnestra, ae, f. window; oop-hole; fig. occasion, temptation.

fēnīlia, v. **fænīlia.**

fēnum, v. **fænum.**

fēnus, v. **fænus.**

fēra, ae, f. wild beast.

fērālis, e, a. funereal; deadly, fatal;— **Fērālia, ium,** n. pl. Feast of the dead.

fērax, ācis, a. fruitful, fertile.

fercŭlum, i, n. litter, bier; dish; course (at dinner); — **pompæ,** litter for carrying spoils of war in procession.

fērē, ad. nearly, almost; about; quite; in general; (with negatives) hardly.

fĕrentārius, ii, m. light-armed soldier, slinger.

fĕretrum, i, n. litter, bier.

fēriae, ārum, f. pl. holidays. [leisure.

fēriātus, a, um, p. & a. keeping holiday, at

fĕrīna, ae, f. game, venison.

fĕrīnus, a, um, a. of wild beasts.

fĕrio, 4. v.a. to strike, to knock; to hit; to slay, to kill; to strike (a bargain); to make (a covenant).

fĕrior, ātus, 1. v.n. dep. to keep holiday.

fĕritas, ātis, f. wildness, savageness.

fermē, ad. nearly, almost, about; (with negat.) scarcely.

fermento, 1. v.a. to cause to ferment;— **fermentor,** pass. to ferment.

fermentum, i, n. yeast, sort of beer; fig. anger, passion.

fĕro, tŭli, lātum, ferre, v.a. ir. to carry; to bring; to bear away; to plunder; to bear with; to lead; to produce, to bring forth; to endure; to extol; to receive; to propose; to exhibit; —, v.n. (of a road, etc.) to lead;—**ferunt,** they say;—**fertur,** it is said;—**legem ferre,** to propose a law;—**ferre prae se,** to pretend. [ness.

fĕrōcia, ae, f. fierceness, ferocity; haughti- **fĕrōcĭtas, ātis,** f. courage, fierceness; ferocity, haughtiness.

fĕrōcĭter, ad. bravely; fiercely; haughtily; cruelly. [haughty; headstrong.

fĕrox, ōcis, a. wild, bold; warlike; cruel;

fĕrrāmentum, i, n. iron tool.

ferrāria, ae, f. iron mine. [iron.

ferrātus, a, um, a. armed or shod with

ferreus, a, um, a. of iron, iron; fig. hard, cruel; firm. [iron-rust, dusky.

ferrūgĭneus, a, um, a. of the colour of **ferrūgo, ĭnis,** f. iron-rust; colour of iron-rust; dusky colour. [weapon; war.

ferrum, i, n. iron; sword; any tool of iron;

ferrūmen, ĭnis, n. glue; cement.

ferrūmĭno, 1. v.a. to glue, to cement.

fertĭlis, e, a. fruitful, fertile; fig. abundant. [abundance.

fertĭlĭtas, ātis, f. fruitfulness, fertility;

fĕrŭla, ae, f. fennel; stick; scourging-rod; goad.

fĕrus, a, um, a. wild, savage; cruel; —, i, m.; —, ae, f. wild beast.

fervĕfăcio, feci, făctum, 3. v.a. to melt; to heat.

fervens, entis, a. boiling hot, glowing, burning; fig. inflamed, impetuous.

ferventer, ad. hotly, warmly.

ferveo, bui, 2. v.n. to be hot; to boil; fig. to rage, to rave.

fervesco, 3. v.n. to grow hot.

fervidus, a, um, a. boiling hot, fiery; torrid; fig. fierce, vehement.

fervo, fervi, 3. v.n., v. **ferveo.** [sion.

fervor, ōris, m. violent heat; ardour, pas- **fessus, a, um,** a. wearied, tired; feeble.

festīnanter, ad. hastily, speedily.

festīnātio, ōnis, f. haste, speed, hurry.

festīno, 1. v.n. & a. to hasten; to accelerate, to hurry;—**festina lente,** hasten slowly.

festīnus, a, um, a. hasty, speedy.

festīvē, ad. joyously, gaily; wittily.

festīvĭtas, ātis, f. merriment, humour, pleasantry.   [humorous; pretty.
festīvus, a, um, a. festive; merry, gay;
festūca, ae, f. straw, stubble, rod.
festum, i, n. holiday, festival; feast.
festus, a, um, a. festal; solemn, merry.
fētiāles, ium, m. pl. Roman college of priests, who ratified treaties, and demanded satisfaction from the enemy before war was declared.
fētĭdus, a, um, a. foul, evil-smelling.
fētor, ōris, m. stench.
fētūra, ae, f. bearing, breeding; *fig.* offspring, brood.
fētus, a, um, a. big with; fertile; full (of); having newly brought forth; —, **ūs,** m. birth; offspring; produce.
fĭber, ri, m. beaver.
fibra, ae, f. fibre, filament; entrails.
fibrīnus, a, um, a. of a beaver.
fĭbŭla, ae, f. clasp, buckle; latchet, brace.
fĭcātum, i, n. liver of animals fattened on figs.
fĭcēdŭla, ae, f. fig-pecker (bird).   [figs.
fĭcētum, i, n. fig-garden.
fictē, ad. feignedly, fictitiously.
fictīcius, a, um, a. artificial.
fictĭlis, e, a. of clay, earthen:—**fictĭle, is,** n. earthen vessel.
fictor, ōris, m. fashioner, counterfeiter.
fictus, a, um, a. feigned, false; counterfeit.
fīcus, i & us, f. fig-tree.
fĭdē, ad. faithfully; loyally.
fĭdēlis, e, a. faithful; loyal; sure.
fĭdēlĭtas, ātis, f. faithfulness, fidelity.
fĭdēlĭter, ad. faithfully; loyally; surely.
fīdens, entis, p. & a. confident; bold.
fīdenter, ad. confidently; boldly.
fīdentia, ae, f. boldness, confidence.
fĭdes, ei, f. faith, trust, confidence: creed, religion; credence; commercial credit; loyalty; honesty; allegiance; promise; security; protection;—**fĭdem fallere,** to break a promise;—**bona fide,** in good faith;—**fĭdes Pūnica,** Carthaginian faith; treachery;—**fĭdei defensor,** defender of the faith.
fĭdes, is, f. pl. **fĭdes, ium,** *fig.* lyre, lute, cithara; (constellation) the Lyre.
fĭdĭcen, ĭnis, m. lute *or* lyre-player.
fīdo, fīsus sum, 3. v.n. to trust (in), to confide.
fĭdūcia, ae, f. trust, confidence; boldness, courage; — **sui,** self-confidence.
fĭdūciārius, a, um, a. holding in trust; held in trust.
fīdus, a, um, a. trusty, faithful, sure;—**fīdus Achates,** a faithful follower (as Achates followed Æneas).
fĭglīnus, a, um, a. of a potter; —**a, ae,** f. pottery *or* the art of pottery; —**um, i,** n. an earthen vessel.

fīgo, xi, xum, 3. v.a. to fix, to fasten; to
fĭgŭlus, i, m. potter.   [transfix; to settle.
fĭgūra, ae, f. shape, figure, form; image.
fĭgūro, 1. v.a. to form, to fashion, to shape; to conceive; to picture.
fīlia, ae, f. daughter; female offspring.
fīliŏla, ae, f. little daughter.
fīliŏlus, i, m. little son.
fīlius, ii, m. son.
fĭlix, ĭcis, f. fern.   [ture; quality; sort.
fīlum, i, n. thread; cord; string; *fig.* tex-
fĭmus, i, m. dung, excrement.
findo, fĭdi, fissum, 3. v.a. to cleave, to split; to divide.
fingo, finxi, fictum, 3. v.a. to shape, to form, to fashion, to make; to feign; to contrive; to invent.
fīnio, īvi & ii, ītum, 4. v.a. to limit; to determine; to define; to end, to finish;—**finiens orbis,** horizon.
fīnis, is, m. & f. boundary, limit; end; purpose; death;—**fīnes, ium,** pl. country, territory.
fīnĭtĭmus, a, um, a. bordering upon, adjoining, neighbouring; *fig.* like.
fīnĭtor, ōris, m. surveyor.
fīo, factus sum, fĭeri, 3. v.n. pass. to be made *or* done; to happen; to become;—**fiat justitia ruat cælum,** let justice be done though the heavens fall.
firmāmen, ĭnis (poet.), **firmāmentum, i,** n. support, prop, stay.
firmē, ad. firmly, steadily.
firmĭtas, ātis, f. firmness, strength.
firmĭter, ad. firmly, strongly; steadfastly.
firmĭtūdo, ĭnis, f. stability; strength.
firmo, 1. v.a. to make firm *or* steady; to strengthen; to harden; to confirm; to establish; to encourage.
firmus, a, um, a. firm; strong; steady; hard; valid; bold.
fiscella, ae, f. small wicker-basket.
fiscĭna, ae, f. small basket of wicker-work.
fiscus, i, m. money-bag, purse; public revenues; Roman Emperor's privy purse.
fissĭlis, e, a. easily split.
fissūra, ae, f. cleft.
fistūca, ae, f. rammer, beetle.
fistŭla, ae, f. pipe, tube; reed-pipe.
fistŭlōsus, a, um, a. full of holes like a shepherd's pipe.
fixus, a, um, a. fixed, fast, immovable.
flăbellum, i, n. fan, fly-flap.
flābra, ōrum, n. pl. blasts, breezes.
flacceo, 2. v.n. to be languid; to droop.
flaccĭdus, a, um, a. flaccid, flabby.
flaccus, a, um, a. flabby; flap-eared.
flăgello, 1. v.a. to lash, to beat.
flăgellum, i, n. whip, scourge; thong; vine-shoot.

flāgĭtātio, ōnis, f. earnest request *or* de-
flāgĭtātor, oris, m. importuner. [mand.
flāgĭtiosē, ad. shamefully, infamously.
flāgĭtiōsus, a, um, a. shameful, infamous,
wicked. [crime.
flāgĭtium, ii, n. shameful *or* base action;
flāgĭto, I. v.a. to demand importunely;
to exact.
flagrans, antis, p. & a. blazing, glowing;
fig. ardent, passionate;—**flagrante de-**
licto, (caught) in the very act of crime.
flagro, I. v.n. to blaze, to flame, to burn;
to be inflamed.
flagrum, i, n. whip, scourge.
flāmen, ĭnis, m. priest of one particular
deity; —, ĭnis, m. blast; gale, wind.
fiamma, ae, f. blaze, flame; star; *fig.*
ardour; glow *or* fire of love.
flammeus, a, um, a. flaming, fiery; fiery
red; —eum, ei, n. bridal veil.
flammĭfer, a, um, a. fiery.
flammo, I. v.n. & a. to flame; to set on
fire; to inflame. [breeze.
flātus, ūs, m. blowing; snorting; breath;
flāveo, 2. v.n. to be yellow *or* gold-
coloured.
flāvesco, 3. v.n. to turn yellow *or* gold.
flāvus, a, um, a. yellow, flaxen, gold-
coloured.
flēbilis, e, a. lamentable; doleful.
flēbĭliter, ad. mournfully.
flecto, xi, xum, 3. v.a. & n. to bend, to
bow, to curve, to turn; *fig.* to persuade; to soften.
flēmĭna, um, n. pl. a swelling at the
ankles caused by excessive exercise.
fleo, flēvi, flētum, 2. v.n. & a. to weep, to
cry.
flētus, ūs, m. weeping; tears.
flexănĭmus, a, um, ad. moving, affecting;
touched, moved. [inconstant.
flexĭbĭlis, e, a. flexible, pliant; fickle,
flexĭlis, e, a. pliant, pliable, supple,
curled. [modulation.
flexio, ōnis, f. bend, turn; (of the voice)
flexuōsus, a, um, a. tortuous.
flexūra, ae, f. winding; turning.
flexus, ūs, m. turning, winding.
flo, flāvi, flātum, I. v.n. & a. to blow; to
sound; to cast (by blowing).
floccus, i, flock (of wool);—**non flocci**
facere, to consider of no importance.
Flōrālia, ium, n. pl. festival of the goddess Flora.
flōreo, ui, 2. v.n. to blossom; to flourish;
fig. to be in one's prime.
flōresco, 3. v.n. to begin to blossom.
flōreus, a, um, a. flowery. [florid.
flōrĭdus, a, um, a. blooming; flowery;
flōrĭfer, a, um, a. flowery.
flōs, ōris, m. blossom, flower; *fig.* prime.

floscŭlus, i, m. little flower, floweret; *fig.*
ornament.
fluctuātio, ōnis, f. wavering, vacillation.
fluctuo, I. v.n. fluctuor, ātus, I. v. dep.
to wave, to float, to undulate; *fig.* to
waver.
fluctus, ūs, m. flood; wave, billow.
fluentum, i, n. stream; river.
fluĭdus, a, um, a. fluid; *fig.* soft, slack,
languid. [waver.
fluĭto, I. v.n. to float; to wave; *fig.* to
flūmen, ĭnis, n. stream, river; *fig.* fluency;
—adverso flumine, against the stream;
—secundo flumine, with the stream.
fluo, xi, xum, 3. v.n. to flow; to stream;
fig. to pass away; to emanate; to arise,
to spring (from).
flŭviālis, e, a., flŭviātĭlis, e, a. river . . .
flŭvius, ii, m. river; running water.
fluxus, a, um, p. & a. flowing, fluid;
loose; transient; frail; dissolute.
fluxus, ūs, m. flow, current.
fōcāle, is, n. neck-cloth.
fōcŭlus, i, m. little hearth; chafing-dish.
fōcus, i, m. fireplace, hearth; funeral
pile; house, family.
fŏdio, fōdi, fossum, 3. v.n. & a. to dig; to
delve; to stab.
foec . . ., v. fec . . .
foedē, ad. foully, basely; horribly.
foederatus, a, um, a. leagued; allied.
foedĭtas, ātis, f. foulness; ugliness.
foedo, I. v.a. to defile; to pollute; to disfigure, to disgrace, to sully.
foedus, a, um, a. foul, filthy; ugly; base,
vile; abominable.
foedus, ĕris, n. league, treaty; covenant.
foen . . ., v. faen . . .
foetĭdus, v. fetidus.
foetor, v. fetor.
foetus, v. fetus.
fōlium, ii, n. leaf. [shell.
follĭcŭlus, i, m. small bag *or* sack; pod;
follis, is, m. pair of bellows; money-bag.
fōmentum, i, n. poultice, fomentation;
fig. alleviation, consolation.
fōmes, itis, m. tinder; fuel.
fons, fontis, m. spring, fountain; *fig.*
source; principal cause;—**fons et ori-**
go, the source and origin.
fontānus, a, um, a. of a spring.
for, fātus, I. v.n. & a. dep. def. to say, to
utter, to speak.
fŏrāmen, ĭnis, n. aperture, hole.
fŏras, ad. out of doors, abroad, forth, out.
forceps, cĭpis, m. & f. pair of tongs,
pincers.
fordus, a, um, a. with young, pregnant.
fŏrensis, e, a. forensic, public; pertaining
to the courts.
forfex, ĭcis, f. shears; scissors.

fŏris, is, fŏres, um, f. pl. door, gate; opening, entrance.

fŏris, ad. out of doors; abroad.

forma, ae, f. form, figure, shape; model; mould; pattern; sort; beauty; set form of words.

formīca, ae, f. ant.

formīdābĭlis, e, a. dreadful.

formīdo, 1. v.a. & n. to dread; to be greatly afraid.

formīdo, ĭnis, f. fear, terror, dread; object producing terror; scarecrow.

formīdōlōsus, a, um, a. fearful; terrible.

formo, 1. v.a. to shape, to fashion, to form; to model; to build; to compose.

formōsus, a, um, a. beautiful, handsome.

formŭla, ae, f. form in law; form of contract; principle, rule, legal process.

fornax, ācis, f. furnace, oven.

fornĭcātus, a, um, a. arched, vaulted.

fornix, ĭcis, m. arch, vault.

fors, fortis, f. fortune, hazard, chance.

forsan, forsit, forsĭtan, fortassĕ, ad. perhaps.

fortĕ, ad. by chance.

fortis, e, a. strong, powerful; stout; hardy; courageous; valiant; manful.

fortĭter, ad. powerfully, strongly, bravely, valiantly.

fortĭtūdo, ĭnis, f. strength; firmness; courage, valour; manfulness.

fortuĭto, ad. by chance, accidentally.

fortuĭtus, a, um, a. casual; accidental.

fortūna, ae, f. fortune; chance; luck; prosperity; condition; estate.

fortūnātē, ad. fortunately.

fortūnātus, a, um, a. lucky, happy, fortunate; rich.

fortūno, 1. v.a. to prosper, to bless.

fŏrum, i, n. market-place; court of justice; Roman forum.

fŏrus, i, gangway in a ship; bee-cell.

fossa, ae, f. ditch, trench.

fossor, ōris, m. digger.

fŏvea, ae, f. pit; pitfall.

fŏveo, fōvi, fōtum, 2. v.a. to keep warm; to favour; to cherish; to maintain, to foster.

fractūra, ae, f. breakage.

fræn . . ., v. fren . . .

frăgă, ōrum, n. pl. strawberries.

frăgĭlis, e, a. brittle, frail; perishable.

frăgĭlĭtas, ātis, f. brittleness; frailty.

fragmen, ĭnis, n. fragment; scrap;— fragmĭna, um, pl. fragments, ruins; chips.

fragmentum, i, n. fragment; remnant.

frăgor, ōris, m. crash; noise.

frăgōsus, a, um, a. fragile; rough; crashing, rushing, roaring.

frăgro, 1. v.n. to emit a scent, to smell.

frango, frēgi, fractum, 3. v.a. to break; to crush; to weaken; to wear out; to vanquish; to tame. [in-law; kinsman.

frāter, tris, m. brother; cousin; brother-frātercŭlus, i, m. little brother.

frāternē, ad. in a brotherly manner, heartily. [friendly.

frāternus, a, um, a. brotherly, fraternal;

frātrĭcīda, ae, m. murderer of a brother.

fraudātio, ōnis, f. deceit, treachery.

fraudo, 1. v.a. to cheat, to beguile, to defraud; to steal. [lent.

fraudŭlentus, a, um, a. deceitful, fraudu-

fraus, fraudis, f. deceit, fraud; artifice; fault; crime; mistake; damage.

fraxĭneus, a, um, fraxĭnus, a, um, a. of ash; ashen.

fraxĭnus, i, f. ash-tree; ashen spear.

freesia (mod. hort.), freesia.

frĕmĕbundus, a, um, a. growling, raging, murmuring.

frĕmĭtus, ūs, m. roaring; shouting; clashing; muttering; blast.

frĕmo, ui, ĭtum, 3. v.n. & a. to roar; to growl; to rage; to murmur; to chafe.

frĕmor, ōris, m. noise, murmur.

frendeo or frendo, ui, fresum, 3. v.a. & n. to gnash the teeth, to grind.

frēno, 1. v.a. to bridle; fig. to curb.

frēnum, i, n. bridle, bit; fig. check.

frĕquens, entis, a. frequent; ordinary, general; crowded; populous.

frĕquenter, ad. often, frequently; by many. [sembly.

frĕquentia, ae, f. frequency; crowd; as-

frĕquento, 1. v.a. to frequent; to repeat; to haunt; to resort to; to throng; to crowd; to celebrate.

frĕtum, i, n. frĕtus, ūs, m. strait, narrow sea, frith; sea.

frĕtus, a, um, a. relying upon, trusting to.

frĭco, ui, ctum, 1. v.a. to rub.

frĭgeo, 2. v.n. to be cold; fig. to flag, to be languid, to be looked on coldly.

frĭgesco, frixi, 3. v.n. to become cold.

frĭgĭdē, ad. coldly; feebly.

frĭgĭdus, a, um, a. cold, cool, chill; faint; slight; dull, flat. [ter.

frĭgus, ōris, n. cold, coldness; frost, win-

fringilla, ae, f. robin.

frio, 1. v.a. to crumble.

fritillāria (mod. hort.), fritillary.

frītillus, i, m. dice-box.

frīvŏlus, a, um, a. frivolous, trifling; silly; worthless.

frondātŏr, ōris, m. hedger; pruner.

frondeo, 2. v.n. to be in leaf, to become green. [to shoot out.

frondesco, dui, 3. v.n. to become leafy,

frondeus, a, um, leafy.

frondōsus, a, um, a. full of leaves, leafy.

frons, dis, f. leafy branch; foliage, leaves·
frons, frontis, f. forehead; human brow; *fig.* forepart. [of horses.
frontālĕ, is, n. ornament for the forehead
fructuōsus, a, um, a. fruitful; profitable.
fructus, ūs, m. fruit; profit; *fig.* result.
frūgālītas, ātis, f. thriftiness, frugality.
frūges, um, frugi, v. **frux.**
frūgīfĕr, a, um, a. fruit-bearing, fertile.
frūmentārius, a, um, belonging to corn *or* forage. [foraging.
frūmentātio, ōnis, f. providing of corn;
frūmentātor, ōris, m. forager.
frūmentor, ātus, I. v.n. dep. to forage.
frūmentum, i, n. corn, grain.
fruor, fructus & fruĭtus, 3. v.n. dep. to enjoy, to have the use of.
frustrā, ad. in vain, to no purpose.
frustrātio, ōnis, f. deceiving, disappointment, frustration.
frustror, atus, I. v. dep. to disappoint, to frustrate; to deceive.
frustum, i, n. morsel, piece.
frŭtex, ĭcis, m. shrub, bush.
frŭtĭcētum, i, n. thicket. [come bushy.
frŭtĭcor, I. v.n. dep. to sprout out, to be·
frŭtĭcōsus, a, um, a. bushy.
frux, frūgis, f., **frūges, um,** pl. fruits (of the earth); food; *fig.* result;—**frugi,** ad. fit; useful; honest; frugal.
fuchsia (mod. hort.), fuchsia, eardrops.
fūco, I. v.a. to colour; to paint; to dye.
fūcōsus, a, um, a. painted; counterfeit, spurious.
fūcus, i, m. purple colour; bee-glue; drone; *fig.* pretence; deceit.
fŭga, ae, flight; fleeing; avoidance; exile.
fŭgax, ācis, a. flying swiftly; swift, fleet; avoiding; *fig.* fading; transitory.
fŭgio, fūgi, fŭgĭtum, 3. v.n. & a. to flee *or* fly, to run away; to go into exile; to shun, to avoid.
fŭgĭtīvus, a, um, fugitive; —, i, m. runaway.
fŭgĭto, I. v.a. & n. to flee hastily, to shun.
fŭgo, I. v.a. to put to flight, to chase away, to rout.
fuit, v. **sum.**
fulcīmen, ĭnis, n. support; prop.
fulcio, fulsi, fultum, 4. v.a. to prop up, to support.
fulcrum, i, n. bedpost, foot of a couch.
fulgeo, fulsi, 2. v.n. to gleam; to glitter, to shine forth, to be bright.
fulgor, ōris, m. lightning; flash; glittering, brightness.
fulgur, ŭris, n. lightning; thunderbolt.
fulgŭro, I. v. imp. to lighten.
fŭlĭca, ae, f. coot (water-fowl).
fūlīgo, ĭnis, f. soot; lamp-black; black paint.

fullo, ōnis, m. fuller.
fullōnius, a, um, a. of a fuller.
fulmen, ĭnis, n. lightning, thunderbolt; *fig.* calamity, destruction.
fulmenta, ae, f. heel of a shoe.
fulmĭneus, a, um, a. of lightning; destructive. [nings.
fulmĭno, I. v.n. to lighten; to hurl light·
fulvus, a, um, a. reddish yellow, tawny.
fūmāria (mod. hort.), fumitory.
fūmeus, a, um, a. smoky.
fūmĭdus, a, um, a. full of smoke, smoky.
fūmĭfer, a, um, a. smoking.
fūmĭgo, I. v.a. to fumigate.
fūmo, I. v.n. to smoke, to reek.
fūmōsus, a, um, a. full of smoke, smoky; smoke-dried.
fūmus, i, m. smoke, steam, vapour.
fūnāle, is, n. cord; thong; torch; chandelier.
fūnālis, e, a. **equus,** trace-horse.
fūnambŭlus, i, rope-walker.
functio, ōnis, f. performance, execution.
funda, ae, f. sling; drag-net.
fundāmen, ĭnis, n. foundation.
fundāmentum, i, n. foundation, groundwork, basis.
fundātor, ōris, m. founder.
funditor, ōris, m. slinger.
fundĭtus, ad. from the very bottom; *fig.* utterly, totally.
fundo, fūdi, fūsum, 3. v.a. to pour out, to shed; to cast (metal); to rout; to display; to scatter; to produce; to bring forth; to utter.
fundo, I. v.a. to found; to fasten, to secure; *fig.* to establish.
fundus, i, m. bottom; land; farm; estate.
fūnebris, e, a. funereal; deadly, mortal; cruel. [structive.
fūnĕreus, a, um, a. funereal; deadly; de·
fūnĕro, I. v.a. to bury, to kill.
fūnesto, I. v.a. to pollute. [cruel.
fūnestus, a, um, a. fatal, deadly; baneful;
fungĭnus, a, um, a. of a mushroom.
fungor, functus, 3. v. dep. to perform, to discharge a duty *or* an office;—**fungi munere,** to do one's duty;—**morte functus,** dead.
fungōsus, a, um, a. spongy.
fungus, i, m. mushroom; 'thief' in a candle.
fūnĭcŭlus, i, m. small rope, cord.
fūnis, is, m. rope, line, cord.
funkia (mod. hort.), plantain lily.
fūnus, ĕris, n. burial, funeral; ruin; death.
fūr, fūris, g.c. thief.
fūrax, ācis, a. thievish.
furca, ae, f. (two-pronged) fork; prop.
furcĭfĕr, i, m. *fig.* jail-bird, rascal.
furfur, ŭris, m. bran.

fŭriæ, ārum, f. pl. fury; Furies, avenging spirits.
fŭriālis, e, a. furious; dreadful.
fŭriāliter, ad. frenziedly.
fŭrĭbundus, a, um, a. raging, mad, furious; inspired.
fŭrio, 1. v.a. to madden.
fŭriōsē, ad. furiously.
fŭriōsus, a, um, a. furious, mad, frantic.
furnus, i, m. oven. [furious; to be wild.
fŭro, ui, 3. v.n. to rage, to be mad or
fŭror, ātus, 1. v.a. dep. to steal, to purloin.
fŭror, ōris, m. fury, rage, madness.
furtim, ad. by stealth, secretly.
furtīvus, a, um, a. stolen; secret, furtive.
furtum, i, n. theft; stolen things; fig. trick, crafty wile, love affair;—furto, by stealth.
fŭruncŭlus, i, m. petty pilferer.
furvus, a, um, a. dark, dusky, gloomy.
fuscina, ae, f. trident.
fusco, 1. v.a. to blacken, to darken.
fuscus, a, um, a. dark, swarthy, dusky; husky; hoarse.
fūsē, ad. at length, diffusely.
fūsĭlis, e, a. molten.
fustis, is, m. cudgel; staff; club.
fustuārium, ii, n. death by beating (a punishment meted out to soldiers).
fūsus, a, um, p. & a. extended, large; diffuse; free; plump.
fūsus, i, m. spindle.
fūtĭlis, e, v. futtilis.
futtĭlis, e, a. empty; vain; worthless.
futtĭlitas, ātis, f. worthlessness.
fŭtūrus, a, um, a future.

Gæsum, i, n. heavy (gallic) javelin.
gaillardia (mod. hort.), gaillardia, blanket-flower.
galanthus (mod. hort.), snowdrop.
galbăneus, a, um, a. of galbanum.
galbănum, i, n. a resinous gum.
gălea, ae, f. helmet, head-piece.
gălēga (mod. hort.), goat's-rue.
galēna, ae, f. silver ore.
gălĕo, 1. v.a. to cover with a helmet.
gălērītus, a, um, a. wearing a furred cap.
gălērum, i, n. furred cap.
gallina, ae, f. hen. [try.
gallināceus, a, um, a. pertaining to poul-
gallinārium, ii, n. hen-coop.
gallinārius, ii, poult-y-keeper.
gallus, i, m. cock.
gănea, ae, f. găneum, i, n. cook-shop.
găneo, ōnis, m. glutton, debauchee.
gannītus, ūs, m. barking, snarling.
gardenia (mod. hort.), Cape jasmine.

gargărizo, 1. v.a. & n. to gargle.
garrio, īvi, & ii, itum, 4. v.a. to chatter.
garrŭlitas, ātis, f. garrulity.
garrŭlus, a, um, a. chattering, garrulous; murmuring.
gărum, i, n. fish-sauce.
gaudeo, gāvīsus sum, 2. v.n. & a. to rejoice, to be glad, to be pleased with.
gaudium, ii, n. joy, gladness; delight.
gausăpa, ae, f., gausăpe, is, n. shaggy woollen cloth.
gāza, ae, f. royal treasure; riches, wealth.
gĕlĭdus, a, um, a. icy cold, frosty.
gĕlo, 1. v.a. & n. to freeze, to stiffen.
gĕlu, ūs, n. icy coldness, frost.
gĕmĕbundus, a, um, a. groaning, sighing.
gĕmellus, a, um, a. twin-born; —, i, m. twin.
gĕmĭnātio, ōnis, f. duplication.
gĕmĭno, i, v.a. to double; to pair.
gĕmĭnus, a, um, a. twin-born; double; both.
Gĕmĭni, the Twins, Castor and Pollux (a constellation). [roaring.
gĕmĭtus, ūs, m. sighing; sigh, groan;
gemma, ae, f. (bot.) bud, eye; jewel; cup; ring.
gemmātus, a, um, a. jewelled. [stones.
gemmeus, a, um, a. set with precious
gemmĭfer, a, um, a. bearing jewels.
gemmo, 1. v.n. & a. to bud; to sparkle; to set or adorn with jewels.
gĕmo, ui, ĭtum, 3. v.n. & a. to sigh, to groan; to lament (over), to bewail.
gĕna, ae, f. cheek, eye.
gĕner, ĕri, m. son-in-law.
gĕnĕrālis, e, a. general.
gĕnĕrāliter, ad. in general, generally.
gĕnĕrātim, ad. by kinds, by tribes; generally.
gĕnĕrātor, ōris, m. engenderer. [engender.
gĕnĕro, 1. v.a. to beget, to procreate, to
gĕnĕrōsē, ad. nobly.
gĕnĕrōsus, a, um, a. of noble birth; noble; generous; brave; good.
gĕnĕsis, is, f. nativity, geniture.
genesta, ae, v. genista.
gĕnĕtrix, īcis, f. mother.
gĕnĕtīvus, a, um, a. native; of a family; —, i, m. the genitive case.
gĕniālis, e, a. pertaining to generation or birth; merry, genial; delightful;—lectus —, bridal bed.
gĕnĭcŭlātus, a, um, a. knotted, jointed.
gĕnista, ae, f. needle, furze.
gĕnĭtālis, e, a. generative; fruitful.
gĕnĭtīvus, a, um, v. genetivus.
gĕnĭtor, ōris, m. begetter; father; creator.
gĕnĭtrix, v. genetrix. [clination; talent.
gĕnius, i, m. tutelary deity or genius; in-
gĕno, ui, ĭtum, 3. v. gigno.

gens, gentis, f. clan; tribe; family; race; nation.

gentiana, ae, f. gentian. [particular clan.

gentīlĭcius, a, um, a. pertaining to a

gentīlis, e, a. of the same clan *or* race; in Late Latin, foreign; heathen.

gentīlĭtas, ātis, f. relationship of the same stock, etc.

gentilitius, v. **gentilicius.**

gĕnu, ūs, n. knee; knee-joint.

gĕnŭīnus, a, um, a. innate, native, natural. [genuinus, a back tooth.

genŭīnus, a, um, a. of the jaw;—**dens**

gĕnus, ĕris, n. birth, descent, origin; noble birth; offspring; race; kind; family; nation; (gr.) gender;—genus, as opposed to species;—**sui generis,** in a class by itself; unique of its kind.

geōgrăphia, ae, f. geography.

geōmetres, ae, m. geometer.

geōmetria, ae, f. geometry.

geōmetrĭcus, a, um, a. geometrical.

georgĭcus, a, um, a. agricultural;—**Georg-ĭca, ōrum,** n. pl. a poem on husbandry by Vergil. [bill.

gerānĭum (mod. hort.), geranium, crane's-

germānĭtas, ātis, f. brotherhood, sister-hood; *fig.* fraternization, union.

germānus, a, um, a. (of brothers & sisters); full; genuine, true; —, **i, m.** brother;—**germāna, ae,** f. sister.

germen, ĭnis, n. branch; sprout, bud; offshoot.

gĕro, gessi, gestum, 3. v.a. to wear, to have; to govern; to carry on; to administer; to achieve; to bring forth;—**se gerere,** to behave oneself; —**gerere personam alicujus,** to re-present one;—**gerere morem alicui,** to humour one;—**res gestæ,** achieve-ments.

gerræ, ārum, f. pl. trifles, nonsense.

gestāmen, ĭnis, n. burden, load; ac-coutrements; sedan-chair.

gestĭcŭlor, 1. v. dep. to posture, to gesticulate.

geum (mod. hort.), geum.

gestio, īvi & ii, ītum, 4. v.n. to leap for joy; to exult; to desire eagerly.

gesto, 1. v.a. & n. to bear, to carry;—**gestāri,** to take the air (in a sedan, etc.).

gestus, ūs, m. carriage of the body, gesture; gesticulation.

gibber, a, um, a. hunch-backed.

gĭgās, antĭs, m. giant.

gigno, gĕnui, gĕnĭtum, 3. v.a. to beget, to bear, to bring forth; to produce.

gingīva, ae, f. gum (in which the teeth are set).

ginnus, v. **hinnus.**

glăber, ra, rum, hairless, smooth.

glăciālis, e, a. icy, frozen, full of ice.

glăcies, ēi, f. ice.

glăcio, 1. v.a. to turn into ice.

glădĭātor, ōris, m. swordsman, fighter.

glădĭātōrius, a, um, a. gladiatorial.

glădĭŏlus, i, m. small sword; the plant gladiolus; sword-lily.

glădius, ĭi, m. sword.

glæba, ae, f. clod; land, soil; lump, mass.

glæbŭla, ae, f. small clod.

glæsum, v. **glesum.**

glans, glandis, f. acorn, beach-nut; chestnut; (mil.) ball of lead *or* clay.

glārea, ae, f. gravel.

glāreōsus, a, um, a. gravelly.

glaucōma, ătis, n. cataract (of the eye).

glaucus, a, um, a. bluish grey.

glēba, v. **glæba.**

glēsum, i, n. amber.

glīs, īris, m. dormouse. [increase.

glisco, 3. v.n. to swell up, to spread; to

glŏbōsus, a, um, a. round as a ball.

glŏbŭlus, i, m. little ball. [crowd.

glŏbus, i, m. ball, sphere, globe; troop,

glŏmĕro, 1. v.a. to form into a ball; to assemble, to crowd.

glŏmus, ĕris, n. ball, clue.

glōria, ae, f. glory, fame, renown; vain-glory, boasting.

glōrĭātĭo, ōnis, f. boasting, vaunting.

glōrĭŏla, ae, f. little glory.

glōrĭor, ātus, 1. v.a. & n. dep. to glory, to boast. [pously.

glōrĭōsē, ad. gloriously; boastfully; pom-

glōrĭōsus, a, um, a. glorious, famous; vainglorious, boasting.

glossa, ae, f. a foreign *or* obsolete word requiring explanation.

glossārium, ĭi, n. a vocabulary of glossae.

gloxinia (mod. hort.), gloxinia.

glūten, ĭnis, n. glue.

glūtĭnātor, ōris, m. bookbinder.

glūtĭno, 1. v.a. to glue (together), to join.

gnārus, a, um, a. skilful, practised, ex-pert; known.

gnascor, v. **nascor.**

gnātus, a, um, v. **natus.**

gnāv . . ., v. **nav . . .**

gnōbĭlis, e, v. **nobilis.**

gnōmon, ōnis, m. rod of the sundial.

gnōtus, a, um, v. **notus.**

gōbius, ĭi, gōbio, ōnis, m. gudgeon.

gorytus, v. **corytus.**

grăbātus, i, m. low couch, pallet, camp, bed.

grăcĭlis, e, a. thin, slender; meagre-lean; scanty, poor; simple, plain.

grăcĭlĭtas, ātis, f. slenderness, thinness meagreness; simplicity, plainness.

grācŭlus, i, m. jay, jackdaw.

grădātim, ad. step by step, by degrees, gradually.   [gradation, climax.

grădātio, ōnis, f. regular progress; *fig.*

grădĭor, **gressus**, 3. v.n. dep. to step, to walk.   [degree; ladder; stair.

grădus, ūs, m. step, pace; position; rank;

græcor, **ātus**, 1. v.n. dep. to imitate the Greeks.

græcŭlus, **a**, **um**, a. Grecian, Greek (mostly in a contemptuous sense); thorough Greek.

grāmen, ĭnis, n. grass; herb.

grāmĭneus, **a**, **um**, a. of grass, grassy.

grammătĭca, **ae**, **grammătĭcē**, **es**, f. grammar; philology.

grammătĭca, **ōrum**, n. pl. grammar; philology.

grammătĭcus, **a**, **um**, a. grammatical; —, **i**, m. grammarian.

grānāria, **ōrum**, n. pl. granary.

grānātum, **i**, n. pomegranate.

grandævus, **a**, **um**, a. of great age, old.

grandesco, 3. v.n. to become great, to grow.

grandĭlŏquus, **i**, m. speaking loftily; grandiloquent.

grandĭnat, 1. v. imp. it hails.

grandio, **ire**, 4. v.a. to enlarge.   [powerful.

grandis, **e**, a. great; grand; tall; lofty;

grandĭtas, **ātis**, f. grandeur, sublimity.

grandĭter, ad. greatly, proudly.

grando, ĭnis, f. hail, hail-storm.

grānum, **i**, n. grain, seed.

grăphĭcē, ad. finely.

grăphĭcus, **a**, **um**, a. fine, skilful.

grăphĭum, **ii**, n. style, writing implement.

grassātor, ōris, m. waylayer, assassin.

grassor, **ātus**, 1. v.n. & a. dep. to go about; to assail, to rob.   [thankfu'ly.

grātē, ad. with pleasure, willingly;

grātēs, f. pl. thanks;—**grātes agere**, to thank.

grātia, **ae**, f. grace; gracefulness; good-will; kindness; favour; obligation; —**s agere**, to thank; (ablat.) for the sake of, in favour of;—**grātiīs**, **grātīs**, gratuitously; gratis.

grātĭfĭcor, **ātus**, 1. v.n. & a. dep. to gratify; to give up as a favour.

grātĭōsus, **a**, **um**, a. in favour; beloved; agreeable.

grātīs, ad., v. gratia.   [to rejoice.

grātor, 1. v. dep. n. & a. to congratulate;

grātŭīto, ad. gratuitously.   [bestowed.

grātŭītus, **a**, **um**, a. gratuitous; freely

grātŭlābundus, **a**, **um**, a. congratulating.

grātŭlātio, ōnis, f. congratulation; re-joicing, joy.   [gratulate; to rejoice.

grātŭlor, **ātus**, 1. v.n. & a. dep. to con-

grātus, **a**, **um**, a. kind; beloved; agree-able; pleasing; thankful.

grăvāmen, ĭnis, n. the heaviest count in an accusation.

grăvātē, ad. with difficulty; grudgingly.

grăvēdo, ĭnis, f. cold in the head, catarrh.

grăvĭdus, **a**, **um**, a. pregnant; full.

grăvis, **e**, a. heavy; weighty, burden-some; burdened; important; solemn; serious; grievous; noisome; difficult; unwholesome; deep (of sound).

grăvĭtas, **ātis**, f. weight, heaviness; dear-ness, pregnancy; severity; authority; majesty.

grăvĭter, ad. heavily, severely; griev-ously; with dignity.

grăvo, 1. v.a. to load, to burden; *fig.* to oppress, to aggravate;—**grăvor**, to take amiss; to chafe at.

grĕgālis, **e**, a. common; ordinary;— **gregales**, **ium**, m. pl. companions.

grĕgārius, **a**, **um**, a. of the common sort, common;—**miles gregarius**, a private soldier.

grĕgātim, ad. in flocks.

grĕmium, **ii**, n. lap, bosom; *fig.* centre.

gressus, ūs, m. going; step; course, way.

grex, **grĕgis**, m. flock, herd; company; crew.

grunnio, **īvi** *or* **ii**, **ītum**, 4. v.n. to grunt.

grunnītus, **us**, 4. m. grunt.

grus, **gruis**, m. & f. crane.

gryps, **grȳphis**, m. griffin.   [government.

gŭbernācŭlum, **i**, n. helm, rudder; *fig.*

gŭbernātio, ōnis, f. steering; *fig.* govern-ment.   [ruler.

gŭbernātor, ōris, m. steersman, pilot;

gŭberno, 1. v.a. to steer (a ship); to govern.

gŭla, **ae**, f. gullet, throat; *fig.* gluttony.

gŭlōsus, **a**, **um**, gluttonous.

gurgĕs, **ĭtis**, m. whirlpool, gulf; *fig.* spendthrift.

gurgŭlio, ōnis, m. gullet, windpipe.

gurgustium, **ii**, n. hovel, hut.

gustātus, ūs, m. the sense of taste; taste, flavour.

gusto, 1. v.a. to taste; to sip.

gustus, ūs, m. tasting; taste.

gutta, **ae**, f. drop; spot; speckle.

guttur, **ŭris**, n. gullet, throat; *fig.* glut-tony.

gūtus, **i**, m. cruet.

gymnăsium, **ii**, n. a school for gymnastic exercises; school, college.

gymnĭcus, **a**, **um**, a. gymnastic.

gȳnæcēum, **i**, n. women's quarter.

gypsātus, **a**, **um**, chalked (in sign of servitude); the feet of slaves intended for sale were chalked.

gypsophĭla (mod. hort.), chalk-plant.

gypsum, **i**, n. white lime, chalk.

gȳrus, **i**, m. circle; circuit; course.

Hăbēna, ae, f. thong; rein; whip.
hăbeo, ui, ĭtum, 2. v.a. & n. to have, to
hold, to possess; to contain; to get,
to acquire; to handle, to use; to
manage; to esteem; to reckon; to
treat; to find; to dwell; to know;—
habeas corpus, you may have the body;
a writ demanding that a person be
liberated from durance;—**habet** or **hoc
habet,** he is hit (an exclamation used
in the gladiatorial games in reference
to a wounded competitor).
hăbĭlis, e, a. handy, manageable; apt,
fit, swift.
hăbĭtābĭlis, e, a. habitable.
hăbĭtātio, ōnis, f. dwelling, habitation.
hăbĭtātor, ōris, m. dweller, inhabitant.
hăbĭto, 1. v.a. & n. to inhabit, to dwell;
to live.
hăbĭtus, ūs, m. condition, state, habit;
attire, dress; feature, appearance;
disposition, feeling.
hāc, ad. by this way or side; here;
hither.
hāctĕnus, ad. to this place; to this extent; hitherto; thus far; thus much.
haedus, i, m. kid.
haemătĭtes, ae, m. iron ore, hematite.
haereditas, v. **hereditas.**
haereo, haesi, haesum, 2. v.n. to stick, to
cling, to adhere, to be fixed; to be at a
stand; to be in difficulties; to doubt;
to linger.
haeres, v. **heres.**
haerĕsis, is, f. school; sect; heresy.
haerĕtĭcus, a, um, a. heretical.
haesĭtātio, ōnis, f. perplexity, hesitation.
haesĭto, 1. v.n. to stick fast; to be at a
stand; to hesitate.
halcedo, halcyon. See **alcedo.**
hālĭtus, ūs, m. breath; steam, vapour.
hālo, 1. v.n. & a. to breathe; to exhale.
hălōs, o, f. circle round the sun or moon,
halo.
hăma, ae, f. water-bucket.   [dryad.
Hāmadryas, ădis, f. wood-nymph, hama-
hăra, ae, f. coop, sty.
hāmātus, a, um, a. hooked, crooked.
hāmus, i, m. hook; fish-hook.
harena, v. **arena.**
hărĭŏlor, 1. v.n. dep. to foretell.
hărĭŏlus, i, m. **hărĭŏla, ae,** f. soothsayer.
harmŏnia, ae, f. harmony.
harpăgo, ōnis, m. grappling-hook.
harpe, es, f. scimitar.
harundo, v. **arundo.**
hăruspex, ĭcis, m. soothsayer.
hasta, ae, f. spear, lance, pike; spear
stuck in the ground at public auctions;
—**sub hasta vendere,** to sell by auction.

hastātus, a, um, a. armed with a spear;
hastati, ōrum, m. pl. first line of a
Roman army.
hastīle, is, n. shaft of a spear; spear.
hau, i. ah!
haud, ad. not, by no means;—**qua-
quam,** not at all.
haurio, hausi, haustum, 4. v.a. to draw
(up or out); to drink; to drain; to
swallow; to exhaust; to derive; to
suffer to the full.
haustus, ūs, m. drawing up; drinking;
drink, draught.
haut, v. **haud.**
have, haveo, v. **aveo.**
Heautontĭmōrūmĕnos, i, m. Self-tor-
mentor, a play of Terence.
hebenus, v. **ebenus.**
hĕbeo, 2. v.n. to be blunt or dull (also
fig.).
hĕbĕs, ĕtis, a. blunt, dull; heavy;
languid; stupid.
hĕbesco, 3. v.n. to grow blunt or feeble.
hĕbĕto, 1. v.a. to blunt, to dull, to weaken.
Hĕcўra, Mother-in-law, a play of Terence.
hĕdĕra, ae, f. ivy.
hĕdĕrōsus, a, um, a. ivied.
hei, i. woe! alas!
heia, i., v. eia.   [choke.
hēlianthus (mod. hort.), sunflower; arti-
hēliotrŏpium, ii, n. heliotrope, cherry-pie.
hellĕbōrum, i, n. **hellĕbōrus, i,** m. hellebore.
hēl(l)uo, ōnis, m. glutton, squanderer.
hēl(l)uor, ātus, 1. v.n. & a. dep. to
glutton; to squander.
hem, i. ha! well! alas!
hēmĕrōcallis (mod. hort), day-lily.
hendĕcăsyllăbi, ōrum, m. verses consisting of eleven syllables.
hendiadys, a figure of speech in which by
means of a conjunction a single expression is expanded into two separate
ones, e.g. **pateris libamus et auro** for
pateris libamus aureis.
hēpătĭca (mod. hort.), liver moss.
hēra, v. **era.**
herba, ae, f. grass; herb.
herbāceus, a, um, a. grassy; green.
herbĭdus, a, um, a. full of grass or herbs;
grassy.
herbārius, ii, m. botanist.
herbĭfer, a, um, a. grassy.
herbōsus, a, um, a. full of grass or herbs.
herbŭla, ae, f. little herb.
hercēus, i, m. an epithet of Jupiter, as the
protector of the house and its enclosure.
hercisco, 3. v.a. to divide an inheritance.
herclĕ, herculĕ, i. by Hercules!
herctum, i, n. an inheritance;—**herctum
ciere,** to divide an estate.

hĕrĕ, v. heri.

hĕrēdĭtārius, a, um, a. hereditary.

hĕrēdĭtas, ātis, f. heirship; inheritance; damnosa hereditas, an inheritance involving loss to the recipient.

hĕrēs, ēdis, m. & f. heir, heiress; ex asse —, sole heir.

hĕrī, ad. yesterday.

hĕrīlis, e, a., v. erilis.

hermăphrōdītus, i, m. hermaphrodite.

hĕrōĭcus, a, um, a. heroic, epic.

hēros, ōis, m. demigod, hero.

hērōus, a, um, a. heroic; epic;—hērōum, i, n. monument to a hero.

hĕrus, i, v. erus.

hespĕris, ĭdis, f. rocket.

Hesperia, ae, f. the western land, Italy.

hesperius, a, um, a. western.

Hespĕrus, i, m. evening-star.

hesternus, a, um, a. of yesterday.

heu! i. oh! alas!

heus! i. ho! ho there! hark!

hexămĕter, tri, m. a verse consisting of six feet, hexameter.

hiātus, ūs, m. opening, cleft; hiatus;— hiatus valde deflendus, a gap (omission) much to be deplored.

hīberna, ōrum, n. pl. hībernacŭlum, i, n. winter-quarters. [in winter-quarters.

hīberno, 1. v.n. to pass the winter; to be

hībernus, a, um, a. of winter; wintry.

hĭbiscum, i, n. hĭbiscus, i, f. rose-mallow.

hibrida, v. hybrida.

hīc, hæc, hoc, pn. this;—ad hoc, for this purpose; an ad hoc authority is one appointed specifically for some particular branch of administration.

hīc, ad. here; in this matter.

hicce, hæcce, hocce, pn. this.

hiccĭne, hæccĭne, hoccĭne, pn. this?

hĭĕmālis, e, a. pertaining to winter, wintry.

hĭĕmo, 1. v.n. & a. to pass the winter; to keep in winter-quarters; to be stormy.

hiems, ĕmis, or hiemps, ĕmis, f. winter; tempest; stormy weather.

hiĕrācium (mod. hort.), hawkweed.

hiĕrātĭcus, a, um, a. reserved for sacred uses.

hiĕroglyphĭcus, a, um, a. hieroglyphic.

hiĕrŏphanta, ae, m. priest; interpreter of mysteries.

hĭlăris, e, hĭlărus, a, um, a. cheerful, lively, gay, merry.

hĭlărĭtas, ātis, f. cheerfulness, gaiety, merriment, hilarity.

hĭlăro, 1. v.a. to gladden.

hinc, ad. hence; henceforth; from this cause; hereupon;—hinc illae lac-rimae, hence those tears.

hinnio, 4. v.n. to neigh.

hinnītus, ūs, m. neighing.

hinnŭleus, ei, m. fawn.

hinnus, i, mule.

hio, 1. v.n. & a. to be open, to gape; fig. to leave a gap; to long for; (poet.) to be amazed.

hippŏcampus, i, m. sea-horse.

hippodrŏmos, i, m. racecourse for horses.

hippŏpŏtămus, i, m. hippopotamus.

hippūris, ĭdis, f. mare's tail.

hircīnus, a, um, a. of a goat.

hircus, i, m. he-goat. [prickly; fig. rude.

hirsūtus, a, um, a. rough, shaggy, bristly,

hirtus, a, um, a. rough, hairy, shaggy; fig. rude.

hīrūdo, ĭnis, f. leech.

hĭrundo, ĭnis, f. swallow.

hisco, 1. v.n. & a. to gape; to mutter.

hispĭdus, a, um, a. rough, shaggy, hairy; bristly; dirty.

histŏria, ae, f. history; tale, story.

histŏrĭcus, a, um, a. historical; —, i, m. historian.

histrio, ōnis, m. stage-player, actor.

hĭulcus, a, um, a. gaping, split, open.

hŏdiē, ad. to-day; at the present day.

hŏdiernus, a ,um, a. of this day; present, actual.

holus, v. olus. [murderess.

hŏmĭcīda, ae, g.c. manslayer, murderer,

hŏmĭcīdium, ii, n. manslaughter, murder.

hŏmo, ĭnis, c. human being, person; man, woman; fellow; (mil.) foot-soldier;—novus homo, nouveau riche, upstart.

hŏmullus, i, m. manikin.

hŏmuncio, ōnis, m. manikin.

hŏmuncŭlus, i, m. dim. little or weakly man, manikin.

hŏnestas, ātis, f. honourableness, honourable feeling; probity; credit; reputation.

hŏnestē, ad. honourably. [grace.

hŏnesto, 1. v.a. to honour; to adorn, to

hŏnestus, a, um, a. worthy; decent; fair; well-favoured.

hŏnor, hŏnos, ōris, m. honour; regard; office, dignity; grace; reward, fee; funeral rites; legacy;—honoris causa, to show respect. [n. fee.

hŏnōrārius, a, um, a. honorary;—ium, ii,

hŏnōrātus, a, um, p. & a. honoured, respected; honourable.

hŏnōrĭficē, ad. respectfully; honourably.

hŏnōrĭficus, a, um, a. honourable.

hŏnōro, 1. v.a. to honour; to adorn.

hŏnōrus, a, um, a. conferring honour.

honos, oris, v. honor.

hōra, ae, f. hour; season (of the year); time;—horæ, pl. clock;—Hōræ, ārum, f. pl. the Seasons (personified).

hordeāceus, a, um, a. of barley.
hordeum, i, n. barley.
hornus, a, um, a. this year's.
hŏrŏlŏgium, ii, n. clock, sundial.
horrendus, a, um, p. & a. dreadful, terrible, horrible.
horreo, 2. v.n. & a. to stand on end, to bristle; to be rough; to shiver and tremble; to dread.
horresco, horrui, 3. v.n. & a. to bristle up, to grow rough; to begin to shake or tremble or shudder.
horreum, i, n. storehouse; barn; beehive. [horrible; astonishing.
horrĭbĭlis, e, a. rough, rugged; terrible, horrĭdē, ad. roughly.
horrĭdŭlus, a, um, a. rough, unkempt.
horrĭdus, a, um, a. rough, bristly; horrible; unkempt, austere.
horrĭfĕr, a, um, horrĭficus, a, um, a. dreadful, horrific.
horrĭsŏnus, a, um, a. sounding dreadfully.
horror, ōris, m. shivering, ague-fit; dread, awe.
hortāmen, ĭnis, n. encouragement.
hortātio, ōnis, f. encouragement; exhortation.
hortātor, ōris, m. encourager; exhorter.
hortātus, ūs, m. exhortation. [encourage.
hortor, ātus, 1. v.a. dep. to exhort; to
hortŭlus, i, m. small garden.
hortus, i, m. garden; vegetables;— hortus siccus, a collection of dried plants;—hortus inclusus, a preserve.
hospĕs, ĭtis, m. guest; visitor; host; stranger.
hospĭta, ae, feminine of hospes. [able.
hospĭtālis, e, a. of or for a guest; hospit-hospĭtālĭter, ad. hospitably, as a guest.
hospĭtium, ii, n. hospitality; entertainment; inn.
hostia, ae, f. victim, sacrifice. [hostile.
hostĭcus, a, um, a. pertaining to an enemy,
hostīlis, e, a. of an enemy, hostile.
hostīlĭter, ad. in a hostile manner.
hostis, is, g.c. stranger, foreigner; enemy.
hoya (mod. hort.), wax-flower.
hūc, ad. hither; to this place; so far.
huccĭne, ad. hitherto?
hūmānĭtās, ātis, f. human nature; humanity; gentleness; good breeding.
hūmānĭter, ad. humanly; humanely; like a gentleman.
hūmānus, a, um, a. human; humane; well-bred, refined.
hūmecto, v. umecto.
hūmĕrus, v. umerus.
hūmesco, v. umesco.
humeo, v. umeo.
hūmi, v. humus.
hūmĭdus, v. umidus.

hŭmĭlis, e, a. low; low-lying; mean; base; feeble; humble. [significance.
hŭmĭlĭtas, ātis, f. lowness; meanness; in-hŭmĭlĭter, ad. basely, meanly.
hŭmo, 1. v.a. to inter, to bury.
hŭmor, ōris, v. umor.
hŭmŭlus (mod. hort.), hop.
hŭmŭs, i, f. earth, soil; land;—humi, ad. on the ground.
hyăcinthus, i, m. hyacinth; jacinth.
Hyădes, um, f. pl. group of seven stars in the head of Taurus.
hyæna, ae, f. hyæna.
hyălus, i, m. glass.
hybrĭda, ae, c. a mongrel; one born of a Roman father and a foreign mother.
hydra, ae, f. water-serpent; water-snake (constellation).
hydrangea (mod. hort.), hydrangea.
hydraulĭcus, a, um, a. of a water-organ.
hydraulus, i, m. water-organ.
hydria, ae, f. jug, urn.
hydrōpĭcus, a, um, dropsical.
hydrops, ōpis, m. dropsy.
hyem . . ., v. hiem . . .
hydrus, i, m. water-snake.
Hўmen, ĕnis, hўmĕnæus, i, m. god of marriage; nuptials, wedding; nuptial song.
hўpallăge, es, f. a. grammatical construction involving the interchange of relations between ideas, e.g. Tyrrhenus tubae clangor for Tyrrhenae tubæ clangor.
hўperbŏle, es, f. exaggeration.
hypericum (mod. hort.), rose of Sharon.
hўpŏcaustum, i, n. a hot room in the baths heated from below.
hyssōpum, i, n. hyssop.

Iambus, i, m. iambic foot; consisting of a short followed by a long syllable; iambic poem.
iaspis, ĭdis, f. jasper.
ibēris (mod. hort.), candytuft.
ibex, ĭcis, m. wild goat.
ĭbĭ, ad. there; on that occasion.
ĭbīdem, ad. in that very place, just there; just then.
ĭbis, ĭdis or s, f. ibis (Egyptian bird).
ichneumon, ōnis, m. ichneumon (Egyptian rat).
ĭco, ĭci, ictum, 3. v.a. to hit, to strike.
ictus, ūs, m. blow, stroke; beat (of beating time); stress.
idcirco, ad. therefore, for that reason.
ĭdem, eădem, ĭdem, pn. the same.
ĭdentĭdem, ad. ever and anon; sundry times; continually.

ĭdeo, ad. for that reason, therefore.
ĭdĭōta, ae, m. layman; inexperienced person.
ĭdōlum, i, n. image; spectre; idol. In Bacon's philosophy **idola tribus** are fallacies that have their origin in human nature itself, **idola specus** fallacies arising from individual aberrations, **idola fori** fallacies due to the ambiguous use of terms, and **idola theatri** fallacies due to false reasoning.
ĭdōneus, a, um, a. fit, suitable; able; meet.
Idus, uum, f. pl. the ides of every month; the eighth day after the nones.
ĭdyllium, ii, idyl; pastoral poem.
ĭgĭtur, ad. therefore.
ignārus, a, um, a. ignorant (of), inexperienced; unknown.
ignāvē, ad. slothfully; in a cowardly way.
ignāvia, ae, f. laziness; cowardice.
ignāvus, a, um, a. idle, sluggish; cowardly.
ignesco, 3. v.n. to take fire, to kindle; *fig.* to glow.
igneus, a, um, a. of fire, on fire; fiery; burning; fervid, vehement.
ignĭfer, a, um, a. fiery.
ignĭpes, ĕdis, a. fiery-footed.
ignĭpŏtens, entis, a. lord of fire.
ignis, is, m. fire; brightness; glow of passion;—**ignis fatuus,** will-o'-the-wisp.
ignōbĭlis, e, a. unknown; ignoble; base; obscure.
ignōbĭlĭtas, ātis, f. obscurity; baseness.
ignōmĭnia, ae, f. ignominy, dishonour.
ignōmĭniōsus, a, um, a. ignominious.
ignōrantia, ae, f. ignorance.
ignōrātio, onis, f. ignorance;—**ignoratio elenchi,** ignorance of the refutation, missing the point.   [ignorant of.
ignōro, 1. v.a. & n. not to know, to be
ignosco, nōvi, nōtum, 3. v.a. to forgive, to pardon.   [ignorant (of).
ignōtus, a, um, a. unknown; low-born;
īlex, ĭcis, f. holm-oak, evergreen-oak, holly.
īlia, ĭum, n. pl. flank; entrails.
īlicet, ad. instantly, forthwith.
īlignus, a, um, a. made of oak.
īllăbĕfactus, a, um, a. unshaken, unimpaired.   [into; to fall down.
īllābor, psus, 3. v.n. dep. to slide *or* flow
īllăcessītus, a, um, a. unprovoked, unattacked.   [exorable.
īllăcrĭmābĭlis, e, a. unlamented; in-
īllăcrĭmo, 1. v.n. **īllăcrĭmor, ātus,** 1. v. dep. to bewail, to lament.
īllæsus, a, um, a. uninjured.
īllætābĭlis, e, a. joyless.
īllăqueo, 1. v.a. to ensnare, to entangle.

ille, a, ud, illĭus, pn. he, she; it; that one, the aforesaid; the very same; the well-known.   [charm; bait.
illĕcebra, ae, f. allurement, enticement;
illĕpĭdus, a, um, a. rude; impolite.
illībĕrālis, e, a. ungenerous, sordid; mean.
illībĕrālĭter, ad. ungenerously.
illĭc, ad. there, yonder.
illĭcio, lexi, lectum, 3. v.a. to allure, to entice.
illĭcĭtus, a, um, a. forbidden, unlawful, illicit.   [immediately.
illĭco, ad. in that very place; there;
illīdo, si, sum, 3. v.a. to strike *or* dash against.   [to entangle.
illĭgo, 1. v.a. to bind *or* tie on, to fasten;
illim, illinc, ad. thence; *fig.* from that side.   [to anoint.
illĭno, lēvi, lĭtum, 3. v.a. to smear over;
illītĕrātus, a, um, a. unlettered, illiterate uneducated, unlearned.
illō, ad. thither; *fig.* to that point.
illōtus, a, um, a. unwashed.
illūc, ad. thither; thereto.
illūcesco, luxi, 3. v.n. & a. to begin to dawn.   [to mock, to jeer (at).
illūdo, si, sum, 3. v.n. & a. to sport with;
illūmĭno, 1. v.a. to light up; to set off; to show up;—**illuminati,** men learned in any subject.
illūsio, ōnis, f. irony.   [noble; evident.
illustris, e, a. clear, bright; famous;
illustro, 1. v.a. to illuminate; to render famous *or* illustrious; to illustrate; to make clear.
illŭvies, ēi, f. dirt, filth.
ĭmāgĭnārius, a, um, a. fancied, imaginary.
ĭmāgĭnātio, ōnis, f. fancy, imagination.
ĭmāgĭnor, atus, 1. v.a. dep. to fancy, to imagine.
ĭmāgo, ĭnis, f. image, likeness; idea; appearance; spectre, vision; echo; semblance.   [imbecility.
imbēcillĭtas, ātis, f. weakness, feebleness;
imbēcillus, a, um, a. weak, feeble; silly.
imbellis, e, a. unwarlike; weak; cowardly.   [liquid.
imber, bris, m. (shower of) rain; (any)
imberbis, e, a. beardless.   [to resolve.
imbĭbo, bi, 3. v.a. to imbibe, to conceive;
imbrex, ĭcis, f. tile.
imbrĭfĕr, a, um, a. rain-bringing, rainy.
imbuo, ui, ūtum, 3. v.a. to wet, to soak; to infect; to inure; to instruct.
ĭmĭtābĭlis, e, a. that may be imitated.
ĭmĭtāmen, ĭnis, n. imitation; resemblance, image.
ĭmĭtāmentum, i, n. imitation.
ĭmĭtātio, ōnis, f. imitation; simulation, pretence.
ĭmĭtātor, ōris, m. imitator.

imĭtātrix, ĭcis, f. female imitator.
imĭtor, ātus, 1. v.a. dep. to imitate; to reproduce; to portray; to counterfeit; to simulate.
immădesco, dui, 3. v.n. to become wet or moist. [strous; inhuman, savage.
immānis, e, a. huge, vast, immense, mon-
immānĭtas, ātis, f. hugeness, vastness; excess; cruelty.
immansuētus, a, um, a. savage.
immātūrus, a, um, a. unripe, immature, untimely.
immĕdĭcābĭlis, e, a. incurable. [heedless.
immĕmor, ŏris, a. unmindful; regardless,
immensĭtas, ātis, f. immensity.
immensus, a, um, a. endless, vast, immense;—immensum, ad. immensely.
immĕrens, tis, a. undeserving; innocent.
immergo, si, sum, 3. v.a. to plunge into, to immerse; to drown.
immĕrĭto, ad. undeservedly.
immĕrĭtus, a, um, a. undeserving; innocent; undeserved.
immigro, 1. v.n. to go or remove into.
immĭneo, 2. v.n. to overhang; to threaten, to be imminent; to have a design upon.
immĭnuo, ui, ūtum, 3. v.a. to diminish; to impair; to encroach upon.
immisceo, scui, xtum & stum, 2. v.a. to mix in, to intermingle.
immītis, e, a. harsh, sour; rough, rude; stern, inexorable.
immitto, mīsi, missum, 3. v.a. to send into; to admit; to throw into; to put in; to give the rein to; to let grow.
immo, ad. on the contrary; nay rather; yes.
immōbĭlis, e, a. immovable; unalterable.
immŏdĕrātē, ad. immoderately.
immŏdĕrātus, a, um, a. immeasurable; immoderate; disorderly.
immŏdĭcē, ad. excessively.
immŏdĭcus, a, um, a. excessive, immoderate.
immŏlātĭo, ōnis, f. sacrificing; sacrifice.
immŏlo, 1. v.a. to sacrifice; to kill.
immŏrior, mortuus, 3. v. dep. to die in or upon. [less.
immortālis, e, a. immortal; eternal, end-
immortālĭtas, ātis, f. immortality.
immōtus, a, um, a. unmoved, immovable; unchangeable. [or at).
immūgio, īvi & ii, 4. v.n. to resound (in
immundus, a, um, a. unclean, impure, filthy.
immūnio, īvi, 4. v.a. to fortify.
immūnis, e, a. free from office; free or exempt from; making no contribution.
immūnĭtas, ātis, f. freedom, exemption.
immūnītus, a, um, a. unfortified.

immurmŭro, 1. v.a. to murmur in or against.
immūtābĭlis, e, a. unchangeable.
immūto, 1. v.a. to change, to alter.
īmo, ad., v. immo.
impăcātus, a, um, adj. restless, warlike.
impar, ăris, a. uneven, unequal; inferior, weaker. [vided, unfurnished.
impărātus, a, um, not ready, unpro-
impătiens, entis, a. impatient.
impătienter, ad. impatiently.
impătientia, ae, f. impatience.
impăvĭdus, a, um, a. fearless, intrepid.
impĕdīmentum, i, n. hindrance, impediment; baggage of an army.
impĕdio, īvi & ii, ītum, 4. v.a. to entangle; to hamper; to hinder.
impĕdītus, a, um, p. & a. blocked up, difficult of passage, encumbered.
impello, pŭli, pulsum, 3. v.a. to push or thrust against; to impel; to incite.
impendeo, 2. v.n. & a. to hang over; to impend; to threaten. [paid on a loan.
impendium, ii, n. cost, expense; interest
impendo, di, sum, 3. v.a. to expend; fig. to devote (to).
impĕnĕtrābĭlis, e, a. impenetrable.
impensa, ae, f. outlay, cost, expense.
impensē, ad. expensively; zealously.
impensus, a, um, p. & a. ample, great; expensive.
impĕrātīvus, a, um, a. — modus, the mood of command; the imperative.
impĕrātor, ōris, m. commander-in-chief; the emperor as commander-in-chief.
impĕrātōrius, a, um, a. pertaining to a general.
impĕrātrix, ĭcis, f. she who commands.
impĕrātum, i, n. command, order.
imperceptus, a, um, a. unperceived.
imperfectus, a, um, a. unfinished, imperfect; incomplete.
impĕriōsus, a, um, a. lordly; powerful; domineering; boisterous. [ness.
impĕrītia, ae, f. inexperience, awkward-
impĕrītē, ad. unskilfully. [govern.
impĕrĭto, 1. v.n. & a. to command, to
impĕrītus, a, um, a. inexperienced in, unskilled, ignorant.
impĕrium, ii, n. command; rule; empire; supreme power;—imperium in imperio, a government within a government.
impĕro, 1. v.a. to command, to rule.
imperterrĭtus, a, um, a. unafraid.
impertio, īvi & ii, ītum, 4. v.a. to impart; to bestow a share on. [turbed.
imperturbātus, a, um, a. calm, undis-
impervius, a, um, a. impassable.
impĕto, 3. v.a. to attack. [tainable.
impetrābĭlis, e, a. easy to be obtained, at-

impetrātio, ōnis, f. an obtaining by re-quest.

impetro, 1. v.a. to accomplish; to get, to obtain by request; to prevail on.

impĕtus, ūs, m. assault, attack; impulse, vigour.

impexus, a, um, a. uncombed.

impĭē, ad. impiously.	[wickedness.

impĭĕtas, ātis, f. impiety; disloyalty,

impiger, gra, grum, a. diligent; quick; courageous.

impigrē, ad. actively, quickly.

impingo, pēgi, pactum, 3. v.a. to thrust, to strike or dash against.	[impious.

impius, a, um, a. irreverent; wicked;

implācābĭlis, e, a. implacable.

implācātus, a, um, a. unappeasable.

implācĭdus, a, um, a. ungentle, rough, savage.	[complish; to fulfil.

impleo, ēvi, ētum, 2. v.a. to fill; to ac-implĭcĭtē, ad. intricately.

implĭco, āvi, ātum & ui, ĭtum, 1. v.a. to in-fold; to involve; to encumber; to entangle;—implĭcor, pass., to be inti-mately connected with.	[implore.

implōro, 1. v.a. to invoke, to entreat, to implūmis, e, a. unfledged, callow.

implŭvium, ii, n. an opening in the roof of the atrium of a Roman house, through which the smoke passed out.

impōlītus, a, um, a. unpolished; rude.

impōno, sui, sĭtum, 3. v.a. to put upon or in; to impose; to assign; to set over.

importo, 1. v.a. to bring or convey into, to import; fig. to bring about.

importūnē, ad. unseasonably.

importūnĭtas, ātis, f. rudeness, insolence.

importūnus, a, um, a. inconvenient; troublesome; urgent; ill-mannered; ill-omened.

importuōsus, a, um, a. harbourless.

impossĭbĭlis, e, a. impossible.

impŏtens, entis, a. powerless, impotent, weak; wild; unruly; headstrong.

impŏtenter, ad. powerlessly, weakly; violently, intemperately.

impŏtentia, ae, f. weakness; insolence; outrageousness.

impraesentiarum, ad. for the moment.

impransus, a, um, a. unbreakfasted.

imprĕcor, ātus, 1. v.a. dep. to call down upon, to imprecate.

impressio, onis, f. attack; impression.

imprīmis, ad. in the first place, chiefly, especially.

imprĭmo, pressi, pressum, 3. v.a. to im-press, to imprint; to press upon; to set a mark; to stamp;—imprimātur, let it be printed; licence to print.

imprŏbē, ad. badly; improperly; dis-honestly.

imprŏbĭtas, ātis, f. wickedness; dis-honesty, improbity.

imprŏbo, 1. v.a. to disapprove, to con-demn.

imprŏbus, a, um, a. bad; wicked; impu-dent, shameless, dishonest; excessive; fierce; presumptuous.

imprŏprius, a, um, a. unsuitable.

imprōvĭdus, a, um, a. improvident; care-less, heedless.

imprōvĭsō, ad. unexpectedly, on a sudden.

imprōvīsus, a, um, a. unforeseen, unex-pected.

imprūdens, entis, a. imprudent; ignorant; foolish; unwarned.

imprūdenter, ad. imprudently; foolishly; heedlessly; before one is aware.	[ance.

imprūdentia, ae, f. imprudence; ignor-impūbes, ēris & is, a. under age; youthful.

impŭdens, entis, a. shameless, impudent.

impŭdenter, ad. shamelessly, impudently.

impŭdentia, ae, f. shamelessness, im-pudence.

impŭdīcĭtia, ae, f. unchasteness, lewdness.

impŭdīcus, a, um, a. unchaste, lewd.

impugno, 1. v.a. to fight against, to at-tack, to assail.	[impulse.

impulsio, ōnis, f. pressure, influence;

impulsor, ōris, m. instigator.

impulsus, ūs, m. shock, impulse; incite-ment.	[scot-free.

impūnē, ad. safely, with impunity;

impūnĭtas, ātis, f. impunity.

impūnītus, a, um, a. unpunished, safe.

impūrĭtas, ātis, f. pollution.

impūrus, a, um, a. unclean, filthy, foul; impure; vile.	[ascribe.

impŭto, 1. v.a. to impute, to charge; to

īmus, a, um, a. inmost, deepest, under-most; last.

in, pr. (with accus.) to; into; against; for; towards; until;—in dies, day after day, every day; (with abl.) at; in; on; within; among;—in camera, in private;—in commendam, in temporary trust;—in esse, in actual existence;—in extenso, in full;—in flagranti delicto, in the very act;—in forma pauperis (to obtain free legal aid) as a pauper;—in loco parentis, in the position of a parent;—in medias res, into the heart of a subject;—in nubibus, in the clouds (of a dreamer); —in posse, in a possible existence;—in propria persona, in one's own per-son;—in puris naturalibus, in a natural state; naked;—in re, in the matter of;—in terrorem, in order to inspire fear;—in toto, entirely;—in vacuo, in an empty space.

ĭnaccessus. a, um, a. inaccessible.

īnædĭfīco, 1. v.a. to build in (a place); to build up; to block up.

īnæquābĭlis, e, a. uneven.

īnæquālis, e, a. uneven, unequal, unlike; *fig.* inconsistent.

īnæquālĭtas, ātis, f. inequality.

īnæstĭmābĭlis, e, a. not to be valued; beyond all price, inestimable.

īnămābĭlis, e, a. not amiable, hateful.

īnambŭlo, 1. v.n. to walk up and down.

īnămœnus, a, um, a. unlovely, gloomy.

īnănĭmus, a, um, a. lifeless, inanimate.

īnānis, e, empty, void; vain, slight; foolish;—īnāne, is, n. the void;— īnānio, īvi *or* ii, ītum, 4. v.a. to empty.

īnānĭtas, ātis, f. uselessness, inanity.

nānĭter, ad. vainly, uselessly.

īnărātus, a, um, a. unploughed, fallow.

īnardesco, rsi, 3. v.n. to kindle, to take fire.

īnāresco, rui, 3. v.n. to become dry.

īnassuētus, a, um, a. unaccustomed.

īnaudio, īvi *or* ii, ītum, 4. v.a. to hear; to overhear. [new.

īnaudītus, a, um, a. unheard of, strange;

īnaugŭro, 1. v.n. & a. to divine by the flight of birds; to inaugurate, to install.

īnauro, 1. v.a. to gild, to make rich.

īnauspĭcātus, a, um, a. inauspicious.

īnausus, a, um, a. unattempted.

inb . . ., v. imb . . .

īncæduus, a, um, a. not felled, unhewn.

incălesco, lui, 3. v.n. to grow hot, to glow; to glow with passion.

incallĭde, ad. unskilfully.

incallĭdus, a, um, a. unskilful, stupid.

incandesco, dui, 3. v.n. to become hot, to glow. [hoary.

incānesco, nui, 3. v.n. to turn grey *or*

incanto, 1. v.a. to chant; to bewitch.

incānus, a, um, a. grey, hoary.

incassum, ad. in vain, to no purpose.

incautē, ad. incautiously, inconsiderately.

incautus, a, um, a. incautious, heedless, improvident.

incēdo, cessi, cessum, 3. v.n. & a. to step, to march along; to move; to go in state; to advance; to befall. [abroad.

incělěbrātus, a, um, a. not spread

incendiārius, ii, m. incendiary.

incendium, ii, n. fire, conflagration; passion; heat.

incendo, di, sum, 3. v.a. to set fire to, to kindle; to inflame; to irritate.

incensus, a, um, a. not assessed, unregistered.

inceptum, i, n. beginning, undertaking.

incertus, a, um, a. uncertain; doubtful, inconstant, vacillating.

incesso, cessīvi & cessi, 3. v.a. to assault, to attack; to reprove, to accuse.

incessus, ūs, m. walking, pace, gait; invasion; entrance.

incestē, ad. impurely, sinfully.

incesto, 1. v.a. to pollute, to defile.

incestus, a, um, a. unchaste; guilty; —, ūs, m. unchastity; incest.

inchoo, v. incoho.

incĭdo, cĭdi, cāsum, 3. v.n. to fall into; to meet with; to befall.

incĭdo, cĭdi, cīsum, 3. v.a. to cut into; to make an end to; to interrupt; to engrave. [to surround.

incingo, xi, ctum, 3. v.a. to gird in;

incĭpio, cēpi, ceptum, 3. v.a. & n. to begin; to attempt; to undertake.

incīsē, incīsim, ad. in short sentences.

incīsio, ōnis, f. incision, clause (of a sentence).

incĭtāmentum, i, n. incitement, incentive.

incĭtātio, ōnis, f. instigation; energy.

incĭtātē, ad. vehemently; hurriedly.

incĭtātus, a, um, p. & a. stirred up, spurred on; speedy;—equo incitato, at full gallop.

incĭto, 1. v.a. to incite; to stir up, to spur on; to hasten.

incĭtus, a, um, a. swift; violent.

inclāmo, 1. v.a. & n. to cry out to, to call upon; to chide, to rebuke.

inclāresco, ui, 3. v.n. to become famous.

inclēmens, entis, a. harsh.

inclēmentia, ae, f. harshness.

inclīnatio, ōnis, f. leaning towards; *fig.* inclination.

inclīno, 1. v.a. & n. to bend down; to lower; to incline; to decay; to grow worse; to set (of the sun).

inclĭtus, a, um, a. renowned, famous, illustrious. [to enclose.

inclūdo, si, sum, 3. v.a. to shut in *or* up;

inclūsio, ōnis, f. confinement.

inclŭtus, a, um, a. inclytus, v. inclitus.

incognĭtus, a, um, a. unknown.

incŏho, 1. v.a. to start; to set going; to begin.

incŏla, ae, c. inhabitant; foreign resident.

incŏlo, lui, 3. v.a. & n. to dwell in, to inhabit.

incŏlŭmis, e, a. uninjured, safe, entire.

incŏlŭmĭtas, ātis, f. soundness, safety.

incŏmĭtātus, a, um, a. unaccompanied.

incommŏdē, ad. incommodiously; unfortunately; unseasonably.

incommŏdĭtas, ātis, f. inconvenience; damage, disadvantage.

incommŏdo, 1. v.a. & n. to inconvenience; to be inconvenient. [fortune; loss.

incommŏdum, i, n. inconvenience; mis-

incommŏdus, a, um, a. inconvenient, troublesome; hurtful; unsuitable.

incompărābĭlis, e, a. not to be equalled.

incompertus, a, um, a. unknown.
incompŏsĭtus, a, um, a. disordered, rude.
incomptus, a, um, a. inelegant, artless, rude.
inconcessus, a, um, a. unlawful.
inconcinnus, a, um, a. awkward, absurd.
inconcussus, a, um, a. unshaken, uninjured.   [rude; artless.
incondĭtus, a, um, a. confused, uncouth,
inconsĭdĕrantia, ae, f. inconsiderateness.
inconsĭdĕrātus, a, um, a. thoughtless, inconsiderate; unconsidered.   [able.
inconsōlābĭlis, e, a. inconsolable; incur-
inconstans, antis, a. changeable, fickle.
inconstanter, ad. inconstantly; inconsistently.
inconstantia, ae, f. inconstancy.
inconsultē, ad. inconsiderately, rashly.
inconsultus, a, um, a. unadvised; indiscreet.
incontĭnens, entis, a. intemperate.
incontĭnentia, ae, f. intemperance.
incŏquo, xi, ctum, 3. v.a. to boil in or down; to boil; to dye.
incorruptē, ad. incorruptibly.
incorruptus, a, um, a. unspoiled, uncorrupted.
increbresco, brui, 3. n. to become frequent; to increase; to grow into vogue.
incrēdĭbĭlis, e, a. incredible, extraordinary.
incrēdĭbĭlĭter, ad. incredibly.
incrēdŭlus, a, um, a. incredulous.
incrēmentum, i, n. growth, increase.
incrĕpĭto, 1. v.a. to challenge; to chide, to rebuke.
incrĕpo, ui, ĭtum, 1. v.n. & a. to make a noise, to rustle; to rebuke; to attack.
incresco, ēvi, 3. v.n. to grow (in or upon).
incruentus, a, um, a. bloodless, without shedding of blood.
incŭbātio, onis, f. hatching, incubation.
incŭbo, ui, ĭtum, 1. v.n. to lie in or upon; to sit upon; to brood over; to cover.
incūdo, di, sum, 3. v.a. to hammer out.
inculco, 1. v.a. fig. to force upon, to inculcate on.
incultus, a, um, a. uncultivated; rude.
incultus, ūs, m. want of cultivation or refinement; filth.
incumbo, cŭbui, cŭbĭtum, 3. v.n. to lay oneself upon, to lean or recline upon; to apply oneself earnestly to;—in gladium incumbere, to fall on one's sword.
incūnābŭla, ōrum, n. pl. swaddling-clothes; cradle; birth-place; (mod.) early printed books;—ab incunabulis, from childhood.
incūria, ae, f. carelessness, negligence.
incūriōsē, ad. negligently.

incūriōsus, a, um, a. careless, negligent; indifferent.
incurro, curri (cŭcurri), cursum, 3. v.n. to run into or towards, to attack, to invade; to meet with; to incur; to befall.
incursio, ōnis, f. incursion; inroad.
incurso, 1. v.a. to run against, to dash against, to attack.
incursus, ūs, m. assault, attack.
incurvo, 1. v.a. to bend, to crook, to çurve.
incurvus, a, um, a. crooked, curved.
incus, ūdis, f. anvil.
incūso, 1. v.a. to accuse; to blame.
incustōdītus, a, um, a. not watched; not attended to.
incŭtio, cussi, cussum, 3. v.a. to strike upon or against; to cast into; to inspire.   [to look for.
indāgo, 1. v.a. to trace out; to explore;
indāgo, ĭnis, f. enclosing with nets; investigation.
indĕ, ad. thence, from that place; from that time; from that cause; thenceforth; afterwards.   [due.
indēbĭtus, a, um, a. that is not owed, not
indĕcōris, e, a. unbecoming; inglorious.
indĕcōro, 1. v.a. to disgrace.
indĕcōrus, a, um, a. unbecoming, indecorous; unseemly.
indēfensus, a, um, a. undefended.
indēfessus, a, um, a. unwearied; indefatigable.
indemnātus, a, um, a. uncondemned.
indeprensus, a, um, a. undiscovered.
index, ĭcis, c. forefinger; mark; proof; discoverer; informer;—index expurgatorius, a cautionary list forbidding the perusal of certain writings.
indĭcātīvus, a, um, a. — modus, the indicative mood.
indĭcium, ii, n. information; token; disclosure; evidence (before a court).
indĭco, 1. v.a. to betray; to reveal; to give information.
indĭco, xi, ctum, 3. v.a. to declare publicly; to name; to appoint; to inflict.
indictus, a, um, a. not said, unsaid; unsung;—indicta causa, without the case being pleaded; unheard.   [thing.
indĭdem, ad. from the same place or
indifferens, entis, a. making no difference; indifferent.
indĭgĕna, ae, g.c. native.
indĭgens, entis, p. & a. needy, indigent.
indĭgentia, ae, f. need; want.
indĭgeo, ui, 2. v.n. to need, to want.
indĭgestus, a, um, a. a chaotic; jumbled.
indĭgĭtes, deified heroes, tutelary deities.
indignātio, ōnis, f. indignation; anger.

indignē, ad. unworthily; basely; indignantly.

indignitas, ātis, f. unworthiness, vileness, insult.

indignor, ātus, 1. v.a. dep. to be displeased at, to be indignant.

indignus, a, um, a. unworthy, undeserving; undeserved; unmeet; shameful; sad, severe.

indigus, a, um, a. lacking; needy.

indiligens, tis, a. careless, negligent.

indiligenter, ad. carelessly, negligently.

indiligentia, ae, f. carelessness, negligence.

indipiscor, deptus, 3. v. dep. to obtain.

indiscrētus, a, um, a. indistinguishable.

individŭus, a, um, a. indivisible; fig. inseparable;—individuum, i, n. atom.

indo, dĭdi, dĭtum, 3. v.a. to put upon; fig. to introduce; to impart or give to.

indŏcĭlis, e, a. unteachable, indocile.

indoctus, a, um, a. untaught; unlearned; ignorant; unskilful. [position.

indōles, is, f. inborn quality; talent, disindōlesco, ui, 3. v.n. to begin to feel pain; to be grieved. [tamable; fierce.

indŏmĭtus, a, um, a. untamed, wild; unindormio, īvi, ītum, 4. v.n. to fall asleep (at, on, over).

indōtātus, a, um, a. undowered.

indŭbĭto, 1. v.n. to doubt of.

indūco, xi, ctum, 3. v.a. to lead or conduct into; to bring in; to introduce; to overspread; to put on; to draw over, to persuade.

inductio, ōnis, f. leading or bringing into; introduction, exhibition; fig. purpose; intention; reasoning from particular instances to a general conclusion.

indulgens, tis, a. indulgent, kind.

indulgenter, ad. indulgently.

indulgentia, ae, f. indulgence, gentleness.

indulgeo, si, tum, 2. v.n. & a. to be kind or indulgent to; to grant; to give way to.

induo, ui, ūtum, 3. v.a. to put on; to dress oneself in; to cover over; to assume.

indūro, 1. v.a. to make hard; fig. to steel.

industria, ae, f. diligence, assiduity, industry;—de or ex —, on purpose.

industriē, ad. diligently, industriously.

industrius, a, um, a. diligent, assiduous, industrious.

indūtiæ, ārum, f. pl. truce, armistice.

inēbrio, 1. v.a. to intoxicate.

inēdia, ae, f. abstaining from food, fasting. [undistinguished.

inēlĕgans, antis, a. lacking in taste;

inēluctābĭlis, e, a. inevitable.

inemptus, a, um, a. unbought.

ĭnēnarrābĭlis, e, not to be related, indescribable. [intricate.

inēnōdābĭlis, e, a. not to be disentangled,

ineo, īvi & ii, ītum, 4. v.a. & n. to go into, to enter (into or upon); to commence; to form; to make.

ineptē, ad. unsuitably; foolishly, absurdly. [absurdities.

ineptiæ, ārum, f. pl. fooleries, trifles,

ineptus, a, um, a. unsuitable; silly, foolish. [unprepared.

inermis,· e, a. unarmed, defenceless; fig.

inerrans, antis, a. stellæ inerrantes, f. pl. fixed stars.

iners,· ertis, a. unskilful; sluggish.

inertia, ae, f. unskilfulness; inactivity, idleness, sloth.

inērŭdītus, a, um, a. unlearned, illiterate; ignorant; awkward.

inesco, 1. v.a. to lay a bait; to allure.

inēvītābĭlis, e, a. unavoidable.

inexcūsābĭlis, e, a. inexcusable. [skilful.

inexercĭtātus, a, um, a. unexercised; un-

inexhaustus, a, um, a. unexhausted; inexhaustible.

inexōrābĭlis, e, a. inexorable, implacable.

inexpectātus, v. inexspectatus.

inexperrectus, a, um, a. unawakened.

inexpertus, a, um, a. inexperienced (in); untried; unproved. [able.

inexpiābĭlis, e, a. inexpiable; irreconcil-

inexplēbĭlis, e, a. insatiable.

inexplētus, a, um, a. insatiable.

inexplĭcābĭlis, e, a. inextricable; intricate, difficult.

inexplōrāto, ad. without examination.

inexplōrātus, a, um, a. unexplored.

inexpugnābĭlis, e, a. impregnable; invincible, firm.

inexspectātus, a, um, a. unexpected.

inexstinctus, a, um, a. inextinguishable.

inexsŭpĕrābĭlis, e, a. insurmountable; invincible.

inextinctus, v. inexstinctus.

inextrĭcābĭlis, e, a. inextricable.

infabrē, ad. bunglingly, rudely, artlessly.

infăcētus, a, um, a. coarse, rude; stupid.

infācundus, a, um, a. ineloquent.

infāmia, ae, f. ill-fame, dishonour, infamy.

infāmis, e, a. disreputable, infamous.

infāmo, 1. v.a. to brand with infamy, to dishonour. [able.

infandus, a, um, a. unutterable; abomin-

infans, antis, a. speechless, mute; childish; silly; —, c. little child.

infantia, ae, f. infancy.

infătŭo, 1. v.a. to make a fool of.

infaustus, a, um, a. unlucky, unfortunate.

infectŏr, ōris, m. dyer.

infectus, a, um, a. not done, unmade; unfinished, impossible.

infēcundĭtas, ātis, f. unfruitfulness.
infēcundus, a, um, a. unfruitful.
infēlīcĭtas, ātis, f. misfortune.
infēlīcĭter, ad. unfortunately.
infēlix, īcis, a. unfruitful; unfortunate, unhappy.
infensē, ad. bitterly, hostilely.
infenso, ĭ. v.a. & n. to treat in a hostile manner; to destroy. [raged.
infensus, a, um, a. hostile, bitter, en-
infĕrĭæ, ārum, f. pl. offerings to the dead.
inferior, v. inferus.
inferius, v. infra.
infernus, a, um, a. lower; infernal.
infĕro, intŭli, illātum, inferre, 3. v.a. to bring into or upon; to apply; to produce, to cause; to inflict; to bury; to draw an inference;—arma inferre, to levy war on.
infĕrus, a, um, a. below, underneath, lower;—inferi, ōrum, m. pl. the dead; —infĕrior, ius, lower; later; latter; younger;—infimus, īmus, lowest, last.
infervesco, ferbui, 3. v.n. to grow hot; to boil.
infestē, ad. hostilely, violently.
infesto, ĭ. v.a. to attack; to molest.
infestus, a, um, a. hostile; dangerous; disturbed;—infestum habere, to infest.
inficio, fēci, fectum, 3. v.a. to dye; to stain; to infect; to imbue; to corrupt.
inficior, v. infitior.
infidēlis, e, a. unfaithful; treacherous.
infidēlĭtas, ātis, f. unfaithfulness; treachery.
infidēlĭter, ad. treacherously.
infidus, a, um, a. faithless; treacherous.
infigo, xi, xum, 3. v.a. to fix, to thrust or fasten in.
infimus, a, um, v. inferus.
infindo, fĭdi, fissum, 3. v.a. to tear; to cut.
infīnĭtas, ātis, f. endlessness, infinity.
infīnĭtē, ad. without end, infinitely.
infīnītīvus, a, um, a. — modus, the infinitive mood.
infīnĭtus, a, um, a. boundless; endless, infinite; countless;—ad infinitum, to infinity. [sickness; inconstancy.
infirmĭtas, ātis, f. weakness; infirmity,
infirmo, ĭ. v.a. to weaken; to diminish; to annul. [sickly; inconstant.
infirmus, a, um, a. weak, feeble; infirm,
infit, v. def. he (or she) begins.
infitĭæ, ārum, f. pl. infitias ire, to deny.
infitĭātĭo, ōnis, f. denial.
infitior, atus, ĭ. v.a. dep. to deny, to disown.
inflammātĭo, ōnis, f. inflammation.
inflammo, ĭ. v.a. to set on fire, to light up, to kindle; fig. to excite; to inflame.

inflātē, ad. haughtily.
inflātĭo, ōnis, f. flatulence.
inflātus, a, um, p. & a. puffed up; fig. inflated; haughty.
inflecto, xi, xum, 3. v.a. to bend; to curve; to change; to move.
infligo, xi, ctum, 3. v.a. to strike against; to inflict, to impose upon.
inflo, ĭ. v.a. to blow into or upon; to blow out, to puff up.
influo, xi, xum, 3. v.n. to flow into; to creep into. [to inter.
infŏdĭo, fōdi, fossum, 3. v.a. to dig in,
informis, e, a. shapeless; deformed, hideous. [fashion; to form an idea of.
informo, ĭ. v.a. to shape, to form; to
infortūnātus, a, um, a. unfortunate.
infortūnĭum, ii, n. misfortune, punishment.
infrā, ad. & p. below, underneath; under; later than; less than;—infra dignitatem (infra dig.), beneath one's dignity.
infractĭo, ōnis, f. breaking to pieces; weakening; fig. despondency.
infractus, a, um, p. & a. broken; broken off; exhausted; disabled.
infrĕmo, ui, 3. v.n. to bellow, to roar.
infrendeo, 2. infrendo, 3. v.n. to gnash.
infrēnis, e, infrēnus, a, um, a. unbridled.
infrēno, ĭ. v.a. to bridle.
infrēquens, tis, a. rare, scanty; few.
infrēquentĭa, ae, f. scantiness; fewness; loneliness.
infringo, frēgi, fractum, 3. v.a. to break; to break off; to quell; to diminish; to dishearten; to affect. [fillet.
infŭla, ae, f. band, bandage; (priest's)
infŭmus, a, um, v. infimus.
infundībŭlŭm (infūd), i, n. a funnel.
infundo, fūdi, fūsum, 3. v.a. to pour into or upon; to administer (a draught, etc.); fig. to impart.
infusco, ĭ. v.a. to make dusky, to darken; to stain, to tarnish. [crease.
ingĕmīno, ĭ. v.a. & n. to redouble; to in-
ingĕmisco, ui, 3. v.a. & n. to groan (over).
ingĕmo, ui, 3. v.a. & n. to mourn over, to bewail.
ingĕnĕro, ĭ. v.a. to implant.
ingĕnĭōsē, ad. cleverly.
ingĕnĭōsus, a, um, a. clever, ingenious; well suited for.
ingĕnĭum, ii, n. innate quality, nature; natural disposition; capacity; talent; genius. [great.
ingens, tis, a. monstrous, vast, huge;
ingĕnŭē, ad. candidly; in a gentlemanly way. [ousness.
ingĕnŭĭtas, ātis, f. good birth; ingenu-
ingĕnŭus, a, um, a. innate, natural; freeborn; candid; generous.

ingĕro, gessi, gestum, 3. v.a. to throw
upon; to heap upon; to inflict; to obtrude. [plant.
ingigno, gĕnui, genitum, 3. v.a. to im-
inglōrius, a, um, a. inglorious; obscure.
inglŭvies, ēi, f. crop, maw; fig. gluttony.
ingrātē, ad. disagreeably; ungratefully.
ingrātiis, ingrātis, ad. unwillingly.
ingrātus, a, um, a. unpleasant; unthankful. [increase.
ingrăvesco, 3. v.n. to grow heavy; fig. to
ingrăvo, 1. v.a. fig. to aggravate, to render worse.
ingrĕdior, gressus sum, 3. v. dep. to step
or go into, to enter; to begin.
ingressio, ōnis, f. ingressus, ūs, m. entering; inroad; walking, gait; fig. beginning. [to fall upon.
ingruo, ui, 3. v.n. to rush into; to assail,
inguen, ĭnis, n. groin.
ingurgĭto, 1. v.a. to flood;--se ingurgi-
tare, to absorb oneself in. [ward.
inhăbĭlis, e, a. unwieldy; unable; awk-
inhăbĭtābĭlis, e, a. uninhabitable.
inhăbĭto, i, v.a. to inhabit, to dwell (in).
inhæreo, hæsi, hæsum, 2. v.n. to stick
in, to cleave to; to inhere in.
inhæresco, hæsi, hæsum, 3. v.n. to inhere; to stick to.
inhălo, 1. v.n. & a. to breathe at or upon.
inhĭbeo, ui, ĭtum, 2. v.a. to restrain, to
curb; to hinder; to employ, to use;—
inhibere (remis), to row backwards.
inhĭbĭtio, ōnis, f. rowing backwards.
inhio, 1. v.n. & a. to gape; to gape at;
to covet.
inhŏnestē, ad. dishonourably.
inhŏnesto, 1. v.a. to disgrace.
inhŏnestus, a, um, a. dishonourable,
shameful. [rewarded.
inhŏnōrātus, a, um, a. unhonoured; un-
inhŏnōrus, a, um, a. unimportant, unsightly, ugly.
inhorreo, 2. v.n. to stand on end, to
bristle; to shudder.
inhorresco, horrui, 3. v.n. to bristle up;
to quiver; to tremble, to shudder
with). [hospitable.
n hospĭtālis, e, inhospĭtus, a, um, a. in-
inhūmānē, ad. cruelly.
inhūmānĭter, ad. discourteously.
inhūmānĭtas, ātis, f. inhumanity, barbarity; incivility; niggardliness.
inhūmānus, a, um, a. inhuman, rude;
unmannerly.
inhūmātus, a, um, a. unburied. [hand.
inĭbi, ad. therein;--inibi esse, to be at
inĭmīcē, ad. in a hostile manner.
inĭmīcĭtia, ae, f. hostility, enmity.
inĭmīcus, a, um, a. hostile, inimical; —,
i, m. enemy, foe.

inĭmĭtābĭlis, e, a. not to be imitated.
inīquē, ad. unequally; fig. unjustly.
inīquĭtas, ātis, f. inequality; difficulty;
injustice.
inīquus, a, um, a. unequal, uneven; disadvantageous; unjust; unkind; hostile. [secrate (to).
inĭtio, 1. v.a. to initiate (into), to con-
inĭtium, ii, n. entrance; beginning;--ab
initio, from the beginning.
inĭtus, ūs, m. advent; beginning.
injĭcio, jēci, jectum, 3. v.a. to throw in or
into; to put on; to inspire; to occasion;--injicere alicui manum, to lay
hands on one.
injūcundus, a, um, a. unpleasant; severe.
injungo, xi, ctum, 3. v.a. to join or fasten
(into); to attach to; to impose (upon);
to enjoin.
injūrātus, a, um, a. unsworn.
injūria, ae, f. wrong, injury; abuse, insult; offence;--injuria (abl.), wrongfully.
injūriōsē, ad. wrongfully. [noxious.
injūriōsus, a, um, a. wrongful, injurious;
injūrius, a, um, a. wrongful, unjust.
injussū, ad. (abl. of injussus, ūs, m.)
without the orders (of).
injussus, a, um, a. unbidden.
injustē, ad. unjustly, wrongfully.
injustĭtia, æ, f. injustice.
injustus, a, um, a. unjust, wrongful; severe; excessive, unsuitable.
innābĭlis, e, a. not to be swum through.
innascor, nātus sum, 3. v. dep. to be born
in. [swim into; to flood.
innăto, 1. v.a. to swim in or upon; to
innātus, a, um, a. p. & a. innate, natural.
innāvĭgābĭlis, e, a. unnavigable.
innecto, xui, xum, 3. v.a. to tie, to fasten
to; to devise. [or rest upon.
innītor, nixus & nīsus, 3. v. dep. to lean
inno, 1. v.n. to swim or float in or upon;
to wash; to sail over.
innŏcens, tis, a. harmless; innocent.
innŏcenter, ad. harmlessly; innocently.
innŏcentia, ae, f. harmlessness; innocence; honesty.
innŏcuus, a, um, a. harmless; safe; uninjured; innocent. [known.
innōtesco, nōtui, 3. v.n. to become
innŏvo, 1. v.a. to renew;--se innovare,
to return to, to recommence.
innoxĭus, a, um, a. harmless, innocuous;
not guilty, innocent; unhurt.
innūbo, nupsi, 3. v.n. to marry into (a
family).
innūbus, a, um, a. unwed.
innŭmĕrābĭlis, e, a. countless.
innŭmĕrābĭlĭter, ad. innumerably.
innŭmĕrus, a, um, a. numberless.

innuo, ŭi, ūtum, 3. v.n. to intimate, to hint.

innuptus, a, um, a. unwed.

inobrŭtus, a, um, a. unburied; safe.

inobservābilis, e, a. baffling.

inobservātus, a, um, a. unobserved.

inoffensus, a, um, a. free from hindrance; uninterrupted.   [duty; disobliging.

inofficiōsus, a, um, a. contrary to one's

inōlesco, ēvi, ŏlĭtum, 3. v.n. to grow in *or* to.   [dearth.

inōpia, ae, f. want, scarcity; indigence;

inōpīnans, ntis, a. not expecting, unaware.

inōpīnāto, ad. unexpectedly.

inōpīnātus, a, um, a. unexpected, sudden.

inōpīnus, a, um, a. unexpected.

inops, ŏpis, a. destitute (of), needy; helpless; poor, meagre.

inordĭnātus, a um, a. disordered, irregular.   [brated.

inornātus, a, um, a. unadorned; uncele-

inp . . ., v. imp . . .

inquam, v. inquio.   [some.

inquies, ētis, a. restless, unquiet; trouble-

inquiēto, 1. v.a. to disturb.

inquiētus, a, um, a. restless, unquiet.

inquilīnus, a, um, a. of foreign birth; —, i, m. inmate, lodger, tenant.

inquĭno, 1. v.a. to bedaub; to stain, to pollute.   [he says.

inquio, 3. v. def., **inquam,** I say;—inquit,

inquīro, quĭsīvi, quĭsītum, 3. v.a. to search for; to examine, to inquire into.

inquīsītio, ōnis, f. search; inquiry.

inquīsītor, ōris, m. searcher, inquirer.

inr . . ., v. irr . . .

insălūbris, e, a. unwholesome.

insānābilis, e, a. incurable.

insānē, ad. madly, insanely.

insānia, ae, f. madness, folly; extravagance.   [or insane.

insānio, īvi, & ii, ītum, 4. v.n. to be mad

insānĭtas, ātis, f. unhealthiness.

insānus, a, um, a. mad, insane; inspired; violent; excessive.

insătiābilis, e, a. insatiable.

insătiābĭlĭter, ad. insatiably.

inscendo, di, sum, 3. v.n. & a. to climb.

insciens, entis, a. not knowing, without knowledge.

inscienter, ad. unknowingly, unskilfully.

inscientia, ae, f., **inscĭtia, ae, f.** ignorance, inexperience.

inscītē, ad. unskilfully.

inscītus, a, um, a. ignorant; unskilful.

inscius, a, um, a. not knowing, ignorant of.

inscrībo, psi, ptum, 3. v.a. to write in *or* upon, to inscribe; to enrol; to superscribe; to mark; to brand.

inscriptio, ōnis, f. inscription, title.

insculpo, psi, ptum, 3. v.a. to carve in *or* upon, to engrave; *fig.* to impress upon.

insĕco, ŭi, ctum, 1. v.a. to cut; to notch; to dissect.

insectātio, ōnis, f. pursuing, pursuit; censuring; insulting.

insectātor, ōris, m. persecutor, censurer.

insecto, 1. v.a., **insector, atus sum,** 1. v.a. dep. to pursue; to chide; to attack.

insectum, i, n. inseçt.

insĕnesco, nui, 3. v.n. to grow old (in *or* at).

insĕpultus, a, um, a. unburied.

insĕquor, cūtus & quutus sum, 3. v.a. dep. to follow after *or* upon; to pursue; to succeed; to reproach.

insĕro, sēvi, sĭtum, 3. v.a. to sow *or* plant in; to ingraft; *fig.* to implant.

insĕro, sĕrui, sertum, 3. v.a. to put into; to insert; to apply; *fig.* **se inserere,** to mingle with.

inserto, 1. v.a. to insert.

inservio, īvi, ītum, 4. v.n. & a. to be a slave *or* vassal; to be devoted to, to serve.

insībĭlo, 1. v.n. to whistle.

insĭdeo, sēdi, sessum, 2. v.n. & a. to sit in *or* upon; to beset; to take possession of; to be deep seated; to occupy.

insĭdiae, ārum, f. pl. ambush; plot, artifice; treachery.

insĭdĭor, ātus sum, 1. v.n. dep. to lie in ambush.

insĭdĭōsē, ad. treacherously.

insĭdĭōsus, a, um, a. deceitful; insidious.

insīdo, sēdi, sessum, 3. v.n. & a. to sit down in *or* on, to settle on; to beset; to take possession of; to be firmly implanted in.

insigne, is, n. mark, token; badge of honour;—**insignia, pl.** ensign; signal.

insignio, īvi ītum, 4. v.a. to mark; to adorn.

insignis, e, a. notable; famous.

insignĭter, ad. notably, extraordinarily, remarkably.

insignītus, a, um, a. & p. clear, plain; remarkable, striking.

insĭlio, ŭi, 3. v.n. to leap into *or* upon, to spring at.

insĭmŭlātio, ōnis, f. accusation, charge.

insĭmŭlo, 1. v.a. to accuse, to charge.

insincērus, a, um, a. insincere, deceitful; putrid.

insĭnuātio, ōnis, f. ingratiating oneself.

insĭnuo, 1. v.a. & n. to put *or* thrust in; to introduce; to insinuate; to creep into; to enter.

insĭpiens, tis, a. unwise, foolish.

insĭpienter, ad. foolishly.

insĭpientia, æ, f. folly.

insisto, stĭti, 3. v.n. & a. to stand or tread upon; to stop; to pursue; to persevere; to set about, to apply oneself (to).

insĭtio, ōnis, f. grafting; time of graft- [ing.

insĭtīvus, a, um a. ingrafted; fig. spurious. [adopted.

insĭtus, a, um, p. & a. inborn, natural;

insōcĭābĭlis, e, a. unsociable.

insŏlens, tis, a. unaccustomed (to); strange; arrogant; insolent; excessive.

insŏlenter, ad. unusually; insolently.

insŏlentia, ae, f. unfamiliarity; strangeness; haughtiness, arrogance.

insŏlesco, 3. to become insolent or haughty. [unusual.

insŏlĭtus, a, um, a. unaccustomed (to);

insomnia, ae, f. pl. sleeplessness.

insomnis, e, a. sleepless.

insomnium, ii, n. vision (in a dream).

insŏno, ui, ĭtum, 1. v.n. to sound loudly, to resound.

insons, tis, a. guiltless; harmless.

insōpītus, a, um, a. sleepless, wakeful.

inspecto, 1. v.a. to look at, to view, to behold.

inspērans, antis, a. not expecting.

inspērātō, ad. unexpectedly.

inspērātus, a, um, a. unhoped for, unexpected; unforeseen.

inspergo, si, sum, 3. v.a. to sprinkle into or upon.

inspĭcio, exi, ectum, 3. v.a. to look into or at, to inspect; to examine; to observe.

inspīro, 1. v.a. & n. to blow into or upon; fig. to inspire; to excite. [stant.

instăbĭlis, e, a. shaky; unstable; inconinstans, p. & a. present; urgent.

instanter, ad. vehemently.

instar, n. indecl. image, likeness; manner;—**instar esse, instar habere.** to be like.

instaurātio, ōnis, f. renewal. [restore.

instauro, 1. v.a. to renew, to repeat; to

insterno, strāvi, strātum, 3. v.a. to spread or strew upon; to cover; to lay over.

instīgo, 1. v.a. to goad on, to stimulate, to instigate.

instillo, 1. v.a. to instil.

instĭmŭlo, 1. v.a. to goad on.

instinctus, ūs, m. impulse; inspiration.

instinctus, a, um, a. instigated; encouraged.

instĭta, ae, f. flounce of a dress.

instĭtor, ōris, m. huckster, hawker.

instĭtuo, ui, ūtum, 3. v.a. to set firmly; to institute; to found; to build; to make; to order; to establish; to begin; to instruct, to educate, to determine.

institūtio, ōnis, f. disposition, arrangement; custom, manner; instruction, education. [law; custom; manner.

institūtum, i, n. regulation; institution;

insto, stĭti, 1. v.n. to stand in or upon; to threaten; to press, to urge; to entreat; to assail.

instrĕpo, ui, ĭtum, 3. v.n. to resound, to rattle, to creak. [ment.

instructio, ōnis, f. construction; arrange-

instrūmentum, i, n. tool, instrument; furniture; provision; stock; dress; means; document.

instruo, xi, ctum, 3. v.a. to build, to construct; to stock; (mil.) to draw up; to set in order; to furnish; to direct, to instruct, to teach.

insuāvis, e, a. unpleasant.

insūdo, 1. v.n. to break out into a sweat.

insuēfactus, a, um, a. accustomed.

insuesco, ēvi, ētum, 3. v.n. & a. to become accustomed (to); to accustom.

insuētus, a, um, a. not accustomed to; unacquainted with; unusual.

insŭla, ae, f. island; house let off in flats.

insulsē, ad. insipidly; absurdly.

insulsĭtas, ātis, f. insipidity; absurdity.

insulsus, a, um, a. insipid; silly; absurd.

insulto, 1. v.n. & a. to leap at or upon; fig. insult; to deride.

insum, fui, esse, v.n. ir. to be in or upon; to dwell in; to belong to; to be involved in.

insūmo, mpsi, mptum, 3. v.a. to apply (to), to bestow (upon); to assume, to take.

insuo, ui, ūtum, 3. v.a. to sew (in) to; fig. to tack or add to.

insŭper, ad. above, overhead; fig. moreover; —, pr. over, above.

insŭpĕrābĭlis, e, a. insurmountable; fig. unconquerable; inevitable.

insurgo, rexi, rectum, 3. v.n. to rise; to rise up against; to grow in power.

insŭsurro, 1. v.n. & a. to whisper into or to; to suggest. [melt away.

intābesco, bui, 3. v.n. to pine away; to

intactus, a, um, a. untouched, intact; unattempted; chaste.

intāmĭnātus, a, um, a. unsullied, undefiled. [open.

intectus, a, um, a. uncovered; fig. frank,

intĕgellus, a, um, a. pretty safe.

intĕger, gra, grum, a. whole, entire; safe; healthful; fresh; undetermined; unbiassed, neutral; heartwhole; innocent; pure; upright;—**ab (de, ex) integro,** afresh, anew.

intĕgo, xi, ctum, 3. v.a. to cover.

intĕgrātio, ōnis, f. renewal.

intĕgrē, ad. wholly; honestly; correctly.

integrĭtas, ātis, f. soundness; honesty; chastity; correctness.

integro, 1. v.a. to renew; to recreate.

intĕgŭmentum, i, n. covering.

intellectus, ūs, m. understanding; perception; meaning.

intelligens, entis, a. capable of understanding; intelligent.

intelligenter, ad. intelligently.

intelligentia, ae, f. intellect, understanding.

intelligo, lexi, lectum, 3. v.a. to understand; to perceive.

intĕmĕrātus, a, um, a. undefiled; chaste.

intempĕrans, tis, a. immoderate, intemperate; dissolute.

intempĕranter, ad. without control.

intempĕrantia, ae, f. want of moderation, intemperance; insolence.

intempĕries, ēi, f. inclemency (of weather); tempest, violence.

intempestīvē, ad. unseasonably.

intempestīvus, a, um, a. unseasonable, inconvenient.

intempestus, a, um, a. unseasonable;—nox intempesta, the dead of night; fig. unhealthy.

intendo, di, tum & sum, 3. v.a. to stretch towards; to strain; to bend; fig. to apply; to design; to exert.

intentātus, a, um, a. untried, unattempted.

intentē, ad. attentively, intently.

intentio, ōnis, f. straining; intention; endeavour, effort.

intento, 1. v.a. to stretch out; to threaten.

intentus, a, um, p. & a. intent upon; eager; strict.

intĕpeo, ui, 2. v.n. to be warm.

intĕpesco, ui, 3. v.n. to become warm.

inter, pr. between, betwixt, among; in; during;—inter alia, among other things;—inter nos, between ourselves.

intercălāris, e, a. intercalary, inserted.

intercălārius, a, um, a. intercalary.

intercălo, 1. v.a. to insert; fig. to put off.

intercăpēdo, inis, f. interruption, pause.

intercēdo, cessi, cessum, 3. v.n. to come between, to intervene; to put a veto on; to interrupt; to go bail (for); to forbid; to oppose; to interfere.

interceptor, ōris, m. usurper, embezzler.

intercessio, ōnis, f. intervention; veto (of a tribune of the people).

intercessor, ōris, m. mediator; surety; hinderer; one who vetoes.

intercĭdo, cidi, 3. v.n. to fall out, to happen; to perish.

intercīdo, cīdi, cīsum, 3. v.a. to cut asunder; to divide; to destroy.

intercino, 3. v.a. to sing between.

intercĭpio, cēpi, ceptum, 3. v.a. to intercept; to steal; to interrupt; to hinder.

interclūdo, ūsi, ūsum, 3. v.a. to shut up, to cut off; to hinder; to blockade.

intercŏlumnium, ii, n. space between columns.

intercurro, cŭcurri & curri, cursum, 3. to run through or between; to intervene; to befall; to intercede.

intercurso, 1. v.n. to run between.

intercursus, ūs, m. intervention, interposition.

intercus, ŭtis, a. under the skin;—aqua intercus, dropsy.

interdīco, xi, ctum, 3. v.a. to interject, to forbid, to interdict; to deprive of.

interdictio, ōnis, f. prohibition.

interdictum, i, n. prohibition; provisional decree of the prætor.

interdiu, ad. by day. [meanwhile.

interdum, ad. sometimes, now and then;

intĕreā, ad. meanwhile; nevertheless.

intĕreo, ii, ĭtum, 4. v.n. to perish, to die; to be ruined; to cease. [between.

intĕrĕquĭto, 1. v.n. & a. to ride among or

interfector, ōris, m. slayer.

interfĭcio, fēci, fectum, 3. v.a. to kill, to slay; to destroy. [tween.

interfluo, fluxi, 3. v.n. & a. to flow be-

interfor, fātus sum, 1. v. dep. to interrupt in speaking; to break in upon a conversation.

interfundo, fūdi, fūsum, 3. v.a. to pour or spread between;—interfūsus, a, um, p. & a. intervening; suffused.

intĕrim, ad. meanwhile; nevertheless.

intĕrĭmo, ēmi, em(p)tum, 3. v.a. to do away with; to kill; to destroy.

intĕrior, ius, ōris, a. inner, more inward; more hidden; deeper.

intĕrĭtus, ūs, m. destruction; ruin.

interjăceo, 2. v.n. to lie between.

interjacio, v. interjicio.

interjectio, ōnis, f. interjection.

interjectus, ūs, m. interposition.

interjĭcio, jēci, jectum, 3. v.a. to throw between; to intermix.

interlĭno, lēvi, lĭtum, 3. to smear at intervals; to erase.

interlūceo, xi, 2. v.n. to shine or glitter forth; fig. to appear.

interlūnium, ii, n. space between the disappearance of the old moon and the appearance of the new.

interluo, 3. v.a. to flow between.

intermĭnātus, a, um, a. unlimited.

interminor, atus, 1. v. dep. to threaten.

intermisceo, scui, xtum & stum, 2. v.a. to intermix.

intermissio, ōnis, f. intermission, interruption; ceasing.

intermitto, mīsi, missum, 3. v.a. & n. to leave off; to discontinue.

intermŏrior, tuus sum, 3. v. dep. to swoon.

intermundia, ōrum, n. pl. distances or spaces between divers worlds.

internascor, nātus sum, 3. v.n. dep. to grow between or among.

internĕcīnus, a, um, v. internecivus.

internĕcio, ōnis, f. massacre; extermination.   [structive.

internĕcīvus, a, um, a. murderous, de-

internōdium, ii, n. the space between joints.

internosco, nōvi, nōtum, 3. v.a. to discern, to distinguish between.

internuntius, i, m. mediator, go-between.

internus, a, um, a. inward, internal; domestic; civil.

interpellātio, ōnis, f. interruption in speaking; hindrance.

interpellātor, ōris, m. interrupter; disturber; hinderer.

interpello, 1. v.a. to interrupt in speaking; to importune; to disturb; to appeal to.   [polate.

interpŏlo, 1. v.a. to furbish up; to inter-

interpōno, pŏsui, pŏsitum, 3. v.a. to put, to lay or set between; to interpose; to insert; to introduce.

interpŏsĭtio, ōnis, f. insertion.

interprĕs, ĕtis, c. explainer, interpreter; go-between, mediator; soothsayer.

interprĕtātio, ōnis, f. interpretation; meaning.

interprĕ or, ātus sum, 1. v. dep. to interpret; .to explain; to decide; to esteem, to judge.   [tuate.

interpungo, nxi, nctum, 3. v.a. to punc-

interquiesco, ēvi, ētum, 3. v.n. to pause.

interregnum, i, n. space between two reigns, interregnum.

interrex, rēgis, m. regent, one who holds office between the demise of an official and the appointment of a successor.

interrĭtus, a, um, a. undaunted, bold.

interrŏgātio, ōnis, f. question; inquiry; interrogation; argument.

interrŏgātīvus, a, um, a. interrogative.

interrŏgo, 1. v.a. to ask, to question; (law) to examine.

nterrumpo, rūpi, ruptum, 3. v.a. to break asunder; to separate; to interrupt.

interruptē, ad. interruptedly.

intersæpio, psi, ptum, 4. v.a. to hedge in; to shut off; to separate.

interscindo, ĭdi, issum, 3. v.a. to cut or hew asunder; to separate.

intersĕro, sĕrui, sertum, 3. v.a. to put between; to insert.   [between.

intersĕro, sēvi, sĭtum, 3. v.a. to plant

intersum, fui, esse, v.n. ir. to be or lie between, to be in the midst; to be present; to take part in; to be different;—interest, it is of interest or importance.   [twine; to intersperse.

intertexo, xui, xtum, 3. v.a. to inter-

intertrīmentum, i, n. dross, refuse, detritus; loss, damage.

intervallum, i, n. space between, interval; distance; respite; fig. difference.

intervĕnio, vēni, ventum, 4. v.n. to come between; to intervene; to interfere; to happen.   [ing; mediation.

interventus, ūs, m. intervention; happen-

interverto, 3. v.a. to embezzle; to cheat.

intestābĭlis, e, a. fig. detestable, abominable.

intestātus, a, um, a. that has made no will, intestate;—intestato, without a will.

intestīna, ōrum, n. pl. entrails, bowels.

intestīnus, a, um, a. inward, internal; fig. domestic, civil.

intexo, xui, xtum, 3. v.a. to inweave; to embroider; to intermingle.

intibum, v. intubum.

intĭmē, ad. most intimately; heartily.

intĭmus, a, um, a. inmost, innermost; most secret; most intimate.

intŏlĕrābĭlis, e, a. intŏlerandus, a, um, a. insupportable, intolerable.

intŏlĕrans, tis, a. impatient, intolerant; intolerable.

intŏlĕranter, ad. intolerably, excessively.

intŏlĕrantia, ae, f. impatience; insolence.

intŏno, ui, 1. v.n. & a. to thunder; to resound; to thunder forth something; to thunder at or upon.

intonsus, a, um, a. unshorn; rough, rude.

intorqueo, torsi, tortum, 2. v.a. to twist, to tùrn round, to sprain; to distort; to wrap round; to brandish; to throw.

intrā, ad. & pr. within; within the compass of; under, fewer than.

intractābĭlis, e, a. unmanageable, intractable.

intrĕmo, ui, 3. v.n. to tremble.

intrĕpĭdē, ad. fearlessly.

intrĕpĭdus, a, um, a. undaunted, intrepid; without disturbance.

intrinsĕcus, ad. on the inside.

intrō, ad. within, into, inside.

intro, 1. v.a. to go into; to enter; to pierce (into), to penetrate.

intrōdūco, xi, ctum, 3. v.a. to lead or bring in; fig. to introduce; to maintain (a thesis).   [enter.

intrŏeo, īvī & ii, ĭtum, 4. v.n. to go into, to

intrōgrĕdior, gressus, 3. v. dep. to enter.

intrōĭtus, ūs, m. going in, entry; passage; beginning; introduction.

intrōmitto, mīsi, missum, 3. v.a. to send into; to admit.   [inside; within.

introrsum, introrsus, ad. towards the

introspĭcio, spexi, spectum, 3. v.a. to examine; to inspect.

intŭbum, i, n., **intŭbus, i,** m. endive.

intueor, ĭtus sum, 2. v. dep. to look at or upon; to consider; to take heed; to reverence.

intŭmesco, mui, 3. v.n. to swell up, to rise; to increase, to grow; to become angry.

intŭmŭlātus, a, um, a. unburied.

inturbĭdus, a, um, a. undisturbed, quiet.

intus, ad. inside, within; at home.

intūtus, a, um, a. defenceless; unsafe.

inŭla, ae, f. elecampane; starwort.

inultŭş, a, um, a. unrevenged; unpunished; unhurt; scot-free.

inumbro, 1. v.a. to cast a shadow.

inundātio, ōnis, f. inundation.

inundo, 1. v.a. & n. to overflow, to inundate, to abound.

inungo, xi, ctum, 3. v.a. to anoint.

inurbānē, ad. boorishly.

inurbānus, a, um, a. rustic; unmannerly.

inŭro, ussi, ustum, 3. v.a. to burn in (with a hot iron); to brand.

ĭnūsĭtātē, ad. unusually.

ĭnūsĭtātus, a, um, a. unusual.   [ful.

inūtĭlis, e, a. useless; unprofitable; hurt-

inūtĭlĭtas, ātis, f. hurtfulness, injuriousness.

invādo, si, sum, 3. v.n. to go into; to invade; to rush into; to assail; to take possession of, to usurp; to seize; to attack; to accost, to address.

invălesco, lui, 3. v.n. to become strong or stronger; to increase, to prevail.

invălĭdus, a, um, a. infirm, weak, feeble; inefficient.   [invective.

invectio, ōnis, f. bringing in, importing;

invĕho, vexi, vectum, 3. v.a. & n. to carry, to bring into; to import;—**invehi,** to ride into; to attack; to enter; to inveigh against.

invĕnio, vēni, ventum, 4. v.a. to invent; to contrive; to find; to discover; to procure.

inventio, ōnis, f. invention; faculty of invention.

inventor, ōris, m. inventor; author, contriver.

inventrix, īcis, f. inventress.

inventum, i, n. invention, device.

invĕnustus, a, um, a. ungraceful; unhappy (in love).

invĕrēcundus, a, um, a. shameless, impudent.

invergo, 3. v.a. to turn to; to pour (upon).

inversio, ōnis, f. inversion.

inverto, verti, versum, 3. v.a. to turn upside down; to overthrow; to pervert; to change; to alter.

investĭgātio, ōnis, f. investigation.

investĭgātor, oris, m. investigator.

investĭgo, 1. v.a. to trace out; to search into, to investigate.

invĕtĕrasco, āvi, 3. v.n. to grow old; to become inveterate.

invĕtĕro, 1. v.a. & n. to keep till a thing be old; to become old; to acquire durability; to keep; to endure.

invicem, ad. by turns, alternately; reciprocally.   [vincible.

invictus, a, um, a. unconquered; in-

invĭdeo, vĭdi, vīsum, 2. v.a. to envy, to grudge; to hate; to hinder; to refuse.

invidentia, ae, f. envy.   [malice.

invĭdia, ae, f. envy, jealousy; spite;

invĭdiōsē, ad. spitefully.

invĭdiōsus, a, um, a. envious; envied, hateful; malicious; spiteful.

invĭdus, a, um, a. envious.   [intent upon.

invĭgĭlo, 1. v.n. to watch over; to be

inviŏlābilis, e, a. sacrosanct, imperishable.

inviŏlātus, a, um, a. unhurt, inviolate; inviolable.

invĭsĭtātus, a, um, a. unvisited, unseen.

inviso, si, sum, 3. v.a. to look after; to view; to go to visit.

invīsus, a, um, a. unseen; hateful, hated.

invītāmentum, i, n. inducement.

invītātio, ōnis, f. invitation.

invītē, ad. unwillingly.

invīto, 1. v.a. to invite; to entertain; to allure, to entice; to summon; challenge.   [reluctant.

invītus, a, um, a. against one's will,

invius, a, um, a. pathless; impassable.

invŏco, 1. v.a. to call upon; to invoke; to call by name; to implore.

invŏlo, 1. v.n. to fly into or at, to rush upon; to attack; to seize.

invŏlucrum, i, n. wrapper, case, envelope.

involvo, volvi, vŏlūtum, 3. v.a. to wrap in, to cover, to involve; to envelop; to roll upon; to entangle.   [evidence.

invulgo, 1. v.a. to publish; to give

invulnĕrātus, a, um, a. unwounded.

iō, interj. oh! come! hurrah!

ipse, a, um, ipsīus, ipsi, pn. he, she, it; self, very, identical;—**ipse dixit,** he himself has said it, i.e. a man's personal assertion;—**ipso facto,** by that very deed or fact;—**ipsissima verba,** the exact words.

ira, ae, f. anger, wrath, rage.

īrācundia, ae, f. irascibility; **wrath,** passion.

īrācundus, a, um, a. irascible, angry.

Irascor, ātus sum, 3. v. dep. to be angry or in a rage.

Irātus, a, um, p. & a. angry; offended.

Iris, ĭdis, f. rainbow; (plant) flag.

Irōnĭa, ae, f. irony.

irrēlĭgatus, a, um, a. unbound.

irrēlĭgiōsus, a, um, a. irreligious, impious.

irrĕmeābĭlis, e, a. from which one cannot return.

irrĕpărābĭlis, e, a. irreparable, irrecoverable. [covered.

irrĕpertus, a, um, a. not found, undis-

irrēpo, psi, 3. v.n. to creep in or into; fig. to steal into; to insinuate oneself.

irrĕprĕhensus, a, um, a. blameless.

irrĕquiētus, a, um, a. disturbed, restless, troubled.

irrēsŏlūtus, a, um, a. unloosed.

irrētio, īvi or **ii, ītum,** 4. v.a. to entangle; to catch in a net.

irrētortus, a, um, a. not turned back.

irrĕvĕrentĭa, ae, f. irreverence.

irrĕvŏcābĭlis, e, a. irrevocable.

irrĭdeo, rīsi, rīsum, 2. v.n. & a. to laugh at; to mock, to scorn.

Irrĭdĭcŭlē, ad. without wit.

irrĭgo, 1. v.a. to water, to irrigate; to inundate; to wet, to moisten; to diffuse. [wet.

irrĭguus, a, um, a. watering; watered;

irrīsio, ōnis, f. mocking, mockery.

irrīsor, ōris, m. mocker, scoffer.

irrīsus, ūs, m. mockery, derision; laughing-stock.

irrĭtābĭlis, e, a. irritable, waspish.

irrītāmen, ĭnis, irrītāmentum, i, n. incitement. [appetite.

irrītātio, ōnis, f. incitement, provocation;

irrīto, 1. v.a. to provoke, to enrage; to irritate. [effect; vain, useless.

irrītus, a, um, a. invalid, void; of no

irrŏgātio, ōnis, f. infliction.

irrŏgo, 1. v.a. to impose, to inflict.

irrōro, 1. v.a. to wet with dew; to besprinkle, to wet.

irrŭbesco, bui, 3. v.n. to grow red.

irrumpo, rūpi, ruptum, 3. v.a. & n. to break or burst or rush into; to interrupt; to attack.

irruo, ui, 3. v.n. & a. to rush or run against; to run hastily in; to attack; to seize on.

irruptio, ōnis, f. irruption, invasion.

is, ea, id, ejus, pn. he, she, it; this, that; **—id genus omne,** all that class of people. [that.

iste, a, ud, istīus, pn. this or that of yours;

isthmus, i, m. isthmus; strait.

istic, aec, oc, (uc), pn. this same.

istic, ad. there; therein.

istinc, ad. thence; thereof.

istĭusmŏdi, a. indecl. of that kind, such.

istō, istūc, ad. to the place where you are; thereinto.

ĭtă, ad. so, thus; even so; yes.

ĭtăquĕ, c. and so; therefore, consequently.

item, ad. just so, likewise; also.

iter, ĭtĭnĕris, n. going, walk; road, way, journey; march; fig. custom, method.

ĭtĕrātio, ōnis, f. repetition.

ĭtĕro, 1. v.a. to do a second time, to repeat; to renew.

ĭtĕrum, ad. again, a second time.

ĭtĭdem, ad. in the same manner, likewise.

ĭtĭnĕrārĭum, ii, n. book of travels.

ĭtio, ōnis, f. going.

ĭto, 1. v.n. to go.

ĭtus, ūs, m. going, gait; departure.

ixia (mod. hort.), ixia.

Jăceo, cui, 2. v.n. to lie; to be situated; to lie sick; to be still; to lie idle; to lie dead; to lie in ruins.

jăcio, jēci, jactum, 3. v.a. to throw, to cast, to hurl; to throw away; to throw up; to utter; to build, to erect; to produce.

jactanter, ad. boastfully.

jactantĭa, ae, f. boasting, ostentation.

jactātio, ōnis, f. shaking; tossing; gestures; fig. boasting; conceit.

jacto, 1. v.a. to throw, to hurl; to toss; to give out; to utter; to boast (of); to torment; to disturb;—**se jactare,** to boast.

jactūra, ae, f. throwing (away, overboard); loss, damage.

jactus, ūs, m. throwing, throw, cast.

jăcŭlātor, ōris, m. darter, shooter.

jăcŭlor, ātus, 1. v. dep. to dart; to throw the dart; to hurl at; to aim at.

jăcŭlum, i, n. dart, javelin, fishing-net.

jam, ad. now, already, presently; ere now; at last.

jamdūdum, ad. long ago; forthwith.

jamprĭdem, ad. some white since.

jānĭtor, ōris, m. door-keeper, porter.

jānua, ae, f. door, house-door; entrance.

Jānŭārĭus, i, m. January.

Jānus, i, m. a Roman god; arcade; arched passage where the moneychangers had their stand (at Rome).

jasmīnum (mod. hort.), jasmine.

jĕcur, jecŏris, jĕcĭnŏris, n. liver.

jējūnē, ad. meagrely, dryly. [poorness.

jējūnĭum, ii, n. fasting; hunger; fig.

jējūnus, a, um, a. fasting; hungry; fig. dry, barren; insignificant; dry; poor, contemptible.

jentācŭlum, i, n. breakfast.

jŏcātio, ōnis, f. joke, joking.

jŏcor, ātus, I. v.n. & a. dep. to jest, to joke.

jŏcōsē, ad. jestingly.

jŏcōsus, a, um, a. jocose, humorous, droll.

jŏcŭlāria, ium, n. pl. jokes, jesting.

jŏcŭlāris, e, a. laughable.

jŏcŭlor, I. v.a. dep. to jest; to joke.

jŏcŭlus, i, m. a small jest.

jŏcus, i, m. jest, joke; pastime, sport.

jŭba, ae, f. mane of a horse; crest (of a helmet).

jŭbar, ăris, n. radiance of the heavenly bodies; brightness; sunshine; luminary.

jŭbeo, jussi, jussum, 2. v.a. to order, to bid, to command; to decree;—**salvere jubeo**, to bid welcome.

jūcundē, ad. agreeably, pleasantly.

jūcundĭtas, ātis, f. pleasantness, delight; mirth.   [joyful.

jūcundus, a, um, a. pleasant, agreeable;

jūdex, ĭcis, c. judge; arbitrator; umpire.

jūdĭcātio, ōnis, f. judicial investigation; judgment.

jūdĭcātum, i, n. decision; verdict.

jūdĭciālis, e, a. judicial, of the courts.

jūdĭciārius, a, um, a. judiciary, of the courts.

jūdĭcium, ii, n. judicial investigation; judgment; verdict; suit; understanding; opinion; discernment.

jūdĭco, I. v.a. to judge, to give sentence; to condemn; to award; to suppose; to decide.

jŭgālis, e, a. yoked together; nuptial.

jŭgĕrum, i, n. acre of land.

jŭgis, e, a. continual, perpetual, perennial.

jŭglans, dis, f. walnut-tree.

jŭgo, I. v.a. to marry; to join, to connect.

jŭgŭlo, I. v.a. to cut the throat, to kill; to butcher.

jŭgŭlum, i, n., jŭgŭlus, i, m. collar-bone; throat.

jŭgum, i, n. yoke (for oxen), collar; team; pair (of horses); ridge (of a mountain);—**sub jugum mittere,** to send under the yoke (as a sign of defeat).

jūmentum, i, n. beast of burden.

junceus, a, um, a. made of rushes.

junctūra, ae, f. juncture, joint; fig. consanguinity; combination.

juncus, i, m. rush.

jungo, nxi, nctum, 3. v.a. to yoke, to harness; to join; to clasp (hands); —**jungere amnem ponte,** to span a river with a bridge.

jūnior, a. younger.

jūnĭpĕrus, i, f. juniper.

Jūnĭus, ii, m. June.

jūre, ad. justly, rightly.

jurgium, i, n. quarrel, dispute.

jurgo, I. v.a. to reproach, to blame, to quarrel.

jūrĭdĭcālis, e, a. pertaining to law.

jūrisconsultus, i, m. lawyer.

jūrisdictio, ōnis, f. jurisdiction, legal authority.

jūrispĕrītus, i, m. lawyer.

jūrisprūdentia, ae, f. science of law.

jūro, i, v.n. & a. to swear, to take an oath; to conspire.

jūs, jūris, n. broth, soup, sauce.

jūs, jūris, n. law, right; equity; reason; authority; court of justice;—**sui juris (homo),** (a man) having authority over himself, i.e. free, independent;— **jus gentium,** international law.

jusjūrandum, i, n. oath.

jussum, i, n. order, command; decree of the people.

jussu, abl. of jussus, by order of.

justē, ad. rightly, justly, lawfully.

justitia, ae, f. justice; equity; righteousness.

justitium, ii, n. cessation of business in the courts; vacation; public mourning.

justus, a, um, a. just, equitable, honest; lawful; legitimate; well grounded; proper; right; regular; impartial;— **justa, ōrum,** n. pl. funeral rites.

jŭvĕnālis, e, a. youthful, juvenile.

jŭvĕnālĭter, ad. youthfully; rashly.

jŭvenca, ae, f. young cow, heifer; girl.

jŭvencus, i, m. young bullock; young man.

jŭvĕnesco, nui, 3. v.n. to grow up; to grow young again; to grow strong.

jŭvĕnīlis, e, a. youthful.

jŭvĕnis, is, a. young, youthful; —, is, c. youth, young man or woman.

jŭventa, ae, f. youth, young age.

jŭventas, ātis, f. youth.

jŭventus, ūtis, f. youth, young folk, warriors.

jŭvo, jūvi, jūtum, I. v.a. & n. to help, to aid, to assist; to delight, to please; to profit;—**juvat,** it delights.

juxtā, pr. hard by, near to; —, ad. close; alike; equally; — **ac,** equally as.

Kal. = Kalendæ.

Kălendae, f. pl. the 1st day of the month.

Kălendārium, ii, n. account-book.

kerria (mod. hort.), Jew's-mallow.

knĭphōfia (mod. hort.), red-hot poker.

L = 50.

lăbasco, 3. v.n. to totter; *fig.* to waver.

lăbĕfăcio, fēci, factum, 3. v.a. to loosen; to shake; to tamper with; to overthrow; to undermine.

lăbĕfacto, 1. v.a. to shake; to overthrow; *fig.* to weaken; to destroy.

lăbellum, i, n. little lip; bathing-tub.

lābes, is, f. downfall; ruin; fault; stain, blemish, dishonour.

lăbia, ae, f., **lăbium, ii,** n. lip.

lăbo, 1. v.n. to totter, to fall, to decay; to fail; to waver.

lăbor, ōris, m. labour, toil, exertion; hardship, distress.

lābor, psus, 3. v.n. dep. to slide *or* glide down; to fall down; to drop; to decay, to err.

lăbōrĭfer, a, um, a. painstaking.

lăbōriōsus, a, um, a. laborious, painstaking; toilsome; burdened with toil.

lăbōro, 1. v.n. & a. to labour, to take pains; to strive; to be sick; to be oppressed *or* troubled; to be in danger; to wo k (at).

lăbos, v. **labor.**

lābrum, i, tub; bath; basin.

labrum, i, n. lip; edge, margin (of a vessel, etc.).

lābrusca, ae, f. wild vine.

lăburnum (mod. hort.), laburnum, golden rain.

lăbyrinthēus, a, um, a. mazy.

labyrinthus, i, m. labyrinth, maze.

lac, lactis, n. milk; milk-white colour; juice.

lăcĕr, a, um, a. mangled, torn to pieces; rending.

lăcĕrātio, onis, f. mangling; tearing.

lăcerna, ae, f. cloak.

lăcĕro, 1. v.a. to tear to pieces, to mangle; to asperse; to torture.

lăcerta, ae, f. lizard. [robust.

lăcertōsus, a, um, a. muscular, brawny,

lăcertus, i, m. lizard; muscular part of the arm; muscle, strength.

lăcesso, īvi & ii, ītum, 3. v.a. to excite, to provoke, to exasperate; to challenge; to urge; to call forth.

lăcinia, ae, f. flap (of a garment); fringe.

lăciniōsus, a, um, fringed; ragged at the edges.

lacrima, ae, f. tear.

lacrĭmābilis, e, a. lamentable, mournful.

lacrĭmo, 1. v.n. & a., **lacrimor, ātus,** 1. v. dep. to shed tears, to weep.

lacrĭmōsus, a, um, a. tearful, weeping; doleful.

lacrŭma, etc., v. **lacrima,** etc. [juicy.

lactens, entis, a. sucking; suckling;

lactes, ium, f. pl. intestines.

lacteus, a, um, a. milky; milk-white;— **circulus** —, Milky Way.

lacto, 1. v.a. to suckle.

lactūca, ae, f. lettuce.

lăcūna, ae, f. pool; cleft; chasm.

lăcūnar, āris, n. carved and gilded ceiling.

lăcus, ūs, m. basin, tank; lake; vat.

lædo, si, sum, 3. v.a. to hurt; to injure; to annoy.

læna, ae, f. lined cloak.

lætābilis, e, a. joyful.

laetē, ad. joyfully.

lætĭfico, 1. v.a. to cheer, to gladden.

lætĭficus, a, um, a. cheering; glad.

lætĭtia, ae, f. joy; gladness. [joyful.

lætor, ātus, 1. v.n. dep. to rejoice, to be

lætus, a, um, a. joyful, cheerful, glad; fortunate; abundant; beautiful; rich.

læva, ae, f. left hand.

lævis, v. **levis.** [lucky.

lævus, a, um, a. left; unfavourable, un

lăgēna, ae, f. flask; bottle. [to wash.

lambo, bi, 3. v.a. to lick; *fig.* to flow by,

lāmentābilis, e, a. doleful; lamentable.

lāmentātio, ōnis, f. lamentation, wailing.

lāmentor, ātus, 1. v.n. & a. dep. to lament; to bewail.

lāmentum, i, n. wailing, lamentation.

lămia, ae, f. witch; sorceress.

lāmina, lamna, ae, f. plate, leaf; veneer; blade (of a sword *or* saw); piece of money.

lampas, ădis, f. torch; lamp.

lāna, ae, f. wool; soft hair; down.

lānātus, a, um, a. woolly.

lancea, ae, f. light spear, lance.

lāneus, a, um, a. woollen. [weary.

langueo, 2. v.n. to be languid; to grow

languesco, gui, 3. v.n. to become faint *or* languid *or* weak.

languidē, ad. feebly, languidly.

languidus, a, um, a. languid, faint, weak; ill; dull; sluggish.

languor, ōris, m. faintness, feebleness; languor; dulness.

lăniātus, ūs, m. mangling; tearing.

lăniēna, ae, f. butcher's shop.

lānĭficium, ii, n. spinning wool.

lānĭficus, a, um, a. wool-working.

lānĭger, a, um, a. wool-bearing, fleecy.

lănio, 1. v.a. to tear to pieces, to mangle, to lacerate.

lănista, ae, m. fencing-master; *fig.* instigator; assassin.

lănius, ii, m. butcher.

lanterna, ae, f. lantern, lamp.

lānūgĭnōsus, a, um, a. downy.

lānūgo, ĭnis, f. woolliness, down.

lanx, lancis, f. plate, dish; scale of a balance; balance.

lăpăthum, i, n., lăpăthus, i, m. *or* f. sorrel.
lăpĭcīdīnae, ārum, f. pl. stone quarry.
lăpĭdātio, ōnis, f. throwing of stones.
lăpĭdeus, a, um, a. of stone; stony.
lăpĭdo, 1. v.a. to throw stones at; to stone;—lapidat, it rains stones.
lăpĭdōsus, a, um, a. full of stones, stony; *fig.* hard as stone.
lăpillus, i, m. little stone, pebble; precious stone, jewel; marble.
lăpĭs, ĭdis, m. stone; stone statue; milestone; landmark; precious stone.
lappa, ae, f. bur.
lapsio, ōnis, f. sliding; *fig.* failure.
lapso, 1. v.n. to slide, to slip, to stumble.
lapsus, a, um, a. ruined.
lapsus, ūs, m. gliding, sliding; flowing; fall; *fig.* error, fault.
lăqueăr(e), āris, n. fretted ceiling.
lăqueātus, a, um, a. panelled.
lăqueus, i, m. noose, snare; *fig.* trap.
lar, lăris, m. tutelary household god; hearth, home.   [ally.
largē, ad. abundantly; bountifully, liber-
largior, ītus, 4. v. dep. to give bountifully, to bribe, to bestow; to grant, to permit.
largĭtas, ātis, f. abundance; munificence.
largĭter, ad. plentifully; liberally; much.
largĭtio, ōnis, f. bountiful largess; bribery.
largītor, ōris, m. liberal giver; spendthrift; briber.   [ful, liberal.
largus, a, um, a. large; plentiful; bounti-
lārĭdum, i, n., lardum, i, n. fat of bacon, lard.
lărix. ĭcis, f. larch-tree.
larva, ae, f. ghost, mask.
larvātus, a, um, a. bewitched.
lascīvia, ae, f. playfulness; wantonness, lasciviousness.
lascīvio, ii, ītum, 4. v.n. to be wanton; to sport; to be insolent.
lascīvus, a, um, a. wanton; frolicsome; sportive; impudent; lascivious, lewd.
lassĭtūdo, ĭnis, f. faintness, weariness.
lasso, 1. v.a. & n. to tire, to weary; to be weary.   [drooping.
lassus, a, um, a. languid, weary, tired;
lātē, ad. widely, far and wide.
lătebra, ae, f. hiding-place, retreat; *fig.* subterfuge.   [porous.
lătebrōsus, a, um, a. full of lurking places;
lătens, entis, p. & a. hidden, secret; unknown.
lătenter, ad. privily.
lăteo, ui, 2. v.n. to lie hid, to lurk; to escape the notice of.
lăter, ĕris, m. brick, tile.
lătĕrāria, ae f. brick-kiln.
lătercŭlus, i small brick or tile.

lătĕrĭcius, a, um, a. made of bricks.
lātex, ĭcis, m. (any) liquid; springwater; juice; wine; oil.
lathўrus (mod. hort.), sweet-pea.
lătĭbŭlum, i, n. hiding-place, den.
lātĭclāvius, a, um, a. wearing a broad purple stripe (a sign of high rank).
Lătīnē, ad. in Latin.
lătīnĭtas, ātis, f. pure Latin style, Latinity.
Lătīnus, a, um, a. Latin.   [law).
lătio, ōnis, f. introduction (of a bill *or*
lătĭto, 1. v.n. to lurk, to be hid.
lătĭtūdo, ĭnis, f. breadth, width; extent, compass.
lātŏmiae, v. lautumiae.   [a law).
lātor, ōris, m. mover *or* proposer (of
lătrātor, ōris, m. barker, dog.
lătrātus, ūs, m. barking.
latro, 1. v.n. & a. to bark; to bark at.
latro, ōnis, m. highwayman, brigand.
lătrōcĭnium, ii, n. highway-robbery; theft; piracy; roguery, fraud; band of robbers.   [highway.
lătrōcĭnor, ātus, 1. v. dep. to rob on the
lătruncŭlus, i, m. highwayman; robber.
lātus, a, um, a. broad, wide; spacious; *fig.* diffuse.
lătus, ĕris, n. side, flank; waist; lungs; (poet.) body;—(milit.) **a latere**, on the flank.
laudābĭlis, e, a. praiseworthy, laudable.
laudābĭlĭter, ad. laudably.
laudātio, ōnis, f. praising, praise; eulogy.
laudātor, ōris, m. praiser;—**laudator temporis acti**, an admirer of the past.
laudātus, a, um, a. praiseworthy, excellent.
laudo, 1. v.a. to praise, to extol; to pronounce a funeral oration; to quote.
laurea, ae, f. laurel-tree; laurel wreath *or* branch; *fig.* triumph.
laureātus, a, um, a. laurelled, laureate;—**laureatæ litteræ**, a despatch reporting a victory.
laureŏla, ae, f. laurel crown; *fig.* triumph.
laureus, a, um, a. laurel . . .
laurĭger, a, um, a. crowned with laurel.
laurus, i, f. bay-tree, laurel; laurel crown; triumph.
laurustīnus (mod. hort.), laurustinus.
laus, laudis, f. praise; glory, fame; merit;—**laus deo**, glory be to God.
lautē, ad. elegantly; finely; cleverly.
lautia, orum, n. pl. hospitality extended to public guests.
lautĭtia, ae, f. splendour, elegance; magnificence of living.   [prison.
lautŭmiae, ārum, f. pl. stone-quarry,
lautus, a, um, a. neat, elegant; rich, grand; glorious; clever.
lavandŭla (mod. hort.), lavender.

lăvātio, ōnis, f. washing; bathing; bath; bathing-place.

lăvo, lāvi & lăvāvi, lautum, lăvātum & lōtum, 1. & 3. v.a. & n. to wash; to bathe; to sprinkle; to wet.

laxāmentum, i, n. respite; alleviation.

laxē, ad. widely, loosely; *fig.* freely.

laxĭtas, ātis, f. roominess.

laxo, 1. v.a. & n. to expand, to extend; to open; to slacken; to release; to relax; to moderate; to relieve.

laxus, a, um, a. wide, loose; roomy; slack; open; lax.

lea, ae, leæna, ae, f. lioness. [hand basin.

lĕbes, ētis, m. kettle, caldron; wash-

lectīca, ae, f. litter; sedan.

lectīcārius, i, m. sedan-bearer, chairman.

lectio, ōnis, f. gathering; reading (aloud); perusal.

lectisternium, ii, n. feast offered to the gods (in which their images were placed on couches before tables covered with viands).

lectĭto, 1. v.a. to read often *or* with eagerness.

lector, ōris, m. reader.

lectŭlus, i, m. small bed or couch.

lectus, a, um, a. select; choice, excellent;—lectus, i, m. couch, bridal-bed.

legalis, e, a. pertaining to the law.

lēgātio, ōnis, f. embassy.

lēgātum, i, n. bequest, legacy.

lēgātus, i, m. ambassador, legate; deputy.

lēgĭfer, a, um, a. law-giving.

lēgio, ōnis, f. Roman legion; army.

lēgĭōnārius, a, um, a. of a legion, legionary.

lēgislātor, ōris, m. lawgiver.

lēgĭtĭmē, ad. lawfully; properly.

ēgĭtĭmus, a, um, a. lawful, right; legitimate; real, genuine; just; meet.

lēgiuncŭla, ae, f. small legion.

lēgo, 1. v.a. to send as ambassador; to choose as deputy; to bequeath.

lĕgo, lēgi, lectum, 3. v.a. to gather; to choose; to furl; to traverse; to read; to survey; to observe; to steal;— legere oram, to coast (by).

lēgŭlēius, i, m. pettifogging lawyer.

lēgūmen, ĭnis, n. pulse, leguminous plant.

lembus, i, m. pinnace, cutter.

lemma, ătis, n. theme; subject; the title of an epigram.

lemniscus, i, m. a ribbon attached to a victor's crown. [the dead.

lĕmŭres, um, m. pl. shades *or* ghosts of

lēna, ae, f. procuress; seductress.

lēnē, ad. softly, mildly, gently.

lēnīmen, ĭnis, n. soothing remedy; solace.

lēnīmentum, i, n. alleviation.

lēnio, īvi & ii, ītum, 4. v.a. & n. to mitigate; to allay, to pacify; to ease.

lēnis, e, a. smooth, soft, mild, gentle, easy, calm.

lēnĭtas, ātis, f. smoothness, softness, gentleness, mildness.

lēnĭter, ad. softly, gently, etc.

lēno, ōnis, m. pander.

lēnōcinium, ii, n. pandering; *fig.* allurement, enticement; cajolery.

lēnōcinor, ātus, 1. v. dep. to cajole; to forward, to serve.

lens, tis, f. lentil.

lentē, ad. slowly; leisurely; calmly; phlegmatically. [slacken.

lentesco, 3. v.n. to become pliant; *fig.* to

lentīgo, ĭnis, f. freckles.

lentiscus, i, m. mastich-tree.

lentĭtūdo, ĭnis, f. slowness; *fig.* dulness.

lento, i, v.a. to bend, to ply.

lentus, a, um, a. pliant; tough; clinging; slow; lazy; calm; backward in paying; prolonged; phlegmatic.

lēnuncŭlus, i, m. skiff.

leo, ōnis, m. lion (also a constellation).

leōnīnus, a, um, a. of a lion; like a lion.

leontopŏdium (mod. hort.), edelweiss.

lĕpĭdē, ad. pleasantly; prettily; smartly.

lepĭdium (mod. hort.), cress.

lĕpĭdus, a, um, a. pleasant; pretty; elegant; dainty; merry; witty.

lĕpor, lĕpos, ōris, m. pleasantness; grace; mirth; wit; humour.

lepræ, ārum, f. pl. leprosy.

lĕpus, ōris, m. hare.

lĕpuscŭlus, i, m. young hare, leveret.

lētālis, e, a. deadly, fatal, mortal.

Lēthæus, a, um, a. of Lethe; causing forgetfulness.

lēthargus, i, m. drowsiness, lethargy.

Lēthe, es, f. Lethe, the river of forgetfulness.

lētĭfer, a, um, a. deadly; mortal.

lēto, 1. v.a. to kill, to slay.

lētum, i, n. death; *fig.* ruin. [drop.

leucōjum (mod. hort.), summer snow-

lĕvāmen, ĭnis, n. alleviation, solace.

lĕvāmentum, i, n. alleviation, mitigation, consolation. [tion.

lĕvātio, ōnis, f. alleviation, relief; diminu-

lĕvis, e, a. light; swift; small; trifling; easy; gentle; capricious; false; light-minded; inconstant.

lēvis e, a. smooth; polished; beardless; bright; spruce.

lĕvĭtas, ātis, f. lightness; agility; *fig.* fickleness; shallowness.

lēvĭtas, ātis, f. smoothness, fluency.

lĕvĭter, ad. lightly; slightly, a little.

lĕvo, 1. v.a. to lighten; to ease; to lift; to help; to lessen; to make easy.

lēvo, 1. v.a. to smooth; to polish.

lex, lēgis, f. law; rule; principle; good order; condition;—**lex talionis**, the law of retaliation, an eye for an eye.

lībāmen, ĭnis, lībāmentum, ī, n. drink-offering; first-fruits.

lībella, ae, f. farthing; water-level.

lībellus, ī, m. little book; journal; memorial; petition; libel; pamphlet; brief.

lībens, p. & a. willing; joyful.

lībenter, ad. willingly; cheerfully, gladly.

lībĕr, a, um, a. free; unimpeded; void of; liberal; at leisure; frank, free-spoken; licentious; unbiassed.

Lībĕr, ī, m. Bacchus; wine.   [work.

līber, brī, m. inner bark of a tree; book;

lībĕrālis, e, a. gentlemanlike; well-bred; liberal; open-handed; generous; lavish.

lībĕrālĭtas, ātis, f. nobleness, kindness; frankness; liberality; gift, present.

lībĕrālĭter, ad. like a gentleman; bountifully, liberally.

lībĕrātio, ōnis, f. (law) acquittal.

lībĕrātor, ōris, m. deliverer, liberator.

lībĕrē, ad. freely; frankly.

lībĕri, ōrum, m. pl. children.   [solve.

lībĕro, 1. v.a. to release, to free; to ab-

lībĕrta, ae, lībertina, ae, f. freedwoman.

lībertas, ātis, f. civil freedom; liberty; frankness.

ĭbertīnus, a, um, a. of a freedman.

lībertĭnus, libertus, ī, m. freedman.

lībet, lĭbuit, lĭbĭtum est, 2. v.n. imp. it pleases, is agreeable; — **mihi**, I like, I will.

lībīdĭnōsē, ad. wantonly; capriciously.

lībīdĭnōsus, a, um, a. sensual, wanton; wilful; capricious.   [caprice.

lībīdo, ĭnis, f. desire; lust; passion;

Lībītina, ae, f. goddess of funerals.

lībo, 1. v.a. to taste, to sip; to pour in offering; to sacrifice; to touch lightly; to pick; to lessen, to impair; to cull, to take out.

lībra, ae, f. Roman pound (12 ounces); level; balance; scales; one of the twelve signs of the zodiac.

lībrāmentum, ī, n. weight; gravity; plane surface; a metal weight.

lībrārium, ii, n. bookcase, book-chest.

lībrārius, a, um, a. pertaining to books; —, ii, m. copyist, secretary.

lībro, 1. v.a. to weigh; to level; to poise; to throw, to sling.

lībum, ī, n. cake; consecrated cake; birthday cake.

lĭburna, ae, f. brigantine.

licens, entis, a. free, unrestrained.

licenter, ad. freely; boldly.

licentia, ae, f. liberty, licence; presumption; impunity; unruliness.

liceo, 2. v.n. to stand at a price; to be on sale.   [auction.

liceor, licĭtus, 2. v. dep. to bid at an

licet, cuit, cĭtum est, 2. v.n. imp. it is lawful or permitted; one may or can.

licĭtātio, ōnis, f. bidding at sales.

licĭtus, a, um, a. lawful.

licium, ii, n. thread, the warp of a web.

lictor, ōris, m. lictor (attendant on a Roman magistrate).

liēn, ēnis, m. spleen.

līgāmen, ĭnis, n. bandage.

līgāmentum, ī, n. band, bandage.

lignārius, ii, m. carpenter; timber-merchant;—**inter lignarios**, in the timber-market.   [wood.

lignātio, ōnis, f. felling or fetching of

lignātor, ōris, m. wood-cutter.

ligneŏlus, a, um, a. made of wood, wooden.

ligneus, a, um, a. of wood, wooden.

lignor, ātus, 1. v. dep. to fetch wood.

lignum, ī, n. wood; firewood; timber; tree.

ligo, 1. v.a. to tie, to bind.

ligo, ōnis, m. mattock, hoe.

ligŭla, ae, lingŭla, ae, f. tongue of a shoe; tongue of land.

ligūr(r)io, ivi & ii, ītum, 4. v.a. to lick; to feed on; fig. to lust after.

līgustrum, ī, n. privet (plant).

līlium, ii, n. lily.

līma, ae, f. file; fig. polishing, revision.

līmātus, a, um, a. polished, refined, elegant.

līmax, ācis, c. slug, snail.

limbus, ī, m. border, hem, edge, selvage, fringe, girdle.

līmen, ĭnis, n. lintel, threshold; fig. entrance; house, dwelling; barrier; beginning.

līmes, ĭtis, m. border, bound; fig. difference, cross-path; by-road; wall (for military purposes).

līmo, 1. v.a. to file; fig. to polish; to file down; to diminish.

līmōsus, a, um, a. miry, muddy.

limpĭdus, a, um, a. clear, limpid.

līmus, a, um, a. askance, squinting.

līmus, ī, m. mud; slime.

līnāria (mod. hort.), toad-flax.

līnea, ae, f. linen thread, string, line; plummet; fishing-line; boundary-line.

līneāmentum, ī, n. line; feature, lineament;—**lineamenta**, pl. designs, drawings.

līneus, a, um, a. made of flax.

lingua, ae, f. tongue; speech, language; eloquence; tongue of land.

lingula, v. **ligula.**
lĭnĭger, a, um, a. wearing linen.
lĭno, lĭvi & lĕvi, lĭtum, 3. v.a. to daub, to besmear, to anoint.
linquo, līqui, 3. v.a. to leave, to quit, to forsake; to cast off.
linter, tris, f. skiff, wherry; trough, vat.
linteum, i, n. linen cloth; linen; sail.
linteus, a, um, a. of linen.
līnum, i, n. flax; linen, lint; thread; rope; drag-net.
lippio, īvi, ītum, 4. v.n. to be blear-eyed.
lippĭtūdo, ĭnis, f. inflammation of the eyes.
lippus, a, um, a. blear-eyed; dim-sighted.
lĭquĕfăcio, fēci, factum, 3. v.a. to make liquid, to melt, to liquefy; *fig.* to enervate.
lĭqueo, licui & līqui, 2. v.n. to be liquid; *fig.* to be clear and plain.
lĭquesco, līcui, 3. v.n. to become liquid, to melt; to become putrid.
liquet, v. imp. it is apparent *or* clear;—**non —,** it doth not appear.
lĭquĭdo, ad. clearly; manifestly.
lĭquĭdus, a, um, a. liquid, fluid; clear; *fig.* manifest.
lĭquo, i. v.a. to melt; to strain, to filter.
lĭquor, 3. v. dep. n. to dissolve; to waste away. [sea.
lĭquor, ōris, m. fluid, liquid; moisture;
līra, ae, f. ridge between furrows.
līs, lītis, f. strife, quarrel; lawsuit; matter in dispute;—**litem lite resolvere,** to explain something obscure by something equally so;—**lite pendente,** while the dispute is unsettled.
lĭtātio, ōnis, f. favourable sacrifice.
lĭtĕra, etc., v. **littera,** etc.
lĭtĭgiōsus, a, um, a. quarrelsome; disputatious. [law.
lĭtĭgo, i. v.n. to quarrel; to dispute at law.
lĭto, i. v.n. & a. to sacrifice under favourable auspices; to appease.
lĭtŏreus, a, um, a. of the seashore.
lĭtŏtes, ĕtis, f. a. rhetorical figure, expressing the opposite of exaggeration, e.g. **non innoxius** for **nocens,** not harmless for harmful.
littĕra, ae, f. letter of the alphabet; word; epistle;—**litteræ, ārum,** pl. letter, learning, literature; writings;—**litteræ humaniores,** polite literature;—**littera scripta manet,** the written letter remains. [cleverly.
littĕrātē, ad. in a clear hand; learnedly;
littĕrātūra, ae, f. alphabet; grammar.
littĕrātus, a, um, a. learned.
littĕrŭlæ, ārum, f. pl. little letter, note; grammatical knowledge; smattering.
lĭtūra, ae, f. smearing; blot.
lītus, ōris, n. seashore, coast.

lĭtuus, i, m. augur's crooked staff; *fig.* instigator; clarion.
līveo, 2. v.n. to be livid; *fig.* to be envious. [livid; *fig.* envious; spiteful.
līvĭdus, a, um, a. bluish; black and blue,
līvor, ōris, m. leaden colour, black and blue spot; *fig.* envy, spite.
lixa, ae, m. sutler; camp-follower.
lobēlia (mod. hort.), lobelia, cardinal flower.
lŏcārius, ii, m. one who occupied a seat at a theatre and let it out before the performance. [tract, lease.
lŏcātio, ōnis, f. letting out, leasing, contractor.
lŏcātor, oris, m. contractor.
lŏco, i. v.a. to place, to lay, to set; to let for hire; to farm out; to put out at interest; to contract (for).
lŏcŭlus, i, m. casket; purse. [worthy.
lŏcŭples, ētis, a. rich, opulent; trust-
lŏcŭplēto, i. v.a. to enrich.
lŏcus, i, m. pl. **loci & loca,** place; position; condition; rank; opportunity; passage (in a book); topic, matter;—**locus standi,** right to appear in court;—**locum tenens,** one who holds office for another;—**locus classicus,** the passage in an author that indirectly sheds most light on some doubtful phrase or custom.
lŏcusta, ae, f. lobster.
lŏcūtio, ōnis, f. speech, discourse; pronunciation.
lōdix, ĭcis, f. blanket; counterpane.
lŏgĭca, ae, lŏgĭcē, es, f. logic.
lŏgĭcus, a, um, a. logical.
lōlīgo, ĭnis, f. cuttle-fish.
lōlium, ii, n. darnel, cockle.
lōmentum, i, n. face-wash.
longævus, a, um, a. of great age, ancient.
longē, ad. far off; far; a great while; very much; a great deal; — **latēque,** far and wide. [tance; duration.
longinquĭtas, ātis, f. length, extent; dis-
longinquus, a, um, a. far off, distant; strange; of long duration;—**e longinquo,** from a distance.
longĭtūdo, ĭnis, f. length; long duration.
longŭrius, ii, m. long pole.
longus, a, um, a. long, tall; lasting long; tedious;—**longa navis,** warship.
lonicēra (mod. hort.), honeysuckle.
lŏquācĭtas, ātis, f. talkativeness.
lŏquax, ācis, a. talkative, loquacious.
lŏquēla, ae, f. speech, discourse; language. [talk, to say; to mention.
lŏquor, cūtus, 3. v.n. & a. dep. to speak, to
lōrīca, ae, f. leather cuirass; breastwork.
lōrĭco, i. v.a. to put on a coat of mail.
lōrum, i, n. thong; bridle; leash; whip.
lōtus, i, f. lotus plant.

lŭbens, etc., v. libens, etc.
lŭbet, v. libet.
lŭbīdo, v. libido.
lūbrĭcus, a, um, a. slippery; smooth; *fig.* inconstant; hazardous; deceitful; difficult.
lūcar, āris, n. pay of actors.
lŭcellum, i, n. small profit.
lūceo, luxi, 2. v.n. to shine; to glitter; to be conspicuous.
lūcerna, ae, f. (oil-)lamp; evening.
lūcesco, 3. v.n. to begin to shine, to grow light.
lūcĭdus, a, um, a. bright, glittering; clear.
lūcĭfĕr, a, um, a. light-bringing; —, i, m. morning-star.
lūcĭfŭgus, a, um, a. avoiding the light.
Lūcīna, ae, f. goddess of childbirth; childbirth.
lucrātĭvus, a, um, a. profitable.
lucrĭfăcio, fēci, factum, 3. v.a. to acquire, to gain;—lucrĭfīo, factus sum, to be won.
lucror, ātus, 1. v.a. dep. to gain, to win; to earn.
lucrōsus, a, um, a. gainful, lucrative.
lucrum, i, n. gain, profit; wealth, riches.
luctāmen, ĭnis, n. struggling, exertion.
luctātĭo, ōnis, f. wrestling; struggle, contest.
luctātor, ōris, m. wrestler.
luctĭfĭcus, a, um, a. doleful, woeful.
luctor, ātus sum, 1. v. dep. to wrestle; to struggle.
luctuōsus, a, um, a. mournful; sad.
luctus, ūs, m. sorrow, mourning, lamentation; mourning apparel; source of grief.
lūcubrātĭo, ōnis, f. nocturnal study; lucubration.
lūcubro, 1. v.n. & a. to work by lamplight; to compose at night.
lūcŭlentus, a, um, a. bright; *fig.* excellent; fine; beautiful; trustworthy.
lŭcŭmo, onis, m. an Etruscan prince.
lūcus, i, m. grove;—lucus, a non lucendo, a derivation of the word lucus from the verb luceo, to be light, because a grove is *not* light. Hence an impossible derivation.
lūdia, ae, f. actress.
lūdĭbrĭum, i, n. mockery; laughing-stock.   [frolicsome.
lūdĭbundus, a, um, a. playful, sportive,
lūdĭcer, cra, crum, lūdĭcrus, a, um, a. sportive, connected with the stage.
lūdĭcrum, i, n. stage-play; show.
lūdĭfĭcātĭo, ōnis, f. mockery.
lūdĭfĭcor, ātus sum, 1. v. dep. to mock; to make sport of; *fig.* to thwart.
lūdĭmăgister, tri, m. schoolmaster.
lūdio, ōnis, lūdius, ii, m. stage-player.

lūdo, si, sum, 3. v.a. & n. to play; to sport; to jeer at; to mock; to cheat.
lūdus, i, m. play, game, pastime; sport, fun; school.
lues, is, f. plague, pestilence; *fig.* calamity, ruin.
lūgeo, xi, ctum, 3. v.n. & a. to mourn, to lament; to wear mourning.
lūgubris, e, a. mourning; mournful; disastrous.
lumbus, i, m. loin.
lūmen, ĭnis, n. light; daylight; day; star; lamp, torch; life; eye; (concretely of a person) glory, ornament.
lūmĭnāria, ium, n. pl. window shutter.
lūmĭnōsus, a, um, a. *fig.* bright, conspicuous.
lūna, ae, f. moon; month; night.
lūnāria (mod. hort.), honesty.
lūnāris, e, a. lunar; crescent-shaped.
lūnātus, a, um, p. & a. crescent-shaped.
lūno, 1. v.a. to crook like a sickle.
luo, lui, 3. v.a. to wash, to lave.
luo, lui, ŭtum & uitum, 3. v.a. to pay; to atone for; to satisfy;—pœnam luere, to suffer punishment.
lŭpa, ae, f. she-wolf; *fig.* prostitute.
lŭpānar, āris, n. brothel.
lŭpātus, a, um, a. furnished with wolf's teeth;—lŭpāti, orum, pl. a curb of wolf's teeth.
Lŭpercālia, ium, n. pl. festival of Pan.
Lŭpercus, i, m. priest of Pan.
lŭpīnus, a, um, a. pertaining to a wolf.
lŭpīnus, i, m., lŭpīnum, *i.* n. lupine.
lŭpus, i, m. wolf; bit (in a horse's mouth); pike (fish);—lupus in fabula, talk of the devil and he'll appear.
lurco, ōnis, m. glutton.
lūrĭdus, a, um, a. sallow, wan, ghastly.
luscinia, ae, f. nightingale.
luscĭtĭōsus, a, um, a. purblind.   [eye.
luscus, a, um, a. one-eyed, blind of one
lūsio, ōnis, f. playing, play.   [mocker.
lūsor, ōris, m. player; wanton writer;
lustrālis, e, a. expiatory.
lustrātĭo, ōnis, f. purification by sacrifice; going *or* wandering about.
lustro, 1. v.a. to purify; to illumine; to go about; to review (an army); to survey, to examine.
lustrum, i, n. purificatory sacrifice; period of five years; den of wild beasts; wood, forest; brothel.
lūsus, ūs, m. play, game; sport, amusement; dalliance;—lusus naturae, a freak.
lūteŏlus, a, um, a. yellow.
lūteus, a, um, a. yellow; saffron.
lŭteus, a, um, a. of mud *or* clay; *fig.* dirty, vile.

lūtra, ae, f. otter.   [*fig.* filthy, vile.
lŭtŭlentus, a, um, a. muddy; turbid;
lŭtum, i, n. mud, mire; loam, clay.
lŭtum, i, n. yellow dye.
lux, lūcis, f. light (of the sun, stars, etc.);
daylight, day; splendour; eye; life;
world; ornament; publicity.
luxo, 1. v.a. put out of joint.
luxŭria, ae, luxŭries, ēi, f. luxury, extravagance, rankness.
luxŭrio, 1. v.n., luxŭrior, ātus, 1. v. dep.
to be rank *or* luxuriant: to have in
abundance; to swell; *fig.* to be luxuriant; to run riot; to wanton, to sport,
to frisk; to be wanton.
luxŭriōsus, a, um, a. luxuriant, exuberant; *fig.* immoderate; wanton; luxurious, voluptuous.   [dour, pomp.
luxus, ūs, m. luxury, debauchery; splen-
Lyæus, i, m. a title of Bacchus; wine.
Lycēum, i, Lycīum, i, n. school in Athens
in which Aristotle taught.
lychnis (mod. hort.), campion.
lychnūchus, i, m. chandelier.
lychnus, i, m. light, lamp.
lycopersicum (mod. hort.), tomato.
lycopōdium (mod. hort.), stag-horn moss.
lympha, ae, f. water; pure *or* spring
water; water-nymph.
lymphāticus, a, um, a. mad, frantic.
lymphātus, a, um, a. crazy, crack-
brained.   [crazy.
lympho, 1. v.a. & n. to make mad; to be
lyncēus, a, um, a. sharp-sighted.
lynx, lyncis, c. lynx.   [(constellation).
lyra, ae, f. lute, lyre; lyric poetry; Lyre
lyricus, a, um, a. lyric.
lysimachia (mod. hort.), creeping jenny.

M = 1000.
măcellum, i, n. provision market.
măcer, cra, crum, a. lean, meagre, poor.
măcěria, ae, f. enclosure, loam- *or* mud-
wall.
măcěro, 1. v.a. to make soft, to soak;
fig. to emaciate; to tease; to distress.
măcesco, 3. v.n. to become thin.
măchĭna, ae, f. machine; engine; *fig.*
trick, artifice.
măchĭnāmentum, i, engine.
măchĭnātĭo, ōnis, f. mechanism; machine; *fig.* machination, artifice.
măchĭnātor, ōris, m. engineer; *fig.* projector.
măchĭnor, ātus, 1. v.a. dep. to devise;
to plot.
măcies, ēi, f. leanness, meagreness;
poverty.   [pine away.
macresco, crui, 3. v.n. to grow lean, to

macrŏcōlum, i, n. paper of the largest
size.
macto, 1. v.a. to honour; to worship; to
sacrifice; to slaughter; to destroy.
mactus, a, um, a. venerated; (used in
voc.) macte, well done! hail! macte
virtute, go on and prosper.
măcŭla, ae, f. spot; stain, blemish;
mesh in a net.
măcŭlo, 1. v.a. to spot, to speckle; to
stain, to pollute; to dishonour.
măcŭlōsus, a, um, a. spotted, speckled;
defiled; infamous.
mădĕfăcio, fēci, factum, 3. v.a. to wet, to
soak;—mădĕfĭo, fĭĕri, to be moistened,
to be made wet.
mădeo, ui, 2. v.n. to be wet *or* moist, to
drip with; to overflow with.   [wet.
mădesco, dui, 3. v.n. to become moist *or*
mădĭdus, a, um, a. moist, wet; drenched;
drunk; boiled soft.
Mæander, dri, m. roundabout way;
winding, meandering; winding border.
Mænas, ădis, f. Bacchante, priestess of
Bacchus.
Mæniānum, i, n. balcony.
mæreo, 2. v.n. & a. to be sad, to grieve,
to lament; to bewail.
mæror, ōris, m. sadness, grief, lamentation.   [choly.
mæstitia, ae, f. sadness, grief, melan-
mæstus, a, um, a. sad, melancholy;
gloomy; woeful.
măga, ae, f. enchantress, witch.
măgālia, ium, n. pl. little dwellings, huts.
măgĕ, ad. = magis.
măgĭcus, a, um, a. magical.
măgĭs, ad. more, rather.
măgister, tri, m. master, chief; president; tutor, teacher; pilot of a ship;
— equitum, dictator's lieutenant; master of the horse.
măgĭstērĭum, ii, n. office of a president,
chief, etc., instruction.
măgistra, ae, f. mistress.
măgistrātus, ūs, m. magistracy; office;
magistrate.
magnănĭmĭtas, ātis, f. magnanimity.
magnănĭmus, a, um, a. magnanimous,
spirited.
magnēs, ētis, m. magnet.
magnĭfĭce, ad. nobly, magnificently,
pompously, proudly.
magnĭfĭcenter, ad. nobly, magnificently.
magnĭfĭcentia, ae, f. greatness, nobleness,
high-mindedness; grandeur; bombast.
magnĭfĭco, i, v.a. to value highly; to
extol.
magnĭfĭcus, a, um, a. noble, eminent,
stately; sumptuous, magnificent, boastful; haughty.

magnĭlŏquentia, ae, f. sublime language, lofty style; brag, rodomontade.

magnĭlŏquus, a, um, a. magniloquent, vaunting. [dance; power.

magnĭtūdo, ĭnis, f. greatness, bulk; abun-

magnōlia (mod. hort.), magnolia.

magnŏpĕrĕ, ad. very much, greatly, exceedingly.

magnus, a, um, a. great, large, tall, broad; loud; much; noble, grand; mighty;—**magni,** at a high price.

măgus, i, m. magician; —, **a, um,** a. magical.

Maius, i, m. May.

măjālis, is, m. barrow hog.

măjestas, ātis, f. majesty; authority; sublimity; honour; sovereign power of the Roman people;—**crimen majestatis,** high treason.

măjor, ōris, a. greater; older, etc., v. magnus;—**măjōres,** pl. ancestors.

māla, ae, f. cheek-bone, jaw.

mălăcia, ae, f. calm at sea, dead calm.

malcōmia (mod. hort.), Virginian stock.

mălĕ, ad. badly, ill, wickedly, unfortunately; amiss; sometimes has the force of a negative, e.g. **male sanus** for **insanus.**

mălĕdĭcē, ad. abusively. [to abuse.

mălĕdĭco, xi, ctum, 3. v.n. to speak ill of,

mălĕdictio, ōnis, f. abuse.

mălĕdictum, i, n. abusive or foul word.

mălĕdĭcus, a, um, a. foul-mouthed, abusive. [or wrong, to injure.

mălĕfăcio, fēci, factum, 3. v.n. to do evil

mălĕfactor, ōris, m. evil-doer.

mălĕficium, ii, n. doing ill; evil or wicked deed, crime; sorcery.

mălĕficus, a, um, a. wicked, mischievous, dangerous.

mălēsuādus, a, um, a. persuading to evil.

mălĕvŏlentia, ae, f. ill-will, spite, malevolence.

mălĕvŏlus, a, um, a. spiteful, malevolent.

mālifer, a, um, a. apple-bearing.

mălignĕ, ad. spitefully, malignantly; stingily. [niggardliness.

mălignĭtas, ātis, f. ill-will, spite, malice;

mălignus, a, um, a. envious, spiteful; morose, niggardly; narrow.

mălitia, ae, f. wickedness; craft; malice.

mălĭtiōsē, ad. wickedly, spitefully.

mălĭtiosus, a, um, a. wicked, malicious.

malleŏlus, i, m. slip; cutting (of a plant); a weapon carrying fire.

malleus, i, m. hammer, mallet.

mālo, mālui, malle, v.a. ir. to wish or choose rather, to prefer. [nut.

mālŏbathrum, i, n. betel; oil of the betel

mălum, i, n. evil, calamity, misfortune.

mălum, i, n. apple; fruit with a kernel.

mălus, a, um, a. bad, evil, wicked; unfortunate; weak; cowardly;—**mala fide,** in bad faith. [pole.

mālus, i, f. apple-tree; mast (of a ship);

malva, ae, f. mallow.

māmilla, ae, breast. [teat.

mamma, ae, f. breast, pap; (of animals)

manceps, ĭpis, m. contractor; purchaser; proprietor; occupier.

mancĭpium, ii, n. formal mode of purchase; property; right of ownership; slave. [sell.

mancĭpo, 1. v.a. to make over (to); to

mancŭp . . ., v. **mancip . . .**

mancus, a, um, a. maimed; infirm; defective.

mandātu, by command (of). [tract.

mandātum, i, n. order, commission, con-

mandĭbŭla, ae, f., **mandĭbŭlum, i,** n. jaw.

mando, 1. v.a. to commit to one's charge, to commission; to command; to intrust (to);—**mandamus,** (we direct) orders given by a superior court to an inferior tribunal.

mando, di, sum, 3. v.a. to chew, to champ; to eat.

mandra, ae, f. cattle-stall.

mandrăgŏras, ae, m. mandrake.

mandūco, 1. v.a. to chew. [morning.

mānĕ, n. indecl. morning; —, ad. in the

măneo, nsi, nsum, 2. v.n. & a. to stay, to remain; to await; to pass the night; to abide by; to last; to endure.

Mānes, ĭum, m. pl. gods of the Lower World; shades or ghosts of the dead; spirit-land.

mango, ōnis, m. broker, dealer.

mănĭbiae, v. **manubiae.**

mănĭca, ae, f. long sleeve of a tunic; fur-glove; handcuff. [sleeves.

mănĭcātus, a, um, a. furnished with long

mănĭfesto, ad. clearly, manifestly.

mănĭfesto, 1. v.a. to manifest. [torious.

mănĭfestus, a, um, a. clear, evident; no-

mănĭpŭlāris, e, a. pertaining to a maniple or company; —, **is,** m. common soldier; comrade. [panies.

mănĭpŭlātim, by handfuls; by com-

mănĭpŭlus, mănĭplus, i, m. handful, bundle; (mil.) company.

manna, ae, f. grain.

mannus, i, m. small Gallic horse, cob.

māno, 1. v.n. to flow, to trickle; to arise or proceed from. [ters.

mansio, ōnis, f. staying, remaining, quar-

mansĭto, 1. v.n. to abide, to dwell.

mansuĕfăcio, fēci, factum, 3. v.a. to tame; fig. to civilize;—**mansuĕffio,** to be made tame.

mansuesco, suēvi, suētum, 3. v.a. & n. tame; to become or grow tame

mansuētūdo, ĭnis, f. *fig.* mildness, gentleness.   [gentle, quiet.
mansuētus, a, um, p. & a. tame; *fig.* mild,
mantēle, is, mantēlĭum, ii, n. towel; napkin.
mantĭca, ae, f. wallet, hand-bag.
mănŭālis, e, a. pertaining to the hand;—
manualia saxa, stones thrown with the
hand;—**mănŭāle, is,** n. book-cover.
mănŭbiae, ārum, f. pl. money obtained
from the sale of booty; booty; spoils
from the enemy.
mănubrium, ii, n. handle, haft.
mănūmissio, ōnis, f. freeing of a slave.
mănūmitto, mīsi, missum, 3. v.a. to set at
liberty, to emancipate (a slave).
mănŭprētium, ii, n. wages; *fig.* pay, reward.
mănus, ūs, f. hand; fist; trunk (of an
elephant); handwriting; power; fight,
combat; band of soldiers; company,
multitude; valour; legal power of a
husband; — **extrema,** finishing touch;
— **ferreæ,** grappling-irons;—**ad manum,** at hand, near;—**conferre manum,**
to encounter;—**dare manus,** to submit, to yield;—**tendere manus,** to entreat, to supplicate.
măpāle, is, n. African hut, cottage;
village.
mappa, ae, f. table-napkin; cloth dropped
as a signal to start a race.
marceo, 2. v.n. to wither; *fig.* to be faint
or languid.   [languish.
marcesco, 3. v.n. to pine away; *fig.* to
marcĭdus, a, um, a. withered, rotten; *fig.*
weak; enervated; languid.
marcor, ōris, m. withering; languor.
marcŭlus, i, hammer.
măre, is, n. sea; salt-water;—**mare
clausum,** a sea closed for traffic.
margărīta, ae, f., **margărītum, i,** n. pearl.
margĭno, 1. v.a. to provide with a border.
margo, ĭnis, m. & f. edge, brink, margin;
boundary.
mărīnus, a, um, a. pertaining to the sea,
marine; sea-born; — **ros,** rosemary.
mărīta, ae, f. married woman, wife.
mărītālis, e, a. nuptial.
mărītĭmus, a, um, a. sea . . ., maritime; (of people) used to the sea;—
maritima, ōrum, n. pl. maritime places,
sea-coast.   [marriage.
mărīto, 1. v.a. to marry; to give in
mărītus, a, um, a. conjugal, matrimonial;
—**, i,** m. husband, suitor.
marmor, ōris, n. marble; marble statue;
sea.   [marble-like.
marmŏreus, a, um, made of marble;
marra, ae, f. hoe.
marrŭbium, ii, n. horehound.

Mars, tis, m. god of war; war, battle;
art of war.
marsŭpium, ii, n. pouch.
Martĭālis, e, a. pertaining or sacred to
Mars.   [to Mars; warlike.
Martĭus, a, um, a. pertaining or sacred
Martius, i, m. March (month).
martŭlus, v. **marcŭlus.**
martyr, yris, c. martyr.
martȳrĭum, ii, n. martyrdom.
mās, măris, m. male; masculine; manly.
mascŭlīnus, a, um, a. male, masculine.
mascŭlus, a, um, a. male; manly; strong.
massa, ae, f. lump, mass; block.
Massicum, i, n. Massic wine.
mastiche, es, f. mastich.
mastīgia, ae, m. rogue.
mastrūca, ae, f. garment of sheepskin.
mastrūcātus, a, um, a. wearing a sheepskin (as a garment).   [source.
māter, tris, f. mother; matron; origin,
mātercŭla, ae, f. little mother.
māterfămĭlias, matrisfămĭlias, f. lady of
the house.
mātĕria, ae, mātĕries, ēi, f. matter, stuff;
timber; subject, theme; occasion,
cause; **materia medica,** drugs used for
healing.
matĕris, is, matĕra, ae, f. Gallic javelin.
māternus, a, um, a. motherly, maternal.
mātertĕra, ae, f. mother's sister, aunt.
māthēmătĭcus, a, um, a. mathematical;
—, i, m. mathematician; astrologer.
mātrĭcīda, ae, m. murderer of one's
mother.
matrĭcīdĭum, ii, n. murder of a mother.
mātrĭmōnium, ii, n. marriage, matrimony.   [living.
mātrimus, a, um, a. having a mother
mātrix, ĭcis, f. female animal kept for
breeding; matrix; origin.
mātrōna, ae, f. wife, matron.
mātrōnālis, e, a. matronly;—**Mātrōnālia,
ium,** n. pl. festival of Mars.
matthiola (mod. hort.), stock.
mātūrē, ad. quickly; soon; seasonably.
mātūresco, rui, 3. v.n. to become ripe,
to ripen.
mātūrĭtas, ātis, f. ripeness.
mātūro, 1. v.a. & n. to make ripe; to
hasten, to accelerate.
mātūrus, a, um, a. ripe; mellow; proper,
seasonable, timely, marriageable; early;
quick.
mātūtīnus, a, um, a. morning . . .
mausōlēum, i, n. tomb, mausoleum.
Mavors, ortis, v. **Mars.**
maxilla, ae, f. jaw-bone.
maxĭmē, ad. in the highest degree, especially; very.   [magnus.
maxĭmus, a, um, a. greatest, etc., v.

me, accusative of **ego.**

meātus, ūs, m. movement, course, orbit.

mecum = cum me.

mĕdens, entis, m. physician.   [correct.

mĕdeor, 2. v.n. dep. to heal, to cure; to

mĕdica, ae, f. lucern (Burgundy clover).

mĕdĭcābĭlis, e, a. curable.

mĕdĭcāmen, ĭnis, n. drug, remedy, medicine; antidote; poisonous drug; paint, cosmetic, dye.   [medicine.

mĕdĭcāmentum, i, n. drug, remedy,

mĕdĭcātus, ūs, m. charm.   [fig. remedy.

mĕdĭcīna, ae, f. medical art; medicine;

mĕdĭco, 1. v.a. to heal, to cure; to medicate; to steep; to colour.

mĕdĭcor, atus, 1. v.a. dep. to heal, to cure.

mĕdĭcus, a, um, a. healing, medical; —, i, m. physician, surgeon.

mĕdimnum, i, n. **mĕdimnus, i,** m. Greek bushel (6 **modii**).

mĕdĭocris, e, a. middling, moderate, tolerable, mediocre.

mĕdĭocrĭtas, ātis, f. medium, moderation; mediocrity;—**aurea mĕdĭocrĭtas,** the golden mean.

mĕdĭocrĭter, ad. moderately, tolerably.

mĕdĭtāmentum, i, n. preparation, exercise.   [tation; preparation.

mĕdĭtātio, ōnis, f. contemplation, medi-

mĕdĭterrāneus, a, um, a. midland, inland.

mĕdĭtor, ātus, 1. v.a. & n. dep. to meditate; to think upon; to reflect; to practise; to compose.

mĕdium, ii, n. middle; public, publicity.

mĕdius, a, um, a. mid, middle; indifferent; neutral; ambiguous; common, middling, ordinary; moderate; middle-aged; —, ii, m. mediator;—**medio tutissimus ibis,** you will fare safest by a middle course.

mĕdulla, ae, f. marrow, kernel; fig. innermost part; quintessence.

mĕdullĭtus, ad. to the very marrow; from the heart.

Mĕgălensia, ium, n. pl. festival in honour of the Magna Mater.

mĕgistānes, um, m. pl. nobles, grandees.

mĕl, mellis, n. honey; fig. sweetness.

mĕlanchŏlĭcus, a, um, a. melancholy.

mĕlĭcus, a, um, a. lyrical; —, i, m. a lyric poet.

mĕlĭlōtos, i, f. melilot (a clover).

mĕlĭmēla, ōrum, n. pl. honey-apples.

mĕlior, ius, ōris, a. comp. better, v. **bonus.**

mĕlisphyllum, i, n. balm.

melleus, a, um, a. of honey.

mellĭfer, a, um, a. honey-producing.

mellĭfĭco, 1. v.a. to make honey.

mellĭtus, a, um, a. of honey; sweetened with honey; fig. darling, lovely.

mēlos, i, n. time, song.

membrāna, ae, f. membrane; skin; parchment.

membrātim, ad. limb by limb; piecemeal.

membrum, i, n. limb, member.

mĕmento, imper. of **memini;**—**memento mori,** keep death in your thoughts.

mĕmet, v. me.   [make mention of.

mĕmĭni, isse, v.n. def. to remember; to

mĕmor, ōris, a. mindful of, remembering; revengeful; grateful; serving as a memorial of.

mĕmŏrābĭlis, e, a. memorable, remarkable;—**memorabilia,** n. pl. reminiscences.

mĕmŏria, ae, f. memory; recollection; time within remembrance; narrative; —**memoria technica,** an artificial system to aid the memory;—**post hominum memoriam,** within human recollection.

mĕmŏrĭter, ad. by heart.

mĕmŏro, 1. v.a. to remind of; to mention; to relate.

menda, ae, f., v. **mendum.**

mendācium, ii, n. lie, untruth.

mendax, ācis, a. lying, false; deceitful; counterfeit.

mendīcĭtas, ātis, f. beggary, pauperism.

mendīco, 1. v.a. to beg, to ask for alms.

mendīcus, a, um, a. beggarly, needy; —, i, m. beggar.

mendōsē, ad. faultily, falsely.

mendōsus, a, um, a. faulty, erroneous; incorrect; blundering.

mendum, i, n. blemish, fault; blunder.

mens, mentis, f. mind, intellect; reason, judgment; thought, feelings; disposition, intention;—**mens (sibi) conscia recti,** a. conscience void of offence;—**mens sana in corpore sano,** a healthy mind in a healthy body.

mensa, ae, f. table; sacrificial table; altar; meal; course (at a meal); bank-counter.

mensārius, ii, m. money-changer, banker.

mensis, is, m. month.

mensor, ōris, m. measurer.

menstruus, a, um, a. monthly.

mensūra, ae, f. measuring; measure.

menta, mentha, ae, f. mint.

mentio, ōnis, f. mention.

mentior, ītus, 4. v.n. & a. dep. to lie, to deceive; to feign; to speak falsely about; to imitate.

mentum, i, n. chin; beard.

meo, 1. v.n. to go along, to pass, to march.

mĕphītis, is, f. pestilential exhalation from the ground.

mĕrācus, a, um, a. pure, unmixed.

mercātor, ōris, m. trader, merchant.

mercātūra, ae, f. trade, commerce.

mercātŭs, ūs, m. trade, buying and selling; market; public festival.

mercēnārius, a, um, a. hired, mercenary; —, ii, m. hireling.

mercēs, ēdis, f. hire, pay, wages, salary; reward; rent, revenue; punishment; stipulation. [to buy.

mercor, ātus, 1. v.n. & a. dep. to trade;

merda, ae, f. dung, excrement.

mērē, ad. purely; merely.

mĕrenda, ae, f. afternoon meal.

mĕreo, ui, ĭtum, mĕreor, ĭtus, 2. v.a. & n. to earn, to get; to deserve; to be rewarded;—merere stipendia, to serve as soldier; to receive pay for war-service.

mĕretrīcius, a, um, a. meretricious.

mĕretrĭcŭla, ae, f. prostitute.

mĕretrix, īcis, f. prostitute, courtesan.

mergae, ārum, f. pl. two-pronged fork.

mergĕs, ĭtis, f. sheaf (of corn); pitchfork.

mergo, si, sum, 3. v.a. to immerse; to plunge; to bury; to hide; to drown; to overwhelm; to ruin;—res mersæ, ruined fortunes.

mergus, i, m. diver, gull.

mĕrīdiānus, a, um, a. pertaining to noon; southern.

mĕrīdies, ēi, m. midday, noon; south.

mĕritō, ad. deservedly, justly.

mĕritōrius, a, um, a. by which money is earned; let for hire.

mĕritum, i, n. desert; service, kindness; blame; fault, hire; reward; value, worth. [due.

mĕritus, a, um, a. deserving; deserved,

mĕrops, ŏpis, f. bee-eater (bird).

merso, 1. v.a. to dip in, to immerse; fig. to overwhelm.

mĕrŭla, ae, f. blackbird; sea-carp.

mĕrum, i, n. pure wine.

mĕrus, a, um, a. pure, unmixed; bare, only, mere; genuine;—merum sal, true wit.

merx, cis, f. goods, merchandise. [plant.

mesēmbryanthĕmum (mod. hort.), ice-

mespīlum, i, n. medlar.

mespĭlus, i, f., mespĭla, ae, f. medlar-tree.

messis, is, f. harvest, crop; harvest time.

messor, ōris, m. reaper, mower.

messōrius, a, um, a. of a reaper.

. . . met = self.

mēta, ae, f. turning-post (at the end of a race-course); limit; end; conical shape; cone.

mĕtallĭcus, a, um, a. of metal.

mĕtallum, i, n. metal; mine.

mĕtămorphōsis, is, f. change of shape.

mĕtăphŏra, ae, f. metaphor.

mĕtăthĕsis, is, f. transposition (of letters) (grammatical term).

mētātor, ōris, m. measurer of land.

mĕtempsychōsis, is, f. transmigration of souls.

mĕtĭcŭlōsus, a, um, fearful; nervous.

mētior, mensus, 4. v.a. dep. to measure; to traverse; to walk or sail through; to estimate, to judge.

mēto, ātum, 1. v.a. to measure.

mĕto, messui, messum, 3. v.a. to reap, to mow, to cut off.

mētor, ātus, 1. v.a. dep. to measure off, to mete out; to define by boundaries.

metrum, i, n. metre, poetical measure.

mĕtuo, ui, ūtum, 3. v.a. & n. to fear; to be afraid of; to beware of.

mĕtus, ūs, m. fear; anxiety; religious awe; object of dread.

meus, a, um, pn. my, mine;—meum est, it is my business;—meum, n. my own property;—meum et tuum, my property and yours;—mei, ōrum, m. pl. my friends or relatives or followers, etc.;—mea culpa, the fault is mine.

mi, voc. of meus.

mīca, ae, f. crumb, morsel.

mico, ui, 1. v.n. to move quickly, to quiver; to leap forth; to palpitate; to flash, to glitter; to sparkle.

migrātio, ōnis, f. removal; changing of one's habitation; fig. (of speech) transferred meaning.

migro, 1. v.n. to remove; to depart (to another place); to emigrate; to change. [diery.

mīlĕs, ĭtis, m. soldier; foot-soldier; sol-

mīlĭtāris, e, a. military; warlike; —, is, m. soldier, warrior.

mīlĭtārĭter, ad. like a soldier.

mīlĭtia, ae, f. military service; warfare; employment;—mīlĭtiæ, at the wars.

mīlĭto, 1. v.n. to be a soldier, to serve as a soldier.

mīlium, ii, n. millet.

mille, pl. millia, or milia, a. thousand; thousands; fig. innumerable; — passus, a mile.

millēsĭmus, a, um, a thousandth.

milliārum (or mīl.), in milestone.

milliārius, a, um (or mīl.), a. containing a thousand.

millies (or mīl.), ad. a thousand times.

milvīnus, a, um, a. of or like a kite; fig. rapacious; insatiable.

miluus, milvus, i, m. kite; gurnard.

mīma, ae, f. female mime. [travagant.

mīmicus, a, um, a. mimic, farcical; ex-

mīmŭla, ae, f., v. mima.

mīmŭlus (mod. hort.), musk.

mīmus, i, m. mimic actor, mime; farce.

mĭna, ae, f. Greek weight (of 100 drachmas).

mĭnācĭter, ad. threateningly.

mĭnæ, ārum, f. pl. threats, menaces.

mĭnātĭo, ōnis, f. threat, menace.

mĭnax, ācis, a. threatening; haughty.

Mĭnerva, ae, f. *fig.* genius, skill, talent, art; weaving; spinning;—**crassa Minerva,** with rude art;—**invita Minerva,** contrary to one's genius.

mĭnĭātus, a, um, a. red.

mĭnĭmē, ad. least, very little, not at all.

mĭnĭmus, a, um, a. least, v. **parvus.**

mĭnister, tri, m. attendant; servant.

mĭnistĕrĭum, ii, n. service, office; servants.   [assistant.

mĭnistrātor, ōris, m. attendant, servant;

mĭnistro, I. v.a. to attend, to serve; to assist; to afford; to furnish; to supply.

mĭnĭtor, ātus, I. v.a. dep. to threaten.

mĭnĭum, ii, n. red oxide of lead, vermilion.   [project; to threaten.

mĭnor, ātus, I. v. dep. to hang over; to

mĭnor, us, ōris, a. lesser, younger, etc., v. **parvus;—mĭnōres, um,** m. pl. descendants.

mĭnŭmē, etc., v. minime, etc.

mĭnuo, ui, ūtum, 3. v.a. & n. to lessen; to impair; to abate; to violate; to grow less.   [if not.

mĭnŭs, ad. less; not so well;—**sin minus,**

mĭnuscŭlus, a, um, a. rather small.

mĭnūtal, ālis, n. minced meat.

mĭnūtātim, ad. piecemeal; bit by bit.

mĭnūtĭæ, ārum, f. pl. trifles.

mĭnūtus, a, um, a. insignificant, petty.

mĭrābĭlis, e, a. wonderful, marvellous, admirable; strange.

mĭrābĭlĭter, ad. wonderfully, marvellously.   [tion, wondering.

mĭrābundus, a, um, a. full of admira-

mĭrācŭlum, i, n. wonder, miracle.

mĭrātĭo, ōnis, f. wondering, admiration.

mĭrātor, ōris, m. admirer.

mĭrē, ad. wonderfully, admirably.

mĭrĭfĭcē, ad. wonderfully; exceedingly.

mĭrĭfĭcus, a, um, a. wonderful; extraordinary.

mirmĭllo, ōnis, m. a gladiator pitted against the rētĭārius, who fought with a net.

mĭror, ātus, I. v.a. & n. dep. to wonder at, to be amazed at; to admire.

mĭrus, a, um, a. wonderful, admirable, prodigious.   [broken meats.

miscellānea, ōrum, n. pl. a mixture of

misceo, miscui, mistum & mixtum, 2. v.a. to mix, to mingle; to embroil; to disorder; to confound.

mĭsellus, a, um, a. poor, wretched.

mĭser, a, um, a. wretched, unfortunate, miserable.

mĭsĕrābĭlis, e, a. pitiable, miserable; wretched.

mĭsĕrābĭlĭter, ad. pitiably, miserably; mournfully.

mĭsĕrātĭo, ōnis, f. pity, commiseration.

mĭsĕrē, ad. wretchedly; desperately.

mĭsĕreor, ĭtus sum, 2. v. dep. to pity.

mĭsĕresco, 3. v.n. to have compassion.

mĭsĕrĕt, mĭsĕrētur, v. imp. it distresses me for; I pity.   [tress; anxiety.

mĭsĕrĭa, ae, f. wretchedness, misery; dis-

mĭsĕrĭcordĭa, ae, f. pity, compassion; mercy; pathos; unhappiness.

mĭsĕrĭcors, dis, a. pitiful, merciful.

mĭsĕror, ātus, I. v. dep. to bewail, to deplore; to pity.   [missĭle, is, n. missile.

missĭlis, e, a. that may be thrown;—

missĭo, ōnis, f. sending (away); release; discharge (of soldiers); cessation; quarter.

missĭto, I. v.a. to send repeatedly.

missus, ūs, m. sending (away); despatch; throw.

mistūra (mix-), ae, f. mixing.

mĭtĕ, ad. mildly, gently.

mĭtella, ae, f. silken head-band.

mĭtesco, 3. v.n. to become mild *or* mellow; to ripen; *fig.* to abate; to grow soft *or* tractable.

mītĭgātĭo, ōnis, f. mitigation.   [to pacify.

mītĭgo, I. v.a.c to soften; *fig.* to assuage;

mītis, e, a. mild; mellow; pliant; good-natured; gracious.

mitra, ae, f. turban, head-band.

mitrātus, a, um, a. turbaned.

mitto, mīsi, missum, 3. v.a. to send, to despatch; to cast, to hurl; to throw away; to dismiss; to omit; to produce; to utter; to cease.

mna, ae, v. **mina.**   [fickle.

mōbĭlis, e, a. movable; quick; pliant;

mōbĭlĭtas, ātis, f. movableness, mobility; *fig.* inconstancy.   [stantly.

mōbĭlĭter, ad. easily; swiftly; incon-

mŏdĕrābĭlis, e, a. moderate.   [ment.

mŏdĕrāmen, ĭnis, n. rudder; *fig.* manage-

mŏdĕrātē, ad. moderately.

mŏdĕrātĭo, ōnis, f. moderation; regularity; guidance, government.

mŏdĕrātor, ōris, m. manager, governor.

mŏdĕratrix, īcis, f. directress.

mŏdĕrātus, a, um, a. moderate; restrained; sober; tolerable; calm.

mŏdĕror, ātus, I. v. dep. to set bounds; to regulate; to govern.

mŏdestē, ad. moderately; modestly.

mŏdestĭa, ae, f. moderation; sobriety; bashfulness; orderly behaviour.

mŏdestus, a, um, a. moderate; bashful, modest; reserved; courteous.

mŏdĭcē, ad. moderately; modestly; little.

mŏdĭcus, a, um, a. moderate; middling; temperate; humble; little.

mŏdĭfĭcātus, a, um, a. measured off.

mŏdius, ii, m. Roman corn-measure, peck.

mŏdŏ, ad. only, merely; just now; a while ago; provided that; if only; at least;—**modo ..., modo ...,** sometimes ..., sometimes ...;—**mŏdŏ nōn,** all but.

mŏdŭlātus, a, um, a. properly measured; melodious, harmonious.

mŏdŭlor, ātus, 1. v. dep. to sing, to play; to dance; to accompany.

mŏdŭlus, i, m. (small) measure; size; rhythm.

mŏdus, i, m. measure; size; rhythm; metre; mode; manner; bound, limit; end; *fig.* moderation;—**modus operandi,** method of working;—**modus vivendi,** way of living; compromise.

mœcha, ae, f. adulteress. [adultery.

mœchor, ātus, 1. v. dep. to commit

mœchus, i, m. adulterer.

mœnia, ium, n. pl. town walls, ramparts.

mœr ..., v. mær ...

mœst ..., v. mæst ...

mōla, æ, f. millstone; mill; meal mixed with salt (for sacrifices).

mōlāris, e, a. pertaining to a mill, grinding; —, **is, m.** millstone, molar tooth.

mōles, is, f. huge, heavy mass; great fabric; pier; crowd; quantity;—difficulty, trouble; effort; *fig.* grandeur; strength;—**mole ruit sua,** it falls by its own weight.

mōlestē, ad. with trouble *or* difficulty.

mōlestia, ae, f. trouble, molestation; discontent; dislike. [affected.

mōlestus, a, um, a. troublesome, offensive,

mōlīmen, ĭnis, n. effort, endeavour.

mōlīmentum, i, n. exertion, labour.

mōlior, ītus, 4, v.n. & n. dep. to toil, to struggle; to manage; to set in motion; to cast; to brandish; to undertake; to build; to design; to plot; to contrive.

mōlītor, ōris, m. author, contriver.

mollesco, 3. v.n. to become soft; *fig.* to become gentle *or* effeminate.

mollio, īvi & ii, ītum, 4. v.a. to soften; *fig.* to mitigate; to render easier; to render effeminate.

mollis, e, a. soft, tender, mild; mellow; pleasant; pliant; easy; weak; effeminate.

mollĭter, ad. softly, gently; effeminately.

mollītia, ae, f., mollītĭes, ēi, f. softness; *fig.* tenderness; weakness; effeminacy.

molītūdo, ĭnis, f. suppleness, softness; susceptibility.

mollusca, ae, f. a kind of nut.

mōlo, ui, ītum, 3. v.a. to grind (in a mill).

mōmen, ĭnis, n. movement; weight; importance.

mōmentum, i, n. balance, equilibrium; alteration; motion; moment; importance; influence;—**momento temporis,** in a moment.

mŏnăchus, i, m. monk.

mŏnēdŭla, ae, f. jackdaw.

mŏneo, ui, ĭtum, 2. v.a. to admonish; to warn; to advise; to rebuke; to teach; to predict. [coin, money.

mŏnēta, ae, f. mint, stamp upon money;

mŏnētālis, e, a. relating to the mint; coined. [a horse).

mŏnīle, is, n. necklace, collar; poitrel (for

mŏnĭmentum, v. monumentum.

mŏnĭtio, ōnis, f. advice; warning.

mŏnĭtor, ōris, m. admonisher, monitor; prompter; preceptor, tutor.

mŏnĭtum, i, n. admonition; prophecy.

mŏnĭtus, ūs, m. warning, admonition; command; foretelling.

mŏnŏpōlium, ii, n. monopoly. [rock.

mons, tis, m. mountain, mount; heap;

monstrātor, ōris, m. inventor, teacher.

monstrĭfer, a, um, a. haunted by monsters.

monstrĭfĭcus, a, um, a. monstrous.

monstro, 1. v.a. to show, to point out; to inform, to teach; to ordain; to denounce; to describe;—**digito monstrari,** to be pointed at with the finger.

monstrum, i, n. monster; evil omen.

monstruōsus, a, um, a. strange, monstrous.

montāna, ōrum, n. mountainous regions.

montānus, a, um, a. mountain ...; mountainous; —, **i, m.** mountaineer.

montbrētia (mod. hort.), montbretia.

montĭcŏla, ae, g.c. mountaineer.

montĭvăgus, a, um, a. mountain-roaming.

montuōsus, a, um, a. mountainous.

mŏnŭmentum, i, n. memorial, monument; tomb; record.

mōra, ae, f. delay; hindrance.

mōrālis, e, a. moral, ethical.

mōrātor, ōris, m. delayer; loiterer.

mōrātōrium, i, n. a legalised suspension of the payment on a debt. [teristic.

mōrātus, a, um, a. mannered; charac-

morbĭdus, a, um, a. sickly, diseased.

morbus, i, m. sickness, disease, illness, distress.

mordācĭter, ad. bitingly. [*fig.* satirical.

mordax, ācis, a. biting, snappish; tart;

mordeo, mŏmordi, morsum, 2. v.a. to bite; to champ; to sting; to hurt; to vex; to satirize; to backbite.

mordĭcus, ad. by biting, with the teeth; tooth and nail; obstinately.

mŏrĭbundus, a, um, a. dying.

mōrĭgĕror, ātus, 1. v. dep. to comply with to humour.

mōrĭgĕrus, a, um, a. obsequious.
mŏrior, mŏrtuus, mŏri, 3. v. dep. to die;
to fail; to become disused.
mŏror, ātus, 1. v.n. & a. dep. to delay, to
stay; to make one wait; to entertain;
—nihil morari, to care nothing about.
mōrōsē, ad. sullenly.
mōrōsĭtas, ātis, f. sullenness.
mōrōsus, a, um, a. peevish, fretful,
morose; overscrupulous; (of things)
stubborn.   [death.
mors, tis, f. death; corpse; weapon of
morsus, ūs, m. bite; sting; *fig.* anguish;
taunt; grief, pain, vexation; prong.
mortālis, e, a. mortal; transient; human;
of this world.
mortālĭtas, ātis, f. mortality; death.
mortārium, ii, n. mortar.
mortĭcinus, a, um, a. dead; carrion.
mortĭfer, mortĭfĕrus, a, um, a. death-
bringing, deadly.
mortuus, a, um, a. dead, deceased.
mōrum, i, n. blackberry, mulberry.
mōrus, a, um, a. foolish.
mōrus, i, f. mulberry-tree.
mōs, mōris, m. custom, fashion; manner;
use, wont; law; temper, humour;—
mores, pl. character; behaviour;
morals;—morem gerere alicui, to comply with one's wishes;—more suo,
after its own fashion.   [Plautus.
Mostellāria, ae, f. Ghost-story, a play of
mōtio, ōnis, f. moving, motion. [about.
mōto, 1. v.a. to keep moving, to move
mōtus, ūs, m. moving, motion; commotion; disturbance; emotion;—motu
proprio, on one's own initiative.
mŏveo, mōvi, mōtum, 2. v.a. & n. to
move, to stir; to brandish; to agitate;
to affect; to provoke; to set in motion; to remove.
mox, ad. soon, presently.
mūcĭdus, a, um, a. mouldy.
mucro, ōnis, m. sharp point, edge;
sharpness; sword.
mūcus, i, mucus.
mūgil, is, mūgĭlis, is, m. mullet.
mūgio, īvi & ītum, 4. v.n. to low, to
bellow.   [ing, loud noise.
mūgītus, ūs, m. lowing, bellowing; roar-
mūla, ae, f. she-mule; mule.
mulceo, si, sum, 2. v.a. to stroke, to
touch lightly; *fig.* to soothe, to appease; to flatter, to delight.
Mulcĭbĕr, ĕris & ĕri, m. Vulcan; *fig.* fire.
mulco, 1. v.a. to beat, to cudgel.
mulcta, v. multa.
mulctra, ae, f. milk-pail.
mulgeo, si, sum & ctum, 2. v.a. to milk.
mūliebris, e, a. womanly, female, feminine; womanish, effeminate.

mūliebrĭter, ad. like a woman, effeminately.
mŭlĭer, is, f. woman; wife.
mŭliercŭla, ae, f. little woman.
mūlīnus, a, um, a. of a mule.
mūlio, ōnis, m. muleteer.
mullus, i, m. red mullet.
mulsum, i, n. mead.   [sweet as honey.
mulsus, a, um, a. mixed with honey;
multa, ae, f. (pecuniary) fine; penalty.
multĭcăvus, a, um, a. porous.   [places.
multĭfāriam, ad. on many sides, in many
multĭfĭdus, a, um, a. split; divided. [form.
multĭformis, e, a. many-shaped, multi-
multĭgĕnus, a, um, a. of many kinds.
multĭjŭgus, a, um, multĭjŭgis, is, yoked
with many; manifold.
multiplex, icis, a. having many windings;
manifold; changeable; sly.
multiplĭcĭter, ad. in manifold *or* various
ways.   [crease.
multiplĭco, 1. v.a. to multiply; to in-
multĭtūdo, ĭnis, f. great number, multitude; crowd; mob.
multo, ad. by much, by far.
multo, 1. v.a. to punish; to fine.
multum, ad. much, very; often.
multus, a, um, a. much, great; many a,
thick, frequent; diffuse;—multi, pl.
many;—multum in parvo, much in a
little; a great quantity packed in a
small space.
mūlus, i, m. mule; *fig.* ass.
mundē, ad. cleanly, neatly.
mundĭtia, ae, mundĭties, ēi, f. cleanness,
neatness; elegance;—simplex mun-
ditiis, simple in elegance.
mundus, a, um, a. clean, neat, elegant;
delicate.   [world; universe.
mundus, i, m. toilet, ornaments; dress;
mūnĕro, 1. v.a. mūnĕror, ātus, 1. v. dep.
to reward, to give, to present to, to
bestow.
mūnia, ōrum, n. pl. duties, functions.
mūnĭceps, ĭpis, c. citizen; burgess;
fellow-countryman.
mūnĭcĭpālis, e, a. municipal; (in contempt) provincial.
mūnĭcĭpium, ii, n. town subject to Rome,
but governed by its own laws; free
town.
mūnĭfĭcē, ad. bountifully, munificently.
mūnĭfĭcentia, ae, f. bountifulness, munificence.   [munificent.
mūnĭfĭcus, a, um, a. bountiful, liberal,
mūnīmen, ĭnis, n. fortification, rampart;
shelter.   [defence.
mūnīmentum, i, n. fortification; bulwark;
mūnio, īvi & ii, ītum, 4. v.n. & a. to
fortify; to build (a road); to enclose;
to strengthen; to secure.

münitio, ōnis, f. fortifying; fortification; wall; building (of roads).

münitor, ōris, m. fortifier; engineer; miner.

münus, ĕris, n. service, office, function, duty; gift; bribe; favour; show, public spectacle.

münusculum, i, n. small present.

müræna, v. murena.

mürālis, e, a. of walls; mural;—corona —, crown given as a reward to him who first scaled the enemy's walls.

mürena, ae, murena, f. kind of eel.

mürex, ĭcis, m. purple-fish; purple dye.

müria, ae, f. brine, pickle.

mürīnus, a, um, adj. of a mouse.

murmur, ŭris, n. murmur(ing); humming; growling; whisper; rustling; roaring (of the sea, a lion *or* the thunder). [to roar.

murmŭro, 1. v.n. to murmur, to mutter;

murra, murrha, ae, f. myrrh-tree; precious stone.

murreus, a, um, a. scented with myrrh.

murrĭnus, a, um, a. made of murra (precious stone).

mürus, i, m. wall; city wall.

müs, müris, c. mouse.

müsa, ae, f. muse; genius; poem; —ae, pl. sciences, poetry.

müsa (mod. hort.), banana.

musca, ae, f. fly.

muscāri (mod. hort.), grape hyacinth.

muscāria, ae, f. muscārium, ii, n. fly-flap.

muscĭpŭla, ae, f. mouse-trap.

muscōsus, a, um, a. mossy.

musculus, i, m. little mouse; (mil.) mantelet.

muscus, i, m. moss.

müsēum, i, n. library; academy; study.

müsica, ae, müsĭcē, ēs, f. music; poetry, artistic *or* scientific culture.

müsĭcus, a, um, a. musical; poetical; scientific; —, i, m. musician.

mussĭto, 1. v.n. & a. to be silent; to mutter.

musso, i, v.n. & a. to say in an undertone, to mutter; to keep silence.

mustēla, mustella, ae, f. weasel.

musteus, a, um, a. of new wine; new; fresh.

mustum, i, n. new wine, must.

mütābilis, e, a. changeable; inconstant.

mütātio, ōnis, f. changing; exchange; — vestis, going into mourning.

mütātor, ōris, m. one who exchanges *or* barters.

mütĭlo, 1. v.a. to maim, to mutilate; to shorten.

mütĭlus, a, um, a. maimed.

müt(t)io, īvi, 4. v.n. to mumble, to mutter.

müto, 1. v.a. & n. to alter, to change; to exchange; to turn; to spoil; to barter; to shift; to dye;—mutare solem, to go into exile;—mutare vestem, to go into mourning;— mutatis mutandis, those things being changed that have to be changed;—mutato nomine, the name being changed.

mütuātio, ōnis, f. borrowing.

mütuō, ad. by turns, mutually.

mütuor, ātus, 1. v.a. dep. to borrow; *fig.* to derive from. [senseless.

mütus, a, um, a. silent, dumb, mute;

mütuus, a, um, a. borrowed, lent; mutual, in return;—mutuum, i, n. loan.

mўŏpăro, onis, m. a piratical craft.

mўŏsōtis, ĭdis, f. forget-me-not.

mўrīca, ae, f. tamarisk.

mўrŏpōla, ae, m. perfumer.

mўrŏpōlium, ii, n. perfumer's shop.

myrrha, ae, f., v. murra.

myrrheus, myrrhĭnus, v. murreus, murrinus.

myrtētum, i, n. myrtle-grove.

myrteus, a, um, a. of myrtle.

myrtum, i, n. myrtle-berry.

myrtus, i, f. myrtle, myrtle-tree.

mystērium, ii, n. divine mystery; secret.

mystĭcus, a, um, a. mystical.

mўthĭcus, a, um, a. fabulous.

Næ, v. ne.

nænia, v. nenia.

nævus, i, m. mole (on the body).

Nāias, ădis, Nāis, ĭdis & ĭdos, f. waternymph. [though; indeed, nay.

nam, c. for, for example, thus; but;

namquĕ, c. for truly *or* for indeed.

nanciscor, nactus sum, 3. v.a. dep. to get, to obtain, to receive; to meet with, to light on, to reach.

nānus, i, m. dwarf.

naphtha, ae, f. naphtha.

nāpus, i, m. turnip.

narcissus (mod. hort.), daffodil.

nardĭnus, a, um, a. of nard.

nardum, i, n. nardus, i, f. nard, spikenard. [trils; nose.

nāris, is, f. nostril;—nares, ium, pl. nos-

narrābĭlis, e, a. that can be narrated.

narrātio, ōnis, f. narration, narrativ͵

narrātor, ōris, m. relater, narrator.

narrātus, ūs, m., v. narratio.

narro, 1. v.a. to tell, to relate, to narrate.

narthēcium, ii, n. medicine-chest.

nascor, nātus, 3. v.n. dep. to be born; *fig.* to proceed (from), to arise.

nassa, ae, f. creel; *fig.* snare, net.

nasturtium, ii, n. cress.

nāsus, i, m. nose; nozzle, spout; handle; *fig.* sense of smelling; sagacity.

nāsūtus, a, um, a. large-nosed; *fig.* sagacious, carping.

nāta, ae, f. daughter.   [birth, natal.

nātālĭcius, nātālĭtius, a, um, a. of one's

nātālis, e, pertaining to birth, natal; —, **is,** m. birthday;—**nātāles, ium,** m. pl. lineage, descent, family.

nātātio, ōnis, f. swimming.

nātātor, ōris, m. swimmer.

nātes, is, f. pl. rump, buttocks.

nātio, ōnis, f. race; nation; people; clan.

nātīvus, a, um, a. innate; natural, native.

nāto, i. v.n. to swim; to be overflowed; to sail; (eyes) to be glassy; to toss about; to be restless; *fig.* to waver.

natrix, īcis, f. water-snake.

nātūra, ae, f. nature; character, habit; instinct; element;—**rerum —,** world, universe.

nātūrālis, e, a. natural; innate.

nātūrālĭter, ad. naturally, by nature, consistently with nature.

nātus, ūs, m. birth; age.

nātus, i, m. son; offspring.

nauarchus, v. navarchus.

naufrăgium, ii, n. shipwreck; *fig.* ruin.

naufrăgus, a, um, a. shipwrecked; causing shipwreck; *fig.* ruined.

naumăchia, ae, f. mock sea-fight.

nausea, ae, f. sea-sickness; vomiting.

nauseo, i. v.n. to be sea-sick; *fig.* to feel disgust.

nauta, ae, m. sailor, seaman.

nautĭcus, a, um, a. nautical;—**nautici, ōrum,** m. pl. seamen.

nāvāle, is, n. dock; arsenal.

nāvālis, e, a. naval;—**corona —,** crown given as the reward of a naval victory; —**navalia, ium,** n. pl. dockyard, naval arsenal.   [miral.

nāvarchus, i, m. captain of a ship, ad-

nāvĭcŭla, ae, f. little ship, skiff.

nāvĭcŭlārius, ii, m. shipowner.

nāvĭfrăgus, a, um, a. wrecking.

nāvĭgābĭlis, e, a. navigable.

nāvĭgātio, ōnis, f. sailing, voyage.

nāvĭger, a, um, a. ship-bearing.

nāvĭgium, ii, n. vessel, ship.

nāvĭgo, i. v.n. & a. to sail, to navigate; to swim;—**naviget Anticyram,** let him voyage to Anticyra (where grows an antidote to madness).

nāvis, is, f. ship; — **longa,** ship of war; — **oneraria,** merchant ship; — **praetoria,** admiral's ship;—**navem solvere,** to set sail.

nāvĭta, v. nauta.

nāvĭter, ad. diligently, zealously; wholly.

nāvo, i. v.a. to do *or* to accomplish with zeal; to exhibit.

nāvus, a, um, a. active, assiduous.

nē, interj. verily; indeed.

nē, ad. & c. not; that not; in order that not; lest; much less;—**ne plus ultra,** nothing further, the utmost;—**ne . . . quidem,** not even;—**ne quid nimis,** (do) nothing in excess;—**ne sutor ultra crepidam,** let the cobbler stick to his last.

nĕ, interrogative enclitic particle;— **videsne,** do you see? (in indirect questions) whether.

nebris, ĭdis, f. fawn-skin.

nĕbŭla, ae, f. mist, vapour, fog; cloud.

nĕbŭlo, ōnis, m. idle rascal.

nĕbŭlōsus, a, um, a. misty, cloudy, dark.

nec, c. neither; nor; and not; — **non,** and also; **nec . . . nec,** neither . . . nor.

necdum, c. nor yet.

nĕcessārio, ad. necessarily.

nĕcessārius, a, um, a. necessary; indispensable; related (to); —, **ii,** m. relative; near friend.

nĕcesse, a.n. indecl. absolutely necessary.

nĕcessĭtas, ātis, f. necessity; fate; constraint; familiarity; tie of friendship; relationship; want.   [intimacy.

nĕcessĭtūdo, ĭnis, f. necessity; need, want;

necnĕ, ad. or not.

necnon, v. nec.

nĕco, i. v.a. to kill, to slay.   [guard.

nĕcŏpīnans, antis, a. not expecting; off

nĕcŏpīnāto, ad. unexpectedly.

nĕcŏpīnātus, a, um, a., **nĕcŏpīnus, a, um,** a. unexpected.   [the dead.

necrōmantĭa, ae, f. necromancy; raising

nectar, ăris, n. nectar, the drink of the gods; anything sweet, pleasant *or* delicious.   [nectar.

nectăreus, a, um, a. nectared; sweet as

necto, xui & xi, xum, 3. v.a. to bind, to tie, to join together (as in chains); to knit; to link; to weave; to contrive.

nĕcŭbĭ, ad. lest anywhere.

nĕcunde, ad. lest from any place.

nēdum, c. much less, still less; not to say, much more.

nefandus, a, um, a. impious, execrable.

nĕfāriē, ad. impiously, abominably.

nĕfārius, a, um, a. impious, abominable, nefarious.

nĕfas, n. indecl. sin, crime (against divine law); wicked action; horrible object; —! interj. horrid! dreadful!

nĕfastus, a, um, a. inauspicious; impious; wicked; unlucky;—**dies nefasti,** days on which judgment could not be pronounced nor assemblies of the people be held.

nĕgātio, ōnis, f. denial, negation.
nĕgĭto, 1. v.a. to deny emphatically.
neglectio, ōnis, f. neglecting, neglect.
neglĕgens, entis, p. & a. heedless, negligent.
neglĕgenter, ad. heedlessly, negligently.
neglĕgentia, ae, f. heedlessness, negligence.
neglĕgo, lexi, lectum, 3. v.a. not to heed, to neglect; to slight; to overlook.
nĕgo, 1. v.n. & a. to say no, to deny; to refuse, to decline.
nĕgōtiālis, e, a. connected with business.
nĕgōtians, antis, m. wholesale dealer; banker.
nĕgōtiātor, ōris, m. banker; tradesman.
nĕgōtior, ātus, 1. v.n. & a. dep. to carry on a banking business; to trade.
nĕgōtiōsus, a, um, a. busy.
nĕgōtium, ii, n. business; affair; difficulty; trouble.
nĕmĕsia (mod. hort.), nemesia.
nēmo, inis, c. no one, nobody; — non, every one; non —, many a one; — unus, no single person;—nemine contradicente (nem. con.), no one opposing, unanimously.   [bell.
nemophĭla (mod. hort.), California blue-
nĕmŏrālis, e, a. woody, sylvan.
nĕmŏrensis, e, a. sylvan.
nĕmŏrĭvăgus, a, um, a. wandering through the glades.
nĕmŏrōsus, a, um, a. woody.
nempĕ, c. certainly; forsooth; of course.
nĕmus, ŏris, n. grove; forest.
nēnia, ae, f. funeral dirge sung in praise of the dead; fig. mournful ditty; lullaby.
neo, nēvi, nētum, 2. v.a. to spin; to weave; to interlace.
nĕpa, ae, f. scorpion.
nĕpos, ōtis, m. grandson; nephew; descendant; spendthrift;—nepotes, pl. posterity.
neptis, is, f. granddaughter.
Neptūnus, i, m. Neptune, (poet.) sea.
nēquam, a. indecl. worthless; vile, bad.
nēquāquam, ad. in no wise, not at all.
nēquĕ, c. not; and not; cf. nec.
nēquĕdŭm, v. necdum.
nēqueo, īvi & ii, ĭtum, 4. v.n. to be unable;—nequeo, I cannot.
nēquicquam or nēquĭquam, ad. in vain.
nēquis, lest any one.
nēquĭter, ad. worthlessly, badly.
nēquĭtia, ae, nēquĭties, ēi, f. (moral) badness; idleness; prodigality; wantonness; villainy.
Nērēis, ĭdos, f. sea-nymph.
Nēreus, ın. Nereus, (poet.) the sea.
nērion, ii, n. oleander.
nervōsē, ad. energetically; strongly.

nervōsus, a, um, a. sinewy, nervous; vigorous.
nervus, i, m. sinew; nerve; bowstring; string (of a lute, etc.); fetter; prison; strength, vigour.
nescio, īvi & ii, ītum, 4. v.a. not to know; to be ignorant.
nescius, a, um, a. not knowing, ignorant.
neu, v. neve.
neuter, tra, trum, a. neither (of two); of neither gender.
neutĭquam, ad. by no means, in no wise.
neutro, ad. to neither side.
nēve, ad. and not, nor, and lest; neve . . . neve, neither . . . nor.   [slaughter.
nex, nĕcis, f. (violent) death, murder,
nexĭlis, e, a. tied together.
nexum, i, n., nexus, ūs, m. binding together; clasp; coil; obligation; condition of a freeman serving for debt.
nexus, i, m. one who has pledged his person as security for a debt; prisoner.
nĭ, ad. & c. if not; unless;—quid ni? why not?
nĭcōtiāna (mod. hort.), tobacco plant.
nicto, 1. v.n. to wink.
nīdĭfĭco, 1. v.n. to build a nest.
nĭdor, ōris, m. savour (of anything roasted); smell; steam.
nīdŭlor, 1. v. dep. a. & n. to build a nest.
nīdŭlus, i, m. little nest.
nīdus, i, m. nest; young birds (in a nest); fig. residence, house.
nigella (mod. hort.), love-in-a-mist.
nĭger, gra, grum, a. black, dark; fig. ill-omened; false; wicked.
nigrans, antis, p. & a. black, dusky.
nigresco, grui, 3. v.n. to become black, to grow dark.
nigro, 1. v.a. & n. to blacken; to be black.
nigror, ōris, m. blackness.
nĭhil, n. indecl. nothing; —, ad. not at all;—nihil ad rem, nothing to do with the case.   [standing.
nĭhĭlōmĭnus, c. nevertheless, notwith-
nĭhĭlum, ad. nothing as yet.
nĭhĭlum, i, n. nothing;—de nihilo, for nothing; for no good reason;—homo nihili, good-for-nothing fellow;—nihili esse, to be good for nought;—ex nihilo nihil fit, nothing is made out of nothing.
nīl, contr. of nihil, nothing, no;—nil admirari, to be surprised at nothing; to adopt a superior attitude.
nimbōsus, a, um, a. stormy, rainy.
nimbus, i, m. rain-storm; thunder-cloud; cloud.
nĭmio, ad. too much.   [forsooth.
nĭmīrum, ad. without doubt, certainly,
nĭmis, ad. too much; beyond measure.
nĭmium, ad. too much, too; very.

nǐmius, a, um, a. excessive, too great, too much.

ningit, nxit, 3. v.n. it snows.

nǐsi, c. if not; unless;—**nisi prius** (unless previously), a writ instructing a sheriff to empanel a jury unless the judges have previously gone away on assize duty.

nīsus, ūs, m. pressure; endeavour; exertion; force; throes (of childbirth).

nĭtēdŭla, ae, f. dormouse.

nĭtella, ae, f. dormouse.

nĭteo, ui, 2. v.n. to shine, to glisten; to be sleek and plump.   [to grow sleek.

nĭtesco, tui, 3. v.n. to shine out *or* forth;

nĭtĭdē, ad. brightly; finely.

nĭtĭdus, a, um, a. shining, glittering, bright; *fig.* polished, fine; spruce; sleek, plump.

nītor, nīsus & nixus, 3. v.n. dep. to lean *or* rest upon; to climb; to endeavour; to exert oneself; *fig.* to rely (upon).

nītor, ōris, m. brightness, splendour; beauty; neatness, elegance.

nivālis, e, a. snowy, snow-covered; snow-like.

nĭveus, a, um, a. snowy; snow-white.

nĭvōsus, a, um, a. full of snow, snowy.

nix, nĭvis, f. snow; white hair.

nixus, ūs, m., v. **nisus.**

no, 1. v.n. to swim; to sail; to float.

nōbĭlis, e, a. famous, celebrated; high-born; *fig.* superior; —, **is,** m. noble-man.

nōbĭlĭtas, ātis, f. renown, glory; high birth; excellence; nobleness.

nōbĭlĭto, 1. v.a. to make known; to render famous; to render notorious; to ennoble.   [jure.

nŏceo, cui, cĭtum, 2. v.n. to hurt, to innŏcīvus, a, um,** a. noxious, hurtful.

noctĭlūca, ae, f. moon.

noctĭvăgus, a, um, a. night-wandering.

noctu, by night.

noctua, ae, f. short-eared owl.

nocturnus, a, um, a. nocturnal, nightly.

nōdo, 1. v.a. to make knotty; to tie in a knot.   [difficult.

nōdōsus, a, um, a. knotty; *fig.* intricate,

nōdus, i, m. knot; knob; joint; *fig.* difficulty; intricacy; bond.

nōlo, nōlui, nolle, v. ir. not to wish; to be unwilling;—**nolens volens,** willy-nilly, whether willing *or* unwilling.

nōmen, ĭnis, n. name; family, house; bond; debt; *fig.* fame; pretence.

nōmenclātor, ōris, m. slave who attended his master in canvassing (for the purpose of telling him the names of those whom he met).

nōmĭnātim, ad. by name, expressly.

nōmĭnātio, ōnis, f. naming; nomination (to an office).

nōmĭnātīvus casus, nominative case.

nōmĭnĭto, 1. v.a. to name.

nōmĭno, 1. v.a. to name; to entitle; to nominate; to accuse, to mention, to make famous.

nōn, ad. not; — **quod,** not that, not as if;—**non cuivis homini,** it is not every man's privilege;—**non possumus,** we cannot do it (a blank negative);—**non sequitur,** it does not follow (a logical fallacy).

Nōnae, ārum, f. pl. the nones; the fifth day of the month, except in March, May, July, and October, when the nones fell on the seventh day.

nōnāgēnārius, a, um, a. containing ninety.

nōnāgēni, ae, a, a. num. ninety each.

nōnāgēsimus, a, um, a. num. ninetieth.

nōnāgies, ad. ninety times.

nōnāginta, a. num. ninety.

nonānus, a, um, a. of the ninth legion.

nondum, ad. not yet, not as yet.

nongenti, ae, a, a. num. nine hundred.

nonnĕ, ad. not? if not, whether not.

nonnēmo, v. nemo.

nonnĭhil, n. indecl. somewhat; a little.

nonnullus, a, um, a. some, several.

nonnunquam, ad. sometimes.

nonnusquam, ad. in some places.

nōnus, a, um, a. num. the ninth.

nōnusdĕcĭmus, a, um, a. num. nineteenth.   [rule, pattern.

norma, ae, f. carpenter's square; *fig.*

nōs, pn. we.   [perceive.

noscĭto, 1. v.a. to know, to recognise; to

nosco, nōvi, nōtum, 3. v.a. to get a knowledge of, to learn to know; to know; to acknowledge;—**nosce teipsum,** know thyself;—**noscitur a sociis,** a man is known by the company he keeps.

noster, stra, strum, pn. a. our, our own, ours; one of us, our friend; favourable to us: dear, good (in addresses).

nostras, ātis, a. of our country, native.

nŏta, ae, f. mark, sign, note; shorthand; token; nod, beck; character; letter; writing; spot, mole; brand, tattoo-mark; censor's condemnation;—**notæ,** pl. letters; secret writing.

nŏtābĭlis, e, a. remarkable, notable; notorious, infamous.

nŏtārius, ii, m. shorthand writer; clerk.

nŏtātio, ōnis, f. marking, noting; anim-adversion (of the censor).

nōtesco, tui, 3. v.n. to become known.

nŏthus, a, um, a. spurious; illegitimate; (animals) mongrel.

nōtio, ōnis, f. idea, notion; investigation.

nōtitia, ae, nōtities, ēi, f. celebrity; knowledge; conception.

nŏto, 1. v.a. to mark; to write down; to observe; to censure; to brand; to find fault with;—**nota bene** (N.B.), mark well.   [familiar.

nōtus, a, um, a. known; notorious;

Nōtus, Nōtos, i, m. south wind.

nŏvācŭla, ae, f. razor.

nŏvālis, is, f. **nŏvāle, is,** n. fallow-land; cultivated field.

nŏvē, ad. newly; strangely.

nŏvellus, a, um, a. young, new; fresh.

nŏvem, a. num. nine.

Nŏvember, Nŏvembris, is, m. November.

nŏvendĕcim, a. num. nineteen.

nŏvendiālis, e, a. of nine days, lasting nine days.

nŏvēnus, a, um, a. num. nine each.

nŏverca, ae, f. stepmother.

nŏvercālis, e, a. of or like a stepmother; fig. hostile, malevolent.

nŏvicius, novītius, a, um, a. new, fresh, recent; (of slaves) newly purchased.

nŏvies, ad. nine times.

nŏvissimē, ad. last of all, finally, recently.

nŏvissimus, a, um, a. last, hindermost, rear; fig. extreme.

nŏvītas, ātis, f. newness, novelty; upstart condition; rareness.

nŏvo, 1. v.a. to make new, to renovate; to alter; to revolutionise.

nŏvus, a, um, a. new; young, fresh, recent;—**novus homo,** a parvenu.

nox, noctis, f. night; darkness; sleep; dream; blindness; death; ignorance; —**nocte, de nocte, noctū,** by night.

noxa, ae, f. hurt, injury; crime; punishment.

noxia, ae, f. offence, trespass, injury.

noxius, a, um, a. hurtful, noxious; guilty, criminal.   [expression.

nūbēcula, ae, f. little cloud; fig. gloomy

nūbēs, is, f. cloud; smoke; swarm; fig. phantom; gloominess; mournful condition; veil, cloak; threatening appearance.

nūbifĕr, a, um, cloud-capped.

nūbigĕna, ae, c. cloud-born.

nūbilis, e, a. marriageable.

nūbilus, a, um, a. cloudy; lowering;— **nūbilum, i,** n. cloudy sky or weather; —**nūbila, ōrum,** n. pl. clouds.   [band).

nūbo, psi, ptum, 3. v.n. to marry (a husband).

nŭceus, a, um, a. of a nut.

nŭcifrangibŭlum, i, n. nutcracker; fig. tooth.   [fruits).

nucleus, i, m. kernel; nut; stone (of

nŭdius tertius, ad. three days ago; the day before yesterday.

nŭdo, 1. v.a. to bare; to strip, to uncover; to plunder; to bereave; fig. to expose.

nūdus, a, um, a. naked, bare; destitute; fig. poor; simple, unabandoned;—**nuda veritas,** truth unadorned.

nūgæ, ārum, f. pl. jokes, jests, trifles, nonsense; a company of jesters.

nūgātor, ōris, m. jester, trifler; swaggerer.

nūgātōrius, a, um, a. trifling, worthless, useless, futile, nugatory.

nūgax, ācis, a. jesting, trifling, frivolous.

nūgor, ātus, 1. v.n. dep. to jest, to play the fool, to talk nonsense.

nullus, a, um, nullīus, a. not any, none, no;—**nulli secundus,** second to none, at the top of the tree.

num, interrog. particle (in direct questions when the answer ' no ' is expected); whether (in indir. questions).

numatus, v. **nummatus.**

nūmen, ĭnis, n. nod; command, will; divine will; inspiration, divine majesty, god, goddess.

nŭmĕrābilis, e, a. that may be numbered; small, little.   [money.

nŭmĕrātus, a, um, a. paid down, in ready

nŭmĕro, 1. v.a. to count, to number; to esteem.

nŭmĕrōsē, ad. numerously; rhythmically; melodiously.

nŭmĕrōsus, a, um, a. numerous; manifold; rhythmical; harmonious; melodious.

nŭmĕrus, i, m. number; measure; rhythm; poetry; tune; order, class, troop; condition, rank.

nummārius, a, um, a. of money; bribed with money.

nummātus, a, um, a. moneyed, rich.

nummŭlus, i, m. small sum.

nummus, i, m. coin, money; fig. farthing.

numquam, v. **nunquam.**

numquis, v. **nunquis.**

nūmus, v. **nummus.**

nunc, ad. now, at present; **nunc . . . nunc,** one time . . . another time.

nunciam = **nunc jam.**

nuncio, v. **nuntio.**

nuncŭpo, 1. v.a. to call, to name; to proclaim; to appoint; to vow.

nundīnæ, ārum, f. pl. the ninth day, market-day; fig. traffic.

nundīnātio, onis, f. trafficking.

nundīnor, ātus, 1. v. dep. to hold a market; to trade; to purchase, to buy; to sell.

nundīnum, i, n. market-time.

nunquam, ad. at no time, never; certainly not.

nunquis, quæ, quid, pn. is there any,
if any.   [to relate, to inform.
nuntio, 1. v.a. to announce, to declare;
nuntius, a, um, a. bringing tidings, reporting; —, ij, m. messenger, courier;
message, tidings.   [in modern times.
nūper, ad. newly, lately, not long ago;
nupta, ae, f. bride; wife.
nuptiæ, ārum, f. pl. marriage, nuptials.
nuptiālis, e, a. nuptial.   [woman.
nŭrus, ūs, f. daughter-in-law; young
nusquam, ad. nowhere, in no place; towards no place; on no occasion; **to** or
for nothing; **— esse,** not to exist.
nūto, 1. v.n. to nod; to sway to and fro;
fig. to waver; to be faithless; to be in
peril.
nūtrīcius, ii, m. tutor.
nūtrīcŭla, ae, f. nurse.
nūtrīmen, ĭnis, n. **nūtrīmentum, i,** n.
nourishment, nutriment.
nūtrio, īvi & ii, **ītum,** 4. v.a. to suckle, to
nourish, to foster, to bring up; to sustain; to feed (a flame).
nūtrix, īcis, f. wet-nurse, nurse.
nūtus, ūs, m. nod; will, command;
pleasure; favour; consent.
nux, nŭcis, f. nut; nut-tree; **— cassa,**
empty nut; *fig.* thing of no value.
nympha, ae, nymphē, ēs, f. nymph, bride,
mistress.
nymphæa, ae, f. water-lily.

Ō, i. oh! **— si,** yet, oh! if only; **—O si sic
omnia,** if only everything were thus; **—
O tempora, O mores,** what an age!
what manners!
ŏb, pr. for; by reason of.   [i, m. debtor.
ŏbaerātus, a, um, a. involved in debt; —,
ŏbambŭlo, 1. v.n. to go past; to walk
about; to prowl around.
ŏbarmo, 1. v.a. to arm.
ŏbăro, 1. v.a. to plough up.
obba, ae, f. beaker.
obc . . ., v. occ . .
obdo, dĭdi, dĭtum, 3. v.a. to put before or
against; to shut; *fig.* to expose; to
oppose.
obdormio, īvi & ii, **ītum,** 4. v.n., **obdormisco,** 3. v.n. to fall asleep.
obdūco, xi, ctum, 3. v.a. to lead or draw
before; to cover or lay over; to overspread; to wrinkle; to hide; to spend,
to pass.
obductio, ōnis, f. veiling (of criminals).
obdūresco, rui, 3. v.n. *fig.* to become
hardened or insensible.
obdūro, 1. v.n. *fig.* to persist, to endure.
obedi . . ., v. obœdi . . .

ŏbĕliscus, i, m. obelisk.
obeo, īvi & ii, **ītum,** 4. v.n. & a. to go to;
to go down; to meet; to set (of stars,
etc.); to fall; to perish; to die; to
traverse; to visit; to survey; to
attend to; to engage in.
ŏbĕquĭto, 1. v.n. to ride towards or up to.
ŏberro, 1. v.n. to wander or ramble about;
fig. to blunder.
ŏbēsus, a, um, a. fat, stout, plump, gross.
ŏbex, obĭcis & **objĭcis,** m. & f. bolt, bar;
barrier; obstacle.
obf . . ., v. off . . .   [cleave to.
ŏbhæresco, hæsi, 3. v.n. to stick; to
ŏbĭter, ad. on or by the way; in passing;
—obiter dictum, a remark made
incidentally.
ŏbĭtus, ūs, m. approaching; approach,
visit; setting (of the sun, etc.); *fig.*
downfall; death, ruin.
objăceo, ui, 2. v.n. to lie before.
objecto, 1. v.a. to throw before or against;
to expose (to); to upbraid one (with).
objectus, a, um, a. opposite, lying before,
situated between.
objectus, ūs, m. placing before; opposing; interposition; barrier.
objex, v. obex.
objĭcio, jēci, jectum, 3. v.a. to throw
before or towards; to present; to
expose (to); to interpose; to lay to
one's charge; **—objici,** to happen.
objurgātio, ōnis, f. chiding; reproof.
objurgātor, ōris, m. chider, blamer,
rebuker.
objurgo, 1. v.a. to chide; to rebuke.
oblectāmen, ĭnis, n., **oblectāmentum, i,** n.
delight, pleasure, amusement.
oblectātio, ōnis, f. delighting, delight.
oblecto, 1. v.a. to delight, to please, to
amuse.
oblīdo, si, sum, 3. v.a. to squeeze together;
to strangle.
obligātio, ōnis, f. bond; obligation.
obligo, 1. v.a. to bind or tie around; to
swathe, to close; *fig.* to oblige; to render liable; to make guilty; to engage.
oblīmo, 1. v.a. to cover with mud; *fig.* to
squander.   [daub; *fig.* to defile.
oblīno, lēvi (līni), lĭtum, 3. v.a. to be-
oblīquē, ad. sideways, athwart; *fig.* indirectly.   [direct.
oblīquus, a, um, a. slanting, oblique; in-
oblītesco, tui, 3. n. to hide.
oblīttěro, 1. v.a. to blot out; *fig.* to cause
to be forgotten.
oblīvio, ōnis, f. oblivion; forgetfulness.
oblīviōsus, a, um, a. forgetful; producing
forgetfulness.
oblīviscor, lītus, 3. v. dep. to forget.
oblīvium, ii, n. forgetfulness, oblivion.

oblo̅ngus, a, um, a. oblong, rather long.
oblŏquor, quūtus & cūtus, 3. v.a. dep. to contradict; (poet.) to sing with; to accompany.
obluctor, ātus sum, 1. dep. to contend with, to struggle against.
obmōlior, lītus sum, 4. v.a. dep. to set against, to oppose; to obstruct.
obmurmŭro, 1. v.n. to murmur or roar at or to.
obmūtesco, mūtui, 3. v.n. to lose one's speech; to be silent; fig. to be out of use.
obnītor, sus, xus, 3. v. dep. to lean against; to struggle against.
obnixus, a, um, a. resolute.
obnoxiē, ad. humbly.
obnoxius, a, um, a. liable (to); addicted (to); exposed to; weak, frail; dangerous; submissive; abject.
obnūbo, psi, ptum, 3. v.a. to veil.
obnuntiātio, ōnis, f. the announcement of evil omens.
obnuntio, 1. v.a. to announce an adverse or evil omen.
ŏbœdiens, entis, a. obedient.
ŏbœdienter, ad. obediently; readily.
ŏbœdientia, ae, f. obedience.
ŏbœdio, īvi or ii, ītum, 4. v.n. to obey; to hearken; to comply with.
ŏbŏrior, ortus, 4. v. dep. to arise, to appear or spring up before; to well up (of tears).
obp . . ., v. opp . . .
obrēpo, psi, ptum, 3. v.n. to creep up to; fig. to steal upon; to take by surprise.
obrigesco, rigŭi, 3. v.n. to become stiff, to stiffen. [a new one.
obrŏgo, 1. v.a. to alter part of a law by
obruo, ui, ŭtum, 3. v.a. to overwhelm; to bury; to sink; to drown; to overthrow; to weigh down.
obsæpio, psi, ptum, 4. v.a. to enclose; to bar.
obscœnē, ad. indecently; lewdly.
obscœnĭtas, ātis, f. lewdness; obscenity.
obscœnus, a, um, a. inauspicious; repulsive; ill-boding; detestable; foul; beastly; obscene. [tion.
obscūrātio, ōnis, f. darkening, obscura-
obscūrē, ad. darkly; indistinctly; privily.
obscūrĭtas, ātis, f. darkness, obscurity; uncertainty; meanness.
obscūro, 1. v.a. to darken, to obscure; to conceal; to make indistinct; to cause to be forgotten.
obscūrus, a, um, a. dark, shady, obscure; gloomy; doubtful; unintelligible;— obscurum per obscurius, to explain the unintelligible by what is more unintelligible.

obsecrātio, ōnis, f. supplication, entreaty; asseveration; public prayer.
obsecro, 1. v.a. to implore; to beg.
obsĕcundo, 1. v.n. to comply with, to submit to.
obsēpio, v. obsæpio. [quiously.
obsĕquenter, ad. with compliance, obse-
obsĕquium, ii, n. compliance, indulgence; obedience.
obsĕquor, cūtus, 3. v. dep. to comply with, to gratify, to submit to.
obsĕro, 1. v.a. to bolt or shut up.
obsĕro, sēvi, sĭtum, 3. v.a. to sow or plant about; to sow with; to fill with.
observantia, ae, f. attention, respect.
observātio, ōnis, f. observation; circumspection, care.
observĭto, 1. v.a. to notice carefully.
observo, 1. v.a. to watch, to observe; to attend to; to respect, to esteem, to court.
obsĕs, ĭdis, c. hostage; security, bail.
obsessio, ōnis, f. besieging, blockade.
obsessor, ōris, m. besieger; frequenter.
obsĭdeo, sēdi sessum, 2. v.n. & a. to besiege, to blockade; to frequent; to surround; to occupy.
obsĭdio, ōnis, f. siege, blockade; fig. imminent danger.
obsĭdium, ii, n. siege, blockade.
obsĭdo, 3. v.a. to besiege; to occupy.
obsigno, 1. v.a. to seal up; to stamp; to impress.
obsisto, stĭti, stĭtum, 3. v.n. to stand in the way; to resist, to oppose; to hinder.
obsĭtus, a, um, p. & a. overgrown, covered.
obsŏlesco, lēvi, lētum, 3. v.n. to grow out of use; to decay. [of use; dirty.
obsŏlētus, a, um, a. worn out; old; out
obsōnātor, ōris, m. caterer.
obsōnium, ii, n. viands, fish.
obsōno, 1. v.a., obsōnor, ātus sum, 1. v. dep. to cater, to purvey; fig. to treat, to give a banquet.
obsorbeo, ui, 2. v.a. to swallow down.
obstetrix, īcis, f. midwife.
obstinātē, ad. firmly; stubbornly.
obstinātio, ōnis, f. firmness; stubbornness.
obstinātus, a, um, a. steady; stubborn.
obstino, 1. v.a. to persist (in), to be obstinate.
obstĭpesco, v. obstŭpesco.
obstĭpus, a, um, a. awry, crooked, bent forwards or to the ground.
obsto, stĭti, ĭtum, 1. v.n. to stand before; fig. to withstand; to hinder.
obstrĕpo, ui, ĭtum, 3. v.n. to roar against; to resound; to disturb; to annoy; to hinder.

obstringo, nxi, ctum, 3. v.a. to bind, to tie
or fasten up; to lay under an obligation.

obstructio, ōnis, f. obstruction, barrier.

obstruo, xi, ctum, 3. v.a. to pile before or
against; to block up; to stop (the ears).

obstŭpĕfăcio, fēci, factum, 3. v.a. to
astonish, to amaze; to rob of one's
senses;—**obstŭpĕfīo, factus, fĭeri,** to be
astonished.

obstŭpesco, pŭi, 3. v.n. to be stupefied;
to grow numb; fig. to be amazed.

obsum, obfui & offui, obesse, v.n. ir. to
hurt, to injure.   [close up.

obsuo, ui, ūtum, 3. v.a. to sew up; to

obsurdesco, dui, 3. v.n. to become deaf.

obtĕgo, xi, ctum, 3. v.a. to cover over;
fig. to conceal; to protect.   [obey.

obtempĕro, 1. v.a. to comply with, to

obtendo, di, tum, 3. v.a. to stretch or
spread before; fig. to pretend; to
conceal; to plead in excuse.   [pretext.

obtentus, ūs, m. spreading before; fig.

obtĕro, trīvi, trītum, 3. v.a. to crush; to
destroy; fig. to trample on, to disparage.

obtestātio, ōnis, f. entreaty, supplication; importunity.

obtestor, ātus, 1. v. dep. to call as a
witness; to protest; to entreat.

obtexo, ui, 3. v.a. to overspread.

obticesco, ticui, 3. v.n. to become silent.

obtineo, tĭnui, tentum, 2. v.a. & n. to hold;
to maintain; to prove; to support;
to obtain; to gain; to last; to prevail.

obtingo, tĭgi, 3. v.n. to fall to one's lot; to
befall.

obtorpesco, pŭi, 3. v.n. to become numb;
to lose feeling.   [twist or turn round.

obtorqueo, si, tum, 2. v.a. to wrench, to

obtrectātio, ōnis, f. detraction, disparagement.

obtrectātor, ōris, m. detractor.

obtrecto, 1. v.n. & a. to detract from; to
decry.   [late; to kill.

obtrunco, 1. v.a. to cut down; to muti-

obtundo, tŭdi, tūsum, 3. v.a. to strike at
or on; to make blunt; to stun; to
weaken.

obturbo, 1. v.a. to disturb, to disorder.

obtūro, 1. v.a. to block up.

obtūsus, a, um, a. blunt; dull; insensible; weak.

obtūtus, ūs, m. gaze; contemplation.

ŏbumbro, 1. v.a. to overshadow; fig. to
darken; to conceal; to defend.

ŏbuncus, a, um, a. bent, hooked.

ŏbustus, burnt; hardened by burning.

obvĕnio, vēni, ventum, 4. v.n. to meet, to
come to one by chance; to happen; to
fall to by lot.

obversor, ātus, 1. v. dep. to appear before
one; to be on the spot.

obverto, ti, sum, 3. v.a. to turn or direct
towards; to turn about.

obviam, ad. in the way; towards, against;
to meet; at hand.

obvius, a, um, a. in the way, meeting;
easy; hindering; hostile; exposed
(to).

obvolvo, vi, ūtum, 3. v.a. to wrap round,
to muffle up, to cover; fig. to cloak.

occæco, 1. v.a. to blind; to darken; to
conceal; to benumb; to make unintelligible.   [(also fig.).

occallesco, lui, 3. v.n. to become callous

occāsio, ōnis, f. opportunity, fit time.

occāsus, ūs, m. sun-setting, west; fig.
ruin, end, death.

occātio, ōnis, f. harrowing.

occidens, entis, m. quarter of the setting
sun, the west.

occidentālis, e, a. western.   [tion.

occīdio, ōnis, f. massacre; utter destruc-

occĭdo, cĭdi, cāsum, 3. v.n. to fall down;
to set (of the sun, etc.); to die, to
perish.   [down; to kill, to slay.

occīdo, cīdi, cīsum, 3. v.n. to strike

occĭduus, a, um, a. going down, setting;
western; fig. sinking, failing.

occĭno, ui, 3. v.n. to croak.   [begin.

occĭpio, cēpi, ceptum, 3. v.a. & n. to

occĭpĭtium, ii, n. the back of the head.

occīsio, ōnis, f. massacre, slaughter.

occlūdo, si, sum, 3. v.a. to shut up.

occo, 1. v.a. to harrow.

occŭbo, 1. v.n. to lie down; to repose in
the grave.

occulco, 1. v.a. to trample down.

occŭlo, cŭlui, cultum, 3. v.a. to cover
over; to conceal.

occultātio, ōnis, f. concealment.

occultē, ad. secretly, privately.

occulto, 1. v.a. to hide.

occultus, a, um, a. hidden, secret.

occumbo, cŭbui, cŭbitum, 3. v.n. to sink
down; to fall upon; to die.

occŭpātio, ōnis, f. taking possession of;
business, occupation.

occŭpo, 1. v.a. to occupy; to seize upon
(forcibly); to attack; to hold; to
overspread; to fill; to engage; to
take up.

occurro, curri, cursum, 3. v.n. to run towards or to meet; to appear before;
to attack; to counteract; to occur.

occursātio, ōnis, f. running to meet,
courting; attention.

occurso, 1. v.a. to run to meet; to rush
against; to attack.

occursus, ūs, m. meeting.

ōcĕănus, i, m. ocean.

ŏcellus, i, m. eye, (*fig.*) darling.
ŏcimum (mod. hort.), basil.
ŏcior, a. swifter, fleeter.
ŏcius, ad. more quickly, sooner.
ocrea, ae, f. greave, leg-covering.
octāvus, a, um, a. num. eighth;—octā-
    vum, for the eighth time.
octies, ad. eight times.   [hundredth.
octingentēsimus, a, um, a. num. eight
octingenti, ae, a, a. num. eight hundred.
octo, a. num. eight.
Octōber, bris, m. October.
octōgēnārius, a, um, a. containing eighty,
    eighty years old.
octōgēni, ae, a, a. num. eighty each.
octōgēsimus, a, um, a. num. eightieth.
octōgies, ad. eighty times.
octōginta, num. eighty.
octōni, ae, a, a. num. eight each.
octōphŏron, i, n. litter carried by eight
    persons.
octuplicātus, a, um, a. octupled, multi-
    plied by eight.
octuplus, a, um, a. eight-fold.
octussis, is, m. eight asses.
ŏcŭlus, i, m. eyesight; bud; luminary;
    ornament; glory; darling.
ŏdi, ŏdisse, v.a. def. to hate; to dislike;
    —oderint dum metuant, let them hate
    as long as they fear.
ŏdiōsē, ad. hatefully.   [troublesome.
ŏdiōsus, a, um, a. hateful, odious;
ŏdium, ii, n. hatred, grudge, ill-will,
    spite;—odio esse, to be hated;—odium
    theologicum, hatred engendered by
    differences of creed.
ŏdor, ŏris, m. smell, scent, odour; per-
    fume; (*fig.*) suspicion; suggestion.
ŏdōrātus, a, um, p. & a. sweet-smelling,
    fragrant; —, ūs, m. smelling; sense of
    smell.
ŏdōrifer, a, um, a. fragrant.
ŏdōro, i. v.a. to perfume.
ŏdōror, ātus, i. v. dep. to smell out, to
    scent; *fig.* to snuff; to seek for; to
    trace out; to get a smattering.
ŏdōrus, a, um, a. odorous, fragrant;
    keen-scented.
ŏdos, v. odor.
œcūmĕnicus, a, um, a. belonging to the
    whole world; ecumenical.
œnŏphŏrum, i, n., us, i, m. wine-flask.
œnothēra (mod. hort.), evening-primrose.
œstrus, i, m. gad-fly.
ŏfella, ae, f. bit, morsel.
offa, ae, f. bit, morsel.
offendo, di, sum, 3. v.a. & n. to strike *or*
    dash against; to light upon; to hurt;
    to stumble; to fail; to offend; to dis-
    please.   [wrong.
offensa, ae, f. offence, displeasure; affront,

offensio, ōnis, f. striking against, stum-
    bling-block; *fig.* offence; discredit;
    hatred; vexaticn; complaint; mis-
    fortune; fault.
offenso, i. v.a. to knock *or* strike against.
offensus, ūs, m. striking; shock; offence.
offĕro, obtŭli, oblātum, 3. v.a. ir. to bring
    before; to offer; to exhibit; to ob-
    trude; to bring forwards; to inflict;
    to cause.   [(of arms).
officīna, ae, f. workshop; manufactory
officio, fēci, fectum, 3. v.a. & n. to stand
    in the way of; to hinder; to oppose;
    to hurt.
officiōsē, ad. obligingly.
officiōsus, a, um, a. obliging, officious;
    dutiful.   [office; submission.
officium, ii, n. service, kindness; duty,
offirmo, i. v.a. to render firm *or* durable;
    —se offirmare, to persist in.
offulgeo, lsi, 2. v.n. to shine upon.
offundo, fūdi, fūsum, 3. v.a. to pour *or*
    spread over or (*fig.*) out.
oh, i. oh! ah!
ohē, i. ho! holloa! ho there!
ŏlea, ae, f. olive-berry; olive-tree.
ŏleāgineus, a, um, ŏleāginus, a, um, a.
    of the olive.
ŏleārius, a, um, a. of oil.
ŏleaster, tri, m. wild olive-tree.
ŏleo, ŏlui, 2. v.n. & a. to smell; to smell
    of; *fig.* to savour of, to betray.
ŏleum, i, n. olive-oil; oil.
olfăcio, fēci, factum, 3. v.a. to smell;
    (*fig.*) to scent out.
olfactus, ūs, m. smelling; sense of smell.
ŏlidus, a, um, a. smelling; stinking, rank.
ŏlim, ad. formerly, in times past; at a
    future time, some day.
ŏlitor, ŏris, m. kitchen-gardener. [tables.
ŏlitōrius, a, um, a. pertaining to vege-
ŏlīva, ae, f. olive; olive-tree; olive-
    branch; staff of olive-wood.
ŏlīvētum, i, n. olive-yard.
ŏlīvifer, a, um, a. olive-bearing.
ŏlīvum, i, n. oil; (*fig.*) wrestling-school.
olla, ae, f. pot, jar.
ollus, v. ille.
ŏlor, ŏris, m. swan.
ŏlōrīnus, a, um, a. of a swan.
ŏlus, ĕris, n. vegetables.
Ōlympias, ădis, f. Olympiad.
ŏmāsum, i, n. bullock's tripe.
ōmen, inis, n. prognostic, sign, token (of
    good *or* bad luck); solemn usage.
ōminor, ātus, i. v. dep. to forebode, to
    presage.
ōmitto, mīsi, missum, 3. v.a. to let go;
    to lay aside; *fig.* to give up; to
    neglect; to disregard; to cease; to over-
    look.

omnĭgĕnus, a, um, a. of all kinds.
omnĭmŏdĭs, ad. in every way.
omnīno, ad. altogether, wholly; utterly; in all; in general; surely; with numbers; just.
omnĭpărens, tis, a. all-producing.
omnĭpŏtens, tis, a. almighty.
omnis, e, a. all, every;—omnes, all men; —omnia, all things;—omne ignotum pro magnifico, everything unfamiliar is glorified.
ŏnăger, ŏnagrus, i, m. wild ass.
ŏnĕrārius, a, um, a. that carries freight or burden;—navis oneraria, merchantship.
ŏnĕro, I. v.a. to load, to burden, to freight; to overload; to cover; to supply; to occupy; to heap up; fig. to weary; to oppress; to aggravate.
ŏnĕrōsus, a, um, a. burdensome, heavy; irksome.
ŏnŏmătŏpœia, ae, f. a rhetorical figure by which the word is made to express the sound, e.g. coccyx, cuckoo.
ŏnus, ĕris, n. load, burden; fig. affliction, trouble, responsibility;—onus probandi, the burden of proof.
ŏnustus, a, um, a. laden, burdened, freighted; filled, full.
ŏnyx, ўchis, c. yellow marble; onyx-box.
ŏpāco, I. v.a. to shade.
ŏpācus, a, um, a. shady; cool; dark; obscure.
ŏpălus, i, m. opal.
ŏpella, ae, f. little business or labour.
ŏpĕra, ae, f. pains, work, labour; task; care, attention, endeavour;—operæ, pl. labourers;—res multæ operæ, a laborious work;—operam dare alicui, to give up oneself to, to attend to; to take care of;—est operæ pretium, it is worth while.
ŏpercŭlum, i, n. cover, lid.
ŏpĕrĭmentum, i, n. cover, lid, covering.
ŏpĕrio, ui, ertum, 4. v.a. to cover (over); to shut; fig. to conceal.
ŏpĕror, ātus, I. v.n. dep. to work; to be engaged in or occupied with; to sacrifice.
ŏpĕrōsē, ad. toilsomely; carefully.
ŏpĕrōsus, a, um, a. painstaking, busy, industrious; troublesome; difficult; costly.   [ous.
ŏpertus, a, um, p. & a. hidden; ambiguŏpes, v. ops.   [fern.
ŏphioglossum (mod. hort.), adder-tongue
ŏphrys (mod. hort.), bee orchid.
ŏpĭcus, a, um, a. rude; barbarous.
ŏpĭfer, a, um, a. helping.
ŏpĭfex, ĭcis, c. maker, fabricator; artisan.
ŏpĭlio, v. ūpĭlio.

ŏpīmus, a, um, a. fruitful; rich; sumptuous; honourable; noble;—spolia opima, arms taken from an enemy's general.
ŏpīnābĭlis, e, a. conjectural.   [fancy.
ŏpīnātio, ōnis, f. supposition, conjecture,
ŏpīnātus, a, um, a. supposed, fancied.
ŏpīnio, ōnis, f. opinion, belief; report, rumour; expectation.
ŏpīnor, ātus, I. v. dep. to be of opinion, to think, to believe.
ŏpīpăre, ad. richly, splendidly.
ŏpīpărus, a, um, a. rich; splendid.
ŏpĭtŭlor, ātus, I. v.n. dep. to bring aid; to help; to relieve.
ŏpium, ii, n. opium.
ŏpŏbalsămum, i, n. balsam juice.
ŏportet, uit, 2. v. impers. it is necessary or proper; it becomes.
oppĕrior, pĕrītus & pertus, 4. v.n. & a. dep. to wait; to await.
oppĕto, īvi & ii, ītum, 3. v.a. to go to meet, to encounter; to perish, to die.
oppĭdānus, a, um, a. of or in a town (other than Rome); provincial, rustic;—oppĭdani, ōrum, m. pl. townsmen, townsfolk.
oppĭdo, ad. very much, exceedingly.
oppĭdŭlum, i, n. village.
oppĭdum, i, n. town.
oppīlo, I. v.a. to stop up.   [up.
oppleo, ēvi, ētum, 2. v.a. to fill or block
oppōno, sui, sĭtum, 3. v.a. to put against or before; to oppose; to offer; to shut; to pledge; to wager; to object, to allege in answer; to speak against.
opportūnē, fortunately; seasonably.
opportūnĭtas, ātis, f. fitness, convenience; fit time; advantage.
opportūnus, a, um, a. fit, convenient; opportune; advantageous; liable to.
oppŏsĭtio, ōnis, f. opposing, opposition.
oppŏsĭtus, a, um, p. & a. standing against, opposite.
oppressio, ōnis, f. crushing; overthrow.
opprĭmo, pressi, pressum, 3. v.a. to press down; to crush; to overpower; to beat down; to surprise; to suppress; to hide, to conceal.   [proach.
opprŏbrium, ii, n. scandal, disgrace; reopprŏbro, I. v.a. to reproach.
oppugnātio, ōnis, f. siege; assault.
oppugnātor, ōris, m. attacker.   [besiege.
oppugno, I. v.a. to attack, to assault; to
ops, ŏpis, f. power, might, strength, ability, help;—ŏpes, um, f. pl. wealth.
opson . . ., v. obson . . .
optābĭlis, e, a. desirable.
optātio, ōnis, f. wish; choice.
optātĭvus, a, um, a. (gram.) optative.
optĭmas, ātis, c. aristocrat.

optĭmē, ad. in the best manner; very well.
optĭmus, a, um, a. best.
optio, ōnis, f. choice; privilege of choosing. [to desire.
opto, I. v.a. to choose; to wish for,
optŭmus, v. optimus.
ŏpŭlenter, ad. richly, splendidly.
ŏpŭlentia, ae, f. riches, wealth; resources, power.
ŏpŭlentus a, um, a. fruitful; rich, wealthy; ample; noble.
opuntia (mod. hort.), prickly pear.
ŏpus, ĕris, n. work, labour; fortification; deed; difficulty.
ŏpus, n. indecl. need, necessity; — est, it is needful; — est mihi, I have need of.
ŏpuscŭlum, i, n. little work.
ōra, ae, f. border, edge; boundary; sea-coast; region, country; earth; life; tone; cable.
ōrācŭlum, i, n. oracle; prophecy.
ōrātio, ōnis, f. speech, harangue; eloquence.
ōrātor, ōris, m. speaker, orator; ambassador. [cal.
ōrātōrius, a, um, a. of an orator; oratori-
ōrbis, is, m. circle; orb; ring; wheel; circuit; the world; roundness;—orbis terrarum, or terræ, the universe.
orbĭta, ae, f. wheel-track, rut, course.
crbĭtas, ātis, f. orphanage; widowhood; bereavement; loss.
orbo, I. v.a. to bereave (of parents, children. etc.), to deprive.
orbus, a, um, a. bereaved; parentless; childless; devoid of; —, i, m. & orba, ae, f. orphan.
orca, ae, f. butt, tun.
orchis, is, f. orchid.
Orcus, i, m. the Lower World; death.
ordĭnārius, a, um, a. orderly; regular; usual. [order.
ordĭnātim, ad. in succession; in good
ordĭnātio, ōnis, f. regulation; ordering.
ordĭno, I. v.a. to set in order, to arrange, to regulate; to ordain; to rule.
ordior, orsus, 4. v. dep. fig. to begin; to undertake; to set about.
ordo, ĭnis, m. row, regular series; order; class of citizens; arrangement; method; degree; train or troop; rank; layer;—ordĭnĕ, duly; regularly;—in ordinem coactus, reduced from an officer to the ranks.
Ŏrēas, ădis, f. mountain-nymph.
orgănĭcus, i, m. musician.
orgănum, i, n. instrument; engine.
orgia, ōrum, n. pl. orgies (of Bacchus).
ōrĭchalcum, i, n. yellow copper ore, brass.
ōriens, entis, m. east, orient; (poet.) day.
ōrĭgănum, i, n. marjoram.

ŏrīgo, ĭnis, f. beginning, source; birth, origin;—fons et origo, the source and starting-point.
ōrior, ortus, 4. v. dep. to rise; to appear; to arise, to proceed. [from.
ōriundus, a, um, a. descended, sprung
ornāmentum, i, n. equipment; ornament, decoration; (mark of) distinction.
ornātē, ad. with ornament, elegantly.
ornātus, ūs, m. military equipment; armour; attire, dress; furniture; decoration, ornament; world.
orno, I. v.a. to adorn; to furnish; to honour; fig. to praise.
ornus, i, f. ash-tree.
ōro, I. v.a. to plead; to speak; to pray.
orsa, ōrum, n. pl. beginning; words, speech. [attempt.
orsus, ūs, m. beginning; undertaking.
orthogrăphia, ae, f. orthography.
ortus, ūs, m. rising, sunrise; birth; fig. beginning, origin.
ōrȳza, ae, f. rice.
ōs, ōris, n. mouth; speech; language; face; impudence; opening; entrance; —ore rotundo, with rounded mouth, grandiloquently.
ŏs, ossis, n. bone; fig. inmost part.
oscĕn, ĭnis, m. bird of omen.
oscillum, i, n. a small mask hung on trees.
oscĭto, I. v.n. to gape; to yawn; to be lazy.
oscŭlātio, ōnis, f. kissing.
oscŭlor, ātus, I. v. dep. to kiss; to value, to prize. [mouth; kiss.
oscŭlum, i, n. little mouth, pretty
osmunda (mod. hort.), flowering fern.
osseus, a, um, a. of bone; bony.
ostendo, di, sum & tum, 3. v.a. to stretch or spread towards; to show; to exhibit; to prove.
ostentātio, ōnis, f. exhibition, display; idle show; pomp, parade. [to offer.
ostento, I. v.a. to show off, to display;
ostentum, i, n. prodigy. [proof, sign.
ostentus, ūs, m. display; show, parade;
ostiā ium, ii, n. door-tax.
ostiārius, ii, m. doorkeeper, porter.
ostiātim, ad. from door to door, from house to house. [trance; exit; door.
ostium, ii, n. mouth (of a river); en-
ostrea, ae, f. oyster; sea-snail.
ostrĭfer, a, um, a. bearing oysters.
ostrum, i, n. purple; anything dyed purple. [leisure.
ōtior, ātus, I. v. dep. to have or enjoy
ōtiōsē, ad. at leisure, at ease; quietly.
ōtiōsus, a, um, a. at leisure, unoccupied; free from public affairs; quiet; indifferent; (of things) free, unemployed; undisturbed (by); superfluous; useless.

ōtĭum, ii, n. leisure; rest; peace; ease; neutrality;—**otium cum dignitate,** ease with dignity.

ŏvātĭo, ōnis, f. triumph, ovation.

ŏvīle, is, n. sheepfold; fold for goats.

ŏvillus, a, um, a. of sheep.

ŏvis, is, f. sheep; wool; *fig.* simpleton.

ŏvo, I. v.n. to celebrate an ovation; to exult, to rejoice.

ŏvum, i, n. egg; wooden balls set up in the Circus, and removed one by one at the completion of each lap;—**ab ovo usque ad mala,** from the hors d'œuvre to the dessert, i.e. from beginning to end.

oxălis, ĭdis, f. wood sorrel.

oxўmōron, a rhetorical figure consisting in the juxtaposition of contradictory expressions, e.g. **splendide mendax,** gloriously untruthful.

Pābŭlātĭo, ōnis, f. pasture; foraging.

pābŭlātor, ōris, m. forager.

pābŭlor, ātus, I. v.n. dep. to forage.

pābŭlum, i, n. food, nourishment; fodder; *fig.* food, sustenance. [ful.

păcālis, e, a. pertaining to peace, peace-

păcātus, a, um, a. peaceful, calm.

păcifer, a, um, a. bringing peace, peaceful.

păcĭfĭcātĭo, ōnis, f. peace-making. [fier.

păcĭfĭcātor, ōris, m. peace-maker; paci-

păcĭfĭco, I. v.a. to conclude a peace; to pacify.

păcĭfĭcus, a, um, a. peace-making, pacific.

păcisco, pactum, 3. v.a., **păciscor, pactus,** 3. v.n. & a. dep. to make a bargain *or* agreement; to agree, to enter into a marriage contract; to betroth; to be betrothed.

păco, I. v.a. to quiet, to pacify, to subdue, to soothe.

pactĭo, ōnis, f. agreement, contract; bargain. [**quo pacto?** how?

pactum, i, n., v. **pactio;** manner, way;—

pæan, ānis, m. hymn; hymn of triumph *or* praise.

pædăgōgus, i, m. pedagogue.

pædor, ōris, m. nastiness, filth.

pælex, v. **pellex.**

pæně, ad. nearly, almost.

pænĭnsŭla, æ, f. peninsula.

pænĭtentĭa, ae, f. repentance.

pænĭtet, uit, 2. v. impers. it repents;— **me paenitet,** I repent; I am displeased.

pænŭla, ae, f. woollen cloak.

pænŭlātus, a, um, a. wearing a pænula.

pænultĭmus, a, um, a. the last but one.

pæōnia, ae, f. pæony.

pætus, a, um, a. having a cast in the eye.

păgānus, a, um, a. rustic; unlearned; heathen.

păgella, ae, f. little page.

păgina, ae, f. page *or* leaf (of a book).

păgus, i, m. village; district, canton; country people.

pāla, ae, f. spade.

pălæstra, ae, f. wrestling-school; gymnastics. [wrestling.

pălæstrĭcus, a, um, a. connected with

păla m, ad. openly, publicly; prep. before.

Pălātīnus, a, um, a. pertaining to the imperial palace, imperial.

Pălātĭum, ii, n. mount Palatine; palace.

pălātum, i, n. palate; *fig.* taste; critical judgment.

pălea, ae, f. chaff.

pălear, āris, n. dewlap. [herd god).

Pălīlĭa, ium, n. pl. Feast of Pales (shep-

pălimpsēstŏs (—us), i, m. (MS.) rewritten on used parchment, cleaned and used again.

pălĭūrus, i, m. Christ's thorn.

palla, ae, f. long and wide upper garment of the Roman ladies; mantle of a tragic actor; undergarment.

Pallădĭum, i, n. image of Pallas Athena, the retention of which in Troy ensured the safety of the city; any protection.

palleo, ui, 2. v.n. to be *or* look pale; to fade; *fig.* to long for, to desire eagerly; to be fearful. [blanch; to fade.

pallesco, pallui, 3. v.n. to grow pale; to

palliātus, a, um, a. cloaked;—**fābŭlæ palliātæ,** comedies in which the figures wore Greek dress (pallium).

pallĭdus, a, um, a. pale.

pallĭŏlum, i, n. small cloak; hood.

pallĭum, i, n. coverlet, pall; cloak; a mantle worn by Greek philosophers.

pallor, ōris, m. paleness, wanness; terror.

palma, ae, f. palm of the hand; hand; palm-tree; date; oar; blade; *fig.* victory.

palmātus, a, um, a. embroidered with palms (of garments worn in triumphal processions). [branch.

palmĕs, ĭtis, m. vine-sprout; young

palmētum, i, n. palm-grove.

palmĭfer, a, um, a. palm-bearing.

palmŭla, ae, f. blade of the oar.

pālor, ātus, I. v. dep. to wander about; to straggle.

palpebra, ae, f. eyelid. [tate.

palpĭto, I. v.n. to throb, to pant, to palpi-

palpo, I. v.a. to stroke, to touch softly; *fig.* to caress, to flatter.

pălūdāmentum, i, n. soldier's cloak; general's cloak. [general's cloak.

pălūdātus, a, um, a. dressed in a

pălūdōsus, a, um, a. fenny, boggy, marshy.

pălumbes, is, c. wood-pigeon, ring-dove.

pālus, i, m. stake, prop, stay, pale.

pălūs, ūdis, f. marsh, morass, pool.
păluster, tris, tre, a. marshy; swampy.
pampīneus, a, um, a. full or consisting of
tendrils or vine-leaves. [leaf.
pampīnus, i, c. tendril of a vine; vine-
pănăcēa, ae, f. (bot.) all-heal.
pandectæ, ārum, m. pl. a treatise com-
prising the whole of any science.
pando, pandi, pansum & passum, 3. v.a.
to spread out, to extend; to unfold;
to discover; to tell.
pandus, a, um, a. bent, crooked, curved.
pango, pēgi & pĕpĭgi, pactum, 3. v.a. to
fasten, to fix; to drive in; fig. to
settle, to stipulate; to conclude; to
compose.
pānĭcŭla, ae, f. down on plants, catkin.
pānĭcum, i, n. millet. [black bread.
pānis, is, m. bread, loaf; — secundus,
pannōsus, a, um, a. ragged, tattered.
pannus, i, m. cloth, garment; patch;
rag;—purpūreus pannus, a purple patch
(a bit of fine writing).
panthēra, ae, f. panther.
pantices, um, m. pl. bowels; sausages.
pantōmīmus, i, m. mime; dancer.
păpāver, ĕris, n. poppy.
păpăvĕreus, a, um, a. of poppy.
păpĭlio, ōnis, m. butterfly.
păpilla, ae, f. breast.
păpŭla, ae, f. pimple, pustule.
păpyrifer, a, um, a. papyrus-bearing.
păpyrus, i, c., păpyrum, i, n. paper-reed;
paper.
păr, păris, a. equal; right; fit; pări
passu, at an equal pace, alongside of;
—par pari referre, to render tit for tat;
—, m. fellow; equal; mate.
păr, păris, n. pair; couple.
părābĭlis, e, a. easy to be had or procured.
părădoxus, a, um, a. paradoxical, contrary to what one expects.
părălўsis, is, f. palsy.
părăsītus, i, m. guest; sponger, parasite.
părātē, ad. preparedly, carefully.
părātus, a, um, a. prepared, ready;
equipped;—victoria parata, easy victory.
părātus, ūs, m. preparation, provision.
parcē, ad. sparingly; thriftily; cautiously; rarely.
parcimōnia, v. parsimonia.
parco, pĕperci (parsi), parcĭtum & par-
sum, 3. v.n. to spare; to save; to
pardon; to forbear; to let alone.
parcus, a, um, a. sparing, economical;
niggardly, parsimonious; infrequent,
moderate; scanty, little.
pardus, i, m. panther.
părens, entis, c. father, mother, parent;
fig. author, inventor.

părentālĭa, ĭum, n. pl. festival in honour
of dead relatives.
părentālis, e, a. parental.
părenthĕsis, is, f. parenthesis.
părento, 1. v.a. to offer a solemn sacrifice
in honour of deceased parents or relatives; to revenge (a person's death by
that of another).
păreo, ui, 2. v.n. to come forth, to appear,
to be visible; to obey; to comply
with; to be subject to; to submit to.
părīcīda, etc., v. parricida, etc.
păries, ĕtis, m. wall (of a house).
păriĕntīnæ, ārum, f. pl. ruins, old fallen-
down walls.
părilis, e, a, like, equal.
părio, pĕpĕri, parĭtum & partum, 3. v.a. to
bring forth, to bear; fig. to produce,
to create; to devise; to procure; to
invent; to obtain.
părĭter, ad. equally, in like manner, as
well; together; — . . .—, as soon as.
parma, æ, f. small round shield; shield.
parnassia (mod. hort.), grass of Parnassus.
păro, 1. v.a. to get ready, to prepare, to
furnish, to provide; to intend; to
plan; to obtain.
păro, 1. v.a. to agree, to arrange with.
părŏcha, ae, f. purveyance.
părŏchus, i, m. purveyor; host.
părŏpsis, ĭdis, f. dessert-dish.
parra, ae, f. owl.
parrīcīda, ae, g.c. parricide (murderer);
murderer of a near relative; traitor;
wretch.
parrīcīdium, ii, n. parricide (murder);
fig. treason, rebellion.
pars, partis, f. part, piece, portion, share;
function, office; species; fig. party;
pars . . . pars, some—others;—partes,
ium, f. pl. party; faction;—ex parte,
partisan; biased.
parsimōnĭa, ae, f. frugality, thrift, parsimony. [participant; —, c. partaker.
particeps, cĭpis, a. sharing, partaking,
particĭpium, ii, n. participle.
particĭpo, 1. v.a. & n. to make partaker of,
to acquaint with, to inform of; to
share with; to partake of. [particle.
particŭla, ae, f. small part, little bit,
partim, ad. partly, in part.
partio, ii & īvi, ītum, 4. v.a., partior, ītus
sum, 4. v. dep. to share, to part; to
divide, to distribute.
partītio, ōnis, f. sharing, parting, partition; division; distribution.
partŭrio, īvi & ii, 4. v.a. to be in travail or
labour; to bring forth; fig. to produce; to brood over, to purpose.
partus, ūs, m. bringing forth, birth;
fetus; embryo; offspring.

părum, ad. too little, not enough; little, not very.

părumper, ad. a little while.

parvŭlus, a, um, a. very small, little, petty, slight. [mean; young; cheap.

parvus, a, um, a. little, small, petty, cheap.

pascha, ae, f. ătis, n. Passover.

pasco, pāvi, pastum, 3. v.a. & n. to drive to pasture; to feed; to fatten; to support; to browse; fig. to feast; to sate.

pascuum, i, n. pasture.

passer, ĕris, m. sparrow.

passiflora (mod. hort.), passion-flower.

passim, ad. here and there, hither and thither; at random, promiscuously.

passio, ōnis, f. suffering; feeling.

passīvus, a, um, a. passive.

passus, ūs, m. step, pace (5 Roman feet); track, trace;—mille passus, a mile.

passus, a, um, a. spread out; dried (of raisins).

passum, i, n. raisin-wine.

pastillus, i, m. lozenge; capsule.

pastināca, ae, f. parsnip.

pastor, ōris, m. herdsman, shepherd.

pastōrālis, e, a. pastoral. [shepherd.

pastōrīcius, a, um, pastōrius, a, um, a. of a

pastus, ūs, m. pasture, fodder, food.

pătĕfăcio, fēci, factum, 3. v.a. to open, to throw open; fig. to disclose, to expose, to bring to light. [dish.

pătella, ae, f. small dish, plate; offering-

pătĕo, ui, v.n. to stand, to lie or to open; to be accessible; to be visible; to be exposed to; to stretch out, to extend; to be attainable; to be evident.

păter, tris, m. father, sire; — familias, head of a family;—patres, patres conscripti, pl. senators; — patres, forefathers.

pătĕra, ae, f. offering-dish, libation-saucer.

păternus, a, um, a. fatherly, paternal.

pătesco, ui, 3. v.n. to be opened; to extend; fig. to become evident.

pătibīlis, e, a. endurable; sensitive

pătibŭlum, i, n. fork-shaped yoke; gibbet.

pătiens, entis, a. bearing, supporting; patient; capable of enduring.

pătienter, ad. patiently; calmly.

pătientia, ae, f. patience; forbearance, indulgence; submissiveness.

pătina, ae, f. dish, pan, stew-pan.

pătior, passus sum, 3. v. dep. to bear, to undergo; to suffer; to allow.

patrātor, ōris, m. achiever, accomplisher.

patria, ae, f. fatherland, native country; fig. home, source. [patriarch.

patriarcha, ae, m. chief of a clan;

patricīda, v. parricida.

patrĭcius, a, um. a. patrician, noble;— patrĭcii, ōrum, m. pl. patricians, Roman nobility. [mony.

patrĭmōnium, ii, n. inheritance, patri-

patrĭmus, a, um, a. having a father still living.

patrius, a, um, a. fatherly, paternal; hereditary, innate; of one's native land.

patro, 1. v.a. to accomplish, to perform, to bring about.

patrōcĭnium, ii, n. protection, defence, patronage, legal defence.

patrōcĭnor, ātus sum, 1. v.n. dep. to protect, to defend, to patronize.

patrōna, ae, f. protectress, patroness.

patrōnus, i, m. protector, patron; pleader, advocate.

patrōnўmĭcus, a, um, a. patronymic, expressing the name of the father or ancestor, e.g. Pelīdes the son of Peleus.

patruēlis, is, c. cousin on the father's side.

patruus, i, m. (paternal) uncle; reprover.

pătŭlus, a, um, a. standing open, open; fig. extended, wide. [scarcity.

paucitas, ātis, f. small number, fewness,

paucŭlus, a, um, a. very little; very few.

paucus, a, um, a. few, little; slight;— pauci, pl. few;—pauca, n. pl. a few words.

paulātim, ad. by degrees, gradually.

paulisper, ad. for a little while, for a short time.

paulo, ad. a little; somewhat.

paulŭlum, ad. a little way or time; —, i, n. little bit, trifle.

paulŭlus, a, um, a. very little, very small.

paulum, ad. a little, somewhat.

paulus, a, um, a. little, small;—paulum, i, n. a little, a trifle. [scanty.

pauper, ĕris, a. poor; needy; feeble,

paupercŭlus, a, um, a. wretchedly poor.

paupĕries, ēi, paupertas, ātis, f. poverty.

pausa, ae, f. halt; stop, cessation.

păvĕfăcio, fēci, factum, 3. v.a. to frighten.

păveo, păvi, 2. v.n. & a. to be much afraid; to become alarmed. [to dread.

păvesco, 3. v.a. & n. to become alarmed;

păvĭdē, ad. timidly; fearfully. [struck.

păvĭdus, a, um, a. fearful, terrified, panic-

păvīmentum, i, n. floor, pavement.

păvio, īvi, ītum, 4. v.a. to beat, to strike, to ram down. [to shiver.

păvĭto, 1. v.n. & a. to be greatly afraid;

păvo, ōnis, m. peacock. [anxiety.

păvor, ōris, m. fear, dread, alarm, terror,

pax, păcis, f. peace; tranquillity of mind; favour, grace; leave;—pace tua, with your good leave; — pax vobiscum, peace be with you; —! i. enough! silence!

peccātum, i, n. fault, error, sin.
pecco, 1. v.n. & a. to err; to commit a fault, to offend, to sin;—**peccavi,** I have sinned (a cry of confession).
pĕcŏrōsus, a, um, a. rich in flocks.
pecten, ĭnis, m. comb; quill wherewith the lyre is struck; *fig.* poem, song.
pectīnātim, ad. like a comb.
pecto, pexi, pexum & pectĭtum, 3. v.a. to comb; to card.
pectus, ŏris, n. breast; breast-bone; *fig.* soul; feeling; courage; understanding.
pĕcu, pl. **pecua,** n. cattle, sheep, pasture.
pĕcuārius, ii, m. grazier. [money.
pĕcūlātor, ŏris, m. embezzler of public
pĕcūlātus, ŭs, m. embezzlement of public money *or* property.
pĕcūliāris, e, a. one's own, belonging to one; proper, special, peculiar; singular; extraordinary.
pĕcūlium, ii, n. small private property; private property of a son, daughter *or* slave, held with the father's *or* master's consent. [money.
pĕcūnia. ae, f. property, riches, wealth;
pĕcūniārius, a, um, a. of money.
pĕcūniōsus, a, um, a. moneyed.
pĕcus, pecŏris, n. cattle; herd, flock.
pĕcus, ŭdis, f. beast, brute, animal; sheep.
pĕdālis, e, a. measuring a foot.
pĕdes, ĭtis, m. pedestrian, foot-soldier;—**pĕdites,** pl. infantry
pĕdester, tris, tre, a. on foot, pedestrian; —**sermo pedestris,** prose;—**pedestres, ium,** m. pl. infantry.
pĕdĕtentim, ad. by trying with the feet; step by step, slowly; *fig.* by degrees.
pēdĭca, ae, f. shackle, fetter; snare.
pēdĭcŭlus, i, m. louse.
pĕdĭsĕquus, pĕdissĕquus, i, m. **pĕdĭsĕqua, ae,** f. footman, page, lackey; waiting-woman; *fig.* follower, attendant.
pĕdĭtātus, ŭs, m. foot-soldiers, infantry.
pēdum, i, n. shepherd's crook.
pegma, ătis, n. bookcase; wooden machines in a theatre for raising and lowering. [forswear oneself.
pēiĕro, 1. v.n. & a. to swear falsely, to
pēior, us, a. worse.
pēius, ad. worse.
pĕlăgus, i, n. open sea.
pēlămis, ĭdis, f. tunny-fish.
pelargonium (mod. hort.), pelargonium.
pellax, ācis, a. seductive, deceitful.
pellĕgo, v. perlĕgo.
pellex, icis, f. concubine (of a married man); kept mistress.
pellĭcio, lexi, lectum, 3. v.a. to allure, to entice. to inveigle, to decoy.
pellĭcŭla, ae, f. small skin *or* hide.
pellis, is, f. skin, hide; tent; shield.

pellītus, a, um, a. covered with skins, clad in skins.
pello, pĕpŭli, pulsum, 3. v.a. to push *or* strike; to drive out, to banish; to move, to touch.
pellūceo, xi, 2. v.n. to shine forth; to be transparent. [cid; very bright.
pellūcĭdus, a, um, a. transparent, pellu-
pēlōris, ĭdis, f. mussel; shell-fish.
pelta, ae, f. small light shield.
peltastae, ārum, m. pl. peltasts; soldiers armed with peltae.
peltātus, a, um, a. armed with the pelta.
pelvis, is, f. basin.
Pēnātes, ium, m. pl. the household gods.
pendeo, pĕpendi, 2. v.n. to hang (down), to be suspended; to hang loose; to be unstable, movable; to float; to linger; to be doubtful; to be in suspense; to depend upon;—**pendente lite,** while the case is undecided.
pendo, pĕpendi, pensum, 3. v.a. & n. to cause to hang down, to suspend; to pay out; *fig.* to ponder.
pendŭlus, a, um, a. hanging down.
pēne, ad., v. pæne. [power of.
pēnes, pr. with *or* in the possession *or*
pĕnetrābilis, e, a. that can be pierced; penetrable; piercing. [sanctuary.
pĕnetrāle, is, n. inner part of a place;
pĕnetrālis, e, a. interior, innermost.
pĕnetro, 1. v.a. & n. to pierce, to penetrate; to enter.
pēnīcillum, i, n., **pēnīcillŭs, i,** m. painter's brush; *fig.* style.
pēninsŭla, v. paeninsula.
pēnĭtus, ad. inwardly; deeply, far within; utterly, altogether.
penna, ae, f. feather;—**pennae,** pl. wing.
pennātus, a, um, a. winged.
pensilis, e, a. hanging down.
pensio, ōnis, f. payment. [consider.
pensito, 1. v.a. to weigh; to pay; to
penso, 1. v.a. to weigh *or* weigh out; to pay *or* punish for; to recompense; to make good; to counterbalance; *fig.* to ponder, to examine.
pensum, i, n. portion weighed out; task; *fig.* charge, duty, office.
pensus, a, um, a. valued, dear;—**nihil pensi habeo,** I care nothing about.
pentstēmon (mod. hort.), pentstemon.
pēnūria, ae, f. want, need.
pēnus, ūs *or* **i,** m. *or* f. provisions, store.
per, pr. through, throughout, all over; during; by (means of); for the sake of; (in compounds) thoroughly, very; —**per capita,** per head;—**per contra,** as a compensation;—**per saltum,** by a leap;—**per se,** in itself.
pēra, ae, f. bag, wallet.

pĕrabsurdus, a, um, a. highly ridiculous.
pĕrācer, cris, cre, a. very sharp.
pĕrăcūtē, ad. very keenly.   [very acute.
pĕrăcūtus, a, um, a. very penetrating,
pĕraequē, ad. equally.
pĕrăgĭto, I. v.a. to drive *or* hunt about
   greatly, to harass; *fig.* to excite.
pĕrăgo, ēgi, actum, 3. v.a. to execute, to
   finish, to accomplish; to pierce
   through; to pass through; to relate.
peragro, I. v.a. to wander *or* travel
   through; *fig.* to go through, to search
   through, to penetrate.
pĕrămanter, ad. very lovingly.
pĕrambŭlo, I. v.a. to walk *or* go through;
   to perambulate.
pĕrangustus, a, um, a. very narrow.
pĕrantīquus, a, um, a. very ancient.
pĕrāro, I. v.a. to write (scratch on a
   waxen tablet).
perbĕātus, a, um, a. very happy.
perbellē, ad. very finely, very well.
perbĭbo, bĭbi, 3. v.a. to drink up.
perca, ae, f. perch (fish).
percallesco, ui, 3. v.n. to become callous;
   to be experienced in.   [mouth.
percĕlebro, I. v.a. to have often in one's
percello, cŭli, culsum, 3. v.a. to throw
   down; to strike; to upset; *fig.* to
   discourage.   [reckon up.
percenseo, ui, 2. v.a. to count over, to
perceptio, ōnis, f. gathering, collecting;
   fig. comprehension, perception.
percieo, 2. percio, civi *or* cii, cĭtum, 4. v.a.
   to excite.
percĭpio, cēpi, ceptum, 3. v.a. to take
   entire possession of; to get, to receive;
   fig. to feel, to conceive; to learn.
percōlo, I. v.a. to filter; to pass through.
percŏlo, lui, cultum, 3. v.a. to respect;
   to pay court to.
percommŏdē, ad. most conveniently.
percommŏdus, a, um, a. most convenient.
percontātio, ōnis, f. question, inquiry.
percontor, ātus sum, I. v.a. & dep. to
   question strictly, to inquire; to investigate.   [to mature.
percŏquo, xi, ctum, to cook thoroughly;
percrēbesco, ui, percrebresco, brui, 3. v.n.
   to become very frequent, to be spread
   abroad.
percurro, percŭcurri & percurri, cursum,
   3. v.a. & n. to run *or* hasten through *or*
   over; to traverse; to mention cursorily.
percursio, ōnis, f. running through *or*
   over; rapid thinking over.
percussio, ōnis, f. beating, striking; beating time; time.
percussor, ōris, m. assassin.
percussus, ūs, m. buffeting; beating.

percŭtio, cussi, cussum, 3. v.a. to strike;
   to fell; to kill; to affright; to shock.
perdisco, dĭdĭci, 3. v.a. to learn by heart.
perdĭtor, ōris, m. destroyer.
perdĭtus, a, um, p. & a. lost; hopeless,
   desperate, ruined, abandoned.
perdiū, ad. for a long while.
perdix, ĭcis, c. partridge.
perdo, dĭdi, dĭtum, 3. v.a. to lose; to destroy; to ruin; to waste; to corrupt.
perdŏceo, ui, ctum, 3. v.a. to teach
   thoroughly.
perdoctus, a, um, a. very learned.
perdŏmo, ui, ĭtum, I. v.a. to tame
   thoroughly, to subjugate completely.
perdūco, xi, ctum, 3. v.a. to lead *or* bring
   through *or* over, to conduct; to besmear; to prolong; to persuade.
perduellio, ōnis, f. treason.
perduellis, is, m. traitor.
perdūro, I. v.a. to endure, to hold out.
pĕrĕdo, ēdi, ēsum, 3. v.a. to eat up, to
   consume.
pĕregre, ad. abroad, from abroad.
pĕregrīnātio, ōnis, f. travel.
pĕregrīnor, ātus, I. v.n. dep. to travel
   about *or* abroad.
pĕregrīnus, a, um, a. outlandish, strange,
   foreign, exotic; —, i, m. foreigner,
   stranger.
pĕrēlĕgans, antis, a. fine; brilliant.
pĕrendiē, ad. the day after to-morrow.
pĕrendĭnus, a, um, a. after to-morrow.
pĕrennis, e, a. perennial, everlasting.
pĕrenno, I. v.a. & n. to preserve long; to
   last long.
pĕreo, ii (īvi), ĭtum, 4. v.n. to go *or* run
   through; to pass away, to vanish, to
   disappear; to be destroyed, to perish;
   to be desperately in love (with);—
   pĕrii, I am undone.
pĕrĕquito, I. v.n. & a. to ride through, to
   ride hither and thither, to ride *or* drive
   about.   [roam *or* ramble over.
pĕrerro, I. v.a. to wander through, to
pĕrexĭguus, a, um, a. very little *or* small.
perfăcilis, e, a. very easy.
perfectio, ōnis, f. finishing, perfection.
perfectus, a, um, p. & a. finished, complete, perfect, exquisite.
perfĕro, tŭli, lātum, v.a. ir. to bear *or*
   carry through; to convey; to report;
   to tell; to endure; to undergo.
perfĭcio, fēci, fectum, 3. v.a. to finish, to
   perform; to complete; to accomplish.
perfĭdia, ae, f. faithlessness, treachery,
   perfidy.
perfĭdiōsē, ad. treacherously.
perfĭdiōsus, a, um, a. treacherous.
perfĭdus, a, um, a. faithless, treacherous,
   perfidious.

perflo, 1. v.a. to blow through or over.
perfluo, xi, 3. v.a. & n. to flow through; to leak.
perfŏdio, fŏdi, fossum, 3. v.a. to dig or pierce through, to transfix. [pierce.
perfŏro, 1. v.a. to bore through; to
perfrico, cui, cătum & ctum, 1. v.a. to rub;—**os** or **frontem perfricare,** to rub one's blushes off, to lose all sense of shame.
perfrīgesco, frixi, 3. v.n. to grow cold.
perfringo, frēgi, fractum, 3. v.a. to break through; to break or dash in pieces, to shatter.
perfruor, ctus, 3. v. dep. to enjoy much.
perfŭga, ae, m. deserter. [to desert.
perfŭgio, fŭgi, 3. v.n. to flee for refuge;
perfŭgium, ii, n. refuge; asylum.
perfundo, fŭdi, fūsum, 3. v.a. to pour over, to wet, to besprinkle.
perfungor, nctus, 3. v.n. dep. to perform, to discharge; to get rid of. [rage.
perfŭro, 3. v.a. & n. to rage through, to
pergo, perrexi, perrectum, 3. v.a. & n. to advance; to continue; to proceed; to undertake.
pergrandis, e, a. very large.
pergrātus, a, um, a. very agreeable or pleasant. [arbour.
pergŭla, ae, f. shed; shop; school;
pĕrhĭbeo, ui, ĭtum, 2. v.a. to exhibit; to bestow; to say, to assert, to name.
pĕrhorresco, rui, 3. v.n. & a. to tremble or shudder greatly; to shudder greatly at.
pĕrīclĭtor, ātus, 1. v.a. & n. dep. to adventure; to risk; to assay; to try, to prove; to test; to be in danger.
pĕrīcŭlōsē, ad. dangerously.
pĕrīcŭlōsus, a, um, a. dangerous, hazardous, perilous.
pĕrīcŭlum, i, n. trial; attempt, proof, essay; danger, peril; risk; lawsuit.
pĕrĭdōneus, a, um, a. very fit or proper.
pĕrillustris, e, a. very brilliant, very notable; highly honoured.
pĕrimo, ēmi, emptum (emtum), 3. v.a. to destroy; to kill; to hinder. [as.
pĕrindĕ, ad. just so equally; — **ac,** just
pĕriŏdus, i, f. completed sentence; period (grammatical term).
pĕriphrăsis, is, f. circumlocution.
pĕrītē, ad. skilfully, expertly, cleverly.
pĕritia, ae, f. experience, practical knowledge, skill. [skilful, expert.
pĕrītus, a, um, a. experienced, practised,
perjūcundē, ad. delightfully.
perjūcundus, a, um, a. delightful.
perjūrium, ii, n. false oath, perjury.
perjūro, v. pejero.
perjūrus, a, um, a. perjured; false, lying.

perlābor, lapsus sum, 3. v.n. dep. to glide over or through, to skim.
perlĕgo, lēgi, lectum, 3. v.a. to view all over; to scan, to survey; to read through.
perlĭcio, v. pellicio. [piciously.
perlĭto, 1. v.n. to sacrifice very ausperluceo, v. pelluceo.
perlucidus, v. pellucidus.
perluo, ui, ūtum, 3. v.a. to wash off or thoroughly; to bathe.
perlustro, 1. v.a. to go or wander all through; to traverse completely; to view all over, to survey.
permagnus, a, um, a. very great.
permăneo, mansi, mansum, 2. v.n. to continue or persist in staying; to persist. [penetrate; to reach.
permāno, 1. v.n. to flow through; to
permansio, ōnis, f. abiding; continuance.
permeo, 1. v.a. to go or pass through, to cross, to traverse; fig. to pervade.
permētior, mensus, 4. v.a. dep. to measure through or out; to travel through.
permisceo, scui, stum & xtum, 2. v.a. to mix or mingle together; to confound; to embroil.
permissio, ōnis, f. unconditional surrender; leave, permission.
permissus, ūs, m. leave; permission.
permitto, mīsi, missum, 3. v.a. to let go through; to launch; to let fly, to hurl; to give up; to entrust; to allow, to permit.
permŏveo, mōvi, mōtum, 2. v.a. to move or stir up thoroughly; fig. to move deeply; to excite; to persuade.
permulceo, si, sum & ctum, 2. v.a. to rub gently, to stroke, to touch gently; fig. to charm, to please, to delight; to soothe, to allay.
permultus, a, um, a. very much, very many. [thoroughly.
permūnio, īvi, or **ii, ĭtum,** to fortify
permūtātio, ōnis, f. change; exchange, barter.
permūto, 1. v.a. to alter or change completely; to exchange, to barter.
perna, ae, f. ham; salted leg.
pernĕcessārius, a, um, a. very necessary; nearly connected.
pernēgo, 1. v.a. to deny altogether or flatly; to refuse or decline altogether.
perniciālis, e, a. ruinous; destructive.
pernicies, ēi, f. destruction, ruin, disaster; death.
perniciōsē, ad. ruinously.
perniciōsus, a, um, a. destructive, ruinous, pernicious. [speed.
pernīcĭtas, ātis, f. swiftness (of foot),
pernio, ōnis, m. chilblain.

pernix, īcis, a. nimble, brisk, agile, quick; persevering.

pernōbĭlis, e, a. very famous.

pernocto, I. v.n. to pass the night.

pernosco, nōvi, nōtum, 3. v.a. to get a thorough knowledge of.   [known.

pernōtesco, tui, 3. v.n. to become well

pernōtus, a, um, a. well known.

pernox, octis, a. lasting all night.

pēro, ōnis, m. boot of raw hide.

pĕrobscūrus, a, um, a. very obscure.

pĕrōdi, ōsus sum, v.a. def. to hate greatly, to detest

pĕrōdiōsus, a, um, a. very grievous.

pĕropportūnē, ad. very conveniently.

pĕropportūnus, a, um, a. very convenient.

pĕrōrātio, ōnis, f. close of an oration, winding up of a speech.

pĕrōro, I. v.a to speak from beginning to end, to plead or argue throughout; to wind up (a speech).

pĕrōsus, a, um, a. hating thoroughly.

perpāco, I. v.n. to bring to complete subjection.   [trifling.

perparvus, a, um, a. very little, very

perpaucus, a, um, a. very little, very few.

perpaulum, ad. very little.

perpello, pŭli, pulsum, 3. v.a. to strike or push violently; fig. to compel, to constrain, to prevail upon.

perpendĭcŭlum, i, n. plummet, plumbline;—**ad perpendĭcŭlum,** perpendicularly.

perpendo, pendi, pensum, 3. v.a. fig.. to weigh carefully, to examine; to ponder.   [truly, falsely.

perpĕram, ad. wrongly, incorrectly, unperpessio, ōnis, f. enduring, suffering.

perpĕtior, pessus, 3. v.n. & a. dep. to bear, to endure.

perpetro, I. v.a. to carry through, to effect, to accomplish, to perpetrate.

perpĕtuĭtas, ātis, f. continuity, perpetuity.

perpĕtuo, ad. constantly, uninterruptedly, perpetually.   [make perpetual.

perpĕtuo, I. v.a. to cause to continue, to

perpĕtuus, a, um, a. uninterrupted; continuous; lasting; universal; constant; —**in perpetuum,** for ever.

perplexus, a, um, a. entangled, confused; intricate, obscure.

perpŏlio, īvi or ii, ītum, 4. v.a. to polish thoroughly; to finish.

perpŏpŭlor, ātus, I. v.a. dep. to lay quite waste, to ravage, to devastate.

perpōto, I. v.a. & n. to drink; to carouse.

perquam, ad. extremely.   [for.

perquīro, sīvi, sītum, to inquire; to search

perrārus, a, um, a. very rare.

perrĭdĭcŭlē, ad. most absurdly.

perrĭdĭcŭlus, a, um, a. utterly absurd.

perrumpo, rūpi, ruptum, 3. v.n. & a. to break or rush through, to force one's way through; to break up; fig. to overcome.

persæpĕ, ad. very often.

perscrībo, psi, ptum, 3. v.a. to write in full or at length; to give a full account or report of in writing; to assign.

perscriptio, ōnis, f. entry; assignment.

perscrūtor, I. v. dep. to search, to examine.

persĕdeo, sēdi, sessum, 2. v.n. to remain sitting, to sit or stay long.

persĕquor, cūtus & quūtus, 3. v.a. dep. to follow perseveringly, to pursue; to pursue with vengeance; to overtake; to strive after; to accomplish.

persĕvērantia, ae, f. steadfastness, constancy, perseverance.   [severe in.

persĕvēro, I. v.n. & a. to persist, to per-

persĭmĭlis, e, a. very like.   [sist.

persisto, stĭti, 3. v.n. to continue, to per-

persolvo, solvi, sŏlūtum, 3. v.a. to unravel, to solve, to explain; to pay; to suffer (punishment).

persōna, ae, f. mask; personage, character, part;—**persona grata,** a popular character.

persōnātus, a, um, a. masked; fig. fictitious.

persōno, ui, ĭtum, I. v.n. & a. to resound, to ring with; to cry out.

perspectus, a, um, a. tried; tested.

perspĕcŭlor, ātus sum, I. v. dep. to examine or explore thoroughly.

perspĭcācĭtas, ātis, f. sharp-sightedness, acuteness, perspicacity.

perspĭcax, ācis, a. sharp-sighted, penetrating, acute, perspicacious.

perspĭcio, exi, ectum, 3. v.a. to look or see through, to look into, to look at, to view, to examine, to inspect.

perspĭcuē, ad. evidently, clearly, manifestly, perspicuously.   [ness.

perspĭcuĭtas, ātis, f. transparency; clear-

perspĭcuus, a, um, a. transparent, clear; evident.

persto, stĭti, stātum, I. v.n. to stand firmly; to last, to endure; fig. to persevere, to persist in.

perstringo, nxi, ctum, 3. v.a. to graze, to graze against; to blunt; to glance at; to reprove.

persuādeo, si, sum, 2. v.a. to persuade, to convince; to induce; to prompt, to prevail upon, to persuade to do.

persuāsio, ōnis, f. persuasion; conviction, belief.   [prance about.

persulto, I. v.n. & a. to leap or skip or

pertædet, tæsum est, 2. v. impers. & n. to be very wearied with.

pertendo, di, sum, 3. v.a. & n. to go on with, to perform; *fig.* to persevere, to persist.   [to affect; to invade.

pertento, 1. v.a. to test, to try; to seize,

pertĕnuis, e, a. very slight.

perterreo, ui, ĭtum, 2. v.a. to frighten *or* terrify thoroughly; to frighten away.

pertĭca, ae, f. pole, long staff, measuring-rod, perch.

pertĭmesco, mui, 3. v.a. to fear greatly.

pertĭnācia, ae, f. obstinacy, pertinacity.

pertĭnāciter, ad. steadily, perseveringly; stubbornly, pertinaciously.

pertĭnax, ācis, a. firm, constant, steadfast, pertinacious.

pertĭneo, ui, 2. v.n. to continue *or* extend through *or* to, to reach; to belong, to pertain to.   [plication to.

pertractātĭo, ōnis. f. busying with, ap-

pertracto, 1. v.a. to handle *or* touch much *or* often; to consider thoroughly, to investigate, to study.

pertrăho, xi, ctum, 3. v.a. to draw *or* drag through *or* to, to bring *or* conduct forcibly to, to entice to.

pertristis, e, a. mournful *or* sad.

pertundo, tŭdi, tūsum, 3. v.a. to bore through.

perturbātĭo, ōnis, f. confusion, disturbance; mental disturbance, perturbation; passion.

perturbo, 1. v.a. to disorder, to confuse; to disturb; to frighten.

pĕrungo, unxi, unctum, 3. v.a. to anoint.

pĕrurbānus, a, um, a. refined; witty.

pĕrūro, ussi, ustum, 3. v.a. to burn up; to nip; to inflame.

pĕrūtĭlis, e, a. very useful.

pervādo, si, sum, 3. v.n. to go *or* come through, to pass *or* press through, to spread through; to penetrate, to pervade.

pervāgor, ātus, 1. v.n. & a. dep. to wander *or* range through, to rove about; to pervade, to spread out, to extend.

pervasto, 1. v.a. to devastate thoroughly.

pervĕho, xi, ctum, 3. v.a. to bear, to carry *or* convey through;—**pervĕhi,** pass. to sail to; to ride to.

pervello, velli, 3. v.a. to twitch; to pinch; to revile.

pervĕnio, vĕni, vĕntum, 4. v.n. & a. to come through to, to arrive at, to reach.

perversē, ad. wrongly; ill.

perversĭtas, ātis, f. perversity.

perversus, a, um, p. & a. askew, awry; *fig.* perverse, evil, bad.

perverto, ti, sum, 3. v.a. to overthrow; *fig.* to subvert; to destroy, to ruin, to corrupt; to silence.   [to investigate.

pervestīgo, 1. v.a. to trace *or* search out;

pervĕtus, ĕris, a. very old.

pervĭcācia, ae, f. stubbornness, obstinacy; firmness steadiness.

pervĭcāciter, ad. obstinately.

pervĭcax, ācis, a. stubborn, obstinate; firm, steadfast.

pervĭdeo, vīdi, vīsum, 2. v.a. to look over *or* on; to look at *or* upon; to view; to consider, to examine; to perceive, to discern.

pervĭgil, is, a. awake; watchful.

pervĭgĭlium, ii, n. wakefulness; vigil.

pervĭgĭlo, 1. v.n. to remain awake, watch all night; to watch.

pervinco, vici, victum, 3. v.a. to conquer *or* defeat completely; to carry a point; to surpass, to exceed; to effect with labour.

pervius, a, um, a. passable, pervious;—**pervium, ii,** n. thoroughfare, passage.

pervŏlito, 1. v.n. to fly *or* flit about.

pervŏlo, 1. v.n. to fly *or* flit about; to fly over.

pervorsus, v. perversus.

pervorto, v. perverto.

pervulgo, 1. v.a. to make publicly known, to spread abroad.

pes, pĕdis, m. foot; metrical foot; measure; foot (of a piece of furniture); sheet (of a sail);—**pedibus merere,** to serve as a foot-soldier.

pessĭmē, ad. very badly.

pessĭmus, a, um, a. the worst.

pessŭlus, i, m. bolt.

pessum, ad. down; — **ire,** to sink; — **dare,** to destroy; to sink.   [tive.

pestĭfer, a, um, a. pestilential; destruc-

pestĭlens, entis, a. pestilential, unhealthy, unwholesome; destructive.

pestĭlentia, ae, f. pest, pestilence, unwholesome atmosphere *or* region; *fig.* plague.

pestis, is, f. plague, pestilence; unhealthy weather; *fig.* destruction, ruin, death.

pĕtāsus, i, m. broad-brimmed hat.

petītĭo, ōnis, f. attack, thrust; pass; request, petition; candidature; lawsuit;—**petitio principii,** begging the question (a logical fallacy).

pĕtītor, ōris, m. seeker, striver after, applicant, candidate; claimant, plaintiff.

pĕto, īvi, ītum, 3. v.a. to go *or* repair to, to travel to; to seek; to fetch; to seek after; to attack; to ask; to desire; to be a candidate for

pĕtorrĭtum, i, n. four-wheeled carriage.

pĕtŭlans, antis, p. & a. pert, saucy, impudent, petulant; wanton, lascivious.

pĕtŭlanter, ad. pertly, wantonly, impudently, petulantly.

pĕtŭlantia, ae, f. sauciness, impudence, wantonness, petulance.

pĕtulcus, a, um, a. butting.

pĕtūnia (mod. hort.), petunia.

peucedănum (mod. hort.), parsnip.

phălangium, ii, venomous spider.

phălanx, angis, f. band of soldiers, host drawn up in close order; battalion.

phălēræ, ārum, f. pl. ornaments worn by the Roman gentlemen and men of arms; trappings of horses.   [pings.

phălērātus, a, um, a. adorned with trap-

phăretra, ae, f. quiver.

phăretrātus, a, um, a. wearing a quiver.

pharmăcŏpōla, ae, m. drug-seller; quack.

phărus, i, f. lighthouse.

phăsēlus, i, c. kidney-bean; light vessel, pinnace.

phiăla, ae, f. shallow drinking-cup.

philadelphus (mod. hort.), syringa.

phĭlŏlŏgia, ae, f. love of letters.

phĭlŏlŏgus, i, m. man of letters.

phĭlŏmēla, ae, f. nightingale.

phœnix (mod. hort.), date-palm.

phĭlŏsŏphia, ae, f. philosophy.   [phize.

phĭlŏsŏphor, ātus, i. v.n. dep. to philoso-

phĭlŏsŏphus, a, um, a. philosophical; —, i, m. philosopher.

philtrum, i, n. love-potion.

phĭlўra, ae, f. linden-tree.

phlox (mod. hort.), phlox.   [calf.

phōca, ae, phōcē, es, f. seal, sea-dog, sea-

phrĕnēsis, is, f. madness.

phrĕnēticus, a, um, a. mad.

phўsĭcus, a, um, a. connected with nature; —, i, m. natural philosopher; —a, orum, n. pl. physics.

phўsiŏlŏgia, ae, f. natural philosophy.

piăcŭlāris, e, a. atoning, expiatory.

piăcŭlum, i, n. sin-offering; victim; crime; remedy.

piāmen, ĭnis, n. atonement

pīca, ae, f. magpie.

pīcea, ae, f. spruce fir.   [black.

pīceus, a, um, a. made of pitch; pitch-

pictor, ōris, m. painter.

pictūra, ae, f. (art of) painting; picture; picturesque description.

pictūrātus, a, um, a. embroidered.

pictus, a, um, a. fig. ornamented, em-broidered.   [conscience.

piē, ad. piously; dutifully; with a good

piĕtas, ātis, f. piety; dutifulness; affec-tion, love; loyalty; gratitude.

pigeo, gui & pĭgĭtum est, 2. v.n. impers. to feel annoyance at;—piget, it irks, it grieves or repents.   [active; benumbed.

piger, gra, grum, a. slow, sluggish, in-piget, v. pigeo.

pigmentum, i, n. colour, paint, pigment; fig. colouring, ornament.

pignĕro, 1. v.a. to pledge, to pawn, to mortgage.

pignĕror, ātus sum, 1. v.a. to take as a pledge; to make one's own.

pignus, ŏris & ĕris, n. pledge, pawn, mort-gage; token, proof; wager.

pigrĭtia, ae, pigrĭties, ēi, f. sloth, sluggish-ness, laziness, indolence.

pīla, ae, f. pillar; pier.

pĭla, ae, f. ball, playing ball.

pīlanus, a soldier of the third rank.

pīleātus, a, um, a. wearing a hat or felt cap.

pĭlentum, i, n. chariot, carriage.

pīleŏlus or um, i, m. or n. small cap.

pīleum, i, n., pīleus, i, m. felt cap, hat; fig. freedom, liberty.

pilleus, v. pileus.

pĭlōsus, a, um, a. hairy.

pīlum, i, n. pestle; javelin.

pĭlus, i, m. hair; trifle.

pīlus, i, m. division of the triarii in a Roman legion;—primum pilum ducere, to be captain of the Triarii.

pĭnăcŏthēca, ae, f. picture-gallery.

pīnētum, i, n. pine-grove.

pīneus, a, um, a. of the pine, piny.

pingo, nxi, pictum, 3. v.a. to paint a pic-ture; to embroider; to embellish.

pinguesco, 3. v.n. to grow fat; to become strong or fertile.

pinguis, e, a. fat; plump; rich; dull; stupid.   [bearing.

pīnĭfer, a, um, pīnĭger, a, um, a. pine-

pinna, ae, f. feather; wing; battlement, pinnacle, fin.

pinnātus, a, um, a. winged; feathered.

pinnĭger, winged; finny.   [pound.

pinso, si or sui, sum or situm, 3. v.a. to

pīnus, ūs & i, f. pine, pine-tree; ship.

pio, 1. v.a. to appease, to propitiate; to celebrate; to purify; (poet.) to avenge, to atone for.

pĭper, ĕris, n. pepper.

pīrāta, ae, m. sea-robber, corsair, pirate.

pīrāticus, a, um, ad. piratical.

pĭrum, i, n. pear.

pĭrus, i, f. pear-tree.

piscārius, ii, m. fishmonger.

piscātor, ōris, m. fisherman, fisher.

piscātōrius, a, um, a. of or for fishing.

piscīna, ae, f. fish-pond.

piscis, is, m. fish.

piscor, ātus, i. v.n. dep. to fish.

piscōsus, a, um, a. full of fish.

pistācia, ae, f. mastich-tree.

pistillus, i, m., um, i, n. pestle.

pistor, ōris, m. baker, miller.

pistrīnum, i, n. pounding-mill.

pistris, is, f. sea monster; whale.

pīsum, i, n. garden pea.

pītuīta, ae, f. slime, phlegm.

pius, a, um, a. pious, religious; kind; dutiful; affectionate;—**pia fraus,** a justifiable deceit.

pix, pīcis, f. pitch.

plācābĭlis, e, a. easily appeased, placable; appeasing, pacifying.   [appeasing.

plācāmentum, i, n. expiation; means of

plācātē, ad. calmly.   [gentle.

plācātus, a, um, a. pacified; calm;

plăcenta, ae, f. cake.

plăceo, cui, cĭtum, 2. v.n. to please, to satisfy;—**plăcet,** it seems good so.

plăcĭdē, ad. gently, calmly, placidly.

plăcĭdus, a, um, a. gentle, calm, mild, peaceful, placid.

plăcĭtum, i, n. that which is pleasing or agreeable; maxim; rule.

plăcĭtus, a, um, a. agreeable, pleasing.

plāco, 1. v.a. to calm, to assuage, to appease, to reconcile.

plāga, ae, f. blow stroke, stripe; thrust, wound; fig. injury, misfortune.

plăga, ae, f. region, tract; zone; snare; hunting-net.   [thief.

plăgiārius, ii, m. kidnapper; literary

plăgōsus, a, um, a. good at flogging.

plăgŭla, ae, f. bed-curtain.

planctus, ūs, m. striking, beating; rustling, roaring; lamentation.

plānē, ad. evidently; quite; altogether.

plănēta, ae, m. wandering star, planet.

plango, nxi, nctum, 3. v.a. to strike, to beat; to lament.   [tation.

plangor, ōris, m. beating, striking; lamen-

plānĭties, ēi, f. flat or even surface, level ground, plain.

planta, ae, f. sprout, shoot, twig, sprig, graft, slip, sole of the foot.

plantāria, ium, n. pl. slips; cuttings.

plānus, a, um, a. level, flat, plane, even; fig. clear.

plătănus, i, f. plane-tree.

plătēa (plătea), ae, f. street.

plaudo, si, sum, 3. v.a. & n. to clap, to strike, to beat; to applaud; to flatter.

plausor, ōris, m. applauder.

plaustrum, i, n. waggon, wain, cart; Charles's Wain.

plausus, ūs, m. clapping; applause.

plēbēcŭla, ae, f. mob; rabble.

plēbēius, a, um, a. pertaining to the common people or commonalty, plebeian; common, vulgar, mean.

plēbes, is & **ēi,** v. plebs.

plēbĭcŏla, ae, g.c. friend of the people, demagogue.   [the people.

plēbiscĭtum, i, n. decree or ordinance of

plebs, plēbēs, is & **ēi** & **i,** f. common people, commons or commonalty, plebeians, populace.

plecto, xi & **xui, ctum,** 3. v.a. to plait, to braid, to interweave; to twist, to bend.

plecto, 3. v.a. to punish; to blame.

plectrum, i, n. quill to strike the strings of a musical instrument.

plēnē, ad. fully; quite.

plēnus, a, um, a. full, filled with; plump, stout; plenteous; entire; whole; mature.

pleonasmus, i, m. pleonasm (grammatical term), employment of redundant words.

plērīque, aeque, ăque, v. plerusque.

plērumque, ad. generally, mostly, commonly, very often.

plērusque, răque, rumque, a. very great part, the greater part, most;—**pleraque,** n. pl. everything, all.

plico, āvi & **ui, ātum** & **icĭtum,** 1. v.a. to fold, to wind together; (of serpents) to coil oneself up.

plodo, v. plaudo.

plōrātus, ūs, m. lamentation.

plōro, 1. v.n. & a. to wail, to weep aloud, to weep over.

plostellum, i, n. small cart.

pluit, v.n. imp. it rains; v. pluo.

plūma, ae, f. feather, soft feather; down; scale.   [wort.

plumbāgo, ĭnis, f. lead ore, (plant) lead-

plumbeus, a, um, a. leaden; blunt, dull; fig. heavy, weighty; stupid.

plumbum, i, n. lead; tin; leaden bullet; leaden pipe.

plūmeus, a, um, a. downy.

plūmo, 1. v.a. to feather.

pluo, plui & **pluvi,** 3. v.n. imp. to rain.

plūmōsus, a, um, a. feathered.

plūrālis, e, a. plural.

plūres, plūra, a. pl. more, many;—**se ad plures penetrare,** to join the majority (to die).

plūrĭmum, ad. very much.

plūrĭmus, a, um, a. very much or many, (the) most, very long or large or big.

plūs, ad. more;—**pluris,** of more value.

pluscŭlus, a, um, a. somewhat more.

plŭteus, m. movable pent-house, shed; parapet; bookcase; couch.

plŭvia, ae, f. rain.

plŭviālis, e, a. rainy.

plŭvius, a, um, a. rainy, causing or bringing rain.   [drinking bout.

pōcŭlum, i, n. cup, goblet, bowl; draught,

pŏdagra, ae, f. gout.

pōdex, ĭcis, m. anus.

pŏdium, ii, n. elevated place; balcony.

poēma, ătis, n. poem.

pœna, ae, f. punishment, penalty; pain; —**dare pœnas,** to pay the penalty.

pœnit . . ., v. pænit . . .

poēsis, is, f. poetry; poem.

poēta, ae, m. poet;—**poeta nascitur, non fit,** a poet is born, not made.

poētica, ae, poēticē, es, f. art of poetry.

poēticus, a, um, a. poetical.

poētria, ae, f. poetess.

pol, i. forsooth, truly.

pŏlĕmōnium (mod. hort.), Jacob's ladder.

pŏlenta, ae, f. pearl barley.

pŏlianthes (mod. hort.), tuberose.

pŏlio, īvi & ii, ītum, 4. v.a. to smooth, to furbish, to polish; to adorn, to embellish; *fig.* to refine, to improve.

pŏlītē, ad. neatly; elegantly.

pŏlīticus, a, um, a. political.

pŏlītus, a, um, a. refined; elegant.

pollen, īnis, m. fine, flour, dust.

pollens, entis, a. strong, able, powerful, potent.

polleo, 2. v.n. to be powerful; to be able, to prevail.

pollex, ĭcis, m. thumb; finger;—**pollice verso,** with thumb turned down (a signal for putting to death a defeated gladiator).

pollĭceor, ĭtus, 2. v.a. dep. to promise.

pollĭcĭtātio, ōnis, f. promise.

pollĭcĭtor, 1. v. dep. to promise.

pollūceo, xi, ctum, 2. v.a. to offer up; to offer.

polluo, ui, ūtum, 3. v.a. to soil, to defile, to pollute; to contaminate, to violate; to dishonour.

pŏlus, i, m. pole; heavens.

polyanthus (mod. hort.), primula.

polygăla (mod. hort.), milkwort.

pŏlўgŏnātum, i, n. Solomon's-seal.

polygŏnum (mod. hort.), knotweed.

pŏlўpŏdium, ii, n. polypody (fern).

pŏlўpŭs, i, m. polypus.

pōmārium, ii, n. orchard.

pōmĕrīdiānus, a, um, a. afternoon, post-meridian.

pŏmerium, v. pomœrium.

pōmifer, a, um, a. fruit-bearing.

pōmœrium, ii, n. space left free from buildings within and without the walls of a town.

pōmōsus, a, um, a. rich in fruit.

pompa, ae, f. solemn *or* public procession; show; pageantry.

pōmum, i, n. fruit; fruit-tree.

pōmus, i, f. fruit-tree.

pondĕro, 1. v.a. to weigh, to consider, to ponder, to examine. [cant.

pondĕrōsus, a, um, a. *fig.* weighty, significant.

pondō, indecl. in *or* by weight.

pondus, ĕris, n. weight; burden; value; importance, gravity, influence; pounds' weight.

pōnĕ, ad. & pr. after, behind, back.

pōno, pŏsui, pŏsĭtum, 3. v.a. to put, to place, to lay; to plant; to lay aside; to appoint; to propose; to assume; to wager; to lay to rest (i.e. to bury); to calm.

pons, ntis, m. bridge; deck (of a ship); floor of a tower;—**Pons Asinorum,** the asses' bridge, the 5th proposition, Bk. I of Euclid.

pontĭcŭlus, i, m. little bridge. [tiff.

pontĭfex, ĭcis, m. Roman high-priest, pontifical.

pontĭfĭcalis, e, pontĭfĭcius, a, um, a. pontifical.

pontĭfĭcātus, ūs, m. pontificate.

pontus, i, m. (poet.) sea; deep; wave.

pōpellus, i, m. mob, populace.

pōpīna, ae, f. cook-shop, tavern.

pōpĭno, ōnis, m. gormandizer.

poplĕs, ĭtis, m. ham, hough; knee.

poplus, v. populus.

pōpŭlābĭlis, e, a. that may be destroyed.

pōpŭlāris, e, a. popular; democratic; of the same country;—**pōpŭlāris aura,** the breeze of popular favour; —, **is,** m. fellow-countryman.

pōpŭlārĭtas, ātis, f. courting of the people.

pōpŭlārĭter, ad. coarsely, vulgarly; popularity.

pōpŭlātĭo, ōnis, f. plundering, devastation; plunder, booty. [plunderer.

pōpŭlātor, ōris, m. devastator, ravager,

pōpŭleus, a, um, a. of a poplar.

pōpŭlo, 1. v.a. pōpŭlor, ātus, 1. v.a. dep. to ravage, to devastate; to plunder.

pōpŭlus, i, m. people, nation; crowd

pōpŭlus, i, f. poplar-tree.

porca, ae, f. sow; boar.

porcīnus, a, um, adj. of a pig; pig's.

porcŭlus, i, m. porker.

porcus, i, m. hog, pig.

porphўrītes, ae, m. porphyry.

porrectus, a, um, a. extended, widespread. [sacrifice.

porrĭcio, ēci, ectum, 3. v.a. to offer in

porrigo, rexi, rectum, 3. v.a. to put forth, to extend; to stretch *or* spread (oneself) out; to offer.

porrīgo, ĭnis, f. scurf, dandruff.

porro, ad. onwards, farther on, afar off; besides; henceforth.

porrum, i, n., porrus, i, m. leek.

porta, ae, f. gate; entrance. [portend.

portendo, di, tum, 3. v.a. to foretell, to

portentōsus, a, um, a. monstrous, portentous, unnatural, revolting.

portentum, i, n. sign, token, omen, portent; monster, monstrosity; fiction.

portĭcus, ūs, f. colonnade, porch, portico.

portĭo, ōnis, f. part, portion, share; relation; proportion;—**pro portione,** proportionally.

portĭtor, ōris, m. ferryman; Charon; receiver of customs.

porto, 1. v.a. to carry or bear, to convey; *fig.* to bear.   [lar's tax.

portōrium, ii, n. dúty, toll, impost; ped-

portŭla, ae, f. small gate.

portŭlāca, ae, f. purslane.   [bours.

portuōsus, a, um, a. abounding in har-

portus, ūs, m. harbour, haven, port; mouth of a river; *fig.* retreat, asylum.

posco, pŏposci, 3. v.n. to ask for, to demand; to desire; to supplicate; to demand in marriage; to demand for punishment.   [tion, site.

pŏsĭtio, ōnis, f. position, posture; situa-

pŏsĭtŏr, ōris, m. builder, founder.

pŏsĭtus, ūs, m. situation, position.

possessio, ōnis, f. possession; estate.

possessor, ōris, m. possessor, owner.

possĭbĭlis, e, a. possible.   [to have.

possĭdeo, sēdi, sessum, 2. v.a. to possess,

possĭdo, sēdi, sessum, 3. v.a. to take possession of, to possess oneself of; *fig.* to occupy.

possum, pŏtui, posse, v.n. ir. to be able; to have power; —, I can, I may.

post, ad. & pr. behind, back; backwards; after; inferior to;—post hoc ergo propter hoc, after this, therefore because of this (a logical fallacy);—post obit, a bond payable after death.

posteā, ad. hereafter, thereafter, afterwards;—quid — ? what then?

posteāquam, ad. after that.

postĕrior, us, a. next in order; later, latter; *fig.* inferior.

postĕrĭtas, ātis, f. future time; posterity.

postĕrus, a, um, a. following, next, ensuing, future;—in postĕrum, for the future;—postĕri, ōrum, m. pl. posterity.

postfĕro, ferre, 3. v.a. to esteem less (than another).

posthăbeo, ui, ĭtum, 2. v.a. to place after, to esteem less, to sacrifice (one thing to another).   [future.

posthāc, ad. hereafter, henceforth, in

posthinc, ad. after this, henceforth.

postĭcus, a, um, a. hinder, back, posterior; postĭcum, i, n. back-door.

postis, is, m. post, door-post; door.

postlĭmĭnium, ii, n. the right to return home and resume lost privileges.

postmŏdo, postmŏdum, ad. afterwards, presently, shortly.

postpōno, pŏsui, pŏsĭtum, 3. v.a. to esteem less, to disregard, to sacrifice (one thing to another).

postquam, c. after that, after, since, as soon as, when.

postrēmō, ad. at last.

postrēmus, a, um, a. last; lowest; worst.

postrīdĭē, ad. on the day after, on the following or next day.   [complaint.

postŭlātio, ōnis, f. petition, request;

postŭlātum, i, n. demand, request; an assumption necessary as a basis of argument.

postŭlo, 1. v.a. to ask, to demand, to require, to request, to desire; to accuse, to prosecute.

postŭmus, a, um, a. last; last born; born after the death of the father.

pōtātio, ōnis, f. drinking-bout, potation.

pōtātor, ōris, m. drinker, toper, bibber.

pōte, a., v. potis,

pŏtens, a. able, mighty, powerful, potent.

pŏtentātus, ūs, m. dominion, empire, rule; pre-eminence.

pŏtenter, ad. powerfully.

pŏtentia, ae, f. might, force, power; efficacy, virtue; *fig.* ability; authority.

potentilla (mod. hort.), cinquefoil.

pŏtesse = posse, v. possum.

pŏtestas, ātis, f. power, faculty, opportunity; authority; efficacy; dominion; command.

pōtio, ōnis, f. drink, draught; poisonous draught; philtre.

pŏtior, ĭtus, 4. v.n. dep. to take possession of, to get, to obtain, to acquire, to receive; to possess.   [preferable.

pŏtior, ius, a. more powerful; better;

pŏtis, pŏte, a. able, capable; possible; powerful.

pŏtissĭmē, pŏtissĭmum, ad. chiefly, principally, especially, above all, most of all.

pŏtissĭmus, a, um, a. principal; most important.

pŏtius, ad. rather, preferably; more.

pōto, ātum & pōtum, 1. v.a. & n. to drink; to drink hard.

pōtor, ōris, m. drinker.   [ing.

pōtōrius, a, um, a. connected with drink-

pōtŭlenta, ōrum, n. pl. drinkables.

pōtus, a, um, a. drunken; —, ūs, m. drinking; drink.

præ, ad. & pr. before, forwards, in front; in comparison with; by reason of;—præ lacrimis non posse loqui, not to be able to speak for tears; — præ se ferre, to show, to exhibit.

præăcūtus, a, um, a. sharpened before or at the end, pointed.   [deep.

præaltus, a, um, a. very high; very

præbeo, ui, ĭtum, 2. v.a. to reach out, to offer; to present; to show; to give.

præcălĭdus, a, um, a. very warm, very hot.   [time; very grey.

præcānus, a, um, a. grey before one's

præcăveo, cāvi, cautum, 2. v.a. & n. to guard against, to beware.

præcēdo, cessi, cessum, 3. v.a. & n. to go before, to precede; to surpass, to excel.

præcellens, entis, p. & a. excellent, surpassing.

præcello, 3. v.a. & n. to excel; to surpass.

præcelsus, a, um, a. very high *or* lofty.

præceps, cipĭtis, a. headlong; hasty; swift; dangerous; steep;—**in præceps,** headlong.

præceptio, onis, f. precept; inculcation.

præceptor, ōris, m. teacher, instructor.

præceptum, i, n. maxim, rule, precept; order, direction.

præcerpo, psi, ptum, 3. v.a. to pluck before a thing is ripe; to impair.

præcīdo, cīdi, cīsum, 3. v.a. to cut off in front; to cut off; to cut in pieces; to destroy; to cut short, to abridge; to refuse *or* deny flatly.

præcingo, nxi, nctum, 3. v.a. to gird (in front); to surround.

præcīno, ui, centum, 3. v.a. & n. to sing before; to predict; to mutter spells.

præcĭpio, cēpi, ceptum, 3. v.a. *fig.* to take *or* obtain in advance, to anticipate; to teach, to direct.

præcĭpĭto, 1. v.a. & n. to throw down headlong, to precipitate; to hasten, to hurry on; to sink down; to fall.

præcĭpuē, ad. especially, chiefly.

præcĭpuus, a, um, a. particular, peculiar, especial; special. [cisely; absolutely.

præcīsē, ad. in short, in few words, con-

præcīsus, a, um, a. broken off, steep, abrupt, precipitous; *fig.* short, brief.

præclārē, ad. very clearly, very plainly; excellently, admirably.

præclārus, a, um, a. very clear, very bright; very beautiful; splendid, noble, excellent, famous.

præclūdo, si, sum, 3. v.a. to shut to, to close; to forbid access to; to hinder.

præco, ōnis, m. crier, herald.

præcōgĭto, 1. v.a. to premeditate.

præcŏlo, lui, cultum, 3. v.a. to cultivate beforehand.

præcōnium, ii, n. office of a public crier; proclaiming; spreading abroad; eulogy; celebration.

præcōnius, a, um, m. of a crier.

præconsūmo, mpsi, mptum, 3. v.a. to spend *or* waste beforehand.

præcordia, ōrum, n. pl. midriff, diaphragm; entrails; stomach; breast, heart.

præcox, cŏcis, præcŏquis, e, præcŏquus, a, um, a. ripened too soon; premature; unseasonable; precocious.

præcurro, cŭcurri (curri), cursum, 3. v.n. & a. to run before, to hasten on before; to precede; to anticipate.

præcursor, ōris, m. forerunner; vanguard; spy.

præda, ae, f. booty, spoil, pillage.

prædābundus, a, um, a. pillaging.

prædātor, ōris, m. plunderer, pillager.

prædātōrius, a, um, a. plundering, rapacious; piratical. [mine in advance.

prædestino, v.a. to predestine, to deter-

prædiātor, ōris, m. one who buys mortgaged estates. [cation; praise.

prædĭcātio, ōnis, f. proclamation, publi-

prædĭco, 1. v.a. to publish; to proclaim; to say, to relate; to own; to acknowledge; to praise.

prædīco, xi, ctum, 3. v.a. to say *or* mention beforehand; to foretell; to advise, to warn; to command. [mand.

prædictum, i, n. prediction; order, com-

prædiŏlum, i, n. small estate.

prædisco, 3. v.a. to learn in advance.

prædĭtus, a, um, p. & a. endowed with.

prædium, ii, n. land, estate.

prædīves, ĭtis, a. very rich.

prædo, ōnis, m. plunderer; robber.

prædor, ātus, 1. v.n. & a. dep. to plunder, to spoil, to rob; to take; to ravish.

prædūco, xi, ctum, 3. v.a. to run (a ditch *or* a wall) in front.

prædulcis, e, a. very sweet. [strong.

prædūrus, a, um, a. very hard; very

præeo, īvi & ii, ĭtum, 4. v.n. & a. to go before, to precede; to recite; to dictate.

præfātio, ōnis, f. saying beforehand; formula; preface, introduction, prologue. [tendence, prefecture.

præfectūra, ae, f. presidency, superin-

præfectus, i, m. prefect, director, president, chief.

præfĕro, tŭli, lātum, v.a. ir. to bear before; to prefer; to display, to reveal, to betray.

præfĕrox, ōcis, a. very fierce; very bold.

præfica, ae, f. woman hired to lament at funerals.

præficio, fēci, fectum, 3. v.a. to set over, to appoint to the command of.

præfīgo, xi, xum, 3. v.a. to fasten before; to fix on the end *or* extremity.

præfīnio, īvi *or* ii, ītum, to fix in advance.

præfluo, 3. v.n. & a. to flow by *or* past.

præfŏdio, fōdi, 3. v.a. to dig before *or* in front of; to bury beforehand.

præfor, fātus, 1. v.n. & a. dep. to say *or* utter beforehand; to preface; to foretell.

præfrīgĭdus, a, um, a. very cold.

præfringo, frēgi, fractum, 3. v.a. to break off before *or* at the end, to shiver.

præfulgeo, si, tum, 2. v.n. to shine in front; to glitter.

praegĕlĭdus, a, um, a. very cold.

praegnans, antis, a. with child; pregnant.

praegrandis, e, a. very large; vast.

praegrăvis, e, a. very heavy; burdensome.

praegrăvo, 1. v.a. to press heavily on; *fig.* to depress.

praegrĕdior, gressus, 3. v.n. & a. dep. to go before, to precede; *fig.* to surpass.

praegusto, 1. v.a. to taste in advance.

praejūdĭcium, ii, n. preceding judicial examination; precedent, example; prejudice.

praejūdĭco, 1. v.a. to prejudge.

praelābor, lapsus sum, 3. v.n. & a. dep. to glide and pass before *or* by.

praelĕgo, lēgi, lectum, 3. v.a. to sail past.

praelĭgo, 1. v.a. to bind *or* tie before, to fasten up.

praelium, v. proelium.

praelongus, a, um, a. very long.

praelŏquor, lŏcūtus, 3. v. dep. to anticipate (in speaking); to preface.

praelūceo, xi, 2. v.n. to shine forth; to outshine, to surpass.

praemando, 1. v.a. to order before.

praemātūrus, a, um, a. too early, untimely.

praemĕdĭtātio, ōnis, f. premeditation.

praemĕdĭtor, ătus sum, 1. v.a. dep. to premeditate.

praelum, v. prelum.

praemĕtuo, 3. v.a. & n. to fear beforehand.

praemitto, mīsi, missum, 3. v.a. to send before, to despatch in advance.

praemium, ii, n. booty; profit, advantage, prerogative; reward; punishment; exploit.

praemŏneo, ui, ĭtum, 2. v.a. to forewarn.

praemŏnĭtus, ūs, m. forewarning.

praemonstro, 1. v.a. to predict, to prognosticate.

praemŏrior, mortuus sum, 3. v.n. dep. to die before *or* prematurely.

praemūnio, īvi, ĭtum, 4. v.a. to fortify *or* defend in front; *fig.* to protect, to secure;—**praemunire**, a writ, a particular kind of writ; the word stands for praemoneri facias, you are to see that so-and-so is forewarned (to appear).

praemūnītio, ōnis, f. defence; *fig.* preparation.

praenăto, 1. v.n. to swim by; to flow by.

praenĭteo, ui, 2. v.n. to shine bright; to outshine.

praenōmen, ĭnis, n. first name.

praenosco, 3. v.a. to foreknow.

praenuntio, 1. v.a. to announce beforehand; to foretell.

praenuntius, a, um, adj. acting as harbinger. [hand; to anticipate.

praeoccŭpo, 1. v.a. to seize upon before-

praeopto, 1. v.a. to choose *or* wish rather, to prefer.

praepărātio, ōnis, f. preparation.

praepăro, 1. v.a. to prepare, to equip; to provide.

praepĕdio, īvi & ii, ĭtum, 4. v.a. to shackle, to fetter; to hinder.

praependeo, 2. v.n. to hand in front.

praepĕs, ĕtis, a. nimble, fleet; winged.

praepinguis, e, a. very rich.

praepollens, entis, a. very powerful.

praepondĕro, 1. v.a. & n. to outweigh; to have more effect; to preponderate.

praepōno, pŏsui, pŏsĭtum, 3. v.a. to put before; to set over; to prefer.

praepŏsĭtio, ōnis, f. preference; (gr.) preposition.

praepostĕrē, ad. in the wrong order.

praepostĕrus, a, um, a. in the wrong order; hind side before; ridiculous.

praepŏtens, entis, p. & a. very powerful.

praeprŏpĕrus, a, um, a. hasty; sudden.

praerĭpio, rĭpui, reptum, 3. v.a. to snatch away, to carry off; to snatch away before the time.

praerŏgātīvus, a, um, a. prerogative;— **praerogativa**, ae, f. tribe which voted first. [off.

praerumpo, rūpi, ruptum, 3. v.a. to break

praeruptus, a, um, p. & a. broken off; steep; *fig.* hasty, rash.

praes, praedis, m. surety, bondsman.

praesaepe, is, n. praesaepes, is, f., praesaepium, ii, n. enclosure; fold; stall; crib; hive; manger; hovel.

praesaepio, psi, ptum, 4. v.a. to fence in front; to block up.

praesāgio, īvi, 4. v.a. to have a presentiment; to presage.

praesāgium, ii, n. prognostication.

praesāgus, a, um, a. foreboding. [scient.

praescius, a, um, a. foreknowing, pre-

praescrībo, psi, ptum, 3. v.a. to write before; *fig.* to order, to prescribe.

praescriptio, ōnis, f. title, preface; order, precept; *fig.* pretext. [rule.

praescriptum, i, n. copy; precept, order,

praesĕco, ui, ctum *or* cātum, 1. v.a. to cut in front, to cut off.

praesens, entis, p. & a. present, in person, at hand, ready; prompt; favourable; effectual; immediate; resolute; present, aiding, favouring, propitious;— **in** —, for the present. [ception.

praesensio, ōnis, f. presentiment; precon-

praesentia, ae, f. presence; readiness.

praesentio, sensi, sensum, 4. v.a. to feel *or* perceive beforehand; to presage.

praesēpĕ, is, v. praesaepe.

praesēpio, v. praesaepio.

praesertim, ad. especially, particularly.

præsĕs, ĭdis, m. president; protector, guardian, defender.

præsĭdeo, sēdi, 2. v.n. to preside (over); *fig.* to guard, to protect, to defend; to superintend.

præsĭdium, ii, n. help, assistance; defence, protection; convoy, escort; garrison; intrenchment.

præsignis, e, a. remarkable; extraordinary. [guished, excellent.

præstābĭlis, e, a. pre-eminent, distin-

præstans, antis, a. excellent; distinguished (for). [ority, excellence.

præstantia, ae, f. pre-eminence, superi-

præstat, v. præsto.

præstigiae, ārum, f. pl. juggling tricks, deceits, delusions; *fig.* mere bombast.

præstigiātor, ōris, m. juggler; cheat.

præstĭtuo, ui, ūtum, 3. v.a. to determine in advance.

præsto, ad. at hand, ready.

præsto, stĭti, stĭtum & **stātum,** 1. v.n. & a. *fig.* to stand out; to be superior, to distinguish oneself; to surpass; to become surety for; to answer for; to fulfil; to maintain; to show.

præstōlor, ātus sum, 1. v.n. & a. dep. to expect, to stand ready for.

præstringo, inxi, ictum, 3. v.a. to bind fast *or* hard, to bind *or* tie up; to graze, to touch; to weaken, to blunt.

præstruo, xi, ctum, 3. v.a. to block up, to stop before; *fig.* to prepare beforehand.

præsul, ŭlis, m. dancer.

præsulto, 1. v.n. to leap *or* dance before.

præsum, fui, v.n. ir. to be before *or* above; to rule (over); to be set over, to preside *or* rule over, to have the charge *or* command of, to superintend;— **præesse classi,** to be admiral.

præsūmo, mpsi & **msi, mptum** & **mtum,** 3. v.a. to take before *or* first; *fig.* to take in advance; to perform beforehand; to spend *or* employ beforehand; to imagine, to picture to oneself beforehand; to presuppose; to foresee.

præsumptio, ōnis, f. anticipation; presupposition; daring.

prætendo, di, tum, 3. v.a. to stretch before; to extend; to pretend, to allege; to urge in excuse.

præter, ad. & pr. past; except; excepting; along; beyond; besides; unless, save.

prætĕrăgo, actum, 3. v.a. to drive past.

prætĕreā, ad. besides; moreover; hereafter.

prætĕreo, ĭvi & **ii, ĭtum,** 4. v.n. & a. to go by *or* past; *fig.* to pass by, to escape; to omit; to neglect; to surpass.

præterfluo, 3. v.n. to flow past.

prætergrĕdior, gressus, 3. v.a. & n. to pass by.

prætĕrĭtus, a, um, a. past.

præterlābor, psus, 3. v.n. & a. dep. to fly *or* run past; *fig.* to slip away. [over.

prætermissio, ōnis, f. omission; passing

prætermitto, mīsi, missum, 3. v.a. to let pass; to omit, to neglect; to pass over, to make no mention of. [cept, save.

præterquam, ad. beyond, besides; ex-

prætervĕhor, ctus sum, 3. v.n. & a. dep. to drive, to ride *or* sail by; *fig.* to pass by. [fly over.

prætervŏlo, 1. v.a. & n. to fly past; to

prætexo, xui, xtum, 3. v.a. to weave in front, to fringe; to adorn; to urge in excuse.

prætexta, ae, f. (toga) Roman tunic (bordered with purple) worn by freeborn children of the higher magistrates;—**prætexta** (fabula), tragedy.

prætextātus, a, um, a. wearing the toga prætexta.

prætextus, ūs, m. excuse; display.

prætor, ōris, m. Roman magistrate who presided over the administration of justice.

prætōriānus, a, um, a. of the emperor's bodyguard; prætorian.

prætōrium, ii, n. general's tent; council of war; imperial bodyguard; country mansion.

prætōrius, a, um, a. pertaining to a prætor; prætorian;—**cohors prætoria,** general's guard; —, ii, m. an ex-prætor.

prætūra, ae, f. prætorship.

præūro, ussi, ustum, 3. v.a. to burn before *or* at the tip.

prævăleo, ui, 2. v.n. to have greater power, influence *or* worth; to prevail.

prævălĭdus, a, um, a. very strong; rich, fertile; *fig.* prevalent.

prævărĭcātio, ōnis, f. shuffling, collusion.

prævărĭcātor, ōris, m. sham accuser, prevaricator.

prævărĭcor, ātus, 1. v. dep. to bring a sham accusation, to prevaricate.

prævĕhor, ctus, 3. v.a. & n. to ride past; to flow past.

prævĕnio, vēni, ventum, 4. v.n. & a. to come before, to get the start of; to anticipate, to prevent.

præverto, ti, 3. v.a. to get before; to anticipate, to preoccupy; to attend to first; to outstrip, to outrun; to surpass.

prævĭdeo, vīdi, vīsum, 2. v.a. to foresee.

prævius, a, um, a. going before, leading the way.

prævŏlo, 1. v.n. to fly before.

pragmătĭcus, a, um, a. belonging to state affairs; skilled in politics; relating to civil law. [(on).

prandeo, di, sum, 2. v.n. & a. to breakfast

prandium, ii, n. breakfast, luncheon.

pransus, a, um, a. having breakfasted; gluttonous.

prăsinus, a, um, green.

prătensis, e, a. of a meadow.

prătŭlum, i, n. little meadow.

prātum, i, n. meadow; plain.

prăvē, ad. wrongly, amiss, ill, badly.

prăvĭtas, ătis, f. impropriety, bad condition; viciousness, perverseness, depravity.

prăvus, a, um, a. crooked; misshapen, deformed; perverse, vicious.

prĕcārio, ad. by prayer, on sufferance.

prĕcārius, a, um, a. obtained by prayer; doubtful, precarious.

prĕcātĭo, ōnis, f. prayer, entreaty.

prĕcor, ātus, 1. v.n. & a. dep. to pray, to beseech, to entreat; to ask for; to invoke; to wish.

prĕhendo, prendo, di, sum, 3. v.a. to take hold of, to seize; to catch in the act.

prĕhenso, prenso, 1. v.a. to seize; to grasp; to solicit.

prĕlum, i, n. wine- or oil-press.

prĕmo, pressi, pressum, 3. v.a. to press; to squeeze; to oppress; to curb; to thrust; to overpower; to cover; to hide; to keep in subjection; to afflict; to depreciate; to pursue; to prune.

pressē, ad. concisely, exactly.

presso, 1. v.a. to press.

pressus, ūs, m. pressing, pressure

pressus, a, um, a. plain; concise; exact, dark (of colour).

prēster, ēris, m. waterspout; hurricane; deadly snake. [costly, dear.

prĕtĭōsus, a, um, a. valuable, precious;

prĕtium, ii, n. price, worth, value; wages, reward; bribe;—**pretium est, or operæ pretium est,** it is worth while.

prex, ĕcis, f. prayer, request, entreaty; curse; wish. [formerly.

prīdem, ad. long since, a long time ago;

prīdĭē, ad. on the day before.

prīmævus, a, um, a. youthful.

prīmārius, a, um, a. chief, principal, excellent. [turion of the **Triarii.**

prīmĭpīlus, primōpilus, i, m. chief cen-

prīmĭtiae, ārum, f. pl. firstlings, first-fruits.

prīmĭtus, ad. for the first time.

prīmō, ad. at first, firstly. [mencement.

prīmordium, ii, n. beginning, origin, com-

prīmōris, is, a. first; foremost, extreme;
—**primores, m.** pl. nobles, men of the first rank.

prīmŭla (mod. hort.), primrose, primula.

prīmum, ad. first, in the first place, in the beginning; for the first time.

prīmus, a, um, a. first, foremost; distinguished;—**prima lux,** early dawn;—**primus inter pares,** first among equals; —**prima facie,** at first sight.

princeps, ĭpis, a. first; —, c. chief; general; prince; prime mover; — **senatus,** senator whose name stood first on the Censor's list;—**principes, um,** pl. soldiers in the second line of a legion.

princĭpālis, e, a. first, original, primitive; chief, principal; princely.

princĭpātus, ūs, m. pre-eminence, preference; supremacy, post of commander-in-chief; rule; sovereignty; beginning, origin.

princĭpium, ii, n. beginning, origin, principle;—**principio,** at first; in the beginning;—**principia,** first principles;— **principiis obsta,** deal sternly with the beginnings (of evil).

prior, prius, ōris, a. former, previous; better;—**priōres, m.** pl. ancestors.

priscus, a, um, a. old, ancient, antique; former, previous.

pristĭnus, a, um, a. former, early, primitive; pristine; old-fashioned.

prius, ad. before, sooner.

priusquam, ad. before that.

prīvātim, ad. in private, privately. [tion.

prīvātĭo, ōnis, f. taking away, depriva-

prīvātus, a, um, p. & a. private.

prīvigna, ae, f. stepdaughter.

prīvignus, i, m. stepson.

prīvilēgium, ii, n. bill or law against an individual; privilege.

prīvo, 1. v.a. to bereave, to deprive of; to free, to release.

prīvus, a, um, a. each; several; one's own, private, peculiar, particular.

prō, pr. before, in front of; from the front of; for, in favour of; instead of; in proportion to;—**pro aris et focis,** in defence of altars and hearths;—**pro bono publico,** for the public good;— **pro forma,** as a formality;—**pro rata,** in proportion;—**pro tanto,** for that much; so far;—**pro tempore,** temporarily.

prō, prōh! i. ah! alas!

proăvia, ae, f. great-grandmother.

proăvītus, a, um, a. ancestral, ancient.

proăvus, i, m. great-grandfather; ancestor. [able, commendable.

prŏbābĭlis, e, a. probable; pleasing, agree-

prŏbābĭliter, ad. probably. [proval.

prŏbātĭo, ōnis, f. trial, examination; ap-

prŏbātor, ōris, m. approver.

prŏbē, ad. rightly, well, properly, fitly, excellently.   [modesty.
prŏbĭtas, ātis, f. honesty, probity;
problēma, ătis, n. problem, puzzle.
prŏbo, 1. v.a. to try, to test; to approve; to recommend; to approve of.
prŏboscis, ĭdis, f. trunk; snout.
probrōsus, a, um, a. shameful, infamous.
prŏbrum, i, n. disgrace; wickedness; lewdness; adultery; abuse, insult; libel.   [able.
prŏbus, a, um, a. good; honest, honour-
prŏcācitas, ātis, f. boldness, shameless-ness, impudence.
prŏcācĭter, ad. impudently; wantonly.
prŏcax, ācis, a. insolent, pert, wanton.
prŏcēdo, cessi, cessum, 3. v.n. to go for-ward or before; to proceed; to ad-vance; to get on; to walk in state; to be successful.
prŏcella, ae, f. storm, hurricane, tempest; tumult, commotion.   [ous, boisterous.
prŏcellōsus, a, um, a. stormy, tempestu-
prŏcer, ĕris, m. great man, nobleman.
prŏcēres, um, v. **procer.**
prŏcērĭtas, ātis, f. height, tallness; length.
prŏcērus, a, um, a. high, tall.
prŏcessio, ōnis, f. advance.
prŏcessus, ūs, m. advance, progress.
prŏcĭdo, cĭdi, 3. v.n. to fall prostrate.
prŏcĭduus, a, um, a. fallen in; prostrate.
prŏcinctus, ūs, m. readiness for battle.
proclāmātor, ōris, m. proclaimer; bawl-ing advocate.   [vociferate.
proclāmo, 1. v.a. to call or cry out, to
prŏclīno, 1. v.a. to bend forward; to totter;—**proclinari,** to be on the verge of ruin.
prŏclīvis, e, a. steep; fig. downward; prone to; ready; easy.
prŏclīvĭtas, ātis, f. steep declivity; fig. tendency, proneness.
prōconsul, is, m. an ex-consul; governor of a province.
prōconsŭlāris, e, a. proconsular.
prōconsŭlātus, ūs, m. proconsulship.
procrastinātio, ōnis, f. putting off; pro-crastination.   [defer.
prōcrastĭno, 1. v.a. to procrastinate, to
prōcreātio, ōnis, f. begetting.
prōcreātor, ōris, m. creator, begetter.
prōcreo, 1. v.a. to bring forth into exist-ence, to beget, to procreate, to pro-duce.   [being.
procresco, 3. v.n. to grow; to come into
prŏcŭbo, 1. v.n. to lie over, to lie stretched out.
prōcūdo, di, sum, 3. v.a. to forge; fig. to cultivate, to form; to produce.
prŏcŭl, ad. far, from afar, far from.
proculco, 1. v.a. to trample upon.

prŏcumbo, cŭbui, cŭbĭtum, 3. v.n. to lean or bend forwards; to sink down, to prostrate oneself.
prōcūrātio, ōnis, f. charge, management; superintendence.
prōcūrātor, ōris, m. manager, overseer; agent; deputy; collector of revenue.
prōcūro, 1. v.a. & n. to attend to; to supervise; to expiate (by sacrifice).
prōcurro, cŭcurri & curri, cursum, 3. v.n. to run forth, to rush forwards; to jut out, to extend.
prōcursātio, ōnis, f. charge, sally, onset.
prōcurso, 1. v.n. to make attacks or sallies.
prōcursus, ūs, m. (mil.) charge.
prōcurvus, a, um, a. curved in front.
prŏcus, i, m. wooer, suitor.
prōdeo, ii, ĭtum, 4. v.n. to go or come forth; to stand out, to project; to appear (on the stage); to advance, to proceed; to come up.
prōdīco, xi, ctum, 3. v.a. to appoint; to put off, to defer.
prōdĭgiōsus, a, um, a. prodigious, strange, wonderful.   [monster.
prōdĭgium, ii, n. omen, portent, prodigy;
prōdĭgo, ēgi, actum, 3. v.a. to squander.
prōdĭgus, a, um, a. wasteful, lavish, prodigal; rich, abounding (in).
prōdĭtio, ōnis, f. betraying, treason; treachery.
prōdĭtor, ōris, m. traitor; betrayer.
prōdo, dĭdi, dĭtum, 3. v.a. to bring forth; to report; to publish; to betray; to hand down.
prōdūco, xi, ctum, 3. v.a. to lead or bring forward; to draw out; to accompany to the tomb; to lengthen; to delay; to bring forth; to promote.   [ing.
prōductio, ōnis, f. lengthening, prolong-
proelior, ātus, 1. v.n. dep. to join battle, to fight; to contend.   [test, strife.
proelium, ii, n. battle, combat; fig. con-
prŏfāno, 1. v.a. to desecrate, to profane.
prŏfānus, a, um, a. secular, profane; wicked; ill-boding.
prŏfectio, ōnis, f. setting out; departure.
prŏfecto, ad. really, surely, certainly.
prŏfectus, us, m. growth; progress; effect.
prōfĕro, tŭli, lātum, v.a. ir. to carry or bring out, to bring forth; to extend; to prolong; to defer; to reveal, to mention; to quote.
prŏfessio, ōnis, f. declaration, promise; public register; business, profession.
prŏfessor, ōris, m. professor; teacher.
prŏfessōrius, a, um, a. professional.
prŏfestus, a, um, a. not kept as a holiday, common, ordinary.

prŏfĭcio, fēci, fectum, 3. v.n. & a. to make way; to advance; to profit; to effect; to help; to conduce.

prŏfĭciscor, fectus, 3. v.n. dep. to set out; to travel, to depart; to proceed, to arise *or* spring from.

prŏfĭteor, fessus, 2. v.a. dep. to declare publicly, to confess, to profess; to promise, to offer.

prŏflĭgātus, a, um, a. abandoned; profligate. [to ruin, to destroy.

prŏflĭgo, 1. v.a. to overthrow, to conquer;

prŏflo, 1. v.a. to breathe forth.

prŏfluenter, ad. flowingly, easily.

prŏfluo, xi, xum, 3. v.n. to flow forth *or* along; to issue, to proceed.

prŏflŭvium, ii, n. flow; outflow.

prŏfor, fātus sum, 1. v. dep. to speak out, to say.

prŏfŭgio, fūgi, 3. v.n. & a. to flee before, to run away; to take refuge with.

prŏfŭgus, a, um, a. fugitive; roving, unsettled; exiled.

prŏfundo, fūdi, fūsum, 3. v.a. to pour out; to bring forth; to cast *or* throw away; to squander; to spend; to vent.

prŏfundus, a, um, a. deep, profound; high; boundless, immoderate; inexhaustible;—**profundum, i,** n. depth, abyss.

prŏfūsē, ad. lavishly, extravagantly, profusely; *fig.* excessively.

prŏfūsus, a, um, a. excessive; lavish.

prōgĕnĕro, 1. v.a. to beget, to engender.

prōgĕnies, ĕi, f. race, family, progeny.

prōgĕnitor, ōris, m. ancestor.

prōgigno, gĕnui, gĕnĭtum, 3. v.a. to beget; to produce. [scended (from).

prognātus, a, um, p. & a. born (of), descended.

progrĕdior, gressus, 3. v.n. dep. to march forwards, to go on, to proceed.

progressio, ōnis, f. going forwards, progression; progress, increase. [course.

progressus, ūs, m. advance, progress;

prōhĭbeo, ui, ĭtum, 2. v.a. to prevent, to restrain; to stop, to forbid; to avert; to defend.

proindĕ, ad. hence, therefore, accordingly, then; just so; — **ac,** just as if.

prōjectio, ōnis, f. stretching out.

prōjectus, a, um, a. jutting out; prostrate; manifest; abject; base; prone to.

prōjĭcio, jēci, jectum, 3. v.a. to throw forth *or* before, to fling down *or* away; to expose, to hold out; to expel, to disdain, to renounce.

prōlābor, lapsus, 3. v.n. dep. to glide *or* slip forwards, to fall down; to fall to decay, to go to ruin; to fail; to go on; to escape.

prōlātio, ōnis, f. postponement; introduction.

prōlāto, 1. v.a. to lengthen, to enlarge; to prolong; to put off, to defer.

prōlecto, 1. v.a. to allure, to entice.

prōlepsis, is, f. prolepsis, grammatical term meaning anticipation, e.g. **tum steriles exurere Sirius agros,** then Sirius burns the barren fields, i.e. so that they shall be barren.

prōlēs, is, f. offspring, progeny, descendants, race.

prōlētārius, ii, m. proletary (citizen of the lowest class); —, a. low, common.

prōlĭcio, lixi, 3. v.a. to allure, to entice.

prōlixē, ad. abundantly; largely.

prōlixus, a, um, a. flowing; extended; obliging.

prōlŏgus, i, m. prologue.

prōlŏquor, cūtus sum, 3. v.n. & a. dep. to speak out, to declare.

prōlūdo, si, sum, 3. v.n. to prelude, to practise beforehand.

prōluo, lui, lūtum, 3. v.a. to wash forth *or* out; to wash off *or* away; to moisten.

prōlūsio, ōnis, f. essay, trial; prelude.

prōlūvies, ei, f. inundation, excrement.

prōmĕreo, ui, ĭtum, 2. v.a., **prōmĕreor, ĭtus sum,** 2. v.a. dep. to deserve, to merit; to deserve well of; to earn; to

prōmĕrĭtum, i, n. guilt; merit. [gain.

prōmĭnens, entis, p. & a. projecting, prominent.

prōmĭneo, ui, 2. v.n. to jut out, to be prominent, to overhang; to extend to.

prōmiscuē, ad. promiscuously.

prōmiscuus, a, um, a. mixed, indiscriminate, promiscuous. [promise.

prōmissio, ōnis, f., prōmissum, i, n.

prōmissus, a, um, a. hanging down, long.

prōmitto, mĭsi, missum, 3. v.a. to send *or* put forth, to let hang down; to let grow; to promise; to foretell.

prōmo, mpsi (msi), mptum (mtum), 3. v.a. to take *or* bring out *or* forth; to disclose; to express, to relate; to exalt.

prōmontūrium, ii, n. promontory, cape; mountain-ridge.

prōmŏveo, mōvi, mōtum, 2. v.a. to move forwards; to advance; to extend; to increase; to reveal. [promptly.

promptē, ad. readily, quickly, willingly,

promptus, a, um, a. visible, evident; at hand, ready, prompt, quick.

promptus, ūs, m., **in promptu esse,** to be visible; to be open; to be at hand; to be easy. [clamation.

prōmulgātio, ōnis, f. promulgation, pro-

prōmulgo, 1. v.a. to make known, to publish.

prōmulsis, ĭdis, f. hors-d'œuvre.

prōmus, i, m. butler; steward.
prōnĕpos, ōtis, m. great-grandson.
prōneptis, is, f. great-granddaughter.
prōnōmen, ĭnis, n. pronoun.   [marriage.
prōnŭbus, a, um, a. presiding over
prōnuntiātio, ōnis, f. publication, pro-
    clamation; delivery; proposition.
prōnuntiātor, ōris, m. narrator, relater.
prōnuntiātum, i, n. logical proposition.
pronuntio, I. v.a. to proclaim, to an-
    nounce; to nominate; to recite, to de-
    claim; to tell, to report; to promise.
prōnŭrus, ūs, f. wife of a grandson.
prōnus, a, um, a. stooping, bending
    down; inclined downwards; setting,
    sinking; disposed, prone to; easy.
prōœmium, ii, n. introduction, preface.
prōpāgātio, ōnis, f. propagation; pro-
    longation.
prōpāgātor, ōris, m. *fig.* enlarger.
prōpāgo, I. v.a. to peg down; to propa-
    gate; to extend, to enlarge, to increase.
prōpāgo, ĭnis, f. set, layer; slip, shoot;
    offspring, children, race, breed.
prōpālam, ad. openly, publicly, no-
    toriously, manifestly.
prōpātŭlus, a, um, a. open, uncovered.
prōpĕ, ad. & pr. near, nigh; hard by; al-
    most.   [few days.
prōpĕdiem, ad. ere long, shortly, within a
prōpello, pŭli, pulsum, 3. v.a. to drive *or*
    push forwards, to hurl, to propel; to
    drive away; to impel.   [almost.
prōpĕmŏdo, prōpĕmŏdum, ad. nearly,
prōpendeo, di, sum, 2. v.n. to hang forth,
    to hang down; *fig.* to have the pre-
    ponderance; to be disposed to; to be
    favourable.
prōpensē, ad. willingly, readily.
prōpensio, ōnis, f. inclination.
prōpensus, a, um, a. hanging forwards,
    projecting; *fig.* approaching; heavy,
    important; inclined, disposed, prone
    to, favourable to.
prōpĕranter, ad. hurriedly, quickly.
prōpĕrātio, ōnis, f. haste.
prōpĕrē, ad. hastily, in haste, speedily.
prōpĕro, I. v.a. & n. to hasten, to acceler-
    ate; to do with haste.   [ing, active.
prōpĕrus, a, um, a. quick, speedy, hasten-
prōpexus, a, um, a. long; flowing.
prōphēta, prōphētēs, ae, m. prophet.
prōpīno, I. v.a. to drink to a person's
    health.
prōpinquĭtas, ātis, f. nearness, proximity;
    relationship, affinity; intimacy, friend-
    ship.   [draw near.
prōpinquo, I. v.a. & n. to bring near, to
prōpinquus, a, um, a. near, neighbouring;
    resembling, similar; **—, i,** m. kinsman.

prōpior, ius, ōris, a. nearer; later; more
    like; more nearly related.
prōpītio, I. v.a. to render favourable, to
    appease, to propitiate.
prōpītius, a, um, a. favourable, well-dis-
    posed, kind, propitious.
prōpius, ad. more nearly, nearer, closer.
prōpōla, ae, f. huckster, retailer.
prōpōno, pŏsŭi, pŏsĭtum, 3. v.a. to put
    forth; to set *or* lay out, to display; to
    imagine; to expose; to report; to
    design; to purpose; to threaten.
prōportio, ōnis, f. analogy, proportion.
prōpŏsĭtio, ōnis, f. setting forth; logical
    proposition.
prōpŏsĭtum, i, n. plan, intention, design,
    purpose; theme, main point; premises
    (of a syllogism).   [common.
prōpŏsĭtus, a, um, a. exposed, laid open;
prōprætor, ōris, m. an ex-prætor; one
    sent to govern a province as prætor.
propriē, ad. specially, peculiarly, pro-
    perly.
propriĕtas, ātis, f. peculiarity, quality;
    ownership, property.
proprius, a, um, a. one's own; personal;
    special; peculiar, proper; fit, suitable;
    strange, singular; certain, sure; last-
    ing;—**proprium, ii,** n. peculiarity;
    characteristic; possession, property;
    —**proprio motu,** on one's own initia-
    tive.
propter, ad. & pr. near, hard by, at
    hand; because of; by reason of.
proptĕrĕa, ad. therefore, on that account.
prōpŭdium, ii, n. *fig.* shameful person,
    villain, shameful act.   [defence.
prōpugnācŭlum, i, n. bulwark, rampart;
prōpugnātio, ōnis, f. *fig.* defending, de-
    fence.   [pion.
prōpugnātor, ōris, m. defender; cham-
prōpugno, I. v.n. & a. to fight; to fight
    in defence of.   [off, to avert.
prōpulso, I. v.a. to drive off; *fig.* to ward
prōpylæum, i, n. gateway, porch.
prōquæstōr, ōris, m. *or* **prō quæstōre,**
    deputy *or* vice-treasurer.
prōra, ae, f. forepart of a ship, prow;
    ship.   [creep forth.
prōrēpo, psi, ptum, 3. v.n. to crawl *or*
prōrĭpio, pui, reptum, 3. v.a. to drag *or*
    snatch away; to rush out.
prōrŏgātio, ōnis, f. prolonging, extension
    (of a term of office); putting off.
prōrŏgo, I. v.a. to prolong, to protract;
    to preserve; to put off, to defer.
prorsus, ad. forwards; right onwards,
    directly; absolutely, wholly; in a
    word.
prōrumpo, rŭpi, ruptum, 3. v.a. & n. to
    send forth; to rush forth, to break out.

prōruo, rui, rŭtum, 3. v.n. & a. to rush forth; to tumble down; to overthrow.

prōsa, ae, f. prose.

prōsāpǐa, ae, f. family, pedigree, race.

proscænium, ii, n. scaffold before the scene for the actors to play on; stage.

proscindo, scǐdi, scissum, 3. v.a. to tear in pieces; to cleave; to reproach; to libel.

proscrībo, psi, ptum, 3. v.a. to announce publicly; to post up, to advertise (for sale); to confiscate: to outlaw, to proscribe.

proscriptio, ōnis, f. advertisement; outlawry; confiscation.   [law.

proscriptus, i, m. proscribed person, out-**prōsectum, i,** n. entrails (for sacrifice).

prōsēlўtus, i, m. a stranger from abroad; a convert.   [spread abroad.

prōsēmǐno, 1, v.a. *fig.* to propagate, to

prōsĕquor, cūtus *or* **quūtus,** 3. v.a. dep. to follow forth *or* after, to follow up, to pursue; to accompany; to wait upon; to honour *or* present with.

prōserpo, 3. v.n. to creep forward.

prōsĭlǐo, ui, 4. v.n. to leap *or* spring forth; to start out; to break forth.

prōsōdǐa, ae, f. prosody.

prōsōpŏpœia, ae, f. personification.

prospecto, 1. v.a. to look forth, to view; to hope; to await.   [prospect.

prospectus, ūs, m. look-out, distant view, **prospĕcŭlor,** v.a. & n. to look out for; to reconnoitre.

prosper, prospĕrus, a, um, a. favourable, fortunate, prosperous; propitious;— **prospera, ōrum,** n. pl. prosperity.

prospĕrē, ad. luckily, prosperously.

prospergo, sparsi, sparsum, 3. v.a. to besprinkle.   [perity, success.

prospĕrĭtas, ātis, f. good fortune, pros-**prospĕro,** 1. v.a. to cause to succeed, to render happy.

prospicientia, ae, f. foresight, care, precaution.

prospĭcǐo, exi, ectum, 3. v.n. & a. to look forwards, to look out; to overlook (geographically); to foresee; to take care of; to discern; to descry; to provide.

prosterno, strāvi, strātum, 3. v.a. to throw to the ground, to overthrow, to prostrate; to subvert, to destroy.

prostĭtuo, ui, ūtum, 3. v.a. to prostitute; to expose.

prosto, stĭti, stătum, 1. v.n. to be set out *or* exposed for sale; to prostitute oneself.   [throw up.

prōsŭbǐgo, ēgi, actum, 3. v.a. to dig up, to **prōsum, fui, prōdesse,** v.n. ir. to do good, to benefit, to profit.

prōtĕgo, xi, ctum, 3. v.a. to cover; to furnish with a projecting roof; to protect; to defend.

prōtendo, di, sum & tum, 3. v.a. to stretch out, to extend; to spread abroad; to put off.

prōtĕnus, ad., v. **protinus.**

prōtĕro, trīvi, trītum, 3. v.a. to crush, to tread under foot; to defeat.

prōterreo, ui, ĭtum, 2. v.a. to frighten.

prōtervē, ad. saucily, boldly.

prōtervĭtas, ātis, f. sauciness; wantonness.

prōtervus, a, um, a. violent, vehement; forward, pert, wanton; impudent.

prōtĭnus, ad. straightforwards; continuously; forthwith.

prōtrăho, xi, ctum, 3. v.a. to drag forth, to bring forth *or* out; to reveal, to expose, to betray; to prolong, to protract.

prōtrūdo, si, sum, 3. v.a. to thrust forwards *or* out; to put off.

prōturbo, 1. v.a. to drive *or* push away, to dislodge.

prout, ad. according as, in proportion, accordingly, just as, as.

prōvectus, a, um, a. advanced, late.

prōvĕho, xi, ctum, 3. v.a. to carry forwards, to transport; to raise; to promote;—**prōvĕhi,** to advance; to go; to proceed.

prōvĕnǐo, vēni, ventum, 4. v.n. to come forth; to come into being; to appear; to arise; to prosper.

prōventus, ūs, m. growth; crop, produce; yield; success; number, supply.

prōverbium, ii, n. adage, proverb.

prōvĭdenter, ad. providentially, prudently.

prōvĭdentia, ae, f. foresight, foreknowledge; precaution, providence.

prōvĭdeo, vīdi, vīsum, 2. v.n. & a. to provide (for); to foresee.   [provident.

prōvĭdus, a, um, a. foreseeing; cautious;

prōvincia, ae, f. command, government, administration; department, office, business.

prōvinciālis, e, a. provincial.

prōvīsio, ōnis, f. foreseeing; foresight, providence; precaution; prevention.

prōvīso, ad. with caution.

prōvīsor, ōris, m. provider; foreseer.

prōvīsus, ūs, m. looking into the distance; foreseeing; precaution.

prōvŏcātio, ōnis, f. calling out, summoning, challenge; appeal.

prōvŏco, 1. v.a. & n. to call forth, to call out; to invite; to challenge, to excite; to appeal.

prōvŏlo, 1. v.n. to fly forth; to rush out.

prŏvolvo, volvi, vŏlūtum, 3. v.a. to roll forwards *or* along, to roll away;—prŏvolvor, to prostrate oneself.

proximē, ad. very near, next;—proxime accessit, he came next (in order of merit); honourable mention in a competition *or* examination.

proxĭmĭtas, ātis, f. nearness; near relationship; resemblance.

proxĭmus, a, um, a. nearest; next; following; next of kin.

prūdens, entis, a. foreseeing, experienced, practised in; aware; intelligent, prudent.

prūdenter, ad. cautiously, prudently; learnedly; intelligently.

prūdentia, ae, f. foresight; intelligence, prudence, discretion.

pruīna, ae, f. hoar-frost, rime.

pruīnōsus, a, um, a. frosty, rimy.

prūna, ae, f. charcoal.

prunella (mod. hort.), self-heal.

prūnum, i, n. plum.

prŭnus, i, f. plum-tree.

prūrĭgo, ĭnis, f. itching. [ton.

prūrio, 4. v.n. to itch; to play the wan-

psallo, li, 3. v.n. to sing to *or* play on the lute.

psalmus, i, psalm.

psaltērium, ii, n. psaltery.

psaltria, ae, f. player on the lute.

Pseudōlus, i, m. The Liar. A comedy of Plautus.

pseudŏthȳrum, i, n. backdoor.

psittăcus, i, m. parrot. [self.

... pte, emphatic suffix of pronouns, = pteris (mod. hort.), bracken. [juicy.

pūbens, ntis, a. pubescent; (*fig.*) rich;

pūber, ĕris, v. pubes. [men.

pūbĕres, um, m. pl. grown-up people,

pūbertas, ātis, f. puberty; virility.

pūbēs, ĕris, a. of ripe age, adult; (of plants) downy.

pūbēs, is, f. young men, people, population.

pūbesco, bui, 3. v.n. to become pubescent, to grow up, to ripen. [taxes.

pūblĭcānus, i, m. farmer of the Roman

pūblĭcātĭo, ōnis, f. confiscation.

pūblĭcē, ad. at the public expense; on behalf of the state.

pūblĭco, 1. v.a. to confiscate; to make public *or* common.

pūblĭcus, a, um, a. public, common;—, i, m. public officer *or* functionary;—publicum, i, n. public territory; public purse, treasury.

pŭdendus, a, um, a. shameful, abominable.

pŭdens, ntis, a. modest; bashful.

pŭdenter, ad. modestly; shyly.

pŭdeo, ui, pŭdĭtum, 2. v.a. & n. to be ashamed; to be a shame;—me pudet, I am ashamed. [ful.

pŭdĭbundus, a, um, a. shamefaced, bash-

pŭdīcē, ad. modestly; chastely.

pŭdīcĭtia, ae, f. chastity, purity.

pŭdīcus, a, um, a. chaste, virtuous.

pŭdor, ōris, m. shame, shyness, modesty; decency.

puella, ae, f. girl, maiden; sweetheart.

puellāris, e, a. girlish, maidenly.

puer, ĕri, m. boy, lad; servant; young man;—a puero, from boyhood.

puĕrīlis, e, a. childish, boyish, youthful; silly.

puĕrītia, ae, f. childhood, boyhood, youth.

puerpĕrium, ii, n. childbirth.

puerpĕra, ae, f. a woman in labour.

pūgil, īlis, m. boxer, pugilist.

pŭgillāres, ium, m. pl. writing-tablets.

pŭgillus, i, a. handful.

pūgio, ōnis, m. dagger, poniard.

pugna, ae, f. fight; battle, combat; contest, dispute. [nately.

pugnācĭter, ad. contentiously; obsti-

pugnātor, ōris, m. fighter, combatant.

pugnax, ăcis, a. combative, warlike, pugnacious; quarrelsome; obstinate.

pugno, 1. v.n. to fight; to give battle; to contradict; to struggle.

pugnus, i, m. fist.

pulcer, cra, crum, pulcher, chra, chrum, a. beautiful, handsome; well-favoured; glorious; illustrious; noble.

pulchellus, a, um, pretty.

pulcrē, pulchrē, ad. beautifully, etc.; —, i. bravo!

pulcrĭtūdo, ĭnis, f. beauty; excellence.

pūlēgĭum, pūlēium, ii, n. pennyroyal; *fig.* agreeableness.

pūlex, ĭcis, m. flea.

pullārius, ii, m. poulterer.

pullātus, a, um, a. clothed in mourning.

pullŭlo, 1. v.n. to put forth, to sprout.

pullus, i, m. young aninal, young; chicken; darling, pet.

pullus, a, um, a. dusky, blackish;—pulla, ōrum, n. pl. weeds, mourning-clothes.

pulmentārium, ii, n. relish, sauce, condiment.

pulmentum, i, n., v. pulmentarium.

pulmo, ōnis, m. lung.

pulpa, ae, f. the fleshy part; flesh.

pulpāmentum, i, n. meat; tit-bits.

pulpĭtum, i, n. scaffold, stage.

puls, pultis, f. pap, pottage.

pulso, 1. v.a. to push, to strike, to beat, to batter; to disquiet. [pulse

pulsus, ūs, m. stroke; beat; pulse; im-

pulvĕreus, a, um, a. full of dust, dusty.

pulvĕrŭlentus, a, um, a. dusty; toilsome.

pulvīnar, āris, n. pulvīnus, i, m. cushion, bolster, pillow.

pulvis, ĕris, m. dust, powder; *fig.* arena, field; labour, toil, effort.

pūmex, ĭcis, m. pumice-stone. [stone.

pūmĭceus, a, um, a. dry *or* soft as pumice-

pūmĭlio, ōnis, m. dwarf.

punctim, ad. with the point.

punctum, i, n. prick, small hole, puncture; small spot; suffrage, vote; applause; — (temporis), a moment.

pungo, pŭpŭgi, punctum, 3. v.a. to prick, to puncture; to bite; to sting, to vex, to trouble, to afflict.

pūnĭceus, a, um, a. purple-coloured.

pūnĭcum, i, n. pomegranate.

pūnio, īvi & ii, ītum, 4. v.a. to punish; to take vengeance for.

pūnītor, ōris, m. punisher; avenger.

pūpa, ae, f. girl; doll. [of the eye.

pūpilla, ae, f. orphan girl, minor; pupil

pūpillāris, e, a. of a ward;—in statu pupillari, in the position of a ward.

pūpillus, i, m. orphan boy, ward.

puppis, is, f. stern, poop; ship.

pūpŭla, ae, f. pupil of the eye.

pūrē, ad. purely, simply; clearly.

purgāmen, ĭnis, n. dirt; filth; sweepings; expiation.

purgāmentum, i, n. offscourings; filth.

purgātio, ōnis, f. purging; justification.

purgo, 1. v.a. to make clean, to clean, to cleanse, to purify; to justify, to excuse, to clear. [atone for.

pūrĭfico, 1. v.a. to cleanse; to clean; to

purpŭra, ae, f. purple colour, purple; purple cloth; purple fan.

purpŭrātus, i, m. high officer at court.

purpŭreus, a, um, a. purple-coloured, purple; beautiful, brilliant.

pūrŭlentus, a, um, a. festering.

pūrum, i, n. unclouded sky.

pūrus, a, um, a. clean, pure, undefiled; clear, chaste, naked, unadorned.

pūs, pūris, n. matter, corruption.

pŭsillus, a, um, a. very little, petty, insignificant; paltry.

pūsio, ōnis, m. little boy. [pimple.

pustŭla, ae, f., pūsŭla, ae, f. blister,

pŭtă, conj. for instance.

pŭtāmen, ĭnis, n. clippings, waste.

pŭtātio, ōnis, f. pruning (of trees).

pŭtātor, ōris, m. pruner.

pŭteal, ālis, n. inclosure surrounding the mouth of a well.

pŭteālis, e, of a well, well . . .

pŭteo, 2. v.n. to stink.

pŭter, tris, tre, a. rotten, decaying; stinking, putrid, crumbling, friable, mellow, flabby.

pŭtesco, pŭtui, 3. v.n. to purify.

pŭteus, i, m. well; pit.

pūtĭdē, ad. affectedly.

pūtĭdus, a, um, a. rotten; stinking; unpleasant; affected, unnatural.

pŭto, 1· v.a. to trim, to prune; to clear up, to settle, to adjust; to reckon, to value, to estimate, to esteem as, to think, to mean, to consider.

pūtor, ōris, m. rottenness; stench.

putrĕfăcio, fēci, factum, 3. v.a. to cause to putrefy;—putrĕfīo, to become rotten. [putrid, to decay.

putresco, 3. v.n. to grow rotten *or*

putrĭdus, a, um, a. rotten, corrupt, decayed.

putris, e, v. puter.

pŭtus, a, um, a. pure, without mixture; genuine; refined.

Pygmæi, ōrum, m. pl. Pygmies.

pȳra, ae, f. funeral pile.

pȳrămis, ĭdis, f. pyramid.

pȳrethrum, i, n. camomile.

pȳrītes, ae, m. flint.

pȳrōpus, i, m. gold-bronze.

Pȳthia, ae, f. Priestess of Apollo. She delivered the oracular responses at Delphi.

Pȳthia, ōrum, n. pl. Pythian games.

pyxis, ĭdis, f. (small) box.

Quā, ad. in which direction; in what manner, how;—qua . . . qua, partly . . . partly *or* as well . . . as, both . . . and, as far as, in so far as.

quācunque, ad. wherever, wheresoever.

quādantĕnus, ad. up to a certain point; to a certain extent. [a morsel.

quadra, ae, f. square; table (for meals);

quadrāgēni, ae, a, a. num. forty each.

quadrāgēsimus, a, um, num. fortieth.

quadrāgies, ad. forty times.

quadrāgintā, a. num. forty.

quadrans, tis, m. fourth part, quarter, fourth part of an as (=3 unciæ).

quadrātus, a, um, a. squared, square; set;—agmen quadratum, army in regular order of battle;—quadratum, i, n. square.

quadrĭduum, i, n. a space of four days.

quadrĭfāriam, ad. four ways, into four parts.

quadrĭfĭdus, a, um, a. split into four.

quadrīgæ, ārum, f. pl. chariot with four horses.

quadrĭjŭgus, a, um, a. four-horsed.

quadrĭmus, a, um, a. of four years, four years old. [dred each.

quadringēnārius, a, um, a. of four hun-

quadringēni. ae. a, a. four hundred each.

quadringentēsimus, a, um, a. the four hundredth.

quadringenti, ae, a, a. four hundred.

quadringenties, ad. four hundred times.

quadripartītus, a, um, a. divided into or consisting of four parts, fourfold.

quadrirēmis, is, galley with four banks of oars. [road.

quadrivium, ii, n. four ways, cross-

quadro, 1. v.a. & n. to make square; to suit.

quadrŭpĕdans, tis, p. & a. galloping.

quadrŭpes, ĕdis, a. four-footed; —, c. quadruped.

quadruplātor, ōris, m. an informer; a cheat.

quadruplex, ĭcis, a. fourfold; quadruple.

quadruplus, a, um, a. fourfold.

quærĭto, 1. v.a. to seek eagerly.

quæro, sīvi & sii, sītum, 3. v.a. to look or search for; to get, to procure; to gain; to seek in vain, to miss; to inquire.

quæsītio, ōnis, f. inquisition.

quæsītor, ōris, m. examiner, inquisitor.

quæsītum, i, n. question.

quæsītus, a, um, a. select, exquisite; affected, far-fetched.

quæso, īvi & ii, 3. v.a. to beg, to pray, to beseech, to entreat.

quæstio, ōnis, f. inquiry, investigation, question; examination by torture;— **quæstiones perpetuæ,** permanent courts for trying special cases.

quæstiuncula, ae, f. small question.

quæstor, ōris, m. quæstor (Roman magistrate), treasurer.

quæstōrius, a, um, a. of a quæstor . . .; —, ii, m. ex-quæstor.

quæstuōsus, a, um, a. gainful, profitable.

quæstūra, ae, f. quæstorship; public money.

quæstus, ūs, m. gaining, acquiring; gain, profit. [where.

quālĭbet, ad. where you will, every-

quālis, e, pn. & a. of what sort, kind or nature, of what a kind.

quāliscunque, quālĕcunque, a. of what quality soever, of whatever kind; any whatever.

quālĭtas, ātis, f. quality, property, nature, state, condition.

quālĭtĕr, ad. just as, as. [wool or fruit.

quālum, i, n., **qualus, i,** m. basket for

quam, ad. in what way; how, how much, as much as, than;—**tam** . . . —, as well . . . as. [how long.

quamdiu, ad. as long as, until, during;

quamlĭbet, ad. as it pleases, at pleasure; how much soever, ever so much.

quamobrem, ad. wherefore? why? for this reason.

quamplūres, a. very many.

quamplūrimus, a, um, a. very much.

quampridem, ad. how long since?

quamprīmum, ad. as soon as possible.

quamquam, c. although, and yet.

quamvis, ad. & c. as much as you will, ever so much, ever so; although; however. [when; at any time.

quandō, ad. & c. at what time? when?

quandōcunque, ad. whenever, as often as, as soon as.

quandōque, ad. whenever, as often as; at one time or other. [seeing that.

quandōquidem, c. since indeed, since,

quanquam, v. **quamquam.**

quantillus, a, um, a. how little.

quantĭtas, ātis, f. quantity.

quantō, ad. by how much.

quantŏpĕrĕ, ad. how greatly, how much.

quantŭlum, ad. how little.

quantŭlus, a, um, a. how little, how small, how trifling.

quantŭluscunque, ăcunque, umcunque, a. however small or insignificant.

quantum, ad. as much, so much, the more, the greater.

quantumvis, ad. how much soever, ever so much, however; very; although.

quantus, a, um, a. how great, as great as; —**quantum sufficet (quantum suff.),** as much as suffices.

quantuscunque, tăcunque, tumcunque, a. how great soever.

quantuslĭbet, tālĭbet, tŭmlĭbet, a. how great soever, ever so great.

quantusvis, tāvis, tumvis, a. however great, ever so great.

quāpropter, ad. wherefore.

quāquā, ad. what way soever; — **versum,** — **versus,** ad. on every side or way.

quārē, ad. by which means, whereby; wherefore, why; to the end that.

quartădĕcŭmānus, i, m. soldier of the fourteenth legion. [fourth legion.

quartāni, ōrum, m. pl. soldiers of the

quartānus, a, um, a. of or belonging to the fourth;—**quartana, ae,** f. quartan ague.

quartārius, ii, m. quart. [time.

quartō, ad. in the fourth place; the fourth

quartum, ad. for the fourth time.

quartus, a, um, a. fourth.

quartusdĕcĭmus, a, um, a. fourteenth.

quăsi, ad. as if, just as, as it were.

quăsillum, i, n. **quăsillus, i,** m. basket (for wool).

quassābĭlis, e, a. to be shaken.

quassātio, ōnis, quassatūra, ae, f. shaking.

quasso, 1. v.a. & n. to shake or toss violently, to shatter; fig. to weaken.

quassus, ūs, m. shaking.

quătĕnus, ad. how far; how long; seeing that, since, as.

quăter, ad. four times.

quăternārius, a, um, a. containing four.

quăterni, ae, a, a. pl. four each, by fours; four together.

quaternio, ōnis, m. number four.

quătio, quassum, 3. v.a. to strike, to shatter; to shake; to drive; *fig.* to agitate, to affect, to excite, to plague, to vex, to harass.

quăttuor, num. four.

quattuordĕcim, fourteen.

quattuorvĭri, ōrum, m. pl. body of four men; board of chief magistrates.

quĕ, c. and (used only as an enclitic particle); **. . . que . . . et,** both . . . and.

quemadmŏdum, ad. in *or* after what manner, how.

queo, ivi & ii, ĭtum, 3. v.n. dep. to be able.

quercētum, i, n. oak-forest.

querceus, a, um, a. of oak, oaken.

quercus, ūs, f. oak, oak-tree; ship.

quĕrēla, ae, f. complaint; plaintive sound; warbling.

quĕrĭbundus, a, um, a. complaining.

quĕrĭmōnia, ae, f. complaint.

quĕrĭtor, 1. v.n. to complain repeatedly.

querneus, a, um, v. querceus.

quernus, a, um, a. of oaks, oaken.

quĕror, questus, 3. v.a. & n. dep. to complain, to lament, to bewail.

querquĕtŭlānus, a, um, a. oak-planted, full of oaks.

querquētum, v. quercetum.

quĕrŭlus, a, um, a. complaining, querulous; cooing, warbling, chirping.

questus, ūs, m. complaint, lamentation.

qui, quæ, quod, pn. who, which, that, as adj. which? any;—**quorum** (of whom), a sufficient number present at a meeting to constitute its legality.

quī, ad. wherewith; why? by what means? how much? how.

quiă, c. because; why? wherefore?

quiănam, ad. wherefore pray?

quicquam, pn. & n. anything.

quīcque, v. quidque.

quīcquid, v. quidquid.

quīcunque, quæcunque, quodcunque, pn. who(so)ever, what(so)ever; all that; each *or* every possible.

quid, v. quis;—**quid nunc,** what now? (a name applied to a person always asking questions);—**quid pro quo,** an equivalent.

quĭdam, quædam, quoddam, pn. a certain one, somebody, something.

quĭdem, ad. indeed, certainly, in truth; at least; for example;—**ne . . . —,** not . . . even.

quidnam, ad. what? how?

quidni, ad. why not?

quidpiam, quidquam, v. **quispiam, quisquam.** [ever.

quidquid, pn. & n. everything, whatsoquidvis, cujusvis, pn. anything.

quies, ētis, f. rest, quiet, repose, peace; sleep; dream; death.

quiesco, ēvi, ētum, 3. v.n. to rest, to keep quiet; to sleep.

quiētē, ad. calmly, quietly.

quiētus, a, um, a. calm, quiet; peaceful, sleeping; undisturbed;—**quieta non movere,** to let sleeping dogs lie.

quīlĭbet, quælĭbet, quodlĭbet & quidlĭbet, pn. any one who will, whom you will, no matter who, any, all.

quĭn, c. that not, but that; indeed; why not? nay more.

quīnārius, a, um, a. containing five; **—, ii,** m. Roman silver coin of five asses.

quincunx, uncis, m. five-twelfths; a pattern in which trees were planted, a row of five alternating with a row of four; interest at 5 per cent.

quincŭpĕdal, ālis, n. five-foot rod.

quindĕcies, ad. fifteen times.

quindĕcim, a. fifteen.

quindĕcimvĭri, ōrum, m. pl. college *or* board of fifteen; college of priests who had charge of the Sibylline books.

quindēni, v. quinideni.

quingēni, ae, a, a. five hundred each.

quingentēsĭmus, a, um, a. five-hundredth.

quingenti, ae, a, a. five hundred.

quingenties, ad. five hundred times.

quīni, ae, a, a. five each; five by five.

quīnīdēni, quindēni, ae, a, a. fifteen each; fifteen.

quīnīvīcēni, ae, a, a. twenty-five each.

quinquāgēnārius, a, um, a. containing fifty.

quinquāgēni, ae, a, a. fifty each.

quinquāgēsĭmus, a, um, a. fiftieth.

quinquāgies, ad. fifty times.

quinquāgintā, a. fifty.

quinquatria, ōrum, ium, n. pl. **quinquatrus, ŭum,** f. pl. feast in honour of Minerva, lasting five days.

quinque, a. five.

quinquĕfŏlium, ii, n. cinquefoil.

quinquĕlibrālis, e, a. of five pounds.

quinquĕmestris, e, a. five months old.

quinquennālis, e, a. quinquennial.

quinquennis, e, a. five years old.

quinquennium, ii, n. (period of) five years.

quinquĕpartīto, ad. in five parts.

quinquĕrēmis, e, a. having five banks of oars; **—, is,** f. galley having five banks of oars. [queviri.

quinquĕvĭrātus, ūs, m. office of the **quin-**

quinquĕvĭri, ōrum, m. pl. board of five.
quinquies *or* **quinquiens,** ad. five times.
quinquĭplĭco, ī, v.a. to make fivefold.
quintădĕcŭmāni, ōrum, m. pl. soldiers of the fifteenth legion.
quintāna, ae, f. market.   [legion.
quintāni, ōrum, m. pl. soldiers of the fifth
quintānus, a, um, a. fifth in order.
quintārius, a, um, containing five.
Quintīlis, is, m. July.
quintō, quintum, ad. for the fifth time.
quintuplex, ĭcis, a. fivefold.
quintus, a, um, a. num. fifth.
quintusdĕcĭmus, a, um, a. fifteenth.
quippe, ad. & c. certainly, to be sure, by all means; since; in as much as; for-sooth.
Quirīnālia, ium, n. pl. a festival in honour of Romulus, celebrated on the 17th of February.
Quirītes, m. pl. citizens of Rome.
quirīto, ī. v.a. to cry for help.
quis, quid, pn. who? which? what? any one; anything; some one; something;—**cui bono?** for whose good? who gains by it?
quisnam, quænam, quidnam, pn. who? which? what pray?
quispiam, quæpiam, quodpiam & **quidpiam** *or* **quippiam,** pn. any one, anybody, anything, any; some one, something, some; in any respect, somewhat.
quisquam, quæquam, quicquam, pn. any, any one, anybody, anything, something.
quisque, quæque, quodque & **quicque** (**quidque**), pn. each, every, everybody, every one, everything;—**optimus quisque,** all the best people.
quisquiliæ, ārum, f. pl. refuse, dregs; scum (of the people).
quisquis, quodquod & **quicquid** (**quidquid**), pn. whoever, whosoever, whatever, whatsoever, every one who, every, all.
quīvis, quævis, quodvis & **quidvis,** pn. who *or* what you please, any one, anything.
quō, ad. & c. whither; whither? *fig.* wherefore; that, because; for what purpose.
quoad, ad. how long? till, until (that); as far as; as long as.
quŏcircā, c. for which reason, wherefore.
quŏcum, pn. with whom.
quŏcunque, ad. whithersoever.
quod, c. that, in that, because; wherefore; as to what; although; since.
quŏdammŏdo, ad. in a certain manner, in some measure.
quoi = **cui.**

quŏjus = **cujus.**
quŏlĭbĕt, ad. whithersoever.   [venting.
quŏmĭnus, c. that not, after verbs of pre-
quŏmŏdŏ, ad. in what manner, in what way, how; in whatsoever manner;—**cunque,** howsoever; —**nam,** how? how, I pray you?
quŏnam, ad. whither pray?
quondam, ad. once, formerly.   [because.
quŏniam, ad. seeing that, whereas, since,
quŏpiam, ad. any whither.   [ever.
quŏquam, ad. to any place, whitherso-
quŏquĕ, c. also, too.
quŏquŏ, ad. whithersoever.
quŏquŏmŏdŏ, ad. howsoever.
quŏquŏversum, quŏquŏversus, ad. on every side, on all sides, all around.
quorsum, quorsus, ad. whither; to what end?   [each, every.
quŏt, a. how many? as many as; all,
quŏtannis, ad. every year.
quotcunque, a. indecl. how many soever.
quŏtēni, ae, a, a. how many.
quŏtīdiānus, a, um, a. every day, daily; usual, common.
quŏtīdiē, ad. daily, every day.
quŏties, ad. how often? how many times? whenever; — **cumque,** as often as.
quotlĭbet, a. indecl. how many soever.
quotquŏt, a. how many soever, as many as.
quŏtŭmus, a, um, a. how many?
quŏtuplex, ĭcis, a. of how many sorts?
quŏtus, a, um, a. of what number; the which (in a series);—**quota,** propor-tion, share.
quŏtusquisque, pn. what one among many? how few?   [how long.
quousquĕ, ad. until what time, till when,
quŏvis, ad. any whither.
quum, c., v. **cum.**

Răbĭdē, ad. madly; furiously.
răbĭdus, a, um, a. furious, enraged, mad.
răbies, em, e, f. rage, madness; *fig.* fury, eagerness; — (**ventris**), ravenous hun-ger; — **civĭca,** fierce civil war.
răbiōse, ad. madly.
răbiōsus, a, um, a. raving, rabid, mad.
răbŭla, ae, m. pettifogger.
răcēmĭfĕr, a, um, a. clustering, crowned with clusters.
răcēmōsus, a, um, a. clustering.
răcēmus, i, m. bunch *or* cluster of grapes, etc.; berry, grape.
rădiātio, ōnis, f. shining, emitting of rays.
rădĭcĭtus, ad. with *or* by the roots; *fig.* utterly.
rādīcor, ī. v. dep. to take root.

rādīcōsus, a, um, a. full of roots.
rādīcŭla, ae, f. small root; radish.
rădio, 1. v.a. & n. to make beaming, to irradiate; to beam, to shine, to radiate.
rădiōsus, a, um, a. emitting rays, brilliant.
rădius, ii, m. staff, rod; spoke (of a wheel); shuttle; beam, ray.
rādix, īcis, f. root; radish; foot of a hill; foundation; origin; primitive word or syllable.
rādo, rāsi, rāsum, 3. v.a. to scrape, to scratch, to shave off; to erase; to graze; to strip off; to hurt, to offend.
rǣda, ae, f. four-wheeled carriage.
rǣdārius, ii, m. coachman.
raia, ae, f. ray (fish).
rāmālĭa, ium, n. pl. brushwood, twigs.
rāmentum, i, n. chip; sawdust; filings; scrapings.
rāmeus, a, um, a. of branches.
rāmex, īcis, m. pectoral vein; rupture; bar, rail.
rāmōsus, a, um, a. having many branches, branching.   [shoot.
rāmŭlus, i, m. twig, sprig; little bough.
rāmus, i, m. branch, bough, twig; tree; branch (of antlers).
rāna, ae, f. frog.
rancens, a. rank.
rancĭdŭlus, a, um, a. somewhat rank; mouldy.   [loathsome.
rancĭdus, a, um, a. rank, rancid; fig.
rānuncŭlus, i, m. little frog, tadpole; (mod. hort.) buttercup.
răpācĭtas, ātis, f. greediness, rapacity.
răpa, ae, f. turnip.
răpax, ācis, a. rapacious; greedy.
răphănus, i, m. radish.
răpĭdē, ad. hastily, quickly, rapidly.
răpĭdĭtas, ātis, f. swiftness, rapidity.
răpĭdus, a, um, a. swift, rapid.
răpīna, ae, f. robbery, plundering, pillage, rapine; booty.
răpio, răpui, raptum, 3. v.a. to snatch, to tear or drag away; to carry off; to plunder; to ravish, to transport.
raptim, ad. hastily, suddenly, hurriedly.
rapto, 1. v.a. to seize and carry off, to hurry away; to ravage.   [ravisher.
raptor, ōris, m. robber, plunderer;
raptum, i, n. booty; plunder.
raptus, ūs, m. violent snatching or dragging away; robbery, carrying off, abduction.
răpŭlum, i, n. little turnip.
răpum, i, n. turnip.
rārē, ad. far apart, scatteredly.
rārĕfăcio, fēci, factum, 3. v.a. to rarefy.
rāresco, 3. v.n. to grow thin, to become rarefied; to grow wider; to die away.

rārĭtas, ātis, f. looseness of texture, rarity, sparseness.
rārō, ad. seldom, rarely.
rārus, a, um, a. thin, loose in texture; scattered, scanty; rare; few; here and there; sporadic.
rāsĭlis, e, a. shaven; smoothed.   [spade.
rastellus, i, m. little rake or harrow,
rastrum, i, n. toothed hoe, rake, mattock.
rāsūra, ae, f. shaving.
rătio, ōnis, f. account, calculation, computation; sum, number; transaction, business; matter, affair; relation; regard, respect; judgment, reason; method, order; system, theory.
rătiōcĭnātĭo, ōnis, f. reasoning, ratiocination; syllogism.
rătiōcĭnātīvus, a, um, a. belonging to reasoning or debating, syllogistic.
rătiōcĭnātŏr, ōris, m. accountant, auditor; reasoner.
rătiōcĭnor, ātus, 1. v.n. & a. dep. to reckon, to compute, to calculate; to reason, to argue; to infer.
rătiōnālis, e, a. reasonable, rational; —, is, m. auditor of the exchequer;— rationale, a statement of reasons.
rătiōnālĭter, ad. rationally.
rătiōnārium, ii, n. account-book.
rătis, is, f. raft, float; boat.
rătus, a, um, p. & a. reckoned, calculated; certain, valid; constant, firm, steady;—pro rata (parte), in proportion, proportionally.   [roaring.
raucĭsŏnus, a, um, a. hoarse-sounding;
raucĭtus, ātis, f. hoarseness.
raucus, a, um, a. hoarse; harsh; disagreeable.   [copper.
raudus, ĕris, n. rude mass; piece of
raudŭscŭlum, i, n. small sum of money; unwrought copper.
rāvis, is, f. hoarseness.
rāvus, a, um, a. greyish, tawny.
rĕ- (before vowels rĕd-), inseparable particle, back again, anew.
rea, v. reus.
rĕapse, ad. in fact, actually, really.
rĕbellātĭo, ōnis, f. revolt, rebellion.
rĕbellatrix, īcis, f. female rebel.
rĕbellĭo, ōnis, f. renewal of war; revolt, rebellion.
rĕbellis, e, a. insurgent, rebellious.
rĕbello, 1. v.n. to wage war again, to revolt, to rebel.
rĕboo, 1. v.n. (poet.) to resound.
rĕbullio, īvi, ītum, 4. v.n. to boil up.
rĕcalcitro, 1. v.n. to kick.
rĕcălĕfăcio, 3. v.a. to warm again.
rĕcăleo, lui, 2., rĕcălesco, 3. v.n. to grow warm again.   [to glow.
rĕcandesco, dui, 3. v.n. to grow white;

rĕcăno, 3. v.a. to sing again; to undo a charm.

rĕcanto, ātum, 1. v.a. to recall, to recant; to charm away; to sing over again.

rĕcēdo, cessi, cessum, 3. v.n. to retire, to withdraw, to retreat; to depart; to recede; to vanish.

rĕcens, ntis, a. fresh, young, recent; vigorous;—recens a vulnere, fresh from a wound; —, ad. lately, just, recently.

rĕcenseo, sui, sum & sītum, 2. v.a. to review, to muster, to survey; fig. to reckon up. [recension.

rĕcensio, ōnis, f. enumeration, reviewing,

rĕcensus, ūs, m. review.

rĕcenter, ad. lately.

rĕceptācŭlum, i, n. reservoir, magazine, receptacle; place of refuge, shelter.

rĕceptātōr, ōris, m. harbourer.

rĕceptio, ōnis, f. reception.

rĕcepto, 1. v.a. to receive back; to recover; to receive, to admit.

rĕceptor, ōris, m. receiver, shelterer; concealer.

rĕceptum, i, n. engagement.

rĕceptus, ūs, m. drawing back; falling back, retreat; refuge;—canere receptui, to sound the retreat.

rĕcessim, ad. in retreating, backwards.

rĕcessus, ūs, m. retiring, retreat; corner; recess.

rĕcīdīvus, a, um, a. recurring; reviving.

rĕcīdo, cidi, cāsum, 3. v.n. to fall back, to recoil; to return; to relapse; to be reduced to.

rĕcīdo, di, sum, 3. v.a. to cut away, to cut down, to cut off; fig. to abridge, to cut short.

rĕcingo, 3. v.a. to ungird, to unloose.

rĕcĭno, 3. v.n. & a. to resound; to cause to resound.

reciper . . ., v. recuper . . .

rĕcĭpio, cēpi, ceptum, 3. v.a. to get back; to retake, to regain, to recover; to withdraw; to admit; to accept; to entertain; to undertake;—se recipere, to retreat, to betake oneself.

rĕcĭprōco, 1. v.a. & n. to fetch back, to draw in; to ebb; fig. to reverse; to reciprocate.

rĕcĭprŏcus, a, um, a. reciprocal, mutual, ebbing and flowing.

rĕcīsāmentum, i, n. piece cut off.

rĕcīsio, ōnis, f. cutting off.

rĕcĭtātio, ōnis, f. recital.

rĕcĭtātor, ōris, m. reciter.

rĕcĭto, 1. v.a. to read out, to recite.

rĕclāmātio, ōnis, f. hostile shout.

rĕclāmĭto, 1. v.a. to gainsay.

rĕclāmo, 1. v.n. & a. to cry out or exclaim against; to resound.

rĕclīnis, e, a. leaning back, reclining.

rĕclīno, 1. v.a. to bend or lean back, to recline.

rĕclūdo, si, sum, 3. v.a. to open; to disclose, to reveal.

rĕclūsio, ōnis, f. opening, disclosure.

rĕcōgĭto, 1. v.a. to consider or think again; to reflect; to recall (to mind).

rĕcognĭtio, ōnis, f. recollection, investigation.

rĕcognosco, gnōvi, gnĭtum, 3. v.a. to know again, to recognize; to recollect; to examine; to inspect.

rĕcolligo, lēgi, lectum, 3. v.a. to gather up again, to recover.

rĕcŏlo, cŏlui, cultum, 3. v.a. to till again; fig. to renew, to resume; to reflect upon.

rĕcommĭniscor, 3. v. dep. to remember.

rĕcompōno, ōsui, ĭtum, 3. v.a. to form anew; to recompose. [ciliation.

rĕconcĭliātio, ōnis, f. renewal; recon-

rĕconcĭliātor, ōris, m. restorer.

rĕconcĭlio, 1. v.a. to restore; to reconcile; to conciliate.

rĕconcinno, 1. v.a. to repair.

rĕcondĭtus, a, um, p. & a. hidden, concealed; abstruse, recondite.

rĕcondo, dĭdi, dĭtum, 3. v.a. to shut up; to hide, to bury, to store up.

rĕcŏquo, coxi, coctum, 3. v.a. to boil over again; to melt or forge again.

rĕcordātio, ōnis, f. remembrance; recollection.

rĕcordor, ātus, 1. v.a. & n. dep. to think over; to call to mind, to remember; to mediate. [to correct anew.

rĕcorrigo, exi, ectum, 3. v.a. to reform;

rĕcreātio, ōnis, f. restoration, recovery.

rĕcreo, 1. v.a. to make anew, to reproduce, to restore; to refresh, to revive.

rĕcrĕpo, ui, 1. v.a. to sound again.

recresco, ēvi, ētum, 3. v.n. to grow up again; to be renewed.

rĕcrūdesco, dui, 3. v.n. to become raw again; to break out afresh.

rectā, ad. right on, directly.

rectē, ad. in a straight line, perpendicularly, uprightly; fig. rightly, correctly, properly, suitably, well; quite; very.

rectio, ōnis, f. direction, management.

rector, ōris, m. guider, director, helmsman; horseman; driver; leader, ruler, governor.

rectrix, īcis, f. directress. [rity, virtue.

rectum, i, n. right line; honesty, integ-

rectus, a, um, p. & a. straight, upright; honest; proper; good;—casus rectus, (gr.) nominative case.

recŭbo, 1. v.n. to recline.

recumbo, cŭbui, 3. v.a. to lie down (again); to recline at table; to fall, to sink down.

recŭpĕrātio, ōnis, f. regaining, recovery.

recŭpĕrātor, ōris, m. recoverer; judge (in lawsuits requiring a speedy decision).

recŭpĕro, 1. v.a. to get again; to regain, to recover.

recŭro, 1. v.a. to refresh; to attend to carefully.

recurro, curri, 3. v.n. to run or hasten back; fig. to recur, to return; to have recourse to.

recurso, 1. v.a. to come back, to return.

recursus, ūs, m. running back, retreat, return.

recurvo, 1. v.a. to bend back.

recurvus, a, um, a. bent back, crooked or curved.

recūsātio, ōnis, f. declining, refusal; objection, protest; counter-plea.

recūso, 1. v.a. to decline, to reject, to refuse; to object; to plead in defence.

recŭtio, cussi, cussum, 3. v.a. to strike back, to reflect, to re-echo.

recŭtītus, a, um, a. circumcised.

reda, v. ræda.

redămo, 1. v.a. to love in return.

redardesco, 3. v.n. to begin to burn again.

redarguo, ui, 3. v.a. to contradict, to refute.

reddo, didi, ditum, 3. v.a. to give back, to return, to restore; to give up, to resign; to offer; to assign; to repeat; to recite; to represent; to render; to make; to answer.

redemptio, ōnis, f. ransoming, redemption; buying up, bribing; farming.

redempto, 1. v.a. to ransom, to buy back.

redemptor, ōris, m. contractor, undertaker, purveyor.

redemptūra, ae, f. taking of a lease; farming of customs.

redeo, ii, itum, 4. v.n. to go or come back; to return; to come to; to reach.

redhibeo, itum, 2. v.a. to give back, to return; to take back.

redhibitio, ōnis, f. returning of a thing to its seller.

redigo, ēgi, actum, 3. v.a. to get back, to call in, to collect, to raise; to receive; to reduce to.   [band.

redimiculum, i, n. fillet, frontlet, head-

redimio, ii, itum, 4. v.a. to encircle, to gird, to crown.

redimo, ēmi, emptum, 3. v.a. to buy back, to repurchase; to ransom, to redeem; to buy off; to release, to rescue; to hire; to obtain; to atone for.

redintegrātio, ōnis, f. renewing.

redintegro, 1. v.a. to restore, to renew, to recruit, to refresh.

reditio, ōnis, f. return(ing).

reditus, ūs, m. returning, return; income, rent, revenue.

redivīvus, a, um, a. renewed, renovated.

redŏleo, ui, 2. v.a. & n. to emit a scent, to diffuse an odour.

redŏno, 1. v.a. to give back again; to give up, to resign; to forgive.

redormio, 4. v.n. to sleep again.

redormītio, ōnis, f. falling asleep again.

redūco, xi, ctum, 3. v.a. to lead or bring or conduct back; to escort; to withdraw; to replace, to restore; to draw back; to bring or reduce to.

reductio, ōnis, f. restoration.

reductor, ōris, m. restorer.

reductus, a, um, p. & a. retired, remote, lonely; low.

reduncus, a, um, a. bent, curved.

redundantia, ae, f. redundancy (of style).

redundātio, ōnis, f. overflow; overturning.

redundo, 1. v.n. to flow back; to overflow; to be superfluous, to abound.

reduvia, ae, f. hangnail; fig. trifle.

redux, ūcis, a. that is led or brought back, returning; bringing back; restoring.

refectio, ōnis, f. fig. refreshment, recreation, recovery.

refello, felli, 3. v.a. to show to be false; to disprove, to confute.

refercio, si, tum, 4. v.a. to fill up, to stuff, to cram.

referio, 4. v.a. to strike back, to reflect.

refero, rettuli, relātum, 3. v.a. ir. to carry, to bring, to draw or put back; to tell; to refer to; to lay before, to propose; to register; to record; to impute; to restore; to repay; to render an account; to answer;—pedem referre, to give ground, to flee.

refert, tulit, v.n. imp. it concerns, is of consequence or importance to;—meā —, it matters to me.   [filled, full.

refertus, a, um, a. stuffed, crammed,

referveo, 2. v.n. to be scalding hot, to boil over.   [to bubble up.

refervesco, vi, 3. v.n. to grow hot again;

reficio, fēci, fectum, 3. v.a. to make again, to restore, to rebuild, to repair, to refit; to re-elect; to refresh.

refigo, xi, xum, 3. v.a. to unfix, to unfasten, to pull out or off.

reflātus, ūs, m. contrary wind.

reflecto, xi, xum, 3. v.a. & n. to bend or turn backwards; to turn about or away.

reflo, 1. v.a. to blow back again; to blow against or contrary.

reflōresco, rui, 3. v.n. to begin to flourish again.

refluo, 3. v.n. to flow *or* run back.

refluus, a, um, a. flowing back, ebbing.

rĕfŏdio, 3. v.a. to dig up *or* out.

rĕformīdātio, ōnis, f. great fear *or* anxiety.

rĕformīdo, ātum, 1. v.a. to fear greatly, to dread, to shun.

rĕformo, 1. v.a. to transform, to remould; *fig.* to reform.

rĕfŏveo, fŏvi, fōtum, 2. v.a. to cherish again; to refresh, to revive.

refractāriŏlus, a, um, a. somewhat stubborn *or* unruly.   [ate.

refractārius, a, um, a. refractory, obstin-

refrāgor, ātus sum, 1. v.n. dep. to gainsay; to oppose; to resist.

refrēno, 1. v.a. to curb, to check; to restrain.   [gall; *fig.* to excite afresh.

refrico, 1. v.a. & n. to scratch open, to

refrīgĕrātio, ōnis, f. coolness.

refrīgĕratōrius, a, um, a. cooling.

refrīgĕro, 1. v.a. to make cool *or* cold; to cool off; *fig.* to cool down, to refresh.

refrīgesco, frixi, 3. v.n. to grow cold *or* cool; to flag; to become obsolete.

refringo, frēgi, fractum, 3. v.a. to break up *or* open; to break in pieces; to destroy.

rĕfŭgio, fŭgi, 3. v.n. & a. to flee back; to run away, to escape; to flee to; to avoid.

rĕfŭgium, ĭi, n. taking refuge; place of refuge.

rĕfŭgus, a, um, a. fleeing back, receding, vanishing; —, m. runaway.

rĕfulgeo, si, 2. v.n. to reflect a light; to shine, to glitter, to glisten.

rĕfundo, fŭdi, fūsum, 3. v.a. to pour back, to overflow.

rĕfūsus, a, um, a. flowing back, overflowing.

rĕfūtātio, ōnis, f. refutation.

rĕfūto, 1. v.a. to check, to drive back, to repress, to disprove; *fig.* to restrain, to oppose.

rēgālis, e, a. kingly, royal, regal; splendid;—regalia, n. pl. trappings of royalty.

rēgāliter, ad. in a kingly manner, royally.

rēgĕlo, 1. v.a. to thaw.

rĕgĕnĕro, 1. v.a. to regenerate, to renew; to represent lineally; to reproduce;—regenerari, to be produced again.

rĕgĕro, gessi, gestum, 3. v.a. to bear, to carry back; to throw back, to retort, to register.

rēgia, ae, f. royal palace, castle, court; royal family; residence.

rēgĭē, ad. royally; imperiously; magnificently.

rēgĭfĭcus, a, um, a. kingly, royal, magnificent.

rēgĭfŭgium, ii, n. festival in commemoration of the expulsion of the Roman kings.

rēgĭmen, ĭnis, n. guidance; rule, command; governor, ruler.

rēgīna, ae, f. queen.

rēgio, ōnis, f. line; tract, territory, region; climate; boundary-line; *fig.* province, sphere;—e regione, in a straight line; over against.

rēgĭus, a, um, a. kingly, royal; splendid; · —morbus —, jaundice.

regnātor, ōris, m. sovereign, ruler, king.

regnātrix, īcis, a. (f.) imperial, ruling.

rēgno, 1. v.n. to have royal power, to reign; —, to govern; *fig.* to prevail.

rēgnum, ĭ, n. kingly government, royalty; sovereignty, tyranny; estate, possession.

rēgo, xi, ctum, 3. v.a. to guide, to conduct, to direct; to govern, to rule; to correct.

regrĕdior, gressus, 3. v.n. dep. to go *or* come back; to return; (mil.) to retire, to retreat.

regressus, ūs, m. going back, return, regress.

rēgŭla, ae, f. ruler, rule, stick, lath; *fig.* pattern, model, example.

rēgŭlus, i, m. petty king; chieftain, prince.

rēgusto, 1. v.a. *fig.* to taste over again.

rējectio, ōnis, f. rejection; vomiting.

rējĭcio, jēci, jectum, 3. v.a. to reject; to refuse; to repulse; to refer to, to make over to; to put off, to defer.

rĕlābor, lapsus, 3. v.n. dep. to slide *or* glide back; to fall back; *fig.* to relapse.

rĕlanguesco, gui, 3. v.n. to grow languid *or* faint again; *fig.* to abate.

rĕlātio, ōnis, f. bringing back; *fig.* throwing back, retorting; motion, proposal, report, narration.

rĕlātor, ōris, m. mover, proposer.

rĕlaxātio, onis, f. relaxation.

rĕlaxo, 1. v.a. to unloose, to loosen; *fig.* to free; to ease, to cheer up, to assuage.

rĕlēgātio, ōnis, f. exiling, banishment.

rĕlēgo, 1. v.a. to send away, to despatch, to remove; to exile; to reject; to ascribe.

rĕlēgo, lēgi, lectum, 3. v.a. to gather together *or* collect again; to read *or* relate again.

rĕlĕvo, 1. v.a. to lift up, to raise; to make light, to lighten; to relieve, to assuage, to abate, to comfort, to refresh.

rĕlictio, ōnis, f. forsaking, abandoning.

rēlĭgĭo, ōnis, f. religion, piety; scrupulousness; sanctity; an object of veneration;—**religio loci,** the hallowed associations of a particular spot.

rēlĭgĭōsē, ad. piously, religiously; scrupulously, conscientiously.

rēlĭgĭōsus, a, um, a. pious, devout, religious; scrupulous. [bind fast.

rēlĭgo, I. v.a. to bind back *or* behind, to

rĕlinquo, līqui, lictum, 3. v.a. to leave behind; to leave; to give up; to forsake; to neglect.

rēlĭqua, ōrum, n. pl. arrears, remains.

rēlĭquiæ, ārum, f. pl. leavings, remains, relics, rest, remnant.

rēlĭquum, i, n. arrear.

rēlĭquus, a, um, a. remaining; future, subsequent.

rellig . . ., v. **relig . . .;**—**relliqu . . .,** v. **reliqu . . .**

rĕlūceo, xi, 2. v.n. to shine back, to shine out; to blaze, to glow.

rĕlūcesco, luxi, 3. v.n. to grow bright again, to shine out.

rĕluctor, ātus, I. v.n. dep. to struggle against, to resist; to oppose.

rĕmăneo, mansi, 2. v.n. to stay behind; to remain, to continue; to abide.

rĕmansio, ōnis, f. remaining, stay.

rĕmĕdĭum, ii, n. cure; remedy; medicine.

rĕmeo, I. v.n. to go *or* come back, to return.

rĕmētĭor, mensus, 4. v.a. dep. to measure again *or* back; *fig.* to reflect upon; to repeat.

rēmex, ĭgis, m. rower, oarsman.

rēmĭgātĭo, ōnis, f. rowing.

rēmĭgĭum, ii, n. rowing; oarage; oarsmen, rowers.

rēmĭgo, I. v.n. to row.

rēmĭgro, I. v.n. to return.

rĕmĭniscor, 3. v.n. & a. dep. to recall to mind, to recollect, to remember; to conceive; to imagine.

rĕmisceo, ui, 2. v. to mix up.

rĕmissē, ad. carelessly; mildly.

rĕmissio, ōnis, f. letting down, lowering; remission, abatement; recreation; mildness.

rĕmissus, a, um, a. slack, loose, languid; *fig.* mild, gentle, indulgent, cheerful, gay.

rĕmitto, mĭsi, missum, 3. v.a. & n. to send back; to relax, to slacken; to relieve; to grant; to concede; to remit; to repay; to give up; to allow, to permit; to abate, to decrease.

rĕmōlĭor, ītus sum, 4. v. dep. to throw off, to remove. [to grow soft.

rĕmollesco, 3. v.n. to become soft again;

rĕmollio, īvi, ītum, 4. v.a. to soften; to enervate.

rĕmōrāmen, ĭnis, n. hindrance, restraint, stop.

rĕmordeo, sum, 2. v.a. to bite again; to cause remorse; to torment.

rĕmŏror, ātus, I. v.n. & a. dep. to stay behind, to linger; to detain, to hinder, to delay, to defer.

rĕmōtē, ad. far off.

rĕmōtus, a, um, a. distant, remote; separate.

rĕmŏveo, mōvi, mōtum, 2. v.a. to move *or* draw back; to take away, to remove; to withdraw.

rĕmūgio, 4. v.n. to bellow again; to resound.

rĕmulceo, si, sum, 2. v.a. to stroke back, to appease; to droop.

rĕmulcum, i, n. tow-rope.

rĕmūnērātĭo, ōnis, f. recompense, reward.

rĕmūnĕro, I. v.a., rĕmūnĕror, ātus, I. v.a. dep. to reward, to recompense, to remunerate.

rĕmurmŭro, I. v.n. to murmur against *or* back. [might and main.

rēmus, i, m. oar;—**velis remisque,** with

rēn, rēnis, v. renes.

rēnarro, I. v.a. to tell over again.

rĕnascor, nātus, 3. v.n. dep. to be born again; to be renewed, to revive.

rĕnāvĭgo, I. v.a. to sail back again.

rĕneo, 2. v.a. to unspin, to unravel.

rēnes, renum, m. pl. kidneys. [to smile.

rĕnīdeo, 2. v.n. to shine back, to glitter;

rĕnītor, 3. v.n. to struggle against.

rēno, I. v.a. & n. to swim back.

rēno, ōnis, m. reindeer-skin, fur.

rĕnōdo, ātum, I. v.a. to unbind, to loosen; to tie in a knot.

rĕnōvāmen, ĭnis, n., rĕnōvātĭo, ōnis, f. renewal.

rĕnōvo, I. v.a. to make new again; to restore, to renovate, to repair; to refresh, to recreate.

rĕnŭmĕro, I. v.a. to count up; to repay.

rēnuntĭātĭo, ōnis, f. declaration, proclamation, announcement.

rēnuntio, I. v.a. to report, to declare, to announce; to revoke, to retract, to renounce.

rēnuntius, ii, m. messenger.

rĕnŭo, ui, 3. v.n. & a. to deny, to disapprove, to reject.

reor, rătus, 2. v.a. dep. to think, to suppose, to imagine, to deem.

rĕpāgŭla, ōrum, n. pl. bar, bolt; *fig.* limits. [up; broad, flat.

rĕpandus, a, um, a. bent backwards, turned

rĕpārābĭlis, e, a. reparable; capable of being regained.

rĕpăro, I. v.a. to recover, to retrieve; to restore, to repair, to renew; to make good; to purchase (with); to refresh.

rĕpecto, xum, 3. v.a. to comb.

rĕpello, reppŭli, pulsum, 3. v.a. to drive or push back; to reject, to repulse, to repel.

rĕpendo, di, sum, 3. v.a. to weigh back; to repay; to purchase, to compensate.

rĕpens, entis, a. sudden, hasty, unexpected; fresh, recent; ad. suddenly, unexpectedly.   [sate.

rĕpenso, I. v.a. to requite; to compen-

rĕpentĕ, rĕpentĭno, ad. suddenly, unexpectedly.   [pected.

rĕpentĭnus, a, um, a. sudden, hasty, unex-

rĕpercussus, ūs, m. repercussion, reflection, reverberating, echo.

rĕpercŭtio, cussi, cussum, 3. v.a. to cause to rebound; to reverberate, to re-echo, to reflect.

rĕpĕrio, reppĕri, rĕpertum, 4. v.a. to find, to meet with, to find out; fig. to discover; to invent.   [author.

rĕpertor, ōris, m. discoverer, inventor,

rĕpertum, i, n. invention.

rĕpĕtitio, ōnis, f. repeating, repetition.

rĕpĕtitor, ōris, m. reclaimer.

rĕpĕto, īvi & ii, ītum, 3. v.a. to return to, to revisit; to fetch back; to demand back; to resume; to repeat; to renew; to derive; to recall; to recollect.

rĕpĕtundæ, ārum, f. pl. money extorted by a provincial governor, which he might be compelled to restore; extortion.

repleo, ēvi, ētum, 2. v.a. to fill again; to fill up, to replenish; fig. to complete.

replētus, a, um, p. & a. filled, full.

replĭcātio, ōnis, f. unfolding; reply.

replĭco, I. v.a. to bend or turn back; fig. to unfold; to open; to repeat; to reply.

rēpo, psi, ptum, 3. v.n. to creep, to crawl.

rĕpōno, pŏsŭi, pŏsĭtum, 3. v.a. to place, to put or lay back; to replace, to restore; to reserve, to preserve; to lay aside; to store up; to substitute.

rĕporto, I. v.a. to carry or bring back; to get, to gain; to carry off (a prize, etc.); to report.

rĕposco, 3. v.a. to demand back, to ask for again; to ask for, to require.

rĕpŏsĭtōrium, ii, n. stand, tray.

rĕpostor, ōris, m. restorer.   [ding-day.

rĕpōtia, ōrum, n. pl. feast after the wed-

repraesentātio, ōnis, f. cash payment.

repraesento, I. v.a. to show, to exhibit, to represent; to pay in ready money; to hasten on.

reprĕhendo, di, sum, 3. v.a. to catch hold of; to restrain; to blame, to censure, to reprove, to reprehend.

reprĕhensio, ōnis, f. checking, check; blame, censure, reprimand, reproof; refutation.

reprĕhensor, ōris, m. blamer, reprover.

rĕprĭmo, pressi, pressum, 3. v.a. to press back; to check, to curb, to restrain; fig. to repress.

reprōmissio, ōnis, f. counter-promise.

reprōmitto, mīsi, missum, 3. v.a. to promise in return, to promise again or anew.   [slowly.

repto, I. v.n. fig. to creep along, to walk

rĕpŭdiātio, ōnis, f. rejection.

rĕpŭdio, I. v.a. to cast off, to divorce, to repudiate; fig. to refuse; to disdain, to scorn.   [pudiation.

rĕpŭdium, ii, n. separation, divorce, re-

rĕpŭĕrasco, 3. v.n. to become a boy again.

rĕpugnantia, ae, f. incompatibility.

rĕpugno, I. v.n. to fight against; to oppose; to resist; to disagree with, to be incompatible.

rĕpullŭlo, I. v.n. to bud again.

rĕpulsa, ae, f. rejection, repulse; denial.

rĕpulso, I. v.a. to strike back; to re-echo.

rĕpulsus, ūs, m. driving back; reflection; reverberation.   [remove.

rĕpurgo, I. v.a. fig. to purge away, to

rĕpŭtātio, ōnis, f. consideration.

rĕpŭto, I. v.a. to count again, to reckon, to calculate; fig. to think over, to meditate, to reflect upon.

rĕquies, ētis, f. repose, rest, relaxation, recreation;—requiem, a hymn praying that the dead may rest in peace.

rĕquiesco, ēvi, ētum, 3. v.a. to rest, to repose;—requiescat in pace, let him rest in peace.

rĕquiētus, a, um, a. having rested, refreshed; untilled.

rĕquiro, quisīvi & sii, quisītum, 3. v.a. to seek again; to search for; to require, to need; to question; to miss.

rēs, rei, f. thing; matter; affair; fact; condition; property; profit, advantage; world, universe, cause (in law), suit; power; valour; exploit;—res novæ, political changes, revolution;—respublica, commonwealth, republic;—res secundæ, prosperity;—re vera, actually; really;—pro re, in accordance with circumstances;—in re, re, in the matter of; concerning;—res angusta domi, poverty in the home;—rem acu tetigisti, you have hit the nail on the head;—re infecta, with one's purpose unaccomplished, unsuccessful;—res judicata, a case decided once for all.

rĕsălūto, 1. v.a. to greet again or in return. [health]·

rĕsānēsco, nui, 3. v.n. to recover (one's

rĕsarcio, sartum, 4. v.a. to mend or patch again; to repair, to make good.

rescindo, scĭdi, scissum, 3. v.a. to cut off, to tear open; to annul, to rescind.

rescisco, īvi & ĭi, ĭtum, 3. v.n. to ascertain, to find out, to learn.

rescrībo, psi, ptum, 3. v.a. to write in return or in answer; to repay.

rescriptum, i, n. imperial rescript.

rĕsĕco, cui, ctum, 1. v.a to cut off; to restrain.

resēda (mod. hort.), mignonette.

rĕsēmĭno, 1. v.a. to beget again.

rĕsĕquor, cūtus sum, 3. v.a. dep. to answer, to reply, to rejoin.

rĕsĕro, 1. v.a. to unlock, to open; to disclose, to reveal.

rĕsĕro, sēvi, 3. v.a. to sow again.

rĕservo, 1. v.a. to keep back, to reserve; to preserve. [sluggish.

rĕsĕs, ĭdis, a. motionless, inactive, idle,

rĕsĭdio, sēdi, 2. v.n. & a. to sit down, to remain behind; to be left.

rĕsĭdo, sēdi, 3. v.n. to sit down; to settle; to abate, to subside, to grow calm.

rĕsĭduus, a, um, a. remaining, residuary; outstanding.

rĕsigno, 1. v.a. to unseal; to reveal; to annul, to cancel; to transfer, to repay; to resign.

rĕsĭlio, ui, 4. v.n. to leap or spring back; to recoil, to retreat; to shrink.

rĕsīmus, a, um, a. turned up, snub.

rēsīna, ae, f. resin.

rēsĭnātus, a, um, a. resined; fig. debauched, effeminate.

rēsĭnōsus, a, um, a. full of resin; clammy.

rĕsĭpio, 3. v.a. to taste or savour (of).

rĕsĭpisco, īvi & ĭi, & uĭ, 3. v.n. to become reasonable again; to recover one's wits.

rĕsisto, stĭti, 3. v.n. to stand still; to remain; to resist, to withstand.

rĕsolvo, solvi, sŏlūtum, 3. v.a. to loosen, to release, to open, to dissolve; to disperse, to melt; to relax; to separate; to abolish; to pay; to perform, to fulfil; to enervate.

rĕsŏnābĭlis, e, a. resounding.

rĕsŏno, 1. v.n. & a. to resound, to re-echo; to repeat.

rĕsŏnus, a, um, a. resounding, re-echoing.

rĕsorbeo, 2. v.a. to suck back, to swallow again.

respecto, 1. v.n. & a. to look at; to regard, to respect; to expect.

respectus, ūs, m. looking back or about; refuge, asylum; respect, regard, consideration.

respergo, si, sum, 3. v.a. to besprinkle, to bestrew.

respersio, ōnis, f. sprinkling.

respĭcio, exi, ectum, 3. v.n. & a. to look about; to look back at, to look to or for; to regard; to consider.

respīrāmen, ĭnis, n. windpipe.

respīrātio, ōnis, f. breathing, fetching breath; exhalation; steam.

respīro, 1. v.a. & n. to breathe out, to exhale; to take breath; to recover, to revive; to abate, to cease.

resplendeo, 2. v.n. to shine brightly; to be resplendent.

respondeo, di, sum, 2. v.a. to answer; to give advice; to answer to; to agree with; to be the counterpart of.

responsio, ōnis, f. answer, reply; refutation.

responsĭto, 1. v.a. to deliver an answer.

responso, 1. v.a. to answer, to reply; to re-echo, to resist.

responsum, i, n. answer, reply; oracle; opinion of one learned in the law.

respublĭca, reipublĭcae, f. commonwealth, republic; state.

respuo, ui, 3. v.a. to spit out; to cast out or off, to expel; to refuse, to reject; to dislike, to disdain.

restagnātio, ōnis, f. overflow(ing).

restagno, 1. v.n. to overflow.

restauro, 1. v.a. to restore, to repair, to rebuild.

restĭbĭlis, e, a. tilled or sown every year.

restĭcŭla, ae, f. little rope.

restinctio, ōnis, f. quenching (of one's thirst).

restinguo, nxi, nctum, 3. v.a. to quench, to extinguish; fig. to allay; to put an end to; to destroy. [or covenant.

restĭpŭlātio, ōnis, f. reciprocal agreement

restĭpŭlor, ātus sum, 1. v. dep. to give a pledge in return

restis, is, f. rope, cord.

restĭtuo, ui, ūtum, 3. v.a. to replace, to restore; to rebuild; to revive; to give back, to return; to reverse (a sentence); to rein ïate.

restĭtūtio, ōnis, f. restoration; recalling; reinstatement.

restĭtūtor, ōris, m. restorer.

resto, stĭti, 1. v.n. to stand still; to stand firm; to withstand, to resist; to remain; to await; to be left.

restrictē, ad. closely, sparingly; strictly, exactly.

restrictus, a, um, a. tight, close; confined; niggardly; stern, rigorous.

restringo, inxi, ictum, 3. v.a. to draw back tightly; to bind back, to bind fast, to tighten; to restrain.

rĕsulto, 1. v.n. & a. to leap back, to re-bound; to resound, to re-echo.

rĕsūmo, mpsi, mptum, 3. v.a. to take up again, to take back, to resume; to recover.

rĕsŭpīno, ātum, 1. v.a. to lay on the back; to bend or turn back.

rĕsŭpīnus, a, um, a. bent back, lying on one's back, supine.

rĕsurgo, surrexi, surrectum, 3. v.n. to rise again, to appear again;—resurgam, I shall rise again.

rĕsuscĭto, 1. v.a. to revive, to resuscitate.

retardātio, ōnis, f. delay, stopping.

rĕtardo, 1. v.a. & n. to retard, to impede; to tarry, to remain behind.

rētĕ, is, n. net; toil, snare.

rĕtĕgo, xi, ctum, 3. v.a. to uncover, to bare, to open; to reveal.   [to slacken.

rĕtendo, di, sum & tum, 3. v.a. to unbend,

rĕtentio, ōnis, f. keeping back.

rĕtento, 1. v.a. to keep back, to hold fast; to preserve.

rĕtento, 1. v.a. to try or attempt again.

rĕtexo, xui, xtum, 3. v.a. to unweave, to unravel; to annul, to cancel; to cor-rect; to revise; to repeat, to renew.

rētĭārius, ĭi, m. net-fighter in the arena.

rĕtĭceo, cui, 2. v.n. & a. to be silent again; to keep silence; to conceal.

rētĭcŭlātus, a, um, a. latticed, net-like.

rētĭcŭlum, i, n., rētĭcŭlus, i, m. little net, reticule, lattice.

rĕtĭnācŭlum, i, n. halter, tether.

rĕtĭneo, ui, tentum, 2. v.a. to hold or keep back; to detain, to retain; to preserve; to maintain, to restrain.

rĕtinnio, 4. v.n. to ring again.

rĕtorqueo, si, tum, 2. v.n. to twist or bend back; to cast back; to wheel round; to drive back; to wrap about.

rĕtorrĭdus, a, um, a. dried up, parched, shrivelled.

retractātio, ōnis, f. refusal, hesitation.

retractātus, a, um, p. & a. corrected, re-vised.

retracto, 1. v.a. to take in hand again, to undertake anew; to draw back, to de-cline; to be reluctant; to reconsider; to withdraw.

retractus, a, um, a. distant, remote.

retrāho, xi, ctum, 3. v.a. to draw back, to withdraw; to call back.

retrĭbuo, ui, ūtum, 3. v.a. to give back, to return, to restore, to repay.

retrō, ad. backwards, behind; on the con-trary; formerly, before.

retrorsum, retrorsus, retrōversus, ad. back, backwards, behind; in reversed order.

retrūdo, si, 3, v.a. to thrust back.

retrūsus, a, um, a. removed, concealed.

rĕtundo, tŭdi, tūsum, 3. v.a. to blunt, to dull; to deaden, to weaken.

rĕtūsus, a, um, p. & a. blunted; dull.

reus, i, m., rea, ae, f. defendant; prisoner; criminal; debtor; surety.   [to recover.

rĕvălesco, lui, 3. v.n. to grow well again;

rĕvĕho, xi, ctum, 3. v.a. to carry or bring back;—revehor, pass; to drive, to ride or sail back; to return.

rĕvello, velli, vulsum, 3. v.a. to pull or tear out; to remove.

rĕvēlo, 1. v.a. to unveil, to bare; to show, to discover.

rĕvĕnio, vēni, ventum, 4. v.n. to come again, to come back, to return.

rĕvērā, ad. truly, in very deed, in reality.

revĕrendus, a, um, p. & a. venerable, re-verent.

rĕvĕrens, entis, a. respectful, reverent.

rĕvĕrenter, ad. respectfully.

rĕvĕrentia, ae, f. respect, regard, fear, awe, reverence.

rĕvĕreor, ĭtus, 2. v.a. dep. to revere; to honour; to stand in awe of.

rĕversio, ōnis, f. turning back, returning.

rĕverto, verti, 3. v.n. to turn back or pass, to come back, to return.

rĕvincio, vinxi, vinctum, 4. v.a. to bind back; to fasten.

rĕvinco, vīci, victum, 3. v.a. to conquer, to subdue; to refute; to disprove; to convict.

rĕviresco, rui, 3. v.n. to grow green again; to grow strong or young again.

rĕvīso, 3. v.a. to revisit.

rĕvīvisco, vixi, 3. v.n. to come to life again, to recover.

rĕvŏcābĭlis, e, a. revocable.

rĕvŏcāmen, ĭnis, n. calling back, recall.

rĕvŏcātio, ōnis, f. recall; fig. revocation, withdrawing.

rĕvŏco, 1, v.a. to call back, to recall; to withhold, to restrain; to apply; to reduce; to refer; to revoke; to retract.

rĕvŏlo, 1. v.n. to fly back.

rĕvŏlūbĭlis, e, a. that may be rolled back.

rĕvŏlūtus, a, um, a. rolled back, wound off; changed; revolving; returning; falling backward.

rĕvolvo, volvi, vŏlūtum, 3. v.a. to roll back; to unroll; to revolve; to read over; to repeat; to ponder.

rĕvŏmo, ui, 3. v.a. to disgorge, to vomit or cast up again.

revort . . ., v. revert . . .

rex, rēgis, m. king, tyrant, despot; master; leader, head; patron; rich man.

rhamnus, i, m. buckthorn.

rhēda, v. ræda.

rhēdārius, v. ræedarius.

rhēno, v. reno.

rhētor, ōris, m. rhetorician.

rhētŏrĭca, ae, rhētŏrĭcē, es, f. rhetoric

rhētŏrĭcē, ad. rhetorically.

rhētŏrĭcus, a, um, a. rhetorical.

rhēum (mod. hort.), rhubarb.

rhīnŏcĕrōs, ōtis, m. rhinoceros.

rhododendron, i, n. rhododendron.

rhombus, i, m. magician's circle; (fish) turbot.

rhus, rhois, m. sumach.

ribes (mod. hort.), currant;—ribes grossularia, gooseberry.

rīca, ae, f. woman's hood.

richardia (mod. hort.), arum lily.

rīcīnium, ii, n. small hood.

rīcīnus, i, m. castor-oil plant.

rictus, ūs, m. mouth wide open; grin.

rīdeo, rīsi, rīsum, 2. v.n. & a. to laugh; to smile; to mock; to laugh at or over.

rīdĭcŭlē, ad. ridiculously; in jest; drolly.

rīdĭcŭlōsus, a, um, a. laughable, facetious droll.

rīdĭcŭlum, i, n. jest, joke.

rīdĭcŭlus, a, um, a. laughable, droll, funny, facetious; silly; —, i, m. buffoon; jester.

rīgeo, 2. v.n. to be stiff or numb; to stand on end; to be cold.

rīgesco, gui, 3. v.n. to grow stiff or numb; to stiffen, to harden; to bristle up.

rīgĭdē, ad. stiffly; rigorously.

rīgĭdus, a, um, a. stiff, hard, rigid; fig. inflexible; stern; rude.

rīgo, 1. v.a. to moisten, to wet, to water.

rīgor, ōris, m. stiffness, rigidity, coldness, numbness, hardness; fig. inflexibility; roughness; severity.

rīguus, a, um, a. wet; watered; watering. [flash of lightning.

rīma, ae, f. cleft, crack, chink, fissure;

rīmor, ātus, 1. v.a. dep. to lay open, to tear or grub up; to rummage about; to examine, to explore; to investigate.

rīmōsus, a, um, a. full of chinks or fissures, leaky. [chafe, to snarl.

ringor, ctus, 3. v.n. dep. to be angry; to

rīpa, ae, f. bank of a stream; shore of the sea. [or shores.

rīpārius, a, um, a. pertaining to the banks

rīsor, ōris, m. laugher, mocker.

rīsus, ūs, m. laughing, laughter, laugh.

rītē, ad. with due form; rightly, fitly.

rītus, ūs, m. religious usage or ceremony, rite; custom, usage; manner, way;— ritu (with the gen.), in the manner of.

rīvālis, is, m. rival.

rīvālĭtas, ātis, f. rivalry in love.

rīvūlus, i, m. rill, rivulet.

rīvus, i, brook; stream.

rixa, ae, f. quarrel, brawl, dispute, strife.

rixor, ātus, 1. v.n. dep. to quarrel, to brawl, to wrangle, to dispute.

Rōbīgālĭa, ium, n. pl. festival in honour of Rōbīgus (on the 25th of April).

rōbīgo, ĭnis, f. rust; mildew, blight.

Rōbīgus, i, m. a god worshipped to keep blasting and mildew from corn.

rōbŏreus, a, um, a. oaken.

rōbŏro, 1. v.a. to strengthen, to invigorate, to confirm.

rōbur, ōris, n. any very hard wood; oak; oak-wood; trunk (of such wood); club; fig. strength, hardness, force, vigour, courage; flower, bloom, best part; part of a prison.

rōbustus, a, um, a. oaken, hard, firm, solid, strong, hardy, robust.

rōdo, si, sum, 3. v.a. to gnaw; to eat away, to corrode, to consume; fig. to backbite. [funeral pile.

rŏgālis, e, a. of a funeral, pertaining to a

rŏgātĭo, ōnis, f. proposed law; entreaty, request; interrogation, question.

rŏgātor, ōris, m. proposer; polling clerk.

rŏgĭto, 1. v.a. to ask or inquire frequently or eagerly; to entreat.

rŏgo, 1. v.a. to ask, to question, to interrogate; to propose (a law, a magistrate); to request, to solicit; (mil.) to administer an oath to the soldiers.

rŏgus, i, m. funeral-pile; fig. grave; destruction.

romneya (mod. hort.), tree poppy.

rōrārii, ōrum, m. pl. skirmishers.

rōrĭdus, a, um, a. dewy, moist.

rōrĭfĕr, a, um, a. bringing dew.

rōro, 1. v.n. & a. to drop or distil dew; to trickle, to drip; to bedew; to wet.

rōrŭlentus, a, um, a. full of dew.

rōs, rōris, m. dew; moisture; juice; —marinus, rosemary. [rose-tree.

rŏsa, ae, f. rose; garland of roses; fig.

rŏsāceus, a, um, a. of roses, rosy.

rŏsārium, ii, n. rose-garden.

roscĭdus, a, um, a. dewy; wet.

rŏsētum, i, n. garden of roses.

rŏseus, a, um, a. of roses; rose-coloured, rosy; ruddy; blooming.

rōsĭo, ōnis, f. gnawing.

rosmărīnum, i, n. rosmarīnus, i, m.; v. ros.

rostrātus, a, um, a. beaked, curved.

rostrum, i, n. snout or muzzle (of an animal), beak, bill; ship's beak;— rostra, ōrum, n. pl. pulpit (for speakers, in the forum);—columna rostrata, a column in the forum adorned with the beaks of ships taken by Duilius in 260 B.C.

rĕta, ae, f. wheel; rack; chariot.
róto, I. v.a. & n. to turn or swing round; to whirl about.
rótŭla, ae, f. little wheel.
rótundē, ad. fig. elegantly, smoothly.
rótundo, I. v.a. to make round, to round off.
rótundus, a, um, a. round, circular; fig. smooth, polished, elegant.   [redden.
rŭbĕfăcio, fēci, factum, 3. v.a. to
rŭbens, entis, a. red; reddish; blushing.
rŭbeo, 2. v.n. to be red, to blush.
rŭber, bra, brum, a. red, ruddy.
rŭbesco, bui, 3. v.n. to grow or turn red, to redden.
rŭbĕta, ae, f. venomous toad.
rŭbētum, i, n. bramble-thicket.
rŭbeus, a, um, a. pertaining to the bramble.
rŭbia, ae, f. madder.
rŭbĭcundus, a, um, a. red, ruddy.
rŭbĭdus, a, um, a. reddish, brownish.
rŭbīgo, v. robigo.
rŭbor, ōris, m. redness; blush; bashfulness, modesty, something to blush at.
rubrīca, ae, f. red chalk; the title of a law.
rŭbus, i, m. bramble-bush, blackberry-bush, raspberry.
ructo, I. v.n. & a., ructor, I. v. dep. to belch, to belch forth; to utter.
ructus, ūs, m. belching.
rudbeckia (mod. hort.), cœne-flower.
rŭdens, entis, m. cable; rope; sheet; the title of a play by Plautus in which a fisherman's rope figures.
rŭdīmentum, i, n. first beginning; principles; rudiments.
rŭdis, e, a. rough, unwrought; raw, wild; ill-made, rudely finished, coarse; ignorant; awkward, clumsy; simple.
rŭdis, is, f. foil (for fencers);—rude donari, to be presented with a staff, i.e. to get one's discharge.
rŭdo, īvi, ītum, 3. v.n. & a. to bellow, to bray, to roar.
rūdus, ĕris, n. old rubbish, rubble.
rūfesco, 3. v.n. to grow red.
rūfo, I. v.a. to make red.
rūfŭlus, a, um, a. reddish.
rūfus, a, um, a. reddish; red-headed.
rūga, ae, f. wrinkle; fold, plait.
rūgōsus, a, um, a. wrinkled, shrivelled, corrugated.
ruīna, ae, f. tumbling down, downfall, ruin; ruins; debris, disaster, destruction.
ruīnōsus, a, um, a. ruinous; fallen, ruined.
rŭmex, ĭcis, f. sorrel.

Rūmĭnālis, e, a. ficus, the fig-tree beneath which the legendary wolf suckled Romulus and Remus.
rūmĭnātio, ōnis, f. chewing of the cud; fig. repetition; thinking over, ruminating.
rūmĭno, I. v.a. & n., rūmĭnor, v. dep. to chew the cud, to ponder over, to ruminate.
rŭmis, is, f. teat.   [tation.
rūmor, ōris, m. hearsay, rumour; reputrumpo, rūpi, ruptum, 3. v.a. to burst asunder, to break down; to force open; to destroy; to violate; to annul; to interrupt.
rūmuscŭlus, i, m. gossip.
rūna, ae, f. dart, javelin.
runcătio, ōnis, f. weeding.
runcĭno, I. v.a. to plane.
runco, I. v.a. to weed; to pluck.
ruo, ui, ŭtum, 3. v.n. & a. to fall down, to go to ruin; to hasten, to hurry, to run, to dash, to rush; to fall, to fail; ruat cælum (let justice be done), though heaven fall; to cast, to turn, to rake up.
rūpes, is, f. rock.
rūpĭcapra, ae, f. wild goat.
ruptor, ōris, m. breaker; fig. violator.
rūrĭcŏla, ae, a. rustic; sylvan.
rūrĭgĕna, ae, m. countryman.
rursum, rursus, ad. backwards; on the contrary; again, anew.
rūs, rūris, n. country; country-seat, farm;—rura, fields;—rus in urbe, country in the midst of a town.
ruscārius, a, um, a. of broom.
ruscum, i, n. broom, furze.
russātus, a, um, a. clad in red (used of the supporters of the red faction in the circus).
russeus, russus, a, um, a. reddish.
rustĭcānus, a, um, rustic; country- . . .
rustĭcātio, ōnis, f. country life; doing of country work.
rustĭcē, ad. awkwardly, clownishly.
rustĭcĭtas, ātis, f. rusticity.
rustĭcor, ātus sum, I. v.n. dep. to rusticate, to live in the country; to do country work.
rustĭcŭla, ae, f. wood-cock.
rustĭcus, a, um, a. rural, rustic, country- . . .; countrified; coarse, awkward; simple; —, i, m. countryman, rustic, peasant;—rustica, ae, f. country-girl; wood-cock.
rŭta (et) cæsa, n. pl. (things dug up and felled), minerals and timber.
rūta, ae, f. (hort.) rue; fig. bitterness.
rŭtābŭlum, i, n. shovel.
rūtāceus, a, um, a. of rue.

rūtātus, a, um, a. flavoured with rue.
rŭtĭlesco, 3. v.n. to grow ruddy.
rŭtĭlo, 1. v.a. & n. to colour red; to be reddish.
rŭtĭlus, a, um, a. red, reddish.
rūtrum, i, n. spade, shovel.

Sabbăta, ōrum, n. pl. the Jewish Sabbath.
săbŭlo, ōnis, m. gravel.
săbŭlōsus, a, um, a. gravelly, sandy.
săburra, ae, f. sand for ballast.
săburro, 1. v.a. to ballast, to load.
sacchăron, i, n. sugar-cane.
sacco, 1. v.a. to filter, to strain.
saccŭlus, i, m. little bag.
saccus, i, m. bag; money-bag.
săcellum, i, n. chapel, sanctuary.
săcer, sacra, sacrum, a. holy, sacred; awful; devoted; cursed; impious, wicked, execrable, infamous;—sacrum, n., v. sacrum.
săcerdos, ōtis, c. priest; priestess.
săcerdōtĭum, ii, n. priesthood.
sacra, n. pl., v. sacrum, n.
sacrāmentum, i, n. oath taken by newly enlisted soldiers; oath, solemn obligation.   [sacred place.
sacrārĭum, ii, n. shrine; chapel; fig.
sacrātus, a, um, a. hallowed, holy, sacred.
sacrĭfĕr, a, um, a. bearing sacred things.
sacrĭfĭcālis, e, a. sacrificial.
sacrĭfĭcĭum, ii, n. sacrifice.
sacrĭfĭco, 1. v.a. to sacrifice, to offer to the gods.
sacrĭfĭcŭlus, i, m. sacrificing priest;—rex —, high-priest.
sacrĭfĭcus, a, um, a. sacrificial.
sacrĭlĕgĭum, ii, n. sacrilege; offence against religion.
sacrĭlĕgus, a, um, a. sacrilegious; profane, impious; —, i, m. sacrilegious person.
sacro, 1. v.a. to consecrate or devote to; to doom; to dedicate; to worship; to immortalize.   [violable.
sacrōsanctus, a, um, a. sacrosanct, insacrum, i, n. sacred thing; consecrated place; temple; beast sacrificed; sacrifice; sacred rite; divine worship;—sacra, pl. mysteries; holy rites; poetry.
saecŭlāris, e, a. of a generation;—ludi saeculares, games celebrated at fixed intervals;—carmen saeculare, hymn sung at the ludi saeculares.
saecŭlum, saeclum, i, n. generation, lifetime; race; century; indefinitely long period; the times.
saepĕ, ad. often, oftentimes, frequently;
saepenŭmĕro, oftentimes, very often.

saepēs, is, f. hedge; fence.
saepĭmentum, i, n. fence; inclosure.
saepio, saepsi, saeptum, 4. v.a. to fence in; to enclose; to cover.
saeptum, i, n. fence, enclosure; voting ground in the Campus Martius.
saeta, ae, f. hair; bristle; fishing-line.
saetĭger, a, um, a. bristly.
saetōsus, a, um, a. bristly.
saevē, ad. fiercely, cruelly, barbarously.
saevio, ii, ītum, 4. v.n. to be fierce or furious, to rage; to be mad or angry.
saevĭter, ad. fiercely, cruelly.
saevĭtĭa, ae, f. rage, fierceness, ferocity; cruelty, barbarity, violence; severity.
saevĭtĭes, ĕi, f. fierceness, cruelty.
saevus, a, um, a. raging, furious, ferocious, barbarous, cruel; severe; violent.
săga, ae, f. female diviner or fortune-teller.
săgācĭtas, ātis, f. acuteness, sagacity.
săgācĭter, ad. keenly; sagaciously.
săgātus, a, um, a. clothed in a mantle.
săgax, ācis, a. sagacious; keen-scented; fig. acute, shrewd.
săgīna, ae, f. meat to cram fowls, fattening, feasting; food, nourishment.
săgīnātĭo, ōnis, f. fattening.
săgīno, 1. v.a. to fatten (animals); to cram, to feast.
săgitta, ae, f. arrow (also as constellation).
săgittārĭus, a, um, a. of or belonging to arrows.   [(constellation).
Săgittārĭus, ii, m. archer, bowman; Archer
săgittĭfer, a, um, a. bearing arrows.
săgŭlum, i, n. small military cloak.
săgum, i, n. coarse woollen blanket or mantle; military cloak;—saga sumere, to prepare for battle.
săgus, a, um, a. prophetic.
sal, sălis, m. salt; sea-water; sea; fig. shrewdness; sarcasm, witticism;—săles, pl. jests, quibbles; pretty conceits.
sălācĭtas, ātis, f. lust.
sălămandra, ae, f. salamander.
sălārĭum, ii, n. salt-money; stipend, allowance, salary.   [ii, m. salter.
sălārĭus, a, um, a. of salt, salt . . . ; —,
sălax, ācis, a. lecherous, salacious; provoking lust.
sălebra, ae, f. rough place; fig. harshness.
săles, ĭum, m. pl., v. sal.
Sălĭāris, e, a. of the Salii, Salian; splendid, sumptuous.
sălictārĭus, a, um, a. of willows; growing among willows.
sălictum, i, n. willow-plantation.
sălientes, ĭum, f. pl. fountains, springs.

sălign(e)us, a, um, a. of willow.
Sălii, ōrum, m. pl. Leapers, Jumpers (college of 12 priests dedicated to the service of Mars).
sălillum, i, n. little salt-cellar.
sălīnae, ārum, f. pl. salt-works, salt-pits.
sălīnum, i, n. salt-cellar.
sălio, 4. v.a. to season with salt; v. salsus.
sălio, ii & ui, saltum, 4. v.n. & a. to leap, to spring, to bound, to jump; to throb.
sălīva, ae, f. spittle; *fig.* taste; flavour; appetite.
sălix, ĭcis, f. willow-tree, willow.
salmo, ōnis, m. salmon.
salpa, ae, f. stockfish.
salpiglossis (mod. hort.), scalloped tube-tongue.   [food.
salsa, ōrum, n. pl. salted things, salted
salsāmentum, i, n. fish-pickle; pickled fish.
salsē, ad. wittily, acutely.
salsĭtūdo, ĭnis, f. saltness.
salsūgo, ĭnis, f. saltness, brine.
salsus, a, um, a. salted; *fig.* acute; witty
saltātio, ōnis, f. dancing, dance.
saltātor, ōris, m. dancer.
saltātōrius, a, um, a. dancing.
saltātrix, ĭcis, f. dancing-girl.
saltātus, ūs, m. dancing.
saltem, ad. at least, at all events;—non or neque —, not *or* nor even.
salto, 1. v.n. & a. to dance, to jump; *fig.* to speak in broken sentences; to represent in a dance.   [forests.
saltuōsus, a, um, a. woody, abounding in
saltus, ūs, m. leaping, leap, spring, bound;—saltus, ūs, m. forest, thicket; dell; ravine.
sălūber, sălūbris, e, a. healthful, wholesome; serviceable; profitable.
sălūbrĭtas, ātis, f. healthfulness, salubrity; health, vigour.
sălūbrĭter, ad. healthfully, salubriously; advantageously.
sălum, i, n. high sea, sea.
sălūs, ūtis, f. health, welfare, safety; greeting, salutation;—salutem dicere, to send greetings (by letter).
sălūtāris, e, a. healthful, salutary; serviceable, advantageous.
sălūtārĭter, ad. salutarily; profitably.
sălūtātio, ōnis, f. greeting, salutation; ceremonial visit.   [tier.
sălūtātor, ōris, m. greeter; visitor; coursălūtĭfer, a, um, a. salubrious.
sălūto, 1. v.a. to greet, to salute; to pay one's respects to.
salveo, 2. v.n. to be well *or* in good health;—salvē! hail! welcome! farewell! good-bye!—salvēre jŭbēre, to greet; to bid welcome.

salvia, ae, f. sage.
salvus, a, um, a. safe, well, sound;—salva lege, without violation of the law.
sambūca, ae, f. dulcimer; sackbut.
sambūceus, a, um, a. of elder (-tree).
sambūcistria, ae, f. female dulcimer-player.
sambūcus, i, f. elder-tree.
sănābĭlis, e, a. curable.
sānātio, ōnis, f. healing.
sancio, xi, ctum, 4. v.a. to consecrate, to establish, to appoint, to ordain; to ratify, to sanction; to forbid solemnly.
sanctē, ad. solemnly; religiously.
sanctĭmōnia, ae, f. sacredness, sanctity; chastity.
sanctio, ōnis, f. ratification; penal statute.
sanctĭtas, ātis, f. sacredness, sanctity; holiness; integrity; chastity.
sanctor, ōris, m. establisher.
sanctus, a, um, p. & a. sacred, inviolable; venerable; holy; divine; just;—sanctum, i, n. a holy place, a private room.
sandix, ĭcis & īcis, f. vermilion colour.
sānē, ad. to be sure, certainly; very, forsooth.
sānesco, 3. v.n. to recover, to grow well.
sanguen, inis, v. sanguis.
sanguĭnārius, a, um, a. *fig.* blood-thirsty.
sanguĭneus, a, um, a. bloody, blood-stained; blood-red.
sanguĭnōlentus, a, um, a. bloody; blood-red; *fig.* sanguinary.
sanguis, ĭnis, m. blood; race, family, consanguinity; *fig.* life; vigour; spirit.
sanguisūga, ae, f. horse-leech.
sănies, em, e, f. bloody matter; venomous slaver.
sānĭtas, ātis, f. health; *fig.* soundness (of mind), good sense; propriety, regularity.
sanna, ae, f. grimace.
sannio, ōnis, m. buffoon, mimic.
sāno, 1. v.a. to make sound *or* healthy, to heal, to cure.
sānus, a, um, a. whole, healthy; sound in mind, rational; correct;—mens sana in corpore sano, a healthy mind in a healthy body.
săpa, ae, f. new wine.
săpiens, entis, p. & a. wise, sensible, well advised, discreet, judicious; wise, philosophical; —, m. philosopher.
săpienter, ad. prudently, judiciously, wisely.
săpientia, ae, f. prudence, wisdom; philosophy; eloquence; statesmanship.
săpīnus, i, f. fir-tree, pine.
săpio, īvi & ii, 3. v.n. & a. to taste; to savour of; to be prudent *or* wise.

săpo, ōnis, m. soap.
săpor, ōris, m. taste, relish, flavour; dainty, delicacy, good taste.
sapphīrinus, a, um, a. of sapphire.
sapphīrus, i, f. sapphire.
sarcina, ae, f. bundle, burthen, load, pack; fig. burden. [gage.
sarcinārius, a, um, a. pertaining to bag-
sarcinŭla, ae, f. little pack; bag.
sarcio, sarsi, sartum, 4. v.a. to patch, to botch, to repair, to restore; fig. to make amends for, to repair;—sarta tecta, buildings in good repair and roofed.
sarcŏphăgus, i, m. grave; tomb.
sarcŭlum, i, n. hoe.
sarda, ae, f. (fish) sprat; cornelian.
sardŏnyx, ўchis, m. & f. sardonyx.
sarissa, ae, f. long spear (of the Macedonians).
sarmentum, i, n. twigs, brush, wood; faggot, fascine.
sarrācum, i, n. cart, waggon.
sar(r)io, ivi & ui, itum, 4. v.a. to weed, to rake, to harrow.
sartāgo, inis, f. frying-pan.
sartor, ōris, m. tailor; cobbler;—sartor resartus, the tailor patched.
sartus, v. sarcio.
sat, v. sătis.
săta, ōrum, n. pl. crops.
sătāgo, ēgi, actum, 3. v.n. to be busy or in distress.
sătellěs, itis, c. attendant, lifeguard, pl. retinue; fig. abettor, accomplice.
sătias, ātis, f. sufficiency, abundance; fig. loathing, disgust.
sătiětas, ātis, f. satiety; disgust.
sătio, i. v.a. to sate, to satiate; fig. to fill; to satisfy; to glut; to disgust.
sătio, ōnis, f. planting, sowing; sown fields.
sătira, v. satura.
sătis, ad. sufficient, satisfactory; enough; —sătius, better, preferable;—sătisaccipio, 3. v.a. to take sufficient bail; —sătisdo, dědi, dătum, i. v.a. to give sufficient securities.
sătisdătio, ōnis, f. giving security.
sătisfăcio, fēci, factum, 3. v.n. & a. to give satisfaction, to satisfy, to content; to make amends; to make excuse; to apologize. [apology.
sătisfactio, ōnis, f. reparation; excuse,
satius, v. satis.
sător, ōris, m. sower, planter; fig. begetter, creator; author.
sătrăpa, ae, m. satraps, ăpis, sătrăpes, ae, m. satrap, Persian governor of a province.
satrăpia, ae, f. satrapy, province.

sătŭr, a, um, a. sated, having eaten enough; fig. rich, abundant, fertile.
sătūra, ae, f. plate of fruit; medley;—hotch-potch; peculiar kind of Roman poetry, satire; per —m, in the gross; confusedly.
sătūreia, ōrum, n. pl. (hort.) savory.
sătūrio, ōnis, m. glutton.
sătūritas, ātis, f. fulness, plenty, abundance, satiety.
Săturnālia, ōrum, ibus, n. pl. festival in honour of Saturn, beginning on the 17th of December.
sătūro, i. v.a. to fill, to cloy, to satiate; to dye; to saturate; fig. to disgust (with).
sătus, i, m. son; —, ūs, m. planting, sowing; begetting, producing; origin; race; seed.
sătyra, v. satura.
Sătўrus, i, m. Satyr; satyric play.
sauciātio, ōnis, f. wounding.
saucio, i. v.a. to wound, to hurt; to prune.
saucius, a, um, a. wounded, hurt; injured, enfeebled, sick, distempered; afflicted, grieved; smitten with love.
sāvium, v. suavium.
saxātilis, e, a. frequenting rocks. [stone.
saxeus, a, um, a. rocky, stony, made of
saxifraga (mod. hort.), London pride.
saxificus, a, um, a. petrifying.
saxifrăgus, a, um, a. breaking stones.
saxōsus, a, um, a. rocky, stony.
saxŭlum, i, n. little stone or rock.
saxum, i, n. stone; rock.
scăbellum, i, n. a. musical instrument played with the foot.
scăber, bra, brum, a. scurfy, mangy.
scăbies, em, e, f. scurf; scab, mange, itch.
scabiōsa (mod. hort.), scabious.
scăbiōsus, a, um, a. scabby, itchy, mangy.
scăbo, scăbi, 3. v.a. to scrape, to scratch.
scabritia, ae, f. roughness; scabbiness.
scæna, ae, f. stage of a theatre; pretext; public view.
scænālis, e, a. pertaining to the stage.
scænicus, a, um, a. theatrical; —, i, m. actor.
scălæ, ārum, f. pl. ladder; stairs.
scalmus, i, m. thole-pin.
scalpellum, i, n. scalpel, lancet.
scalpo, psi, ptum, 3. v.a. to curve, to scrape, to scratch, to engrave; fig. to tickle.
scalprum, i, n. chisel; penknife.
scalptor, ōris, m. engraver.
scalptōrium, i, n. back-scratcher.
scalptūra, ae, f. engraving.
scammōnea, ae, f. scammony.

scamnum, i, n. bench.

scando, di, sum, 3. v.a. & n. to climb, to mount, to ascend; *fig.* to rise.

scandŭla, ae, f. lath, shingle.

scansĭlis, e, a. that may be climbed.

scăpha, ae, f. light boat, skiff.

scăphium, ii, n. drinking-vessel.

scăpŭlæ, ārum, f. pl. shoulder-blades; shoulders.

scăpus, i, m. stalk; shaft; tongue (of a balance); post; pillar.

scărăbæus, i, m. beetle.

scărĭfico, 1. v.a. to scarify, to lancet.

scărus, i, m. (fish), char.

scătebra, ae, f. bubbling, gushing up.

scăteo, 2. v.n. to bubble, to gush out; to be plentiful; to abound; to swarm with.

scătūrīgo, ĭnis, f. spring water, spring.

scaurus, i, m. bow-legged.

scĕlĕrātē, ad. wickedly, basely.

scĕlĕrātus, a, um, a. polluted; wicked, vicious; hurtful.

scĕlĕro, 1. v.a. to defile.   [accursed.

scĕlĕrōsus, a, um, a. vicious, abominable,

scĕlestē, ad. wickedly; infamously.

scĕlestus, a, um, a. wicked, villainous, infamous, abominable.

scĕlus, ĕris, n. crime, sin, enormity; rascal.

scēna, v. **scæna.**

scēnālis, v. **scænalis.**

scēnĭcus, v. **scænicus.**

sceptrĭfĕr, a, um, sceptrĭgĕr, a, um, a. bearing a sceptre.   [thority.

sceptrum, i, n. sceptre; kingdom; au-

schĕda, ae, f. leaf *or* sheet of paper.

schĕdula, ae, small sheet of paper.

schēma, ae, f. & **ătis,** n. shape, figure, form; fashion, manner; figure of speech.

schizanthus (mod. hort.), fringe-flower.

schœnŏbătes, ae, m. acrobat, rope-dancer.   [of distance.

schœnus, i, m. bulrush; Persian measure

schŏla, ae, f. lecture, dissertation; school, sect.

schŏlasticus, a, um, a. scholastic; —, i, m. lecturer; rhetorician.

schŏlĭon, i, schŏlĭum, i, n. short comment, gloss.

scibĭlis, e, a. knowable.

sciens, entis, a. knowing, having knowledge; expert (in).

scienter, ad. knowingly, wisely, skilfully, expertly.

scientia, ae, f. knowledge, science; expertness; theory.

scīlicet, ad. of course, evidently, certainly; namely, to wit, that is to say; (*iron.*) of course, forsooth.

scilla, ae, f. shrimp; sea-onion.

scindo, scĭdi, scissum, 3. v.a. to split, to cleave, to tear, to cut asunder; to break down; to tear open; to separate.

scintilla, ae, f. spark.

scintillo, 1. v.n. to sparkle, to flash.

scintillŭla, ae, f. little spark.

scio, īvi & ii, ītum, 4. v.a. to know, to understand, to perceive; to decree;— **quod sciam,** for aught I know.

scīpio, ōnis, m. staff; cudgel.

Scīron, ōnis, m. north-west wind.

scirpeus, a, um, a. made of rushes.

scirpea, ae, f. wicker-work body of a cart.

scirpĭcŭlus, i, n. basket of rushes.

scirpus, i, m. rush, reed-grass;— **in scirpo nodum quærere,** to look for a knot in a bulrush, i.e. to find difficulties where none exist.

sciscĭtor, ātus, 1. v.a. dep. to inform oneself; to ask, to inquire, to examine.

scisco, scīvi, scītum, 3. v.a. to learn, to ascertain, to know; to assent, to approve; to decree, to ordain.

scissūra, æ, f. cleft, rent.

scītāmentum, i, n. pleasant food, dainty.

scītē, ad. cunningly; cleverly; elegantly.

scītor, 1. v.a. dep. to seek to know; to ask, to inquire.

scītū, ad. by decree.

scītum, i, n. ordinance, statute, decree.

scītus, a, um, a. knowing, shrewd, acute, experienced, skilful; proper, fit; judicious; witty; fine, elegant.

sciūrus, i, m. squirrel.

scŏbis, is, f. sawdust, filings.

scolopendrium (mod. hort.), hartstongue fern.

scomber, bri, m. mackerel.

scōpæ, ārum, f. pl. twigs, broom.

scŏpŭlōsus, a, um, a. craggy, rocky.

scŏpŭlus, i, m. rock, cliff, crag; *fig.* danger, difficulty; evil.

scŏria, ae, f. dross.

scorpio, ōnis, scorpios, scorpius, ii, m. scorpion.

scortea, ae, f. leather-coat.

scorteus, a, um, a. of hide, leathern.

scortillum, i, n. young slut.

scortum, i, n. whore, harlot, prostitute.

scrība, ae, m. public clerk, writer; secretary, notary.

scrībo, psi, ptum, 3. v.a. to write; to compose; to describe; to draw up (a law, etc.); to appoint, to designate; (mil.) to enroll, to levy.

scrīnium, ii, n. book-case; writing-desk.

scriptio, ōnis, f. (act of) writing; composition.   [pose in writing.

scriptĭto, 1. v.a. to write often; to com-

scriptor, ōris, m. writer, scribe, secretary; author; compiler;—**rerum** —, historian.

scriptum, i, n. something written *or* drawn, line; book, work; treatise; law.   [testamentary provision.

scriptūra, ae, f. writing; composition;

scrōbis, is, c. ditch; grave.

scrōfa, ae, f. sow.

scrūpeus, a, um, a. rugged, rough; steep.

scrūpŭlōsē, ad. scrupulously, exactly.

scrūpŭlōsus, a, um, a. rough, rugged; *fig.* exact, careful, scrupulous.

scrūpŭlus, i, m. scruple (weight); *fig.* trouble, anxiety, doubt, scruple.

scrūta, ōrum, n. pl. frippery, trash.

scrūtātor, ōris, m. searcher, scrutinizer, examiner, investigator.

scrūtor, ātus, I. v.a. dep. to search carefully, to examine thoroughly, to explore; to find out.

sculpo, psi, ptum, 3. v.a. to carve, to grave, to chisel.

sculptĭlis, e, a. carved, graven.

sculptor, ōris, graver, sculptor.

sculptūra, ae, f. carving, sculpture.

scurra, ae, m. buffoon, jester; dandy.

scurrīlis, e, a. buffoon-like, jeering, scurrilous.

scurrīlĭtas, ātis, f. buffoonery.

scurror, I. v.n. dep. to play the buffoon; to flatter, to cringe.

scūtāle, is, n. thong of a sling.

scūtātus, a, um, a. armed with a long shield.

scŭtĭca, ae, f. lash, whip.

scutra, ae, f. chafing-dish.

scŭtŭla, ae, f. wooden roller, cylinder; rhomb, lozenge.

scŭtŭlātus, a, um, a. check-patterned.

scŭtŭlum, i, n. little shield.

scūtum, i, n. (oblong) shield, buckler; *fig.* defence, shelter.

scȳphus, i, m. cup, goblet.

sē, pn., v. **sui.**

sēbōsus, a, um, a. of tallow, tallowy.

sēbum, i, n. suet, tallow.

sēcēdo, cessi, cessum, 3. v.n. to step aside, to withdraw, to retire; to secede, to revolt.

sēcerno, crēvi, crētum, 3. v.a. to sunder, to sever, to separate; *fig.* to discern, to distinguish.   [secession.

sēcessio, ōnis, f. going aside; schism,

sēcessus, ūs, m. departure; separation; solitude; retreat.

sēcius, v. **secus.**

sēclūdo, si, sum, 3. v.a. to shut off, to shut up, to seclude; to remove; to exclude.

seclum, v. **sæculum.**

sēclūsus, a, um, a. remote.

sēco, cui, ctum, I. v.a. to cut, to cut off; to amputate; to separate; to divide; to fly *or* sail through.

sēcrētio, ōnis, f. separation.

sēcrēto, ad. apart, separately; in secret.

sēcrētus, a, um, a. separate, apart; private, secret; remote; hidden;— secretum, i, n. secret, mystery, place of retreat.

secta, ae, f. way, mode, manner, method; sect, school.   [adherent.

sectātor, ōris, m. follower, attendant,

sectĭlis, e, a. cut; carved;—**sectilia pavimenta,** pavement of small stones; mosaic.

sectio, ōnis, f. cutting off; parcelling out; confiscation; selling by auction of forfeited goods.

sector, ātus, I. v.a. dep. to follow continually *or* eagerly; to pursue; to hunt, to chase; *fig.* to strive after.

sector, ōris, m. cutter; cut-throat; sequestrator; buyer of confiscated goods.

sectūræ, ārum, f. pl. mines.

sēcŭbĭtus, ūs, m. sleeping alone.

sēcŭbo, ui, I. v.n. to sleep alone; *fig.* to live in solitude.

sēc . . ., v. **sæc . . .**

secum = cum se.

sēcunda, ōrum, n. pl. prosperity.

sēcundæ, ārum, f. pl. second *or* inferior parts (in plays).

sēcundāni, ōrum, soldiers of the second legion.   [ling, inferior.

sēcundārius, a, um, a. second-rate, midd-

sēcundo, ad. secondly.   [to promote.

sēcundo, I. v.a. to favour, to further,

sēcundum, ad. & pr. after, behind; along; next to; in favour of; according to.

sēcundus, a, um, a. second; following; next; inferior, secondary; favourable;—**res secundæ,** prosperity.

sēcūrē, ad. carelessly, indifferently.

sēcūrĭfĕr, sēcūrĭgĕr, a, um, a. armed with an axe.   [sovereignty.

sēcūris, is, f. axe, hatchet; authority,

sēcūrĭtas, ātis, f. unconcern; carelessness; safety, security.

sēcūrus, a, um, a. unconcerned; careless, reckless; safe, secure; serene, tranquil; untroubled; easy, offhand.

sēcŭs, ad. & pr. otherwise; amiss;— **non** —, just so; (comparative) **sēcius; —non sēcius,** none the less;—**nihilo sēcius,** nevertheless.

sēcūtor, ōris, m. follower, attendant.

sĕd, c. but; however; yet; but also; — **enim,** but truly; — **etiam,** but also.

sēdātē, ad. calmly.

sēdātio, ōnis, f. (act of) calming, allaying.

sēdātus, a, um, a. calm, sedate.

sēdĕcim, a. num. sixteen.

sēdentārius, a, um, a. sedentary.

sēdeo, sēdi, sessum, 2. v.n. to be seated, to sit; to remain; to linger; to keep the field; to be firmly fixed; to strike home (of a weapon); to sit in court; to settle; to subside.

sēdēs, is, f. seat, bench, chair, throne; abode; residence; temple; place; situation, foundation.

sēdīle, is, n. seat, bench, stool, chair.

sēdītio, ōnis, f. separation; mutiny, sedition; dissension, quarrel.

sēdītiōsē, ad. seditiously.

sēdītiōsus, a, um, a. factious, mutinous, seditious; quarrelsome.

sēdo, 1. v.a. & n. to settle, to allay, to appease; to check, to stop.

sēdūco, xi, ctum, 3. v.a. to lead aside or apart; to separate.

sēductio, ōnis, f. leading aside, seducing.

sēductus, a, um, a. distant.

sēdūlĭtas, ātis, f. assiduity, zeal, sedulousness; officiousness.

sēdŭlo, ad. diligently, industriously, assiduously; sedulously; on purpose.

sēdŭlus, a, um, a. diligent, industrious, assiduous, sedulous; officious.

sēdum, i, n. stonecrop.

sĕgĕs, ĕtis, f. corn-field; crop; field, soil.

segmentum, i, n. slice, geographical zone, pl. strips of tinsel, flounces, trimmings.

segmentātus, a, um, a. embroidered, flowered.

segnē, ad. sluggishly, lazily;—non segnius, haud segnius, none the less keenly.

segnis, e, a. slow, sluggish, inactive, unenergetic; cowardly; unfruitful.

segnĭter, ad. slowly, sluggishly, unenergetically. [gishness; inactivity.

segnĭtia, ae, f., segnĭties, ēi, f. sluggishness; inactivity.

sēgrĕgo, 1. v.a. to separate from the flock; to separate, to remove; to divide.

sējŭgis, is, m. team of six horses; chariot drawn by six horses.

sējunctim, ad. separately.

sējunctio, ōnis, f. separation.

sējungo, nxi, nctum, 3. v.a. to disunite, to separate.

sēlectio, ōnis, f. choice, selection.

sēlibra, ae, f. half-pound. [choose.

sēlĭgo, lēgi, lectum, 3. v.a. to select, to

sella, ae, f. seat, chair, stool; sedan;— sella curulis, magistrate's chair.

sellāria, ae, f. sitting-room.

sellisternia, ōrum, n. pl. religious banquet for female deities.

sellŭla, ae, f. little stool; sedan.

sellŭlārius, ii, m. sedentary worker.

sĕmel, ad. once, a single time; once for all; the first time; at any time, once, ever; — atque iterum, once and again.

sēmen, ĭnis, n. seed; shoot; graft; progeny, posterity; element; cause; occasion; origin; author, instigator.

sēmentis, is, f. sowing; young corn; seed-time.

sēmentĭvus, a, um, a. pertaining to sowing; occurring at seed-time.

sēmento, 1. v.n. to run to seed.

sēmestris, e, a. half-yearly.

sēmēsus, a, um, a. half-eaten, half-consumed.

sēmet, pn. himself; herself; themselves.

sēmi, inseparable particle = half, demi . . .

sēmiădăpertus, a, um, a. half-opened.

sēmiambustus, a, um, a. half-burned, scorched.

sēmiănĭmis, e, sēmiănĭmus, a, um, a. half-alive, half-dead.

sēmiăpertus, a, um, a. half-open.

sēmibarbărus, a,um, a. semi-barbarous.

sēmibōs, bŏvis, m. half-bull (i.e. the Minotaur).

sēmicăper, pri, m. half-goat (Pan).

sēmicoctus, a, u n, a. parboiled.

sēmicrēmātus, a, um, a., sēmicrĕmus, a, um, a. half-b urned.

sēmideus, a, um, a. half-divine.

sēmidoctus, a, um, a. half-learned.

sēmiermis, e, sēmiermus, a, um, a. half-armed.

sēmifactus, a, um, a. half-finished.

sēmifĕr, a, um, a. half-bestial, half-savage.

sēmigræcus, i, m. half a Greek.

sēmigro, 1. v.n. to go or wander away.

sēmihians, tis, a. half-open.

sēmihŏmo, ĭnis, m. half man and half beast; half-wild.

sēmihōra, ae, f. half an hour.

sēmiĭnānis, e, a. half-full.

sēmilăcĕr, a, um, a. half-torn.

sēmimărīnus, a, um, a. amphibious.

sēmimas, āris, m. hermaphrodite; —, a. gelded, castrated.

sēmĭnārium, ii, n. nursery-garden, seed-plot.

sēmĭnātor, ōris, m. sower; producer, author. [dead.

sēmĭnĕcis, a. (without nominative) half-dead.

sēmĭnium, ii, n. race, stock, breed; kind.

sēmĭno, 1. v.a. plant, beget, propagate, sēmĭnūdus, a, um, a. half-naked.

sēmiorbis, is, m. semicircle.

sēmĭpĕdālis, e, a. measuring half a foot.

sēmĭpēs, pĕdis, m. half a foot.

sēmĭplēnus, a, um, a. half-full; half-manned.

sēmǐpūtātus, a, um, a. half-pruned.
sēmǐrēductus, a, um, a. half bent back.
sēmǐrēfectus, a, um, a. half-repaired.
sēmǐrūtus, a, um, a. half-ruined or demolished. [half an acre of land.
sēmis, issis, m. half an as; half; 6%;
sēmǐsēpultus, a, um, a. half-buried.
sēmǐsomnus, a, um, a. half-asleep, drowsy.
sēmǐsūpǐnus, a, um, a. half-raised.
sēmǐta, ae, f. footpath, lane.
sēmǐustǔlo, v. semustulo.
sēmǐustus, a, um, a., v. semustus.
sēmǐviētus, a, um, a. half-withered.
sēmǐvir, i, m. half man and half beast, hermaphrodite; —, effeminate.
sēmǐvīvus, a, um, a. half-alive, almost dead.
sēmǐvōcālis, e, a. half-sounding.
sēmǒdius, ii, m. half a peck.
sēmōtus, a, um, a. distant, remote.
sēmōveo, mōvi, mōtum, 2. v.a. to move or put aside; to separate.
semper, ad. always, ever, for ever.
sempervīvum, i, n. houseleek.
sempǐternus, a, um, a. everlasting, perpetual, eternal.
sēmuncia, ae, f. half an ounce; twenty-fourth part (of a pound, etc.).
sēmunciālis, e, sēmunciārius, a, um, a. of half an ounce.
sēmustǔlo, 1. v.a. to char, to singe.
sēmustus, a, um, half-burnt.
sěnācǔlum, i, n. parliament-house, council-chamber.
sěnārius, ii, m. verse consisting of six feet.
sěnātor, ōris, m. member of the Senate, senator.
sěnātōrius, a, um, a. senatorial.
sěnātus, ūs, m. Senate.
sěnātusconsultum, i, n. decree of the Senate.
sěněcio, onis, m. ragwort; cineraria.
sěnecta, ae, sěnectūs, f. ūtis, old age, senility.
sěneo, ui, 2. v.n. to be old; to grow old.
sěnesco, nui, 3. v.n. to grow old; to grow hoary; fig. to grow weak, to waste away; to decline; to become exhausted.
sěnex, sěnis, c. old man; old woman; —, a. old, aged.
sěnī, ae, a, a. num. six each; six.
sěnīdēni, ae, a, a. num. sixteen each.
sěnīlis, e, a. aged, senile.
sěnio, ōnis, m. (the number) six.
sěnior, ōris, a. elder;—seniores priores, let elders go first.
sěnium, ii, n. weakness of age; decline, decay; fig. old fellow; moroseness; trouble, vexation. [ideas.
sensa, ōrum, n. pl. sentiments, thoughts,

sensǐbilis, e, a. perceptible by the senses.
sensǐfěr, a, um, causing feeling.
sensilis, e, a. sensible, possessing sense.
sensim, ad. perceptibly; slowly, gently, gradually.
sensus, ūs, m. · faculty of feeling, perception, sensation, sense; affection, emotion; disposition; mind, reason; meaning, signification (grammatical sentence);—communis —, human feelings, conscience of mankind.
sententia, ae, f. opinion, sentiment; determination, decision; idea; judgment; advice; vote; meaning; period; sentence; axiom; aphorism;—ex sententia, satisfactorily, to one's liking.
sententiǒla, ae, f. short sentence.
sententiōsus, a, um, a. sententious.
senticētum, i, n. place full of briers.
sentīna, ae, f. sink in the hold of a ship; bilgewater; fig. dregs of the people, rabble.
sentio, si, sum, 4. v.a. to discern by the senses; to feel, to hear, to see; to suffer, to undergo; to perceive, to notice; to think, to deem; to vote, to declare.
sentis, is, m. (rarely f.) thorn, brier, bramble.
sentisco, 3. v.n. to begin to know.
sentus, a, um, a. rough, rugged.
seorsum, seorsus, ad. asunder, separately, apart.
sēpar, ǎris, a. separate.
sēpǎrābilis, e, a. separable.
sēpǎrātim, ad. asunder, apart, separately.
sēpǎrātio, ōnis, f. severing, separation.
sēpǎro, 1. v.a. to put apart; to separate, to divide; fig. to distinguish; to except.
sēpělio, ivi & ii, pultum, 4. v.a. to bury, to inter; fig. to ruin, to destroy.
sēpes, v. saepes.
sēpia, ae, f. cuttle-fish; ink.
sēpio, v. saepio.
sēplāsia, ae, f. perfumer's shop.
sēpōno, pōsui, pōsǐtum, 3. v.a. to put apart or aside; to separate, to pick out; to banish.
seps, sēpis, m. venomous serpent.
septem, a. num. seven.
September, bris, a. pertaining to the seventh month of the old Roman year or to September.
septemděcim, v. septendecim.
septemflǔus, a, um, a. running in seven streams.
septemgěmǐnus, a, um, a. sevenfold.
septempědālis, e, a. seven feet long.
septemplex, adj. sevenfold.
septemtrio, v. septentrio. [temviri.
septemvǐrātus, ūs, m. office of the sep-

septemvĭri, ōrum, m. pl. college *or* board of seven men.

septēnārius, a, um, a. containing seven; septenary.

septendĕcim, a. num. seventeen.

septēni, ae, a, a. num. seven each; seven.

septennis, v. septuennis.

septentrio, ōnis, m. north, northern regions.

septentriōnālis, e, a. northern.

septentriōnes, um, m. pl. Great Bear; Little Bear; *fig.* north, northern region; north wind.

septicus, a, um, a. putrefactive.

septies, ad. seven times.

septĭmāni, ōrum, m. pl. soldiers of the seventh legion.

septĭmus, a, um, a. num. seventh;—**septĭmum,** ad. the seventh time.

septĭmusdĕcĭmus, a, um, a. seventeenth.

septingēnārius, a, um, a. of seven hundred.   [hundredth.

septingentēsĭmus, a, um, a. num. seven-

septingenti, a, a, a. num. seven hundred.

septingenties, ad. seven hundred times.

septuāgēni, ae, a, a. seventy each.

septuāgēsĭmus, a, um, a. num. seventieth.

septuāgies, ad. seventy times.

septuāḡintā, a. num. seventy.

septuennis, e, a. seven years old.

septunx, uncis, m. seven-twelfths.

sēpulcrālis, e, a. sepulchral.

sēpulcrētum, ĭ, n. burying-place.

sēpulcrum, ĭ, n. grave, sepulchre; monument.

sēpultūra, ae, f. burial, interment.

sēquax, ācis, a. (poet.) following *or* seeking after, pursuing; clinging; (of flames) lambent, darting.

sēquēla, ae, f. sequel, consequence.

sēquester, tris, m. mediator; go-between, agent; —**, tra, trum,** a. intermediate.

sēquestra, ae, f. female go-between, mediatress.

sēquestrum, ĭ, n. arbitration, reference of a dispute to a mediator.

sēquius, v. secius.   [wood.

sequoia (mod. hort.), Californian red-

sēquor, sĕcūtus, 3. v.a. dep. to follow, to come *or* go after, to attend; to pursue; to aim at; to result; to comply (with), to conform (to); to succeed.

sēra, ae, f. bar (for fastening doors).

sērēnĭtas, ātis, f. serene weather.

sērēno, 1. v.a. to make clear *or* serene, to clear up.

sērēnum, ĭ, n. fair weather.

sērēnus, a, um, a. clear, fair, bright, serene, cloudless; cheerful, glad, joyous, tranquil, serene.

sēresco, 3. v.n. to grow dry.

sēresco, 3. v.n. to curdle.

sēria, ae, f. large jar.

sēria, ōrum, n. pl. serious affairs.

sēriātim, ad. in series.

sērica, ae, f. silken garment.

sērĭcātus, a, um, a. clothed in silk.

sērĭcus, a, um, a. silken.

sēries, em, e, f. row, succession, series, chain; lineage.

sēris, ĭdis, f. endive.

sērium, ii, n., **sēria, ōrum,** pl. serious affairs;—**sērio,** ad. seriously, in earnest.

sērius, a, um, a. grave, earnest, serious.

sērius, ad. later, too late;—**serius aut citius,** sooner *or* later.

sermo, ōnis, m. conversation, discourse; disputation; report, rumour; diction, style; dialect; satire.

sermōcĭnātio, ōnis, f. discourse, conversation.   [talk with; to dispute.

sermōcĭnor, 1. v.n. dep. to converse, to

sermuncŭlus, ĭ, m. common talk, tittle-tattle.

sērō, ad. late, at a late hour; too late.

sēro, sĕrui, sertum, 3. v.a. to put in a row, to join; to plait, to interweave, to entwine; *fig.* to combine, to contrive; to engage (in).

sēro, sēvi, sātum, 3. v.a. to sow, to plant; *fig.* to beget; to produce; to disseminate, to propagate; to cause, to occasion.

sērōtĭnus, a, um, a. backward.

serpens, entis, f. snake, serpent.

serpĕrastra, ōrum, n. pl. knee-splints; *fig.* (jest.) martinets.

serpo, psi, ptum, 3. v.n. to creep, to crawl; *fig.* to spread abroad; to increase, to prevail.

serpyllum, ĭ, n. wild thyme.

serra, ae, f. saw.

serrātus, a, um, a. serrated; notched.

serrŭla, ae, f. little saw.

serta, ae, f. chaplet.

sertum, ĭ, n. garland, wreath (of flowers).

sērum, ĭ, n. watery part of curdled milk, whey.

sērum, ĭ, n. late hour, late time.

sērus, a, um, a. late; too late.

serva, ae, f. female slave.

servābĭlis, e, a. that may be saved.

servans, antis, a. keeping; observing.

servātor, ōris, m. watcher, deliverer, preserver; saviour.

servātrix, ĭcis, f. female preserver.

servilis, e, a. slavish, servile.

servilĭter, ad. slavishly, servilely.

servio, ĭvi & ĭi, ĭtum, 4. v.n. to be a slave, to serve, to be in service; to be of use (to); to gratify; to be subject (to).

servĭtium, ii, n. slavery, servitude; *fig.* subjection; servants, slaves.

servĭtūdo, ĭnis, f. slavery, servitude.

servĭtūs, ūtis, f. slavery, serfdom; (law) liability (of lands, etc.); servants, slaves; *fig.* subjection.

servo, 1. v.a. to save, to preserve; to deliver; to protect; to keep, to retain, to uphold; to lay up; to pay attention to; to observe, to watch; (poet.) to dwell in.

servŭla, ae, f. servant-girl.

servŭlus, i, m. servant-lad.

servus, i, m. slave, servant, serf; —, a, um, a. slavish, servile; subject; (law) liable (to).

sēsăma, ae, f. sesame.

sescēni, ae, a, a. six hundred each.

sescentēsĭmus, a, um, a. six hundredth.

sescenti, ae, a, a. six hundred; any large number.

sescenties, ad. six hundred times; an indefinite number of times.

sescuncia, ae, f., sescunx, uncis, m. ounce and a half.

sescŭplum, i, n. the whole and half as much.

sēse, pn. himself, herself; themselves.

sesqui . . ., ad. more by a half.

sesquialter, a, um, a. one and a half.

sesquihōra, ae, f. an hour and a half.

sesquijūgĕrum, i, n. an acre and a half.

sesquĭmensis, is, m. a. month and a half.

sesquĭmōdius, ii, m. a peck and a half.

sesquĭpĕdālis, e, a. of a foot and a half; *fig.* (of words) half a yard long.

sesquĭpēs, pĕdis, m. a foot and a half.

sesquitertius, a, um, a. one and a third.

sessĭlis, e, a. fit for sitting upon; sitting low.

sessio, ōnis, f. sitting; seat; loitering, tarrying; session.

sessĭto, 1. v.a. to sit often.

sessiuncŭla, ae, f. little company.

sestertium, n. (originally gen, pl. after milia), a thousand sesterces;—decies centena milia sestertium, a million sesterces.

sestertius, a, um, a. two and a half; —, ii, m. two asses and a half, sesterce.

set, v. sed.

sēta, v. saeta.

sētĭger, a, um, v. saetiger.

sētōsus, v. saetosus.

seu, v. sive.

sĕvērē, ad. gravely, seriously, austerely, severely.

sĕvērĭtas, ātis, f. gravity, sternness, strictness, severity.

sĕvērus, a, um, a. grave, strict, austere, stern, severe; (of wine) tart.

sēvŏco, 1. v.a. to call apart *or* aside, to call away to; *fig.* to withdraw, to remove.

sex, num. six.

sexāgēnārius, a, um, a. of *or* containing sixty; sixty years old; —, ii, m. sexagenarian.

sexāgēni, ae, a, a. num. sixty each.

sexāgēsĭmus, a, um, a. num. sixtieth.

sexāgies, ad. sixty times.

sexāgintā, a. num. sixty.

sexangŭlus, a, um, a. hexagonal. [dred.

sexcēnārius, a, um, a. containing six hun-

sexc . . ., v. sesc . . .

sexdĕcim, v. sedecim.

sexennis, e, a. six years old.

sexennium, ii, n. (period of) six years.

sexies, ad. six times.

sextādĕcĭmāni, ōrum, m. pl. soldiers of the sixteenth legion.

sextans, antis, m. sixth part; two ounces.

sextantārius, a, um, a. of two ounces weight. [*or* weight; pint.

sextārius, ii, m. sixth part of a measure

Sextīlis, e, a. pertaining to the sixth month of the old Roman year; —, m. (month) August.

sextŭla, ae, f. sixth part of an ounce.

sextus, a, um, a. num. sixth;—sextum, ad. the sixth time.

sextusdĕcĭmus, a, um, a. num. sixteenth.

sexus, ūs, m. sex.

sī, c. if.

sībĭlo, 1. v.n. & a. to hiss, to whistle; to hiss at;—sībĭlor, 1. v. dep. to be hissed at.

sībĭlus, i, m. sībĭlum, i, n. hissing, whistling; hissing at (*or* off); —, a, um, a. hissing, whistling.

Sĭbylla, ae, f. prophetess, Sibyl.

Sĭbyllīnus, a, um, a. sibylline.

sĭc, ad. in this *or* in such a manner, so; thus; to such a degree; as things stand; just so; yes.

sīca, ae, f. poniard, dagger.

sīcārius, ii, m. assassin; ruffian.

siccē, ad. *fig.* solidly; plainly.

siccesco, 3. v.n. to grow dry.

siccĭtas, ātis, f. dryness; drought; *fig.* solidity; dryness. [haust.

sicco, 1. v.a. to dry up; (poet.) to ex-

siccŏcŭlus, a, um, a. having dry eyes.

siccŭlus, a, um, a. dryish.

siccum, i, n. dry ground.

siccus, a, um, a. dry; rainless; firm, solid; vigorous; thirsty; abstemious, sober; insipid; jejune.

sicīlicus, i, m. ¼ of an ounce or inch.

sĭcīlio, 4. v.a. to mow again.

sicĭnē, ad. so? thus?

sĭcŭbi, ad. if anywhere, wheresoever.

sĭcundĕ, ad. if from any place.
sĭcŭt, sĭcŭtī, ad. so as, just as, as; as it really is; as it were; as for instance; just exactly; (just) as if.
sīdĕrālis, e, a. of the stars.
sīdĕrātio, ōnis, f. blight.
sīdĕreus, a, um, a. pertaining to the stars; starry; bright; excellent; high; heavenly.
sīdĕrītes, ae, m. sīdĕrītis, is, f. loadstone.
sīdĕror, 1. v.a. to be blasted or suffer sunstroke.
sīdo, sīdi, 3. v.n. to settle; to sink down; to sit fast; to be stranded; to disappear; to vanish.
sīdus, ĕris, n. star, constellation; climate, season, weather; storm, tempest; fig. glory, pride; height; destiny.
sĭgilla, ōrum, n. pl. little images; seal.
sĭgillātim, ad. v. singillatim.
sĭgillātus, a, um, a. adorned with figures.
sigma, ătis, n. crescent-shaped couch for seven persons to sit on.
signātor, ōris, m. sealer, signer, witness (to a will).
signĭfer, a, um, a. bearing signs or images; starry; —, i, m. ensign, standard-bearer; fig. leader.
signĭficanter, ad. significantly.
signĭficantia, ae, f. significancy.
signĭficātio, ōnis, f. signifying; expression, indication, sign, token; assent, applause; sense, meaning; emphasis.
signĭficātus, ūs, m. prognostic.
signĭfico, 1. v.a. to show, to point out, to indicate; to intimate, to signify; to portend, to prognosticate; (of words) to mean.
signo, 1. v.a. to mark (out), to designate; to imprint; to seal up; to coin, to stamp; to adorn; to remark; to observe; to prescribe.
signum, i, n. mark, token, sign; standard, ensign; cohort; signal, watchword; prognostic, symptom; image, picture, statue; seal, signet; constellation;—signa ferre, to break camp;—ab signis discedere, to break the ranks.
sĭlācĕus, a, um, a. yellow, ochre-coloured.
sĭlēnē (mod. hort.), campion.
sĭlens, entis, p. & a. still, calm, quiet, silent;—silentes, um, c. the dead.
sĭlentium, ii, n. stillness, silence; repose, tranquillity.
sĭleo, ui, 2. v.n. & a. to be silent, to keep silence; not to speak of; to cease, to rest.
sĭler, ĕris, n. willow.
sĭlesco, ui, 3. v.n. to be hushed.
sĭlex, ĭcis, c. pebble-stone, flint; rock; fig. hard-hearted person.

sĭlĭcernium, ii, n. funeral supper; fig. skeleton.
sĭlīgĭneus, a, um, a. wheaten.
sĭlīgo, ĭnis, f. fine flour.
sĭlīqua, ae, f. pod, husk (of leguminous plants);—siliquæ, pl. pulse.
sĭlūrus, i, m. (fish) shad.
silva, ae, f. wood, forest; grove; orchard; crop, growth; trees; fig. abundance, quantity.
silvāni, ōrum, m. pl. sylvan deities.
silvātĭcus, a, um, a. of or belonging to woods.
silvesco, 3. v.n. to run to wood.
silvestris, e, a. pertaining to a wood or forest; woody; wild; pastoral, rural.
silvĭcola, ae, g.c. inhabitant of forests.
silvōsus, a, um, a. woody.
sīmia, ae, f. ape; sometimes fig. m.
sĭmĭla, ae, sĭmĭlāgo, ĭnis, f. flour.
sĭmĭlis, e, a. like, resembling, similar.
sĭmĭlĭter, ad. in like manner, similarly.
sĭmĭlĭtūdo, ĭnis, f. likeness, resemblance, similitude; comparison, simile.
sīmĭŏlus, i, m. little ape.
sĭmĭtū, ad. at the same time; together.
sīmius, ii, m. ape; mimic.
simplex, ĭcis, a. simple, unmixed; fig. ingenuous, frank, honest; straightforward.   [frankness, honesty.
simplĭcĭtas, ătis, f. simplicity; plainness,
simplĭcĭter, ad. simply, plainly, naturally, directly; candidly.
simplus, a, um, a. simple.
simpŭvium, ii, n. chalice or cup used in sacrifices.
sĭmul, ad. at once, together, at the same time.
sĭmŭlāc, sĭmŭlatquĕ, ad. as soon as.
sĭmŭlācrum, i, n. likeness, image, form, portrait; phantom, shade; emblem, type; fig. appearance.
sĭmŭlāmen, ĭnis, n. copy, imitation.
sĭmŭlātĕ, ad. feignedly, pretendedly, not sincerely.   [feint, deceit.
sĭmŭlātio, ōnis, f. feigning, pretence,
sĭmŭlātor, ōris, m. imitator; pretender, hypocrite.
sĭmŭlatque, v. simulac.
sĭmŭlo, 1. v.a. to imitate, to copy, to represent; to simulate, to counterfeit, to pretend, to feign.
sĭmultas, ătis, f. hostile encounter, dissension, enmity, rivalry, jealousy; grudge.
sĭmŭlus, a, um, sīmus, a, um, a. flat-nosed, snub-nosed.
sīn, c. if not, if however, if on the contrary, but if.
sĭnāpe, is, n., sĭnāpis, is, f. mustard-seed,

sincērē, ad. sincerely, honestly.
sincēritas, ātis, f. cleanness, soundness, honesty.
sincērus, a, um, a. clean, sound, whole, real, genuine; *fig.* pure, chaste; uncorrupted; sincere.
sinciput, ĭtis, m. brain.
sindon, ōnis, f. fine linen, lawn.
sĭnĕ, pr. without;—sine die, without a day being fixed, an indefinite adjournment;—sine qua non, (a condition) without which it is impossible to come to terms.
singillātim, ad. singly, one by one.
singŭlāris, e, a. alone, single, solitary, singular; the singular (number); *fig.* matchless, unique, excellent.
singŭlārĭter, ad. particularly, exceedingly, in the singular number.
singŭl(ā)tim, v. singillatim.
singŭli, ae, a, a. one to each, separate, single; individual.
singultim, ad. sobbingly.
singulto, ātum, 1. v.n. & a. to sob, to hiccup; to rattle in the throat; to breathe out with sobs.
singultus, ūs, m. sobbing.
sinister, tra, trum, a. left, on the left; *fig.* awkward; wrong; unlucky, bad; auspicious, lucky, favourable.
sinistērĭtas, ātis, f. unluckiness.
sinistra, ae, f. left hand *or* side.
sinistrā, ad. on the left hand.
sinistrē, ad. badly, unfairly, wrongly, perversely; unluckily.
sinistrorsum, sinistrorsus, ad. to the left.
sĭno, sĭvi, sĭtum, 3. v.a. to let, to leave; to allow, to permit;—sine, so be it; granted;—ne Juppiter sirit, God forbid!
sīnum, i, n. sīnus, i, m. bowl, milk-pail; large drinking-vessel.
sinuo, 1. v.a. to wind, to curve; to bow.
sinuōsus, a, um, a. winding, sinuous; *fig.* diffuse.
sinus, ūs, m. curve; fold; hollow; bosom (of a garment, etc.); lap; curl, ringlet; bay, gulf; purse, money; point of land; love; asylum; inmost part; hiding-place. [v. supparum.
sīpārium, ii, n. drop-curtain in a theatre;
sīpho, ōnis, m. siphon; funnel; syringe.
sīquando (si quando), ad. if ever, if at any time.
sīquĭdem, c. if indeed, if at least, if only; although; inasmuch as, since.
sīquis, qua, quid, pn. if any one, if any person. [tress; melody, music.
Sīrēn, is, f. Siren, mermaid; *fig.* seduc-
Sīrius, ii, m. dog-star, Sirius;—, a, um, a. of the dog-star; sultry.

sīrus, i, m. pit (for preserving corn).
sisto, stĭti, stătum, 3. v.a. & n. to set, to put, to place; to stay, to stop; to arrest; to support; to build, to erect; to stand still; to last; to endure; to decide (upon); to appear, to present oneself;—vadimonium sistere, to make good one's bail (by appearing in court).
sistrum, i, n. timbrel, metallic rattle.
sĭtella, ae, f. ballot-box (partly filled with water).
sĭtĭcŭlōsus, a, um, a. arid, parched.
sĭtiens, entis, a. thirsting, thirsty, athirst; arid, dry, parched; *fig.* greedy, thirsting for.
sĭtienter, ad. thirstily; greedily.
sĭtio, 1vi & ii, 4. v.n. & a. to thirst, to be thirsty; *fig.* to long for, to covet.
sĭtis, is, f. thirst; aridity, dryness; greediness.
sĭtŭla, ae, f. pail, ballot-box.
sĭtus, a, um, a. situate(d); built, founded; buried.
sĭtus, ūs, m. situation, position, site; structure; rust; filth; wasting away; dulness.
sīvĕ, c. or if; — ... —, whether ... or, whether.
smăragdus, i, m. emerald; beryl, jasper.
smăris, ĭdis, f. anchovy.
smīlax, ăcis, f. bindweed, sarsaparilla.
smyrna, ae, f. myrrh.
sŏbŏles, v. suboles.
sōbrĭē, ad. soberly, frugally.
sōbrĭĕtas, ātis, f. sobriety; gravity.
sōbrīnus; i, m. sobrīna, ae, f. cousin-german.
sōbrius, a, um, a. sober; *fig.* continent, moderate, temperate; prudent, reasonable.
soccŭlus, i, m. little shoe.
soccus, i, m. shoe, slipper, sock; shoe worn by comic actors; *fig.* comedy.
sŏcer, ĕri, m. father-in-law;—sōcĕri, parents-in-law.
sōcia, f., v. socius.
sōcĭābĭlis, e, a. sociable.
sōcĭālis, e, a. sociable, social; confederate, conjugal.
sōcĭālĭter, ad. socially, in a social manner.
sōcĭĕtas, ātis, f. association, company; (com.) partnership; trading company; society; alliance, confederacy.
sōcĭo, 1. v.a. to associate; to share with; —sōcĭāri, to take part (in).
sōcĭus, i, m. sōcia, ae, f. sharer, partner, companion, associate; consort, spouse; ally, confederate.
sōcĭus, a, um, a. sharing, partaking, associated; allied, confederate.

sōcordia, ae, f. carelessness, indolence.
sōcorditer, ad. carelessly.
sōcors, ordis, a. silly, stupid, thoughtless; careless, sluggish.
socrus, ūs, f. mother-in-law.
sōdālicium, ii. n. fellowship, intimacy, companionship; secret society.
sōdālis, is, m. mate, fellow, comrade, boon-companion; member (of a corporation); accomplice.
sōdālitas, ātis, f. fellowship, brotherhood, intimacy; association; club; unlawful society.
sōdālitium, v. sodalicium.
sōdes (=si audes, si audies), if you please, pray. [place, heat of the sun; day.
sōl, sōlis, m. sun; east; sunlight; sunny
solacium, v. solatium.
sōlāmen, inis, n. comfort, solace.
sōlānum, i, n. (mod. hort.), potato.
sōlāris, e, a. solar.
sōlārium, ii, n. sundial; clock; balcony.
sōlātiōlum, i, n. little comfort or solace.
sōlātium, ii, n. solace, comfort, relief.
sōlātor, ōris, m. comforter.
sōlea, ae, f. sole, sandal; horseshoe.
sōleārius, ii, m. sandal-maker.
sōleātus, a, um, a. wearing sandals.
sōlemnis, etc., v. sollennis, etc. [to use.
sōleo, itus sum, 2. v.n. to be accustomed,
sōlers, etc., v. sollers, etc.
sōllicito, v. sollicito.
solidāgo (mod. hort.), golden-rod.
sōlidē, ad. solidly; really; perfectly, fully.
sōlidesco, 3. v.n. to grow solid or sound.
sōlidipes, ēdis, a. whole-hoofed.
sōliditas, ātis, f. solidity.
sōlido, 1. v.a. to make solid; to make whole or sound; to strengthen; to fasten together.
sōlidum, i, n., v. solidus.
sōlidus, a, um, a. solid, firm, dense, compact; complete, entire; fig. sound; genuine, real, true;—solidum, i, n. firm ground.
sōlidus, i, m. a pound (in money).
sōlitārius, a, um, a. alone, lonely, solitary.
sōlitūdo, inis, f. loneliness, solitariness; desert, wilderness; fig. deprivation, destitution.
sōlitus, a, um, p. & a. wonted, accustomed, usual, habitual, ordinary.
sōlium, ii, n. seat; throne; fig. rule, dominion. [tary.
sōlivāgus, a, um, a. roving alone; solisollemnis, e, a. solemn; festive, religious; common, wonted, usual;—sollemne, is, n. usual custom, common way, ceremony, solemnity.

sollemniter, ad. solemnly; according to custom. [sagacious.
sollers, tis, a. skilful, clever; intelligent,
sollerter, ad. skilfully; sagaciously, shrewdly.
sollertia, ae, f. shrewdness, ingenuity; skill; expertness; quickness.
sollicitātio, ōnis, f. instigation.
sollicitē, ad. carefully, earnestly, urgently, diligently.
sollicito, 1. v.a. to move violently; to stir, to shake, to agitate; to disturb; to frighten; to distress; to provoke; to incite; to instigate; to persuade, to solicit.
sollicitūdo, inis, f. care, anxiety, solicitude.
sollicitus, a, um, a. stirred up, agitated, disturbed; fig. uneasy, troubled, anxious, solicitous; watchful; timid, vacillating.
solliferreum, an iron javelin.
sōlo, 1. v.a. to lay waste.
sōloecismus, i, m. (gr.) solecism; a grammatical fault in construction.
sōlor, ātus, 1. v.a. dep. to comfort, to console, to solace; (of things) to relieve, to soothe.
solstitiālis, e, a. solstitial; midsummer; solar.
solstitium, ii, n. solstice; summer-time.
sōlum, i, n. bottom; earth, ground, soil; sole of the foot or shoe, country, region, land; foundation; vault of heaven.
sōlum, ad. alone, only, merely;—non — ... sed, not only ... but.
sōlus, a, um, a. alone, only, single, sole; solitary.
sōlūtē, ad. freely; carelessly; loosely; fig. fluently.
sōlūtio, ōnis, f. loosening; dissolution; payment; explanation.
sōlūtus, a, um, a. loose, unbound; thin, free; wild, dissolute; lawless; cheerful; fluent; loosely flowing; unbiassed.
solvo, solvi, sōlūtum, 3. v.a. to loosen, to unbind; to separate, to disengage; to dissolve; to melt; to open; to fulfil, to perform; to explain, to solve; to banish; to deliver, to release; to acquit; to cancel;—solvere navem, to set sail;—solvendo esse, to be solvent; —solvitur, the question is solved.
somniculōsus, a, um, a. drowsy, sleepy; sluggish.
somnifer, a, um, somnificus, a, um, a. soporific.
somnio, 1. v.a. to dream; to dream of or see in a dream; to fancy, to talk idly or foolishly.

somnium, ii, n. dream; *fig.* fancy, nonsense.

somnus, i, m. sleep; *fig.* sloth, night; death. [sounding.

sŏnābĭlis, e, sŏnax, ācis, a. noisy,

sŏnĭpes, ĕdis, m. (poet.) horse, steed.

sŏnĭtus, ūs, m. noise, sound, din.

sŏno, ui, ĭtum, 1. v.n. & a. to make a noise, to sound, to resound; to utter, to speak; to cry out, to sing.

sŏnor, ōris, m. sound, noise, din.

sŏnōrus, a, um, a. noisy, loud, resounding, sonorous. [malefactor, criminal.

sons, sontis, a. guilty, criminal; —, m.

sŏnus, i, m. noise, sound.

sŏphistēs, ae, m. sophist.

sŏphus, i, m. wise man, scholar.

sōpio, īvi & ii, ītum, 4. v.a. to lull to sleep; to stun; *fig.* to calm, to quiet; to kill.

sŏpor, ōris, m. stupefaction; lethargy; *fig.* laziness; sleeping-draught.

sŏpōrĭfer, a, um, a. bringing sleep; drowsy, sleepy.

sŏpōro, ātum, 1. v.a. to put asleep; *fig.* to stupefy, to overpower; to render soporific.

sŏpōrus, a, um, a. sleepy, drowsy.

sorbeo, ui, 2. v.a. to suck in, to drink down, to swallow; *fig.* to absorb, to swallow up, to put up with.

sorbillo, 1. v.a. to sip.

sorbĭlo, ad. sippingly; *fig.* bit by bit.

sorbĭtio, ōnis, f. draught; pottage; potion.

sorbum, i, n. sorb-apple, service-berry.

sorbus, i, f. service-tree.

sordeo, 2. v.n. to be dirty, filthy, foul, nasty; *fig.* to be despised.

sordēs, is, f. dirt, filth, nastiness, squalor; *fig.* baseness, lowness; sordidness, niggardliness. [filthy.

sordesco, dui, 3. v.n. to become dirty *or*

sordĭdātus, a, um, a. shabbily dressed.

sordĭdē, ad. meanly; poorly, stingily.

sordĭdŭlus, a, um, a. dirty.

sordĭdus, a, um, a. dirty, foul, filthy; *fig.* base, low; vile; poor; small; paltry, niggardly, sordid.

sordĭtūdo, ĭnis, f. dirt, filth.

sŏrex, ĭcis, m. mouse. [mouse.

sŏrĭcīnus, a, um, a. pertaining to the

sŏrītēs, is, m. vicious syllogism.

sŏror, ōris, f. sister;— sŏrōres, pl. (poet.) the Muses; the Fates.

sŏrōrĭcīda, ae, g.c. murderer of a sister.

sŏrōrius, a, um, a. sisterly.

sors, tis, f. lot, drawing of lots; decision by lot; prophecy; answer of an oracle; fate, destiny; part; share; capital (bearing interest).

sortĭlĕgus, a, um, a. prophetic, foretelling; —, i, m. fortune-teller, diviner.

sortior, ītus sum, 4. v.n. & a. dep. to cast *or* draw lots; to assign, to allot; to obtain by lot; to divide, to share; to choose, to receive.

sortītio, ōnis, f. drawing of lots; choosing by lots.

sortīto, ad. by lot.

sortītor, ōris, m. caster of lots.

sortītus, ūs, m. casting *or* drawing of lots.

sospĕs, ĭtis, a. saving; safe and sound, uninjured; lucky, fortunate; auspicious.

sospĭta, ae, f. female preserver.

sospĭtālis, e, health-bringing.

sospĭto, 1. v.a. to save, to preserve.

spādix, ĭcis, m. nut-brown.

spādo, ōnis, m. eunuch.

spargo, sparsi, sparsum, 3. v.a. to strew, to scatter; to bestrew, to sprinkle, to bedew, to moisten; to disperse; to spread abroad; to distribute; to intersperse, to insert; to report.

sparsim, ad. here and there.

sparsio, ōnis, f. sprinkling.

spartārium, ii, broom-field.

spartārius, a, um, a. of broom.

spartum, i, n. Spanish broom.

spărus, i, short hunting-spear.

spasmus, i, m. cramp.

spastĭcus, a, um, a. affected with the cramp.

spătha, ae, f. a. wooden spoon, broad (two-edged) sword.

spătior, ātus, 1. v.n. dep. to walk about, to promenade; to expand, to spread out. [at large.

spătiōsē, ad. spaciously, widely, largely,

spătiōsus, a, um, a. roomy, ample, spacious; large, long; *fig.* prolonged.

spătium, ii, n. room, space; place for walking, open space; distance, interval; period; length; leisure; time; opportunity; measure; quantity.

spĕciālis, e, a. particular, proper, special.

spĕciālĭter, ad. specially; particularly.

spĕcies, ĕi, f. figure, shape; mien; semblance; pretence; display, splendour, beauty; vision; image, likeness; statue; quality, species.

spĕcillum, i, n. (surgical) probe; looking-glass.

spĕcĭmen, ĭnis, n. example, instance, specimen, proof; model, pattern.

spĕcio, exi, ectum, 3. v.a. to behold, to see, to regard. [well.

spĕciōse, ad. handsomely; splendidly;

spĕciōsus, a, um, a. showy, handsome, beautiful, splendid, brilliant; specious, plausible.

spectābĭlis, e, a. remarkable; admirable.

spectăcŭlum (āclum), i, n. show, sight, spectacle; (stage-)play; theatre.

spectāmen, ĭnis, n. essay, proof.

spectātē, ad. notedly; bravely.

spectātio, ōnis, f. sight, view; testing (of money); *fig.* respect.

spectātor, ōris, m. looker-on, spectator; critic, judge.

spectātrix, ĭcis, f. female beholder *or* observer.

spectio, ōnis, f. right of observing the auspices.

spectātus, a, um, a. tried, proved; worthy; excellent.

specto, I. v.a. to look at, to behold; to watch, to observe; (geographically) to lie, to face; to examine; to try; to consider, to have regard to; to judge (of).

spectrum, i, n. appearance, spectre.

spĕcŭla, ae, f. look-out, watch-tower; height.

spēcŭla, ae, f. slender hope.

spĕcŭlābĭlis, e, a. visible.

spĕcŭlābundus, a, um, a. on the watch.

spĕcŭlāria, ōrum, n. window; casement.

speculāria (mod. hort.), Venus's looking-glass.

spĕcŭlātor, ōris, m. spy, scout; *fig.* examiner, explorer.

spĕcŭlātōrius, a, um, a. spy . . ., relating to spies, watching.

spĕcŭlātrix, ĭcis, f. female spy, female watcher.

spĕcŭlor, ātus, I. v.a. dep. to behold, to view, to observe, to spy out, to watch, to examine, to explore; to wait for.

spĕcŭlum, i, n. looking-glass, mirror; copy, imitation.

spĕcus, ūs, m. f. or n. cavern, den; ditch, drain; pit; cavity, hollow (of any kind).

spēlæum, i, n. cavern, cave, den.

spēlunca, ae, f. cave; den, hole.

spērābĭlis, e, a. that may be hoped for.

spērātus, i, m. lover, bridegroom;—spērāta, ae, f. bride, sweetheart.

spernax, ācis, a. slighting, scornful.

sperno, sprēvi, sprētum, 3. v.a. to scorn, to despise, to contemn.

spēro, I. v.a. to expect, to look for.

spēs, spei, f. hope; expectation; object of hope; joy; anxiety, apprehension (of evil);—puer optimæ spei, a boy of the highest promise.

sphæra, ae, f. sphere, globe, ball; orb (of the heavenly bodies).

sphæristērium, ii, n. tennis-court; bowling-green.

spīca, ae, f. point; ear (of corn); spike; tuft.

spīceus, a, um, a. consisting of ears of corn.

spīco, I. v.a. to shoot out (as an ear of corn); to spike, to point the end.

spīcŭlātor, ōris, m. archer, spearman.

spīcŭlo, I. v.a. to sharpen the point.

spīcŭlum, i, n. sting; javelin; arrow.

spīna, ae, f. thorn; spine; backbone; fish-bone; quill;—spīnæ, pl. *fig.* difficulties, subtleties.

spīnācia (mod. hort.), spinach.

spīnētum, i, n. thorn-hedge.

spīneus, a, um, a. of thorns, thorny.

spīnifer, a, um, a. prickly, thorny.

spīnōsus, a, um, a. thorny, prickly; crabbed, obscure, difficult.

spīnus, i, f. blackthorn, bullace-tree, sloe-tree.

spīra, ae, f. fold, spire, circle; coil, twist.

spīrābĭlis, e, a. good to breathe; living vital.   [hole.

spīrācŭlum, , n. air-hole, breathing-

spīræa, ae, f. meadowsweet.

spīrāmen, ĭnis, spīrāmentum, i, n. breathing-hole, vent; pore; breathing-space; pause.

spīrĭtus, ūs, m. breath of air, breeze; breath, breathing; soul, mind; life; sigh; inspiration; spirit, courage; haughtiness, pride.

spīro, I. v.n. & v.a. to breathe, to blow, to respire; to live; to blow favourably; to be arrogant; to breathe out; to emit; to savour, to smell; to aim at, to aspire, to seek for.

spissāmentum, i, n. bung.

spissātio, ōnis, f. thickening.

spissē, ad. *fig.* slowly; with much ado.

spissesco, 3. v.n. to grow thick.

spissĭtas, ātis, spissĭtūdo, ĭnis, f. thickness.

spisso, I. v.a. to thicken, to condense.

spissus, a, um, a. thick, close, dense; crowded; difficult; slow; late.

splen, ēnis, m. milt *or* spleen.

splendeo, 2. v.n. to shine, to be bright; to glitter, to glisten; *fig.* to be illustrious.

splendesco, dui, 3. v.n. to become bright, to begin to shine; to display itself.

splendĭdē, ad. brightly; *fig.* brilliantly, nobly;—splendĭdē mendax, superbly untruthful.

splendĭdus, a, um, a. bright, shining, glittering, brilliant; splendid, sumptuous; illustrious, noble; fine, showy.

splendor, ōris, m. brilliance, splendour; magnificence; sumptuousness; honour, eminence.

splēnĭcus, a, um, a. splenetic.

splēnĭum, ii, n. spleenwort; plaster.

spŏdium, ii, n. cinders; slag.

spōliātio, ōnis, f. robbing, plundering, spoliation.

spōliātor, ōris, m. plunderer, robber.

spōlio, 1. v.a. to strip or rob of clothing; to plunder, to spoil, to rob.

spōlium, ii, n. skin, hide (of an animal stripped off); booty, spoil;—spōlia ōpīma, spoils taken by a general after a single combat with the opposing general.

sponda, ae, f. bed, couch, sofa.

spondæus, i, v. spondeus.

spondālium, ii, n. hymn.

spondeo, spŏpondi, sponsum, 2. v.a. to promise, to vow; to engage oneself; to assure; to betroth.

spondēus, i, m. spondee (metrical foot of 2 long syllables).

spondўlus, i, m. vertebra.

spongia, ae, f. sponge; asparagus-root; coat of mail.

spongiōsus, a, um, a. spongy.

sponsa, ae, f. bride.

sponsālia, ōrum, n. pl. betrothal.

sponsio, ōnis, f. solemn promise; guarantee, security; wager at law.

sponsor, ōris, m. bondsman, surety.

sponsum, i, n. agreement, covenant; engagement, promise.

sponsus, i, m. betrothed, bridegroom; suitor.

sponsus, ūs, m. betrothal; bail, bond.

sponte, ad. of one's own accord, freely, voluntarily, spontaneously; by oneself, alone.

sporta, ae, f. basket, pannier, sieve.

sportella, ae, f. little basket, fruit-basket.

sportŭla, ae, f., v. sportella; alms; gratuity.

sprētor, ōris, m. despiser, contemner.

spūma, ae, f. foam, froth, scum, spume.

spūmātus, ūs, m. foaming; froth.

spūmesco, 3. v.a. to begin to foam.

spūmeus, spūmĭfer, a, um, a. foaming, frothy.

spūmo, 1. v.n. & a. to foam; to cover with foam.

spūmōsus, a, um, a. foaming.

spuo, ui, ūtum, 3. v.n. & a. to spit, to spit out. [scenely.

spurcē, ad. fig. basely, villainously; obscenely.

spurcĭtia, ae, f. spurcĭties, ēi, f. filthiness, dirtiness; slovenliness; filth; dross; baseness; villainy.

spurco, 1. v.a. to defile, to pollute.

spurcus, a, um, a. dirty, nasty, impure; foul, base, low, mean.

spŭrius, a, um, a. of illegitimate birth.

spūtātor, ōris, m. spitter.

spūto, 1. v.a. to spit often, to sputter.

spūtum, i, n. spittle.

squāleo, ui, 2. v.n. to be stiff or rough; to be squalid; to mourn (in squalid clothes).

squālĭdē, ad. dirtily, roughly.

squālĭdus, a, um, a. dirty, filthy, squalid; fig. rude, unadorned.

squālor, ōris, m. dirtiness, filthiness, mourning-garments.

squālus, i, m. (fish) ray, skate.

squāma, ae, f. scale; scale-armour.

squāmātim, ad. like scales.

squāmĕus, squāmĭger, squāmōsus, a, um, a. scaly.

squilla, ae, f., v. scilla.

st, i. hist! whist! hush!

stăbĭlīmentum, i, n. stay, support; assurance.

stăbĭlio, īvi, ītum, 4. v.a. to make stable; to establish, to fix; to repair; to settle.

stăbĭlis, e, a. firm, steady, stable; fig. steadfast; intrepid.

stăbĭlĭtas, ātis, f. steadfastness, stability; constancy.

stăbĭlĭtor, ōris, m. establisher.

stăbŭlo, 1., stăbŭlor, ātus sum, 1. v.n. dep. to kennel, to stable; to roost.

stăbŭlum, i, n. abode, habitation; stall, stable; bee-hive; inn; brothel; retreat, shelter.

stacta, ae, stactē, ēs, f. cinnamon-oil, myrrh-oil.

stădium, ii, n. furlong, stade; race-course. [undate.

stagno, 1. v.n. & a. to stagnate; to instagnum, i, n. pool, pond; lake; water.

stāmen, ĭnis, n. warp (in the loom); flax (on the distaff, to spin); yarn, thread; string (of a musical instrument); fig. thread of the Fates; life.

stāmĭneus, a, um, a. full of threads.

stanneus, a, um, a. of tin.

stannum, i, n. tin.

stăphis, ĭdis, f. wild vine.

stăphўlīnus, i, f. carrot; parsnip.

stătārius, a, um, a. standing firm, stationary, steady; calm, tranquil;—comœdia stataria, comedy with quiet acting; —statarii, ōrum, m. pl. actors in the aforesaid comedy.

stăter, ēris, m. Grecian coin (worth about 3s. 4d.).

stătēra, ae, f. steelyard; balance.

stătĭcē, es, f. sea-lavender.

stătĭcŭlum, i, n. little statue.

stătim, ad. firmly, steadily, uniformly; forthwith, at once, immediately, instantly.

stătio, ōnis, f. standing (still); abode, residence; post, station, place; anchorage;—stătiōnes, pl. sentinels; bodyguard.

stătiōnālis, e, a. fixed, stationary.

stătiōnārius, a, um, a. stationary.

stătīvus, a, um, a. stationary;—castra stătīva, n. pl. pitched camp.

stător, ōris, m. magistrate's attendant, servant, messenger; surname of Jupiter (the supporter).

stătua, ae, f. image, statue.

stătuăria, ae, f. (art of) sculpture.

stătuārius, a, um, a. of or relating to statues; —, ii, m. statuary.

stătūmen, ĭnis, n. ship's rib; support.

stătūmĭno, 1. v.a. to prop up, to support.

stătuo, ui, ūtum, 3. v.a. to put, to place, to set; to build, to erect; to appoint; to settle; to determine, to resolve; to pass judgment, to decide; to dictate. [posture; size, stature.

stătūra, ae, f. standing upright, upright

stătus, a, um, a. set, fixed, appointed, stated, certain.

stătus, ūs, m. standing, position; attitude, posture; condition, circumstance, state; constitution; public order;—status quo (ante), the position in which things stood before.

stēla, ae, f. pillar; tombstone.

stella, ae, f. star; constellation; sun; starfish; — errans, planet.

stellans, antis, p. & a. starry; shining, bright.

stellātus, a, um, p. & a. starry; sparkling; many-eyed.

stellĭfer, stelliger, a, um, a. starry.

stellio, ōnis, m. lizard; knave, rascal.

stemmă, ătis, n. genealogy; stem.

stěphănōtis (mod. hort.), clustered wax-flower.

stercŏro, 1. v.a. to manure.

stercus, ōris, n. dung, excrements, ordure.

stěrĭlesco, 3. v.n. to grow barren.

stěrĭlis, e, a. barren, sterile; fruitless; unprofitable, unproductive; useless, vain. [unfruitfulness; scarcity.

stěrĭlĭtas, ătis, f. barrenness, sterility;

sternax, ācis, a. throwing its rider (of a horse).

sterno, strāvi, strātum, 3. v.a. to spread out, to strew; to stretch out, to extend; to smooth; to prostrate; to throw down; to bring low; to pave.

sternūmentum, i, n. sneeze.

sternuo, ui, 3. v.n. & a. to sneeze; to sputter, to crackle; to sneeze out.

sterquĭlīnium, ii, n. dunghill.

sterto, ui, 3. v.n. to snore.

stĭbium, ii, n. antimony used to black the eyebrows. [infamy.

stigma, ătis, n. brand, burned mark; fig.

stĭgmătias, ae, m. branded rogue or slave.

stilla, ae, f. drop.

stillātĭcius, a, um, stillātīvus, a, um, a. dropping, trickling.

stillātim, ad. by drops.

stillĭcĭdium, ii, n. falling water; trickling of the rain.

stillo, 1. v.n. & a. to drop, to drip, to trickle, to distil; to let fall in drops; to whisper.

stilus, i, m. pointed stick for writing on wax; style; manner, mode; composition.

stĭmŭlātĭo, ōnis, f. stimulation; incentive.

stĭmŭlo, 1. v.a. to prick with a goad, to urge on; to torment, to vex, to trouble, to disturb; to incite, to stimulate.

stĭmŭlus, i, m. goad; spur; pointed stake; fig. incitement; incentive.

stinguo, 3. v.a. to extinguish, to quench.

stīpa, ae, v. stuppa.

stīpātĭo, ōnis, f. crowding; retinue, suite.

stīpātor, ōris, m. attendant;—stīpātōres, pl. retinue, train.

stīpendiārius, a, um, a. tributary; mercenary.

stīpendium, ii, n. tax, tribute, contribution; pay; military service; campaign;—stipendia mereri, to be or serve as a soldier.

stīpĕs, ĭtis, m. log, stock, trunk (of a tree); stake; block, dolt, dunce.

stīpo, 1. v.a. to crowd, to press together, to compress, to fill with; to surround.

stips, stĭpis, f. gift, donation, contribution. [straw.

stīpŭla, ae, f. stalk, stem, blade, halm;

stīpŭlātĭo, ōnis, f. agreement, bargain, covenant, stipulation.

stīpŭlātiuncŭla, ae, f. small bargain.

stīpŭlor, ātus, 1. v. dep. to stipulate, to agree; to make a bargain; to engage or pledge oneself.

stīria, ae, f. icicle.

stirpēs, stirps, pis, f. trunk, stock, stem, stalk; root; plant, shrub; fig. foundation, ground; origin, source; kindred, lineage, race; offspring, progeny.

stirpĭtus, ad. by the roots; utterly.

stīva, ae, f. plough-tail.

sto, stĕti, stătum, 1. v.n. to stand; to stand still; to be fixed; to stand on end or upright; to endure, to stand out; to persist; to remain; to tarry; to adhere (to); to be one's fault; to please, to succeed;—stare cum (abl.), to take part with;—per te stetit quominus vincerem, it was due to you that I did not conquer;—multo sanguini iis victoria stetit, the victory cost them much blood.

Stoa, ae, f. the porch at Athens in which Zeno taught philosophy.

Stŏĭcē, ad. like a Stoic.

Stŏĭcĭ, ōrum, m. pl. Stoics (philosophers).

Stŏĭcus, a, um, a. Stoic.

stŏla, ae, f. gown, long robe, stole.

stŏlātus, a, um, a. wearing a long robe with a train.

stŏlĭdē, ad. stolidly, foolishly.

stŏlĭdĭtas, ātis, f. dulness, stupidity.

stŏlĭdus, a, um, a. dull, stupid.

stŏlo, ōnis, m. shoot, sucker.

stŏmăchĭcus, a, um, a. sick in the stomach.

stŏmăchor, ātus, 1. v.n. & dep. to be angry; to fume, to fret.

stŏmăchōsus, a, um, a. angry, irritable, peevish, pettish.

stŏmăchus, i, m. gullet; stomach; *fig.* taste, liking, dislike, displeasure, irritation. [straw), carpet.

stŏrea, stŏria, ae, f. mat (of rush *or*

străbo, ōnis, m. squint-eyed person.

străgēs, is, f. defeat, overthrow; massacre, slaughter, cutting down; havoc; confused heap.

străgŭlum, i, n. carpet, blanket, rug; coverlet; litter.

străgŭlus, a, um, a., **stragula vestis,** coverlet; rug; carpet.

strāmen, ĭnis, n. straw, litter. [cloth.

strāmentum, i, n. straw, litter; coverlet,

strāmĭneus, a, um, a. made of straw.

strangŭlātĭo, ōnis, f. strangling.

strangŭlo, 1. v.a. to throttle, to choke; *fig.* to torture.

strangūria, ae, f. strangury.

strătēgēma, ătis, n. stratagem, trick.

strătēgus, i, m. commander-in-chief; master of a feast.

strātum, i, n. coverlet, quilt, blanket, pillow; bed, couch; horse-cloth.

strātūra, ae, f. paving.

strātus, a, um, a. paved.

strēna, ae, f. New Year's gift. [ously.

strēnuē, ad. eagerly, quickly, strenu-

strēnuĭtas, ātis, f. briskness, activity.

strēnuus, a, um, a. brisk, active, vigorous, strenuous; resolute; busy, restless.

strĕpĭto, 1. v.n. to make a great noise.

strĕpĭtus, ūs, m. noise, din; crashing, rustling, clattering sound (of a musical instrument).

strĕpo, ui, ĭtum, 3. v.n. & a. to make a noise; to rattle, to rumble, to murmur, to roar; to bawl, to vociferate.

stria, ae, f. channel. [superficially.

strictim, ad. tightly, briefly; *fig.* slightly,

strictūra, ae, f. iron bar.

strictus, a, um, a. close, strait, tight; brief, concise.

strīdeo, di, 2., **strīdo, di,** 3. v.n. to creak, to hiss, to whistle, to buzz, to rattle.

strīdor, ōris, m. hissing, buzzing, rattling, whistling.

strīdŭlus, a, um, a. noisy, crackling, creaking. [scraper.

strĭgĭlis, is, f. currycomb; flesh-brush,

strigmentum, i, n. parings, scrapings.

strĭgōsus, a, um, a. lean, thin, meagre; *fig.* dry, insipid.

stringo, inxi, ictum, 3. v.a. to draw *or* tie tight; to draw *or* press together; to graze; to pluck off, to strip off; to prune; to unsheath; *fig.* to abridge; to affect, to touch; to pain.

strio, 1. v.a. to channel.

strix, strĭgis, f. screech-owl.

strombus, i, m. snail.

strŏphium, ii, n. breast-band; head-band.

structor, ōris, m. builder, mason, carpenter, carver.

structūra, ae, f. building, construction; structure; mines; (gr.) arrangement, order.

struēs, is, f. heap, pile; funeral pile; a heap of sacrificial cakes.

strūma, ae, f. scrofulous tumour, wen.

strūmōsus, a, um, a. having a wen.

struo, xi, ctum, 3. v.a. to pile up, to build, to construct; to arrange; to prepare; to contrive; to excite, to instigate.

strūthiŏcămēlus, i, m. ostrich.

stŭdeo, ui, 2. v.a. & n. to be eager *or* zealous, to strive after; to take care of, to favour; to study; to be a student.

stŭdĭōsē, ad. eagerly, zealously, carefully, studiously.

stŭdĭōsus, a, um, a. eager, zealous, assiduous, anxious after, studious (of); affectionate, fond; devoted.

stŭdĭum, ii, n. assiduity, zeal, eagerness, fondness; endeavour, study, application; attachment, devotion.

stultē, ad. foolishly, sillily.

stultĭlŏquentia, ae, f., **stultĭlŏquĭum, ii,** n. babbling, prating, tittle-tattle.

stultĭlŏquus, a, um, a. talking foolishly.

stultĭtia, ae, f. silliness, stupidity.

stultus, a, um, a. foolish, silly.

stŭpa, ae, v. **stuppa.**

stŭpĕfăcio, fēci, factum, 3. v.a. to stun, to stupefy;—**stŭpĕfio,** to be astonished.

stŭpeo, ui, 2. v.n. & a. to be stunned *or* benumbed; to be astonished *or* stupefied; to stop; to wonder at.

stŭpesco, 3. v.n. to become amazed.

stŭpeus, a, um, a., v. **stuppeus.**

stŭpĭdĭtas, ātis, f. stupidity.

stŭpĭdus, a, um, a. struck senseless, amazed; dull, stupid.

stŭpor, ōris, m. numbness, dulness, stupefaction; astonishment, amazement, stupidity.

stuppa, ae, f. oakum, tow.

stuppeus, a, um, a. of tow.

stuprātor, ōris, m. ravisher, violator.

stupro, 1. v.a. to debauch, to deflower, to ravish.

stuprum, i, n. dishonour, disgrace; debauchery, lewdness; violation.

sturnus, i, m. starling.

stȳlŏbăta, ae, m. pedestal, of a column.

stȳlus, i, v. **stilus.**

stypticus, a, um, a. astringent.

suadēla, ae, f. fair speaking, persuasion.

suădeo, si, sum, 2. v.n. & a. to **advise,** to recommend, to exhort, to urge.

suādus, a, um, a. tending to persuade.

suāsio, ōnis, f. advice, recommending; persuasive eloquence.

suāsor, ōris, m. adviser, counsellor.

suāsōrius, a, um, a. exhortative.

suāveŏlens, tis, a. sweet-smelling.

suāviātio, ōnis, f. kissing.

suāvĭdĭcus, a, um, a. sweet-speaking.

suāvĭlŏquens, tis, a. fair-spoken, agreeable, courteous.

suāvĭlŏquentia, ae, f. sweet language.

suāvĭlŏquus, a, um, a., v. **suaviloquens.**

suāvĭŏlum, i, n. tender kiss.

suāvior, ātus sum, 1. v.a. dep. to kiss, to caress.   [delightful.

suāvis, e, a. sweet, pleasant, agreeable,

suāvĭtas, ātis, f. sweetness, pleasantness, agreeableness.

suāvĭter, ad. sweetly, agreeably, pleasantly, delightfully;—**suaviter in modo, fortiter in re,** gently in manner, firmly in act.

suāvium, ii, n. kiss; sweetheart.

sŭb, pr. (with abl.) under, below, beneath; under the power of; (with accus.) near to; about; next after; a little before; towards; (in compounds) under, secretly, a little;—**sub divo,** in the open air;—**sub rosa,** in secret; —**sub silentio,** in silence.

sŭbabsurdus, a, um, a. somewhat or rather absurd.   [somewhat.

sŭbaccūso, 1. v.a. to blame or accuse

sŭbăcĭdus, a, um, a. sourish.

sŭbactus, ūs, m. kneading.

sŭbagrestis, e, a. somewhat rustic, rather boorish.

sŭbalbĭdus, a, um, sŭbalbus, a, um, a. somewhat white.

sŭbalpīnus, a, um, a. under the Alps.

sŭbāmārus, a, um, a. somewhat bitter.

sŭbăquĭlus, a, um, a. somewhat brown.

sŭbăro, 1. v.a. to plough up.

sŭbarrŏganter, ad. somewhat arrogantly.

sŭbausculto, 1. v.a. to listen secretly, to overhear.

subbibo, 3. v.a. to drink a little, to tipple.

subblandior, 4. v. dep. to wheedle, to fawn.

subc . . ., v. succ . . :

subdiālis, e, a. in the open air.

subdifficilis, e, a. somewhat difficult.

subdiffīdo, 3. v.n. to distrust a little.

subdītīvus, a, um, a. supposititious, spurious.

subdiū, ad. in the daytime.

subdo, dĭdi, dĭtum, 3. v.a. to put or lay under; to substitute; to subject; to supply; to apply; to forge, to counterfeit.

subdŏceo, 2. v.a. to teach as an assistant.

subdŏlē, ad. craftily.   [deceitful.

subdŏlus, a, um, a. somewhat crafty, sly,

subdŏmo, 1. v.a. to tame.

subdŭbĭto, 1. v.n. to doubt a little or in some measure.

subdūco, xi, ctum, 3. v.a. to draw from under or from below; to withdraw; to draw off; to draw up; to steal (away); to hide; to haul up; to cast up, to reckon; to deliberate.

subductio, ōnis, f. reckoning; hauling up; drawing on shore.

subdulcis, e, a. sweetish.

subdūrus, a, um, a. somewhat hard.

sŭbēdo, ēdi, 3. v.a. to eat away underneath.

sŭbeo, ii & īvi, ĭtum, 4. v.n. to come or go under; to sink; to come up to; to succeed; to spring up; to occur, to suggest itself; —, v.a. to approach; to enter; to steal upon or into; to suffer, to sustain, to undergo.

sūber, ĕris, n. cork-tree.

subf . . ., v. suff . . .

subg . . ., v. sugg . . .   [favoured.

sŭbhorrĭdus, a, um, a. rather rough; ill-

sŭbigo, ēgi, actum, 3. v.a. to bring under; to conquer, to subjugate; to plough, to cultivate; to work; to compel, to force; to discipline; to train.

sŭbimpŭdens, entis, a. somewhat impudent; overbold.

sŭbinānis, e, a. somewhat vain.

sŭbindĕ, ad. immediately after, presently, thereupon; continually, frequently.

sŭbinsulsus, a, um, a. somewhat insipid or silly.   [little.

sŭbinvĭdeo, invīsum, 2. v.n. to envy a

sŭbinvīsus, a, um, a. somewhat odious.

sŭbinvīto, 1. v.a. to invite coldly.

sŭbīrascor, atus, 1. v.n. dep. to be somewhat angry.

sŭbĭtārius, a, um, a. speedily raised; sudden, hasty.

sŭbĭto, ad. suddenly, unexpectedly; extempore.

sŭbĭtus, a, um, p. & a. sudden, unexpected;—sŭbĭtum, i, n. sudden occurrence.

subjăceo, 1. v.n. to lie under; to be subject to, to appertain to.

subjectē, ad. humbly, submissively.

subjectio, ōnis, f. laying or putting under; forgery, substitution.

subjecto, 1. v.a. to put under, to throw up; to apply.

subjector, ōris, m. forger.

subjectus, a, um, a. bordering on; submissive; subject to.

subjĭcio, jēci, jectum, 3. v.a. to lay or throw under; to throw or plough up; to forge; to substitute; to subordinate; to subject, to submit; to suggest; to add, to subjoin.   [(gram.).

subjunctīvus, a, um, a. subjunctive

subjungo, xi, ctum, 3. v.a. to yoke to; to add to, to annex, to subjoin; to subdue, to subjugate.

sublābor, lapsus sum, 3. v.n. dep. to fall or sink down or under; to glide away.

sublātē, ad. fig. sublimely.

sublātio, ōnis, f. fig. exaltation, cancellation.

sublātus, a, um, a. elated, haughty.

sublĕgo, lēgi, lectum, 3. v.a. to gather up, to catch up by stealth; to substitute.

sublestus, a, um, a. weak; slender, thin; of no value.

sublēvātio, ōnis, f. alleviation.

sublēvo, 1. v.a. to lift up, to raise up, to support; fig. to lighten, to alleviate; to assist; to encourage.

sublica, ae, f. pile, stake, prop.

sublĭcius, a, um, a. consisting of or resting upon piles;—pons —, pile bridge.

subligācŭlum, i, n. drawers, waist-band.

subligar, āris, n., v. subligaculum.

sublīgo, 1. v.a. to bind or tie below, to bind on.

sublīmē, ad. aloft, loftily, on high.

sublīmis, e, a. high, lofty, exalted; tall; fig. haughty; sublime; aspiring; eminent.

sublīmitas, ātis, f. height, sublimity.

sublīmus, a, um, a., v. sublimis.

sublīno, lēvi, litum, 3. v.a. to anoint, to grease; fig. to deceive; to mock.

sublūcānus, a, um, a. just before daybreak.   [feebly.

sublūceo, 2. v.n. to glitter, to shine

subluo, lūtum, 3. v.a. fig. to wash or bathe the base or foot of.

sublustris, e, a. glimmering.

subm . . ., v. summ . . .

subnascor, natus sum, 3. v.n. dep. to grow out of; to grow after; to succeed.

subnăto, 1. v.a. to swim under.

subnecto, nexui, xum, 3. v.a. to bind or tie under, to bind on beneath; to add, to join; to subscribe.

subnĕgo, avi, 1. v.a. to half deny.

subniger, gra, grum, a. blackish.

subnixus, a, um, a. underpropped, supported by; fig. relying on.

subnūba, ae, f. second wife, intruder, rival.

subnūbĭlus, a, um, a. somewhat cloudy.

sŭbobscēnus, a, um, a. somewhat obscene.   [scure.

sŭbobscūrus, a, um, a. somewhat ob-

sŭbŏdiōsus, a, um, a. somewhat odious.

sŭboffendo, 3. v.n. to offend or displease a little.

sŭboleo, ui, ĭtum, 2. v.n., subolet mihi, I have an inkling.

sŭbŏlēs, is, f. sprout, offshoot; fig. issue, race, offspring.

sŭbŏlesco, 3. v.n. to grow up gradually.

sŭbŏrior, ortus sum, 4. v. dep. to arise.

sŭborno, 1. v.a. to fit out, to furnish, to equip, to adorn; to suborn, to instruct privately or secretly.

sŭbortus, ūs, m. rising.

subp . . ., v. supp . . .

subr . . ., v. surr . . .

subscrībo, psi, ptum, 3. v.a. to write underneath; to subscribe, to sign; to accuse; to assent (to), to approve (of); to note down.

subscriptio, ōnis, f. subscription; signature; noting down; list, register.

subscriptor, ōris, m. undersigner; favourer; prompter.

subsĕcīvus, v. subsicivus.

subsĕco, cui, ctum, 1. v.a. to cut away below, to clip, to pare, to pluck.

subsellium, ii, n. bench, seat; court, tribunal.   [out, to surmise.

subsentio, si, 4. v.a. to perceive, to smell

subsĕquor, cūtus, 3. v.n. & a. dep. to follow close after; to follow, to succeed; to comply with.   ‸

subservio, 4. v.n. to be subject to; to comply with, to humour.

subsessor, ōris, m. lier in wait.

subsĭcīvus, a, um, a. spare; extra; done in overtime (of work);—tempora subsiciva, spare moments.

subsidiārius, a, um, a. subsidiary;—subsidiarii, ōrum, m. pl. auxiliaries, reserves.

subsĭdium, ii, n. body in reserve; relief, aid; support; protection.

subsīdo, sēdi, sessum, 3. v.n. & a. to squat; to settle down; to settle; to subside; to remain; to stay; to lie in ambush; to waylay; to abase, to decrease.

subsignāni, ōrum, m. pl. legionary soldiers kept in reserve (under the standard).   [register.
subsigno, 1. v.a. to sign, to subscribe; to
subsilio, lui, 4. v.n. to leap up, to start up.
subsīmus, a, um, a. flattish-nosed.
subsisto, stiti, 3. v.n. & a. to stand still,
to stop, to halt; to stay, to abide; to
stand firm, to withstand, to resist; to
cease to continue; to subsist; to sustain; to encounter.
subsōlānus, a, um, a. eastern; —, i, m.
east wind.
subsortior, ītus sum, 4. v.a. dep. to substitute (another judge instead of the
rejected one).   [tuting by lot.
subsortītio, ōnis, f. choosing or substi-
substantia, ae, f. substance, matter; essence; estate, wealth.
substantīvum, i, n. substantive, noun.
substerno, strāvi, strātum, 3. v.a. to
strew, to scatter, to spread or lay
under;—substrātum, i, n. a foundation.
substituo, ui, ūtum, 3. v.a. to set under,
to substitute, to put in the place of;
(law) to appoint as next or second heir.
substrāmen, ĭnis, substrāmentum, i, n.
litter.
substrictus, a, um, a. girt in; plucked
up; slender; close.
substringo, nxi, ctum, 3. v.a. to bind
beneath; to bind, to tie or truss up;
to check, to restrain; to contract;
—aurem substringere, to prick up the
ear.   [ture; underpinning.
substructio, ōnis, f. foundation, substruc-
substruo, xi, ctum, 3. v.a. to build beneath, to lay a foundation, to pave.
subsultim, ad. by leaps or jumps.
subsulto, 1. v.n. to leap; to jump; to
pant.
subsum, v.n. ir. to be under, among; to
be near or at hand; to lurk privily;
to remain; to help.
subsūtus, a, um, a. sown beneath,
stitched about, trimmed around at the
bottom.
subtardus, a, um, a. rather slow.
subtē(g)men, ĭnis, n. woof; thread;
fig. threads of the Fates.
subtěnuis, e, a. somewhat slender.
subter, ad. & pr. below, beneath, under,
underneath; close to, near; (in composition) under; privily.
subterduco, xi, ctum, 3. v.a. to steal
away, to withdraw.   [under.
subterfluo, uxi, uxum, 3. v.n. to flow
subterfūgio, fūgi, 3. v.n. & a. to flee
secretly, to get off; to escape, to evade,
to shun.

subterlābor, 3. v.n. dep. to glide or flow
underneath; to slip away, to escape.
subtěro, trīvi, trītum, 3. v.a. to bruise, to
pound, to break.
subterrāneus, a, um, a. underground,
subterranean.
subtersěco, 1. v.a. to cut underneath, to
part.
subtexo, xui, xtum, 3. v.a. to weave under
or below; to interweave; to veil; to
compose, to prepare; to add, to annex,
to subjoin.
subtīlis, e, a. fine-spun, fine; subtle;
slender, delicate, nice; exact; exquisite; small; (of style) plain; acute,
sharp; shrewd; witty.
subtīlitas, ātis, f. fineness, slenderness;
acuteness, penetration, subtlety; (of
style) plainness, simplicity.
subtīliter, ad. finely, minutely; acutely;
subtly; plainly, simply.
subtīmeo, ui, 3. v.n. to be half-afraid.
subtrāho, xi, ctum, 3. v.a. to draw away
from underneath or by stealth; to
take away, to remove; to withdraw;
to subtract, to diminish; to keep from.
subturpĭcŭlus, a, um, a. rather mean.
subturpis, e, a. somewhat base or disgraceful.
subtus, ad. below, beneath, underneath.
sŭbūcŭla, ae, f. shirt, under-garment of
a man.
sŭbŭla, ae, f. awl, bodkin.
sŭbulcus, i, m. swineherd.
sŭbŭlo, ōnis, m. flute-player; hart.
Sŭbūra, ae, f. a quarter of Rome where
the principal provision market was
situated.
Sŭbūrānus, a, um, a. relating to a quarter
in Rome called the Subura.
sŭburbānitas, ātis, f. neighbourhood;
nearness (to Rome).
sŭburbāni, ōrum, m. pl. inhabitants of
the suburbs.
sŭburbānum, i, n. suburban villa,
country- or summer-house.
sŭburbānus, a, um, a. suburban.
sŭburbium, ii, n. suburb.
sŭburgeo, 2. v.a. to drive or urge close to,
to push forward.   [ance.
subvectio, ōnis, f. transporting, convey-
subvecto, 1. v.a. to carry; to transport.
subvectus, ūs, m. carrying, conveyance.
subvěho, vexi, vectum, 3. v.a. to carry;
to bring or convey up.
subvěnio, vēni, ventum, 4. v.n. to come
up, to aid, to relieve; to succour.
subvěreor, 2. v.n. dep. to be somewhat
fearful.
subverso, 1. v.a. to overthrow, to ruin.
subversor, ōris, m. overthrower, subverter.

subverto, ti, sum, 3. v.a. to turn upside down; to upset, to overthrow; to destroy, to ruin, to subvert.

subvĭrĭdis, e, a. greenish.

subvexus, a, um, a. inclined, sloping up.

subvŏlo, 1. v.n. to fly upwards.

subvolvo, 3. v.a. to roll up *or* along.

succēdāneus, a, um, a. succeeding, substituted.

succēdo, cessi, cessum, 3. v.n. & a. to go below *or* under; to go from under; to mount, to ascend; to succeed; to follow; to submit to; to approach, to advance; to prosper, to thrive; to happen; to take the place of; to succeed to.

succendo, di, sum, 3. v.a. to kindle from below; *fig.* to inflame.

succenseo, sui, sum, 2. v.n. to be angry.

succentŭrio, ōnis, m. under-centurion.

succerno, crēvi, crētum, 2. v.a. to sift through.

successio, ōnis, f. succession.

successor, ōris, m. follower, successor.

successus, ūs, m. advance (up a hill), approach; succession (of time); *fig.* success, good result.

succīdāneus, v. succedaneus.

succīdia, ae, f. flitch of bacon.

succĭdo, cĭdi, 3. v.n. to sink down; to fail; to totter.

succīdo, cīdi, cīsum, 3. v.a. to cut from below, to cut off, to cut down, to fell.

succĭdus, v. sucidus. [ing down.

succĭduus, a, um, a. (poet.) failing, sink-

succinctus, a, um, a. girt; ready; succinct, well-set; compendious.

succĭnĕus, v. sucineus.

succingo, nxi, nctum, 3. v.a. to gird below, to tuck up, to gird; *fig.* to equip with; to surround.

succingŭlum, i, n. belt; truss.

succĭno, 3. v.n. to accompany, to chime in.

succĭnum, v. sucinum.

succĭpio, v. suscipio.

succīsīvus, v. subsicivus.

succlāmātio, ōnis, f. acclamation, shouting. [to cry out.

succlāmo, 1. v.a. to shout, to exclaim to,

succollo, 1. v.a. to bear on the shoulders.

succontŭmēliōsē, ad. somewhat insultingly.

succōsus, a, um, v. sūcōsus.

succresco, 3. v.n. to grow under; to grow up; to increase; to grow up to; reach by growing.

succrispus, a, um, a. somewhat crisped.

succumbo, cŭbui, cŭbĭtum, 3. v.n. to lie down; to fall *or* sink down; to succumb, to yield, to give way.

succurro, curri, cursum, 3. v.n. to run under; to succour, to help; be an antidote for; *fig.* to come into one's mind.

succus, i, v. sucus.

succŭtio, cussi, cussum, 3. v.a. to toss.

sūcĭdus, a, um, a. sappy; fresh, plump.

sūcĭneus, a, um, a. of amber.

sūcĭnum, i, n. amber.

sūcōsus, a, um, a. juicy, succulent.

suctus, ūs, m. licking, sucking.

sŭcŭla, ae, f. windlass.

sūcŭlentus, a, um, a. succulent.

sūcus, i, m. juice, sap; draught, potion; strength, vigour; energy.

sūdārium, ii, n. handkerchief, napkin, towel. [stove.

sūdātio, ōnis, f. sweating; hot-house,

sūdātōrium, ii, n. hot bath, stove.

sūdātōrius, a, um, a. belonging to sweating; sweating.

sūdēs, sūdis, is, f. stake, pile.

sūdo, 1. v.n. & a. to sweat, to perspire; to distil (from), to drip, to exude; to labour, to toil; to perform carefully.

sūdor, ōris, m. sweat, perspiration; fatigue, labour, toil.

sūdum, i, n. bright *or* fair weather.

sūdus, a, um, a. clear, dry, fair.

suesco, suēvi, suētum, 3. v.n. to become used *or* accustomed; to be wont.

suētus, a, um, a. wont, customary.

sūfes, ētis, m. chief magistrate of the Carthaginians.

suffarcĭno, 1. v.a. to stuff.

suffĕro, sustŭli, sublātum, sufferre, v.a. ir. to carry under, to put *or* lay under; to bear, to suffer.

suffervĕfăcio, factum, 3. v.a. to warm up.

suffes, ētis, v. sufes.

sufficio, fēci, fectum, 3. v.a. & n. to put under *or* among; to suffuse, to dye; to furnish, to supply; to choose in the place of another; to substitute; to suffice *or* be sufficient.

suffīgo, xi, xum, 3. v.a. to fasten beneath, to affix.

suffīmen, inis, suffīmentum, i, n. incense.

suffĭo, īvi & ii, ītum, 4. v.a. to fumigate, to perfume.

suffītio, ōnis, f. perfuming; fumigation.

suffītor, ōris, m. perfumer.

suffītus, ūs, m. perfuming. [stop.

sufflāmen, inis, n. drag on a wheel; delay,

sufflātio, ōnis, f. blowing up. [bombastic.

sufflātus, a, um, a. puffed up, inflated;

sufflāvus, a, um, a. yellowish.

sufflo, 1. v.a. to blow *or* puff up.

suffōcātio, ōnis, f. suffocation.

suffōco, 1. v.a. to choke, to stifle, to strangle, to suffocate.

suffŏdio, fŏdi, fossum, 3. v.a. to sap, to undermine; to stab.

suffrāgātio, ōnis, f. suffrage, voting.

suffrāgātor, ōris, m. voter; partisan, supporter.

suffrāgātōrius, a, um, a. belonging to a voter; recommendatory.

suffrāgium, ii, n. voting-tablet, ballot; vote, suffrage; right of voting; favour, support; approbation; decision, judgment.

suffrāgo, ĭnis, f. ham, hock.

suffrāgor, ātus, 1. v.n. dep. to vote for; to favour, to recommend, to support.

suffringo, 3. v.a. to break below *or* underneath, to break (in the middle).

suffŭgio, fŭgi, 3. v.n. to flee away.

suffŭgium, ii, n. refuge, shelter.

suffulcio, si, tum, 4. v.a. to underprop; to strengthen.

suffūmigo, 1. v.a. to suffumigate.

suffundo, fŭdi, fūsum, 3. v.a. to pour underneath, into *or* upon; to pour *or* spread through, to suffuse; to tinge; to intermingle.

suffūror, 1. v. dep. to pilfer.

suffuscus, a, um, a. somewhat dusky.

suffūsio, ōnis, f. cataract (of the eyes).

suggĕro, gessi, gestum, 3. v.a. to carry up; to heap up; to erect; to furnish, to supply.

suggestio, ōnis, f. prompting;—**suggestio falsi,** the suggestion of untruth; asserting as fact what one knows to be false.

suggestum, i, n., **suggestus, ūs,** m. raised place; platform, stage.

suggrandis, e, a. rather large.

suggrĕdior, gressus sum, 3. v.n. & a. dep. to approach; to come upon, to surprise; to attack.

suggrunda, ae, f. eaves.

sūgillātio, ōnis, f. livid spot, black mark; slander, taunt, insult.

sūgillātum, i, n. black eye.

sūgillo, 1. v.a. to beat black and blue; to defame, to insult, to revile, to taunt.

sūgo, xi, ctum, 3. v.a. to suck; *fig.* to take in.

sui, sĭbi, sē (sēsē), pn. of himself; of herself; of itself; of themselves;—**apud se,** at his house; with him;—**apud se esse,** to be in one's senses;—**per se,** of itself;—**propter se,** for its own sake;—**pro se quisque,** each for himself.

suillus, a, um, a. of swine.   [rower.

sulcātor, ōris, m. ploughman; ferryman,

sulco, 1. v.a. to furrow, to plough; to pass through; to sail over.

sulcus, i, m. furrow; ditch, trench; ploughing; rut, track; trail of a meteor.

sulfŭr, ŭris, n. brimstone, sulphur.

sulfŭrātus, a, um, a. impregnated with sulphur.

sulfŭreus, a, um, a. sulphureous.

sulphur, v. **sulfur.**

sum, fui, esse, v. auxil. to be, to exist: to live; to happen; to remain;—**est** (with genitive) it belongs to, it is the nature *or* duty, etc., of;—**sunt qui,** there are some who;—**fuit,** it is no more, it is gone;—**fuimus,** *fig.* we are lost *or* ruined.

sūmen, ĭnis, n. udder of a sow; breast (of a woman); tit-bit.

summa, ae, f. main thing, chief point; (mil.) main body; command-in-chief; sum total; whole; summit, chief power; perfection;—**in** —, in all;—**ad** —**m,** in a word, on the whole.

summās, ātis, c. grandee, lord, lady.

summātim, ad. summarily, briefly.

summātus, ūs, m. supremacy.

summē, ad. in the highest degree, extremely.

summergo, si, sum, 3. v.a. to plunge; to submerge; to overwhelm; to drown.

sumministro, 1. v.a. to furnish, to supply.

summissē, ad. softly; in a low voice; humbly.

summissio, onis, f. dropping (of the voice); depression.

summissus, um, a. low; soft; gentle; abject.

summitto, mīsi, missum, 3. v.a. to send up; to produce; to let down; to drop; to lower; to send secretly; to supply, to let grow.   [ing.

summŏlestus, a, um, a. somewhat annoy-

summŏneo, ui, itum, 2. v.a. to warn secretly.

summŏrōsus, a, um, a. somewhat peevish.

summōtor, ōris, m. lictor; beadle.

summŏveo, mōvi, mōtum, 2. v.a. to remove; to clear off; to draw back; to banish.

summŭla, ae, f. little sum.

summus, a, um, a. highest, greatest, very great; chief, principal; the farthest, utmost, last, extreme; very deep;—**summus mons,** the top of the mountain;—**summum,** ad. at the utmost;—**summum, i,** n. sum, whole; height, top;—**summum bonum,** the greatest good.

sūmo, sumpsi, sumptum, 3. v.a. to take, to lay hold of, to assume; to receive; to get; to buy; to procure; to bestow, to spend; to choose; to undertake; to employ, to use; to take for granted; to demand; to cite, to mention; to inflict.

sumptio, ōnis, f. *fig.* assumption.
sumptĭto, 1. v.a. to take often.
sumptŭārius, a, um, a. sumptuary, pertaining to expenses.
sumptŭōsē, ad. lavishly.
sumptŭōsus, a, um, a. expensive, costly, sumptuous; lavish; extravagant.
sumptus, ūs, m. expense, cost, charge.
suo, sui, sūtum, 3. v.a. to sew, to stitch, to join *or* to tack together.
suŏvĕtaurīlia, ium, n. pl. sacrifice of a hog, a sheep, and a bull.
sŭpellex, lectĭlis, f. household stuff, furniture, outfit.
sŭper, ad. & pr. above, on, over; beyond; on the top, thereupon; moreover; about; concerning; (in composition) above; in addition;—**omnia,** above *or* before all, during;—**satis superque,** enough and more than enough.
sŭpĕrā, v. **supra.**
sŭpĕra, ōrum, n. pl. heaven.
sŭpĕrābĭlis, e, a. that may be got over *or* surmounted; *fig.* that may be overcome *or* subdued.
sŭpĕraddo, dĭtum, 3. v.a. to add besides.
sŭpĕrātor, ōris, m. conqueror.
sŭperbē, ad. haughtily, proudly.
sŭperbia, ae, f. loftiness, haughtiness, pride; (in a good sense) high-mindedness.
sŭperbĭbo, 3. v.a. to drink upon another thing.
sŭperbĭlŏquentia, ae, f. haughty speech *or* language.
sŭperbio, 4. v.n. to be haughty, to take pride in; to be magnificent.
sŭperbus, a, um, a. haughty, proud, arrogant; magnificent, splendid; noble, distinguished, superb; delicate, fastidious, squeamish. [cilious.
sŭperciliōsus, a, um, a. haughty, super-
sŭpercilium, ii, n. eyebrow; ridge, summit; *fig.* arrogance, pride, superciliousness.
sŭpercurro, 3. v.n. to exceed.
sŭperēdo, 3. v.a. to eat besides.
sŭperēmĭnĕo, 2. v.a. to overtop, to rise above, to be higher.
sŭperēmŏrior, 3. v. dep. to die upon.
sŭperfĕro, tŭli, lātum, ferre, v.a. to carry over; to lift.
sŭperfēto, 1. v.n. to superfetate.
sŭperfĭcies, ei, f. upper side, surface; outside; building, superficies.
sŭperfio, 3. v.n. to be left, to remain.
sŭperfixus, a, um, a. fixed on the top.
sŭperfluo, 3. v.n. to run over, to overflow; *fig.* to s'perabound; to be excessive *or* extravagant.

sŭperfluus, a, um, a. superfluous, unnecessary.
sŭperfoeto, 1., v. **superfeto.** [over.
sŭperfŭgio, ūgi, fŭgĭtum, 3. v.n. to flee
sŭperfulgeo, si, 2. to shine above.
sŭperfundo, fūdi, fūsum, 3. v.a. to pour over *or* upon; to spread over;—**se superfundere,** to overflow; to extend.
sŭpergrĕdĭor, gressus, 3. v.a. & n. dep. to get *or* pass over; to excel, to surpass.
Sŭpĕri, ōrum, m. pl. the gods above, deities.
superillino, lĭtum, 3. v.a. to smear over.
sŭperimmĭnĕo, 2. v.n. to hang over, to overhang. [lay upon.
sŭperimpōno, pŏsĭtum, 3. v.a. to put *or*
sŭperincĭdens, entis, a. falling from above, falling down.
sŭperincŭbans, antis, a. lying over *or* upon.
sŭperincumbo, cŭbui, 3. v.n. to lay *or* cast oneself upon.
sŭperingĕro, gestum, 3. v.a. to heap on.
sŭperinjicio, jēci, jectum, 3. v.a. to throw on *or* above, to cast over *or* upon, to add.
sŭperinsterno, strāvi, 3. v.a. to spread over, to cover *or* lay over.
sŭperior, ius, a. higher, upper, superior, better; past, previous; elder, stronger; victorious.
sŭperjăcio, jēci, jectum, 3. v.a. to cast *or* throw over *or* upon, to spread over; to add; to exaggerate, to overdo; to overtop. [bole.
sŭperlātio, ōnis, f. exaggeration, hyper-
sŭperlātīvus, a, um, a. superlative.
sŭperlātus, a, um, a. exaggerated, extravagant.
superlīno, lĭtum, 3. v.a. to smear over.
sŭpernās, ātis, a. lying above, upper, northern. [the top.
sŭpernāto, 1. v.n. to swim upon *or* at
sŭpernē, ad. from above, above, upwards.
sŭpernus, a, um, a. that is above, upper; high-standing; celestial.
sŭpero, 1. v.n. & a. to go over; to overtop, to surmount; to cross; to survive; to abound; to exceed; to go past *or* beyond; to double, to sail past; to be superior, to overcome, to surpass; to vanquish.
sŭperobruo, 3. v.a. to overwhelm.
sŭperpendens, entis, a. overhanging.
sŭperpōno, pŏsui, pŏsĭtum, 3. v.a. to put *or* lay over *or* upon, to set over; to postpone.
sŭperscando, 3. v.a. to climb *or* step over.
sŭpersĕdeo, sēdi, sessum, 2. v.n. & a. to sit upon; to be above; to omit, to forbear, to cease; to desist from.

sǔperstagno, 1. v.n. to spread out into a lake, to overflow.

sǔpersterno, strātum, 3. v.a. to strew or cover or lay over.

sǔperstěs, itis, a. outliving, surviving; —, c. survivor.

sǔperstītio, ōnis, f. superstition; religious awe; religious rite; object of dread.

sǔperstītiōsē, ad. superstitiously.

sǔperstītiōsus, a, um, a. superstitious, prophetic.

sǔpersto, 1. v.n. & a. to stand upon or over.

sǔperstruo, xi, ctum, 3. v.a. to build upon or over.

sǔpersum, fui, esse, v.n. ir. to be over and above; to be left, to remain, to exist still; to outlive, to survive; to abound; to be superfluous.

sǔpertěgo, 3. v.a. to cover over.

sǔpertrǎho, 3. v.a. to draw over.

sǔpěrus, a, um, a. above, high; divine; heavenly;—superum mare, the Adriatic Sea;—see also superior; supremus.

sǔpervǎcāneus, a, um, a. needless, superfluous, done in leisure moments.

sǔpervǎcuō, ad. superfluously.

sǔpervǎcuus, a, um, a. superfluous, redundant, useless, needless.

sǔpervādo, 3. v.a. to go or climb over, to surmount.

sǔpervěhor, vectus sum, 3. v.n. dep. to go, to ride, to sail, etc., over or past.

sǔpervěnio, věni, ventum, 4. v.n. & a. to come over or upon, to come in addition to; to arrive; to follow after, to press upon, to surpass.

sǔperventus, ūs, m. arrival.

sǔpervīvo, ixi, 3. v.n. to outlive, to survive.

sǔpervǒlito, 1. v.a. to fly over often.

sǔpervǒlo, 1. v.a. & n. to fly over.

sǔpīnē, ad. supinely; negligently.

sǔpīno, 1. v.a. to throw or lay on the back; to upturn.

sǔpīnum, i, n. (gr.) supine.

sǔpīnus, a, um, a. lying on the back, supine; backwards, retrograde; sloping; stretching out; lifted up, haughty; careless, negligent.

suppar, ǎris, a. nearly equal.

suppǎrāsītor, ātus sum, 1. v.n. dep. to flatter a little, to sponge.

suppǎrum, i, n., suppǎrus, i, m. (any) garment of linen; topsail, streamer.

suppědītātio, ōnis, f. supply; abundance.

suppědīto, 1. v.n. & a. to be at hand in abundance; to suffice; to give or procure in abundance; to supply; to aid; to serve.

suppětiæ, ārum, f. pl. aid, assistance,

succour; supplies; suppětias ire, to go to the assistance (of anyone).

suppětior, ātus sum, 1. v.n. dep. to come to the aid of, to assist, to succour.

suppěto, ivi & ii, ītum, 3. v.n. to be at hand or in store; to suffice; fig. to be equal to.

suppīlo, ātum, 1. v.a. to steal underhand, to pilfer.

suppingo, pactum, 3. v.a. to fasten underneath.

supplanto, 1. v.a. to trip up; to overthrow.

supplaudo, etc., v. supplodo, etc.

supplēmentum, i, n. supplement; (mil.) recruiting; reinforcements.

suppleo, ěvi, ētum, 2. v.a. to complete, to fill up, to supply; (mil.) to recruit, to reinforce.

supplex, icis, a. humble, suppliant.

supplicātio, ōnis, f. public prayer, supplication; day of prayer or thanksgiving.

suppliciter, ad. humbly, suppliantly.

supplicium, ii, n. supplication; public prayer; punishment; torture.

supplico, 1. v.n. to pray or beg humbly, to implore, to supplicate; to worship.

supplōdo, si, 3. v.a. to stamp with the feet.

supplōsio, ōnis, f. stamping with the feet.

suppœnītet, 2. v. imp. to be rather sorry.

suppōno, pōsui, pōsitum, 3. v.a. to put or set under; to substitute; to forge, to counterfeit; to apply; to add, to annex; to subject, to submit; to hold in less esteem.

supporto, 1. v.a. to carry, to bring or to convey up to.

suppōsitĭcius or tius, a, um, a. false; counterfeit.

suppōsitio, ōnis, f. substitution, forgery.

suppressio, ōnis, f. suppression; embezzlement;—suppressio veri, suppression of the truth.

suppressus, a, um, a. suppressed; hidden; drowned; sunk; short; (voice) subdued, low.

supprīmo, pressi, pressum, 3. v.a. to press down or under; to suppress; to keep back, to restrain; to conceal; to drop (the voice).

supprōmus, i, m. under-butler.

suppǔdet, 2. v. imp. to be somewhat ashamed.

suppūrātio, ōnis, f. suppuration.

suppūrātōrius, a, um, a. suppurative.

suppūrāta, orum, n. pl. festering matter.

suppūro, 1. v.n. to come to a head, to fester, to suppurate.

suprā, ad. & pr. above, over, on the upper side; beyond; more; before, formerly.

suprascando, 3. v.a. to climb over, to surmount.

suprēma, ōrum, n. pl. last moments, death; funeral; last will, testament.

suprēmo, suprēmum, ad. for the last time.

suprēmus, a, um, a. highest; topmost; last, extreme; latest; dying; greatest; utmost; fig. manus suprema, finishing touch.

sūra, ae, f. calf of the leg.

surcŭlārius, a, um, a. belonging to shoots; set with shoots.

surcŭlōsus, a, um, a. full of shoots.

surcŭlus, i, m. shoot, sprout, twig; cutting, graft.

surdaster, tra, trum, a. somewhat deaf.

surdĭtas, ātis, f. deafness.

surdus, a, um, a. deaf; inexorable; insensible; unwilling to hear; not understanding; dull-sounding; silent, mute; imperceptible; faint, dim.

surēna, ae, m. Parthian grand vizier.

surgo, surrexi, surrectum, 3. v.a. & n. to lift or raise up, to erect; to arise; to grow up; to spring; to increase; to ascend; to appear; to occur.

surrancĭdus, a, um, a. somewhat rancid.

surraucus, a, um, a. somewhat hoarse.

surrēmigo, 1. v.n. to row along.

surrēpo, psi, ptum, 3. v.n. & a. to crawl under; to creep from under; to crawl along; to creep softly; to steal over insensibly.

surreptĭcius or tius, a, um, a. stolen; secret.

surrĭdeo, si, 2. v.n. to smile.

surrĭdĭcŭlē, ad. rather absurdly.

surrĭgo, v. surgo.

surrĭguus, a, um, a. wet.

surringor, 3. v.n. dep. to be somewhat vexed.

surrĭpio, rĭpui, reptum, 3. v.a. to snatch away secretly, to steal, to pilfer, to purloin.

surrogo, 1. v.a. to choose in place of another.

surrostrāni, orum, people who hang round the Forum.

surrŭbeo, 2. v.n. to blush.

surrŭbicundus, a, um, a. reddish.

surrŭfus, a, um, a. reddish.

surrŭmus, a, um, a. sucking, suckling.

surruo, ui, ŭtum, 3. v.a. to undermine; to overthrow.

surrusticus, a, um, a. somewhat boorish.

surrŭtilus, a, um, a. reddish.

sursum, ad. upwards, on high; above; — deorsum, up and down, to and fro.

sūs, suis, g.c. swine, hog, pig, sow.

susceptio, ōnis, f. taking in hand, undertaking.

suscĭpio, cēpi, ceptum, 3. v.a. to take or catch up; to raise up; to prop, to support, to sustain; to beget, to conceive, to bear (children); to undertake; to incur; to usurp; to acknowledge (a new-born child); to resume (a speech); to suffer, to undergo.

suscĭto, 1. v.a. to lift up, to raise; to build, to erect; to awake, to arouse; to provoke, to stir up; to produce; to cause.

suspecto, 1. v.a. to look up at, to watch; to distrust, to suspect.

suspectus, a, um, a. suspected, mistrusted; critical, dangerous.

suspectus, ūs, m. looking up; regard, esteem; height.

suspendiōsus, a, um, a. connected with hanging; —, i, one who has hanged himself.

suspendium, ii, n. hanging; halter.

suspendo, di, sum, 3. v.a. to hang up, to suspend; to hang, to gibbet; to dedicate (votive offerings); to build upon arches; to prop up; to depend upon; to keep in suspense; to stop, to interrupt; to hang or fix upon.

suspensūra, ae, f. vaulting.

suspensus, a, um, a. raised; vaulted; wavering, uncertain; in suspense; dependent; attentive; suspended.

suspĭcax, ācis, a. distrustful, suspicious, causing mistrust.

suspĭcio, spexi, ctum, 3. v.a. & n. to look upwards; to look up at; to esteem, to respect; to suspect. [picion.

suspĭcio, ōnis, f. mistrust, distrust, suspicion.

suspĭciōsē, ad. suspiciously.

suspĭciōsus, a, um, a. mistrustful, suspicious; dangerous.

suspĭcor, ātus, 1. v.a. dep. to mistrust, to suspect; to suppose, to believe, to surmise. [ing.

suspīrātio, ōnis, f. fetching breath, sigh-

suspīrātus, ūs, m. sighing, sigh.

suspīriōsus, a, um, a. breathing short.

suspīritus, ūs, deep breath, sigh.

suspīrium, ii, n. deep breath, sighing, sigh.

suspīro, 1. v.n. & a. to draw a deep breath, to sigh; to exhale, to long or sigh for.

susquē dēquē, ad. up and down;—susque deque habere, to regard with indifference.

sustentācŭlum, i, n. prop, stay, support.

sustentātio, ōnis, f. delay; forbearance.

sustento, 1. v.a. to uphold, to support; to keep up, to sustain, to maintain, to nourish; to preserve; to bear, to endure, to suffer; to defer, to put off.

sustĭneo, tĭnui, tentum, 2. v.a. to hold up, to uphold, to support, to sustain; to nourish; to maintain; to defend, to protect; to suffer, to bear, to undergo; to oppose, to resist, to withstand; to restrain, to keep back or in; to defer, to put off; to have patience, to permit; to have the heart to, to dare; to represent.

sustollo, 3. v.a. to lift up, to raise; to take away, to remove; to destroy.

sūsum, v. sursum.

sŭsurro, 1. v.n. & a. to hum, to buzz, to murmur; to mutter, to whisper.

sŭsurrus, i, m. humming, murmuring, muttering, whispering, whisper.

sŭsurrus, a, um, a. muttering, whispering.

sūta, ōrum, n. pl. joints, coat of mail.

sūtēla, ae, f. craft, subtlety.

sūtĭlis, e, a. sewed together, stitched.

sūtor, ōris, m. shoemaker; cobbler; ne — ultra or supra crepidam, let the cobbler stick to his last.

sūtōrius, a, um, sūtrīnus, a, um, a. belonging to a shoemaker or cobbler.

sūtrīna, ae, f. cobbler's shop.

sūtrīnum, i, n. shoemaker's trade.

sūtūra, ae, f. suture, seam.

suus, a, um, pn. his own, her own, its own, their own; proper, peculiar; favourable, kind; due, lawful; (law) free, independent; in one's right mind;—suum, i, n. one's own, property, possession; — cuique, to every one what belongs to him;—sui, ōrum, m. pl. one's own people; followers, party, troops;—sui generis, in a class by itself; unique of its kind.

sȳcăminus, i, f. mulberry-tree.

sȳcŏmŏrus, i, f., v. sycaminus.

sȳcŏphanta, ae, m. tale-bearer, slanderer, cheat.

sȳcŏphantia, ae, f. treachery, deceit.

sȳcŏphantor, 1. v.n. dep. to cheat, to trick.

syllăba, ae, f. syllable;—auceps syllabarum, word-catcher, caviller.

syllăbātim, ad. syllable by syllable.

syllŏgismus, i, m. syllogism.

sylva, sylvānus, etc., v. silva, etc.

symbŏla, ae, f. share (in a reckoning).

symbŏlus, i, m. symbŏlum, i, n. symbol, ring, seal.

symmetria, ae, f. proportion, symmetry.

symphōnia, ae, f. harmony, symphony.

symphōniăcus, a, um, a. belonging to harmony;—pueri symphoniaci, singing-boys.

Sympŏsium, ii, n. the Banquet (title of one of Plato's dialogues).

sȳnecdŏchē, ēs, f. (gr.) putting a part for the whole or the whole for a part.

syngrăpha, ae, f. writing under hand and seal, bond, indenture.

syngrăphus, i, m. contract; passport.

sȳnizēsis, is, f. (gr.) contraction of two vowels into one syllable.

sȳnōnȳmum, i, n. (gr.) a word having the same meaning as another; a synonym.

syntaxis, is, f. (gr.) syntax.

synthēsis, is, f. a service of plate; a suit of clothes; a loose gown.

syringa (mod. hort.), lilac.

syrma, ătis, n. a trailing robe.

Syrtis, is, f. quicksand.

Tăbānus, i, m. horse-fly.

tăbella, ae, f. tablet; voting-tablet; bill, letter; writing; bond; contract; public record; last will; little gaming-board; small boat; votive-tablet; little picture; picture-book; painter's board.

tăbellārius, ii, m. letter-carrier, courier; —, a, um, a. of or belonging to voting.

tābeo, 2. v.n. to waste away, to be consumed.

tăberna, ae, f. hut, shed; booth, workshop, inn, tavern; — (libraria), bookseller's shop.

tăbernācŭlum, i, n. tent.   [man.

tăbernārius, ii, m. shopkeeper; tavern-

tăbernŭla, ae, f. small tavern.

tābēs, is, f. wasting away, consumption; putrefaction; plague; corruption; gore; poisonous matter; pestilence.

tābesco, bui, 3. v.a. to waste away; to decay, to languish; to pine.

tābidus, a, um, a. wasting away, putrefying, rotten; consumptive; consuming, corrupting, infectious.

tābificus, a, um, a. melting; corrupting, infectious; posionous.

tābitūdo, ĭnis, f. wasting away.

tablīnum, v. tabulinum.

tăbŭla, ae, f. board, plank; votive-tablet; writing-tablet; letter, will; account-book; panel; picture; map; pedigree; auction;—tabulæ, pl. register; — (testamenti), last will, testament; —manum de —, enough! hold!— novæ tabulæ, a revolution, a demand for new account-books and the cancelling of old debts;—tabula rasa, a clean sheet.

tăbŭlārium, ii, n. archives, register-office; exchequer-office.

tăbŭlārius, ii, m. scrivener; accountant; public notary.

tăbŭlātio, ōnis, f. planking, flooring; floor, story.

tăbŭlātum, i, n. flooring; floor, story.
tăbŭlātus, a, um, a. floored; planked.
tăbŭlīnum, i, n. place where archives
were kept.
tābum, i, n. corrupt matter, foul blood;
plague, pestilence.
tăceo, cui, cĭtum, 2. v.n. & a. to be silent,
to hold one's tongue; to be still *or*
quiet; to pass over in silence, to be
silent about.
tăcĭtē, ad. silently, secretly.
tăcĭtum, i, n. secret.
tăcĭturnĭtas, ātis, f. silence, taciturnity.
tăcĭturnus, a, um, a. close, reserved,
taciturn.
tăcĭtus, a, um, a. silent; still, noiseless, dumb, mute; secret, hidden;
unmentioned.
tactĭlis, e, a. tangible.
tactio, ōnis, f. touching; (sense of)
touch.
tactus, ūs, m. touch, handling; (sense of)
touch; *fig.* effect, influence.
tæda, ae, f. resinous fir; pine-torch; *fig.*
marriage, wedding.
tædet, duit, tæsum est, 2. v.n. imp. it
wearies *or* disgusts.
tædĭfĕr, a, um, a. bearing a torch.
tædĭum, ii, n. weariness, irksomeness,
tediousness; loathing, disgust, loathsome object.
tænia, ae, f. band, fillet, ribbon; head-
band.
tæter, tra, trum, foul; hideous; loathsome; shameful.
tætrē, ad. foully. [severe; harsh.
tætrĭcus, a, um, a. gloomy; sour;
tăgax, ăcis, a. light-fingered. [sandals.
tālărĭa, ium, n. pl. ankles; winged
tālāris, e, a. reaching to the ankles.
tālārius, a, um, a. pertaining to dice.
tălasio, ōnis, f., tălassius, ii, m. congratulatory exclamation addressed to a
bride.
tālea, ae, f. stake, rod; graft.
tălentum, i, n. talent (Grecian weight = 60
minæ, about £250).
tālio, ōnis, f. retaliation similar to the
injury dealt; an eye for an eye.
tālis, e, a. such, of such a kind; so good
or great. [manner.
tālĭter, ad. in such a manner; in like
talpa, ae, c. (animal) mole.
tālus, i, m. ankle, ankle-bone; heel;
foot; die (to play with).
tam, ad. so; so much, so very; in so far;
as, as much, as well;—non — . . .
quam, not so much . . . as, less . . .
than.
tămărīce, ēs, tămărix, īcis, f. tamarisk.
tămărindus (mod. hort.), tamarind.

tamdiū, ad. so long (as).
tămen, c. notwithstanding, neverthelsss,
however, yet, still.
tămĕnetsi, c. although.
tămetsi, c. although, though.
tamquam, ad. as if; just as if.
tănăcētum (mod. hort.), tansy.
tandem, ad. at length, at last, in the end,
finally; (interrogatively) pray, now,
then.
tango, tĕtĭgi, tactum, 3. v.a. to touch; to
lay hands on; to handle; to strike; to
take; to taste; to reach, to be near,
to arrive (at); to besmear; to besprinkle; to wash; *fig.* to affect, to
move; to dupe; to cheat; to touch
upon, to mention;—(rem) acu tangere,
to hit the nail on the head;—de cælo
tactus, struck by lightning.
tanquam, v. tamquam.
tantillum, ad. (ever) so little.
tantillus, a, um, a. so little.
tantisper, ad. for so long a time, so long;
meanwhile. [greatly.
tantō, ăd. so much, by so much, so
tantŏpĕrĕ, ad. so greatly, so very, so
much.
tantŭlus, a, um, a. so little, so small;
—tantulum, ad. such a trifle, ever so
little.
tantum, ad. so much, so greatly, to such
a degree, so; so long; only, but, just;
— non, all but.
tantummŏdo, ad. only.
tantundem, tantĭdem, n. just so much,
just as much.
tantus, a, um, a. so great;—tantum, ad.
so much; so many; so little, so few;
—in tantum, so far, to such a degree;—
tanti, worth so much; for so much;—
tanti esse, to be worth while;—tanto,
by so much, so greatly; so much the . . .
tantusdem, tantadem, tantundem, a. just
so great; just as much.
tăpes, ētis, m., tăpēte, ĭs, tăpētum, i, n.
carpet, tapestry, hangings; coverlet.
tăraxăcum (mod. hort.), dandelion.
tardē, ad. slowly, tardily.
tardesco, 3. v.n. to become slow.
tardĭgrādus, a, um, a. slow-paced.
tardĭlŏquus, a, um, a. slow-spoken.
tardĭpes, ĕdis, a. slow-footed.
tardĭtas, ātis, tardĭtūdo, ĭnis, f. slowness,
tardiness; *fig.* dulness, stupidity.
tardĭuscŭlus, a, um, a. somewhat slow *or*
dull (of apprehension).
tardo, 1. v.a. & n. to make slow, to retard; to hinder, to delay; to loiter, to
tarry.
tardus, a, um, a. slow, sluggish, tardy; *fig.*
deliberate; dull, stupid.

tarpessīta, ae, tarpezīta, ae, m. v. **trapezīta.**

Tartăreus, a, um, a. Tartarean, infernal.

Tartărus, i, m., **Tartăra, ōrum,** n. pl. infernal regions, Tartarus.

taura, ae, f. barren cow.

taurea, ae, f. leather whip.

taureus, a, um, a. of a bull *or* ox, of oxen; —**terga taurea,** bulls' hides; *fig.* drum.

taurĭfer, a, um, a. bull-bearing.

taurĭformis, e, a. bull-shaped.

Taurii ludi, games at Rome, held in honour of the infernal gods.

taurīnus, a, um, a. pertaining to bulls *or* oxen, bull's . . .

taurus, i, m. bull, bullock, ox; Bull (constellation).

tautŏlŏgia, ae, f. tautology.

taxātĭo, ōnis, f. estimation, valuation.

tāxeus, a, um, a. of yew.

taxo, i. v.a. *fig.* to rate, to value, to appraise, to estimate; to reproach, to tax with a fault.

tāxus, i, f. yew-tree.

tē, v. tu.

techna, ae, f. ruse, stratagem.

technici, ōrum, m. pl. teachers of art.

technicus, a, um, a. technical.

tectē, ad. covertly, privily, cautiously.

tector, ōris, m. plasterer.

tectōriŏlum, i, n. plaster, rough-cast.

tectōrium, ii, n. plaster, stucco, rough-cast, coating.

tectōrius, a, um, a. pertaining to a plasterer's work.

tectum, i, n. roof; house; abode, dwelling; shelter.   [cautious.

tectus, a, um, a. disguised, reserved,

tēda, etc., v. **tæda, etc.**   [coverlet.

tēges, ĕtis, f. rush mat; coarse rug;

tēgillum, i, n. hood.

tēgīmen, ĭnis, n. covering, cover. [tum.

tēgīmentum, tegmentum, i, v. **tegumen-**

tegmen, ĭnis, v. **tegimen.**

tēgo, xi, ctum, 3. v.a. to cover; to hide, to conceal; to keep secret; to defend, to guard, to protect.

tēgŭla, ae, f. tile;—**tegulæ,** pl. tiled roof.

tēgŭmen, ĭnis, v. **tegimen.**

tēgŭmentum, i, n. covering, cover.

tēla, ae, f. woven stuff, web; warp; loom; design, plan.

tellūs, ūris, f. earth; globe; land, ground; country, territory, region.

tēlum, i, n. missile, dart, spear, javelin; sword; arrow; (any offensive) weapon; sunbeam, ray.

tēmĕrārius, a, um, a. accidental; rash, foolhardy, thoughtless, imprudent, inconsiderate.

tēmĕrātor, ōris, m. defiler, polluter.

tēmĕrē, ad. by chance, at random, rashly, heedlessly, inconsiderately;—**non** *or* **haud temere est,** it is no accident;—**non —,** not easily.   [temerity.

tēmĕrĭtas, ātis, f. rashness, heedlessness;

tēmĕro, i. v.a. to violate; to profane, to defile, to pollute.   [drink.

tēmētum, i, n. strong wine; intoxicating

temno, tempsi, temptum, 3. v.a. to slight, to scorn, to despise, to contemn.

tēmo, ōnis, m. beam *or* pole of a carriage; wagon; Charles's Wain.

tempĕrāmentum, i, n. measure, mean, moderation; temperature.

tempĕrans, antis, a. moderate, temperate; sober; sparing; abstaining.

tempĕranter, ad. moderately.

tempĕrantia, ae, f. moderateness, moderation, sobriety, temperance.

tempĕrātē, ad. moderately, temperately.

tempĕrātĭo, ōnis, f. fit proportion, symmetry; organization, constitution; temper.   [composition.

tempĕrātūra, ae, f. climate, temperature,

tempĕrātus, a, um, a. temperate; moderate; sober.   [seasonably.

tempĕri, ad. at the right time, in time,

tempĕries, ei, f. mixture, tempering; temperature; temperateness; moderation.

tempĕro, i. v.a. & n. to temper, to mix *or* mingle; to moderate, to dilute, to allay, to calm; to regulate; to govern, to rule; to restrain; to be moderate *or* temperate; to abstain, to forbear; to spare.

tempestas, ātis, f. space of time, season, period; weather; storm, tempest; calamity, misfortune; disturbance; destruction.   [fitly.

tempestīvē, ad. seasonably, opportunely;

tempestīvitas, ātis, f. timeliness, seasonableness.

tempestīvus, a, um, a. timely, seasonable, opportune, fitting; early, mature, ripe.

templum, i, n. temple; (in augury) open place for observation, marked out with the augur's staff; sanctuary; asylum; shrine; sepulchral monument; any open space.

tempŏrārius, a, um, a. temporary.

tempŏri, ad. in good time.

temp . . ., tempt . . ., v. **tent.**

tempus, ōris, n. time, season; occasion, opportunity; season (of the year); measure, quantity; climate; condition, state; affair, case;—**tempora,** pl. times, circumstances; temples of the head;—**tempore** & **tempori,** in time, seasonably, betimes;—**ad —,** in time, at the right time; for a time, for the moment;—**ex tempore,** instantane-

ously, ex tempore, on the spur of the
mome' -in tempore, at the right
time, in time;—in —, for a time;—
pro tempore, according to circumstances.
tēmŭlentia, ae, f. drunkenness.
tēmŭlentus, a, um, a. drunk, intoxicated,
tipsy.
tĕnācītas, ā+is, f. tenacity; niggardliness.
tĕnācĭter, ad. tenaciously.
tĕnax, ācis, a. holding fast, tenacious;
firm; sparing, niggardly; persistent,
steadfast; stubborn, obstinate.
tendĭcŭla, ae, f. little snare.
tendo, tĕtendi, tentum & tensum, 3. v.a.
& n. to stretch, to stretch out, to extend; to pitch (a tent); to lay (a
snare); to bend (a bow); to aim, to
strain, to aggravate; to strive; to go,
to tend; to encamp; to endeavour; to
advance, to reach.
tĕnebræ, ārum, f. pl. darkness, obscurity;
night; swoon; blindness; death; dark
place; haunt; nether world; *fig.*
gloom; low birth; baseness; mysteries.
tĕnebrīcōsus, a, um, a. dark, gloomy.
tĕnebrĭcus, tĕnebrōsus, a, um, a. dark,
gloomy.
tĕnellŭlus, a, um, a. tender, delicate.
tĕnellus, a, um, a. somewhat tender *or*
delicate; young.
tĕneo, tĕnui, tentum, 2 v.a. & n. to hold,
to hold fast; to seize; to keep, to
have, to possess, to dwell in; to
occupy; to retain, to stop, to hinder;
to engage; to amuse; to embrace; to
support; to defend; to guard, to preserve; to reach; to understand; to
remember; to contain; to prevail; to
continue, to last, to hold out; to
keep one's course; to steer; to hold a
position.
tĕner, ĕra, ĕrum, a. soft, delicate, tender;
effeminate; young; gentle; inexperienced; weak; merciful.
tĕnĕrasco, 3. v.n. to grow tender.
tĕnĕrē, ad. tenderly, delicately, softly.
tĕnĕresco, 3. v.n., v. tenerasco.
tĕnĕrĭtas, ātis, f. softness, tenderness.
tĕnĕrĭtūdo, ĭnis, f. softness.
tĕnor, ōris, m. holding on, holding fast;
course, career, tenor; accent;—**uno
—e,** in one course, uniformly.
tensa, ae, f. chariot on which the images
of the gods were carried in the games
in the Circus.
tensus, v. tentus.
tentābundus, a, um, a trying, making
attempts.
tentāmen, ĭnis, n trial, essay, attempt.

tentāmentum, i, n. trial, proof, essay,
attempt.
tentātio, ōnis, f. trial, proof; attack.
tentātor, ōris, m. trier, tempter.
tento, 1. v.a. to handle, to touch, to feel;
to attempt, to try; to prove; to test;
to attack; to urge; to excite, to disturb.
tentōrium, ii, n. tent.
tentus, a, um, a. stretched out, strained,
tense.
tĕnuĭcŭlus, a, um, a. slight, poor.
tĕnuis, e, a. thin, slender; slight; small;
mean; poor, trifling; fine, nice;
subtle; weak; insignificant; low.
tĕnuĭtas, ātis, f. thinness, slenderness,
smallness, tenuity; poverty, scarcity;
fineness, acuteness, subtlety.
tĕnuĭter, ad. thinly; finely, exactly,
subtly; lightly.
tĕnuo, 1. v.a. to make thin; to dilute; to
reduce, to lessen; to enfeeble.
tĕnŭs, pr. reaching to, as far as, up to.
tĕpĕfăcio, fēci, factum, 3. v.a. to make
lukewarm; to warm; **tĕpĕfio, factus,
fĭĕri,** 3. v.n. pass. to be lukewarm.
tĕpeo, 2. v.n. to be (luke)warm; *fig.* to be
indifferent; to be enamoured.
tĕpesco, pui, 3. v.a. to become lukewarm,
to become warm, to grow cool.
tĕpĭdārium, ii, n. hot bath.
tĕpĭdo, 1. v.a. to warm.
tĕpĭdus, a, um, a. lukewarm, tepid; faint,
languid.
tĕpor, ōris, m. gentle warmth, lukewarmness; coldness.
tĕr, ad. three times, thrice.
terdĕcies, ad. thirteen times.
tĕrēbinthĭna, ae, f. turpentine.
tĕrēbinthĭnus, a, um, a. of *or* belonging
to turpentine.
tĕrēbinthus, i, f. terebinth tree
tĕrebra, ae, f. borer, gimlet.
tĕrebro, 1. v.a. to bore, to perforate.
tĕrēdo, ĭnis, f. boring beetle; moth.
tĕrēs, ĕtis, a. round, rounded off; smooth,
polished; slender, well-made; elegant.
tergĕmĭnus, a, um, a. threefold, triple.
tergeo, tergo, si, sum, 2. *or* 3. v.a. to rub
off, to wipe clean *or* dry, to cleanse;
to polish.
tergĭversātio, ōnis, f. subterfuge, tergiversation.
tergĭversor, ātus sum, 1. v.n. dep. to turn
one's back; to decline, to refuse; to
shuffle, to tergiversate.
tergum, i, tergus, ōris, n. back; hide,
skin; body; shield, target; surface;—
terga dare *or* **terga vertere,** to turn tail,
to flee.
termēs, ĭtis, f. bough *or* twig cut off.

Terminalia, ium, n. pl. festival of the god of boundaries (Terminus).

terminatio, onis, f. bounding, end; conclusion, determination; arrangement.

termino, 1. v.a. to set bounds to, to limit; to define; to end, to terminate.

terminus, i, m. boundary, bound, limit; end, term; — **terminus ad quem,** the end at which one aims;—**terminus a quo,** the place from which one starts.

terni, ae, a, a. three each; three.

terni deni, ae, a, a. num. thirteen each.

ternio, onis, m. (the number) three.

tero, trivi, tritum, 3. v.a. to rub, to bruise, to grind; to thrash out; to polish, to smooth; to wear out or away; to handle constantly; to visit frequently; to pass, to spend (the time); to waste.

terra, ae, f. earth; land, ground, soil; country; territory; — **marique,** by land and sea;—**orbis terræ** or **orbis terrarum,** the world;—**terræ motus, us,** m. earthquake;—**terræ filius,** a son of the soil;—**terra firma,** solid earth;— **terra incognita,** an unexplored region.

terrenus, a, um, a. earthen; earthly; mortal;—**terrenum, i,** n. land, ground.

terreo, ui, itum, 2. v.a. to frighten, to terrify; to scare away; to deter.

terrestris, e, a. by or on land, terrestrial.

terreus, a, um, a. earthen.

terribilis, e, a. frightful, terrible.   [bear.

terricula, orum, n. pl. scarecrow, bug-

terrifico, 1. v.a. to terrify.

terrificus, a, um, a. frightful, terrific.

terrigena, ae, c. (poet.) earth-born.

terriloquus, a, um, a. speaking terrible things.

territo, 1. v.a. to frighten frequently; to alarm, to terrify.

territorium, ii, n. domain, district, territory.

terror, oris, m. dread, alarm, terror.

tersus, a, um, a. clean, neat.

tersus, us, m. scouring, wiping.

tertiadecimani, orum, m. pl. soldiers of the thirteenth legion.

tertianus, a, um, a. tertian;—**tertiana, ae,** f. tertian fever;—**tertiani, orum,** m. pl. soldiers of the third legion.

tertio, ad. for the third time; thirdly, in the third place.

tertium, ad. for the third time.

tertius, a, um, a. third;—**tertium quid,** a third body resulting from the union of two other bodies;—**tertius gaudens,** a third party gleefully watching the struggle between his two competitors.

tertiusdecimus, a, um, a. num. thirteenth.

teruncius, ii, m. farthing; trifle.

tesca, orum, n. pl. wild regions, deserts.

tesqua, v. tesca.

tessella, ae, f. small square stone.

tessellatus, a, um, a. checkered, tessellated.

tessera, ae, f. square piece of stone; square tile; die; tablet on which the watchword was written; watchword; tally; billet, ticket.

tesserarius, ii, m. he who gives the watchword from the commander.

tesserula, ae, f. small square bit of stone for paving.

testa, ae, f. earthen pot, pitcher, jug; pottery, brick, potsherd; shell; shellfish; crust.

testaceus, a, um, a. testaceous; made of earth, baked, covered with shell.

testamentarius, a, um, a. testamentary; —, ii, m. forger of a testament; notary.

testamentum, i, n. will, testament.

testamur (mod.), we bear witness (that so-and-so has successfully passed an examination); a certificate of proficiency.

testatio, onis, f. invoking as witness.

testator, oris, m. one who makes a will or testament.

testatrix, icis, f. testatrix.

testatus, a, um, a. published, public.

testiculus, i, m. testicle.

testificatio, onis, f. bearing witness, giving testimony; attestation, proof, evidence.

testificor, atus sum, 1. v.a. dep. to call to witness; to bear witness, to attest, to testify; to declare; to publish, to show.

testimonium, ii, n. attestation, testimony; evidence, proof.

testis, is, c. witness; spectator.

testis, is, m. testicle.

testor, atus sum, 1. v.a. dep. to be a witness, to testify, to attest; to prove; to declare; to invoke as witness; to make a will.   [earthen pot.

testu, indecl., **testum, i,** n. earthen pot lid,

testudineus, a, um, a. pertaining to a tortoise; made of tortoiseshell.

testudo, inis, f. tortoise; tortoiseshell; lute, lyre; arch, vault; penthouse; roof of a house; (mil.) a covering formed of the shields of the soldiers held over their heads.

testum, i, n. earthen pan.

tetanicus, a, um, a. suffering from spasms.

tetanus, i, m. spasm.

teter, v. tæter.

tetradrachmum, i, n. silver coin of four drachmas (about 3s. 4d.).

tetrao, ōnis, m. black-cock.
tetrarchēs, ae, m. tetrarch; ruler of the fourth part of a country.
tetrarchia, ae, f. tetrarchy.
tĕtrē, v. tætre.
tetrĭcus, v. tætricus.
texo, xui, xtum, 3. v.a. to weave; to plait; to fabricate, to make; to build; to compose.
textĭlis, e, a. woven, wrought, textile; —textile, is, n. web, stuff, fabric, piece of cloth, canvas.
textor, ōris, m. weaver.
textrīnum, i, n. weaving.
textrix, īcis, f. female weaver; spinster.
textum, i, n. texture, fabric; framework; web.
textūra, ae, f. texture, web, structure.
textus, ūs, m. texture, tissue; structure; construction.
thălămus, i, m. bedchamber; bridal-bed; marriage, wedlock; dwelling-room, chamber.
thălictrum, i, n. (mod. hort.), tufted columbine.
theātrālis, e, a. theatrical, of the stage.
theātrum, i, n. playhouse, theatre; scaffold; theatrical audience, spectators; place of exhibition, show.
thĕca, ae, f. envelope, cover, case, sheath.
thĕma, ătis, n. theme, subject; horoscope, nativity.
thensaurus, v. thesaurus.
theobrōma (mod. hort.), cocoa-tree.
theŏlŏgus, i, m. theologian.
theŏrēma, ătis, n. theorem.
theŏrēticus, a, um, a. theoretical.
theŏria, ae, f. theory.
thēriăca, ae, f. an antidote against poisonous bites.   [baths.
thermæ, ārum, f. pl. warm springs, warm
thermŏpōlium, ii, n. tavern (where warm drinks were sold).
thermŏpōto, 1. v.a. to refresh with warm potations.
thermŭlæ, ārum, f. pl. little hot baths.
thēsaurārius, ii, m. treasurer; —, a, um, a. of treasure.
thēsaurus, i, m. treasure, provision, store; treasury; treasure-vault; fig. collection, magazine, repository.
Thĕtĭs, ĭdis, f. a. sea-nymph; the sea.
thiăsus, i, n. Bacchic dance; fig. frantic revel.
thŏlus, i, m. cupola; rotunda.
thŏrax, ācis, m. breast; breastplate, cuirass; bust.
Thrascias, ae, m. north-west wind.
Thrax, ācis, m. fencer, gladiator.
thrŏnus, i, m. throne.
thus, thūris, v. tus.

thuya (mod. hort.), arbor vitæ.
thyăsus, v. thiasus.
thymbra, ae, f. (bot.) savory.
thymōsus, a, um, a. full of thyme.
thymum, i, n. thyme.
thynnus, i, m. tunny-fish.
thyrsus, i, m. Bacchic staff (wound with ivy and vine-leaves).
tiāra, ae, f., tiāras, ae, m. turban, tiara.
tībia, ae, f. shin-bone; pipe, flute.
tībiăle, is, n. legging, stocking.
tībiālis, e, a. relating to the flute.
tībĭcen, ĭnis, m. flute-player.
tībĭcĕna, ae, f. female flute-player.
tigillum, i, n. little beam or rafter; funnel of a chimney.
tignārius, a, um, a. relating to beams, etc.;—faber —, carpenter.
tignum, i, n. timber, building-material; trunk of a tree, log, beam; vine-prop.
tigridia (mod. hort.), tiger-flower.
tigrīnus, a, um, a. like a tiger.
tigris, is, & ĭdis, c. tiger; tigress.
tĭlia, ae, f. linden-tree, lime-tree.
timĕfactus, a, um, a. frightened, alarmed, scared.
timeo, ui, 2. v.a. & n. to fear, to dread, to be fearful; to be afraid of.
timĭdē, ad. fearfully, timidly.
timĭdĭtas, ātis, f. fearfulness, timidity, cowardice.
timĭdus, a, um, a. fearful, afraid, timid, cowardly.
timor, ōris, m. fear, dread, terror; anxiety; awe; reverence; object exciting fear.
tinctĭlis, e, a. impregnated.
tinctūra, ae, f. dye, colour, tincture.
tinctus, ūs, m. dyeing; dipping.
tinea, ae, f. moth, book-worm, silk-worm.
tingo (tinguo), nxi, nctum, 3. v.a. to wet, to bathe; to dye, to tinge; to sprinkle.
tinnio, īvi & ii, ītum, 4. v.n. & a. to jingle, to tinkle; to scream.
tinnītus, ūs, m. jingling, tingling; fig. jingle of words.
tinnŭlus, a, um, a. ringing, tinkling, shrill-sounding.
tintinnābŭlum, i, n. little bell.
tintinno or tintĭno, 1. v.n. to jingle, to tingle.
tīnus, i, m. laurustinus (kind of bay-tree).
tippŭla, ae, f. water-spider.
tĭro, ōnis, m. recruit; beginner, apprentice, novice.
tīrōcĭnium, ii, n. inexperience in service; first campaign; recruits; fig. first beginning, first trial; mere novice.
tīruncŭlus, i, m. young beginner.
Tītan, ānis, m. fig. sun.
tītillātio, ōnis, f. tickling, titillation.

titillo, 1. v.a. to tickle, to titillate; to provoke; to move pleasantly.

titŭbanter, ad. hesitatingly, falteringly.

titŭbantia, ae, f. stammering; hesitation.

titŭbātio, ōnis, f. staggering.

titŭbo, 1. v.n. & a. to stagger, to totter, to reel; to hesitate, to waver.

titŭlus, i, m. title; ticket, bill; notice, (title of) honour; glory, renown; pretence.

tmēsis, is, f. the division of a word and the interposition of another word between the parts, e.g. hanc ego nunc ignaram . . . inque salutatam linquo for insalutatamque.

tŏcul(l)io, ōnis, m. usurer.

tōfus, i, m. tufa.

tŏga, ae, f. outer garment of a Roman citizen in time of peace, toga; *fig.* peace; management of civil affairs; — candida, toga worn by candidates for office; — prætexta, toga worn by magistrates and freeborn children, seamed with purple; — virilis, toga worn by adults (without the purple seam).

tŏgātus, a, um, a. dressed in *or* wearing a toga;—togata, ae, f. national (Roman) drama; prostitute;—togati, ōrum, m. pl. Roman citizens; —, i, m. client; citizen.

tŏgŭla, ae, f. little toga.

tŏlĕrābĭlis, e, a. that may be borne with, tolerable, patient.

tŏlĕrābĭliter, ad. tolerably, patiently.

tŏlĕrans, antis, a. tolerating, tolerant.

tŏlĕranter, ad. tolerantly, patiently.

tŏlĕrantia, ae, f. endurance, sufferance.

tŏlĕrātio, ōnis, f. toleration.

tŏlĕro, 1. v.a. to bear, to endure, to sustain, to tolerate; *fig.* to nourish, to support.

tollēno, ōnis, m. swingbeam.

tollo, sustŭli, sublātum, 3. v.a. to lift *or* raise up; to animate; to accept, to acknowledge (a new-born child); to beget; to bring up, to educate; to defer; to put up; to cut off; to annul, to abolish; to destroy; to remove; to kill.

tŏlūtim, ad. fast, full trot; amblingly.

tŏmācŭlum, i, n. sausage.

tōmentum, i, n. stuffing for cushions.

Tŏnans, antis, m. thunderer.

tondeo, tŏtondi, tonsum, 2. v.a. to shear, to shave; to clip; to prune; to crop, to browse (upon); to gather; to cull; to pluck; to fleece, to plunder.

tŏnĭtrus, ūs, m. tŏnitruum, i, n. thunder.

tŏno, ui, ĭtum, 1. v.n. & a. to thunder; to roar; to thunder forth, to speak with a thundering voice.

tonsa, ae, f. oar.

tonsĭlis, e, a. shorn; clipped.

tonsillæ, ārum, f. pl. tonsils.

tonsĭto, 1. v.a. to shear.

tonsor, ōris, m. shearer, shaver; hair-cutter; barber.   [—, razor.

tonsōrius, a, um, a. of a barber;—culter

tonstrīcŭla, ae, f. female hair-cutter.

tonstrīna, ae, f. barber's shop.

tonstrix, īcis, f. female hair-cutter *or* barber.

tonsūra, ae, f. shearing, clipping.

tonsus, ūs, m. shearing; cut *or* mode of dressing the hair.

tŏnus, i, m. sound, tone (also of colour).

tŏpazus, i, f. topaz.

tophus, v. tofus.   [gardening.

tŏpiāria, ae, f. topiary art, ornamental

tŏpiārius, a, um, a. connected with ornamental gardening; —, ii, m. ornamental gardener.

tŏrāl, is, n. valance (of a bed).

torcŭlar, is, n. oil- *or* wine-press, cellar.

torcŭlārius, a, um, belonging to a press.

torcŭlum, i, n. press.

torcŭlus, a, um, a., v. torcularius.

tŏreuma, ātis, n. embossed work.

tŏreuta, ae, m. graver.

tŏreutice, es, f. the art of graving.

tormentum, i, n. twisted rope; engine to cast stones *or* darts; missile; instrument of torture; rack; torture, anguish, pain, torment.

tormina, um, n. pl. colic.   [or colic.

torminōsus, a, um, a. subject to the gripes

torno, 1. v.a. to turn (in a lathe); to round off; *fig.* to fashion, to smooth.

tornus, i, m. (turner's) lathe.   [fleshy,

tŏrōsus, a, um, a. muscular, brawny,

torpēdo, ĭnis, f. numbness, torpidity; sluggishness; cramp-fish.

torpeo, 2. v.n. to be numb *or* torpid; *fig.* to be stupefied.

torpesco, pui, 3. v.n. to grow numb, to become torpid; *fig.* to slacken.

torpĭdus, a, um, a. benumbed, torpid; stupefied.

torpor, ōris, m. numbness, torpor, stupefaction; inactivity, listlessness, sluggishness.   [wreathed.

torquātus, a, um, a. wearing a collar,

torqueo, torsi, tortum, 2. v.a. to turn, to twist, to turn about *or* away; to twist awry, to whirl; to hurl; to put upon the rack, to torture; to distort; to pervert; to vex.

torquēs, torquis, is, m. & f. collar, chain, necklace; wreath; garland (of flowers).

torrens, entis, a. burning hot; parching; sultry; boiling; roaring, rushing; *fig.* impetuous, violent.

torrens, entis, m. torrent (also *fig.*).
torreo, torrui, tostum, 2. v.a. to parch, to roast, to scorch, to burn; to dry up.
torresco, 3. v.n. to be dried *or* roasted.
torridus, a, um, a. parched, torrid, dried up, dry; shrivelled up; sultry; nipped (with cold).
torris, is, m. firebrand.
tortilis, e, a. twisted, winding.
tortivus, a, um, a. squeezed, put through a press.
tortor, ōris, m. executioner; tormentor, torturer.
tortuōsus, a, um, a. winding, tortuous; *fig.* entangled, involved; complicated; painful.
tortūra, ae, f. twisting; torturing; torture.
tortus, a, um, a. crooked, twisted.
tortus, ūs, m. twisting, winding; wreath.
tōrŭlus, i, m. tuft of hair.
tōrus, i, m. knot; bulge; muscle, brawn; raised ornament; swelling; bed, couch, sofa; marriage-bed, marriage; bank of earth. [verity.
torvitas, ātis, f. sourness, sternness, se-
torvus, a, um, a. stern, wild, fierce, grim; gloomy; cruel, savage.
tōt, a. indecl. so many.
tŏtĭdem, a. indecl. just so many, just as many;—**totidem verbis,** in so many words.
tŏtiens, tŏtiēs, ad. so often, so many times, as often, as many times.
tōtus, a, um, tōtīus, a. all, the whole, entire, total;—**ex toto,** totally, wholly; —**in toto,** in general, upon the whole; —**in totum,** wholly, entirely;—**toto cælo,** by the whole sky, entirely.
toxĭcum, i, n. poison.
trăbālis, e, a. pertaining to beams; beam-like, strong as a beam.
trăbea, ae, f. robe of state.
trăbeātus, a, um, a. clad in *or* wearing a robe of state.
trăbēs, is, trabs, trăbis, f. beam, timber; ship; roof; obelisk; weapon.
tractābilis, e, a. manageable, tractable; *fig.* pliant, gentle.
tractātio, ōnis, f. management, treatment; handling; discussion.
tractātus, ūs, m. handling, treating; management; treatise.
tractim, ad. by degrees, little by little; slowly; lingeringly; at length.
tracto, 1. v.a. to touch, to handle, to manage; to exercise, to practise, to transact, to perform; to conduct, to lead; to represent; to treat, to use; to discuss; to wield.
tractum, i, n. flock of wool.
tractus, a, um, a. flowing, fluent.

tractus, ūs, m. trailing; train; drawing, draught; creeping; region, tract, territory; coast; climate; space, place; track; current; course, progress; lapse (of time), period; extension, length; drawling (of words).
trādĭtio, ōnis, f. giving up, surrender instruction, teaching.
trādĭtor, ōris, m. betrayer, traitor.
trādo, dĭdi, dĭtum, 3. v.a. to give over, to deliver, to surrender; to consign; to commit, to confide; to betray; to give up, to intrust; to transmit; to bequeath; to narrate, to relate; to teach.
trādūco, xi, ctum, 3. v.a. to lead *or* bring across *or* over; to lead along *or* parade; to hand down, to transmit; to transfer; to remove; to draw over; to disgrace; to dishonour; to pass; to spend.
trāductio, ōnis, f. leading along; course, passage; scandal; disgrace; passing, spending; removal.
trādux, ŭcis, m. vine-branch, vine-layer.
trăgĭcē, ad. tragically.
trăgĭcŏcōmœdia, ae, f. tragicomedy.
trăgĭcus, a, um, a. tragic; grand, sublime; horrible, terrible; **—, i,** m. tragic poet, tragedian.
trăgœdia, ae, f. tragedy; tragical event; spectacle.
trăgœdus, i, m. tragedian; tragic actor.
tragopōgon (mod. hort.), salsafy.
trăgŭla, ae, f. large javelin; drag-net; attack; plot; snare.
trăhea, ae, f. drag, sledge.
trăho, xi, ctum, 3. v.a. to draw, to drag, to haul; to drag along; to trail; to draw *or* stretch out; to extend; to contract; to drink; to snuff up; to carry off, to plunder; to attract, to allure; to influence; to ascribe; to divert, to draw off; to bring, to fetch; to lead; to derive; to get; to assume, to claim; to distract; to protract; to guess; to defer, to delay; to describe.
trăjectio, ōnis, f. crossing *or* passing over, passage; (of stars) shooting; exaggeration.
trăjectus, ūs, m. crossing, passage; ferry.
trăjicio, jēci, jectum, 3. v.a. to throw, to cast *or* shoot over *or* across; to convey across, to transport; to pierce, to stab; to transfer;— v.n. to pass over.
trālātīcius, v. **translaticius.**
trālūceo, v. **transluceo.**
trāma, ae, f. weft, woof.
trāmeo, v. **transmeo.**
trămĕs, ĭtis, m. crossway, bypath, footpath; road, path, way; flight; course; method.

t: ā migro, v. transmigro.

trāmitto, v. transmitto. [over.

trānăto, 1. v.n.; to swim across; to swim

trāno, 1. v.a. to swim over *or* across *or* through; to pierce through; to fly over.

tranquillē, ad. calmly, tranquilly.

tranquillĭtas, ātis, f. quietness, tranquillity; (of weather) calm; *fig.* calmness, serenity.

tranquillō, ad. quietly.

tranquillo, 1. v.a. to calm, to still; to tranquillize; to brighten, to clear up.

tranquillum, ĭ, n. calm, calmness; fine weather.

tranquillus, a, um, a. quiet, calm, still, tranquil; serene, settled.

trans, pr. across, over, beyond;˙ (in composition) across; through.

transăbeo, ĭi, 4. v.a. to transfix, to go beyond.

transactor, ōris, m. manager, broker.

transădĭgo, ădēgi, ădactum, 3. v.a. to thrust *or* pierce through.

Transalpīnus, a, um, a. Transalpine; —Transalpini, ōrum, m. pl. Transalpine nations.

transcendo, di, sum, 3. v.n. & a. to climb *or* step over, to surmount; to exceed, to surpass; to transcend; to transgress.

transcrībo, psi, ptum, 3. v.a. to copy off, to transcribe; to transfer, to assign; to remove.

transcurro, curri & cŭcurri, cursum, 3. v.n. & a. to run over *or* across; to pass by; to run *or* hasten through; to touch upon; to elapse.

transcursus, ūs, m. running *or* flying through; brief touching upon, cursory mention.

transdūco, etc., v. traduco, etc. [trap.

transenna, ae, f. lattice, casement; snare,

transeo, ĭi & īvi, ĭtum, 4. v.n. & a. to go over *or* across, to pass over; to pass by; to go through; to go over (to a party, etc.); to exceed, to surpass; to transgress; to omit, to say nothing of; to excel; to elapse, to pass away; to be transformed.

ransĕro, 3. v.a. to transplant.

transfĕro, tŭli, lātum, v.a. ir. to carry *or* bring over; to transport; to transfer, to transplant; to copy, to transcribe; to change; to transform; to remove, to convey, to direct; to put off, to postpone; to use metaphorically.

transfigo, xi, xum, 3. v.a. to thrust *or* pierce through, to transfix.

transfigūrātio, ōnis, f. transfiguration, change.

transfigūro, 1. v.a. to transform, to transfigure, to metamorphose.

transfŏdio, fōdi, fossum, 3. v.a. to thrust *or* stab through.

transformis, e, a. transformed.

transformo, 1. v.a. to change in shape, to transform.

transfŏro, 1. v.a. to bore through.

transfrēto, 1. v.n. & a. to cross a strait, to pass over the sea.

transfŭga, ae, c. deserter.

transfŭgio, fūgi, 3. v.n. to go over to the enemy, to desert.

transfŭgium, ĭi, n. desertion.

transfundo, fūdi, fūsum, 3. v.a. to pour out, to pour off, to decant, to transfuse; to transfer.

transfŭsio, ōnis, f. pouring out, decanting; *fig.* transmigration (of a people).

transgrĕdior, gressus, 3. v.a. & n. dep. to step over, to go *or* pass over, to cross; to surpass; to omit; to go over (to another party). [position.

transgressio, ōnis, f. passage; *fig.* trans-transgressus, ūs, m. passing over, passage.

transĭgo, ēgi, actum, 3. v.a. to thrust *or* run through, to pierce through; to conclude, to finish, to settle; to dispatch, to come to an agreement; to spend; to lead.

transĭlio, īvi & ui, 4. v.n. & a. to leap, to jump *or* spring across *or* over; to neglect, to skip over; to transgress.

transĭtio, ōnis, f. passing over, passage; desertion; infection, contagion.

transĭtus, ūs, m. passage; transition; desertion.

transj . . ., v. traj . . .

translātīcius (*or* ītius), a, um, a. transmitted, hereditary; customary; common, usual.

translātio, ōnis, f. transferring; transplanting; metaphor; shifting off.

translātor, ōris, m. transferrer, conveyer.

translūceo, 2. v.n. to shine through; to be transparent.

translucĭdus, a, um, a. transparent.

transmărinus, a, um, a. transmarine.

transmeo, 1. v.n. & a. to go over *or* across, to go through.

transmigro, 1. v.n. to transmigrate, to move. [ing over.

transmissio, ōnis, f. sending across, pass-transmissus, ūs, m. passing over, passage.

transmitto, mĭsi, missum, 3. v.a. & n. to let go through *or* across; to send *or* convey across; to dispatch, to transmit; to omit, to pass by; to leave unmentioned; to spend; to cross; to traverse. [mountains.

transmontānus, ĭ, a. (m.) beyond the

transmŏveo, mōvi, mōtum, 2. v.a. to remove; to transfer.

transmūto, 1. v.a. to change, to shift, to transmute.

transnăto, 1., v. trānăto.

transno, v. trano.

transpĭcio, 3. v.a. to look or see through.

transpōno, pŏsui, pŏsĭtum, 3. v.a. to set over or across; to remove, to transfer.

transportātio, ōnis, f. transportation.

transporto, 1. v.a. to carry across; to remove, to transport; to convey over; to banish.

transscendo, v. transcendo.

transscribo, v. transcribo.

transsilio, v. transilio.

transsulto, v. transulto.

transtrum, i, n. cross-beam; seat or bench in a boat.

transulto, 1. v.n. to leap over or across.

transūmo, mpsi, mptum, 3. v.a. to adopt from another.

transuo, ui, ūtum, 3. v.a. to sew or stitch through; to pierce through.

transvectio, ōnis, f. carrying or transporting across; riding past, review.

transvĕho, trăvĕho, xi, ctum, 3. v.a. to carry over, to convey across, to transport; to conduct or lead along;— transvehi, to sail, ride or travel over; to elapse, to pass.

transverbĕro, 1. v.a. to thrust or pierce through, to transfix.

transversārius, a, um, a. transverse, lying across.

transversus, a, um, p. & a. across, athwart, crosswise; transverse; contrary, opposite;—digitus transversus or unguis transversus, a. finger's-breadth.

transvŏlĭto, 1. v.n. to fly over or through.

transvŏlo, 1. v.a. & n. to fly over or across; to hasten across or through, to hasten through; to neglect.

trăpētus, i, m. oil-mill.

trăpēza, ae, f. banker's table.

trăpēzīta, ae, m. money-changer, banker.

trăvectio, trăvĕho, v. transv . . .

trăvŏlo, v. transvolo.

trĕcēni, ae, a, num. three hundred each; three hundred.

trĕcentēsĭmus, a, um, num. three-hundredth.

trĕcenti, ae, a, a. & num. three hundred.

trĕcenties, ad. three hundred times.

trēdĕcim, a. num. thirteen.

trĕmēbundus, a, um, a. trembling, quivering, shaking.

trĕmĕfăcio, fēci, factum, 3. v.a. to cause to tremble, to make tremble.

trĕmendus, a, um, a. fearful, formidable, terrible, tremendous.

trĕmisco, 3. v.n. & a. to begin to tremble, to tremble for fear; to tremble at.

trĕmo, ui, 3. v.n. & a. to shake, to quiver, to tremble; to tremble at, to dread.

trĕmor, ōris, m. shaking, quivering, trembling, tremor; great fear; earthquake.

trĕmŭlus, a, um, a. shaking, quivering, trembling, tremulous; causing a shiver.

trĕpĭdanter, ad. tremblingly, anxiously.

trĕpĭdātio, ōnis, f. confusion, trepidation, fear.

trĕpĭdē, ad. hastily; in alarm.

trĕpĭdo, 1. v.n. & a. to hurry about anxiously, to be in alarm; to quiver, to tremble; to palpitate; to move noisily or irregularly; to be afraid of, to tremble at.

trĕpĭdus, a, um, a. alarmed, anxious; trembling; frighted; timorous; hasty, swift; alarming; perilous; critical.

trĕpondo, n. indecl. three pounds.

trēs, tria, a. num. three;—tria juncta in uno, three joined in one.

tresdĕcim, v. tredecim.

tressis, is, m. three asses.

tresvĭri, ōrum, m. pl. board of three.

triangŭlum, i, n. triangle.

triangŭlus, a, um, a. three-cornered, triangular.

triārii, ōrum, m. pl. the Roman soldiers in the third line of battle.

trĭbuārius, a, um, a. of a tribe.

trĭbūlis, is, m. fellow-tribesman; plebeian.

trĭbŭlum, i, n. thrashing-sledge.

trĭbŭlus, i, m. caltrop; iron spike.

trĭbūnal, ālis, n. judgment-seat, tribunal; monument, embankment.

trĭbūnātus, ūs, m. tribuneship, office of a military tribune.

trĭbūnĭcius, trĭbūnĭtius, a, um, a. belonging to a tribune, tribunitial; —, ii, m. ex-tribune.

trĭbūnus, i, m. tribune; military tribune.

trĭbuo, ui, ūtum, 3. v.a. to attribute, to assign, to impose; to give, to bestow; to grant; to yield; to divide, to distribute; to devote (to).

trĭbus, ūs, f. (division of the people) tribe.

trĭbūtārius, a, um, a. tributary; concerning tribute.

trĭbūtim, ad. tribe by tribe, by tribes.

trĭbūtum, i, n. tribute; tax, toll; subsidy.

trĭbūtus, a, um, a. formed into tribes.

trīcæ, ārum, f. pl. trifles, toys, gewgaws; fig. nonsense; tricks.

trĭcēni, ae, a, a. thirty each.

trĭceps, cĭpĭtis, a. three-headed, triple.

trĭcēsĭmus, a, um, a. thirtieth.

tricessis, is, m. weight of 30 pounds.
trichila, ae, f. bower, arbour; summer-house.
trichomanes (mod. hort.), bristle fern.
tricies, ad. thirty times.
tricliniaria, ium, n. pl. dining-room hangings.   [room.
tricliniaris, e, a. belonging to a dining-
triclinium, ii, n. couch for the guests to sit upon at meals, table-couch; dining- or supper-room.
trico, onis, m. trifler, deceiver.
tricor, atus sum, I. v.n. dep. to trifle, to dally, to play tricks; to baffle.
tricornis, e, a. three-horned.
tricorpor, oris, a. three-bodied.
tricuspis, idis, a. three-pointed.
tridens, entis, a. three-pronged; —, m. trident.
tridentifer, tridentiger, i, tridentipotens, tis, m. trident-bearer (epithet of Neptune).
triduum, ii, n. space of three days.
triennia, ium, n. pl. triennial festival.
triennium, ii, n. space of three years.
triens, entis, m. third part, third; third part of an as.
trientabulus, i, n. land given by the state as an equivalent for one-third of the sum which the state owed.
trientalis, e, a. four inches thick.
trierarchus, i, m. trierarch; commander of a trireme.
trieris, m, f. a boat with three banks of oars.
trietericus, a, um, a. triennial; —, a, orum, n. pl. festival of Bacchus.
trieteris, idis, f. three years; triennial festival.
trifariam, ad. in three different ways, triply; in three places.
trifaux, cis, a. triple-throated, three-mouthed.   [year.
trifer, a, um, a. bearing fruit thrice a
trifidus, a, um, a. three-forked.
trifolium, ii, n. trefoil.   [threefold.
triformis, e, a. of three forms, triple,
trifur, uris, m. arrant or very noted thief.
trifurcifer, i, m. arrant knave.
trigarium, ii, n. chariot-course.
trigeminus, a, um, a. three born at a birth; v. tergeminus.
triginta, a. num. thirty.
trigon, onis, m. play-ball.
trigonum, i, n. a triangle.
trilibris, e, a. of three pounds weight.
trilinguis, e, a. triple-tongued.
trilix, icis, a. triple-twilled.
trimestris, e, a. of three months.
trimetrus, i, m. (verse) trimeter, containing six feet.

trimus, a, um, a. three years old.
trini, ae, a, a. num. three each; three, triple.
trinoctium, ii, n. three nights.
trinodis, e, a. three-knotted.
Trinummus, i, m. The three pieces of money. A comedy by Plautus.
triobolus, i, m. half a drachm; fig. trifle.
Triones, um, m. pl. Wain, the Two Bears (constellation).
tripartito, ad. in or into three parts.
tripartitus, a, um, p. & a. divided into three parts; threefold.
tripedalis, e, a. three feet long.
tripedaneus, a, um, a. of three feet.
tripertitus, v. tripartitus.
tripes, edis, a. three-legged.
triplex, icis, a. threefold, triple.
triplices, um, m. pl. memorandum-books.
triplico, I. v.a. to treble.
triplo, ad. trebly.
triplus, a, um, a. threefold, triple.
tripodes, um, m. pl., v. tripus.
tripudio, I. v.n. to leap, to jump, to dance, to caper.
tripudium, ii, n. solemn religious dance; favourable omen (when the sacred chickens ate so greedily that the food dropped to the ground).
tripus, odis, m. three-footed seat, tripod; fig. oracle (at Delphi).
triquetrus, a, um, a. three-cornered, triangular.   [—, is, f. trireme.
triremis, e, a. with three banks of oars;
tris, v. tres.
triscurria, orum, n. pl. buffooneries.
triste, ad. sadly, sorrowfully; harshly, severely.
tristiculus, a, um, a. rather sad, pensive.
tristificus, a, um, a. making sad, saddening.
tristis, e, a. sad, sorrowful, mournful, dejected, melancholy; miserable; gloomy, ill-humoured, stern, harsh, severe; sullen; angry; bitter.
tristitia, ae, f. sadness, grief, melancholy; sullenness; gloominess; harshness, severity; disgust.
trisulcus, a, um, a. forked, three-pointed; threefold, triple.
trisyllabus, a, um, a. trisyllabic.
trittavus, i, m. great-grandfather's great-grandfather.
triticeus, a, um, a. wheaten.
triticum, i, n. wheat.
tritoma (mod. hort.), red-hot-poker.
tritor, oris, m. grinder; thrasher.
tritura, ae, f. thrashing (of corn).
tritus, a, um, a. frequented, beaten, worn; common; familiar; commonplace, trite; fig. expert, practised.

trītus, ūs, m. rubbing, grinding; wearing off. [ornaments of a triumph.

triumphālia, ium, n. pl. solemnities or

triumphālis. e, a. triumphal;—vir triumphālis, man who has been honoured by a triumph;—imagines triumphales images of generals who had celebrated a triumph.

triumphātus, a, um, a. triumphed over, conquered.

triumpho, 1. v.n. & a. to triumph; to celebrate a triumph; *fig.* to exult, to triumph over. [triumph (also *fig.*).

triumphus, i, m. triumphal procession.

triumvir, v. triumviri.

triumvirālis, e, a. triumviral.

triumvirātus, ūs, m. triumvirate.

triumviri, ōrum & um, m. pl. board of three, triumvirate; — capitales, superintendents of public prisons.

triviālis, e, a. common, commonplace, vulgar, ordinary, trivial

trivium, ii, n. place where three roads meet, cross-road; *fig.* public street, highway; *fig.* ex trivio, out of the street, from the mob.

trivius, a, um, a. having a temple at a spot where three roads met.

trŏchæus, i, m. trochee (a long foot followed by a short).

trŏchaïcus, a, um, a. trochaic.

trochlea, ae, f. pulley, windlass.

trŏchus, i, m. child's hoop.

Trōjŭgĕna, ae, c. Trojan, Trojan born.

trŏpæŏlum (mod. hort.), nasturtium; flame flower.

trŏpæum, 1. n. trophy; monument, victory, mark, token.

trŏpĭcus, a, um, a. figurative.

trŏpus, i, m. trope; figurative use of a word.

trŭcīdātio, ōnis, f. slaughtering, massacre.

trŭcido, 1. v.a. to slaughter, to butcher, to massacre; to cut up, to slash; to destroy, to ruin.

trŭcŭlentē, ad. cruelly; roughly; sourly.

trŭcŭlentia, ae, f. cruelty, savageness; inclemency (of weather).

trŭcŭlentus, a, um, a. savage, ferocious, stern, grim, harsh, cruel.

trŭdis, is, f. waterman's pole, pike.

trŭdo, si, sum, 3. v.a. to thrust, to push, to shove; to press on, to drive, to force; to put forth (plants).

trulla, ae, f. dipper, scoop, fire-pan, a basin.

trulleum, i, n., trullio, ōnis, m. washhand-basin. [cut off.

trunco, 1. v.a. to maim, to mutilate; to

truncus, i, m. stem, stock, trunk (of a tree); body; *fig.* blockhead, dunce.

truncus, a, um, a. maimed, mutilated, disfigured; broken; imperfect, wanting. [*fig.* judgment.

trŭtina, ae, f. balance, pair of scales;

trŭtinor, 1. v. dep. to examine, to consider well, to weigh.

trux, ŭcis, a. wild, rough, harsh, savage, ferocious, grim, stern.

tryblium, ii, n. plate, salver, saucer.

tū, tui, tĭbi, te, pn. thou;—tu quoque, you also; a retort accusing an opponent of the same delinquencies as oneself is accused of.

tuātim, ad. as you are wont.

tŭba, ae, f. (straight) trumpet; war-trumpet; *fig.* instigator.

tŭber, ĕris, n. bump, swelling, tumour; knot of a tree; mushroom, truffle.

tŭber, ĕris, m. *or* f. fruit of the tuber-tree (a kind of apple).

tŭbĭcen, ĭnis, m. trumpeter.

tŭbĭlustrĭum, ii, n. feast of trumpets (on the 23rd of March and 23rd of May).

tŭbŭlātus, a, um, a. hollowed.

tŭbŭlus, i, m. little pipe; bar of metal.

tŭbus, i, m. pipe, tube.

tūcētum, i, n. sausage.

tūdĭtans, a. hammering, bustling.

tueor, tuĭtus sum, 2. v.a. dep. to look at; to behold, to watch; to guard; to defend, to protect, to maintain, to uphold; to keep in good order *or* in repair;—torva tueri, to look grim.

tŭgŭrium, ii, n. hut, cot, cottage (of shepherds).

tuitio, ōnis, f. defence, preservation.

tulipa (mod. hort.), tulip.

tum, ad. then; at that time; besides; afterwards; in that case; at that moment;—quid —? what then? what further?; tum . . . tum, both . . . and; as well . . . as; first . . . then, now . . . now;—cum . . . tum, both . . . and especially; not only . . . but also; —tum dēmum, tum dēnĭque, then and not till then;—tum prīmum, then for the first time.

tŭmĕfăcio, fēci, factum, 3. v.a. to cause to swell; *fig.* to puff up, to inflate (with pride).

tŭmeo, 2. v.n. to swell, to be tumid, to be puffed up *or* inflated (of speech); to be bombastic; to be violent *or* excited, to burst out.

tŭmesco, mui, 3. v.n. to begin to swell, to swell up; *fig.* to break out, to burst forth.

tŭmĭdē, ad. *fig.* proudly.

tŭmĭdus, a, um, a. swollen, swelling, tumid; violent; elated, haughty; bombastic.

tŭmor, ōris, m. swelling; tumour; commotion, excitement; anger; haughtiness, pride; crisis; bombast.

tŭmŭlo, 1. v.a. to bury, to inter, to entomb. [locks.

tŭmŭlōsus, a, um, a. hilly, full of hil-

tŭmultuārius, a, um, a. tumultuary; done in haste; raised in a hurry; disorderly, confused. [tumult.

tŭmultuātio, ōnis, f. bustling, hurrying,

tŭmultŭo, 1. v.a., tŭmultuor, ātus sum, 1. v.n. dep. to make a tumult, to be in an uproar; to mutiny.

tŭmultŭōsē, ad. tumultuously. [tuous.

tŭmultuōsus, a, um, a. turbulent, tumul-

tŭmultus, ūs, m. tumult, uproar, disturbance; turbulence; alarm; mutiny; sedition; roar of thunder; insurrection, civil war; agitation (of the mind or feelings), disquietude.

tŭmŭlus, i, m. mound, hillock; grave, tomb; sepulchral monument; urn.

tunc, ad. then, at the very time, immediately, at that time; v. tum.

tundo, tŭtŭdi, tunsum & tūsum, 3. v.a. to beat, to knock, to smite, to strike, to thump; to bruise, to pound; to stun, to weary.

tŭnĭca, ae, f. tunic; fig. coating, skin, membrane; wrapper; peel.

tŭnĭcātus, a, um, a. coated; clothed only in a tunic, poor.

tŭnĭco, ātum, 1. v.a. to clothe with a tunic.

tŭnĭcŭla, ae, f. little coat or skin.

tuor, 3. v.a., v. tueor.

turba, ae, f. uproar, disorder, tumult, riot; multitude, crowd; band, train; rabble; confusion, disturbance, quarrel.

turbāmentum, i, n. means of disturbing.

turbātē, ad. confusedly; m. disorder.

turbātio, ōnis, f. confusion, disorder, disturbance.

turbātor, ōris, m. troubler, disturber.

turbatrix, īcis, f. female disturber.

turbātus, a, um, a. disorderly, confused; stormy.

turbellae, ārum, f. pl. bustle, stir.

turben, ĭnis, v. turbo, ĭnis.

turbĭdē, ad. in disorder, confusedly.

turbĭdus, a, um, a. wild, confused, disordered; muddy, thick, turbid; foggy; boisterous, troubled, turbulent; confused; angry; gloomy; vexatious; dangerous, vehement; mutinous. [concave.

turbĭnātus, a, um, a. made like a top;

turbĭneus, a, um, a. conical.

turbo, 1. v.a. to disturb, to confuse, to trouble, to disorder; to make thick or turbid.

turbo, ĭnis, m. whirl, rotation; circle; whirlwind, tornado; whirlpool; whipping-top; reel, wheel.

turbŭlentē, turbŭlenter, ad. in a turbulent manner, confusedly; boisterously; in a hurry.

turbŭlentus, a, um, a. confused, disturbed; boisterous, stormy, tempestuous; troublesome, turbulent; muddy; seditious, factious.

turda, ae, f. turdus, i, m. thrush, throstle.

tūreus, a, um, a. of frankincense.

turgeo, tursi, 2. v.n. to swell out, to be swollen or tumid; fig. to be enraged; (of speech) to be inflated or bombastic.

turgesco, 3. v.n. to begin to swell, to swell up; fig. to swell with passion; (of speech) to be inflated.

turgĭdŭlus, a, um, a. somewhat swollen.

turgĭdus, a, um, a. swollen, inflated, turgid.

tūrĭbŭlum, i, n. censer.

tūrĭcrĕmus, a, um, a. for burning incense.

tūrĭfer, a, um, a. that bears or produces incense.

tūrĭlĕgus, a, um, a. incense-gathering.

turma, ae, f. troop, squadron (of horse); fig. crowd, throng; band; company.

turmālis, e, a. belonging to a troop or squadron.

turmātim, ad. by troops or squadrons; in troops, in bands.

turpĭcŭlus, a, um, a. somewhat filthy.

turpĭfĭcātus, a, um, a. debased, corrupted; polluted.

turpĭlucrĭcŭpĭdus, a, um, a. covetous of base or dishonest gain.

turpis, e, a. ugly; foul; disfigured; base, shameful, infamous; scandalous.

turpĭter, ad. in an ugly manner; basely, shamefully, disgracefully.

turpĭtūdo, ĭnis, f. ugliness; foulness; baseness, shamefulness, disgrace, infamy, turpitude.

turpo, 1. v.a. to make ugly; to defile, to pollute, to disfigure.

turrĭcŭla, ae, f. turret; dice-box.

turrĭger, a, um, a. turreted, wearing a turreted crown. [citadel; palace.

turris, is, f. tower; turret; castle;

turrĭtus, a, um, a. turreted; crowned with towers; tower-shaped; towering, high, lofty.

turtur, ŭris, m. turtle-dove.

tūs, tūris, n. frankincense.

tussĭcŭla, ae, f. little cough.

tussĭlāgo, ĭnis, f. (bot.) colt's-foot.

tussio, 4. v.n. to cough.

tussis, is, f. cough.

tūtāmen, ĭnis, n. (means of) defence, protection.

tūtāmentum, i, n. defence, support, safeguard.

tūtĕ, pn., v. tu.

tūtĕ, ad. safely, without danger.

tūtēla, ae, f. safeguard, defence, protection; guardianship, tutelage; guardian, protector; image or sign of a ship; care, charge.

tūtēlārius, ii, m. guard, warden.

tūtĕmĕt, pn. thou thyself.   [security.

tūtō, ad. safely, without danger; in

tūto, ı. v.a., v. tutor, ı.

tūtor, oris, m. protector, defender; guardian, curator, tutor.

tūtor, ātus sum, ı. v.a. dep. to guard, to protect, to defend; fig. to ward off.

tūtus, a, um, a. safe, secure, out of danger; careful, watchful; prudent, trustworthy.

tuus, a, um, pn. a. thy, thine, your, yours; favourable; suitable.

tympănum, i, n. drum, tambour, tambourine; drum, wheel for lifting weights.

typhon, ōnis, m. whirlwind.

typus, i, m. type; figure; image (on a wall); pattern.

tyrannicē, ad. tyrannically.

tyrannicīda, ae, m. killer of a tyrant.

tyrannicīdium, ii, n. tyrannicide.

tyrannicus, a, um, a. tyrannous, tyrannical.

tyrannis, ĭdis, f. tyranny.

tyrannus, i, m. despot, tyrant; monarch.

tyrianthĭna, orum, n. pl. purple garments.

tyro, ōnis, v. tiro.

tyrōtărĭchos, i, m. dish of salt-fish prepared with cheese.

Ūber, ĕris, n. teat, pap, udder; fig. fruitfulness, richness.

ūber, ĕris, a. fruitful, fertile, plentiful, copious; great, large, ornate.

ūbĕrius, ad. more fruitfully, more copiously.

ūbertas, ātis, f. fruitfulness, fertility; abundance, plenty; richness; fulness.

ūbertim, ad. plentifully, copiously.

ŭbĭ, ad. where; where? when, as soon as; after that; by or in which; by or with whom; wherewith.

ŭbĭcumquĕ, ŭbĭcunquĕ, ad. wherever; wheresoever; everywhere.

ŭbĭlĭbet, ad. wheresoever you please.

ŭbĭnam, ad. where? in what place?

ŭbĭquāquĕ, ad. wheresoever, everywhere.

ŭbĭquĕ, ad. everywhere, anywhere, wheresoever.

ŭbĭvis, ad. where you will, anywhere everywhere; fig. in any matter or affair.   [drunk.

ūdus, a, um, a. wet, moist, damp, humid,

ulex (mod. hort.), furze.

ulcĕro, ı. v.a. to make sore, to ulcerate.

ulcĕrōsus, a, um, a. ulcerous, sore; fig. wounded (with love).

ulciscor, ultus, 3. v.a. dep. to take vengeance (on) or revenge (for); to avenge; to punish.

ulcus, ĕris, n. ulcer, sore; fig. sore spot; delicate subject.

ūlĭgĭnōsus, a, um, a. moist, wet, swampy.

ūlĭgo, ĭnis, f. moisture; ooziness; marshiness.

ullus, a, um, ullīus, a. any, any one.

ulmārium, ii, n. elm-grove.

ulmeus, a, um, a. of elm.

ulmus, i, f. elm, elm-tree.

ulna, ae, f. elbow; arm; ell; fathom.

ulpĭcum, i, n. wild garlic.   [more.

ultĕrĭor, us, a. farther, beyond; past;

ultĕrĭus, ad. beyond, farther on, further.

ultĭmum, ad. the last time.

ultĭmus, a, um, a. last; utmost; furthest; greatest; lowest, meanest; highest; latest; earliest; oldest;—ultima ratio, the last resort;—ultimum supplicium, the punishment of death;—ad ultimum, finally;—ultima Thule (remotest Thule), the furthest limit.

ultio, ōnis, f. revenge, vengeance.

ultor, ōris, m. avenger, revenger; punisher.

ultrā, ad. beyond, farther, over, more, besides; —, pr. beyond, past; above; more than;—ultra vires, beyond one's powers or authority.

ultrix, ĭcis, fem. a. avenging, vengeful.

ultro, ad. beyond; moreover; willingly, voluntarily; gratuitously; of its own accord;—ultro citroque, on this side and on that; to and fro;—ultro tributa, state expenditure for public works.

ŭlŭla, ae, f. screech-owl.

ŭlŭlātus, ūs, m. howling, wailing, shrieking; war-whoop; shouting.

ŭlŭlo, ı. v.n. & a. to howl, to yell, to shriek; to shout; to resound; to wail; to fill with cries.

ulva, ae, f. (bot.) sedge.   [parasol.

umbella, ae, f. fan, screen, sunshade,

umbĭlīcātus, a, um, a. navel-shaped.

umbĭlīcus, i, m. navel; end of a stick on which a book was rolled; seacockle; gnomon of a sundial; fig. middle, centre.

umbo, ōnis, m. boss (of a shield); shield; knob, top; swelling; elbow.

umbra, ae, f. shade, shadow; ghost (of a dead person); shady place; shelter; protection; *fig.* faint appearance, semblance; trace; unbidden guest; (fish) umber.

umbrācŭlum, i, n. bower, arbour; shady place; sunshade, umbrella; *fig.* school.

umbrātĭcŏla, ae, m. *fig.* lounger.

umbrātĭcus, a, um, a. *fig.* keeping at home, retired; effeminate.

umbrātĭlis, e, a. shady; keeping private, retired; contemplative; lazy; (of speech) in the manner of the schools; academic.

umbrĭfer, a, um, a. casting a shade, shady.

umbro, i. v.a. to shade, to shadow; to cover.

umbrōsus, a, um, a. shady.

ūmecto, i. v.a. to moisten, to wet.

ūmectus, a, um, a. moist, damp.

ūmeo, 2. v.n. to be wet; to be moist.

ūmĕrus, i, m. shoulder.

ūmesco, 3. v.n. to become moist.

ūmĭdŭlus, a, um, a. somewhat moist.

ūmidus, a, um, a. damp; moist.

ūmor, ōris, m. moisture; liquid; dew; milk; tears.

umquam, v. unquam.

ūnā, ad. at the same time, in company, together, all at once.

ūnănĭmĭtas, ātis, f. unanimity, concord.

ūnănĭmĭter, ad. unanimously.

ūnănĭmus, a, um, a. unanimous, loving.

uncia, ae, f. twelfth part, twelfth; ounce; inch; *fig.* bit; trifle.

unciālis, e, a. weighing an ounce or measuring an inch;—**litterae unciales,** text *or* capital letters.

unciārius, a, um, a. of an ounce *or* inch; —**faenus unciarium,** eight and a third per cent.

unciātim, ad. by ounces or inches; *fig.* little by little.

unctio, ōnis, f. anointing.

unctĭto, i. v.a. to anoint often.

unctor, ōris, m. anointer.

unctōrium, ii, n. the anointing-room (in a bath).

unctum, i, n. ointment; splendid banquet *or* feast; good fare.

unctūra, ae, f. anointing (of the dead).

unctus, a, um, p. & a. anointed; greasy, fat; *fig.* luxurious, rich; copious, plentiful; elegant; polished; gay.

uncus, i, m. hook, barb; anchor; drag; a hook used to drag criminals to the Tiber. [barbed.

uncus, a, um, a. hooked, crooked, curved;

unda, ae, f. wave, billow, surge; fluid; water; air; *fig.* crowd, stream.

undātim, ad. like waves.

undĕ, ad. whence; whence?; of *or* from whom; out of which; wherewith how, by what means;—**unde unde** from whatever quarter.

undĕcentēsimus, a, um, a. ninety-ninth.

undĕcentum, a. indecl. ninety-nine.

undĕcies, ad. eleven times.

undĕcim, a. num. eleven.

undĕcĭmus, a, um, a. num. eleventh.

undĕcunquĕ, ad. from what part *or* place soever.

undēni, ae, a, a. num. eleven each; eleven.

undēnōnāgintā, eighty-nine.

undēoctōgintā, a. num. (indecl.) seventy-nine.

undēquadrāgies, ad. thirty-nine times.

undēquadrāgintā, a. num. thirty-nine.

undēquinquāgēsimus, a, um, a. num. forty-ninth.

undēquinquāgintā, a. num. forty-nine.

undēsexāgintā, a. num. fifty-nine.

undētrĭcēsimus, undētrĭgēsimus, a, um, a. num. twenty-ninth.

undēvīcēni, ae, a, a. num. nineteen each.

undēvīcēsimus, undēvīgēsimus, a, um, a. num. nineteenth.

undēvīginti, a. num. nineteen.

undīquĕ, ad. from all sides or places, from every quarter; on all sides, everywhere.

undĭsŏnus, a, um, a. roaring *or* resounding with waves.

undo, i. v.n. & a. to rise in waves; to surge, to swell; to undulate; to foam; to deluge, to overflow; to abound; *fig.* to hang loosely.

undōsus, a, um, a. wavy, billowy, surgy.

ūnetvīcēsimāni, ōrum, m. pl. soldiers of the twenty-first legion.

ūnetvīcēsimus, a, um, a. num. twenty-first, one-and-twentieth.

ungo *or* **unguo, unxi, unctum, 3.** v.a. to smear, to anoint; to daub; to dress with oil; to perfume.

unguen, ĭnis, n. fat; ointment.

unguentāria, ae, f. female perfumer; art of making ointments *or* perfumes.

unguentārius, a, um, a. of ointments; —, ii, m. perfumer, dealer in ointments *or* perfumes.

unguentātus, a, um, a. perfumed.

unguentum, i, n. ointment; perfume.

unguĭcŭlus, i, m. little finger-nail; soft nail; *fig.* **a teneris unguiculis,** from early childhood.

unguĭnōsus, a, um, a. unctuous, oily.

unguis, is, m. nail (of a human finger *or* toe); claw, talon, hoof; white mark; *fig.* **ad (in) unguem,** to a hair; exactly; highly accomplished;—**ex ungue leonem,** *fig.* from small incidents you

may infer to great ones;—**de tenero
ungui**, from early childhood;—**transversum unguem**, a finger's breadth.
ungŭla, ae, f. claw, talon, hoof; horse;
fig. **omnibus ungulis**, with might and
main, tooth and nail.
unguo, v. **ungo.**
ūnĭcaulis, e, a. having a single stalk.
ūnĭcē, ad. alone, solely, singularly.
ūnĭcŏlor, ōris, a. of one colour. [unicorn.
ūnĭcornis, e, a. one-horned; —, **is,** m.
ūnĭcus, a, um, a. only, sole, single; *fig.*
unique, uncommon, unmatched.
unĭformis, e, a. uniform.
ūnĭgĕna, ae, a. only-begotten, only;
(poet.) of one parent; of the same
family.
ūnĭjŭgus, a, um, a. coupled together.
ūnĭmănus, a, um, a. one-handed.
ūnĭo, ōnis, m. large pearl.
ūnĭtas, ātis, f. oneness, unity, uniformity.
ūnĭter, ad. in one, together.
ŭnĭusmŏdi, a. indecl. of one sort.
ūnĭversālis, e, a. universal.
ūnĭversē, ad. in general, generally.
ūnĭversĭtas, ătis, f. whole; universality;
fig. universe, guild; university.
ūnĭversus, a, um, a. whole, general, universal;—**universum, i,** n. whole world,
universe;—**in universum,** as a whole,
generally.
ūnŏcŭlus, a, um, a. one-eyed.
unquam, ad. at any time, ever.
ūnus, a, um, a. num. one; a, an; only;
single, alone, sole; (the very) same;
certain one; some one;—**in unum,**
into one, together;—**unus aut alter** *or*
unus et alter, one or two;—**ad unum,**
to a man; all together; **uno ore,**
unanimously; with one voice.
unusquisque, unăquæque, unumquodque
or **unumquidque,** pn. everyone.
ūpĭlio, ōnis, m. shepherd.
upŭpa, ae, f. hoopoo; mattock.
urbāne, ad. courteously, politely, ur-
banely; elegantly; wittily.
urbānĭtas, ātis, f. city-life; politeness;
refinement, delicacy; pleasantry; wit;
knavery; roguery.
urbānus, a, um, a. of *or* belonging to a
city; courteous, polite; pleasant;
witty; polished, refined; elegant.
urbĭcăpus, i, m. winner of cities.
urbĭcus, a, um, a. of a city, civic.
urbs, urbis, f. walled town, city; (city of)
Rome; citizens;—**urbi et orbi,** to
Rome and the world.
urceŏlus, i, m. little pitcher.
urceus, i, m. water-pot, pitcher, ewer.
ūrēdo, ĭnis, f. blight (of plants); burning
in the skin.

urgeo, ursi, 2. v.a. to press on, to urge,
to push, to drive; to enforce; to
aggravate; to hasten on; to press
upon, to crowd; to confine; to
solicit; to ply hard, to stick to; to
oppress; to be close upon one's heels.
ūrīnātor, ōris, m. diver.
ūrīnor, 1. v.n. dep. to plunge, to dive.
urna, ae, f. water-jar; urn; cinerary
urn; money-jar; ballot-box, voting-
urn; *fig.* urn of fate; a liquid measure
about 24 pints.
urnālis, e, a. holding an urna, about 24
pints.
urnŭla, ae, f. little pitcher.
ūro, ussi, ustum, 3. v.a. to burn; to burn
up; to destroy by fire; to set on fire;
to scorch; to burn in; to gall, to rub
sore; to pain *or* sting sharply; to nip,
to blast; to pinch (with cold); to
inflame; to harass; to oppress.
ursa, ae, f. she-bear; bear; — **Mājor,**
Great Bear. [bear.
ursīnus, a, um, a. of *or* belonging to a
ursus, i, m. bear.
urtīca, ae, f. stinging-nettle.
ūrus, i, m. aurochs.
ūsĭtātē, ad. in the customary way.
ūsĭtātus, a, um, p. & a. usual, customary,
common, accustomed, familiar.
uspiam, ad. anywhere, somewhere; in
any matter.
usquam, ad. at *or* in any place, anywhere;
to any place; in anything at all.
usquĕ, ad. continuously, constantly; all
along, all the way; all the while, as
long *or* as far as, until;—**usque ad,**
right up to; — **eo . . . ut,** to such
an extent that . . . that; **usque ad
nauseam,** till disgust is produced.
usquĕquāque, ad. continually.
usta, ae, f. red-colour.
ustio, ōnis, f. burning.
ustor, ōris, m. burner of dead bodies.
ustŭlo, 1. v.a. to scorch, to singe; to
burn up.
ūsūcăpio, cēpi, captum, 3. v.a. to acquire
by prescription *or* long use.
ūsūcăpio, ōnis, f. acquisition of ownership by long use *or* possession, prescription.
ūsūra, ae, f. usage, use; enjoyment;
usury, interest.
ūsūrārius, a, um, a. fit for use; relating
to interest *or* usury; paying interest.
ūsurpātio, ōnis, f. using, use.
ūsurpo, 1. v.a. to make use of; to use,
to employ, to practise, to exercise; to
acquire, to obtain; to usurp; to
assume; to mention often; to call,
to name.

ūsus, ūs, m. usage, use, employment; service, benefit, profit, utility, usufruct; practice, exercise, custom; habit; experience; familiarity, intimacy; need, necessity; opportunity; —**ūsus est, ūsus vĕnit,** it is necessary.

ūsusfructus, ūs, m. usufruct.

ŭt, ŭti, ad. & c. in what manner, how; in the manner that, as; however; **s**uch as; for, as being, inasmuch as; how much or greatly; when, as soon as;—**ut . . . ita,** not only . . . but also; although . . yet; the more . . . the more; —, c. so that; to the end that, in order that; as if; as if it were; to wit, namely; albeit, although; as is usual; **(fac)** —, in case that, supposing, even if;—**uti possidetis,** to remain in your present possessions; as you are.

utcumquĕ, utcunquĕ, ad. howsoever, however; whenever. [necessaries.

ūtensīlia, ium, n. pl. utensils; materials;

ūtensīlis, e, a. useful, of use.

ūter, tris, m. leather bottle for wine, oil, etc.; bladder.

ūter, utra, utrum, a. whether or which of the two, either one.

ŭtercunquĕ, utracunque, utrumcunque, pn. whichever of the two.

ŭtĕrīnus, a, um, a. born of the same mother.

ŭterlĭbet, utrălĭbet, utrumlĭbet, pn. which of the two you please; either of the two.

ŭterquĕ, utrăque, utrumque, pn. both the one and the other; both, each.

ŭtĕrus, i, m. womb; fruit of the womb, child (in the womb); belly.

ŭtervis, utrăvis, utrumvis, pn. which of the two you will, either of the two; both.

ūtĭbĭlis, e, a. fit, serviceable.

ūtĭlis, e, a. useful, serviceable, fit, suitable, advantageous.

ūtĭlĭtas, ātis, f. use, usefulness, utility, profit, advantage, expediency.

ūtĭlĭter, ad. usefully, profitably, advantageously. [that!

ŭtĭnam, ad. oh that! I wish that! would

ŭtĭquĕ, ad. anyhow; in any case, at any rate, certainly, by all means.

ūtor, ūsus, 3. v. dep. to use, to make use of, to employ, to apply, to enjoy; to practise, to exercise; to take advantage of; to experience; to be familiar with; to be in possession of, to have; to find;—**utendum dare,** to lend;—**untendum recipere,** to borrow.

utpŏtĕ, ad. namely, as being, as, seeing that, inasmuch as, since.

ūtrārius, ii, m. water-carrier.

utrimquĕ, utrinque, ad. from or on both sides or parts; by both persons.

utrō, ad. which way, to which side.

utrŏbi, ad., v. utrubi.

utrŏbīdem, ad., v. utrubidem.

utrŏbīque, ad., v. utrubique. [tions.

utrŏquĕ, ad. to both sides, in both directions.

utrŭbi, ad. at which of two places, on which of the two sides, where.

utrŭbĭdem, ad. on both sides.

utrŭbīquĕ, ad. on both parts or sides.

utrum, ad. whether; whether?

ūva, ae, f. grape; bunch, cluster; swarm of bees; uvula.

ūvens, entis, a. moist.

ūvesco, 3. v.n. (poet.) to grow moist or humid; to refresh oneself.

ūvĭdŭlus, a, um, a. a little wet.

ūvĭdus, a, um, a. moist, wet, damp, dank, humid.

ūvĭfer, a, um, a. bearing grapes.

uxor, ōris, f. wife, spouse, consort.

uxorcŭla, ae, f. pretty little wife.

uxōrius, a, um, a. of or belonging to a wife; excessively fond of one's wife.

Văcātio, ōnis, f. exemption, immunity; dispensation; freedom; exemption from military service.

vacca, ae, f. cow.

vaccīnium, ii, n. whortleberry.

vaccīnus, a, um, a. of cows.

vaccŭla, ae, f. little cow or heifer.

văcēfīo, fĭĕri, v.n. pass. to become empty.

văcillātio, ōnis, f. rocking to and fro, reeling motion.

văcillo, 1. v.n. to stagger, to reel, to totter; fig. to waver, to vacillate.

văcīvē, ad. at leisure, leisurely.

văcīvĭtas, ātis, f. emptiness, want.

văcīvus, a, um, a. empty, void; destitute (of).

văco, 1. v.n. to be empty, void of or free from; to lack, to want; to be at leisure or disengaged or at liberty; to be intent upon, to apply, to study; to be unoccupied; to have no owner.

văcuĕfăcio, fēci, factum, 3. v.a. to make empty, to clear, to free.

văcuĭtas, ātis, f. freedom, absence, exemption. [to empty.

văcuo, 1. v.a. to make empty or void;

văcuum, i, n. void, empty place or space, vacuity.

văcuus, a, um, a. empty, void; wanting, without; vacant; at leisure; idle; single, unmarried; calm, careless; vain; unmarried; ownerless; free.

vădĭmōnium, ii, n. bail, security.
vădo, 3. v.n. to go, to walk; to march.
vădor, ătus sum, 1. v.a. dep. to bind over by bail.
vădōsus, a, um, a. shallow, fordable.
vădum, i, n. shallow, ford; narrow passage of the sea; sea; bottom, depths.
væ, i. ah! alas! woe!—væ victis, alas! for the conquered.
væn . . ., v. ven . . . [subtle.
văfer, fra, frum, a. sly, cunning, crafty,
văfrāmentum, i, n. trick, wile.
văfrē, ad. slyly, cunningly.
văfrĭtia, ae, f. craftiness, slyness.
văgātio, ōnis, f. (practice of) strolling about, straying.
văgē, ad. far and wide, at random.
văgīna, ae, f. scabbard, sheath; husk.
văgīnŭla, ae, f. little sheath; small husk.
văgio, īvi & ii, 4. v.n. to cry as an infant, to squeak, to squall.
văgītus, ūs, m. crying, squalling (of young children); bleating.
văgor, ătus sum, 1. v.n. dep. to stroll about, to wander, to roam, to rove; to be unsteady; to digress; to be diffused.
văgŭlus, a, um, a. wandering.
văgus, a, um, a. strolling about, roving, wandering; vagrant; unsteady, wavering; uncertain, doubtful, vague, indefinite.
vah, vaha, i. bravely! rarely! out upon it! [ingly; vehemently.
valdē, ad. very very much, exceed-
vāle, v. valeo. [adieu.
vălēdīco, 3. v.n. to say farewell, to bid
vălens, entis, a. strong, stout, vigorous; healthy; fig. powerful; valiant. [energetically.
vălenter, ad. strongly, stoutly; violently;
vălentŭlus, a, um, a. somewhat strong.
văleo, ui, ĭtum, 2. v.n. to be in health, to fare well; to be strong or vigorous; to be able or capable; to take effect; to be powerful; to prevail; to do good; to have influence; to be worth; to mean, to signify;—valere jubere or dicere, to bid farewell or good-bye;—vale, farewell! adieu!;—valeat, let me have nothing to do with him!
valeriāna (mod. hort.), valerian.
vălesco, 3. v.n. to grow strong.
vălētŭdĭnārium, ii, n. infirmary.
vălētŭdĭnārius, a, um, a. sickly, infirm; —, ii, m. invalid, valetudinarian.
vălētŭdo, ĭnis, f. health, soundness; good health; ill health, malady, sickness; feebleness; indisposition.
valgĭter, ad. with a wry mouth.

valgus, a, um, a. bow-legged, bandy-legged. [much.
vălĭdē, ad. strongly, stoutly, vehemently;
vălĭdus, a, um, a. strong, stout, sturdy, powerful, able; healthy, sound, well; active; brisk; fig. effective, influential.
vallāris, e, a. belonging to the walls;—corona —, crown given to him who first scaled the enemy's rampart.
vallis, or vallēs, is, f. valley, vale; hollow.
vallo, 1. v.a. to circumvallate, to intrench, to fortify; fig. to defend, to protect.
vallum, i, n. earthen wall, rampart, intrenchment, circumvallation; fig. fortification.
vallus, i, m. stake, pale; palisade; palisaded rampart; tooth of a comb.
valvæ, ārum, f. pl. folding-door.
valvātus, a, um, a. furnished with folding-doors.
vānesco, 3. v.n. to pass away, to disappear, to vanish; to come to nothing; to wear off.
vānĭdĭcus, a, um, a. vain-speaking.
vanilla (mod. hort.), vanilla.
vānĭlŏquentia, ae, f. idle talk, prating.
vānĭlŏquus, a, um, a. talking idly, lying; boastful.
vānĭtas, ātis, f. emptiness; untruth; vainglory, vanity; falsehood.
vannus, i, f. fan (to winnow corn), seed-hopper.
vānus, a, um, a. empty, void, vacant; vain, useless; insignificant; foolish, trifling; silly; false; lying; deceitful; groundless.
văpĭdē, ad. poorly, ill.
văpĭdus, a, um, a. flat, vapid; spoiled.
văpor, ōris, m. steam, exhalation, vapour; heat; smoke. [baths.
văpōrārium, ii, n. steam-pipe in Roman
văpōrātio, ōnis, f. steaming, emitting of vapours.
văpōrĭfer, a, um, a. steam-producing.
văpōro, 1. v.n. to emit steam or vapour; to glow, to burn; —, v.a. to fill with steam; to steam; to heat, to warm; to perfume.
vappa, ae, f. flat wine; —, m. a good-for-nothing.
văpŭlo, 1. v.n. to get a flogging; to be beaten or defeated; to be squandered; fig. to be lashed or attacked;—vapula! you be hanged!
vărĭantia, ae, f. diversity, variety.
vărĭātio, ōnis, f. difference, variation.
vārĭco, 1. v.n. to straddle.
vărĭcōsus, a, um, a. varicose.
vārĭcus, a, um, a. straddling.

vărĭē, ad. variously; differently; in various ways.

vărĭĕtas, ātis, f. difference, variety; change, vicissitude; inconstancy.

vărĭo, ɪ. v.a. & n. to variegate; to alter, to change, to vary; to alternate; to differ; to be variegated; to be different *or* various; to fluctuate.

vărĭus, a, um, a. variegated; diverse; various; changeable, inconstant; wavering;—**varĭorum** (an edition with annotations) of various authors.

vărix, ĭcis, f. dilated *or* swollen vein.

vărus, a, um, a. crooked; knock-kneed; *fig.* different, diverse, various.

vărus, i, m. spot, speckle; pimple.

văs, vădis, m. bail, surety.

văs, văsis, n., **vasa, ōrum,** n. pl. vessel, dish; utensil; baggage.

vāsărĭum, ii, n. money given to a provincial governor to furnish his house.

vascŭlārĭus, ii, m. worker in metals; goldsmith.

vascŭlum, i, n. small vessel.   [tion.

vastātĭo, ōnis, f. laying waste, devasta-

vastātor, ōris, m. destroyer, ravager.

vastē, ad. vastly, hugely; widely; harshly, rudely.

vastĭtas, ātis, f. waste, desert; devastation; destruction, ruin; vastness.

vastĭtĭes, ēi, f. ruin, destruction.

vasto, ɪ. v.a. to empty; to deprive (of inhabitants); to lay waste; to ruin, to destroy; to harass; to vex.

vastus, a, um, a. empty; desolate; vast, huge, enormous; rough, rude; insatiable;—**vastum dare,** to lay waste.

vātes, is, c. foreteller, prophet; prophetess; poet, poetess; specialist, authority in any art.

vātĭcĭnātĭo, ōnis, f. prophesying, prediction.

vātĭcĭnātor, ōris, m. soothsayer, prophet.

vātĭcĭnĭum, ii, n. prophecy.

vātĭcĭnor, ātus, ɪ. v.n. & a. dep. to foretell; to prophesy; to sing, to celebrate; to rave, to talk foolishly.

vātĭcĭnus, a, um, a. prophetical.

vātĭus, a, um, a. bow-legged.

vĕ, enclitic c. or, either.

vēcordĭa, ae, f. madness.

vēcors, dis, a. mad, frantic; foolish.

vectātĭo, ōnis, f. carrying; riding.

vectīgal, ālis, n. toll, impost; income, revenue.

vectīgālis, e, a. tributary; bringing in revenue *or* income.

vectĭo, ōnis, f. conveyance; riding.

vectis, is, m. crowbar, lever; bolt.

vecto, ɪ. v.a. to carry, to convey about; pass; to be carried; to ride.

vector, ōris, m. bearer, carrier; passenger; rider; sailor.

vectōrĭus, a, um, a. serving for carriage of burden, passenger;—**navigia vectoria,** transport-ships.

vectūra, ae, f. transportation (by carriage or by ship); riding; transport, conveyance; passage-money, fare.

vĕgĕtus, a, um, a. lively, animated, vigorous, active.   [meagre, poor.

vēgrandis, e, a. little, small, diminutive;

vĕhĕmens, entis, a. violent, impetuous, ardent, vehement; vigorous, powerful, strong.

vĕhĕmenter, ad. impetuously, ardently, violently, vehemently; strongly, powerfully; exceedingly, very much.

vĕhĕmentia, ae, f. vehemence; strength.

vĕhes, vĕhis, is, f cart.

vĕhĭcŭlum, i, n. carriage, conveyance; cart, car, wagon, vehicle, ship.

vĕho, xi, ctum, 3. v.a. & n. to carry, to convey;—**vehi,** to go; to ride; to sail; to travel, to journey.

vĕl, c. or; even; at least; for instance; (with superlatives) the utmost possible; — ... —, either ... or.

vēlāmen, ĭnis, n. covering, clothing, veil.

vēlāmentum, i, n. cover, covering; veil; curtain;—**velamenta,** pl. olive-branches carried by suppliants.

vēlārĭs, e, a. of *or* belonging to a sail *or* curtain.   [the top of a theatre).

vēlārĭum, ii, n. covering; awning (on

vēlāti, ōrum, m. pl. reserve troops (who took the place of those who fell).

vēles, ĭtis, m. light-armed soldier; skirmisher.

vēlĭfer, a, um, a. sail-bearing.

vēlĭfĭcātĭo, ōnis, f. making sail, sailing.

vēlĭfĭco, ɪ. v.n. to make sail, to sail.

vēlĭfĭcor, ātus sum, ɪ. v.n. dep. to spread *or* hoist sail, to sail; *fig.* to seek to obtain; to court.

vēlĭfĭcus, a, um, a. with sails, sailing.

vēlĭtārĭs, e, a. of *or* belonging to the light troops of the **velites**.

vēlĭtes, um, v. **veles.**

vēlĭtor, ātus sum, ɪ. v.n. dep. to skirmish; to brawl, to wrangle.

vēlĭvŏlans, antis, a. flying with sails.

vēlĭvŏlus, a, um, a. wĭngᵉd with sails; navigable.

vellĭco, ɪ. v.a. to pluck, to twitch; *fig.* to carp, to rail at.

vello, velli, vulsum, 3. v.a. to pluck *or* pull (out), to tear out *or* away; to pinch.

vellus, ĕris, n. wool shorn off, fleece; hide, fell, pelt; down.

vēlo, ɪ. v.a. to wrap up, to envelop, to veil; to hide, to conceal.

vēlōcĭtas, ātis, f. swiftness, rapidity, velocity.

vēlōcĭter, ad. swiftly, quickly, speedily.

vēlox, ōcis, a. swift, rapid, speedy.

vēlum, i, n. sail; curtain, veil, cloth; hangings; awning; *fig.* **remis velisque,** with might and main;—**vela dare,** to set sail.

vĕlut, vĕlŭtī, ad. even as, just as, like as; for example; like, as it were; as if, as though.

vemens, v. vehemens.

vēna, ae, f. blood-vessel, vein; artery; pulse; vein of metal; watercourse; grain in wood; rill; *fig.* innate quality of a thing; disposition, genius.

vēnābŭlum, i, n. hunting-spear.

vēnālĭcius, vēnālĭtius, a, um, a. exposed for sale; —, **ii, m.** slave-trader, dealer in slaves.

vēnālis, e, a. to be sold, for sale; venal; —, **is, m.** slave put up for sale.

vēnālĭtius, v. venalicius.

vēnātĭcus, a, um, a. for hunting.

vēnātĭo, ōnis, f. hunting, chase; battue; combat of wild beasts; beasts hunted, game.

vēnātor, ōris, m. hunter; hound; *fig.* tracer, explainer, interpreter.

vēnātōrius, a, um, a. of hunting, relating to the chase.

vēnātrix, īcis, f. huntress; — **dea,** Diana.

vēnātūra, ae, f. chase, hunting.

vēnātus, ūs, m. chase, hunting; fishing; game.   [agreeable; popular.

vendĭbĭlis, e, a. saleable; *fig.* acceptable;

vendĭco, v. vindico.

vendĭtātĭo, ōnis, f. boasting; ostentation.

vendĭtātor, ōris, m. boaster, braggart.

vendĭtĭo, ōnis, f. selling, sale.

vendĭto, 1. v.a. to offer for sale; *fig.* to cry up, to recommend, to praise; to advertise; to curry favour with; to boast (of).

vendĭtor, ōris, m. seller, vender.

vendo, dĭdi, dĭtum, 3. v.a. to sell, to vend; *fig.* to betray, to give up; to cry up, to praise, to recommend.   [ess, witch.

vĕnēfĭca, ae, f. female poisoner; sorcer-

vĕnēfĭcium, ii, n. poisoning; magic, sorcery.

vĕnēfĭcus, a, um, a. poisoning, poisonous; magical; —, **i, m.** poisoner; sorcerer.

vĕnēnārius, ii, m. poisoner.

vĕnēnātus, a, um, p. & a. poisonous, venomous; *fig.* biting, harming; bewitched, enchanted.

vĕnēnĭfer, a, um, a. poisonous, venomous.

vĕnēno, 1. v.a. to poison; *fig.* to injure.

vĕnēnum, i, n. poison; potion; magical potion; charm; dye, paint, colouring matter; sorcery, witchcraft.

vēneo, īvi & ii, ītum, 4. v.n. to go for sale, to be sold.

vĕnĕrābĭlis, e, a. reverend, venerable; worshipful.

vĕnĕrābĭliter, ad. reverentially.

vĕnĕrābundus, a, um, a. venerating, reverential.

vĕnĕrātĭo, ōnis, f. reverence, veneration.

vĕnĕrātor, ōris, m. reverencer, venerator.

Vĕnēreus, Vĕnĕrius, a, um, a. of Venus.

Vĕnēreus, Vĕnĕrius, ii, m. Venus throw *or* highest throw (at dice).

vĕnĕror, ātus sum, 1. v.a. dep. rarely;— **vĕnĕro, 1. v.a.** to reverence, to worship, to revere, to venerate; to honour; to supplicate, to implore.

Vĕnĕtus, a, um, a. bluish, sea-coloured;— **Veneta factio,** the Blues (a political party).

vĕnia, ae, f. pardon, forgiveness; leave, permission; favour, indulgence, grace, courtesy;—**bona tua venia,** with your good leave.

vĕnĭcŭla, v. venucula.

vĕnio, vēni, ventum, 4. v.n. to come; to go; to arrive; to accrue; to arise, to grow; to come to pass; to proceed; to come *or* fall into; to return.

vēnor, ātus sum, 1. v.n. & a. dep. to hunt, to chase; *fig.* to hunt after, to pursue, to seek (for).

vēnōsus, a, um, a. veiny; dry, meagre.

venter, tris, m. belly; paunch; maw; stomach; *fig.* gluttony; womb; fœtus; protuberance, swelling.

ventĭlātĭo, ōnis, f. fanning, winnowing.

ventĭlo, 1. v.a. to fan, to wave, to toss, to swing; *fig.* to disturb, to disquiet.

ventĭo, ōnis, f. coming.

ventĭto, 1. v.n. to come often, to be wont to come; to haunt.

ventōsus, a, um, a. full of wind, windy; swift (as the wind); light; blustering, stormy; *fig.* fickle, changeable; conceited, vain; puffed up; proud.

ventrāle, is, n. waist-band.

ventrĭcŭlus, i, m. belly; stomach.

ventriōsus, a, um, a. pot-bellied.

ventŭlus, i, m. little wind, breeze.

ventus, i, m. wind; storm; breath of fortune.

vēnŭcŭla, ae, f. kind of grape (for preserving).

vēnum, i, v. vēnus.

vēnumdo, dĕdi, dătum, 1. v. *or* vēnundo, a. to put up for sale, to expose to sale; to sell.

Vĕnus, ĕris, f. goddess of love; beloved person; object of love; loveliness; beauty; charm; (planet) Venus; highest *or* Venus throw at dice.

vēnus, ŭs, m. **vēnum, i,** n. sale.

vĕnustas, ātis, f. loveliness, comeliness, charm, grace, beauty.   [beautifully.

vĕnustē, ad. charmingly, gracefully,

vĕnustŭlus, a, um, a. lovely, charming, delightful.

vĕnustus, a, um, a. lovely, charming, graceful, beautiful.

vēpallĭdus, a, um, a. very pale.

veprēcŭla, ae, f. little brier-bush.

vepres, is, m. thorn-bush, brier, bramble-bush.

vēr, vēris, n. spring; spring-time *or* prime of life;—**ver sacrum,** an offering made from the firstlings of the spring.

vērātrum, i, n. hellebore.

vērax, ācis, a. true of speech, veracious.

verbascum, i, n. Aaron's rod.

verbēna, ae, f. vervain.

verbēnæ, ārum, f. pl. sacred boughs (of laurel, myrtle, olive, etc.); altar-herbs.

verbēnātus, a, um, a. crowned with vervain *or* a garland of sacred branches.

verber, ĕris, n. lash, whip, scourge, rod; thong (of a sling); lashing, scourging; blow, stroke.

verbĕrātio, ōnis, f. chastisement, punishment.

verbĕreus, a, um, a. deserving of stripes.

verbĕro, 1. v.a. to lash, to scourge, to whip, to flog; to harass, to chastise.

verbĕro, ōnis, m. scoundrel, rascal.

verbōsē, ad. verbosely.

verbōsus, a, um, a. verbose, wordy, prolix; tedious.

verbum, i, n. word; language; discourse, speech; phrase, sentence; proverb; (gr.) verb;—**verba,** mere words; pretence;—**verba dare (alicui),** to deceive (one);—**ad verbum** *or* **de (e, pro) verbo,** to a word, literally; exactly;—**uno verbo,** in a word; briefly;—**verbi causa** *or* **gratia,** for example, for instance;—**verbum sapienti (verb. sap.,** a word to the wise.

vērē, ad. truly, really, indeed, verily; justly, rightly.

vĕrēcundē, ad. bashfully; modestly.

vĕrēcundia, ae, f. bashfulness, coyness, modesty; respect; reverence; shame.

vĕrēcundor, 1. v.n. dep. to be bashful *or* ashamed, to be modest.

vĕrēcundus, a, um, a. shamefaced, bashful, modest.

vĕrēdus, i, m. post-horse.   [terrible.

vĕrendus, a, um, a. awful, venerable;

vĕreor, ĭtus, 2. v.a. & n. dep. to stand in awe of, to regard reverently; to fear, to be afraid.

Vergĭliæ, ārum, f. pl. Pleiades (constellation).

vergo, 3. v.a. & n. to turn, to incline; to bend; to pour out; to mix; to be inclined, to lie, to trend; to sink.

vērīdĭcus, a, um, a. speaking the truth, veracious.

vērīsĭmĭlis, e, *or* **vērī sĭmĭlis,** a. likely, credible, probable.   [ably.

vērīsĭmĭlĭter, *or* **vērī sĭmĭlĭter,** ad. probably.

vērīsĭmĭlĭtūdo, *or* **vērī sĭmĭlĭtūdo, ĭnis,** f. likelihood, probability; true likeness.

vērĭtas, ātis, f. truth, verity; reality; honesty.

vermĭcŭlātus, a, um, p. & a. inlaid, chequered, vermiculated.

vermĭcŭlor, ātus sum, 1. v.n. dep. to be worm-eaten.

vermĭcŭlus, i, m. little worm, grub.

vermĭna, um, n. pl. gripes.   [wormy.

vermĭnōsus, a, um, a. full of worms,

vermis, is, m. worm.

verna, ae, c. home-born slave; *fig.* native; —, a. native.

vernācŭlus, a, um, a. native, domestic, indigenous, vernacular, innate; —, i, m. home-born slave.

vernātio, ōnis, f. skin, slough.

vernīlis, e, a. slavish, fawning; pert.

vernīlĭtas, ātis, f. servility; pertness.

vernīlĭter, ad. slavishly, servilely.

verno, 1. v.n. to be *or* grow verdant; to sprout out; to cast the skin; to bloom; to grow young.

vernō, ad. in the spring-time.

vernŭla, ae, g.c. young home-born slave; —, a. native, indigenous.

vernus, a, um, a. of the spring, vernal.

vēro, ad. in truth, in fact, certainly, to be sure, surely; —, c. but, nay, rather; yet.

veronica (mod. hort.), speedwell.

verres, is, m. boar-pig.

verrīnus, a, um, a. of a boar-pig.

verro, verri, versum, 3. v.a. to sweep, to brush, to scour; to draw along; to rake; to carry off; to skim over.

verrūca, ae, f. steep place, hillock; wart; *fig.* little fault.

verrūcōsus, a, um, a. full of warts, warty; *fig.* rough, rugged, uneven.

verrunco, 1. v.a. & n. to prosper; to turn out.   [versatile.

versābĭlis, e, a. movable; *fig.* changeable;

versābundus, a, um, a. revolving.

versātĭlis, e, a. revolving, movable; *fig.* versatile.

versātio, ōnis, f. turning, change.

versĭcŏlor, ōris, a. changing colour; parti-coloured.

versĭcŭlus, i, m. little line; little verse.

versĭfĭcātio, ōnis, f. versifying, versification.

versīfĭcātor, ōris, m. versifier.

versīfĭco, 1. v.a. to put into verse, to versify.

versĭpellis, e, a. changing its skin or form; *fig.* sly, crafty, cunning; —, is, m. werwolf.

verso, 1. v.a. to turn; to turn often; to turn over or up; to wheel about; to bend, to roll, to tumble; *fig.* to stir about; to agitate; to disturb, to vex; to think over, to consider.

versor, ātus sum, 1. v.n. dep. to be turned; to dwell, to live, to remain; *fig.* to be; to behave; to be circumstanced or situated; to be engaged (in).

versōria, ae, f. sheet;—capere versoriam, to tack.

versum, ad. & pr., v. versus.

versūra, ae, f. turning around; borrowing; loan.

versus, ūs, m. line; row; furrow; written line; verse; dancing-step.

versus, ad. & pr. towards, facing.

versūtē, ad. craftily.

versūtia, ae, f. cunning, subtlety.

versūtus, a, um, a. clever, versatile; crafty, sly; shrewd, deceitful; quick-witted, ready. [spine.]

vertebra, ae, f. joint; vertebra (of the

vertebrātus, a, um, a. jointed with, or in the form of, vertebræ.

vertex, ĭcis, m. whirl; whirlwind; whirlpool; crown of the head; head; peak, top, summit (of anything).

verticillus, i, m. little whirl for the spindle.

verticōsus, a, um, a. whirling, eddying, full of whirlpools.

vertīgĭnōsus, a, um, a. dizzy.

vertīgo, ĭnis, f. turning or whirling around; *fig.* giddiness, dizziness.

verto, ti, sum, 3. v.a. & n. to turn, to turn around or about; to turn upside down; to overthrow; to put to flight; to alter, to change; to transform; to translate; to impute; to turn out; to result;—quod di bene vertant, may the gods prosper it;—verti, to be engaged (in); to depend (upon).

vĕru, ūs, n. spit, broach; dart, javelin.

vĕrŭcŭlum, i, n. little spit or javelin.

vĕrŭīna, ae, f. small javelin.

vĕrum, i, n. spit; v. veru.

vĕrum, i, n. truth, reality; justice, reason.

vērum, c. but, but yet; truly; just so; yes; yes indeed.

vērumtămen, vēruntămen, c. nevertheless, but yet.

vērus, a, um, a. true, real, genuine; just; right; proper; reasonable; speaking the truth, veracious.

veri similis, v. verisimilis.

vĕrūtum, i, n. dart, javelin.   [dullard.

vervex, ēcis, m. wether; (term of abuse)

vēsānia, ae, f. madness, insanity.

vēsāniens, entis, a. furious, raging.

vēsānus, a, um, a. mad, insane; furious, wild.

vescor, 3. v.n. dep. to take food, to eat; to live upon; to enjoy; to have; to use.

vescus, a, um, a. little, small; lean; weak.

vēsīca, ae, f. bladder; cap; lantern; purse; football.

vēsīcŭla, ae, f. little bladder.

vespa, ae, f. wasp.

vesper, ĕris & ĕri, m. evening, eventide; evening - star; west; — sub vesperum, towards evening; —e or —i, in the evening.

vespertĭlio, ōnis, m. bat.

vespĕra, ae, f. evening, eventide.

vespĕrasco, avi, 3. v.n. to become evening, to grow towards evening.

vespertīnus, a, um, a. evening . . ., of the evening; western.

vespĕrūgo, ĭnis, f. evening-star.

vespillo, ōnis, m. bearer (who carried the bodies of the poor for burial at night).

Vestālis, e, a. vestal; —, is, f. Vestal, priestess of Vesta.

vester, tra, trum, pn. a. your.

vestiārium, ii, n. wardrobe.

vestĭbŭlum, i, n. fore-court, entrance-court; entrance; *fig.* beginning, opening, rudiment.

vestīgātor, ōris, m. hunter, tracer.

vestīgium, ii, n. footstep; footprint, track; sole of the foot; *fig.* trace, mark, vestige; moment, instant;—e vestigio, instantly, forthwith.

vestīgo, 1. v.a. to follow in a track, to track, to trace; to inquire after or into, to investigate; to trace out.

vestīmentum, i, n. clothing, garment, vestment.

vestio, īvi & ii, ītum, 4. v.a. to dress, to clothe; to cover; to adorn, to deck; to surround.

vestiplica, ae, f. lady's-maid.

vestis, is, f. garment, clothing, dress; coat; robe; *fig.* skin, slough; beard; spider's web; carpet, curtain; tapestry;—mutare vestem, to put on mourning.

vestītus, ūs, m. clothing, clothes, dress; apparel, ornament;—redire ad suum vestitum, to go out of mourning.

vestras, ātis, pn. of your country or kindred, etc.

vĕtĕrānus, a, um, a. old, veteran; —, i, m. old soldier, veteran.

vĕtĕrasco, āvi, 3. v.n. to grow old.

vĕtĕrātor, ōris, m. old in deceit, crafty fellow.

vĕtĕrātōriē, ad. craftily, slyly.

vĕtĕrātōrius, a, um, a. crafty, sly.

vĕtĕrina, ōrum, n. pl. & veterīnæ, ārum, f. pl. beasts of burden.

vĕtĕrīnārius, ii, m. farrier; veterinary surgeon; —, a, um, a. of or belonging to a farrier.

vĕtĕrīnus, a, um, a. bearing burdens.

vĕternōsus, a, um, a. lethargic; sleepy, drowsy, dreamy; languid.

vĕternus, m. lethargy; drowsiness; sloth.

vĕtĭtum i, n. forbidden or prohibited thing; prohibition, protest.

vĕto, ui, ĭtum, I. v.a. to forbid; to prohibit, to hinder.

vettōnica, ae, f. betony.

vĕtŭla, ae, f. little old woman.

vĕtŭlus, a, um, a. oldish; stale; —, i, m. little old man; fig. old fellow.

vĕtus, ĕris, a. aged, old;—vĕtĕres, um, m. pl. ancients; ancestors; old authors or writers.

vĕtustas, ātis, f. old age; antiquity; long duration; posterity.

vĕtustē, ad. anciently; of long standing.

vĕtustus, a, um, a. aged, old, ancient.

vexāmen, ĭnis, n. vexātio, ōnis, f. shaking, quaking, violent movement; trouble, vexation, distress.

vexātor, ōris, m. troubler, disturber.

vexillārius, ii, m. standard-bearer, ensign;—vexillarii, pl. soldiers who had served in a legion, and who during their last years of service formed a distinct body under a flag of their own (under the emperors).

vexillātio, ōnis, f. company of soldiers under one ensign; battalion, corps; cavalry of an army.

vexillum, i, n. ensign, standard, banner, flag; company, troop.

vexo, I. v.a. to move violently, to shake; to twist (the hair); fig. to injure, to trouble, to maltreat, to abuse, to vex, to disturb, to disquiet, to torment.

via, ae, f. way; highway, road, path, street; passage; channel, pipe; lane (in a camp); windpipe; gullet; cleft; march; journey; fig. manner, method, mode; right method, true way;—viā, rightly, properly;—via media, a middle course.

viālis, e, a., Lares viales, images of gods placed or worshipped by the roadside.

viātĭcātus, a, um, a. provided with travelling-money.

viātĭcum, i, n. travelling-money, provision for a journey; prize-money; extreme unction.

viātĭcus, a, um, a. relating to a journey.

viātor, ōris, m. wayfarer, traveller; summoner.   [lers.

viātōrius, a, um, a. belonging to travel-

vībex, īcis, m. mark of a stripe, weal.

vibro, I. v.a. to brandish, to shake; to hurl; to dart, to throw, to curl, to frizzle; to fling, to launch; —, v.n. to vibrate, to quiver; to glitter, to sparkle.

vīburnum, i, n. guelder-rose.

vīcānus, a, um, a. of or dwelling in a village; —, i, m. villager.

vĭcārius, a, um, a. instead of another, vicarious; —, ii, m. substitute, deputy; vicar; underslave.

vĭcātim, ad. from street to street, through the streets; from village to village, in hamlets.

vīcēnārius, a, um, a. belonging to the number twenty; twentieth.

vīcēni, ae, a, a. num. twenty each; twenty.

vīcēsima, ae, f. twentieth part (as a tax); 5 per cent. of the value of a manumitted slave; export-duty.

vīcēsĭmāni, ōrum, m. pl. soldiers of the twentieth legion.   [part.

vīcēsĭmārius, a, um, a. of the twentieth

vīcēsĭmus, a, um, num. twentieth.

vicia, ae, f. vetch.

vĭcies, ad. twenty times.

vīcīna, ae, f. female neighbour.

vīcīnālis, e, a. neighbouring, near.

vīcīnia, ae, f. neighbourhood; nearness; likeness, resemblance.

vīcīnĭtas, ātis, f. neighbourhood, nearness; neighbours; fig. congeniality; resemblance.

vīcīnum, i, n. neighbourhood, neighbouring place.

vīcīnus, a, um, a. neighbouring, in the neighbourhood, near; fig. like, resembling; kindred; —, i, m. neighbour

vĭcis, genit., no nom., f. change; alternation; succession; course; place, stead; office; part; duty; exchange, retaliation, return; case, condition; state; fortune; vicissitude;—in vicem or in-vicem, by turns; reciprocally; instead of;—vicem, instead of, on account of, for; like, after the manner of;—vice, for, instead of, in the place of, like;—per vices, alternately;—pro hac vice, for this particular turn;—vice versa, the position being reversed.

vĭcissātim, ad. again, in return, by turns.

vĭcissim, ad. by turn, in turn; on the other hand.   [vicissitude.

vĭcissĭtūdo, ĭnis, f. change, alternation

victĭma, ae, f. beast for sacrifice; sacrifice, victim.

victĭmārius, a, um, a. belonging to victims; —, **ii, m.** assistant at sacrifices; seller of beasts for sacrifice.

victĭto, I. v.n. to live poorly.

victor, ōris, m. conqueror, vanquisher, victor;—**currus —,** triumphal car.

victōria, ae, f. victory; success.

victōriātus, i, m. silver coin stamped with the image of Victory, half a denarius.

Victōriŏla, ae, f. little statue of Victory.

victrix, īcis, f. female conqueror; —, a. (f.) victorious.

victus, ūs, m. livelihood, sustenance, nourishment, provisions, victuals; mode of living.

vīcŭlus, i, m. little village, hamlet.

vīcus, i, m. quarter of a city; street; village, hamlet; country-seat.

vidēlicet, ad. it is easy to see; evidently; to wit, that is to say; (sarcastically) of course; forsooth.

vĭdeo, vīdi, vīsum, 2. v.a. to see; to look at, to behold, to observe, to perceive; to understand; to know; to regard, to take care, to have an eye to; to consider; to provide; to live; to see.

vĭdeor, 2. v. dep. & pass. to appear, to seem; to be seen; to be looked upon or regarded;—**vidētur,** it seems good.

vĭdua, ae, f. widow.

vĭduĭtas, ātis, f. bereavement, want; widowhood.

vĭdŭlum, i, n. vĭdŭlus, i, m. portmanteau, knapsack.

vĭduo, ātum, I. v.a. to make a widow; to deprive or bereave of.

vĭduus, a, um, a. bereft, deprived; widowed; void; destitute (of); solitary.

vĭeo, (ēvi), ētum, 2. v.a. to bind with twigs, to tie up, to tie fast; to plait, to weave.

vĭētor, ōris, m., v. **vitor.**

vĭētus, a, um, p. & a. stooping with age, bent; shrunken, wrinkled, withered.

vĭgeo, 2. v.n. to be strong or vigorous; to thrive, to flourish, to bloom; to be brisk or lively; to be in vogue; to be esteemed.

vĭgesco, gŭi, 3. v.n. to become lively or vigorous; to thrive; to begin to bloom.

vĭgēsĭmus, v. **vicesimus.**

vĭgessis, is, m. twenty asses.

vĭgil, ilis, a. awake, on the watch, alert; inextinguishable, perpetual; fig. wakeful, active; attentive, diligent; —, c. watchman, sentinel.

vĭgĭlans, antis, watchful, anxious, careful, vigilant.

vĭgĭlanter, ad. watchfully, carefully, vigilantly.

vĭgĭlantia, ae, f. wakefulness; fig. watchfulness, vigilance.

vĭgĭlax, ācis, a. watchful.

vĭgĭlia, ae, f. wakefulness, lying awake; watch, guard, sentry; nightly vigils; fig. watchfulness, vigilance.

vĭgĭlo, I. v.n. & a. to watch; to be wakeful; to be vigilant or watchful; to watch through; to burn bright; to spend in watching; to make by sleepless labour.

vĭginti, a. num. twenty.

vĭgintĭvīrātus, ūs, m. the office of twenty men.

vĭgintĭvīri, ōrum, m. pl. board of twenty men.

vĭgor, ōris, m. liveliness, activity, vigour.

vĭlic . . , v. **villic . . .**

vīlĭpendo, 3. v.a. to despise, to slight.

vīlis, e, a. cheap; base, vile; paltry, trifling; abundant.

vīlĭtas, ātis, f. cheapness; meanness, baseness; trifling value; worthlessness; contempt, disregard.

vīlĭter, ad. cheaply.

villa, ae, f. country-house, country-seat; farm.

villāris, e, villātĭcus, a, um, a. of a country-house.

villĭca, ae, farmer's wife; female overseer.

villĭco, I. v.a. to manage an estate or farm in the country.

villĭcus, i, m. steward, bailiff.

villōsus, a, um, a. shaggy, rough.

villŭla, ae, f. little country-house or villa; little farm.

villus, i, m. shaggy hair, tuft of hair.

vīmen, ĭnis, n. twig, switch, withe, osier, plaited work.

vīmentum, i, n. osier, withy.

vīmĭnālis, e, a. of osiers or twigs.

vīmĭnētum, i, n. osier-bed.

vīmĭneus, a, um, a. made of osiers.

vin = visne, from **volo.**

vīnāceus, a, um, a. of wine, winy.

Vīnālia, ium, n. pl. wine-festival (on the 22nd of April and the 19th of August).

vīnāria, ōrum, n. pl. wine-pots, wine-vessels.

vīnārius, a, um, a. of wine; —, **ii, m.** wine-dealer, vintner.

vinca, ae, f. periwinkle.   [fetter.

vincio, vinxi, vinctum, 4. v.a. to bind, to

vinclum, v. **vinculum.**

vinco, vici, victum, 3. v.a. to conquer, to vanquish; to overcome; to defeat; to subdue; to win; fig. to surmount; to exceed, to excel; to prove; to prevail, to carry the day.

vincŭlum, i, n. band, bond, cord, rope, fetter; band; prison; imprisonment; obligation. [tage; grapes, wine.
vindēmia, ae, f. grape-gathering; vin-
vindēmiātor, ōris, m. vintager; star in the constellation Virgo.
vindēmiātōrius, a, um, a. of or belonging to vintage.
vindēmio, 1. v.n. to gather grapes.
vindēmiŏla, ae, f. little vintage.
vindēmĭtor, ōris, v. vindemiator.
vindex, ĭcis, c. claimant; defender; protector; avenger, revenger; champion; punisher; redresser, liberator.
vindĭcātio, ōnis, f. protection, avenging, punishment; vindication.
vindĭciæ, ārum, f. pl. legal claim; assertion.
vindĭco, 1. v.n. to vindicate, to lay legal claim to; to defend, to maintain; to excuse; to save, to preserve; to deliver, to free; to avenge, to revenge; to punish; to restore;—rempublicam in libertatem vindicare, to assert the freedom of the state.
vindicta, ae, f. manumission-staff (laid upon a slave when made free); revenge, vengeance; punishment, defence, protection.
vīnea, ae, f. vineyard; vine; shed (of timber and hurdles, for sheltering besiegers).
vīnētum, i, n. vineyard.
vīnĭtor, oris, m. vine-dresser.
vīnŏlentia, ae, f. drunkenness, intoxication from wine. [intoxicated.
vīnŏlentus, a, um, a. drunk with wine;
vīnōsus, a, um, a. full of wine, fond of wine; given to wine; drunk (with wine).
vīnum, i, n. wine.
vĭŏla, ae, f. violet; violet colour; pansy.
vĭŏlābĭlis, e, a. that may be hurt or profaned; violable.
vĭŏlāceus, a, um, a. of a violet colour.
vĭŏlārium, ii, n. bed or bank of violets.
vĭŏlārius, ii, m. dyer of violet colour.
vĭŏlātio, ōnis, f. injury, profanation, violation. [lator.
vĭŏlātor, ōris, m. injurer, profaner, vio-
vĭŏlens, entis, a. impetuous, vehement, furious, violent.
vĭŏlenter, ad. impetuously, forcibly, vehemently, violently.
vĭŏlentia, ae, f. violence, vehemence, impetuosity, ferocity.
vĭŏlentus, a, um, a. violent, forcible, vehement; impetuous, boisterous.
vĭŏlo, 1. v.a. to injure, to profane; to defile, to pollute; to deflower; to break, to transgress, to violate.

vīpĕra, ae, f. viper; adder, snake, serpent. [poisonous.
vīpĕreus, vīpĕrĭnus, a, um, a. of vipers;
vir, vĭri, m. man; male; husband, honourable man; hero; soldier; fig. manhood. [warrior, heroine.
vĭrāgo, ĭnis, f. heroic maiden, female
vĭrectum, i, n. greensward, glade.
vĭreo, ui, 2. v.n. to be green or verdant; to bloom, to flourish; fig. to be fresh, lively or vigorous.
vīres, ium, f. pl. strength.
vĭresco, 3. v.n. to grow green or verdant; fig. to prosper.
vĭrētum, i, v. virectum.
virga, ae, f. twig, switch, rod; limetwig; switch (for flogging); staff; magic wand; coloured stripe.
virgātor, ōris, m. flogger; beadle.
virgātus, a, um, a. made of twigs or osiers; beaten with rods; streaked, striped.
virgētum, i, n. thicket of osiers, osierplot.
virgeus, a, um, a. of rods or twigs;—flamma virgea, brushwood set on fire.
virgĭdēmia, ae, f. fig. harvest of rods, sound flogging.
virgĭliæ, v. vergiliæ.
virgĭnālis, e, a. maidenly, virgin, virginal.
virgĭnārius, a, um, a. of a virgin.
virgĭneus, a, um, a. maidenly, virgin.
virgĭnĭtas, ātis, f. maidenhood, virginity.
virgo, ĭnis, f. maid, maiden, virgin; girl; Virgo (constellation); aqueduct (at Rome.
virgŭla, ae, f. little twig, small rod, wand; divining-rod. [shrubbery.
virgultum, i, n. bush, thicket, copse,
virguncŭla, ae, f. little maid, young girl.
vĭriæ, ārum, f. pl. bracelet.
vĭrĭcŭlum, i, n. graving tool.
vĭrĭdans, tis, a. verdant.
vĭrĭdārium, ii, n. pleasure-garden, green plot or walk, pleasaunce.
vĭrĭdia, ium, n. pl. herbs, green plants.
vĭrĭdĭcātus, a, um, a. become green; made green or fresh.
vĭrĭdis, e, a. green, grassy; fresh, blooming, sappy; lusty, vigorous; young, youthful; lively.
vĭrĭdĭtas, ātis, f. green colour, greenness, verdure; vigour.
vĭrĭdo, 1. v.a. & n. to make green; to grow green; to be green.
vĭrīlis, e, a. male, masculine; of a man; full-grown; manly; bold; firm; vigorous;—pro virili parte, with the utmost effort; as far as a man may;—toga —, v. toga.

vĭrīlĭtas, ātis, f. manhood; manliness.
vĭrīlĭter, ad. manfully, courageously.
vĭrĭŏla, ae, f. small bracelet.
vĭrītim, ad. man by man, singly; individually.
vĭrōsus, a, um, a. stinking.
virtūs, ūtis, f. manliness, manhood; virtue; bravery, courage; strength; merit; value, worth.
vīrus, i, n. slime; poison; stench.
vis, vis, vim, vi, f., vīres, ium, pl. strength, force; vigour, power, energy; violence; fury; importance; meaning, signification; nature; efficacy, virtue (of drugs, etc.); abundance, plenty;—vires, strength; power; military forces, troops;—vis a fronte, a push from in front;—vis a tergo, a push from behind. [lime.
viscātus, a, um, a. smeared with bird-
viscĕra, um, n. pl., v. viscus.
viscĕrātio, ōnis, f. public distribution of meat; good cheer.
viscum, i, n. mistletoe; bird-lime.
viscus, ĕris, n., viscĕra, um, n. pl. internal organs; entrails, bowels; fig. flesh; child, offspring; fig. inward or inmost part.
viscus, i, v. viscum. [idea, notion.
vīsio, ōnis, f. appearance, apparition;
vīsĭto, i. v.a. to go to see, to visit.
vīso, si, sum, 3. v.a. to view, to behold, to survey; to look after; to visit.
vīsum, i, n. sight, appearance, vision; dream.
vīsus, ūs, m. look, glance; sight, vision; appearance, apparition.
vīta, ae, f. life; living, subsistence; mode or manner of life; career; mankind, world.
vĭtābĭlis, e, a. to be avoided.
vĭtābundus, a, um, a. shunning, avoiding.
vītālis, e, a. of life; vital; long-lived;—vitalia, ium, n. pl. vital parts, vitals.
vītālĭtas, ātis, f. vitality; liveliness.
vītālĭter, ad. vitally.
vītātio, ōnis, f. avoiding, avoidance.
vĭtellus, i, m. little calf; yolk (of an egg).
vīteus, a, um, a. belonging to the vine.
vītex, ĭcis, f. willow.
vĭtĭārium, ii, n. vine plantation.
vītĭcŭla, ae, m. little vine tendril.
vītĭfer, a, um, a. vine-bearing.
vītĭgĕnus, a, um, a. produced from the vine.
vītĭgĭneus, a, um, a. of the vine.
vĭtīlĭgo, ĭnis, f. leprosy.
vītīlis, e, a. made of wicker.
vĭtio, i. v.a. to spoil, to mar, to corrupt, to infect, to vitiate; to pollute; to deflower, to violate, to render void.

vĭtĭōsē, ad. faultily, defectively, corruptly, badly, ill.
vĭtĭōsĭtas, ātis, f. faultiness, corruption.
vĭtĭōsus, a, um, a. faulty, defective, bad, corrupt; wicked, vicious. [staff.
vītis, is, f. vine; vine-branch; centurion's
vītĭsātor, ōris, m. vine-planter.
vĭtĭum, ii, n. fault, defect, blemish; error; offence, crime, vice; sin;—vitio vertere, to impute as a fault.
vĭto, i. v.a. & n. to avoid, to shun, to evade.
vītor, ōris, m. basket-maker.
vĭtrea, ōrum, n. pl. drinking-glasses; glass-ware.
vĭtreārius, ii, m. worker in glass.
vĭtreus, a, um, a. of glass, glassy; transparent; brilliant, beautiful.
vītrīcus, i, m. stepfather.
vĭtrum, i, n. glass, woad.
vitta, ae, f. chaplet, fillet, headband.
vittātus, a, um, a. wearing a fillet.
vĭtŭla, ae, f. cow-calf.
vĭtŭlīna, ae, f. veal, calf's flesh.
vĭtŭlīnus, a, um, a. of a calf; of veal.
vĭtŭlor, i. v.n. dep. to rejoice, to be joyful; to bring a thank-offering.
vĭtŭlus, i, m. (bull-)calf; foal; seal; young.
vĭtŭpĕrābĭlis, e, a. blameable, blameworthy.
vĭtŭpĕrātio, ōnis, f. blame, vituperation.
vĭtŭpĕrātor, ōris, m. blamer.
vĭtŭpĕro, i. v.a. to blame, to find fault with, to vituperate.
vīvācĭtas, ātis, f. long life; vivacity.
vīvārium, ii, n. park, preserve.
vīvātus, a, um, a. lively, vivid.
vīvax, ācis, a. long-lived, vivacious, lively, vigorous; durable.
vīverra, ae, f. ferret.
vīvesco, vixi, 3. v.n. to become alive; to shoot up; to get life; to grow lively or vigorous.
vīvĭdus, a, um, a. living; true to the life, vivid, lively, vigorous.
vīvĭrādix, īcis, f. a quickset.
vīvisco, v. vivesco.
vīvo, vixi, victum, 3. v.n. to live, to be alive; to live on or upon; to dwell; to be; to live well; to last; to endure; to be kindled, nourished or increased.
vīvus, a, um, a. alive, living; lively, quick; fresh, green; running; burning; true to life;—ad vivum, to the quick;—viva voce, orally, as opposed to in writing.
vix, ad. hardly, scarcely, with difficulty.
vixdum, ad. scarcely yet.
vŏcābŭlum, i, n. word, appellation, designation, name; substantive, noun.

vōcālis, e, a. vocal; endowed with voice; singing; loud, sonorous; speaking.
vōcālis, is, f. vowel.
vŏcāmen, ĭnis, n. designation, name.
vŏcātio, ōnis, f. citing; summons; invitation to dinner.
vŏcātīvus, i, m. vocative case.
vŏcātor, ōris, m. inviter.
vŏcātus, ūs, m. calling upon, summoning; invitation to dinner.
vōcĭfĕrātio, ōnis, f. vociferation, outcry.
vōcĭfĕrātus, ūs, m. clamour.
vōcĭfĕror, ātus sum, 1. v.n. & a. dep. to cry aloud, to scream, to bawl, to vociferate, to resound.
vŏcĭto, ātum, 1. v.a. & n. to call often, to name; to call loudly.
vōcīvus, a, um, a., v. vacivus.
vŏco, 1. v.a. & n. to call; to call upon, to summon; to name; to bid, to invite; to challenge; to cite, to incite; to demand; to bring, to draw, to put; to reduce; to refer.
vōcŭla, ae, f. low voice; weak voice.
vŏla, ae, f. palm of the hand; sole of the foot.
vŏlæmum, i, n. a kind of pear.
vŏlantes, ium, m. pl. birds.
vŏlātĭcus, a, um, a. flying, winged; volatile, transitory.
vŏlātĭlis, e, a. flying, winged; swift, rapid; fleeting, transitory.
vŏlātūra, ae, f. flight.
vŏlātus, ūs, m. flying, flight.
Volcānus, v. Vulcānus.
vŏlēmum, v. vŏlæmum.
vŏlens, entis, a. willing, voluntary, ready; favourable;—si vobis volentibus est, if it is your wish.
volgiŏlus, i, n. roller, rolling-stone.
volgo, volgus, v. vulgus.
vŏlĭto, 1. v.n. to fly about, to flutter; to hasten, to hover about, to get excited.
volnus, etc., v. vuln.
vŏlo, vŏlui, velle, v.n. & a. ir. & def. to will, to be willing; to wish, to desire; to want; to wish well; to have to say, to wish to speak; to think, to suppose; to mean, to signify; (law) to ordain, to will.
vŏlo, 1. v.n. to fly; fig. to hasten along.
vŏlo, ōnis, m. volunteer.
volpes, is, v. vulpes.
volsella, ae, or volsilla, f. tweezers.
volsus, a, um, v. vulsus.
voltŭrius, ii, v. vulturius.
voltus, us, v. vultus.
vŏlūbĭlis, e, a. whirling, rolling, revolving, turning; voluble; gliding swiftly; fluent, rapid; changeable; inconstant.

vŏlūbĭlĭtas, ātis, f. whirling motion; roundness; fluency, volubility; changeableness.
vŏlūbĭlĭter, ad. fluently, volubly.
vŏlŭcer, cris, e, a. flying, winged; fig. swift; light; unstable.
vŏlŭcre, is, n. a. caterpillar that devours vines.
vŏlucris, is, f. bird.
vŏlūmen, ĭnis, n. roll, volume; book; spire, turn; wreath, fold; revolution, vicissitude.
vŏluntārius, a, um, a. of his or its own free will, voluntary;—voluntarii, ōrum, m. pl. volunteers.
vŏluntas, ātis, f. will, wish, choice, desire, inclination; favour, good-will; last will, testament; meaning, sense, signification.
vŏlŭp, ad. agreeably, pleasantly, to one's satisfaction.
vŏluptābĭlis, e, a. pleasurable.
vŏluptārius, a, um, a. pleasant, agreeable; sensual, voluptuous.
vŏluptas, ātis, f. voluptuousness, sensuality; delight; pleasure; charmer, sweetheart;—voluptates, pl. sports or spectacles (given to the people).
vŏluptuōsus, a, um, a. pleasant; delightful.
vŏlūta, ae, f. leaves wreathed about the capital of a pillar.
vŏlūtābrum, i, n. place where swine wallow.
vŏlūtābundus, a, um, a. wallowing about.
vŏlūtātio, ōnis, f. rolling about, wallowing; restlessness, disquiet.
vŏlūtātus, ūs, m. wallowing.
vŏlūto, 1. v.a. to roll, to wallow, to tumble; to spread; to revolve in the mind, to consider, to ponder.
volva, ae, f., v. vulva.
volvo, volvi, vŏlūtum, 3. v.a. to roll, to turn about or round, to tumble; fig. to toss; to consider, to ponder.
vōmer, ĕris, m. ploughshare.
vŏmĭca, ae, f. sore, ulcer, abscess; fig. curse, plague.
vōmis, ĕris, v. vomer.
vŏmĭtio, ōnis, f. vomiting.
vŏmĭto, 1. v.n. to vomit often.
vŏmĭtor, ōris, m. vomiter.
vŏmĭtōrius, a, um, a. producing sickness;—vŏmĭtōria, n. pl. entrances to the blocks of seats in the amphitheatre.
vŏmĭtus, ūs, m. vomiting.
vŏmo, ui, ĭtum, 3. v.n. & a. to vomit, to throw out; to discharge, to emit.
vŏrācĭtas, ātis, f. voracity; greediness.
vŏrāgo, ĭnis, f. gulf, whirlpool, chasm; spendthrift.

vŏrax, ăcis, a. voracious; ravenous; devouring; greedy.

vŏro, I. v.a. to swallow up, to eat greedily, to devour; *fig.* to overwhelm; to pursue eagerly, to pore over (a book).

vors . . ., v. vers . . .

vortex, etc., v. **vert.**

voster, tra, trum, v. **vester.**

vŏtĭfer, a, um, a. votive.

vŏtīvus, a, um, a. votive.

vŏtum, i, n. vow; votive offering; prayer; desire, wish, ideal.

vŏveo, vŏvi, vŏtum, 2. v.a. to vow; to devote, to wish (for).

vox, vōcis, f. voice, sound, tone, cry, call; word; speech; sentence; proverb; language; accent; style; dialect.

Vulcānālis, e, a. of Vulcan;—**Vulcānālia, ium,** n. pl. Feast of Vulcan on the 23rd of August.

Vulcānius, a, um, a. of Vulcan; connected with fire.

Vulcānus, i, m. the god of fire; *fig.* fire.

vulgāris, e, a. vulgar, usual, common, commonplace.

vulgārĭter, ad. commonly, vulgarly.

vulgātor, ōris, m. publisher, divulger, tell-tale.

vulgātus, a, um, a. generally known, notorious; common, usual.

vulgĭvăgus, a, um, a. roving, wandering everywhere.

vulgo, I. v.a. to make common; to publish; to spread abroad, to divulge; to prostitute.

vulgō, ad. generally, everywhere, commonly, publicly.

vulgus, i, n. promiscuous crowd, the multitude, the people, public.

vulnĕrārius, a, um, a. connected with wounds; —, **ii,** m. surgeon.

vulnĕrātio, ōnis, f. wounding; wound; *fig.* injuring. [injure.

vulnĕro, I. v.a. to wound, to hurt, to

vulnĭficus, a, um, a. wound-inflicting.

vulnus, ĕris, n. wound, rent, cut, notch; *fig.* remorse, sting; pain, sorrow, defeat.

vulpēcŭla, ae, f. little fox.

vulpes, is, f. fox; *fig.* cunning, craftiness.

vulsus, a, um, a. smooth; hairless; *fig.* effeminate.

vultĭcŭlus, i, m. look, mien.

vultum, i, v. **vultus.**

vultuōsus, a, um, a. full of emotional expression; affected.

vultur, ŭris, m. vulture.

vultŭrīnus, a, um, a. of or like a vulture.

vultŭrius, ii, m. vulture; extortioner; unlucky throw at dice.

vultus, ūs, m. countenance, visage, grim visage, stern look; appearance; mien, expression.

vulva, ae, f. wrapper, womb, matrix.

Weigēlia (mod. hort.), weigelia.

wellingtonia (mod. hort.), sequoia.

wistāria (mod. hort.), wistaria, grape-flower vine.

X = 10.

xĕnium, ii, n. gift, present (to friends, guests).

xĭphias, ae, m. sword-fish.

xystici, ōrum, m. pl. athletes, wrestlers.

xystum, i, n. **xystus, i, m.** colonnade, portico.

Zēa, ae, f. maize.

zēlŏtȳpus, a, um, a. jealous.

Zĕphȳrus, i, m. western breeze, zephyr.

zeugma, ătis, n. zeugma, a grammatical figure in which a word stands in the same relation to two others but in a different sense in each case.

zmăragdus, i, v. **smaragdus.**

zōdiăcus, i, m. zodiac.

zōna, ae, f. belt, girdle; zone.

zōnārius, ii, m. girdle-maker; —, **a, um,** a. belonging to girdles;—**sector** —, cut-purse.

zingiberi, n. ginger.

zinnia (mod. hort.), zinnia, youth-and-old-age.

zȳthum, i, n. beer.

LIST OF HISTORICAL AND
MYTHOLOGICAL PROPER NAMES

Acastus, i, king of Iolcos and one of the Argonauts, was killed by Peleus.

Accius, v. Attius.

Achæi, ōrum, the ruling nation among the Greeks in Homeric times.

Achæmĕnes, is, ancestor of the old Persian kings.

Achæus, i, son of Xuthus, ancestor of the Achæans.

Achātēs, ae, bosom-friend of Æneas;—**fidus —,** *fig.* faithful friend.

Achilles, is, son of Peleus and of Thetis.

Acīdălia, ae, f. a surname of Venus (from a fountain in Bœotia).

Acis, idis, son of Faunus, beloved of Galatea; slain by the jealous Polyphemus.

Actæon, ŏnis, a huntsman torn to pieces by his own dogs for having seen Diana bathing.

Admētus, i, king of Thessaly, husband of Alcestes.

Adōnis, is & **idis,** son of Cinyras, king of Cyprus, beloved by Venus; *fig.* beautiful young man; Lovelace.

Adrastus, i, king of Argos, one of the seven heroes before Thebes.

Æäcīdes, ae, a. descendant of Æacus; his grandson Achilles.

Æēta, Æētes, ae, king of Colchis, father of Medea.

Ægeus, ei, father of Theseus.

Ægisthus, i, the paramour of Clytemnestra and murderer of Agamemnon.

Ænēas, ae, son of Anchises and Venus.

Ænēis, idis & **idos,** f. Æneid (epic poem of Virgil).

Æŏlus, i, god of the winds.

Æschīnes, is, famous Greek orator.

Æschўlus, i, one of the three great tragic poets among the Greeks.

Æscŭlāpius, ii, god of the medical art, son of Apollo.

Æsŏnīdes, ae, Jason, son of Æson.

Æsōpus, i, Greek writer of fables.

Afrĭcānus, i, a surname of the two Scipios.

Agămemnon, ŏnis, king of Mycenæ, commander-in-chief of the Greek forces before Troy.

Agāvē, es, mother of Pentheus; being driven mad by Bacchus she tore her son in pieces. [Cadmus.

Agēnor, ŏris, ancestor of Dido, father of

Agesilāus, i, victorious Spartan king.

Agis, idis, name of several kings of Sparta.

Aglaia, ae, one of the Graces.

Agrippa, ae, general of Augustus.

Agrippīna, ae, wife of Tiberius, the Emperor.

Ajax, ācis, — Telamonius & — Oileus, two Greek heroes in the Trojan war.

Alcæus, i, famous lyric poet of Mitylene.

Alcămĕnes, is, Greek sculptor, the most celebrated disciple of Phidias.

Alcestē, ēs, Alcestis, is, wife of Admetus; she died for her husband.

Alcĭbiādes, is, Athenian nobleman and general in the Peloponnesian war.

Alcīdes, ae, Hercules (grandson of Alceus).

Alcĭnŏus, i, king of the Phæacians.

Alcmæōnĭdæ, arum, a celebrated Athenian family.

Alcmēnē, ēs, mother of Hercules.

Alcўŏne, es, wife of Ceyx; she was changed into a kingfisher.

Alecto, ūs, f. a Fury.

Alexander, dri, — Magnus, son of Philip, king of Macedonia.

Amalthēa, ae, a nymph, the nurse of Jupiter; name of the goat with the milk of which Jupiter was fed.

Amāsis, i, king of Egypt, 570-526 B.C.

Amazŏnes, um, f. pl. warlike women living on the south coast of the Black Sea.

Ambrŏsius, ii, a Christian Father, strong opponent of the Arians.

Amilcar, v. Hamilcar.

Ammōn, ŏnis, Æthiopian god, supposed to be identical with Jupiter.

Amphiãrãus, i, Greek seer.

Amphĭon, ŏnis, king of Thebes, husband of Niobe.

Amphĭtrīte, es, wife of Neptune, goddess of the sea.

Amphĭtryo, ōnis, husband of Alcmene.

Amūlĭus, ii, king of Alba, grandfather of Romulus and Remus.

Ãmyclæ, arum, f. pl. an old town of Laconia. [Teos.

Ãnacreōn, ontis, famous lyric poet of

Ãnaxãgŏras, ae, Greek philosopher, teacher of Euripides and Pericles.

Ãnaxĭmander, dri, Greek philosopher.

Anchīses, ae, father of Æneas.

Ancus Martĭus, fourth king of Rome.

Andōcĭdes, ae, Athenian orator.

Andrŏmãcha, ae, Andrŏmãchē, ēs, wife of Hector.

Andrŏmĕda, ae, daughter of Cepheus and Cassiope; rescued by Perseus from a sea-monster.

Andrŏnīcus, i, Roman surname;—T. Livius —, first dramatic poet of the Romans.

Anna, ae, sister of Dido.

Annĭbal, v. Hannĭbal.

Antæus, i, Libyan giant, slain by Hercules. [Padua.

Antēnor, ŏris, noble Trojan, founder of

Antĭgŏnē, ēs, daughter of Œdipus.

Antĭgŏnus, i, general of Alexander.

Antĭŏchus, i, king of Syria.

Antĭpãter, tri, general under Alexander the Great.

Antĭphōn, ontis, Athenian orator.

Antōnīnus Pius, Roman emperor, A.D. 138-161.

Antōnĭus, a, um, Roman gentile name;— M. —, one of the triumvirs.

Ãnūbis, is & ĭdis, Egyptian dog-headed god. [Socrates.

Ãnȳtus, i, one of the three accusers of

Ãpelles, is, renowned Greek painter.

Ãpis, is, the Bull, an Egyptian god.

Ãpollo, ĭnis, the sun-god, son of Jupiter and Latona.

Ãpollōnĭus, ii, (1) Rhodius, wrote a poem on the Argonauts; (2) a philosopher of Tyãna in Cappadocia credited with magic powers.

Archĕlãus, i, king of Macedonia, protector of Euripides. [Cicero's time.

Archĭas, ae, Greek poet of Antioch in

Archĭlŏchus, i, Greek poet of Paros, inventor of the iambic verse.

Archĭmēdes, is, mathematician and mechanical inventor at Syracuse.

Archȳtas, ae, Pythagorean philosopher at Tarentum, Plato's friend.

Argo, ŭs, f. ship in which the Greek heroes under Jason sailed to Colchis to obtain the golden fleece.

Argŏnautæ, ãrum, m. pl. the heroes who sailed in the *Argo*.

Argōus, a, um, a. relating to the Argo.

Argus, i, the hundred-eyed keeper of Io.

Ãrĭadnē, ēs, daughter of Minos, king of Crete.

Ãrīon, ŏnis, lyric poet and cithara-player of Lesbos; saved from death by a dolphin. [Cæsar's time.

Ãrĭovistus, i, chief of a German tribe in

Ãristãgŏras, ae, of Miletus; fomented the revolt of Ionia against the Persians.

Ãristarchus, i, critic of Alexandria.

Ãristīdes, is, noble Athenian and statesman.

Ãristippus, i, philosopher and founder of the Cyrenaic school.

Ãristŏgīton, onis, m. conspired with Harmodius to murder Hipparchus.

Ãristŏphãnes, is, the greatest comic poet of Greece.

Ãristŏtĕles, is & i, the greatest natural philosopher of antiquity.

Ãristoxĕnus, i, writer on music in Aristotle's time.

Arius, ii, of Alexandria; preached against doctrine of the Trinity; flourished A.D. 315.

Artaxerxes, is, name of several Persian kings. [Alba Longa.

Ascãnĭus, ii, son of Æneas; founder of

Asclēpĭãdes, is, Greek lyric poet, inventor of the metre named after him.

Asdrubal, v. Hasdrubal.

Aspãsia, ae, f. mistress of Pericles.

Astartē, ēs, Syro-Phœnician moon-goddess.

Astræa, ae, goddess of Justice.

Astyãges, is, king of Media, grandfather of Cyrus.

Astyãnax, actis, m. son of Hector and Andromache.

Ãtãlanta, (1) daughter of Iasius; took part in the hunt of the Calydonian boar; (2) daughter of Schœneus; very swift of foot; engaged in a race with Hippomenes and was defeated by a ruse.

Ãthãmas, antis, king of Thessaly, father of Phrixus and Helle.

Ãthãnãsĭus, ii, Christian Father, born 296, archbishop of Alexandria; the upholder of orthodoxy against the Arians;— Athanasius contra mundum, Athanasius against the world.

Atlãs, antis, a giant who supported the heavens on his shoulders.

Atreus, ei, king of Mycenæ, father of Agamemnon and Menelaus.

Atrīdes, ae, descendant of Atreus.

Ātrŏpos, i, f. one of the three Fates.

Attălus, i, king of Pergamus.

Attĭla, ae, king of the Huns and scourge of the Roman Empire; died A.D. 453.

Attĭus, a, um, Roman gentile name;—**P. Varus,** Roman poet, contemporary with Pacuvius.   [loved of Cybele.

Ătys *or* **Attys,** a Phrygian shepherd be-

Augĭas, ae, king of Elis (whose stable was cleansed by Hercules).

Augustus, i, surname of Octavianus and subsequently of all the Roman emperors.   [275.

Aurēlianus, Roman emperor, A.D. 270-

Aurēlius, M. Aurelius Antoninus, Roman emperor, A.D. 161-180.

Autŏlўcus, i, an arrant thief endowed with the power of transforming himself into various shapes.

Baccha, ae, Bacchis, ĭdis, f. Bacchante, priestess of Bacchus.

Bacchĭcus, a, um, Bacchius, a, um, a. of Bacchus, Bacchic.   [and Semele.

Bacchus, i, god of wine, son of Jupiter

Bacchўlĭdes, ae, a Greek lyric poet born in Ceos.

Barcas, ae, a noble Carthaginian, ancestor of the family to which Hannibal belonged.

Băthyllus, i, m. a youth beloved by Anacreon; a freedman of Mæcenas, inventor of the pantomime at Rome.

Battus, i, founder of Cyrene.

Baucis, ĭdis, the wife of Philemon.

Băvius, ii, m. a bad poet, contemporary of Virgilius.

Bēlĭdes, um, f. pl. daughters of Danaus.

Belisārius, ii, general of Justinian; defeated the Goths in Italy; died A.D. 565.

Bellĕrŏphōn, ontis, slayer of the Chimæra; rode the winged horse Pegasus.

Bellōna, ae, goddess of war.

Bēlus, i, ancient king of Egypt.

Bias, antis, Greek philosopher (one of the seven wise men), contemporary of Crœsus.

Bion, ōnis, a pastoral poet contemporary with Moschus.

Bœōtia, ae, f. a district of Greece north of Attica, having Thebes as capital.

Boēthius, i, m. a Stoic philosopher.

Bŏmilcar, ăris, a Carthaginian general during the second Punic war.

Bona Dea, f. a goddess, worshipped by the Roman ladies as goddess of Fertility and Chastity on the 1st of May.

Bŏreas, ae, the north wind.

Brasĭdas, ae, a famous Spartan who captured Amphipolis from the Athenians in 424 B.C.

Brennus, i, m. a chief of the Gauls who conquered Rome, 390 B.C.

Briăreus, ei, m. a hundred-armed giant.

Brŏmius, ii, Bacchus.

Brūtus, i, Roman surname;—**M. Junius** —, one of Cæsar's murderers in 44 B.C.

Būcĕphălas, ae, m. horse of Alexander the Great.

Būsĭris, ĭdis, king of Egypt, slain by Hercules.

C. = Caius.

Cācus, i, a giant, son of Vulcan, slain by Hercules.   [Agenor.

Cadmus, i, founder of Thebes, son of

Cæsar, ăris, surname of the gens Julia;— **C. Julius** —, a great Roman general, orator, statesman, dictator, and author; murdered 44 B.C.

Cāius, i, a Roman first name.

Calchas, antis, high priest and seer among the Greeks before Troy.

Călĭgŭla, ae, the third Roman emperor.

Callĭmăchus, i, famous Greek poet, 250 B.C.   [poetry, 700 B.C.

Callīnus, i, the father of Greek elegiac

Calliŏpē, ēs, one of the Muses, goddess of epic poetry.

Callisto, ūs, daughter of the Arcadian king Lycaon; (as constellation) the Greater Bear.

Calpurnius, a, um, Roman gentile name.

Călypso, ūs, f. a nymph, daughter of Oceanus, ruling over the island Ogygia.

Cambўses, is, father of the elder Cyrus; son of him.   [(later) the Muses.

Cămēnæ, ārum, prophetic nymphs;

Cămillus, i, M. Furius —, defeated the Gauls in 390 B.C.

Căpăneus, ei, one of the seven heroes who attacked Thebes.

Cărăcalla, ae, m. emperor of Rome, A.D. 211-217.

Carneădes, ae, m. a philosopher of Cyrene, founded the New Academy at Athens, 213-129 B.C.

Cassander, dri, son of Antipater, king of Macedonia after Alexander's death.

Cassandra, ae, prophetess, daughter of Priam and Hecuba.   [Andromeda.

Cassiŏpe, ēs, wife of Cepheus, mother of

Cassius, a, um, Roman gentile name.

Castor, ŏris, twin-brother of Pollux, son of Tyndareus.   [conspirator.

Cătĭlīna, æ, m. noble Roman, the ill-famed

Căto, ōnis, (1) the censor, author of the phrase, **delenda est Carthago** (Carthage must be destroyed); born 234 B.C.; (2) an opponent of Cæsar; committed suicide at Utica when his cause was defeated, 49 B.C.

Cătullus, i, Roman lyric poet (in Cicero's time).

Caurus, i, m. the north-west wind.

Cecrops, ŏpis, first king of Attica, founder of Athens.

Cĕleus, i, king of Eleusis, whom Ceres taught agriculture and the Mysteries.

Centauri, ōrum, m. pl. a wild race of Thessaly, half-man, half-horse.

Cĕphălus, i, husband of Procris.

Cĕphēis, ĭdis, f. Andromeda.

Cĕpheus, i, king of Ethiopia, father of Andromeda.

Cerbĕrus, i, three-headed dog, guarding the entrance to Hell.

Cĕrēs, ĕris, Roman goddess of agriculture.

Chabrias, ae, Athenian general.

Chărĭtes, um, f. pl. (Greek name of) the Graces.

Chăron, ontis, ferryman of the Lower World.

Chĭmæra, ae, f. fire-breathing monster in Lycia, daughter of Typhon and Echidna, slain by Bellerophon.

Chiron, ōnis, a Centaur who tutored Æsculapius, Hercules and Achilles.

Chrȳsēis, ĭdis, daughter of Chryses.

Chrȳses, ae, priest of Apollo.

Chrȳsippus, i, a Stoic philosopher; born 280 B.C.

Chrysostŏmus, i, Chrysostom, born at Antioch, A.D. 347; a famous preacher, made Archbishop of Constantinople, 397.

Cĭcĕro, ōnis, surname in the gens Tullia; —**M. Tullius** —, great Roman orator.

Cĭmon, ōnis, father of Miltiades; son of Miltiades, Athenian general.

Cincinnātus, i, Roman dictator.

Cingĕtŏrix, ĭgis, a king of Kent in Cæsar's time.

Cinna, m. leader of the popular party during Sulla's absence from Rome, 87-84 B.C.

Circē, ēs & ae, a famous sorceress.

Cisseus, ei, king of Thracia, father of Hecuba.

Clælĭa, ae, a Roman maiden, escaped by swimming from captivity of Porsena.

Claudiānus, i, last of the classical Roman poets; flourished about A.D. 400.

Claudius, Roman emperor, A.D. 41-54.

Cleōn, onis, a famous Athenian demagogue attacked by Aristophanes; died in action, 422 B.C.

Clĕŏpātra, ae, queen of Egypt, daughter of Ptolemy Auletes; loved by Anthony.

Clīo, ūs, f. Muse of History.

Clītus, i, friend and general of Alexander the Great, by whom he was killed.

Clōdius, a patrician demagogue, enemy of Cicero.

Clōthō, us, f. one of the Fates (who span the thread of Fate).

Clūsium, ii, a famous Etruscan town; the residence of Porsena.

Clȳtæmnestra, æ, wife of Agamemnon.

Cnæus, i, a Roman first name.

Cocles, ĭtis, surname of a Roman Horatius, who excelled in the war against Porsena.

Cōdrus, i, last king of Athens.

Collātīnus (a, um), surname of L. Tarquinius, husband of Lucretia.

Cŏlŭmella, ae, m. a writer on agriculture contemporary with Seneca. [192.

Commŏdus, i, Roman emperor, A.D. 180-

Cōnon, ōnis, Athenian general.

Constantīnus, i, Roman emperor, surnamed "the Great"; reigned A.D. 306-337.

Cŏrinna, ae, Greek poetess in Pindar's time.

Cŏriŏlānus, surname of C. Marcius, who took Corioli; became an enemy of his countrymen, the Romans.

Cornēlia, the mother of the Gracchi.

Cŏrȳbantes, um, m. pl. priests of Cybele.

Crătīnus, i, comic Athenian poet, contemporary of Aristophanes.

Creon, ontis, king of Corinth.

Creūsa, ae, daughter of Creon, wife of Jason; daughter of Priam, wife of Æneas.

Crĭtias, ae, one of the Thirty Tyrants.

Crœsus, king of Lydia; fig. a rich man.

Ctēsĭphon, tis, Athenian statesman, friend of Demosthenes.

Cŭpīdo, ĭnis, Cupid, son of Venus, the god of Love.

Cŭriātii, ōrum, an Alban family, fought the Horatii.

Curtius, ii, leaped with his horse into a chasm in the Roman Forum and saved the city.

Cўbĕlē, ae & ēs, Phrygian goddess.

Cyclops, ōpis, Cyclops;—**Cyclopes, um,** m. pl. one-eyed giants, workmen in Vulcan's smithy.

Cȳrus, i, founder of the Persian monarchy.

Cўthĕrēa, ae, f. Venus.

Dædălus, i, father of Icarus; built the Labyrinth in Crete.

Dāmocles, is, m. a flatterer of Dionysius of Syracuse; a sword was suspended by a hair over his head.

Dănaĕ, ēs, mother of Perseus.

Dănaïdes, um, daughters of Danaus; they murdered their cousins who sought their hand in marriage and were compelled in the underworld to pour water through a sieve.

Dănaus, i, son of Belus, father of 50 daughters.

Daphnē, ēs, daughter of the river-god Peneus, loved by Apollo.

Dardănus, i, ancestor of the Trojan dynasty.

Dārius, i, king of Persia, 521-485 B.C.

Daunus, i, king of Apulia, ancestor of Turnus.

Dāvus, i, a slave in the Andria of Terence; —Davus sum, non Œdipus, I'm a slave, not a reader of riddles like Œdipus.

Dĕcius Mūs, consul 340 B.C.; devoted himself to death to save his country.

Dēiănīra, ae, wife of Hercules.

Dēiphŏbus, i, a son of Priam.

Dēmētrius, ii, — Poliorcetes, king of Macedonia, son of Antigonus.

Dēmocrĭtus, i, of Abdera; called " the laughing philosopher."

Dēmosthĕnēs, is, great Athenian orator.

Deucălion, ōnis, king of Phthia in Thessaly, son of Prometheus; with his wife Pyrrha was the only mortal saved from flood.   [Apollo.

Diāna, ae, goddess of hunting, sister of

Dictynna, ae, name of Diana, as goddess of the chase.

Dīdŏ, ūs & ōnis, f. foundress of Carthage.

Diespĭter, tris＝Jupiter.

Dindymēnē, ēs, Cybele.   [305.

Dioclētiānus, i, Roman emperor, A.D. 284-

Diŏdōrus Sĭcŭlus, historian; wrote in Greek; contemporary of Julius Cæsar.

Diŏgĕnes, is, Cynic philosopher.

Diŏmēdes, is, son of Tydeus, one of the heroes before Troy.

Dion, ōnis, brother-in-law of the elder Dionysius of Syracuse, friend of Plato.

Dion Cassius, historian, born A.D. 155.

Diōnē, ēs, mother of Venus, daughter of Oceanus.   [Syracuse.

Diŏnȳsius, ii, name of two tyrants of

Dĭs, Dītis＝Pluto.

Dŏmĭtiānus, i, Roman emperor, son of Vespasian; reigned A.D. 81-96.

Drūsus, i, Roman family name (in the gentes Livia & Claudia).

Dryădes, um, f. pl. wood-nymphs.

Duellius, Duīlius, ii, Roman consul, victorious over the Carthaginians at sea, 260 B.C.

Ĕchidna, ae, f. Lernæan hydra, killed by Hercules.

Ĕcho, ūs, a nymph, metamorphosed to an echo.   [father of Andromache.

Ēĕtion, ōnis, king of Thebæ in Cilicia,

Ēgĕria, ae, a nymph, the instructress of Numa Pompilius.

Ĕleātes, um, m. pl. Eleatic school (philosophers).   [Clytemnestra.

Ēlectra, ae, daughter of Agamemnon and

Ēlis(s)a, ae, another name of Dido.

Empĕdocles, is, natural philosopher of Agrigentum; flourished about 440 B.C.

Encĕlădus, i, hundred-handed giant, made war on the gods.   [loved by Diana.

Endymion, ōnis, a beautiful youth, be-

Ēnīpeus, i, river of Thessaly.

Ennius, ii, early Roman poet.

Ēnȳo, us, f. the goddess of war.

Ĕpămīnondas, ae, Theban general, defeated the Spartans.

Ēpēus, i, constructor of the Wooden Horse at Troy.   [about 340 B.C.

Ēphŏrus, i, Greek historian; flourished

Ĕpicharmus, i, a Greek comic poet.

Ĕpictētus, i, m. Stoic philosopher under the early empire.

Ĕpicūrus, i, Greek philosopher, originator of the Epicurean philosophy.

Ĕpigŏni, ōrum, m. pl. sons of the seven heroes before Thebes.   [of Prometheus.

Ĕpimētheus, ei, son of Iapetus, brother

Ērăto, f. the Muse of lyric amatory poetry.   [born 276 B.C.

Ĕrătosthĕnes, is, a savant of Alexandria,

Ĕrĕbus, i, god of darkness; *fig.* the Lower World.

Ĕrechtheus, ei, mythical king of Attica.

Ĕrichthŏnius, ii, king of Athens, son of Vulcan.   [porary with Sappho.

Ĕrinna, ae, Lesbian poetess, contem-

Ĕrīnys, ȳos, a Fury;—**Erinyes, um,** pl. the Furies.

Ĕteocles, is, son of Œdipus, brother of Polynices; the brothers fell in fight by each other's hand.

Euclīdes, is, mathematician and geometrician of Alexandria.

Euhēmĕrus, i, a sceptical philosopher, flourished about 320 B.C.

Euius, i, surname of Bacchus.

Eumĕnides, um＝the Furies.

Eupŏlis, idis, Athenian comic poet, contemporary with Aristophanes.

Eurīpĭdes, is, one of the three great tragic poets of Athens.

Eurōpa, ae, Eurōpē, ēs, daughter of Agenor, king of Phœnicia; carried off by Jupiter in the form of a bull.

Eurўdĭcē, ēs, wife of Orpheus.

Eurysthĕnes, is, king of Sparta; twin-brother of Procles.

Eurystheus, ei, son of Sthenelus, king of Mycenæ; imposed labours on Hercules.

Euterpē, ēs, the Muse of lyric poetry.

Eutrŏpĭus, ii, Roman historian under Constantine.

Ēvan, Ēvĭus, ii, surname of Bacchus.

Evander, dri, emigrated from Arcadia to Italy 60 years before the Trojan war.

Făbĭus, a, um, Roman gentile name; 306 Fabii were killed at the battle on the Cremera, 477 B.C.

Fabrĭcĭus, a, um, Roman gentile name.

Fauni, ōrum, n. pl. Fauns.

Faunus, i, grandson of Saturn.

Faustīna, ae, (1) wife of Antoninus Pius; (2) wife of M. Aurelius.

Fĕretrĭus, ii, surname of Jupiter, to whom the spolia opima were conse-crated.

Fimbria, ae, m. Roman family surname.

Flaccus, i, Roman surname;—Horatius Flaccus, v. Horatius;—Valerius Flac-cus, Roman poet under Vespasian, wrote the Argonautica.

Flāmĭnĭus, a, um, Roman gentile name.

Flāvĭus, name of the gens to which Vespasian belonged.

Flōra, ae, goddess of the flowers and spring.

Fortūna, ae, f. the Goddess Fortune.

Fronto, ōnis, the tutor of Marcus Aurelius.

Fūfĭus, a, um, Roman gentile name.

Fulvĭus, a, um, Roman gentile name.

Fūrĭus, a, um, Roman gentile name.

Găbīnĭus, a, um, Roman gentile name.

Gaius=Caius.

Gălătēa, ae, a sea-nymph, beloved by Acis.

Galba, ae, Roman emperor on the death of Nero, A.D. 68.

Gălēnus Claudĭus, famous medical writer, born A.D. 130.

Gallĭus, a, um, Roman gentile name.

Gallus, i, Roman surname.

Gănўmēdes, is, Jupiter's cupbearer.

Gellĭus, a, Roman gentile name.

Gĕlon, ōnis, king of Syracuse; defeated the Carthaginians at Himera in 480 B.C.

Gensĕric, king of the Vandals; captured Rome, A.D. 455.

Gēryon, ŏnis, Gerўŏnes, ae, m. a king of Spain having three heads; his oxen were carried off by Hercules.

Gĭgantes, um, the Giants.

Glaucus, i, son of Sisyphus; Lycian com-mander in the Trojan war.

Gordĭus, ii, king of Gordium; he owned a waggon, the pole of which was at-tached to the yoke by a knot of bark; Alexander the Great cut the Gordian knot.

Gorgĭas, ae, Greek sophist of Leontini in Sicily, contemporary of Socrates.

Gorgo, ŏnis, or ūs, f. Medusa, daughter of Phorcus, and her two sisters were called the Gorgons.

Gracchus, i, Roman family name; two famous brothers of this family, Tiberius and Gaius, tried to solve the agrarian difficulty; the former was tribune in 133 B.C., the latter in 123 and 122 B.C.

Grādīvus, i, surname of Mars.

Grĕgŏrĭus, ii, Gregory of Nazianzus in Cappadocia; Bishop of Constantinople, A.D. 380; the champion of orthodoxy against the Arians.

Gўges, is & ae, rich king of Lydia.

Hămadrўas, ădis, wood-nymph.

Hămilcar, ăris, father of Hannibal.

Hannĭbal, ălis, Punic surname; great Carthaginian general during the second Punic war, son of Hamilcar.

Hanno, ōnis, Punic surname; antagonist of Hannibal.

Harmŏdĭus, ii, and Aristogīton, the mur-derers of Hipparchus, tyrant of Athens.

Harmŏnĭa, ae, daughter of Mars and Venus.

Harpyĭæ, ārum, mythical rapacious mon-sters, half-bird, half-woman.

Hasdrūbal, ălis, (1) brother of Hannibal; (2) son-in-law of Hamilcar.

Hēbē, ēs, goddess of youth, cupbearer to the gods.

Hĕcătæus, a historian; flourished in Miletus about 500 B.C.

Hĕcătē, ēs, a goddess of the Lower World, worshipped as goddess of spells and enchantments.

Hector, ŏris, son of Priam and Hecuba.

Hĕcŭba, ae, wife of Priam.

Hĕlĕna, ae, Hĕlĕnē, ēs, (1) daughter of Jupiter and Leda, wife of Menelaus; (2) mother of Constantine the Great.

Hĕlĕnus, i, soothsayer, son of Priam.

Hellānĭcus, a historian, born in Mitylene about 496 B.C.

Hellē, ēs, f. daughter of Athamas, king of Bœotia, was drowned in the narrow sea (Hellespont) called after her.

Hēraclīdæ, ārum, m. pl. descendants of Hercules.

Hēraclītus, i, Greek philosopher; flourished about 510 B.C.

Hercūles, is & **i,** son of Jupiter and Alcmene, a demigod and divine hero.

Hermĭŏne, ēs, daughter of Menelaus and Helena, married to Orestes.

Hēro, ūs, priestess of Aphrodite in Sestos, beloved by Leander of Abydos.

Hērōdes, is, king of Judæa.

Hērŏdŏtus, i, Greek historian, born at Halicarnassus, 484 B.C.

Hersĭlia, ae, wife of Romulus.

Hēsiŏdus, i, ancient Greek poet.

Hespĕrĭdes, um, f. pl. daughters of Erebus and the Night; they lived in an island garden beyond Mt. Atlas and guarded the golden apples which Juno received on her wedding.

Hespĕrus, i, son of Atlas, or of Cephalus, and Aurora; planet Venus as evening-star.

Hēsўchius, ii, a grammarian of Alexandria; flourished about A.D. 380.

Hiĕro, ōnis, king of Syracuse.

Hipparchus, i, brother of Hippias, son of Pisistratus. [stratus; a sophist.

Hippias, ae, tyrant of Athens, son of Pisi-

Hippŏcrātes, is, Greek physician, born about A.D. 460.

Hippŏdămia, ae, (1) daughter of Œnomaus; won by Pelops in a chariot race; (2) daughter of Adrastus, married to Pirithous; at her wedding occurred the fight between the Centaurs and the Lapithæ.

Hippŏlўta, ae, Hippŏlўtē, ēs, an Amazon, taken captive and married by Theseus.

Hippŏlўtus, i, son of Theseus and Hippolyte, stepson of Phædra.

Hippōnax, actis, Greek poet of Ephesus; flourished about 530 B.C.

Hŏmērus, i, the earliest Greek (epic) poet.

Hŏnōrius, ii, Roman Emperor of the West, A.D. 395-423.

Hōræ, ārum, f. pl. the Hours, goddesses of the seasons.

Hŏrātius, a, um, Roman gentile name;—
Q. — Flaccus, Roman lyric poet.

Hortensius, a, um, Roman gentile name.

Hostīlius, a, um, Roman gentile name.

Hyăcinthus, i, beautiful youth beloved by Apollo, and accidentally killed by him.

Hyădes, um, f. pl. daughters of Atlas; a group of seven stars. [by Hercules.

Hўdra, ae, f. seven-headed serpent, killed

Hўgēa, Hўgīa, goddess of health.

Hўlas, ae, beautiful youth who accompanied Hercules on the Argonautic expedition.

Hўmen, ĕnis, Hўmĕnæus, i, Hymen, god of marriage.

Hўpătia, ae, female philosopher of Alexandria; torn to pieces by Christians, A.D. 415.

Hўpĕrĭdes, ae, Attic orator, friend of Demosthenes.

Hўpĕrĭon, ŏnis, son of a Titan and the Earth; the Sun.

Hўpĕrĭŏnis, ĭdis, f. Aurora, daughter of Hyperion.

Hypsipўle, of Lemnos; saved Thoas, her father, when the Lemnian women sought to slay all the men in the island.

Hystaspes, is, father of the Persian king Darius.

Iacchus, i, Bacchus.

Iamblĭchus, i, a Neoplatonist philosopher under Constantine the Great.

Iăpĕtus, i, a Titan, father of Prometheus.

Iāpyx, ўgis, son of Dædalus, founder of colony in southern Italy.

Iarba, Iarbas, ae, king of Mauretania, rival of Æneas.

Iāson, ōnis, son of Æson, king of Thessaly, Grecian hero.

Ibўcus, i, Greek lyric poet of Rhegium; flourished about 540 B.C.

Īcărus, i, son of Dædalus; tried to fly from Crete and fell into the sea.

Īdŏmĕneus, i, son of Deucalion; led the Cretans against Troy.

Īlia, ae, Rhea Silvia, mother of Romulus and Remus.

Īliăs, ădis, f. the Iliad.

Īlīthyia, ae, the goddess of childbirth.

Īlium, ii, n. Troy.

Īlus, i, founder of Ilium, son of Tros.

Īnăchus, i, first king of Argos.

Īno, ūs, daughter of Cadmus and Hermione, stepmother of Phrixus and Helle.

Īo, ūs, daughter of Inachus; beloved of Zeus, turned into a cow and pursued by Argus.

Iŏcastē, ēs, wife of Œdipus.

Iŏlāus, i, the constant companion of Hercules.

Ion, ōnis, son of Apollo by Creusa.

Iphĭgĕnia, ae, daughter of Agamemnon and Clytemnestra.

Īrēnæus, i, early Christian Father; flourished about A.D. 180.

Īris, Ĭdis, daughter of Thaumas and Electra, messenger of the gods.

Īsæus, Athenian orator; taught Demosthenes.

Īsis, Ĭdis & is, Egyptian goddess, wife of Osiris.

Īsocrătes, is, Athenian orator, 436-338 B.C.

Īsthmĭa, ōrum, n. pl. games celebrated on the Isthmus of Corinth.

Ĭtys, yos, son of Tereus and Procne; made into pie and served up to father.

Iūlus, i, son of Æneas, called also Ascanius.

Ixīon, ŏnis, son of Phlegyas, king of the Lapithæ in Thessaly; made love to Juno and was fastened on a wheel.

Jānus, i, old Italian deity, with two faces.

Jāson, v. Iason.

Jocasta, v. Iocaste.

Josephus, i, Jewish historian, born A.D. 37.

Jŭba, ae, king of Numidia in Pompey's time.

Jŭgurtha, ae, king of Numidia, nephew of Micipsa.

Jūliānus, i, surnamed the Apostate; Roman emperor, A.D. 361-363.

Jūlius, a, um, Roman gentile name.

Jūnius, a, um, Roman gentile name.

Jūno, ōnis, goddess and wife of Jupiter.

Jūpĭter, Jŏvis, Jupiter, the chief Roman god.

Justīniānus, i, emperor of the East, 527-565; drew up a complete body of law.

Justīnus, i, early Christian martyr, born A.D. 103.

Jūturna, ae, nymph of a fountain in Latium, sister of Turnus.

Jŭvĕnālis, is, Roman satiric poet.

K.=Kæso, v. Cæso.

L.=Lucius.   [Fabii, Antistii, etc.).

Lăbeo, ōnis, Roman surname (of the

Lăbĕrius, a, Roman family name.

Lăbiēnus, i, Roman proper name;— **Titus** —, general of Cæsar, deserted to Pompey.

Lăchĕsis, is, f. one of the three Fates.

Lælius, a, Roman family name;—**C. —,** friend of Scipio Africanus.

Lāertes, is, father of Ulysses.

Lāis, ĭdis, celebrated courtesan in Corinth.

Lāius, i, father of Œdipus.

Lāmus, i, mythical king of the Læstrygones, founder of Formiæ.

Lāŏcoon, ontis, a Trojan priest of Apollo.

Lāŏdămĭa, wife of Protesilaus.

Lāŏmĕdon, ontis, father of Priam, king of Troy, killed by Hercules.

Lăpĭthæ, ārum, m. pl. Thessalian tribe, fought with the Centaurs.

Lăsus, i, Greek lyric poet, teacher of Pindar.

Lătĕranus, a, um, Roman family name.

Lătīnus, i, king of the Laurentians.

Lātōna, ae, mother of Apollo and Diana,

Lăverna, ae, goddess of rogues and thieves.   [of Æneas.

Lāvīnia, ae, daughter of Latinus, wife

Lēander, dri, the lover of Hero.

Lēda, ae, Lēde, ēs, f. wife of Tyndareus, mother of Clytemnestra, Helen, Castor and Pollux.

Lēnæus, a, um, a. Bacchic.

Lentŭlus, i, Roman surname.

Leōnĭdas, ae, heroic king of Sparta, died at Thermopylæ.

Lĕpĭdus, i, Roman surname.

Leucōthea, ae, Ino, a sea-goddess.

Līber, ĕri, Bacchus.

Lībĕra, ae, Proserpine.

Lībĕrālĭa, ĭum, n. pl. festival in honour of Liber.

Lībēthrĭdes, um, f. pl. the Muses, from Libethrum in Macedonia, where they were worshipped.

Lĭbĭtīna, ae, goddess of funerals.

Lĭcinius, a, um, Roman gentile name.

Linus, i, son of Apollo, instructor of Orpheus.

Līvia, mother of the Emperor Tiberius.

Līvius, a, um, Roman gentile name;—**Titus** —, Roman historian, born at Padua, 59 B.C.

Lollius, a, um, Roman gentile name.

Lūcānus, M. Annæus, Roman poet, born A.D. 39; wrote the *Pharsalia*.

Lūciānus, Greek writer, born about A.D. 120; wrote humorous dialogues.

Lūcĭfĕr, i, m. planet Venus as morning-star.

Lūcīlius, ii, first Roman satirist, born 148 B.C.

Lūcīna, ae, goddess of childbirth.

Lūcius, i, Roman first name.

Lūcrētius, a, T. — Carus, Roman poet, born 95 B.C.; wrote *De Rerum Natura*.

Lūcullus, i, L. —, conqueror of Mithridates.

Lŭpercālĭa, ĭum & ōrum, n. pl. festival of the god Lŭpercus on the 15th of February.

Lŭpercus, i, m. Pan.

Lūna, ae, f. the goddess of the Moon.

Lyæus, i, surname of Bacchus.

Lўcāon, ŏnis, king of Arcadia, transformed into a wolf.

Lўcŏmēdes, is, king of Scyros; at his court Achilles was left disguised as a maiden that he might not be taken to the Trojan war.

Lўcophron, ŏnis, Greek poet; wrote a poem called *Cassandra* full of obscure myths.

Lўcurgus, i, lawgiver of the Spartans.

Lўcurgus, i, king of the Edonian Thracians; persecutor of Bacchus. [naut.

Lynceus, ei, a very sharp-sighted Argo-

Lўsander, dri, Spartan general.

Lўsias, ae, Athenian orator, born 458 B.C.

Lўsĭmăchus, i, one of the generals of Alexander the Great and afterwards king of Thrace.

Lўsippus, i, famous Greek sculptor.

M. = Marcus; M'. = Manius; Mam. = Mamercus.

Măcer, cri, Roman surname.

Măchāon, ŏnis, son of Æsculapius, surgeon of thē Greeks before Troy.

Macrŏbius, ii, a grammarian who lived under Honorius and Theodosius.

Mæcēnas, ātis, friend of Augustus, and patron of Horace and Virgil.

Mælius, a, um, Roman gentile name;—Sp. Mælius, killed in 440 B.C. on a charge of aspiring to be king of Rome.

Mænădes, um, f. pl. Bacchantes.

Mænius, a, um, Roman gentile name.

Mæŏnĭdes, ae, Homer. [miserable poet.

Mævius, ii, Roman proper name; a

Măgo, ōnis, a brother of Hannibal.

Maia, ae, mother of Mercury.

Mămĭlius, a, um, Roman family name.

Mănĕtho, onis, an Egyptian priest; wrote in Greek a history of Egypt; lived under the first Ptolemy.

Mănīlius, a, um, Roman gentile name.

Manlius, a, um, Roman gentile name;—M. Manlius, drove the Gauls from the Capitol in 390 B.C.

Marcellus, a, um, Roman family name;—M. Claudius —, captured Syracuse, 212 B.C.

Manto, ūs, (1) daughter of Tiresias, prophetess of Thebes; (2) daughter of Hercules, founded Mantua.

Marcius, a, um, Roman gentile name.

Marcus, i, Roman first name.

Mardŏnius, ii, Persian general, defeated at Platæa, 479 B.C.

Mărius, a, um, Roman gentile name;—C. —, conquered Jugurtha; crushed the Cimbri and Teutons; consul seven times.

Măro, ōnis, surname of Virgil.

Mărŏbŏduus, i, king of the Suevi, enemy of Arminius.

Mars, tis, the god of war.

Marsўa, Marsyas, ae, a satyr and fluteplayer; challenged Apollo and was flayed alive.

Martiālis, is, M. Valerius, Roman poet, born A.D. 43; wrote epigrams.

Măsĭnissa, ae, king of Numidia, grandfather of Jugurtha.

Mātūta, ae, f. goddess of the early hours or the dawn.

Mausōlus, i, king of Caria, died 353 B.C.; his tomb was a costly monument called the Mausōlēum.

Māvors, ortis, v. Mars.

Maxĭmus, Q. Fabius, surnamed Cunctātor; commanded against Hannibal, 217-214 B.C.

Mēdēa, ae, daughter of Æetes, king of Colchis; deserted by Jason, killed her own children.

Mědūsa, ae, daughter of Phorcus; one of the Gorgons; turned those who looked on her to stone.

Měgæra, ae, f. a Fury.

Měla, ae, m. Pompōnius —, a Roman geographer, under Claudius.

Mělěăger, gri, son of Œneus, king of Calydon; took part in the hunt of the Calydonian boar.

Melpŏměnē, ēs, the Muse of tragic poetry.

Memmius, a, um, Roman gentile name.

Memnon, ŏnis, son of Tithonus and Aurora, king of the Ethiopians.

Měnander, Měnandros, dri, a Greek comic poet.

Měnělāus, i, brother of Agamemnon.

Měnēnius, a, um, Roman family name; Agrippa — reconciled the Patricians and Plebeians, 493 B.C.

Mentor, ōris, faithful friend of Ulysses.

Měriŏnes, ae, a Cretan; charioteer of Idomeneus.

Mercŭrius, ii, son of Jupiter and Maia, the messenger of the gods; the god of eloquence and of merchants and thieves.

Měrŏpe, es, daughter of Atlas, wife of Sisyphus.

Messāla, ae, Roman surname.

Messālīna, ae, wife of Emperor Claudius.

Mětellus, a, um, Roman family name.

Měton, ōnis, an Athenian astronomer; flourished about 440 B.C.

Mezentius, king of Etruscans; friend of Turnus; killed by Æneas.

Mĭcipsa, ae, king of Numidia, son of Masinissa.

Mīdas, ae, king of Phrygia; all he touched was turned into gold.

Mīlo, Mīlon, ōnis, m. athlete of Crotona.

Miltiădes, is, Athenian general; defeated the Persians at Marathon, 490 B.C.

Mĭmallōnes, um, f. pl. Bacchantes.

Mĭmnermus, i, Greek poet from Asia Minor, inventor of the erotic elegy, 594 B.C.

Minerva, ae, daughter of Zeus, goddess of wisdom, of the arts and sciences.

Mīnos, ōis, son of Zeus and Europa, king of Crete.

Mīnōtaurus, i, monster with the head of a bull in the Labyrinth of Crete.

Mĭnŭcius, a, um, Roman gentile name.

Mĭnyæ, ārum, m. pl. ancient race whose capital was the Bœotian Orchomenos.

Mithras, ae, Persian sun-god.

Mithrĭdātes, king of Pontus.

Mnēmŏsўnē, ēs, f. mother of the Muses.

Mŏnēta, ae, surname of Juno; money was coined in her temple at Rome.

Mopsus, i, name of two soothsayers; a shepherd.

Morpheus, ei & eos, god of dreams.

Moschus, i, a pastoral poet; flourished about 250 B.C.

Mūcius, a, um, Roman gentile name.

Mummius, a, um, Roman gentile name;— **L. —,** notorious for the sack of Corinth, 146 B.C.

Murcia, ae, surname of Venus.

Mūsa, ae, f. a. Muse.

Mūsæus, i, Greek poet in Orpheus' time.

Mўcēnis, ĭdis, f. Iphigenia.

Myrmĭdōnes, um, m. pl. the followers of Achilles; they lived in Phthiotis in Thessaly.

N.=Numerius.

Nævius, a, um, Roman family name;—**Cn. —,** Roman poet; produced a play, 235 B.C.; attacked Scipio and the Metelli.

Narcissus, i, son of Cephissus, turned into a flower named after him.

Narses, is, general of Justinian; crushed the Goths in Italy, A.D. 552.

Nāso, ōnis, Roman surname;—**P. Ovidius —, v. Ovidius.** [friended Ulysses.

Nausicaa, ae, daughter of Alcinous; be-

Nāvius, Attus, an augur under Tarquinius Priscus; cut a whetstone with a razor. [Great.

Nearchus, i, an admiral of Alexander the

Nēleus, ei & eos, king of Pylos, father of Nestor. [revenge.

Nĕmĕsis, is & ios, goddess of justice and

Neoptŏlĕmus, i, Pyrrhus, son of Achilles.

Nĕphĕlē, ēs, mother of Phrixus and Helle.

Nĕpos, ōtis, Roman surname;—**Cornelius —,** Roman historian and writer of biographies; died under Augustus.

Neptūnus, i, the god of the sea.

Nēreus, ei & eos, a sea-god, son of Oceanus and Thetys.

Nēro, ōnis, Roman surname;—**Nero Claudius Cæsar,** emperor, A.D. 54-68.

Nerva, ae, m. Roman family name;— **M. Cocceius —,** Roman emperor, A.D. 96-98.

Nessus, i, a Centaur, killed by Hercules.

Nestor, ōris, king of Pylos, one of the oldest of the heroes before Troy.

Nestŏrius, ii, a heretical theologian denounced at the Council of Ephesus, A.D. 431. [man.

Nĭcias, ae, Athenian general and states-

Nīnus, i, first king of Assyria, son of Belus.

Nĭŏba, ae, Nĭŏbē, ēs, f. wife of Amphion, king of Thebes, and daughter of Tantalus; her children were slain by Apollo and Diana, and Niobe was changed into a rock.

Nīsus, i, king of Megara, father of Scylla.

Nŭma, ae, Roman proper name; **— Pompilius,** the second king of Rome.

Nŭmĭtor, ōris, king of Alba, father of Ilia, grandfather of Romulus and Remus.

Nymphæ, arum, f. pl. spirits inhabiting trees, rivers, mountains, woods, etc.

Nўseus, ei & eos, Bacchus.

O.M.=Optimus Maximus, title of Jupiter.

Ōceănus, i, father of the rivers and nymphs, son of Heaven and Earth.

Octāviānus, i, surname of the Emperor Augustus.

Octāvius, a, um, Roman gentile name.

Ŏdyssēa, ae, f. the Odyssey (of Homer).

Œagrus, i, king of Thrace, father of Orpheus.

Œbălus, i, king of Sparta, father of Tyndareus, grandfather of Helen.

Œdĭpūs, i & ŏdis, son of Laius, king of Thebes; murdered his father and married his mother.

Œneus, ei or eos, king of Calydon, father of Meleager and Tydeus.

Ōgўges, is, mythical founder of Thebes.

Oïleus, ei & eos, king of Locris, father of Ajax the Less. [at Olympia.

Ŏlympia, ōrum, n. pl. the Olympic games

Ŏlympias, ădis, mother of Alexander the Great. [Hercules.

Omphălē, ēs, queen of Lydia, beloved of

Ŏpīmius, a, um, Roman gentile name.

Oppius, a, um, Roman family name.

Ops, Ŏpis, goddess of plenty, wife of Saturn.

Ŏrestes, ae & is, son of Agamemnon; killed his mother Clytemnestra.

Ŏrigĕnes, is, Origen, an early Christian author; born at Alexandria, A.D. 186.

Ŏrīon, ŏnis & ōnis, son of Hyrieus, a hunter; the constellation Orion.

Ŏrīthyīa, ae, daughter of Erechtheus; carried away to Thrace by Boreas.

Ŏrōdes, i & is, Parthian king.

Orpheus, ei, son of Œagrus and Calliope, husband of Eurydice.   [of Isis.

Ŏsīris, is & idis, Egyptian god, husband

Ōtho, ōnis, Roman surname;—M. Salvius —, Roman emperor, A.D. 69.

Ŏvīdīus, a, um, Roman gentile name;—P. — Naso, Ovid, Roman poet under Augustus.

P.=Publius.

Păcŭvīus, ii, Roman tragic poet; born about 220 B.C.

Pæan, ānis, Apollo, the Healer.

Pălămēdes, is, king of Eubœa, son of Nauplius; joined the expedition to Troy; falsely accused of treason.

Păles, is, tutelar goddess of shepherds and cattle.

Pălinūrus, i, the pilot of Æneas.

Pallădium, statue of Pallas in the citadel of Troy; captured by Ulysses and Diomed.

Pallas, ădis & ădos, Minerva.

Pallās, antis, son of Evander; slain by Turnus.

Păn, Pānos, son of Mercury, the god of woods and shepherds.

Pănætius, ii, Stoic philosopher; friend of the younger Scipio.

Pandărus, i, a famous archer; fought for the Trojans.

Pandīon, ŏnis, king of Athens, father of Procne and Philomela.

Pandōra, ae, first woman; created by Vulcan, and endowed with gifts by all the gods; wife of Epimetheus.

Păpīrius, a, um, Roman family name.

Păpius, a, um, Roman family name.

Parca, ae, one of the Fates;—Parcæ, pl. the Fates, three sisters.

Păris, idis, a son of Priam and Hecuba; carried off Helen, wife of Menelaus.

Parmĕnides, is, Greek philosopher of Elea; born about 513 B.C.

Parmĕnio, onis, general of Alexander the Great.

Parrhăsius, ii, famous Greek painter.

Parthĕnŏpæus, i, one of the seven against Thebes.

Pāsĭphaē, ēs, daughter of Helios, wife of Minos, and sister of Circe.

Pătercŭlus, C. Velleius, Roman historian, lived under Tiberius.

Patroclus, i, friend of Achilles, slain by Hector.

Paulus, Paullus, i, Roman surname;— L. Æmīlius —, defeated King Perses at Pydna, 168 B.C.

Pausānias, ae, (1) Spartan general; defeated the Persians at Platæa, 479 B.C.; (2) a geographer, wrote an *Itinerary of Greece*, lived under M. Aurelius.

Pausias, ae, painter of Sicyon.

Pēgăsus, i, a winged horse, sprung from the blood of the slain Medusa; by the aid of Pegasus Bellerophon slew the Chimæra.

Pēleus, ei & eos, king of a part of Thessaly, husband of Thetis, father of Achilles.

Pēlias, ae, king of Iolcos, son of Neptune; was boiled by his daughters in an unfortunate attempt to restore him to youth.

Pēliădes, um, daughters of Pelias.

Pēlīdes, is, son of Peleus, i.e. Achilles.

Pēlŏpĭdas, ae, Theban general; defeated Alexander of Pheræ at Cynoscephalæ in 364 B.C.,

Pĕlops, ŏpis, king of Phrygia, son of Tantalus, father of Atreus and Thyestes.

Pēnĕlŏpē, ēs, wife of Ulysses.

Pēnĕus, i, river-god.

Penthĕsilĕa, ae, queen of the Amazons, fighting before Troy against the Greeks.

Pentheus, ei & eos, king of Thebes, grandson of Cadmus; opposed the worship of Bacchus and was torn in pieces by his mother.

Pĕrenna, Anna —, a Roman goddess, a sister of Dido.

Pĕriander, dri, tyrant of Corinth, 625-585 B.C.

Pĕricles, i & is, Athenian orator and statesman, died 429 B.C.

Perses, is, king of Macedon; defeated by Æmilius Paulus, 168 B.C.

Perseus, ei & eos, son of Jupiter and Danae, killer of the Medusa, husband of Andromeda.

Persius, ii, Roman surname; Roman satiric poet in Nero's time.

Petronius Arbiter, friend of Nero; wrote a book called *Satyricon*.

Phædra, ae, daughter of Minos, and second wife of Theseus; fell in love with Hippolytus. [Latin fables.

Phædrus, i, a freedman and author of

Phaëthon, ontis, son of Helios and Clymene; tried to drive the chariot of the sun. [Tarentum.

Phālanthus, i, a Spartan, founder of

Phălaris, ĭdis, tyrant of Agrigentum.

Phaon, ōnis, beautiful Lesbian youth beloved by Sappho.

Pharnăces, is, grandfather of Mithridates; son of Mithridates.

Phĕrecrătes, is, poet of the Old Comedy, contemporary with Aristophanes.

Phīdias, ae, a great Athenian sculptor; designed the Parthenon; died 432 B.C.

Philæni, ōrum, two brothers of Carthage, who out of patriotism suffered themselves to be buried alive.

Philădelphus, i, surname of Ptolemy, king of Egypt.

Philēmon, ōnis, Greek comic poet contemporary with Menander.

Philippus, i, king of Macedonia, son of Amyntas, father of Alexander the Great.

Philo, ōnis, (1) Academic philosopher; taught Cicero; (2) Jewish philosopher under the early empire; tried to reconcile Jewish and Greek systems of thought.

Philoctētes, ae, son of Pœas, a famous archer; sailed against Troy, but being wounded was marooned on Lemnos.

Philŏmēla, ae, daughter of Pandion, sister of Procne; turned into a nightingale.

Philŏpœmen, ĕnis, general of the Achæan league; born about 252 B.C.

Phīneus, ei & eos, king of Salmydessus in Thrace; tormented by the Harpies.

Phlĕgyas, ae, son of Mars, father of Ixion.

Phōcion, ōnis, Athenian general in the time of Demosthenes.

Phœbē, ēs, f. moon-goddess, sister of Phœbus, i, Apollo. [Phœbus.

Phœnix, ĭcis, son of Amyntor; tutor of Achilles.

Phorcus, i, Phorcys, ўos, son of Neptune, father of Medusa and the Gorgons, afterwards a sea-god.

Phorcys, ўdos, a female descendant of Phorcus. [Parthia.

Phraātes, is, name of several kings of

Phrixus, i, son of Athamas, brother of Helle; fell into the Hellespont and was drowned.

Phrỹnē, ēs, a celebrated courtesan at Athens.

Phrynĭchus, i, Athenian tragedian, gained first prize, 511 B.C.

Pīcumnus, i, brother of Pilumnus.

Pīcus, i, son of Saturn, grandfather of Latinus; changed by Circe into a woodpecker.

Piērĭdes, um, the Muses.

Pīlumnus, i, an old god of marriage.

Pimplēa, ae, Pimplēis, ĭdos, a Muse.

Pindărus, i, Theban lyric poet; began to write about 500 B.C.

Pīrĭthous, i, king of the Lapithæ, son of Ixion; helped Theseus to carry off Persephone.

Pīsander, dri, an Athenian; helped to establish the Four Hundred in 412 B.C.

Pīsistrătĭdæ, ārum, sons of Pisistratus: Hippias and Hipparchus.

Pīsistrătus, i, tyrant of Athens; seized the tyranny, 560 B.C.

Pīso, ōnis, Roman surname. [Greece.

Pittăcus, i, one of the seven wise men of

Plăto, Plătōn, ōnis, Athenian philosopher, disciple of Socrates.

Plautius, a, um, Roman family name.

Plautus, i, Roman comic poet; born about 254 B.C.

Plēĭădes, um, the seven daughters of Atlas and Pleione.

Plēĭŏnē, ēs, daughter of Oceanus, wife of Atlas, and mother of the Pleiades.

Plīnĭus, a, um, Roman gentile name;—**C. — Secundus,** author of a natural history; born A.D. 23;—**C. — Cæcilius Secundus,** the Younger, author of Letters; born A.D. 61.

Plōtīnus, i, founder of the Neoplatonic school of Philosophy; born A.D. 203.

Plŭtarchus, i, of Bœotia; wrote *Parallel Lives* of Greeks and Romans; flourished under Domitian. [World.

Plūto, Plūton, ōnis, the god of the Lower

Plūtus, i, god of wealth.

Pollio, ōnis, Roman surname.

Pollux, ūcis, son of Tyndareus and Leda, brother of Castor. [204 B.C.

Pŏlўbius, ii, Greek historian; born about

Pŏlўcarpus, i, of Smyrna; said to have been disciple of St. John; one of the earliest martyrs.

Pŏlyclētus, i, Greek sculptor in the time of Pericles. [B.C.

Pŏlycrătes, is, tyrant of Samos; died 522

Pŏlўdōrus, i, son of Priam; entrusted to Thracian king during Trojan war; killed by his host.

Pŏlygnōtus, i, Greek painter.

Pŏlўhymnia, ae, Muse of lyric poetry.

Pŏlўmnestor, ōris, king of the Thracian Chersonese; killed Polydorus.

Pŏlўphēmus, i, a Cyclops; son of Neptune.

Pŏlyxĕna, ae, daughter of Priam; sacrificed to Achilles after the Trojan war.

Pōmōna, ae, the goddess of fruits.

Pompēius, a, um, Roman gentile name;—
Cn. — Magnus, one of the triumvirs; defeated at Pharsalia by Cæsar, 48 B.C.

Pompīlius, a, um, Roman gentile name;
v. Numa.

Pompōnius, a, um, Roman gentile name.

Popīlius, a, um, Roman gentile name.

Poplĭcŏla, ae, Roman surname.

Poppæus, a, um, Roman gentile name.

Porcius, a, um, Roman gentile name.

Porsĕna, Porsenna, ae, king of Clusium in Etruria; tried to restore Tarquinius Superbus to the throne of Rome.

Portumnus, Portūnus, i, tutelar god of harbours.

Pŏsīdōnius, i, Stoic philosopher; teacher of Cicero.

Postŭmius, a, Roman gentile name.

Praxĭtĕles, is, a great Athenian sculptor; flourished about 360 B.C.

Priămīdes, ae, a son of Priam.　　[don.

Priămus, i, king of Troy, son of Laome-

Priāpus, i, god of fruitulness.

Priscĭānus, i, grammarian of Cæsarea; flourished about A.D. 450.

Prŏcas, ae, king of Alba, father of Numitor and Amulius.　　[Tereus.

Procnē, ēs, daughter of Pandion, wife of

Procris, is & ĭdis, daughter of Erechtheus, wife of Cephalus.

Procrustes, is, highwayman in Attica, slain by Theseus; had a bed which all his victims were made to fit.

Prŏcŭlus, i, Roman surname.

Prŏdĭcus, i, sophist; contemporary with the Peloponnesian war; author of the fable The Choice of Hercules.

Prognē, v. Procne.

Prŏmētheus, ei & eos, son of Iapetus and Clymene; stole fire from heaven and gave it to mortals.

Prŏmēthiădes, ae, Deucalion.

Prŏpertius, ii, Roman elegiac poet; born about 51 B.C.　　[of Pluto.

Prŏserpĭna, ae, daughter of Ceres, wife

Prŏtăgŏras, ae, sophist of Abdera; born about 480 B.C.

Prŏtēsĭlāus, i, husband of Laodamia; the first of the Greek expedition to land at Troy and the first killed.

Prōteus, ei & eos, a sea-god and prophet.

Prōtŏgĕnes, is, Greek painter, 300 B.C.

Prūdentius, Christian poet; born A.D. 348.

Prūsias, ae, king of Bithynia.

Ptŏlĕmæus, i, name of the Egyptian dynasty.

Publĭcius, a, um, Roman gentile name.

Publĭcŏla, v. Poplicola.

Publius, ii, Roman first name.

Pūpius, a, um, Roman gentile name.

Pygmălion, ōnis, king of Cyprus; fell in love with a statue he had made himself.

Pȳlădes, is & ae, son of Strŏphius, bosom-friend of Orestes.

Pȳrămus, i, the lover of Thisbe.

Pyrrha, ae, wife of Deucalion, daughter of Epimetheus.

Pyrrho, ōnis, Greek philosopher, founder of the sceptic school.

Pyrrhus, i, (1) son of Achilles and Deidamia; (2) king of Epirus, who waged war against the Romans.

Pȳthăgŏras, ae, Greek philosopher of Samos; flourished about 520 B.C.

Pytheas, ae, a geographer; born at Marseilles; contemporary with Alexander the Great.　　[Apollo near Delphi.

Pȳthon, ōnis, m. a serpent slain by

Q.=Quintus.

Quintĭliānus, i, Roman surname;—M. Fabius —, an orator and critic; born A.D. 40.

Quintĭlius, a, um, Roman gentile name.

Quintius, a, um, Roman gentile name.

Quirīnus, i, name of Romulus after his deification.

R.=Rufus.

Răbīrius, a, um, Roman gentile name.

Rēgŭlus, i, Roman surname;—M. Atilius —, Roman consul during the first Punic war.

Rĕmŭlus, i, a king of Alba.

Rĕmus, i, brother of Romulus.

Rhădămanthus, i, son of Jupiter, brother of Minos, judge in the Lower World.

Rhĕa, ae, Cybele.

Rhĕa Sylvia, daughter of Numitor, mother of Romulus and Remus.

Rhēsus, i, a Thracian king, friend of the Trojans, killed by Diomedes and Ulysses.　　[slave of Æsop.

Rhŏdōpis, ĭdis, famous courtesan; fellow-

Rōmŭlĭdæ, ārum, m. pl. the Romans.

Rōmŭlus, i, founder and first king of Rome.

Roscius, a, Roman gentile name;—Q. —, famous actor; friend of Cicero.

Roxānē, ēs, wife of Alexander the Great.

Rūfus, i, Roman surname.

Rŭpĭlius, a, um, Roman gentile name.

Rŭtĭlius, a, um, Roman gentile name.

S. or Sex.=Sextus.

Săbazius, ii, surname of Bacchus.

Săbīna, Poppæa, wife of Nero.

Săbīnus, i, Roman poet; friend of Ovid.

Sallustius, a, um, Roman gentile name;—C. — Crispus, Roman historian; born

Sancus, i, Sabine god. [86 B.C.

Sapphō, ūs, f. lyric poetess of Mytilene; contemporary of Alcæus.

Sardănăpălus, i, the last king of Assyria.

Sarpēdon, ŏnis, son of Jupiter, king of Lycia; killed before Troy.

Sassănīdæ, Persian dynasty; ruled A.D. 226-651.

Săturnīnus, i, Roman surname;—L. Appuleius —, demagogue; tribune, 100 B.C.

Săturnia, ae, Juno.

Săturnus, i, father of Jupiter, originally a mythical king of Latium.

Sătўri, ōrum, Satyrs; companions of Bacchus.

Scævŏla, ae, surname of C. Mucius, a Roman who burned off his own right hand to convince Porsenna of his courage.

Schœneus, ei, king of Bœotia, father of Atalanta, according to some accounts.

Scīpio, ōnis, Roman surname in the gens Cornelia; Scipio Africanus Major defeated Hannibal at Zama, 202 B.C.; Scipio Africanus Minor took Carthage, 146 B.C.

Scōpas, ae, Greek sculptor of Paros; flourished about 370 B.C.

Scrībōnius, a, um, Roman gentile name.

Scylla, ae, f. a sea-monster; lived on the Italian side of the Straits of Messina, opposite Charybdis.

Sējānus, Ælius, corrupt favourite of the Emperor Tiberius.

Sēleucus, i, a general of Alexander the Great, later king of Syria.

Sĕmĕlē, ēs, daughter of Cadmus, mother of Bacchus, by Jupiter.

Sĕmīrămis, is & ĭdis, queen of Assyria, wife of Ninus.

Sēmo, ōnis, another name of Sancus.

Semprōnius, a, um, Roman gentile name.

Sĕnĕca, ae, Roman surname;—M. Annæus —, rhetorician; born about 61 B.C.; L. Annæus —, philosopher and poet, tutor to Nero.

Septimius, a, um, Roman gentile name.

Sĕrāpis, is & ĭdis, m. an Egyptian god.

Sergius, a, um, Roman gentile name.

Serrānus, i, surname in the gens Atilia.

Sertōrius, ii, Roman general and adherent of Marius.

Servīlius, a, um, Roman gentile name.

Servius, a, Roman proper name (in the gens Sulpicia); Roman first name.

Sĕsostris, is & ĭdis, an Egyptian king.

Sestius or Sextius, Roman gentile name.

Sĕvērus, L. Septimius, Roman emperor A.D. 193-211.

Sextus, i, Roman first name.

Sĭbylla, ae, a prophetess of Cumæ consulted by Æneas.

Sĭchæus, i, husband of Dido.

Sĭdōnius Ăpollīnāris, Christian poet; born A.D. 431. [Junia).

Sĭlānus, i, Roman surname (in the gens Silenus, i, tutor of Bacchus.

Sĭlius, a, um, Roman gentile name;—C. Silius Itălicus, Roman poet; born about A.D. 25; wrote Punica, History of the Punic War.

Silvānus, i, m. god of the woods.

Silvius, ii, name usual among the kings of Alba Longa.

Sĭmōnides, is, lyric poet of Ceos; born 556 B.C.

Sinis, is, of Corinth; a robber.

Sĭnon, ōnis, friend of Ulysses; persuaded the Trojans by treachery to introduce the Wooden Horse within their walls.

Sīrēnes, um, sea-nymphs enchanting by their songs.

Sĭsўphus, i, son of Æolus, king of Corinth; punished in Hell by having to roll a stone up a hill.

Smintheus, ei, Apollo.

Sōcrătes, is, Athenian philosopher; born 469 B.C.

Sōlon, ōnis, Athenian lawgiver, one of the seven wise men of Greece.

Sŏphocles, is, the second of the three great Athenian tragic poets; born 495 B.C.

Sōphron, ōnis, Greek poet, contemporary with Euripides; wrote mimes.

Sōsius, a, um, Roman gentile name.

Sp.=Spurius.

Spartăcus, i, a Thracian gladiator, leader of the gladiators in their war against Rome; killed 71 B.C.

Spūrius, ii, Roman first name.

Stăgīrītes, ae, Aristotle (born at Stagira).

Stătīra, ae, wife of Darius, the opponent of Alexander the Great.

Stătius, ii, Roman surname;—P. Papinius —, a Roman poet under Domitian; wrote Thebaid.

Stentor, ŏris, Greek herald, famed for his loud voice. [B.C.

Stēsichŏrus, i, Greek lyric poet, 600

Sthĕnĕlus, i, king of Mycenæ, father of Eurystheus.

Stĭlicho, ōnis, general of Honorius.

Strābo, ōnis, Roman surname; a geographer; born 54 B.C.

Strătŏnīce, es, wife of Seleucus; beloved of her stepson Antiochus.

Strŏphius, ii, king of Phocis, father of Pylades.

Suētōnius, a, um, Roman gentile name;—C. — Tranquillus, historian and biographer of the early Roman emperors.

Suidas, ae, Greek lexicographer; date uncertain.

Sulla, ae, Roman surname (in the gens Cornelia);—L. Cornelius —, famous Roman dictator; born 138 B.C.

Sulpicius, a, um, Roman gentile name.

Summānus, i, an Etruscan, later also a Roman deity: the god of nocturnal lightnings.

Sўchæus, i, v. Sichæus.   [reed.

Sўrinx, ingis, f. a nymph changed into a

T.=Titus.

Tăcĭtus, i, C. Cornelius —, a great Roman historian; born A.D. 61.

Talthўbius, ii, herald of Agamemnon.

Tănăquĭl, ĭlis, wife of the elder Tarquin.

Tantălĭdes, ae, male descendant of Tantalus.

Tantălus, i, son of Jupiter, father of Pelops and Niobe; divulged the secrets of the gods; was punished in Hell by a raging thirst which he could not quench.

Tarpēius, a, Roman proper name;—Tarpeia, Roman maiden, who treacherously opened the citadel to the Sabines.

Tarquĭnius, ii, Priscus, the fifth king of Rome; Superbus, the last king of Rome.

Tātius, ii, king of the Sabines, contemporary with Romulus.

Tĕlămon, ōnis, an Argonaut, king of Salamis, son of Æacus, father of Ajax and Teucer.

Tĕlĕgŏnus, i, son of Ulysses and Circe; killed her father.   [elope.

Tĕlĕmăchus, i, son of Ulysses and Penelope.

Tĕrentia, ae, wife of Cicero.

Tĕrentius, a, um, Roman gentile name;—M. — Afer, Terence, Roman comic poet; born 195 B.C.

Tēreus, ei & eos, king of Thrace, husband of Procne, and father of Itys; cut out the tongue of his wife's sister Philomela; Procne, in revenge, killed Itys and served him up to her husband in a dish.

Termĭnus, i, m. god of boundaries.

Terpander, dri, Greek musician; flourished about 675 B.C.

Terpsĭchŏrē, ēs, the Muse of dancing.

Tertulliānus, Q. Septimius Florens, the earliest of the Latin fathers; flourished about A.D. 200.

Tēthys, yos, a sea-goddess, wife of Oceanus.

Teucer, cri, king of Salamis, son of Telamon, brother of Ajax.

Thāis, ĭdis, a celebrated courtesan, mistress of Alexander the Great.

Thăles, is & ētis, Greek philosopher and one of the Seven Sages.

Thălīa, ae, f. the Muse of Comedy.

Thămўras, ae, Thracian poet blinded by the Muses.

Thaumantis, ĭdis, f. Iris.

Thaumas, antis, father of Iris.

Thĕmis, ĭdis, goddess of justice.

Thĕmistocles, is, Athenian general and statesman; born about 514 B.C.

Theocrĭtus, i, pastoral poet of Syracuse; flourished about 280 B.C.

Theŏdōrĭcus, i, king of the Visigoths, A.D. 418-451.

Theŏdōsius, ii, Roman emperor of the East, A.D. 378-395.

Theognis, ĭdis, elegiac poet; flourished about 550 B.C.

Theophrastus, i, Greek philosopher; pupil of Aristotle.   [about 378 B.C.

Theŏpompus, i, Greek historian; born

Thērămĕnes, is, member of the oligarchical government at Athens, 411 B.C.

Thēron, ōnis, tyrant of Agrigentum, 488-472 B.C.

Thersītes, ae, an ugly, hump-backed and scurrilous Greek before Troy.

Thēseus, ei & eos, king of Athens, son of Ægeus.

Thēsĭdes, ae, Hippolytus.   [tragedy.

Thespis, is, actor and founder of Greek

Thĕtis, ĭdis & ĭdos, a sea-nymph, daughter of Nereus, wife of Peleus, and mother of Achilles.   [by Pyramus.

Thisbē, ēs, maiden of Babylon, beloved

Thoas, antis (1) king of Tauris; (2) king of Lemnos, father of Hypsipyle.

Thrăsўbūlus, i, Athenian who liberated his native city from the Thirty Tyrants.

Thrăsyllus, i, an Athenian; assisted Thrasybulus to put down the Thirty Tyrants.

Thūcўdĭdes, is, Greek historian.

Thyestes, ae, son of Pelops, brother of Atreus, father of Ægisthus.

Ti.=Tiberius, Roman first name.

Tibĕrius Claudius Nero, emperor of Rome, A.D. 14-37.

Tĭbullus, i, Albius —, Roman elegiac poet; died 18 B.C.

Tigrānes, is, king of Armenia, son-in-law of Mithridates.

Tĭmŏleon, ontis, Corinthian general; saved Sicily from the Carthaginians, 339 B.C.

Timon, ónis, Athenian misanthrope.

Timótheus, ei, Athenian general, son of Conon.

Tirésias, ae, a blind soothsayer of Thebes.

Tirĭdătes, is, name of several kings of Armenia.

Tisĭphŏnĕ, ĕs, a Fury.

Titan, ănis, Phœbus, the sun-god.

Titănĕs, um, m. pl. giants, sons of Uranus and Ge, precipitated by Jupiter into Tartarus.

Tithŏnus, i, son of Laomedon, husband of Aurora.

Titius, a, um, Roman gentile name.

Titus, i, Roman first name.

Tityos, a giant of Eubœa; offered violence to Latona and was killed.

Tŏmўris, a Scythian queen; defeated and killed Cyrus, 529 B.C.

Torquătus, i, Roman surname (in the gens Manlia).

Trājānus, i, Roman emperor, A.D. 98-117.

Trĕbellius, a, um, Roman gentile name.

Trĕbŏnius, a, um, Roman gentile name.

Triptŏlĕmus, i, king of Eleusis, the inventor of agriculture.

Triton, ónis, a sea-god, son of Neptune.

Tritōnis, ĭdis & ĭdos, Minerva.

Trōilus, i, son of Priam.

Trōs, óis, king of Phrygia, after whom Troy was named.

Tullia, ae, daughter of Cicero.

Tullius, a, um, Roman gentile name;— Servius —, the sixth king of Rome.

Tullus Hostĭlius, third king of Rome.

Turnus, i, king of the Rutuli; killed by Æneas.

Tŷdeus, ei & eos, father of Diomedes.

Tŷdĭdes, ae, Diomedes.

Tyndăreus, ei, king of Sparta, husband of Leda.

Tyndărĭdes, ae, male descendant of Tyndareus.

Tyndăris, ĭdis, Helen.

Tŷphŏeus, ei & eos, a giant, struck with lightning by Jupiter, and buried under Ætna.

Tŷrannio, ōnis, m. a grammarian and geographer of Amisus in Pontus; captured by Lucullus, 72 B.C.; gave lessons at Rome.

Ŭlixes, is, Ulysses, is & ei, king of Ithaca, one of the Grecian heroes before Troy.

Ulpiānus Domitius, jurist under Caracalla.

Ŭrănia, ae, the Muse of Astronomy.

Urănus, i, father of Saturn.

Văcūna, ae, a Sabine deity, the goddess of rural leisure.

Vălens, entis, Roman emperor of the East, A.D. 364-378.

Vălentĭniānus, i, emperor of Rome, A.D. 364-375.   [260.

Vălĕriānus, emperor of Rome, A.D. 253-

Vălĕrius, a, um, Roman gentile name; — Maximus, writer of historical anecdotes under Tiberius.

Valgius, a, um, Roman gentile name;—C. — Rufus, Roman poet, contemporary with Vergil.

Varro, ōnis, Roman surname (in the gens Terentia);—M. Tĕrentius —, writer of many treatises, contemporary with Cicero.

Vărus, i, Roman surname (in the gens Quintilia);—P. Quintilius —, destroyed with three legions by Arminius, A.D. 7.

Vătĭnius, a, um, Roman gentile name.

Vējŏvis, is, m. an Etruscan deity of the underworld.

Vĕlĕda, ae, a German virgin and prophetess.

Vellēius, a, um, Roman gentile name;—C. — Paterculus, historian under Augustus and Tiberius.   [wife of Janus.

Vĕnīlia, ae, a nymph, mother of Turnus;

Ventĭdius, a, um, Roman gentile name.

Vĕnus, ĕris, goddess of Love.

Vergilius Maro, P., Roman poet; born 70 B.C.; wrote Æneid, Georgics, etc.

Vergĭnia, ae, a beautiful maiden, beloved by Appius Claudius.

Verres, is, governor of Sicily, 73-71 B.C.; denounced by Cicero for his rapacity.

Vertumnus, i, god of the seasons.

Vespăsiānus, Roman emperor, A.D. 69-79.

Vesta, ae, daughter of Saturn and Rhea, goddess of the hearth-fire and of domestic life.

Virgĭlius, v. Vergilius.

Virgĭnia, v. Verginia.

Vitellius, a, um, Roman gentile name;— Aulus —, Roman emperor, A.D. 69.

Vŏcōnius, a, um, Roman gentile name.

Volcānus, v. Vulcanus.

Vŏlumnia, ae, wife of Coriolanus.

Vŏlumnius, a, um, Roman gentile name.

Vortumnus, v. Vertumnus.

Vulcānus, i, lame son of Juno, god of fire and furnaces.

Xanthippe, ĕs, wife of Socrates.

Xanthippus, i, father of Pericles.

Xĕnocrătes, is, philosopher, disciple of Plato.

Xĕnŏphănes, is, Greek philosopher, 530 B.C.; founder of the Eleatic school.

Xĕnŏphon, tis, Greek historian and general, disciple of Socrates.

Xerxes, is, king of Persia, 485-465; marched against Greece and was defeated at Salamis.

Zēno, Zēnon, ōnis, Greek philosopher, founder of the Stoics.

Zēnŏbia, ae, queen of Palmyra; defeated by Aurelian, A.D. 273.

Zēnŏdŏtus, i, grammarian; flourished about 200 B.C.

Zĕphȳrus, i, the west wind.

Zētes, ae, an Argonaut; brother of Calais, son of Boreas.

Zeuxis, is, a famous Greek painter, 400 B.C.

Zōroastres, is, lawgiver among the Persians.

Zōsĭmus, Greek historian, A.D. 420.

LIST OF GEOGRAPHICAL NAMES

Abæ, ārum, f. pl. town in Phocis, where Apollo had a temple.

Abantes, um, m. pl. aborigines of Eubœa.

Abătos, i, f. a rocky island in the Nile, near Philæ, where Osiris was entombed.

Abdēra, ae, f. town on the Thracian coast (noted for the stupidity of its inhabitants). [tant of Abdera.

Abdērīta, ae, Abdērītēs, ae, m. inhabi-

Abdērītīcus, a, um, a. of Abdera.

Abella, ae, f. town in Campania, the modern Avellino.

Abnŏba, ae, m. (the modern) Black Forest.

Abrŏtŏnum, i, n. town in Africa between the two Syrtes, the modern Sabert.

Abȳdēnus, a, um, a. of Abydos.

Abȳdus, Abydos, i, f. & m. town in Asia on the Hellespont, opposite Sestos.

Acădēmĭa, ae, a gymnasium near Athens in which Plato taught.

Acarnān, ānis, a. Acarnanian.

Acarnānia, ae, f. most western province of Greece. [Acre.

Acē, ēs, f. town in Phœnicia, the modern

Acerræ, ārum, f. pl. the modern Acerra, (town near Naples).

Acěsīnēs, ae, m. the modern Chenab (affluent of the Indus).

Achæus, a, um, a. Achæan.

Achāia, ae, f. Achæa, the northern coast of the Peloponnese.

Achāīcus, a, um, a. Achæan, Grecian.

Acharnæ, ārum, f. pl. town in Attica.

Acharnānus, i, m. native of Acharnæ.

Achělŏŭs, i, m. the largest river in Greece, rises in Mt. Pindus and flows into the Ionian Sea.

Achěron, ntis, m. river in the Lower World; fig. Lower World.

Achěruns, untis, m., v. Acheron.

Achěrūsius, a, um, a. of Acheron.

Achillēum, i, n. town near Sigeum, in Troas.

Achillis insula, f. an island in the Black Sea before the mouth of the Dnieper.

Achīvus, a, um, a. Achæan, Grecian.

Achrădīna, ae, f. part of the city of Syracuse.

Acrăgās, antis, m. mountain on the south-west coast of Sicily; town of Agrigentum, modern Girgenti.

Acrŏcěraunia, ōrum, n. pl. mountain range in Epirus; the extremity of the Ceraunian Mountains where they reach the sea.

Acrŏcŏrinthus, i, f. citadel of Corinth.

Actium, i, n. promontory and town in Epirus; celebrated for the victory of Augustus over Antony, 31 B.C.

Addua, ae, m. the modern Adda, a river, North Italy.

Adria, etc., v. Hadria, etc.

Adŭātĭci, ōrum, m. pl. a Cimbrian tribe in Gallia Belgica.

Æa, ae, f. old name of a part of Colchis.

Ææa, ae, f. island of Circe.

Ææus, a, um, a. Circean; Colchian.

Ædui, ōrum, m. pl. a tribe in Gallia Celtica (between the Arar [Saône] and the Liger [Loire]).

Ægæum, i, n. mare —, the Aegean Sea.

Ægātes, um, f. pl. islands in the Mediterranean (near the promontory of Lilybæum).

Ægīna, ae, f. island near Attica.

Ægīnēta, ae, m. native or inhabitant of Ægina.

Ægos Potami, n. river in the Thracian Chersonnesus; the Athenians were defeated here by Lysander, 405 B.C.

Ægyptius, a, um, a. Egyptian.

Ægyptus, i, f. Egypt.

Æmonia, v. Hæmonia.

Æōlēs, um, m. pl. Æolians (one of the branches of the Greek race).

Æōlia, ae, f. province of Asia Minor.

Æōliæ Insŭlæ, the Lipari Islands off north-east Sicily.

Æōlis, ĭdis, f. province in Asia Minor.

Æōlius, a, um, a. Æolian.

Æqui, ōrum, m. pl. people of ancient Italy, in the neighbourhood of the Volsci.

Æsēpus, i, m. river flowing into the Propontis from Mt. Ida.

Æthălia, ae, f. an island, also called Ilva, the modern Elba.

Æthiopia, ae, f. a country of Africa, S. of Egypt.

Æthiops, ŏpis, m. Ethiopian.

Ætna, ae, Ætnē, ēs, f. volcano in Sicily, the modern Monte Gibello.

Ætōlia, ae, f. province in Greece (between Locris and Acarnania).

Ætōlĭcus, Ætōlius, Ætōlus, ă, um, a. Ætolian.

Äfer, fra, frum, a. African.

Afri, ōrum, m. pl. Africans.

Africa, ae, f. Africa; Libya.

Africānus, Afrĭcus, a, um, a. African.

Ăgănippē, ēs, f. sacred fountain at the foot of Helicon out of which the Muses drank.

Ăgăthyrsi, ōrum, m. pl. Sarmatian people on the banks of the Hungarian river Maris.

Agrĭgentīni, ōrum, m. pl. inhabitants of Agrigentum.

Agrĭgentum, i, n., v. Acragas.

Ăgylla, ae, f. town in Etruria, later Cære, the modern Cervetri.

Ăgўrinensis, e & is, a. & s. of Agyrium; inhabitant of Agyrium.

Ăgўrium, ii, n. town in Sicily.

Ălăbanda, ae, f. town in Caria.

Ălāni, ōrum, m. pl. Scythian (or Sarmatian) tribe.

Alba, Alba Longa, ae, f. mother city of Rome (between the Alban Lake and Mons Albanus).

Albani, ōrum, m. pl. inhabitants of Alba Longa.

Albis, is, m. Elbe.

Albŭla, Albŭnea, ae, f. spring near Tibur, consisting of several sulphureous fountains.

Ălēius, a, um, a. of Ale (in Lycia);— Ălēii campi, m. pl. a plain in Cilicia, where Bellerophon, after being thrown off by Pegasus, roamed about.

Ălĕmanni, ōrum, m. pl. a German confederacy between the Danube and the Rhine.

Ălĕsia, ae, f. town in Gallia Lugdunensis; besieged and taken by Cæsar.

Ălexandrīa, ae, f. town on the north coast of Egypt, founded by Alexander the Great.

Algĭdus, i, m. a mountain near Rome.

Ălīso, ōnis, m. fortress on the Lippe, the modern Elsen.

Allia, ae, an affluent of the Tiber; the Romans were defeated on its banks by the Gauls in 390 B.C.　　　[nium.

Allīfæ, ārum, Alīfa, ae, f. town of Sam-

Allobrŏges, gum, m. pl. a people of the modern Savoy.

Allobrŏgĭcus, a, um, of or belonging to the Allobroges.

Almo, ōnis, m. affluent of the Tiber.

Alpes, ium, f. pl. the Alps.

Alphēus, Alphēos, i, m. chief river of Peloponnesus.

Alpīnus, a, um, a. of the Alps.

Alsium, ii, n. town in Etruria.

Altīnum, i, n. a town near Venice.

Aluntĭum, i, n. town on the north coast of Sicily.　　　[ing to the Taurus.

Ămānus, i, m. a mountain-chain pertain-

Ămărynthus, i, f. town of Eubœa with a temple of Diana.

Ămāsēnus, i, m. river in Latium, the modern Amaseno.　　[coast of Cyprus.

Ămăthūs, untis, f. town on the southern

Ămăzŏnius Mons, mountain-range in Pontus.　　[neighbours of the Ædui.

Ambarri, ōrum, m. pl. a Gallic people,

Ambiāni, ōrum, m. pl. a people on the coast of Gallia Belgica.

Ambĭvărĭti, ōrum, m. pl. a Gallic people on the Meuse.　　　[modern Arta.

Ambrăcia, ae, f. town of Epirus, the Ambrăcius Sinus, a gulf in the Ionian Sea between Epirus and Acarnania.

Ambrōnes, um, m. pl. a Celtic tribe.

Ambrўsus, i, f. town in Phocis.

Ămĕnānus, i, m. river in Sicily.

Ămĕria, ae, f. town in Umbria, the modern Amelia.

Ămĕrīnus, a, um, a. of Ameria.

Ămestrătus, i, f. town on the north coast of Sicily.

Ămīsia, ae, m. Ems (river in Germany).

Ămĭsus, i, f. town in Pontus, the modern Samsun.　　　[country.

Ămĭternum, i, n. town in the Sabine

Amphĭpŏlis, is, f. town in Macedonia on the Strymon.　　[near Delphi.

Amphissa, ae, f. a town of Locris Ozolis,

Amphrўsus, f. a river of Thessaly flowing into the Pagasæan Gulf.

Amsanctus, is, m. a lake of Samnium, famous for its mephitic vapours.

Ămўclæ, ārum, f. pl. (1) town in Laconia; (2) town in Latium.

Ănactŏrium, ii, n. promontory upon the gulf of Ambracia.　　　[Anagni.

Ănagnia, ae, town in Latium, the modern

Ănāpus, i, Ănăpis, is, m. river in Sicily.

Ănas, ae, m. Guadiana (river in Spain).

Ancon, ōnis, Ancōna, ae, f. a town of Picenum on the Adriatic; f. the modern Ancona.

Ancўra, ae, f. chief town of Galatia, the modern Angora.

Andria, the girl from Andros; the title of a play by Terence.

Andros, Andrus, i, f. one of the Cyclades, the modern Andro.

Angli, ōrum, m. pl. a German tribe on the left bank of the Elbe; afterwards crossed over to Britain.

Anio, ēnis, m. river of Latium, affluent of the Tiber, the modern Teverone.

Antandros, i, f. town in Mysia, at the foot of Ida. [bine country.

Antemnæ, ārum, f. pl. town in the Sa-

Anthēdon, ōnis, f. town with a seaport, in Eubœa.

Antĭcўra, ae, f. (1) town of Phocis, the modern Aspra Spitia; (2) town in Thessaly; both towns were famous for hellebore, which was regarded as a cure for madness.

Antĭgŏnēa, ae, f. (1) town in Epirus; (2) town in Macedonia.

Antĭlĭbănus, i, m. mountain-range in Phœnicia, parallel to Libanus.

Antiŏchĭa, ae, f. Antioch; (1) in Syria on the Orontes; (2) in Pisidia.

Antissa, ae, f. town in Lesbos. [Antissa.

Antissæi, ōrum, m. pl. inhabitants of

Antium, ii, n. the modern Anzio (town on the coast of Latium); it contained a famous temple to Fortune.

Antron, ōnis, f. town in Thessaly.

Anxur, ŭris, m. or n. town of Latium; later called Terracina.

Aŏnes, um, m. pl. aborigines of Bœotia.

Aŏnia, ae, f. country of Bœotia.

Aŏnĭdes, um, f. pl. the Muses.

Aornos, i, m. Lake of Avernus.

Aŏus, i, m. river in Illyria.

Apămēa, ae, f. (1) town in Syria; (2) town in Bithynia; (3) town in Phrygia.

Apennīnus, i, m. Apennines.

Apĭdănus, i, m. river in Thessaly.

Apollōnia, ae, f. (1) town in Macedonia; (2) town in Illyria.

Apūlia, ae, f. the modern Puglia; a district of lower Italy. [Apulia.

Apūlicus, a, um, Apŭlus, a, um, a. of

Aquīlēia, ae, f. capital of Venetia.

Aquīlōnia, ae, f. town of Samnium.

Aquīnum, i, n. a town in Latium, the birthplace of Juvenal, the modern Aquino. [Gaul.

Aquītānia, ae, f. province in southern

Ărăbia, ae, f. Arabia.

Ărăbicus, Ărăbus, a, um, a. Arabian.

Ărabs, ăbis, a. Arabian; —, c. Arab.

Ărăcynthus, i, m. mountain-range on the south coast of Ætolia.

Ărădus, i, f. town in Phœnicia.

Ărar, is, m. affluent of the Rhone, the modern Saône.

Ărausio, ōnis, f. a town of Gallia Narbonensis, now Orange. [in Persia.

Ăraxes, is, m. (1) river in Armenia, (2) river

Arbēla, ōrum, n. pl. town in Assyria; near here Darius was defeated by Alexander the Great in 331 B.C.

Arcădia, ae, f. district of the Peloponnesus. [Arcadia.

Arcădĭcus, a, um, Arcădĭus, a, um, a. of

Arcas, ădis, m. Arcadian. [Ardea.

Ardea, ae, f. town of Latium, still called

Arduenna, ae, f. Ardennes (mountain-range and forest in Gaul).

Ărĕlās, ātis, f. town in Gallia Narbonensis, the modern Arles.

Ărĕōpăgītes, ae, m. member of the court of the Areopagus.

Ărĕōpăgus, i, m. Mars' Hill at Athens, chief criminal tribunal at Athens.

Ărĕthūsa, ae, f. celebrated fountain near Syracuse. [modern Arezzo.

Ărētium, ii, n. city of Etruria, the

Argentōrātus, i, f. (the modern) Strasbourg.

Argĭlētum, i, n. quarter of the city of Rome, inhabited chiefly by mechanics and booksellers.

Argĭnūsæ, ārum, f. pl. three small islands in the Ægean Sea off Lesbos; the Athenians won a victory over the Lacedæmonians here in 406 B.C.

Argīvus, a, um, a. of Argos.

Argŏlis, ĭdis, f. district of the Peloponnesus.

Argos, n. (no genitive), **Argi, ōrum,** m. pl. capital of Argolis.

Argos Amphilochium, n town in Acarnania.

Aria, ae, f. a province of Persia.

Arīcia, ae, f. town in Latium.

Arīmĭnum, i, town in Umbria, the modern Rimini.

Arisba, ae, f. town in Troas.

Arměnia, ae, f. Armenia. [a. Armenian.

Arměnĭăcus, a, um, Arměnĭus, a, um,

Armŏrĭcæ, ārum, f. pl. the modern Brittany. [modern Arno.

Arnus, i, m. river in Etruria, the

Arpi, ōrum, m. pl. city in Apulia.

Arpīnas, ātis, a. & s. of Arpinum; inhabitant of Arpinum.

Arpīnum, i, n. town in Latium, birthplace of Marius and Cicero.

Arretium, v. Aretium.

Artaxăta, ōrum, n. pl. capital of Armenia.

Artěmĭsium, ii, n. promontory of Eubœa with a town of the same name.

Arverni, ōrum, m. pl. a people of Gaul, in the country of the modern Auvergne.

Ascălo, ōnis, f. one of the chief cities of Philistia.

Ascănia, ae, f. lake in Bithynia.

Ascra, ae, f. village in Bœotia, the birth-place of Hesiod.

Ascŭlum, i, n. capital of Picenum, the modern Ascoli.

Ăsia, ae, f. (1) Asia; (2) the Roman province of Asia Minor.

Ăsiānus, Ăsiātĭcus, a. Asiatic.

Ăsōpus, i, m. (1) river in Bœotia; (2) river in Peloponnesus.

Aspendus, i, f. town in Pamphylia.

Assўria, ae, f. country in Asia, between Media, Mesopotamia, and Babylonia.

Assўrius, a, um, a. Assyrian.

Asta, ae, f. (1) town in Liguria, the modern Asti; (2) town in Hispania Bætica.

Astăcus, i, f. a town of Bithynia.

Astăpa, ae, f. town in Hispania Bætica.

Astūra, ae, m. river in Latium.

Astūres, um, m. pl. people in the north-west of Spain.

Astŷpălæa, ae, f. one of the Sporades, the modern Stampalia.

Ătella, ae, f. town of Campania, the home of a particular kind of farce.

Ătellānus, a, um, a. of Atella.

Ăthămă iia, ae, f. district in Epirus.

Ăthēnæ. ārum, f. pl. Athens.

Ăthēnæus, a, um, Ăthēniensis, e, a. Athenian.

Ăthĕsis, is, m. the Adige (river).

Ăthos, (no genitive) m. high mountain in Macedonia, the modern Monte Santo.

Atlas, antis, m. mountain-range in the north-west of Africa.

Atlantis, ĭdis, f. a fabulous island beyond the pillars of Hercules.   [Thessaly.

Atrax, ăcis, m. river in Ætolia; town in

Attĭca, ae, f. district of Greece, the capital of which was Athens.

Attĭcus, a, um, a. Attic, Athenian; fig. eloquent; fine, neat; elegant.

Aufĭdus, i, m. principal river of Apulia, the modern Ofanto.

Augusta, name of several towns and cities; — **Gaditana,** (the modern) Cadiz; — **Emerita,** (the modern) Merida (in Estremadura); — **Raura-corum,** capital of the Rauraci near Basle; — **Suessonum,** (the modern) Soissons; — **Taurinorum,** (the modern) Turin; — **Trevirorum,** (the modern) Treves; — **Vindelicorum,** Augsburg.

Augustŏdūnum, i, n. town of the Ædui in Gallia Lugdunensis, (the modern) Autun.

Aulis, is & Ĭdis, f. seaport town in Bœotia from which the Greek fleet sailed for Troy.   [in Calabria.

Aulon, ōnis, m. vine-bearing mountain

Ausōnes, um, m. pl. the Ausonians (ancient name of the primitive inhabi-tants of central Italy).

Ausōnia, ae, f. land of the Ausonians; (poet.) Italy.

Ausōnius, a, um, a. Ausonian; Italian.

Auximum, i, n. town of the Piceni, the modern Osimo.

Avărĭcum, i, n. chief town of the Bitu-riges, the modern Bourgĕs.

Avella, v. **Abella.**

Ăventīnus, i, m. Aventine (one of the seven hills of Rome); —, a, um, a. relating to the Aventine.

Ăvernus (lacus), i, m. Lago d'Averno, a lake near Naples that gave off mephitic vapours, considered to be the entrance to Hell.

Axius, ii, m. chief river of Macedonia.

Axōna, ae, f. r iver in Gaul, the modern Aisne.

Băbўlon, ōnis, f. Babylon, a town on the Euphrates.   [a. Babylonian.

Băbўlōnius, a, um, Băbўlōnĭcus, a, um,

Băcēnis, is, f. the western part of the Thuringian Forest.

Bactra, ōrum, n. pl. chief city of Bactria, the modern Balkh.

Bactrus, i, m. river near Bactra.

Baduhennæ lucus, m. a forest in Frisia.

Bæcŭla, ae, f. town in Spain, the modern Baylen.

Bætĭca, ae, f. a province of Spain, the modern Andalusia and a part of Granada.

Bætis, is, m. river in southern Spain, the modern Guadalquivir.

Băgrăda, ae, m. river in North Africa, the modern Mejerdah.

Băiæ, ārum, f. pl. town on the coast of Campania, near Naples, known for its warm baths.

Băleāres, ium, f. pl. Balearic Islands (in the Mediterranean).

Bandūsia, ae, f. fountain near Venusia.

Bantia, ae, f. town in Apulia.

Bantīnus, a, um, a. of Bantia.

Barcæi, ōrum, m. pl. inhabitants of Barce.

Barcē, es, f. city of Cyrenaica.

Bargūsii, ōrum, m. pl. a people in the north-east of Spain.

Bărium, ii, n. town in Apulia, the modern Bari.   [Galicia.

Bastarnæ, ārum, m. pl. German tribe in

Bătāvi, ōrum, m. pl. inhabitants of the country now called Holland.

Bătŭlum, i, n. town in Campania.

Bauli, ōrum, m. pl. a place near Baiæ, the modern Bacolo.

Bebrÿces, um, m. the Bithynians.

Bĕbrÿcia, ae, f. (later) Bithynia.

Bēdriăcum, i, n. village in northern Italy (between Verona and Cremona), famous for two battles, in which, first, Otho and, later, Vitellius, were defeated, A.D. 69.

Belgæ, ārum, m. pl. the Belgians.

Belgĭcus, a, um, a. Belgian, Belgic.

Belgium, ii, n. the land of the Belgians.

Bellocassi, ōrum, v. **Velocasses.**

Bēnācus, i, m. Lago di Garda, a lake of North Italy.

Bĕnĕventum, i, n. a town of Samnium (the modern) Benevento.

Bĕrĕcyntus, i, m. mountain in Phrygia (sacred to Cybele).

Bergŏmum, i, n. a town of North Italy, the modern Bergamo.

Bĕrœa, ae, f. (1) town in Macedonia; (2) town in Syria, the modern Aleppo.

Bērÿtus, i, f. the modern Beirût.

Bessi, ōrum, m. pl. a Thracian tribe.

Bibracte, is, n. chief town of the Ædui, the modern Autun.

Bibrax, actis, f. a town of the Remi, the modern Bièvre.

Bigerriōnes, um, m. pl. Gallic tribe in Aquitania.

Bilbĭlis, is, m. affluent of the Ebro, with a town of the same name; the latter was the birthplace of Martial.

Bingium, ii, n. the modern Bingen on the Rhine.   [near the Strymon.

Bisaltæ, ārum, m. pl. a Thracian tribe

Bistŏnes, um, m. pl. Thracian people.

Bĭthÿnia, ae, f. district of Asia Minor between the Propontis and the Black Sea.   [Bithynian.

Bĭthÿnĭcus, a, um, Bĭthÿnus, a, um, a.

Bĭtŭriges, um, m. pl. a people of Aquitania.

Blandæ, ārum, f. pl. town in Lucania.

Bŏdotria, ae, f. the modern Firth of Forth.

Bœbē, ēs, f. town in Thessaly.

Bœbēis, idis, f. a lake of Thessaly.

Bœōtia, ae, f. district of Greece, the capital of which was Thebes.

Bœōtius, a, um, Bœōtus, a, um, a. Bœotian.   [Bavarians.

Boii, ōrum, m. pl. old name of the

Bōla, ae, f. town of the Æqui in Latium.

Bōlānus, a, um, a. of Bola.

Bolbe, es, f. a lake in Macedonia.

Bonna, ae, f. Bonn, a town on the Rhine.

Bonnensis, e, a. of Bonn.

Bŏnōnia, ae, f. Bologna.

Bŏnōniensis, e, a. of Bologna.

Bŏrysthĕnes, is, m. river of Sarmatia, the modern Dnieper.

Bospŏrus, i, *or* **Bosphŏrus, m. — Thracius,** Bosphorus; **— Cimmerius,** strait between the sea of Azof and the Black Sea.   [modern Bojano.

Bōviānum, i, n. city of Samnium, the

Bōvillæ, an old town of Latium, ten miles from Rome.

Braurōn, ōnis, m. a town in Attica containing a temple of Artemis.

Breuci, ōrum, m. pl. a Pannonian tribe.

Breuni, ōrum, m. pl. people of Rhætia.

Brĭgantes, um, m. pl. people in Britain.

Britannia, ae, f. Great Britain.

Brĭtannus, a, um, Brĭtannĭcus, a, um, a. British.

Brixellum, i, n. a town on the Po, the modern Brescello.

Brixia, ae, f. Brescia, a town of Cisalpine Gaul.   [about the Ems.

Bructĕri, ōrum, m. pl. German tribe

Brundĭsium, ii, n. Brindisi, a seaport of Calabria.

Bruttii, ōrum, m. pl. inhabitants of the most southern part of Italy.

Bŭthrōtum, i, n. maritime town in Epirus.

Byrsa, ae, f. citadel of Carthage.

Bÿzantium, ii, n. Constantinople.

Bÿzantius, a, um, a. of Byzantium.

Căbillōnum, i, n. town in Gallia, the modern Châlons-sur-Saône.

Cadmēa, ae, f. citadel of Thebes.

Cădurci, ōrum, m. pl. Gallic tribe in Aquitania.

Cæcŭbum, i, n. marshy tract in southern Latium (producing the most excellent kind of Roman wine).   [Rome.

Cælius Mons, one of the seven hills of

Cære, n. indecl. a town of Etruria, the modern Cervetri.

Cærītes, um, *or* **Cærētes, um,** m. pl. inhabitants of Cære.

Cæsărēa, ae, f. (1) capital of Cappadocia; (2) maritime town in Palestine, the modern Kaisaryeh; (3) town in Mauritania; (4) town in Phœnicia.

Cæsena, ae, f. town in Gallia Cispadana.

Cæsia Silva, f. forest in the north-east of Germany.

Caïcus, i, m. river of Mysia.

Caïēta, ae, f. town on the coast of Latium.

Călăber, bra, brum, a. Calabrian.

Călabria, ae, f. a district of south-east Italy, the modern Terra di Otranto.

Călacta, ae, f. the modern Caronia (in Sicily).

Călăgŭr(r)is, is, f. a town in Spain.

Călătia, ae, f. the modern Galazze (in Campania).

Călauria, ae, f. the modern Poro (island), off the coast of Argolis.

Călēdŏnia, ae, f. northern part of Britain.

Călēdŏnius, a, um, a. of Caledonia.

Căles, ium, f. pl. the modern Calvi (town in Campania), celebrated for its wine.

Callĭpŏlis, is, f. town on the Thracian Chersonesus, the modern Gallipoli.

Calpē, es, f. Gibraltar.　　　　[in Cilicia.

Călўcadnus, i, m. river and promontory

Călўdon, ōnis, f. town in Ætolia, the home of Atalanta.

Cămărīna, ae, f. a town on the south-west coast of Sicily.

Căměria, ae, f. town in Latium.

Căměrīnum, i, n. the modern Camerino (in Umbria).

Cămertes, ium, m. pl. the people of Căměrīnum.

Campānia, ae, f. a district of Italy south of Latium, the modern Terra di Lavoro.　　　[modern Colchester.

Cămŭlŏdūnum, i, n. town in Britain, the

Cannæ, ārum, f. pl. village in Apulia; the scene of the defeat of the Romans by Hannibal in 216 B.C.

Cannensis, e, a. of or relating to Cannæ.

Cănŏpītæ, ārum, m. pl. inhabitants of Canopus.

Cănōpus, i, m. town in Lower Egypt.

Cantăber, bri, m. Cantabrian.

Cantabria, ae, f. province of Spain, the modern Biscaya.　　　　[cayan.

Cantabricus, a, um, a. of Cantabria, Bis-

Cantium, ii, n. Kent.

Cănŭsium, ii, n. town in Apulia, the modern Canosa.

Căpēna, ae, f. a town of Etruria, the modern S. Martino.

Căphāreus, ei, m. (promontory) of Eubœa.

Cappădŏcia, ae, f. province of Asia Minor, north of Cilicia.

Cappădŏx, ŏcis, m. Cappadocian.

Căprěæ, ārum, f. pl. island near Naples.

Capsa, ae, f. town in Numidia.

Căpua, ae, f. capital of Campania.

Car, Căris, m. Carian.

Cărălis, is, f., **Carales, um,** f. pl. chief city of Sardinia, the modern Cagliari.

Cardia, ae, f. town on the Thracian Chersonesus.　　　　[Asia Minor.

Căria, ae, f. country in the south-west of

Carmānia, ae, f. a province of Persia.

Carmēlus, i, m. mountain in Palestine, the modern Carmel.

Carnuntum, i, n. town in Pannonia on the Danube, the modern Hainburg.

Carnūtes, um, m. pl. people of Gaul living near the Loire.

Carpăthus, i, f. (an island) between Crete and Rhodes.　　　　[centre of Spain.

Carpētāni, ōrum, m. pl. people in the

Carseŏli, ōrum, m. pl. town of the Æqui, in Latium.　　　　[raltar.

Cartēia, ae, f. ancient town near Gib-

Carthāgo, inis, f. Carthage; — **Nova,** the modern Cartagena.

Cărystus, i, f. town in Eubœa.

Căsĭlīnum, i, n. town in Campania.

Căsīnum, i, n. city of Latium, the modern San Germano.

Caspium mare, n. Caspian Sea.

Caspius, a, um, a. Caspian.

Cassandrēa, ae, f. town in Macedonia, the former Potidæa.

Castālia, ae, f. fountain on Parnassus sacred to Apollo and the Muses.

Castālius, a, um, a. Castalian.

Castŭlo, onis, f. town in Spain on the Guadalquivir.

Cătăbathmos, i, m. steep slope between Lybia and Egypt, which causes the Cataracts.

Cătadūpa, ōrum, n. pl. First Cataract.

Catana, ae, v. Catina.

Cătaŏnia, ae, f. a part in Cappadocia.

Cătĭna, ae, f. the modern Catania, a town on the east coast of Sicily.

Catti, ōrum, v. Chatti.

Caucăsius, a, um, a. Caucasian.

Caucăsus, i, m. chain of mountains between the Black and Caspian Seas.

Caudīnus, a, um, a. relating to Caudium; —**Caudīnæ Fauces,** a narrow pass where the Romans were defeated by the Samnites in 321 B.C.

Caudium, ii, n. town in Samnium.

Caunus, i, f. city of Caria.

Cayster, tri, Caystros, i, m. river in Lydia.

Cēa, ae, f. one of the Cyclades.

Cēi, ōrum, m. pl. inhabitants of Cea.

Cĕbenna, ae, f. the Cevennes.

Cĕlænæ, ārum, f. pl. town in Phrygia.

Cĕletrum, i, n. town in Macedonia.

Celtæ, ārum, m. pl. the Celts.

Celticus, a, um, a. Celtic.

Celtĭbēri, ōrum, m. pl. people in central Spain.

Celtĭbēria, ae, f. the land of the Celtiberi.

Celtĭbēricus, a, um, a. of or relating to the Celtiberi.　　　　[Corinth.

Cenchreæ, ārum, f. pl. a harbour of

Cĕnŏmāni, ōrum, m. pl. a Celtic tribe of Cisalpine Gaul.

Centum Cellæ, an Etruscan seaport, now Civita Vecchia.

Centŭrĭpæ, ārum, f. pl. the modern Centorbi (town in Sicily at the foot of Ætna).

Cĕphălēnia, ae, f. the modern Cephalonia (island in the Ionian Sea).

Cĕphălœdis, is, f. the modern Cefali (in Sicily).

Cĕphīsus, Cĕphissus, i, m. (1) river in Phocis and Bœotia; (2) river of Attica.

Cĕraunia, ōrum, n. pl. mountains in Epirus.

Chærōnēa, ae, f. Bœotian town, the modern Kapurna.

Chalcēdon, ŏnis, f. town in Bithynia, opposite to Byzantium.

Chalcĭdĭce, es, f. a peninsula of Macedonia. [modern Egripo.

Chalcis, ĭdis, f. chief town of Eubœa, the

Chaldæi, ōrum, m. pl. a people of Assyria. [Chaldæan.

Chaldæus, a, um, Chaldaĭcus, a, um, a.

Chălўbes, um, m. pl. people of Pontus.

Chāŏnes, um, m. pl. people in the northwest part of Epirus.

Chāŏnia, ae, f. land of the Chaones.

Chărybdis, is, f. dangerous whirlpool between Italy and Sicily opposite to Scylla.

Chatti, ōrum, m. pl. a German tribe.

Chauci, ōrum, m. pl. tribe of Germany, between the Ems and the Elbe.

Cherrōnēsus, Chersŏnēsus, i, f. Chersonese; (1) Thracian; Gallipoli peninsula; (2) Tauric, between the Black Sea and the Sea of Azof.

Chĕrusci, ōrum, m. pl. the most celebrated of all the German tribes.

Chios, ii, f. the modern Scio (island in the Ægean Sea).

Chĭus, a, um, a. of Chios, Chian.

Choaspes, is, m. (1) river in Susiana, the modern Kerah *or* Kara-su; (2) river in India, the modern Attock.

Cibўra, ae, f. town in Phrygia.

Cĭcōnes, um, m. pl. Thracian people.

Cĭlĭces, um, m. pl. Cilicians. [Asia Minor.

Cĭlĭcia, ae, f. province in the south-east of

Cĭlix, ĭcis, a. of Cilicia.

Cimbri, ōrum, m. pl. people of northern Germany.

Cimbrĭcus, a, um, a. Cimbrian, Cimbric.

Cĭmĭnus *or* **Cĭmĭnius lacus,** a lake in Etruria near Tarquinii.

Cimmĕrii, orum, m. pl. (1) Thracian people in the Crimea; (2) a fabulous people of the farthest West.

Cĭmōlus, i, f. the modern Cimoli, one of the Cyclades celebrated for fuller's earth. [tory in Latium.

Circēii, ōrum, m. pl. town and promontory

Cirrha, ae, f. ancient town near Delphi.

Cirta, ae, f. city in Numidia, the modern Constantine.

Cithæron, ŏnis, m. mountain-range between Bœotia and Attica.

Cĭtium, ii, n. (1) town in Cyprus; (2) town in Macedonia.

Clănis, is, m. river in Etruria.

Clăros, i, f. town in Ionia, containing a temple of Apollo.

Clāzŏmĕnæ, ārum, f. pl. town on the coast of Ionia. [(river in Umbria).

Clĭtumnus, i, m. the modern Clitunno

Clŭpeæ, ārum, f. pl. town on the coast of Africa, east of Carthage.

Clŭsium, ii, n. town of Etruria, residence of Porsena, the modern Chiusi.

Cnĭdus, i, f. city on the south-western coast of Caria.

Cnōsus, v. Gnosus.

Cōcўtus, i, m. river in the Lower World.

Cœlē Sўria, Cœlēsўria, ae, f. country between Libanus and Antilibanus.

Cœlius, ii, m., v. Cælius.

Colchis, ĭdis, f. country in Asia, east of the Black Sea; —, Colchian woman.

Colchus, a, um, Colchĭcus, a, um, a. of Colchis. [near Rome.

Collātia, ae, f. ancient town of Latium,

Cŏlōnæ, ārum, f. pl. town in Troas.

Cŏlōnus, i, m. an Attic deme containing the tomb of Œdipus.

Cŏlŏphon, ŏnis, m. Ionian town in Lydia.

Cŏlossæ, ārum, f. pl. town of Phrygia.

Cŏmāna, ōrum, n. pl. (1) (— Pontica) town in Pontus; (2) (— Chryse) town in Cappadocia.

Commăgēnē, ēs, f. province of Syria.

Cōmum, i, n. Como, town of North Italy.

Confluentes, ium, f. pl. Coblenz, situated at the confluence of the Rhine and the Moselle.

Consentia, ae, f. a town of the Bruttii, the modern Cosenza.

Constantīnŏpŏlis, is, f. Constantinople.

Cōpæ, arum, f. pl. town in Bœotia.

Cōpāis lacus, m. lake of Copæ.

Cŏra, ae, f. town of the Volsci in Latium.

Corcўra, ae, f. the modern Corfu, an island in the Ionian Sea.

Cordŭba, ae, f. Cordova, a town in southern Spain. [a. Corinthian.

Cŏrinthĭăcus, a, um, Cŏrinthĭus, a, um,

Cŏrinthus, i, f. a city of Greece, on the Corinthian isthmus.

Cŏriŏli, ōrum, m. pl. town in Latium.

Cornĭcŭlum, i, n. town in Latium.

Cŏrōnē, ēs, f. town in Messenia.

Cŏrōnēa, ae, town in Bœotia.

Corsĭca, ae, f. island in the Mediterranean Sea.

Corsus, a, um, Corsĭcus, a, um, a. Corsican.

Cortōna, ae, f. town in Etruria.   [Cilicia.

Cŏrўcos, Cŏrўcus, i, f. promontory in

Cŏrўthus, i, m. town in Etruria, later Cortona.

Cōs, Cous, f. island in the Ægean Sea.

Cōs(s)a, ae, f. Cossæ, ārum f. pl. town in Etruria.   [Sicily.

Cossўra, ae, f. island between Africa and

Cōus, a, um, a. of Cos.   [culum.

Crabra (aqua), f. an aqueduct near Tus-

Crāgus, i, m. mountainous tract in Lycia.

Crān(n)on, ōnis, f. a town of Thessaly.

Crĕmōna, ae, f. town in Gallia Cisalpina.

Crĕmōnensis, e, a. of Cremona.

Crēs, ētis, m., Cressa, ae, f. Cretan.

Crēta, ae, f. Crete.

Crētæus, a, um, Crētensis, e, Crētĭcus, a, um, a. Cretan.   [Phocis.

Crīs(s)a, ae, f. an ancient seaport of

Crŏton, ōnis, m. or f. town on the east coast of Bruttium.

Crustŭmĕria, ae, f., Crustŭmĕrium, ii, n. town in the Sabine country.

Cūmæ, ārum, f. pl. city on the coast of Campania.   [Cumæ.

Cūmānus, a, um, Cūmæus, a, um, a. of

Cŭres, ium, m. & f. pl. chief town of the Sabines.

Cūrētes, um, m. pl. mythical people in the entrance of the Black Sea.

Cўăneæ, ārum, f. pl. two rocky islands at Crete.

Cyclădes, um, f. pl. group of islands in the Ægean Sea.   [of Crete.

Cўdōnia, ae, f. town on the north coast

Cyllēnē, ēs & ae, f. mountain in Pelopon- nesus.   [a gymnasium on it.

Cўnŏsarges, is, n. a hill near Athens with

Cўnŏsūræ, ārum, f. pl. promontory in Attica.

Cynthius, a, um, a. relating to Cynthus.

Cynthus, i, m. mountain of Delos.

Cўnūria, ae, f. a district between Argolis and Laconia.

Cyprius, a, um, a. of Cyprus.

Cyprus, i, f. island in the Mediterranean Sea south of Cilicia.

Cўrēnaĭcus, a, um, Cўrēnæus, a, um, a. of Cyrene.

Cўrēnē, ēs, Cўrēnæ, ārum, f. Greek city in north-eastern Africa.

Cyrnos, i, f. (Greek name of) Corsica.

Cўtæ, ārum, f. pl. town in Colchis.

Cўthēra, ōrum, m. pl. island in the Ægean Sea, the modern Çerigo.

Cўthērēus, a, um, Cўthērēius, a, um, Cўthēriăcus, a, um, a. of Cythera.

Cythnos, i, f. island in the Ægean Sea.

Cўtōrus, i, m. mountain in Paphlagonia.

Cўzicum, i, n. Cyzicus, i, f. Greek city on an island of the Propontis.

Dāci, ōrum, m. pl. the Dacians.

Dācia, ae, f. country of the Dacians on the north of the Danube.

Dācus, a, um, a. Dacian.

Dalmătæ, ārum, m. pl. people of Illyria.

Dalmătia, ae, f. land of the Dalmatæ.

Dalmătĭcus, a, um, a. Dalmatian.

Dămascēnus, a, um, a. of Damascus.

Dămascus, i, f. capital of Cœlesyria.

Dănai, ōrum, m. pl. the Greeks.

Dănaus, a, um, a. of Danaus; Grecian, Greek.

Dānŭvius, ii, m. Danube.

Daphne, es, f. a grove near Antioch in Syria.   [pont; (2) Troy.

Dardănia, ae, (1) a city on the Helles-

Daulis, idis, f. town in Phocis.

Daunias, ădis, f. (poet.) Apulia.

Dĕcĕlēa, ae, f. town in Attica.

Dĕcetia, ae, f. town of the Ædui in Gallia Lugdunensis, the modern Decize.

Dēliăcus, a, um, v. Delius.

Dēlium, ii, n. town on the coast of Bœotia.

Dēlius, a, um, a. of Delos.

Dēlos, i, f. the smallest of the Cyclades, famous for the worship of Apollo.

Delphi, ōrum, m. pl. Delphi (in Phocis), the modern Kastri, containing a famous oracle of Apollo; —, inhabi- tants of Delphi.

Delphĭcus, a, um, a. of Delphi.

Derbē, ēs, f. town in Lycaonia.

Dertōna, ae, f. city in Liguria, the modern Tortona.

Dēva, ae, f. Chester.

Dīa, ae, f. (old name of) Naxos.

Dictæus, a, um, a. of Dicte.

Dictē, ēs, f. mountain in Crete.

Dĭgentia, ae, f. the modern river Licenza, a tributary of the Anio.

Dindўmus, i, m. mountain in Mysia (sacred to Cybele).

Dircē, ēs, f. fountain in Bœotia.

Dōdōna, ae, f. town in Epirus with a famed oracle of Jupiter.

Dōdōnæus, a, um, a. of Dodona.

Dŏlŏpes, um, m. pl. a people in Thessaly.

Dŏlŏpia, ae, f. country where the Dolopes dwelled.

Dōres, um, m. pl. the Dorians.   [Dorian.

Dōricus, a, um, Dōrius, a, um, a. Doric,

Dōris, idis, f. a district of Greece south of Thessaly.

Dōriscus, i, m. a town of Thrace near the mouth of the Hebrus.

Dŏrўlæum, i, n. town in Phrygia.

Drĕpăna, ōrum, n. pl., Drĕpănum, i, n. the modern Trapani, a seaport of Sicily.

Drўŏpes, um, m. pl. people of Epirus.

Dūbis, is, m. the modern Doubs (river).

Dubræ, ārum, f. pl. Dover.
Dūlĭchia, ae, f., Dūlĭchium, ii, n. island of
the Ionian Sea.
Dūrŏcortŏrum, i, n. capital of the Remi in
Belgic Gaul, the modern Rheims.
Dȳmē, ēs, f. town on the coast of Achaia.
Dyrrhăchium, ii, n. the modern Durazzo,
a coast town of Illyria.

Ebŏrăcum, i, n. town in Britain, the
modern York.
Ebūrōnes, um, m. pl. people in Gallia
Belgica, between Liége and Aix-la-
Chapelle.
Ėbusus, i, f. the modern Iviza (island) off
the east coast of Spain.
Ecbătăna, ōrum, n. pl. capital of Media.
Ėchīnădes, um, f. pl. group of islands in
the Ionian Sea.
Ėdessa, ae, f. ancient capital of Mace-
donia; city of Mesopotamia.
Ėdōni, ōrum, m. pl. Thracian people.
Ėlăver, ėris, n. the modern Allier (river).
Ėlea, ae, f. city of Lucania, called also
Velia; the home of the Eleatic school.
Ėlĕphantīnē, ēs, f. island and town on the
Nile in Upper Egypt.
Ėlēus, a, um, a. of Elis.
Ėleusīnus, a, um, a. of Eleusis.
Ėleusis, ĭnis, f. city of Attica.
Ėli, ōrum, m. pl. the Eleans.
Ėlis, ĭdis, f. country in the Peloponnesus.
Ėlȳsium, ii, n. the abode of the blessed in
the Lower World.
Ėlȳsius, a, um, a. Elysian.
Ėmăthia, ae, f. district of Macedonia.
Ėnīpeus, i, m. river in Thessaly.
Enna, ae, f., v. Henna.
Entella, ae, f. town in Sicily.
Ėphĕsius, a, um, a. of Ephesus.
Ėphĕsus, i, f. Ionian city in Asia Minor.
Ėphȳra, ae, f. (ancient name of) Corinth.
Ėpĭdamnus, i, f. (old name of) Dyrrha-
chium.
Ėpĭdaurus, i, f. city in Argolis.
Ėpīrōtĭcus, a, um, a. of Epirus.
Ėpīrus, Ėpīros, i, f. country in the north-
west of Greece.
Ėpŏrĕdĭa, ae, f. town of Cisalpine Gaul,
the modern Ivrea.
Ėrĕbus, i, m. *fig.* the Lower World.
Ėrechthīdae, ārum, m. pl. the Athenians.
Ėretria, ae, f. town of Eubœa.
Ėrētum, i, n. town of the Sabines.
Ėrĭdănus, i, m. (Greek name of the river)
Padus or Po.

Ėrȳmanthus, i, m. mountain-chain in
Arcadia.
Ėrythræ, ārum, f. pl. (1) city of Ionia;
(2) city of Bœotia.
Ėrythræum mărĕ, n. Persian Gulf, Red Sea.
Ėryx, ȳcis, m. mountain in Sicily on
which stood a temple of Venus.
Esquĭliæ, ārum, f. pl. one of the seven
hills of Rome.
Esquĭlīnus, a, um, a. of the Esquiline hill.
Etrūria, ae, f. country on the west coast of
central Italy.
Etruscus, a, um, a. Etrurian.
Eubœa, ae, f. island in the Ægean Sea,
the modern Negroponte.
Euēnus, i, m. river of Ætolia.
Euphrātes, is, m. river of Syria, the
modern Frat.   [and Eubœa.
Eurīpus, i, m. channel between Bœotia
Eurōpa, ae, f. (the continent of) Europe.
Eurōpæus, a, um, a. European.
Eurōtas, ae, m. principal river of Laconia.
Euxīnus pontus, m. Black Sea.
Evēnus, v. Euenus.

Făbăris, is, m. a small affluent of the
Tiber, the modern Farfa.
Fabrătĕria, ae, f. town in Latium.
Fæsŭlæ, ārum, f. pl. city of Etruria, the
modern Fiesole.
Fălērii, orum, m. pl. city in Etruria.
Fălernus ager, m. a vine-producing
district of Campania.
Fălisci, ōrum, m. pl. people of Etruria.
Farfărus, i, m., v. Fabaris.
Făventia, ae, f. a town of Cisalpine Gaul,
the modern Faenza.
Fĕrentīnum, i, n. (1) a town of Etruria;
(2) a town of Latium.
Fescennia, ae, f. town of Etruria.
Fescennīnus, a, um, a. of Fescennia.
Fibrēnus, i, m. the modern Fibreno (river
in Latium).
Fĭdēnæ, ārum f. pl. town of Latium, near
Rome.
Firmum, i, n. city of Picenum, the
modern Fermo.
Flāvīna, ae, f. town in Etruria.
Flōrentia, ae, f. city of Etruria, the
modern Florence.
Flōrentīnus, a, um, a. of Florence.
Fŏrentum, i, n. town in Apulia.
Formiæ, ārum, f. pl. city of Latium,
Mola di Gaeta.   [Formiæ.
Formiāni, ōrum, m. pl. inhabitants of
Fortūnātæ Insŭlæ, fabled islands in the
Western Ocean; the home of the
blessed.
Fŏrŭli, ōrum, m. pl. village of the Sabines,
the modern Civita Tommasa.

Fŏrum Appii, town in Latium.

Fŏrum Aurēlium, town of Etruria, the modern Alto.

Fŏrum Cornēlium, a town of Gallia Cispadana, the modern Imola.

Fŏrum Gallōrum, a town of Gallia Cispadana, the modern Castel Franco.

Fŏrum Jūlii, a town on the Mediterranean coast near Cannes, the modern Fréjus.

Franci, ōrum, m. pl. a confederacy of German tribes on the Rhine.

Frĕgellæ, ārum, f. pl. a town of Latium, the modern Ceprano.   [tribe.

Frīsii, ōrum, m. pl. a northern German

Frūsĭno, ōnis, m. a town of Latium, the modern Frosinone.

Fūcĭnus, i, a lake in Latium, m. the modern Lago di Celano.

Fundi, ōrum, m. pl. town of Latium, the modern Fondi.

Găbii, ōrum, m. pl. ancient city of Latium.

Gādes, ĭum, f. pl. Cadiz.

Gādītānus, a, um, of Gades.

Gætūli, ōrum, m. pl. a people of Africa, in the modern Morocco.

Gætŭlus, a, um, a. belonging to the Gætuli.   [modern Galese.

Gălæsus, i, m. river near Tarentum, the

Gălātæ, ārum, m. pl. the Galatians.

Gălătia, ae, f. country of the Galatians; a district of Asia Minor.

Gălīlæi, ōrum, m. pl. inhabitants of Galilee; a district of Palestine.

Gallæcia, ae, f. country of the Gallæci in Hispania and Lusitania.

Galli, ōrum, m. pl. the Celts or Gauls.

Gallia, ae, f. France.

Gallĭcus, a, um, Gallĭcānus, a, um, a. Celtic, Gallic.

Gangărĭdæ, ārum, m. pl. an Indian people.

Ganges, is, m. river of India.

Gărămantes, um, m. pl. a nation of Africa (in the modern Fezzan).

Gargānus, i, m. mountain and promontory in Apulia.

Gargăphie, es, f. a fountain of Bœotia.

Gargăra, ōrum, n. pl. (1) summit of Mt. Ida; (2) a city at the foot of Mt. Ida.

Gargettus, i, m. a place in Attica, birthplace of Epicurus.

Gărumna, ae, m. river of Gaul, (the modern) Garonne.

Gaurus, i, m. mountain in Campania.

Gaza, ae, f. town in Palestine.

Gĕbenna, v. Cebenna.

Gedrōsia, ae, f. part of the modern Baluchistan.

Gĕla, ae, f. town on the south coast of Sicily.   [Ubii, on the Rhine.

Geldŭba, ae, f. fortified place of the

Gĕlōni, ōrum, m. pl. Scythian people.

Gĕnābum, i, n. capital of the Carnutes, on the Liger, the modern Orléans.

Gĕnauni, ōrum, m. pl. a Rætian people.

Gĕnāva, ae, f. town of the Allobroges, on the frontiers of the Helvetii, the modern Geneva.

Gĕnua, ae, f. a town of Liguria, Genoa.

Gĕnŭsus, i, m. river of Illyria.   [Eubœa.

Gĕræstus, i, f. town and promontory of

Gĕrānēa, ae, f. a mountain-range near Corinth.

Gergis, Ĭthis, f. a town of the Troad.

Gergŏvia, ae, f. a town of the Arverni.

Germāni, ōrum, m. pl. the Germans.

Germānia, ae, f. Germany.

Germānĭcus, a, um, Germānus, a, um, a. German.

Gĕrōnium, ii, n. town in Apulia.

Gesoriăcum, i, n. a town of Gallia Belgica, Boulogne.

Gĕtæ, arum, m. pl. Thracian people on the Danube.

Gĕtĭcus, a, um, a. of the Getæ.

Glēvum, i, n. Gloucester.

Gnīdus, Gnīdos, v. Cnidus.

Gnōssus, Gnōssos, i, f. capital of Crete, residence of Minos.

Gomphi, ōrum, m. pl. town in Thessaly.

Gonni, ōrum, m. pl. town in Thessaly.

Gordium, ii, n. city of Phrygia.

Gortyn, ӯnis, Gortӯna, ae, Gortӯnē, ēs, f. city of Crete.

Gŏthi, ōrum, Gŏthōnes, um, m. pl. German people on the northern Vistula.

Græci, ōrum, m. pl. the Grecians or Greeks.

Græcia, ae, f. Greece.

Græcus, a, um, a. Greek.

Grāii, ōrum, m. pl. Greeks.

Graius, a, um = Græcus.

Grājŭgĕna, ae, c. Greek by birth.

Grampius or Graupius mons, m. mountain in Caledonia, the modern Grampian Hills.

Grānĭcus, i, m. river in Mysia.

Gyărus, i, f., Gyăra, ōrum, n. pl. an island in the Ægean.

Gyndes, is, m. river in Assyria.

Gythēum, Gythĭum, i, n. town and harbour in Laconia.

Hadria, ae, f. (1) city in Picenum; (2) city in northern Italy, the modern Adria.

Hadria, ae, m. Adriatic Sea.

Hadrūmētum, i, n. city of North Africa.

Hædui, v. **Ædui.**

Hæmŏnia, ae, f. (poetical name of) Thessaly.

Hæmus, Hæmos, i, m. range of mountains in Thrace, Balkan range.

Hălæsa, Hălēsa, ae, f. town in Sicily.

Hăliacmon, ŏnis, m. river of Macedonia, the modern Vistritza (river).

Hăliartus, i, f. city of Bœotia.

Hălĭcarnassus, Halĭcarnassos, i, f. city in Caria, birthplace of Herodotus.

Hălĭcyæ, ārum, f. pl. town in Sicily.

Hălys, yos, m. river of Asia Minor, the modern Kisil-Irmak.

Hebræi, ōrum, the Hebrews.

Hebrus, i, m. river of Thrace, the modern Maritza.

Hĕcătompўlos, i, f. capital of Parthia.

Hĕlĭcē, ēs, f. town on the coast of Achaia.

Hĕlĭcon, ŏnis, m. mountain in Bœotia (sacred to Apollo and the Muses).

Hĕliŏpŏlis, is, f. (1) city of Egypt; (2) city of Syria.

Hellespontus, i, m. the Dardanelles.

Hĕlōrus, i, m. river of Sicily; town of Sicily, f.

Hĕlōtes, um, m. pl. original inhabitants of Laconia, the Helots.

Helvĕtii, ōrum, m. pl. a Gallic people, in modern Switzerland.

Helvĕtius, a, um, Helvĕtĭcus, a, um, a. Swiss. [Provence

Helvii, ōrum, m. pl. Gallic people in Hĕnĕti, v. **Veneti.**

Hēniŏchi, ōrum, m. pl. a people of Colchis.

Henna, ae, f. city in the centre of Sicily.

Hēphæstia, ae, f. town of Lemnos.

Hēraclēa, Hēraclĭa, ae, f. (1) seaport of Lucania, the modern Policoro; (2) maritime town of Pontus; (3) city of Thessaly.

Hēraclēum, i, n. town in Macedonia on the frontiers of Thessaly.

Hercŭlāneum, ei, n. town of Campania.

Hercŭlāneus, a, um, Hercŭlānensis, e, a. of Herculaneum.

Hercўnia silva, f. Hercynian forest, a mountain-range of Germany.

Herminius mons, m. mountain in Lusitania. [time town of Argolis).

Hermĭŏnē, ēs, f. the modern Kastri (mari-

Hermĭōnes, um, m. pl. German tribe between the Elbe and Vistula.

Hermundŭri, ōrum, m. pl. German tribe on the Elbe.

Hermus, i, m. a river of Asia Minor.

Hernĭci, ōrum, m. pl. a people of Latium.

Hespĕria, ae, f. the Occident; Italy; Spain.

Hiberia, etc., v. **Iberia,** etc.

Hibernia, ae, f. Ireland.

Hiĕrŏsŏlўma, ōrum, n. pl. Jerusalem.

Hīlōtæ, v. **Helotes.**

Hīmĕra, ae, m. river in Sicily; —, **ae,** f. city of Sicily.

Hippo, ōnis, m. (1) city of Numidia; (2) city of Spain; (3) town in Africa, near Utica.

Hippocrēnē, ēs, f. fountain near Mount Helicon (sacred to the Muses).

Hirpīni, ōrum, m. pl. a people in the south of Samnium.

Hispālis, is, f. (the modern) Seville.

Hispāni, ōrum, m. pl. the Spaniards.

Hispānia, ae, f. Spain.

Hispāniensis, e, Hispānĭcus, a, um, Hispānus, a, um, a. Spanish.

Hister, v. **Ister.**

Hŏmŏlē, ēs, f. mountain in Thessaly.

Hortānum, i, n. city of Etruria.

Hunni, ōrum, the Huns, a Tartar tribe.

Hyantes, um, m. pl. (old name of the) Bœotians.

Hybla, ae, Hyblē, ēs, f. town in Sicily, famous for honey.

Hўdaspes, is, m. tributary of the Indus, the modern Jelum.

Hydrus, untis, f. city of Calabria, the modern Otranto.

Hўmettus, Hymettos, i, m. mountain near Athens, famous for its honey.

Hўpănis, is, m. river of Sarmatia, the modern Boug.

Hўpāsis, Hўphăsis, is, m. tributary of the Indus, the modern Sutlej.

Hўperbŏrei, ōrum, m. pl. a fabulous people living in the extreme north.

Hўperbŏreus, a, um, a. far north northernmost. [the Caspian Sea.

Hyrcāni, ōrum, m. pl. a people near

Hўriē, ēs, f. town in Bœotia.

Iălўsus, i, m. a town of Rhodes.

Iāpўges, um, m. pl. a people in Illyria.

Iāpўgia, ae, f. southern part of Apulia.

Iassus, Iāsus, i, f. city of Caria.

Iazўges, Jazyges, um, m. pl. a Sarmatian people.

Ĭbēres, um, m. pl. Iberians, Spaniards.

Ĭbēria, ae, f. Spain.

Ĭbērĭcus, a, um, Ĭbērus, a, um, a. Spanish.

Ĭbērus, i, m. Ebro.

Ĭcăria, ae, f. an island in the Ægean Sea.

Icēni, ōrum, m. pl. a people of Britain.

Ida, ae, Idē, ēs, f. (1) mountain in Crete; (2) mountain-range near Troy.

Idæus, a, um, a. of the Ida.

Īdălia, ae, f., **Īdălium, ii,** n. city in Cyprus.

Ĭdūmæa, ae, f. a region of southern Palestine.

Ĭgŭvĭum, ĭi, n. city of Umbria, the modern Gubbio.

Ĭlerda, ae, f. city in Spain, the modern Lerida.

Ĭlergĕtes, um, m. pl. a people in the north-east of Spain.

Ĭlĭăcus, a, um, v. Ilius.

Ĭlissus, i, m. river of Attica.

Ĭlĭum, Ĭlĭon, ĭi, n., Ĭlĭos, i, f. (poet.) Troy.

Ĭlĭus, a, um, a. of Troy, Trojan.

Illўria, ae, country of the Illyrians on the Adriatic, the modern Dalmatia.

Illўrii, ōrum, m. pl. the Illyrians.

Illўrĭus, a, um, Illўrĭcus, a, um, a. Illyrian.

Ilva, ae, f. Elba (island of the Mediterranean).

Ĭnărĭmē, ēs, f. Ischia, an island off the coast of Campania.

India, ae, f. India.

Indĭcus, a, um, Indus, a, um, a. Indian.

Indus, i, m. river in India.

Insubres, ĭum, m. pl. a people in Gallia Cisalpina.

Intĕramna, ae, f. (1) city in Umbria, the modern Terni; (2) town in Latium.

Internum mare, the Mediterranean.

Iolcos, Iolcus, i, f. town in Thessaly.

Ĭōnes, um, m. pl. the Ionians.

Ĭōnia, ae, f. Ionia, a district of Asia Minor.

Ĭōnĭcus, a, um, Ĭōnĭus, a, um, a. Ionian, Ionic.

Ĭōnĭum mare, part of the Mediterranean between Italy and Greece.

Ĭsăra, ae, f. river in Gaul, the modern Isère.

Ĭsauria, ae, f. a country of Asia Minor.

Ĭsmărus, i, m., Ismăra, ōrum, n. pl. a mountain and town of Thrace.

Ismēnus, i, m. river of Bœotia, flowing through Thebes.   [Sea.

Issa, ae, f. small island in the Adriatic

Issus, i, f. city of Cilicia; scene of the defeat of Darius by Alexander in 333 B.C.

Ister, tri, m. (lower part of the) Danube.

Isthmus, i, m. isthmus; the Isthmus of Corinth.   [Istria.

Istri, ōrum, m. pl. the inhabitants of

Istria, ae, f. Istria, a district on the north of the Adriatic.

Istrĭcus, a, um, a. of Istria.

Ĭtălia, ae, f. Italy.

Ĭtălĭcus, a, um, Ĭtălus, a, um, a. Italian.

Ĭthăca, ae, f. island in the Ionian Sea, the kingdom of Ulysses.

Ĭthōmē, ēs, f. a city of Messenia.

Itius portus, m. a seaport of Gaul, opposite Britain.

Ĭtōnus, i, m. town in Bœotia.

Ĭtūræi, ōrum, m. pl. a tribe inhabiting Ituræa, a country of Cœlesyria.

Ĭverna, ae, Ireland.

Jānĭcŭlum, i, n. mons Jānĭcŭlus, m. one of the seven hills of Rome.

Jaxartes, is, m. river of Central Asia.

Joppē, es, a town on the Palestine coast, the modern Jaffa.

Jordānes, is, m. chief river of Palestine.

Jūdæa, ae, f. the country of the Jews.

Jūdæus, a, um, Jūdaĭcus, a, um, a. Hebrew, Jewish.

Jūra, ae, m. a chain of mountains extending from the Rhine to the Rhone.

Jūverna, ae, f. Ireland.

Lăbĭci, ōrum, m. pl. town of Latium.

Lăbўrinthus, i, m. the Labyrinth in Crete; a building with many winding passages.

Lăcæna, ae, f. Lacedæmonian woman.

Lăcĕdæmon, ŏnis, f. Sparta, a town of Peloponnese.

Lăcĕdæmŏnius, a, um, a. Spartan.

Lăcĕtānia, ae, f. country in the north of Spain.

Lăcĭnium, ĭi, n. promontory in Bruttium, the modern Capo delle Colonne.

Lăco, Lăcon, ŏnis, m. Lacedæmonian, Spartan.

Lăcōnia, Lăcōnĭca, ae, f. Laconia, a district of Peloponnese.

Lăcōnĭcus, a, um, a. Laconian, Spartan.

Læstrўgŏnes, um, m. pl. a fabulous race of giants in Sicily.   [modern Zeitun.

Lămia, ae, f. town in Thessaly, the

Lampsăcum, i, n. Lampsăcus, i, f. city of Mysia, on the Hellespont.

Lānŭvium, ĭi, n. a town of Latium.

Lăpĭthæ, ārum, m. pl. a mythical people inhabiting the mountains of Thessaly.

Lārīnum, i, n. Larino, a town of Samnium.

Lārissa, ae, f. (1) city in Thessaly; (2) a fortress in Argos.   [North Italy.

Lārius, i, m. Lago di Como, a lake of

Lătĕrĭum, ĭi, n. a country seat of Cicero near Arpinum.

Lătium, ĭi, n. a district of Italy in which Rome was situated.

Lătius, a, um, Lătīnus, a, um, a. Latin.

Latmus, i, m. mountain in Caria frequented by Endymion.

Latobrigi, ōrum, m. pl. a Gallic tribe, neighbours of the Helvetii.

Laurentum, i, n. town in Latium near the coast.

Lāvīnium, ii, n. a city of Latium.
Lĕbădia, ae, f. town in Bœotia, the modern Livadhia.
Lĕbĕdus, i, f. a city on the coast of Ionia.
Lĕchæum, i, n. seaport of Corinth, on the Corinthian Gulf.
Lĕlĕges, um, m. pl. a Pelasgian tribe in Asia Minor and Greece.
Lĕmannus (lacus), i, m. Lake of Geneva.
Lemnos, Lemnus, i, f. island in the Ægean Sea, the modern Stalimene.
Lĕmŏvīces, um, m. pl. Gallic people in Aquitania, about the modern Limoges.
Leon, tis, m. a town in Sicily.
Leontīni, ōrum, m. pl. the modern Lentini (in Sicily).
Lĕpontii, ōrum, m. pl. an Alpine tribe in North Italy.
Lepreum, i, n. maritime town of Elis.
Leptis, is, f. — magna, a town in Africa, situated on the Great Syrtis; — parva, a town in Africa near Hadrumetum, the modern Lempta.
Lerna, ae, Lernē, ēs, f. a forest and marsh near Argos.
Lesbos, i, f. island in the Ægean Sea, the modern Mitylene.
Lēthē, ēs, f. river in the infernal regions.
Leucădia, ae, Leucas, ădis, f. island in the Ionian Sea, the modern S. Maura.
Leucāta, Leucātes, ae, m. promontory of Leucadia.
Leucē, ēs, f., v. Achillis insula.
Leuci, ōrum, m. pl. a people in Gallia Belgica, near Liége.
Leucōpetra, ae, f. in Bruttium (the modern promontory) Capo dell' Armi.
Leucōsia, ae, f. an island near Pæstum.
Leuctra, ōrum, n. pl. a small town in Bœotia, famous for the victory of the Thebans over the Spartans in 371 B.C.
Lǐbēthrum, i, n. town in Thessaly, near the fountain Libethra, sacred to the Muses.
Lǐbui, ōrum, m. pl. a Celtic people in Gallia Transpadana.
Liburni, ōrum, m. pl. an Illyrian people.
Lǐbya, ae, Lǐbyē, ēs, f. Libya; Africa.
Lǐbȳcus, a, um, a. Libyan.
Lǐbȳphœnīces, um, m. pl. a people in Libya, descendants of the Phœnicians.
Lǐger, Lǐgĕris, is, m. the modern Loire.
Lǐgŭres, um, m. pl. a people in the northern part of Italy.
Lǐgŭria, ae, f. country of the Ligures.
Lǐlȳbæum, i, n. promontory of Sicily, the modern Capo Bœo; a town of the same name.
Lǐmȳrē, ēs, f. town of Lycia.
Lindos, Lindus, i, f. town in Rhodes.
Lindum, i, n. Lincoln.

Lingŏnes, um, m. pl. a Celtic people near the Vosges, later on the banks of the Padus.
Lǐpăra, ae, Lǐpărē, ēs, f. Lipari (island) situated north of Sicily.
Lǐris, is, m. a river of Latium, the modern Garigliano.
Lissus, i, f., Lissum, i, n. a city in southern Dalmatia, the modern Alessio.
Lǐtāna (silva), f. a forest on the Apennines, near Mutina.
Lǐternum, i, n. a city on the coast of Campania, the modern Patria.
Lǐternus, i, m. river in Campania.
Locri Epizĕphȳrii, an ancient Greek city of Bruttium.
Locri, ōrum, m. pl. a people of Greece.
Locris, ǐdis, f. the name of two districts in Greece; (1) Eastern, extending along the coast from Thermopylæ to Bœotia; (2) Western, a country between Doris and the Corinthian Gulf.
Londǐnium, ii, n. London.
Lūca, ae, f. Lucca, a town of Etruria.
Lūcāni, ōrum, m. pl. a people of southern Italy.
Lūcānia, ae, f. country of the Lucani.
Lūcĕria, ae, f. city of Apulia, the modern Lucera.
Lucrīnus, i, m. lake in the neighbourhood of Baiæ.
Lugdunensis, e, a. of Lyons.
Lugdūnum, i, n. Lyons.
Lugdūnum Batavorum, Leyden.
Lūna, ae, f. city of Etruria.
Lūpercal, ālis, n. grotto on the Palatine Hill, sacred to god Lupercus.
Lūpia, ae, f. river in Germany, the modern Lippe.
Lūsǐtānia, ae, f. Portugal.
Lūsǐtānus, a, um, a. Portuguese.
Lutētia, ae, f. the modern Paris.
Lȳcæus, i, m. a mountain in Arcadia.
Lȳcăŏnes, um, m. pl. a people of Asia Minor.
Lȳcăŏnia, ae, a district of Asia Minor.
Lȳcēum, i, n. a gymnasium at Athens.
Lȳcia, ae, f. a country in the south of Asia Minor.
Lȳcius, a, um, a. Lycian.
Lȳcormas, ae, m. a river of Ætolia.
Lyctus, i, f. a city of Crete.
Lȳcus, i, m. (1) a river in Bithynia; (2) a river in Phrygia.
Lȳdia, ae, f. a country in Asia Minor, the capital of which was Sardes.
Lȳdius, a, um, Lȳdus, a, um, a. Lydian.
Lyrnē(s)us, i, f. a town in Troas.
Lȳsǐmăchǐa, æ, f. (1) a city in Thrace; (2) town in Ætolia.

Măcĕdŏnes, um, m. pl. the Macedonians.

Măcĕdŏnia, ae, f. country of the Macedonians, a large district in the north of Greece.   [a. Macedonian.

Măcĕdŏnĭcus, a, um, Măcĕdŏnĭus, a, um,

Macra, ae, m. river between Liguria and Etruria, the modern Magra.

Mæander, Mæandros, Mæandrus, dri, m. river of Asia Minor noted for its windings.

Mæandrius, a, um, a. of Mæander.

Mædi, ōrum, m. pl. a Thracian people.

Mæōnia, ae, f. (ancient name of) Lydia.

Mæōnius, a, um, a. Lydian.

Mæōtis, ĭdis, ĭdos & ĭs, f. the Sea of Azof.

Magnēsia, ae, f. (1) a city in Lydia; (2) city in Ionia on the Mæander; (3) district of Thessaly.

Magnētes, um, m. pl. the Magnesians.

Magontiăcum, i, n. Mayence, on the Rhine.   [Malaga.

Mălăca, ae, f. town in Spain, the modern

Măleă, Mălēa, ae, f. south-eastern promontory of Laconia.   [ventum.

Mălĕventum, i, n. (old name of) Bene-

Mălĭăcus Sĭnus, m. a gulf between Thessaly and Phocis, the modern Gulf of Zeitun.

Malli, ōrum, m. pl. an Indian people.

Māmertĭni, ōrum, m. pl. the inhabitants of Messana.   [country.

Mandēla, ae, f. a place in the Sabine

Mandūbii, ōrum, m. pl. a Gallic tribe.

Mandūria, ae, f. a town in Calabria.

Mantĭnēa, ae, f. a city of Arcadia.

Mantua, ae, f. a town of Transpadane Gaul; Vergil was born in a village near Mantua.

Mărăcanda, ōrum, n. pl. capital of Sogdiana, the modern Samarkand.

Mărăthon, ōnis, f. a village on the eastern coast of Attica, famous for the victory of the Athenians over the Persians, 490 B.C.

Mărăthōnius, a, um, a. of Marathon.

Mărăthos, i, f. a town in Phœnicia.

Marcŏmăn(n)i, ōrum, m. pl. a German people.

Mardi, ōrum, m. pl. a tribe dwelling in the highlands south of the Caspian Sea.

Mărĕa, ae, f. a town in Egypt.

Mărĕōtis, ĭdis, f. a lake of Lower Egypt.

Margiāna, ae, f. a country between Bactria and Hyrcania.

Marmărĭca, ae, f. a country in north-eastern Africa.

Mărōnēa, Mărōnĭa, ae, f. town of Thrace.

Marpēs(s)us, i, f. a town in the Troad.

Marpēssus, i, f. a mountain in the island of Paros.

Marrŭbium, Marrŭvium, ii, n. capital of the Marsians, a city of Latium.

Marrŭcīni, ōrum, m. pl. a people of Italy, whose chief city was Teate.

Marsi, ōrum, m. pl. nation of central Italy.   [March.

Marus, i, m. river in Dacia, the modern

Massăgĕtæ, ārum, m. pl. a Scythian people.

Massĭcus, i, m. Monte Massico, a mountain of Campania celebrated for its wine.

Massĭlia, ae, f. Marseilles.

Massȳli, ōrum, m. pl. a people of Numidia.

Mătīnus, i, m. a mountain in Apulia.

Matisco, ōnis, m. town of the Ædui on the Arar, the modern Mâcon.

Matrŏna, ae, m. river of Gaul, Marne.

Mattiăcum, i, n. Wiesbaden.

Mauri, ōrum, m. pl. the Moors.

Maurītānia, ae, f. country of the Moors, Morocco.

Maurus, a, um, a. Moorish.

Mēdi, ōrum, m. pl. the Medes.

Mēdia, ae, f. country of the Medes, situated between Armenia, Parthia, Hyrcania and Assyria.

Mēdĭcus, a, um, Mēdus, a, um, a. of the Medes.

Mēdĭōlānensis, e, a. Milanese.

Mēdĭōlānum, i, n. Milan, a town of North Italy.

Mēdĭōmatrĭci, ōrum, m. pl. Gallic people on the banks of the Moselle.

Medullia, ae, f. a town in Latium.

Mĕgălŏpŏlis, is, f. a city of Arcadia.

Mĕgăra, ae, f. **Mĕgăra, ōrum,** n. pl. capital of Megaris.

Mĕgărĕus, a, um, Mĕgărĭcus, a, um, Mĕgărus, a, um, a. of Megara.

Mĕgăris, ĭdis, f. a country of Greece, between Attica and Corinth.   [Italy.

Mēla, Mella, ae, m. a river in northern

Meldi, ōrum, m. pl. a Gallic people between Meaux and Melun.

Mĕlĭbœa, ae, f. a maritime town of Thessaly.   [in the Mediterranean.

Mĕlĭta, ae, Mĕlĭtē, ēs, f. Malta; island

Mĕlodūnum, i, n. town in Gaul, the modern Melun.

Mēlos, i, f. island in the Ægean Sea, one of the Cyclades.   [Egypt.

Memphis, is & ĭdos, f. a city of Middle

Mĕnăpii, ōrum, m. pl. a people in Gallia Belgica, between the Meuse and the Scheldt.

Mendes, ētis, m. a town in Egypt.

Mĕninx, ngis, f. island on the coast of Africa.

Mĕroē, ēs, f. an island in the Nile.

Mĕsŏpŏtămia, ae, f. a country of Asia, between the Euphrates and Tigris.

Messāna, ae, f. Messina, a town on the north-east coast of Sicily.

Messāpia, ae, f. (the Greek name of) Calabria.

Messēnē, ēs, Messēna, ae, f. capital of Messenia, in the Peloponnesus.

Messēnia, ae, f. a district of Peloponnese west of Laconia.

Mētăpontum, i, n. town of Lucania.

Mētaurus, i, m. a river in Umbria; on its banks Hasdrubal was defeated, 207 B.C.

Mēthymna, æ, f. a city in Lesbos.

Mētrŏpŏlis, is, f. a city in Thessaly.

Mēvānia, ae, f. a city in Umbria, the modern Bevagna.

Midaïum, i, n. town in Phrygia.

Mīlētus, i, m. city of Asia Minor.

Mīlēsius, a, um, a. of Miletus.

Mīmas, antis, m. a promontory in Ionia, opposite Chios.   [Gaul.

Mincius, ii, m. Mincio, a river of Cisalpine

M nio, ōnis, m. the modern Mignone, river of Etruria.

Minturnæ, arum, f. pl. a city of Latium.

Mīsēnum, i, n. promontory and town in Campania.

Mĭtÿlēnē, i, Mÿtĭlēnē, ēs, f. **Mĭtÿlēnæ, ārum,** f. pl. capital of Lesbos.

Mœnis, is, Mœnus, i, m. the Main, a river of Germany.

Mœris, idis, f. a lake in Middle Egypt.

Mœsi, ōrum, m. pl. a people who dwelt between Thrace and the Danube.

Mœsia, ae, f. Bulgaria and Servia.

Mogontiăcum, v. **Magontiacum.**

Mŏlossi, ōrum, m. pl. a people in the southern part of Epirus.

Mŏna, ae, f. (1) Isle of Man; (2) Isle of Anglesey.

Mopsuestia, ae, f. town in Cilicia.

Mŏrīni, ōrum, m. pl. a people of Belgic Gaul (in Picardy).

Mŏsa, ae, m. Meuse (river of Belgic Gaul).

Mŏsella, ae, m. & f. Moselle, a river of Belgic Gaul.

Mostēna, ae, f. a town in Lydia.

Mulucha, ae, m. river between Numidia and Mauritania.

Munda, ae, f. a city in the south of Spain.

Mūnÿchia, ae, f. a port of Athens.

Murgantia, ae, f. (1) a city in Samnium; (2) a city in Sicily, also called Murgentia.

Mŭtĭna, ae, f. Modena, a town of Cisalpine Gaul.   [country.

Mŭtusca, ae, f. town in the Sabine

Mŭtÿce, ēs, f. town in Sicily.

Mÿcălē, es, f. a promontory in Ionia, opposite Samos.

Mÿcălessus, i, m. a mountain and town of Bœotia.

Mÿcēnæ, ārum, Mycēnē, es, f. a city in Argolis, the city of Agamemnon.

Mÿcŏnos, i, f. island in the Ægean Sea.

Mygdŏnes, m. pl. Phrygians.

Mygdŏnis, idis, Mygdŏnius, a, um, a. Phrygian.

Mÿlăsa, ōrum, m. pl. town in Caria.

Myndus, i, f. town and harbour in Caria.

Myrīna, ae, f. a seaport in Mysia.

Myrmidŏnes, um, m. pl. a people of Thessaly, ruled by Achilles.

Myrtos, i, island in the Ægean Sea.

Myrtŏum mare, n. Myrtoan Sea, a part of the Ægean Sea.   [of Asia Minor.

Mÿsia, ae, f. a country in the north-west

Mytilenæ, v. **Mitylenæ.**

Myus, untis, f. town in Caria.

Năbătæi, ōrum, m. pl. a nomadic tribe in Arabia.

Namnētes, ium, m. pl. a Gallic tribe about the modern Nantes.

Nantuātes, um, m. pl. a people of Gallia Narbonensis.   [the modern Nera.

Nār, Nāris, m. a tributary of the Tiber,

Narbo, onis, m. Narbonne, a town on the south of Gaul, capital of the province of Gallia Narbonensis.

Narnia, ae, f. town in Umbria (on the Nar).   [the Opuntian Locri.

Nārÿcion, ii, n., **Nāryx, ÿcis,** f. a city of

Năsāmōnes, um, m. pl. a people of northern Africa.

Naupactus, i, f., **Naupactum, i,** n. city of Ætolia on the Corinthian Gulf.

Naxos, i, f. the largest of the Cyclades.

Neāpŏlis, is, f. Naples, a city of Campania.

Neāpŏlītānus, a, um, a. Neapolitan.

Nĕmausum, i, n., **Nĕmausus, i,** f. town in Gallia Narbonensis, the modern Nîmes.

Nĕmea, ae, Nĕmeē, es, f. a city in Argolis.

Nĕmētes, um, m. pl. a people in Gallia Belgica about the modern Spire.

Nemetocenna, ae, f. town in Gallia Belgica, (the modern) Arras.

Nĕpēte, is, n. a city in Etruria.

Nērītos, i, m. (1) a mountain in Ithaca, (2) f. little island near Ithaca.

Nerŭlum, i, n. town in Lucania.

Nervii, ōrum, m. pl. a people of Belgic Gaul.

Nēsis, ĭdis, f. a little island opposite Misenum, the modern Nisita.

Nessus, i, m. a river of Thrace.

Nētum, i, n. a town in Sicily.

Nīcæa, ae, f. (1) a city in Bithynia; (2) a city in Locris; (3) a city on the Hydaspes; (4) a city of Liguria, Nice.

Nĭcŏmēdīa, ae, f. capital of Bithynia.
Nĭcŏpŏlis, is, f. (1) town in Epirus; (2) town in Armenia.
Nīlus, i, m. the Nile.
Nīnus, i, m. Nineveh.
Nĭphātes, ae, m. mountain-range in Armenia.
Nĭsībis, is, f. town in Mesopotamia.
Nĭtĭobrīges, um, m. pl. a people of Aquitania.
Nōla, ae, f. a city in Campania.
Nōmentum, i, n. a Sabine town near Rome.   [in Arcadia.
Nōnăcris, is, f. a mountain and town
Nōra, ōrum, n. pl. (1) citadel in Cappadocia; (2) town in Sardinia.
Norba, ae, f. a town in Latium.
Nōrēia, ae, f. town of the Norici, the modern Neumarkt, in Styria.
Nōrĭcum, i, n. a country between the Danube and the Alps, west of Pannonia.
Nōrĭcus, a, um, a. of Noricum.
Nŏvesium, ii, n. town on the Rhine, the modern Neuss.
Nŏvĭŏdūnum, i, n. (1) a city of the Bituriges, the modern Nouan; (2) a city of the Ædui, the modern Nevers; (3) a city of the Suessones, the modern Soissons.
Nŭcĕria, ae, f. a city in Campania, the modern Nocera.
Nŭmantia, ae, f. a city in the north of Spain.
Nŭmantīnus, a, um, a. of Numantia.
Nŭmīdæ, ārum, m. pl. a people of northern Africa.
Nŭmīdia, ae, f. country of the Numidians.
Nŭmīdĭcus, a, um, a. Numidian.
Nursia, Nurtia, ae, f. a Sabine town.
Nymphæum, i, n. promontory and harbour of Illyria.
Nȳsa, ae, f. (1) city in Caria; (2) a city in India, the birthplace of Bacchus.

Oaxes, Oaxis, is, m. a river in Crete.
Ocrĭcŭlum, i, n. a town in Umbria.
Octŏdūrus, i, m. town of the Veragri, (the modern) Martigny.
Octogēsa, ae, f. town in Spain.
Odrȳsæ, ārum, m. pl. a people of Thrace, on the Hebrus.
Ŏdyssēæ portus, m. a promontory of Sicily.   [Tripoli.
Œa, ae, f. town in Africa, the modern
Œbălia, ae, f. Tarentum.
Œchălia, ae, f. a town in Eubœa.
Œnŏnē, ēs, f. the island of Ægina.
Œnŏpia, ae, f. (ancient name of) Ægina.

Œnōtria, ae, f. (old name of the) southeastern part of Italy; (poet.) Italy.
Œta, ae, Œtē, ēs, f. a mountain-range in the south of Thessaly.
Olbia, ae, f. (1) a city in Sardinia; (2) a city of Bithynia.
Ŏleăros, Ŏliărus, i, f. one of the Cyclades.
Ŏlēnos, i, f. (1) a city in Achaia; (2) a city in Ætolia.
Ŏlympia, ae, f. a district in Elis Pisatis, where the Olympian games were held.
Ŏlympiăcus, a, um, Ŏlympĭcus, a, um, Ŏlympius, a, um, a. Olympian, Olympic.
Ŏlympium, ii, n. temple of the Olympic Jupiter.
Ŏlympus, i, m. (1) a mountain on the boundary of Macedonia and Thessaly, seat of the gods; (2) a mountain in Mysia.
Ŏlynthus, i, f. a city of Macedonia.
Onchestus, i, f. a city of Bœotia.
Opici, v. Osci.
Ŏpuntius, a, um, a. of Opus.
Ŏpus, untis, f. a town of Locris.
Orcădĕs, um, f. pl. the modern Orkneys.
Orchŏmĕnus, i, m. & f. (1) a city in Bœotia; (2) a city in Arcadia.
Ŏrestæ, ārum, m. pl. a people of Epirus.
Ōrĭcos, Ōrĭcus, i, f. Ōrĭcum, i, n. a seaport of Epirus.
Ŏroanda, ae, f. town in Pisidia.
Ŏrontes, is or ae, m. river of Syria.
Ortōna, ae, f. town in Latium.
Ortȳgia, ae, Ortȳgiē, ēs, f. (1) (ancient name of) Delos; (2) island near Syracuse and a quarter of that city.
Osca, ae, f. a town in Spain, the modern Huesca.
Osci, ōrum, m. pl. a tribe of Italy in Campania and Samnium.
Ossa, ae, f. a high mountain in the northeast of Thessaly.
Ostia, ae, f. a seaport town in Latium, at the mouth of the Tiber.   [Thessaly.
Othrys, yos, m. a mountain in southern
Oxos, Oxus, i, m. river of Asia flowing into the Caspian.

Păchȳnum, i, n. Păchȳnus, i, m. & f. the modern Capo Passaro, a promontory of Sicily.   [Lydia.
Pactōlus, i, m. an auriferous river in
Pactyē, ēs, f. town in Thrace.
Pădæi, ōrum, m. pl. a people of India.
Pădus, i, m. the Po.
Pădūsa, ae, f. a canal flowing from the Po through Ravenna.
Pæligni, ōrum, v. Peligni.

Pæŏnes, um, m. pl. a people of northern Macedonia.

Pæŏnia, ae, f. country of the Pæones.

Pæstum, i, n. a city of Lucania, near the Gult of Salerno.

Păgăsa, ae, f., Păgăsæ, ārum, f. pl. a maritime town of Thessaly.

Pălæstĭna, ae, Pălæstĭnē, ēs, f. Palestine.

Pălæstĭnus, a, um, a. of Palestine.

Pălātium, ii, n. one of the seven hills of Rome.

Pălĭnūrus, i, m. a promontory of Lucania. [Macedonia.

Pallēnē, ēs, f. a peninsula and town of

Palmȳra, ae, f. a city of Syria.

Pamphȳlia. ae, f. a country of Asia Minor, between Lycia and Cilicia.

Panchăia, ae, f. a region in Araby the Blest. [rhenian Sea.

Pandātăria, ae, f. island in the Tyr-

Pangæus, i, m. a mountain of Thrace.

Pannŏnia, ae, f. a country between the Danube and the Alps, east of Noricum.

Pannŏnĭ(c)us, a, um, a. of Pannonia.

Pănormītănus, a, um, a. of Palermo.

Pănormus, i, f. Pănormum, i, n. Palermo, a city of Sicily.

Panticăpēum, i, n. town in the modern Crimea.

Paphlăgo, ŏnis, m. Paphlagonian.

Paphlăgŏnia, ae, f. a province of Asia Minor on the Black Sea.

Păphos, Paphus, i, f. a city in Cyprus (sacred to Venus). [Africa.

Pārætōnium, ii, n. a seaport in northern

Părīsii, ōrum, m. pl. a people of Gaul; living about Paris.

Părius, a, um, a. Părian, of Paros.

Parma, ae, f. a town in Gallia Cispadana.

Parmensis, e, a. of Parma.

Parnăs(s)ius, a, um, a. of Parnassus.

Parnăs(s)os, Parnăs(s)us, i, m. a high mountain in Phocis sacred to Apollo, and to the Muses.

Parnes, ēthis, m. a mountain-range of Attica. [Central Asia.

Paropamīsus, i, m. mountain-range of

Păros, i, f. one of the Cyclades, noted for its marble.

Parrhăsia, ae, f. a district of Arcadia.

Parthēni, Parthīni, ōrum, m. pl. a people in Illyria.

Parthĕnius, ii, m. (1) a mountain in Arcadia; (2) river of Paphlagonia.

Parthĕnŏpē, ēs, f. Greek name of Naples.

Parthĕnŏpŏlis, is, f. town in Mœsia.

Parthi, ōrum, m. pl. a Scythian people, the Parthians.

Parthia, ae, f. country of the Parthians.

Parthĭcus, a, um, Parthus, a, um, a. Parthian.

Parthus, i, f. a city in Illyria.

Păsargădæ, ārum, f. pl. ancient royal city of Persia.

Pătăra, ae, f. seaport town of Lycia, containing an oracle of Apollo.

Pătăvium, ii, n. Padua.

Pătăvinus, a, um, a. of Padua.

Patræ, ārum, f. pl. a city in Achaia, the modern Patras.

Pēdum, i, n. an ancient town of Latium, near Rome.

Pĕlăgŏnes, um, m. pl. a people in northern Macedonia.

Pĕlasgi, ōrum, m. pl. the oldest inhabitants of Greece; the Greeks.

Pĕlasgus, a, um, a. Pelasgian.

Pēligni, ōrum, m. pl. a people of central Italy, descendants of the Sabines.

Pēlion, ii, n. a mountain in eastern Thessaly.

Pella, ae, Pellē, ēs, f. a city in Macedonia, birthplace of Alexander the Great.

Pēllēnē, ēs, f. a city of Achaia.

Pĕlŏponnēsiăcus, a, um, Pĕlŏponnēsius, a, um, a. of the Peloponnesus.

Pĕlŏponnēsus, i, f. the modern Morea; the southern peninsula of Greece.

Pēlōrus, i, m. Pēlōrum, i, n. the modern Capo di Faro (a promontory in Sicily).

Pēlūsium, ii, n. a city at the mouth of the Nile.

Pēnēus, i, m. river of Thessaly, flowing through the Valley of Tempe.

Pēnius, ii, m. river in Colchis.

Pennīnus (mons), m. the Great St. Bernard. [Sea.

Pēpărēthos, i, f. an island in the Ægean

Perga, ae, f. a city of Pamphylia.

Pergămum, i, n., Pergămos, Pergămus, i, f., Pergăma, ōrum, n. pl. the citadel of Troy; Troy.

Pergămum, i, n. a city in Mysia.

Pĕrinthus, i, f. a city of Thrace.

Permessus, i, m. a river in Bœotia, sacred to Apollo and the Muses.

Perrhæbia, ae, f. a country of Thessaly.

Perrhæbi, ōrum, m. pl. a people of Thessaly.

Persæ, ārum, m. pl. the Persians.

Persēpŏlis, is, f. a city of Persia.

Persis, idis, f. Persia.

Persĭcus, a, um, a. Persian.

Pĕrūsia, ae, f. Perugia, a city of Etruria.

Pes(s)ĭnūs, untis, f. a town in Galatia noted for the worship of Cybele.

Pĕtēlia, ae, f. Greek town on the coast of Bruttium.

Pĕteon, ŏnis, f. a town of Bœotia.

Pĕtrŏcŏrii, ōrum, m. pl. a Gallic tribe in Aquitania, about the modern Périgueux.

Peucĕtia, ae, f. a region in Apulia.

Phæăces, um, m. pl. a fabulous people, on the Isle of Scheria.

Phæācia, ae, f. Scheria.

Phæācus, a, um, a. of the Phæaces.

Phæstum, i, n. a town of Crete.

Phălăra, ōrum, n. pl. seaport-town in Thessaly.

Phălērum, i, n. a harbour of Athens.

Phănæ, ārum, f. pl. a vine-producing promontory in Chios.

Pharsālius, a, um, a. of Pharsalus.

Pharsālos, Pharsālus, i, f. a town in Thessaly, noted for the defeat of Pompey by Cæsar, 48 B.C.

Phărus, Phăros, i, f. an island near Alexandria, famous for its lighthouse.

Phăsēlis, ĭdis, f. a town on the coast of Lycia.

Phāsis, ĭdis & ĭdos, m. a river in Colchis.

Phĕneos, Pheneus, i, f. town and lake in Arcadia. [(2) a city in Messenia.

Phĕræ, ārum, f. pl. (1) a city of Thessaly; Philădelphĭa, ae, f. town in Lydia.

Philænōn aræ, f. pl. harbour on the frontiers of Cyrene, the southernmost place of the Great Syrtis, where altars in honour of the brethren Philæni were erected. [donia.

Philippi, ōrum, m. pl. a city in Macedonia.

Philŏmēlium, ii, n. a city of Phrygia.

Phlĕgĕthon, ontis, m. a river in the Lower World.

Phlegra, ae, f. a country of Macedonia, afterwards Pallene.

Phliūs, untis, f. a city of Peloponnesus between Sicily and Argolis.

Phōcæa, ae, f. a maritime town of Ionia, the mother-town of Massilia.

Phōcæi, orum, m. pl. the Phocæans.

Phōcaïcus, a, um, a. Phocæan.

Phōcenses, ium, Phōcii, ōrum, m. pl. the Phocians.

Phōcēus, a, um, a. of Phocis.

Phōcis, ĭdis, f. a country of Greece west of Bœotia.

Phœnīcē, ēs, Phœnīcia, ae, f. a maritime country of Asia.

Phœnīces, um, m. pl. the Phœnicians.

Phœnissa, ae, f. a Phœnician woman.

Phŏloē, ēs, f. (1) a mountain in Arcadia; (2) mountain in Thessaly.

Phrȳges, um, m. pl. Phrygians; Trojans.

Phrȳgia, ae, f. Phrygia. [Trojan.

Phrȳgius, a, um, Phryx, ȳgis, a. Phrygian; Phthīa, ae, Phthĭōtis, ĭdis, f. a district of Thessaly.

Phthīōtes, ae, m. inhabitant of Phthia.

Phthĭōtĭcus, a, um, Phthĭus, a, um, a. Phthian.

Phȳlăcē, es, f. a city of Thessaly.

Phȳlē, ēs, f. a fortress in Attica on the frontiers of Bœotia.

Pīcēnum, i, n. a district of central Italy, bounded by the Adriatic.

Pictōnes, m. pl. a people of Gaul, in the modern Poitou.

Pĭeria, ae, f. (1) a district of Macedonia, famous for the worship of the Muses; (2) a district of Syria.

Pimplēa, ae, f. a fountain of Pieria sacred to the Muses. [Pincio.

Pincius, ii, m. a hill at Rome; Monte Pindĕnissus, i, m. a town of Cilicia.

Pindus, Pindos, i, m. a mountain-range between Thessaly and Epirus.

Pīræeus, Pīræus, i, m. the principal harbour of Athens.

Pīræus, a, um a. of or belonging to the Piræus. [Corinth.

Pīrēnē, ēs, f. a fountain in the citadel of Pīsa, ae, Pīsæ, ārum, f. a city of Elis, near which the Olympic games were held.

Pisaurum, i, n. a city of Umbria, the modern Pesaro.

Pĭsīdæ, ārum, m. pl. a people of Asia Minor, bordering on the Phrygians.

Pĭsīdia, ae, f. a district in the south of Asia Minor. [modern Pistoia.

Pistōrium, ii, n. town in Etruria, the Pĭtănē, ēs, f. town on the coast of Mysia.

Pĭthēcūsa, ae, f. (also pl.) island near Cumæ, the modern Ischia.

Plăcentia, ae, f. Piacenza, a town of Cispadane Gaul.

Plăcentīnus, a, um, a. of Piacenza.

Planasia, ae, f. island south of Elba, the modern Pianosa.

Plătææ, ārum, f. pl. a city in Bœotia.

Plemmȳrium, ii, n. a promontory of Sicily, near Syracuse. [Belgica.

Pleumoxii, ōrum, m. pl. a people in Gallia Pleurōn, ōnis, f. city of Ætolia.

Pœni, ōrum, m. pl. the Carthaginians.

Pœnŭlus, i, the young Phœnician; the title of a play by Plautus.

Pœnus, a, um, v. Punicus.

Pollentia, ae, f. (1) a city in Picenum; (2) a city in Liguria. [town of the Volsci.

Pōmētia, ae, f., Pōmĕtii, ōrum, m. pl. a Pompeii, ōrum, m. pl. a maritime city in the south of Campania, near Vesuvius.

Pompēiānum, i, n. a country-seat of Cicero, near Pompeii.

Pompēiŏpŏlis, is, f. town in Cilicia; v. Soli.

Pomptīnæ paludes, the Pontine Marshes, a district of Latium.

Pontia, ae, f. an island in the Tuscan Sea.

Ponticus, a, um, a. of the Pontus.

Pontus, i, m. (1) the Black Sea; (2) northeastern province of Asia Minor.

Pŏpŭlōnia, ae, f., Pŏpŭlōnium, ii, n., Pŏpulōnii, ōrum, m. pl. a town on the coast of Etruria.

Potniæ, ārum, f. pl. a village in Bœotia.

Præneste, is, n. a town in Latium, the modern Palestrina, famous for an oracle and temple of Fortune.

Prætūtii, ōrum, m. pl. a people in Picenum.

Priēnē, ēs, f. a maritime town of Ionia.

Privernum, i, n. a town of Latium, the modern Piperno.

Prŏchўta, ae, Prŏchўtē, ēs, f. Procida, an island off the coast of Campania.

Prŏconnēsus, i, f. an island in the Propontis.   [Marmora.

Prŏpontis, ĭdos & ĭdis, f. the Sea of

Prūsa, ae, f. town in Bithynia.

Ptĕleum, i, n., Pteleos, i, f. town in Thessaly.

Ptŏlĕmāis, ĭdis, f. (1) a city in Egypt; (2) a city in Phœnicia.

Pūnĭcus, a, um, a. Punic, Carthaginian.

Pupinia, ae, f., Pupinius, ii, Pupiniensis ager, m. a barren tract of land near Rome.

Pŭteŏli, ōrum, m. pl. town on the coast of Campania (with mineral springs); the modern Pozzuoli.

Pydna, ae, f. a city in Macedonia, noted for the defeat of Perseus by Æmilius Paulus in 168 B.C.

Pўlæ, ārum, f. pl. (1) — Tauri, a narrow pass between Cappadocia and Cilicia; (2) Pass of Thermopylæ.

Pўlos, Pўlus, i, f. (1) a city in Elis; (2) a city in Messenia, the modern Navarino; (3) a city in Arcadia.

Pўrāmus, i, m. large river in Cilicia.

Pўrēnē, ēs, f. the Pyrenees.

Pўrēnæus, a, um, a. of the Pyrenees.

Pyrgi, ōrum, m. pl. town in Etruria.

Pyrrha, ae, f. town in the island of Lesbos.

Pўthĭcus, a, um, Pўthĭus, a, um, a. Pythian.

Pўtho, ūs, f. old name of Delphi.

Quādi, ōrum, m. pl. a German people in the modern Moravia.

Ræti, ōrum, m. pl. a people between the Alps and the Danube.   [Tyrol.

Rætia, ae, f. the modern Grisons and the Ræti(c)us, Rætus, a, um, a. Rætian.

Raudii campi, m. pl. a plain near Vercellæ, famous for the defeat of the Cimbrians by Marius in 101 B.C.

Raurăci, Raurĭci, ōrum, m. pl. a Gallic people, neighbours of the Helvetii.

Răvenna, ae, f. a city in Gallia Cispadana on the Adriatic, Ravenna.

Răvennas, ātis, a. of Ravenna.

Reāte, is, n. a town of the Sabines, the modern Rieti.

Rĕdŏnes, um, m. pl. a Gallic people in Brittany, about the modern Rennes.

Rēgillus, i, m. (1) a town of the Sabines; (2) a lake in Latium.

Rēgium, (1) a town in Gallia Cisalpina, the modern Reggio; (2) a city of Calabria opposite Messina in Sicily.

Reudigni, ōrum, m. pl. a people in northern Germany.

Rhæti, etc., v. Ræti, etc.

Rhăgæ, ārum, f. pl. a city of Media.

Rhamnūs, untis, f. a town on the east coast of Attica, famous for its temple of Nemesis.

Rhēgĭum, v. Regium.

Rhēnānus, a, um, a. of the Rhine.

Rhēnus, i, m. the Rhine.

Rhĭnŏcŏlūra, ae, f. town on the southern coast of the Mediterranean between Egypt and Palestine, the modern El-Arish.

Rhion, Rhium, ii, n. promontory in Achaia, opposite Antirrhium.

Rhĭpæi, Rhĭphæi montes, a range of mountains in northern Scythia.

Rhŏdănus, i, m. the Rhone.

Rhŏdiensis, e, Rhŏdius, a, um, a. of Rhodes.   [Thrace.

Rhŏdŏpē, ēs, f. a mountain-range in

Rhŏdos, i, Rhŏdus, i, f. Rhodes; town of the same name in the island of Rhodes.

Rhœtēum, i, n. town and promontory in Mysia, on the Hellespont.

Rhōsos, i, f. town in Cilicia.

Rigŏdŭlum, i, n. town in the country of the Treviri.

Rōma, ae, f. capital of the Roman empire, Rome.

Rōmānus, a, um, a. Roman.

Rōsea, Rōsia, ae, f. a fertile district near Reate.   [the modern Ruvo.

Rŭbi, ōrum, m. pl. a town in Apulia,

Rŭbĭco, ōnis, m. a small boundary-stream between Italy and Cisalpine Gaul; the crossing of the Rubicon by Cæsar, 49 B.C., was the prelude to the civil war.

Rŭdiæ, ārum, f. pl. a town in Apulia, birthplace of Ennius.

Rŭdīni, ōrum, m. pl. inhabitants of Rudiæ.

Rufræ, ārum, f. pl. town in Campania.

Rugii, ōrum, m. pl. a German tribe on the Baltic.

Ruscīno, ōnis, f. town in Gallia Narbonensis, the modern la Tour de Roussillon.

Rūsellæ, ārum, f. pl. a town of Etruria.

Rūtēni, ōrum, m. pl. a Celtic tribe in Aquitania.

Rŭtŭli, ōrum, m. pl. a people of Latium, whose capital was Ardea.

Rŭtŭpiæ, ārum, f. pl. a town in Kent, now Richborough.

Săba, ae, a town in Araby the Blest.

Săbæus, a, um, a. of Saba, Sabean.

Săbāria, ae, f. a town in Pannonia.

Săbātē, ēs, f. a town in Etruria, **near a** lake called Lacus Sabatinus.

Săbelli, ōrum, m. pl. (ancient name for) the Sabines.   [Sabine.

Săbellus, a, um, Săbellĭcus, a, um, a.

Săbīni, ōrum, m. pl. the Sabines, an ancient Italian stock.

Sabis, is, m. river in Gallia Belgica, the modern Sambre.

Săcæ, ārum, m. pl. a Scythian tribe.

Sacri-portus, ūs, m. a place in Latium.

Sætābis, is, f. a town of Spain, near Valencia.   [Asia Minor.

Săgăris, is, Sangărius, ii, m. a river of

Săguntum, i, n., Săguntus, i, f. Murviedro, a town of Spain, near Valencia.

Sălămīnĭus, a, um, a. of Salamis.

Sălămis, īnis, f. (1) island in the Saronic Gulf, the modern Koluri; (2) a city in Cyprus.

Sălăpia, ae, f. a town in Apulia.

Salassi, ōrum, m. pl. a people of Transpadane Gaul occupying the modern Savoy.   [Calabria.

Săl(l)entīni, ōrum, m. pl. a people in

Sălernum, i, n. the modern Salerno, a town on the coast of Campania.

Salmăcis, ĭdis, f. a fountain in Caria.

Salmўdessus, i, f. a town in Thrace on the Black Sea.

Sălōnæ, ārum, f. pl. capital of Dalmatia.

Salpia, v. Salapia.

Sămāria, ae, f. a district in Palestine.

Sămărobrīva, ae, f. the modern Amiens, a town of Belgic Gaul.

Sămē, ēs, f. (1) ancient name of the island of Cephallenia; (2) capital of this island.

Samnium, ii, n. a country of central Italy, inhabited by the Samnites.

Samnis, ītis, a. Samnite.

Samnītes, ium, m. pl. the Samnites.

Samnītĭcus, a, um, a. of the Samnites.

Sămos, i, f. an island on the coast of Asia Minor opposite Ephesus.

Sămothrācē, ēs, Sămothrācia, ae, f. an island in the Ægean Sea off the Thracian coast.

Samus, v. Samos.

Santōni, orum, m. pl. a people of Aquitania.   [on the Propontis.

Săpæi, orum, m. pl. a Thracian people

Sapriportus, us, m. harbour between Sybaris and Tarentum.

Sardes, ium, f. pl. capital of Lydia.

Sardi, ōrum, m. pl. the inhabitants of Sardinia.

Sardinĭa, ae, an island in the Mediterranean between Spain and Italy.

Sardōus, a, um, Sardiniensis, e, Sardus, a, um, a. Sardinian.

Sarmătæ, ārum, m. pl. a barbarous people who occupied great tracts of the modern Poland and Russia.

Sarmătia, ae, f. country inhabited by the Sarmatae.   [—um, the Black Sea.

Sarmătĭcus, a, um, a. Sarmatian;—**mare**

Sarnus, i, m. a river in Campania, the modern Sarno.

Sărōnicus Sīnus, the Saronic Gulf, between Attica and the Peloponnese.

Sarra, ae, f. the city of Tyre.

Sarrastes, um, m. pl. a people in Campania.   [place of Plautus.

Sarsina, ae, f. a town in Umbria, birth-

Sătĭcŭla, ae, f. a town of Samnium.

Satrĭcum, i, n. a town in Latium.

Sătŭræ palus, f. a lake in Latium.

Sătŭrēiānus, a, um, a. Apulian.

Săturnia, ae, f. town on the Capitoline Hill.

Saurŏmătæ, Saurŏmătes, v. Sarmatæ.

Săvus, i, m. Save, a tributary of the Danube.

Saxōnes, um, m. pl. the Saxons.

Scæa porta, ae, f. the Scæan *or* western gate of Troy.

Scaldis, is, m. river in northern Gallia, the modern Scheldt.

Scămander, dri, m. a river near Troy.

Scaptia, ae, f. town in Latium.

Scepsis, is, f. a town in Mysia.

Schěria, ae, ancient name of Corcyra.

Scodra, ae, f. the modern Scutari, a town of Illyria.

Scordisci, ōrum, m. pl. (1) a people in Pannonia; (2) a people of Illyria.

Scōti, ōrum, m. pl. Scots, a people in Ulster; later in Scotland.

Scōtĭcus, a, um, a. Scottish.

Scўlăcēum, i, n. a town on the coast of Bruttium, the modern Squillace.

Scylla, æ, f. a rock between Italy and Sicily, opposite Charybdis.

Scȳros, Scȳrus, i, f. one of the Sporades, the modern Scyro.

Scÿthæ, ārum, m. pl. the Scythians, people dwelling north and east of the Black Sea.

Scÿthia, ae, f. country inhabited by the Scythians.

Scÿthĭcus, a, um, a. Scythian.

Scÿthis, ĭdis, f. a Scythian woman.

Sēbēthos, i, m. river in Campania.

Sedūni, ōrum, m. pl. a Helvetian tribe, about the modern Sion.

Sĕgesta, ae, f. a city on the north-western coast of Sicily.

Segni, ōrum, m. pl. a people in Belgium.

Sĕgobrīga, ae, f. a town in Spain, the capital of the Celtiberi.

Sĕgūsiāvi, ōrum, m. pl. a Gallic tribe.

Sĕleucĭa, ae, f. (1) a city in Syria, the modern Kepse; (2) a town in Babylonia, the capital of the Parthians; (3) a city of Cilicia.

Sĕlīnūs, untis, f. a town on the south-west coast of Sicily.

Semnŏnes, um, m. pl. German people between the Elbe and Vistula.

Sēna, ae, f. a town of Umbria, Senigaglia.

Sēnŏnes, um, m. pl. (1) a people of Gaul, whose chief city was Agendicum, the modern Sens; (2) a people in Gallia Cisalpina.

Sēplăsia, ae, f. a street in Capua, where perfumes were sold.

Sēquăna, ae, f. a river of Gaul, the Seine.

Sēquăni, ōrum, m. pl. a Gallic tribe about the banks of the Sequana.

Sēres, um, m. pl. the Chinese.

Sēricus, a, um, a. Chinese.

Sĕrīphus, i, f. one of the Cyclades, the modern Serpho.

Sestos, Sestus, i, f. a town in Thrace, on the Hellespont, opposite Abydos.

Sētābis, is, f., v. Saetabis.

Sētia, ae, f. a town in Latium, the modern Sezza. [country.

Sĕvērus mons, a mountain in the Sabine

Sibuzātes, um, m. pl. a people in Aquitania, in the modern Sobusse.

Sīcambri, v. Sigambri.

Sīcāni, ōrum, m. pl. a people of Italy, partially emigrated to Sicily.

Sīcānia, ae, f. Sicily.

Sīcānius, a, um, a. Sicilian.

Sicca, ae, f. a town of Numidia.

Sicīlia, ae, f. Sicily.

Sīcŏris, is, m. river in the north-east of Spain. [Sicani.

Sicŭli, ōrum, m. pl. another name for the

Sicŭlus, a, um, a. Sicilian.

Sicyōn, ōnis, f. the capital of Sicyonia, a town of the Peloponnese, near Corinth.

Sĭda, ae, f. a town in Pamphylia.

Sidīcīni, ōrum, m. pl. a people in Campania, whose chief town was Teanum.

Sīdōn, ōnis & ŏnis, f. a Phœnician city, the mother-city of Tyre, the modern Saida.

Sīdŏnius, a, um, Sīdōnĭcus, a, um, a. of or relating to Sidon.

Sĭgambri, ōrum, m. pl. a people of Germany.

Sĭgēum, i, n. a promontory in Troas.

Signia, ae, f. a town in Latium, the modern Segni. [the Bruttii.

Sila, ae, f. a forest in the country of

Sĭlārus, i, m. a boundary river between Lucania and Campania.

Simoīs, entis, m. a river in Troas, which falls into the Scamander.

Sĭnōpē, ēs, f. a Greek colony in Paphlagonia, the modern Sinoub.

Sĭnuessa, ae, f. a city of Latium, on the confines of Campania.

Siphnos, i, f. one of the Cyclades, the modern Sifanto.

Sĭpontum, i, n. a maritime town in Apulia.

Sĭpўlus, i, m. a mountain of Lydia.

Sirmio, ōnis, m. peninsula of Lake Garda.

Sĭsăpo, ōnis, f. town in Hispania Bætica.

Sīthōnii, ōrum, m. pl. a Thracian people; the Thracians.

Smyrna, ae, f. a maritime city of Ionia, still called Smyrna.

Smyrnæus, a, um, a. of Smyrna.

Sŏdŏma, ōrum, n. pl. Sodom, a town of Palestine.

Sogdiana, f. a region between the Jaxartes and the Oxus.

Sōli, ōrum, m. pl. town in Cyprus; v. Pompeiopolis. [trict in Latium.

Sōlonium, ii, n. Sōlonius ager, m. a dis-

Sōlўma, ōrum, n. pl. a mountain-range of Lycia. [Lycia.

Sŏlўmi, ōrum, m. pl. the aborigines of

Sōra, ae, f. a town in Latium.

Sōracte, is, n. Monte di S. Oreste, a mountain of Etruria.

Sparta, ae, f. the capital of Laconia, in the Peloponnese. [Spartan.

Spartānus, a, um, Spartīcus, a, um, a.

Spartiātes, ae, m. a Spartan.

Sperchēos, Sperchĭus, i, m. a river of southern Thessaly.

Spōlētium, ii, Spōlētum, i, n. a city of Umbria, Spoleto.

Spŏrădes, um, f. pl. a group of islands in the Ægean.

Stăbiæ, ārum, f. pl. a town on the coast of Campania near Pompeii.

Stăgīra, ōrum, n. pl. a town in Macedonia, the birthplace of Aristotle.

Statielli, ōrum, m. pl. a people in Liguria.

Stellātis ager *or* **campus,** m. a district in northern Campania, near Cales.

Strătŏnīcēa, ae, f. a city of Caria.

Strŏphădes, um, f. pl. two islands off the coast of Messenia, the residence of the Harpies.

Strȳmon, ŏnis, m. boundary-river between Macedonia and Thrace, the modern Struma. [Styx.

Stȳgius, a, um, a. of *or* belonging to the

Stymphālus, i, m., **Stymphālum, i,** n. a district in Arcadia, with a town and lake of the same name.

Styx, ȳgis & ȳgos, f. the principal river in the infernal regions, by which the gods swore.

Sucro, ŏnis, m. (1) a river of Spain, the modern Jucar; (2) a town at the mouth of this river.

Suēbi, ōrum, v. **Suevi.**

Suessa, ae, f. (1) a town in Latium, called also Suessa Pometia; (2) a town of Latium, near the borders of Campania, the modern Sessa.

Suessiōnes, um, m. pl. a people of Gaul, near the modern Soissons.

Suessŭla, ae, f. a town of Campania.

Suēvi, ōrum, m. pl. a German tribe.

Suēvia, ae, f. the country of the Suevi.

Suēvicus, a, um, Suēvus, a, um, a. of the Suevi. [Scandinavia.

Suiōnes, um, m. pl. the aborigines of

Sulmo, ŏnis, m. a town of the Peligni, the birthplace of Ovid.

Sūnion, Sūnium, ii, n. a promontory and town of Attica, the modern Capo Colonni.

Surrentum, i, n. Sorrento, a town of Campania, in the Bay of Naples.

Sūsa, ōrum, n. pl. ancient capital of Persia.

Sūtrium, ii, n. Sutri, a town of Etruria.

Sȳbăris, is, f. a town of Lucania on the Gulf of Tarentum.

Syēnē, ēs, f. a town in Upper Egypt, the modern Assouan.

Sȳmæthus, i, m. (1) a river in the vicinity of Ætna; (2) a town situated upon it.

Symplēgădes, um, f. pl. two floating islands at the entrance of the Euxine.

Synnăda, ōrum, n. pl. a town in Phrygia.

Sȳrācūsæ, ārum, f. pl. Syracuse, ancient capital of Sicily. [Syracusan.

Sȳrācūsānus, a, um, Sȳrācūsius, a, um, a.

Sȳria, ae, f. Syria.

Sȳrius, a, um, Sȳrus, a, um, Sȳriăcus, a, um, Sȳriscus, a, um, a. Syrian.

Sȳros, i, f. one of the Cyclades.

Syrtes, ium, f. pl. two great very dangerous gulfs on the north coast of Africa.

Syrtis, Major and **Minor,** the modern Gulf of Sidra and Gulf of Cabes.

Tænărus, i, c. **Tænărum, i,** n. the most southern point of the Peloponnesus, Cape Matapan. [modern Tajo.

Tăgus, i, m. a river in Lusitania, the

Tămăsus, i, f. a town of Cyprus.

Tămĕsis, is, m. the Thames.

Tănăger, gri, m. a river in Lucania.

Tănagra, ae, f. town in Bœotia.

Tănais, is, m. a river of Sarmatia, the modern Don.

Taprŏbănē, ēs, f. Ceylon.

Tapŭri, ōrum, m. pl. a nomad tribe in Media. [tania.

Tarbelli, ōrum, m. pl. a people in Aqui-

Tărentīnus, a, um, a. of Tarentum.

Tărentum, i, n. Taranto, a city of Calabria.

Tărichēa, ae, f. Sea of Galilee.

Tarquinii, ōrum, m. pl. a town of Etruria.

Tarrăcĭna, ae, f. a town on the coast of Latium, formerly called Anxur.

Tarrăco, ōnis, f. Tarragona, a town in Spain.

Tarsus, i, f. the capital of Cilicia.

Tartessus, i, f. a maritime town in the south of Spain.

Taunus, i, m. a mountain-range in western Germany. [the Crimea.

Tauri, ōrum, m. pl. a barbarous people in

Tauricus, a, um, a. of the Tauri.

Taurīni, ōrum, m. pl. a people of northern Italy, near the modern Turin.

Tauris, ĭdis, f. the modern Crimea.

Taurois, entis, m. a sea-surrounded citadel near Massilia (Marseilles), the modern Tarento.

Taurŏmĕnium, ii, n. Taormina, a town of Sicily. [Minor.

Taurus, i, m. a mountain-chain of Asia

Tȳgĕtus, i, m. a mountain-chain in Laconia.

Teānum, i, n., — Apulum, a town in Apulia; **— Sidicinum,** a town in Campania, the modern Teano.

Teāte, is, n. a town of the Marrucini near the Adriatic coast.

Tectŏsăges, um, m. pl. a people in Gallia Narbonensis.

Tĕgea, ae, f. a town in Arcadia.

Tĕlĕboæ, ārum, m. pl. the inhabitants of several small islands on the coast of Acarnania, and also of Capreæ.

Tĕlēsia, ae, f. town in Samnium.

Telmessus, Telmissus, i, f. a town of Lycia.

Tĕmĕsa, ae, Tĕmĕsē, ēs, Tempsa, ae, f. a town in Bruttium.

Temnos, i, m. a town of Æolia.

Tempē, n. indecl. a valley in Thessaly, through which ran the River Peneus.

Tempȳra, ōrum, n. pl. a town in Thrace.

Tenc(h)tĕri, ōrum, m. pl. a German people on the Rhine.

Tĕnĕdos, Tĕnĕdus, i, f. an island in the Ægean Sea off the Troad.

Tĕnos, i, f. one of the Cyclades, the modern Tino.

Tentȳra, ōrum, n. pl. a city in Upper Egypt, the modern Denderah.

Teos, Teus, i, f. a town in Ionia, the birth-place of Anacreon.

Tĕrentus, i, f. a place in the Campus Martius, where the Ludi Sæculares were held.

Tergeste, is, n. (the modern) Trieste, a town of Istria at the head of the Adriatic.

Tergestīni, ōrum, m. pl. inhabitants of Tergeste.

Tĕrīna, ae, f. town in Bruttium.

Teucria, ae, f. Troyland.

Teucrus, a, um, a. Trojan.

Teutoburgiensis saltus, a forest of Germany in which Varus was defeated and killed in A.D. 9.

Teutŏnes, um, Teutŏni, orum, m. pl. a people of Germany.

Teutŏnicus, a, um, a. Teutonian.

Thala, ae, f. town in Numidia.

Thapsus, i, f. (1) a city in Sicily; (2) a city in Africa.

Thăsus, Thasos, i, f. an island in the Ægean Sea off the coast of Thrace, the modern Thaso.

Thēbæ, ārum, f. pl. (1) a city in Upper Egypt; (2) the capital of Bœotia.

Thēbānus, a, um, a. Theban.

Thĕmiscȳra, ae, f. town in Pontus, in the country of the Amazons.

Thēra, ae, f. one of the Sporades islands.

Thĕrapnæ, ārum, f. pl. a town in Laconia, birthplace of Helen.

Thermæ, ārum, f. pl. a town in Sicily.

Therme, es, f. a town of Macedonia, afterwards Thessalonica.

Thermōdōn, ōntis, m. a river of Pontus, on which dwelt the Amazons.

Thermŏpȳlæ, ārum, f. pl. the famous pass between Thessaly and Locris, where Leonidas fell, 480 B.C.

Thespiæ, ārum, f. pl. a town in Bœotia.

Thesprōtia, ae, f. a district in Epirus.

Thessălia, ae, f. Thessaly, a district in the north of Greece.

Thessălicus, a, um, Thessălus, a, um, a. Thessalian, Thessalic.

Thessălŏnīca, ae, f. a maritime city of Macedonia, the modern Salonica.

Thisbē, ēs, f. a town of Bœotia.

Thrāca, ae, Thrācē, ēs, Thrācia, ae, f. Thrace, a district of North Greece.

Thrācius, a, um, a. Thracian.

Thrax, ācis, m. a Thracian.

Thrōnium, ii, n. town in Locris.

Thūlē, es, f. an island in the extreme north of Europe.

Thūrii, ōrum, m. pl. a city of Lucania, on the Tarentine Gulf.

Thyāmis, is, m. a river in Epirus.

Thyătīra, ae, f. a town in Lydia. [Troas.

Thymbra, ae, Thymbrē, es, f. a city in

Thȳni, ōrum, m. pl. a Thracian people who emigrated to Bithynia.

Thȳrea, ae, a town on the borders of Argolis and Laconia.

Thȳreum, i, n. town in Acarnania.

Tibarăni, ōrum, m. pl. a people in Cilicia.

Tibĕris, is, Tibris, is & ĭdis, m. a river of Latium, on which Rome stood, the Tiber.

Tĭbur, ŭris, n. a town of Latium on the Anio, the modern Tivoli.

Tĭcīnum, i, n. Pavia, a town of Cisalpine Gaul.

Tĭcīnus, i, m. a river of Cisalpine Gaul, the modern Ticino.

Tĭfāta, ōrum, n. pl. a mountain near Capua. [town in Samnium.

Tĭfernum, i, n. (1) town in Umbria; (2)

Tigrănŏcerta, ae, f. or **ōrum,** n. pl., capital of Great Armenia.

Tigris, ĭdis, m. a river of western Asia.

Tigurīni, ōrum, m. pl. a people in the modern canton of Zurich.

Tīmāvus, i, m. river in Istria, between Aquileia and Tergeste, the modern Timavo.

Tīmōlus, v. Tmolus.

Tīryns, nthis & nthos, f. town in Argolis.

Tisse, es, f. a small town in Sicily.

Tissenses, ium, m. pl. inhabitants of Tisse in Sicily. [Epirus.

Tmăros, Tmărus, i, m. a mountain in

Tmōlus, i, m. a mountain of Lydia in which the Pactolus rises.

Tolbiācum, i, n. town in Belgic Gaul, the modern Zulpich.

Tŏlēnus, i, m. river in the Sabine country.

Tŏlētum, i, n. town in Spain, the modern Toledo.

Tŏlōsa, ae, f. a town of Gallia Narbonensis, Toulouse.

Tŏmis, is, f., **Tŏmi, ōrum,** m. pl. a town of Mœsia, on the Euxine, to which Ovid was banished.

Tŏrōnē, ēs, f. a town in Macedonia.

Trăchas, ntis, f., v. **Tarracina.**

Trāchīn, īnis, Trāchȳn, ȳnos, f. a town in southern Thessaly.

Trāchōnītis, īdis, f. a district of Palestine.

Tralles, ium, f. pl. a city of Lydia, near the Mæander.

Trăpezus, untis, f. Trebizond.

Trăsŭmēnus (lacus), i, m. a lake of Etruria, famous for the victory of Hannibal over the Romans in 217 B.C.

Trĕbia, ae, m. the modern Trebbia (river), a river of Cisalpine Gaul famous for the defeat of the Romans by Hannibal in 218 B.C.

Trĕbŭla, ae, f. (1) town in the Sabine country, called also Mutusca; (2) town in Campania.

Trĕvīri, ōrum, m. pl. a people in Gallia Belgica, about the modern Treves.

Triballi, ōrum, m. pl. a Thracian people in Mœsia.

Triboc(c)i, ōrum, m. pl. German tribe in the modern Alsace.

Tricca, ae, f. ancient town in Thessaly.

Trīnăcria, ae, f. Sicily.

Trīnăcrius, a, um, a. Sicilian.

Trinŏbantes, um, m. pl. a people in the eastern part of Britain.

Trĭpŏlis, is, f. (1) a district of Thessaly; (2) town in Africa, on the Syrtis Minor, the modern Tripoli; (3) town and harbour in Phœnicia, the modern Tarablus; (4) a district of Arcadia.

Trītŏn, ōnis, m. a river and lake in Africa, near the Lesser Syrtis, near which Minerva was born.

Trivĭcum, i, n. town in the Hirpine country, the modern Trevico.

Trœzēn, ēnis, f. a city of Argolis.

Trōas, ădis & **ădos,** f. a Trojan woman; the region about Troy, the Troad.

Troglŏdȳtæ, ārum, m. pl. the Troglodytes, cave-dwellers of Æthiopia.

Trōĭcus, a, um, Trōius, a, um, Trōjānus, a, um, a. Trojan.

Trōja, Trōia, ae, f. (1) a city of Asia Minor; (2) a town founded by Æneas in Italy; (3) a town settled by Helenus in Epirus.

Trōjŭgĕna, ae, g.c. Trojan.

Trōs, ōis, m. a Trojan.

Tulliānum, i, n. the dungeon of a prison in Rome standing on the Capitoline Hill.

Tūnes, ētis, m. town on the coast of Africa, (the modern) Tunis.

Tungri, ōrum, m. pl. a people in the country of the modern Liége, with a capital of the same name, the modern Tongres.

Tūria, ae, m. a river in Spain.

Tŭrŏnes, um, m. pl. a people of Gallia, near the modern Tours.

Tusci, ōrum, m. pl. (another name for) Etrusci.　　　　　　[a. Tusculan.

Tuscŭlānensis, e, Tuscŭlīnus, a, um, Tuscŭlānum, i, Cicero's villa at Tusculum.

Tuscŭlŭm, i, a town of Latium, the modern Frascati.

Tuscus, a, um, a. Etrurian, Tuscan.

Tyăna, ōrum, n. pl. a city in Cappadocia (birthplace of Apollonius the wonderworker).

Tȳcha, ae, f. a quarter of Syracuse.

Tȳras, ae, m. a river in Sarmatia, the modern Dniester.

Tyrrhēni, ōrum, m. pl. a Pelasgian people from whom sprung the Etrurians.

Tyrrhēnia, ae, f. Etruria.

Tyrrhenus, a, um, a. Etrurian, Tuscan.

Tȳrius, a, um, a. Tyrian; Carthaginian.

Tȳros, Tȳrus, i, f. a maritime city of the Phœnicians.

Ubii, ōrum, m. pl. a German people on the Rhine;—**Ara Ubiorum,** a place near the modern Bonn.

Ŭfens, tis, m. the modern Uffente, a river of Latium.

Ŭlŭbræ, ārum, f. pl. town of Latium, near the Pontine Marshes.

Umber, bra, brum, a. Umbrian.

Umbri, ōrum, m. pl. a people in Umbria.

Umbria, ae, f. country of the Umbri, a district of Italy on the Adriatic, north of Picenum.

Unelli, v. **Venelli.**

Urbīnum, i, n. town in Umbria, the modern Urbino.

Uscāna, ae, f. town in Illyria.

Ŭsĭpētes, um, m. pl. German people on the Lippe and on the Rhine.

Ustĭca, ae, f. a hill near Horace's Sabine villa.　　　　　　[Carthage.

Ŭtĭca, ae, f. a town in Africa, near

Utĭcensis, e, a. of Utica.

Uxellŏdūnum, i, n. a fortified town of the Cadurci in western Gaul.

Văcălus, i, Văhălis, is, m. the modern Waal (the main western affluent of the Rhine).　　　　　[modern Beja.

Vacca, ae, f. a town of Numidia, the

Vaccæi, ōrum, m. pl. a people of Spain.

Vada, ae, f. citadel in Gallia Belgica.

Văda, ōrum, n. pl. (1) town in Liguria; (2) — **Volaterrana,** town and harbour in Etruria.

Vădĭmōnis lacus, m. a lake in Etruria, the modern Lago di Bassano.

Vaga, v. **Vacca.**

Văhălis, is, v. **Vaculus.**

Vălentia, ae, f. town in Hispania Tarraconensis.

Vandăli, Vandălii, ōrum, m. pl. a people in the northern part of Germany, the Vandals.

Vangiōnes, um, m. pl. a German people, about the modern Worms.

Vardæi, ōrum, m. pl. a people in Dalmatia.

Văria, ae, f. a small town in the Sabine country, the modern Vicovaro.

Varīni, ōrum, m. pl. a German tribe on the Baltic.   [ern Spain.

Vascōnes, um, m. pl. a people of north-

Vătĭcānus (mons, collis), i, m. one of the seven hills of Rome.

Vectis, is, f. the modern Isle of Wight.

Vectōnes, Vettōnes, um, m. pl. a people of Lusitania.

Věii, ōrum, m. pl. a city in Etruria.

Vělābrum, i, n. a district in Rome on the Palatine, where provision dealers dwelt.

Velauni, ōrum, v. Vellavi.

Vělia, ae, f. (1) a part of the Palatine Hill, at Rome; (2) a town on the coast of Lucania, called also Elea.

Vělīnus, i, m. a river in the Sabine territory; a lake formed by it.

Vělĭtræ, ārum, f. pl. Velletri, a town of Latium.

Vellaunŏdūnum, i, n. town in the country of the Senones in Gaul.

Vellavii, ōrum, m. pl. a Celtic tribe, about Le Puy in the old Velay.

Velocasses, Veliocasses, ium, ōrum, m. pl. a people on the right bank of the Seine.

Věnāfrum, i, n. a town of the Samnites, the modern Venafri.

Věnelli, ōrum, m. pl. a people in Armorica in Normandy.

Věněti, ōrum, m. pl. a people in the north-east of Italy; a people of the north-west of Gaul.

Věnětia, ae, f. country of the Veneti.

Věnětus, a, um, a. Venetian.

Věnŭsia, ae, f. a town of Apulia, the modern Venosa.

Veragri, ōrum, m. pl. an Alpine people in Gallia Narbonensis.   [alpina.

Vercellæ, ārum, f. pl. town in Gallia Cis-

Veromandui, ōrum, m. pl. a people of Belgic Gaul, in the modern Vermandais.

Vērōna, ae, f. a town of Transpadane Gaul, still called Verona.

Vērōnensis, e, a. of Verona.

Verulamium, ii, n. St. Albans.

Vesbius, ii, m. Vesuvius.

Vescia, ae, f. a town on the river Liris.

Vesěris, is, m. a river in Campania, with a town of the same name.   [Vesuvius.

Věsēvus, a, um, a. of or belonging to

Věsontio, ōnis, m. capital of the Sequani, (the modern) Besançon.

Vestīni, ōrum, m. pl. a people of central Italy on the Adriatic Sea.

Věsŭlus, i, m. a mountain of Liguria, (the modern) Monte Viso.

Věsŭvius, ii, m. a volcano in Campania.

Vettōnes, v. Vectones.

Vibo, ōnis, f. town and harbour on the western coast of Bruttium.   [Vicenza.

Vīcētia, ae, f. a town of Transpadane Gaul,

Vienna, ae, f. capital of the Allobroges in Gallia Narbonensis, (the modern) Vienne.

Viennensis, e, a. of Vienne.

Vīmĭnālis collis, m. one of the seven hills of Rome.   [ern Germany.

Vindělĭci, ōrum, m. pl. a people of south-

Vindŏbŏna, ae, f. Vienna.

Vistŭla, ae, f. the Vistula (river).

Visurgis, is, m. the Weser (river).

Vitellia, ae, f. town in Latium.

Vŏcontii, ōrum, m. pl. a people of Gallia Narbonensis.

Vŏlăterræ, ārum, f. pl. a town of Etruria, Volterra.

Volcæ, ārum, m. pl. a people in Gallia Narbonensis.   [of Latium.

Volsci, ōrum, m. pl. a people in the south

Volscus, a, um, a. of the Volsci.

Volsinii, ōrum, m. pl. a town of Etruria, Bolsena.   [Alsace.

Vŏsěgus, i, m. the Vosges mountains in

Vulsci, v. Volsci.

Vultur, ŭris, m. a mountain in Apulia.

Vulturnum, i, n. town in Campania.

Vulturnus, i, m. Volturno (river of Campania).

Xanthus, i, m. (1) a river of Troas; (2) a river in Lycia.

Xȳniæ, ārum, f. pl. town in Thessaly on the lake Xynias.

Zăcynthus, i, f. Zante, an island of the Ionian Sea.

Zăma, ae, f. a town in Numidia, famous for Scipio's victory over Hannibal, 202 B.C.

Zanclē, ēs, f. old name of Messana.

Zēla, ae, f. town on the border of Armenia.   [of Cilicia.

Zěphȳrium, ii, n. town and promontory

Zērynthus, i, f. a town in Thrace.

Zeugma, ătis, n. a town in Syria.

Zmyrna, v. Smyrna.

Zōstēr, ēris, m. promontory and seaport town of Attica.

ENGLISH—LATIN

A, indefinite article, generally unexpressed in Latin; unus (a, um); quidam; is (ea, id); —, a particle, e.g. **a-bed,** in lecto.

Aaron's rod, s. verbascum (mod. hort.).

aback, ad. a tergo ; retro ; **taken —,** *fig.* stupefactus, attonitus, consternatus.

abaft, ad. in puppi.

abandon, v.a. (de)relinquo, desero, destituo, abjicio, omitto, neglěgo, 3.

abandoned, a. derelictus; desertus; *fig.* flagitiosus, perditus.

abandoning, abandonment, s. derelictio, destitutio, f.

abase, v.a. deprimo; demitto; *fig.* reprimo, 3. minuo.

abasement, s. demissio; dejectio, f.

abash, v.a. confundo; pudore afficio, 3.

abashed, p. & a. pudibundus.

abate, v.a. (to make lower) imminuo, 3; (to slacken) laxo, 1; (price) remitto, detraho, 3; (to lighten) levo, sublevo, 1; —, v.n. (to lessen) imminuo, decresco; (to decline, etc.) cado, decedo, 3.

abatement, s. remissio; detractio, f.

abbess, s. abbatissa, f.

abbey, s. abbatia, f.

abbot, s. abbas, atis, m.   [contraho, 3.

abbreviate, v.a. abbrevio, 1; imminuo,

abbreviation, s. contractio, f.; compendium, n.

abdicate, v.a. & n. abdico, 1 (se, with abl.); depono, 3.

abdication, s. abdicatio, f.

abdomen, s. abdomen, n.

abduct, v.a. rapio, 3.

abduction, s. raptus, us, m.

aberration, s. error, m.

abet, v.a. adjuvo, instigo, 1; faveo, 2.

abetter, s. instigator, impulsor, m.

abeyance, s. **in —,** vacuus.   [sor, 1.

abhor, v.a. abhorreo, 2; detestor, aver-

abhorrence, s. odium, n.

abhorrent, a. perosus; odiosus; alienus.

abide, v.a. patior, 3; tolero, 1; subeo, 4; expecto, 1; —, v.n. habito, 1; maneo, 2; **to — by,** sto (abl.) 1; (defend) defendo, 3.

abiding, a. mansūrus; constans, fidus; —, s. commoratio, f.

abidingly, ad. constanter.

ability, s. facultas; peritia, f.; ingenium, n.; **to the best of one's —,** summa ope.

abject, a. abjectus, vilis; humilis.

abjectly, ad. humiliter; abjecte.

abjectness, s. humilitas, f.; sordes, f. pl.

abjuration, s. ejuratio, f.; (avoidance) fuga . . . f.

abjure, v.a. abjuro, ejuro, 1; (avoid) renuntio, 1.

ablative (case), s. ablativus, m.

able, a. potens; capax, peritus; ingeniosus; **to be — (to),** posse, valere, 2; quire, 4; sufficere, 3.

able-bodied, a. validus, robustus, firmus.

ablution, s. ablutio, lavatio, f.

ably, ad. ingeniose.

abnegation, s. contemptio, f.; rejectio, f.

abnormal, a. abnormis.

aboard, ad. in nave; **to go — a ship,** navem conscendere, 3.

abode, s. domicilium, n.; sedes, f.; (sojourn) commoratio; mansio, f.

abolish, v.a. aboleo, 2; exstinguo, tollo rescindo, 3.

abolition, s. abolitio, dissolutio, f.

abominable, a. detestabilis, execrabilis, infandus; odiosus.

abominably, ad. odiose.   [sor, 1.

abominate, v.a. abominor, detestor, aver-

abomination, s. detestatio, f.; odium, n.; **abominations,** (vile acts) nefaria, n.pl.

aborigines, s. aborigines, indigenæ, m. pl.

abortion, s. abortus, us, m.

abortive, a. abortivus; *fig.* irritus.

abortively, ad. *fig.* frustra.

abound, v.n. abundo, redundo, 1; supersum; supero, 1; **to — in,** abundo, 1; (with abl.).

abounding, a. abundans; copiosus, largus; creber.

about, pr. circa, circum (with acc.) ad, apud; circiter; fere; sub; de; super; —, ad. circiter; ferme; (as it were) quasi; **to be — to . . .** (f.e. write, etc.), scripturus, etc.; **to go —,** aggredior, incipio, 3; **to bring about,** efficio, 3.

251

above, pr. (higher) super, supra; (beyond, more than) ante; præter, ultra; (superior), superior; —, ad. supra; insuper; plus, magis; (upwards) sursum; **from** —, desuper, superne; **to be** —, emineo, 2; *fig.* dedignor, 1; fastidio, 4; **over and** —, insuper.

above-board, ad. *fig.* aperte, candide.

above-mentioned, a. quod supra dictum est.

abrade, v.a. abrado, 3.

abrasion, s. attritus, us, m.; ulcus, n.

abreast, ad. ex adverso.

abridge, v.a. contraho, 3.

abridgment, s. contractio, f., compendium, n.

abroach, ad. terebratus; **to set** —, relino, 3.

abroad, ad. foris; (out of doors) foras; (in foreign parts) peregre; (here and there) passim, undique; **from** —, extrinsecus; peregre; **to be** (*or* **live**) —, peregrinor, 1; patria careo, 2; **to get** —, *fig.* divulgari, 1.

abrogate, v.a. abrogo, 1; rescindo, 3.

abrogation, s. abrogatio, f.

abrupt, a. præruptus; præceps; *fig.* subitus, repentinus; improvisus; (of style) abruptus.

abruptly, ad. abrupte; raptim.

abruptness, s. declivitas; celeritas, festinatio, f.

abscess, s. ulcus, n.

abscond, v.n. me clam subduco, me abdo, lateo, 2; latito, 1.

absence, s. absentia; peregrinatio, f.; *fig.* (of mind) forgetfulness, oblivio, f.

absent, a. absens; **to be** —, abesse, peregrinari; *fig.* animo vagari.

absent, v.r. **to** — **oneself,** non comparere, 2.

absentee, s. peregrinator, m.

absinth, s. absinthium, n.

absolute, a. absolutus; summus; *fig.* (frank) sincerus.

absolutely, ad. absolutē; prorsus; (entirely) penitus.

absolution, a. absolutio; indulgentia, f.

absolve, v.a. veniam do, 1; absolvo, 3; libero, 1; dimitto, 3.

absorb, v.a. absorbeo, 2; haurio, 4; combibo, 3; *fig.* teneo, 2.

absorbent, a. (of stones, etc.) bibulus; —, s. absorbens, n.

abstain, v.n. abstineo, 2.

abstemious, s. abstemius; sobrius; —**ly,** ad. sobrie, temperate.

abstemiousness, s. continentia, temperantia, f.

abstinence, s. abstinentia, *fig.* (fasting) jejunium, n.

abstinent, a. abstinens; —**ly,** ad. abstinenter, continenter.

abstract, v.a. abstraho, 3; separo, 1; sejungo, excludo, 3.

abstract, a. abstractus; ab oculis sevocatus, (in the abstract, in thought) cogitatione.

abstract, a. compendium, n.

abstracted, a. (in mind) parum attentus; —**ly,** ad. parum attente.

abstraction, s. separatio, f.; (concept of the mind) imago, f.

abstruse, a. abstrusus; reconditus; obscurus, occultus; —**ly,** ad. abdite, occulte.

abstruseness, s. obscuritas, f.

absurd, a. absurdus, insulsus; ineptus, ridiculus; —**ly,** ad. inepte, absurde.

absurdity, s. ineptia; insulsitas; res inepta, f. [tas, f.

abundance, s. abundantia, copia, uber-

abundant, a. abundans; amplus; copiosus, plenus; uber; **to be** —, abundo, 1.

abundantly, ad. abunde, abundanter, copiose; effuse; (fruitfully) feliciter.

abuse, v.a. (to misuse) abutor, 3; *fig.* (to insult, etc.) maledico, 3; convicior, lacero, 1; (to deceive) decipio, 3.

abuse, s. (wrong use) abusus; perversus mos, m.; (insult) injuria, f., convicium, n.; violatio, f.

abuser, s. conviciator, m.

abusive, a. contumeliosus; maledicus; —**ly,** ad. contumeliose; maledice.

abut, v.n. adjaceo, immineo, 2.

abutting, a. confinis, conterminus.

abyss, s. abyssus, f. profundum, n.; (whirlpool) gurges, m.; *fig.* vorago, f.

acacia, s. acacia, f.

academic, a. academicus; —**ally,** ad. ut solent academici.

academy, s. Academia; collegium, f. c

accede, v.n. accedo, annuo, 3; assentior, 4. [pero, 1.

accelerate, v.a. accelero, festino, appro-

acceleration, s. festinatio, f.

accent, s. accentus; tenor; *fig.* sonus, m.; lingua, f. [writing) fastigo, 1.

accent, v.a. (in speaking) acuo, 3; (in

accentuation, s. accentus, m.

accept, v.a. accipio; recipio, 3; (approve of) probo, 1; (agree to) assentior, 4.

acceptable, a. acceptus, gratus; jucundus.

acceptably, ad. grate; (opportunely) opportune.

acceptance, s. acceptio; approbatio.

acceptation, s. acceptio, f.; *fig.* sensus, f.; significatio, f.

access, s. aditus; accessus, m.; (of fever, etc.) accessio, f.; **to have** —, admitti, 3.

accessible, a. patens; *fig.* affabilis, facilis.

accession, s. (increase) accessio, f.; incrementum, n.; cumulus, m.; (to the throne) regni principium, n.

accessory, a. adjunctus; (of crimes) conscius; —, s. particeps, c., conscius, m.

accidence, s. grammaticēs elementa, n. pl.

accident, s. casus; (by accident) casu, fortuito, temere.

accidental, a. fortuitus; —**ally,** ad. casu; fortuito.

acclamation, s. acclamatio, f., clamor, consensus, plausus, m.

acclimatize, v.a. assuefacio, 3.

acclivity, s. acclivitas, f.

accommodate, v.a. accommodo, apto, 1; *fig.* (have room for) capio, 3; **to — oneself,** obsequor, 3.

accommodation, s. accommodatio, f.; (convenience) commoditas, f.; (money) commodum; (lodgment) deversorium, n.; (space) locus, m.; spatium, n.

accompany, v.a. comitor, 1; (escort) deduco, 3; (mus.) concino, 3.

accomplice, s. particeps, conscius (rei); (of crimes *or* vices) satelles, m.

accomplish, v.a. exequor, perficio; perago, 3; impleo, 2.

accomplished, a. *fig.* eruditus; doctus; (eloquent) disertus.

accomplishment, s. exsecutio, effectio; (skill) ars, f.

accord, s. consensus, m., concordia, f.; **of one's own —,** sponte; ultro; **with one —,** uno ore.

accord, v.a. (grant) concedo, 3; v.n. congruo, 3; concordo, 1; convenio, 4.

accordance, s., v. **accord,** s.; **in — with,** secundum.

.ccording, pr. — **to,** de, ex, pro, secundum; — **as,** prout.

accordingly, ad. itaque; ita; (therefore) igitur, ergo.

accost, v.a. appello; compello, 1; alloquor, 3.

account, s. (reckoning, of money) ratio, f.; (narrative) memoria; narratio, f.; (esteem) reputatio, f.; (advantage) commodum, n.; *fig.* **on — of . . .,** ob, propter, causa; **on that —,** propterea; ideo; **to call to —,** rationem poscere, 3; **of little** *or* **no —,** nullius pretii, vilis.

account, v.a. (to esteem) æstimo, 1; habeo, 2; pendo, pono, 3; —, v.n. rationem reddo; causam affero, 3; **to — for,** rationem reddere, 3.

accountable, a. reus, rationem reddere debens.

accountant, s. calculator, m.; tabularius.

account-book, s. tabulæ, f. pl.

accoutre, v.a. apparo, 1; instruo, 3.

accoutrement, s. arma; insignia, n. pl., ornatus; apparatus, m.

accrue, v.a. orior; accresco, 3; provenio, 4.

accumulate, v.a. accumulo, coacervo, 1; congero, 3; —, v.n. cresco, 3; congeror.

accumulation, s. (heap, etc.) cumulus; acervus; *fig.* congestus, m.

accumulator, s. accumulator, m.

accuracy, s. cura; subtilitas, f.

accurate, a. accuratus; subtilis; —**ly,** ad. accurate, subtiliter.

accursed, a. exsecratus; scelestus; sceleratus.

accusation, s. accusatio, f.; crimen, n.

accusative (case), s. accusativus, m.

accusatory, a. accusatorius.

accuse, v.a. accuso; criminor, 1; (to blame) reprehendo, 3; **to — falsely,** calumniari, 1.

accuser, s. accusator; (informer) delator; **false —,** calumniator.

accustom, v.a. assuefacio, 3; **to — oneself,** assuefieri, consuescere, 3; **to be —ed,** solitus esse.

accustomed, a. assuetus, consuetus, solitus.

acerbity, s. acerbitas; *fig.* severitas, f.

ache, v.n. doleo, 2; **my head —s,** caput mihi dolet.

ache, s. dolor, m.

achieve, v.a. patro, 1; consequor, conficio, perficio, 3.

achievement, s. res gesta, f.; facinus, n.

aching, s. dolor, m.

acid, a. acidus; acidulus.

acid, s. acidum, n.

acidity, s. aciditas, f.

acidulous, a. acidulus.

acknowledge, v.a. agnosco, recognosco, 3; fateor, confiteor, 2.

acknowledgment, s. agnitio; confessio, f.

acme, s. fastigium, n.; (the acme of folly) summa dementia.

aconite, s. aconitum, n.

acorn, s. glans, f.; — **-bearing,** a. glandifer.

acquaint, v.a. certiorem facio, 3; **to — oneself** (with), noscere, cognoscere, 3.

acquaintance, s. scientia; (intimacy with) familiaritas; notitia, f.; (as person) familiaris, c.

acquainted, a. gnarus (rei); (with) prudens (locorum, etc.); peritus (rei *or* re); **to become —,** noscere, cognoscere.

acquiesce, v.n. (in) acquiesco, 3; assentior, 4; probo, 1.

acquiescence, s. assensus, m.; approbatio, f.

acquire, v.a. comparo, 1; nanciscor, consequor, pario, adipiscor, 3; *fig.* disco, 3.

acquirement, s. adeptio, f.; eruditio, f.; comparatio.

acquisition, s. (acquiring) conciliatio, comparatio, f.; (thing acquired) quæsitum, n.

acquit, v.a. absolvo, 3; libero, purgo, 1; **to — oneself,** se gerere, 3.

acquittal, s. absolutio, f.

acquittance, s. acceptilatio, f.

acre, s. jugerum, n.; **by —,** jugeratim.

acrid, a. acerbus, acer.

acridity, s. acerbitas, f.   [culentus.

acrimonious, a. acerbus; *fig.* asper, tru-

acrimony, s. acrimonia; amaritudo, f.

acrobat, s. funambulus, m.

across, pr. trans.; ad. ex transverso, in transversum.

act, v.n. ago, facio; gero, 3; (behave) me gero, 3; (exert force) vim habeo, 2; (on the stage) in scænam prodeo, 4; —, v.a. (as actor) (comœdiam, primam partem) ago, 3.

act, s. (deed, action) factum; gestum, n.; (exploit) facinus, n.; (decree) decretum, m.; (in a play) actus, m.; **— of indemnity,** lex oblivionis, f.; **be caught in the very —,** deprehendi; **—s,** pl. acta, n. pl.

acting, s. actio; f.

action, s. actio, f.; actus, m.; (battle) pugna, f.; (gesture) gestus, m.; (law) actio, f.; **to bring an — against one,** actionem alicui intendere, 3.

actionable, a. (judicio) obnoxius.

active, a. agilis; impiger, industrius, operosus; strenuus; vividus; (gr.) activus; **—ly,** ad. impigre; strenue; (gr.) active.   [gnavitas, f.

activity, s. agilitas, mobilitas; industria,

actor, s. (in a play) comœdus, histrio; mimus; artifex scænicus; (doer) auctor; qui agit, m.

actress, s. mima, f.

actual, a. verus, ipse; **—ly,** ad. re vera, re ipsa.

actuality, s. (reality) veritas, f.

actuary, s. tabularius, m.

actuate, v.a. moveo, 2; impello, 3; incito, 1.

acumen, s. sagacitas, f.; ingenium, n.

acute, a. acutus; acer; (of the understanding) sagax, subtilis; (witty) salsus; **—ly,** ad. acute; acriter; (shrewdly) sagaciter.

acuteness, s. acies, f.; *fig.* acumen, n. subtilitas, f.; **—shrewdness,** sagacitas.

adage, s. proverbium, n.

adamant, f. adamas, m.   [tinus.

adamantine. a. adamanteus; adaman-

adapt, v.a. accommodo, apto, 1.

adaptation, s. accommodatio, f.

adapted, a. aptus.

add, v.a. addo; appono, adjungo, adjicio, 3; (in speaking) adjicio, 3; (to reckon) adscribo; (in writing) subjungo, 3; **to — up,** computo, 1; **to be —ed,** accedo, 3.

adder, s. coluber, m., vipera, f.

adder-tongue fern, s. ophioglossum (mod. hort.).

addict, to be —ed (to), v.r. deditus esse (be wont) solitus esse.

addicted, a. deditus, studiosus.

addition, s. additamentum, n.; adjectio; accessio.

additional, a. additicius.

addled, a. (of eggs) (ovum) irritum, zephyrium.   [stultus.

addle-headed, a. *fig.* inanis, vanus, fatuus,

address, v.a. (to direct to) inscribo, 3; (to speak to) alloquor, aggredior, 3. *See* **accost.**

address, s. (speaking to) alloquium, n. allocutio; (direction) inscriptio, f.; (petition) libellus supplex, m.; *fig.* dexteritas, f. ars; (speech) oratio, contio, f.

adduce, v.a. (witnesses) profero, 3; (to quote) cito, 1; adduco, 3.

adept, a. peritus; —, s. (master in a thing) peritus (with genitive), m.

adequacy, s. sufficientia, f.

adequate, a. sufficiens, par.

adhere, v.n. adhæreo; cohæreo, 2; *fig.* sto (in), 1.

adherence, s. adhæsio, f.

adherent, s. assectator; fautor; particeps, socius; (dependent) cliens, m.

adhesion, s. adhæsio, f.

adhesive, a. tenax, lentus.

adhesiveness, s. lentitia; tenacitas, f.

adieu, i. ave, salve, vale; **to bid —,** valedico, 3; valere jubeo, 2.

adjacent, a. confinis, conterminus; vicinus.

adjective, s. adjectivum (nomen), n.

adjoin, v. adjaceo, 2.

adjoining, a. adjacens, confinis, vicinus.

adjourn, v.a. comperendino, 1; differo, profero, 3; —, v.n. differri.

adjournment, s. dilatio, prolatio, f.

adjudge, v.a. addico, 3; adjudico, 1.

adjudicate, v.a. addico, decerno, 3.

adjudication, s. addictio; (verdict) sententia, f., arbitrium, n.

adjunct, s. accessio, f.

adjuration, s. obtestatio; obsecratio, f.

adjure, v.a. obsecro, obtestor, 1.

adjust, v.a. apto, 1; dispono, 3; (settle) compono, 3; ordino 1.

adjustment, a. accommodatio, compositio, ordinatio, f.

adjutancy, s. optionatus, m.

adjutant, s. optio, m.

admeasurement, s. mensura, f.

administer, v.a. (to manage, etc.) administro, curo, procuro, 1; (medicine, etc.) adhibeo, 2; (an oath) adigo, 3; (justice) exerceo, 2; reddo, 3; (to contribute) suppedito, 1.

administration, s. administratio; cura; procuratio, f.; magistratus, m.; (task of managing public affairs) summa rerum. [curator, m.

administrator, s. administrator; pro-

admirable, a. admirabilis; mirabilis, admirandus; insignis.

admirableness, s. admirabilitas, f.

admirably, ad. admirabiliter; præclare, insigniter.

admiral, s. præfectus classis, m.

admiralty, s. qui rei maritimæ præpositi sunt. [abiliter.

admiration, s. admiratio, f.; to —, admir-

admire, v.a. admiror; amo, 1.

admirer, s. admirator; mirator; laudator; amans, m. [dendus.

admissible, a. accipiendus, aptus, conce-

admission, s. admissio, f.; aditus, accessus, m.

admit, v.a. admitto; recipio; introduco; (adopt) ascisco, 3; (confess) fateor, confiteor, 2; it is —ted, constat. [m.

admittance, s. admissio, aditus, accessus,

admixture, s. admixtio, f.

admonish, v.a. moneo, commoneo, 2.

admonisher, s. monitor, admonitor, m.

admonition, s. monitio, admonitio, f.; adhortatio; (the contents of an admonition) monitum, n.

admonitory, a. monitorius.

ado, s. tumultus, m.; with much —, ægre, vix; without more —, statim.

adolescence, s. adolescentia, f.

adolescent, a. adolescens.

adopt, v.a. (a minor) adopto, (an adult) arrogo, 1; fig. ascisco; assumo, 3; (a policy, etc.) capio, 3; ineo, 4.

adoption, s. adoptio, adoptatio; (of an adult) arrogatio; fig. assumptio, f.

adoptive, a. adoptivus.

adorable, a. adorandus, venerandus; (lovable) amandus.

adoration, s. adoratio, f.; (love) amor, m.

adore, v.a. adoro, veneror, fig. admiror, amo, 1.

adorer, s. cultor, m.; (lover) amator, m.

adorn, v.a. orno, decoro, distinguo, illustro, 1; excolo, como, 3.

adornment, s. exornatio, f.; ornatus, m.; ornamentum, n.

Adriatic Sea, s. Hadria, m. [fluctuor, 1.

adrift, ad. in salo fluctuans; be —, v.

adroit, a. callidus, dexter, sollers, peritus, ingeniosus; —ly, ad. callide, sollerter, perite, ingeniose.

adroitness, s. dexteritas, f.

adulation, s. adulatio, assentatio, f.

adulator, s. assentator, m.

adulatory, a. adulatorius, blandus.

adult, a. adultus; pubes; —, s. adultus homo, puber; (youth collectively) pubes, f.

adulterate, v.a. adultero, vitio, 1; corrumpo, 3; (mix) commisceo, 2.

adulteration, s. adulteratio, (mixture) admixtio, f.

adulterer, s. adulter; mœchus, m.

adulteress, s. adultera; mœcha, f.

adulterous, a. adulterinus; —ly, ad. adulterio, per adulterium.

adultery, s. adulterium; stuprum, n.; to commit —, mœchor, 1.

adumbrate, v.a. adumbro, 1.

advance, v.a. promoveo, 2; (to lift up) tollo, attollo, 3; exalto, 1; erigo; (an opinion) exhibeo, 2; profero, 3; (lend) commodo, 1; (accelerate) maturo, 1; (advance a person's interests) alicui consulo, 3; rebus alicujus studeo, 2; —, v.n. procedo, progredior, incedo, 3; (mil.) gradum (pedem) infero, 3; fig. proficio, 3.

advance, s. progressus; (step) passus, m.; (attack) incursio, f.; (in rank) accessio dignitatis, f.; (increase, rise) incrementum, n.

advanced, a. provectus; (of age) grandis.

advance-guard, s. antecursores, m. pl., primum agmen, n.

advancement, s. dignitatis accessio.

advantage, s. lucrum, commodum, emolumentum, n.; utilitas, f.; fructus; usus, m.; (blessings) bona, n. pl.; to have an — of, præsto, 1; superior sum; to make or take — of, utor, 3; to be of —, prosum. [expedit, 4.

advantage, v.a. prosum; (it advantages)

advantageous, a. fructuosus; utilis; commodus; —ly, ad. utiliter; bene; commode. [astically).

advent, s. adventus, us, m. (also ecclesi-

adventitious, a. adventicius.

adventure, s. casus, m.; (as action) facinus, n. [trial) periclitor, 1.

adventure, v.a. & n. audeo, 2; (put to

adventurer, s. (mil.) latro, pirata, m.

adventurous, a. audax; —ly, ad. audacter.

adverb, s. adverbium, n.

adverbial, a. adverbialis; —ly, ad. adverbialiter.

adversary, s. adversarius, m.; inimicus, m.; adversatrix, inimica, f.

adverse. a. adversus, infestus; *fig.* asper; —ly, ad. secus, infeliciter.

adversity, s. res adversæ, f. pl.; calamitas, f.; res asperæ, f. pl.

advert (to), v.n. (to speak of) attingo, 3; (to look at) considero, 1; animum adverto, 3.

advertence, s. consideratio, cura, f.; respectus, m.

advertise, v.a. (warn) commonefacio, certiorem facio, 3; (to publish) divulgo, 1; (try to sell) vendito, 1.

advertisement, s. venditatio, 1.

advertiser, s. venditator, m.

advice, s. consilium, n.; **to ask** —, consulo, 3; **to give** —, moneo, 2; (information, intelligence) indicium, n.

advisable, a. commodus, utilis; **it is** —, expedit, 4.

advisableness, s. utilitas, f.

advise, v.a. moneo; (persuade) suadeo, 2; (with) consulo, 3; (to the contrary) dissuadeo, 2; (exhort) hortor, 1.

advisedly, ad. consulto, consilio.

advisedness, s. cautela, prudentia, f.

adviser, s. consultor, monitor, suasor, auctor, m.

advocacy, s. patrocinium, n.

advocate, s. advocatus, causidicus; patronus; (one who persuades) suasor, m.; (defender) defensor, m.

advocate, v.a. suadeo, 2.

adze, s. ascia, f.

ædile, s. ædilis, m.

ægis, s. ægis, f.

aerial, a. aerius, aethereus.

aerolyte, s. lapis de cœlo missus, m.

afar, ad. procul, longe; **from** —, e longinquo.

affability, s. comitas, affabilitas, facilitas, f.

affable, a. affabilis, comis, facilis.

affably, ad. comiter.

affair, s. res, f.; negotium, n.

affect, v.a. afficio, 3; commoveo, 2; percutio, 3; (with joy) gaudio afficio, 3; (aim at) affecto, 1; expeto, sequor, 3; (pretend) simulo, 1.

affectation, s. simulatio; affectatio, f.

affected, a. simulatus, fictus; (in style, etc.) putidus; quæsitus.

affectedly, ad. putide.

affectingly, ad. misere, miserabiliter.

affection, s. (state of mind *or* body) affectus, m.; affectio, f.; (love) amor, m.; gratia; benevolentia, f.; (feeling) affectus, impetus, motus; sensus, m.

affectionate, a. amans, benevolus, pius; blandus; —ly, ad. amanter; pie, blande.

affectionateness, s. pietas, f.

affiance, s. sponsalia, ium, n. pl.

affiance, v.a. spondeo, despondeo, 2.

affidavit, s. jusjurandum, n., fides, f.

affinity, s. affinitas; cognatio, proximitas, f.

affirm, v.a. affirmo, assevero, testificor, 1.

affirmation, s. affirmatio, f.; asseveratio, n. [—, v. aio.

affirmative, a. aiens; **to answer in the affix,** v.a. affigo, 3.

afflatus, s. afflatus, m.; numen, n.

afflict, v.a. torqueo, 2; vexo, crucio, 1.

affliction, s. miseria, f.; res adversæ, f. pl.

affluence, s. abundantia, copia, f.; divitiæ, f. pl.

affluent, a. abundans, affluens; dives; —ly, ad. abundanter.

afford, v.a. præbeo, 2; (to yield) reddo, fero, fundo, 3; (supply) sufficio, 3; (buy) emo, 3.

affray, s. rixa, f.

affright, v.a. terreo, 2; pavefacio, 3.

affright, v. **fright.**

affront, v.a. irrito, 1; contumelia afficio, 3; —, s. contumelia, injuria, f.

afoot, ad. pedibus, pedes; **to set** —, in medium proferre, molior; **to be** —, parari.

aforesaid, a. supra dictus.

afraid, a. timidus, pavidus; **to be** — (**of**), timeo, 2; (much) pertimesco, 2; expavesco, 3; **to make** —, terreo, 2; territo, 1; **not** —, impavidus, intrepidus. [denuo.

afresh, ad. de integro, ab integro, iterum, **aft,** ad. a puppi; *fig.* a tergo.

after, pr. post; a, de, e, ex; (one after another) alius ex alio; (following immediately upon) sub; (of degree *or* succession) juxta; secundum; (in imitation of) ad; (afterwards) exinde, postea, posterius; post; — **all,** tamen; saltem; **a little** —, paulo post; **the day** —, postridie; — **that,** (when) postquam, posteaquam.

after, a. futurus, posterus.

after-ages, s. posteritas, f.

afternoon, s. post meridiem, n.; —, a. postmeridianus, pomeridianus.

after-thought, s. posterior cogitatio, f.

afterwards, ad. post; postea; deinde, deinceps, dehinc.,

again, ad. iterum, denuo, rursum, rursus; (hereafter) post, postea, posthac; jam; porro; (likewise, in turn) invicem, mutuo, vicissim; contra; (besides) præterea; (after verbs) re . . .; **as high** —, duplo altior; **over** —, ab integro; **to and** —, ultro citroque; — **and** —, iterum atque iterum.

against, pr. (opposite to), contra; adversus; (denoting attack) in; (by, at) ad, ante; (relating to time) ante; **to be —,** adversor, oppugno, 1; **fight —,** pugno cum.

agapanthus, s. agapanthus (mod. hort.).

agape, a. hians, attonitus.

agaric, s. agaricum, n.

agate, s. achates, ae, m. & f.

age, s. ætas, f.; (century) sæculum; (time in general) tempus, n.; (old —) senectus, f.; **of full —,** maturus, adultus; **under —,** impubis; **of the same —,** æquævus.

aged, a. ætate provectus; senilis; (of a certain age) natus (with accus. of annus). [curatio, f.

agency, s. (medium) opera; (office) pro-

agent, s. actor; auctor; (assistant) satelles, c.; administer, m.

agglomerate, v.a. glomero, agglomero, 1; —, v.n. glomeror, agglomeror, 1.

agglutinate, v.a. agglutino, 1.

aggrandize, v.a. amplifico, 1; attollo, 3; augeo, 2. [crementum, n.

aggrandizement, s. amplificatio, f.; in-

aggravate, v.a. augeo, 2; exaggero, 1.

aggravation, s. exaggeratio, f.

aggregate, v.a. confero, 3; congrego, 1.

aggregate, a. totus.

aggregate, s. summa, f.; v. **aggregation.**

aggregation, s. congregatio, f.

aggression, s. incursio, f.

aggressive, a. arma (ultro) inferens; (pugnacious) pugnax.

aggressor, s. qui bellum infert; qui alterum prior lacessit, m.

aggrieve, v.a. dolore afficio; injuriam infero, 3; **feel oneself —d,** ægre fero, 3.

aghast, a. attonitus, consternatus.

agile, a. agilis; pernix.

agility, s. agilitas; pernicitas, f.

agio, s. collybus, i, m.

agitate, v.a. agito, 1; commoveo, 2; perturbo, 1; **—d,** a. tumultuosus; turbulentus; (anxious) sollicitus.

agitation, s. agitatio; commotio; jactatio, f.; *fig.* tumultus, m.; trepidatio, f.

agitator, s. concitator; turbator (populi *or* vulgi), m.

agnail, s. reduvia, f.

agnate, s. agnatus, i., m.

ago, ad. abhinc; **long —,** jamdudum; **a while —,** haud ita pridem; **how long — ?** quamdudum; **some time —,** pridem.

agog, ad. cupidus; (astonished) attonitus.

agoing, a. **to set —,** moveo, cieo, 2.

agonize, v.n. discrucior, crucior, 1.

agonizing, a. crucians.

agony, s. dolor, m.; cruciatus, m.

agrarian, a. agrarius.

agree, v.n. in opinion; (to be in harmony) congruo, 3; concordo, 1; concino, 3; consentio, 4; (to make a bargain) paciscor, 3; (to answer to) respondeo, 2; (to be agreeable) placeo, 2; (to assent) annuo, 3; assentior, 4; **it is —d,** constat; **it is —d upon,** convenit.

agreeable, a. gratus, acceptus; amabilis; (consistent) congruens, conveniens; **very —,** pergratus.

agreeableness, s. dulcedo, suavitas; gratia, f.; (grace) lepor, m.

agreeably, ad. grate, jucunde; suaviter; (to) congruenter (with dat.).

agreement, s. consensus, m.; (covenant) pactum, n.; stipulatio, f.; conventum; (bargain) condicio, f.; (harmonious arrangement) concinnitas, f.; (*fig.* harmony) consensio, f.; (in time) concentus, m.

agricultural, a. rusticus.

agriculture, s. agri cultura, f.; res rustica, f.

agriculturist, s. agricola, m.

agrimony, s. agrimonia (mod. hort.).

aground, ad.; **to run —,** in terram appellere, 3; (be stranded) ejicior, 3; **be —,** (touch bottom) sido, 3.

ague, s. febris, f.

aguish, a. febriculosus.

ah, i. ah! eia! vah! væ!

ahead, ad. ante, (get ahead of) prætereo, 4.

aid, s. auxilium; subsidium, n.; **by the — of,** opera.

aid, v.a. adjuto, juvo, 1; succurro, 3; subvenio, 4.

aide-de-camp, s. optio, m.

aider, s. particeps, c.; adjutor, m.

ail, v.a. doleo, 2.

ailing, a. ægrotus.

ailment, s. malum, n.; morbus, m.; ægritudo, ægrotatio, f.

aim, s. propositum, n.

aim, v.a. intendo; dirigo, tendo, 3; *fig.* (to — at) affecto; specto; expeto, 3; molior, 4; (— at by insinuations) designo, 1.

air, s. aer, m., aura, f.; (sky) cœlum, n.; *fig.* habitus; gestus, m.; (appearance) species, f.; (tune) numeri, m. pl., modus, m.; **in the open—,** sub divo; **to take the —,** deambulo. 1.

air, v.a. sicco, 1; (— opinions) profero, 3.

air-hole, s. spiraculum, spiramentum, n.

airing, s. ambulatio, f.; **to take an —,** deambulo, 1.

airy, a. s. aerius; apertus, patens, ventosus; *fig.* levis.

aisle, s. ala, f.
ait, s. insula, f.
ajar, a. (of doors) semiapertus; semi-adapertus.
akin, a. cognatus; propinquus; *fig.* finitimus, cognatus.
alabaster, s. alabaster, m.
alack, v. **alas.**
alacrity, s. alacritas, f.; studium, n.
alarm, s. (signal in war, etc.) classicum, n.; (sudden fright) trepidatio, f.; tumultus, m.
alarm, v.a. terreo, 2; consterno, territo, 1; **be —ed,** perturbor.
alarming, a. terribilis.
alarum, s. (bell) tintinnabulum.
alas, i. eheu! heu, hei mihi misero! (alas for the conquered!) væ victis!
albatross, s. diomedea, f.
albeit, c. etsi, quamquam, quamvis, licet.
albugo, s. albugo, f.
albumen, s. albumen, n.
alchemist, s. alchemista, m.
alchemy, s. alchemia, f.
alchohol, s. spiritus vini, m.
alcove, a. (corner) angulus, m.; (cabinet) zotheca, f.
alcyon, s. alcyon, f.; alcedo, f.
alder, s. alnus, f.
ale, s. cerevisia, f.
ale-house, s. caupona, f.
ale-house-keeper, s. caupo, m.
alert, a. alacer, promptus, vigil.
alertness, s. alacritas, f.
alibi, s. (law) absentia rei, f.
alien, a. & s. peregrinus; alienigena, c.
alienable, a. quod abalienari potest.
alienate, v.a. alieno; abalieno, 1; *fig.* averto, 3.
alienation, s. abalienatio; alienatio; (estrangement) disjunctio, alienatio, f.
alight, v.n. descendo, 3; (from a horse) desilio, 4; (as of birds, etc.) insido, 3.
alike, a. æquus, par, similis; —, ad. pariter, similiter.
aliment, s. alimentum, nutrimentum, n.
alimentary, a. alimentarius.
alimony, s. alimonium, n.
alive, a. vivus; *fig.* vividus, alacer; **to be —,** vivo, 3; supersum.
alkanet, s. anchusa (mod. hort.).
all, a. omnis, cunctus; universus; (whole) totus; (every one in particular) unusquisque; **— in general,** universi, m. pl.; **by — means,** quoquomodo; **on — sides,** ubique, passim, undique; **— this while,** usque adhuc; **— the better,** tanto melius; **—the more,** eo plus; **it is — over with,** actum est de; **it is — one to me,** nihil mea interest.

all, s. omnia, n. pl.; **at —,** omnino; **not at —,** nihil *or* nullus, etc., admodum; **in —,** in summa.
allay, v.a. lenio, 4; mitigo, 1; (to mingle) diluo, 3; tempero, 1; (quench) restinguo, 3; sedo, 1.
allaying, allayment, s. lenimen, levamen, n.
allegation, s. affirmatio, f.
allege, v.a. arguo, 3; affirmo, 1; (bring forward) affero, 3.
allegiance, s. fides.
allegorical, a. allegoricus; **—ly,** ad. allegorice.
allegory, s. allegoria, f.
alleviate, v.a. levo, allevo, sublevo, 1.
alleviation, s. levamen, n.
alley, s. (walk in a garden) xystus, m.; (narrow street) angiportus, m.; ambulatio, f.
alliance, s. (by blood) consanguinitas; (by marriage) affinitas, f.; (of states) fœdus, n.; (mutual connection) societas. [states) fœderatus, socius.
allied, a. & p. cognatus; propinquus; (of
alligation, s. alligatio, f.
alligator, s. crocodilus, m.
all-mighty, all-powerful, a. omnipotens.
allocution, s. allocutio, f.
allodial, a. immunis.
allot, v.a. distribuo, 3; assigno, 1; tribuo, 3; do, 1.
allotment, s. assignatio, portio, f.; pars.
allow, v.a. concedo, permitto, 3; (permit) patior, sino, 3; **to — of,** admitto, 3; (confess) fateor, confiteor, 2; **to — for,** indulgeo, 2; **it is —ed,** licet.
allowable, a. licitus, concessus.
allowably, ad. jure.
allowance, s. (permission) licentia, venia; **an — for support,** cibarium, n.; **make —s for,** indulgeo.
alloy, s. mixtura, f.; **without —,** a. sincerus.
alloy, v.a. misceo, 2; vitio, 3; adultero, 1.
all-seeing, a. omnituens.
all-spice, s. calyanthus (mod. hort.).
allude, v.n. (to) attingo, 3; designo, denoto; specto, 1.
allure, v.a. allicio, 3; allecto, 1.
allurement, s. illecebra; *fig.* blandimentum, n.; blanditiæ, f. pl.
allurer, s. allector, m.
alluring, a. blandus; **—ly,** ad. blande.
allusion, s. significato, f.
allusive, a. obliquus; **—ly,** ad. oblique.
alluvial, a. alluvius.
alluvium, s. alluvio, f.; alluvies, f.
ally, s. socius.
ally, v.a. socio, 1.
almanac, s. fasti, m. pl.

almightiness, s. omnipotentia, f.
almighty, a. omnipotens.
almond, s. amygdala, f.; amygdalum, n.
almond-tree, s. amygdalus, f.
almost, ad. fere, pæne, prope; tantum
non. [syna, f.
alms, s. stips; (in Christianity) eleemo-
alms-giver, s. qui (quæ) stipem dat.
aloe, s. aloe, f., agave (mod. hort.).
aloft, ad. sublime.
alone, a. solus; unus; solitarius; —, ad.
solum; tantum; **to leave** —, desero,
3; **to let** —, omitto, mitto, 3.
along, pr. secundum; præter; — **with,**
cum; —, ad. porro, protinus.
aloof, ad. procul; **to stand** —, discedo,
3; removeo (me ab), 2; non attingo, 3.
aloud, ad. clara voce, clare.
alphabet, s. alphabetum, n.; _fig._ elementa
prima, n. pl.
alpine, a. alpinus.
already, ad. jam.
also, ad. etiam; item, quoque, necnon;
(moreover) præterea, porro, insuper.
altar, s. ara, f. altare, n.
alter, v.a. muto, commuto; vario, novo,
1; verto, 3; —, v.n. mutor, commu-
tor, etc.
alterable, a. mutabilis, commutabilis.
alteration, a. mutatio; commutatio, f.
altercation, s. altercatio, f., jurgium, n.
alternate, alternative, a. alternus.
alternate, v.a. & n. alterno, vario, 1.
alternately, ad. invicem, per vices;
alternis.
alternation, s. vicissitudo, f.; vices, f. pl.
alternative, s. (middle course) medium,
n.; (condition) condicio, f.; (refuge) refugium, n.; **I have no** —, nihil mihi
reliqui est. [quamvis, licet.
although, c. etsi, tametsi, quamquam,
altitude, s. altitudo, sublimitas, f.
altogether, ad. omnino; prorsus; plane,
penitus.
alum, s. alumen, n.
alyssum, s. alyssum (mod. hort.).
always, ad. semper; in æternum.
am, sum, v. **to be.**
amain, ad. vi, strenue.
amalgamate, v.a. misceo, 2; v.n. coeo.
amalgamation, s. mixtura, f.; (combination) coitus, m.
amanuensis, s. librarius; a manu, ab
epistolis (servus); amanuensis, m.
amaranth, s. amarantus, i, m.
amass, v.a. coacervo, cumulo, 1.
amateur, s. (unskilful) rudis, imperitus.
amatory, a. amatorius.
amaze, v.a. obstupefacio, 3.
amazed, a. attonitus, stupefactus; —**to
be** —, stupeo, 2; obstupesco, 3.

amazement, s. stupor, m.
amazing, a. mirus, mirabilis, mirandus;
—**ly,** ad. (ad)mirabiliter.
Amazon, s. Amazon, f.; _fig._ virago, f.
Amazonian, a. Amazonius.
ambassador, s. legatus, m., (pleader) orator.
ambassadress, s. oratrix, f.
amber, s. sucinum, electrum, n.; —,
a. sucineus.
ambient, a. circumfusus.
ambiguity, s. ambiguitas, f., ambages,
f. pl. [—**ly,** ad. ambigue.
ambiguous, a. ambiguus, dubius, anceps;
ambit. a. ambitus, m.
ambition, s. ambitio, f.
ambitious, a. laudis _or_ gloriæ, etc., cupidus; ambitiosus; —**ly,** ad. ambitiose.
amble, v.n. tolutim incedo, 3.
ambler, s. equus gradarius, m.
amblingly, ad. tolutim.
ambrosia, s. ambrosia, f.
ambrosial, a. ambrosius.
ambuscade, ambush, s. insidiæ, f. pl.;
to lie in —, insidior, 1.
ameliorate, v.a. & n. meliorem _or_ melius
facere; melior _or_ melius fio.
amelioration, s. amplificatio, f.
amen, ad. amen; fiat, esto.
amenable, a. obediens, docilis, (exposed
to) obnoxius.
amend, v.a. emendo, 1; corrigo, 3; —,
v.n. proficio, 3.
amendment, s. correctio, emendatio, f.
amends, s. expiatio, compensatio, satisfactio, f.; **to make** —, expio, 1; satisfacio, luo, 3; compenso, 1.
amenity, s. amœnitas, f.
amerce, v.a. multo, 1.
amercement, s. multa, f.
amethyst, s. amethystus, f.
amiability, s. lenitas, humanitas, suavitas, f. [manus.
amiable, a. amabilis, suavis, lenis, hu-
amiableness, v. **amiability.**
amiably, ad. amabiliter, suaviter, leniter,
humaniter. [nignus.
amicable, a. pacatus; benevolus; be-
amicably, ad. pacate; amice, benevole.
amid(st), pr. in medio, inter.
amidships, ad. media navi.
amiss, ad. perperam, prave, male; secus;
to do —, pecco, 1; offendo, 3.
amity, s. amicitia, f.
ammonia, s. salammoniacus.
ammoniac, s. ammoniacum, n.
ammunition, s. arma, n. pl.; apparatus
bellicus, m.
amnesty, s. impunitas, venia, oblivio, f.
among, amongst, pr. in, inter; apud;
ad; **from** —, e, ex.

amorous, a. amatorius; amore captus; —ly, ad. amatorie.

amorousness, s. libido, f.

amount, s. summa, f.

amount, v.n. (to) sum, expleo, 2; **it amounts to the same thing,** idem est, par est.

amour, s. amores, m. pl.; res amatoria.

ampelopsis, s. ampelopsis (mod. hort.).

amphitheatre, s. amphitheatrum, n.

amphitheatrical, a. amphitheatricus.

ample, a. amplus; copiosus; largus; (enough) satis.

ampleness, a. magnitudo, amplitudo, f.

amplification, s. amplificatio, f.

amplifier, s. amplificator, m.

amplify, v.a. dilato; amplifico, 1; (advance) promoveo, 2; profero, 3.

amplitude, s. amplitudo, f.

amply, ad. ample, abunde, satis.

amputate, v.a. amputo; seco, 1.

amputation, a. amputatio; sectio, f.

amuck, ad. (run amuck), furo, 3.

amulet, s. amuletum, n.

amuse, v.a. oblecto, delecto, 1; (mock) ludo, 3; **to — oneself,** ludo, 3; mihi placeo, 2.

amusement, s. delectatio, oblectatio, f.; delectamentum, oblectamentum, n.; (game) ludus, m.

amusing, a. festivus.

amusingly, ad. festive.

anæsthetic, a. soporifer.

analogical, a. ex analogia.

analogous, a. analogus; (like) similis.

analogy, s. analogia; (likeness) similitudo, f.

analysis, s. explicatio, f.

analyse, v.a. enodo, explico, 1.

anapæst, s. anapæstus, m.

anapæstic, a. anapæsticus.

anarchical, a. *fig.* turbulentus.

anarchist, s. civis seditiosus et turbulentus, m.

anarchy, s. licentia, f.

anathema, s. anathema, n.

anathematize, v.a. anathematizo, 1.

anatomical, a. anatomicus.

anatomist, s. anatomicus, m.

anatomize, v.a. disseco, 1.   [ossa, n. pl.

anatomy, s. anatomia; (frame, bones)

ancestor, s. avus, proavus, atavus; auctor, m.; **-s,** pl. majores; priores, m. pl.

ancestral, a. avitus, proavitus.

ancestry, s. prosapia; stirps, f.; genus; v. **ancestors.**

anchor, s. ancora, f.; **to weigh —,** ancoram tollere *or* solvere, 3; **cast —,** ancoram jacere; **ride at —,** in ancoris consistere.

anchor, v.a. & n. ancoras jacere, 3; (of ships) stare, 1.

anchorage, s. statio, f.

anchorite, s. anachoreta, ae, m.

ancient, a. antiquus, vetus, vetustus; priscus; (former) pristinus; **from — times,** antiquitus; **the —s,** s. pl. (forefathers, ancestors) veteres, priores, m. pl.; (authors) antiqui, m. pl.; (abstractly) antiquitas, f.

ancient, s. (flag) insigne; (flag-bearer) signifer, m.

anciently, ad. olim, quondam.

and, c. et, ac, atque; (enclitic) que; necnon, n.

anecdote, s. fabella; narratiuncula, f.

anemone, s. anemone (mod. hort.).

anew, ad. denuo; ab integro.

angel, s. angelus, m.; —, a. angelicus.

angelic, a. angelicus.

anger, s. ira; iracundia; bilis, f.; furor, m.

anger, v.a. irrito, exacerbo, 1; commoveo, 2.

angle, s. angulus, m.

angle, v.a. hamo piscor, 1.

angler, s. piscator, m.

angling-rod, s. arundo, f.; calamus, m.

angrily, ad. iracunde, irate.

angry, a. iratus, iracundus; **to be —,** irascor, 3; succenseo, 2; stomachor; **to make —,** irrito, exacerbo, 1.

anguish, s. angor, dolor, m.

anguished, a. animo fractus.

angular, a. angularis; (full of angles) angulosus.

angulated, a. angulatus.

animadversion, s. animadversio, f.

animadvert, v.a. (to remark) animadverto, 3; (upon) castigo, 1.

animal, s. animal, n.; animans, c.; (wild beast) fera, f.; (beast) pecus, f.

animal, a. animalis.

animate, v.a. (to give life to) animo; *fig.* hortor; excito, 1; erigo, 3.

animate, a. (living) animans; (of nature) vividus.

animated, a. (lively) vividus, alacer.

animation, s. alacritas f.; ardor; spiritus, m.

animosity, s. (grudge) simultas, acerbitas, malevolentia, f.; odium, n.

animus, s. malevolentia, f.

anise, s. anisum, n.

ankle(-bone), s. talus, m.; **reaching to the ankle,** a. talaris.

annalist, s. annalium scriptor, m.

annals, s. annales, fasti, m. pl.

annex, v.a. annecto, adjungo, suppono, 3; (seize) rapio, 3.

annexation, s. adjectio, f.

annexed, a. adjectus, additus.

annihilate, v.a. deleo, 2; extinguo, everto, 3.   [(ruin) excidium, n.
annihilation, s. exstinctio; internecio, f.;
annihilator, s. exstinctor, m.
anniversary, a. anniversarius; annuus;
—, s. festus dies anniversarius, m.
annotate, v.a. annoto, commentor, 1.
annotation, s. annotatio;. nota, f.
announce, v.a. nuntio; (to report) renuntio, 1; (of laws, etc.); promulgo, 1.
announcement, s. nuntiatio; renuntiatio,
f.; (news) nuntius, m.
announcer, s. nuntius, m.
annoy, v.a. incommodo, 1; male habeo,
2; (vex) irrito, 1; to be —ed, stomachor, 1; offensus sum.
annoyance, s. molestia, f.; (anger) ira, f.
annoying, a. molestus, incommodus.
annual, a. anniversarius, annuus; —ly,
ad. quotannis.
annual, s. annales, m. pl.
annuity, s. annuum, n.
annul, v.a. abrogo, 1; rescindo, tollo, 3.
annulet, s. anulus, m.
annulment, s. abolitio; abrogatio, f.
anodyne, s. anodynon medicamentum,
n.; —, a. anodynos.
anoint, v.a. ungo, inungo, perungo, 3.
anointer, s. unctor, m.
anointing, s. unctio, f.
anomalous,   a.   anomalus;   (irregular)
enormis.
anomaly, s. anomalia; enormitas, f.
anon, ad. statim, illico; mox; ever and
—, identidem.
anonymous, a. —ly, ad. sine nomine.
another, a. alius; —'s, alienus; one —,
alius alium, inter se.
answer, v.a. respondeo, 2; (of written an-
swers) rescribo, 3; (to correspond to)
respondeo, 2; congruo, 3; to — for,
rationem reddo, 3; præsto, 1; —,
v.n. (to succeed) bene cedere, prospere
cedere.
answer, s. responsio, f., responsum, n.;
(of an oracle) sors, f.; (solution of a
problem) explicatio, f.
answerable,   a.   cui   responderi   potest;
(correspondent)   congruens,   consentaneus; (responsible) reus; obnoxius;
to be —, præsto, 1; (to make answerable) obligo, 1.
answerably, ad. congruenter.
answering,   a.   congruens;   (echoing)
resonus.
ant, s. formica, f.
ant-hill, s. formicarum cuniculus, m.
antagonism,   s.   adversitas,   f.;   (dislike)
inimicitia, f.
antagonist,   s.   adversarius,   m.;   adversatrix, f.; æmulus, hostis, inimicus, m.

antarctic, a. antarcticus.
antecedent, a. antecedens, prior.
antecedents, s. (past life) vita jam acta.
ante-chamber, s. vestibulum, n.
antediluvian, a. qui ante diluvium fuit;
(old-fashioned) obsoletus.
antelope, s. dorcas, f.
antenuptial, a. antenuptialis.
antepenult, s. syllaba antepænultima, f.
antepenultimate, a. antepænultimus.
anterior, a. prior, superior.
ante-room, s. vestibulum, n.
anthem, s. canticum, n.
anthology, s. anthologica, f.
Anthony's fire, s. pusula, f.
anthracite, s. anthracites, ae, m.
antic, s. histrio, mimus, m.; (buffoonery)
motus ridiculi, m. pl.
antic, a. ridiculus.
antichrist, s. antichristus, m.
anticipate, v.a. anticipo, 1; præsumo, 3;
(forestall) prævenio, 4.
anticipation, s. anticipatio; præsumptio.
anticlimax, s. (gr.) climax inversa, f.
antidote, s. antidotum, n.; antidotus, f.;
remedium, n.
antimony, s. stibium, stimmi, n.
antipathy,   s.   antipathia,   f.;   odium,
fastidium, n.
antipodes, s. antipodes, um, m. pl.
antipope, s. antipapa, m.
antiquarian,   antiquary,   s.   antiquarius,
rerum antiquarum studiosus; rerum
antiquarum peritus, m.
antiquated, a. obsoletus.
antique, a. antiquus.
antique, s. opus antiqui artificis; monumentum antiquitatis, m.
antiquity, s. antiquitas; vetustas, f.
antithesis, s. antitheton, n.
antler, s. ramus, m.
anvil, s. incus, f.
anxiety, s. anxietas; sollicitudo, trepidatio, f.
anxious, a. anxius; sollicitus; trepidus;
to be — (to), laboro (ut or ne), 1;
anxium esse de aliqua re.
anxiously, ad. anxie; sollicite; trepide.
any, anybody, pn. quisquam, quivis,
quilibet; (interrogatively) ecquis;
(all) omnis; — longer, diutius; —
more, amplius; at — time, unquam.
anyhow, ad. quoquomodo.
anything,   s.   quicquam,   quidpiam,
quodvis.
anywhere, ad. ubilibet, alicubi, ubivis.
apace, ad. celeriter; cito, propere.
apart, ad. seorsum, separatim; dis . . .;
to stand —, disto, 1; set —, sepono.
apartment, s. conclave, n.
apathetic, a. lentus, socors.

apathy, s. stupor, m.; ignavia, socordia, lentitudo, f.

ape, s. simius, m.; simia, f.; —, v.a. imitor, 1. [a. apertivus.

aperient, s. (med.) catharticum, n.; —,

aperture, s. apertura, f.; foramen, n.

apex, s. cacumen, n.; apex, m.

aphorism, s. sententia, f.

apiary, s. alvearium, apiarium, n.

apiece, ad. singuli, ae, a; quisque.

apish, a. mimicus; — trick, s. ineptia, f.

apishness, s. cacozelia, f.

apocalypse, s. apocalypsis, f.

apocrypha, s. libri apocryphi, m. pl.

apocryphal, a. apocryphus; (false) fictus.

apodosis, s. apodosis, f.

apologetic(al), a. apologeticus.

apologist, s. apologiæ scriptor; *fig.* defensor, m.

apologize, v.a. excuso, 1; defendo, veniam peto, 3.

apologue, s. apologus, m.; fabula, f.

apology, s. excusatio; defensio; (written treatise) apologia, f.; to make an — for, excuso, 1. [tentia, f.

apophthegm, s. apophthegma, n.; sen-

apoplectic, a. apoplecticus.

apoplexy, s. apoplexia, f.

apostasy, s. apostasia, f.; (falling away) defectio, f.

apostate, s. apostata, m.

apostatize, v.n. apostato, 1.

apostle, s. apostolus, m.

apostleship, s. apostolatus, m.

apostolic, a. apostolicus. [phus, f.

apostrophe, s. apostrophe; (gr.) apostro-

apostrophize, v.a. compello, 1; affari.

apothecary, s. medicamentarius, m.; —'s shop, s. medicina, f.

apotheosis, s. apotheosis, f.; consecratio, f.

appal, v.a. exterreo, 2; percello, 3.

apparatus, s. apparatus, m.

apparel, s. vestis, f., vestitus, m.

apparel, v.a. vestio, 4; induo, 3.

apparent, a. manifestus; (feigned as opposed to real) simulatus, fictus; to be —, appareo, 2.

apparently, ad. (plainly) aperte, manifeste; (pretendedly) per speciem; he is — dead, mortuus esse videtur.

apparition, s. spectrum, simulacrum, n.

apparitor, s. apparitor, m.

appeal, v.n. appello; provoco; obsecro, 1; (call to witness), testor, 1.

appeal, s. (law) appellatio; provocatio; (entreaty) obsecratio, f.

appear, v.n. appareo, compareo, 2; se ostendare, 3; (to seem) videor, 2; (to arise) exorior, 4; surgo, 3; (appear before a court) me sisto, 3; it —s, patet, liquet.

appearance, s. (becoming visible) aspectus, m.; (outward show) species; (vision) spectrum, n.; arrival, adventus, m.; first —, exortus, m.; to all —, he has been killed, occisus esse videtur.

appease, v.a. placo; mitigo; expio; (hunger, etc.) sedo, 1.

appellant, s. appellator, m.

appellation, s. vocabulum, n.

appellative, a. appellativus.

append, v.a. addo, 3.

appendage, s. appendix; accessio; appendicula, f.

appendix, s. appendix, f.

appertain, v.a. pertineo, attineo, 2; specto, 1.

appetence, s. appetitio; cupiditas, f.

appetite, s. appetitus, m. cupiditas, f.; to have —, esurio, 4.

applaud, v.a. applaudo, 3; laudo, 1; plaudo. [laudator, m.

applauder, s. plausor, applausor; *fig.*

applause, s. plausus, applausus, m., laus, f.

apple, s. malum, pomum, n.; (of the eye) pupula, pupilla, f.

apple-loft, s. pomarium, n.

apple-tree, s. malus, f. [tum, n.

appliance, s. (instrument) instrumen-

applicable, a. commodus, conveniens; (not to be applicable) alienum esse.

applicant, s. petitor.

application, s. (use) usus, m.; usurpatio, f.; (zeal) studium, n., sedulitas, diligentia, cura, f.

apply, v.a. adhibeo; admoveo, 2; appono, 3; apto, accommodo, 1; —, v.n. pertineo, 2; (— to a person for aid) aggredior, 3.

appoint, v.a. creo, 1; facio, 3; designo; destino, 1; constituo, 3.

appointment, s. creatio, f.; (order) mandatum; (rendezvous) constitutum, n.

apportion, v.a. divido, distribuo, 3.

apportioner, s. distributor, m.

apportionment, s. divisio, distributio, f.

apposite, a. aptus, idoneus; appositus; —ly, ad. apte; apposite.

apposition, s. appositio, f.

appraise, v.a. æstimo, 1.

appraisement, s. æstimatio, f.

appraiser, s. æstimator, m.

appreciable, a. quod æstimari potest.

appreciate, v.a. æstimo, 1; (value highly) magni facio. [laus, f.

appreciation, s. æstimatio; (praise)

apprehend, v.a. comprehendo, apprehendo; percipio, 3; (fear) timeo, 2; (suspect) suspicor, 1; (to seize) capio, 3; (to take unawares) intercipio, 3; (arrest) comprehendo, 3.

apprehension, a. ingenium, n.; intelligentia; (suspicion) suspicio; (seizing) comprehensio; (fear) timor, m.

apprehensive, s. timidus.

apprentice, s. discipulus; tiro, m.

apprenticeship, s. tirocinium, n.

apprise, v.a. doceo, 2.

approach, v.a. & n. appropinquo, 1; accedo, 3; adeo, 4; (threaten) immineo, 2; insto, 1.

approaching, s. appropinquatio, f.

approachable, a. v. accessible.

approbation, s. approbatio, laus, f.

appropriate, v.a. mihi arrogo, 1; mihi assero, 3; vindico, 1; assumo, 3.

appropriate, a. proprius; congruens.

appropriately, ad. apte, congruenter.

appropriateness, s. convenientia.

approvable, a. laudabilis.

approval, s. approbatio, f.

approve, v.a. approbo, probo, laudo, 1..

approver, s. approbator, probator, laudator, m.

approving, s. approbatio, f.

approximate, a. propinquus.

approximate, v.n. non multum absum; prope accedo.

appurtenance, s. appendix, f.

apricot, s. malum Armeniacum, n.

April, s. Aprilis, m.

apron, s. subligaculum, n.

apt, a. aptus, idoneus; (inclined, prone) pronus, propensus, proclivis.

aptitude, s. habilitas, f.; ingenium, n.

aptly, ad. apte, apposite.

aptness, s. convenientia, congruentia; (tendency, propensity) proclivitas, f.

aquamarine, beryllus, m.

aquatic, a. aquatilis; aquaticus.

aqueduct, s. aquæ ductus, aquarum ductus, m.

aqueous, a. aquatilis, aquosus.

aquiline, a. aquilinus; (of the nose) aduncus.

arable, a. arabilis; — land, s. arvum, novale, n.; novalis, f.

arbalist, s. arcuballista, m.

arbiter, s. arbiter; dominus, m.

arbitrarily, ad. ad arbitrium; ad libidinem.

arbitrariness, s. dominatio, libido, f.

arbitrary, a. imperiosus; superbus.

arbitrate, v.a. & n. discepto, 1.

arbitration, s. arbitrium, n.

arbitrator, s. arbiter; (private) disceptator, m.

arbitrement, s. arbitratus, m., arbitrium, n.

arbor vitæ, s. thuya (mod. hort.).

arbour, s. umbraculum, n.; pergula, f.

arbute, s. (tree) arbutus, f.; (fruit) arbutum, n.; — -berry, s. arbutum, n.

arc, s. arcus, m.

arcade, s. porticus, f.

arch, s. arcus, fornix, m.

arch, v.a. arcuo, 1.

arch, a. petulans, protervus, lascivus; (eminent in any art, good or bad) summus.

archæology, s. scientia antiquitatis, f.

archaic, a. obsoletus.

archaism, s. verbum priscum et obsoletum, n.; locutio obsoleta, f.

archangel, s. archangelus, m.

archbishop, s. archiepiscopus, m.

archbishopric, s. archiepiscopatus, m.

archdeacon, s. archidiaconus, m.

archdeaconry, archdeaconship, s. archidiaconatus, m.

arched, a. curvus.

archer, s. sagittarius; (constellation) Arcitenens, m.

archery, s. ars sagittandi, f.

archetype, s. archetypum, exemplum, n.

architect, s. architectus, m.; artifex, c.

architectural, a. architectonicus.

architecture, s. architectura, f.

architrave, s. epistylium, n.

archives, s. tabulæ, f. pl.; tabularium, n.

archly, ad. petulanter, proterve, lascive.

archness, s. petulantia, lascivia, protervitas, f.

archpriest, s. pontifex maximus, m.

archway, s. porticus, f.

archwise, ad. arcuatim, fornicatim.

arctic, a. arcticus; arctous.

ardent, a. ardens, fervidus; —ly, ad. ardenter.

ardour, s. ardor, fervor, m.

arduous, a. altus, celsus; (difficult) arduus; difficilis; —ly, ad. difficulter.

arduousness, s. difficultas, f.

area, s. area; superficies, f.

arena, s. arena, f.

argonaut, s. argonauta, m.

argue, v.a. & n. disputo, discepto, 1; dissero, 3; (prove) arguo, evinco, 3; probo, 1.

arguer, s. disputator, m.

argument, s. disceptatio, disputatio, f.; (subject) argumentum, n.

argumentation, s. argumentatio, f.

argumentative, a. (fond of dispute) litigiosus.

arid, a. aridus, siccus.

aridity, s. ariditas, siccitas, f.

aright, ad. recte bene.

arise, v.n. surgo, 3; orior, 4; (to proceed from) nascor, 3.

aristocracy, s. optimates, nobiles, m. pl.

aristocrat, s. optimas, patricius, m.

aristocratic, a. patricius; —ally, ad. more patricio.

arithmetic, s. arithmetica, n. pl.
arithmetical, a. arithmeticus.   [m.
arithmetician, s. arithmeticorum peritus,
ark, s. arca; cista, f.
arm, s. bracchium, n.; lacertus, m.; (of
the sea) sinus, m.; fretum, n.; (of a
tree) ramus, m.; (weapon) telum, n.;
v. **arms.**
arm, v.a. armo, 1; —, v.n. armor;
arma capio; bellum paro, 1.
armada, s. classis, f.   [bellicus, m.
armament, s. armatura, f.; apparatus
arm-hole, s. ala, f.
armistice, s. indutiæ, f. pl.
armless, a. mancus, truncus.   [chiale, n.
armlet, s. armilla, f.; (bracelet) brac-
armorial, a. — **bearings,** s. insignia.
armour, s. armatura, f.; armatus, m.;
arma, n. pl.; — **bearer,** s. armiger, m.
armoury, s. armamentarium, n.
arm-pit, s., v. **arm-hole.**
arms, s. arma; *fig.* bellum, n.; **to lay
down —,** ab armis discedere; arma
dedere; **to take, take up —,** sumere
arma; **to be under —,** in armis esse.
army, s. exercitus, m.; (in battle array)
acies, f.; (on the march) agmen, n.;
(forces) copiæ, f. pl.
aroma, s. odor, m.; (of wine) flos, m.
aromatic, a. fragrans.   [undique.
around, pr. & ad. circum, circa; **all —,**
arouse, v.a. suscito, excito, concito, 1;
(produce) cieo, moveo, 2; conflo, 1;
(encourage) erigo, 3; **to — oneself,**
expergisci, 3.
arraign, v.a. accuso, 1.
arraignment, s. accusatio, f.
arrange, v.a. instruo, struo, (battle) instituo, 3; ordino, 1; dispono, 3;
address, etc.) colloco, 1; (make a
plan) constituo, 3.
arrangement, s. collocatio, compositio;
dispositio; (of battle) ordinatio, f.;
(plan) consilium, n.
arrant, a., v. **arch,** a.; — **thief,** trifur, m.
arras, s. tapete, is, n.
array, s. (of battle) acies, f.; (clothing)
vestitus, m.; (arrangement, order)
ordo, m.; dispositio, compositio, f.
array, v.a. vestio, 4; adorno, 1; compono, instruo, 3.
arrear, arrears, s. reliqua, n. pl. residuæ
(of taxes, vectigalium), f. **pl.; be in
—,** reliquor, 1.
arrest, s. comprehensio, f.
arrest, v.a. comprehendo, 3; (stay) detineo, 2.
arrival, s. adventus, m.
arrive, v.n. advenio, pervenio, 4; (as a
ship) advehor, appellor; (to attain)
adipiscor, 3.

arrogance, s. arrogantia; superbia, insolentia, f.
arrogant, a. arrogans; superbus; insolens; —**ly,** ad. arroganter; insolenter.
arrogate, v.a. arrogo, vindico, 1; assero,
assumo, 3.
arrow, s. sagitta, arundo, f.; telum, n.
arsenal, s. armamentarium, n.; navalia,
n. pl.
arsenic, s. arsenicum.
arson, s. incendium, n.
art, s. ars, f.; (cunning) artificium, n.;
(skill) sollertia, f.; **fine** *or* **liberal —s,**
artes elegantes *or* ingenuæ, pl.;
black —, magice, f.
artery, s. arteria; vena, f.
artful, a. callidus, subtilis; subdolus;
—**ly,** ad. callide, subtiliter, subdole.
artfulness, s. artificium, n.; calliditas, f.
arthritic, a. arthriticus.
arthritis, s. arthritis, f.
artichoke, s. (glove) cynara, (Jerusalem)
helianthus (mod. hort.).
article, s. (head, chapter) caput, n.; (condition) condicio; pactio; (for sale)
merx, f.; (gr.) articulus, m.; — **by —,**
articulatim.
article, v.a. addico.
articular, a. articularis.
articulate, a. distinctus; dilucidus; —**ly,**
ad. articulatim, distincte, dilucide.
articulate, v.a. articulo, enuntio, 1;
(utter) profero, eloquor, 3.
artifice, s. artificium, n.; ars, f.; dolus,
m.; fraus, f.
artificer, s. artifex; opifex, c.
artificial, a. artificiosus; facticius; —**ly,**
ad. arte.
artillery, s. tormenta, n. pl.
artisan, s. faber, m.; artifex; opifex, c.
artist, s. artifex, c.
artistic, a. artificiosus; —**ally,** ad. artifi-
ciose; affabre.
artless, a. incomptus; incompositus; ingenuus, simplex; —**ly,** ad. incompte;
ingenue.
artlessness, s. simplicitas, f.
arum lily, s. richardia (mod. hort.).
as, c. & ad. (of time) dum, cum; (of
manner) ut; quam; ita ut; sicut;
velut; — **far —,** quoad, usque ad,
quantum; — **if,** quasi, perinde ac si;
ita ut si; — **it were,** ceu, tanquam; —
long —, quamdiu; — **many —,** quot
quot, quotcunque; — **much,** tantum;
— **often —,** quoties; — **soon —,** cum
primum, simul atque; — **yet,** adhuc;
not — yet, nondum.
ascend, v.a. & n. ascendo, conscendo
scando, 3.
ascendant, to be in the, superior esse.

ascendency, s. (victory) victoria; (superiority) præstantia, f.

ascension, s. ascensio, f.; ascensus, m.

ascent, s. ascensio, f.; ascensus, m.; acclivitas, f. [4; cognosco, 3.

ascertain, v.a. comperio, pro certo scio,

ascertainable, a. quod comperiri potest.

ascertainment, s. cognitio, f.

ascetic, a. asceticus; —s, asceta, m.

asceticism, s. temperantia, f.

ascribable, a. ascribendus.

ascribe, v.a. imputo, 1; ascribo, tribuo, 3.

ash, s. (tree) fraxinus, f.; (cinders) cinis, c.; v. **ashes;** —, a. fraxineus.

ashamed, a. pudibundus; **to be** —, erubesco, 3; **I am** — **of,** use me pudet, 2 (with genitive or infinitive).

ash-coloured, a. cinereus.

ashen, a. fraxineus; (pale) pallidus.

ashes, s. cinis, m.; (hot —) favilla, f.

ashlar, s. cæmenta, m. pl.

ashore, ad. in terram, ad litus; **be cast** —, ejicior, 3; **go** —, egredior; **put** —, expono, 3.

ashy, a. cineraceus; (pale) pallidus.

Asiatic, a. Asiaticus, Asius.

aside, ad. seorsum, oblique; **to call** —, sevoco, 1; **to lay** or **set** —, sepono, 3; **to speak** —, in aurem dicere.

asinine, a. asininus.

ask, v.a. rogo, 1; posco, peto, quæro, 3; (a question) interrogo, 1.

askance, ad. oblique; **looking** —, a. limus.

askew, ad. in obliquum.

aslant, ad. oblique, in obliquum.

asleep, a. dormiens; **to be** —, dormio, 4; **to fall** —, obdormio, 3; **to lull** —, sopio, conspio, 4.

aslope, ad. in obliquum.

asp, s. aspis, idis, f.

asparagus, s. asparagus, m.

aspect, s. aspectus; prospectus; vultus, us, m., facies, f.

aspen, s. populus, f.; a. populeus.

asperity, s. acerbitas, f.

asperse, v.a. aspergo, 3; fig. calumnior, 1.

aspersion, s. approbrium, n.; calumnia, f.

asphalt, s. bitumen, n.

asphodel, s. asphodelus, m.

asphyxia, s. suffocatio, f.

aspirant, s. appetens, m.

aspirate, v.a. (gr.) aspiro, 1 (with dative).

aspirate, s. aspiratio, f.

aspiration, s. (gr.) aspiratio; (desire) affectatio, f.; (longing) votum, n.

aspire, v.a. affecto, aspiro, 1; peto, annitor, 3.

aspiring, a. appetens (with genitive).

asquint, ad. **to look** —, limis oculis intueri.

ass, s. asinus, m., asina, f.; (wild —) onager; — -**driver,** s. asinarius, m.

assail, v.a. aggredior, 3; oppugno, 1; invehor, 3.

assailable, a. qui (quod) oppugnari potest.

assassin, s. sicarius, m.

assassinate, v.a. insidiis interficio, 3.

assassination, s. cædes, f.

assault, s. impetus, m.; oppugnatio; (violence) vis, f.; v. **attack; to take by** —, expugno, 1.

assault, v.a. adorior, 4; oppugno, 1; manus infero, 3.

assay, v.a. experior, 4; tento, 1.

assay, s. (trial of gold) obrussa; (in general) experimentum, tentamentum, n. [multitudo, f.

assemblage, s. congregatio; (multitude)

assemble, v.a. congrego, convoco, 1; contraho, 3; —, v.n. convenio, 4.

assembling, s. convocatio, f.

assembly, s. cœtus, conventus, m.; concilium; (in politics) comitia, n. pl.; contio, f.; (small) conventiculum, n.; (of people standing round) corona, f.

assembly-room, s. curia, f.

assent, v.a. assentior, 4; annuo, 3.

assent, s. assensus, us, m.

assert, v.a. 3; affirmo, assevero, 1; (to vindicate) defendo, 3; tueor, 2.

assertion, s. affirmatio, asseveratio; sententia, f.

assertor, s. (maintainer) assertor; vindex, m. [æstimo, 1.

assess, v.a. (to tax) censeo, 2; (to value)

assessment, s. census, m.; æstimatio, f.; (tax) vectigal; tributum, n.

assessor, s. (judge) assessor; (of taxes) censor, m.

assets, s. bona, n. pl.

asseverate, v.a. assevero, affirmo, 1.

asseveration, s. asseveratio, f.

assiduity, s. assiduitas, diligentia, f.

assiduous, a. assiduus, sedulus; —**ly,** ad. assidue, sedulo.

assign, v.a. attribuo, 3; delego, assigno, 1; (determine) statuo, constituo, 3; (appoint) indico; (to allege) suggero; affero, 3.

assignation, s. constitutum, n.

assignment, s. assignatio; attributio, f.

assimilate, v.a. assimulo; (make equal) æquo, 1; (digest) concoquo, 3.

assimilation, s. assimilatio; (digestion) concoctio, f.

assist, v.a. juvo, adjuvo; auxilior, 1; succurro, 3; subvenio, 4. [sing.

assistance, s. auxilium, n., opis, f., gen.

assistant, s. adjutor, m., adjutrix, f., administer; auxiliator; advocatus, m., (colleague) collega, m.

assize, s. (law) conventus, m.

associate, v.a. consocio, 1; adscisco, 3; (impute) ascribo; —, (associate with) v.n. versor cum, 1.

associate, a. socius.

associate, s. socius, m.; consors, c.; particeps, c.

association, s. societas; communitas; consociatio; congregatio, f.; (corporation) collegium, n.; (intercourse) commercium, n.

assort, v.a. digero; v.n. congruo, 3.

assortment, s. digestio; dispositio; (abundance) copia, f.

assuage, v.a. allevo, levo, 1; lenio, 4; (check) sedo, 1; (relieve) remitto, 3.

assuagement, s. remissio, allevatio, f.

assume, v.a. induo; assumo, 3; (claim) arrogo, 1; (pretend) simulo, 1; (take for granted) pono, 3.

assuming, a. arrogans.

assumption, s. arrogantia, f.; (postulate) sumptio, f.

assurance, s. fiducia; audacia, impudentia; (warrant) cautio; (pledge) pignus, n.

assure, v.a. confirmo, affirmo, 1; promitto, 3; (encourage) adhortor, 1; **to be —d,** confido, 3.

assuredly, ad. profecto, certe. [hort.].

aster, s. aster, (Mexican) cosmos (mod.

asterisk, s. asteriscus, m.

astern, ad. in puppi; a puppi.

asthma, s. dyspnœa, f.

asthmatic, a. asthmaticus.

astonish, v.a. obstupefacio, 3; **to be —ed,** miror, 1; obstupesco, 3.

astonishingly, ad. admirabiliter.

astonishment, s. admiratio, f.; stupor, m.

astound, v.a. (ob)stupefacio, 3.

astragal, s. astragalus, m.

astray, a. **to go —,** erro, 1; **to lead —,** via recta abducere, transversum agere, 3.

astride, ad. use a. varicus.

astringent, a. astrictorius. [m.

astrologer, s. astrologus; mathematicus,

astrological, a. Chaldaïcus.

astrology, s. astrologia; mathematica, f.

astronomer, s. astrologus; astronomus, m.

astronomical, a. astronomicus.

astronomy, s. astrologia; astronomia, f.

astute, a. callidus, astutus, sagax.

astutely, ad. callide, astute, sagaciter.

astuteness, s. calliditas, sagacitas, f.

asunder, ad. seorsum, separatim; (in two) dis . . .; **to cut —,** disseco, 1; **to pull —,** distraho, 3.

at, pr. ad, apud; in; (during) inter; (of time) use abl., (of cost) use gen. or abl.

atheist, s. atheus, m.

athirst, ad. sitiens.

athlete, s. athleta, m. [transversum.

athwart, prep. trans; ad. transverse, in

atmosphere, s. aër, m.; cœlum; inane, n.

atmospheric, a. aëris, cœli (genitive).

atom, s. atomus, f. corpus individuum, corpus insecabile, n.; fig. mica, particula, f.; (not an atom of) nihil omnino (gen.). [amends.

atone, v.a. pio; expio, 1; solvo, luo, 3; v.

atonement, s. piaculum, n. expiatio; compensatio, satisfactio, f.

atrabilious, a. melancholicus.

atrocious, a. nefarius, nefandus; (enormous) immanis; (of crimes) dirus; atrox; **—ly,** ad. nefarie; fœde.

atrocity, s. atrocitas, f.; nefas, facinus, n.

atrophy, s. atrophia, f.

attach, v.a. annecto, adjungo, 3; applico (win over) concilio, 1; (seize) comprehendo, 3; (belong to) attineo (ad.); **to be —ed** (to), hæreo, adhæreo, 2.

attachment, s. (affection) amor, m., caritas; (arrest, seizure) comprehensio, f.

attack, s. (onset) impetus, m.; oppugnatio, f.; incursus, m.; fig. (of a disease, etc.) tentatio, f.

attack, v.a. (the enemy) aggredior, irruo, 3; (a town) oppugno; fig. provoco, 1; lacesso, 3; **— in words,** invehor, 3; (of diseases) corripio, invado, 3; tento, 1.

attacker, s. oppugnator; provocator, m.

attain, v.a. adipiscor, consequor, 3; pervenio, ad. 4.

attainable, a. impetrabilis.

attainment, s. comparatio, impetratio, f.; v. **learning, knowledge, accomplishment.**

attaint, s. fig. macula, f.

attaint, v.a. accuso, f.

attar, s. rosaceum, n.

attemper, v.a. tempero, 1.

attempt, s. conatus; inceptum, ausum, periculum, n.; **a first —,** tirocinium, n.

attempt, v.a. conor, 1; nitor, 3; molior, 4; audeo, 2; tento, 1.

attend, v.a. (to accompany) comitor, 1; (to escort) deduco, 3; **to — at,** (to be present) intersum; (be present at) adesse (dat.); **to — on,** appareo, 2; assector, 1; **to — to,** curo, procuro, 1; servio, 4; (to comply with) obtempero; invigilo, 1; (pay attention) animum adverto, 3.

attendance, s. (service) obsequium; officium, ministerium, m.; (care) cura, diligentia, f.; (retinue) comitatus, m.

attendant, s. comes; assectator, assecla apparitor; famulus, m.; famula, f.; **—s,** pl. comitatus, m.

attention, s. animus attentus, m.; intentio; sedulitas, f.; cultus, m.; observantia, f.; **to pay —,** observo, 1; operam do, 1; colo, 3; studeo, 2.

attentive, a. attentus; sedulous; officiosus; **—ly,** ad. attente, intento animo; sedulo; officiose.

attenuate, v.a. attenuo; extenuo, 1.

attenuation, s. attenuatio, extenuatio, f.

attest, v.a. testor, testificor, 1.

attestation, s. testificatio, f.; (evidence) testimonium, n.

attire, s. ornatus; vestitus, m.

attire, v.a. adorno, 1; vestio, 4.

attitude, s. habitus; status, m.; (opinion) sententia, f.

attorney, s. cognitor, causidicus, advocatus.

attract, v.a. traho, attraho; allicio, 3.

attraction, s. illecebra, f.; v. **charm.**

attractive, a. lepidus, blandus; **—ly,** ad. lepide, blande.,

attractiveness, s. lepor, m.

atributable, a. imputandus.

attribute, v.a. tribuo, attribuo, ascribo, 3; (falsely) affingo, 3; imputo, 1.

attribute, s. (characteristic) proprium.

attrition, s. attritus, m.

attune, v.a. modulor, 1.

auburn, a. flavus; aureus.

auction, s. auctio, f.; **to sell by —,** auctionor, 1; sub hasta vendo, 3.

auction-mart, auction-room, s. atrium auctionarium, n.

auctionary, a. auctionis (genitive).

auctioneer, s. præco, m.

audacious, a. audax; confidens; **—ly,** ad. audacter; confidenter.

audacity, s. confidentia, audacia, f.

audible, a. quod audiri potest.

audibly, ad. clara voce, ut omnes exaudire possint.

audience, s. aditus, m.; colloquium, n. (hearers); auditores, m. pl.; (bystanders) corona, f.

audit, v.a. rationes inspicio, 3.

auditor, s. (hearer) auditor, m.

auditory, a. auditorius.

auditory, s. auditorium, n.; auditores, m. pl.

auger, s. terebra, f.

augment, v.a. augeo, 2; amplio, 1; **—,** v.n. (to be augmented) augeor, 2; cresco, accresco, 3.

augmentation, s. incrementum, n.

augur, s. augur, c.; hariolus, haruspex, m.

augur, v.n. & a. auguror; vaticinor, hariolor, 1.

augural, a. auguralis.

augury, s. augurium, auspicium, n.; auguratio, f.

august, a. augustus; magnificus.

August, s. (month) Sextilis, Augustus, m.; **on the first of —,** Kalendis Sextilibus.

aulic, a. (of or belonging to the court) aulicus, regius.

aunt, s. (on the father's) amita; (on the mother's side) matertera, f.

auricle, s. (of the ear) auricula, f.

auriferous, a. aurifer.

aurist, s. medicus auricularius.

aurochs, s. urus, bison, m.

auspices, s. auspicium, n.; **under your —,** te auspice.

auspicious, a. faustus; secundus, prosperus; auspicatus; **—ly,** ad. auspicato; feliciter; prospere.

austere, a. austerus, severus.

austerely, ad. austere, severe.

austerity, s. austeritas, severitas, f.

austral, a. australis.

authentic, a. certus; verus; fide dignus.

authentically, ad. certo auctore; cum auctoritate.

authenticate, v.a. recognosco, 3; firmo, confirmo, 1.

authentication, s. auctoritas; confirmatio, f.

authenticity, s. auctoritas; fides, f.

author, s. auctor; scriptor; (inventor) conditor, inventor; (beginner) princeps, m.; (of a crime) caput (sceleris), n.

authoress, s. (poetess) poetria, f.

authoritative, a. auctoritate firmatus; (imperious) imperiosus.

authoritatively, (imperiously) ad. imperiose.

authority, s. auctoritas; potestas; (leave) licentia, f.; (power) jus; imperium, n.; (office or official) magistratus, m.; (witness) testis, c.

authorization, s. confirmatio, licentia, f.

authorize, v.a. potestatem or copiam do, 1; (excuse) excuso; (approve) probo, 1.

autocrat, s. dominus, m.

autograph, s. chirographum, n.

autographic, a. autographus (a, um).

autography, s. chirographum, n.

automatic, a. automatarius.

automaton, s. automaton, i, n.

autumn, s. auctumnus, i, m.

autumnal, a. auctumnalis.

autumn crocus, s. colchicum (mod. hort.).

auxiliary, a. auxiliaris, auxiliarius; —, s. adjutor, m.; **—auxiliaries,** s. pl. (mil.) auxilia, n. pl.

avail, v.n. prosum, proficio, confero, 3; valeo, 2; **to — oneself of,** utor, 3.

avail, s. **to be of no —,** usui non esse.

available, a. utilis; efficax; (at hand) præsto.

availableness, s. utilitas, f.
availably, ad. (at hand) præsto.
availing, a., v. **available.**
avalanche, s. nivis casus, m.
avarice, s. avarita, parcimonia, sordes, f.
avaricious, a. avarus, sordidus; —ly, ad. avare, sordide.
avaunt, i. apage! abi!
avenge, v.a. vindico, 1; ulciscor, 3.
avenger, s. ultor, m., ultrix, f.; vindex, c.
avenging, a. ultrix, vindex.
avenue, s. aditus, introitus; (of trees) xystus, m.
aver, v.a. affirmo, assevero, 1.
average, s. medium inter maximum et minimum, n.; æqua distributio, f.; (on the average) peræque; (about) circiter.
average, a. medius inter maximum minimumque.
averment, s. affirmatio, asseveratio, f.
averse, a. alienus; aversus, abhorrens; to be —, abhorreo, 2.
aversion, s. odium, fastidium, n.; — to, tædium (gen.), n.; (flight from) fuga (gen.), n.
avert, v.a. amoveo, 2; averto, depello, 3; (beg off) deprecor, 1.
aviary, s. aviarium, n.
avid, a. avidus.
avidity, s. aviditas, f.
avocation, s. officium, n.; negotia, munia, n. pl.
avoid, v.a. fugio, 3; (de)vito, 1; (to quit) discedo, 3; (turn aside, decline) declino, detrecto, 1.
avoidable, a. evitabilis, quod effugi potest.
avoidance, s. vitatio; declinatio; (flight from) fuga (gen.), f.
avouch, v.a. affirmo, assevero, 1; (for another) spondeo, 2.
avow, v.a. profiteor, confiteor, 2.
avowal, s. professio, confessio, f.
avowedly, ad. ex professo, aperte.
await, v.a. exspecto, 1.
awake, a. vigil, vigilans; (sleepless) exsomnis; to be —, vigilo, 1.
awake, awaken, v.a. excito, suscito, 1; expergefacio, 3; —, v.n. expergiscor, 3.
award, s. sententia, f.; judicium, arbitrium, n.
award, v.a. adjudico, 1; addico; tribuo, 3; assigno, 1.
awarder, s., arbiter, m.
aware, a. gnarus, sciens; not —, ignarus nescius; to be — (of), sentio, scio, 4.
away, ad. procul, 1; abi! apage! to be —, abesse; to go —, abeo, 4; to take —, aufero, tollo, 3.
awe, s. reverentia, f.; (fear) metus, terror, m., formido, f.; to stand in —, metuo, 3; timeo, 2.

awe, v.a., v. **frighten.**
awe-struck, a. pavefactus.
awful, a. pavefactus; (awe-inspiring) verendus; (dreadful) formidolosus, terribilis, dirus; —ly, ad. formidolose.
awfulness, s. (majesty) majestas, f.; (horribleness) atrocitas, f.
awhile, ad. paulisper.
awkward, a. ineptus; rusticus, rudis, inscitus; (things) incommodus; —ly, ad. inepte; rustice; inscite.
awkwardness, s. imperitia, rusticitas, f.; (inconvenience) incommoditas, f.
awl, s. subula, f.
awn, s. (of corn) arista, f.
awning, s. velarium, n.
awry, a. obliquus; —, ad. oblique; perverse; prave, perperam; to turn —, distorqueo, 2.
axe, s. securis, ascia; (battle-axe) bipennis; (pick-axe) dolabra, f.
axiom, s. axioma, pronuntiatum, n.
axis, s. axis, m.
axle(-tree), s. axis, m.
ay, ad. & i. immo, sane, maxime.
aye, ad. (always) semper; (for ever) in æternum.
azalea, s. azalea (mod. hort.).
azure, a. cæruleus; cærulus, s.

Ba, baa, s. balatus, m.
ba, v.n. (like a sheep) balo, 1.
babble, s. garrulitas, f.
babble, v.n. blatero, 1; garrio, 4.
babbler, s. garrulus, m.
babbling, a. garrulus, loquax.
babbling, s. garrulitas, f.
babe, baby, s. infans, parvulus, m.; (doll) pupa, f.
baboon, s. cynocephalus, m.
babyhood, s. infantia, f.
babyish, a. puerilis.
bacchanal, s. baccha, f.; bacchanalis; bacchantes, m. pl.
bacchanalian, a. bacchanalis.
bacchic, a. bacchicus; baccheus.
bachelor, s. cœlebs; (academically) baccalaureus, m.
bachelor's button, s. silene (mod. hort.).
back, s. tergum; dorsum; (to wound in the back) aversum vulnero; (hinder part) pars postica.
back, ad. retro; retrorsum; re . . .
back, v.a. adjuvo, 1; faveo, 2; (to back water) navem remis inhibere; — v.n. retrogradior, me recipio; (back out of) evado, 3.
backbite, v.a. maledico, calumnior, dente carpo, 3.

backbiter, s. maledicus, obtrectator, m.
backbiting, s. obtrectatio, f.
backbone, s. spina, f.
back-door, s. posticum ostium, m.
backer, s. adjutor, m.
back-ground, s. scæna; *fig.* recessus, us, m.; (keep in the background) abscondo.
backslide, v.n. deficio, 3; desum.
backslider, s. defector, m.
backsliding, s. defectio, f.
backward(s), ad. retro; retrorsum; (with the back turned towards the beholder) aversus.
backward, a. (lying on the back) supinus; (slow) piger, tardus, segnis; (averse to) alienus; **to be —,** cunctor, 1.
backwardness, s. tarditas; pigritia, f.
bacon, s. lardum, n.; **flitch of —,** succidia, f.
bad, a. maius, pravus, nequam; improbus; (ill) æger; (unfortunate) malus, tristis; **— weather,** tempestas adversa, f.
badge, s. insigne, signum, indicium, n.
badger, s. meles, melis, f.
badger, v.a. vexo, inquieto, 1.
badly, ad. male, prave; improbe.
badness, s. nequitia; improbitas, f.
baffle, v.a. decipio, fallo, eludo, 3.
bag, s. saccus; crumena, f.; (of leather) uter, m.; (of network) reticulum, n.
bag, v.a. capto, 1. [n. pl.
baggage, s. sarcinæ, f. pl.; impedimenta,
bagnio, s. balneum; lupanar, n.
bagpiper, s. utricularius, m.
bail, s. vadimonium, n.; (surety) vas (vadis); (for debt) præs, dis, m.
bail, v.a. (to give — for) spondeo, 2; fidepromitto, 3; (to accept — for) vador, 1.
bailiff, s. (manager of a farm) villicus; (serjeant of a court of justice) apparitor, m.
bailiwick, s. jurisdictio, f.
bait, s. esca, f.; *fig.* incitamentum, n.
bait, v.a. inesco, 1; (to tease) lacesso, 3.
bake, v.a. torreo, 2; coquo, 3; igne obduro, 1.
bakehouse, bakery, s. pistrina, f.
baker, s. pistor, m.; **—'s shop,** s. pistrina, f. pistrinum, n.
balance, s. libra, statera, trutina, f.; (equipoise) æquipondium, n.; (in bookkeeping) reliquum, n.; (to lose one's —) labi.
balance, v.a. libro; pendo; (weigh one thing against another) penso; compenso, 1; (accounts) dispungo, 3.
balcony, s. mæniana, n. pl.
bald, a. calvus, glaber; *fig.* jejunus, aridus; **—ly,** ad. jejune.

balderdash, s. farrago, f.
baldness, s. calvitium, n.
baldric, cingulum, n.
bale, s. sarcina, f., fascis, m.
baleful, a. funestus; perniciosus, exitialis, noxius.
balk, s. (of land) limes, m.; (of wood) tignum, n.
balk, v.a. frustror, 1; eludo, decipio, fallo, 3.
ball, s. globus, globulus, m.; (to play with) pila, f.; (clue) glomus, n.
ballad, s. nenia, f.; carmen triviale, n.
ballast, s. saburra, f.
ballast, v.a. saburro, 1.
ballet, s. pantomimus, i, m.; embolium, n.
ballet-dancer, s. pantomimus, m., pantomima, f.
ballot, s. (used in voting) tabella, f.; (voting) suffragatio, f.
ballot, v.n. tabella *or* tabellis suffragari, 1.
ballot-box, s. cista, f.
balm, s. balsamum, n.; *fig.* solatium, n.
balm of Gilead, s. cedronella (mod. hort.).
balmy, a. ambrosius, suavis; mollis.
balsam, balsamum, n.
balsamic, a. balsaminus.
baluster, balustrade, s. (for stairs) epimedion, i, n.; (between pillars) pluteus, m.; (rails inclosing a place) cancelli, m. pl.
bamboo, s. bambusa (mod. hort.).
bamboozle, v.a. decipio, 3.
ban, s. interdictio, f.
ban, v.a. interdico.
banana, s. musa (mod. hort.).
band, s. vinculum; (headband) redimiculum, n.; (troop) caterva, f.; (chorus) grex, m.; *fig.* catena, copula, f.; vinculum, n.; **by —s,** turmatim.
band, v.a. socio, consocio; v.n. (league together) conjuro, 1.
bandage, s. fascia, f.
bandage, v.a. deligo, 1.
bandbox, s. capsula, f.
bandit, s. latro, m.
bandy, v.a. permuto, 1; (bandy words) rixor, 1.
bandy-legged, a. loripes, valgus.
bane, s. venenum, n.; pestis; pernicies, f.
baneful, a. pestifer; perniciosus; funestus; exitialis.
bang, v.a. & n. crepo, 1.
bang, s. crepitus, sonitus, m.; (blow) plaga, f.; (shock) percussus, m.
banish, v.a. in exilium mitto, pello, 3; relego, 1; *fig.* pono, 3.
banishment, s. (act) ejectio; relegatio, f.; (state) exilium, n.; fuga.
banister, s., v. **baluster.**

bank, s. (hillock) tumulus, i, m.; (of a river) ripa, f.; (bench for rowers) transtrum; scamnum, n.; (for money) argentaria taberna, f.

bank, v.a. exstruo, 3.

banker, s. argentarius, mensarius, trapezita, m.

bankrupt, a. decoctor, m.; **to be — or to become —,** rationes conturbare, 1; decoquo, 3.

bankruptcy, s. novæ tabulæ.

banner, s. vexillum, n.   [f. pl.

banquet, s. convivium, n.; epulæ, dapes,

banquet, v.n. convivor; epulor, 1; —, v.a. convivio excipio, 3.

banqueter, s. epulo, conviva, m.

banqueting, s. epulatio, f.

banter, s. jocus, m.; cavillatio, f.

banter, v.a. cavillor, 1; derideo, 2.

banterer, s. cavillator; risor, m.

bantering, s. cavillatio, f.

banteringly, a. per ludibrium.

bantling, s. infans, c.

baptism, s. baptisma, n., baptismus, i, m.

baptistery, s. baptisterium, n.

baptize, v.a. baptizo, 1.

bar, s. vectis; (of a door) obex, m.; repagulum, n.; pessulus, m.; *fig.* impedimentum, ·n.; (ingot) later, m.; (in a court of justice) cancelli, m. pl.; claustra, n. pl.; (barristers) advocati, m. pl.; (supremacy at the bar) regnum judiciale.

bar, v.a. obsero, 1; excludo, 3; prohibeo, 2; veto, 1.

barb, s. (horse) sonipes; (hook) uncus; hamus, m.

barbacan, s. turris; specula, f.

barbarian, a. & s. barbarus, m.

barbaric, a. barbaricus.

barbarism, s. barbaria, barbaries; feritas, f.; (of language) barbarismus, m.

barbarity, s. barbaries; feritas, truculentia, f.

barbarous, a. barbarus; ferus; immanis; sævus, truculentus; (uncultivated) rudis, barbarus; **—ly,** ad. barbare; sæve.

barbarousness, s. barbaria, barbaries, f.

barbed, a. hamatus.

barber, s. tonsor, m. tonstrix, f.; **—'s shop,** tonstrina, f.

barberry, s. berberis (mod. hort.).

bard, s. vates, c.; (Celtic poet) bardus, m.

bare, a. (unclothed) nudus; (mere) merus; (of style) pressus; (of money) inops; (threadbare) tritus; (lean) macer; (plain) manifestus.

bare, v.a. nudo, denudo, 1; aperio, 4.

barefaced, a. impudens; audax; **—ly,** ad. impudenter.

barefacedness, s. audacia, impudentia, f.

barefoot, barefooted, a. nudo pede, nudis pedibus; discalceatus.

bareheaded, a. nudo capite.

barely, ad. vix, ægre.

bareness, s. (of hair) calvitium, n.; (of money) tenuitas; *fig.* sterilitas, f.; (thinness) macies.

bargain, s. pactio, f., pactum, n.

bargain, v.n. stipulor, 1; paciscor, 3.

bargainer, s. pactor.

barge, s. actuariolum, n., navicula, f.

bargeman, s. portitor, m.

bark, s. (of trees) cortex, c.; (inner bark) liber; (of dogs) latratus, us, m.; (ship) ratis, f.

bark, v.a. (to peel) decortico, 1; —, v.n. latro, 1; **to — at,** allatro, 1 (also *fig.*).

barking, s. latratus, m.

barley, s. hordeum, n.; **(of barley)** a. hordeaceus; **-water,** s. ptisanarium, n.

barmaid, s. ministra cauponæ, f.

barn, s. granarium, horreum, n., area, f.; **- -door fowls,** s. pl. gallinæ, f. pl.

barnacle, s. (in farriery) postomis, f.

barque, s. navicula, ratis, linter, f.

barracks, s. castra (stativa), n. pl.   [m.

barrack-master, s. præfectus castrorum,

barrel, s. (cask) cadus, m., dolium, n.; orca, f.; (cylinder) cylindrus, m.

barren, a. sterilis; infecundus.

barrenness, s. sterilitas, infecunditas, f.

barricade, s. agger, m.; vallum, n.

barricade, v.a. obstruo, 3.

barrier, s. cancelli, m. pl.; sæpta, n. pl.; (in the circus) carcer, m.; claustra, m. pl.; *fig.* impedimentum, n.

barrister, s. advocatus, causidicus, m.

barrow, s. (castrated hog) majalis, m.; (vehicle) ferculum, n.; (mound) tumulus, m.

barter, s. permutatio, f.; commercium, n.

barter, v.a. & n. (per)muto, (com)muto, 1; paciscor, 3.

basalt, s. basaltes, m.

base, a. humilis, ignobilis, obscurus; inferior; infamis, vilis, turpis; fœdus; **—ly,** ad. abjecte; turpiter.

base, s. basis, f.; fundus, m.; fundamentum, n.

baseless, a. vanus, inanis; falsus.

basement, s. basis, f. fundamentum, n.

baseness, s. humilitas; turpitudo; nequitia, f.

bashaw, s. satrapes, m.

bashful, a. pudens; pudicus, pudibundus, modestus; verecundus; **—ly,** ad. timide; modeste, verecunde; pudenter.

bashfulness, s. pudor; rubor, m.; vere-cundia, modestia, f.

basil, s. ocimum, n.

basilica, s. (church) basilica, f.

basilisk, s. basiliscus, m.

basin, s. (for washing the hands) pelvis trulleum, f.; (tub) labrum, n.; (lake) lacus, m.; (dock) navalia, n. pl.

basis, s. fundamentum, n.; (cause) causa.

bask, v.n. apricor, 1.

basket, s. corbis, f.; canistrum; qualum, n.; calathus, m.; (large basket) cophinus, m.

bason, s. v. basin. [anaglypta, n. pl.

bas-relief, s. cælamen, n.; cælatura, f.;

bass, s. sonus gravis.

bast, s. tilia, f.

bastard, s. nothus, spurius, m.; *fig.* fictus, falsus; —, a. spurius.

baste, v.a. perfundo, conspergo, 3.

bastinado, s. fustuarium, n.

bastinado, v.a. verbero, 1.

bastion, s. propugnaculum, castellum, n.

bat, s. vespertilio, m.; (club) clava, f.

batch, s. (troop) turma, f.; **in —es,** ad. turmatim.

bate, v.a. minuo, remitto, 3.

bath, s. balneum, n.; lavatio, f.; (tub) alveus, m., labrum, n.

bathe, v.a. lavo; (steep) macero, 1; (sprinkle) perfundo, 3; —, v.n. lavor,

bathing, s. lavatio, f. [1.

bathing-place, s. lavatio, f.

bathing-tub, s. alveus, m.; labrum, n.

bath-keeper, s. balneator, m.

bating, pr. præter, præterquam; nisi.

battalion, s. cohors, f.; (army in battle-array) acies, f.

batten, v.a. & n. pascor, 3.

batter, v.a. verbero, pulso, 1; percutio, obtundo, diruo, 3; ferio, 4.

battering-ram, s. aries, m.

battery, s. (mound for artillery), agger, m.; (artillery) tormenta, 1. pl.; (assault) vis, f.

battle, s. prœlium, n., pugna; (in array) acies, f.

battle, v.n. prælior, pugno, 1; (with one) contendo, 3.

battle-array, s. acies, f.

battle-axe, s. bipennis, f.

battlement, s. pinna, f.

bauble, s. tricæ, nugæ, f. pl.

bavin, s. fascis, m.

bawd, s. lena, f.; leno, m.

bawl, v.n. clamito, vociferor, 1.

bawler, s. clamator, m.

bawling, s. vociferatio, f.; clamor, m.

bay, s. (of the sea) sinus, m.; (tree) laurus, laurea, f.; **at —,** ad pugnam paratus; **stand at —,** consisto, s.

bay, a. (light —) helvus; (dark —) spadix.

bay, v.a. & n. allatro, 1.

bazaar, s. forum.

be, v.n. sum, fui, esse; (exist) existo, 3; how are you? quid agis? **to — against,** adversor, 1; abhorreo, 2; **to — amongst** or **between,** intersum; **to — away,** absum; **to — for** (one), faveo, 2; cum aliquo sto, 1; **to — in,** inesse; **so — it,** ita fiat, esto! let —, mitto; **to — present,** adsum; **to —without,** careo, 2.

beach, s. litus, n.; (coast) ora, f.

beach, v.a. ad litus appello, 3.

beacon, s. specula, f.; (lighthouse) pharus, m.; (fire) ignis, m.

bead, s. globus, globulus, m.

beadle, s. apparitor, m.

beagle, s. canis venaticus, m. [n. pl.

beak, s. rostrum, n.; (of ships) rostra,

beaked, a. rostratus.

beaker, s. poculum, carchesium, n.

beam, s. tignum, n., trabs, f.; (of ships) transtrum, n.; (of a balance) scapus; (sunbeam) radius, m.

beam, v.n. radio, 1; refulgeo, niteo, 2.

beaming, a. nitens, lucidus; —, s. nitor,

beau, s. faba, f., phaselus, c. [m.

bear, v.a. fero; *fig.* patior; gero, 3; subeo, 4; sustineo, 2; tolero, 1; (of children) pario, (bring forth) fero, effero, fundo, profundo, 3; **to — away** or **off,** aufero, 3; **to — down,** *fig.* opprimo, 3; **to — out,** effero, 3, *fig.*; præsto, 1; **to — up,** sustineo, 2, resisto, 3; **to — with,** indulgeo, 2; **to — witness,** testor, 1.

bear, s. ursus, m., ursa, f.; (constellation) septentriones, m. pl.

bearable, a. tolerandus, tolerabilis.

beard, s. barba; (of corn) arista, f.

bearded, a. barbatus; intonsus.

beardless, a. imberbis.

bearer, s. (porter) bajulus; (of litters, etc.) lecticarius; (of corpses) vespillo, m.

bearing, s. gestus, m.; **to have a — on,** pertinere, ad.

bear's foot, s. acanthus (mod. hort.).

beast, s. belua; (wild beast) bestia, f.; (cattle) pecus, m.; **wild —,** fera, f.; **— of burden,** jumentum, n.

beastly, a. obscenus.

beat, v.a. verbero; (to knock) pulso, 1; cædo, 3; (conquer) vinco; (to bruise) tero, 3; (excel) supero, 1; —, v.n. palpito, 1; **to — back (off),** repello, 3; **to — down,** demolior, 4; sterno, prosterno, 3; **to — upon** (of waves) illidor, 3.

beat, s. pulsus, m.
beaten, a. victus; (of a road) tritus.
beatify, v.a. beatifico, beo, 1.
beating, s. verberatio, f.; (blow) ictus, m.; verbera, n. pl.; (of time, mus.) percussio, f.; (of the heart) palpitatio, f.; (of veins) pulsus, m.
beatitude, s. beatitudo, f.
beautiful, a. pulcher, cra, crum; (of form) formosus.
beautifully, ad. pulchre.
beautify, v.a. decoro, orno, 1; excolo, 3.
beauty, s. pulcritudo; forma; (grace, etc.) venus, f.
beaver, s. castor, fiber, m.; (of a helmet) buccula, f.
becalm, v.a. paco, sedo, 1; —ed, vento destitutus.
because, c. quia, quod; — of, ob, propter, gratia; — (of preventive causes) præ.
beck, s. nutus, m.
beckon, v.a. nuto, 1; annuo, innuo, 3.
become, v.n. ir. fio, 3; —, v. imp. deceo, 2; it —s, decet.
becoming, a. decorus; decens; conveniens; —ly, ad. decenter; honeste.
becomingness, s. decor, m.
bed, s. lectus, torus, m.; cubile, n.; (in a garden) areola, f.; (of a river) alveus, m.; to be brought to —, parturio, 4.
bed, v.a. (plant) sero, 3.
bedaub, v.a. lino, perunguo, 3; inquino, conspurco, 1.
bedchamber, s. cubiculum, n.
bedclothes, bedding, s. stragulum, n.; vestis, f.   [excolo, 3.
bedeck, v.a. decoro, orno, exorno, 1;
bedevil, v.a. (to enchant) fascino, 1.
bedew, v.a. irroro, umecto, 1; perfundo, 3.
bed-fellow, s. socius (m.) or socia (f.) tori.
bed-hangings, s. aulæa, n. pl
bedim, v.a. obscuro, 1.
bedizen, v.a. exorno, 1; distinguo, 3.
bedpost, s. fulcrum, n.
bed-ridden, a. lecto affixus.
bedroom, s., v. **bedchamber.**
bedstead, s. sponda, f.
bed-time, s. hora somni, f.
bee, s. apis, f.; — -eater, s. merops, f.; — -hive, s. alveus, m.; apiarium, alvearium, n.; — -keeper, — -master, s. apiarius, m.
beechen, a. faginus, fagineus, fageus.
beech-nut, s. glans, f.
beech-tree, s. fagus, f.
beef, s. bubula (caro), f.
bee orchid, s. ophrys (mod. hort.).
beer, s. cervisia, f.   [m.
beet, s. beta, f.; — -root, s. pes betaceus,

beetle, s. scarabæus, m.; (rammer) fistuca, f.
beetle, v.n. promineo, 2.
beeves, s. pl. boves, m. pl.
befall, v.n. contingo, accido, 3; evenio, 4.
befit, v.a. convenio, 4; it —s, par est, convenit, 4; decet, 2.
befitting, a. decens; conveniens, idoneus.
befool, v.a. ludificor, 1; ludo, 3.
before, pr. ante; præ; pro; (in presence of) coram; apud; —, ad. ante; antea prius; — all things, imprimis; — now, antehac; — that, antequam, priusquam; — then, antea; long —, jamdudum; a little —, paulo ante.
before, a. prior.
beforehand, ad. ante, prius; præ . . .; (ready at hand) præsto.
befoul, v.a. inquino, spurco, 1.
befriend, v.a. sublevo, adjuvo, 1; faveo, 2.
beg, v.a. & n. peto, posco, 3; oro, precor, obsecro, flagito, rogo, 1; (to ask alms) mendico, 1; I beg, quæso; —ging the question, petitio principii.
beget, v.a. gigno, 3; procreo, creo, genero, 1.
beggar, s. mendicus, m., mendica, f.
beggar, v.a. ad inopiam redigere, 3.
beggarliness, s. paupertas; inopia, miseria, f.
beggarly, a. mendicus; vilis, abjectus; (wretched) exilis.
beggary, s. mendicitas, egestas, paupertas, f.   [mendico, 1.
begging, s. mendicitas, f.; to go a- —,
begin, v.a. & n. initium facio, 3; incoho, 1; ordior, 4; cœpi, incipio, 3; (to take rise) exorior, 4.
beginner, s. auctor; fig. tiro, m.
beginning, s. inceptio, f.; initium; principium, exordium, n.; origo, f.; fig. (of learning, etc.) rudimentum, n.
begone, i, apage!
begonia, s. begonia (mod. hort.).
begrime, v.a. inquino, polluo; be —d, squaleo, 2.
beguile, v.a. fraudo, frustror, 1; fallo, 3; circumvenio, 4.
beguiler, s. fraudator, m.
behalf, s. in — of, pro, propter, causa.
behave, to — oneself, v.n. & r. me gero; (towards) utor, 3.
behaviour, s. mores, m. pl.; (actions) facta, n. pl.; good —, urbanitas, f.; ill —, rusticitas, f.
behead, v.a. decolio, 1; securi percutio.
behest, s. jussum, n.
behind, ad. pone, a tergo, post; (remaining) reliquus; to be (left) —. relinquor, 3; pr. post.

behindhand, ad. reliquus; **be —,** (make too little advance) parum progredior.

behold, v.a. conspicio, 3; obtueor, 2; specto, 1; cerno, 3; aspicio, 3.

behold, i. ecce! en! aspice!

beholden, a. obnoxius; **to be —,** obligor, 1; gratiam debere.

beholder, s. spectator, m.

behoof, s. commodum, n., gratia, f.

behove, v. imp. **it —s,** oportet; convenit; decet.

being, s. natura; (essence) essentia, f.; (man) homo, m.; **supreme —,** numen, n.

belabour, v.a. verbero, pulso, 1.

belch, v.n. ructo; eructo, 1.

belch, belching, s. ructus, m.

beldam, s. vetula, f.

beleaguer, v.a. obsideo, 2.

belie, v.a. mendacii coarguo (aliquem), 3; (— one's hopes) fallo, 2; (counterfeit) imitor, 1.

belief, s. fides; opinio; persuasio; religio, f.; (teaching) doctrina, f.; **hard of —,** incredulus.

believe, v.a. credo, 3; (to trust to) confido, 3; (think) existimo, opinor, arbitror, puto, 1; **— in the gods,** deos esse credo.

believer, s. qui (quæ) credit.

believing, ad. credulus.

bell, s. (large) campana, f.; (a little one) tintinnabulum, n.

belladonna lily, s. amaryllis (mod. hort.).

bellman, s. præco, m.

bell-shaped, a. curvus.

belle, s. formosa puella, f.

belles-lettres, s. litteræ, f. pl.

belligerent, a. & s. qui bella gerit.

bellow, v.n. rugio, mugio, 4.

bellowing, s. mugitus, m.

bellows, s. (a pair of —) follis, m.

belly, s. venter, m.; abdomen, n.; alvus f.; stomachus, uterus, i, m.; (womb) vulva, f.

belly, v.n. turgeo, tumeo, 2.

belly-ache, s. tormina, um, n. pl.

belly-band, s. ventrale, cingulum, n.

belong, v.n. (to) pertineo ad, 2.

beloved, a. delectus, carus; amatus.

below, pr. infra; subter; **—,** ad. infra; deorsum, subter; **from —,** ab inferiore parte.

belt, s. cingulum, n.; zona, f.; (sword-belt) balteus, m.

bemoan, v.a. ingemo, 3; deploro, 1; defleo, 2.

bench, s. scamnum; sedile; (of the Senate) subsellium, n.; (court of justice) subsellia, n. pl.; **— of rowers,** transtrum, n.; **—-table,** mensa, f.

bend, v.a. flecto, 3; curvo; inclino, 1; *fig.* domo, 1; **to — down,** deflecto, 3; **—,** v.n. use pass. of verbs given.

bend, s. sinus, flexus, m., curvamen, n.; *fig.* inclinatio, f.

bending, s. flexura; curvatura; inclinatio, f.

beneath, v. below; **it is — me to . . .** me indignum est.

benediction, s. benedictio, f.

benefaction, s. largitio, f.; beneficium n.

benefactor, s. patronus, m.

benefactress, s. patrona, f.

benefice, s. beneficium (ecclesiasticum), n.

beneficed, a. beneficiarius.

beneficence, s. beneficentia, f.

beneficent, a. beneficus, benignus, liberalis; **—ly,** ad. benefice, benigne, liberaliter.   [**—ly,** ad. utiliter.

beneficial, a. utilis, commodus; salutaris;

benefit, s. beneficium, n., gratia, f.

benefit, v.a. juvo, 1; prosum, proficio, 3; **—,** v.n. lucror, 1.

benevolence, s. benevolentia; largitio, f.

benevolent, a. benevolus; benignus; **—ly,** ad. benevole, benigne.

benighted, a. nocte deprehensus; *fig.* incultus.

benign, benignant, a. benignus.

benignity, s. benignitas, f.

bent, a. curvus, flexus; (backwards) recurvus; (forwards) pronus; (inwards) camur; (winding) sinuosus.

bent, s. *fig.* (inclination) ingenium, n.; animus, m.; voluntas, f.

benumb, v.a. obstupefacio, 3.

bepraise, v.a. laudo, 1.

bequeath, v.a. lego, 1; relinquo, 3.

bequest, s. legatum, n.

bereave, v.a. (of) orbo, spolio, privo, 1.

bereaver, s. orbator, m.

bereavement, s. orbitas; spoliatio; (loneliness) solitudo, f.

berry, s. baca, f.; acinus, i, m.

berth, s. (nav.) statio, f.; (sleeping-place) cubiculum, n.; (place, office) munus, n.

beryl, s. beryllus, m.

beseech, v.a. obsecro, imploro, supplico, obtestor, 1.

beseem, v.a. deceo, 2; **it —s,** decet.

beset, v.a. circumdo, 1; obsideo; circumsideo; urgeo, 2; vexo, 1.

beside, besides, pr. (in addition to) ad, (outside) extra, (near) juxta, (except) præter; (along) secundum; **—,** ad. porro, præterea, præterquam; insuper; **to be — oneself,** deliro, 1.

besiege, v.a. circumsedeo, obsideo, 2.

besieger, s. obsessor, m.   [sessio, 1.

besieging, s. obsidio, obsessio, circum-

besmear, v.a. illino, perlino, lino, 3; (to soil) inquino, 1.

besom, scopæ, f. pl.

besot, v.a. infatuo; inebrio, 1.

bespangle, v.a. adorno, decoro, 1.

bespatter, v.a. aspergo, 3.

bespeak, v.a. (order beforehand) præmando, 1; (give proof of) arguo, 3; — a person's attention, rogare (aliquem) ut animum advertat, 1; (to address) alloquor, 3.

besprinkle, v.a. conspergo, 3.

best, a. optimus, præstantissimus; — of all, ad. optime, potissimum; to the — of one's ability, pro viribus.

best, ad. optime.

bestial, a. obscenus; —ly, ad. obscene.

bestir, to — oneself, v.r. expergiscor, 3; (make an effort) incumbo.

bestow, v.a. tribuo; confero, 3; dono, 1; largior, 4; (to give in marriage) colloco, 1; (place) pono, repono, 3.

bestower, s. largitor, dator, m.

bestrew, v.a. spargo, diffundo, 3.

bestride, v.a. insideo, 2.

bet, s. pignus; sponsio, f.; v. wager.

bet, v.a. pignore contendo, 3.

betake, to — oneself, v.r. sese conferre; (have recourse to) confugio, 3; to — oneself to flight, se in fugam dare, 1.

bethink, to — oneself, v.r. delibero, 1; consulo, 3; reputo, 1.

betide, v.a. evenio, 4; accido, 3.

betoken, v.a. indico, 1; portendo, 3.

betray, v.a. trado, prodo, 3; (leave in the lurch) desum; fig. oleo, 2 (with accus.); (show forth) profero; (give proof of) arguo, 3.

betrayal, proditio, f.

betrayer, s. proditor.

betroth, v.a. spondeo, despondeo, 2.

betrothal, s. sponsalia, n. pl.

betrothed, a. & s. sponsus, m.; sponsa, f.

better, a. melior, potior, f.

better, a. melior, potior, præstantior; superior; to get the —, supero, 1; vinco, 3; prævaleo, 2; it is —, præstat.

better, ad. melius, potius; rectius, satius; to grow —, (in health) convalesco, 3.

better, v.a. emendo, 1; corrigo, 3; —, v.n. melior fio, 3.

betters, s. pl. superiores, m. pl.

between, pr. inter, in medio; — whiles, interim.

beverage, s. potio, f., potus, m.

bevy, s. grex, f.

bewail, v.a. deploro, 1; ingemo, queror, 3; lamentor, 1; defleo, 2.

beware, v.n. caveo, præcaveo, 2.

bewilder, v.a. perturbo, 1; confundo, 3.

bewilderment, s. perturbatio, f.

bewitch, v.a. fascino, 1; (to charm) demulceo, 2; capio, 3.

bewitching, a. (met.) venustus.

beyond, pr. ultra, supra; præter; (across) trans; —, ad. supra, ultra; ulterius.

bias, s. inclinatio, f.; momentum, n.; impetus, m.

bias, v.a. inclino, 1.

bibber, s. potor, m.

bicker, v.n. altercor, rixor, 1.

bibulous, a. bibulus, vinosus.

bickering, s. altercatio, rixa, f.; jurgium, n.

bid, v.a. jubeo, 2; impero, mando; (invite) invito, rogo; (money for wares) licitor, 1; liceor, 2; to — adieu, valedico, 3.

bid, s. licitatio, f.

bidding, s. jussum, mandatum, n.; (at the bidding of) jussu (gen.), f.; (auction) licitatio, f.

bide, v.a. expecto, 1; maneo, 2; opperior, 4; (endure) fero, 3; tolero, 1; sustineo, 2; —, v.n., v. abide.

biennial, a. biennalis, bimus.

bier, s. feretrum, n., sandapila, f.

biestings, s. colostra, f.

bifurcated, a. bifidus; scissus.

big, a. ingens, immanis, vastus, grandis; (in bulk) crassus; (with young) prægnans; fig. potens; (with pride) tumidus; to talk —, ampullari, 1.

bigamist, s. bimaritus, m.; bigamus, m.

bight, s. sinus, m., v. bay, s.

bigly, ad. fig. tumide.

bigness, s. amplitudo, magnitudo, moles, f.

bigoted, a. superstitiosus; (obstinate) pervicax.

bigotry, s. superstitio, f.; (obstinacy) pervicacia, f.

bilberry, s. vaccinium.

bile, s. bilis, f.

bilge-water, s. sentina, f.

bilious, a. biliosus.

bill, s. (of a bird) rostrum, n.; (axe) securis; falx, f.; (in writing) libellus, m.; (law proposed) rogatio; lex, f.; plebiscitum, n.; (account) syngrapha.

billet, s. epistula, f.; libellus, codicilli, m. pl.; (— doux) notæ blandæ, f. pl.; (log of wood) stipes, m.; (ticket) tessera, f.

billet, v.a. milites per hospitia disponere, 3.

bill-hook, s. falx, falcula, f.

billow, s. fluctus, m.

billowy, a. fluctuosus, undabundus.

bin, s. (in a wine-cellar) loculus, m.; (for corn) cista, f., panarium, n.

bind, v.a. ligo, 1; necto, stringo, 3; vincio, 4; *fig.* astringo, 3; (legibus) obligo, 1; devincio, 4; to — down, deligo, 1; to — over, obligo; vador, 1; to — together, colligo, 1; to — up, ligo; alligo; colligo, 1; substringo, 3; (be bound up in) *fig.* contineri, 2.

binding, a. obligatorius.

binding, s. religatio, f.; (wrapper) involucrum, n., v. fringe.

bindweed, s. convolvulus, m.

biographer, s. vitæ rerumque gestarum alicujus scriptor, m.

biography, s. vitæ descriptio, f.

biped, a. bipes.

birch-tree, s. betula, f.

birch-rod, s. virga, f.

bird, s. avis, volucris, ales, f.; (bird of omen) præpes, f.; oscen, m.

bird-cage, s. cavea, f.

bird-catcher, s. auceps, cupis, m.

bird-catching, s. aucupium, n.

bird-lime, s. viscum, n.

bird's-nest, s. nidus, m.

birth, s. partus; ortus, m.; (race) stirps, f., genus, n., natales, m. pl.

birthday, s. dies natalis, m.

birth-place, s. solum natale *or* genitale, n.

birth-right, s. jus ex genere ortum, n.

biscuit, s. buccellatum, n. [secare, 1.

bisect, v.a. in duas partes æquales

bishop, s. episcopus, m.

bishopric, s. (district) diœcesis, f.; (office) episcopatus, m.

bison, s. bison, m.

bit, s. (for a horse) frenum; (little piece) frustum, n., offa, offula, f.

bit, v.a. frenos equo adhibeo, 2.

bitch, s. canis, f.

bite, s. morsus, m.

bite, v.a. mordeo, 2; (as pepper, etc.) uro.

biting, a. mordax; *fig.* asper; —, s. morsus, m.

bitter, a. amarus; acerbus; asper; gravis; infensus; —ly, ad. amare; acerbe, aspere; graviter; infense.

bittern, s. ardeola, f.

bitterness, s. amaritudo; acerbitas; asperitas, gravitas, f.

bitumen, s. bitumen, n.

bituminous, a. bituminosus, bitumineus.

bivouac, s. excubiæ, f. pl.

bivouac, v.n. excubo, 1.

blab, v.n. garrio, 4; deblatero, 1; —, v.a. profero, effero, 3.

blab, s. garrulus; vulgator, m.

black, a. niger; ater; *fig.* (gloomy) tristis; scelestus, improbus; — and blue, lividus; — eye, sugillatio, f.

black, s. nigrum, n.; (negro) Æthiops, m.; dressed in —, pullatus.

blackberry, s. morum, n.; — -bush, s. rubus, m.

blackbird, s. merula, f.

black-cock, s. tetrao, m.

black-death, s. pestis, f.

blacken, v.a. nigro; denigro (also *fig.*), 1.

blackguard, s. nebulo; homo perditus, m.

blacking, s. atramentum, n.

blackish, a. subniger.

blacklead, s. plumbago, f.

blackness, s. nigritia, nigrities, nigritudo, f.

blacksmith, s. ferrarius faber, m.

blackthorn, s. prunus silvestris, f.

bladder, s. vesica, f.

blade, s. lamina, f.; (of grass, etc.) caulis, m.; herba, f.; culmus, m.; (of an oar) palma, palmula, f.

blade-bone, s., v. shoulder-blade.

blain, s. pustula, f., ulcus, n. [pandus.

blamable, a. vituperabilis; culpabilis; culblamably, ad. culpabiliter.

blame, v.a. reprehendo, 3; culpo, vitupero, 1.

blame, s. reprehensio; culpa, f.

blameless, a. integer, innoxius; innocens, innocuus; irreprehensus; —ly, ad. integre, innocenter.

blamelessness, s. integritas; innocentia, f.

blamer, s. reprehensor; vituperator, m.

blanch, v.n. expallesco, palleo, 2; pallesco, 3.

bland, a. blandus.

blandishment, s. blanditiæ, f. pl., blandimentum; (charm) lenocinium, n.

blank, a. (empty) vacuus; (unwritten on) purus; (depressed) demissus, tristis; (surprised) attonitus; to look —, confundor, 3.

blank, s. inane, n.; res vana, f.

blanket, s. stragulum, n.; lodix, m.

blanket-flower, s. gaillardia (mod. hort.).

blare, s. sonus, strepitus, m.

blarney, s. adulatio, f.

blaspheme, v.a. & n. blasphemo, 1.

blasphemer, s. blasphemus, m.

blasphemous, a. blasphemus, impius.

blasphemy, s. blasphemia, impietas, f.

blast, s. (of wind) flatus, m.; flamen, n.; flabra, m. pl.; (blight) sideratio, rubigo, f.; (sound) clangor, m.

blast, v.a. (corn) uro; (overthrow) everto, 3; (ruin) deleo, 2; (tear up) eruo, 3; (a reputation, etc.) infamo, 1.

blaze, s. flamma, f.; fulgor, m.; incendium, n.

blaze, v.n. flagro, 1; ardeo, 2; ardesco, 3; —, v.a. to — abroad, divulgo, 1.

blazon, v.a. enarro; vendito, 1; (adorn) orno, 1.

blazon s. insignia, n. pl.

bleach, v.a. candefacio, 3; v.n. albesco.
bleak, a. algidus, frigidus; immitis.
bleakness, s. algor, m.; frigus, n.
blear-eyed, a. lippus; **to be** —, lippio, 4.
bleat, v.n. (as a sheep) balo.
bleating, s. balatus, m.
bleed, v.n. (of blood) fluere, 3; (emit blood) sanguinem effundo.
bleeding, s. (of wounds) crudus.
bleeding, s. (flowing of blood) sanguinis profluvium, n.
bleeding heart, s. dielytra (mod. hort.).
blemish, s. (flaw) vitium, n., labes, macula, f.
blemish, v.a. maculo, 1.
blend, v.a. misceo, immisceo, commisceo, 2.
bless, v.a. benedico, 3; (to consecrate) consecro; (with good success) bene verto, 3; prospero, aspiro, secundo, 1.
blessed, a. beatus; pius; (fortunate) felix, fortunatus; (the islands of the blessed) Fortunatæ Insulæ.
blessedness, s. beatitudo, beatitas, f.; felicitas.
blessing, s. benedictio; (good wish) fausta precatio, f.; (benefit) beneficium, bonum, munus, n.
blight, s. lues; (of corn, etc.) robigo, uredo; sideratio, f.
blight, v.a. uro, 3; (ruin) deleo, 2; (frustrate) frustror, 1; fallo, 3.
blind, a. cæcus; (dark) obscurus, opacus; (false) falsus.
blind, s. (screen of cloth) velum, n.; fig. prætextum, n.
blind, v.a. cæco, occæco, 1; (to deceive) fallo, 3.
blindly, ad. temere.
blindness, s. cæcitas, f.; tenebræ, f. pl.
blink, v.n. conniveo, 2; nicto, 1.
bliss, s. beatitudo, f.
blissful, a. beatus; **—ly,** ad. beate.
blister, s. pustula, f.
blister, v.a. & n. pustulo, 1.
blithe, a. hilaris, hilarus, lætus.
blithely, ad. hilare, læte.
bloated, a. sufflatus; inflatus, tumefactus, tumidus; (immense) immanis.
block, s. truncus; stipes, m.; massa, f.; caudex, m.
block, v.a. **to — up,** obstruo, intercludo, 3.
blockade, s. obsidium, n.; obsidio, f.; —, v.a. obsideo, 2.
blockhead, s. caudex, m.
blockhouse, s. arx, f.
blood, s. sanguis, m.; (gore) cruor, m.; (corrupted blood) sanies, f.; fig. (slaughter) cædes; (lineage) natura, f. genus, n.; (death) mors, f.

blood-guiltiness, s., v. **murder,** s.
bloodless, a. exsanguis; (without bloodshed) incruentus.
blood-red, a. cruentus; sanguineus, sanguinolentus.
bloodshed, s. cædes, f.
blood-shot, a. cruore suffusus.
blood-stained, a. cruentus, cruentatus, sanguinolentus.
blood-stone, s. hæmatites, ae, m.
blood-sucker, s. sanguisuga, hirudo, f.
blood-thirstily, ad. crudeliter.
blood-thirsty, a. sanguinarius; sanguinolentus; sanguineus; cruentus.
blood-vessel, s. arteria, vena, f.
blood-wort. s. sanguinalis herba, f.
bloody, a. sanguineus; sanguinolentus; sanguinarius; cruentus.
bloom, s. flos, m. (also fig.); robur, n.
bloom, v.n. floreo, vigeo, 2; (also fig.).
blooming, a. florens; floridus; nitidus.
bloomy, a., v. **blooming.**
blossom, s. & v.n., v. **bloom.**
blot, s. macula, litura; fig. labes, f., dedecus, n.
blot, v.a. maculo, 1; (soil) conspurco, 1; **to — out,** deleo, 2; extinguo; (to erase) oblittero, 1.
blotch, s. varus, m.
blow, s. (stroke) plaga, f., ictus, m.; (with the fist) colaphus, m.; plaga, f.; vulnus, n.; (it came to blows) res ad pugnam venit.
blow, v.n. flo; (to breathe) spiro, 1; (musical instruments) cano, 3; (to pant) anhelo, 1; (to blossom) floreo, 2; —, v.a. flo, afflo; (a wind instrument) inflo; (glass) conflo, 1; (blow the nose) emungo, 3.
blower, s. flator; (of a horn) cornicen, m.
blowing, s. sufflatio, f.; flatus, m.; (of the nose) emunctio, f.
blubber, s. (fat) adeps, m.
blubber, v.n. lachrimas effundo, 3.
bludgeon, s. fustis, m.
blue, a. cæruleus, cærulus; (dark blue) cyaneus; —, s. cæruleum.
bluebell, s. scilla (mod. hort.).
blue-bottle, s. (flower) cyanus, m.; (fly) musca, f. [n.; livor, m.
blueness, s. cæruleus color, m., cæruleum,
blues, s. melancholia, f.
blue-eyed, a. cæruleus; glaucus.
blue-gum, s. eucalyptus (mod. hort.).
bluff, a. rusticus; (steep) declivis; (windy) ventosus; (hearty) vehemens.
bluish, a. lividus, livens. [m.
blunder, s. mendum, erratum, n.; error,
blunder, v.n. offendo, 3; erro, 1.
blunderer, blunderhead, s. homo ineptus or stupidus, m.; stipes, m.

blunt, a. hebes; obtusus; retusus; *fig.* inurbanus, rusticus; (plain) planus; —ly, ad. plane, libere.

blunt, v.a. hebeto, 1; obtundo, retundo, 3.

bluntness, s. hebetatio, f.

blur, s. macula, labes, f.

blur, v.a. maculo, 1; (darken) obscuro, 1.

blurt, v.a. **to — out,** divulgo, vulgo, 1.

blush, v.n. erubesco, rubesco, 3; rubeo, 2.

blush, blushing, s. rubor, m.

blushing, a. —ly, ad. rubens, erubescens.

bluster, v.n. me jacto; glorior, 1; fremo, strepo, 3. [tus, m.

bluster, s. jactatio; fremitus, strepi-

boa, s. boa, f.

boar, s. aper; verres, m.

board, s. (plank) tabula; (table) mensa, f.; (food, etc.) victus; (playing-table) abacus, alveus lusorius, m.; (council, etc.) collegium; consilium, n.; **on —,** in nave.

board, v.a. contabulo, 1; navem ascendo *or* conscendo, 3; (feed) alo, 3; **—,** v.n. victito, 1.

boarder, s. convictor; hospes, m.

boast, v.n. jacto, glorior, 1.

boast, s. jactantia, jactatio, gloriatio, vanitas, f.

boaster, s. jactator, m. [quus.

boastful, boasting, a. gloriosus, vanilo-

boasting, s., v. **boast,** s.

boastingly, ad. jactanter.

boat, s. linter, scapha, navicula, **cymba,** f.

boat-hook, s. contus, m.

boatman, s. nauta, intrarius, m.; (ferry-man) portitor, m.

boatswain, s. magister, m.

bode, v.a. portendo, 3; præsagio, 4; præmonstro, 1.

bodiless, a. incorporalis; sine corpore.

bodily, a. corporeus; corporalis; **—,** ad. corporaliter.

bodkin, s. subula, f.

body, s. corpus; (corpse) cadaver, n.; (trunk) truncus, (mil.) numerus, m., vis, f.; (collection of people) societas; multitudo, f.; collegium, n.

bodyguard, s. stipatores, satellites, m. pl.; cohors prætoria, f.

bog, s. palus, f.

boggle, v.n. dubito, hæsito, f.

boggy, a. paludosus, palustris. ·

boil, v.n. ferveo, 2; effervesco, 3; æstuo, exæstuo, 1; **—,** v. a. fervefacio; coquo, 3.

boil, s. furunculus, m.; ulcus, n.

boiler, s. (vessel) aenum, caldarium, n.; (kettle) lebes, m.

boisterous, a. procellosus; violentus; turbidus; —ly, ad. turbide: turbu-lente; tumultuose.

bold, a. audax; fortis; impavidus; (free) liber; (rash) temerarius; (saucy) insolens; procax; (stout) intrepidus.

boldly, ad. audacter; libere; insolenter; fortiter.

boldness, s. audacia; fidentia; (of speech) libertas; impudentia; (rash-ness), temeritas, f.

bolster, s. pulvinus, m.; (of a bed) cervical, n.

bolster, v.a. **to — up,** fulcio, 4.

bolt, s. (of a door) pessulus, m.; claus-trum, n.; obex, m.; (dart) jaculum, pilum; (of thunder) fulmen, n.; (pin) clavus, m.

bolt, v.a. obsero, 1; occludo, 3; **to — out,** excludo, 3; (to sift) cribro, 1.

bolter, s. cribrum, n.

bombard, v.a. tormentis verbero, 1.

bombast, s. ampullæ, f. pl.

bombastic, a. inflatus, tumidus.

bombazine, s. bombycina; Coa vestis, f.

bond, s. vinculum, n.; nodus, m.; copula; catena; (imprisonment) custodia, f.; (obligation) necessitas, necessitudo, f.; (legal document), syngrapha, f.; **to give —,** satisdo, 1.

bond, a. servus, m., serva, f.

bondage, s. servitus, f., servitium, n.; captivitas, f. [c.

bondsman, s. servus; addictus, 4; verna,

bone, s. os (ossis), n.; (of fish) spina, f.

bone, v.a. exosso, 1.

boneless, a. exos, exossis.

bonfire, s. ignes festi, m. pl.

bon-mot, s. dictum, n.

bonnet, s. mitra, f.

bonny, a. hilarus; lepidus, pulcher.

bony, a. osseus; (thin) macer.

booby, s. stultus, m.

book, s. liber, libellus, m.; volumen, n.; codex, m.

book, v.a. in tabulas (*or* codicem, libel-lum, etc.) refero, 3.

bookcase, s. foruli, m. pl.

bookish, a. libris deditus.

bookseller, s. bibliopola, librarius, m.; **—'s shop,** taberna (libraria).

bookshelf, s. pluteus, m.

bookworm, s. tinea, blatta, f.; *fig.* **be a —,** libris helluari.

boom, s. (of a ship) longurius, m.; (of harbour) obex, catena, f.; (noise) stri-dor, m.

boom, v.n. resono, 1.

boon, s. bonum, donum, n.; gratia, f.

boon, a., **companion,** s. compransor; compotor, m.

boor, s. rusticus, m. [rustice.

boorish, a. agrestis, rusticus; —ly, ad.

boorishness, s. rusticitas, f.

boot, v.a. prosum; **what —s it?** cui bono?

boot, to, ad. insuper.

boot, s. calceus, m.; caliga, f.

booted, a. calceatus.

booth, s. taberna, f., tabernaculum, n.

bootless, a. irritus, inutilis.

booty, s. præda, f.; spolia, n. pl.; (arms stripped from a foe) exuviæ, f. pl.

borage, s. borago (mod. hort.).

border, s. (edge) margo, c.; (of dress) limbus, m.; (boundary) finis, terminus, m.; confinium, n.

border, v.n. tango, attingo, 3; circumjaceo, 2; —, v.a. prætexo, 3. [confinis.

borderer, s. accola, finitimus, m.; vicinus,

bordering, a. affinis, finitimus. [fatigo, 1.

bore, v.a. terebro, perforo; cavo, 1; *fig.*

bore, s. (hole) foramen, n.; (borer, i.e. tool) terebra, f.; *fig.* importunus, molestus, odiosus, i, m.

borer, s. (tool) terebra, f.

boring, s. terebratio, f.

born, p. & a. natus; genitus; **to be —,** nascor, gigni, 3; *fig.* orior, 4; **a — soldier,** aptus militiæ.

borough, s. municipium, n.

borrow, v.a. mutuor; mutuum sumo; *fig.* imitor, 1.

borrowed, a. mutuatus, mutuus; alienus.

borrower, s. qui mutuatur.

borrowing, s. mutuatio, f.

bosom, s. (breast) pectus, n., sinus, m.; gremium, n.; **— friend,** amicus conjunctissimus.

Bosphorus, s. Bosphorus, m.

boss, s. bulla, f.; (of a shield) umbo, m.; (of a book rolled up) umbilicus.

botanist, s. herbarius, m.

botany, s. herbarum scientia, f.

botch, v.a. *fig.* male gero, 3.

botcher, s. sartor imperitus, m.

both, a. ambo; (pair) geminus; duo; uterque; **— ways,** bifariam.

both, c. — ... **and,** et ... et, cum ... tum; (enclitic) que ... que ...; (enclitic) que ... et.

bother, v.a. vexo, 1.

bother, s. vexatio, sollicitudo, cura, f.

bottle, s. ampulla; (with handles) lagena, f.; (of hay) fasciculus, m.

bottle, v.a. in ampullas infundo, 3.

bottle-nosed, a. nasutus.

bottom, s. fundus, i, m.; (of a ship) carina, f.; (dregs) fæx, f.; (of a mountain) radix, f.; (depth of a thing) profundum, n.; (ship) navis; (valley) vallis, f.; **at —,** ad imum (imam) ...; (go to the —) subsido, resido, 3; (sink) mergor, 3; (from top to —) funditus, penitus; (get to the — of) scrutor, 1.

bottom, a. imus, infimus. [profundus.

bottomless, a. fundo carens, immensus;

bough, s. ramus, m., bracchium, f.

bounce, v.n. resilio, 4; resulto, 1.

bouncing, a. pinguis, robustus; valens.

bound, s. finis, terminus, limes, m.; meta, f.; (leap) saltus, m.; *fig.* modus, m.

bound, v.a. finio, definio, 4; termino, 1; (set —s to) circumscribo, 3; —, v.n. salio, exsilio, 4.

boundary, s. finis, terminus, limes, m.; confinium, n.

boundless, a. infinitus; immensus.

boundlessness, s. infinitas, f.; immensitas.

bounteous, bountiful, a. benignus, largus, munificus; **—ly,** ad. benigne, large, munifice.

bountifulness, s. benignitas, f.

bounty, s. largitas; benignitas, munificentia, f.; præmium, munus, n.

bouquet, s., v. nosegay; (of wine) flos, m.

bovine, a. bubulus.

bow, v.a. flecto, 3; inclino, 1; (one's head) demitto, 3; *fig.* submitto, 3; —, v.n. flector, 3; (yield) cedo, 3.

bow, s. arcus, m.; (of a ship) prora, f.

bowels, s. intestina, viscera, n. pl.; *fig.* misericordia, f.

bower, s. trichila, pergula, f., umbraculum, n.

bowl, s. cratera; patera, phiala, f.; (basin) pelvis, f.

bowl, v.a. volvo.

bow-legged, a. valgus.

bowman, s. sagittarius, m.

bowstring, s. nervus, m.

box, s. arca; cista, f.; loculus, m.; capsa, f.; (— for letters, etc.) scrinium, n.; (— for ointments, etc.) pyxis, f.; — **on the ear,** alapa, f.

box, s. (tree) buxus, i, f.

box, v.n. pugnis certo, 1.

boxer, s. pugil, m.

boxing-match, s. pugilatio, f.

boy, s. puer, i; (little —) puerulus, m.

boyhood, s. pueritia; ætas puerilis, f.

boyish, a. puerilis; **—ly,** ad. pueriliter.

brace, s. (strap) fascia, f.; copula, f.; (couple) par, n.; (hook) uncus, m.; (ship's rope) rudens, m.; (in architecture) fibula, f.

brace, v.a. ligo, alligo, 1; (exert oneself), contendo, 3.

bracelet, s. armilla, f., bracchiale, n.

bracken, s. pteris (mod. hort.).

bracket, s. mutulus, m.

brackish, a. subsalsus.

brad, s. clavulus, m.; — **-awl,** s. subula, f.

brag, v.n. jacto, 1.

braggadocio, braggart, s. jactator, salaco, m.

braggart, a. gloriosus.

bragging, s. jactantia (sui), jactatio, f.

braid, s. limbus, m.; (of hair) cincinnus, m.

braid, v.a. plecto, texo, prætexo, 3.

brain, s. cerebrum; (sense) cor, n.; (understanding) mens, f.

brain, v.a. excerebro, 1.

brainless, a. *fig.* stolidus, inconsultus, vecors.

braising-pan, s. foculus, m.

brake, s. (fern) filix, f.; (thicket) dumetum, n.; (horse-bit) lupi, m. pl.; lupata, n. pl.

bramble, s. (blackberry-bush) rubus, m.; (thicket of it) rubetum, n.; (thorny bush) sentis, vepris, m. [mus.

bran, s. furfur, n.; — **-new,** a. recentissi-

branch, s. (of a tree) ramus, m.; bracchium; (of mountains) bracchium, n.; (of a river) cornu, n.; (of a pedigree) stemma, n.; *fig.* pars, f.; (vine —) palmes, m.; pampinus, f.

branch, v.n. (of trees) germino, 1; floresco, 3; *fig.* dividor, scindor, diffundor, 3. [spreading) patulus.

branchy, a. ramosus; frondosus; (wide-

brand, s. (mark) nota, f.; (torch) torris, m.; fax, tæda, f. [n.

branding-iron, s. cauter, m.; cauterium,

brand-new, a., v. **bran-new.**

brandish, v.a. vibro, libro, corusco, 1.

brass, s. orichalcum, æs, n.

brassy, a. aēnus, æreus, aēneus, æratus.

brat, s. infans, c.

brave, a. fortis; strenuus; animosus; (splendid) splendidus, speciosus; præstans, præclarus.

brave, v.a. provoco, 1; lacesso, 3.

bravely, ad. fortiter; animose; eximie; splendide, speciose.

bravery, s. fortitudo; virtus; magnanimitas, f.; splendor, m.

bravo, i, eu! euge!

bravo, s. sicarius, m.

brawl, v.n. rixor, jurgo, 1.

brawl, s. rixa; jurgium, n.

brawler, s. rixator; rabula, m.

brawling, a. litigiosus.

brawn, s. callum aprugnum, n.; (muscle) lacertus, torus, m.

brawniness, s. callositas, f.

brawny, a. lacertosus, torosus.

bray, v.a. contundo, 3; —, v.n. (of asses) rudo, 3; (to cry out) vociferor, 1.

bray, braying, s. tritura, f.; (noise) strepitus, m.

braze, v.a. ferrumino, 1.

brazen, a. (of brass) aēnus, aēneus, æreus, æratus; *fig.* — **-faced,** impudens.

brazier, s. ærarius, m.; (coal-pan) foculus, m.

breach, s. ruptura; ruina; (of a treaty) violatio, f.; (falling out) discidium, n.; discordia, f.

bread, s. panis; *fig.* victus, m.

bread-basket, s. panarium, n.

bread-making, s. panificium, n.

breadth, s. latitudo, f.

break, v.a. frango; rumpo, 3; *fig.* violo, 1; (to bruise) tero, 3; v.n. frangor, 3; (cease) desino; **to —asunder,** diffringo, dirumpo, 3; **to — down,** demolior, 4; destruo, 3; **to — forth,** erumpo, 3; **to — in,** domo, 1; subigo, 3; **to — into,** irrumpo; invado, 3; **to — loose,** eluctor, 1; **to — off,** abrumpo; (friendship) dirumpo; (a conference) dirimo; (a conversation) interrumpo, 3; v.n. præfringor; **to — open,** effringo, 3; **to — out,** erumpo; (a calamity, etc.) prorumpo, 3; (a war) exorior, 4; (to be known) innotesco, 3; **to — through,** perrumpo, 3; **to — up,** frango, effringo, dissolvo; (an army, assembly) dimitto; (ground) fodio, 3; **to — with,** dissideo, 2.

break, intermissio, f.; intervallum; (of day) diluculum, n.

breakage, s. fractura, f.

break-down, s. calamitas; frustatio, f.

breaker, s. (wave) fluctus, m.

breakfast, s. prandium, jentaculum, n.

breakfast, v.a. prandeo, 2; jento, 1.

breaking, s. fractura, f.; (discontinuance) intermissio; — **up,** dissolutio; *fig.* violatio, f.

break-up, s. dissolutio, f.

breakwater, s. moles, pila.

bream, s. sparus, m.; phagrus, m.

breast, s. pectus, n.; (of a woman) mamma, papilla, f.; (full of milk) uber, n.; *fig.* præcordia, n. pl., pectus, cor, n.

breast-bone, s. os pectorale, n.

breastplate, s. lorica; thorax, m.

breastwork, s. lorica, f.; pluteus, m.

breath, s. halitus, spiritus, flatus, m.; anima; (of air) aura, f.; **to take —,** respiro, 1.

breathe, v.a. duco, 3; (to pant) anhelo; (to whisper) susurro, 1; **to — out,** exspiro; (the life) exhalo, 1; —, v.n. spiro, respiro, 1.

breathing, s. respiratio, f.; (gr.) spiritus, m.

breathing-hole, s. spiraculum, spiramen, spiramentum, n.

breathing-time, s. pausa, f.

breathless, a. exanimis, exanimus; exanimatus; (panting) anhelus.

bred, a. well —, humanus, urbanus.

breech, s. clunes, m. pl., podex, m.

breeches, s. bracæ, f. pl.

breed, v.a. pario, gigno, 3; genero, creo, 1; (to cause) produco, 3; (to engender) procreo, 1; (horses, etc.) pasco, 3; alo, 3; nutrio, 4; (bring up) educo, 1; alo, 3.

breed, s. genus, n.

breeder, s. generator; (of cattle) nutritor; (stallion) admissarius, m.

breeding, s. fetura; (education) educatio, f.; **good —,** humanitas, urbanitas, f.

breeze, s. aura, f.

breezy, a. ventosus.

brethren, s. pl. fratres, m. pl.

brevet, s. rescriptum, n.

breviary, s. summarium, breviarium, n.

brevity, s. brevitas, f.

brew, v.a. coquo, 3; *fig.* concito, conflo, 1; —, v.n. excitor, concitor, 1; **be —ing,** immineo, 2.

briar, s., v. **bramble.**

bribe, s. pretium, n., merces, pecunia, f., v. **bribery.**

bribe, v.a. corrumpo, 3.

briber, s. corruptor, largitor, m.

bribery, s. corruptio, corruptela, largitio, f.; ambitus, m.

brick, s. later, m.

brickbat, s. testa, f.

brick-clay, s. terra lateraria, f.

brick-kiln, s. lateraria, f.

brick-layer, s. cæmentarius, m.

brick-maker, s. laterarius, m.

brick-work, s. latericium, n.   [lamium, n.

bridal, a. nuptialis; — **song,** s. epitha-

bridal-chamber, s. thalamus, m.

bride, s. sponsa; nupta, nympha, f.

bridecake, s. mustaceus, m.

bridegroom, s. sponsus; novus maritus, m.

bride's-maid, s. pronuba, f.

bridewell, s. carcer, m.

bridge, s. pons, m.; (of an instrument *or* nose) jugum, n.

bridge, v.a. **to — over,** flumen ponte jungo, 3.

bridle, s. frenum, n. (also *fig.*); habena, f.

bridle, v.a. freno; *fig.* infreno, refreno, 1; coerceo, 2.

brief, s. litteræ, f. pl.; (account) summarium, n.

brief, a. brevis, concisus.

briefly, ad. breviter; paucis (verbis).

briefness, s. brevitas, f.

brier, s., v. **bramble.**

brig, s. navicula, f.

brigade, s. (of infantry) legio; (of cavalry) turma, f.

brigadier, s. tribunus militum, m.

brigand, s. latro, latrunculus, m.

brigantine, s. Liburna, f.

bright, a. clarus; lucidus, splendidus; nitidus; candidus; (flashing) fulgidus; (smart, clever) argustus, sollers; (cloudless) serenus.

brighten, v.a. polio, 4; —, v.n. lucesco; splendesco; claresco, 3; (gladden) hilaro, exhilaro, 1.

brightly, ad. lucide, clare, splendide, nitide.

brightness, s. splendor; nitor; fulgor, m.; (of the sun) lumen, n.; *fig.* hilaritas, f.; (of intellect) sollertia, f.

brill, s. (fish) psetta, f.

brilliancy, s. splendor, m.; *fig.* (of style) lumen, n.

brilliant, a. splendidus; nitens; nitidus; *fig.* luculentus; præclarus; **to be —,** splendeo, niteo, 2.

brilliantly, ad. splendide; luculenter, nitide.

brim, s. ora, f., margo, c., labrum, n.

brimstone, s. sulfur, n.

brindled, a. (particoloured) discolor; maculosus; varius.

brine, s. muria, f., salsamentum; (sea) salum, n.

bring, v.a. ir. fero, affero, infero; gero, duco, 3; porto, 1; (by carriage; etc.) adveho, 3; *fig.* (persuade) persuadeo, 2; adduco, 3; **to — about,** efficio, 3; **to — again, to — back,** refero, reduco, 3; reporto; *fig.* revoco, 1; (by force) redigo, 3; **to — before,** defero; produco, 3; **to — down,** defero; deduco; (by force) dejicio, 3; **to — forth,** prodo; depromo; pario; (to yield) fero, effero, 3; **to — forward,** profero, effero; ago, 3; **to — in(to),** infero; inveho; induco; (as income) reddo, 3; **to — off,** præsto, 1; (carry through) perficio, 3; **to — on,** affero; adduco; *fig.* objicio, 3; **to — out,** effero; produco, 3; excio, 4; **to — over,** perduco, traduco; *fig.* perduco, traho, 3; concilio, 1; **to — to,** adduco; appello, 3; *fig.* persuadeo, 2; **to — together,** confero; (to assemble, etc.) contraho, 3; *fig.* concilio, 1; **to — to pass,** efficio, 3; **to — under,** subigo, subjicio, 3; **to — up,** subduco, 3; (children) educo, 1; (to vomit) evomo, 3.

bringer, s. (of tidings) nuntius.

bringing, s. advectio, f.; — **forth,** s. prolatio, f.; partus, m.; — **in,** s. inductio; — **together,** s. collatio, f.; — **up,** s. educatio, f.

brink, s. margo, c.; **be on the — of,** in eo esse ut.

briny, a. salsus; subsalsus.

brisk, a. alacer, agilis, vividus; lætus; impiger acer; —**ly,** ad. alacriter, acriter impigre; **to be** —, vigeo, 2.

brisket, s. pectus (agninum, bovinum, etc.), n.

briskness, s. alacritas, f., vigor, m.

bristle, s. sæta, f.

bristle fern, s. trichomanes (mod. hort.).

bristle, v.n. **to** — **up,** horreo, 2; horresco, 3.

bristly, a. sætiger, sætosus; hirsutus.

Britain, s. Britannia, f.

British, a. Britannicus.

brittle, a. fragilis, caducus.

brittleness, s. fragilitas, f.

broach, s. veru, n.

broach, v.a. (a cask) (dolium) relino, 3; (to publish) in medium profero, 3.

broacher, s. auctor, m.

broad, a. latus, largus, amplus; *fig.* manifestus, apertus.

broadly, ad. late.

broadness, s. amplitudo, latitudo; (of expressions) rusticitas, f.

broadsword, s. gladius, m.

brocade, s. vestis picta, f.

broccoli, s. brassica, f.

brogue, s. (shoe) pero, m.; (of pronunciation) latitudo, peregrinitas, f.

broil, s. rixa, f.; jurgium, n.; altercatio, f.

broil, v.a. torreo, 2.

broken, p. & a. fractus; intermissus; dirutus; (off) abruptus; (open) effractus; (in pieces) contusus; (up) dismissus; violatus; (of the heart) vulneratus.

broken-hearted, a. abjectus, spe dejectus, afflictus.

broken-winded, a. anhelus.

broker, s. (in old goods) scrutarius, m.; proxeneta, pararius, m.; (money-changer) nummularius, m.

brokerage, s. proxeneticum, n.

bronze, s. æs, n.

bronze, a. aënus, aëneus, æreus, æratus.

brooch, s. fibula.

brood, s. proles; progenies; suboles; (of chickens) pullities, f.

brood, v.a. & n. (as a hen) incubo, 1; *fig.* (upon) foveo, 2; agito, 1.

brook, s. amniculus, rivulus, m.

brook, v.a. fero, patior, 3; tolero, 1.

broom, s. genista, f.; ruscum, n.; (besom) scopæ, f. pl.

broomstick, s. scoparum manubrium, n.

broth, s. jus, n.

brothel, s. lupanar, lustrum, n.

brother, s. frater, germanus, m.; — **-in-law,** s. levir, sororis maritus, m.

brotherhood, s. germanitas; fraternitas, f.; *fig.* sodalitium, collegium, n.

brotherly, a. fraternus; —, ad. fraterne.

brow, s. supercilium, n.; frons, f.

browbeat, v.a. terreo, 2; deprimo, 3.

browbeating, s. minæ, f. pl.

brown, a. fulvus, fuscus, pullus, spadix; —, s. fulvus color, m.

brownish, a. subniger, suffuscus.

brownness, s. fulvus color, m.

browse, v.a. carpo, depasco, 3; tondeo, 2.

browse-wood, s. virgultum, n.

bruise, v.a. contundo, 3; sugillo, 1; infringo, 3.

bruise, s. contusio; sugillatio, f.

bruit, v.a. vulgo, divulgo, 1.

brunette, s. puella suffusca, f.

brunt, s. vis, f., impetus, m.; (blow) ictus, m.

brush, s. scopula, f.; (painter's —) penicillus, m.; (bushy tail) muscarium, n.; (fray, skirmish) concursatio, f.

brush, v.a. verro, 3; tergeo; detergeo; **to**— **away,** amoveo, 2; — **up,** orno, 1; reficio, 3.

brushwood, s. sarmenta, virgulta, ramalia, n. pl.

brushy, a. (shaggy) hirsutus, setosus.

brutal, a. ferus; immanis; inhumanus; sævus; furiosus; —**ly,** ad. inhumane; sæve.

brutality, s. feritas; ferocitas, sævitia; immanitas, f.

brutalize, v.a. effero, 1.

brute, s. bestia, pecus, f.

brute, a. brutus; stupidus.

brutish, a. ferus; fatuus, stupidus.

bryony, s. bryonia, f.

bubble, s. bulla; *fig.* fraus, f. [2.

bubble, v.n. bullio, 4; (to gush up) scateo, 3.

bubbling, s. bullitus, m.; scatebra, f.

buccaneer, s. pirata, prædo, m.

buck, s. cervus; (he-goat) hircus.

bucket, s. hama, situla, f.; (on a wheel) modiolus, m.

buckle, s. fibula, f.

buckle, v.a. fibula necto, 3; — **on,** accomodo, 1.

buckler, s. parma, f., v. **shield.**

buckskin, s. pellis cervina, f.

buckthorn, s. rhamnus, f.

bucolic, a. bucolicus, pastoralis, pastorius, rusticus, agrestis.

bud, s. gemma, f., germen, n.; (of a flower) calyx; (in grafting) oculus, m.

bud, v.n. gemmo, germino, 1; —, v.a. oculos insero, 3.

budding, s. germinatio, f.

budge, v.n. me moveo, 2; cedo, loco cedo, 3.

budget, s. saccus; publicæ pecuniæ accepti atque expensi ratio, f.

buff, a. luteus.

buffalo, s. bubalus, urus, m.

buffet, s. alapa, f.; colaphus, m.; (sideboard) abacus, m.

buffet, v.a. (strike) ferio, 4.

buffoon, s. scurra; sannio, balatro, m.; to play the —, scurror, 1.   [jocus, m.

buffoonery, s. scurrilitas, f.; lascivia, f.;

bug, s. cimex, c.

bugbear, s. terricula, f.; *fig.* formido, f.

bugle, s. bucina, f.; cornu, n.; (plant) ajuga (mod. hort.).

build, v.a. ædifico, 1; struo, construo, exstruo, condo, 3; fabrico, 1; (upon) inædifico, 1; *fig.* (to rely) nitor, 3.

builder, s. ædificator; conditor, structor; *fig.* auctor, fabricator, m.

building, s. (act) ædificatio, exstructio, f.; (structure) ædificium, n.

bulbous, a. bulbosus.

bulge, v.n. tumeo, turgeo, 2; procurro, 3; to — out, tumesco, 3.

bulk, s. amplitudo; moles, f.

bulkiness, s. magnitudo, f.

bulky, a. crassus; ingens; gravis; onerosus; (fat) pinguis.

bull, s. taurus, bos, m.; (edict) edictum, n.

bullace, s. prunum, n.

bull-dog, s. canis molossus, m.

bullet, f. glans (plumbea), f.

bulletin, s. libellus, m.

bullion, s. aurum argentumve infectum, n.; massa, f.

bullock, s. taurus castratus; juvencus, m.

bully, s. salaco, rixator, m.

bully, v.a. insulto, 1; lacesso, 3.

bulrush, s. scirpus; juncus, m.

bulwark, s. agger, m.; propugnaculum, n.; mœnia, munimenta, n. pl.; *fig.* præsidium, propugnaculum, n.

bump, s. (swelling) tuber, n.; (thump) plaga, f.

bump, v.a. offendo, 3; pulso, 1.

bumpkin, s. rusticus, m.

bun, s. libum, crustulum, n. placenta, f.

bunch, s. (bundle) fasciculus; — of grapes, racemus, m.   [2.

bunch, v.n. to — out, exto, 1; promineo,

bundle, s. fascis, fasciculus, m.; (wallet) sarcina, f.; (of rods) fasces, m. pl.

bundle, v.a. colligo, 1; to — out, foras extrudo, 3.

bung, s. obturamentum, m.

bung, v.a. obturo, 1.

bung-hole, s. foramen, n.

bungle, v.a. rem inscite gero, inscite ago, 3; v.n. erro, 1.

bungler, s. homo rudis; imperitus, m.

bunglingly, ad. infabre, inscite.

buoy, v.a. (up) attollo, 3; sustineo, 2; sustento, 1; fulcio, 4.

buoyancy, s. levitas; *fig.* hilaritas, f.

buoyant, a. levis; *fig.* hilaris.

bur, s. lappa, f.

burden, s. onus, n.; fascis, m.; sarcina, f.; (of a song) versus intercalaris.

burden, v.a. onero, gravo, 1; opprimo, 3; ship of —, navis oneraria; a ship of 100 tons —, navis centum amphorarum; beast of —, jumentum, n.

burdensome, a. onerosus, gravis, molestus, iniquus.

burdock, s. lappa, f.

bureau, s. armarium, scrinium, n.

burgess, s. civis, municeps, c.

burgher, s. civis, c.

burglar, s. effractarius, perfossor parietum, m.

burglary, s. effractura, f.

burial, s. (act of burning) sepultura, f.; funus, n.; exsequiæ, f. pl.

burial-place, s. locus sepulturæ, m.; sepulcrum, n.   [imitatio, f.

burlesque, a. ridiculus;   s. ridicula

burlesque, v.a. (ridicule) imitari, 1; in risum verto, 3.

burly, a. corpulentus, robustus, lacertosus.

burn, v.a. uro, 3; cremo, 1; (to set on fire) incendo; (to bake) coquo, 3; —, v.n. flagro, 1; ardeo, 2; — with love, etc., ardeo, 2; flagro, 1; caleo, 2; calesco, 3; to — down, deuro, 3; to be burnt down, deflagro, 1; to — out, exuro; (v.n.) extinguor, 3; to — up, concremo, 1.

burn, s. adustio, f.; combustum, ambustum, n.

burner, s. ustor, m.

burning, s. ustio, adustio; deflagratio, f., incendium, n.

burning, a. ardens; *fig.* fervens.

burning-bush, s. dictamnus, f.

burnish, v.a. polio, expolio, 4; levigo, 1.

burnisher, s. politor, m.

burnishing, s. expolitio, politura, f.

burrow, s. cuniculus, i, m.; cubile, n.

burrow, v.n. (dig down) defodio, 3.

bursar, s. promus, m.

burst, v.a. rumpo, dirumpo; (with a noise) displodo, 3; to — forth, v.n. erumpo, prorumpo, 3; (of tears) prosilio, 4; — into tears, in lacrimas effundor; to — open, effringo, 3; —, v.n. dirumpor, 3; dissilio, 4.

burst, s. impetus, m.; eruptio, f.; (noise) fragor, m.

bury, v.a. sepelio, 4; humo, 1; (to hide, etc.) abdo, condo; (to attend to the grave) effero; (put into the ground) infodio, defodio, 3.

bush, s. frutex, dumus, sentis, vepres, m.

bushel, s. medimnus, modius, m.
bushy, a. dumosus; fruticosus; (of hair) hirsutus, horridus.
busily, ad. industrie, sedulo.
business, s. negotium, n.; (calling, trade) ars; (matter) res; (employment) occupatio, f.; studium; (duty) officium; (work) opus, n.
buskin, s. pero; cothurnus, m.
buss, s. suavium, n.
bust, s. statua, effigies, f.
bustard, s. otis, f.
bustle, s. festinatio; (alarm) trepidatio, f., tumulus, m.
bustle, v.n. (to hurry) festino; (to be in an alarm) trepido, 1; (to run to and fro) discurro, 3.
bustling, a. operosus.
busy, a. occupatus; negotiosus; (industrious) strenuus, industrius, navus; (meddling) curiosus, molestus; (active, laborious) operosus.
busybody, s. ardelio, m.
but, c. & pr. sed, ast, at; autem; ceterum; vero, verum; — for, absque; (except) præter, nisi; (only) modo, solum, tantum; — if, sin, sin autem; — if not, sin aliter, sin minus; —that, nisi, nisi quod; — yet, nihilominus, veruntamen; I cannot —, facere non possum quin.
butcher, s. lanius; fig. carnifex, m.; —'s shop, s. macellum, n.
butcher, v.a. cædo, 3; trucido, 3.
butcher's broom, s. ruscum, n.
butchery, s. cædes, trucidatio, f.
butler, s. promus, m.
butt, s. (mark) meta, f.; (cask) dolium, n.; (bank, mound) agger, m.; fig. (laughing-stock) ludibrium, n.
butt, v.n. arieto, 1; butting, petulcus.
butter, s. butyrum, n.
buttercup, s. ranunculus (mod. hort.).
butterfly, s. papilio, m.
butter-milk, s. (lactis) serum, n.
buttery, s. cellarium, n.
buttock, s. clunis, c.; natis, f.
buttress, s. erisma, n.
buttress, v.a. ulcio, suffulcio, 4.
buxom, a. alacer, hilaris, lætus, lascivus, procax; (fat) pinguis.
buy, v.a. emo, 3; mercor, 1; to — back or off, redimo, 3; to — up, emercor, 1; coemo, 3.
buyer, s. emptor, m.
buying, s. emptio, mercatura, f.
buzz, v.n. murmuro, susurro, 1; (in the ear) insusurro, 1.
buzz, buzzing, s. bombus, i, murmur, n.; susurrus, m.
buzzard, s. buteo, m.

by, pr. (of place) ad, apud; sub; (along) secundum, præter; (near) propter, juxta; (of time) sub; (denoting the instrument or cause) per; (of the living agent) a, ab; (in adjurations) per; — oneself, solus, solum; — and —, mox, brevi, postmodo; to go —, prætereo, 4.
bygone, a. præteritus; priscus.
by-law, s. præscriptum, n.
bypath, s. semita, f.; trames, m.
by-road, s., v. bypath.
bystander, m.; —s, pl. circumstantes, m. pl.
by-way, v. bypath.
byword, s. proverbium, n.; fig. fabula, f.

Cab, s. cisium, n.
cabal, s. consilium clandestinum, n.; (intrigue) doli, m. pl.
caballer, s. doli machinator, m.
cabbage, s. brassica, f., caulis, m.; crambe, f.
cabin, s. (little cottage) tugurium, n.; (small room) cellula, f.
cabinet, s. conclave; (little room) zotheca, f.; (piece of furniture) scrinium, armarium, n., cistula, f.; (government) summum principis consilium, n.
cabinet-maker, s. faber intestinarius, m.
cable, s. ancorale, n., rudens, m.
cabman, s. cisiarius, m.
cabriolet, s. cisium, n.; birota, f.
cachinnation, s. cachinnus, m., cachinnatio, f.
cackle, v.n. strepo, 3; clango, 3; (of hens) gracillo, 1; fig. garrio, 4.
cackle, s. strepitus, clangor, m.; fig. gerræ, f. pl.
cackler, s. nugator, m.
cackling, s., v. cackle, s.
cactus, s. cactus, m.
cadaverous, a. cadaverosus; (thin) macer.
cadence, s. (mus.) intervallum, n.; numerus, m.
cadet, s. frater minor; filius junior; discipulus militaris, m.
cæstus, s. cæstus, m.
cæsura, s. cæsura, f.
cage, s. cavea, f., avarium, n.; (prison) carcer, m.; (for greater beasts) sæptum, n.
cage, v.a. includo, 3.
cairn, s. lapidum acervus, m.
caitiff, s. scelus, n.; furcifer, m.
cajole, v.a. adulor, 1; illicio, 3; blandior, 4.
cajoler, s. homo blandus, adulator, m.
cajolery, s. blanditiæ, f. pl.; adulatio, f.

cake, s. placenta, f., libum, n.; (doughy mass) massa, f.

cake, v.n. concresco, 3.

calamine, s. cadmia, f.

calamint, s. calamintha (mod. hort.).

calamitous, a. calamitosus; lacrimosus; funestus; gravis; infelix; —**ly,** ad. calamitose, infeliciter.

calamity, a. calamitas; clades, f.; malum, n.; res adversa, f. [verti, 3.

calcine, v.a. exuro, 3; —, v.n. in calcem

calculate, v.a. & n. computo, supputo, 4; æstimo, existimo, 1.

calculated, a. aptus, accommodatus; (intentional) meditatus.

calculation, s. computatio, ratio, f., calculus, m.; *fig.* ratiocinatio, f.

calculating-machine, s. abacus, m.

calculator, s. computator, m. [tina, f.

caldron, s. aēnum, n., lebes, m.; cor-

calendar, s. kalendarium, n., fasti, m. pl.; (diary) ephemeris, f.

Calends, s. Kalendæ, f. pl.

calf, s. vitulus, m.; (of the leg) sura, f.; (sea-calf) phoca, f.

calibre, s. *fig.* ingenium, n., indoles, f.

calico, s. byssus, f.; (of —) byssinus.

calk, v.a. (to pitch) pico, 1.

call, v.a. voco, 1; (to name) appello, nomino, 1; **to — apart** *or* **aside,** sevoco, 1; **to — away,** avoco, 1; *fig.* devoco, 1; **to — back,** revoco, 1; **to — down,** devoco, 1; **to — for,** postulo, 1; flagito; **to — forth,** evoco, provoco, 1; *fig.* excieo, 2; elicio, 3; **to — in,** introvoco, 1; (money) cogo, 3; **to — out,** evoco, 1; (v.n.) exclamo, 1; **to — over,** recito, 1; **to — off,** avoco, revoco, 1; **to —, on** *or* **upon,** inclamo, 1; cieo, 2; appello, 1; (to visit) viso, 3; saluto, 1; **to — over,** recenseo, 2; **to — to,** advoco, 1; **to — to mind,** recordor, 1; **to — to witness,** testor, 1; **to — together,** convoco, 1; **to — up,** excito; suscito, 1; elicio, 3.

call, s. vocatio; (sound of the voice) vox, f.; (shout) clamor, m.; (short visit) salutatio, f.; (requisition) postulatio, f.

caller, s. salutator, m.

calling, s. vocatio, f.; (profession) studium, n.; ars, f.; (bent) impetus; (rank, position) condicio, f.; — **back,** revocatio, f.; — **in** (of money), coactio, f.; — **together,** convocatio, f.; — **out,** evocatio, f.; — **upon,** invocatio, f.

callosity, s. callum, n.

callous, a. callosus; *fig.* (insensible) durus; **to become —,** occallesco; obduresco, 3.

callousness, s. duritia, f.

callow, a. implumis.

calm, a. tranquillus, placidus, sedatus, placatus, quietus, serenus.

calm, s. tranquillitas, quies, f.; (a calm sea) tranquillum, n.

calm, v.a. paco, placo, sedo, 1; mulceo, 2; tranquillo, 1.

calmly, ad. placide, sedate, tranquille.

calmness, s. tranquillitas; serenitas, quies, f.; **bear with —,** æquo animo fero, 3.

calorific, a. calorificus.

caltrop, s. (thistle) carduus, m.; tribulus; (instrument) murex, m.

calumniate, v.a. calumnior, infamo, obtrecto, 1.

calumniation, s. calumnia, obtrectatio, f.

calumniator, s. obtrectator, m.

calumnious, a. calumniosus, criminosus; —**ly,** ad. criminose.

calumny, s. maledictum, n., criminatio, f.

calve, v.n. parere, 3.

calyx, s. calyx, m.

cambric, s. carbasus, f.; **of —,** carbaseus.

camel, s. camelus, m.

camellia, s. camellia (mod. hort.).

camelopard, s. camelopardalis, m.

camomile, s. anthemis, f.

camp, s. castra, n. pl.; **winter —,** hiberna, n. pl.; **summer —,** æstiva, n. pl.; **to break up a —,** castra movere, 2.

camp, v.n. castra pono, 3.

camp-follower, s. lixa, m.

campaign, s. expeditio, f.; (service) militia, f.; stipendium; (war) bellum, n.; *fig.* **one's first —,** tirocinium, n.

campaign, v.a. expeditioni interesse.

campaigner, s. veteranus, i, m.

campion, s. lychnis; silene (mod. hort.).

can, s. hirnea, hirnula, f.

can, v.n. possum, ir.; queo, 4; **I —no** nequeo; nescio, 4.

canal, s. fossa, f.; canalis, m.

canary-bird, s. fringilla, f.

cancel, v.a. deleo, 2; rescindo, 3; abrogo, 1; tollo, 3.

cancer, s. (disease, and sign of the zodiac) cancer, m.

cancerous, a. canceraticus.

candelabrum, s. candelabrum, n.

candid, a. candidus; apertus; sincerus; —**ly,** ad. candide; sincere; sine fraude.

candidate, s. candidatus, i, m.

candidateship, a. petitio, f.

candle, s. candela, f.

candle-light, s. lucerna, f.; **to study by —,** lucubro, 1.

candlestick, s. candelabrum, n.

candour, s. candor, m., sinceritas, f.

candy-tuft, s. iberis (mod. hort.).
cane, s. canna, arundo, f.; baculus, i,
calamus, m.; (rod for striking) ferula, f.
cane, v.a. ferula ferio, 4.
canine, a. caninus.
canister, s. pyxis, f.
canker, s. (of plants) robigo, f.; fig. lues, f.;
pestis, f.
canker, v.a. corrumpo, peredo, 3; vitio, 1.
cannibal, s. anthropophagus, m.
cannon, s. tormentum, n.
canoe, s. linter, f.
canon, s. (rule) canon, m.; regula,
norma, f.; (prebendary) canonicus, m.;
— law, jus canonicum, n.
canoness, s. canonica, f.
canonical, a. canonicus; —ly, ad.
canonice.
canonize, v.a. in sanctorum numero collo-
care.   [aulæa, n. pl.
canopy, s.ˊconopeum, n.; vela; (curtain)
cant, s. (parade) ostentatio, f.
cant, v.n. fictam pietatem ostento.
cantankerous, a. difficilis, morosus, v.
headstrong, stubborn.
canteen, s. caupona, f.
canter, v.n. curro, 3; volo, 1; —ing,
quadrupedans.
canter, s. cursus incitatus.
Canterbury bell, s. campanula (mod.
hort.).
cantharides, s. cantharides, f. pl.
canticle, s. canticum, n.
canto, s. (of a poem) liber, m.
canton, s. pagus, m.; tribus, civitas, f.
cantonment, s. stativa, n. pl.
canvas, s. linteum, n.; carbasus, f. (for
sails); (for painters) textile, n.
canvass, s. ambitio, petitio, f.; (unlawful)
ambitus, m.
canvass, v.a. ambio; circumeo, 4;
prenso, 1; (be a candidate) peto, 3; (to
sift a business) vestigo, scrutor, 1.
cap, s. pilleus, galerus, m.; mitra, f.
capability, s. facultas, f.
capable, a. capax; idoneus, potens.
capacious, a. capax; amplus.
capaciousness, s. capacitas; amplitudo,
f., spatium, n.
capacity, s. (measure) mensura, f.; modus,
m.; (intelligence) ingenium, n.; facultas, f.
caparison, s. stratum, stragulum, n.
caparison, v.a. insterno, 3.
cape, s. promonturium; (garment) umer-
ale, n.; lacerna, f.
Cape lily, s. crinum (mod. hort.).
caper, s. saltus, m., exsultatio, f.
caper, s. (plant) capparis, is, f.
caper, v.n. tripudio, exsulto, 1.
capillary, a. capillaris.

capital, a. præcipuus, princeps; (of crimes)
capitalis; (of letters) grandis; fig. insignis, eximius.
capital, s. (in archit.) capitulum; (chief
city) caput; (money) caput, sors, f.
capitalist, s. dives, m.
capitally, ad. egregie, insigniter, bene.
capitation, s. tributum in singula capita
impositum, n.
capitol, s. capitolium, n.
capitulate, v.n. arma trado, me dedo, 3.
capitulation, a. deditio, f.
capon, s. capus, capo, m.
caprice, s. libido; inconstantia, f.
capricious, a. levis, inconstans; mobilis;
ventosus; —ly, ex libidine; inconstanter.
capricorn, s. capricornus, m.
capstan, s. sucula, f.
capsule, s. (bot.) vasculum, n.; (anat.)
capsula, f.
captain, s. (of infantry) centurio; (of
cavalry) præfectus; (of a merchant-
ship) navicularius, magister, m.; (general) dux, imperator, m.
captaincy, captainship, s. centuriatus, m.
captious, s. captiosus; fallax; morosus;
—ly, ad. captiose.
captiousness, s. morositas; cavillatio, f.
captivate, v.a. mulceo, 2; capto, 1;
capio, allicio, 3.
captive, s. captivus, m.; a. captivus,
a, um.
captivity, s. captivitas, f.; (confinement)
custodia, f.; (chains) vincula, n. pl.
captor, s. expugnator, m.
capture, s. captura; expugnatio, f.
capture, v.a. capio, excipio, 3; expugno, 1.
car, s. carrus, currus, m.; carpentum, n.;
ræda, f.
caravan, s. commeatus, comitatus, m.
caravansary, s. deversorium, m.
caraway, s. careum, n.
carbuncle, s. (tumour) carbunculus, furunculus, i; (precious stone) carbunculus, m.
carcass, s. cadaver, n.
card, s. (paper) charta; (for combing
wool) pecten, m.
card, v.a. (wool) pecto, carpo, 3; carmino, 1.
carder, s. carminator, m.
cardinal, a. cardinalis; (chief) præcipuus, —, s. cardinalis, m.
carding, s. carminatio, f.
care, s. cura, sollicitudo; (heed) cautio;
(diligence) diligentia; (anxiety) anxietas; (tuition) tutela; (management)
procuratio; curatio; custodia, f.; to
take —, caveo, 2; to take — of,
curo, 1.

care, v.n. curo, 1; **to — for,** provideo, 2; invigilo, 1; **I don't —,** non mihi curæ est.

career, s. curriculum, n.; cursus, decursus, m.; (life) vita, f.

careful, a. (troubled) sollicitus, anxius; (diligent) diligens; attentus; (cautious) cautus, providus; (of things) accuratus; **—ly,** ad. anxie, caute; diligenter; accurate, exquisite.

carefulness, s. cura; (anxiety) sollicitudo; (diligence) diligentia; (caution) cautio, f.

careless, a. securus; neglegens; imprudens; (loose) dissolutus; **—ly,** ad. neglegenter; secure; incuriose; (loosely) solute.

carelessness, s. incuria; neglegentia; imprudentia; securitas, f.

caress, s. blanditiæ, f. pl.; complexus, m.

caress, v.a. blandior, 4; foveo, permulceo, 2; osculor, 1.

cargo, s. onus, n.

caries, s. caries, f.

carious, a. cariosus.

carking, a. mordax.

carman, s. vecturarius, m.

carmine, s., v. **scarlet.**

carnage, s. cædes, strages, trucidatio, f.

carnal, a. libidinosus, voluptarius, carnalis; **—ly,** ad. libidinose, carnaliter.

carnality, s. libido, carnalitas, f.

carnation, s. dianthus, m. (mod. hort.).

carnival, s. saturnalia, n. pl.; festum, n.

carnivorous, a. carnivorus.

carol, s. cantus, m.

carol, v.n. canto, cantillo, 1.

carousal, carouse, s. comissatio, potatio, f.   [bacchor, 1.

carouse, v.a. & n. comissor, poto; per-

carouser, s. comissator, m.

carp, s. (fish) cyprinus, m.

carp, v.a. (at) carpo, rodo, 3; vellico, 1; mordeo, 2.

carpenter, s. faber tignarius.

carpentry, s. ars fabrilis, opera fabrilis, f.

carper, s. cavillator, censor, objurgator, m.

carpet, s. tapete, n.; stragulum, n.

carpet, v.a. tapetibus sterno, 3.

carping, a. fig. mordax.

carping, s. cavillatio, f.

carriage, s. (act of carrying) vectura, f.; (vehicle) vehiculum, n.; ræda, f.; currus, m.; carpentum, n.; fig. habitus, gestus, incessus, m.

carriage-horse, s. equus rædarius, m.

carrier, s. bajulus; (of letters) tabularius; (messenger) nuntius, m.

carrion, s. cadaver, n., caro morticina, f.

carrot, s. pastinaca, f.; daucus, m.

carroty, a. (red-haired) rufus.

carry, v.a. porto, 1; fero; gero, 3; gesto, 1; (by carriage) veho; (to lead) duco, conduco, 3; **to — away,** aufero; aveho; fig. rapio, 3; **to — along,** perduco; ago, 3; **to — back,** refero; reveho, 3; **to — from,** asporto, 1; **to — in,** importo, 1; inveho, 3; **to — off,** aufero; rapio; abstraho, 3; **to — on,** promoveo, 2; perduco, 3; fig. exerceo, 2; gero, 3; **to — out,** effero, 3; exporto, 1; eveho; fig. exsequor, 3; **to — over,** transfero, 3; transporto, 1; **to — round,** circumfero, 3; **to — together,** comporto, 1; confero, 3; **to — through,** perfero, 3; fig. exsequor; **one's point,** evinco, 3; **— by storm,** expugno, 1.

cart, s. carrus, m., plaustrum, vehiculum, n.; **to put the — before the horse,** fig. præposteris consiliis uti, 3.

cart, v.a. plaustro veho, 3; **to — away,** aufero, 3.

cartage, s. vectura, f.

carter, s. auriga; plaustrarius, m.

cart-grease, s. axungia, f.

cart-horse, s. caballus, m.; jumentum, n.

cartilage, s. cartilago, f.

cartilaginous, a. cartilagineus.

carting, s., v. **cartage.**

cart-load, s. vehes, f.

cartouche, (in archit.) helix, f.

cart-wright, s. faber, carpentarius, m.

carve, v.a. sculpo, exsculpo, 3; cælo, 1; incido, 3; (at table) seco, 1.

carver, s. (artist) cælator; (of meat) carptor; scissor, m.; (knife) cultellus, m.

carving, s. cælatura, f.; **— -knife,** s. cultellus, m.

Caryatides, Caryatides, f. pl.

cascade, s. aquæ lapsus or dejectus, m.

case, s. (sheath) involucrum, n., theca; vagina; (matter) res; (in law) causa; (condition, state, etc.) condicio, f., status, m., quæstio, f.; (event) eventus, m.; (gr.) casus, m.; **in no —,** haudquaquam; **it is often the —,** sæpe accidit; **nothing to do with the —,** nihil ad rem.

case, v.a. includo, tego, 3.

cash, s. pecunia numerata; (— down) præsens pecunia, f.; (— payment) repræsentatio, f.

cash, v.a. pecunia numerata solvo, 3.

cash-book, s. codex, m.

cashier, v.a. exauctoro, 1; dimitto, 3.

cashmere, s. lana, f.

cask, s. cadus, m.; dolium, n.

casket, s. arca, arcula; pyxis, cista, cistula, f.

cassia, s. casia, cassia, f.

cast, v.a. jacio; conjicio; mitto, 3; jaculor, jacto, 1; (metal) fundo, 3; *fig.* damno, 1; **to — about,** circumjacio, 3; **to — away,** abjicio, rejicio, 3; **to — down,** dejicio; *fig.* affligo, 3; **to — in one's teeth,** objicio, 1; **to — in,** injicio, 3; **to — off,** (the skin) exuo, 3; *fig.* amoveo, 2; pono, 3; repudio, 1; **to — out,** ejicio, expello; (to vomit forth) exspuo, 3; **to — over,** trajicio, 3; **to — up,** (of accounts) subduco, 3; **to — upon,** superinjicio; *fig.* aspergo; confero, 3.

cast, s. (throw and distance) jactus; missus, m.; (pattern) imago, f.; **having a — in the eye,** a. limus.

castanet, s. crotalum, n.

castaway, s. perditus, m.; (shipwrecked) naufragus.   [genero, 1.

caste, s. ordo, m.; **to lose —,** de-

castellan, s. castelli præfectus, m.

caster, s. jaculator; (of metals) flator, m.; (rowel) rotula, f.

castigate, v.a. castigo, 1.

castigation, s. castigatio, f.

casting, s. (of metals) fusura, f.; (throwing) jactatus, jactus, m.; (reckoning) computatio, f.

casting-net, s. jaculum, rete jaculum, n.

castle, s. castellum, n.; turris, arx, f.; (—s in the air) somnia, n. pl.; votum, n.

castled, a. turritus.

castor, s., v. **beaver.**

castor-oil, (plant) s. ricinus (mod. hort.).

castrate, v.a. castro, exseco, 1; excido, 3.

castration, e. castratio, castratura, f.

casual, a. fortuitus; **—ly,** ad. fortuito; temere; (by the way) obiter.

casualty, s. casus, m.

casuistical, a. captiosus, fallax.

casuistry, s. captio, f.   [lum, n.

cat, s. feles, f.; (scourge, whip) flagel-

catacombs, s. puticuli, m. pl.

catalepsy, s. catalepsis, f.

catalogue, s. index, m.; tabula, f.

cataplasm, s. cataplasma, n.

catapult, s. catapulta, f.

cataract, s. cata(r)racta, f., catarractes, m.; (disease of the eye) glaucoma, n.

catarrh, s. gravedo, f.

catastrophe, s. exitus, eventus, m.; (ruin) pernicies, f.; exitium, n.

catch, v.a. capio, 3; capto, 1; (by surprise) deprehendo; (understand) intellego, 2; comprehendo, 3; (a falling person) suscipio, 3; (in a net) illaqueo; (with bait) inesco, 1; (fire) concipio; (of diseases) contraho, 3; **to — at,** arripio, 3; *fig.* capto, 1; **to — away,** abripio, rapio, 3; **to — up,** excipio, 3.

catch, s. (prize) captura, f.; (advantage) commodum, n.; (of locks, etc.); ansa, f.

catching, s. captura, f.; *fig.* aucupium, n.

catching, a. contagiosus.

catchup, v. **catsup.**

catechism, s. catechismus.

catechist, s. catechista, m.

catechize, v.a. catechizo, 1.

catechumen, s. catechumenus, m., catechumena, f.

categorical, a. categoricus.

category, s. categoria, f.; (class) genus, n.

cater, v.n. obsonor; cibos suppedito, 1.

caterer, s. obsonator, m.

caterpillar, s. eruca, f.

caterwauling, s. ululatus, m.

catholic, a. catholicus.

catkin, s. iulus, m.

cat's-eye, s. lapis specularis, m.

catsup, s. garum, n.

cattle, s. boves, m. pl.; (in a wider sense, also sheep, etc.) pecus, n.; (a single animal) pecus, f.

cattle-market, s. forum boarium, n.

caudle, s. sorbito, f.

caul, s. (membrane in the abdomen) omentum, n.; (membrane on the heads of new-born infants) pilleus, m.

cauliflower, s. brassica, f.

cause, s. causa, (material) materia, f.; (source) fons; origo, f.; (matter) res; (reason) ratio; (action at law) actio, lis, f.

cause, v.a. facio, efficio, 3; creo, 1; excito; moveo, 2; (induce) suadeo, 2; adduco, 3.   [sine causa.

causeless, a. sine causa; vanus; **—ly,** ad.

causeway, s. agger viæ, m.

caustic, a. causticus; *fig.* mordax, acerbus.

cauterism, cauterization, s. caustio, f.

cauterize, v.a. ferro aduro, 3.

cautery, s. ustio, f.; cauterium, n.

caution, s. cautio; cura; prudentia; (warning) monitio, f.

caution, v.a. (ad)moneo, 2.

caution-money, s. arrhabo, m.

cautious, a. cautus, consideratus; circumspectus; providus, prudens; **—ly,** ad. caute; pedetentim.

cautiousness, s. cautus animus, m.; cautio, f.

cavalcade, s. pompa equestris, f.

cavalier, s. eques, m.

cavalry, s. equitatus, m., equites, m. pl., copiæ equestres, f. pl.

cave, s. specus, m. f. *or* n., antrum, n.; caverna, spelunca, f.

caveat, s. cautio, f.

cavern, s. spelunca, caverna, f., antrum, n.; specus, m. f. *or* n.

cavernous, a. cavus.
cavil, v.a. cavillor, 1; carpo, 3.
cavil, s. argutiola, cavillatio, f.
caviller, s. cavillator, m.
cavity, s. caverna, f.; cavum, n.
caw, v.n. crocio, 4; crocito, 1.
cawing, s. crocatio, f.
cayenne pepper, s. capsicum (mod. hort.).
cease, v.a. desino; omitto; intermitto; v.n. (with infin.) mitto, desino; desisto; omitto, 3; cesso, 1; (come to an end) desino, desisto, 3; cesso, 1.
ceaseless, a. perpetuus; assiduus; **—ly,** ad. perpetuo; assidue; usque; continenter.
cedar, s. cedrus, f.
cedar, a. cedreus.
cede, v.a. cedo, dedo, 3; v.n. cedo, decedo, 3.
ceiling, s. lacunar, laquear, n.
celandine, s. chelidonia, f.
celebrate, v.a. celebro, laudo, 1; (solemnize) ago, 3; agito, celebro, 1.
celebrated, a. celeber; nobilis; clarus, præclarus, illustris.
celebration, s. celebratio, f.
celebrity, s. fama, celebritas, f.
celerity, s. celeritas, f.
celery, s. apium, n.
celestial, a. cœlestis; divinus; —, s. cœles, m.; cælicola, c.
celibacy, s. cælibatus, m., cælebs vita, f.
cell, s. cella, f.
cellar, s. cella, f., cellarium, n.
cellarage, s. cellarum spatium, n.; merces cellarum, f.
cellarer, s. cellarius, promus, m.
cement, s. ferrumen, cæmentum, m.
cement, v.a. conglutino; ferrumino, 1; fig. (confirm) firmo, confirmo, 1.
cemetery, s. sepulcretum, n.
cenobite, s. cœnobita, m.
cenotaph, s. tumulus inanis, m.; cenotaphium, n.
censer, s. turibulum, n.
censor, s. censor; (one who blames) reprehensor, castigator, m.
censorius, a. austerus, severus.
censoriously, ad. austere, severe.
censoriousness, s. austeritas, severitas, f.
censorship, s. censura, f.
censurable, a. culpandus.
censure, s. vituperatio, censura, reprehensio, f.
censure, v.a. animadverto, reprehendo, 3; vitupero, improbo, 1.
censurer, s. censor; vituperator, m.
census, s. census, m.
cent, s. 12 **per** — **per annum,** centesimæ usuræ, f. pl.; **24 p.c.,** centesimæ binæ.
centaur, s. centaurus, m.

centaury, s. centaureum, n.
centenary, a. centenarius; —, s. centenarius numerus; centesimus annus, m.
centipede, s. centipeda, f.
central, a. medius; —ly, ad. in medio.
centralize, v.a. in unum contraho, 3.
centre, s. centrum, n.; medius locus; (the centre of the line) media acies.
centre, v.n. fig. positus esse, situs esse; (depend) pendere.
centuple, a. centuplex.
centurion, s. centurio, m.
century, s. (political division, subdivision of a legion) centuria, f.; (number of years) sæculum, n.
cereal, a. cerealis.
ceremonial, a. sollemnis; —ly, ad. rite; sollemniter.
ceremonial, s. ritus, m.; sollemne, n.
ceremonious, a. sollemnis; —, ad. sollemniter.
ceremony, s. cærimonia, f.; sollemne, officium, n.; ritus; (pomp) apparatus, m.
certain, a. certus; compertus; **a —,** quidam; **for —,** certe, pro certo; **it is —,** constat.
certainly, ad. certe, certo; profecto.
certainty, s. certum, n., veritas, fides, f.
certify, v.a. confirmo, affirmo, 1.
cerulean, a. cæruleus.
cerumen, s. sordes, aurium, f.
ceruse, s. cerussa, f.
cessation, s. cessatio; intermissio, f.; (end) finis, c.; **— of arms,** indutiæ, f. pl.
cession, s. traditio; (of property) cessio, f.
cesspool, s. cloaca, f.
cestus, s. cæstus, m.
cetacean, s. balæna, f.
chafe, v.a. calefacio, 3; foveo, 2; (with the hand) frico, 1; (to gall) attero, 3; (to vex) vexo, 1; —, v.n. (to be vexed) ægre fero, 3; indignor, 1.
chafer, s. scarabæus, m.
chaff, s. palea, f.; acus, n.; fig. quisquiliæ, f. pl.; (mocking) ludificatio, f.
chaff, v.n. ludificor, 1.
chaffer, v.n. de pretio ambigo, 3; mercor, 1.
chaffinch, s. fringilla, f.
chafing-dish, s. foculus, m.
chagrin, s. vexatio, f.
chagrin, v.a. vexo, 1.
chain, s. catena, f.; vinculum, n.; (ornament) torques, c.; fig. series, f.; (of mountains) jugum, n.
chain, v.a. catenis constringo; catenas alicui injicio, 3.
chair, s. sella; cathedra, sedes, f.; sedile, n.; (sedan) lectica, f.

chairman, s. (of a club, etc.) præses; (carrier) lecticarius, m.
chaise, s. cisium, n.
chalice, s. calix, m.
chalk, s. creta, f.
chalk, v.a. creta noto, 1; creta illino, 3; to — out, designo, 1.
chalked, a. cretatus.
chalk-pit, s. cretifodina, f.
chalk-plant, s. gypsophila (mod. hort.).
chalky, a. (chalk-like) cretaceus; (full of chalk) cretosus.
challenge, s. provocatio; (law) rejectio, f.
challenge, v.a. provoco, 1; lacesso; (law) rejicio, 3; (to claim) arrogo, 1.
challenger, s. provocator, m.
chalybeate, a. ferrugineus.
chamber, s. cubiculum, conclave, n.; (bedroom) thalamus, m.
chamberlain, s. cubicularius, m.
chamber-maid, s. ancilla, f.
chameleon, s. chamæleon, m.
chamois, s. capreolus, m., rupicapra, f.
champ, v.a. & n. mando, 3; mordeo, 2.
champaign, a. campester.
champaign, s. campus, m.
champion, s. propugnator; defensor, m.; vindex, c.; (of a party) antesignanus, m.
chance, s. (accident) casus, m.; fors, fortuna, fig. alea; (probability) spes, f.; (opportunity) occasio, f.; by —, casu, fortuito, forte.
chance, v.n. accido, contingo, 3; evenio, 4; (light upon) incido in.
chance, a. fortuitus; inexpectatus.
chancel, s. cancelli, m. pl.
chancellor, s. cancellarius, m.
chandelier, s. candelabrum, n.
change, v.a. muto, commuto; novo, vario; (one's place) demigro, 1; (money) permuto; —, v.n. mutor, vario; (of the moon) renovor, 1.
change, s. mutatio; commutatio; vicissitudo, f.; vices, f. pl.; (variety) varietas, f.; (small money) nummuli, m. pl.; (revolution) res novæ, f. pl.
changeable, a. mutabilis; inconstans; levis; (of colour) versicolor.
changeableness, s. mutabilitas; mobilitas, inconstantia, levitas, volubilitas, f.
changeless, a. immutabilis, immutatus.
changeling, s. subditus, suppositus, m.
changer, s. mutator, m.
channel, s. canalis; (of rivers) alveus, m.; (arm of the sea) fretum, n.; fig. cursus, m.; via, f.
channel, v.a. sulco; excavo, 1.
chant, s. cantus, m.
chant, v.a. & n. canto, 1.
chanter, s. cantor, m.

chanticleer, m. gallus, m.; vigil ales, f.
chaos, s. chaos, n.; fig. confusio, f.
chaotic, a. confusus; indigestus.
chap, s. rhagades, f. pl.
chapel, s. sacellum, sacrarium, n.
chaplet, s. sertum, n.; corona, f.
chapman, s. caupo; emptor, m.
chapter, s. caput, n.; (cathedral body) use collegium, m.
char, v.a. amburo, 3.
char-woman, s. operaria, f.
character, s. mores, m. pl.; indoles, f.; ingenium, n.; habitus, m.; natura; proprietas, f.; good or bad —, bona or mala fama, f.
characteristic, a. proprius (with genitive); -ally, ad. ex more (tuo, suo, etc.).
characteristic, s. proprium, n.
characterize, v.a. describo, 3.
charcoal, s. carbo, m.
charge, v.a. accuso, 1; arguo, 3; criminor, 1; (to attack) adorior, 4; aggredior, 3; (to burden) onero; (to command) impero, 1; —, v.n. irruo, invado, 3; (entrust) committo, credo, 3; mando, 1; (exact) exigo, 3.
charge, s. accusatio, f.; crimen, n.; (attack) impetus, incursus, m.; (command) mandatum, n.; (trust) cura, custodia, f.; (office) munus, n.; (cost) impensa, f., sumptus, m.
chargeable, a. (liable) obnoxious.
charger, s. (large dish) patera, f.; (warhorse) equus bellator, sonipes, quadrupedans, m.
chariot, s. currus, m., curriculum, n.; (for war purposes) essedum, n.
charioteer, s. auriga, c.
charitable, a. benignus, beneficus; fig. mitis; (put a — construction on) in meliorem partem accipere.
charitableness, s. benignitas, liberalitas, f.
charitably, ad. benigne; indulgenter, in meliorem partem.
charity, s. (Christian love) caritas; (alms) stips, f.; (good-will) benevolentia, f.; (indulgence) indulgentia, venia, f.
charlatan, s. pharmacopola circumforaneus; fig. ostentator, jactator, m.
charlatanry, ostentatio, f.
Charles'-wain, s. plaustrum, n.
charlock, s. lapsana, f.
charm, s. cantus, m.; carmen, n.; cantio, f.; incantamentum, n.; fig. illecebra; gratia, f.; (physical charms) venustas, f.; veneres, f. pl.; (amulet) amuletum, n.
charm, v.a. incanto, fascino, canto, 1; (to delight) capio, 3; delecto; to — away, recanto, 1.

charmer, s. magus, m.; (sweetheart) deliciæ, f. pl.   [blandus.

charming, a. venustus, amœnus, lepidus,

charmingly, ad. lepide, blande.

charnel-house, s. ossuarium, n.

chart, s. tabula, f.

charter, s. (privilege) licentia, f.

charter, v.a. conduco, 3.

chary, a. parcus, cautus.

chase, v.a. persequor, 3; venor, sector, 1; (drive) pello, ago, 3; agito, 1.

chase, s. (hunting) venatio, f.; venatus, m.

chase, v.a. (to engrave) cælo, 1.

chaser, s. (hunter) venator; (engraver) cælator, m.

chasing, s. cælatura, f.

chasm, s. hiatus, m.; specus, m. f. *or* n.

chaste, a. castus, pudicus; purus; **—ly,** ad. caste, pudice; pure.

chasten, v.a. castigo, 1.

chasteness, s. castitas, continentia, pudi-

chastise, v.a. castigo, 1.   [citia, f.

chastisement, s. castigatio; animadver-sio, f.

chastiser, s. castigator, m.

chastity, s. pudicitia, castitas, f.; (modesty) pudor, m.

chat, v.n. fabulor, 1; garrio, 4.

chat, s. sermo, m.; **to have a —,** fabu-lor, 1; garrio, 4.

chattel, s. bona, n. pl.; res, f.

chatter, v.n. nugor, 1; garrio, effutio, 4; (of the teeth) crepito, 1.

chatter, chattering, s. strepitus, m.; (idle talk) garrulitas, f.; nugæ, f. pl.; (of the teeth) crepitus, m.

chatter-box, s. lingulaca, f.

chatterer, s. garrulus, loquax, m.

chattering, a. garrulus.

chatty, a. garrulus.

cheap, a. vilis.

cheaply, ad. bene, vili.

cheapness, s. vilitas, f.   [fraudo, 1.

cheat, v.a. decipio, fallo, eludo, 3;

cheat, s. fraus, ars, f., dolus, m.; (cheater) fraudator, m.

check, v.a. (to restrain) cohibeo, inhibeo, 2; reprimo, 3; (to stop) retardo, tardo, 1; (to bridle) refreno, 1; (accounts) dis-pungo, 3.

check, s. (hindrance) impedimentum, n.; (reprimand) reprehensio, f.; (bridle) frenum, n.; (disadvantage) detrimen-tum, n.; (delay) mora, f.; (admission-ticket) tessera, f.

checker, v.a., v. **chequer.**

checkered, a., v. **chequered.**

check-mate, v.a. ad incitas redigere, 3.

cheek, s. gena, bucca, f.; **— -bone,** s. mala, maxilla, f.; **— -tooth,** s. dens maxil-laris, m.

cheeky, a. impudens.

cheer, v.a. hilaro, exhilaro, 1; (to en-courage) hortor, adhortor, 1; (to com-fort) solor, 1; (applaud) plaudo, 3.

cheer, s. (shout) clamor, plausus, m.; (cheerfulness) hilaritas, f.; (food) cibus, m.; epulæ, f. pl.; mensa, f.; (be of good —) bono animo esse.

cheerful, a. hilaris, alacer, lætus; **—ly,** ad. hilare, læte; (willingly) libenter.

cheerfulness, s. alacritas, hilaritas, f.

cheering, s. acclamatio, f., plausus, m.

cheerless, a. illætabilis.

cheery, a., v. **cheerful.**

cheese, s. caseus, m.

cheese-cake, s. savillum, n.

chemise, s. indusium, n.

chemist, s. pharmacopola, m.

cheque, s. (ticket) tessera, f.

chequer, v.a. distinguo, 3; vario, 1; *fig.* misceo, 2; vario, 1.

chequered, a. tessellatus, distinctus; varius.

chequer-work, s. tessellatum (opus), n.

cherish, v.a. (to nourish) alo, 3; (to keep warm) calefacio, 3; (to treat tenderly) foveo, 2; *fig.* colo, 3.

cherry, s. cerasus, f.; cerasum, n.; **— -tree,** s. cerasus, f.

cherry-pie, s. heliotropium, n.

cherub, s. cherub, pl. cherubim.

chervil, s. cærefolium, n.

chess, s. ludus latruncularius; **— -board,** s. tabula latruncularia; **— -man,** s. latrunculus, calculus, m.

chest, s. (breast) pectus, n.; (box) cista, arca, capsa, f.; (for clothes) vestiarium, n.; (cabinet) scrinium, n.

chestnut, s. castanea, f.; **— -tree,** s. castanea, f.

chestnut, a. badius, spadix.

chevalier, s. eques; nobilis, m.

chevaux de frise, s. ericius, cervus, m.

chew, v.a. mando, 3; manduco, 1; (the cud) rumino, 1; *fig.* meditor, 1.

chicane, chicanery, s. calumnia, præ-varicatio, f.; (deceit) fraus, f.

chick, s. pullus (gallinaceus), m.

chicken, s., v. **chick;** **— -hearted,** a.

chickling, s. pullus, m.   [timidus.

chick-pea, s. cicer, n.

chick-weed, s. alsine, f.

chicory, s. cichorium, n.; intubus, c.

chide, v.a. & n. objurgo, vitupero, 1; reprehendo, 3; (sharply) corripio, 3.

chider, s. objurgator, m.

chiding, s. objurgatio, reprehensio, f.

chief, s. primus; præcipuus, summus, supremus.   [caput, n.

chief, s. princeps, procer, dux, auctor, m.,

chiefly, ad. præcipue, imprimis.

chieftain, s. dux, ductor, m.
chilblain, s. pernio, m.
child, s. infans, c.; puer, filius, m.; puella, filia, f.; (children) liberi, m. pl.;
  to bear a —, parturio, 4; with —,
  gravida.
child-bearing, s. partus, m.
child-bed, s. puerperium, n.; woman in
  —, puerpera, f.   [bores, m. pl.
child-birth, s. partus, m.; Lucinæ la-
childhood, s. infantia; pueritia, f.;
  from —, a puero or pueris; a parvo.
childish, a. puerilis, infans; —ly, ad.
  pueriliter.
childishness, s. puerilitas, f.
childless, a. orbus.
childlike, a. puerilis.
chill, s. frigus, n.; algor, m.; horror, m.;
  (fever) febris, f.
chill, a. frigidulus.
chill, v.a. refrigero, 1.
chilliness, s. algor, m.
chilling, a. algificus; frigidus, gelidus.
chilly, a. alsiosus; frigidulus.
chime, s. (harmony) concentus.
chime, v.n. (of bells) cano, 3; to — in,
  succino, 3.
chimera, s. chimæra, f.; fig. portentum
  monstrum, n.; (fiction) commentum, n.
chimerical, a. fictus.
chimney, s. caminus.
chimney-corner, s. focus, m.
chin, s. mentum, n.
china, s. murrha, f.; murrhina, n. pl.
chine, s. tergum, n., spina, f.
chink, s. rima, fissura, f.; (sound) tinnitus, m.
chink, v.n. tinnio, 4.
chinky, a. rimosus.
chip, s. segmen, n., assula, f.; (for lighting
  fire) fomes, m.; (fragment) fragmentum, fragmen, n.
chip, v.a. dolo, dedolo, 1.
chirp, chirrup, v.n. (of birds) pipio, 4;
  pipilo, 1; (of crickets) strideo, 2.
chirp, chirping, chirrup, s. pipatus, m.
chisel, s. scalprum, cælum, n.
chisel, v.a. scalpo, 3.
chit, s. infans, c.
chit-chat, s. garrulitas, f.; nugæ, f. pl.
chitterlings, s. lactes, f. pl.
chivalrous, a. magnanimus, nobilis.
chivalry, s. equestris dignitas, f.; ordo
  equestris, m.; virtus, f.
choice, s. delectus, m.; electio; (the power
  of choosing) optio; (diversity) varietas, f.   [eximius.
choice, a. electus, exquisitus, præstans,
choicely, ad. exquisite.
choiceness, s. excellentia, præstantia, f.
choir, s. chorus, m.; (of a church) apsis, f.

choke, v.a. suffoco; strangulo, 1; fauces
  elido, 3; fig. præcludo; —, v.n. suffo-
  cor; strangulor, 1.
choking, s. suffocatio; strangulatio, f.
choler, s. ira, bilis, f.
cholera, s. cholera, f.
choleric, a. biliosus, iracundus.
choose, v.a. eligo, deligo, lego, 3; opto, 1;
  —, v.n. (to prefer) malo; (be willing)
choosing, s. rictus, m.   [volo.
chop, v.a. abscido, 3; trunco; to — off,
  detrunco, 1; abscido; to — up, concido, 3.
chop, s. (of meat) ofella; — and change,
  vicissitudo, f.
chop-house, s. popina, caupona, f.
chopping-block, s. caudex, m.
chopping-knife, s. dolabra, f.
chops, s. rictus, m.
chord, s. (string) chorda, f., nervus, m.
chorister, s. canentium choro ascriptus, m.
chorus, s. chorus, m.; concentus, m.
Christ, s. Christus, m.
christen, v. to baptize.
Christendom, s. cuncti Christiani, m. pl.
Christian, a. Christianus; fig. pius.
Christianity, s. Christiana religio, f.; fig.
Christ's thorn, s. paliurus, m.   [pietas.
chromatic, a. (mus.) chromaticus.
chronic, a. chronicus.
chronicle, s. annales, fasti, m. pl.
chronicle, v.a. in annales refero, 3.
chronicler, s. annalium scriptor, m.
chronology, s. ætatum ordo, m.; ratio
  temporum, f.
chrysalis, s. chrysallis, f.
chrysanthemum, s. chrysanthemum (mod.
  hort.).
chrysolite, s. chrysolithus, c.
chrysoprase, s. chrysoprasus, m.
chub, s. (fish) perca, f.
chubby, a. bucculentus.
chuckle, v.n. cachinno, 1.
chum, s. contubernalis, m.
chump, s. stipes, truncus, m.
church, s. ecclesia, f.
churchman, s. ecclesiasticus, m.
church-yard, s. cæmeterium, sepulcretum, n.
churl, s. homo rusticus, homo illiberalis, m.
churlish, a. inhumanus; agrestis; —ly,
  ad. inhumaniter.
churlishness, s. inhumanitas, rusticitas, f.
chyle, s. chylus, m.
chyme, s. chymus, m.
cicatrice, s. cicatrix, f.
cicerone, s. dux, mystagogus, m.
cincture, s. cinctus, m.; cingulum, n.
cinder, s. cinis, m.; favilla, f.

cineraria, s. senecio (mod. hort.).
cinnabar, s. minium, n.
cinnamon, s. cinnamomum, cinnamum, n.
cinquefoil, s. quinquefolium, n., potentilla (mod. hort.).
cipher, s. (nought, zero) nihil, n.
cipher, v.n. computo, 1.
circle, s. circulus, orbis; (whirling motion) gyrus, m.; (of persons) corona, f.; (social meeting) circulus, m.
circle, v.a. circumdo, 1; cingo, 3; v.n. (move round) circumvolvor, 3.
circlet, s. armilla, f.
circuit, s. circuitus; ambitus, m.; circumscriptio, f.; (of judges) conventus, m.; **to make a —,** circumire, 4.
circuitous, a. devius.
circular, a. orbiculatus, rotundus; —ly, ad. in orbem.
circulate, v.a. spargo, differo, 3; —, v.n. circulor, 1.
circulation, s. circumactus, m.; **come into —,** in usum venire.
circumcise, v.a. circumcido, 3.
circumcision, s. circumcisio, f.
circumference, s. peripheria, f., circulus, orbis, m.
circumflex, a. circumflexus; —, s. (accent) circumflexus, m.
circumjacent, a. circumjacens, circumjectus.
circumlocution, s. circumlocutio, f.; ambages, f. pl.
circumnavigate, v.a. circumvehor, 3.
circumnavigation, s. periplus, m.
circumscribe, v.a. finio, 4; termino, 1; circumscribo, 3.
circumspect, a. circumspectus, cautus.
circumspection, s. circumspectio, cautio, f.
circumstance, s. res, f.; tempus, n.; condicio, f.; status, m.; **under these —,** cum res ita se habeant.
circumstanced, a. situs, positus.
circumstantial, a. adventicius; (detailed) accuratus; (of evidence) conjecturalis.
circumvallate, v.a. circummunio, 4.
circumvallation, s. circummunitio, f.
circumvent, v.a. circumvenio, 4; (in a bad sense) circumscribo, 3.
circumvention, s. circumscriptio; fraus, f.
circus, s. circus, m.
cistern, s. cisterna, f.; puteus, m.
citadel, s. arx, f.
citation, s. vocatio, prolatio, f.
cite, v.a. (law) cito, evoco, 1; (to quote) profero, 3.
citizen, s. civis, c.; (townsman) oppidanus, m.
citizenship, s. civitas, f.
citron, s. citreum, n.; — -tree, s. citrus, f.

city, s. urbs, f.
city, a. urbanus; urbicus.
civic, a. civilis, civicus.
civil, a. civilis; (polite) comis, urbanus; —ly, ad. comiter, urbane.
civilian, s. juris peritus, juris consultus; (non-military person) togatus.
civility, s. urbanitas, f.
civilization, s. cultus, m.
civilize, v.a. excolo, 3; expolio, emollio, 4.
clad, a. vestitus, indutus, amictus.
claim, v.a. postulo; flagito, 1; exposco, exigo, 3; (aim at) affecto; (demand for oneself) vindico, 1.
claim, s. vindicatio; postulatio, f.; postulatum, n.; **legal —,** vindiciæ, f. pl.
claimant, s. petitor, m.
clamber, v.n. scando, conscendo, 3.
clamminess, s. lentitia, f.
clammy, a. lentus, viscidus.
clamorous, a. tumultuosus; —, ad. tumultuose.
clamour, s. clamor, tumultus, m.
clamour, v.a. exclamo; clamo, vociferor, 1; strepo, 3; **—for,** flagito, efflagito, 1.
clamp, s. confibula, f.
clan, s. gens, f.
clandestine, a. clandestinus, furtivus; —ly, ad. clam, furtim, clanculum.
clang, s. clangor, m.
clang, v.n. clango; strepo, 3.
clank, s. crepitus, m.
clank, v.n. crepo, 1.
clansman, s. gentilis, m.
clap, v.n. (to beat) percutio, 3; pulso, 1; (hands) plaudo, 3; **— on,** *fig.* impono, 3.
clap, s. (blow) ictus; (noise) crepitus, (of thunder) fragor; (wtih the hands) plausus, m.
clapper, s. (person) plausor; (of a bell) malleus, m.; (rattle) crepitaculum, sistrum, n.
clap-trap, s. fraus, f.
clarify, v.a. deliquo, defæco, 1.
clarion, s. lituus, m.; tuba, f.
clash, s. crepitus, m.; concursus, m.; (opposition) repugnantia, f.
clash, v.n. crepito, 1; concurro, 3; *fig.* confligo, 3; repugno, 1.　　[m.
clasp, s. fibula, f.; (embrace) amplexus,
clasp, v.a. fibulo, 1; (to embrace) amplector; (to grasp) comprehendo, 3.
clasper, s. (of a vine) clavicula, f.
class, s. classis, f.; ordo, m.; genus, n.
class, v.a. in classes distribuo, 3; (value) æstimo, 1.
classic(al), a. (pre-eminent) optimus, præstantissimus; (ancient) antiquus; (well known) notissimus; —(al)ly, ad. optime; ad optimorum auctorum exemplum.

classification, s. distributio, f.
classify, v.a. in classes distribuo, 3.
clatter, v.n. crepo, crepito, 1.
clatter, clattering, s. strepitus, crepitus, m.
clause, s. (part of a sentence) articulus, i, m.; clausula, f.; (in a will) elogium, n.
clavicle, s. (shoulder-blade) scapulæ, f. pl.
claw, s. unguis, m.; ungula, f.; (of a crab) bracchium, n.
claw, v.a. (to scratch) scalpo, 3; lacero, 1; to — away or off, diripio, 3.
clay, s. argilla; creta, f.; lutum, n.
clayey, clayish, a. argillaceus, argillosus, lutosus.
clean, a. mundus, purus; nitidus.
clean, ad. omnino, prorsus, funditus.
clean, v.a. mundo, purgo, 1; (sweep) verro.
cleanliness, s. munditia, f.; nitor, m.
cleanly, a. & ad. mundus; purus; munde, pure.   [centia, f.
cleanness, s., v. cleanliness; fig. inno-
cleanse, v.a. purgo, depurgo, expurgo, purifico, 1; (by wiping, brushing or rubbing) tergeo, detergeo, 2; (by wash- ing) abluo, 3.
cleansing, s. purgatio, f.
clear, a. (bright) lucidus, clarus; (of fluids) limpidus; (transparent) liqui- dus; (clean) purus; (fair) serenus; (of voice) candidus; (clear and shrill) acu- tus, sonorus; (manifest) conspicuus, manifestus; (of space) apertus, patens; (without mixture) merus; (without in- fection) integer; (of style) lucidus; (free of deduction) solidus; fig. (in the head) sagax; — of (free from), solutus, liber; keep — of, caveo, 2; with a — conscience, pie.
clear, ad. prorsus, omnino.
clear, v.a. purgo, 1; (to acquit) absolvo, 3; (a doubt) explano; (from) libero; (land, forests) extrico; (to profit) luc- ror; (to exculpate) purgo (de aliqua re), 1; to — away, detergeo; amoveo, 2; to — off, amolior, 4; (a debt) solvo, 3; to — out, emundo, 1; to — up, (v.a.) enodo; explano, illustro; (v.n.) (of the weather) sereno, 1; it —s up, disserenat.
clearly, ad. clare; (of sounds) liquide; fig. dilucide; plane; aperte, haud dubie, manifesto.   [fig. candor, m.
clearness, s. claritas; (of sky) serenitas, f.;
clear-sighted, a. perspicax; fig. sagax.
cleave, v.a. findo, 3; diffindo; — v.n. dehisco, 3; dissilio, 4; (to adhere to) hæreo, adhæreo, 2.
cleaver, s. dolabra, f.
cleft, s. rima, fissura, f.

clemency, s. clementia, mansuetudo, in- dulgentia, f.; (of weather) cœlum sudum, n.   [—ly, ad. clementer.
clement, a. clemens, mitis, mansuetus;
clench, v. clinch.
clergy, s. clerus, m.
clergyman, s. clericus, ecclesiasticus, m.
clerical, a. clericus, clericalis, ecclesiasti- cus.
clerk, s. (clergyman) clericus, i; (scholar) doctus; (accountant) actuarius; scriba, m.
clever, a. sollers; dexter; ingeniosus; (knowing) scitus; (quick) versutus; (sly, cunning) callidus, astutus.
cleverly, ad. sollerter, perite; ingeniose; scite; astute; callide.
cleverness, s. dexteritas, sollertia, astutia, calliditas, f.
click, v.n. crepito, 1.
click, s. crepitus, tinnitus, m.
client, s. cliens, c.; (one who consults another) consultor, m.
clientship, s. clientela, f.
cliff, s. (sharp rock) cautes, rupes, f., scopulus; (hill) collis, m.
cliffy, a. abruptus, declivis.
climacteric, a. climactericus; —, s. cli- macter, m.
climate, s. regio, f.; aer, m.; cælum, n.; a mild —, temperies, f.
climax, s. gradatio, f.; (critical point) discrimen, n.
climb, v.a. & n. ascendo, conscendo, scando, enitor, evado, 3.
clime, s. regio, f., v. climate.
clinch, v.a. (the fist) contraho; (an argu- ment) astringo, 3.
clinch, clincher, s. clavus; uncus, m.
cling, v.n. adhæreo, hæreo, 2; amplector, 3; (remain) maneo, 2.
clinical, a. clinicus.
clinging, a. lentus, tenax, sequax.
clink, v.n. tinnio, 4.
clink, s. tinnitus, m.
clip, v.a. (circum)tondeo, 2; circumcido, præcido, 3; amputo, 1; (words) mutilo, 1; (embrace) amplector, 3.
clipper, s. (ship) celox, f.
clipping, s. tonsura, f.; —s, pl. reseg- mina, n. pl.
clique, s. factio, f.
cloak, s. pallium, sagum, n.; lacerna, læna, chlamys, f.; amictus, m. (pre- text) species, simulatio, f.; prætex- tum, n.
cloak, v.a. pallio vestio, 4; fig. dis- simulo, 1; prætendo, tego, 3.
clock, s. horologium, n.; what o'— is it? quota hora est?
clod, s. glæba, f.

cloddy, a. (of clods) glæbalis; (full of clods) glæbosus.

clodhopper, s. rusticus, m.

clodpated, a. stupidus.

clodpoll, s., v. blockhead.

clog, s. (heavy shoe) sculponeæ, f. pl.; (fetter) compes, f.; *fig.* impedimentum, n.; mora, f.

clog, v.a. impedio, præpedio, 4; onero, 1.

cloister, s. monasterium, cœnobium; (portico) porticus, f.; (asylum) asylum, n.

cloistered, a. inclusus.

close, v.a. claudo, 3; operio, 4; (end) finio, 4; termino, 1; —, v.n. (to come together) coeo, 4; (end) terminor, 1; **to — up,** præcludo, occludo; **to — with,** (of fighting) consero (manum); (of bargains) accipio, 3.

close, a. (shut) occlusus; (thick) densus; (narrow) angustus; artus; (fast) firmus; (near to) contiguus; (dark) tenebrosus; (secret) arcanus; *fig.* taciturnus, tectus; (niggardly) avarus; tenax; **—by,** vicinus, propinquus; **— together,** confertus, continuus.

close, ad. dense; (near) prope, proxime.

close, s. sæptum, n.; (end) finis, c.; (— of a speech) peroratio, f.; **to bring to a —,** finio, 4; termino, 1; **to draw to a —,** terminor, 1.

close-fisted, a. parcus.   [clanculum.

closely, ad. dense; exacte; (secretly)

closeness, s. densitas; angustiæ; *fig.* parsimonia, f.; silentium, n.; (nearness) proximitas, f.   [vestiarium, n.

closet, s. cella, f., conclave; (for clothes)

closet, v.a. includo, 3.

closing, a. ultimus.   [m.

clot, s. glæba, massa, f.; (of blood) cruor,

clot, v.n. concresco, 3.

cloth, s. pannus, m.; (linen) linteum; (for horses) stragulum, n.

clothe, v.a. vestio, amico, 4; induo, 3; velo, 1.

clothes, s. vestis, f.; vestitus, m., vestimenta, n. pl.; (of bed) stragulum, n.

clothier, s. vestiarius, m.

clothing, s. vestitus, m., vestimenta, n. pl.; (covering, etc.) velamen, n.

cloud, s. nubes, nebula, f.; nubila, n. pl.

cloud, v.a. *fig.* contristo, 1; v.n. nubilo, 1.

cloudless, a. serenus, sudus.

cloudy, a. nubilus; (of liquids) turbidus; **to grow —,** nubilo, 1.

clout, s. panniculus; (blow) ictus, m.

clout, v.a. sarcio, 4; (strike) ferio, 4.

clove, s. caryophyllum, n.

cloven, a. bisulcus, bifidus.

clover, s. trifolium, n.

clown, s. (countryman) rusticus; homo agrestis; (buffoon) scurra, m.

clownish, a. rusticus; agrestis; **—ly,** ad. rustice.

clownishness, s. rusticitas, f.

cloy, v.a. satio, exsaturo, 1.

club, s. (cudgel) clava, f. fustis, m.; (of persons) sodalicium, n.; sodalitas, f.; circulus, m.

club, v.a. confero, 3.

club-footed, a. scaurus, loripes.

cluck, v.n. glocio, 4.

clue, s. glomus, n.; (trace, mark) indicium, n.

clump, s. massa, f.; globus, m.; **— of bushes,** dumentum, n.

clumsily, ad. crasse; rustice; inscite, ineleganter, male.

clumsiness, s. rusticitas, f.

clumsy, a. inhabilis; inelegans; inscitus; rusticus, agrestis.

cluster, s. (of grapes, etc.) racemus; (of flowers) corymbus, m.; **— of islands,** celebritas insularum, f.

cluster, v.n. congregor, conglobor, 1.

clutch, v.a. arripio, 3.

clutch, s. (hand) manus, f.; *fig.* **in one's —es,** in sua potestate.

clyster, s. clyster, m.

coach, s. currus, m., ræda, f.; pilentum, petoritum, n.

coachman, s. rædarius, m., auriga, c.

coadjutor, s. adjutor, auxiliator, administer, socius, collega, m.

coagulate, v.a. coagulo, 1; —, v.n. concresco, 3.

coagulation, s. coagulatio, f.

coal, s. carbo, m.; (burning) pruna, f.; **to carry —s to Newcastle,** in silvam ligna ferre.

coal mine, s. fodina, f.

coalesce, v.n. coalesco, 3; *fig.* coeo, 4.

coalition, s. societas; (plot) coïtio, f.

coarse, a. crassus; *fig.* incultus; rudis, rusticus, infacetus, illiberalis; **—ly,** ad. crasse; infacete.

coarseness, s. crassitudo; rusticitas, f.

coast, s. ora, f., litus, n.

coast, v.n. (oram) lego, 3.

coaster, coasting-vessel, s. navis oraria, f.

coat, s. vestis; tunica, f.; **— of arms,** insignia, n. pl.; **— of mail,** lorica; (skin) pellis, f.; corium, n.; tegumentum, n.

coat, v.a. illino, induco, 3.

coating, s. (skin) tegumentum, n.; pellis, f.; corium, n.

coax, v.a. mulceo, 2; blandior, 4; (persuade) adduco.

coaxing, s. blandimenta, n. pl.; blanditiæ, f. pl.

coaxing, a. blandus.

coaxingly, ad. blande.

cobble, v.a. resarcio.

cobbler, s. sutor, veteramentarius, m.
cobweb, s. aranea tela, aranea, f.; aranea texta, n. pl.
cochineal, s. coccum, n.
cock, s. gallus, m.
cock, v.a. attollo, erigo, 3.
cockatoo, s. psittacus, m.
cockatrice, s. basiliscus, m.
cock-boat, s. scapha, f.
cockchafer, s. blatta, f.
cockcrow, s. gallicinium, n.   [chema, f.
cockle, s. (plant) lolium, n.; (shell-fish)
cock-loft, s. granarium, n.
cockney, a. urbanus, oppidanus.
cockroach, s. blatta, f.
cockscomb, s. crista, f.; fig. (fop) homo putidus; nugator, m.; (plant) celosia (mod. hort.).
cocoanut palm, s. cocos (mod. hort.).
cocoa-tree, s. theobroma (mod. hort.).
cocoon, s. globulus, m.
coddle, v.a. indulgeo, f.
codicil, s. codicilli, m. pl.
codify, v.a. digero, 3.
coequal, a. æqualis.
coerce, v.a. coerceo, 2; refreno, 1; cogo, 3.
coercion, s. coercitio, f.; (force) vis, f.; (necessity) necessitas.
coeval, a. æqualis.
coexist, v.n. simul or uno tempore esse or existere, 3.   [hort.).
coffee, s. (plant and drink) coffea (mod.
coffer, s. arca, cista, f.
coffin, s. arca, f.; loculus, m.
cog, s. (of a wheel) dens, m.
cogency, s. vis, f.; pondus, momentum, n.
cogent, a. gravis, efficax; —ly, ad. efficaciter, graviter.
cogitate, v.n. meditor, reputo, 1.
cogitation, s. reputatio, f.
cognate, a. cognatus, affinis.
cognizance, s. cognitio; jurisdictio; (legal inquiry) quæstio, f.
cohabit, v.n. concumbo, 3.
cohabitation, s. concubitus, m.
coheir, coheiress, s. coheres, c.
cohere, v.n. cohæreo, 2; fig. consentio, 4; concordo, 1.
coherence, s. contextus, m.; (order) ordo, m.   [clarus.
coherent, a. contextus, continens; (clear)
coherently, ad. constanter; (clearly) clare.
cohesion, s. cohærentia, f.; contextus, m.
cohesive, a. tenax, lentus.
cohort, s. cohors, f.
coif, s. mitra, mitella, f.
coil, s. spira, f.; volumen, glomus, n.
coil, v.a. & n. glomero; glomeror, 1; (wind) volvo, volvor.
coin, s. nummus, i, m.; (collectively) pecunia, f.; a little —, nummulus, m.

coin, v.a. (money) cudo, 3; ferio, 4; fig. (to invent) fingo, 3.
coinage, s. res nummaria; (coined money) pecunia publice signata, moneta; (invention) fictio, f.
coincide, v.n. congruo, 3; convenio, 4.
coincidence, s. concursio fortuitorum; (agreement) consensus, m.; it happens by a lucky —, peropportune accidit.
coiner, s. cusor, monetarius; (false stamper) qui nummos adulterinos cudit; fig. novator, m.
coining, s., v. coinage.
colander, s. colum, n.
cold, a. frigidus, gelidus; (met.) lentus, frigidus; to be —, frigeo, algeo, 2; to become —, frigesco, 3.
cold, s. frigus, n., algor, m.; (catarrh) gravedo, f.; to catch —, perfrigesco, algesco, 3.
coldish, a. frigidulus.
coldly, ad. fig. frigide, gelide, lente.
coldness, s. frigus, n. algor, m.; fig. lentitudo, f.
colewort, s. brassica, f.
colic, s. tormina, um, n. pl.; colum, n.
collapse, v.n. collabor; concido, corruo, 3.
collapse, s. lapsus, casus, m.; labes, ruina, f.
collar, s. (of a garment) collare, n.; (ornament) torques, c.; monile, n.; (for horses) helcium, n.; (for dogs) mellum, f.
collar, v.a. comprehendo, 3.   [n.
collar-bone, s. jugulum, n.
collate, v.a. confero, 3.
collateral, a. (of relationship) transversus, ex transverso (cognatus); fig. adventicius; — relationship, latus, n.; —ly, ad. a latere, ex transverso.
collation, s. collatio, f.; (luncheon) merenda, f.
colleague, s. collega, m.; consors, c.
collect, v.a. lego, colligo, confero, 3; (an army) comparo, convoco, 1; (to gather) cogo, 3; comporto, 1; (money) exigo, 3; (heap up) coacervo, 1; — oneself, se or animum colligere; v.n. convenio, coeo, 3; congregor, 1.
collected, a. præsens; intentus.
collection, s. collectio; conquisitio; (of money) collatio, f.; (out of authors) collectanea, n. pl.
collective, a. collectivus; —ly, ad. una simul.   [actor, m.
collector, s. qui colligit; (of taxes) ex-
college, s. collegium, n.; academia, f.
collegian, s. alumnus, m.
collegiate, s. academicus.
colliery, s. fodina, f.
collision, s. conflictio, f.; concursus, m.
collop, s. offa, ofella, f.

colloquial, a. communis (sermo), m.

colloquy, s. colloquium, n.

collusion, s. collusio; prævaricatio, f.

collusive, a. dolosus, fallax, fictus; —ly, ad. fallaciter, ficte.

colocynth, s. colocynthis, f.

colon, s. (punctuation) colon, n.

colonel, s. dux, tribunus, m.

colonial, a. colonicus.

colonist, s. colonus, m.

colonize, v.a. coloniam deduco (in, with acc.).

colonnade, s. porticus, f., xystus, m.

colony, s. colonia, f.

colossal, a. (of statues) colossicus, colosseus; ingens, immanis.

colossus, s. colossus, m.

colour, s. color, m., pigmentum, n.; (standard) vexillum, signum, n.; *fig.* prætextus, m.; prætextum, n.

colour, v.a. coloro, 1; (to dye) tingo, inficio, imbuo, 3; *fig.* (to palliate) obtego, prætendo, 3; —, v.n. erubesco, 3.

colourable, a. speciosus.

coloured, a. coloratus.

colouring, s. color; *fig.* ornatus, m.

colour-sergeant, s. vexillarius, m.

colt, s. equulus, pullus equinus, m.; **ass's** —, pullus asininus, m.

colter, s. culter, m.

colt's-foot, s. tussilago, f.

columbine, s. aquilegia (mod. hort.); **tufted** —, thalictrum, n.

column, s. columna, f.

comb, s. pecten, m.

comb, v.a. pecto, 3; (to dress the hair) como, 3.   [men, n.

combat, s. pugna, f., prœlium; certa-

combat, v.a. & n. pugno, prœlior, 1; certo, dimico, 1; contendo, 3; (oppose) repugno, impugno, adversor, 1.

combatant, s. miles, c.; pugnator, prœliator, m.

combination, s. conjunctio, junctura, f.; concursus, m.; (plot) conspiratio, f.

combine, v.a. conjungo, 3; misceo, 2; —, v.n. (plot) conspiro, 1; coeo, 4.

combustion, s. crematio, deflagratio, f.

come, v.n. venio, 4; (to arrive) pervenio, 4; (to happen) fieri; **to — about,** evenio, 4; **to — after,** sequor, 3; **to — again,** revenio, 4; **to — along,** procedo, 3; **to — away,** abscedo, 3; abeo, 4; **to — back,** revenio; redeo, 4; **to — before,** prævenio, 4; **to — by,** prætereo, 4; (to get) acquiro, 3; **to — down,** descendo, 3; (to fall down) decido, 3; **to — forth,** exeo, 4; egredior, 3; *fig.* exorior, 4; **to — forward,** procedo, 3; **to — in(to),** introeo, 4; **to — near,** appropinquo, 1; accedo, 3;

to — of, originem traho (de, e); **to — off,** recedo; *fig.* discedo, 3; (of hair, etc.) cado, 3; **to — on,** procedo, pergo, 3; **— on!** agite! **to — out,** v. **to — forth** & **to — off;** (to be published) edi, emitti, 3; (to become known) evulgor, 1; **to — over,** supervenio, obeo, 4; (to go over to) transgredior, 3; transeo, f.; **to — round,** circumagi; *fig.* adduci, 3; **to — short,** deficio, 3; desum; **to — to,** advenio, 4; pervenio; *fig.* **to — to pass,** evenio, 4; fio, 3; **to — together,** convenio, coeo, 4; **to — up,** subvenio, 4; (to spring up) provenio, 4; **to — upon,** supervenio, 4; (to attack) ingruo, invado, 3; (to surprise) deprehendo, 3.

come! i. age! eia!

comedian, s. comœdus; comicus, m.

comedy, s. comœdia, f.; soccus, m.

comeliness, s. decentia, forma; venustas, f.; decor, m.

comely, a. decens, pulcher, venustus.

comer, s. (new-comer) advena, c.

comet, s. cometes, m., stella crinita, f.

comfit, s., v. **sweet-meat.**

comfort, v.a. consolor, solor, 1.

comfort, s. solatium, solamen, n., consolatio, f.

comfortable, a. consolatorius; (commodious) commodus.

comfortableness, s. commoditas, f.

comfortably, ad. commode.

comforter, s. consolator, m.

comfortless, a. inconsolabilis; (inconvenient) incommodus.

comic(al), a. comicus; ridiculus.

comically, ad. comice; ridicule.

coming, a. adventus, m.

coming, a. venturus, futurus.

comma, s. (mod.) comma, n.

command, v.a. impero, 1; jubeo, 2; præcipio, 3; (to look towards a situation) specto, 1; (overhang) immineo, 2.

command, s. mandatum, præceptum, imperium, n.; (order) jussus, m.; jussum, n.; (office, place) præfectura, f., imperium, n.

commander, s. dux, præfectus, imperator, m.

commanding, a. eximius.

commandment, s. imperium, n.

commemorate, v.a. celebro, 1.

commemoration, s. celebratio, f.

commence, v.a. & n. incipio, 3; incoho, 1; ordior, 4; cœpi, 3.

commencement, s. initium, principium, n.

commend, v.a. (to commit) commendo, 1; committo, 3; (approve) approbo, laudo, probo, 1.

commendable, a. commendabilis, probabilis, laudabilis.

commendably, ad. laudabiliter.

commendation, s. commendatio, laus, f.

commendatory, a. commendaticius.   [m.

commender, s. laudator, commendator,

commensurable, a. par, conveniens.

commensurate, a. par, conveniens.

comment, v.a. & n. commentor, interpretor, 1; (remark) animadverto, 3.

comment, commentary, s. commentarius, m., commentarium, n.; (censure) animadversio, f.

commentator, s. interpres, c.

commerce, s. commercium, n.; mercatus, m.; mercatura, f.

commingle, v.a. misceo, commisceo, 2.

commiserate, v.a. miseror, commiseror, 1; miseresco, 3.

commiseration, s. miseratio, f.

commissariat, res frumentaria, f.; commeatus, m.

commissary, s. procurator; curator, m.

commission, s. mandatum, n.; (in the army) tribunatus, m.; (umpires) arbitri; **a — of two,** duumviri, m. pl.

commission, v.a. delego.

commissioner, s. arbiter, m.   •

commit, v.a. do, 1; (to trust) committo, 3; (to be guilty of) patro, perpetro, 1; admitto, 3; (to imprison) in custodiam do, 1.

commitment, comprehensio, f.

committee, s. delecti; **a — of ten,** decemviri, m. pl.

commodious, a. commodus; expeditus; (convenient) opportunus, idoneus; (large) amplus; **—ly,** ad. commode; (conveniently) opportune.

commodity, s. res venalis, merx, f.

common, a. communis; publicus; (ordinary, etc.) vulgaris; (well known) pervulgatus; *fig.* tritus; mediocris; (gr.) promiscuus; (low class) plebeius.

common, s. ager publicus *or* compascuus, m.

common, in —, ad. in medium, in commune; communiter; promiscue.

commonage, s. jus agri publici, n.

commonality, s. plebs, f., plebeius ordo, m.

commoner, s. plebeius, m.

commonly, ad. vulgo, fere plerumque.

commons, s. plebs, f., plebeius ordo, m.; (food) victus, m.

common-crier, s. præco, m.

common-law, s. jus translaticium, jus consuetudinis, n.

commonplace, s. locus communis, m.; **—,** a. (hackneyed) vulgaris, pervulgatus, tritus; **—-book,** s. commentarius, m.

commonwealth, s. respublica, civitas, f.

commotion, s. agitatio, f. tumultus, motus, concursus, m.

commune, v.n. colloquor, 3.

communicable, a. fandus.

communicate, v.a. & n. impertio, 4; communico, 1.

communication, s. communicatio, f.; commercium; colloquium, n.; (message) nuntius, m.; (mil.), **to cut off —s,** omnes aditus intercludere.

communicative, a. affabilis, apertus.

communicativeness, s. affabilitas, f.

communion, s. communio; societas, f.

community, s. communitas; (partnership) societas; (state) civitas, respublica, f.

commutation, s. permutatio, mutatio, f.

commute, v.a. remitto, 3.

compact, s. densus, spissus; solidus; (of style) pressus; **—ly,** ad. dense, spisse; presse.   [fœdus, n.

compact, s. pactum, n.; conventio, f.;

compactness, s. densitas, spissitudo; soliditas, f.

companion, s. socius, sodalis; comes; (as soldier) contubernalis; (at play), collusor, m.; **boon —,** compotor, m.; (accessory) socius, m.; consors, c.

companionable, a. affabilis, facilis.

companionship, s. sodalitas, f.; contubernium, n.

company, s. societas, sodalitas; (of soldiers) cohors, f., manipulus, m.; (at table) convivium, n.; (troop) caterva; turba, manus, f.; (animals) grex, m.; (corporation) collegium, n.

comparable, a. comparabilis.

comparative, a. comparativus.

comparative, s. (gr.) gradus comparativus, m.

comparatively, ad. use the comparative; **— slow,** tardior.

compare, v.a. comparo, æquo, 1; confero, 3.

comparison, s. comparatio, collatio, f.; **in — with,** ad. adversus; præ (with ablative).

compartment, s. loculus, m., cella, f.

compass, s. (circuit) ambitus, circuitus, m.; (limits) fines, m. pl.; (pair of compasses) circinus, m.

compass, v.a. circumdo, 1; cingo, 3; ambio, 4; (gain) consequor, 3; (accomplish) patro, perpetro, 1.

compassion, s. misericordia, miseratio, f.

compassionate, a. misericors; **—ly,** ad. misericorditer.   [recr, 2.

compassionate, v.a. miseresco, 3; mise-

compatibility, s. congruentia; (conformity) convenientia, f.

compatible, a. congruus, conveniens.

compatriot, s. civis, popularis, m.

compeer, s. par; æqualis, c.

compel, v.a. cogo, compello, 3.

compendious, a. brevis, succinctus; —ly, ad. breviter, summatim.

compendium, s. summarium, n., breviarium.

compensate, v.a. penso, compenso; —, v.n. (to repay) compensor, 1.

compensation, s. compensatio, f.

compete, v.n. contendo, 3; certo, 1.

competence, competency, s. facultas, f.; (legal capacity) jus, n.; (property) opes, f. pl.

competent, a. capax; (suitable) congruens, idoneus; (of authorities) locuples; —ly, ad. idonee, satis.

competition, s. contentio, æmulatio, f., certamen, n.

competitor, s. æmulus, rivalis, m. [n. pl.

compilation, s. collectio, f.; excerpta,

compile, v.a. colligo, conscribo, compono, 3.

compiler, s. auctor; conscriptor, m.

complacency, s. delectatio, f.; (self-love) amor sui.

complacent, a. (contented) contentus, (civil) comis, humanus.

complacently, ad. æquo animo; (civilly) comiter, humaniter.

complain, v.a. queror, conqueror, 3; ploro, 1; —, v.n. gemo, 3; lamentor, 1.

complainant, s., v. **plaintiff.**

complaining, a. querulus.

complaint, s. querela, querimonia, f.; (charge) crimen, n.; lamentatio, f.; (disease) morbus, i, m.

complaisance, s. obsequium, n.; comitas, humanitas, f.

complaisant, a. officiosus, comis, facilis, humanus; —ly, ad. comiter, humaniter, officiose.   [mentum, n.

complement, s. complementum, supple-

complete, a. plenus; integer; perfectus; —ly, ad. plane, prorsus.

complete, v.a. compleo; suppleo; expleo, 2; (to accomplish) perficio, 3.

completeness, s. integritas; perfectio, f.

completion, s. (accomplishment) perfectio, f.

complex, a. multiplex.

complexion, s. (of the skin) color, m.; (of the body) natura; indoles, f.; temperament) ingenium, n.

complexity, s. ambages, f. pl.; difficultas, f.   [quium, n.

compliance, s. obtemperatio, f., obse-

compliant, a. officiosus; facilis.

complicate, v.a. impedio, 4; confundo, 3; turbo, 1.

complicated, a. nodosus, difficilis, perplexus.

complication, s. nodus, m.; ambages, f. pl.; difficultas, f.

complicity, s. conscientia, f.

compliment, s. verba honorifica, n. pl.; blanditiæ, f. pl.; **to pay one's —s** (to), saluto, 1.

compliment, v.a. laudo, 1.

complimentary, a. honorificus; blandus.

comply, v.n. (with) concedo (with dat.); cedo, 3; pareo, 2; (to humour) morigeror; (me) accommodo, 1; (accept) accipio, 3.

component, s. pars, f., elementa, n. pl.

comport, v.n. (to agree) convenio, 4; (to behave oneself) se gerere, 3.

compose, v.a. compono; (arrange) digero, dispono, 3; (to calm) sedo; **to — oneself,** tranquillor, 1.

composed, a. quietus, tranquillus; —ly, ad. quiete, æquo animo.

composer, s. scriptor.

composite, a. compositus.

composition, s. compositio; confectio, f.; (book) liber, m.; (covenant) pactum, n.

compost, s. stercus, n.   [æquus, m.

composure, s. tranquillitas, f., animus

compound, v.a. compono, 3; misceo, 2; —, v.n. convenio, 4; paciscor, 3.

compound, a. compositus; concretus.

compound, s. farrago, f.

comprehend, v.a. contineo, 2; complector; (to understand) capio, percipio, comprehendo, intelligo, 3.

comprehensible, a. comprehensibilis.

comprehension, s. intellectus, m., intelligentia, comprehensio, f.

comprehensive, a. amplus; —ly, ad. ample.

comprehensiveness, s. amplitudo, f.

compress, v.a. comprimo, astringo, 3 coarto, 1.

compression, s. compressio, f.

comprise, v.a. contineo, cohibeo, 2; comprehendo, complector, 3.

compromise, s. compromissum, n.; (agreement) pactum, n.

compromise, v.a. compromitto, 3; (bring into odium) in invidiam adduco; —, v.n. paciscor, 3.

compulsion, s. vis, necessitas, f.

compulsorily, ad. vi, per vim.

compunction, s. pænitentia, f.; (pity) misericordia, f.

computation, s. ratio, computatio, f.

compute, v.a. computo, 1.

computer, s. calculator, m.

comrade, s. sodalis, socius; (military) contubernalis, m.

con, v.a. edisco, recenseo, 3.

concatenation, s. series, f.

concave, a. cavus; concavus.

conceal, v.a. celo, occulto, 1; abdo, condo, occulo, 3; (dissemble) dissimulo, 1.

concealer, s. occultator, m.

concealment, s. occultatio; dissimulatio, f.

concede, v.a. concedo, permitto, 3; do, 1.

conceit, s. opinio; arrogantia, superbia, f.; (invention) inventum, n.; (image) imago, f.; **witty —,** lepor, m.; (be) **out of — with,** fastidio.

conceited, a. arrogans, superbus, tumidus; **—ly,** ad. arroganter, superbe.

conceivable, a. comprehensibilis.

conceive, v.a. concipio; (comprehend) percipio, intelligo, 3; (picture in the mind) fingo, 3; (harbour) concipio, 3.

concentrate, v.a. in unum locum contraho; *fig.* animum intendo (in aliquid), 3.

concentration, s. in unum locum contractio, *fig.* animi intentio, f.

conception, s. (in the womb) conceptus, m.; (idea) imago, species, notio, f.

concern, s. (affair) res, f., negotium, n.; cura, f.; (importance) momentum, n.; (anxiety, trouble) sollicitudo, f.

concern, v.a. pertineo, 2; **it —s,** interest, refert; **to be —ed,** occupor, 1; particeps sum; (be anxious) sollicitus sum; **it does not — me,** non mihi curæ est. [quod ad.

concerning, pr. (about) de; (as to)

concert, v.a. statuo, 3; delibero, 1; (consult) consulo, 3; **—,** v.n. consentio, 4.

concert, s. (agreement) pactum, n.; (mus.) concentus, m.

concession, s. concessio, f.; (thing) concessum, n.; (allowance) venia, f.

couch, s. concha, f. [1; capio, 3.

conciliate, v.a. concilio; (to gain) paro,

conciliation, s. conciliatio, f.

conciliatory, a. pacificus; pacificatorius.

concise, a. brevis, concisus; (style) pressus; **—ly,** ad. breviter, concise.

conciseness, s. brevitas, f.

conclave, s. conclave, consilium, n.

conclude, v.a. & n. concludo, 3; finio, 4; (to end) perficio; (to settle) statuo, 3; (to infer) concludo, 3.

conclusion, s. (end) conclusio, f.; finis, m.; (of a speech) peroratio, f.; epilogus, m.; (inference) conclusio, f.

conclusive, a. (of arguments) certus.

concoct, v.a. concoquo, 3; (to contrive) excogito, machinor, 1.

concomitant, a. adjunctus, conjunctus; quod sequitur.

concord, s. concordia; conspiratio, f.; consensus, m.; (mus.) concentus, m.

concordant, a. concors, consonus, consentiens. [frequentia, f.

concourse, s. concursus; conventus, m.;

concrete, a. concretus.

concrete, concretion, s. concretus, m.

concubinage, s. concubinatus, m.

concubine, s. concubina, f.

concupiscence, s. libido, f.

concur, v.n. convenio; (to agree) consentio, 4.

concurrence, s. concursus, consensus, m.

concurrently, ad. una, simul.

concussion, s. concussio, f.

condemn, v.a. damno, condemno; (blame) vitupero, 1. [andus.

condemnable, a. condemnandus; vituper-

condemnation, s. damnatio, condemnationatio, f.

condemnatory, a. damnatorius. [natio, f.

condensable, a. quod spissari *or* condensari potest.

condensation, s. densatio, spissatio, f.

condense, v.a. (con)denso, spisso, 1; *fig.* coarto, 1.

condescend, v.n. dignor, 1; descendo, me summitto, 3.

condescending, a. comis, facilis, officiosus.

condescendingly, ad. comiter, officiose.

condescension, s. obsequium, n., comitas, f.

condign, a. dignus, meritus, debitus.

condiment, s. condimentum, n.

condition, s. condicio, f., status, m.; pactum, n., lex, f.; (rank) ordo, m.

conditional, a. condicionalis; **—ly,** ad. (law) condicionaliter.

condole, v.n. cum aliquo doleo, 2; (pity) misereor, 2. [ignosco, 3.

condone, v.a. condono, veniam do, 1;

conduce, v.n. conduco; proficio (ad), 3.

conducive, a. bonus, utilis, aptus.

conduct, s. vita, ratio, f.; mores, m. pl.; administratio, cura, f.; (deeds) facta, n. pl.

conduct, v.a. adduco; deduco; perduco, 3; administro, 1; (to direct) dirigo, 3; (preside over) præsum.

conductor, s. dux; administrator, m.

conduit, s. canalis, c., aquæductus, m.

cone, s. conus, i, m.; (in the circus) meta, f.

cone-flower, s. rudbeckia (mod. hort.).

coney, cony, s. cuniculus, m.

confection, s. conditura, f. [rius, m.

confectioner, s. crustularius, pistor dulcia-

confectionery, s. cuppedia, n. pl.

confederacy, s. (alliance) fœdus, n.; societas, f.; (plot) conspiratio, f.

confederate, s. socius; conjuratus, m.

confederate, v.a. & n. socio; conspiro; socior, 1.

confederation, s. fœdus, n.; societas, f.

confer, v.a. (to bestow) confero, 3; (to compare) comparo, 1; **to — with,** colloquor, 3; convenio, 4.

conference, s. colloquium, n.; congressus, m.

confess, v.a. fateor, confiteor, 2. [aperte.

confessedly, ad. ex confesso; manifesto,

confession, s. confessio.

confidant, s. familiaris, c., conscius, a, m. & f.

confide, v.a. confido, committo; credo, 3; (to trust) confido, fido, 3; (rely on) fretus sum.

confidence, s. fides; fiducia; confidentia; (boldness) audacia, f.; (self-confidence) sui fiducia, f.; **in —,** (secretly) clam.

confident, a. confidens; securus; (bold) audax; **—ly,** ad. confidenter.

confidential, a. candidus; (secret) arcanus.

configuration, s. forma, figura, f.

confine, s. confinium, confine, n.

confine, v.a. claudo, includo, 3; coerceo, cohibeo, 2; circumscribo, 3; termino, 1; **to be —d,** pario, 3.

confinement, s. inclusio; (imprisonment) custodia, f.; carcer, m.; (lying-in) puerperium, n.

confirm, v.a. confirmo; firmo; (to prove) comprobo, 1; (to ratify) sancio, 4.

confirmation, s. confirmatio, f.

confirmed, a. inveteratus.

confiscate, v.a. proscribo, 3; publico, confisco, 1. [proscriptio, f.

confiscation, s. publicatio, confiscatio,

conflagration, s. incendium, n.

conflict, s. contentio; controversia, f.; certamen, n.; pugna, f.

conflict, v.n. contendo, 3; (to struggle) luctor, 1; (be at variance) discrepo, 1.

conflicting, a. contrarius, adversus.

confluence, s. confluens, m.

conform, v.a. conformo, accommodo, 1; —, v.n. (to comply with) obtempero, 1.

conformable, a. congruens, consentaneus, accommodatus.

conformably, ad. convenienter, accommodate. [forma, f.

conformation, s. conformatio; figura,

conformity, s. convenientia, congruentia, f.; **in — with,** secundum.

confound, v.a. confundo, 3; permisceo, 2; perturbo, 1; (overthrow) everto, 3; (destroy) deleo, 2; perimo, 3.

confraternity, s. societas, f., sodalicium, n.

confront, v.a. (meet) congredior; (match) committo, 3.

confuse, v.a. confundo, 3; perturbo, 1.

confused, a. confusus, perplexus; indistinctus; pudibundus.

confusedly, ad. confuse, perplexe; perturbate.

confusion, s. confusio; perturbatio, f.; tumultus; pudor, n.; (ruin) labes, i, pernicies, f.

confutation, s. refutatio, f.

confute, v.a. confuto, refuto, 1; refello, redarguo, 3.

congeal, v.a. congelo, glacio, 1; —, v.n. consisto, concresco, 3.

congelation, s. congelatio, f.

congenial, a. consentaneus; concors; (pleasant) gratus.

conger, s. (eel) conger, m.

congestion, s. congestus, m.

congratulate, v.a. gratulor, grator, 1.

congratulation, s. gratulatio, f.

congratulatory, a. gratulatorius.

congregate, v.a. colligo, cogo, 3; congrego, 1; —, v.n. congregor, conglobor, 1; convenio, 4.

congregation, s. contio, f.; cœtus, m.; auditores, m. pl.

congress, s. congressus, m.

congruity, s. congruentia, convenientia, concordia, f. [veniens.

congruous, a. congruens, congruus, con-

conical, a. turbineus.

conifer, s. arbor conifera, f.

conjectural, a. opinabilis, conjecturalis; **—ly,** ad. ex conjectura.

conjecture, s. conjectura, f.

conjecture, v.a. conjecto, 1; conjicio, 3.

conjoin, v.a. conjungo, 3.

conjoint, a. conjunctus, communis; **—ly,** ad. conjunctim.

conjugal, a. conjugalis; conjugialis; **—ly,** ad. conjugaliter.

conjugate, v.a. (gr.) declino, 1.

conjugation, s. (gr.) conjugatio, f.

conjunction, s. conjunctio, f.; concursus, m.; (gr.) conjunctio, convinctio, f.

conjuncture, s. tempora, n. pl.; (crisis) discrimen, n. [men, n.

conjuration, s. obtestatio; (sorcery) car-

conjure, v.a. obtestor; (enchant) fascino, incanto, 1; —, v.n. præstigiis utor, 3.

conjurer, s. magus; (juggler) præstigiator, m.

conjuring, s. (juggling) præstigiæ, f. pl.

connect, v.a. connecto, 3; copulo, 1; (in a series) sero, 3.

connected, a. conjunctus; continuus; **to be —,** cohæreo, 2.

connection, s. conjunctio, f.; contextus, m.; (relation) affinitas; cognatio, f.; **have a — with,** pertineo ad, 2.

connivance, s. indulgentia, f.

connive, v.n. conniveo, indulgeo, 2; (leave unpunished) prætermitto, 3.

connoisseur, s. homo doctus, peritus, intelligens, elegans.

connubial, a. conjugalis.

conquer, v.a. vinco, 3; supero; domo, 1; (to gain) capio, 3; potior, 4.

conqueror, s. victor; domitor, m., victrix, f.

conquest, s. victoria, f.; (what is gained) partum, n. [tas, f.

consanguinity, s. cognatio, consanguini-

conscience, s. conscientia, f.; with a good —, pie.

conscientious, a. religiosus; sanctus; —ly, ad. bona fide, pie, religiose.

conscientiousness, s. æqui reverentia, religio, fides, f.

conscious, a. conscius; —ly, ad. use a. sciens, prudens.

consciousness, s. conscientia, f.; (feeling) sensus, m.; lose —, concido, 3; exanimor, 1.

conscript, s. tiro, m.

conscription, s. (of soldiers) delectus, m.

consecrate, v.a. sacro, consecro; dedico, 1; —d ground, terra sacra, f.

consecration, s. consecratio; dedicatio, f.

consecutive, a. continuus; —ly, ad. per ordinem; continenter; deinceps.

consent, v.n. assentior, consentio, 4.

consent, s. consensus, m., consensio, f.; without my —, me invito.

consequence, s. consequentia, consecutio; (logical) conclusio, f.; (issue) exitus, m.; (advantage) utilitas, f.; (importance) momentum, n.

consequent, a. consequens, consectarius; —ly, ad. ergo, igitur, proinde.

consequential, a. arrogans; —ly, ad. superbe, arroganter.

conservation, s. conservatio, f.

conservative, a. (moderate) mediocris; a — in politics, optimatium fautor.

conservator, s. (con)servator, m.; (guardian) procurator, m.

conserve, v.a. conservo, servo, 1.

consider, v.a. considero, contemplor, 1; intueor, contueor, 2; (turn over in the mind) volvo, 3; verso, voluto, reputo, 1; (to regard) æstimo; (to reckon) numero, 1. [plus.

considerable, a. aliquantus; (of size) am-

considerably, ad. aliquantum; multum, maxime.

considerate, a. consideratus, prudens; (kind) humanus; —ly, ad. considerate; (kindly) humaniter.

considerateness, s. humanitas, f.

consideration, s. consideratio; contemplatio; prudentia, f.; (regard) respectus, m.; (kindness) humanitas, f.; to take into —, rationem habere (gen.); without —, inconsulte.

considering, pr. — that, pro, utpote, (since) quoniam, quando.

consign, v.a. confido, 3; assigno, 1; trado, 3.

consist, v.n. consto, 1; consisto, 3; (be) sum; (to be consistent with) congruo, 3.

consistency, s. convenientia; constantia, f.; (hardness) firmitas, f.; (thickness) densitas, f.

consistent, a. constans; congruens; consentaneus; —ly, ad. constanter; congruenter.

consistory, s. consistorium, n.

consolable, a. consolabilis.

consolation, s. consolatio, f.; solamen, solacium, n.

consolatory, a. consolatorius.

console, v.a. solor, consolor, 1.

console, s. ancon, m.

consoler, s. consolator, m.

consolidate, v.a. consolido, firmo, 1; stabilio, 4; to become —d, solidesco, 3.

consonance, s. consonantia; fig. concordia, convenientia, f.

consonant, a. consonus; congruus, consentaneus.

consonant, s. consonans (littera), f.

consort, s. conjux, c.; maritus, m., uxor, f.

consort, v.n. — with, vivo cum (abl.); familiariter utor (abl.).

conspicuous, a. conspicuus; insignis; manifestus; —ly, ad. manifesto.

conspiracy, s. conjuratio, conspiratio, f.

conspirator, s. conjuratus, conspiratus, m.

conspire, v.n. conjuro, conspiro, 1.

constable, s. vigiles, m. pl.; lictor, apparitor, m.

constabulary, s. vigiles, m. pl.

constancy, s. constantia, firmitas; perseverantia, f.

constant, a. constans, firmus; perpetuus; assiduus; fidelis; fidus; —ly, ad. constanter, fideliter; perpetuo, assidue.

constellation, s. sidus, astrum; (of the Zodiac) signum, n.

consternation, s. consternatio, trepidatio, f., pavor, m.

constipate, v.a. comprimo, astringo, 3.

constipation, s. alvus astricta or compressa, f.

constituents, s. elementa, n. pl.

constitute, v.a. constituo, facio, 3, creo, 1; (be) sum.

constitution, s. (of the body, etc.) habitus, m., constitutio, f.; (body) corpus; (political) civitas, f.; fig. condicio, natura, f.

constitutional, a. legitimus, e republica; natura insitus; —ly, ad. natura.

constitutional, s. ambulatio, f.

constrain, v.a. cogo, compello, 3.

constrained, a. coactus, invitus.
constrainedly, ad. vi, invite.
constraint, s. vis, coercitio, necessitas,
construct, v.a. construo, struo, exstruo,
3; ædifico, 1.
construction, s. constructio, ædificatio;
figura, forma, f.; (meaning, sense)
sensus; **put a bad — on,** in malam
partem accipio.
constructor, s. structor, fabricator, m.
construe, v.a. interpretor, 1; (gr.) construo, 3.
consul, s. consul, m.
consular, a. consularis.
consulate, consulship, s. consulatus, m.
consult, v.a. & n. consulo, 3; consulto; delibero, 1; **— a person's interests,** consulo (dat.).
consultation, consulting, s. consultatio;
consilium; deliberatio, f.
consulter, s. consultor, m.
consumable, a. (of eatables) edulis; (de-
structible) delebilis.
consume, v.a. (to destroy, to use up)
consumo, absumo, conficio; (squander) effundo, 3; dissipo, 1; —, v.n. (to
waste away) tabesco, 3.
consumer, s. consumptor, m.　　　　[1.
consummate, v.a. (to finish) consummo,
consummation, s. (accomplishment) con-
summatio, f.; (end) finis, c.
consumption, s. consumptio; (disease)
tabes; phthisis, f.　　　　[phthisicus.
consumptive, a. tabidus; (of the lungs)
contact, s. contactus, m.; (infection)
contagium, n.
contagion, s. contagium, n.
contagious, a. pestilens, pestifer, contagiosus.　　　　　　　[tagia, n. pl.
contagiousness, s. vis tabifica, f.; con-
contain, v.a. contineo, habeo, 2; comprehendo, 3; **— oneself,** se tenere.
contaminate, v.a. inquino, 1; polluo,
inficio, 3; fœdo, violo, 1.
contamination, s. contagium, n.
contemn, v.a. temno, contemno, sperno,
despicio, 3; fastidio, 4.
contemner, s. contemptor, spretor, m.
contemplate, v.a. & n. contemplor, 1; intueor, contueor, 2.
contemplation, s. contemplatio, meditatio, f.
contemplative, a. contemplativus.
contemplator, s. contemplator, m.
contemporaneous, contemporary, a. æqualis (tempori), contemporaneus.
contemporary, s. æqualis, æquævus, m.
contempt, s. contemptio, f., contemptus,
m.; fastidium, n.
contemptible, a. contemnendus; abjectus; sordidus.

contemptibly, ad. humiliter, abjecte;
sordide.
contemptuous, a. fastidiosus, superbus;
—ly, ad. fastidiose, contemptim.
contend, v.n. contendo, 3; pugno, certo,
1; (to struggle) luctor, 1; (to dispute)
verbis certo, 1; (to maintain) confirmo, affirmo, 1; **to — against,** repugno, adversor, 1.
contending, a. adversus; rivalis.
content, a. contentus.
content, v.a. satisfacio, 3; placeo, 2.
content, s. æquus animus, m.
contented, a., v. **content,** a.
contentedly, ad. æquo animo, placide.
contentedness, s. æquanimitas, f., æquus
animus, m.　　　　　　　　　　[n.
contention, s. contentio, lis, f.; certamen,
contentious, a. litigiosus; pugnax.
contentiousness, s. pugnacitas, f.
contentment, s., v. **content,** s.
contents, s. quod inest; (of a book) argumentum, n.
contest, v.a. & n. (oppose) repugno, 1.
contest, s. certatio, contentio; controversia; lis, f.; certamen, n.
contestable, a. dubitabilis.
context, s. contextus, m.
contexture, s. contextus, m.
contiguity, s. propinquitas, f.
contiguous, a. contiguus, conterminus,
adjunctus.
continence, s. continentia; pudicitia, f.
continent, a. abstinens, continens; castus, pudicus; **—ly,** ad. temperanter.
continent, s. continens, f.
continental, a. continentem incolens; in
continenti positus, ad continentem
pertinens.
contingency, s. casus, eventus, m.
contingent, a. (accidental) fortuitus; **be
— on,** pendere ex (abl.); **—ly,** ad. fortuito.
contingent, s. numerus, m.
continual, a. continuus; perpetuus; assiduus; perennis; **—ly,** ad. continenter;
perpetuo; semper; assidue.
continuance, s. continuatio; perpetuitas;
assiduitas; (abode) mansio, f.
continuation, s. continuatio; series, f.
continue, v.a. persevero in (abl.), 1; (prolong) produco, 3; (propagate) propago,
1; —, v.n. (re)maneo, 2; duro, 1; persisto, 3; (go on) pergo, 3.
continuity, s. continuitas; perpetuitas, f.
continuous, a. continens; continuus; perpetuus; **—ly,** ad. continenter, perpetuo.
contort, v.a. distorqueo, 2.
contortion, s. distortio, f.
contour, s. lineamenta, n. pl.
contraband, a. illicitus, vetitus.

contract, v.a. contraho, astringo, 3; (a disease, etc.) contraho, — **for,** loco, 1; (to undertake) redimo, 3; —, v.n. (to bargain) paciscor, 3; stipulor, 1; (to shrink) contrahor, 3.

contract, s. (bargain) locatio, f.; pactum, n. [dium, n.

contraction, s. contractio, f.; compen-

contractor, s. (of works) susceptor; redemptor, conductor, m.

contradict, v.a. contradico, obloquor, 3; adversor, 1.

contradiction, s. contradictio; (of things) repugnantia, f.

contradictorily, ad. contrarie.

contradictory, a. contrarius, repugnans.

contrariety, s. natura contraria or diversa; (inconsistency) repugnantia, f.

contrarily, ad. contrarie.

contrary, a. (opposite) contrarius; diversus; adversus; repugnans.

contrary, ad. & pr. — **to,** contra; præter.

contrary, s. contrarium, n., contraria pars, f.; **on the** —, contra, e contrario; immo.

contrast, s. diversitas; varietas; dissimilitudo, f. [—, v.n. discrepo, 1.

contrast, v.a. comparo, 1; confero, 3;

contravene, v.a. violo, 1; frango, 3.

contravention, s. violatio, f.

contribute, v.a. confero, 3; (give) do, 1; *fig.* prosum.

contribution, s. collatio; (of money) collecta, f.; (gift) donum, n.

contrition, s. pænitentia, f.

contrivance, s. inventio, machinatio, f.; (thing contrived) inventum, n.; machina, f.

contrive, v.a. (to invent) fingo, 3; excogito, 1; invenio, 4; machinor, 1; —, v.n. (to succeed) evenio, pervenio, 4; — **to,** efficio ut.

contriver, s. inventor; artifex; machinator, m.

control, s. (power) potestas, dicio, f.; (command) imperium, regimen, n.; (management) administratio, f.; **self-**—, moderatio, f.; (check) coercitio, f.

control, v.a. (to check) reprimo, 3; (to restrain) coerceo, 2; (be at the head of) præsum; (manage) administro, moderor, 1; (rule) rego, 3.

controller, s. dominus, moderator, m.

controversial, a. controversus.

controversy, s. controversia, f.; concertatio; (debate) disceptatio; (disagreement) dissensio.

controvert, v.a. refello, redarguo, 3; refuto, 1.

contumacious, a. contumax; pertinax; —**ly,** ad. contumaciter.

contumaciousness, contumacy, s. contumacia, f.; contumax animus, m.

contumelious, a. contumeliosus, probrosus; —**ly,** ad. contumeliose.

contumely, s. contumelia, probrum, opprobrium, n.

contuse, v.a. contundo, 3; sugillo, 1.

contusion, s. contusio, f., contusum, n.

convalescent, a. convalescens.

convene, v.a. convoco, 1.

convenience, s. commoditas, f.; commodum, n.; utilitas, f.

convenient, a. commodus, idoneus, opportunus; —**ly,** ad. commode; opportune.

convent, s. cœnobium, monasterium, n.

conventicle, s. conventiculum, n.

convention, s. conventus, m.; (agreement) pactum, conventum, n.; (custom) mos, m.

conventional, a. usitatus, translaticius.

converge, v.n. vergo, 3.

conversable, a. affabilis.

conversableness, s. comitas, affabilitas, f.

conversant, a. peritus, exercitatus.

conversation, s. colloquium, n., sermo, m.; (intercourse) commercium, n.

conversazione, s. circulus, m.

converse, v.n. colloquor, 3.

converse, s. (intercourse) congressus, m.; colloquium, n.; sermo, m.

converse, a. contrarius.

conversely, ad. retrorsum.

conversion, s. conversio, f.

convert, v.a. converto, 3; commuto, 1; reduco, transfero, 3.

convert, s. neophytus, m.

convertible, a. commutabilis.

convex, a. convexus.

convexity, s. convexitas.

convey, v.a. veho, asporto, deporto, 1; adveho, 3; porto, vecto; (to transfer) abalieno; *fig.* significo, 1.

conveyance, s. (act) advectio, vectura, f.; (vehicle) vehiculum, n.; (law) abalienatio, f.

conveyancer, s. (notary) tabellio, m.

convict, v.a. convinco, 3; (to detect) comperio, 4; (by sentence) condemno, 1.

convict, s. convictus, ad pœnam damnatus, i, m.

conviction, s. damnatio; persuasio, f.

convince, v.a. suadeo, persuadeo, 2; deduco, 3.

convincing, a. gravis; —**ly,** ad. graviter.

convivial, a. hilaris, lætus.

conviviality, s. hilaritas, f. [vocatio, f.

convocation, s. (act & assemblage) con

convoke, v.a. convoco, 1.

convolvulus, s. convolvulus, m.

convoy, v.a. comitor, 1; deduco, 3.

convoy, s. (escort) præsidium, n.; (train) commeatus, m.

convulse, v.a. concutio, convello, 3.

convulsed, a. convulsus.

convulsion, s. convulsio, f., spasmus, m.

convulsive, a. spasticus.

cony, s., v. **coney.**

coo, v.n. gemo, 3.

cooing, s. genitus, m.; *fig.* **billing and —,** exosculatio, f.

cook, s. coquus, m., coqua, f.

cook, v.a. & n. coquo, 3.

cookery, s. ars coquinaria, f.

cooking, s. coctura, f.; —, a. coquinarius.

cook-shop, s. popina, f.

cool, a. frigidus; frigidulus; (shady) opacus; *fig.* sedatus; immotus; impavidus; (indifferent) lentus; (impudent) impudens.

cool, s., v. **coolness.**

cool, v.a. & n. refrigero; refrigeror, 1; *fig.* frigesco, defervesco, languesco, 3.

cooling, a. refrigeratorius.

coolly, ad. frigide; *fig.* sedate; æquo animo; lente; impudenter.

coolness, s. frigus, n.; (a pleasant —) refrigeratio, f.; (shadiness) opacum, n.; *fig.* lentitudo; cautela, f.; æquus animus, m. [ing in) saginarium, n.

coop, s. (for hens) cavea, f.; (for fatten-

coop, v.a. **to — up,** includo, 3.

cooper, s. vietor, m.

co-operate, v.n. una ago, 3; adjuvo, cooperor, 1. [co-operatio, f.

co-operation, s. auxilium, adjumentum, n.,

coot, s. fulica, f.

co-partner, s. socius, m.

co-partnership, s. societas, f.

cope, v.n. **to — with,** certo, 1; contendo, 3; (manage) gero, 3; tracto, administro, 1.

coping, s. (of a wall) corona; lorica, f.

copious, a. copiosus, abundans, uber; **—ly,** ad. abundanter, copiose.

copiousness, s. copia; ubertas, f.

copper, s. æs; cyprium; (copper vessel) aënum, n.

copper, a. aëneus, aënus, cypreus.

copper-smith, s. faber ærarius, m.

coppery, a. ærarius.

coppice, copse, s. dumetum, fruticetum, n.

copy, s. exemplar, exemplum, n.; imitatio; imago, f.

copy, v.a. & n. transcribo, 3; imitor, 1; (to follow) sequor, 3.

copyhold, s. emphyteusis, f.

copyholder, s. emphyteuta, m.

copying-clerk, s. scriba, m.

copyist, s. librarius, m.

coquetry, s. protervitas, petulantia, f.

coquettish, a. petulans, protervus, procax.

coral, s. coralium, n.; —, a. corallinus.

coralline, a. corallinus.

cord, s. funis, m.; (— of wood) strues, f.

cord, v.a. constringo, 3; circumligo, 1.

cordage, s. rudentes, m. pl.

corded, a. funibus *or* funiculis circumligatus; (of stuffs) striatus.

cordial, a. benignus; sincerus; **—ly,** ad. ex animo; benigne; sincere.

cordiality, s. animus benignus, m.; comitas, f.

cordon, s. corona, f.

core, s. (of fruit) vulva, f.

coreopsis, s. coreopsis (mod. hort.).

coriander, s. coriandrum, n.

cork, s. (tree) suber, n.; (bark) cortex, c.

cork, a. subereus.

cork, v.a. obturo, 1.

corn, s. frumentum, n.; (cereals) fruges, f. pl.; annona, f.; (of salt, etc.) granum, n.; mica, f.; (on the toes) callus, m.

corn-chandler, s. frumentarius, m.

corn-chest, s. cumera, f.

cornel-berry, cornum, n.

cornel(-tree), s. cornus, f.

cornelian, s. sardachates, m.

corner, s. angulus, m.; (lurking-place) latebra, f., recessus, m.; (of a street) compitum, n.

corner-stone, s. lapis angularis, m.

cornet, s. (wind-instrument) bucina, f.; (officer) vexillarius, m.

cornfield, s. seges, f., arvum, n.; **—s,** pl. sata, n. pl.

corn-flower, s. centaureum, n.

cornice, s. sima, f.; (over doors) hyperthyrum, n.

corn-law, s. lex frumentaria, f.

corn-merchant, s. frumentarius, m.

corn-mill, s. mola frumentaria, f.

cornucopia, s. cornu copiæ, n.

corollary, s. corollarium, n.

coroner, s. quæstor, m.

coronet, s. diadema, n.

corporal, s. decurio, m.

corporal, corporeal, a. corporeus, corporalis.

corporation, s. societas, f., sodalicium, n.

corps, s. legio, f.

corpse, s. cadaver, n.

corpulence, s. obesitas, f.

corpulent, a. corpulentus, pinguis, obesus.

corpuscle, s. corpusculum, n.

correct, a. amendatus; rectus; accuratus; elegans; **—ly,** ad. emendate; recte; accurate; eleganter.

correct, v.a. corrigo, 3; emendo, 1; *fig.* animadverto, 3; castigo, 1.

correction, s. correctio, emendatio; *fig.* animadversio; castigatio, f.

corrective, s. temperatio, f.

correctness, s. elegantia, accuratio, f.

corrector, m. corrector; emendator, castigator, censor, m.

correlative, a. mutuus, reciprocus.

correspond, v.n. congruo, 3; respondeo, 2.

correspondence, s. congruentia; (letters) epistulæ, f. pl. [eus.

correspondent, a. congruens, consentan-

correspondent, s. scriptor, m.

corridor, s. andron, m.

corrigible, a. corrigendus, emendandus, emendabilis.

corroborate, v.a. confirmo, 1.

corrode, v.a. erodo; peredo, 3.

corroding, a. *fig.* mordax.

corrosion, s. rosio, f.

corrosive, a. mordax.

corrupt, v.a. corrumpo, 3; depravo, 1; —, v.n. putresco, 3.

corrupt, a. corruptus, putridus; *fig.* pravus; impurus; venalis; **—ly,** ad. corrupte; inceste; turpiter.

corrupter, s. corruptor, m., corruptrix, f.

corruptibility, s. corruptibilitas; (by bribes) venalitas, f.

corruptible, a. corruptibilis; venalis.

corruption, s. corruptio; putredo, f.; *fig.* depravatio, pravitas; (by money) corruptela, f.

corruptress, s. corruptrix, f.

corsair, s. pirata, prædo, m.

corslet, s. lorica, f.; thorax, m.

cortege, s. pompa, f.

coruscation, s. fulgor, m.

corvette, s. celox, f. [phæus, m.

corypheus, s. magister (chori); cory-

cosily, ad. commode.

cosmetic, s. medicamen, n.

cosmographer, s. cosmographus, m.

cosmopolitan, a. cosmicus.

cost, s. (price) pretium, n.; (expense) impensa, f.

cost, v.a. & n. consto, sto, 1.

costive, a. astrictus.

costiveness, s. alvus astricta, f.

costliness, s. caritas, f.

costly, a. pretiosus, carus, sumptuosus.

costume, s. vestitus, m.

cosy, a. commodus.

cot, s. tugurium, n., casa, f.; (bed) lectulus, m.; (for doves) columbarium; (for sheep) ovile, n.

cottage, s. casa, f., tugurium, n.

cottager, s. casarius; rusticus, m.

cotton, s. (tree) gossypium, xylon, n.; (wool) lana, f.

couch, s. cubile; pulvinar, n.; lectus, torus, m.; (haunts) lustra, n. pl.

couch, v.n. cubo, 1; (to stoop down) subsido, 3; —, v.a. in insidiis colloco, 1; **a —ed spear,** infesta hasta.

cough, s. tussis, f.; **to have a bad —,** male tussire, 4.

cough, v.n. tussio, 4.

coulter, s. culter, dens, m.

council, s. concilium, consilium, n., senatus, m.

councillor, s. consiliarius, m.

counsel, s. (advice) consilium, n.; (person) advocatus, m.

counsel, v.a. consulo, 3; moneo, 2.

counsellor, s. consiliarius, consiliator; advocatus, m.

count, s. comes, m.

count, v.a. & n. numero, 1; censeo; (consider, deem) habeo, 2; **existimo,** 1; duco, 3; **to — upon,** confido, 3.

count, s. computatio, f.

countenance, s. (face, look) facies, f., vultus, aspectus; (encouragement) favor, m.; **to put out of —,** confundo, 3; perturbo, 1. [indulgeo, 2.

countenance, v.a. faveo, 2; adjuvo, 1;

counter, s. (for a shop) mensa, f.; (at play) calculus, m.

counter, ad. contra; **run — to,** adversor, repugno, 1.

counteract, v.a. renitor, obsisto, 3.

counterbalance, v.a. exæquo, penso, compenso, 1. [ulo, 1.

counterfeit, v.a. imitor; adultero; simulo, 1.

counterfeit, a. ficticius; simulatus; fictus; adulterinus.

counterfeit, s. simulatio; imitatio, f.

counterfeiter, s. imitator; falsarius, m.

countermand, v.a. renuntio, 1.

countermarch, v.n. signa converto, 3.

countermine, s. cuniculus transversus, m.

counterpane, s. lodix, f.; stragulum, n.

counterplot, v.a. fraudem fraudi opponere, 3.

counterpoise, v.a. compenso, exæquo, 1.

counterpoise, s. æquipondium, n.

counterscarp, s. crepido, f.

countersign, s. tessera, f.

countervail, v.a. æquo, compenso, 1.

countess, s. comitissa, f.

counting, s. dinumeratio, f.

counting-house, s. tabularia, f.

countless, a. innumerabilis, **innumerus,** infinitus.

countrified, a. agrestis, rusticior.

country, s. rus, n.; regio; terra, f.; loca, n. pl.; **native —,** solum natale, n.

country-house, s. villa, f.

countryman, s. rusticus; civis, popularis; indigena, m.

county, s. comitatus, m.

county-town, s. municipium, n.

couple, s. par, n.

couple, v.a. copulo, 1; connecto, conjungo, 3; —, v.n. (of animals) coeo, 4.

couplet, s. distichon, n.

courage, s. animus, m., virtus; audacia; fortitudo, f.

courageous, a. animosus, ferox; audax; fortis; —ly, ad. ferociter; audacter; fortiter.

courier, s. cursor; nuntius; (letter-carrier) tabellarius; (on horseback) veredarius, m.

course, s. (running) cursus; (of water) ductus, m.; (turn) vicissitudo; (way) iter, n., via; (means) ratio; (order) series, f., ordo, m.; (custom) mos, m.

course, v.a. venor; sector, 1; —, v.n. curro, 3; propero, 1.

courser, s. sonipes, m.

coursing, s. venatio, f.

court, s. (of a house) area, f., atrium, n.; (palace) regia domus, aula, f.; (retinue) comitatus, m.; (in law) forum, tribunal, n.; judices, m. pl.; (civility) observantia, f.

court, v.a. colo, 3; ambio, blandior, 4; observo, 1; (of a suitor) peto, 3.

courteous, a. comis, humanus, benignus; affabilis; —ly, ad. comiter, humaniter, benigne, affabiliter.

courteousness, s. comitas, affabilitas, humanitas, f.

courtesan, s. meretrix, f.

courtesy, s. urbanitas; (bow) salutatio, f.

courtier, s. aulicus, purpuratus.

courtlike, courtly, a. aulicus.

court-martial, s. judicium castrense, n.

court-plaster, s. emplastrum, n.

courtship, s. amor, m.   [patruelis, c.

cousin, s. consobrinus, m.; consobrina, f.;

cove, s. (small bay) sinus, m.

covenant, s. pactum, n.; conventio, f.

covenant, v.n. paciscor, 3; stipulor, 1.

cover, v.a. tego, 3; operio, 4; celo, 1; instruo, 3; fig. protego, 3.

cover, s. tegmen; (lid) operculum; (wrapper) involucrum; (shelter) praesidium, n.; (for game) operimentum; lustra, n. pl.; fig. praetextus, m.

covering, s. (act) obductio, f.; (cover) tegmen, velamen; (wrapper) involucrum; (lid) operculum; (of a bed) stragulum; (of a house) tectum, n.; (clothing) vestitus, m.

coverlet, s. stragulum, n.

covert, s. perfugium, latibulum, lustrum; (thicket) dumentum, n.

covert, a. tectus; occultus; (indirect) obliquus; —ly, ad. tecte, occulte; oblique.   [peto, 3.

covet, v.a. & n. concupisco, cupio, ap-

coveting, s. cupido, concupiscentia, f.

covetous, a. avidus, avarus, appetens, cupidus; —ly, ad. avide, avare; appetenter.   [itas, f.

covetousness, s. avaritia, aviditas, cupid-

covey, s. grex, m.

cow, s. vacca, bos, f.

cow, v.a. domo, 1; stupefacio, 3.

coward, s. ignavus, timidus, m.

cowardice, s. ignavia; timiditas, f.

cowardly, a. ignavus, timidus; —, ad. ignave, timide.

cower, v.n. subsido, 3.

cow-herd, s. bubulcus, armentarius, m.

cow-hide, s. corium vaccinum, n.

cow-house, s. bubile, n.

cowl, s. cucullus, m.

coxcomb, s. nitidus atque elegans.

coy, a. modestus; timidus; verecundus; —ly, ad. verecunde, timide.

coyness, s. modestia; timiditas, f.

cozen, v.a. fallo, 3; ludificor, 1.

cozenage, s. fraus, f., dolus, m.

cozener, s. ludificator, fraudator, m.

cozily, v. **cosily.**

cozy, v. **cosy.**   [silvestre.

crab, s. cancer, m.; (wild apple) malum

crabbed, a. morosus; (sour) acerbus; —ly, ad. morose.

crabbedness, s. morositas; importunitas, f.

crack, v.a. findo; frango, 3; (a whip) flagello insono, 1; —, v.n. dehisco, displodor, 3; dissilio, 4.

crack, s. fissura, rima, f.; (noise) crepitus, m.

crack-brained, a. cerritus, delirus, vecors.

cracked, a. cerritus, delirus, (of walls, etc.) rimosus.

crackle, v.n. crepito, 1.

crackling, s. crepitus, m.

cradle, s. cunae, f. pl.; fig. cunabula, incunabula, n. pl.

craft, s. (cunning) astutia, f.; astus, m.; (trick) dolus, m.; (calling, trade) ars, f.; (ship) navicula, linter, f.

craftily, ad. astute, callide.

craftiness, s. astutia, calliditas; (skill) sollertia, f.

crafty, a. astutus, callidus; (deceitful) subdolus, fallax, dolosus.

craftsman, s. artifex, m.

crag, s. scopulus, m.   [asper.

cragged, craggy, a. scopulosus; (rough)

cram, v.a. farcio, 4; (poultry) sagino, 1; **to — together,** constipo, 1.

cramp, s. (disease) spasmus, m.; (tool) uncus, m.

cramp, v.a. fig. comprimo, 3; coarto, 1.

crane, s. (bird) grus, c.; (machine) tolleno, f.

crannied, a. rimosus.

cranny, s. rima, fissura, f.
crape, s. (mourning) vestis pulla.
crash, s. fragor, strepitus, m.   [do, 1.
crash, v.n. strepo, 3; sono, fragorem
crass, a. crassus.
crater, s. (of a volcano) crater, m.
craunch, v.n. dentibus frango, morsu divello, 3.
cravat, s. focale, n.
crave, v.a. rogo, imploro, efflagito, 1;
  posco, expeto, 3.
craven, s. & a. ignavus, timidus.
craving, s. desiderium, n.; appetitus, m.;
  sitis, fames, f.
crawfish, s. cancer, m.
crawl, v.n. repo, serpo, 3; repto, 1.
crawler, s. serpens, f.
crawling, a. reptabundus.
crayfish, v. crawfish.
craze, v.a. obstupefacio, 3; alieno (mentem), 1.
craziness, s. imbecillitas, vesania, insania, f., furor, m.
crazy, a. imbecillus, insanus, vesanus.
creak, v.n. strideo, 2; crepito, 1.
creaking, s. stridor, crepitus, m.
creaking, a. stridulus.
cream, s. flos lactis, m.; fig. flos, m.;
  robur, n.
cream, v.n. spumo, corusco, 1.
crease, s. ruga, f.
crease, v.a. corrugo, rugo, replico, 1.
create, v.a. creo, 1; pario, gigno, 3;
  fig. formo, 1; fingo, 3; invenio, 4;
  (elect) creo, 1.
creation, s. (act) creatio, f.; (origin) origo,
  f.; (whole world) mundus, m.; fig.
  (work of art) opus, n., ars, f.
creative, a. creatrix; effectrix.
creator, s. creator, procreator; fig. fabricator; auctor, m.
creature, s. res creata, f.; animal, n.;
  (person) caput, n.; (dependant, tool)
  minister, m.   [credo, 3.
credence, s. (belief) fides, f.; to give —,
credentials, s. auctoritates, litterae, f. pl.
credibility, s. fides, probabilitas, f.
credible, a. credibilis; (of persons) locuples.
credibly, ad. credibiliter.
credit, s. (authority) auctoritas; (belief,
  faith) fides; (reputation) fama, existimatio; (praise) laus, f.; (com.) fides, f.
credit, v.a. credo; (com.) acceptum refero
  (alicui), 3.
creditable, a. honorificus, honestus.
creditably, ad. honeste.
creditor, s. creditor, m.
credulity, s. credulitas, f.
credulous, a. credulus.
creed, s. fides, doctrina, opinio, f.

creek, s. aestuarium, n.
creep, v.n. repo, serpo, 3; repto, 1;
  — over, fig. surrepo, 3; me insinuo, 1.
creeper, s. serpens, f.; (plant) herba, f.
creeping, s. reptatio, f., reptatus, m.
creeping jenny, s. lysimachia (mod. hort.).
crepuscular, a. sublustris.
crescent, s. luna crescens, f.
crescent-shaped, a. lunatus.
cress, s. lepidium, n. (mod. hort.);
  water- —, nasturtium, n.; rock- —,
  arabis (mod. hort.).
crest, s. (of animals) crista; (of a horse)
  juba; (of a helmet) crista, f.; (device)
  insigne, n.
crested, a. cristatus.
crest-fallen, a. fig. demissus, dejectus.
crevice, s. rima, rimula, f.
crew, s. grex, m., turba, multitudo, f.; (of
  a ship) remiges, nautae, m. pl.
crib, s. (manger) praesaepe; (ox-stall)
  bubile, n.; (little bed) lectulus, m.
crick, s. spasmus, tetanus, m.
cricket, s. gryllus, m., cicada, f.
crier, s. praeco, m.
crime, s. crimen, delictum, maleficium;
  facinus; (shameful deed) flagitium, n.
Crimea, s. Tauri, n. pl.
criminal, s. nocens.
criminal, a. scelestus, sceleratus, nefarius;
  (of a charge) capitalis.
criminality, s. improbitas, f.
criminally, ad. nefarie, sceleste, scelerate.
criminate, v.a. criminor, 1.
crimination, s. criminatio, f.
crimp, v.a. crispo, 1.   [coccinus.
crimson, s. coccum, n.; —, a. coccineus,
cringe, v.a. adulor, 1.
cringing, s. adulatio, f.
cringing, a. demissus, supplex.
cripple, s. claudus, m.
cripple, v.a. aliquem claudum facio, 3;
  fig. debilito, 1; accido, 3.
crisis, s. discrimen, momentum, n.
crisp, a. crispus; (brittle) fragilis.
crisp, v.a. crispo, 1.
criterion, s. signum, insigne; indicium, n.
critic, s. existimator; judex; criticus, censor, m.
critical, a. criticus; (careful) accuratus;
  fastidiosus; (censorious) mordax;
  (doubtful) anceps, dubius, incertus,
  periculosus.   [quisite; periculose.
critically, ad. fastidiose; accurate; ex-
criticism, s. ars critica, f.; judicium, n.;
  censura, reprehensio, f.
criticize, v.a. judico, examino, 1; carpo,
  reprehendo, 3.
croak, v.n. (as frogs) coaxo, 1; (as ravens)
  crocio, 4; fig. queritor, 1.

croak, croaking, s. crocitus, m.; *fig.* querimonia, f.

crockery, s. (vasa) fictilia, n. pl.

crocodile, s. crocodilus, m.

crocus, s. crocus, m., crocum, **n.**

croft, s. sæptum, n.

crone, s. anicula, vetula, f.

crony, s. amicus familiaris, m.

crook, s. curvamen; (of shepherds) pedum, n.; **by hook or by —,** quocunque modo.

crook, v.a. curvo, incurvo, 1; flecto, 3; *fig.* depravo, 1.

crook-backed, a. gibber.

crooked, a. curvatus, curvus, incurvus, flexus; *fig.* pravus; dolosus; **—ly,** ad. torte; prave.

crookedness, s. curvatura, f., curvamen, n.; *fig.* pravitas, f.

crook-legged, a. valgus.

crop, s. (of a bird) ingluvies; (of corn) messis, f.; (yield) reditus, m.

crop, v.a. abscido, decurto, 1; tondeo, 2; (to harvest) meto; (to browse) carpo, depasco, 3; tondeo, 2.

crosier, s. lituus, m.

cross, s. crux; *fig.* molestia, f.; cruciatus, m.; infortunium, n.

cross, a. transversus; (contrary) adversus; *fig.* (peevish) morosus; (boorish, rude) rusticus; **—ly,** ad. morose; rustice.

cross, v.a. (to cancel) deleo; (breeds) misceo, 2; (to pass over) transeo, 4; transmitto, transgredior, trajicio, 3; (to surmount) supero; *fig.* (to thwart) adversor, frustror, 1; **— one's mind,** subeo, 4; succurro, 3; **—,** v.n. **to — over,** transcendo, trajicio, transgredior, 3.

cross-bar, s. repagulum, n.

cross-beam, s. transtrum, n.

cross-bow, s. arcuballista, f.

cross-bowman, s. arcuballistarius, m.

cross-examination, s. interrogatio, percontatio, f.

cross-examine, v.a. percontor, 1.

cross-grained, a. *fig.* difficilis, morosus.

crossing, s. transitus; trajectus, m.; (of roads) bivium; (of three *or* four roads) trivium, quadrivium, n.

crossness, s. morositas, f.

cross-piece, s., v. **cross-beam.**

cross-question, v.a. percontor, 1.

cross-road, s. trames, m.

cross-wise, a. decussatim; in quincuncem.

crotchet, s. libido, f.

crotchety, a. morosus.

crouch, v.n. me demitto, subsido, 3; (lie hid) delitesco, 3.

croup, s. (disease) cynanche, t.

crow, s. (bird) cornix, f.; (lever) vectis; (voice of the cock) cantus, m.; gallicinium, n.

crow, v.n. (of cocks) cano, 3; canto; *fig.* (to boast) jacto, 1.

crowd, s. turba; frequentia, caterva, multitudo, f.; concursus, m.; (heap) cumulus, acervus, m.

crowd, v.a. arto, stipo, 1; premo, 3; **—,** v.n. (around) circumfundor, 3; (together) convolo, congregor, 1; concurro, confluo, 3.   [quens; celeber.

crowded, a. condensus, confertus; frecrow-foot, s. ranunculus, m.

crowing, s. (of the cock) gallicinium, n., cantus, m.

crown, s. corona, f., diadema, n.; (top) vertex, m.; (completion) cumulus, m.; *fig.* (royal power) regnum, n.

crown, v.a. corono, 1; (with a garland, etc.) cingo, 3; (make perfect) cumulo, 1; **be —ed with success,** felicem exitum habere.

crucible, s. catinus, m.

crucifixion, s. summum supplicium, n.

crucify, v.a. cruci suffigo, 3.

crude, a. crudus; *fig.* rudis; incultus; **—ly,** ad. imperfecte, inculte.

crudity, s. (undigested food) crudita; *fig.* imperitia, rusticitas, f.

cruel, a. crudelis, atrox, sævus; immanis; barbarus, durus, ferus; **—ly,** ad. crudeliter, sæve; dure; atrociter.

cruelty, s. crudelitas; atrocitas, sævitia, f.

cruet, s. guttus, m.; acetabulum, **n.**

cruise, v.n. pervagor, circumvector, 1.

cruise, cruising, s. navigatio.

cruiser, s. speculatoria, navis.

crumb, s. (of bread) mica, f.; frustum, n.

crumble, v.a. frio, 1; comminuo, contero, 3; **—,** v.n. frior, 1; collabor, corruo, 3.

crumbling, a. puter; friabilis.

crumple, v.a. rugo, corrugo, 1.

crunch, v craunch.

crupper, s. postilena, f.

crush, v.a. contundo, contero; (press) premo, comprimo, 3; elido; *fig.* opprimo; affligo, 3; (bring low) debilito, 1.

crush, s. contusio, f.; (crowd) turba, f.

crust, s. crusta, f.

crust, v.a. crusto, incrusto, 1.

crustaceous, a. crustatus.

crusty, a. crustosus; *fig.* morosus.

crutch, s. baculum, n.; (support) fulcrum, n.

cry, v.a. & n. clamo, exclamo, conclamo; (to weep) lacrimo, 1; fleo, 2; **to — against,** objurgo, 1; **to — down,** detrecto, 1; **to — out,** exclamo, vociferor, 1; **to — up,** vendito; (to boast) prædico, 1.

cry, s. clamor, m., vox, exclamatio, f.; (of infants) vagitus; (weeping) ploratus, m.

crying, s. fletus, ploratus, m.; — down, s. detrectatio, f.

crypt, s. crypta, f.

crystal, s. crystallum, n. [dus.

crystal, a. crystallinus, vitreus; pelluci-crystalline, a. crystallinus.

cub, s. catulus, m.

cub, v.n. pario, 3.

cube, s. cubus, m.

cubic(al), a. cubicus.

cubit, s. cubitum, n., ulna, f.

cuckoo, s. coccyx, cuculus, m.

cuckoo-flower, s. cardamine (mod. hort.).

cuckoo-pint, s. arum (mod. hort.).

cucumber, s. cucumis, m.

cud, s. chew the —, rumino.

cudgel, s. fustis, m., baculum, n.

cudgel, v.a. fustibus verbero, 1.

cudgelling, s. fustuarium, n.

cue, s. (hint) nutus, m.; (watchword) signum, n.; tessera, f.

cuff, s. (blow) colaphus, m.; alapa, f.

cuirass, s. lorica, f.; thorax; cataphracta, m. [tus, m.

cuirassier, s. eques loricatus, cataphrac-

culinary, a. culinarius; coquinarius.

cull, v.a. carpo, lego, decerpo, 3.

culminate, v.n. ad summum fastigium pervenire, 4.

culpability, s. culpa, f.

culpable, a. culpandus; nocens.

culpably, ad. male.

culprit, s. (person accused) reus, m., rea, f.; (person convicted of a crime) nocens, noxius, m.

cultivate, v.a. colo, 3; (develop) formo, 1; fingo, excolo, 3; (train) exerceo; (show attentions to) foveo, 2; observo, 1.

cultivation, s. cultura, f., cultus, m.

cultivator, s. cultor; colonus, m.

culture, s. cultura, f., cultus, m.; (of the mind) humanitas, f.

cumber, v.a., v. encumber.

cumbersome, cumbrous, a. iniquus, gravis, incommodus, onerosus.

cumin, s. cuminum, n.

cunning, a. doctus, peritus; sollers; (in a bad sense) astutus, vafer.

cunningly, ad. docte, perite, sollerter; astute, vafre, dolose.

cunning, s. peritia; astutia, calliditas, ars, f.

cup, s. poculum, n., calix, m.; (breaker) patera, f.; (of a flower) calyx, m.

cup-bearer, s. pocillator, minister, m.

cupboard, s. armarium, n.

Cupid, s. Cupido, Amor, m.

cupidity, s. cupiditas. f.

cupola, s. tholus, m.

cupping, s. cucurbitatio, f.

cupping-glass, s. cucurbita, f.

cur, s. canis, c.

curable, a. medicabilis, sanabilis.

curative, a. medicabilis.

curator, s. curator; custos, m.

curb, s. frenum, n.; fig. coercitio, f.

curb, v.a. freno, refreno, 1; compesco, comprimo, 3; coerceo, 2.

curd, s. coagulum, n.

curdle, v.a. cogo, 3; coagulo, 1; —, v.n. coeo, 4; concresco, 3.

cure, s. (of wounds) sanatio, f.; (remedy) remedium, n., medicina, f.

cure, v.a. (to heal) sano, 1, medeor, 2; (to preserve in pickle) salio, 4.

cureless, a. insanabilis.

curer, s. (of fish) salarius, m.

curiosity, s. curiositas; audiendi or spectandi studium, n.; old —, res rara, raritas, f.

curious, a. curiosus; elaboratus; rarus; mirus; —ly, ad. curiose; mirabiliter; arte (abl. of ars).

curl, v.a. (hair) crispo, 1; torqueo, 2; —, v.n. crispor, 1.

curl, s. (natural) cirrus; (artificial) cincinnus, m.; (curve) flexus, m.

curling-iron, s. calamister, m., ferrum, n.

curly, a. crispus. [dus, m.

curmudgeon, s. homo avarus or sordi-

currant, s. ribes (mod. hort.).

currency, s. cursus, tenor, m.; (money) moneta; nummi, n. pl.

current, a. vulgaris, usitatus; (be —) valeo, 2; (present) hic; —ly, ad. vulgo.

current, s. flumen, n.; (of the sea) aestus; (of air) afflatus, m.; aura, f.; fig. cursus, m.

currier, s. coriarius, m.

currish, a. caninus.

curry, v.a. (leather) macero; (a horse) defrico, 1; rado, 3; fig. (to beat) caedo; — favour with, morem gerere (dat.) 3.

curry-comb, s. strigilis, f.

curse, s. exsecratio, f., maledictum, n.; (plague) pestis, pernicies, f.

curse, v.a. exsecror, detestor, 1; devoveo, 2.

cursed, a. exsecrabilis.

cursing, s., v. curse, s. [tim, obiter.

cursorily, ad. breviter, summatim; stric-

cursory, a. brevis, properatus.

curt, a. brevis, abruptus; —ly, ad. breviter. [3; fig. coarto, 1; minuo, 3.

curtail, v.a. decurto, mutilo, 1; praecido,

curtailing, curtailment, s. decurtatio, f.

curtain, s. velum, conopaeum; (in a theatre) aulaeum, n.; (for beds, etc.) plagula, f.

curtly, ad., v. **curt.**
curtness, s. brevitas, f.
curtsy, s., v. **courtesy.**
curvature, s. curvatura, f.
curve, s. curvamen, n., flexus; sinus, m.; (thing curved) curvatura, f.; —ed, a. curvus, incurvus, recurvus; curvatus; sinuosus; (as the sickle) falcatus.
curve, v.a. (in)curvo, sinuo, 1; flecto, 3.
curvet, s. (of a horse) saltus, m.
curvet, v.n. insulto, 1.
cushion, s. pulvinar, n., pulvinus, m., culcita, f.; (in a carriage) sedularia, n. pl.   [ment) carcer, m.
custody, s. custodia, tutela, f.; (imprison-
custom, s. (use) usus, mos, m., consuetudo, f.; (fashion) institutum, præscriptum, n.; (rite) ritus, m.; (duty) portorium, vectigal, n.
custom-house, s. telonium, n.; — -officer, s. portitor, m.   [laticius.
customary, a. usitatus, consuetus, trans-
customer, s. emptor, m.
cut, v.a. seco, 1; (to fell) cædo; (to mow) succido, meto, 3; **to — asunder,** intercido, 3; disseco, 1; **to — away,** recido, abscindo, 3; (to amputate) amputo, 1; **to — down,** cædo; (to kill) occido, 3; **to — in pieces,** concido, 3; **to — off,** præcido; abscindo, 3; (to amputate) amputo, 1; (the head) detrunco, 1; (to intercept) intercludo, 3; prohibeo, 2; *fig.* (to destroy, etc.) extinguo, perimo, adimo, 3; **to — open,** incido, 3; **to — out,** exseco, 1; (out of a rock, etc.) excido, 3; **to — short,** intercido; (to abridge) præcido, 3; *fig.* (to interrupt) intermitto, 1; **to — through,** disseco, 1; (the enemy) perrumpo, 3; **to — up,** minutatim concido, 3; (the enemy) trucido, 1; (to inveigh) invehor, 3.
cut, s. incisura, f.; (slice) segmentum; (wound) vulnus, n., plaga, f.; (ditch) fossa, f.; (a short cut) via compendiaria, f.
cuticle, s. cuticula, f.
cutlass, s. ensis, gladius, m.
cutlery, s. ferramenta, n. pl.
cutlet, s. offa, f., frustum, n.   [m.
cutpurse, s. saccularius, sector zonarius,
cutter, s. sector, m.; (ship) celox, f.
cut-throat, s. sector collorum, sicarius, m.
cutting, a. (sharp) acutus; *fig.* mordax.
cutting, s. (act) sectio; (to pieces) consectio; (out) exsectio; (excavation) fossa, f.; (piece cut off) segmen, n.; (of a plant) propago, talea, f.
cuttle-fish, s. loligo, sepia, f.
cyclamen, s. cyclamen (mod. hort.).

cycle, s. orbis, m.
cylinder, s. cylindrus, m.
cylindrical, a. cylindratus.
cymbal, s. cymbalum, n.
cynic, a. & s. cynicus, m.
cynical, a. mordax, difficilis, severus; —ly, ad. cynice, mordaciter, severe.
cynosure, s. cynosura, f.
cypress, s. cupressus, cyparissus, f.

Dab, v.a. illino, 3.
dabble, v.a. aspergo, oblino, 3; —, v.n. strictim attingo, 3.
dactyl, s. dactylus, m.
dactylic, a. dactylicus.
daffodil, s. narcissus, m.
dahlia, s. dahlia (mod. hort.).
dagger, s. pugio, m., sica, f.
daily, a. diurnus; quotidianus; —, ad. quotidie, in dies.
daintily, ad. fastidiose, delicate, molliter.
daintiness, s. fastidium, n.
dainty, a. (of persons) fastidiosus; elegans; (of things) delicatus; exquisitus, mollis.
dainty, s. cuppediæ, f. pl.
daisy, s. bellis, f.
dale, s. vallis, convallis, f.
dalliance, s. blanditiæ, f. pl.
dallier, s. nugator, cunctator, m.
dally, v.n. moror; (to trifle) nugor; (with one) ludificor, 1; blandior, 4.
dam, s. (of animals) mater, f.; (mole) moles, pila, f., agger, m.; (barrier) ♀ex, m.
dam, v.a. coerceo, 2; obstruo, 3; oppilo, 1.
damage, s. damnum, incommodum; (loss) detrimentum, n.; (injury) injuria, noxa, f.
damage, v.a. lædo, 3; (impair) obsum.
dame, s. domina, era, matrona, f.
damn, v.a. damno, condemno, 1; *fig.* (to hiss off) explodo, 3.
damnable, a. sceleratus, impius.
damnably, ad. scelerate, impie.
damnation, s. damnatio.
damp, a. umidus, udus.
damp, s. umor, m.; (vapour) exhalatio, f.
damp, v.a. umecto, 1; *fig.* infringo; restinguo, 3.
dampish, a. humidulus.
dampness, s. uligo, f.; umor, m.
damsel, s. puella, virgo, f.
damson, s. prunum Damascenum, n.
dance, s. saltatus, m., saltatio, f.; chorus, m.; chorea, f.
dance, v.n. salto, 1.
dancer, s. saltator, m.
dancing, s. saltatio, f., saltatus, m.

dancing-g·rl, s. saltatrix, f.
dandelion, taraxacum (mod. hort.).
dandle, v.a. in bracchiis gesto; moto, 1.
dandruff, s. furfur, m.; porrigo, f.
dandy, s. homo bellus.
danger, s. periculum, discrimen, n.
dangerous, a. periculosus, gravis; —ly, ad. periculose; graviter.
dangle, v.n. pendeo, dependeo, 2; fluctuo, 1.
dangler, s. assecla, assectator, m.
dangling, a. pendulus.
dank, a. umidus, uvidus, udus.
dapper, a. nitidus.
dapple, v.a. maculo, vario, 1.
dappled, a. variatus, varius.
dare, v.n. audeo, 2; —, v.a. provoco, 1.
daring, a. audens; ferox; audax; animosus; —ly, ad. audenter, audacter, animose.
dark, a. obscurus; opacus; niger; cæcus; tenebrosus; caliginosus; (as mourning-dress) pullus; fig. obscurus, ambiguus, dubius, anceps; (gloomy) atrox.
dark, s. tenebræ, f. pl.; obscurum, n.; nox, f. [fusco; fig. occæco, 1.
darken, v.a. obscuro; (of colours) in-
darkening, s. obscuratio, f.
darkish, a. subniger, suffuscus.
darkly, ad. obscure; fig. per ambages.
darkness, s. obscuritas, caligo, f.; (shadiness) opacitas, f.; tenebræ, f. pl.; color fuscus, m.
darksome, a. subnubilus, subobscurus.
darling, s. deliciæ, f. pl.; amores, m. pl.; corculum, n.; —, a. suavis, mellitus; amatus.
darn, v.a. resarcio, 4.
darnel, s. lolium, n.
dart, s. jaculum, spiculum, missile, n.; hasta, lancea, f.
dart, v.a. jaculor, 1; mitto, conjicio, 3; —, v.n. provolo, 1; se injicere, 3.
dash, v.a. (against) allido, illido; offendo, 3; (sprinkle) aspergo, respergo, 3; (frustrate) frustror, 1; (confound) confundo; (to overthrow) everto, 3; to — in pieces, discutio, 3; to — out, (v.a.) elido, 3; (v.n.) ruo, feror, 3; —, v.n. (to rush) ruo, feror; (to be dashed in pieces) frangor, 3.
dash, s. (shock) percussus; (onset) impetus, m.
dashing, a. acer, alacer; splendidus.
dastard, s. homo ignavus, m.
dastardly, a. ignavus.
data, s. facta; (points agreed upon) concessa, n. pl.
date, s. (of time) dies, m. & f.; tempus, n.; (fruit) balanus, c.; palma, f.; out of —, obsoletus, desuetus.

date, v.a. diem ascribo, 3; —, v.n. (from) incipio, originem traho, 3.
date-tree, s. palma, f., phœnix (mod. hort.).
dative (case), s. (gr.) dativus, m.
daub, v.a. oblino, illino.
daub, s. litura.
dauber, s. pictor malus, m.
daughter, s. filia, f.
daughter-in-law, s. nurus, f.
daunt, v.a. pavefacio, 3; terreo, perterreo, 2. [ad. impavide.
dauntless, a. impavidus, intrepidus; —ly,
daw, s. monedula, f.
dawdle, v.n. (to loiter) moror, cesso, 1.
dawdler, s. cessator, m.
dawn, v.n. illucesco, dilucesco, 3; fig. eluceo, 2; — upon, fig. subeo, 4; succurro, 3.
dawn, dawning, s. aurora, prima lux, f., diluculum, n.
dawning, a. incipiens, primus.
day, s. dies, c.; lux, f., sol, m.; tempus, n.; fig. victoria, f.; before —, antelucanus; the — before, pridie; the — after, postridie.
day, a. diurnus. [tarius, m.
day-book, s. ephemeris, f.; commen-
daybreak, s. lux prima, f. [m.
day-labourer, s. operarius, mercenarius,
daylight, s. lux, f., dies, m. & f.
day-lily, s. hemerocallis (mod. hort.).
day-star, s. Lucifer, Phosphorus, m.
day's-work, s. opera, f.
day-time, s. tempus diurnum, n.
dazzle, v.a. præstringo, 3; fig. capio, 3.
dazzling, a. fulgidus, splendidus.
deacon, s. diaconus, m.
deaconate, deaconship, s. diaconatus, m.
deaconess, s. diaconissa, f.
dead, a. mortuus; vita defunctus; (lifeless, senseless) exanimis; fig. torpidus; (dull) segnis.
dead, s. manes, m. pl.; (of night) intempesta (nox), f.
dead, ad. omnino.
dead-drunk, s. madidus, m.
deaden, v.a. hebeto, 1; obtundo, 3; (weaken) debilito enervo, 1; (lessen) imminuo, 3. [implacabilis.
deadly, a. mortifer, letalis; fig. capitalis,
deadness, s. torpor; stupor, m., inertia; (dullness) insulsitas, f.
deaf, a. surdus.
deafen, v.a. exsurdo, 1; obtundo, 3.
deafish, a. surdaster.
deafness, s. surditas, f.
deal, s. (quantity) numerus, m.; vis, copia, f.; (business) negotium, n.; a great —, multum; (wood) abies, f.; made of —, abiegnus.

deal, v.a. distribuo, 3; (handle) tracto, 1; — **in**, (sell) vendo; — **with**, utor, 3; —, v.n. mercor, negotior, 1.

dealer, s. mercator, negotiatior.

dealing, s. (trade) negotiatio, mercatura; (intercourse) commercium, n.; usus, m.; (doing) factum, n.; (treatment) tractatio, f.

dean, s. decanus, m.

deanery, s. decanatus, m.

dear, a. (costly) carus, pretiosus; (pleasant) dulcis, gratus; (beloved) dilectus, carus; —**ly**, ad. care; valde; **to buy** —, magni emere, 3.

dear, i, heu! eheu!

dearness, s. caritas, f.

dearth, s. inopia, penuria; fames, f.

death, s. mors, f.; letum, n.; interitus, obitus, m.; **violent** —, nex, f.; funus, n.

death-bed, s. **on the** —, moriens.

deathless, a. immortalis.

debar, v.a. excludo, 3; prohibeo, arceo, 2; (to deprive) privo, 1.

debase, v.a. depravo; adultero; vitio, 1; corrumpo, 3; *fig.* dedecoro, 1.

debasement, s. adulteratio, f.; *fig.* dedecus, n.; ignominia, f.   [dubius.

debatable, a. disputabilis, controversiosus.

debate, v.a. disputo, discepto, 1; dissero, 3; —, v.n. cogito, meditor, 1.

debate, s. controversia, disceptatio; (friendly) colloquium, n.

debater, s. disputator, m.   [rumpo, 3.

debauch, v.a. stupro; vitio, 1; cor-

debauch, s. comissatio, f.

debauchee, s. ganeo, helluo, scortator; homo dissolutus, m.

debaucher, s corruptor, stuprator, m.

debauchery, s. libido, luxuria, f., stuprum, n.

debilitate, v.a. debilito, infirmo, 1.

debility, s. debilitas, infirmitas, f.

debit, s. debitum, n.

debit, v.a. expensam pecuniam alicui ferre.   [*fig.* debitum, n.

debt, s. (of money) debitum, æs alienum;

debtor, s. debitor (also *fig.*), m.

decalogue, s. decalogus, m.

decamp, v.n. castra moveo, 2; *fig.* fugio, 3.

decampment, s. profectio, f., discessus, m., fuga, f.

decant, v.a. transfundo, 3.

decanter, s. lagena, ampulla, f.

decay, v.n. (of buildings) dilabor, labor; (of flowers) defloresco; (to rot) putresco; (to grow old) senesco; (to waste away) tabesco, 3; (to grow obsolete) obsolesco, 2; *fig.* deficio, 3; declino, 1.

decay, s. tabes, caries; *fig.* defectio; deminutio, f.

decease, s. decessus, obitus, m.

deceased, a. mortuus, defunctus.

deceit, s. fraus, fallacia, f., dolus, m.

deceitful, a. fallax; dolosus; fraudulentus; falsus; (of things) vanus; —**ly**, ad. fallaciter; fraudulenter; dolose; per fallacias.

deceitfulness, s. fallacia, (emptiness) vanitas, f.

deceive, v.a. decipio, fallo, 3; (to cheat) fraudo, 1; circumduco, 3; circumvenio, 4; (mock) deludo, 3; —, v.n. *fig.* mentior, 4.

deceiver, s. fraudator, m.

December, s. December, m.

decency, s. decorum, n.; pudor, m.

decennial, a. decennalis, decennis.

decent, a. decens; decorus; pudicus; honestus; —**ly**, ad. decore, decenter, honeste.

deception, s. fraudatio, fraus, fallacia, f.

deceptive, a. fallax, vanus; (of persons) falsus, fraudulentus.

decide, v.a. & n. discepto, dijudico, 1; decerno; constituo, 3.

decided, a. firmus, constans; (of things) certus; —**ly**, ad. certe.

decider, s. disceptator, arbiter, m.; judex, c.

deciduous, a. deciduus, caducus.

decimate, v.a. decimo; *fig.* depopulor, 1.

decimation, s. decimatio, f.

decipher, v.a. explico, 1.

decision, s. sententia, f., arbitrium, judicium, n.

decisive, a. decretorius, haud dubius, certus; —**ly**, ad. haud dubie.

deck, v.a. exorno, 1; ponte struo, 3.

deck, s. pons, m.; transtra, n. pl.

decking, s. ornatus, m.

declaim, v.a. & n. declamo, declamito, 1; invehor (in . . .), 3.

declaimer, s. declamator.

declamation, s. declamatio, f.

declamatory, a. declamatorius.

declaration, s. professio; (of war) denuntiatio, f.; (speech) oratio, f.; (opinion) sententia, f.

declare, v.a. declaro, 1; aperio, 4; profiteor, 2; (war) denuntio; (as a judge) judico, 1; —, v.n. affirmo, 1; (for) *fig.* faveo, 2.

declension, s. (gr.) declinatio, f.

declinable, a. declinabilis.

declination, s. declinatio; (decay) defectio, f.

decline, v.a. detrecto; (to refuse) recuso, 1; (gr.) flecto, 3; —, v.n. vergo, 3; inclino, 1; (to decay) deficio, minuor, 3; (of prices: to abate) laxo, 1.   [tabes, f.

decline, s. defectio; (consumption)

declivity, s. declive, n.
decoction, s. decoctum, n.
decompose, v.a. dissolvo; v.n. dissolvor,
  putresco, 3.   [tabes, f.
decomposition, s. dissolutio; (decay)
decorate, v.a. orno, exorno, decoro, 1.
decoration, s. (act) ornatio, exornatio, f.;
  ornatus, m.; (ornament) ornamentum;
  (distinction) decus, n.
decorator, s. exornator, m.
decorous, a. decorus; —ly, ad. decore.
decorum, s. decorum, quod decet, n.
decoy, v.a. inesco, 1; *fig.* allicio, illicio,
  pellicio, 3.
decoy, s. illecebra, f., illicium, n.; —
  -bird, s. allector, m.
decrease, v.a. minuo, imminuo, deminuo,
  3; v.n. decresco, minuor, 3; minor fio.
decrease, s. deminutio, imminutio, f.
decree, s. decretum, edictum, n.; (judgment) sententia, f.; (purpose) propositum; (award) arbitrium, n.
decree, v.a. impero, 1; statuo; decerno,
  edico, 3.
decrepit, a. decrepitus, debilis, enervatus.
decrepitude, s. ætas decrepita, senectus,
  defectio virium, f.
decrial, s. obtrectatio, f.
decrier, s. obtrectator, m.
decry, v.a. detrecto, obtrecto, 1.
decuple, a. decemplex.   [2.
dedicate, v.a. dedico; consecro, 1; voveo,
dedication, s. dedicatio; consecratio; (of
  a book) nuncupatio, f.
deduce, v.a. (to infer) concludo, 3.
deducible, a. consectarius.
deduct, v.a. detraho, subtraho, deduco, 3.
deduction, s. deductio, f.; (in logic) conclusio, f.
deed, s. factum; facinus, n.; (law) syngrapha, f., instrumentum, n.; in —,
  re vera, re.
deem, v.a. judico, puto, existimo, 1;
  duco, 3.
deep, a. altus, profundus; (of sounds)
  gravis; (of colours) satur; *fig.* callidus;
  dolosus; —, ad., v. deeply.
deep, s. profundum; (sea) mare, n.
deepen, v.a. excavo, 1; defodio, deprimo, 3; —, v.n. altior fio; (night,
  etc.) densor, 1.
deep-laid, a. occultus.
deeply, ad. alte, profunde; (inwardly)
  penitus; *fig.* graviter, valde.
deepness, s. altitudo, profunditas, f.;
  (craft) fraus, fallacia, f.
deer, s. cervus, m.; cerva, f.; (fallow-deer)
  dama, m. & f.
deface, v.a. deformo, turpo, 1.
defaced, a. deformis.
defacement, s. deformitas, deformatio, f.

defalcation, s. (embezzlement) peculatus, m.
defamation, s. obtrectatio, f.
defamatory, a. probrosus.   [to, 1.
defame, v.a. diffamo, calumnior, obtrec-
defamer, s. calumniator, obtrectator, m.
default, s. (deficiency) defectus, m.
default, v.n. (fail) deficio, 3; (law) ad
  vadimonium non venio, 4.
defaulter, s. (embezzler) peculator, m.
defeat, s. clades, calamitas; (frustration)
  frustratio, f.
defeat, v.a. (to baffle) frustror, 1; (to conquer) vinco, 3; supero, 1; (put to
  flight) fundo, 3; fugo, 1.
defect, s. vitium, mendum, n.; menda, f.;
  (want) defectus, m.
defection, s. defectio, f.
defective, a. mancus, vitiosus; imperfectus; (gr.) defectivus; —ly, ad. vitiose; imperfecte.
defectiveness, s. vitiositas, f.
defence, s. (act) defensio; (excuse) excusatio; (means of) tutela, f.; tutamen; (defences), munimentum, n.
defenceless, a. inermis; defensoribus
  nudatus.
defend, v.a. defendo, 3; (at law) patro-
  cinor, 1.
defendant, s. reus, m., rea, f.; the —, iste.
defender, s. defensor; patronus, m.
defensible, a. quod defendi potest; excusabilis.
defer, v.a. differo, profero, produco, 3;
  —, v.n. obsequor, 3.
deference, s. observantia; reverentia, f.
defiance, s. provocatio, f.; to bid — to,
  provocare, 1, *or* contemnere, 3, (aliquem); in — of, contra; in — of
  your friends, amicis invitis.
deficiency, s. defectio, f., defectus, m.;
  pars relicta; (want) lacuna, f.
deficient, a. mancus; (deficient in) inops
  (gen.); to be — in, deficio, 3.
deficit, s. lacuna, f.
defile, v.a. contamino, inquino, maculo,
  commaculo; *fig.* fœdo; incesto, violo,
  1; —, v.n. iter facio, 3.   [saltus, m.
defile, s. fauces, angustiæ, f. pl.;
defilement, s. violatio, macula, labes, f.;
  (of a woman) stuprum, n.
defiler, s. violator; stuprator, m.
define, v.a. circumscribo, 3; termino, 1;
  definio, 4.
definite, a. certus, status, definitus; —ly,
  ad. definite, certe.
definition, s. definitio, f.
definitive, a. definitivus, decretorius.
deflect, v.a. & n. deflecto, 3; declino, 1.
deflection, s. deflexus, m.; declinatio, f.
deflower, v.a. strupro, 1; corrumpo, 3.

deform, v.a. deformo, 1.
deformed, a. deformis; deformatus; distortus.
deformity, s. deformitas; pravitas, f.
defraud, v.a. fraudo, defraudo, 1.
defrauder, s. fraudator, m.
defray, v.a. præbeo, 2; suppedito, 1.
deft, a. habilis.
defunct, a. vita defunctus, defunctus, mortuus.
defy, v.a. provoco, 1; contemno, 3.
degeneracy, s. mores corrupti, m. pl.
degenerate, v.n. degenero, 1.
degenerate, a. degener.
degradation, s. ignominia; gradus dejectio, f.
degrade, v.a. dejicio, 3; loco moveo, 2; *fig.* ignominia afficio, 3.
degree, s. gradus, ordo, m.; **in the highest —,** summe; **by —s,** paulatim, sensim, pedetentim, gradatim.
deification, s. apotheosis, consecratio, f.
deify, v.a. divum habeo, 2; in numero deorum colloco, 1.
deign, v.n. dignor; non aspernor, non gravor, 1; sustineo, 2.
deity, s. numen, n.; deus, m.; dea, f.
deject, v.a. affligo, 3.
dejected, a. demissus, tristis.
dejectedly, ad. demisse.
dejection, s. animi demissio, f.; animus afflictus, m.
delation, s. delatio, f.
delay, s. mora, cunctatio; dilatio, retardatio, f.
delay, v.a. detineo, 2; tardo; retardo; (to keep back) remoror, 1; **—,** v.n. cunctor; moror, cesso, 1.
delectable, a. amœnus.
delectably, ad. amœne, jucunde.
delectation, s. delectatio, f.
delegate, s. legatus, m.
delegate, v.a. (to depute) delego; (to commit) commendo, 1.
delegation, s. delegatio, f.
deleterious, a. perniciosus, noxius.
delft, s. fictilia, n. pl.
deliberate, a. deliberatus, consideratus, cautus, prudens; lentus; **—ly,** ad. deliberate, cogitate; lente; consulto.
deliberate, v.n. consulto, delibero, considero, reputo, verso, voluto, 1; volvo, 3.
deliberateness, s. circumspectio, f.
deliberation, s. deliberatio, f.
deliberative, a. deliberativus.
delicacy, s. subilitas, tenuitas; elegantia, f.; (flavour) sapor, m.; (dainty) cuppediæ, f. pl.; (modesty) verecundia, f.; (weakness) infirmitas.

delicate, a. delicatus; mollis, tener; exquisitus; elegans; fastidiosus; (of texture) subtilis; (in taste) suavis; (modest) verecundus; (weak) infirmus; **—ly,** ad. delicate; exquisite; subtiliter; molliter.
delicious, a. delicatus, suavis; exquisitus; **—ly,** ad. suaviter, delicate; exquisite.
deliciousness, s. suavitas, dulcedo, f.
delight, s. delectatio, f.; deliciæ, f. pl.; gaudium, n.; voluptas, f.
delight, v.a. delecto, 1; **—,** v.n. gaudeo, 2; lætor, 1.
delightful, a. suavis, jucundus, amœnus; **—ly,** ad. jucunde, suaviter.
delightfulness, s. suavitas, jucunditas, amœnitas, f.
delineate, v.a. describo, 3; delineo, adumbro, 1; exprimo, expono, 3.
delineation, s. designatio; descriptio, f.
delinquency, s. delictum, n.
delinquent, s. nocens, m.
delirious, a. non sui compos, mente alienatus.
delirium, s. mentis alienatio, f.; delirium, n.
deliver, v.a. do, 1; (to hand over) trado, 3; (to free) libero, 1; (to surrender) prodo, 3; (a speech) habeo, 2; (sentence) dico (jus), 3; (an opinion) promo, 3; (a message) perfero, 3; (of childbirth) parienti adsum; (be —ed of) pario, edo, 3; (to — up) cedo, 3.
deliverance, s. liberatio, f.
deliverer, s. liberator, conservator, m.; vindex, c.
delivery, s. liberatio; (of goods) traditio; (utterance) pronuntiatio, f.; (childbirth) partus, m.
dell, s. vallis, convallis, f.
delude, v.a. decipio, deludo, 3; derideo, 2.
deluder, s. fraudator, m.   [n.
deluge, s. diluvies, inundatio, f., diluvium,
deluge, v.a. inundo, 1.
delusion, s. error, m.; fraus, f.
delusive, a. fallax; vanus, falsus.
delve, v.a., v. dig.
demagogue, s. plebicola, contionator, m.
demand, v.a. postulo, flagito, 1; posco, deposco, peto, 3.
demand, s. postulatio, petitio, f.; **be in —,** a multis expetor.
demander, s. flagitator, m.
demarcation, s. designatio, f.; (boundary) confinium, n.
demean, v.r. **to — oneself,** gero, 3; (condescend to) descendo ad, 3.
demeanour, s. mores, m. pl.; (deportment) gestus, m.
demerit, s. culpa, f.; delictum, vitium, n.
demesne, s. ager, m.
demi, a. semi. . . .

demise, s. (lease) locatio, f.; decessus, obitus, m.; mors, f.

demise, v.a. (bequeath) lego; (lease) loco, 1.

democracy, s. civitas popularis, f.; liber populus, m.

democrat, s. plebicola, homo popularis, m.

democratical, a. popularis; —ly, ad. populi voluntate, per populum.

demolish, v.a. demolior, 4; everto, disjicio, 3.

demolisher, s. eversor, m.

demolition, s. demolitio, eversio, f.

demon, s. dæmon, m.

demoniac, s. dæmoniacus, m.

demoniacal, a. dæmonicus; exsecrandus.

demonstrable, a. demonstrabilis, manifestus.

demonstrably, ad. clare, manifeste.

demonstrate, v.a. demonstro, firmo, 1; convinco, 3.

demonstration, s. demonstratio, f.

demonstrative, a. demonstrativus.

demonstratively, ad. demonstrative.

demoralization, s. depravatio (morum), f.; mores corrupti, m. pl.; pravitas, f.

demoralize, v.a. mores depravo, 1; corrumpo, 3.

demur, v.n. hæsito, dubito, 1; (in law) excipio, 3; to — to, nego, repudio, 1.

demur, s. mora; (objection) exceptio, f.

demure, a. modestus, gravis, severus; —ly, ad. modeste.

demureness, s. modestia, f.

demurrer, s. (in law) exceptio, f.

den, s. specus, m. f. & n.; (of beasts) latibulum, n.; spelunca, latebra, f.; lustra, n. pl.

deniable, a. infitiandus.

denial, s. negatio; infitiatio; (refusal) repudiatio; repulsa, f.

denizen, s. incola, c., civitate donatus, m.

denominate, v.a. nomino, indico, 1.

denomination, s. nominatio, f., nomen, n.

denote, v.a. significo, 1.

denounce, v.a. (to declare solemnly) denuntio, 1; defero, 3; (accuse) accuso; (blame) culpo, 1.

denouncer, s. accusator, m.

dense, a. densus, spissus, confertus; —ly, ad. dense; crebro.

density, s. densitas, f.

dent, s. (mark) nota, f.; (wound) vulnus, n.

dent, v.a. (mark) noto; (wound) vulnero, 1.

dentifrice, s. dentifricium, n.

dentist, s. dentium medicus, m.

dentistry, s. dentium medicina, f.

denudation, s. nudatio, spoliatio, f.

denude, v.a. denudo, nudo, 1; detego, 3; (rob) spolio, 1.

denunciation, s. denunciatio; accusatio, f.

deny, v.a. nego, infitior; (refuse) nego, recuso, denego, 1; renuo, abnuo, 3.

depart, v.n. abeo; exeo, 4; (to leave) discedo, 3; (move) demigro, 1; (to set out) proficiscor; fig. (to die) morior, 3.

departed, p.a. mortuus; vita defunctus.

department, s. provincia, f.; cura, f.; munus, n.; (branch) genus, n.

departure, s. abitus, discessus, m., profectio; (deviation) digressio; (death) mors, f., obitus, m.

depend, v.n. (to hang down) dependeo; (to hang upon) pendeo, 2; — upon, (trust) confido, fido.

dependant, v. dependent.

dependence, dependency, s. servitus; (reliance) fiducia; fides; (authority) dicio, f.; (duty) officium, n.; (poverty) inopia, f.

dependent, s. cliens; assecla, m.; —, a. subjectus; (poor) inops.

depict, v.a. (de)pingo; effingo; describo; exprimo, 3.

depletion, s. exinanitio, f.

deplorable, a. miserabilis, flebilis, lugendus, plorabilis, calamitosus.

deplorably, ad. misere, miserabiliter.

deplore, v.a. deploro, 1; defleo, 2; lamentor, 1; ægre fero, 3.

deploy, v.a. explico, 1.

deponent, s. testis, c.

deponent, a. (gr.) deponens.

depopulate, v.a. desolo, vasto, 1.   [tas, f.

depopulation, s. vastatio; (state) vasti-

deportment, s. gestus, habitus, m.

depose, v.a. abrogo, 1; amoveo, 2; (as witness) testor, 1.   [mendo, 1.

deposit, v.a. depono, 3; (to commit) com-

deposit, s. depositum; (pledge) pignus, n.; (earnest money) arrhabo, m.

depositary, s. depositarius, m.; custos, c.

deposition, s. (evidence) testimonium, n.

depositor, s. depositor, m.   [m.

depository, s. receptaculum, n.; thesaurus,

depravation, s. depravatio, corruptio, f.

deprave, v.a. depravo, vitio, 1; corrumpo, 3.

deprecate, v.a. deprecor, 1.

depreciation, s. deprecatio, f.

deprecatory, a. supplex.

depreciate, v.a. detrecto, obtrecto, 1.

depreciation, s. obtrectatio, f.   [m.

depreciator, s. detrectator, obtrectator,

depredate, v.a. prædor, 1.

depredation, s. prædatio, spoliatio, f.; latrocinium, n.

depredator, s. prædator, prædo, latro, m.

depress, v.a. deprimo; fig. infringo; affligo, 3.   [low) cavus.

depressed, a. afflictus; (flat) planus; (hol-

depressing, a. tristis.

depression, s. *fig.* animi demissio, f.; animus afflictus, m.

deprivation, s. (act) privatio; spoliatio; (state) orbitas; inopia, f.

deprive, v.a. privo; spolio; orbo, 1; adimo, eripio, 3.

deprived, a. expers, exsors.

depth, s. altitudo, f.; profundum, n.; (sea) pontus, i; (bottom) fundus, m.; *fig.* (acuteness) ingenium, n.

deputation, s. legati; (spokesmen) oratores, m. pl.

depute, v.a. lego, mando, 1.

deputy, s. legatus; vicarius, m.

derange, v.a. (per)turbo, 1; confundo, 3.

deranged, a. (of persons) mente captus, delirus.

derangement, s. perturbatio, confusio; (of mind) mens alienata, mentis alienatio, f.

dereliction, s. derelictio, f.

deride, v.a. rideo, derideo, irrideo, 2.

derider, s. derisor, irrisor, m.

derision, s. risus, derisus, m.; irrisio, f.

derisive, a. acerbus.

derivation, s. derivatio; etymologia, f.

derivative, s. derivativus.

derive, v.a. duco, deduco, 3; —, v.n. proficiscor, 3; orior, 4.

derogate, v.n. derogo, 1; imminuo, 3; (with dative) detraho, 3.

derogation, s. derogatio, imminutio, f.

derogatory, a. inhonestus, turpis, f.

descant, v.n. decanto, 1.

descend, v.a. & n. descendo; (to fall suddenly) delabor, 3; **be —ed from**, orior ab (abl.), 4; originem traho ab (abl.), 3.

descendant, s. progenies, proles, stirps, f.

descent, s. descensus, m.; descensio; (slope) declivitas, f.; *fig.* lapsus, m.; (origin) origo, f.; genus, n.   [1.

describe, v.a. describo; depingo, 3; narro,

describer, s. narrator, m.

description, s. descriptio; narratio, f.

descry, v.a. exploro, 1; conspicio, cerno, 3.

desecrate, v.a. profano, violo, 1; polluo, 3.

desecration, s. violatio, f.

desert, a. desertus, solus.

desert, s. (wilderness) desertum, n., vastitas, solitudo, f.

desert, s. meritum, n.; (goodness) virtus, f.

desert, v.a. desero, relinquo, destituo, 3; —, v.n. transfugio, signa relinquo, 3.

deserter, s. desertor; transfuga, m.

desertion, s. derelictio; (betrayal) proditio, f.   [sum.

deserve, v.a. & n. mereo, mereor, 2; dignus

deservedly, ad. merito, jure.   [bus.

deserving, a. dignus; bonus, optimus, pro-

desideratum, s. res expetenda, f.

design, v.a. describo, 3; *fig.* machinor, excogito, 1; molior, 4; (destine) destino, 1.

design, s. (drawing) descriptio, f.; *fig.* (purpose) consilium, propositum, n.

designate, v.a. designo; nomino, 1.

designation, s. designatio, f.; (name) nomen, n.

designedly, ad. consulto, consilio; (purposely) de industria.   [ator.

designer, s. inventor; fabricator; machin-

designing, a. callidus, subdolus.

desirable, a. optabilis, expetendus.

desire, v.a. desidero, opto, 1; expeto, cupio, 3; (to request) oro, 1; peto, 3.

desire, s. desiderium, n.; cupido, f.; appetitus, m.; appetitio, f.

desirous, a. cupidus, appetens.

desist, v.n. desisto; absisto; (to cease) desino, 3.

desk, s. scrinium; pulpitum, n.

desolate, a. solus, desertus, vastus, desolatus; *fig.* (of persons) afflictus.

desolate, v.a. devasto, desolo, 1.

desolation, s. vastitas; solitudo, f.; (bereavement) orbitas, f.

despair, s. desperatio, f.

despair, v.n. despero (de aliqua re), 1.

despairingly, ad. desperanter.

despatch, v.a. mitto; dimitto, 3; (a deputy) lego, 1; (to finish) absolvo; exsequor; (to settle) transigo; conficio; (to kill) interficio, 3.

despatch, s. mandatum, n., epistula, f.; (hasty execution) properatio, f.

despatch-box, s. scrinium, n., capsa, f.

desperado, s. perditus civis; sicarius, m.

desperate, a. exspes, desperatus; extremus; periculosus; **—ly**, ad. ita ut spes amittatur; **to be —ly in love**, perdite amare, 1.

desperation, s. desperatio, f.

despicable, a. aspernandus, vilis.

despicably, ad. turpiter.

despise, v.a. despicio, sperno, temno, contemno, 3; aspernor, 1.

despiser, s. contemptor, spretor, m.

despite, s., v. **spite**.

despoil, v. **spoil**, v.a.

despond, v.n. despondeo, 2; animum demitto, 3.

despondency, s. animi demissio, f.

despondent, a. demissus.

despondingly, ad. animo demisso.

despot, s. dominus; tyrannus, m.

despotic, a. imperiosus, superbus, tyrannicus; **—ally**, ad. tyrannice.

despotism, s. dominatio, regia potestas, f.

dessert, s. secunda mensa, f.; bellaria, n. pl.

destination, s. destinatio, f.; propositum, n.; (goal) meta, f.
destine, v.a. destino; (to mark out) designo, 1.
destiny, s. fatum, n.; sors, f.
destitute, a. egens, egenus, inops; destitutus, expers; viduus.
destitution, s. inopia; egestas, f.; mendicitas, f.
destroy, v.a. destruo, perdo, everto, tollo, consumo, 3; aboleo, deleo, 2; vasto, 1; **to be —ed,** intereo, 4.
destroyer, s. exstinctor; eversor; (of lands) vastator, m.
destruction, s. eversio, f.; exitium, n. clades, f.
destructive, a. exitialis, perniciosus; calamitosus; **—ly,** ad. perniciose.
desuetude, s. desuetudo, f.
desultorily, ad. cursim.
desultory, a. inconstans; volaticus; vagus.
detach, v.a. sejungo; solvo, secerno, 3.
detached, a. sejunctus.
detachment, s. separatio; (of troops) manus, f.; (fairness) æquitas, f.
detail, v.a. enumero, 1; singillatim dico, 3. [n. pl.
detail, s. singulæ res, f. pl.; singula, n. pl.
detain, v.a. definio, 4; retineo, 2; retardo, 1.
detect, v.a. comperio, 4; deprendo, 3.
detection, s. deprehensio, f.; indicium, n.
detective, s. inquisitor, m.
detention, s. mora, f. [to, 3.
deter, v.a. deterreo, absterreo, 2; averdeteriorate, v.a. corrumpo, 3; depravo, 1; —, v.n. deterior fio, in pejus mutor.
deterioration, s. depravatio, corruptio, f.
determinate, a. certus; **—ly,** ad. certe.
determination, s. definitio, f.; arbitrium, judicium, n.; mens, voluntas, f.; (purpose) consilium, n.; (resoluteness) constantia, f.
determine, v.a. determino, 1; definio, 4; statuo, constituo, decerno, 3; dijudico, 1; **I am —d,** certum est mihi; v.n. finem habeo, 2.
detest, v.a. abominor, detestor, 1; odi, perodi, 3.
detestable, a. detestabilis, fœdus, odiosus.
detestably, ad. odiose.
detestation, s. odium, n.; detestatio, f.
dethrone, v.a. regno expello, 3.
detonate, v.n. crepo, 1; dissilio, 4.
detonation, s. fragor, m.
detract, v.a. detraho, imminuo, 3; (to slander) detrecto, obtrecto, 1.
detraction, s. obtrectatio, f.
detractor, s. obtrectator, m.
detriment, s. detrimentum, damnum, n.
detrimental, a. damnosus, injuriosus, iniquus.

deuce, s. (in dice) binio, m.; **take it!** malum! **the —!** papæ.
devastate, v.a. vasto, populor, depopulor, 1. [(state) vastitas, f.
devastation, s. (act) vastatio, populatio;
develop, v.a. evolvo, 3; explico, 1; fig. excolo, 3. [exitus, m.
development, s. explicatio, f.; (issue)
deviate, v.n. aberro, 1; digredior, 3.
deviation, s. aberratio; declinatio; digressio, f.; fig. error, m.
device, s. (emblem) insigne, is, n.; (motto) inscriptio, f.; (contrivance) artificium, n.; machina, f.
devil, s. diabolus.
devilish, a. diabolicus; fig. nefandus; **—ly,** ad. diabolice; nefande.
devious, a. devius; vagus; erraticus; **— course,** ambages, f. pl.
devise, v.a. fingo, 3; excogito, 1; concoquo, 3; molior, 4; machinor, 1; (to bequeath) lego, 1.
deviser, s. inventor, auctor, machinator, m.
devoid, a. inanis, vacuus; liber; expers.
devoir, s. officium, munus, n.
devolve, v.a. defero; (to intrust) committo, 3; —, v.n. pervenio (ad); redeo, 4.
devote, v.a. devoveo, 2; consecro, dico, 1; (set apart) sepono, 3; (doom) destino, 1; **to — oneself to,** studeo, 2; incumbo, 3.
devoted, a. studiosus; (loving) pius.
devotedly, ad. studiose, summo studio.
devotedness, s. pietas, f.
devotee, s. homo religiosus, cultor, m.
devotion, s. devotio, f.; (affection) pietas, f.; (zeal) studium, n.; diligentia, f.
devotional, a. pius.
devour, v.a. voro, devoro, 1; haurio, 4; consumo, 3.
devourer, s. helluo, m.; fig. vorago, f.
devout, a. pius, devotus; **—ly,** ad. pie, religiose, sancte.
devoutness, s. pietas, f.
dew, s. ros, m.
dew-drop, s. gutta roscida, f.
dew-lap, s. palear, n.
dewy, a. roscidus, roridus, rorulentus.
dexterity, s. calliditas, sollertia, f.
dexterous, a. callidus, sollers, sciens, habilis; **—ly,** ad. callide, scienter, sollerter.
diabolical, a. diabolicus.
diadem, s. diadema, n.; (fillet) tænia, vitta, f.
diagnosis, s. (examination) exploratio, f.; (judgment) sententia, f.
diagonal, a. diagonalis; —, s. diagonalis linea, f.; **—ly,** ad. in quincuncem, in transversum.

diagram, s. forma; forma geometrica, f.

dial, s. solarium, n.

dialect, s. dialectus, f.; sermo, m.

dialectical, a. dialecticus.

dialogue, s. sermo, m.: colloquium, n.; (written discussion) dialogus, m.

diameter, s. diametros, dimetiens, f.

diametrical, a. diametrus; —**ly,** ad. per medium; *fig.* prorsus, omnino.

diamond, s. adamas, m.

diaphragm, s. præcordia, n. pl.

diarrhœa, s. profluvium, n.

diary, s. diarium, n.; ephemeris, f.

diatribe, s. libellus, m.

dibble, s. pastinum, n.   [game] alea, f.

dice, s. pl. tali, m. pl.; tesseræ, f. pl.; (the

dice-box, s. fritillus, phimus, m.

dictate, v.a. dicto, 1; præscribo, 3; (command) impero; (lord it over) dominor, 1.

dictate, s. præscriptum, jussum, præceptum, n.

dictation, s. dictatum, n.; (command) imperium, præscriptum, n.

dictator, s. dictator, m.

dictatorial, a. dictatorius; arrogans; imperiosus.

dictatorship, s. dictatura, f.

diction, s. dictio, f.

dictionary, s. lexicon, n.; thesaurus, m.

die, s. tessera, f.; (for gaming) talus, m.; the — **is cast,** alea jacta est.

die, v.n. morior; *fig.* exstinguor; (to decay) labor, 3; pereo, intereo, 4; (to fade) cado, 3.

diet, s. (food) victus, m.; (med.) diæta, f.; (assembly) conventus, m.

diet, v.a. cibos præscribo, 3.

differ, v.n. differo, 3; discrepo, disto, 1; (in opinion, etc.) dissentio, 4; dissideo, 2.

difference, s. differentia; diversitas; varietas, f.; discrimen, n.; (of opinion) discrepantia; dissensio, f.

different, a. diversus; alius; dispar; (unlike) dissimilis; (various) diversus, varius; —**ly,** ad. aliter; diverse.

difficult, a. difficilis; arduus.

difficulty, s. difficultas, f.; (dilemma, need) angustiæ, f. pl.; **with** —, ægre.

diffidence, s. diffidentia; (modesty) verecundia, modestia, f.

diffident, a. diffidens; verecundus, timidus; modestus; —**ly,** ad. diffidenter; verecunde, timide, modeste.

diffuse, v.a. diffundo, differo, 3.

diffuse, a. diffusus; longus; *fig.* verbosus; —**ly,** ad. effuse, latius.

diffuseness, s. longitudo, f.

diffusion, s. diffusio, prolatio, f.

diffusive, a. redundans, exundans, largus.

dig, v.a. & n. fodio; — **up,** eruo, effodio, 3.

digest, v.a. & n. (to arrange) digero, dispono; (food) concoquo, 3; (also *fig.*).

digest, s. digesta, n. pl.

digestion, s. (of food) concoctio, f.; (stomach) stomachus, m.

digestive, a. digestorius.

digger, s. fossor, m.

digging, s. fossio, fossura, f.

digit, s. digitus, numerus, m.

dignified, a. gravis.

dignify, v.a. honesto, honoro, orno, 1.

dignity, s. dignitas, gravitas, f., honor, m.

digress, v.n. digredior, 3; aberro, 1.

digression, s. digressio, f.   [agger, m.

dike, s. (ditch) fossa, f.; (dam, mound)

dilapidated, a. ruinosus, prolapsus.

dilapidation, s. ruina; **free from** —**s,** sartus tectus.

dilate, v.a. & n. dilato; dilator, 1; —**on,** uberius dico de (abl.).

dilatoriness, s. cunctatio, tarditas, f.

dilatory, a. cunctabundus, lentus, tardus.

dilemma, s. dilemma, n.; *fig.* (difficulty) angustiæ, f. pl.

diligence, s. diligentia, sedulitas, f.

diligent, a. diligens, sedulus; —**ly,** ad. diligenter, sedulo.

dill, s. anethum, n.

dilute, v.a. diluo, 3; misceo, 2; tempero, f.   [ture) dilutum, n.

dilution, s. temperatio, mixtura, f.; (mix-

dim, a. hebes; obscurus; **to be** —, hebeo, 2; **to become** —, hebesco, 3.

dim, v.a. hebeto; obscuro; (to prevent from seeing) occæco, 1.

dimension, s. dimensio, mensura, f.

diminish, v.a. minuo, imminuo, deminuo, 3; (to reduce) extenuo, 1; —, v.n. minuor, 3; extenuor, 1.

diminution, s. imminutio, deminutio, f.

diminutive, a. parvus, exiguus; (gr.) deminutivus.

diminutive, s. (nomen) deminutivum, n.

diminutiveness, s. exiguitas, f.

dimly, ad. obscure.

dimness, s. hebetatio; obscuritas; caligo, f.

dimple, s. lacuna, f.; gelasinus, m.

dim-sighted, a. lippus.

din, s. strepitus, sonitus, fragor, m.

din, v.a. (to deafen) obtundo, 3; **to make a** —, strepo, 3.

dine, v.n. ceno, 1; prandeo, 2.

dingle, s. convallis, f.; nemus, n.

dingy, a. fuscus, squalidus, sordidus, subniger.

dining-room, s. cenatio, f.

dinner, s. cena, f.

dinner-party, s. convivium, n.

dint, s. (blow) ictus, m.; (mark of it) nota, f.; (wound) vulnus, n.; **by** — **of,** per.

diocese, diœcesis, f.
dip, v.a. immergo; tingo, 3; —, v.n. mergor; tingor; (to sink) premor, vergo, 3; declino, 1.
dip, s. declivitas, f.
diphthong, s. diphthongus, f.
diploma, s. diploma, n.
diplomacy, s. *fig.* ars, astutia, f.
diplomatist, s. (ambassador) legatus.
dire, a. dirus, terribilis.
direct, a. rectus, directus; —ly, ad. directe, recta (via); (immediately) statim, confestim.
direct, v.a. dirigo; (turn) flecto, verto; (to address) inscribo, 3; (to order) jubeo, 2; (to rule) guberno; (manage) curo, procuro, 1.
direction, s. (act) directio, f.; (way) iter, n., via; (quarter) regio; (ruling) gubernatio; (management) administratio, f.; (order) præceptum, n.; in which —, quo? in both —s, utroque.
director, s. rector; magister; præses, præfectus; gubernator; (manager) curator, m.
directory, s. (office of director) curatio, f.; magisterium, n.; (body of directors) magistri, curatores, m. pl.   [trix, f.
directress, s. gubernatrix, magistra, rectdireful, a. dirus.
dirge, s. nenia, carmen funebre, n.
dirk, s. pugio, m.   [limus, m.
dirt, s. sordes, f.; cænum, lutum, n.;
dirtily, ad. sordide, spurce, obscene.
dirtiness, s. spurcitia; *fig.* obscenitas, f.
dirty, a. spurcus, sordidus, immundus, lutulentus, cænosus; (unwashed) illotus; *fig.* obscenus.
dirty, v.a. fœdo, spurco, maculo, commaculo, 1.
disability, s. impotentia, f.
disable, v.a. debilito; enervo, 1.
disabled, a. debilis; mancus.
disablement, s. debilitatio, f.
disabuse, v.a. dedoceo, 2; errorem alicui eripio, 3.
disaccustom, v.a. desuefacio, 3.
disadvantage, s. incommodum, detrimentum, damnum, n.; (unfavourable character) iniquitas, f.   [quus.
disadvantageous, a. incommodus; inidisadvantageously, ad. incommode; inique.
disaffect, v.a. alieno, 1; animum, animos averto, abduco, 3; (tamper with) sollicito, 1.   [sus.
disaffected, a. alienatus; aversus; seditiodisaffection, s. alienatus animus, m.; seditio, f.
disagree, v.n. discrepo, 1; dissideo, 2; dissentio, 4.

disagreeable, a. injucundus; ingratus; molestus; insuavis; gravis; (of persons) difficilis, morosus.
disagreeableness, s. injucunditas, gravitas, molestia, morositas, f.
disagreeably, ad. injucunde, ingrate.
disagreement, s. dissensio, discordia, f.
disallow, v.a. & n. veto; improbo, 1.
disappear, v.n. vanesco; evanesco; dilabor, 3.   [m.
disappearance, disappearing, s. exitus,
disappoint, v.a. fallo, 3; frustror, fraudo, 1.
disappointment, s. frustratio, f.; (inconvenience) incommodum, n.; (rejection) repulsa, f.
disapprobation, disapproval, s. improbatio, reprehensio, f.
disapprove, v.a. reprehendo, 3; improbo, 1.   [*fig.* mitigo, 1.
disarm, v.a. exarmo, 1; armis exuo, 3;
disarray, v.a. perturbo, 1; confundo, 3.
disarray, s. perturbatio, f.
disaster, s. calamitas, clades, f.; incommodum, n.
disastrous, a. calamitosus, funestus; pestifer; —ly, ad. calamitose; pestifere.
disavow, v.a. diffiteor, 2; infitior, 1; abnuo, 3.
disavowal, s. infitiatio, f.
disband, v.a. dimitto, 3; missum facio, 3.
disbanding, s. dimissio, f.
disbelief, s. diffidentia; incredulitas, f.
disbelieve, v.a. fidem non habeo, 2; non credo, 3.
disbelieving, a. incredulus.
disburden, v.a. exonero, 1; solvo, 3.
disburse, v.a. erogo, 1; expendo, solvo, 3.
disbursement, s. erogatio; solutio, f.
disc, s. orbis (solis, lunæ), m.
discard, v.a. repudio, 1; rejicio, excutio, 3.
discern, v.a. discerno, distinguo, 3.
discerning, a. perspicax, acutus.
discernment, s. perspicientia, f.; (faculty) prudentia, f.; acumen, n.
discharge, v.a. & n. (to unload) exonero, 1; (to dismiss) dimitto, 3; (of rivers) effundo, 3; (to perform) fungor, perfungor, 3; (to pay) solvo, 3; (to shoot, to let fly) mitto, immitto; (acquit) absolvo, 3.
discharge, s. (unloading) exoneratio; (dismissal) missio; (acquittal) absolutio; (payment) solutio, f.; (efflux) profluvium, effluvium, n.
disciple, s. discipulus, m.; discipula, f.; *fig.* sectator, m.
discipline, s. disciplina, f.
discipline, v.a. instituo; assuefacio, 3.
disciplined, a. optima disciplina institutus.

disclaim, v.a. infitior, 1; diffiteor, 2; nego, 1; (let go) remitto, dimitto, 3.

disclaimer, s. negatio, infitiatio, f.

disclose, v.a. patefacio, pando, detego, 3; aperio, 4; enuntio, vulgo, 1.

disclosure, s. indicium, n.

discolour, v.a. decoloro, 1.

discomfit, v.a. fundo, 3; profligo, 1.

discomfiture, s. clades, f.

discomfort, s. incommoda, n. pl.; molestiæ, f. pl.; vexatio, f.

discomfort, v.a. perturbo, agito, sollicito, 1. [*fig.* vexo, 1.

discompose, v.a. confundo, 3; perturbo;

discomposure, s. perturbatio, sollicitudo, f. [(frustrate) frustror, 1.

disconcert, v.a. conturbo, perturbo, 1;

disconnect, v.a. disjungo, sejungo, 3.

disconsolate, a. afflictus, tristis; —ly, ad. insolabiliter; triste.

discontent, v.a. displiceo, 3.

discontent, s. animus parum contentus, m.; (anger) ira, f.; (hatred) odium, n.

discontented, a. parum contentus; (disagreeable) morosus. [parum contento.

discontentedly, ad. animo iniquo, animo

discontinuation, s. intermissio, f.

discontinue, v.a. & n. intermitto; desino, desisto, 3.

discord, s. discordia, f.

discordance, s. discrepantia, dissensio, f.

discordant, a. discors; discrepans; dissonus; absonus.

discount, v.a. deduco, 3; repræsento, 1.

discourage, v.a. deterreo, 2; examino, 1; (dissuade) dissuadeo, 2; be —d, animum demitto, 3.

discouragement, s. animi demissio, f.; (dissuasion) dissuasio.

discouraging, a. adversus, incommodus.

discourse, s. sermo, m.; colloquium, n.; (written) libellus, m.

discourse, v.n. dissero, 3; sermocinor, 1; verba facio, 3.

discourteous, a. inurbanus; inhumanus; —ly, ad. inurbane; inhumaniter.

discourtesy, s. inhumanitas, f.

discover, v.a. comperio, 4; (disclose) detego, patefacio, 3; (search out) exploro, investigo, 1; (to descry) conspicor, 1.

discoverer, s. inventor; repertor, m.; inventrix, repertrix, f.; (searcher) investigator, m.

discovery, s. inventio; (searching out) investigatio, f.; (thing found out) inventum, n.; (making known) patefactio, f.

discredit, s. dedecus, n., macula, f.

discredit, v.a. fidem non habeo (alicui), 2; infamo, dehonesto, 1.

discreditable, a. inhonestus, indecorus.

discreditably, ad. inhoneste.

discreet, a. cautus, prudens; —ly, ad. caute, prudenter.

discrepancy, s. discrepantia, f.

discrepant, a. discrepans, discors.

discretion, s. prudentia. circumspectio, f.; **years of** —, ætas adulta; **at the** — **of,** arbitrio (gen.), ad arbitrium (gen.).

discretionary, a. — power, arbitrium, n.

discriminate, v.a. dijudico, 1; distinguo, 3.

discriminating, a. proprius; (intelligent) acutus, perspicax, sagax.

discrimination, s. (distinguishing) distinctio, f.; (discernment) judicium; (distinction) discrimen, n.

discursive, a. vagus.

discuss, v.a. disputo, 1; dissero, ago, 3.

discussion, s. disputatio, disceptatio, controversia, f.

disdain, v.a. dedignor, aspernor, 1; despicio, sperno, contemno, 3; fastidio, 4.

disdain, s. contemptus, m.; fastidium, n.; superbia, f.

disdainful, a. fastidiosus, superbus; —ly, ad. fastidiose, contemptim, superbe.

disease, s. morbus, m., malum, n.; (plague) pestilentia, pestis, lues, f.

diseased, a. ægrotus, æger.

disembark, v.a. & n. e navi (navibus) expono; e navi egredior (in terram), 3.

disembarkment, disembarkation, s. egressus, m.

disembarrass, v.a. solvo, exsolvo, 3; libero, exonero, 1; expedio, 4.

disembodied, (of ghosts, etc.) inanis, corporis expers.

disembody, v.a. dimitto, 3; exauctoro, 1.

disembogue, v.n. (of rivers) in mare deferri, effundi, 3.

disembowel, v.a. eviscero, 1.

disenchant, v.a. fascinatum exsolvo; *fig.* errorem demo (alicui), 3. [solvo, 3.

disencumber, v.a. exonero; laxo, 1; ex-

disencumbrance, s. liberatio, f.

disengage, v.a. solvo, exsolvo, 3; avoco, 1.

disengaged, a. (at leisure) otiosus; (not occupied) vacuus.

disengagement, s. (freeing) liberatio, f.; (leisure) otium, n. [pedio, 4.

disentangle, v.a. extrico, explico, 1; ex-

disfavour, s. invidia, f.

disfavour, v.a. improbo, 1.

disfigure, v.a. deformo, turpo, mutilo, 1.

disfigurement, s. deformatio; deformitas, fœditas, f.; (blemish) vitium, n.; labes, f. [mo, 3.

disfranchise, v.a. (alicui) civitatem adi-

disgorge, v.a. revomo, evomo, 3.

disgrace, s. (shame) infamia; ignominia, f.; dedecus, n.; (disfavour) offensa, invidia, f.
disgrace, v.a. dedecoro, dehonesto, 1.
disgraceful, a. turpis, inhonestus, ignominiosus; —ly, ad. turpiter, inhoneste, ignominiose.
disgracefulness, s. turpitudo, ignominia, f.
disguise, s. (mask) persona, f.; *fig.* dissimulatio, f.; (false appearance) species, f.; (pretence) praetextum, n.
disguise, v.a. vestem muto; *fig.* celo; dissimulo, 1; —d **as a boy,** puerili ornatu.
disguiser, s. dissimulator, m.
disgust, s. (loathing) fastidium, taedium, odium, n.
disgust, v.a. fastidium moveo, 2; **to be** —ed, piget (me rei), 2; aegre fero, 3.
disgusting, a. foedus; *fig.* odiosus.
disgustingly, ad. foede; *fig.* odiose.
dish, s. catinus, m.; (flat —) patina; (a large one) lanx, f.; (course) mensa, f.
dish, v.a. **to — up,** appono, 3.
dish-clout, s. peniculus, m.
dish-cover, s. operculum, n.
dishearten, v.a. animum frango, 3; exanimo, 1; **be** —ed, animum demitto.
dishevelled, a. passus, effusus, irreligatus.
dishonest, a. improbus, malus, perfidus, fradulentus; —ly, ad. improbe, dolo malo, fraude ac dolo.
dishonesty, s. improbitas, fraus, f.; dolus malus, m. [ignominia, f.
dishonour, s. infamia, f.; dedecus, n.;
dishonour, v.a. dehonesto; dedecoro; (a woman) stupro, 1.
dishonourable, a. inhonestus, turpis.
dishonourably, ad. inhoneste, turpiter.
dishonoured, a. inhonoratus; ignominiosus. [odium, n.
disinclination, s. aversatio, fuga, f.;
disincline, v.a. abduco, abstraho, 3; avoco, 1.
disincorporate, v.a. exauctoro, 1.
disingenuous, a. parum candidus; dolosus; —ly, ad. dolose.
disinherit, v.a. exheredo, 1.
disinter, v.a. eruo, effodio, 3.
disinterested, a. aequus, integer; —ly, ad. integre; gratuito.
disinterestedness, s. integritas, aequitas, f.
disjoin, v.a. segrego, 1; disjungo, 3.
disjointed, a. intermissus.
disjunction, s. disjunctio, f.
disk, s. discus, m., v. **disc.**
dislike, v.a. aversor, non amo, 1.
dislike, s. aversatio, f.; odium, fastidium, n.
dislocate, v.a. luxo, 1.
dislocation, s. luxatura, f.
dislodge, v.a. deturbo, 1; depello, 3.

disloyal, a. infidelis, perfidus, perfidiosus; —ly, ad. perfide, perfidiose.
disloyalty, s. infidelitas, perfidia, f.
dismal, a. tristis, miser; moestus; (dreadful) dirus; —ly, ad. misere, moeste.
dismalness, s. tristitia, f.
dismantle, v.a. diruo, 3; (of ships) exarmo, 1. [pavor, m.
dismay, s. consternatio, perturbatio, f.;
dismay, v.a. perterrefacio, 3; territo, consterno, perturbo, 1.
dismember, v.a. lacero, mutilo, 1.
dismemberment, s. mutilatio, f.
dismiss, v.a. dimitto, 3; demoveo, 2.
dismissal, s. missio, demissio, f.
dismount, v.n. ex equo desilio, 4; —, v.a. ex equo excutio, 3.
disobedience, s. contumacia, f.
disobedient, a. non obediens; contumax; —ly, ad. contra (alicujus) jussum.
disobey, v.n. non pareo (2) *or* obedio, 4; neglego, 3; detrecto, 1.
disoblige, v.a. offendo, 3.
disobliging, a. inofficiosus.
disorder, s. confusio; (disturbance of the peace) tumultus, m.; (distemper) aegrotatio; (of mind) perturbatio (animi); (licence) licentia, f.
disorder, v.a. perturbo, 1; confundo, 3.
disordered, a. turbatus; tumultuosus.
disorderly, a. inordinatus, turbatus; turbidus; incompositus; tumultuosus.
disorganization, s. dissolutio, f.
disorganize, v.a. dissolvo, 3.
disown, v.a. diffiteor, 2; infitior, 1.
disparage, v.a. obtrecto, detrecto, 1.
disparagement, s. obtrectratio, f.
disparity, s. inaequalitas, diversitas, f.
dispassionate, a. sedatus, tranquillus; —ly, ad. sedate, aequo animo.
dispel, v.a. dispello, depello, solvo, 3.
dispensation, s. (immunity) immunitas, f.; (institution) institutum, n.; (lot, fortune) sors, f.; **by divine —,** divinitus.
dispense, v.a. distribuo; (to release) solvo, remitto, 3; **to — with,** careo (abl.), 2.
dispenser, s. dispensator, m.
dispeople, v.a. vasto, 1.
disperse, v.a. spargo, dispergo, 3; dissipo, 1; (put to flight) fundo, 3; fugo, 1; —, v.n. dilabor; diffugio, 3.
dispersion, s. dissipatio, f.
dispirit, v.a. animum frango, 3; exanimo, 1. [fractus.
dispirited, a. abjectus, dismissus, animo
displace, v.a. summoveo, 2; (a person) loco moveo, 2; (transpose) transfero, 3.
displacement, s. translatio, f.
display, s. (show) ostentus, m.; *fig.* jactatio, ostentatio, f.

display, v.a. (to expose) expono; (to spread) expando, 3; *fig.* jacto, ostento, 1; (exercise) præsto, 1; exhibeo, 2.

displease, v.a. displiceo, 2.

displeasure, s. offensa; offensio; (grudge) ira, f. [oblector, 1.

disport, v.n. to — oneself, lascivio, 4;

disposable, a. in promptu.

disposal, s. arbitrium, n.; (use) usus, m.

dispose, v.a. dispono, 3; ordino; (induce) adduco, 3; (turn, direct) verto, 3; to — of, (sell) vendo, 3; (get rid of) tollo, 3.

disposed, a. inclinatus (ad); propensus (ad); pronus (ad); well- —, æquus; ill- —, malevolus, iniquus.

disposer, s. rector, moderator, m.

disposition, s. (arrangement) dispositio; (nature) natura, indoles, f.; ingenium, n.; mens, f.; animus, m.

dispossess, v.a. ejicio, detrudo, pello, 3.

dispraise, v. blame.

disproof, s. refutatio, f.

disproportion, s. inæqualitas, f.

disproportionate, a. inæqualis, impar; —ly, ad. inæqualiter, impariter.

disprove, v.a. confuto, refuto, 1; refello, redarguo, 3.

disputable, s. disputabilis; (doubtful) dubius, ambiguus.

disputant, s. disputator, m.

disputation, s. disputatio, f. [ter.

disputatious, pugnax; —ly, ad. pugnaci-

disputatiousness, s. pugnacitas, f.

dispute, s. disputatio, disceptatio, contentio; controversia, f.; (quarrel) rixa, f.; jurgium, n.

dispute, v.a. & n. disputo, 1; contendo, 3; it is —d, ambigitur.

disqualification, s. impedimentum, n.

disqualify, v.a. impedimento esse (dat.).

disquiet, v.a. inquieto, vexo, sollicito, 1.

disquiet, disquietude, s. sollicitudo, inquies, f.

disquisition, s. commentatio, f.

disregard, s. incuria, neglegentia, f.; contemptus, m.

disregard, v.a. neglego; parvi facio, 3.

disregardful, a. neglegens.

disrelish, s. fastidium, tædium, n.

disrelish, v.a. fastidio, 4.

disreputable, a. infamis.

disrepute, s. infamia, f.

disrespect, s. neglegentia, irreverentia, f.

disrespectful, a. irreverens; —ly, ad. irreverenter.

disrobe, v.a. vestitu exuo, 3.

disruption, s. diruptio, f.; *fig.* discidium, n.

dissatisfaction, s. tædium, fastidium, n.; indignatio, f.

dissatisfied, a. male (parum) contentus.

dissatisfy, v.a. non (parum) satisfacio, 3.

dissect, v.a. disseco, 1; incido, 3.

dissection, s. sectio, incisio, anatomia, f.

dissector, s. anatomicus, m.

dissemble, v.a. & n. dissimulo, 1.

dissembler, s. dissimulator, m.

dissemblingly, ad. dissimulanter.

disseminate, v.a. spargo, sero, 3; dissemino; *fig.* divulgo, 1.

dissension, s. dissensio, f.; dissidium, n.

dissent, v.n. dissentio, 4; dissideo, 2.

dissent, s. dissensio, f. [lus, m.

dissertation, s. commentatio, f.; libel-

disservice, s. damnum, malum, n.

dissever, v.fi. separo, 1; sejungo, 3.

dissimilar, a. dissimilis, dispar.

dissimilarity, s. dissimilitudo, f.

dissimulation, s. dissimulatio, f.

dissipate, v.a. & n. dissipo; dissipor, 1.

dissipation, s. dissipatio, f.; (licentiousness) libido, luxuria, f.

dissipated, a. perditus, dissolutus.

dissoluble, dissolvable, a. dissolubilis.

dissolute, a. dissolutus, corruptus, immoderatus; —ly, ad. dissolute, immoderate, prodige.

dissoluteness, s. mores dissoluti, m. pl.

dissolution, s. dissolutio; mors, f.

dissolve, v.a. dissolvo; (to melt) liquefacio, 3; liquo, 1; (break up) dirimo, 3; —, v.n. liquesco, 3; (to break up) dissolvor, 3.

dissonant, a. dissonus, absonus.

dissuade, v.a. dissuadeo, 2; abduco, 3.

dissuasion, s. dissuasio, f.

distaff, s. colus, f.

distance, s. distantia, f.; intervallum, (space) spatium, n.; (remoteness) longinquitas, f.; at a —, procul, longe.

distance, v.a. supero, 1; præcurro, 3.

distant, a. distans, disjunctus, longinquus, remotus, amotus; *fig.* frigidus; —ly, ad. procul; *fig.* frigide.

distaste, s. fastidium, n.

distasteful, a. (of taste) tæter; *fig.* odiosus, molestus, gravis.

distemper, s. morbus, m.; (paint) pigmentum, n.

distemper, v.a. perturbo; (whitewash) dealbo, 1.

distend, v.a. distendo, 3.

distended, a. tumidus, tumefactus.

distention, s. distentio, f.; distentus, m.; (swelling) tumor, m.

distich, s. distichon, n.

distil, v.n. & n. destillo, destillo; exsudo, 1.

distillation, s. destillatio, f.; stillicidium, n.; (moisture) umor, m.; gutta, f.

distinct, a. (different) diversus, alius; (clear) clarus; distinctus; —ly, ad. clare, distincte.

distinction, s. distinctio, f.; (difference) differentia, f.; discrimen, n.

distinctive, a. proprius, f.

distinctness, s. claritas.

distinguish, v.a. distinguo, discerno, 3; **to — oneself,** eniteo, 2; præcello, 3.

distinguishable, a. qui (quæ, quod) secerni, internosci potest.

distinguished, a. insignis; clarus, præclarus, celeber, notus, eximius.

distort, v.a. distorqueo; detorqueo, 2; depravo, 1.

distortion, s. distortio, depravatio, f.

distract, v.a. distraho, 3; (to divert) avoco; (to madden) furio, 1.

distracted, a. —**ly,** ad. amens, demens, mente alienatus, vesanus, vecors.

distraction, s. dementia, f.; amentia, f.

distrain, v.a. pigneror, 1; bona vendo, 3.

distrainer, s. pignerator, m.

distraint, s. bonorum venditio.

distress, s. dolor, m.; miseria, tristitia, f.; angustiæ, f. pl.; (poverty) inopia, f.

distress, v.a. affligo, ango, 3.

distressing, a. molestus, gravis.

distribute, v.a. distribuo, divido, 3; dispertio, 4.

distributer, s. divisor, m.

distribution, s. distributio, f.

distributive, a. (gr.) distributivus.

district, s. regio, f.

distrust, s. diffidentia, f.

distrust, v.a. diffido, 3; fidem non habeo, 2.

distrustful, a. diffidens, suspicax, suspiciosus; —**ly,** ad. diffidenter.

disturb, v.a. perturbo; sollicito, inquieto, 1; (break up) dirimo, 3.

disturbance, s. perturbatio; confusio, f.; tumultus, m.; seditio, f.

disturber, s. turbator; concitator, m.

disunion, s. disjunctio; *fig.* dissensio, f.; dissidium, n.

disunite, v.a. sejungo; *fig.* dirimo, 3; —, v.n. separor, 1.

disuse, s. desuetudo, f.

disuse, v.a. desuesco, 3.

ditch, s. fossa, f.

dittany, s. dictamnus, f.; dictamnum, n.

ditty, s. canticum, n.

diuretic, a. diureticus.

diurnal, a. diurnus; quotidianus.

divan, s. (sofa) lectulus, m.

dive, v.n. mergor, 3; *fig.* investigo, exploro, penetro, 1.

diver, s. urinator; (bird) mergus, m.

diverge, v.n. deflecto, 3; declino, 1.

divergence, s. declinatio; *fig.* discrepantia, f.

divergent, a. diversus; (contrary) contrarius.

divers, diverse, a. alius, varius, diversus.

diversely, ad. diverse.

diversification, s. variatio, f.; vices, f. pl.

diversify, v.a. vario, 1; distinguo, 3.

diversion, s. (turning aside) derivatio; *fig.* oblectatio, f.; oblectamentum, n.

diversity, s. diversitas, varietas, f.

divert, v.a. diverto, 3; *fig.* oblecto, 1; (call away) avoco, 1.

divertisement, s. oblectatio, f.

divest, v.a. exuo, 3; nudo, spolio, 1.

divide, v.a. divido, 3; partior, 4; distribuo, 3; —, v.n. discedo; (to gape open) dehisco, 3.

divider, s. divisor, m.

divination, s. divinatio, vaticinatio, f.

divine, a. divinus; cælestis; —**ly,** ad. divine.

divine, s. theologus, m.   [divine.

divine, v.a. auguror, vaticinor, 1; divino, 1; (to guess) conjicio, 3; conjecto, 1.

diviner, s. haruspex, vatidicus, m.; vates, augur, c.

divinity, s. divinitas; numen, n.; (god) deus, m.; (theology) theologia, f.

divisible, a. dividuus, divisibilis.

division, s. divisio, distributio, partitio; pars; *fig.* seditio, discordia, f.; dissidium, n.

divorce, s. divortium, discidium, n.

divorce, v.a. repudio, 1; dimitto, 3.

divulge, v.a. vulgo, divulgo, 1; palam facio, in medium profero, 3.

dizziness, s. vertigo, f.

dizzy, a. vertiginosus; (precipitous) præceps.

do, v.a. ago, facio, efficio, 3; **to — away with,** tollo, perdo, 3; **to — for,** conficio, 3; **to — up,** (bind) constringo, 3; **what am I to — with?** quid faciam? (abl., dat.); v.n. (be suitable) convenio, 4.

docile, a. docilis; tractabilis.

docility, s. docilitas, f.; facile ingenium, n.

dock, s. navale, n.; (law) cancelli, m. pl.

dock, v.a. (ships) subduco, 3; (to curtail) curto, 1.

docket, s. index, m.

dockyard, s. navalia, n. pl.

doctor, s. (teacher) doctor, m.; (physician) medicus, m.

doctor, v.a. curo, medicor, 1.

doctrine, s. doctrina, f.

document, s. litteræ, f. pl.

dodge, v.n. tergiversor, 1; —, v.a. eludo, 3.

dodge, s. dolus, m.; fraus, f.; tricæ, f. pl.

dodger, s. veterator, m.

doe, s. cerva, f.

doer, s. actor; effector, m.; auctor, c.

dog, s. canis, c.; *fig.* scelus, n.

dog, v.a. indago, 1.

dog-collar, s. mellum, n.
dog-day, s. dies canicularis, m.   [ter.
dogged, a. pervicax; —ly, ad. pervicaci-
doggedness, s. pervicacia, f.
doggerel, s. versus inculti, m. pl.
doggish, a. caninus.
dog-grass, s. triticum caninum, n.
dog-kennel, s. (canis) cubile, n.
dogma, s. dogma, placitum, præceptum, n.
dogmatical, a. imperiosus; (obstinate)
  pertinax; —ly, imperiose.
dogmatism, s. (obstinacy) pertinacia, f.
dogmatist, s. dogmatistes, m.
dog-rose, s. cynosbatos, f.
dog-star, s. canicula, f.; Sirius, m.
dogtooth violet, s. erythronium (mod.
  hort.).
dogwood, s. cornus, f.
doily, s. (table-napkin) mappa, f.
doing, s. factum, facinus, n.
dole, v.a. to — out, metior, 4.
dole, s. donatio, f.; congiarium, n.; diurnus victus, m.
doleful, a. miser, tristis, flebilis, lugubris,
  mœstus; —ly, ad. mœste, misere.
dolefulness, s. miseria, mœstitia, f.;
  mœror, m.
doll, s. pupa, f.
dolphin, s. delphinus, delphin, m.
dolt, s. caudex, stipes, m.
doltish, a. stultus, stolidus.
domain, s. ager, m.
dome, s. tholus, fornix, m.
domestic, a. domesticus, familiaris; intestinus; (private) privatus.
domestic, s. famulus, m.; famula, f.
domesticate, v.a. assuefacio; (tame)
  mansuefacio, 3.
domicile, s. domicilium, n.; domus, f.
dominant, a. prævalens.
domination, s. dominatio, f.
domineer, v.n. dominor, 1; imperito, 1.
domineering, a. arrogans, imperiosus.
dominion, s. imperium, n.; potestas, f.;
  dicio, f.; regnum, n.
donation, s. donum, munus, n.; stips, f.
donkey, s. asinus, asellus, m.
donor, s. donator, dator, m.; donatrix, f.
doom, s. fatum, exitium; judicium, n.
doom, v.a. damno, condemno, 1; — to,
  destino (dat.).
door, s. janua, foris, f.; ostium n.;
  folding —, valvæ, f. pl.   [custos, c.
doorkeeper, s. janitor, m.; janitrix, f.;
door-post, s. postis, m.
doorway, s. janua, f.; ostium, n.
Doric, a. Doricus.   [latens.
dormant, a. (lying idle) reses; (hidden)
dormitory, s. cubiculum, dormitorium, n.
dormouse, s. glis, m.

dorsal, a. dorsualis.
dose, s. portio, f.
dose, v.a. medicamenta do, 1.
dot, s. punctum, n.
dot, v.a. punctum impono, 3.
dotage, s. deliratio, f.; (old age) senium,
  n.; senectus, f.
dotard, s. senex delirus, m.
dote, v.n. deliro, 1; to — upon, depereo,
  4; deamo, 1.
dotingly, ad. insane.
double, a. duplex; (of pairs) geminus;
  (as much again) duplus; fig. fallax,
  ambiguus.
double, s. duplum, n.; fig. fallacia, f.
double, v.a. duplico, 1; (a cape) prætervehor, 3; —, v.n. duplicor; fig. tergiversor, 1.
double-dealer, s. homo duplex, m.
double-dealing, s. fraus, fallacia, f.;
  dolus, m.
double-tongued, a. bilinguis.
doubly, ad. dupliciter; bis.
doubt, s. dubitatio, f.; scrupulus, m.;
  there is no —, non est dubium.
doubt, v.a. dubito, suspicor; (distrust)
  diffido, 1; —, hæsito, dubito.
doubtful, a. (of persons) dubius; (of
  things) incertus; ambiguus; anceps;
  —ly, ad. (of persons) dubie; (of things)
  ambigue.
doubtless, a. sine dubio, haud dubie.
douceur, s. munusculum, n.
dough, s. farina ex aqua subacta, f.
doughty, a. strenuus, armipotens.
douse, v.a. mergo, immergo, 3; —, v.n.
  immergor, 3.
dove, s. columbus, m.; columba, f.
dove-coloured, a. columbinus.
dove-cot, s. columbarium, n.   [cula, f.
dove-tail, s. (term in carpentry) securi-
dove-tailed, a. securiculatus.
dowdy, a. squalidus, f.
dower, v. dowry.
dower, v.a. doto, 1.
dowerless, a. indotatus.
down, s. pluma; (of hair) lanugo, f.; (of
  plants) pappus, m.   [humi.
down, ad. deorsum; (on the ground)
down, pr. de; — to, usque ad; up and
  —, sursum deorsum.
down, a. declivis; (sad) tristis.
downcast, a. (of the eyes or head) dejectus, demissus; fig. afflictus.
downfall, s. occasus, m.; ruina, f.;
  exitium, n.
downhill, a. declivis.
downright, a. directus, sincerus; merus.
downright, ad. sincere; (positively) prorsus; (candid) candidus; plane.
downward, a. declivis; pronus.

downwards, ad. deorsum. [sus.
downy, a. plumosus; plumeus; lanugino-
dowry, s. dos, f.
doze, v.n. dormito; (with mouth wide
open) oscito, 1.
dozen, s. duodecim, duodeni, a.
drab, a. cinereus; pullus.
drachm, s. drachma, f.
draft, v. **draught.**
drag, s. (harrow) rastrum, n.; (hook)
harpago, m.; (break) sufflamen, n.;
(sledge) traha, trahea, f.
drag, v.a. traho; (seize) rapio, 3; —, v.n.
(on the ground) trahor, 3.
draggle, v.a. & n. traho, trahor, 1.
draggled, a. squalidus.
drag-net, s. tragula, f.; everriculum, n.
dragoman, s. interpres, c.
dragon, s. draco; anguis, serpens, m.
dragon plant, s. dracæna (mod. hort.).
drain, s. cloaca; fossa, f.
drain, v.a. sicco; (to drink off) exhaurio,
4; ebibo, 3; epoto, exsicco, 1.
drake, s. (mas) anas, m.
dram, s. (in weight) drachma, f.; (drinking) haustus, m.
drama, s. drama, n.; fabula, f.
dramatic, a. dramaticus, scænicus; **—ally,**
ad. scænice.
dramatist, s. poeta scænicus, m. [pono, 3.
dramatize, v.a. fabulam ad scænam com-
drape, v.a. induo, 3; amicio, 4; velo, 1.
drapery, s. (cloth) vestis, f.
draught, s. (of drink) haustus, m.; (first
copy) exemplar, n.; (pull) tractus; (of
a net) jactus, m.; (of air) aura, f.
draughts, s. lusus duodecim scrip-
torum, m.
draught-horse, s. equus rædarius, m.
draughtsman, s. (piece in the game) calculus, m.
draw, v.a. traho; duco, 3; (a picture, etc.)
delineo, 1; describo, 3; (the sword)
stringo, destringo; (teeth) extraho, 3;
(water) haurio, 4; **to — along,** per-
traho, 3; **to — aside,** abduco, seduco,
3; **to — away,** averto, distraho, 3;
to — back, (v.a.) retraho; (v.n.) pedem
refero, cedo; *fig.* recedo, 3; **to — in,**
fig. illicio, 3; **to — near,** v.n. appropinquo; insto, 1; **to — off,** v.a. detraho; abduco; (wine) promo; (v.n.)
cedo, 3; **to — on,** v.a. (clothes, etc.)
induco, 3; (v.n.) appropinquo, f.; **to
— out,** extraho; (sword, etc.) educo;
fig. elicio, 3; **to — over,** induco, 3;
fig. (on the other side) concilio, 1; corrumpo, 3; sollicito, 1; **to — to,** v.n.
(of ships) appeto, 3; **to — together,**
contraho, 3; **to — up,** subduco;
scribo; (troops) instruo, constituo, 3.

drawback, s. impedimentum; detrimentum; incommodum, n.; mora, f.; retardatio, f.
drawer, s. (sliding box) loculus, m.;
(chest) armarium, n.
drawers, s. subligaculum, subligar, n.
drawing, s. (art) pictura linearis; (picture) tabula, imago, f.
drawing-room, s. exedra, f.
drawl, v.a. decanto, tractim pronuntio, 1.
dray, s. plaustrum, plostellum, n.
drayman, s. plaustrarius, m.
dread, s. terror, pavor, m.; formido, f.
dread, a. terribilis, v. **dreadful.**
dread, v.a. timeo, 2; metuo, expavesco,
3; formido, 1.
dreadful, a. terribilis, horribilis; dirus;
(violent) atrox; **—ly,** ad. fœde, atrociter.
dreadless, a. impavidus.
dream, s. somnium, n.; quies, f.
dream, v.a. & n. somnio; *fig.* dormito, 1.
dreamer, s. somniator.
dreamy, a. somniculosus.
drearily, ad. triste.
dreariness, s. solitudo, vastitas; (sadness)
tristitia, f. [dus; tristis.
dreary, a. vastus, solus, incultus; horri-
dredge, s. everriculum, n.
dregs, s. fæx; sentina, f.
drench, v.n. madefacio, 3; irrigo, 1.
dress, s. habitus, vestitus, m.; vestis, f.;
ornatus, m.
dress, v.a. vestio, 4; induo, 3; (ex)orno;
(wounds) curo; (to bind up) obligo, 1;
(to cook) coquo, 3.
dresser, s. mensa culinaria, f.
dressing, s. ornatus, m.; (of food) coctura; (wounds, etc.) curatio, f.; (poultice) fomentum, n.
dribble, v.n. stillo, 1.
driblet, s. stilla; gutta; summula, f.
drift, s. propositum, n.; (purpose) consilium; (of sand) cumulus, m.; (of
snow) vis, f. [fluito, 1.
drift, v.a. defero, 3; —, v.n. feror, 3;
drill, v.a. terebro, perforo, 1; (troops)
exerceo, 2; (to discipline) instituo, 3.
drill, s. terebra; (of troops) exercitatio, f.
drilling, s. terebratio; (mil.) exercitatio, f.
drink, v.a. & n. bibo, 3; poto, 1; **to —
in,** absorbeo, 2; bibo, 3; **to — off,**
out, *or* up, ebibo, 3; haurio, 4; epoto, 1;
to — to, propino, 1.
drink, s. potus, m.; potio, f.
drinkable, a. potabilis.
drinker, s. potor, potator, m.
drinking, a. (given to drink) bibulus.
drinking, s. (act) potatio; (drunkenness)
ebrietas, f.; **-bout,** s. compotatio, f.;
—-cup, s. poculum, n.

drip, v.n. stillo; roro, mano, 1.
drip, s. stillicidium, n.
dripping-pan, s. sartago, f.
drive, v.a. ago; pello; impello; (to force) compello, cogo, 3; (a trade) exerceo, 2; (horses, carriages) ago, 3; —, v.n. (in a carriage) vehor; (to be carried along) defero, 3; **to — about,** jacto; (a carriage) verso, 1; **to — along,** v. **to — on; to — away,** abigo; depello, 3; fugo, 1; (to dislodge) dejicio, 3; **to — back,** repello, 3; **to — in(to),** (a nail, etc.) infigo; (sheep, etc.) cogo; *fig.* compello, 3; **to — off,** abigo; (v.n.) avehor, 3; **to — on,** impello; **to — out,** expello, 3; **— past,** prætervehor, 3.
drive, s. (riding in a carriage) vectio, f.
drivel, s. saliva, f.; *fig.* ineptiæ, f. pl.
driveller, s. *fig.* homo ineptus, m.
driver, s. agitator; agaso, m.; (of carriages) auriga, c.
drizzle, v.n. roro, irroro, 1.
drizzle, s. pluvia, f.
droll, a. facetus, jocosus; ridiculus.
droll, s. scurra, sannio; (comic actor) mimus, m.
drollery, s. facetiæ, f. pl.; ludus, jocus, m.
dromedary, s. camelus dromas, m.
drone, s. fucus; (person) deses; (noise) bombus, m.
drone, v.n. murmuro, susurro.
droop, v.n. langueo, 2; marcesco; tabesco, 3; —, v.a. demitto, 3.
drooping, s. languor, m.
droopingly, ad. languide.
drop, s. gutta, stilla, f.; v. **ear-ring; (a little bit) paululum, n.; by —s,** guttatim.
drop, v.a. stillo, 1; (to let slip) omitto, 3; (pour out) effundo; (dismiss) dimitto, 3; —, v.n. stillo, 1; (to fall *or* glide down) delabor, 3.
dropping, s. stillicidium, n.
dropping, a. caducus; stillaticius.
drop-scene, s. siparium, n.
dropsical, a. hydropicus.
dropsy, s. hydrops, m.
dross, s. scoria; spurcitia, f.; ˈaqua intercus, f.; *fig.* quisquiliæ, f. pl.; fæx, f.
drought, s. siccitas, ariditas; (thirst) sitis, f.   [sitiens.
droughty, a. siccus, aridus; (of persons)
drove, s. grex, m.
drover, s. pecuarius, armentarius, m.
drown, v.a. immergo, demergo; *fig.* opprimo, 3; **his voice was —ed by shouts,** vox præ clamoribus audiri non potuit.
drowsily, ad. somniculose.
drowsiness, s. somni cupiditas; *fig.* ignavia, f.; veternus, m.

drowsy, a somniculosus; (causing sleep) soporifer, somnifer; *fig.* ignavus.
drub, v.a. verbero, 1.
drubbing, s. verberatio, f.
drudge, v.n. me exerceo, 2; laboro, 1.
drudge, s. (a slave) mediastinus; *fig.* homo clitellarius, m.
drudgery, s. opera servilis, f.
drug, s. medicamentum, medicamen, n.; medicina, f.
drug, v.a. medico, 1.
druggist, s. medicamentarius, m.
Druids, s. pl. Druidæ, m. pl.
drum, s. tympanum, n.
drummer, s. tympanista, m.
drunk, a. ebrius, potus.
drunkard, s. (use adj.) temulentus, ebriosus, vinolentus, m.
drunken, v. **drunk.**
drunkenness, s. ebrietas, temulentia, f.
dry, a. aridus, siccus; (thirsty) siticulosus; *fig.* jejunus; insulsus; (reserved) taciturnus.
dry, v.a. sicco, desicco, 1; arefacio, 3; (in the sun) insolo, 1; —, v.n. aresco, 3.
Dryad, s. Dryas, f.   [facete.
dryly, ad. sicce; *fig.* insulse; (of jokes)
dryness, s. ariditas, siccitas, f.
dry-nurse, s. nutrix assa, f.
dry-shod, a. siccis pedibus.
dub, v.a. creo; (name) nomino, 1.
dubious, a. dubius; **—ly,** ad. dubie.
ducal, a. ducalis.
ducat, s. ducatus, m.
duchess, s. ducissa, f.
duchy, s. ducatus, m.
duck, s. anas, f.; *fig.* v. **darling.**
duck, v.a. mergo, submergo, demergo, 3.
duckling, s. anaticula, f.
ductile, a. ductilis, lentus, flexilis.
dudgeon, s. ira, indignatio, f.   [aptus.
due, a. debitus; justus; meritus; idoneus,
due, ad. recta (via).
due, s. debitum; jus; (tax) vectigal, n.
duel, s. singulare certamen, n.
duet, s. bicinium, n.
dug, s. uber, n.; papilla, f.
duke, s. dux, m.
dukedom, s. ducatus, m.
dull, a. hebes; obtunsus; surdus; (cloudy) caliginosus; nebulosus; *fig.* tardus; languidus; tristis; segnis; insulsus; stupidus.   [facio, 3.
dull, v.a. hebeto, 1; obtundo; stupe-
dullard, s. homo brutus, bardus, m.
dully, ad. languide; insulse; frigide; (of sounds) surde; (dimly) indistincte.
dulness, s. hebetatio; stupiditas; tarditas; *fig.* insulsitas, f.; languor, m.
duly, ad. rite; recte.
dumb, a. mutus; **to be —,** obmutesco, 3.

dumbfound, v.a. obstupefacio, 3.
dumb-show, s. (mutus) gestus, m.
dummy, s. *fig.* muta persona, f.
dumpy, a. brevis atque obesus.
dun, a. fuscus, furvus, subniger.
dun, s. flagitator, m.
dun, v.a. flagito; efflagito, 1.
dunce, s. homo stupidus, stipes, m.
dun-fly, s. tabanus, m. [merda, f.
dung, s. stercus, n.; fimus, m.; (of birds)
dung, v.a. stercoro, 1.
dungeon, s. carcer, m.; ergastulum, n.
dung-hill, sterquilinium, fimetum, n.
dupe, s. homo credulus, m.; victima, f.
dupe, v.a. decipio, 3; ludifico, 1; fallo, 3.
duplicate, a. duplex. [graphum, n.
duplicate, s. exemplum, exemplar, apo-
duplicity, s. fraus; fallacia, f.
durability, a. stabilitas, f. [constans.
durable, a. stabilis; durabilis; solidus;
durably, ad. stabiliter, solide.
durance, s. custodia, f.; carcer, m.
duration, s. spatium (temporis), n.; diuturnitas, f.
during, pr. per; inter.
dusk, s. crepusculum, n.
duskiness, s. color suffuscus, m.
dusky, a. obscurus, tenebrosus; fuscus.
dust, s. pulvis, m.; (of filing *or* sawing)
scobis, f.
dust, v.a. detergeo, 2.
duster, s. peniculus, m.
dustman, s. scoparius, m.
dusty, a. pulverulentus, pulvereus.
Dutchman's pipe, s. aristolochia (mod.
hort.).
dutiful, a. (affectionate) pius; officiosus,
obediens, obsequens; **—ly,** ad. pie;
officiose; obedienter.
dutifulness, s. pietas; obedientia, f.
duty, s. officium; munus; (tax) vectigal,
n.; (mil.) statio, f.; **it is a man's —
to . . .** viri est (infin.).
dwarf, s. nanus, pumilio, m.
dwarf, v.a. (diminish) imminuo, 3; (overtop) superemineo, 2.
dwarfish, a. pumilus, exiguus.
dwell, v.n. habito, 1; incolo, 3; *fig.*
(upon) commoror, 1.
dweller, s. incola, c.; habitator, m.
dwelling-place, s. domicilium, n.; sedes,
domus, habitatio, f.
dwindle, v.n. decresco, imminuor, 3.
dye, v.a. tingo, inficio, imbuo, 3; coloro, 3.
dye, s. tinctura, f.; color, m.
dyeing, s. tinctura, f.
dyer, s. infector, m.
dying, a. moriens, moribundus; (last) extremus, ultimus. [trix, f.
dynasty, s. imperium, n.; domus regna-
dysentery, s. dysenteria, f.

Each, a. (every) quisque; (every one)
unusquisque; **— other,** alter alterum,
invicem; **— of two,** uterque; **one —,**
singuli.
eager, a. acer, studiosus, cupidus, avidus;
(fierce) ferox; (earnest) vehemens;
—ly, ad. acriter; avide, cupide.
eagerness, s. aviditas, cupiditas; *fig.*
alacritas, f.; impetus, m.; studium, n.
eagle, s. aquila, f. (also as standard).
ear, s. auris; (of a pot, etc.) auricula,
ansa; (of corn) spica, f.; (hearing)
aures, f. pl.
earache, s. aurium dolor, m.
earl, s. comes, m.
earldom, s. comitatus, m.
ear-lap, s. auricula, f.
earliness, s. maturitas, f.
early, a. (in the morning) matutinus; (of
early date) antiquus; (beginning) novus; (forward) maturus, præmaturus,
præcox.
early, ad. (in the morning) mane; (untimely) mature; (too —) præmature;
(quickly, soon) cito.
earn, v.a. lucror, 1; mereo, 2; consequor,
quæro, 3.
earnest, a. intentus; impensus; vehemens; ardens; (important) gravis; (serious) serius; **—ly,** ad. acriter; impense,
intente.
earnest, s. **in —,** serio; bona fide; **—
-money,** s. arrha, f.; arrhabo, m.
earnestness, s. assiduitas, f.; ardor, m.;
gravitas, f.
ear-prick, s. auriscalpium, n.
ear-ring, s. inaures, f. pl.
ear-shot, s. unde quis exaudiri potest.
earth, s. terra, tellus, f.; orbis, m.; (of
a fox) specus, m. f. *or* n.; (ground)
solum, n.; humus, f.
earth, v.a. defodio; (to hide) condo, 3.
earth-born, a. terrigenus; *fig.* terrenus,
mortalis; (low) vilis.
earthen, a. fictilis; terrenus.
earthenware, s. fictilia, n. pl.
earthly, a. terrenus; terrestris; humanus.
earthquake, s. terræ motus, m.
earth-work, s. agger, m.
earthy, a. terrosus; *fig.* terrenus.
ease, s. otium, n.; quies, requies, f.; *fig.*
(grace) lepor, m.; facilitas; (pleasure)
voluptas, f.; **with —,** (use abl.) facile.
ease, v.a. levo, exonero, laxo, 1.
easily, ad. facile.
east, a. orientalis.
east, s. oriens; ortus, m.
easter, s. pascha, f.
easterly, eastern, a. orientalis; ad orientem vergens.

eastward, a. orientem versus.

east wind, s. eurus, m.

easy, a. facilis; solutus; expeditus; (at leisure) otiosus; quietus; (graceful) lepidus; (of temper) facilis.

eat, v.a. & n. edo, comedo, vescor; *fig.* rodo, 3; **to — away,** peredo; *fig.* corrodo, 3; **to — up,** comedo, 3; voro, devoro, 1.

eatable, a. esculentus, edulis.

eatables, s. pl. edulia, n. pl.

eater, s. qui edit; **a great —,** homo edax, m.

eating, s. esus, m.; **— -house,** s. popina, f.

eaves, s. suggrunda, n. pl.

eaves-drop, v.n. subausculto, 1.

eaves-dropper, s. auceps, m.

ebb, s. recessus, m.

ebb, v.n. recedo; *fig.* decresco, 3.

ebony, s. (tree) hebenus, f.

ebullition, s. æstus, impetus, m.

eccentric, a. insanus.

eccentricity, s. insania, f.

ecclesiastic(al), a. & s. ecclesiasticus.

echo, s. imago, echo; resonantia, f.

echo, v.a. repercutio, 3; resono, 1; —, v.n. resulto 1; (re—, be loud) sono, resono, persono, 1.

eclipse, s. defectus, m.; defectio, f.

eclipse, v.a. obscuro, obumbro, 4; **be —d,** deficio, 3.

eclogue, s. ecloga, f.

ecod, i. mehercle!

economic(al), a. œconomicus; (sparing) parcus; **—ly,** ad. parce.

economize, v.a. & n. parco, 3. [simonia, f.

economy, s. œconomia; (stinginess) parcecstasy, s. ecstasis, insania, f.; furor, m.

ecstatic, a. furibundus, lymphatus.

eddy, s. vortex, m.

eddy, v.n. circumferri.

edelweiss, s. leontopodium (mod. hort.).

edge, s. (brink) margo, c.; (of a knife, etc.) acies; (of a forest, etc.) ora, f.; lip, labrum, n.

edge, v.a. (to sharpen) acuo; (to border) prætexo, 3; *fig.* exacerbo, 1.

edged, a. acutus.

edging, s. limbus, m.

edible, a. esculentus, edulis.

edict, s. edictum, decretum, n.

edification, s. *fig.* confirmatio, f.

edifice, s. ædificium, n.

edify, v.a. *fig.* confirmo, 1; (exhort) hortor.

edit, v.a. edo, 3.

edition, s. editio, f.

editor, s. editor, m.

educate, v.a. educo, 1; erudio, 4.

education, s. educatio; eruditio; disciplina, f.

educational, a. scholasticus.

educator, s. præceptor, magister, m.

educe, v.a. elicio, 3.

eel, s. anguilla, f.

eerie, nidus.

efface, v.a. deleo, 2; exstinguo, 3; oblittero, 1.

effect, s. vis, f.; effectus, m.; **in —,** revera; etenim; **to take —,** bene succedere, 3; efficax, esse; **have —,** (avail) proficio, 3; (help forward) promoveo, 2.

effect, v.a. efficio, exequor, 3.

effective, a. efficax; potens.

effects, s. pl. bona, n. pl.

effectual, a. efficax, valens, **potens; —ly,** ad. efficaciter, potenter.

effeminacy, s. mollitia, f.

effeminate, a. effeminatus, mollis, muliebris; **ly,** ad. effeminate; muliebriter.

effervesce, v. n. effervesco, 3.

effervescence, s. fervor, m.

effete, a. effetus.

efficacious, a. efficax; **—ly,** ad. efficaciter.

efficacy, efficiency, s. efficacitas, vis, f.

efficient, a. efficiens; efficax; **—ly,** ad. efficaciter.

effigy, s. imago, effigies, f.

effluvium, s. halitus, m.   [m.

effort, s. conatus, nisus, impetus, labor,

effrontery, s. audacia, impudentia, f.

effulgence, s. fulgor, splendor, m.

effulgent, a. fulgidus.

effusion, s. effusio; (of blood) cædes, f.

eft, s. lacerta, f.

egg, s. ovum, n.; **to lay —s,** ova parere, 3.

egg on, v.a. impello, incendo, 3; excito, 1.

egg-shell, s. ovi putamen, n.; ovi testa, f.

eglantine, s. rosa canina, f.

egotism, s. sui jactantia, f.

egregious, a. egregius, insignis; **—ly,** ad. egregie; valde.

egress, s. egressus, exitus, m.

eight, a. octo; **— times,** octies; **— each,** octoni.

eighteen, a. duodeviginti.

eighteenth, a. duodevicesimus.

eightfold, a. octuplus.

eighth, a. octavus; **—,** s. octava pars, f.

eight hundred, a. octingenti.

eight hundredth, octingentesimus.

eightieth, a. octogesimus.

eightly, ad. octavum.

eighty, a. octoginta.

either, pn. alteruter; uter; alter; **— of two,** utervis, uterlibet; **not either,** neuter.

either, c. **either . . . or,** aut . . . aut: vel . . . vel.

ejaculate, v.n. clamo, 1.

ejaculation, s. vox, f.
eject, v.a. ejicio; expello, 3.
ejection, ejectment, s. ejectio; (law) dejectio.
eke, v.a. **to — out,** suppleo, 2; (livelihood) colligo, 3.
elaborate, v.a. elaboro, evigilo, 1.
elaborate, a. elaboratus; accuratus; **—ly,** ad. accurate.
elaboration, s. nimia diligentia, f.
elapse, v.n. prætereo, 4; labor, 3.
elastic, a. lentus.
elasticity, s. lentitia, f.
elate, a. elatus, inflatus.
elate, v.a. inflo, 1; effero, 3; **be —d,** intumesco, 3.
elation, s. superbia, f.; animus elatus, m.
elbow, s. cubitum, n.; ulna, f.
elbow-room, s. *fig.* spatium, n.
eld, s. senectus, f.; senium, n.
elder, a. major natu; (in date) prior.
elder, s. (tree) sambucus. f.; **— -berry,** s. sambucum, n.
elderly, a. ætate provectior.
eldest, a. maximus natu; antiquissimus.
elect, v.a. eligo, 3; creo.
elect, a. electus; designatus.
election, s. electio, f., delectus, m.; (political) comitia, n. pl.
electioneering, s. petitio, ambitio, prensatio, f.; **—,** a. candidatorius.
elector, s. suffragator, m.
electoral, a. suffragatorius.
electrify, v.a. *fig.* percello, 3.
electuary, s. ecligma, n.
elegance, s. elegantia, f.; nitor, m.
elegant, a. elegans; nitidus; lautus; concinnus; **—ly,** ad. eleganter, nitide, laute.
elegiac, a. elegiacus; (elegiac verses) elegi, m. pl.
elegy, s. elegia, f.; elegi, m. pl.
element, s. elementum, n.; **—s,** pl. principia rerum; *fig.* rudimenta, n. pl.
elemental, elementary, a. simplex, puerilis, primus.
elephant, s. elephantus, elephas, m.
elevate, v.a. levo, 1; effero, attollo, 3; *fig.* inflo, 1.
elevation, s. elatio; (loftiness) altitudo, f.; (rising ground) locus superior, m.
eleven, a. undecim; **— times,** undecies.
eleventh, a. undecimus.
elf, s. nympha, f.; Dryas, f.
elfin, a. (enchanted) incantatus, cantatus.
elicit, v.a. elicio, 3; evoco, 1.
eligible, a. dignus.
eliminate, v.a. amoveo, **2.**
elision, s. elisio, f.
elixir, s. potio, f.
elk, s. alces, 1.

ell, s. ulna, f.; cubitum, n.
ellipse, ellipsis, s. detractio, ellipsis, f.
elliptical, a. (cut short) præcisus; **—ly,** ad. præcise.
elm, s. ulmus, f.
elocution, s. elocutio, f.
elogy, s. carmen, n.
elongate, v.a. produco, 3.
elope, v.n. (domo) clam fugio, aufugio, 4.
elopement, s. fuga clandestina, f.
eloquence, s. eloquentia, facundia, f.; eloquium, n.
eloquent, a. eloquens, disertus, facundus; **—ly,** ad. diserte, eloquenter.
else, a. alius; **no one —,** nemo alius; nemo alter.
else, ad. præterea; (otherwise) aliter; (if not) si non.
elsewhere, ad. alibi.
elucidate, v.a. illustro, explico, 1.
elucidation, s. explicatio, f.
elude, v.a. eludo, effugio, 3; frustror, 1; evito, 1.   [campi, m. pl.
Elysian, a. Elysius; **— fields,** s. pl. Elysii
emaciate, v.a. emacio, macero, 1.
emaciated, a. macer, macilentus.
emaciation, s. macies; tabes, f.
emanate, v.n. emano, 1; orior, 4.
emanation, s. emanatio, f.
emancipate, v.a. emancipo, 1; manumitto, 3; *fig.* libero, 1.
emancipation, s. (of a slave) manumissio; emancipatio (of a son); *fig.* liberatio, f.
emasculate, v.a. castro, exseco; *fig.* enervo, 1.
embalm, v.a. condio, pollingo, 3.
embalmer, s. pollinctor, m.
embank, v.a. exstruo, 3.
embankment, s. agger, m.; moles, f.
embark, v.a. in navem impono, 3; **—,** v.n. in navem conscendo, 3.
embarkation, s. (in navem) conscensio, f.
embarrass, v.a. impedio, 4; implico; *fig.* perturbo, 1.
embarrassment, s. implicatio, f.; angustiæ, f. pl.; scrupulus, m.; perturbatio, f.; (hindrance) impedimentum, n.; mora, f.
embassy, s. legatio, f.; legati, m. pl.
embattle, v.a. aciem instruo, 3.
embellish, v.a. orno, exorno, 1.
embellishment, s. ornamentum, decus, insigne, n.   [villa, f.
embers, s. cinis, c.; (live coals) fa-
embezzle, v.a. averto, 3.
embezzlement, s. peculatus, m.
embezzler, s. interceptor, perculator, m.
embitter, v.a. exacerbo, 1.
emblazon, v.a. insignio, 4; orno, 1.
emblem, s. signum, n.; imago, f.; (example) exemplum, n.

embody, v.a. intertexo, 3; (unite) conjungo.

embolden, v.a. animo, confirmo, 1.

emboss, v.a. cælo, 1.

embrace, v.a. complector; (contain) contineo, 2; amplector, 3; (also *fig.*: an opportunity).

embrace, s. amplexus, complexus, m.

embrocation, s. fomentum, n.

embroider, v.a. acu pingo, 3.

embroidery, s. (art) ars plumaria, f.

embroil, v.a. confundo, 3; permisceo, 2; *fig.* implico, 1; impedio, 4; (match, set to fight) committo, 3.

embroilment, s. implicatio; perturbatio, f.; (disturbance) rixa, f.; tumultus, m.

embryo, s. semen, n.

emendation, s. correctio, emendatio, f.

emendator, s. corrector, emendator, m.

emerald, s. smaragdus, c.

emerge, v.n. emergo; (to arise) exsisto, 3.

emergency, s. (accident) casus, m.; (crisis) discrimen, n.; necessitas, f.

emetic, s. vomitorium, n.; —, a. vomitorius.

emigrant, s. colonus, m.

emigrate, v.n. migro, 1.

emigration, s. migratio (in alias terras), f.

eminence, s. præstantia, f.; (height) tumulus, m.

eminent, a. eminens; egregius, eximius, insignis, præstans; —ly, ad. eximie, insigniter.

emir, s. phylarchus Arabum, m.

emissary, s. emissarius, legatus, m.

emission, s. emissio, f.

emit, v.a. emitto, 3; (breathe out) exhalo, 1.

emmet, s. formica, f.

emollient, s. mollimentum, n.; —, a. mollificus.

emolument, s. lucrum, emolumentum, n.; quæstus, m.

emotion, s. animi motus, affectus, m.; commotio; perturbatio, f.

empanel, v.a. cito, 1.

emperor, s. imperator, m.

emphasis, s. vis, f.; pondus, n.; (gr.) emphasis, f.

emphatic, a. gravis; —ally, ad. graviter.

empire, s. imperium, regnum, n.

empiric, s. empiricus, m.

empirical, a. empiricus; —ly, ad. ex usu tantum.

empiricism, s. empirice, f.

employ, v.a. adhibeo; exerceo, 2; occupo, 1; (use) utor, 3; usurpo, 1.

employ, s. usus; m.; (service) ministerium, m.

employer, s. conductor; dominus, m.

employment, s. occupatio, f.; (business) negotium, studium, n., v. **employ,** s.

emporium, s. emporium, forum, n.

empower, v.a. potestatem (alicui) facio, 3; copiam (alicui) do, 1.

empress, s. imperatrix, f.

emptiness, s. inanitas; *fig.* vanitas, f.

empty, a. vacuus, inanis; *fig.* vanus.

empty, v.a. vacuo, 1; vacuefacio, 3; exinanio, 4; (to drink off) haurio, exhaurio, 4.

empyrean, s. æther, m.

emulate, æmulor; imitor, 1.

emulation, s. æmulatio, f.

emulous, a. æmulus; —ly, ad. certatim.

enable, v.a. facultatem (alicui) facio, 3.

enact, v.a. decerno, 3; sancio, 4.

enactment, s. sanctio; (law) lex, f.; decretum, n.

enamoured, a. to be —, amo, deamo, 1.

encage, v.a. in caveam includo, 3.

encamp, v.a. castra pono, 3.

encampment, s. castra, n. pl.

encaustic, a. encausticus, encaustus.

enchant, v.a. fascino, 1; *fig.* capio, 3; delecto, 1.

enchanted, a. cantatus, incantatus.

enchanter, s. magus; (met.) deliciæ.

enchanting, a. *fig.* venustus, suavissimus, pulcherrimus.

enchantment, s. incantamentum, n.; *fig.* illecebræ, f. pl.; (magic) carmen, n.

enchantress, s. maga; cantatrix, f.; (beloved one) amata, f. [circumdo, 1.

encircle, v.a. circumplector; cingo, 3;

enclose, v.a. sæpio, 4; includo; (encircle) cingo, 3; circumdo, 1.

enclosure, s. sæptum, n.

encomiast, s. laudator, m.

encomium, s. laudatio, f.

encompass, v.a. complector, cingo, 3.

encore, v.a. (an actor) revoco, 1.

encounter, s. (meeting) congressus, m.; (fight) certamen, n.; pugna, f.

encounter, v.a. & n. congredior, 3; obviam eo, 4; incurro, 3.

encourage, v.a. hortor, cohortor, animo, confirmo, 1. [tio, confirmatio, f.

encouragement, s. hortatus, m.; cohorta-

encourager, s. hortator, impulsor, m.

encroach, v.n. usurpo, 1; præsumo, 3; (steal upon) obrepo, 3.

encroachment, s. usurpatio, f.

encumber, v.a. onero, 1; impedio, 4; (to weight down) prægravo, 1.

encumbrance, s. impedimentum; onus, n.; (trouble) molestia, f.; (children) liberi, m. pl.

end, s. finis, c.; terminus; exitus, m.; (aim, design) propositum, n.; (death) mors, f.; obitus, m.

end, v.a. finio, 4; termino, 1; concludo, 3; —, v.n. (to cease) desino, 3; finior, 4.
endanger, v.a. periclitor, 1; in periculum deduco, 3.
endear, v.a. carum reddo, 3; benevolentiam concilio, 1.
endearing, a. carus. [menta, n. pl.
endearment, s. blanditiæ, f. pl.; blandi-
endeavour, v.n. tempto, conor, 1; nitor, enitor, 3; contendo, 3. [men, n.
endeavour, s. conatus, nisus, m.; cona-
ending, s. exitus, m.
endive, s. intubum, n.
endless, a. infinitus; perpetuus; æternus; sempiternus; —ly, ad. sine fine, perpetuo; in æternum.
endow, v.a. doto, 1; instruo, 3; orno, 1; —ed with, præditus (abl.).
endowment, s. dos, f.
endurable, a. tolerabilis.
endurance, s. patientia; (stability) stabilitas, f.; (duration) diuturnitas.
endure, v.a. tolero, 1; patior, perpetior, fero, 3; sustineo, 2; —, v.n. duro, 1; permaneo, 2.
enduring, a. tolerans; durabilis.
enema, s. clyster, m.
enemy, s. hostis, inimicus, m.
energetic, a. strenuus; alacer, acer; —ally, ad. strenue; acriter.
energy, s. vis; alacritas; vehementia, f.; impetus, m.
enervate, v.a. enervo; debilito, 1.
enfeeble, v.a. debilito, infirmo, labefacto, 1.
enfeeblement, s. infirmitas, debilitas, f.
enforce, v.a. (compel) cogo, 3; (of arguments) confirmo, 1; (put in force), exerceo, 2.
enfranchise, v.a. libero, 1; manumitto, 3; civitatem do, 1.
enfranchisement, s. manumissio, liberatio; civitatis donatio, f.
engage, v.a. (put under obligation) obligo, 1; devincio, 4; (to hire) conduco, 3; (to involve, to entangle) implico, 1; (one's honour) fidem interpono, 3; (occupy) occupo, 1; —, v.n. (in battle) confligo, 3; (to promise) spondeo, 2; (to undertake) suscipio, 3.
engaged, a. (to wed) sponsus.
engagement, s. stipulatio, f.; pactum, n.; (occupation) occupatio, f.; (battle) prœlium, n.; (betrothal) pactio nuptialis, f.; (promise) fides, f.
engaging, a. amabilis, blandus; —ly, ad. amabiliter, blande.
engender, v. beget.
engine, s. machina; machinatio, f.; (mil.) tormentum, n.
engineer, s. machinator; architectus, m.

England, s. Anglia, f.
English, a. Anglicus, Britannicus.
Englishman, s. Anglus, m.
engrave, v.a. scalpo, sculpo; incido, 3; cælo, 1.
engraver, s. scalptor, sculptor, m.
engraving, s. (art) scalptura, sculptura.
engross, v.a. in me transfero; (occupy) occupo; —ed in, deditus (dat.).
enhance, v.a. augeo, 2; amplifico, orno, 1; (to raise) accendo, 3.
enhancement, s. amplificatio, accessio, f.; incrementum, n.
enigma, s. ænigma, n.; ambages, f. pl.
enigmatical, a. ænigmaticus, ambiguus; —ly, ad. ambigue.
enjoin, v.a. jubeo, 2; injungo, præcipio, præscribo, 3.
enjoy, v.a. percipio, fruor, 3; (to rejoice in) gaudeo; (possess) possideo, 2; — oneself, me oblecto, 1.
enjoyment, s. fructus, m.; gaudium, n.; possessio, f.; oblectatio; voluptates, f. pl.
enlarge, v.a. amplifico; dilato; (to release) libero, 1; —, v.n. amplificor, 1, etc.; to — upon (a subject), uberius dico de (abl.), 3.
enlargement, s. amplificatio; (of prisoners) ex custodia missio, f.; (increase) auctus, m.
enlighten, v.a. illustro, 1; fig. erudio, 4; doceo, 2.
enlightened, a. (cultivated) cultus.
enlightenment, s. illustratio; fig. eruditio, f.; (culture) humanitas, f.
enlist, v.a. conscribo, 3; (win over) concilio, 1; —, v.n. sacramentum dico, 3.
enlistment, s. delectus, m.
enliven, v.a. animo; incito; exhilaro, 1.
enmity, s. inimicitia, f.; odium, n.
ennoble, v.a. nobilito; fig. illustro, 1.
ennui, s. lassitudo, f.
enormity, s. immanitas; fig. atrocitas, f.
enormous, a. ingens, enormis, immensus; vastus, immanis; —ly, ad. admodum, multum, mire.
enough, ad. satis, sat, affatim; — of this, sed hæc hactenus.
enquire, v. inquire.
enrage, v.a. irrito; exaspero, 1.
enraged, a. iratus, furens.
enrapture, v.a. capio, 3.
enrich, v.a. locupleto, dito, 1.
enrol, v.a. inscribo, 3.
ensconce, v.a. (place) loco, 1.
enshrine, v.a. consecro, 1; includo; condo, recondo, 3.
ensign, s. (flag) vexillum; (mark) insigne, n.; (officer) signifer, m.; — -bearer, s. signifer, vexillarius, m.

enslave, v.a. subigo, in servitutem redigo, 3.   [tium, n.
enslavement, s. servitus, f.; servi-
enslaver, s. domitor, m.; *fig.* domina, f.
ensnare, v.a. illaqueo, 1; irretio, 4; (*fig.*) illicio, capio, 3.
ensue, v.n. sequor, insequor, 3.
ensuing, a. sequens, insequens, posterus, proximus.
ensure, v.a. (guarantee) præsto, 1; (see to it that) curo ut (subj.).
entail, v.a. *fig.* derivo, 1; affero, 3.
entangle, v.a. implico, illaqueo, 1; irretio; impedio, 4.
entanglement, s. implicatio; confusio, f.; nodus; error, m.
enter, v.a. intro, 1; ineo, 4; ingredior, 3; — **in a book,** refero, 3; **to — on** *or* **upon,** (to undertake) incipio, suscipio, 3.
entering, s. introitus, m., v. **entrance. entry.**
enterprise, s. (undertaking) inceptum; ausum; (in a bad sense) facinus, n.; (boldness) audacia, f.
enterprising, a. audax, strenuus, acer.
entertain, v.a. (to keep) alo, 3; sustento, 1; (to treat) accipio, excipio, 3; (an opinion) habeo, 2; (to amuse) oblecto, 1.
entertainer, s. hospes, convivator, m.
entertainment, s. (by a host) hospitium; (feast) convivium, n.; (amusement) oblectatio, delectatio, f.
enthusiasm, s. fervor, m.; alacritas, f.
enthusiast, s. fanaticus, m.
enthusiastic, a. fervidus, fanaticus; —**ally,** ad. fanatice.
entice, v.a. allicio, 3; allecto, 1.
enticement, s. allectatio; illecebra, f.
enticer, s. allector, m.
enticing, a. blandus.
entire, a. integer, totus; —**ly,** ad. omnino; penitus, prorsus.
entireness, entirety, s. integritas, f.
entitle, v.a. appello, nomino, 1; inscribo (titulum), 3; (to give a right) potestatem do (dat.), 1.
entity, s. ens, n.; res, f.
entomb, v.a. humo, 1; sepelio, 4.
entombment, s. sepultura, f.
entrails, s. viscera, n. pl.
entrance, s. aditus; introitus, m.; (beginning) principium, n.
entrance, v.a. rapio, capio, 3.
entrance-hall, s. vestibulum, n.
entrap, v.a. illaqueo; inesco, 1; (by net) irretio, 4; *fig.* capio, 3.
entreat, v.a. obsecro; oro; deprecor, obtestor, 1; (to beg) peto, 3.
entreaty, s. obsecratio, f.; preces, f. pl.
entrust, v. **intrust.**

entry, s. (act of entering) introitus, m.; (of a house) vestibulum, n.; (in a book) nomen, n.
entwine, v.a. implico; circumplico, 1; necto, 3.
enumerate, v.a. enumero, 1; recenseo, 2.
enumeration, s. enumeratio; recensio, f.
enunciate, v.a. (to predicate) enuntio, 1; (to utter) fundo, mitto, 3.
enunciation, s. enunciatio, f.
envelop, v.a. involvo, 3; amicio, 4.
envelope, s. involucrum, n.
envenom, v.a. veneno; *fig.* exaspero, 1.
enviable, a. dignus cui invideatur, fortunatus.
envious, a. invidus, invidiosus; —**ly,** ad. invidiose.   [orator, m.
envoy, s. nuntius, legatus; (spokesman)
envy, s. invidia; malignitas, f.; livor, m.
envy, v.a. invideo (alicui), 2.
ephemera, s. ephemeris, f.
ephemeral, a. *fig.* brevis; caducus.
epic, a. epicus; — **poem,** epos, n.
epicure, s. helluo, m.
Epicurean, a. Epicureus.
epidemic, a. epidemus.
epidermis, s. epidermis, f.
epigram, s. epigramma, n.
epigrammatic, a. epigrammaticus.
epigrammatist, s. epigrammatista, m.
epigraph, s. inscriptio, f.
epilepsy, s. morbus comitialis, morbus caducus, m.; epilepsia, f.
epileptic, a. epilepticus.
epilogue, s. epilogus, m.
epiphany, s. epiphania, n. pl.
episcopacy, s., v. **episcopate.**
episcopal, episcopalian, a. episcopalis.
episcopate, s. episcopatus, m.
episode, s. embolium; (affair) res, f.
epistle, s. epistula, f.; litteræ, f. pl.
epistolary, a. epistularis.
epitaph, s. epitaphium; carmen, n.
epithet, s. epitheton, n.
epitome, s. epitome, f.; breviarium, n.
epitomize, v.a. epitomo, abbrevio, 1.
epoch, s. sæculum, n.; ætas, f.; tempus, n.
equal, a. æqualis, æquus, par.
equal, s. par, c.
equal, v.a. æquo, adæquo, æquiparo, 1; assequor, 3.
equality, s. æqualitas, f.; æquum, n.
equalization, s. (act) æquatio; (state) æqualitas, f.
equalize, v.a. æquo, adæquo, exæquo, 1.
equally, ad. æque; æqualiter; pariter.
equanimity, s. æquus animus, m.
equator, s. æquinoctialis circulus, m.
equatorial, a. æquinoctialis.
equerry, s. equiso, m.
equestrian, a. equestris; —, s. eques, c.

equilateral, a. æquilateralis.
equilibrate, v.a., v. counterbalance, v.a.
equilibrium, s. æquilibrium, n.
equinoctial, a. æquinoctialis.
equinox, s. æquinoctium, n.
equip, v.a. armo; exorno, 1; instruo, 3.
equipage, s. instrumentum, n.; apparatus; ornatus, m., v. carriage. [tura, f.
equipment, s. armamenta, n. pl.; arma-
equipoise, s. æquipondium, n.
equitable, a. æquus, justus.
equitably, ad. æque, juste.
equity, s. æquitas, f.; æquum, n.
equivalent, a. tantusdem; par. [bigue.
equivocal, a. ambiguus; —ly, ad. am-
equivocate, v.a. tergiversor, 1.
equivocation, s. tergiversatio; ambiguitas, f. [lum, n.
era, s. æra, f.; tempus, n.; ætas, f.; sæcu-
eradicate, v.a. eradico, exstirpo, 1; tollo, 3.
eradication, s. exstirpatio, f.; excidium, n.
erase, v.a. erado, 3; deleo, 2.
erasure, s. litura, f.
ere, pr. priusquam; — long, brevi, mox,
postmodo; — now, ante hoc tempus.
erect, a. erectus, arrectus.
erect, v.a. (to raise) erigo, educo; (to
build up) exstruo; fig. statuo, (found)
condo, 3.
erection, s. exstructio; ædificatio, f.
erotic, a. amatorius. [quo, 3.
err, v.n. (ab)erro; fig. pecco, 1; delin-
errand, s. mandatum, n.
errand-boy, s. nuntius, m.
errant, a. errabundus, erraticus, vagus.
erratic, a. erraticus; fig. inconstans.
erroneous, a. falsus, vanus; —ly, ad.
falso.
erroneousness, s. vanitas, f.
error, s. error, m.; (fault) delictum, peccatum, erratum, n.; (mistake) fraus, f.
erudite, a. eruditus, doctus.
erudition, s. eruditio, f.
eruption, s. (of a volcano) eruptio; (of
the skin) scabies, f.
erysipelas, s. erysipelas, n.
escalade, s. scalæ, f. pl.
escapade, s. ausum, n.
escape, v.a. & n. evado, effugio, elabor, 3;
(secretly) subterfugio, 3; (with difficulty or by struggling) eluctor, 1.
escape, s. fuga, f.; effugium, n.
escheat, v.n. (law) ad fiscum devolvi; (in
general) revertor, 3.
escheat, s. hereditas caduca, f.
eschew, v.a. evito, 1; fugio, 3.
escort, s. comitatus, m.; (protection) præsidium, n.; custodia, f. [quor, 3.
escort, v.a. comitor, 1; deduco, 3; prose-
esculent, a. esculentus, edulis.
escutcheon, s. insigne, n.

especial. v. special.
especially, ad., v. specially.
esplanade, s. ambulacrum, n.
espousals, s. sponsalia, n. pl.
espouse, v.a. spondeo, 2; nubo; fig. (an
opinion) amplector, 3; (a cause) suscipio, sequor, 3.
espy, v.a. conspicor, 1; aspicio, 3; video,
2; —, v.n. speculor, 1.
esquire, s. armiger, m.
essay, v.a. conor, tento, 1.
essay, s. experimentum, tentamentum,
n.; (treatise) libellus, tractatus, m.
essence, s. essentia; natura, vis, f.
essential, a. proprius, necessarius; —ly,
ad. natura, necessario.
establish, v.a. status; constituo, 3;
firmo, confirmo, 3; stabilio, 4.
establishment, s. (arrangement) constitutio, f.; (house) familia, domus, f.
estate, s. (state) status, m.; conditio, f.;
(landed property), fundus, ager, m.;
(means, wealth) bona, n. pl.; divitiæ,
f. pl.; (class, in politics) ordo, m.;
dignitas, f.; man's —, pubertas, f.
esteem, v.a. æstimo, puto, 1; habeo, 2;
(to judge) existimo, 1; (to respect)
magni facio, 3. [entia, f.
esteem, s. æstimatio, f.; honor, m.; rever-
estimable, a. æstimandus, venerabilis,
venerandus. [seo, 2.
estimate, v.a. æstimo, 1; (to assess) cen-
estimate, s. (valuation) æstimatio, f.;
pretium; judicium, n.
estimation, s. æstimatio; opinio, f.
estimator, s. æstimator, m.
estrange, v.a. alieno, abalieno, 1.
estrangement, s. alienatio, f.; discidium, n.
estuary, s. æstuarium, n.
eternal, a. æternus, sempiternus, immortalis; —ly, ad. in æternum, semper.
eternity, s. æternitas; immortalitas, f.
eternize, v.a. æterno, 1.
ether, s. æther, m.
ethereal, a. æthereus.
ethics, s. ethice, f.
etymological, a. etymologicus.
etymology, s. etymologia; etymologica
ratio, f.
eucharist, s. eucharistia, f.
eulogist, s. laudator, m.
eulogistic, a. panegyricus, laudativus.
eulogize, v.a. collaudo, 1.
eulogy, s. laus, laudatio, f.; panegyricus,
m. [spado, m.
eunuch, s. eunuchus; (in contempt)
euphony, s. euphonia, vocalitas, f.
European, a. & s. Europæus, m.
Euxine, s. Euxinus pontus, m.
evacuate, v.a. vacuo, 1; vacuefacio, 3;
(leave) relinquo, 3.

evacuation, s. (departure) excessus, m.
evade, v.a. subterfugio, eludo, 3.
evanescent, a. evanidus, caducus, brevis,
evangelical, a. evangelicus.
evangelist, s. evangelista, m.
evangelize, v.a. & n. evangelizo, 1.
evaporate, v.n. evaporor, 1; evanesco, 3;
—, v.a. evaporo, exhalo, 1.
evaporation, s. evaporatio, exhalatio, f.
evasion, s. effugium, n.; fuga; tergiversatio, f.
evasive, a. vafer; subdolus; ambiguus;
—ly, ad. vafre; subdole; ambigue.
eve, s. vesper, m.; (of a feast) vigiliæ,
f. pl.; be on the — of, in eo esse ut.
even, a. æqualis, æquus; (level) planus;
(of numbers) par.
even, ad. etiam, quoque; (with superlatives) vel; (namely) scilicet; not —,
ne . . . quidem; — as, perinde ac si,
quemadmodum.
even-handed, a. æquus, justus.
evening, s. vesper, m.
evening, a. vespertinus.
evening-primrose, s. œnothera (mod.
hort.).
Evening-star, s. Vesper, Hesperus, m.
evenly, ad. æqualiter, æquabiliter.
evenness, s. (levelness) æqualitas; (justness) æquitas, f.; æquus animus, m.
event, s. eventus, exitus, casus, m.
eventful, a. memorabilis.
even-tide, s. vespertinum tempus, n.
eventually, ad. denique, aliquando, tandem.
ever, ad. unquam; aliquando; semper;
for —. in æternum; whoso—, qui-
cumque.
evergreen, a. semper viridis. [æternum.
everlasting, a. sempiternus; —ly, ad. in
evermore, ad. semper.
every, a. quisque, quæque, quodque;
omnis.
everybody, pn. quisque; unusquisque;
nemo non; omnes; quivis; quilibet.
everyday, a. quotidianus; usitatus; —,
ad. quotidie; in dies.
everything, s. omnia; quidvis; quidlibet.
everyway, ad. quoquoversus.
everywhere, ad. ubique, ubivis, undique.
evict, v.a. (law) evinco, 3.
eviction, s. (law) evictio, f.
evidence, s. (proof) argumentum; (in
law) testimonium, n.; (witness) testis,
c.; (information) indicium, n.
evidence, v.a. testor, probo, 1.
evident, a. apertus, manifestus, clarus,
liquidus; it is —, apparet, liquet;
—ly, ad. aperte, manifesto, liquide.
evil, a. malus, pravus, improbus; —, s.
malum, incommodum, n.

evil, ad. male.
evil-doer, s. maleficus, m.
evilly, ad. male, prave.
evil-minded, a. malevolus, malignus.
evil-speaking, a. maledicus; —, s. male-
dicentia, f.; maledicta, n. pl.
evince, v.a. præsto, 1.
evoke, v.a. evoco, 1; elicio, 3.
evolution, s. (mil.) decursus, m.
evolve, v.a. evolvo, 3.
ewe, s. ovis femina, f.
ewer, s. urceus, m.
exact, a. diligens; subtilis; (of things)
exactus; —ly, ad. exacte, ad unguem.
exact, v.a. exigo, 3.
exaction, s. exactio, f.
exactor, s. exactor, m.
exaggerate, v.a. exaggero, aggravo, 1;
augeo, 2.
exaggeration, s. amplificatio, f.; immoderatio, f.
exalt, v.a. extollo; (in rank) eveho, 3;
(in speaking) amplifico, 1.
exaltation, s. elatio, f.
exalted, a. celsus, altus, sublimis.
examination, s. investigatio; inspectio;
(of witnesses) interrogatio, f.
examine, v.a. investigo; exploro, 1; inspicio, 3; (witnesses) interrogo, 1.
examiner, s. examinator, m.
example, s. exemplum, exemplar, documentum, n.; for —, verbi gratia.
exasperate, v.a. exaspero, exacerbo,
irrito, 1.
exasperation, s. ira, f.; animus iratus, m.
excavate, v.a. excavo, 1; effodio, 3.
excavation, s. excavatio, f.
exceed, v.a. excedo, 3; supero, 1.
exceedingly, ad. valde, egregie, magnopere; vehementer.
excel, v.a. supero, præsto (alicui), 1; —,
v.n. excello, 3.
excellence, s. excellentia, præstantia, f.
excellent, s. excellens, præstans, egregius, eximius; —ly, ad. egregie,
optime; excellenter, eximie.
except, v.a. excipio, eximo, 3.
except, excepting, pr. (unless) nisi; (save)
extra, præter; — that, nisi quod, nisi si.
exception, s. exceptio; take — to, reprehendo, 3; culpo, 1; with the — of,
excepto (excepta) (ablat. absol.).
exceptional, a. rarus; —ly, ad. raro; (in
an eminent degree) eximie; (contrary
to custom) præter solitum.
excess, s. exsuperantia, immoderatio;
(licence) intemperatia, licentia, f.; to
—, nimis.
excessive, a. nimius; immodicus; immoderatus; —ly, ad. nimis; immodice;
immoderate.

exchange, s. (barter) mutatio, permutatio, f.; (of money) collybus, m.; (building) basilica, f.

exchange, v.a. muto, permuto, 1.

exchequer, s. ærarium, n.; fiscus, m.

excise, s. vectigal, portorium, n.

excitable, a. irritabilis; fervidus.

excitation, s. incitatio, f.

excite, v.a. excito, incito, stimulo, 1; (to inflame) incendo, 3; (thus produce) cieo, moveo, 2; conflo, 3.

excitement, s. commotio; perturbatio, f.; (thing exciting) incitamentum, n.

exciter, s. concitator, m.

exclaim, v.a. exclamo; (several voices) conclamo; (against) acclamo (alicui), 1.

exclamation, s. vox; exclamatio; (of several persons) conclamatio, f.

exclude, v.a. excludo, 3; arceo; prohibeo; removeo, 2.

exclusion, s. exclusio, f.

exclusive, a. (one's own) proprius; (especial) præcipuus.

exclusively, ad. (only) solum.

excommunicate, v.a. excommunico, 1.

excommunication, s. excommunicatio, f.

excoriate, v.n. desquamo.

excoriation, s. intertrigo, f.

excrement, s. excrementum, stercus, n.; proluvies, f.

excrescence, s. tuber, n.

excretion, s. excrementum, n.

excruciate, v.a. excrucio, 1; torqueo, 2.

exculpate, v.a. (ex)purgo; excuso, 1; absolvo, 3.

exculpation, s. purgatio, f.

excursion, s. excursio, incursio; *fig.* digressio, f.

excursive, a. errans, devius.

excusable, a. excusabilis.

excusably, ad. excusate.

excuse, v.a. excuso; (to exculpate) purgo, 1; (to pardon) ignosco, 3; condono, 1.

excuse, s. excusatio, f.; causa, f.; (pretence) prætextum, n.

execrable, a. nefarius, detestabilis; (bad) malus.

execrably, ad. nefarie; (badly) male.

execrate, v.a. exsecror, detestor, 1.

execration, s. exsecratio, f.

execute, v.a. (to fulfil, to perform) exsequor, persequor, perficio, perago, 3; (as punishment) securi ferio, 4.

execution, s. exsecutio; (punishment) supplicium, n.; (death) mors, f.; (law) bonorum venditio, f.; **place of —,** furca, f.

executioner, s. carnifex, m.

executive, a. — **power,** s. administratio, f.

exemplar, s. (pattern) exemplar, n.

exemplary, a. egregius, eximius, excellens.

exemplification, s. expositio, f.; (example) exemplum, n.

exemplify, v.a. (give example of) exemplum do (gen.).   [do, 1.

exempt, v.a. eximo, 3; immunitatem

exempt, a. immunis.

exemption, s. vacatio, immunitas, f.

exercise, s. exercitatio, f.; (of soldiers) exercitium, n.; (task) pensum, n.

exercise, v.a. exerceo, 2; (an office) fungor, 3; —, v.n. exerceor, 2.

exert, v.a. exhibeo, exerceo, 2; **to — oneself,** contendo, nitor, 3.

exertion, s. contentio, f.; nisus, m.

exhalation, s. exhalatio, f.; vapor, m.

exhale, v.a. exhalo, exspiro, 1; spargo, emitto, 3; —, v.n. exhalor, 1.

exhaust, v.a. exhaurio, 4; conficio, 3; debilito, infirmo, 1.

exhausted, a. fessus, defessus, confectus, languidus.

exhaustion, s. *fig.* languor, m.; lassitudo, defectio (virium) f.

exhibit, v.a. exhibeo, 2; expono, propono, profero, ostendo, 3; (qualities) præsto, 1.   [lum, n.

exhibition, s. prolatio, f.; (show) spectacu-

exhilarate, v.a. exhilaro, 1.

exhilaration, s. hilaritas, f.

exhort, v.a. hortor, 1.

exhortation, s. hortatio, f.

exhume, v.a. eruo, 3.

exigency, s. necessitas, f.; angustiæ, f. pl.

exile, s. (banishment) ex(s)ilium, n.; fuga, f.; (person banished) ex(s)ul, extorris, c.

exile, v.a. relego, 1; in exilium pello, 3.

exist, v.n. sum, exsisto; vivo, 3.

existence, s. vita, f.   [est.

existing, a. verus, qui (quæ, quod) nunc

exit, s. exitus, m.; effugium, n.

exonerate, v.a. culpa libero, excuso, 1.

exorable, a. exorabilis.

exorbitant, a. nimius, immodicus.

exorcise, v.a. exorcizo, 1.

exorcism, s. exorcismus, m.

exorcist, s. exorcista, m.

exordium, s. exordium; principium, n.

exoteric, a. exotericus.

exotic, a. externus, peregrinus.

expand, v.a. expando; extendo, 3; dilato, 1; augeo, 2; —, v.n. expandor, extendor, cresco, 3; dilator, 1.

expanse, s. spatium.

expatiate, v.n. exspatior, 1; — **on,** amplifico, 1 (acc.).

expatriate, v.a. expello, 3.

expatriation, s. ex(s)ilium, n.

expect, v.a. & n. exspecto; spero, 1.

expectancy, s. spes, exspectatio, f.

expectation, s. exspectatio; spes, f.

expectorate, v.a. exscreo, 1; exspuo, 3.
expectoration, s. exscreatio, f.; sputum, n.
expediency, s. utilitas, f.
expedient, a. utilis, commodus, salutaris; **it is —,** expedit; **—ly,** ad. apte, commode.
expedient, s. modus, m.; ratio, f.
expedite, v.a. maturo, 1.
expedition, s. (mil.) expeditio; (speed) celeritas, f.   [celeriter, mature.
expeditious, a. celer, promptus; **—ly,** ad.
expel, v.a. expello, ejicio, 3.
expend, v.a. expendo, impendo; consumo, 3.
expenditure, s. sumptus, m.; impensa, f.
expense, s. impensa, f.; sumptus, m.
expensive, a. sumptuosus, pretiosus, carus; **—ly,** ad. sumptuose, pretiose, care.
expensiveness, s. caritas, f.; magnum pretium, n.
experience, s. experientia; peritia, f.; usus, m.   [co, 3.
experience, v.a. experior, 4; utor, cognos-
experienced, a. peritus, experiens; callidus.
experiment, s. experimentum, periculum.
experiment, v.a. experimentum facio, 3.
experimental, a. usu comparatus; **—ly,** ad. usu, experimentis.
expert, a. callidus, sciens; **—ly,** ad. callide scienter.
expertness, s. ars, calliditas, sollertia, f.
expiable, a. piabilis.
expiate, v.a. expio, 1; luo, 3.
expiation, s. expiatio, f.; piaculum, n.
expiatory, a. piacularis, c.   [tus, m.
expiration, s. exspiratio, f.; finis, c.; exi-
expire, v.n. (die) exspiro, 1; (terminate) exeo, 4; intercedo, conficior, 4.
explain, v.a. explano, explico, 1; expono, 3.
explainer, s. explanator, m.
explanation, s. explanatio, explicatio, f.
expletive, a. expletivus.
explicit, a. explicatus; apertus; **—ly,** ad. aperte, plane, nominatim.
explode, v.a. (to blow up) displodo; *fig.* explodo, rejicio; **—,** v.n. displodor, 3; **be —d,** *fig.* obsolesco, 3.
exploit, s. res gesta, f.; facinus, n.
exploration, s. indagatio, investigatio, f.
explore, v.a. exploro; perscrutor; vestigo, indago, 1.
explorer, s. explorator, m.
explosion, s. crepitus, fragor, m.
exponent, s. interpres, c.
export, v.a. eveho, 3; exporto, 1.
export, exportation, s. exportatio, f.
expose, v.a. expono, retego, 3; nudo, 1; **— to,** objicio, 3; objecto, 1.

exposition, s. explicatio, expositio; interpretatio, f.; (show) spectaculum, n.
expositor, s. interpres, c.
expostulate, v. **remonstrate.**
expostulation, s. expostulatio, querela, deprecatio, f.
exposure, s. expositio; (disclosure) indicium, n.; (cold) frigus, n.
expound, v.a. expono, 3; interpretor, 1.
expounder, s. interpres, c.
express, v.a. exprimo, loquor, dico, 3; significo, 1.
express, a. clarus; certus; expressus; **—ly,** ad. expresse, nominatim.
express, s. nuntius, m.
expressible, a. fandus.
expression, s. (word) vox; (sentence) sententia, f.; *fig.* (of the feature) vultus, m.
expressive, a. significans; *fig.* (of) index; (speaking) loquax; (clear) argutus; **—ly,** ad. significanter.
expressiveness, s. argutiæ, f. pl.
expulsion, s. exactio, f.
expunge, v.a. deleo, 2; oblittero, 1.
expurgate, v.a. expurgo, 1.
exquisite, a. conquisitus; exquisitus; elegans, subtilis, eximius; **—ly,** ad. exquisite, eximie, eleganter.
exquisite, s. homo elegans, m.
exquisiteness, s. elegantia; subtilitas; (violence) vis, f.
extant, a. superstes; **be —,** v.n. exsto.
extemporary, a. extemporalis.
extempore, ad. subito; ex tempore.
extemporize, v.a. ex tempore dico.
extend, v.a. extendo; produco, 3; propago, 1; **—,** v.n. extendo; porrigor, 3.
extension, s. extensio; propagatio; (of boundaries, etc.) prolatio, f.; (space) spatium, n.
extensive, a. late patens, amplus, diffusus; **—ly,** ad. late.
extensiveness, s. latitudo, f.
extent, s. spatium, n.; (of a country) tractus, m.; fines, m. pl.; (compass) circuitus, m.; (amount) vis, f.
extenuate, v.a. mitigo, extenuo, elevo, 1; (to lessen) minuo, 3.
extenuation, s. imminutio; (pardon) venia, f.
exterior, a. externus, exterior.
exterior, s. species, facies, forma, f.
exterminate, v.a. exstirpo, extermino, 1; deleo, 2; tollo, exstinguo, 3.
extermination, s. exstirpatio, f.
exterminator, s. exstinctor, m.
external, a. externus; extraneus; **—ly,** ad. extrinsecus.
extinct, a. exstinctus; obsoletus; **to become —,** exstinguor, obsolesco, 3.

extinction, s. exstinctio, f.; interitus, m.
extinguish, v.a. exstinguo, 3.
extirpate, v.a. exstirpo, 1.
extirpation, s. exstirpatio, exstinctio, f.
extol, v.a. laudibus effero, 3; laudo, 1.
extort, v.a. extorqueo, 2; exprimo, 3.
extortion, s. repetundæ, f. pl.   [tor, m.
extortioner, s. exactor, extortor, rap-
extra, ad. insuper, præterea; —, s. supplementum, n.
extract, v.a. extraho; (teeth, roots, etc.).
extract, s. (juice) sucus, m.; (literary)
   excerptum; (epitome) compendium, n.
extraction, s. (birth) stirps; origo, f.;
   genus, n.
extraneous, a. extraneus; alienus.
extraordinarily, a. extra modum; præter
   solitum.
extraordinary, a. extraordinarius, insolitus, mirabilis.
extravagance, s. intemperantia, effusio;
   luxuria, f.
extravagant, a. immodicus, nimius; profusus; effusus; luxuriosus; (dissolute)
   perditus; —ly, ad. immodice; effuse;
   prodige; nimis.
extreme, a. extremus; ultimus; summus;
   fig. ingens; —ly, ad. summe.
extreme, s. extremum, summum, n.
extremity, s. extremitas, f.; extremum, n.;
   (distress) miseria, f.; (danger) discrimen, periculum, n.; (difficulty) angustiæ, f. pl.   [libero, 1.
extricate, v.a. expedio, 4; extraho, 3;
extrinsic, a. extraneus.
extrude, v.a. extrudo, expello, 3.
exuberance, s. luxuria, redundantia;
   ubertas, f.   [effusus.
exuberant a. luxuriosus; redundans; fig.
exude, v.a. & n. exsudo, 1.
exult, v.n. exsulto, ovo, 1; gestio, 4.
exultant, a. lætus, ovans.
exultation, s. lætitia, f.; gaudium.
exultingly, ad. læte.
eye, s. oculus, ocellus, m.; lumen, n.;
   (loop) ansula, f.; (of a needle) foramen,
   n.; (of a plant) gemma; (sight) acies,
   f.; (presence) conspectus, m.
eye, v.a. aspicio, 3; intueor, 2; contemplor, 1.
eyeball, s. pupula, f.
eyebright, s. euphrasia (mod. hort.).
eyebrow, s. supercilium, n.
eyelet-hole, s. foramen, n.
eyelid, s. palpebra, f.
eye-salve, s. collyrium, n.
eyesight, s. acies oculi, f.
eyesore, s. res odiosa, f.
eye-tooth, s. dens caninus, m.
eye-witness, s. arbiter, m.; testis, c.;
   spectator, m.

Fable, s. fabula, f.
fabric, s. (building) ædificium; (woven
   stuff) textile, textum, n.
fabricate, v.a. fabrico, 1; struo, 3.
fabrication, s. fabricatio, f.; fig. mendacium, n.
fabricator, s. structor, m.
fabulist, s. fabricator; (story-teller)
   fabulator, m.
fabulous, a. fictus, commenticius; fabulosus; —ly, ad. fabulose; ficte.
face, s. facies, f.; os, n.; vultus; fig. conspectus, m.; (boldness) audacia, impudentia, f.; (appearance) species, f.;
   — to —, coram.
face, v.a. aspicio, 3; intueor, 2; (of position) specto ad (acc.), 1; (meet) subeo,
   obeo, 4; (cover in part) prætexo, 3;
   to — about, (mil.) signa converto, 3.
facetious, a. facetus, lepidus; —ly, ad.
   facete, lepide.
facetiousness, s. facetiæ, f. pl.; lepor, m.
facile, a. facilis.
facilitate, v.a. facilius reddo, 3.
facility, s. facilitas, f.; (opportunity)
   copia, facultas, f.
facing, pr. adversus, ante, pro, e regione.
facing, a. contrarius, adversus.
facsimile, s. imago scripturæ, f.
fact, s. factum, n.; res, f.; in —, re ipsa;
   revera, enim.
faction, s. (party) factio, f.
factious, a. factiosus; seditiosus; —ly,
   ad. seditiose; per factionem.
factiousness, s. (party-spirit) studium
   partium, n.
factitious, a. facticius.
factor, s. procurator, m.; (element) pars, f.
factory, s. (manufactory) officina, f.
faculty, s. facultas; vis, f.; ingenium, n.
fade, v.a. marcesco, defloresco, 3; langueo, 2; (to decay) deficio, 3.
fag, v.n. desudo, laboro, 1; v.a. fatigo, 1.
faggot, s. fascis, m.; sarmenta, n. pl.
fail, v.a. (to disappoint) deficio, desero,
   3; —, v.n. succumbo, 3; (of duty)
   delinquo, 3; (to become bankrupt) decoquo, 3; (to be unsuccessful) cado, 3;
   male cedo, 3.
fail, s. without —, certo.
failing, s. (deficiency) defectus, m.;
   (fault) culpa, f.; delictum n.; (disappointment) frustratio; (ceasing) remissio, f.
failure, s. defectio, f.; defectus, m.;
   (fault) culpa, f.; delictum, n.; meet
   with —, male cedo, 3.
fain, a. libens; —, ad. (willingly) libenter.

faint, a. (weary) defessus; (drooping) languidus; (of sight, smell, etc.) hebes; (of sound) surdus; (slack) remissus; (unenthusiastic) frigidus; (timid) demissus; **—ly,** ad. languide; timide.

faint, v.n. langueo, 2; (to swoon) collabor, 3. [imbellis; v. **cowardly.**

faint-hearted, a. animo demisso; ignavus,

faint-heartedness, s. ignavia; demissio animi, f.

faintness, s. defectio, f.; languor, m.

fair, a. (of complexion) candidus; (beautiful) formosus, pulcher; (of weather) serenus, sudus; (of winds) secundus, idoneus; *fig.* æquus; mediocris; modicus; **— play,** s. æquitas, f.

fair, s. mercatus, m.

fairly, ad. juste; (moderately) mediocriter.

fairness, s. (of complexion) candor, m.; (beauty) forma, pulchritudo, f.; (justice) æquitas, f.; candor animi, m.

fair-spoken, a. blandiloquus, blandus.

fairy, s. nympha, Dryas, f.

faith, s. (trust) fides, (confidence) fiducia, (religion) religio, f.; **in —!** mehercle !

faithful, a. fidelis; fidus; **—ly,** ad. fideliter, fide.

faithfulness, a. fides, fidelitas, integritas, f.

faithless, a infidus, infidelis, perfidus; perfidiosus; **—ly,** ad. perfide, infideliter, perfidiose.

faithlessness, perfidia, infidelitas, f.

falchion, s. (scimitar) acinaces, m.

falcon, s. falco, m.

fall, v.n. cado; concido; (to die) occido; (of the wind) pono; (to abate) decresco; (as hair) defluo; (violently and completely) corruo, 3; **to — asunder,** dilabor, 3; **to — away,** deficio, 3; **to — back,** recido; relabor; (to retreat) pedem refero; *fig.* recurro, 3; **to — down,** decido; (completely) concido, 3; **to — forwards,** procido; procumbo; prolabor, 3; **to — foul of,** (of ships) incurro, 3; **to — in(to),** incido; (of rivers) influo, 3; exeo, 4; (in a passion) exardesco, 3; **to — in with,** (to meet) incido, 3; (to find) invenio, 4; (to agree) assentior, 4; **to — in love with,** adamo, 1; **to — off,** decido; (as hair) defluo; (to grow lean) macresco, 3; *fig.* mutor in deterius, 1; **to — on,** v. **to — upon; to — out,** excido; (to happen) contingo, accido, 3; evenio, 4; (with one) dissideo, 2; **to — short of,** non contingo, 3; **to — sick,** in morbum incido, 3; **to — to,** (of inheritances, etc.) obvenio, 4; obtingo, 3; **to — under,** succumbo, 3; (to be reckoned) pertineo (ad), 2; (to be subjected) patior, 3; **to — upon,** accido; incido; (to assail) invado, ingruo, incurro, 3; occupo, 1; (to come to as portion) obtingo, 3; **to let —,** demitto; (out of the hand) emitto, 3.

fall, s. casus; lapsus, m.; (ruin) ruina, f.; labes, f.; (of ground, etc.) libramentum, n.; (waterfall) cataracta; (diminution) deminutio, f.; (autumn) auctumnus, m.; (death) mors, f.

fallacious, a. fallax, fictus, falsus; **—ly,** ad. fallaciter, ficte, falso.

fallacy, s. (sophism) captio, f.

fallible, a. errori obnoxius.

falling, s. casus, lapsus, m.; (of water) cataracta, f.; **— away,** defectio; (decline) deminutio; (wasting) tabes, f.; **— in,** labes, f.; **— off,** deminutio, (desertion) defectio, f.; **— out,** dissensio, f.

falling-sickness, s. morbus caducus, m.

fallow, a. (of colour) gilvus, helvus, fulvus; (of land) inaratus; (never having been ploughed) novalis; **(— land)** novalis, m.; novale, n.

false, a. falsus; fictus (counterfeit) adulterinus; **—ly,** ad. falso, perperam, ficte.

falsehood, s. (untrue story) commentum; (lie) mendacium, n.

falseness, s. perfidia, f.; dolus, m.

falsification, s. adulteratio, corruptio, f.

falsify, v.a. (liquids) adultero, 1; (other things) suppono, corrumpo, 3; depravo, (documents) vitio, 1; interlino, 3.

falsity, v. **falseness.**

falter, v.n. hæreo, 2; hæsito, labo; (to reel, to totter) titubo, 1.

falteringly, ad. titubanter; timide.

fame, s. fama; laus, gloria, f.; nomen, decus, n.; (famousness) claritas; celebritas, f.

famed, a. clarus, illustris.

familiar, a. a familiaris; solitus; notus; intimus; **—ly,** ad. familiariter.

familiarity, s. familiaritas; necessitudo, notitia; (in bad sense) licentia, f.

familiarize, v.a. assuefacio, 3.

family, s. familia; domus, f.; genus, n.; cognatio, f.; (clan) gens, f.

family, a. familiaris; (relating to families *or* races) gentilis, gentilicius; familiæ (genitive); (of home) domesticus.

famine, s. fames, f.; (fast) jejunium, n.; *fig.* inopia, f.

famish, v.n. fame necor, 1.

famished, a. famelicus; fame enectus.

famous, a. clarus, præclarus, notus, celeber, inclitus; **—ly,** ad. præclare; insigniter.

fan, s. flabellum, n.; (for corn) vannus, f.

fan, v.a. ventilo, 1; (fire) accendo, 3; *fig.* excito, conflo, 1.

fanatic, a. fanaticus; —ally, ad. fanatice.

fanaticism, s. furor religiosus, m.

fancier, s. (dealer) mercator, m.

fanciful, a. vanis imaginibus deditus; (capricious) inconstans, levis; libidinosus; —ly, ad. inconstanter.

fancy, s. opinio, imaginatio; (mind) animus, m.; (sense) sensus, m.; (caprice) libido, f.; (dream) somnium, n.; (liking, inclination) voluntas, f.; (as faculty) phantasia, f.

fancy, v.a. & n. imaginor; somnio; (to like) amo, 1.

fang, s. dens; (claw) unguis, m.

fantastic(al), a. vanus; (absurd) absurdus.

far, a. longinquus, remotus.

far, ad. procul, longe; — off, procul; by —, multo; from —, procul; how —, quousque? as — as, quantum; quatenus; so —, thus —, eousque, hactenus; . — be it from me, longe absit; — and near, longe lateque; so — from . . . that, adeo non . . . ut.

farce, s. mimus, m.

farcical, a. mimicus; —ly, ad. mimice.

farcy, s. farciminum, n.

fare, s. (food) cibus, victus, m.; (money) vectura, f.; naulum, n.; (person) vector, m.

fare, v.n. ago, 3; habeo (me) 2; cedo, 3; — well, valeo, 2.

farewell, ad. & i. vale; salve! bid —, valere *or* salvere jubeo, valedico.

far-fetched, a. quæsitus; longe petitus.

farm, s. fundus, agellus, m.; prædium, n.

farm, v.a. (to till) aro, 1; colo; (to hire) conduco, 3; (to lease) loco, 1.

farmer, s. agricola; colonus; (of revenues) publicanus, m.

farm-house, s. villa, f.

farming, s. agricultura, f.; res rusticœ, f. pl.; (taking on lease) conductio, f.

farrago, s. farrago, f.

farrier, s. veterinarius, m.

farriery, s. ars veterinaria, f.

farrow, v.n. (of swine) pario, 3.

farther, a. ulterior; —, ad. longius, ulterius.

farthest, a. ultimus, extremus.

farthing, s. quadrans, m.; (smallest copper coin) raudusculum, n.; to a —, ad assem.

fascinate, v.a. fascino, 1; *fig.* capio, 3.

fascination, s. fascinatio, f.; illecebræ, f. pl.; gratia, f.

fascine, s. cratis, f.; fasciculus, m.

fashion, s. (form) figura, forma, f.; (manner) mos, modus; ritus, m.; (custom) consuetudo, f.; usus, m.

fashion, v.a. (to shape) formo, informo, fabrico, 1; effingo, 3.

fashionable, a. elegans; concinnus; be —, in usu esse, valere, 2.

fashionably, ad. ad morem; eleganter.

fast, a. (firm) firmus, stabilis; (tight) astrictus; (swift) celer; (of sleep) profundus; (shut) occlusus, m.

fast, ad. firmiter; (quickly) celeriter.

fast, v.n. cibo abstineo, 2; jejuno, 1.

fast, s. jejunium, n.

fasten, v.a. astringo, affigo; *fig.* infero; (down) defigo; (to) annecto; impingo, 3; (together) colligo, 1; configo, 3; —, v.n. (to) hæreo, 2; (upon) arripio, 3.

fastening, s. vinculum, n.

fastidious, a. fastidiosus; delicatus; elegans; morosus; —ly, ad. fastidiose; morose.

fastidiousness, s. fastidium, n.; morositas, f.

fastness, s. firmitas, f.; (stronghold) arx, f.; munimentum, n.; locus munitus, m.

fat, a. pinguis, obesus; opimus; (productive) fertilis.

fat, s. adeps, c.; pingue, n.; arvina, f.; (suet) sebum, n.; (of a hog) lardum, n.; (in general) pinguitudo, f.

fatal, a. mortifer, letifer; exitialis; funebris; funestus; —ly, ad. fataliter; fato; (be mortally wounded) vulnus mortiferum accipere.

fatality, s. fatum, n.; (misfortune) infortunium, malum, n.

fate, s. latum, n.; sors, f.; the Fates, pl. Parcæ, f. pl.; (fortune) fortuna, f.; (chance) casus, m.

fated, a. fatalis; ill— —, infaustus.

father, s. pater, genitor, parens, m.; — of a family, paterfamilias, m.

father, v.a. adopto, 1; (on, upon) addico, 3.

fatherhood, s. paternitas, f.

father-in-law, s. socer, m.

fatherless, a. orbus.

fatherly, a. paternus, patrius.

fathom, s. ulna, f.

fathom, v.a. comperio, 4; exploro; investigo, 1.

fathomless, a. profundus; immensus.

fatigue, s. (de)fatigatio, lassitudo.

fatigue, v.a. fatigo, defatigo, delasso, 1.

fatness, s. pinguitudo, sagina, f.

fatten, v.a. sagino, 1; farcio, 4; —, v.n. pinguesco, 3.

fattening, s. saginatio; (cramming of fowls), fartura, f.

fatty, a. pinguis.

fatuity, s. fatuitas, stultitia, f.

fatuous, a. stultus, fatuus.

fatuously, ad. stulte, fatue.

fault, s. delictum, mendum, vitium, n.; culpa, f.; (mistake) error, m.; (in writing) erratum, n.; (blemish) menda, labes, macula, f.; **to find — with,** vitupero, 1; carpo, 3.

faultily, ad. mendose; vitiose.

faultiness, s. vitiositas; pravitas, f.

faultless, a. perfectus; integer; (corrected) emendatus.

faulty, a. vitiosus; mendosus.

Faun, s. Faunus, m.

favour, s. favor, m.; gratia; (goodwill) benevolentia, f.; beneficium, n.; (present) munus, n.; **by** or **under (the) — of,** beneficio (with genitive).

favour, v.a. faveo, 2; secundo, 1.

favourable, a. prosperus, felix, faustus; commodus, idoneus; benignus; (as the gods) propitius, æquus, secundus.

favourably, ad. prospere, feliciter, fauste; benigne, opportune.

favourer, s. fautor, m.; fautrix, f.

favourite, a. dilectus, gratus; (popular) gratiosus; —, s. (darling, etc.) deliciæ, f. pl.

favouritism, s. ambitio; gratia; (partiality) iniquitas, f.

fawn, s. hinnuleus, m.

fawn, a. (of colour) gilvus.

fawn, v.n. (on, upon) adulor, 1.

fawner, s. adulator, m.

fawning, a. adulatorius, blandus; **—ly,** ad. adulatorie, blande.

fawning, s. adulatio, f.

fealty, s. fides, f.; **swear — to,** in verba juro (gen.), f.

fear, s. timor, metus, m.; formido, f.

fear, v.a. & n. timeo, paveo, 2; metuo, 3; formido, 1; (reverentially), vereor, 2.

fearful, a. timidus, pavidus; (terrible) dirus; formidolosus; **—ly,** ad. timide, formidolose.

fearfulness, s. timiditas, f.

fearless, a. impavidus, intrepidus; **—ly,** ad. impavide.

fearlessness, s. audacia, audentia, f.

feasible, quod fieri potest.

feast, s. (holiday) dies festus, m.; sollemne, n.; (banquet) convivium, n.; epulæ, dapes, f. pl.

feast, v.n. epulor, convivor, 1; —, v.a. (to treat) excipio, 3; fig. feast (one's eyes on) pasco, 3.

feaster, s. epulo; (entertainer) hospes, m.

feat, s. facinus; factum, n.; res gesta, f.

feather, s. (great or wing —) penna; (small, downy) pluma, f.

feather, v.a. pennis adorno, 1.

feathered, a. pennatus; plumosus, penniger.

feathery, a. plumeus; plumosus.

feature, s. lineamentum, n.; vultus, m.; os, n.; fig. (part) pars, f.; (disposition) ingenium, n.

febrile, a. febriculosus.

February, s. Februarius, m.

fecund, a. fecundus.

fecundate, v.a. fecundo, 1.

fecundity, s. fecunditas, f.

federal, a. fœderatus.

federation, s. societas, f.

fee, s. (pay) merces, f.; præmium, pretium, n.

fee, v.a. muneror, 1.

feeble, a. infirmus, debilis, languidus; **to grow —,** languesco, 3.

feebleness, s. infirmitas, debilitas, f.; languor, m.

feebly, ad. infirme; languide.

feed, v.a. (animals) pasco; (to nourish) alo, 3; (support) sustento, 1; fig. (one's eyes, etc.) pasco; —, v.n. pascor; vescor, 3.

feed, s., v. **food.**

feel, v.a. & n. (to touch) tango, 3; (handle) tracto, 1; (perceive) sentio, 4; concipio, percipio, 3; (be moved, affected) moveor, commoveor; **how do you —?** quid agis? 2; **to — for,** doleo (cum aliquo), misereor (alicujus), 2.

feel, s. tactus, m.

feeler, s. (of an insect) crinis, m.; fig. tentamen, n.

feeling, a. misericors.

feeling, s. (touch) tactus; (sensibility in general) sensus; (emotion) affectus, m.; (anger) ira, f.; (pity) miseratio, f.; (taste) judicium, n.

feelingly, a. (compassionately) cum miseratione.

feign, v.a. & n. fingo, comminiscor, 3; (to pretend) dissimulo, simulo, 1; (to lie) mentior, 4.

feignedly, ad. ficte, simulate.

feint, s. simulatio; (in fencing) captatio, f.

felicitate, v.a. grator, gratulor, 1.

felicitation, s. gratulatio, f.

felicitous, a. felix; **—ly,** ad. feliciter.

felicity, s. felicitas, f.

feline, s. felin(e)us.

fell, s. (skin) pellis, f.

fell, a. atrox, sævus, crudelis, dirus.

fell, v.a. (trees) cædo; (to knock down) sterno, prosterno, everto, 3.

fellmonger, s. pellio, m.

felloe, v. **felly.**

fellow, s. (companion) socius; (in office) collega; (any individual) homo; (equal) par, m. 　　　　　　　　　　　[civis.

fellow-citizen, **fellow-countryman,** s.

fellow-creature, s. homo, m.

fellow-feeling, s. (pity) misericordia, f.
fellow-labourer, s. consors laboris, m.
fellow-servant, s. conservus, m.; conserva, f.
fellowship, s. societas, communitas, f.; sodalicium, n.
fellow-soldier, s. commilito, m.
fellow-student, s. condiscipulus, m.
fellow-sufferer, laborum socius.
fellow-traveller, s. convector; socius itineris, m.
felly, s. (of a wheel) curvatura rotæ, f.
felon, s. noxius, scelestus, m.
felonious, a. nefarius, scelestus.
felony, s. scelus, maleficium, n.
felt, s. coactilia, n. pl.
female, s. femina, mulier, f.
female, a. femineus, muliebris.
feminine, a. femineus, muliebris; femininus.
fen, s. palus, f.
fence, s. sæpes, f.; sæptum; *fig.* (protection) tutamen, n.
fence, v.a. sæpio, 4; defendo, 3; —, v.n. battuo, 3.
fenceless, a. apertus. [ta, m.
fencer, s. gladii peritus, gladiator, lanis-
fencing, s. ars gladii, f. [ista, m.
fencing-master, s. gladii magister, lan-
fencing-school, s. ludus gladiatorius, m.
fend, v.a. defendo, 3; — for oneself, suis opibus niti.
fennel, s. fæniculum, n.
fenny, a. paluster, paludosus, uliginosus.
ferment, s. fermentum, n.; *fig.* æstus, m.
ferment, v.a. & n. fermento; fermentor, 1.
fermentation, s. *fig.* æstus, fervor, m.
fern, s. filix, f.; flowering- —, osmunda (mod. hort.).
fernery, fern-plot, s. filictum, n.
ferocious, a. ferus, truculentus, sævus, atrox; —ly, ad. truculente, sæve, atrociter.
ferociousness, ferocity, s. sævitia, feritas, atrocitas, f.
ferret, s. viverra, f.
ferret, v.a. to — out, rimor, expiscor, 1.
ferruginous, a. ferrugineus.
ferry, s. trajectus, m.
ferry, v.a. trajicio, transveho, 3.
ferry-boat, s. scapha, cymba, f.
ferry-man, s. portitor, m.
fertile, a. fertilis, fecundus, ferax, uber.
fertility, s. fertilitas, ubertas, f.
fertilize, v.a. fecundo, 1.
ferule, s. ferula, f.
fervency, s. fervor, impetus, m.
fervent, a. ardens, fervidus; vehemens; —ly, ad. ardenter; vehementer.
fervid, a. fervidus, ardens; —ly, ad. ardenter.

fervour, s. ardor, fervor, impetus, m.
fester, v.n. suppuro, ulceror, 1.
festival, s. dies festus, m.; sollemne, n.
festive, a. festus, festivus.
festivity, a. sollemnia, n. pl.; (gaiety) festivitas, f. [adorno, 1.
festoon, s. sertum, n.; —, v.a. corono,
fetch, v.a. adduco, affero; arcesso, peto, 3; to — away, abduco, 3; to — back, reduco, 3; to — down, deveho; to — in, importo, 1; to — off, aufero, 3; to — out, depromo; (to cause to appear) elicio, 3.
fetid, a. fetidus; graveolens.
fetidness, s. fetor, m.
fetlock, s. cirrus, m.
fetter, v.a. compedes impingo (alicui), 3; colligo, 1; vincio, 4; *fig.* impedio, 4; illaqueo, 1.
fetter, s. compes, pedica,. f.
feud, s. lis, simultas; inimicitia, f.; odium, n.
fever, s. febris, f.; to be in —, febrio, 4.
feverish, a. febriculosus; *fig.* ardens.
few, a. pauci, perpauci; —, aliquot, (indecl.); in a — words, paucis, breviter.
fewness, s. paucitas, raritas, f.
fib, s. mendaciolum, mendaciunculum, n.
fibre, s. fibra, f.; filum, n.
fibrous, a. fibratus. [levis.
fickle, a. inconstans, mobilis; instabilis;
fickleness, s. inconstantia; mutabilitas; mobilitas, levitas, f.
fiction, s. fictio, f.; commentum, n.; fabula, f.
fictitious, a. fictus, commenticius; (simulated), simulatus; —ly, ad. ficte.
fiddle, s. fides, f.
fiddle-faddle, s. nugæ, gerræ, f. pl.
fiddler, s. fidicen, m.
fiddle-string, s. chorda, fides, f.
fidelity, s. fidelitas; constantia, fides, f.
fidget, s. agitatio; (running to and fro) cursitatio, f.; (restlessness) inquies, f.
fidget, v.a. vexo, 1; —, v.n. cursito, 1.
fidgety, a. inquietus.
fie, i. phu, proh!
field, s. campus, ager, m.; arvum, rus, n.; — of grass, pratum; (battle) prœlium, n.; *fig.* (scope) area, f.
fieldfare, s. turdus, m.
field-marshal, s. imperator, m.
field-mouse, s. mus agrestis, m.
field-piece, s. tormentum, n.
field-sports, s. venatio, f.
fiend, s. diabolus, m.; *fig.* Erinys, f.
fiendish, a. diabolicus.
fierce, a. atrox; sævus; vehemens; —ly, ad. atrociter; sæve; ferociter; vehementer.

fierceness, s. atrocitas; sævitia; ferocitas; ferocia; vehementia, f.

fieriness, s. iracundia, f.   [cundus.

fiery, a. igneus; *fig.* ardens, fervidus, ira-

fife, s. tibia, f.

fifer, s. tibicen, m.

fifteen, a. quindecim; — **times,** quindecies; — **each,** quindeni.

fifteenth, a. quintus decimus.   [quinto.

fifth, a. quintus; **for the — time,** quintum,

fifth, s. quinta pars, f.

fifthly, a. quintum, quinto.

fiftieth, a. quinquagesimus.

fifty, a. quinquaginta; — **each,** quinquageni.

fig, s. (fruit and tree) ficus, f.

fig-tree, s. ficus, f.

fig-pecker, s. ficedula, f.

fight, s. pugna, f.; prœlium, n.; (struggle) contentio, f.

fight, v.a. & n. pugno; dimico, 1; contendo, 3; (in battle) prœlior; (with sword) digladior; (hand to hand) comius pugno, 1; **to — against,** repugno, 1.

fighter, s. pugnator, prœliator, m.

fighting, s., v. **fight,** s.

fighting-cock, s. gallinaceus pyctes, m.

figment, s. commentum, n.

figurative, a. translatus; **—ly,** ad. per translationem, tropice.

figure, s. figura; forma; (shape) imago, f.; (delineation) descriptio, f.; (appearance) species, f.; (in speech) tropus, m.

figure, v.a. delineo, 1; fingo, 3; figuro, 1.

figured, a. sigillatus; (chased) cælatus.

filament, s. fibræ, f. pl.; filum, n.

filbert, s. nux avellana, f.; — **-tree,** corylus, f.

filch, v.a. surripio, 3; suffuror, 1.

file, s. (tool) lima, f.; (for *or* of papers) scapus; (line, string, row) ordo, m.; series, f.; **the rank and —,** milites gregarii, m. pl.

file, v.a. limo, 1; **to — off,** v.n. (mil.) decurro, 3.

filial, a. pius; **—ly,** ad. pie.

filigree, s. diatreta, n. pl.

filings, s. scobis, f.

fill, v.a. compleo; impleo, expleo; (to supply) suppleo, 2; **to — out,** impleo, 2; **to — up,** expleo; (completely) compleo, 2; (to heap) cumulo, 1.

fill, s. satietas, f.; **have one's — of,** satior (abl.).

fillet, s. vitta; fascia; tænia, f.

fillip, s. talitrum, n.; *fig.* (give a — to) promoveo, 2 (acc.).

filly, s. equula, f.

film, s. membranula; *fig.* caligo, f.

filmy, a. membranaceus; *fig.* obscurus.

filter, s. colum, n.

filter, v.a. & n. percolo; percolor, 1.

filtering, s. percolatio, f.

filth, s. sordes, colluvies, illuvies, f.; (personal shabbiness) squalor, m., v. **dirt.**   [obscenitas, f.

filthiness, s. fœditas, f.; squalor, m.; *fig.*

filthily, ad. fœde, spurce.   [obscenus.

filthy, a. sordidus, fœdus, spurcus; *fig.*

filtration, s. percolatio, f.

fin, s. pinna, f.

final, a. ultimus, extremus, postremus; **—ly,** ad. postremo; denique.

finance, s. res familiaris, fiscus, ærarii reditus, m.

finch, s. fringilla, f.

find, v.a. invenio, reperio, 4; (to hit upon) offendo, 3; (catch in the act) deprehendo; **to — out,** comperio, 4; (to discover) rescisco, 3; (to guess) conjecto, 1.

finder, s. inventor, repertor, m.; inventrix, repertrix, f.

fine, a. (of texture) subtilis; (thin) tenuis; (of gold) purus; (handsome) bellus; elegans; (serene) serenus; (ironically) bonus, egregius, præclarus.

fine, s. mul(c)ta, f.

fine, v.a. mul(c)to, 1.

finely, ad. subtiliter; tenuiter; *fig.* pulchre; egregie.

fineness, s. subtilitas; tenuitas; *fig.* pulchritudo; elegantia, præstantia, f.

finery, s. ornatus, cultus, m.; (trimness) lautitia, f.; (meretricious adornment) lenocinium, n.

finger, s. digitus, m.

finger, v.a. tango, 3; tracto, 1.

finical, a. putidus; **—ly,** ad. putide.

finicalness, s. putida elegantia, f.

finish, v.a. conficio, perficio, 3; (to put an end to) termino, 1; finio, 4; **to — off,** consummo, 1; ultimam manum operi impono, 3.

finish, s. perfectio, f.

finishing, s. perfectio, absolutio, f.; **— -touch,** s. ultima manus, f.

finite, a. caducus, moriturus.

finny, a. pinniger.

fir(-tree), s. abies, pinus, f.; (of fir) a. abiegnus, pineus.

fire, s. ignis, m.; (conflagration) incendium, n.; *fig.* fervor, ardor, impetus, us, m.; **to catch** *or* **take —** ignem concipere, 3; **to set on —,** incendo, 3; **on —,** incensus, inflammatus.

fire, v.a. accendo, incendo; **—,** v.n. ignem concipio; (to be in a passion) excandesco, 3; ardeo, 2; exardesco, 3.

firebrand, s. torris, m.; *fig.* (person) fax, f.

fire-engine, s. sipho, m.

firemen, s. excubiæ vigilesque adversus incendia, m. pl.

fireplace, s. caminus; focus, m.

fireproof, a. ignibus impervius.

fire-ship, s. navis ad incendium præparata, f.

fire-shovel, s. batillum, n.

fireside, s. focus, m.

firestone, s. pyrites, m.

fire-wood, s. lignum, n.

firkin, s. dolium, n.

firm, a. firmus; solidus; (of purpose) tenax; **to be —,** persevero, persto, 1.

firm, s. (com.) societas, f.

firmament, s. cælum, firmamentum, n.

firmly, ad. firme, firmiter; solide; (of purpose) tenaciter.

firmness, s. firmitas; constantia, f.

first, a. primus; princeps; **— but one,** a primo proximus.

first, ad. primum; **at —,** primo; **— of all,** imprimis.

first-fruits, s. primitiæ, f. pl.

firth, v. frith.

fisc, s. fiscus, m.

fiscal, a. fiscalis.

fish, s. piscis, m.

fish, v.a. & n. piscor; *fig.* expiscor, 1.

fish-bone, s. spina piscis, f.

fisher, fisherman, s. piscator, m.

fish-hook, s. hamus, m.

fishing, s. piscatus, m.; piscatio, f.

fishing-boat, s. piscatoria navis, f.

fishing-line, s. linum, n.

fishing-net, funda, f.; jaculum, everriculum, n.

fishing-rod, s. arundo, f.; calamus, m.

fishing-tackle, s. (mod.) instrumenta piscatoria, n. pl.

fish-market, s. forum piscarium, n.

fish-monger, s. cetarius, piscarius, n.

fish-pond, s. piscina, f.; vivarium, n.

fishy, a. piscosus, pisculentus; *fig.* suspectus. [pectus.

fissure, s. rima, fissura, f.

fist, s. pugnus, m.

fistula, s. fistula, f.

fit, s. (of a disease) accessio, m.; **epileptic —,** morbus caducus; (whim) libido, f.; **by —s and starts,** carptim.

fit, a. aptus, idoneus; conveniens, opportunus; habilis; (becoming) decens; (ready) paratus.

fit, v.a. accommodo, apto; (to apply) applico, 1; (to furnish) instruo, 3; orno, 1; **—,** v.n. (of dress) sedeo, 2; *fig.* convenio, 4; **to — out,** instruo, 3; orno, adorno, 1; suppedito, 1.

fitful, a. mobilis, mutabilis, inconstans.

fitly, ad. apte; convenienter; decenter.

fitness, s. convenientia.

fitted, a. accommodatus, aptatus.

fitting, a. decens, v. **fit.**

five, a. quinque; **— times,** quinquies; **— each,** quini.

fix, v.a. figo, 3; (the eyes, etc.) intendo, 3; (establish) stabilio, 4; (on, upon) eligo, 3; (appoint) statuo, constituo, 3; (be fixed, stick) inhæreo, 2.

fixed, a. fixus, firmus; certus; (intent upon) intentus; **—ly,** ad. firmiter, constanter.

fixedness, fixity, s. firmitas, f.

fixture, s. affixum, n.

fizz, fizzle, v.n. sibilo, 1.

fizz, fizzle, s. sibila, n. pl.

flabby, a. flaccidus, flaccus; fluidus; (drooping) marcidus.

flaccid, a. flaccidus. [(plant) iris, f.

flag, s. (banner) vexillum; insigne, n.;

flag, v.n. languesco; refrigesco, remittor, 3; laxor, 1.

flageolet, s. fistula, f.

flagitious, a. flagitiosus, turpis; **—ly,** ad. flagitiose, turpiter.

flagitiousness, s. turpitudo, f.

flagon, s. lagena, f. [tas, f.

flagrancy, s. nequitia, infamia, immani-

flagrant, a. immanis, insignis; atrox, nefarius; (open) apertus.

flagrantly, ad. atrociter, nefarie; (openly) aperte.

flag-ship, s. navis prætoria, f.

flail, s. pertica, f.; tribulum, n.

flake, s. floccus, m.; frustum, n.; squama, f.; **snow —s,** nives, f. pl.

flaky, a. squameus.

flambeau, s. fax, tæda, f.; torris, m.

flame, s. flamma, f.; ardor, m.

flame, v.n. flammo, flagro, 1; **to — up,** *fig.* exardesco, 3.

flame-coloured, a. flammeus; rutilus.

flamingo, s. (bird) phœnicopterus, m.

flank, s. (of an animal) ilia, n. pl.; (of an army) latus, n.

flap, s. (of a dress) lacinia; (blow) alapa, f.; (fly-flap) muscarium, n.

flap, v.a. & n. alis plaudere, 3; (to hang loosely) fluito, 1; dependeo, 2.

flare, v.n. flagro, 1; fulgeo, 2.

flash, s. fulgor, m.; (of lightning) fulmen, n.; **— of wit,** sales, m. pl.

flash, v.n. fulgeo, splendeo, 2; corusco, 1.

flashy, a. speciosus.

flask, s. ampulla, laguncula, f.

flat, a. (even, level) planus; (not mountainous) campester; (lying on the face) pronus; (sheer) merus; (insipid, of drinks) vapidus; *fig.* frigidus; insulsus; jejunus.

flat, s. (level surface) planities, f.; æquor, n.; campus, m.

flatly, ad. aperte, plane.

flatness, s. planities; (evenness) æqualitas; (of a discourse, etc.) jejunitas; (of drinks) vappa, f.

flat-nosed, a. simus.

flatten, v.a. complano, æquo, 1. [dior, 4.

flatter, v.a. adulor, assentor, 1; blan-

flatterer, s. adulator, assentator, m.

flattering, a. adulans, blandus, adulatorius.

flatteringly, ad. blande. [ditiæ, f. pl.

flattery, s. adulatio, assentatio, f.; blan-

flatulency, s. inflatio, ventositas, f.

flaunt, v.a. objicio, 3; v.n. (to flutter) volito, 1; fig. tumeo, 2; spatior, 1.

flavour, s. sapor, m.

flavour, v.a. condio, 4.

flavouring, s. condimentum, n.

flaw, s. (defect) vitium, n.; menda, macula, labes, f.; (chink) rima, f.

flawless, a. sine mendo, perfectus, integer.

flax, s. linum, n.

flaxen, flaxy, a. lineus; (of colour) flavus.

flay, v.a. pellem detraho, 3.

flea, s. pulex, m.

flea-bane, s. erigeron (mod. hort.).

fleck, s. macula, f.

fleck, v.a. maculo, 1.

fledged, a. plumatus.

flee, v.a. & n. fugio, 3; **to — away,** aufugio, 3; **to — back,** refugio, 3; **to — to,** confugio, 3.

fleece, s. vellus, n.

fleece, v.a. (to shear) tondeo, 2; fig. spolio; privo; expilo, 1.

fleecy, a. laniger.

fleer, v.a. & n. ludificor, 1; irrideo, 2.

fleet, s. classis, f. [(winged) volucer.

fleet, a. celer; velox, rapidus, pernix;

fleeting, a. fugax; fluxus; lubricus; caducus. [f.

fleetness, s. velocitas, pernicitas, celeritas,

flesh, s. (meat) caro, f.; viscera, n. pl.; fig. (body) corpus, n.; (sensuality) libido, f.

flesh-coloured, a. carnosus.

fleshliness, s. (sensuality) carnalitas, f.

fleshly, a. carnalis.

fleshy, a. (abounding in flesh) carnosus.

flexibility, s. mollitia, facilitas, f.

flexible, a. flexibilis, flexilis, mollis, lentus; fig. exorabilis.

flexion, s. curvatura, f.; flexus, m.

flicker, v.n. (to flutter) volito; (to flash) corusco, 1.

flight, a. fuga, f.; (escape) effugium n.; (of birds) volatus; (covey) grex (avium), m.; (of stairs) scala, f.; **to put to —,** in fugam impello, 3; fugo, 1; fundo, 3; **to take to —,** aufugio, 3.

flightiness, s. levitas, inconstantia, f.

flighty, a. levis; volaticus; inconstans.

flimsiness, s. tenuitas, exilitas, f.

flimsy, a. tenuis, prætenuis; fig. frivolus.

flinch, abhorreo, 2.

fling, v.a. jacio, mitto, 3; **to — away,** abjicio, 3; **to — down,** dejicio, 3; **to — off,** rejicio, 3; **to — up,** fig. depono, 3.

fling, s. jactus, m.

flint, s. silex, c.

flinty, a. siliceus.

flippancy, s. levitas, protervitas, f.

flippant, a. levis, protervus, petulans; **—ly,** ad. proterve, petulanter.

flirt, v.n. ludo, 3.

flirtation, s. lusus, m.

flit, v.n. volito, circumvolito, 1.

flitch, s. (— of bacon) succidia, f.

float, s. (raft) ratis, f.; (of a fishing-line) cortex, m.

float, v.n. fluito, (in)nato; fluctuor, 1; pendeo, 2; (to hang loosely) volito, 1; v.a. (to launch) deduco, 3.

flock, s. (of wool) floccus; (of sheep, birds, etc.) grex, m.; **in —s,** gregatim.

flock, v.n. (together) coeo, convenio, congregor, 4; convolo, 1.

flog, v.a. verbero, 1; cædo, 3.

flogging, s. verberatio, f.; verbera, n. pl.

flood, s. (inundation) diluvies, f.; (stream) flumen, n.; (tide) æstus, m.; fig. flumen, n.

flood-gate, s. emissarium, n.

floor, s. solum, n.; (paved —) pavimentum, n.; (of a barn) area; (story) contignatio, f.; tabulatum, n.

floor, v.a. pavimentum struo, 3; (with planks) contabulo, 1; (to throw down) sterno, 3; (to silence) confuto, 1.

flooring, s. contabulatio, f., v. **floor,** s.

floral, a. florens. [(of style) floridus.

florid, a. (of complexion) rubicundus; fig.

floss-flower, s. ageratum (mod. hort.).

flotilla, s. classicula, f. pl.

flounce, a. fimbriæ, f.; instita, f.

flounder, v.n. voluto, titubo, 1.

flour, s. farina, f.; (finest) pollen, n.

flourish, v.a. vibro, roto, 1; (to sound a trumpet) cano, 3; —, v.n. floreo; vireo, 2; floresco, 3; (to boast) jacto, 1.

flourish, s. ornamentum, n.; (of style) calamistri, flosculi, m. pl.; (of a trumpet) cantus, m.

flourishing, a. florens.

floury, a. farinulentus.

flout, v.a. derideo, 2; repudio, 1.

flow, v.n. fluo, feror, 3; mano, 1; (of the tide) affluo, accedo, 3.

flow, s. fluxus, m.; (gliding motion) lapsus; (of the tide) accessus, m.; (stream) flumen, n.; (course) cursus, m.

flower, s. flos, flosculus, m.; *fig.* (the best) flos; (of troops) robur, n.; (of age) adolescentia, f.

flower, v.n. floreo, 2; floresco, 3.

flower-bed, s. area, f.

floweret, s. flosculus, m.

flower-garden, s. hortus, m.

flower-stalk, s. calamus, m.

flowery, a. floreus; floridus; florifer.

fluctuate, v.a. fluctuo; fluito, jactor, 1.

fluctuation, s. fluctuatio; *fig.* mutatio, f.

flue, s. cuniculus fornacis, m.

fluency, s. volubilitas linguæ; copia verborum, f.

fluent, a. volubilis; profluens; (eloquent) disertus; —ly, ad. volubiliter.

fluid, a. fluidus, liquidus.

fluid, s. liquor, umor, latex, m.

flummery, s. *fig.* (flattery) blanditiæ, f. pl.

flunkey, s. servus, m.

flurry, s. perturbatio, f.; tumultus, m.

flurry, v.a. perturbo; inquieto, sollicito, 1.

flush, s. (sudden access) impetus, m.; (abundance) copia, f.; (blush) rubor, m.

flush, v.n. erubesco, 3; —, v.a. rubefacio, 3. [licito.

fluster, v.a. perturbo; inquieto, 1; solflute,** s. tibia; (in architecture) stria, f.

flute, v.a. strio, 1.

flutist, s. tibicen, m.

flutter, v.a. agito, perturbo, sollicito, 1; —, v.n. (of birds) volito; (with alarm) trepido, 1. [trepidatio, f.

flutter, fluttering, s. plausus, m.; (alarm) flux,** s. fluxus, m.; profluvium, n.

fly, s. musca, f.

fly, v.n. volo, volito, 1; (to flee) fugio, 3; **to — asunder,** dissilio, 4; (with noise) displodor, 3; **to — off,** avolo, 1; **to, — open,** dissilio, 4; **to — out,** provolo, 1; *fig.* excandesco, 3; **to — up,** subvolo, 1.

fly-catcher, s. (bird) melancoryphos, m.

fly-flap, s. muscarium, n.

flying, a. volatilis; volucer; ales.

foal, s. pullus; (of asses) asellus; (of the horse) equulus, m.

foal, v.n. (of horses and asses) pario, 3.

foam, s. spuma, f.

foam, v.n. spumo; (to boil) æstuo, exæstuo, 1. [spumifer.

foamy, a. spumans; spumeus, spumosus, fodder,** s. pabulum, n.

fodder, v.n. pabulum præbeo, 2.

foe, s. hostis, inimicus, m.

fog, s. caligo, nebula, f.

foggy, a. caliginosus, nebulosus.

foible, s. vitium, n.; error, m.

foil, s. (for fencing) rudis, f.; (leaf of metal) lamina; (very thin) bractea, f.; (contrast) exemplum contrarii.

foil, v.a. frustror, 1; repello, 3; **be —ed,** spe dejici.

foist, v.a. suppono, subdo, 3.

fold, s. sinus, m.; (wrinkling) ruga, f.; (for cattle) stabulum; (for sheep) ovile, n. [stabulo, 1; includo, 3.

fold, v.a. plico, complico; (sheep) folding-doors,** s. valvæ, f. pl.

foliage, s. frons, coma, f.; folia, n. pl.

folks, s. homines, m. pl.

follow, v.n. sequor, insequor, consequor, 3; (close) insto, sector, assector, 1; (on) persequor; (out) exsequor, prosequor; (up) subsequor, 3.

follower, s. sectator, assectator; *fig.* discipulus, i, m.

following, a. (in)sequens; posterus, proximus; (uninterruptedly) continuus;— **on the following day,** postridie.

folly, s. stultitia; insipientia; (madness) dementia, f.

foment, v.a. foveo, 2; (disorder, etc.) stimulo, 1; cieo, 2.

fomentation, s. fomentum, n.

fomenter, s. concitator, auctor, m.

fond, a. amans; deditus; cupidus; (indulgent) indulgens; (foolishly infatuated) demens; **to be — of,** amo, 1.

fondle, v.a. permulceo, foveo, 2.

fondling, s. deliciæ, f. pl.

fondly, ad. amanter, peramanter; (foolishly) stulte.

fondness, s. amor, m.; indulgentia; caritas; (foolishness) dementia, f.

font, s. baptisterium, n.

food, s. (for cattle, etc.) pabulum; (any nourishing substance) alimentum, n.; (of men) cibus, m.; esca, f.

fool, s. stultus, insipiens; (idiot) fatuus; (in a play) sannio, m.; **to make a — of,** ludificor (aliquem), 1; **to play the —,** ineptio, 4; nugor, 1.

fool, v.a. ludificor, 1; ludo, illudo, 3; (to disappoint) frustror, 1; **— away,** dissipo, 1; profundo, 3.

foolery, s. ineptiæ, nugæ, f. pl.

foolhardiness, s. temeritas, f.

foolhardy, a. temerarius.

foolish, a. stultus, fatuus, ineptus, stolidus; —ly, ad. stulte, inepte.

foot, s. pes, m.; (of a mountain) radix, f.; (of a pillar, etc.) basis, f.; (mil.) peditatus, m.; **on —,** pedester (tris, tre). [(to dance) salto, 1.

foot, v.n. (to tread) pulso (tellurem); football,** s. pila, f.

footbath, s. lavacrum, n.

footboy, s., v. **footman.**

footing, a. (mod.) locus in quo firmiter insisti possit; (condition) status, m.; condicio, f.

footpad, s. latro, grassator, m.
footpath, s. semita, f.; callis, trames, m.
footprint, s. vestigium, n.
foot-race, s. cursus, m.
foot-soldier, s. pedes, m.
footstep, s. vestigium, n.
footstool, s. scabellum, n.
fop, s. bellus homo, putidus homo, m.
foppery, s. elegantia, f.
foppish, a. elegans putidus; nitidus, delicatus; —ly, eleganter, putide, delicate.
foppishness, s. elegantia, f.
for, pr. pro; causa; per; (because of) ob, propter (with accusative); (after negatives) prae; —, c. nam, enim; — **some time,** aliquandiu; — **the sake of,** causa; — **that,** propterea quod, siquidem, quoniam; **food — a day,** cibus unius diei; — **the future,** in posterum.
forage, s. pabulum, n.
forage, v.a. & n. pabulor; frumentor, 1; fig. rimor.
forager, s. pabulator; frumentator, m.
foraging, s. pabulatio; frumentatio, f.
forasmuch, c. cum, quoniam.
foray, v.a. incursio, populatio, f.
forbear, v.a. parco, mitto, 3; —, v.n. abstineo, 2; (to leave off) desisto; (to spare) parco, 3.
forbearance, s. patientia; indulgentia, f.
forbearing, a. patiens, tolerans.
forbid, v.a. veto, 1; prohibeo, 2; interdico, 3.
forbidding, a. insuavis, odiosus; (ugly) deformis; (frightful) immanis.
force, s. vis; (law) manus, f.; (mil.) copiæ, f. pl.; (weight) momentum, pondus, n.; (strength) vires, f. pl.; robur, n.; **by main —,** vi et armis; **in —,** valens, validus.
force, v.a. cogo; (a door, a wall, etc.) perrumpo; (to drive away) expello, 3; **to — down,** detrudo, 3; **to — in,** (a nail, etc.) infigo, 3; **to — out,** extorqueo, 2; depello, 3; **to — open,** rumpo, 3; **to — up,** subigo, 3.
forced, a. (unnatural) arcessitus, quæsitus; — **march,** magnum or maximum iter, n.
forceful, a. validus.
forcemeat, s. insicium, n.
forceps, s. (in surgery) forceps, c.; volsella, f.
forcible, a. per vim factus; (strong) validus; (violent) vehemens; (weighty) gravis; (compulsory) coactus.
forcibly, ad. per vim, vi; violenter; graviter.
ford, s. vadum, n.
ford, v.a. vado transire, 4.

fordable, a. quod vado transiri potest.
fore, a. prior; anticus, adversus.
fore-arm, s. bracchium, n.
forearm, v.a. præcaveo, 2; præmunio, 4.
forebode, v.a. portendo, 3; præsagio, 4; (to forewarn) moneo, 2; (conjecture) auguror, 1.
foreboding, s. portentum, præsagium, n.; (prophetic feeling) præsensio, f.
foreboding, a. præsagus.
forecast, v.a. prævideo, 2; prospicio, 3; auguror, 1.
forecast, s. providentia, f.; augurium, n.
forecastle, s. prora, f.
foredoom, v.a. destino, 1.
forefather, s. atavus, m.; —s, pl. majores, m. pl.
forefend, v.a. prohibeo, 2.
fore-finger, s. digitus index, m.
foregoing, a. prior, proximus.
forgo, v.a. renuntio, 1; dimitto, 3; (not to meddle with) abstineo, 2; (to lose) amitto, 3.
forehead, s. frons, f.
foreign, a. externus, alienus, peregrinus.
foreigner, s. (not a fellow-citizen) peregrinus, externus; (stranger) advena, m.
foreknow, v.a. prænosco, 3; præscio, 4.
foreknowledge, s. providentia; (of God) præscientia, f.
foreland, s. promontorium, n.; lingua, f.
forelock, s. cirrus, m.; **to take time by the —,** occasionem præcipio, 3.
foreman, s. præfectus, m.
forementioned, a. supra dictus.
foremost, a. primus; princeps, præcipuus.
forenoon, a. dies antemeridianus; **in the —,** ante meridiem.
forensic, a. forensis.
fore-part, s. prior pars, f.
fore-quarter, s. (of an animal) armus, m.
forerunner, s. prænuntius, antecursor, m.
foresaid, a. supra dictus.
foresee, v.a. prævideo, 2; prospicio, 3.
foreseeing, a. providus.
foresight, s. providentia, prospicientia, prudentia; (precaution) provisio, f.
forest, s. silva, f.; nemus, n.; saltus, m.; —, a. silvestris, nemorensis.
forestall, v.a. anticipo, 1; præcipio, 3.
forester, s. silvarum incola; (keeper of forest) saltuarius, m.
foretaste, s. gustus, m.
foretaste, v.a. prægusto, 1.
foretell, v.a. prædico, 3; vaticinor, 1.
foreteller, s. vates, c.; fatidicus, m.
forethought, s. providentia, prospicientia, f.
foretoken, v.a. portendo, 3; præsignifico, 1.
foretop, s. antiæ, f. pl.

forewarn, v.a. præmoneo; moneo, 2.

forewarning, s. præmonitus, monitus, m.

forfeit, s. mul(c)ta, pœna, f.

forfeit, v.a. mul(c)tor, 1; (to lose) amitto, 3.

forfeiture, s. (lost) amissio; (of goods) publicatio, f.

forge, v.a. (as a smith) cudo, procudo, 3; fabricor, 1; (to devise) fingo; (counterfeit) corrumpo, 3; (a document) interlino, 3; v.n. — **ahead,** progredior, 3.

forge, s. fornax, f.

forger, s. fabricator; (of writings) falsarius, m.

forgery, s. (of documents) subjectio; litteræ falsæ, f. pl.

forget, v.a. obliviscor; (to unlearn) dedisco, 3.

forgetful, a. obliviosus, immemor.

forgetfulness, s. oblivio, f.; oblivium, n.

forget-me-not, s. myosotis, f.

forgive, v.a. condono, 1; ignosco, 3.

forgiveness, s. venia, f.

forgiving, a. ignoscens; clemens.

fork, s. furca, f.; (of roads) bivium, trivium, quadrivium, n.

fork, v.n. scindor, 3.

forked, forky, a. bifurcus, bicornis.

forlorn, a. solus, desertus, miser.

form, s. forma, figura, f.; (bench) scamnum, n.; (rite) ritus, m.; (class in a school) classis, f.; **in due —,** rite.

form, v.a. formo, 1; fingo; (to produce) efficio; (troops) instruo, 3; (constitute) sum.

formal, a. formalis; *fig.* frigidus; (stiff) rigidus, durus; —**ly,** ex formula; *fig.* frigide.

formality, s. ritus, m.

formation, s. conformatio; forma, figura, f.

former, a. prior, priscus, pristinus; (immediately preceding) superior; —**ly,** ad. antea, prius, antehac; olim; quondam.

formidable, a. formidabilis, formidolosus, metuendus.

formidably, ad. formidolose.

formless, a. informis; *fig.* rudis.

formula, s. formula, f.; exemplar, n.; **recite a —,** verba præeo.

forsake, v.a. desero, derelinquo, relinquo, destituo, 3.

forsooth, ad. (indeed) vere, enimvero; (ironically) nempe; nimirum, scilicet.

forswear, v.a. abjuro; repudio; (to swear falsely) pejero, 1.

fort, s. castellum, n.; arx, f.

forth, ad. foras; (of time) inde; **and so —,** et cetera.

forthcoming, a. promptus; in promptu.

forthwith, ad. extemplo, protinus, statim, continuo.

fortieth, a. quadragesimus.

fortification, s. munitio, f.; munimen, munimentum, n.

fortify, v.a. munio, circummunio, 4.

fortitude, s. fortitudo, virtus, f.

fortnight, s. semestrium, n.; dies quatuordecim, m. pl.

fortress, s. arx, f.; castellum, n.

fortuitous, a. fortuitus; —**ly,** ad. fortuito.

fortunate, a. fortunatus, felix, prosperus; —**ly,** ad. fortunate, prospere, feliciter.

fortune, s. fortuna, fors, sors, f.; casus, m.; **good —,** fortuna, f.; (estate) divitiæ, opes, f. pl.; (of a woman) dos, f.; **to tell —s,** hariolor, 1.

fortune-hunter, s. captator, m.

fortune-teller, s. hariolus, m.; hariola, f.

forty, a. quadraginta; — **times,** quadragies; — **each,** quadrageni.

forum, s. forum, n. [prorsum.

forward, forwards, ad. porro, prorsus,

forward, a. (early, soon ripe) præcox; (ready) promptus; (bold) audax; (saucy) protervus; (inclined) propensus.

forward, v.a. (to despatch) mitto, 3; (to promote); promoveo, 2; consulo (dat.), 3.

forwardness, s. (speed) celeritas, f.; (sauciness) protervitas; (earliness) maturitas, f.

fosse, s. fossa, f.

fossil, a. fossilis.

foster, v.a. foveo, 2; nutrio, 4; alo, 3.

foster-brother, s. collacteus, collactaneus, m.

foster-child, s. alumnus, m.; alumna, f.

fosterer, s. nutritor; *fig.* patronus, m.

foster-father, s. nutricius, nutritor, m.

foster-mother, s. nutrix, altrix, educatrix, f.

foster-sister, s. collactea, collactanea, f.

foster-son, s. alumnus, m.

foul, a. (dirty) fœdus, lutulentus, squalidus; (ugly) deformis; (of language) obscenus; (of weather, stormy) turbidus; *fig.* turpis; **to fall — of,** incurro, collidor, 3.

foul, v.a. fœdo, inquino, 1.

foully, ad. fœde, turpiter, obscene.

foul-mouthed, a. maledicus.

foulness, s. fœditas; (dirt) squalor, m.; (of a crime) atrocitas; (in appearance) deformitas; *fig.* turpitudo; obscenitas, f.

found, v.a. fundo, 1; condo, constituo, construo, 3.

foundation, s. fundamentum, fundamen, n.; substructio, sedes, f.

founder, s. fundator, conditor; auctor; (of metals) fusor, m.

founder, v.n. (as ships) submergor, deprimor, 3.
foundling, s. expositicius, m.
foundress, s. conditrix, fundatrix, f.
fount, fountain, s. fons, m.
fountain-head, s. origo fontis, f.
four, a. quattuor; — **times,** quater; — **each,** quaterni; **on all —s,** repens.
fourfold, a. quadruplex, quadruplus; —, s. quadruplum, n.
four-footed, a. quadrupes.
four-in-hand, s. quadriga, f.
four-oared, a. quadriremis.
fourscore, a. octoginta.
fourteen, a. quattuordecim.
fourteenth, a. quartus decimus.
fourth, a. quartus; **—ly,** ad. quarto.
fowl, s. avis, volucris, f.; **domestic —,** gallina, f.
fowler, s. auceps, c.
fowling, s. aucupium, n.
fox, s. vulpes, vulpecula, f.; *fig.* homo astutus; **an old —,** veterator, m.
foxglove, s. digitalis (mod. hort.), m.
foxhound, s. catulus, m. [fragmen, n.
fraction, s. pars exigua; fragmentum,
fractious, a: difficilis, morosus.
fractiousness, s.; morositas, f.
fracture, s. fractura, f.; —, v.a. frango, 3.
fragile, a. fragilis; *fig.* caducus.
fragility, s. fragilitas, f.
fragment, s. fragmentum, fragmen, n.
fragrance, s. odor, m.
fragrant, a. suaveolens, odorus; odorifer.
frail, a. fragilis; caducus; infirmus.
frailty, s. fragilitas; infirmitas, f.
frame, s. (in general, of a building, of the world) compages; (of body) figura; (of a window, etc.) forma; (of a bed) sponda, f.; (edge) margo, c.; *fig.* habitus animi, m.
frame, v.a. formo; (to build) fabrico, 1; (to join together) compingo, 3; (to contrive) molior, 4.
framer, s. fabricator; creator; auctor, m.
framework, s. compages, f.
France, s. Gallia, f.
franchise, s. civitas, f.; jus suffragii, n.
frank, a. candidus, liber, ingenuus, sincerus, simplex.
frankincense, s. tus, n.
frankly, ad. candide, libere, ingenue, sincere, simpliciter.
frankness, s. libertas; candor, m.; ingenuitas; simplicitas; sinceritas, f.
frantic, a. fanaticus, furens, insanus, amens; **—ly,** ad. insane.
fraternal, a. fraternus; **—ly,** ad. fraterne.
fraternity, s. germanitas; (association) sodalitas, f.
fraternize, v.n. amice convenio.

fratricide, s. (murderer) fratricida, m.; (murder) fraternum parricidium, n.
fraud, s. fraus, fallacia, f.; dolus, m.
fraudulent, a. fraudulentus, dolosus; **—ly,** ad. fraudulenter, dolo malo.
fraught, a. oneratus, plenus.
fray, s. rixa, pugua, f.; certamen, n.
fray, v.a. territo, 1; (wear away) attero, 3.
freak, s. (whim) libido, f.; (monster) monstrum, portentum, n.
freakish, a. levis, (monstrous) prodigiosus.
freckle, s. lentigo, f.
freckled, a. lentiginosus.
free, a. liber; (from business) otiosus; (not bound by . . .) solutus; (of space) vacuus; (immune) immunis; (gratuitous) gratuitus; (impudent) procax; *fig.* candidus, sincerus; **— from,** expers, vacuus, liber.
free, v.a. libero, 1; (a slave) manumitto, 3; (a son) emancipo, 1. [m.
freebooter, s. prædo, latro; (at sea) pirata,
freebooting, s. latrocinium, n.
freeborn, a. ingenuus.
freedman, s. libertus, libertinus, m.
freedom, s. libertas; immunitas; (from) vacuitas, f.; (franchise) civitas, f.; (candour) candor, m.
freedwoman, s. liberta, libertina, f.
freehold, s. prædium liberum, n.
freely, ad. libere; (of one's own accord) sponte; (liberally) large; copiose; liberaliter, munifice; (far and wide) late; (for nothing) gratis.
freeman, s. liber, m.
freeness, s. libertas, f.
freesia, s. freesia (mod. hort.).
freespoken, a. ingenuus, candidus, simplex. [bitrium, n.
free-will, s. voluntas, f.; liberum ar-
freeze, v.a. congelo, gelo, glacio, 1; —, v.n. consisto, rigesco, 3; **it —s,** gelat.
freight, s. onus, naulum, n.
freight, v.a. onero, 1.
French, a. Gallicus; **the —,** s. Galli, m. pl.; **in —,** Gallice.
french-bean, s. phaseolus, m.
Frenchman, s. Gallus, m.
frenzied, a. furens, lymphatus.
frenzy, s. furor, m.; insania, f.
frequency, s. crebritas; frequentia, f.
frequent, a. creber; frequens: **—ly,** ad. crebro; frequenter, sæpe.
frequent, v.a. frequento, celebro, 1.
frequentative, a. frequentativus.
frequenter, s. frequentator, obsessor, m.
fresco, s. tectorium, n.; **al —,** sub divo.
fresh, a. (new) recens, novus; (cool) frigidulus; (lusty) vigens; (not tired) integer; (green) viridis; (not salt) dulcis.

freshen, v.a. recreo, 1; v.n. increbresco, 3.

freshly, ad. recenter.

freshman, s. novicius, m.

freshness, s. (newness) novitas, f.; (vigour) vigor, m.

fret, v.a. (to rub) frico, 1; attero, erodo; *fig.* ango, 3; vexo, 1; —, v.n. (to grieve) doleo, 2; crucior, 1; ægre fero, 3.

fret, s. ira; sollicitudo, f.

fretful, a. morosus; difficilis; **—ly,** ad. morose.

fretfulness, s. morositas, f.

fretwork, s. cælatum opus, n.

friable, a. friabilis; puter.

friar, s. cœnobita, monachus, m.

friary, s. monasterium, n.

friction, s. frictio, f.; tritus, attritus, m.

Friday, s. dies Veneris, m.

friend, s. amicus, m.; amica, f.; familiaris, c.; necessarius, m.; sodalis, c.; (of a thing) amator, m.; **—s,** pl. (relations) genus, n.; parentes, c.

friendless, a. amicorum inops, desertus.

friendliness, s. benevolentia; comitas, affabilitas, f.

friendly, a. benevolus; comis; amicus.

friendship, s. amicitia, sodalitas, necessitudo, familiaritas, f.

frieze, s. (in architecture) zoophorus, m.

frigate, s. navis longa, f.

fright, s. pavor, terror, metus, m.; formido, f.; (scarecrow) terricula, f.

frighten, v.a. (per)terreo, 2; **to —away,** absterreo, 2.

frightful, a. terribilis, terrificus; dirus; **—ly,** ad. terribilem in modum.

frigid, a. frigidus; **—ly,** ad. frigide.

frigidity, s. frigiditas, f.

fringe, s. fimbriæ, f. pl.; limbus, m.; **-maker,** a. limbolarius, m.

fringe, v.a. prætexo, 3.

fringe-flower, s. schizanthus (mod. hort.).

frippery, s. (old clothes) scruta, n. pl.; *fig.* (rubbish, trifles) quisquiliæ, f. pl.

frisk, v.n. lascivio; salio, exsilio, 4; luxurio, 1.

frisky, a. lascivus, procax, protervus.

frith, s. æstuarium; (narrow sea) fretum, n.

fritillary, s. fritillaria (mod. hort.).

fritter, v.a. **to — away,** contero; comminuo, 3; *fig.* dissipo, 1.

frivolity, s. levitas, inconstantia, f.

frivolous, a. levis; frivolus, futilis; **—ly,** ad. nugatorie, tenuiter.

friz(zle), v.a. crispo; (to broil) asso, 1.

fro, ad. **to and —,** huc illuc; ultro citroque.

frock, s. palla, stola, f.

frog, s. rana, f. [m.

frolic, s. lascivia, f.; (play, prank) ludus,

frolic, v.n. exsulto, 1; lascivio, 4.

frolicsome, a. ludibundus, lascivus.

frolicsomeness, s. lascivia, f.

from, pr. a, ab; de; ex; (owing to) propter; **— abroad,** peregre; **— above,** desuper; **— day to day,** de die in diem; **— time to time,** continuo; **— within,** intra; **— without,** extra.

front, s. frons, prior pars, f.; (mil.) primum agmen, n.; *fig.* audacia, impudentia, f.

front, a. prior, primus; (of the forefront) anticus; (mil.) primoris; **in —,** ex adverso.

front, v.a., v. **face.**

frontage, s. frons, f.

frontier, s. finis, terminus, m.,

fronting, pr. adversus.

frontlet, s. (for horses) frontalia, n. pl.

frost, s. gelu, n.; (hoar-frost) pruina, f.

frost-bitten, a. frigore adustus.

frost-bound, a. gelu concretus; rigidus.

frosty, a. gelidus, glacialis; *fig.* (indifferent) frigidus.

froth, s. spuma, f.; *fig.* (empty words) vaniloquentia, f.

froth, v.n. spumo, 1.

frothy, a. spumeus, spumosus; *fig.* tumidus.

froward, a. pertinax, perversus, difficilis; **—ly,** ad. perverse, pertinaciter.

frowardness, s. perversitas, f.

frown, s. contractio frontis, f.; vultus severus, m.

frown, v.n. frontem contraho, 3; *fig.* (— upon) aversor.

frowning, a. *fig.* præruptus.

frozen, a. conglaciatus, gelatus, gelu rigens, concretus.

frugal, a. abstinens, parcus, frugalis; **—ly,** ad. frugaliter, parce.

frugality, s. parsimonia; frugalitas, f.

fruit, s. fructus, m.; frux, f.; (of the womb) fetus, m.; *fig.* (gain) lucrum, n.; (result) fructus, m.

fruit-bearing, a. frugifer, pomifer.

fruiterer, s. pomarius, m.

fruitful, a. fecundus, fertilis; ferax, uber; **—ly,** ad. fecunde, feraciter.

fruitfulness, s. fecunditas, fertilitas, ubertas, f.

fruit-garden, s. pomarium, n.

fruition, s. fructus, m.

fruitless, a. sterilis; infecundus; *fig.* irritus; **—ly,** ad. frustra; re infecta.

fruit-tree, s. pomum, n.

frustrate, v.a. frustror, 1; (to baffle) decipio, fallo, 3; (to break off) dirimo, 3.

frustration, s. frustratio, f.

fry, v.a. frigo, 3.

frying-pan, s. sartago, f.

fuchsia, s. fuchsia (mod. hort.).
fuddle, v.a. inebrio, 1.
fudge, i. gerræ!
fuel, s. fomes, m.; ligna, n. pl.; nutrimen, n.
fugitive, a. fugitivus; fugax.
fugitive, s. profugus, m.; profuga, f.
fulcrum, s. (of a lever) pressio, f.
fulfil, v.a. expleo, 2; exsequor, 3; (answer to) respondeo, 2.
fulfilment, s. exsecutio, perfectio, f.; (result) exitus, m.
full, a. plenus; (filled up) expletus; (entire) integer; solidus; (satiated) satur; (of dress) fusus; —, ad. v. **fully.**
full-blown, a. (of flowers) apertus; *fig.* tumidus.
full-grown, a. adultus.
full-moon, s. plenilunium, n.
fuller, s. fullo, m.; **—'s earth,** s. creta fullonica, f.
fully, ad. plene; copiose; omnino, prorsus.
fulminate, v.a. intono, 1.
fulmination, s. *fig.* verborum fulmina, n. pl.; minæ, f. pl.
fulness, s. plenitas; satietas, f.
fulsome, a. putidus, molestus, servilis; —ly, ad. serviliter.
fumble, v.n. *fig.* erro, 1.
fume, s. vapor, habitus, m.
fume, v.a. & n. exhalo, 1; irascor, 3.
fumigate, v.a. fumigo, 1; suffio, 4.
fumigation, s. suffitus, m.; suffitio, f.
fumitory, s. fumaria (mod. hort.).
fun, s. jocus, ludus, m.; ludibrium, n.
function, s. munus, officium, n.
functionary, s. magistratus, m.
fund, s. pecunia, f.; opes, f. pl.; *fig.* copia, f.
fundament, s. podex, anus, m.; natis, f.; clunis, c.
fundamental, a. primus, simplex, necessarius, stabilis; ad. (by nature) natura; (essentially) necessario; (altogether) penitus, omnino.
funeral, s. funus, n.; exsequiæ, f. pl.
funer(e)al, a. funebris, funereus; **— rites,** justa funebria, n. pl.; **— pile,** s. rogus, m.; pyra, f.
fungous, a. fungosus, funginus.
fungus, s. fungus, m.
funnel, s. infundibulum, n.
funnily, ad. ridicule, festive.
funny, a. ridiculus, festivus.
fur, s. villi, m. pl.; pellis, f.
fur, a. pellicius, 3.
furbish, v.a. polio, 4; detergeo; renovo, 1.   [ad. furiose, furenter.
furious, a. furialis, furiosus, furens; **—ly,**
furl, v.a. contraho, lego, 3.
furlong, s. stadium, n.
furlough, s. commeatus, m.

furnace, s. fornax, f.; (fireplace) caminus, m.   [exorno, 1; instruo, 3.
furnish, v.a. ministro, suppedito; orno,
furniture, s. supellex, f.; apparatus, m.
furrier, s. pellio, m.
furrow, s. sulcus, m.; (groove) stria, f.
furrow, v.a. sulco; aro, 1.
furry, a. pellicius.   [a. ulterior.
further, ad. ultra, longius, ulterius; —,
further, v.a. promoveo, 2; proveho, consulo (dat.) 3; (to aid) adjuvo, 1.
furtherance, s. auxilium, n.
furtherer, s. adjutor, m.
furthermore, ad. porro, insuper.
furthest, a. extremus, ultimus.
furtive, a. furtivus; **—ly,** ad. clam, furtim, furtive.
fury, s. furor, m.; ira, rabies, f.
furze, s. ulex (mod. hort.); **needle —,** genista, f.
fuse, v.a. fundo, liquefacio, 3; conflo, 1.
fusible, a. liquabilis.
fusion, s. fusura, f.
fuss, s. tumultus, m.; turba, f.
fusty, a. mucidus.
futile, a. futilis, frivolus, vanus.
futility, s. futilitas, f.
future, a. futurus.
future, s. futura, n. pl.; posterum tempus, n.; **for the —,** in posterum.
futurity, s. futurum tempus, n.; posteritas, f.

Gab, s. lingua, f.; **gift of the —,** volubilitas linguæ, f.
gabble, v.n. blatero, 1; garrio, 4.
gabble, s. garrulitas, verbositas, stultiloquentia, f.
gabbler, s. garrulus, m.
gable(-end), s. fastigium, n.
gad, v.n. vagor; cursito, 1.
gadder, s. homo vagus, m.
gad-fly, s. tabanus, œstrus, asilus, m.
gag, s. oris obturamentum, n.
gag, v.a. os obturo, præligo, 1; obstruo, 3.
gage, s. pignus, n.
gaiety, s. festivitas, hilaritas, f.; nitor, splendor, m.
gaily, ad. festive, hilare.
gain, v.a. lucror, 1; consequor, acquiro, 3; (get possession of) potior, 4; (to prevail) prævaleo, 2; **to — over** *or* **upon,** concilio, 1; (to encroach) usurpo, 1; **— the day,** vinco, 3.
gain, s. lucrum, emolumentum, n.; quæstus, m.
gainful, a. lucrosus.
gainsay, v.a. contradico, 3.
gait, s. incessus, ingressus, m.

gaiter, s. ocreæ, f. pl.
gala-day, s. dies festus, m.
galaxy, s. via lactea, f.; *fig.* cœtus, m.
gale, s. ventus, m.; aura, tempestas, procella, f.
gall, s. bilis, f.; fel, n.
gall, v.a. attero, uro, 3; *fig.* (to irritate) mordeo, 2.
gallant, a. nitidus, elegans; urbanus; (brave) fortis; —, s. amator, m.
gallantly, ad. fortiter.
gallantry, s. virtus, f.; (politeness) urbanitas, elegantia, f.
galleon, s. navis oneraria.
gallery, s. porticus, f.; (open) peristylium, n.; (top seats) summa cavea, f.; (in mines) cuniculus, m.
galley, s. navis longa, biremis, triremis, f.
galley-slave, s. homo remo publicæ navis affixus, m.
Gallic, a. Gallicus, Gallicanus.
galling, a. (irritating) mordax, molestus.
gall-nut, s. galla, f.
gallon, s. congius, m.
gallop, s. cursus citatus, m.
gallop, v.n. citato equo contendo, 3; (of the horse) quadrupedo, 1.
gallows, s. patibulum, n.
gallows-bird, s. furcifer, m.
gamble, v.n. alea ludo, 3; **to — away,** ludo amitto, 3.
gambler, s. aleator; lusor, m.
gambling, s. alea, f.
gambling-house, s. aleatorium, n.
gambling-table, s. alveus, m.
gambol, s. saltus; lusus, m.; exsultatio, f.
gambol, v.n. lascivio, 4; ludo, 3; exsulto, 1.
game, s. ludus; (act of playing) lusus, m.; (in hunting) feræ, f. pl.; (venison) ferina caro, f.; **— of hazard,** alea, f.; **to make — of,** ludificor, 1.
game-cock, s. gallinaceus pyctes, m.
gamekeeper, s. saltuarius, m.
gamesome, a. ludibundus, petulans.
gamesomeness, s. petulantia, f.
gamester, s. aleator, m.
gaming, v. **gambling.**
gammon, s. perna, f.; —! gerræ!
gander, s. anser, m.
gang, s. grex, m.; (troop) caterva, f.; sodalicium, n.
ganger, s. dux (catervæ), m.
gangrene, s. gangræna, f.
gangway, s. (in a ship) forus, m.
gaol, etc., v. **jail,** etc.   [m.
gap, s. rima, fissura; lacuna, f.; hiatus,
gape, v.n. hio, 1; dehisco, 3; (with mouth open) oscito, 1; *fig.* stupeo, 2; **to — after** *or* **at,** inhio, 1.
gaping, a. hians, hiulcus; *fig.* stupidus.

gaping, s. (aperture) hiatus, m.; (yawning) oscitatio, f.
garb, s. vestitus, m.
garbage, s. quisquiliæ, f. pl.
garble, v.a. vitio, 1; corrumpo, 3.
garden, s. hortus, m.
gardener, s. hortulanus; **market- —,** holitor, m.; **fancy —,** topiarius, m.
gardenia, s. gardenia (mod. hort.).
gardening, s. hortorum cultus, m.
garden-stuff, s. holus, n.
gargle, v.n. gargarizo, 1; —, s. gargarisma, n.
gargling, s. gargarizatio, f.
garland, s. sertum, n.; corona, f.
garland-flower, s. daphne (mod. hort.).
garlic, s. allium, n.
garment, s. vestimentum, n.; vestitus, m.
garner, s. horreum, n.
garner, v.a. condo, 3.
garnet, s. carbunculus, m.
garnish, v.a. decoro, orno, 1; (season) condio, 4; —, s. ornamentum, n.
garotte, v.a. laqueo strangulo, 1.
garret, s. cenaculum, n.
garrison, s. præsidium, n.; —, v.a. præsidium colloco, 1.
garrulity, s. garrulitas, loquacitas, f.
garrulous, a. garrulus, loquax.
garter, s. periscelis, f.; genualia, n. pl.
gash, s. vulnus, n.; plaga, f.; v.a. seco, vulnero, 1.
gasp, s. anhelitus, m.
gasp, v.n. anhelo, 1.
gasping, s., v. **gasp,** s.
gastronomy, s. gula, f.
gate, s. janua, f.; ostium, n.; fores, f. pl.; (of a town) porta, f.
gate-keeper, s. janitor, m.
gate-post, s. postis, m.
gate-way, s. porta, f.
gather, v.a. (to assemble) congrego, 1; (to bring together) colligo; (of fruits) decerpo, lego; (to pluck) carpo; (in logic) concludo, 3; (to suspect) suspicor, 1; —, v.n. (to assemble) convenio, 4; (of purulent matter) suppuro, 1; **to — round,** v.n. convolo, 1; confluo, 3; **to — up,** colligo; (to pick up) sublego, 3.
gatherer, s. (of toll) publicanus; (of grapes) vindemiator, m.
gathering, s. collectio; (of grapes) vindemia; (of matter) suppuratio; (assembling) congregatio, f.; (assembly) cœtus, m.
gaudily, ad. laute, splendide, speciose, f.
gaudiness, s. ornatus, nitor, m.; lautitia, f.
gaudy, a. lautus, splendidus, speciosus.
gauge, v.a. metior, 4.
gauge, s. modulus, m.

gaunt, a. macer.

gauze, s. Coa, n. pl.; sindon, f.

gawky, a. ineptus, stolidus.

gay, a. lætus, hilaris; floridus; splendidus.

gaze, s. conspectus; (fixed look) obtutus, m. [plor, 1.

gaze, v.n. intueor, 2; specto, contem-

gazelle, s. dorcas, f.

gazette, s. acta diurna, n. pl.

gazetteer, s. (book) itinerarium, n.

gear, s. instrumenta, n. pl.; arma, n. pl.; supellex, f.

gelatine, s. gluten, n.

gelatinous, a. glutinosus.

geld, v.a. castro, exseco, 1.

gelder, s. castrator, m.

gelding, s. castratio, f.; (horse gelded) canterius, m.

gem, s. gemma; baca, f. [gemmo, 1.

gem, v.a. gemmo, 1; —, v.n. germino,

gender, s. genus, n.

genealogist, s. genealogus, m.

genealogy, s. genealogia, f.; (origin) genus, n.; stirps, f.

general, a. generalis; vulgaris, publicus, universus; **in** —, in universum; (in the most part) plerumque.

general, s. dux, imperator.

generality, s. plerique, m. pl.

generally, ad. generatim; universe; (commonly) plerumque, vulgo.

generalship, s. ductus, m.; (skill of a commander) ars imperatoria, n.

generate, v.a. genero, procreo, 1; gigno, 3.

generation, s. generatio, f.; (lineage) genus, n.; (age) sæculum, n.

generosity, s. liberalitas, generositas, f.; munificentia.

generous, a. generosus; liberalis; munificus; magnanimus.

generously, ad. liberaliter, munifice.

genial, a. genialis, hilaris; **—ly,** ad. (gaily) genialiter.

geniality, s. geniale ingenium, n.

genitals, s. genitalia, um, n. pl.

genitive, s. genitivus, m.

genius, s. ingenium, n.; indoles, f.; vir ingeniosus, m.

genteel, a. elegans, urbanus; **—ly,** ad. eleganter, urbane.

gentian, s. gentiana, f.

gentile, s. homo gentilis, m.

gentility, s. nobilitas; elegantia, f.

gentle, a. (well-born) generosus; nobilis; (mild) lenis, mitis, clemens; (gradual) mollis; (tame) mansuetus; (polite) comis.

gentleman, s. homo nobilis; *fig.* vir honestus; (well-bred man) homo liberalis, m. [manus.

gentlemanly, a. liberalis, honestus, hu-

gentleness, s. lenitas, clementia; (tameness) mansuetudo, f.

gentlewoman, s. mulier libera, ingenua, f.

gently, ad. leniter; clementer; placide; (gradually) sensim; paulatim; pedetemptim.

gentry, s. nobiles, optimates, m. pl.

genuine, a. sincerus; purus; verus; germanus; **—ly,** ad. sincere, vere.

genus, s. genus, n.

geographer, s. geographus, m.

geographical, a. geographicus.

geography, s. geographia, f.

geometrical, a. geometricus.

geometrician, s. geometres, m.

geometry, s. geometria, f.

geranium, s. geranium (mod. hort.).

germ, s. germen, n. [Germanus.

german, a. germanus; (of Germany)

germane, a. aptus, appositus.

Germanic, a. Germanicus.

Germany, s. Germania, f.

germinate, v.n. germino, pullulo, 1.

germination, s. germinatio, f.; germinatus, m.

gesticulate, v.n. gestum ago, 3.

gesticulation, s. gestus, m.

gesture, s. gestus, motus, m.

get, v.a. adipiscor, consequor, acquiro, 3; (by entreaty) impetro, 1; **— something done,** curo aliquid faciendum; **—,** v.n. (to become) fio; (to arrive at) pervenio, 4; **to — abroad,** (to spread, v.n.) palam fio, 3; emano, 1; **to — along,** procedo, 3; **to — at,** attingo, 3; **to — away,** aufugio, 3; **to — back,** (v.a.) recupero, 1; (v.n.) reverto, 3; **to — the better of,** *fig.* supero, 1; prævaleo, 2; **to — down,** (v.a.) depromo; (v.n.) descendo, 3; **to — hold of,** prehendo, 3; occupo, 1; **to — off,** (v.a.) expedio, 4; (v.n.) aufugio; dimittor, 3; absolvor; **to — on,** procedo, proficiscor, 3; (to succeed) bene cedo, succedo, 3; **to — out,** (v.n.) exeo, 4; (e curru) descendo 3; **to — over,** trajicio, transgredior, 3; supero, 1; **to — rid of,** amoveo, 2 tollo, 3; **to — through,** pervenio, 4 *fig.* perago, perficio, 3; **to — together** (v.a.) colligo, cogo, 3; (v.n.) congrego, 1; **to — up,** surgo, 3.

gewgaw, s. nugæ, f. pl.

ghastliness, s. pallor, m.; *fig.* fœditas, f.

ghastly, a. luridus; (pale) pallidus, pallens; (horrid, shocking) fœdus.

ghost, s. (phantom) larva, f.; (shade of a dead person) umbra, f.; manes, m. pl.; give up the **—,** animam expiro, 1.

ghostly, a. (of the soul) animæ; (unsubstantial) inanis.

giant, s. gigas, m.; **—,** a. prægrandis.

gibberish, s. inanis strepitus, m.
gibbet, s. furca, f. ; patibulum, n. ; —, v.a.
suspendo, 3.
gibe, s. sanna, f. ; (mockery) ludibrium, n. ;
—, v.a. illudo, 3.
giblets, s. gigeria, n. pl.
giddily, a. inconsiderate.
giddiness, s. vertigo, f. ; *fig.* levitas, inconstantia, f.
giddy, a. vertiginosus ; *fig.* levis, inconstans. [nature, dos, f.
gift, s. donum ; beneficium, munus, n. ; —
gift, v.a. dono, 1. [sus.
gifted, a. (endowed) præditus ; *fig.* ingenio-
gig, s. (carriage) cisium, n.
gigantic, a. prægrandis, ingens.
giggle, v.n. cachinno, 1.
gild, v.a. inauro, 1.
gilding, s. (art) auratura, f.
gill, s. (of fishes) branchiæ, f. pl.
gillyflower, s. cheiranthus (mod. hort.).
gimlet, s. terebra, f.
gin, s. (snare) pedica, f. ; laqueus, m.
ginger, s. zinziberi, n. indecl.
gingerbread, s. crustula, n. pl.
giraffe, s. camelopardalis, f.
gird, v.a. cingo, accingo, 3 ; to — up,
succingo, 3.
girder, s. trabs, f.
girdle, s. cingulum, n. ; balteus, m. ; (of
women) zona, f.
girdle, v.a., v. gird.
girl, s. puella, virgo, f.
girlhood, s. puellaris ætas, f.
girlish, a. puellaris ; virginalis ; virgineus.
girt, girth, s. fascia ; (of a horse) cingula,
f. ; (circuit) ambitus, m.
gist, s. (main point) summa, f.
give, v.a. do, dono, 1 ; confero, 3 ; præbeo,
2 ; (yield) reddo, fero, 3 ; (to deliver)
trado, 3 ; to — away, dono, 1 ; to —
back, reddo, 3 ; to — forth, emitto, 3 ;
to — in, (v.a.) refero ; (v.n.) (to yield)
cedo, 3 ; to — out, edo ; emitto, 3 ;
nuntio, 1 ; distribuo, 3 ; (v.n.) (fail)
deficio ; to — over, transfero ; relinquo, 3 ; to — up, (v.a.) trado ; (to
betray) prodo ; (to abandon) dimitto,
3 ; to — oneself up to, sese addicere,
3 ; to — way, (mil.) pedem refero ; (to
yield) cedo ; (to comply with) obsequor, 3.
giver, s. donator, dator, m.
giving, s. datio, donatio, largitio, f. ; (gift)
donum, n.
gizzard, s. ventriculus, m.
glad, a. lætus, contentus ; hilaris, libens ;
to be —, gaudeo, 2 ; lætor, 1.
gladden, v.a. lætifico, hilaro, exhilaro, 1.
glade, s. nemus, n. ; saltus, m.
gladiator, s. gladiator, m.

gladly, ad. læte ; libenter.
gladness, s. gaudium, n. ; lætitia, f.
gladsome, a. festivus, lætus.
glance, s. aspectus, obtutus, m.
glance, v.n. aspicio ; (gleam) mico, corusco, 1 ; *fig.* to — at, stringo, per-
gland, s. glandula, f. [stringo, 3.
glare, s. fulgor, ardor, m.
glare, v.n. fulgeo, ardeo, 2 ; torvis oculis
aspicio, 3.
glaring, a. fulgens ; *fig.* manifestus.
glass, s. vitrum ; (mirror) speculum, n. ;
(for drinking) calix, m. ; (glassware)
vitrea, n. pl.
glass, a. vitreus.
glass-maker, s. vitrearius, m.
glassy, a. vitreus.
gleam, s. fulgor, splendor, m. jubar, n.;
fig. aura, f.
gleam, v.n. corusco, mico, 1 ; fulgeo, 2.
gleaming, a. coruscus, renidens.
glean, v.a. spicas colligo, 3 ; (grapes) ra-
cemor, 1.
gleaning, s. spicilegium, n. ; racematio, f.
glebe, s. glæba, f. ; solum, n.
glee, s. lætitia, f. ; gaudium, n.
gleeful, a. lætus.
glen, s. vallis, convallis, f. ; nemus, n.
glib, a. lubricus ; *fig.* volubilis ; —ly, ad.
volubiliter.
glide, v.n. labor, prolabor, 3.
glimmer, s. lux dubia, f. ; crepusculum,
n., v. gleam.
glimmer, v.n. subluceo, 2.
glimmering, a. sublustris.
glimpse, s. aspectus, m. ; *fig.* (a little) aliquantulum, n. ; to have a — of, dis-
picio, 3.
glisten, v.n. luceo, fulgeo, 2 ; radio, 1.
glitter, s. fulgor, m.
glitter, v.n. fulgeo, 2 ; radio, mico, corusco, 1.
gloat, v.n. (on, over, upon) oculos pasco, 3.
globe, s. globus ; *fig.* orbis terræ or ter-
globular, a. globosus. [rarum, m.
globule, s. globulus, m. pilula, f.
gloom, s. tenebræ, f. pl. ; caligo ; *fig.*
tristitia, f.
gloomily, ad. mœste.
gloominess, s., v. gloom.
gloomy, a. tenebrosus, nubilus ; (of colour)
pullus ; *fig.* mœstus, tristis.
glorification, s. laudatio, glorificatio, f.
glorify, v.a. celebro, glorifico, 1.
glorious, a. gloriosus, illustris ; splendidus ; eximius ; —ly, ad. gloriose ;
eximie ; splendide.
glory, s. gloria ; laus, fama, f.
glory, v.n. glorior, 1 ; superbio, 4.
gloss, s. interpretatio, f. ; (of stuff's)
nitor, m.

gloss, v.a. (stuff's) levigo, 1 ; polio, 4 ; *fig.* coloro, 1.

glossary, s. glossarium, n.

glossiness, s. nitor, m.

glossy, a. nitidus ; expolitus ; levis.

glove, s. digitabulum, n.

glow, s. ardor, fervor, calor, m.

glow, v.n. candeo, caleo, 2 ; excandesco, 3.

glowing, a. candens, fervens ; *fig.* fervidus.

glow-worm, s. cicindela, lampyris, f.

gloxinia, s. gloxinia (mod. hort.).

gloze, v.n. blandior, 4 ; adulor, 1.

glue, s. gluten, glutinum, n.

glue, v.a. glutino, conglutino, 1.

gluey, a. glutinosus ; viscosus, viscidus.

glum, a., v. **sullen.**

glut, s. satietas, f.   [pasco, 3.

glut, v.a. satio, saturo, 1 ; (to feast)

glutinous, a. glutinosus, viscosus.

glutton, s. helluo, homo gulosus, m.

gluttonize, v.n. helluor, 1.

gluttonous, a. gulosus, edax ; **—ly,** ad. gulose.

gluttony, s. gula, f.

gnarled, a. nodosus.

gnash, v.a. frendeo, infrendeo, 2 ; dentibus strido, 3.

gnashing, s. stridor dentium, m.

gnat, s. culex, m.

gnaw, v.a. & n. rodo, 3.

gnawing, a. mordax.

go, v.n. eo, 4 ; proficiscor, incedo, 3 ; (succeed) cedo, succedo, 3 ; **to —
about,** circumeo, 4 ; *fig.* aggredior, 3 ;
to — abroad, peregre abeo, 4 ; **to —
after,** sequor, 3 ; **to — aside,** discedo,
3 ; **to — astray,** aberro, vagor, 1 ; **to
— away,** abeo, 4 ; **to — back,** revertor,
3 ; **to — before,** præeo, 4 ; antecedo, 3 ;
to — between, intervenio, 4 ; **to —
beyond,** egredior ; *fig.* excedo, 3 ; **to
— by,** prætereo, 4 ; *fig.* (to adhere to)
sto, 1 ; **to — down,** descendo ; (of the
sun) occido, 3 ; **to — for,** peto, 3 ; (to
be considered) habeor, 2 ; putor, 1 ; **to
— forth,** exeo, 4 ; **to — in** (to), ineo, 4 ;
to — off, abeo, 4 ; **to — on,** pergo ;
(to happen) fio ; (to succeed, to thrive)
succedo, 3 ; **to — out,** exeo, 4 ; *fig.* (of
fire) extinguor, 3 ; **to — over,** transgredior ; *fig.* (a subject) percurro, 3 ;
to — round, circumeo (locum), 4 ; **to
— through,** transeo ; obeo, 4 ; pertendo,
3 ; **to — to,** adeo, 4 ; accedo, 3 ; **to —
towards,** peto, 3 ; **to — under,** subeo,
4 ; **to — up,** ascendo, 3 ; **to let —,**
dimitto ; (to let fall) omitto, 3.

goad, s. pertica, f. ; stimulus, m.

goad, v.a. instigo ; *fig.* stimulo ; (to exasperate) exaspero, 1.

goal, s. (in the Roman circus) meta,
calx, f. ; *fig.* finis, c.

goat, s. caper, m. ; (she- —) capra, f.

goat-herd, s. caprarius, m.

goat's-rue, s. galega (mod. hort.).

gobble, v.n. voro, devoro, 1 ; exsorbeo, 2.

go-between, s. internuntius, m. ; inter-
nuntia, f. ; conciliator, m. ; conciliatrix, f.   [cup.

goblet, s. poculum, n. ; scyphus, m., v.

goblin, s. larva, f. ; monstrum, n.

god, s. deus, m. ; divus, m.; numen, n.

goddess, s. dea, diva, f.

godhead, s. numen, n.

godless, a. atheus ; improbus.

godlike, a. divinus ; cælestis.

godliness, s. pietas (erga Deum), f.

godly, a. pius, sanctus.

going, s. incessus, m. ; **— about,** circumi-
tio, f. ; **— back,** reditus, m. ; **— in,**
ingressus, m. ; **— to,** aditus, m.

gold, s. aurum, n. ; **—,** a. aureus.

gold-coin, s. nummus aureus, m.

golden, a. aureus ; (yellow) flavus.

golden-rain, s. laburnum (mod. hort.).

golden-rod, s. solidago (mod. hort.).

goldfinch, s. carduelis, f.

goldfish, s. hippurus, m.

gold-leaf, s. bractea auri, f.

gold-mine, s. aurifodina, f.

goldsmith, s. aurifex, m.

good, a. bonus ; (for) efficax ; salutaris ;
utilis ; (kind-hearted) benevolus ; **— for
nothing,** nequam ; **to do —,** prodesse ;
to make —, compenso, 1 ; restituo, 3 ;
sano, 1.

good, s. (profit) commodum, lucrum, n. ;
salus ; utilitas, f. ; (in abstract sense)
bonum, n.

good, i. bene ! euge !

good-humoured, a. facilis.

goodliness, s. pulchritudo, f.

goodly, a. pulcher.

good-natured, a. comis, benignus, facilis.

goodness, s. bonitas ; probitas ; benignitas, f.

goods, s. bona, n. pl. ; res, f.

good-temper, s. facilitas, f.

good-temperedly, ad. suaviter.

good-will, s. benevolentia ; gratia, f.

goose, s. anser, m.

gooseberry, s. ribes grossularia (mod.
hort.).

gordian-knot, s. Gordius nodus, m.

gore, s. cruor, m. ; sanies, f.

gore, v.a. cornu ferio, 4.

gorge, s. fauces ; (defile) angustiæ, f. pl.

gorge, v.n. devoro, ingurgito, 1.

gorgeous, a. nitidus, lautus, splendidus ;
magnificus ; **—ly,** ad. laute, magnifice,
splendide.

gorgeousness, s. magnificentia, lautitia, f. splendor, m.

gorget, s. colli armatura, f.

gormandize, v.a. helluor, 1.

gormandizer, s. helluo, m.

gorse, s. ulex, m.

gory, a. cruentus, cruentatus, sanguineus, sanguinolentus.

goshawk, s., v. **hawk.**

gosling, s. anserculus, m.

gospel, s. evangelium, n.

gossamer, s. aranea, f. ; a. tenuis.

gossip, s. (idle talk) nugæ, gerræ, f. pl. ; (person) homo garrulus, m. ; mulier loquax, f. ; (boon companion) compotor, m.

gossip, v.n. garrio ; (to blab out) effutio, 4.

Goth, s. Gothus, m.

Gothic, a. Gothicus.

gouge, v.a. evello, eruo, 3.

gourd, s. cucurbita, f.

gout, s. morbus articularis, m. ; (in the feet) podagra ; (in the hands) chiragra, f.

gouty, a. arthriticus ; podagricus.

govern, v.a. impero, imperito, dominor, 1 ; rego, 3 ; (check) coerceo, 2 ; moderor, 1.

governable, a. tractabilis.

governess, s. magistra, f.

government, s. gubernatio (civitatis) ; administratio, f. ; imperium, regnum, n. ; provincia, f.

governor, s. gubernator ; præfectus ; dominus, m.

governorship, s. præfectura, f.

gown, s. (woman's garment) stola ; (of a Roman citizen) toga, f.

grace, s. gratia ; (elegance, etc.) venustas, f. ; veneres, f. pl. ; decor, lepor, m. ; (pardon) venia, f. ; **Graces,** pl. Gratiæ, f. pl.

grace, v.a. exorno ; honesto, 1.

graceful, a. elegans ; lepidus, venustus ; —ly, ad. venuste ; eleganter, lepide.

gracefulness, s. venustas, f. ; lepor, m.

graceless, a. deformis ; (of persons) improbus.

gracious, a. benignus ; clemens, humanus ; (propitious) æquus, propitius ; —ly, ad. benigne ; humane.

graciousness, s. benignitas, humanitas, clementia, f. [gradatio, f.

gradation, s. gradus, m. ; (in speech)

grade, s. gradus, ordo, m.

gradient, s. clivus, m.

gradual, a. per gradus ; —ly, ad. gradatim, pedetemptim, paulatim.

graft, s. insitum, n. ; surculus, m.

graft, v.a. insero, 3.

grain, s. granum, n. ; fig. particula, 1. ; **against the —,** fig. invita Minerva.

grammar, s. grammatica, f.

grammarian, s. grammaticus, m.

grammatical, a. grammaticus ; —ly, ad. grammatice.

granary, s. horreum, granarium, n.

grand, a. grandis, magnificus ; præclarus, splendidus.

grandchild, s. nepos, m. ; neptis, f.

grand-daughter, s. neptis, f.

grandee, s. nobilis, m.

grandeur, s. magnificentia ; granditas ; sublimitas ; majestas, f. ; splendor, m.

grandfather, s. avus, m.

grandiloquent, a. magniloquus ; tumidus.

grandly, ad. magnifice, splendide.

grandmother, s. avia, f.

grandson, s. nepos, m.

grange, s. villa, f.

grant, v.a. concedo, permitto, 3 ; (to acknowledge) fateor, 2 ; do, 1 ; præbeo, 2.

grant, s. concessio, f.

grape, s. acinus, m. ; uva, f. ; **bunch of —s,** racemus, m.

grape-hyacinth, s. muscari (mod. hort.).

graphic, a. expressus ; —ally, ad. expresse.

grapnel, s. harpago, m. ; manus ferrea, f.

grapple, v.a. complector, 3 ; —, v.n. luctor, 1 ; manu ferrea injecta navem retineo, 2.

grasp, v.a. prehendo, corripio, 3 ; affecto, 1 ; (understand) teneo, 2 ; **to — at,** capto, 1 ; fig. appeto, 3.

grasp, s. complexus, m. ; (power) potestas ; (hand) manus, f.

grasping, a. avidus, cupidus ; avarus.

grass, s. gramen, n. ; herba, f. ; **— of Parnassus,** parnassia (mod. hort.).

grass-green, a. herbidus.

grasshopper, s. grillus, m.

grassy, a. graminosus, gramineus, herbosus, herbidus. [focus, m.

grate, s. clathri, cancelli, m. pl. ; (hearth)

grate, v.a. (to grind) tero, contero ; —, v.n. strideo, 2.

grateful, a. gratus, jucundus ; —ly, ad. grate ; (thankfully) grato animo.

gratefulness, s. jucunditas ; (thankfulness) gratia, f.

gratification, s. expletio ; gratificatio ; (pleasure ; delight) voluptas ; oblectatio, f.

gratify, v.a. (to indulge) indulgeo, 2 ; gratificor, 1 ; morem gero, 3.

gratifying, a. gratus.

grating, s. clathri, cancelli, m. pl. ; (sound) stridor, m.

grating, a. (shocking) mordax ; molestus.

gratis, ad. gratuito, gratis.

gratitude, s. gratia, f. ; gratus animus, m.

gratuitous, a. gratuitus ; —ly, ad. gratuito.

gratuity, s. stips, f. ; munus, præmium, n.
grave, a. gravis, serius ; (stern) severus ;
(of sounds) gravis ; **—ly,** ad. graviter ;
severe.   [lus, m.
grave, s. sepulcrum, bustum, n. ; tumu-
grave, v.a. sculpo, insculpo, 3.
grave-clothes, s. tunica funebris, f.
grave-digger, s. tumulorum fossor, m.
gravel, s. glarea, f. ; sabulo, m. ; (disease)
calculus, m.
gravel, v.a. *fig.* in angustias adduco, 3.
gravelly, a. glareosus, sabulosus.
gravely, ad. graviter, serio, severe.
graver, s. sculptor, m. ; (tool) cælum, **n.**
grave-stone, s. monumentum, n.
gravitate, v.n. deferri, 3.
gravity, s. gravitas, f. ; pondus, n. ; (personal) severitas ; dignitas ; tristitia, f.
gravy, s. (broth) jus, n. ; (juice) sucus, m.
gray, a. cinereus ; (blue-gray) glaucus ;
(with age) canus ; **to become —,**
canesco, 3.
gray-eyed, a. cæsius.
gray-headed, a. canus.
grayish, a. canescens.
grayness, s. canities, f.
graze, v.a. (to pasture) pascor ; **(to touch
lightly)** stringo, perstringo, 3.
graze, s. vulnus, n.
grazier, s. pecuarius, m.
grease, v.a. ungo, perungo, illino, 3.
grease, unguen, pingue, n. ; arvina, f. ;
(for wheels) axungia, f.   [dus.
greasy, a. pinguis ; unctus ; (dirty) squali-
great, a. magnus ; ingens ; amplus, grandis ; (powerful) potens ; **so —,** tantus ;
as — as, tantus, quantus.
great-coat, s. lacerna, pænula, f. ; pallium, n.
great-grandfather, s. proavus, m.
great-hearted, a. magnanimus.
greatly, ad. magnopere, valde.
greatness, s. magnitudo, f.
greaves, s. ocreæ, f. pl.
Grecian, a. Græcus.
greedily, ad. avide, cupide.
greediness, s. aviditas ; voracitas, f.
greedy, a. avidus, avarus, cupidus ; vorax.
Greek, a. & s. Græcus.
green, a. viridis ; virens ; prasinus ; *fig.*
recens ; (unripe) crudus, immaturus ;
to become —, viresco, 3 ; **—,** s. color
viridis ; (lawn) locus *or* campus herbidus, m. ; **—s,** holera, n. pl.
greenfinch, s. fringilla, f.
green-grocer, s. holerum venditor, m.
greenhorn, s. tiro, m.
greenish, a. subviridis.
greenness, s. color viridis, m. ; (in abstract sense) viriditas, f. ; *fig.* immaturitas, f.

greensward, s. cæspes, m.
greet, v.a. saluto, 1 ; salutem dico, 3.
greeting, s. salutatio, salus, f.
gregarious, a. gregalis.
grey, v. **gray.**
greyhound, s. vertagus, m.
gridiron, s. craticula, f.
grief, s. dolor, mœror ; luctus, **m.** ; ægritudo ; molestia, tristitia, f.
grievance, s. querimonia, querela, injuria, f. ; malum, n.
grieve, v.a. dolore afficio (aliquem), 3 ;
excrucio, sollicito, 1 ; **—,** v.n. doleo,
lugeo, 2.
grievous, a. gravis, durus, atrox, acerbus ;
—ly, ad. graviter ; atrociter, acerbe.
grievousness, s. gravitas, atrocitas, f.
griffin, s. gryps, m.
grill, v.a. torreo, 2.
grim, a. torvus ; trux, truculentus, horridus ; **—ly,** ad. horride.
grimace, s. vultus distortus, m. ; oris depravatio, f.
grime, s. squalor, v. **dirt.**
grimness, s. torvitas, f.
grimy, a. squalidus.
grin, v.n. ringor, 3 ; (laugh) rideo, 2.
grin, s. rictus, m.
grind, v.a. (corn) molo, 3 ; (in a mortar)
contundo, 3 ; (on a whetstone) exacuo,
3 ; (colours) tero, 3 ; (the teeth) dentibus frendeo, 3.
grinder, s. (molar tooth) molaris, m.
grindstone, s. cos, f.
gripe, s., v. **grasp; —s,** pl. (in the bowels)
tormina, n. pl.
gripe, v.a. (to take hold of) prenso, 1 ;
(of the bowels) torminibus afficio, 3.
grisly, a. horrendus, horridus ; (shaggy)
hirsutus.
grist, s. farina, f.
gristle, s. cartilago, f.
gristly, a. cartilagineus, cartilaginosus.
grit, s. glareà, f. ; arena, sabulo, m. ; (of
corn) far, n.
gritty, a. arenosus, sabulosus.
grizzled, grizzly, a. canus.
groan, v.n. gemo, ingemo, 3.
groan, groaning, s. gemitus, m.
grocer, s. condimentarius, m.
groin, s. inguen, n.
groom, s. agaso, equiso, m.
groom, v.a. (equum) curo, 1.
groove, s. canalis, m. ; stria, f.
groove, v.a. strio, 1.
grope, v.n. prætento, 1.
gropingly, ad. pedetentim.
gross, a. crassus, densus ; pinguis ; (coarse)
rusticus, incultus ; (dreadful) atrox ;
(whole) totus ; **—ly,** ad. graviter ;
crasse ; turpiter.

grossness, s. crassitudo; (coarseness) rusticitas, f.; (dreadfulness) atrocitas, f.

grot(to), s. antrum; (made of rock-work) museum, n.

grotesque, a. absurdus, ridiculus; —**ly,** ad. absurde, ridicule.

ground, s. solum, n. terra; humus, f.; (place) locus, m.; *fig.* causa, f.; **on the** —, humi; **gain** —, proficio, 3; **lose** —, recedo, 3; **grounds, sediment,** fæx, f.

ground, v.a. fundo, 1; (to teach) instruo, 3; (to establish) sancio, 4; —, v.n. (of a ship), sido, 3; **be grounded on,** innitor, 3.

groundless, a. vanus, falsus; fictus; —**ly,** ad. falso, ex vano.

groundlessness, s. vanitas, f.

ground-rent, s. solarium, f.

groundsel, s. senecio, m. [mentum, n.

groundwork, s. subtructio, f.; *fig.* fundagroup, s. corona, turba, f.; globus, circulus, m.

group, v.a. dispono, 3; —, v.n. circulor, 1.

grouse, s. lagopus, tetrao, m.

grove, s. lucus, saltus, m.; nemus, n.

grovel, v.n. provolvor, 3; *fig.* servio, 4.

grovelling, a. humilis, supplex, servilis.

grow, v.n. cresco, 3; (to increase) augeor, 2; adolesco, 3; (to become) fio; —, v.a. (to cultivate) sero, 3; (a beard, etc.) promitto, 3; **to** — **again,** renascor, 3; **to** — **out,** excresco, 3; **to** — **out of,** *fig.* orior, 4; nascor, 3; **to** — **up,** accresco, 3; (in stature) adolesco, 3.

grower, s. cultor, m.

growing, s. cultura, f.; v. **growth.**

growl, s. fremitus, m. [1.

growl, v.n. fremo, 3; mussito, murmuro,

grown, a. (up) adultus; puber.

growth, s. incrementum, n.; auctus; (produce) fructus, m.; **full** —, maturitas, f.

grub, s. vermiculus, m.

grub, v.a. eradico, runco, 1; effodio, 3; (rummage about) rimor, 1.

grubbing-hoe, s. runco, m.

grudge, s. odium, n. simultas, f.; **to owe a** — **against one,** succenseo (alicui), 2.

grudge, v.a. invideo, 2.

grudgingly, ad. invitus, gravate.

gruel, s. ptisanarium, n. [aspere.

gruff, a. asper, tætricus, torvus; —**ly,** ad.

gruffness, s. asperitas, f.

grumble, v.n. murmuro, mussito, 1; queror, 3.

grumbler, s. homo querulus, m.

grumbling, s. querela, f.; questus, m.

grunt, v.n. grunnio, 4.

grunt, s. grunnitus, m.

guarantee, s. fides, satisdatio, f.; (person) fidejussor, vas, m.

guarantee, v.a. satisdo, præsto, 1; (promise) spondeo, 2.

guard, s. custodia; tutela, f.; (mil.) præsidium, n.; (person) custos, c.; — **duty,** excubiæ, f.m.; vigilia, statio, f.; (of a sword) capulus, m.; **to be on one's** —, caveo, 2.

guard, v.a. custodio, 4; defendo, protego, 3; munio, 4; —, v.n. (against) caveo, 2.

guarded, a. cautus, circumspectus.

guardian, s. custos; præses, c.; defensor; (of orphans) tutor; curator, m.

gudgeon, s. gobius, m.

guelder-rose, s. viburnum (mod. hort.).

guess, v.a. & n. conjicio, 3; divino, suspicor, 1; (solve) solvo, 3.

guess, s. conjectura, f.

guesser, s. conjector, m.

guest, s. hospes; (stranger) advena; (at a feast) conviva, c.

guest-chamber, s. hospitium, n.

guidance, s. ductus, m.; cura, curatio, administratio, f.

guide, s. dux; ductor, m.

guide, v.a. duco, 3; (to rule) guberno, 1; rego, 3.

guide-book, s. itinerarium, n.

guild, s. collegium, n.

guild-hall, s. prytaneum, conciliabulum, n.; curia, f.

guile, s. dolus, astus, m.; astutia, f.

guileful, a. dolosus, subdolus, astutus.

guileless, a. simplex, sincerus, integer.

guilt, s. culpa, noxa, f.; crimen, peccatum, n.

guiltless, a. innocens, insons, innocuus.

guilty, a. sons, nocens, noxius (with ablative *or* genitive); sceleratus.

guinea-fowl, guinea-hen, s. meleagris, f.

guinea-pig, s. mus porcellus, m.

guise, s. modus; mos, m.; (appearance) species, f.

guitar, s. cithara, f.

gulf, s. sinus, m.; (abyss) vorago, f.

gull, s. larus marinus; (person cheated) stultus, m.

gull, v.a. lacto, ludificor, 1.

guller, s. fraudator, m.

gullet, s. gula, f.; fauces, f. pl.

gullibility, s. credulitas, f.

gullible, a. credulus.

gully, s. fossa, f.

gulp, v.a. absorbeo, 2; haurio, 4; voro ingurgito, 1.

gum, s. (of the mouth) gingiva, f.; **adhesive** —, gummi, n.; indecl.

gum, v.a. glutino, 1.

gummy, a. gummosus.

gun, s. sclopetum, n.

gun-powder, s. pulvis pyrius, m.

gurgle, v.n. murmuro, susurro, 1.

gurgling, s. murmur, n. ; susurrus, m.
gush, v.n. (out) effluo, profluo, 3 ; prosilio, 4 ; scateo, 2.
gush, gushing, s. scatebra, f.
gust, s. flatus, m. ; flamen, n.
gusty, a. procellosus.
gut, s. intestinum, n. ; **great —,** colon, n. ; **—s,** viscera, n. pl.
gut, v.a. exentero, 1 ; *fig.* exinanio, 4.
gutter, s. canalis, m. ; (of streets) colliciæ, f. pl.
gutter-tile, s. imbrex, c.
guzzle, v.n. helluor, 1.
guzzler, s. helluo, m.   [f.
gymnasium, s. gymnasium, n. ; palæstra,
gymnastic, a. gymnicus, gymnasticus.
gymnastics, s. palæstrica, f.
gypsum, s. gypsum, n.
gyrate, v.n. volvor.
gyration, s. gyrus, m.
gyves, compes, pedica, **f.**

Ha ! i. ah !
ha ! ha ! i. ha, ha, he !
habiliment, s. vestimentum, n. ; vestis, f.
habit, s. (custom) consuetudo, f. ; mos, m. ; (dress) vestitus, m. ; (state) habitus, m.   [habitabilis.
habitable, a. habitabilis ; **not —,** in-
habitation, s. habitatio, domus, f.
habitual, a. inveteratus, assuetus, consuetus, solitus ; **—ly,** ad. de (ex) more.
habituate, v.a. assuefacio, 3.
hack, v.a. concido, 3 ; mutilo, 1.
hackneyed, a. tritus ; pervulgatus.
haddock, s. gadus, m.
haft, s. manubrium, n.
hag, s. anus ; venefica, f.
haggard, a. macer, exsanguis.
haggle, v.a. cavillor ; (to bargain) licitor, 1.
hail, s. grando, f.   [v.n. grandino, 1.
hail, v.a. (to salute) saluto, 1 ; **—,**
hail, i. salve !
hailstone, s. grando, f.
hair, s. capillus, crinis, cæsaries, coma, f. ; (single) pilus ; (of animals) villus, m.
hair-cloth, s. cilicium, n.
hair-dresser, s. capitis et capilli concinnator, m. ; ornatrix, f.
hairless, a. (of the head) calvus ; (of the body) glaber.
hairpin, s. crinale, n.
hair-splitting, s. subtilitas, f. ; disserendi spinæ, f. pl.
hairy, a. pilosus ; crinitus ; comatus ; (shaggy) hirsutus.
halberd, s. bipennis, f.
halcyon, s. alcedo, alcyon, **f.**

hale, a. validus, robustus, viridis, crudus.
half, a. dimidius ; **—,** s. dimidia, pars, f. ; dimidium, n.
half . . ., in comp. semi . . .
half-dead, a. semianimis.
half-eaten, a. semiesus.   [lunula, f.
half-moon, s. luna dimidiata ; (shape)
halfpenny, s. obolus, m.
half-pound, s. semis, m.
half-yearly, a. semestris.
hall, s. atrium ; (entrance- —) vestibulum ; (for business) conciliabulum, n. ; (of the senate) curia, f.
halloo, i. heus ! ohe !
halloo, v.n. inclamo ; vociferor, 1.
hallow, v.a. consecro, dedico, 1.
hallucination, a. alucinatio, f. ; error, m. ; somnium, n.
halo, s. corona, f.
halt, v.n. (to limp) claudico, 1 ; (of troops) consisto, 3 ; *fig.* hæsito, 1.
halt, s. pausa, mora, f.
halt, a. claudus.
halter, s. capistrum, n. ; funis, m.
halting, s. claudicatio, f.
halve, v.a. ex æquo divido, 3.
ham, s. perna, f. ; (of men) poples, **m.**
hamlet, s. viculus, m.
hammer, s. malleus, m.
hammer, v.a. cudo, 3.
hammock, s. lectus suspensus, m.
hamper, s. qualus, m. ; fiscina, f.
hamper, s. impedio, 4 ; implico, retardo, 1.
hamstring, s. poplitis nervus, m. ; **—,** v.a. poplitem alicui succido, 3.
hand, s. manus, palma, f. ; (handwriting) chirographum, n. ; (of a dial) gnomon, m. ; **at —,** ad manum ; præ manibus ; præsto ; **by —,** manu ; **— in —,** junctis manibus ; **— to —,** comminus ; **in —,** (of money) præ manu ; **on the other —,** altera parte ; **on the right —,** ad dextram ; **out of —,** illico, confestim.   [cumfero, 3.
hand, v.a. trado, 3 ; **to — round,** cir-
hand-barrow, s. ferculum, n.
handbell, s. tintinnabulum, n.
hand-bill, s. libellus, m.
hand-book, s. libellus, m.
hand-breadth, s. palmus, m.
handcuffs, s. pl. manicæ, f. pl.
handful, s. manipulus, pugillus, m.
handicraft, s. ars, f. ; artificium, **n.**
handicraftsman, s. artifex, c.
handily, ad. habiliter.
handiness, s. habilitas ; sollertia, f.
handiwork, s. opus, n. ; opera, f.
handkerchief, s. sudarium, n.
handle, v.a. tracto, 1.
handle, s. manubrium, n. ; ansa, f. ; (of a sword) capulus, m. ; *fig.* occasio, f.

handling, s. tractatio, f.

handsome, a. pulcher, formosus; honestus; elegans, bellus; —ly, ad. pulchre, honeste, eleganter, belle.

handsomeness, s. forma, pulchritudo, elegantia, f.

hand-writing, s. manus, f.; (manuscript) chirographum, n.

handy, a. habilis; sollers; (useful) utilis.

hang, v.a. suspendo; (to let — down) demitto, 3; —, v.n. pendeo, dependeo; — back, hæsito, 1; — over, immineo, 2.

hanger, s. pugio, m.; — -on, s. assecla, fig. parasitus, m.

hanging, a. pensilis; pendulus; (down) demissus; (loose) fluens.

hanging, s. suspendium, n.; (curtains, etc.) tapete, n.

hangman, s. carnifex, m.

hank, s. (of thread) glomus, n.

hanker, v.n. desidero, 1; expeto, 3.

haphazard, s. fors, f.; quod casu fit.

hapless, a. infortunatus, infelix.

haply, ad fortasse; v. perhaps.

happen, v.n. accido, 3; evenio, 4; contingo, 3; fio.

happily, ad. beate; feliciter.

happiness, s. vita beata; (good fortune) felicitas, f.

happy, a. felix, fortunatus, faustus; beatus.

harangue, s. contio, f.; —, v.a. & n. contionor, 1.

haranguer, s. contionator, m.

harass, v.a. fatigo; vexo; inquieto, 1; lacesso, 3.

harbinger, s. prænuntius, antecursor, m.

harbour, s. portus, m.; fig. refugium, perfugium, n.

harbour, v.a. excipio, 3; (feelings, etc.) habeo, 2; afficior, 3 (abl.); v.n. obsideo, 2; stabulor, 1.

harbourer, s. receptor, m.

harbourless, a. importuosus.

hard, a. durus; fig. (difficult) arduus; (unjust) iniquus; (severe) acer, rigidus; (hard-hearted) crudelis; — of belief, incredulus; —, ad. vix; ægre.

harden, v.a. duro; induro, 1; —, v.n. duresco; obduresco, 3.

hard-hearted, a. durus, ferreus, inhumanus, crudelis.

hard-heartedness, s. crudelitas, f.; ingenium durum, n.

hardihood, s. audacia, f.

hardily, ad. duriter.

hardiness, s. robur, m.

hardly, ad. dure; crudeliter; (with difficulty, scarcely) vix; ægre.

hardness, s. duritia fig. iniquitas; acerbitas, f.

hardship, s. ærumna; difficultas, f.; labor, m.; dura, n. pl.

hard-ware, s. ferramenta, n. pl.

hardy, a. durus; robustus.

hare, s. lepus, m.

hare-bell, s. campanula (mod. hort.).

hare-brained, a. temerarius; insanus, demens.

harem, s. gynæceum, n.

hare's-foot fern, s. davallia (mod. hort.).

hark, i. heus!

harken, v.n. audio, 4.

harlequin, s. sannio, m.

harlot, s. meretrix, f.; scortum, n.

harm, s. damnum, n.; injuria; fraus, noxa; calamitas, f.

harm, v.a. lædo, 3; noceo, 2.

harmful, a. noxius, perniciosus.

harmless, a. (things) innocuus; innoxius; (person) innocens; —ly, ad. innocue; innoxie, innocenter.

harmlessness, s. innocentia, f.

harmonic, a. harmonicus.

harmonics, s. harmonice, f.

harmonious, a. concors, consonus; canorus; fig. concors, consentiens; —ly, ad. consonanter; fig. concorditer.

harmonize, v.a. compono, 3; —, v.n. concino, 3; fig. consentio, 4.

harmony, s. harmonia, f.; concentus, m.; fig. concordia, f.

harness, s. ornatus, m.

harness, v.a. adjungo, jungo, subjungo, 3; (to saddle) insterno, 3.

harp, s. lyra, f.; —, v.n. psallo, 3; fig. to — the same string, eandem incudem tundo, 3.

harper, harpist, s. psaltes, m.; psaltria, f.

harpoon, s. jaculum, n.; —, v.a. jaculo transfigo, 3.

harpy, s. harpyia, f.; fig. homo rapax, m.

harridan, s. anus, vetula, f.

harrier, s. catulus, m.

harrow, s. rastrum, n.; irpex, m.; —, v.a. occo, 1; fig. crucio, excrucio, 1.

harsh, a. asper; (in sound) discors, stridulus; (hoarse) raucus; (in taste) acer; fig. gravis; severus, durus; —ly, ad. aspere; graviter, acerbe, duriter.

harshness, s. asperitas; acerbitas; sævitia; severitas, f.

hart, s. cervus, m.; cerva, f.

hart's-tongue fern, s. scolopendrium (mod. hort.).

harvest, s. messis, f.; —, v.a. meto, 3.

harvester, s. messor, m.

hash, v.a. (to mince) comminuo, 3.

hash, s. minutal, n.; fig. make a — of, male gero (acc.).

hasp, s. fibula, f.

hassock, s. scabellum, n.

haste, s. celeritas ; festinatio, properatio, f. ; **in** —, propere; properanter ; **to make** —, propero, 1 ; festino.

hasten, v.a. accelero, propero ; (hurry away) rapio, abripio ; (to hurry on) præcipito, 1 ; —, v.n. propero, festino, 1.

hastily, ad. propere ; raptim.

hastiness, s. celeritas ; *fig.* iracundia, f.

hasty, a. properus ; præceps ; *fig.* iracundus.

hat, s. pilleus, galerus, petasus, m.

hatch, v.n. pullos excludo ; *fig.* coquo, 3 ; machinor, 1 ; molior, 4.

hatchet, s. ascia, securis, bipennis, f.

hatching, s. fetura, pullatio, f.

hate, v.a. odi, perodi, 3 ; destestor, 1.

hate, s., v. **hatred.**

hateful, a. odiosus, invisus ; inamabilis ; —ly, ad. odiose.

hatred, s. odium, n. ; invidia, simultas, inimicitia, f.

hauberk, s. lorica, f.

haughtily, ad. superbe, arroganter.

haughtiness, s. superbia ; arrogantia, f. ; fastidium, n.

haughty, a. superbus ; arrogans ; fastidiosus.

haul, v.a. traho, subduco, 3.

haul, s. tractus, m. ; (draught of the net) jactus, m.

haulm, s. stipula, f. ; culmus, m.

haunch, s. clunis, coxa, f.

haunt, v.a. frequento ; *fig.* (of spirits) adsum ; (disturb) agito, 1.

haunt, s. latebra, f. ; lustra, n. pl. ; cubile, n.

haunter, s. frequentator.

have, v.a. habeo ; possideo, teneo, 2 ; **to — on,** gero, 3 ; **I would — you know,** velim scias.

haven, s. portus, m.

havoc, s. strages, cædes, f.

hawk, s. accipiter, m.

hawk, v.a. vendito, 1.

hawker, s. caupo, m.

hawk-eyed, a. lynceus.

hawkweed, s. hieracium (mod. hort.).

hawser, s. retinaculum, n. ; rudens, m.

hawthorn, s. cratægus oxyacantha, f.

hay, s. fænum, n.

hay-harvest, s. fænisecia, f.

hay-loft, s. fænilia, n. pl.

hay-maker, fænisex, m. ; fæniseca, f.

hazard, s. periculum, discrimen, n. ; (chance) alea, f.   [ad. periculose.

hazardous, a. periculosus ; anceps ; —ly,

haze, s. nebula, f. ; vapor, m.

hazel, s. (tree) corylus, f.

hazel, a. colurnus ; (of colour) spadix, flavus.

hazel-nut, s. nux avellana, f.

hazy, a. nebulosus, caliginosus ; *fig.* (doubtful) dubius, ambiguus.   [mas, m.

he, pn. hic, is, ille ; — . . ., (of animals)

head, s. caput, n. ; vertex, m. ; (also *fig.*) (mental faculty) ingenium, n. ; (chief) princeps, c. ; (top) culmen, cacumen, n.

head, a. princeps, summus.

head, v.a. dux sum (gen.).

headache, s. capitis dolor, m.

head-band, s. vitta, f.

head-dress, s. comptus comæ, m.

header, s. **to take a** —, præcipitem me do, 1.

heading, s. titulus, m.

headland, s. promontorium, n.

headless, a. truncus.

headlong, a. præceps ; temerarius.

head-piece, s. (helmet) cassis, f. ; (understanding) ingenium, n.

head-quarters, s. prætorium, n.

headship, s. principatus, m.

headstrong, a. pervicax, contumax, v. **stubborn.**

headwind, s. ventus adversus, m.

heady, a. temerarius, præceps ; (of wine) inebrians.

heal, v.a. sano, 1 ; medeor, 2 ; —, v.n. sanesco ; (wounds) coalesco, 3 ; coeo, 4.

healer, s. medicus, m.

healing, a. salutaris, saluber ; —, s. sanatio, f.

health, s. sanitas, valetudo, salus, f.

healthful, a. salutaris, saluber ; —ly, ad. salutariter, salubriter.

healthily, ad. salubriter, salutariter.

healthiness, s. firma valetudo ; (of place *or* things) salubritas, f.

healthy, s. sanus ; **integer** ; (places *or* things) saluber.   [geries, f.

heap, s. acervus, cumulus, m. ; conheap, v.a. acervo, coacervo, accumulo, 1.

hear, v.a. & n. audio ; exaudio, 4 ; ausculto, 1 ; (to learn) certior fio.

hearer, s. auditor ; discipulus, m.

hearing, s. (act) auditio, f. ; (sense) auditus, m.

hearken, v.n. ausculto, 1 ; v. **hear.**

hearsay, s. fama, f. ; rumor, m.

hearse, s. feretrum, n.

heart, s. cor, n. ; *fig.* (feeling) pectus, n. ; (courage) animus, m. ; (endearing term) corculum, n. ; (of a tree) medulla, f. ; **have the — to,** sustineo, audeo, 2.

heart-ache, s. *fig.* angor, m.

heart-break, s. angor, m.

heart-breaking, a. miserabilis.

heart-broken, a. angoribus confectus, afflictus.

heart-burning, s. *fig.* (grudge) simultas, invidia, ira, f.

heartfelt, a. verus.

hearth, s. focus, m.
heartily, ad. sincere ; effuse; valde ; vere;
ex animo.
heartiness, s. sinceritas, f.
heartless, a. ferreus, crudelis, inhumanus ;
—ly, ad. inhumane, crudeliter.
heartlessness, s. inhumanitas, sævitia, f.
heart-rending, a. acerbissimus.
heart's-ease, s. viola tricolor, f.
heart-whole, a. (free from love) vacuus.
hearty, a. verus, sincerus.
heat, s. calor, ardor ; fervor, æstus, m.
heat, v.a. calefacio, incendo, 3 ; —, v.n.
calesco, 3.
heath, s. (plant) erice, f. ; loca (humilibus
virgultis) obsita, n. pl.
heath-cock, s., v. grouse.
heathen, s. paganus, m. ; —, a. ethnicus.
heathenish, a. ethnicus.
heating, s. calefactio, f.
heave, v.a. attollo, 3 ; levo, 1 ; (sighs, etc.)
traho, duco, 3 ; —, v.n. tumeo, 2 ; fluctuo, 1.
heaven, s. cælum, n. ; fig. di, superi, m. pl.
heaven-born, a. divinus ; cælestis.
heavenly, a. cœlestis, divinus.
heavily, ad. graviter ; (slowly) tarde.
heaviness, s. gravitas ; (slowness) tarditas ;
(dulness) stultitia, f. ; (drowsiness)
sopor, m.
heavy, a. gravis ; onerosus, ponderosus ;
fig. tardus, segnis, iners.
Hebraic, a. Hebraicus.
Hebrew, s. Hebræus, m. ; (language)
Hebræa lingua, f.
hecatomb, s. hecatombe, f.
hectic, a. tabidus.
hector, v. bully.
hedge, s. sæpes, f. ; sæpt 1m, n. ; —, v.a.
sæpio, 4.
hedge-hog, s. erinaceus, ericius, m.
heed, s. cura, cautela, f. ; to take —,
(præ)caveo, 2.
heed, v.n. caveo, 2 ; prospicio ; attendo, 3 ;
—, v.a. curo, 1 ; animum adverto, 3.
heedful, a. cautus, circumspectus.
heedless, a. incautus ; temerarius ; —ly,
ad. incaute ; temere.
heedlessness, s. neglegentia, f.
heel, s. calx, f.
heft, s. manubrium, n.
heifer, s. juvenca, f.
height, s. altitudo ; (tallness) proceritas,
f. ; (top) culmen, n. ; (hill) clivus, collis,
tumulus, m.
heighten, v.a. altius effero, 3 ; fig. amplifico ; exaggero, 1.
heinous, a. atrox ; nefarius ; fœdus ; —ly,
ad. atrociter, nefarie, fœde.
heinousness, s. atrocitas, f.
heir, heiress, s. heres, c.

heirloom, s. res hereditaria, f.
heirship, s. hereditas, f.
heliotrope, s. heliotropium, n.
hell, s. Tartarus, m.
Hell-hound, s. Furia, Erinys, f.
hellebore, s. helleborus, m.
Hellenic, a. Hellenicus, Græcus.
Hellenism, s. Hellenismus, m.
Hellenist, s. Hellenista, m.
hellish, a. infernus, nefarius.
helm, s. gubernaculum, n ; calvus, m.
helmet, s. cassis, galea, f.
helmsman, s. gubernator, rector navis, m.
Helots, s. pl. Helotes, m. pl.
help, s. auxilium, n. ; opem, f. acc. sing. ;
(remedy) remedium, n. ; medecina, f.
help, v.a. (ad)juvo, 1 ; succurro, 3 ; subvenio, 4 ; auxilior, sublevo, 1.
helper, s. adjutor, auxiliator, m.
helpful, utilis.
helpless, a. inops.
helplessness, s. inopia, f.
helpmate, s., v. helper.
helter-skelter, ad. confuse, turbate.
hem, s. ora, f. ; limbus, m.
hem, v.a. prætexo ; fig. cingo, 3 ; to —
in, circumsideo, 2.
hem, i. hem ! ehem !
hemisphere, s. hemisphærium, n.
hemistich, hemistichium, n.
hemlock, s. cicuta, f.
hemorrhage, s. hæmorrhagia, f.
hemp, s. cannabis, f.
hempen, a. cannabinus.
hen, s. gallina, f.
henbane, s. hyoscyamus, m.
hence, ad. hinc ; —, i. procul ! apage !
henceforth, ad. posthac ; dehinc, in posterum.
hen-coop, s. cavea, f.
hen-house, s. gallinarium, n.
hen-pecked, a. uxorius.
her, pn. suus, f.
herself, pn. ipsa, f.
herald, s. caduceator ; (crier) præco, m.
herald, v.a. nuntio, 1.
herb, s. herba, f. ; (collectively) holus, n.
herbage, s. herbæ, f. pl. ; gramen, n.;
cæspes, m.
herbalist, s. herbarius, m.
herbarium, s. herbarium.
herd, s. grex ; fig. (in contempt) vulgus, m.
herd, v.n. congrego, 1. [cus, m.
herdsman, s. pastor ; armentarius ; bubul-
here, ad. hic ; — and there, raro.
hereabouts, ad. hic alicubi.
hereafter, ad. posthac ; in posterum.
hereat, ad. hic.
hereby, ad. ex hoc, ex hac re.
hereditarily, ad. jure hereditario.
hereditary, a. hereditarius.

herein, ad. in hoc, in hac re.
heresiarch, s. hæresiarcha, m.
heresy, s. hæresis, f.
heretic(al), a. hæreticus ; falsus, pravus ;
—**ly,** ad hæretice.
hereupon, ad. hic ; deinde.
herewith, ad. una cum hac re.
heritage, s. hereditas, f.
hermaphrodite, s. androgynus, Herma-
phroditus, semimas, m.
hermetically, ad. arte.
hermit, s. eremita, anachoreta, m.
hermitage, s. eremitæ cella, f.
hernia, s. hernia, f. ; ramex, m.
hero, s. heros, vir fortis ; (in a play) qui
primas partes agit, m.
heroic, a. heroicus ; —**ally,** ad. fortiter.
heroine, s. heroina ; virago ; (of a play)
quæ primas partes agit, f.
heroism, s. virtus, fortitudo, f.
heron, s. ardea, f.
herring, s. harenga, f.
hers, pn. ejus, illius (gen. of ea, illa).
herself, s. ipsa ; (reflexive) se.   [cesso, 1.
hesitate, v.n. dubito, hæsito, cunctor,
hesitating, a. hæsitans ; —**ly,** ad. cunctanter.
hesitation, s. dubitatio ; hæsitatio, f.
Hesperia, s. Hesperia.
Hesperian, a. Hesperius.
heteroclite, a. heteroclitus.
heterodox, a. impius.
heterodoxy, s. impietas, f.
hew, v.a. dolo, 1 ; cædo, 3 ; seco, 1.
hey, i. ohe !
heyday, s. flos (juventutis), m.
hiatus, s. hiatus, m. ; v. **gap.**
hiccough, hiccup, s. singultus, m.
hiccough, hiccup, v.n. singulto, 1.
hickory, s. carya (mod. hort.).
hide, s. pellis, f. ; corium, n.
hide, v.a. abdo, condo, occulo, abscondo,
3 ; celo, 1 ; (dissemble) dissimulo, 1 ; —,
v.n. lateo, 2.
hide-bound, a. inveteratus.
hideous, a. fœdus, turpis, deformis ; —**ly,**
ad. fœde ; turpiter.   [formitas, f.
hideousness, s. fœditas, turpitudo, de-
hiding, s. verberatio, f.
hiding-place, s. latebra, f. ; latibulum, n.
hie, v.n., v. **go, hasten.**
hierarchy, s. sacerdotium, collegium, n.
hieroglyphical, a. hieroglyphicus.   [f. pl.
hieroglyphics, s. hieroglyphicæ litteræ,
higgle, v.n. vendito.
high, a. altus, excelsus ; sublimis ; (tall)
procerus ; (of price) pretiosus ; carus ;
fig. magnus ; amplus ; —, ad. alte ;
sublime ; valde ; vehementer ; **to aim**
—, magnas res appeto, 3.
high-born, a. summo loco natus ; nobilis.

high-flown, a. inflatus, tumidus.
highland, s. regio aspera *or* montuosa, f.
highlander, s. montanus, m.
highly, ad. (much) valde, multum ; (value)
magni, permagni.
high-minded, a. magnanimus.
highness, s. altitudo, f.
high-priest, s. summus sacerdos, pontifex
maximus, m.
high-road, s. via, f.
high-spirited, a. generosus, animosus.
high-treason, s. crimen læsæ majestatis,
n. ; perduellio, f.
highway, s. via, f.
highwayman, s. latro, grassator, m.
hilarious, a. hilaris, festivus.
hilarity, s. hilaritas, festivitas, f.
hill, s. collis ; tumulus ; (slope) clivus, m.
hillock, s. tumulus ; (heap of earth, etc.)
grumus, m.
hilly, a. montuosus, clivosus.
hilt, s. (of a sword) capulus, m.
him, pn. eum, hunc, illum ; **of** —, ejus,
hujus ; illius ; de illo.
himself, pn. ipse ; (reflexive) se.
hind, s. cerva, f.   [posticus.
hind, hinder, a. posterior, aversus ; (back)
hinder, v.a. impedio, 4 ; obsto, 1 ; officio,
3 ; retardo, 1 ; (prevent) prohibeo, 2.
hind(er)most, a. postremus, ultimus.
hindrance, s. impedimentum, n.
hinge, s. cardo, m.
hinge, v.n. (depend) pendeo, dependeo, 2.
hint, s. indicium, n. ; nutus, m.
hint, v.a. & n. innuo, suggero, 3 ; sum-
moneo, 2 ; **to — at,** perstringo, 3.
hip, s. coxa, coxendix, f.
hippodrome, s. hippodromos, m.
hippopotamus, s. hippopotamus, m.
hire, s. merces, f. ; stipendium, n.
hire, v.a. conduco, 3 ; loco, 1.
hired, a. conductus, conducticius ; mercenarius.
hireling, a. & s. mercenarius, m.
hirer, s. conductor, m.
hirsute, a. hirsutus, pilosus.
his, pn. ejus, hujus ; illius, ipsius ; **— own,**
suus, proprius.   [off, explodo, 3.
hiss, v.a. & n. sibilo, 1 ; strideo, 2 ; **to —**
hiss, hissing, s. sibilus ; stridor, m.
historian, s. historicus, m.
historic(al), a. historicus ; —**(al)ly,** ad.
historice.
historiographer, s. historiarum scriptor, m.
history, s. historia, memoria rerum gestarum, f. ; res, f. ; (narrative) narratio, f.
histrionic, a. histrionalis.
hit, v.a. ferio, 4 ; percutio, 3 ; —, v.n.
bene succedo, 3 ; **to — upon,** offendo,
3 ; (discover) invenio, reperio, 4.

hit, s. plaga, f. ; ictus, m.
hitch, s. impedimentum, n. ; mora, f.
hither, ad. huc.
hither, a. citerior.   [huc usque.
hitherto, ad. (of time) adhuc ; (of place)
hive, s. alvus, f. alvearium, n.
hoar, a. canus, v. hoary.
hoard, s. acervus, m. ; —, v.a. coacervo, 1.
hoarder, s. accumulator, m.
hoarfrost, s. pruina, f.
hoariness, s. canities, f.
hoarse, a. raucus ; to get —, irraucesco, 3.
hoarsely, ad. rauca voce.
hoarseness, s. raucitas, f.
hoary, a. albescens ; (with age) canus ;
(with frost) pruinosus.
hoax, s. ludificatio, f. ; fraus, f. ; dolus, m. ;
—, v.a. ludificor, 1.
hob, s. focus, m.
hobble, v.n. claudico, 1.
hobby, s. studium, n. ; cura, f.
hobby-horse, s. (for children) arundo, f. ;
fig. voluptas, f. ; studium, n.
hobgoblin, s. larva, f.
hob-nail, s. clavus, m.
hob-nob, v.n. propino, 1.
hock, s. poples, m.
hocus-pocus, s., v. jugglery.
hodge-podge, s. farrago, f. ; miscellanea,
n. pl.
hoe, s. sarculum, pastinum, n. ; —, v.a.
sarculo, 1 ; ligo, m. ; pastino, 3 ; (weeds)
pecto, 3.   [cina, f.
hog, s. sus, porcus, m. ; —'s flesh, por-
hoggish, a. inquinatus, fœdus.
hogshead, s. dolium, n.
hoiden, s. puella proterva, f.
hoist, v.a. sublevo, 1 ; tollo, 3.
hold, v.a. teneo ; possideo, habeo, 2 ; (to
contain) capio, 3 ; —, v.n. permaneo,
2 ; (to think) existimo, 1 ; censeo, 2 ;
to — back, retineo, 2 ; (v.n.) cunctor,
1 ; **to — forth,** (v.a.) porrigo, extendo,
3 ; (to offer) præbeo, 2 ; *fig.* ostendo, 3 ;
(v.n.) contionem habeo, 2 ; **to — in,**
inhibeo, cohibeo, 2 ; **to — off,** abstineo, 2 ; **to — out,** v. **to — forth;**
(to endure) duro, 1 ; (to persevere) obduro, persevero, 1 ; **— together,** contineo, 2 ; **to — up,** (to lift up) attollo,
3 ; sustineo, 2 ; **to — with,** consentio, 4.
hold, s. manus ; custodia, f. ; (support)
fulcrum, n. ; (influence) momentum,
n. ; potestas, f. ; (of a ship) alveus, m.
holder, s. possessor, m. ; colonus, m. ;
(handle) manubrium, n.
holding, s. possessio, f. ; (farm) fundus,
agellus, m. ; (back) retentio, f.
hole, s. foramen, n. ; rima, f. ; *fig.* latebra,
f. ; (of mice, etc.) cavum, n.

holiday, s. dies festus, m. ; —s, pl. feriæ, f. pl.
holily, ad. sancte.
holiness, s. sanctitas, religio, pietas, f.
hollo, holloa, v. halloo.
hollow, a. cavus ; concavus ; *fig.* vanus.
hollow, s. caverna, f. ; cavum, n. ; (depression) lacuna, f.
hollow, v.a. cavo, excavo, 1.
hollowness, s. *fig.* vanitas, f.
holly, s. ilex (mod. hort.).
holly-hock, s. althæa, f.
holm-oak, ilex, f.
holocaust, s. holocaustum, n.
holy, a. sanctus ; sacer, religiosus ; (pious)
pius.
holy-day, v. holiday.
homage, s. obsequium, n. ; cultus, m. ;
observantia, f.
home, s. domicilium, n. ; domus, f. ; at
—, domi.
home, a. domesticus ; —, ad. (homewards) domum ; (strike —, of weapons)
sedeo, 2.
home-bred, a. domesticus, vernaculus.
homeless, a. tecto carens, profugus.
homeliness, s. rusticitas, f.
homely, a. domesticus, simplex ; rudis ;
incompositus ; rusticus.
home-made, a. domesticus, vernaculus.
homespun, a. domi factus.
homestead, s. villa, f.
homeward, ad. domum.
homicidal, a. cruentus, sanguinolentus.
homicide, s. (person) homicida, m. ; (deed)
homicidium, n.
homily, s. sermo, tractatus, m.
homogeneous, a. ejusdem generis.
hone, s. cos, f.
honest, a. probus ; sincerus ; integer,
verus ; —ly, ad. probe, sincere, integre,
vere.
honesty, s. probitas, sinceritas, integritas, f. ; (plant) lunaria (mod. hort.).
honey, s. mel, n. ; —, a. melleus.
honey-bee, s. apis mellifera, f.
honey-comb, s. favus, m.
honeyed, honied, a. mellitus.
honeysuckle, s. caprifolium lonicera
(mod. hort.).
honorary, a. hononarius.
honour, s. honos, m. ; fama, laus, gloria ;
honestas, fides, f. ; (high position)
dignitas, f.
honour, v.a. honoro ; celebro, 1 ; (hold in
—) in honore habeo, 2 ; (court) colo, 3 ;
observo, 1.
honourable, a. honestus ; honorificus ;
bonus.
honourably, ad. honorifice ; honeste.
hood, s. cucullus, m. ; palliolum.

hoodwink, v.a. occæco ; *fig.* ludificor, 1.
hoof, s. ungula, f.
hook, s. hamus ; uncus, m. ; (of shepherds) pedum, n.
hook, v.a. inunco, 1 ; *fig.* capio, 3.
hooked, a. hamatus ; (crooked) curvatus, aduncus, curvus, recurvus.   [m.
hoop, s. circulus ; (for children) trochus,
hooping-cough, s. tussis clamosa, f.
hoopoe, hoopoo, s. upupa, f.
hoot, v.a. & n. gemo, queror, 3 ; acclamo, 1 ; explodo, 3.
hoot, hooting, s. gemitus, m. ; acclamatio, f.
hop, s. (plant) lupus humulus (mod. hort.).
hop, v.n. salio, 4 ; subsulto, 1.
hope, s. spes, f.
hope, v.a. spero, 1 ; **to — for,** exspecto, 1.   [magna spe.
hopeful, a. bonæ spei ; **—ly,** ad. cum
hopeless, a. exspes ; desperatus ; **—ly,** ad. sine spe, deperanter.
hopelessness, s. (of things) desperata condicio ; (of persons) desperatio, f.
hopper, s. (of a mill) infundibulum, n.
horde, s. turba, f. ; v. **crowd.**
hore-hound, s. marrubium, n.
horizon, s. orbis finiens, m.
horizontal, a. libratus ; **—ly,** ad. ad libram.
horn, s. cornu, n. ; (to blow on) bucina, f. ; cornu, n.
horn, a. corneus.
hornbeam, s. carpinus, f.
horn-blower, s. cornicen, m.
horned, a. cornutus, corniger.
hornet, s. crabro, m.   [durus.
horny, a. corneus ; (callous) callosus,
horoscope, s. horoscopus, m. ; genesis, f.
horrible, a. horribilis, fœdus, nefarius ; (excessive) immoderatus.
horribly, ad. horribili modo, fœde, nefarie.   [**—ly,** ad. horride.
horrid, a. horridus, horrens, immanis ;
horridness, s. horror, m. ; atrocitas, f.
horrific, a. horrificus, terribilis.
horrify, v.a. horrifico, 1 ; terreo, exterreo, 2.
horror, s. horror, pavor, m. ; (hatred) odium, n.
horse, s. equus, m. ; equitatus, m.
horseback, s. **on —,** (in) equo, ex equo ; **ride on —,** equito, 1.
horse-breaker, s. domitor equorum, m.
horse-chestnut, s. æsculus, f.
horse-cloth, s. stragulum, n.
horse-fly, s. tabanus, asilus, m.
horse-hair, s. pilus equinus, m.
horse-laugh, s. cachinnus, m.
horse-leech, s. sanguisuga, hirudo, f. ; medicus equarius, m.

horseman, s. eques, c.
horsemanship, s. ars equitandi, f.
horse-race, s. curriculum equorum, n. ; certatio equestris, f.
horse-radish, s. armoracia, f. ; cochlearia (mod. hort.).
horse-shoe, s. solea, f.
horse-soldier, s. eques, m.
horse-whip, s. virga, scutica, f. ; **—,** v.a. verbero, 1.
hortatory, a. hortativus.
horticulture, s. hortorum cultus, m.
hose, s. tibiale, n. ; feminalia, n. pl. ; (pipe) tubulus, m.
hosiery, s. feminalia, n. pl.
hospitable, a. hospitalis, liberalis, munificus.   [munifice.
hospitably, ad. hospitaliter, liberaliter,
hospital, s. valetudinarium, n.
hospitality, s. hospitium, n. ; hospitalitas ; liberalitas, f.
host, s. (entertainer) hospes, m. ; (at an inn) caupo, m. ; (crowd) multitudo, f. ; (army) exercitus, m. ; (among the Catholics) hostia, f.
hostage, s. obses, c.
hostess, s. hospita ; (at an inn) caupona, f.
hostile, a. hostilis, hosticus, inimicus, infestus ; **—ly,** ad. hostiliter, inimice, infeste.
hostility, s. inimicitia ; **hostilities,** (war) bellum, n.
hot, a. calidus ; fervens, candens ; fervidus ; (of spices) acer ; (furious) furens, iratus ; (keen) vehemens, acer ; **to grow —,** excandesco, 3.
hot-bath, s. balneum fervens, n. ; thermæ, f. pl.   [n. pl.
hotch-potch, s. farrago, f. ; miscellanea,
hotel, s. hospitium, n. ; caupona, f. ; deversorium, n.
hot-headed, a. præceps, temerarius.
hotly, ad. acriter, ardenter, vehementer.
hough, s., v. **hock.**
hound, s. catulus, m. ; canis, c.
hour, s. hora, f. ; **half an —,** semihora, f. ; **three-quarters of an —,** dodrans horæ, m.
hour-glass, s. horarium, n.
hourly, a. & ad. in singulas horas ; in horas, singulis horis.
house, s. domus, sedes, f. ; tectum ; domicilium, n. ; *fig.* familia ; domus, gens, f. ; (in politics) (senatorum, etc.) ordo, m.
house, v.a. domo excipio ; (to store) condo, 3.   [m.
house-breaker, s. effractarius, effractor,
house-breaking, s. effractura, f.
house-dog, s. canis domus custos, c.
household, s. domus, familia, f. ; **—,** a. domesticus, familiaris.

household-god, s. Lar, m. ; —s, pl. Penates, m. pl.

householder, s. paterfamilias, m.

housekeeper, s. promus ; dispensator, m. ; (female) dispensatrix, f.

housekeeping, s. cura rei familiaris, f.

houseleek, s. sempervivum, n.

housemaid, s. ancilla, f. [f.

house-rent, s. merces habitationis annua,

house-tax, s. tributum in singulas domos impositum, n.

housewife, s. materfamilias, f.

housewifery, s. cura rei familiaris, f.

housings, s. (for a horse) strata, stragula, n. pl.

hovel, s. tugurium, n. ; casa, f.

hover, v.n. pendeo, 2 ; volito, 1 ; libror, 1 ; (over) immineo, 2.

how, ad. quomodo ; ut ; (to what degree) quam ; — many, quot, quam multi ; — often, quoties ; — much, quantum.

how, (inter.) ut ! quam !

however, ad. cumque, quamvis, utcumque ; quantumvis ; —, c. nihilominus, tamen.

howl, v.n. ululo, 1 ; —, s. ululatus, m.

hubbub, s. tumultus, m. ; turba, f.

huckle-bone, s. talus, m.

huckster, s. propola, m.

huddle, v.n. confercio, 4 ; — away, raptim effero, 3.

huddle, s. confusio ; turba, f. [tio, f.

hue, s. color, m. ; — and cry, conclama-

huff, s. ira, f.

huff, v.a. arroganter tracto, 1 ; —, v.n. stomachor, 1.

hug, s. complexus, amplexus, m.

hug, v.a. complector, amplector, 3 ; fig. amplexor, 1 ; — (the shore), lego, 3.

huge, a. ingens ; vastus ; immanis ; —ly, ad. immaniter, egregie.

hugeness, s. vastitas, immanitas, moles, f.

hulk, s. navis, alveus, m.

hull, s. (of beans, etc.) siliqua, f. ; folliculus, m. ; (of a ship) alveus, m.

hum, v.n. susurro ; murmuro, 1.

hum, s. bombus, m. ; fremitus, m. ; murmur, n. ; susurrus, m.

hum, i. hem, ehem !

human, a. humanus ; mortalis ; —ly, ad. humanitus.

humane, a. humanus, misericors ; —ly, ad. humaniter ; misericorditer.

humanity, s. humanitas ; misericordia, f. ; (men) homines, mortales, m. pl.

humanize, v.a. excolo, 3 ; emollio, 4.

humble, a. humilis ; summissus, supplex ; (mean) obscurus.

humble, v.a. infringo, deprimo, 3 ; — myself, me demitto.

humbleness, s. humilitas ; obscuritas, f.

humbly, ad. humiliter, summisse ; — born, humili loco natus.

humbug, s. nugæ, gerræ, tricæ, f. pl.

humbug, v.a. verba do, 1 ; fallo, decipio, 3.

humbug, s. fraus, fallacia, f.

humble-bee, s. apis terrestris, f.

humdrum, a. tardus, somniculosus.

humid, a. umidus.

humidity, s. umor, m.

humiliate, v.a. humilio, 1 ; deprimo, 3.

humiliation, s. humiliatio, f. ; dedecus, n. ; ignominia, turpitudo, f.

humility, s. animus summissus, m. ; modestia, f.

humorist, s. homo lepidus, festivus.

humorous, a. facetus ; lepidus ; ridiculus ; —ly, ad. facete, lepide, ridicule.

humour, s. (frame of mind) ingenium, n. ; (whim) libido, f. ; (pleasantry) festivitas, f. ; lepor, m. ; facetiæ, f. pl.

humour, v.a. obsequor, morem gero, 3 ; indulgeo, 2.

humoursome, a. morosus, difficilis.

hump, s. gibber, gibbus, m.

hump-backed, a. gibber.

hunch-backed, v. hump-backed.

hundred, a. centum ; —, s. centuria, f. ; — each, centeni ; — times, centiens.

hundred-fold, a. centuplex ; —, s. centuplum, n.

hundredth, a. centesimus.

hundred-weight, s. centumpondium, n.

hunger, s. fames, f. ; jejunium, n. ; —, v.n. esurio, 4 ; fig. cupio, 3.

hungrily, ad. voraciter. [vorax.

hungry, a. esuriens ; jejunus ; fig. avidus,

hunt, v.n. venor, 1.

hunt, hunting, s. venatio, f. ; venatus, m.

hunter, s. venator ; (hunting horse) equus venaticus, m.

hunting-horn, s. cornu, n.

hunting-knife, s. culter venatorius, n.

hunting-spear, s. venabulum, n.

huntress, s. venatrix, f.

huntsman, s. venator, m.

hurdle, s. crates, f.

hurl, v.a. jacio, projicio, 3 ; jacto, 1 ; jaculor, 1.

hurly-burly, s. tumultus, m.

hurra, hurray, euge !

hurricane, s. procella, tempestas, f. ; turbo, m.

hurriedly, ad. raptim ; festinanter.

hurry, v.n. festino, propero, præcipito, 1 ; curro, 3 ; —, v.a. urgeo, 2 ; festino, propero, præcipito, 1 ; to — along, rapto, 1 ; (v.n.) curro, 3 ; to — away, v.n. propero, 1 ; aufugio, 3 ; to — on, maturo, 1 ; (v.n.) curro, 3.

hurry, s. festinatio, properatio, f. ; in a —, festinanter.

hurt, v.a. lædo, 3 ; noceo, 2 ; *fig.* offendo, 3 ; —, v.n. doleo, 2.

hurt, s. vulnus ; damnum, n. ; injuria, f.

hurtful, a. noxius, perniciosus ; —**ly,** ad. nocenter.   [m., 1.

husband, s. maritus, vir, uxor, conjux,

husband, v.a. parco, 3.

husbandman, s. agricola, m.

husbandry, s. agricultura, res rustica, f.

hush, i. st ! tace, tacete.

hush, v.a. paco, 1 ; comprimo, 3 ; *fig.* celo, 1 ; —, v.n. taceo, 2.

husk, s. folliculus, m. ; siliqua, f. ; (of corn) gluma, f.

husky, a. (of voice) surraucus.

hustings, s. suggestum, n. ; comitia, n. pl.

hustle, v.a. proturbo, 1.

hut, s. tugurium, n. ; casa, f.

hutch, s. cavea, f. ; mapalia, n. pl.

huzza, i. euge !

hyacinth, s. hyacinthus, m.

hydra, s. hydra, f.

hydrangea, s. hydrangea (mod. hort.).

hydraulic, a. hydraulicus.

hydraulics, s. hydraulica, n. pl.

hydromel, s. hydromeli, n.

hydrophobia, a. hydrophobia, f.

hyena, s. hyæna, f.

Hymen, s. Hymen, Hymenæus, m.

hymeneal, a. nuptialis.

hymn, s. hymnus, m.

hyperbole, s. hyperbole, f.

hyperbolic, a. hyperbolicus.

hypercritical, a. nimis acer atque subtilis.

hyphen, s. hyphen, n.

hypochondria, s. atra bilis, f.

hypochondriacal, a. melancholicus.

hypocrisy, s. simulatio, dissimulatio ; pietas ficta, f.

hypocrite, s. simulator, dissimulator ; hypocrita, m.

hypocritical, a. simulatus, fictus.

hypocritically, ad. simulate, ficte.

hypothesis, s. (guess) conjectura ; (opinion) sententia, f.

hypothetical, a. hypotheticus.

hyssop, s. hyssopum, n.

hysterical, a. hystericus.

I, ego ; — **myself,** egomet, ipse ego.

iambic, a. iambicus, iambeus ; — **verse,** iambus, m.

ice, s. glacies, f. ; gelu, n.

ice, v.a. glacio.

iced, a. nivatus.

ice-plant, s. mesembryanthemum (mod. hort.).

icicle, s. stiria, f.

icy, a. glacialis ; gelidus.

idea, s. species, forma ; imago ; notitia ; notio ; (opinion) opinio, sententia ; (suspicion) suspicio ; (guess) conjectura, f.

ideal, a. perfectus ; mente conceptus.

ideal, s. exemplar (perfectum), n.

identical, a. idem ; unus atque idem.

identify, v.a. (equalize) exæquo, 1 ; (in law) agnosco, 3 ; — **oneself with,** sto cum (abl.).

idiocy, v. **idiotcy.**

idiom, s. (habit) consuetudo, f. ; (tongue, talk) lingua, f. ; sermo, m.

idiomatic, a. proprius linguæ ; vernaculus.

idiosyncrasy, s. proprium, n.   [m.

idiot, s. fatuus ; stupidus, stultus ; excors,

idiotcy, s. fatuitas, stultitia, f.

idiotic, a. fatuus.

idle, a. otiosus ; vacuus ; (of persons) ignavus, piger, segnis, desidiosus, iners ; *fig.* vanus.

idle, v.n. cesso, 1 ; tempus tero, 3.

idleness, s. otium, n. ; ignavia, segnitia, desidia, f.

idler, s. cessator, homo ignavus, m.

idly, ad. otiose ; segniter ; *fig.* frustra, incassum.

idol, s. idolum, simulacrum, n. ; *fig.* deliciæ, f. pl.

idolator, s. idololatres, m.

idolatry, s. idololatria, f.

idolize, v.a. *fig.* depereo, 4 ; (with acc.).

idyl, s. idyllium, n.

if, c. si ; **as** —, quasi, tanquam ; **but** —, sin (autem) ; **even** —, etiamsi ; — **only,** dummodo ; — **not,** ni, nisi, si non.

igneous, a. igneus.

ignite, v.a. accendo ; —, v.n. exardesco, excandesco, 3.

ignoble, a. ignobilis ; (of birth) obscurus ; *fig.* inhonestus, turpis.

ignobly, ad. inhoneste, turpiter.

ignominious, a. contumeliosus, ignominiosus, turpis ; —**ly,** ad. contumeliose, ignominiose, turpiter.   [dedecus, n.

ignominy, s. ignominia, turpitudo, f. ;

ignoramus, s. expers omnibus litteris.

ignorance, s. ignoratio, ignorantia, inscitia, f.

ignorant, a. inscius, ignarus, nescius ; (unlearned) indoctus, inscitus ; **to be** —, ignoro, 1 ; nescio, 4.

ignorantly, ad. (not knowing) per ignorantiam ; *fig.* indocte ; inscienter.

ignore, v.a. *fig.* prætereo, 4.

Iliad, s. Ilias, f.

ill, a. malus ; (in health) ægrotus ; **to be** —, ægroto, 1 ; **to fall** —, in morbum incido, 3.

ill, s. malum, n. ; —, ad. male, prave ; **take it** —, ægre fero, 3.

ill-advised, a. inconsideratus, inconsultus, temerarius.
ill-affected, a. malevolus.
ill-bred, a. agrestis, inurbanus.
ill-disposed, a. malevolus, malignus.
illegal, a. quod contra leges fit ; illicitus ; —ly, ad. contra leges ; illicite.
illegible, a. quod legi non potest.
illegitimacy, s. (of birth) ortus infamia, f.
illegitimate, a. haud legitimus ; spurius ; nothus ; (wrong) vitiosus.
ill-gotten, a. male partus.
illiberal, a. illiberalis ; —ly, ad. illiberaliter.
illiberality, s. illiberalitas, f.
illicit, a. illicitus ; —ly, ad. illicite.
illimitable, a. infinitus, immensus.
ill-natured, a. malevolus, malignus.
illness, s. morbus, m. ; aegrotatio, f.
illogical, a. vitiosus.
ill-omened, a. dirus, infaustus.
ill-temper, s. iracundia, morositas, f.
ill-tempered, a. iracundus, acerbus, stomachosus ; difficilis.
illuminate, v.a. illustro ; illumino, 1 ; (decorate) decoro, 1.   [ignes, m. pl.
illumination, s. lux, f. ; lumen, n. ; festi
illusion, s. error, m.
illusive, illusory, a. fallax.
illustrate, v.a. illustro ; fig. explano, 1 ; patefacio, 3.   [plum, n.
illustration, s. illustratio, f. ; fig. exem-
illustrative, a. aptus ad rem.
illustrious, a. clarus, illustris, praeclarus, inclitus, insignis ; —ly, ad. praeclare ; insigniter.
ill-will, s. malevolentia, malitia, malignitas.
image, s. simulacrum, n. ; (likeness, portrait) effigies, imago, f. ; (form) species forma, f.
image, v.a. effigiem pingo, 3 ; v. imagine.
imagery, s. imagines, f. pl.
imaginable, a. quod animo concipi potest.
imaginary, a. (unreal) imaginarius, fictus, falsus.
imagination, s. cogitatio ; imaginatio ; (dream) somnium, n. ; (opinion) opinio, f. ; power of —, vis ingenii.
imaginative, a. ingeniosus.
imagine, v.a. imaginor, 1 ; fingo, 3 ; (to think) existimo, arbitror, 1 ; (guess) conjicio, 3 ; (dream) somnio, 1.
imbecile, a. (weak) imbecillus ; (of mind) fatuus ; —, s. fatuus, m.
imbecility, s. imbecillitas animi, f.
imbibe, v.a. imbibo, bibo, 3 ; absorbeo, 2 ; fig. inficior, 3.
imbrue, v.a. imbuo, madefacio, 3.
imbue, v.a. imbuo, tingo, 3.
imitable, a. imitabilis.

imitate, v.a. imitor, assimulo, 1.
imitation, s. imitatio, f. ; imitamentum, n.
imitative, a. ad imitandum aptus.
imitator, s. imitator, m. ; imitatrix, f. ; aemulus, aemulator, m.
immaculate, a. castus, integer, inviolatus.
immaterial, a. simplex, incorporalis ; (unimportant) levis.
immature, a. immaturus.
immaturity, s. immaturitas.
immeasurable, a. immensus, infinitus.
immediate, a. praesens ; —ly, ad. confestim, extemplo, protinus ; continuo.
immemorial, a. from time —, ex omni memoria aetatum.
immense, a. ingens, immensus, enormis ; —ly, ad. immensum, multum.
immensity, s. immensitas ; vastitas, f.
immerge, immerse, v.a. mergo, demergo, immergo, 3.
immersion, s. immersio, f.
imminent, a. instans, praesens.
immobility, s. immobilitas, f.
immoderate, a. immodicus, nimius, immoderatus ; —ly, ad. immoderate, nimie ; immodice.
immodest, a. immodestus ; impudicus ; inverecundus ; —ly, ad. immodeste, inverecunde.
immodesty, s. immodestia, f.
immolate, v.a. immolo, macto, sacrifico, 1.
immolation, s. immolatio, f.
immoral, a. corruptus, pravus, improbus ; —ly, ad. prave ; improbe.
immorality, s. improbitas morum, f.
immortal, a. immortalis ; aeternus ; —ly, ad. in aeternum.
immortality, s. immortalitas, f.
immortalize, v.a. aeterno, 1 ; immortalem reddo, 3.
immovable, a. immobilis ; immotus.
immune, a. immunis.
immunity, s. immunitas, f.
immure, v.a. includo, 3.
immutability, s. immutabilitas ; immobilitas, f.
immutable, a. immutabilis ; immobilis.
immutably, ad. immutabiliter.
imp, s. (child) infans, c.
impair, v.a. laedo ; imminuo ; attero, 3 ; debilito, 1.
impalpable, a. intactilis.
impannel, v.a. eligo, 3.
impart, v.a. impertio, 4 ; communico, 1.
impartial, a. aequus ; —ly, ad. sine ira et studio.
impartiality, s. aequitas, aequabilitas, f.
impassable, a. insuperabilis, invius, impervius.
impassioned, a. vehemens, ardens.
impatience, s. impatientia, f.

impatient, a. impatiens ; iracundus ; **—ly,**
ad. impatienter.
impeach, v.a. accuso, 1.
impeachment, s. accusatio, f.
impede, v.a. impedio, 4 ; retardo, 1.
impediment, s. impedimentum, n. ; mora,
f. ; (in speech) hæsitatio, f.
impel, v.a. impello, 3 ; excito, stimulo, 1 ;
cieo, 2.
impend, v.n. impendeo, immineo, 2 ;
insto, 1.
impending, a. præsens.
impenetrability, s. soliditas, f.
impenetrable, a. impenetrabilis, impervius ; *fig.* occultus.   [cia, f.
impenitence, s. impænitentia ; pervica-
impenitent, a. impænitens ; pervicax.
imperative, a. imperiosus ; imperativus ;
—, s. (gr.) modus imperativus, m.
imperceptible, a. quod sensu percipi non
potest.   [obscure.
imperceptibly, ad. sensim ; pedetentim ;
imperfect, a. imperfectus, mancus ;
(faulty) mendosus ; vitiosus ; **—ly,** ad.
imperfecte ; mendose, vitiose.
imperfection, s. defectus, m. ; vitium, n.
imperial, a. imperatorius ; imperialis ;
—ly, ad. regie.
imperil, v.a. in periculum adduco, 3.
imperious, a. imperiosus ; superbus ; arrogans ; **—ly,** ad. imperiose ; superbe ;
arroganter.
imperiousness, s. superbia ; insolentia, f.
imperishable, a. perennis ; *fig.* immortalis.
impermeable, a. impervius.
impersonal, (gr.) impersonalis ; **—ly,** ad.
impersonaliter.
impersonate, v.a. partes (alicujus) sustineo, 2.
impersonation, s. partes (actoris), f. pl.
impertinence, s. insolentia, f.
impertinent, a. insolens ; (things) ineptus,
absurdus ; **—ly,** ad, insolenter.
impervious, a. impervius.   [m.
impetuosity, s. vehementia, f. ; impetus,
impetuous, a. vehemens, fervidus ; **—ly,**
ad. vehementer.
impetus, s. vis, f. ; impetus, impulsus, m.
impiety, s. impietas, f. ; scelus, nefas, n.
impious, a. impius ; scelestus, sceleratus ; nefandus, nefarius ; **—ly,** ad.
impie ; sceleste, scelerate ; nefarie.
implacable, a. implacabilis, inexorabilis.
implacably, ad. implacabiliter.
implant, v.a. ingigno ; insero, 3.
implement, s. instrumentum, n. ; arma,
n. pl.   [particeps sum.
implicate, v.a. implico, 1 ; **am implicated,**
implication, s. **by —,** tacite.
implicit, a. tacitus ; (unconditional) absolutus ; **—ly,** ad. tacite.

implore, v.a. imploro, obsecro, supplico,
obtestor, 1.
imply, v.a. significo, 1 ; **be implied,**
subesse.
impolicy, s. inconsulta ratio, f.
impolite, a. inurbanus ; **—ly,** ad. inurbane.
impoliteness, s. rusticitas, importunitas, f.
impolitic, a. imprudens.   [pondere.
imponderable, a. ponderis expers ; sine
import, v.a. importo, 1 ; inveho, 3 ; (to
mean) significo, 1 ; **it —s,** refert.   [f.
import, s. significatio ; (of goods) invectio,
importance, s. *fig.* momentum, pondus, n. ;
gravitas, f.
important, a. magni momenti, gravis.
importation, s. invectio, f.
importer, s. qui merces peregrinas invehit.
importunate, a. importunus, molestus ;
—ly, ad. importune.
importune, v.a. flagito, efflagito.
importunity, s. efflagitatio, f.
impose, v.a. (to enjoin) injungo, impono,
3 ; (to deceive) fraudo, 1.
imposer, s. fraudator, m.
imposition, s. (tax) vectigal ; tributum,
n. ; (punishment) pensum, n. ; (cheat)
fraus, f.
impossibility, s. impossibilitas, f.
impossible, a. impossibilis.
impost, s. vectigal, tributum, n.
impostor, m. fraudator, præstigiator, m. ;
planus, m.
imposture, s. præstigiæ, f. pl. fraus, f.
impotence, s. infirmitas, f.
impotent, a. infirmus, impotens ; (crippled)
claudus ; **—ly,** ad. infirme.
impound, v.a. confisco, 1 ; (beasts) includo, 3.
impoverish, v.a. pauperem reddo, 3 ; *fig.*
vitio.
impracticable, a. quod fieri non potest.
imprecate, v.a. imprecor, exsecror, 1.
imprecation, s. exsecratio, f.
impregnable, a. inexpugnabilis ; (of
persons) firmus.
impregnate, v.a. gravidam facio, 3 ; fecundo, 1 ; impleo, 2.
impress, v.a. imprimo, 3 ; (to mark) signo,
1 ; *fig.* inculco, 1 ; (to move) moveo, 2.
impress, impression, s. impressio ; (track,
footstep) vestigium, n. ; (of a book)
editio, f. ; *fig.* animi motus ; (effect)
momentum, m.
impressive, a. gravis ; **—ly,** ad. graviter.
imprint, v.a. imprimo, 3.
imprison, v.a. includo, in vincula conjicio, 3.
imprisonment, s. captivitas, custodia, f.
improbable, a. haud, verisimilis.
improbably, ad. haud verisimiliter.
impromptu, a. ex tempore dictum.

improper, a. indecorus ; indignus ; —**ly,** ad. indecore ; indigne.

impropriety, s. improprietas, f. ; indecorum, n.

improve, v.a. emendo, 1 ; excolo, corrigo, 3 ; —, v.n. melior fio, proficio, 3.

improvement, s. cultura, f. ; (progress) profectus, m.

improver, s. corrector ; emendator, m.

improvident, a. improvidus ; imprudens ; —**ly,** ad. improvide ; imprudenter.

improvise, v.a. ex tempore dico or compono, 3.

imprudence, s. imprudentia, f.

imprudent, a. imprudens, incautus, inconsultus ; —**ly,** ad. imprudenter, inconsulte.

impudence, s. impudentia, procacitas, protervitas, f.

impudent, a. impudens ; procax, protervus ; —**ly,** ad. impudenter ; procaciter, proterve.

impugn, v.a. impugno ; culpo, 1.

impulse, impulsion, s. impulsus, impetus, m. [rius.

impulsive, a. vehemens, ardens, temera-

impunity, s. impunitas, f. ; **with** —, impune.

impure, a. impurus ; incestus ; impudicus ; —**ly,** ad. impure ; inceste.

impurity, s. impuritas ; (lewdness) impudicitia, f.

imputable, a. imputandus.

imputation, s. criminatio, f.

impute, v.a. (to ascribe) attribuo, 3 ; do, 1 ; verto, 3 ; (as a fault) imputo, 1.

in, pr. in. ; ad, apud ; inter ; intra ; de, ex ; per ; præ, pro ; sub ; tenus ; secundum ; —, ad. intro, intus ; —, a. internus, insitus.

inaccessible, a. inaccessus, difficilis aditu.

inaccuracy, s. neglegentia, f. ; error, m.

inaccurate, a. parum accuratus, minime exactus ; falsus ; —**ly,** ad. parum accurate ; falso.

inaction, s. otium, n.

inactive, a. iners, ignavus, otiosus.

inactivity, s. inertia, socordia ; cessatio, f.

inadequate, a. impar ; mancus ; —**ly,** ad. haud satis.

inadmissible, a. illicitus.

inadvertence, s. imprudentia, f.

inadvertently, ad. imprudenter.

inalienable, a. quod alienari non potest.

inanimate, a. inanimus.

inanition, s. inanitas, f. [pl.

inanity, s. inanitas (absurdity), ineptiæ, f.

inapplicable, a. **be** —, non pertineo ad.

inappreciable, a. tam parvus ut æstimari non possit.

inapproachable, a. inaccessus.

inappropriate, a. haud idoneus, parum aptus ; —**ly,** ad parum apte ad rem.

inaptitude, s. ingenium inhabile (ad aliquam rem), n.   [ad. confuse.

inarticulate, a. indistinctus, confusus ; —**ly,**

inasmuch, ad. quandoquidem, quoniam.

inattention, s. animus parum attentus, m. ; neglegentia, incuria, f.

inattentive, a. haud or parum attentus ; neglegens ; —**ly,** ad. animo parum attento ; neglegenter.

inaudible, a. quod audiri nequit.

inaudibly, s. ita ut exaudiri non possit.

inaugurate, v.a. inauguro, 1.   [f.

inauguration, s. inauguratio, consecratio,

inauspicious, a. infaustus ; infelix, funestus ; —**ly,** ad. malo omine ; infeliciter.

inborn, inbred, a. ingenitus, innatus, insitus.

incalculable, a. quod æstimari nequit ; *fig.* immensus ; incredibilis.

incantation, s. carmen, n. ; cantus, m.

incapable, a. inhabilis, imperitus.

incapacitate, v.a. lædo, 3 ; noceo, 2.

incapacity, s. imperitia, inscitia, f.

incarcerate, v.a., v. **imprison.**

incase, v.a. includo, 3.

incautious, a. incautus ; —**ly,** ad. incaute.

incendiarism, s. incendium, n.

incendiary, s. incendiarius, m.

incense, s. tus, n.

incense, v.a. fumigo ; *fig.* exaspero, 1 ; incendo, 3.   [m.

incentive, s. incitamentum, n. ; stimulus,

incessant, a. continuus, assiduus, perpetuus ; —**ly,** ad. assidue ; perpetuo.

incest, s. incestum, n. ; incestus, m.

incestuous, a. incestus ; —**ly,** ad. inceste.

inch, s. uncia, f. ; — **by** —, unciatim ; *fig.* paulatim, sensim.

inchoate, a. incohatus.

incident, s. (event) eventus, m. ; res, f. ; casus, m.

incidental, a. fortuitus ; —**ly,** ad. fortuito.

incipient, a. nascens ; primus.

incised, a. incisus.

incision, s. incisura, f. ; incisus, m.

incisive, a. *fig.* acer, acerbus.

incisor, s. dens acutus, m.

incite, v.a. incito, stimulo, 1 ; impello, 3.

incitement, s. incitamentum, n. ; incitatio, f. ; stimulus, m.

inciter, s. impulsor, incitator, m.

incivility, s. rusticitas, inhumanitas, f.

inclemency, s. inclementia ; asperitas, f.

inclement, a. inclemens ; asper.

inclination, s. (act) inclinatio ; (slope) a:-clivitas ; *fig.* voluntas, inclinatio, f.

incline, v.a. inclino, 1 (also *fig.*) ; *fig.* adduco, 3 ; —, v.n. propendeo, 2 ; inclino, 1.

incline, s. acclivitas, f.
inclined, a. proclivis ; propensus.
include, v.a. includo, comprehendo, 3.
incognito, ad. dissimulato nomine.
incoherence, s. confusio, f.
incoherent, a. confusus ; —ly, ad. confuse, nullo ordine.
income, s. reditus ; fructus, m. ; (of the State) vectigal, n.
incoming, s. reditus, m.
incommode, v.a. incommodo, 1.
incommodious, a. incommodus, molestus ; —ly, ad. incommode.
incomparable, a. incomparabilis, unicus.
incomparably, ad. unice ; longe . . .
incompatibility, s. repugnantia, f.
incompatible, a. discors, repugnans, contrarius.
incompetence, incompetency, s. inscitia, imperitia, f.
incompetent, a. inhabilis ; inscitus, imperitus.
incomplete, a. imperfectus, incohatus ; mancus ; —ly, ad. imperfecte.
incompleteness, s. imperfectio, f.
incomprehensible, a. quod comprehendi non potest.
inconceivable, a. quod cogitari *or* mente percipi non potest.
inconclusive, a. levis ; infirmus.
incongruity, s. repugnantia, f.
incongruous, a. inconveniens, male congruens ; —ly, ad. parum apte.
inconsequent, a. confusus.
inconsequently, ad. confuse ; temere.
inconsiderable, a. levis, parvi momenti.
inconsiderate, a. inconsideratus ; —ly, ad. inconsiderate.   [sideratus, m.
inconsiderateness, s. animus parum con-
inconsistency, s. inconstantia, mutabilitas ; repugnantia, f.
inconsistent, a. inconstans ; contrarius, absonus ; —ly, ad. inconstanter.
inconsolable, a. inconsolabilis.
inconstancy, s. levitas, inconstantia, f. ; mutabilitas, mobilitas.
inconstant, a. inconstans, levis, mutabilis, mobilis.
incontestable, a. certus, haud dubius.
incontinence, s. incontinentia ; intemperantia ; (unchastity) impudicitia, f.
incontinent, a. incontinens, intemperans ; impudicus ; —ly, ad. incontinenter, intemperanter.
incontrovertible, a. certus.
inconvenience, s. incommodum, n. ; —, v.a. incommodo, 1.
inconvenient, a. incommodus ; molestus ; —ly, ad. incommode.
incorporate, v.a. adjungo, 3 ; admisceo, 2 ; (politically) contribuo, 3.

incorporeal, a. incorporalis, inanis.
incorrect, a. mendosus, falsus ; —ly, ad. mendose, prave, falso, perperam.
incorrectness, s. vitium, n. ; pravitas, f.
incorrigible, a. insanabilis.
incorrupt, a. incorruptus, integer.
incorruptibility, s. incorruptibilitas, f. ; incorrupti mores, m. pl.
incorruptible, a. incorruptus ; integer.
increase, v.a. augeo, 2 ; amplifico, 1 ; —, v.n. augeor, 2 ; cresco, 3 ; ingravesco.
increase, s. incrementum, n. ; auctus, m.
incredible, a. incredibilis.
incredibly, ad. incredibiliter, **incredibile** quantum ; ultra fidem.
incredulity, s. incredulitas, f.
incredulous, a. incredulus.
incriminate, v.a. accuso, 1.
incrust, v.a. crusto, incrusto, 1.
incrustation, s. crusta ; incrustatio, f.
incubate, v.n. incubo, 1.
incubation, s. incubatio, f. ; incubitus, m.
incubus, s. incubo, m.
inculcate, v.a. inculco, 1 ; præcipio, 3.
incumbent, a. **it is —,** oportet (with accus. and infinitive).
incur, v.a. incurro (in), 3 ; mereor, 2.
incurable, a. insanabilis, immedicabilis.
incursion, s. incursio, f.
indebted, a. obæratus ; (for) obnoxius ; **I am — to you for this,** hoc tibi debeo.
indecency, s. indecorum, n. ; indignitas, f.
indecent, a. indecens, indecorus ; —ly, ad. indecenter, indecore.
indecision, s. hæsitatio, dubitatio, f.
indecisive, a. dubius, incertus, anceps, ambiguus.
indeclinable, a. indeclinabilis.
indecorous, a., v. **indecent.** [—? itane ?
indeed, ad. (it is true) re vera, profecto ;
indefatigable, a. indefessus, indefatigabilis, assiduus, impiger.
indefatigably, ad. impigre, assidue.
indefeasible, a. quod infringi non potest.
indefensible, a. non excusandus ; (mil.) qui teneri non possit.
indefinite, a. incertus ; anceps, obscurus ; —ly, ad. indefinite.
indelible, a. indelebilis.
indelicacy, s. indecorum, n.
indelicate, a. turpis, fœdus, putidus.
indemnification, s. compensatio, f.
indemnify, v.a. damnum sarcio, 4.
indemnity, s. indemnitas, f. ; **act of —,** impunitas, f.
indent, v.a. incido, 3.
indentation, s. incisura, f.
independence, s. libertas, f.
independent, a. sui potens ; liber ; *fig.* sui juris ; —ly, ad. libere ; suis legibus ; (each by itself) singillatim.

indescribable, a. inenarrabilis, infandus.
indestructible, a. quod dirui non potest.
indeterminate, a. indefinitus; —ly, ad. indefinite.
index, s. (of a book) index, (of a dial) gnomon, m.; *fig.* indicium, n.
Indian, s. Indus, m.; —, a. Indicus.
indicate, v.a. indico; significo, 1.
indication, s. signum, indicium, n.
indicative, a. indicativus; —, s. (gr.) modus indicativus, m.
indict, v.a. accuso, 1; defero, 3.
indictment, s. libellus, m.; (accusation) accusatio, f.
indifference, s. (neutrality) æquus animus; (carelessness) neglegentia, f.; (contempt) contemptus, m.
indifferent, a. æquus, medius; remissus, neglegens, frigidus; —ly, ad. æquo animo; (carelessly) frigide.
indigence, s. egestas, inopia, f.
indigenous, a. indigena.
indigent, a. egens, inops.
indigestible, a. crudus.
indigestion, s. cruditas, f.
indignant, a. indignans, indignabundus, iratus; —ly, ad. indignanter.
indignation, s. indignatio; ira, f.
indignity, s. indignitas; contumelia, ignominia, f.
indigo, s. indicum, n.
indirect, a. obliquus; —ly, ad. oblique; to touch on —, perstringo, 3.
indiscreet, a. inconsultus; —ly, ad. inconsulte, temere.
indiscretion, s. imprudentia, f.
indiscriminate, a. promiscuus; —ly, ad. promiscue.
indispensable, a. necessarius.
indispensably, ad. necessario.
indispose, v.a. alieno, 1; averto, 3; deduco. [valens.
indisposed, a. aversus; (in health) minus
indisposition, a. (illness) ægrotatio, commotiuncula, f.; (aversion) animus alienus, m.
indisputable, a. certus; haud dubius.
indisputably, ad. haud dubie.
indissoluble, a. indissolubilis.
indissolubly, ad. indissolubiliter.
indistinct, a. indistinctus, obscurus; —ly, ad. indistincte, obscure.
indite, v.a. compono, scribo, 3.
individual, a. individuus, proprius; —ly, ad. singillatim.
individual, s. homo, c.
individuality, s. proprium ingenium, n.
indivisible, a. individuus.
indocile, a. indocilis; intractabilis.
indocility, s. indocilis natura, f.; indocile ingenium, n.

indolence, s. inertia, desidia, ignavia, socordia, f.
indolent, a. iners, ignavus, deses, socors, segnis; —ly, ad. ignave, segniter.
indomitable, a. indomitus, invictus.
indubitable, a. indubitabilis, haud dubius, certus.
indubitably, ad. haud dubie.
induce, v.a. adduco, impello, 3; persuadeo, 2; incito, 1.
inducement, s. incitamentum, n.; causa, f.; stimulus, m.
induction, s. inductio, f.
indue, v. endow.
indulge, v.a. indulgeo, 2; servio, 4.
indulgence, s. indulgentia; venia; (kindness) clementia, f.
indulgent, a. indulgens, facilis, clemens; —ly, ad. indulgenter, clementer.
industrious, a. industrius; diligens; sedulus; strenuus; —ly, ad. industrie, diligenter, sedulo, strenue.
industry, s. industria; sedulitas; diligentia, f.; studium, n.
inebriate, v. intoxicate.
ineffable, a., v. unspeakable.
ineffective, ineffectual, a. inefficax, inutilis.
ineffectually, ad. frustra, nequiquam.
inefficiency, s. inutilitas, f.
inefficient, a. inefficax; inhabilis; inutilis.
inelegance, s. inconcinnitas, f.
inelegant, a. inelegans; inconcinnus.
inept, a. ineptus.
inequality, s. inæqualitas, f.
inert, a. iners, segnis; —ly, ad. segniter.
inertia, inertia, f.
inertness, s. inertia, f.
inestimable, a. inæstimabilis.
inevitable, v. unavoidable.
inexcusable, a. inexcusabilis.
inexcusably, ad. nulla excusatione.
inexhaustible, a. inexhaustus.
inexorable, a. inexorabilis, durus, implacabilis.
inexpediency, s. inutilitas, f.
inexpedient, a. inutilis.
inexperience, s. imperitia, inscitia, f.
inexperienced, a. imperitus; inexpertus inscitus; rudis.
inexpert, a. inscitus, imperitus.
inexpiable, a. inexpiabilis.
inexplicable, a. inexplicabilis, inenodabilis.
inexpressible, a. inenarrabilis, infandus.
inexpugnable, a. inexpugnabilis.
inextinguishable, a. inexstinctus.
inextricable, a. inextricabilis.
infallible, a. qui errare non potest; certus, haud dubius.
infallibly, ad. haud dubie.

infamous, a. infamis ; turpis, inhonestus, fœdus, ignominiosus ; —**ly,** ad. turpiter, inhoneste, fœde, ignominiose.

infamy, s. infamia, ignominia, f. ; opprobrium, probrum, n.

infancy, s. infantia, ætas iniens, f.

infant, s. infans, c. ; (law) pupillus, m.

infant, a. infans ; puerilis.

infanticide, s. (person) infanticida, m. ; (murder) infanticidium, n.

infantine, a. infantilis, puerilis.

infantry, s. peditatus, m. ; pedestres copiæ, f. pl.

infatuate, v.a. infatuo, 1 ; (deceive) decipio ; (entice) allicio, 3.

infatuation, s. dementia, cæcitas mentis, f.

infect, v.a. inficio, 3 ; contamino, 1.

infection, s. contagium, n. ; contagio, f. ; contactus, m.

infectious, a. contagiosus.

infer, v.a. conjicio, infero, colligo, 3.

inference, s. conjectura, conclusio, f.

inferior, a. inferior, deterior, minor ; —, s. impar, c.

infernal, a. infernus ; *fig.* nefandus.

infertility, s. sterilitas, f.

infest, v.a. infesto, vexo, 1 ; infestum, habeo, 2.

infidel, a. & s. infidelis.

infidelity, s. infidelitas, f.

infinite, a. infinitus ; immensus ; —**ly,** ad. infinite ; infinito.

infinitive, s. infinitivus (modus), m.

infinitude, infinity, s. infinitas, infinitio, f.

infirm, a. infirmus, debilis, imbecillus.

infirmary, s. valetudinarium, n.

infirmity, s. infirmitas, imbecillitas, debilitas, f.

inflame, v.a. inflammo, 1 ; incendo, 3.

inflammation, s. inflammatio, f.

inflammatory, a. *fig.* turbulentus, seditiosus.

inflate, v.a. inflo, 1 ; (also *fig.*) : **to be —d,** tumeo, 2.

inflation, s. inflatio, f. ; tumor, m.

inflect, v.a. inflecto, 3 ; curvo, 1.

inflection, s. inflexio, f. ; inflexus, m.

inflexibility, s. rigor, m.

inflexible, a. rigidus ; *fig.* obstinatus.

inflexibly, ad. obstinate ; rigide.

inflict, v.a. infligo ; impono, 3 ; irrogo, 1.

infliction, s. irrogatio, f. ; (punishment) pœna, f.

influence, s. momentum, pondus, n. ; auctoritas, gratia, f. ; impulsus, m.

influence, v.a. moveo, 2 ; impello, 3 ; valeo, 2.

influential, a. (auctoritate) gravis, potens ; (popular) gratiosus.

influx, s. influxio, f.

infold, v.a. involvo, amplector, 3.

inform, v.a. (to teach) doceo, 2 ; instruo ; (to give intelligence) certiorem facio ; (against) defero, 3 ; — **oneself,** disco, 3.

informal, a. privatus.

informality, s. vitium, n.

informant, s. auctor ; (law) delator, m. ; (messenger) nuntius, m.

information, s. (news) nuntius, m. ; (law) delatio, f.

informer, s. delator, m.

infraction, s. violatio, f.

infringe, v.a. violo, 1.

infringement, s. violatio.

infringer, s. violator, m.

infuriate, v.a. effero, exaspero, 1.

infuse, v.a. infundo ; *fig.* (to inspire) injicio, 3.

infusion, s. infusio, f. ; decoctum, n.

ingathering, s. perceptio, f.

ingenious, a. sollers ; subtilis ; ingeniosus ; —**ly,** ad. sollerter ; subtiliter ; ingeniose.

ingenuity, s. ingenium, n.

ingenuous, a. ingenuus, apertus.

ingenuously, ad. ingenue, aperte.

inglorious, a. inglorius ; obscurus ; turpis ; —**ly,** ad. sine gloria ; obscure ; turpiter.

ingot, s. later, m.

ingraft, v.a. insero, 3.

ingrained, a. insitus, inveteratus.

ingratiate, to — oneself, v.r. gratiam ineo apud (aliquem), 4 ; gratiam (mihi) concilio, 1.

ingratitude, s. animus ingratus, m. ; beneficii oblivio, f.

ingredient, s. pars, f.

ingress, s. ingressus, initus, m.

ingulf, v.a. devoro, ingurgito, 1.

inhabit, v.a. colo, incolo, 3 ; habito, 1.

inhabitable, a. habitabilis.

inhabitant, s. incola, c. ; habitator, colonus, m.

inhale, v.a. duco, 3 ; haurio, 4.

inharmonious, a. dissonus, absonus.

inhere, v.n. inhæreo, 2 ; insum.

inherent, a. inhærens, proprius.

inherit, v.a. hereditate accipio, 3.

inheritance, s. hereditas ; patrimonium, n.

inheritor, s. heres, c.

inhospitable, a. inhospitalis, inhospitus.

inhospitably, ad. inhospitaliter.

inhospitality, s. inhospitalitas, f.

inhuman, a. inhumanus ; crudelis ; —**ly,** ad. inhumane ; crudeliter.

inhumanity, s. inhumanitas ; crudelitas, f.

inhume, v.a. inhumo, 1.

inimical, a. inimicus.

inimitable, a. inimitabilis.

iniquitous, a. improbus, iniquus.

iniquity, s. improbitas, f.   [tera, f.

initial, a. primus ; —, s. prima verbi lit-

initiate, v.a. initio, 1.
initiation, s. initiatio, f. ; initiamenta, n. pl.
initiative, a. take the —, initium capio, 3.
inject, v.a. infundo, immitto, 3.
injection, s. (act) infusio, f. ; infusus, m.
injudicious, a. inconsultus ; —ly, ad. inconsulte.
injunction, s. mandatum, imperatum, n.
injure, v.a. noceo, 2 ; lædo ; offendo, 3.
injurious, a. noxius ; damnosus ; malus ; —ly, ad. male.
injury, s. injuria, f. ; damnum, detrimentum, n.   [f.
injustice, s. injustitia ; iniquitas ; injuria,
ink, s. atramentum, n.
inkling, s. (hint) rumusculus, m. ; (suspicion) suspicio, f.
inkstand, s. atramentarium, n.
inland, a. mediterraneus.
inlay, v.a. distinguo, 3 ; cælo, 1 ; (inlaid work) opus intestinum, n.
inlet, s. accessus, aditus, m. ; (of the sea) æstuarium, n.
inmate, s. incola, inquilinus, m.
inmost, a. intimus, imus ; — recesses, penetralia, n. pl.
inn, s. caupona, taberna, f. ; deversorium, hospitium, n.
innate, a. innatus ; insitus ; ingenitus.
innavigable, a. innavigabilis.
inner, a. interior.
innermost, a. intimus ; imus.
innkeeper, s. caupo, m.
innocence, s. innocentia ; integritas ; castitas, f.
innocent, a. innocuus ; innocens ; insons ; (chaste) castus ; —ly, ad. innocue ; innocenter ; caste.
innocuous, a. innocuus ; —ly, ad. innocue.
innovate, v.a. novo, innovo, 1.
innovation, s. res novæ, f. pl.
innovator, s. rerum novarum cupidus, m.
innoxious, a. innoxius.
innuendo, s., v. hint.
innumerable, a. innumerabilis, innumerus.
innumerably, ad. innumerabiliter.
inoculate, v.a. (in gardening) inoculo, 1 ; fig. insero, 3.
inoculation, s. inoculatio, f.
inoffensive, a. innocens, innoxius.
inopportune, a. intempestivus ; —ly, ad. intempestive.
inordinate, a. immoderatus ; —ly, ad. immoderate.
inquest, s. inquisitio, f.
inquire, v.a. & n. quæro, inquiro, 3 ; investigo, 1.
inquiry, s. inquisitio, f.
inquisition, s. quæstio, inquisitio, f.
inquisitive, a. curiosus ; —ly, ad. curiose.

inquisitiveness, s. curiositas, f.
inquisitor, s. quæsitor, inquisitor, m.
inroad, s. incursio, irruptio, f.
insalubrious, a. insalubris.
insane, a. insanus ; vecors ; amens ; demens ; —ly, ad. insane, dementer.
insanity, s. insania, dementia, amentia, vecordia, f.
insatiable, a. insatiabilis, inexplebilis, inexpletus.
insatiably, ad. insatiabiliter.
inscribe, v.a. inscribo ; insculpo ; incido, 3.
inscription, s. inscriptio, f. ; titulus, m. ; carmen, n.
inscrutable, a. obscurus, cæcus.
insect, s. insectum, n.
insecure, intutus, periculosus ; infestus lubricus.
insecurity, s. periculum, n.
insensate, a., v. mad.
insensibility, s. hebetatio, f. ; frigus, n. ; languor, m.
insensible, a. insensilis ; fig. durus, lentus, frigidus.
insensibly, ad. (gradually) sensim.
inseparable, a. inseparabilis.
insert, v.a. insero ; ascribo, interpono, 3.
inside, s. interior pars, f. ; interiora, n. pl.
inside, a. interior ; —, ad. intrinsecus ; intra, intro, intus ; — (of) pr. intra.
insidious, a. insidiosus ; subdolus ; —ly, ad. insidiose ; subdole.
insight, s. prudentia, cognitio, f.
insignia, s. insignia, n. pl.
insignificance, s. exiguitas, f. ; levitas.
insignificant, a. exiguus ; nullius momenti ; levis.
insincere, a. insincerus, simulatus ; fallax ; dolosus ; —ly, ad. haud sincere ; simulate ; dolose.
insincerity, s. fallacia ; simulatio, f.
insinuate, v.a. insinuo, 1 ; instillo, 1 ; — oneself into, irrepo, 3.
insinuation, s. insinuatio, f. ; (suspicion) suspicio, f. ; make —s against, oblique perstringo.
insipid, a. insulsus ; fig. hebes ; frigidus ; —ly, ad. insulse ; frigide.
insipidity, s. insulsitas, f.
insist, v.n. insto, 1 ; urgeo, 2 ; exigo, 3.
insnare, v. ensnare.
insolence, s. insolentia, arrogantia, superbia, f.
insolent, a. insolens, arrogans, superbus ; —ly, ad. insolenter ; impudenter ; superbe.
insoluble, a. inexplicabilis, inextricabilis.
insolvent, a. be —, non esse solvendo.
inspect, v.a. inspicio, introspicio, 3.
inspection, s. inspectio ; cura, f.
inspector, s. curator, f. ; præfectus.

inspectorship, s. cura, f.

inspiration, s. (divine) afflatus, m.; numen, n.; instinctus, m.

inspire, v.a. inspiro, 1; injicio, 3; (kindle) incendo, 3; excito, 1.

inspirit, v.a. hilaro, exhilaro, 1.

instability, s. instabilitas, inconstantia, f.

install, v.a. inauguro, 1; constituo, 3.

instalment, s. (payment in part) pensio, portio, f.

instance, s. exemplum, n.; (request) flagitatio, f.; for —, exempli gratia.

instance, v.a. exemplum do, 1.

instant, a (earnest) impensus; (of date) præsens; —ly, ad. impense; (at once) statim.

instant, s. momentum, punctum temporis, n.; this —, statim, actutum.

instantaneous, a. quod momento temporis fit; —ly, ad. continuo; statim.

instead, ad. — of, loco, vice; pro.

instigate, v.a. instigo, stimulo, incito, 1; cieo, 2.

instigation, s. incitatio, f.; stimulus, m.

instigator, s. impulsor, auctor, m.

instil, v.a. instillo, 1.

instinct, s. natura, f.

instinctive, a. naturalis; —ly, ad. naturaliter.

institute, v.a. instituo, constituo, 3.

institution, s. (act) institutio, f.; (thing instituted) institutum, n.

instruct, v.a. (to teach) doceo, 2; instruo, instituo, 3; erudio, 4; (to order, to command) mando, 1.

instruction, s. institutio, disciplina, f.; (to ambassadors, etc.) mandatum, n.

instructive, a. ad docendum aptus.

instructor, s. præceptor, magister, m.; magistra, f.

instrument, s. instrumentum, n.; (law) tabula, syngrapha, f.

instrumental, a. aptus, utilis.

instrumentality, s. (service, agency) ministerium, n.; opera, f.

insubordinate, a. seditiosus. [m.

insubordination, s. seditio, f.; tumultus,

insufferable, a. intolerandus, intolerabilis.

insufficiency, s. inopia, egestas, f.

insufficient a. non or parum sufficiens, impar; —ly, ad. haud satis.

insular, a. insulanus.

insult, s. opprobrium, probrum, convicium, n.; contumelia, f.

insult, v.a. insulto, 1; maledico, 3.

insulter, s. conviciator, m.

insulting, a. contumeliosus.

insultingly, ad. contumeliose.

insuperable, a. insuperabilis.

insupportable, a. intolerabilis.

insupportably, ad. intolerabiliter.

insurgent, a. & s. rebellis.

insurmountable, a. inexsuperabilis, insuperabilis.

insurrection, s. rebellio, seditio, f.; tumultus, m. [sus.

insurrectionary, a. seditiosus, tumultuo-

intact, a. integer; incolumis.

integral, a. necessarius.

integrity, s. integritas, probitas; sinceritas, innocentia, f.

integument, s. integumentum, n.

intellect, s. intellectus, m.; intelligentia, mens, f.

intelligence, s. ingenium, n.; (cleverness) sollertia, f.; (news) nuntius, m.

intelligent, a. intelligens; sollers; —ly, ad. intelligenter.

intelligible, a. intelligibilis.

intelligibly, ad. ita ut intelligi possit.

intemperance, s. intemperantia, impotentia, f.

intemperate, a. intemperans; immodicus; immoderatus; (ungovernable) impotens; —ly, ad. intemperanter; immodice; immoderate.

intend, v.a. destino, 1; (resolve) constituo, decerno, 3; (set on foot) paro, 1; molior, 4.

intended, a. destinatus; (of the future husband or wife) sponsus, sponsa.

intense, a. acer, vehemens; (excessive) nimius; —ly, ad. acriter; vehementer; valde; magnopere.

intensity, s. vehementia, vis, f.; (of winter, etc.) asperitas, f.

intent, a. intentus, attentus; —ly, ad. intente.

intent, intention, s. consilium, propositum, n.; (meaning) significatio, f.

intentionally, ad. de industria, consilio, consulto.

inter, v.a. humo, 1; sepelio, 4.

intercalary, a. intercalarius.

intercalation, s. intercalatio, f.

intercede, v.n. intercedo, 3; deprecor, 1.

interceder, s. deprecator, m.

intercept, v.a. intercipio, intercludo, 3; deprehendo.

intercession, s. deprecatio, f.

intercessor, s. deprecator, m.

interchange, v.a. permuto, commuto, 1.

interchange, s. permutatio; vicissitudo, f.

intercourse, s. commercium, n.; (social) consuetudo, f.; (talk) colloquium, n.

interdict, v.a. interdico, 3; prohibeo, 2; veto, 1.

interdiction, s. interdictio, f.; interdictum, n.

interest, v.a. teneo, 2; capio, 3; delecto, 1; to — oneself, incumbo (rei), 3; studeo, 2.

interest, s. (advantage) emolumentum, n.; utilitas, f.; (for money) fænus, usura, f.; *fig.* studium, n.

interfere, v.n. intercedo, 3; intervenio, 4; (hinder) obsto, 1.

interference, s. intercessio, f.; interventus, m.

interim, s. intervallum, n. [interior, f.

interior, a. interior, internus; —, s. pars

interjection, s. interjectio, f.

interlace, v.a. intexo, intertexo, 3.

interlard, v.a. infercio, 4; *fig.* vario, 1.

interline, v.a. interscribo, 3.

interlinear, a. interscriptus.

interloper, s. qui alienis negotiis intervenit.

interlude, s. embolium, n.

intermarriage, s. connubium, n.

intermeddle, v.n., v. interfere.

intermediate, a. medius.

interment, s. sepultura, humatio, f.; exsequiæ, f. pl.; funus, n.

interminable, a. infinitus.

intermingle, v.a. intermisceo, immisceo, 2.

intermission, s. intermissio; cessatio, remissio, f.

intermit, v.a. intermitto, 3; —, v.n. cesso, 1.

intermittent, a. rarus.

intermix, v.a. intermisceo, 2.

internal, a. intestinus, domesticus; —ly, ad. intus.

international, a.; — law, s. jus gentium, n.

interpolate, v.a. interpolo, 1; interlino, 3; corrumpo, 3; vitio, 1.

interpose, v.a. interpono, 3; v.n. intervenio, 4; intercedo, 3; (beg off) deprecor, 1.

interposer, s. deprecator, m.

interposition, s. (interference) interventus, m.

interpret, v.a. interpretor, 1; conjicio, 3.

interpretation, s. interpretatio, conjectio, f.

interpreter, s. interpres, c.

interregnum, s. interregnum, n.

interrogate, v.a. interrogo, percontor, 1.

interrogation, s. interrogatio, percontatio, f.

interrogative, interrogatory, a. interrogativus; —ly, ad. interrogative.

interrupt, v.a. interrumpo, intermitto, 3; interpello, 1.

interruptedly, ad. interrupte.

interrupter, s. interpellator, m.

interruption, s. interruptio; interpellatio, f.

intersect, v.a. interseco, 1.

intersection, s. decussatio, f.

intersperse, v.a. intermisceo, immisceo, 2.

interstice, s. lacuna, rima, f.

intertwine, v.a. intertexo, 3.

interval, s. intervallum, spatium, n.

intervene, v.n. (to be between) interjaceo, 2; (to come between) intercedo, 3; (to prevent) intervenio, 4.

intervening, a. medius. [tus, m.

intervention, s. interventus, interjec-

interview, s. colloquium, n.; congressus, m.

interview, v.a. convenio, 4.

interweave, v.a. intertexo; intexo, 3.

intestate, a. intestatus.

intestate, ab intestato.

intestine, a. intestinus; —s, s. pl. intestina; viscera, n. pl.

inthral, v.a. mancipo, 1; servum facio, 3; *fig.* capio, 3.

inthralment, s. servitium, n.

intimacy, s. familiaritas, consuetudo, f.

intimate, a. familiaris, intimus; —ly, ad. familiariter, intime.

intimate, v.a. indico, 1; innuo, 3.

intimation, s. indicium, n.; nutus, m.; signum, n.

intimidate, v.a. metum injicio, 3; terreo, 2; minor, 1.

intimidation, s. minæ, f. pl.

into, pr. in (with accusative).

intolerable, a. intolerabilis, intolerandus.

intolerably, ad. intoleranter.

intolerance, s. intolerantia, impatientia, f.

intolerant, a. intolerans, impatiens.

intonation, s. accentus, m.

intoxicate, v.a. ebrium reddo, 3.

intoxication, s. ebrietas, f.

intractable, a. intractabilis.

intrench, v.a. munio, 4; vallo, 1; *fig.* (on, upon) violo, 1; invado (jus alienum), 3.

intrenchment, s. vallum, n.; agger, m.

intrepid, a. intrepidus, impavidus; —ly, ad. intrepide, impavide.

intrepidity, s. animus intrepidus, m.

intricacy, s. ambages, f. pl.

intricate, a. contortus, perplexus; —ly, ad. contorte; perplexe.

intrigue, s. consilium clandestinum, n.; fraus, ars, f.; (amour) amores, m. pl.

intrigue, v.n. vafre ago, dolis contendo, 3; — with, sollicito (acc.).

intriguer, s. fallaciarum peritus, m.

intrinsic, a. internus; innatus; —ally, ad. intrinsecus. [instituo, 3.

introduce, v.a. introduco; (set on foot)

introduction, s. inductio; (to a person) introductio; (preface) præfatio, f.; exordium, procemium, n.

introductory, a. introductorius.

intrude, v.a. & n. immitto, me immitto, 3; molestus sum.

intruder, s. molestus homo, m.
intrusion, s. importunitas ; usurpatio, f.
intrusive, a. molestus ; —ly, ad. moleste.
intrust, v.a. committo, credo, 3 ; mando,
commendo, 1.
intuition, s. vis mentis, f.
intuitively, ad. mentis propria vi ac
natura.
inundate, v.a. inundo, 1.
inundation, s. inundatio, f. ; diluvium, n.
inure, v.a. assuefacio, 3.
inurement, s. consuetudo, f.   [fero, 3.
invade, v.a. invado, irrumpo, bellum in-
invader, s. invasor, m.
invalid, a. infirmus, vitiosus, nugatorius,
irritus.   [m.
invalid, s. æger, ægrotus, valetudinarius,
invalidate, v.a. irritum reddo ; rescindo, 3.
invaluable, a. inæstimabilis.   [mobilis.
invariable, a. constans, immutabilis, im-
invariably, ad. immutabiliter ; semper.
invasion, s. incursio, irruptio, f.
invective, s. convicium, n. ; male dicta,
n. pl.   [sector, 1.
inveigh, v.n. invehor, 3 ; maledictis in-
inveigle, v.a. illicio, pellicio, 3.
invent, v.a. invenio, reperio, 4 ; (to contrive) excogito, 1 ; fingo, 3.
invention, s. (act) inventio, f. ; (thing in-
vented) inventum, n. ; (lie, etc.) commentum, n.
inventive, a. habilis, ingeniosus.
inventor, s. inventor, repertor, m.
inventory, s. inventarium, n.
inventress, s. inventrix, f.
inverse, v.a. inversus, conversus.
inversion, s. inversio, conversio, f.
invert, v.a. inverto, 3.
invest, v.a. do, mando ; (money) colloco,
1 ; pono, 3 ; (to besiege) obsideo, 2.
investigate, v.a. investigo, indago, scrutor, 1 ; inquiro, cognosco, 3.
investigation, s. investigatio, inquisitio, f.
investigator, s. investigator, indagator ;
quæsitor, m.
investment, s. (of a town) obsessio, obsidio, f. ; (of money) pecunia in fænore
posita.
inveterate, a. inveteratus.
invidious, a. invidus, malignus, invidiosus ; —ly, ad. invidiose ; maligne.
invidiousness, s. invidia, f.
invigorate, v.a. corroboro, confirmo, 1.
invincible, a. invictus ; insuperabilis.
invincibly, ad. ita ut vinci non possit.
inviolability, s. sanctitas, religio, f.
inviolable, a. inviolatus, sanctus, religiosus, f.
inviolably, ad. inviolate ; sancte.
inviolate, a. inviolatus, intactus, integer,
incolumis.

invisible, a. invisibilis.
invisibly, ad. ita ut videri non possit.
invitation, s. invitatio, f.
invite, v.a. invito, voco, 1.
inviting, a. gratus, blandus, suavis ; —ly,
ad. suaviter, blande.
invocation, s. obtestatio, f.
invoice, s. libellus, m.
invoke, v.a. invoco, imploro, obtestor, 1.
involuntarily, ad. invite.
involuntary, a. invitus, coactus.
involve, v.a. (to wrap up) involvo, 3 ; (to
contain) contineo, 2 ; (to entangle)
implico, 1 ; (imply) habeo.
involved, a. (in debt) obæratus ; (intricate) perplexus.
invulnerable, s. invulnerabilis.
inward, a. interior.
inwardly, inwards, ad. intus, intrinsecus,
introrsus.
Ionian, Ionic, s. Ionicus.
irascible, a. iracundus.
ire, s. ira, iracundia, f.
Ireland, s. Hibernia, f.
iris, s. (plant) iris, f.
Irish, a. Hibernicus.
irk, v.a. ; it —s, tædet, 3.
irksome, a. molestus, odiosus.
irksomeness, s. tædium, n.
iron, s. ferrum, n. ; —s, pl. vincula, n. pl.
iron, a. ferreus ; fig. durus.
ironclad, s. navis longa, f.
ironical, a. deridens ; —ly, ad. ironice.
ironmonger, s. negotiator ferrarius, m.
ironmongery, s. ferramenta, n. pl.
irony, s. ironia, dissimulatio, f.
irradiate, v.a. illustro, 1 ; illumino.
irradiate, v.a. illustro, 1 ; illumino.
irrational, a. rationis expers, irrationalis ;
—ly, ad. irrationaliter.
irreclaimable, a. perditus.
irreconcilable, a. implacabilis ; (incompatible) repugnans.
irrecoverable, a. irreparabilis.
irrecoverably, ad. ita ut reparari non
possit.
irrefragable, a. certissimus.
irrefutable, a. quod confutari non potest.
irregular, a. enormis, abnormis ; (disorderly) tumultuarius ; (gr.) anomalus ;
(spasmodic) rarus, infrequens ; —ly,
ad. enormiter ; sine ordine.
irregularity, s. enormitas ; (gr.) anomalia,
f. ; (of conduct) luxuria, f.
irrelevant, a. non pertinens, alienus.
irreligion, s. impietas, neglegentia deorum, f.
irreligious, a. impius, irreligiosus, religio-
nis neglegens ; —ly, ad. impie, irreligiose.
irreligiousness, s., v. irreligion.
irremediable, a. insanabilis, immedicabilis.

irreparable, a. irreparabilis ; irrevocabilis.
irreproachable, a. irreprehensus, integer.
irresistible, a. invictus ; cui nullo modo
  resisti potest. [resisti possit.
irresistibly, ad. (mod.) it aut nulla vi
irresolute, a. incertus animi ; dubius ; (of
  permanent character) parum firmus ;
  —**ly,** ad. dubitanter.
irresolution, s. dubitatio, **f. ;** animus
  parum firmus, m.
irretrievable, a. irreparabilis.
irretrievably, ad., v. **irreparably.**
irreverence, s. irreverentia, f.
irreverent, a. irreverens, parum reverens.
irrevocable, a. irrevocabilis.
irrigate, v.a. rigo, irrigo, 1.
irrigation, s. irrigatio, inductio aquæ, f.
irritability, s. iracundia, f. [cundus.
irritable, a. irritabilis, stomachosus, ira-
irritably, ad. stomachose ; iracunde.
irritate, v.a. irrito ; inflammo, 1.
irritation, s. irritatio, f. ; stomachus, m. ;
  ira, f.
irruption, s. incursio, irruptio, f.
isinglass, s. ichthyocolla, f.
island, s. insula, f.
islander, s. insulanus, m.
islet, s. parva insula, f.
isolate, v.a. sejungo, secerno, 3.
Israelite, s. Israelita, m.
issue, s. (outlet) egressus, m. ; (result)
  eventus, exitus, m. ; (end) finis, c. ;
  (success) successus, m. ; (offspring)
  liberi, m. pl. ; (discharge) profluvium,
  n. ; (of money) erogatio, f. ; (profit)
  reditus, m.
issue, v.a. (to give forth) edo ; (to post up)
  propono, 3 ; (money) erogo, 1 ; —, v.n.
  emano, 1 ; egredior, 3 ; (to end)
  evenio, 4.
isthmus, s. isthmus, m.
itch, s. scabies, prurigo, f.
itch, v.n. prurio ; fig. gestio, 4.
itching, s. pruritus, m. ; prurigo, f.
itchy, a. scabrosus.
iteration, s. iteratio, f.
itinerant, a. circumforaneus.
itinerary, s. itinerarium, n.
ivory, s. ebur, n.
ivory, a. eburneus ; eburnus.
ivy, s. hedera, f.
ixia, s. ixia (mod. hort.).

Jabber, v.n. blatero, 1.
jabberer, s. blatero, m.
jack, s. (leather bottle) uter, m. ; (fish)
  lucius, m. ; (flag of a ship) vexillum, n. ;
  (frame) machina, f.
jackal, s. canis aureus, m.

jackanapes, s. homo ineptus, m.
jackass, s. asinus ; fig. stultus, m.
jackdaw, s. monedula, f.
Jacob's ladder, s. polemonium (mod.
  hort.).
jade, s. (horse) caballus, m. ; fig. (woman)
  importuna mulier, f.
jaded, a. defessus.
jaggy, a. dentatus, serratus.
jail, s. carcer, m.
jail-bird, s. furcifer, m.
jailer, s. custos, m.
jamb, s. postis, m.
jangle, v. **wrangle.**
janissary, s. janissarius, m.
January, s. Januarius, m.
jar, s. (pitcher, bottle, cask) olla ; amphora, f. ; urceus ; (of sound) sonus
  discors, m. ; fig. (disagreement) rixa, f. ;
  jurgium, n. ; (shaking) tremor, m.
jar, v.n. discrepo, discordo, 1.
jargon, s. confusæ voces, f. pl. ; barbarus
  sermo, m.
jarring, a. dissonus, discors.
jasmin, s. jasminum, n. (mod. hort.).
jasper, s. iaspis, f.
jaundice, s. morbus regius, icterus, m.
jaundiced, a. ictericus ; fig. morosus ;
  invidiosus.
jaunt, s. excursio, f.
javelin, s. pilum, jaculum ; telum, veru,
  n.
jaw, s. mala ; maxilla, f. ; fig. fauces, f. pl.
jawbone, s. maxilla, f.
jaw-tooth, s. dens maxillaris, m.
jay, s. corvus glandarius, m.
jealous, a. invidus ; æmulus ; invidiosus ;
  —**ly,** ad. invidiose.
jealousy, s. invidia ; æmulatio, f. ; livor, m.
jeer, v.n. derideo, irrideo, 2.
jeer, jeering, s. risus ; irrisus, m.
jeerer, s. derisor, irrisor, m.
jeeringly, ad. per ludibrium.
jejune, a. jejunus, frigidus ; —**ly,** ad.
  jejune, frigide.
jelly, s. cylon, quilon, s.
jelly-fish, s. pulmo, halipleumon, m.
jeopardize, v.a. in periculum adduco, 3.
jeopardy, s. periculum, discrimen, n.
jerk, s. impetus, subitus motus, m.
jerk, v.a. subito moveo, 2.
jessamine, s., v. **jasmin.**
jest, s. jocus, lusus, m. ; facetiæ, f. pl. ; in
  —, joco, jocose.
jest, v.n. jocor, 1 ; ludo, 3.
jester, s. joculator ; (buffoon) scurra, m.
jestingly, ad. per jocum.
Jesuit, s. Jesuita, m.
jesuit's-bark, s. cinchona, f.
Jesus, s. Jesus, m. [(mineral) gagates, m.
jet, s. (spout of water) scatebra, f. ;

jet-black, a. nigerrimus.
jetty, s. moles, pila, f.
Jew, s. Judæus, m.
jewel, s. gemma, f.
jewel, v.a. gemmo, 1.
jewelled, a. gemmeus, gemmifer.
jeweller, s. gemmarius, m.
jewelry, s. gemmæ, f. pl.
Jewess, s. Judæ, mulier Judaica, f.
Jewish, a. Judaicus.
Jew's mallow, s. kerria (mod. hort.).
jig, s. saltatio, f.
jilt, v.a. fallo, 3.
jingle, v.n. tinnio, 4.
jingle, jingling, s. tinnitus, m.
job, s. negotiolum, n. ; res lucrosa, **f.**
jockey, s. agaso, m.
jockey, v.a. decipio, 3 ; fraudo, 1.
jocose, a. jocosus ; **—ly,** ad. jocose.
jocular, a. jocularis, jocosus, facetus ;**—ly,**
    ad. joculariter, facete, jocose.
jocularity, s. facetiæ, f. pl., animus joco-
    sus, m.
  ocund, a. festivus, hilaris.
jog, v.a. concutio, quatio, 3 ; **—,** v.n. (to
    shake) contremisco, 3 ; **—along,** repo; 3.
jog-trot, s. lentus gressus, m.
join, v.a. jungo, conjungo, 3 ; (to be near)
    contingo ; (battle) confligo, consero, 3 ;
    (meet) congredior ; **—,** v.n. adjungor,
    3 ; cohæreo, 2 ; (to take part in) parti-
    ceps *or* socius sum (alicujus rei).
joiner, s. lignarius.
joint, s. commissura, f. ; articulus, m. ;
    vertebra ; junctura, f. ; (of plants)
    geniculum.
joint, v.a. deartuo, 1.
joint, a. communio.
jointed, a. vertebratus ; (of plants) geni-
    culatus.
joint-heir, s. coheres, c.
jointly, ad. conjuncte, conjunctim, una,
    communiter.
joint-stock company, s. societas, f.
jointure, s. dos, f.
joist, s. tignum transversarium, n.
joke, s. jocus, m. ; sales, m. pl. ; facetiæ, f.
    pl. ; **in —,** per jocum.
joke, v.a. & n. jocor, 1 ; ludo, 3 ; irrideo, 2.
joker, s. joculator, m.
jollity, s. festivitas, hilaritas, **f.**
jolly, a. festivus, hilaris.
jolt, v.a. & n. concutio, 3 ; jacto, quasso,
    1 ; concutior, 3 ; jactor, quassor, 1.
jolt, jolting, s. jactatio, f.
jostle, v.a. pulso, deturbo, 1.
jot, s. punctum, n.
journal, s. ephemeris, f. ; diarium, **n. ;**
    (newspaper) acta diurna, n. pl.
journey, s. iter, n. ; profectio, f. ; via, f.
journey, v.n. proficiscor, 3 ; peregrinor, 1.

journeyman, s. mercenarius, m.
Jove, s. Jupiter, m.
jovial, a. hilaris, festivis.
joviality, s. hilaritas, festivitas, **f.**
jowl, s., v. **cheek.**
joy, s. gaudium, n. ; lætitia, f. ; **to give or**
    wish —, gratulor, 1.
joyful, joyous, a. lætus, hilaris ; **—ly,** ad.
    læte, hilare ; libenter.
joyless, a. illætabilis, tristis, mæstus.
jubilant, a. lætitia exsultans ; ovans.
jubilation, s. triumphus, m. ; gaudium, n.
jubilee, s. jubilæus, m.
Judaic, a., v. **Jewish.**
Judaism, s. Judaismus, **m.**
judge, s. judex ; quæsitor, arbiter ; **—,**
    (a critic) existimator, censor, m.
judge, v.a. & n. judico ; existimo, 1 ;
    censeo, 2 ; (to value) æstimo, 1.
judgment, s. sententia, f. ; arbitrium ; *fig.*
    (opinion & faculty of judging) judicium
    n.   [justice) tribunal, n.
judicature, s. jurisdictio, f. ; (court of
judicial, a. judicialis ; **—ly,** ad. judiciali-
    ter.   [sapienter, prudenter.
judicious, a. sapiens, prudens ; **—ly,** ad.
judiciousness, s. prudentia, **f.** ; consil-
    ium, n.
jug, s. urceus, m.
juggle, v.a. præstigias ago, 3.
juggle, juggling, s., v. **jugglery.**
juggler, s. præstigiator ; pilarius, m.
jugglery, s. præstigiæ, f. pl.
jugular, a. jugularis ; **—,** s. vena jugu-
    laris, f.
juice, s. sucus, m.
juiciness, s. suci abundantia, f.
juicy, a. sucosus.   [zizyphus, f.
jujube, s. (fruit) **zizyphum,** n. ; (tree)
July, s. Quintilis, m.
jumble, v.a. confundo, 3 ; permisceo, 2.
jumble, s. confusio, congeries, strages, f.
jump, v.n. salio, exsilio, 4 ; exsulto, 1.
jump, s. saltus, m.
junction, s. conjunctio, junctura, f.
June, s. Junius, m.
jungle, s. locus virgultis obsitus, m.
junior, a. & s. junior, minor.
juniper, s. juniperus, f.
junket, v.n. commissor, epulor, 1.
juridical, a. juridicalis.
jurisconsult, s. jurisconsultus, m.
jurisdiction, s. jurisdictio, f.
jurisprudence, s. jurisprudentia, f.
jurist, s. jurisconsultus, m.
juror, s. judex, m.
jury, s. judices, m. pl.
just, a. justus ; meritus ; æquus.
just, ad. (a moment ago) modo ; (on'y)
    modo ; **— as, — so,** haud secus.
justice, s. justitia, æquitas, f.

justifiable, a. excusandus.
justifiably, ad. jure ; cum causa, excusate.
justification, s. excusatio, purgatio, f.
justify, v.a. purgo ; excuso, 1 ; (approve) approbo, 1.
justly, ad. juste ; jure ; merito.
justness, s. justitia, æquitas, f.
jut, v.n. procurro, 3 ; **to — out,** promineo, 2.
jutting, a. procurrens, projectus.
juvenile, a. juvenilis, puerilis.

Kale, s. crambe, f.
kangaroo, s. halmaturus, m.
keel, s. carina, f.
keen, a. acer ; alacer ; sagax ; acutus ; **—ly,** ad. acute, acriter ; sagaciter.
keenness, s. sagacitas, subtilitas ; (of the eye) perspicacitas ; *fig.* acerbitas, f.
keen-scented, a. sagax.
keen-sighted, a. perspicax.
keen-sightedness, s. perspicacitas, f.
keep, v.a. teneo ; habeo, 2 ; (to preserve) servo, conservo, 1 ; (to guard) custodio, 4 ; (to store) recondo ; (to support) alo, 3 ; sustineo, 2 ; (animals) pasco, 3 ; (a holiday) celebro, 1 ; ago, 3 ; (reserve) reservo, 1 ; (one's word, law, etc.) servo, 1 ; —, v.n. maneo, 2 ; duro, 1 ; **to — away,** arceo, prohibeo ; (v.n.) abstineo, 2 ; **to — back,** retineo, cohibeo, 2 ; (to conceal) celo, 1 ; (to hold one's tongue) reticeo, 2 ; **to — company,** comitor, 1 ; **to — down,** comprimo, 3 ; **to — from,** (v.a.) prohibeo, 2 ; (v.n.) abstineo, 2 ; **to — in,** includo, 3 ; **to — off,** v. **to — away** ; **to — together,** contineo, cohibeo, 2 ; **to — under,** compesco, supprimo, 3 ; **to — up,** (to maintain) tueor, 2 ; sustineo, 2 ; (v.n.) subsequor, 3.
keep, s. (citadel) arx, f. ; (food) cibus, m.
keeper, s. custos, c.
keeping, s. tutela ; custodia ; cura, f.
keepsake, s. monumentum, pignus, n.
keg, s. cadus, m. ; testa, f.
ken, s. conspectus, m.
kennel, s. cubile, n. ; stabulum, n.
kennel, v.n. stabulor, 1.
kerb-stone, s. crepido, f.
kernel, s. (of a fruit) nucleus, m. ; *fig.* medulla, f.
kettle, s. lebes, m. ; aënum, n.
kettle-drum, s. tympanum, n.
key, s. clavis, f. ; (of a position) claustra, n. pl. ; *fig.* cardo, m.
keystone, s. saxum medium, n.
kibe, s. pernio, m.
kick, v.n. calcitro, 1 ; calce ferio, 4.

kick, s. calcitratus, m.
kid, s. hædus, m.
kidnap, v.a. surripio, 3.
kidnapper, s. plagiarius, m.
kidney, s. ren, m.
kidney-bean, s. phaselus, m.
kill, v.a. interficio, cædo, occido, interimo, perimo, 3 ; neco, 1.
killer, s. interfector.
kiln, s. fornax, f.
kin, s. consanguinitas, f. ; genus, n. ; v. **relation.**
kind, s. genus, n. ; modus, m. ; species, f. ; **of what —,** qualis, cujusmodi.
kind, a. amicus ; benignus ; benevolus ; comis ; humanus ; suavis.
kind-hearted, a. benignus.
kindle, v.a. accendo, 3 ; *fig.* inflammo, 1 ; —, v.n. exardesco, 3. [comitas, f.
kindliness, s. benignitas ; humanitas ;
kindly, a., v. **kind** ; —, ad. amice ; benigne ; humane ; comiter ; **will you — answer,** velim respondeas.
kindness, s. benignitas ; humanitas, f. ; beneficium, n. ; v. **kindliness.**
kindred, s. consanguinitas, f. ; genus, n.
kindred, a. consanguineus, cognatus.
king, s. rex, m.
kingdom, s. regnum, n.
kingfisher, s. alcedo, f.
kingly, a. regius, regalis, regificus ; —, ad. regie, regaliter.
kinsman, s. necessarius, cognatus, consanguineus, m. [necessaria, f.
kinswoman, s. consanguinea, cognata,
kiss, s. suavium, osculum, basium, n.
kiss, v.a. suavior, osculor, basio, 1.
kissing, s. osculatio, f. ; **— -crust,** a. (sweetmeats) crustulum, n.
kitchen, s. culina, f.
kitchen-garden, s. holitorius hortus, m.
kitchen-gardener, s. holitor, m.
kitchen-herbs, s. holus, n.
kitchen-maid, s. culinaria, f.
kite, s. (bird) milvus, m.
kitten, s. catulus felinus, m.
knack, s. ars sollertia, f.
knapsack, s. sarcina, f.
knave, s. homo nequam, nebulo, m.
knavery, s. fraus, f. ; dolus, m. ; malitia, f.
knavish, a. scelestus, nefarius ; (mischievous) malitiosus ; **—ly,** ad. sceleste, nefarie, malitiose.
knead, v.a. depso, subigo, 3.
kneading, s. subactio, f. ; **— -trough,** s. magis, f.
knee, s. genu, n. ; v. **joint.**
knee-pan, s. patella, f.
kneel, v.n. in genua procumbo, genibus nitor, 3.

knife, s. culter, cultellus, m.

knight, s. eques, m.

knighthood, s. equestris dignitas, f.

knightly, a. equester.

knit, v.a. to — the brow, supercilium (frontem) contraho, 3.

knob, s. tuber, n. nodus, m. ; (of a shield) umbo, m. ; (of a door) bulla, f.

knobbed, knobby, a. nodosus.

knock, v.a. & n. pulso, 1 ; ferio, 4 ; tundo, 3 ; to — against, (one's head, etc.) offendo, 3 ; — at (a door), pulso, 1 ; ferio, 4 ; to — down, (to overthrow) dejicio, sterno, 3 ; fig. (at an auction) addico (bona alicui), 3 ; to — off, excutio ; decido, 3 ; fig. termino, 1 ; perficio, 3 ; to — out, excutio, 3 ; to — under, sese subjicere, succumbo, 3 ; to — up, (to awake) suscito, 1 ; (to weary) defatigo, 1.

knock, knocking, s. pulsatio, f.

knock-kneed, a. varus.

knoll, s. tumulus, m.

knot, s. nodus, m. ; geniculum, n. ; fig. (of people) circulus, m. ; fig. difficultas, f.

knot, v.a. nodo, 1.

knotted, a. nodatus ; nodosus.

knotty, a. nodosus ; fig. spinosus, difficilis.

knotweed, s. polygonum (mod. hort.).

know, v.a. scio, 4 ; (to learn, to become acquainted with) cognosco, 3 ; (to be acquainted with) nosco, 3 ; not to —, ignoro, 1 ; to — again, recognosco, 3.

knowing, a. sciens, prudens ; (cunning) astutus ; —ly, ad. scienter ; prudenter ; (cunningly) astute.

knowledge, s. scientia, cognitio ; (skill) peritia ; (learning) eruditio, f. ; (understanding) intellectus, m.

known, p.a. notus ; to be —, enotesco, 3 ; it is —, constat ; to become —, emano, 1 ; to make —, palam facio, 3 ; divulgo, 1 ; well —, (famous) celeber ; (common) tritus.

knuckle, s. condylus, articulus, m. ; —-bones, pl. (game) tali, m. pl.

knuckle, v.n. to — down, succumbo, 3.

Koran, s. Coranus, m.

Labarum, labarum, n.

label, s. titulus, m.

label, v.a. titulum affigo, 3.

labial, a. labialis.

laborious, a. laboriosus ; (difficult) operosus ; —ly, ad. laboriose ; operose ; multo labore.

laboriousness, s. labor, m. ; difficultas, f.

labour, s. labor, m. ; (manual) opera, f. ; (work) opus, n. ; (of child-birth) partus, m.

labour, v.a. & n. laboro, operor, 1 ; (to struggle, etc.) contendo, 3 ; (under) laboro, 1.

labourer, s. operarius, m. ; opifex, c.

laburnum, s. cytisus, c. ; laburnum, n.

labyrinth, s. labyrinthus, m.

labyrinthine, a. labyrinthicus ; fig. inextricabilis. [tringo, 3.

lace, v.a. prætexo, 3 ; (to tie) necto, aslacerate, v.a. lacero, lanio, 1.

laches, s. neglegentia, f.

lack, v.a. & n. egeo, careo, 2 ; vaco, desidero, 1.

lack, s. inopia, egestas, f.

lackey, s. pedisequus, m.

laceration, s. laceratio, f. [breviter.

laconic, a. Laconicus, brevis ; —ally, ad.

lad, s. puer, adulescens, m.

ladder, s. scala, f.

lade, v.a. onero, 1 ; to — out, exonero, 1.

lading, s. (freight) onus, n.

ladle, s. ligula, spatha, f. ; coclear, n.

lady, s. domina ; matrona, era, f.

lady's-maid, s. ornatrix, f.

lady's-slipper, s. cypripedium (mod. hort.).

lag, v.n. cesso, cunctor, moror, 1.

laggard, lagger, s. cessator, m.

lagoon, s. lacuna, f.

lair, s. cubile ; latibulum, lustrum, n.

laity, s. laici, m. pl.

lake, s. lacus, m. ; stagnum, n.

lamb, s. agnus, m. ; agna, f.

lamb, v.n. agnellum parere, 3.

lambkin, s. agnellus, m.

lame, a. claudus, debilis ; (imperfect) imperfectus ; fig. inconcinnus, ineptus ; to walk —, claudico, 1.

lame, v.a. mutilo ; debilito, 1. [inepte.

lamely, ad. fig. imperfecte ; inconcinne ;

lameness, s. clauditas ; fig. infirmitas, f.

lament, v.a. & n. lamentor ; deploro, 1 ; fleo, 2.

lament, s., v. lamentation.

lamentable, a. miserandus ; lamentabilis ; luctuosus, flebilis, miser.

lamentably, ad. misere miserabiliter ; flebiliter.

lamentation, s. lamentatio, f. ; lamenta, n. pl. ; (act) ploratus, fletus, m. [m.

lamp, s. lucerna, lampas, f. ; lychnus,

lamp-black, s. fuligo, f.

lamp-stand, s. lychnuchus, m.

lampoon, s. carmen, n. ; libellus, m.

lampoon, v.a. diffamo, 1.

lamprey, s. muræna, f.

lance, s. lancea, hasta, f.

lancer, s. hastatus, m. [phlebetomus, m.

lancet, s. scalpellum, n. ; (for bleeding)

land, s. (soil) terra, tellus ; (country) regio, f. ; (estate) fundus, m. ; prædium, n. ; (field) ager, m.

land, v.a. in terram expono, 3 ; —, v.n.
egredior, 3. [sessiones, f. pl.
landed, a. — property, s. agri, m. pl. ; pos-
land-forces, s. pl. copiæ terrestres, f. pl.
landing, s. egressus, m.
landlady, s. (innkeeper) caupona ; domina, f. [of land) dominus, m.
landlord, s. (innkeeper) caupo ; (owner
landmark, s. limes, m.
landscape, s. forma et situs agri ; (picture)
topia, f.
landscape-gardener, s. topiarius, m.
landslip, s. lapsus terræ, m.
land-surveyor, s. decempedator.
land-tax, s. vectigal, n.
landward, ad. terram versus.
lane, s. angiportus, m.
language, s. lingua, oratio, f. ; sermo, m. ;
verba, n. pl.
languid, a. languidus ; —ly, ad. languide.
languidness, s. languor, m.
languish, v.n. langueo, 2 ; languesco, 3.
languishing, a. languidus ; —ly, ad.
languide.
languor, s. languor, m
lank, lanky, a. macer.
lankness, s. macies, f.
lantern, s. laterna, lanterna, f.
lantern-bearer, s. lanternarius, m.
lap, s. sinus, m. ; fig. gremium, n. ; (in a
racecourse) spatium, n.
lap, v.a. (to lick) lambo, 3 ; (to wrap up)
obvolvo, 3.
lap-dog, s. catellus, m.
lapful, s. gremium, n.
lapidary, s. sculptor, m.
lappet, s. lacinia, f. [peccatum, n.
lapse, s. lapsus, m. ; fig. (error) erratum,
lapse, v.n. labor, 3 ; (come to an end)
exeo, 4 ; (to err) pecco, 1.
lapwing, s. fringilla vanellus, f.
larceny, s. furtum, n.
larch(-tree), s. larix, f.
lard, s. laridum, lardum, n.
larder, s. carnarium, n. ; cella, f.
large, a. magnus, amplus, grandis, largus ;
—ly, ad. ample, large.
largeness, s. amplitudo, f.
largess, s. largitio, f. ; donativum, n.
lark, s. alauda, f.
larkspur, s. delphinium (mod. hort.).
larynx, s. arteria, f. ; guttur, n.
lascivious, s. salax ; lascivus, petulans ;
—ly, ad. lascive ; petulanter .
lasciviousness, s. salacitas, lascivia ; petulantia, f.
lash, s. (stripe) verber, n. ; (whip) scutica,
f. ; flagellum, n.
lash, v.a. (to whip) verbero, flagello ; (to
fasten) alligo ; fig. castigo, 1.
lashing, s. verberatio, f.

lass, s. puella, f.
lassitude, s. lassitudo, f. ; languor, m.
last, a. postremus, ultimus ; summus,
extremus, novissimus ; — but one,
pænultimus ; at —, demum, tandem ;
denique, postremo.
last, ad. postremum ; novissime.
last, v.n. duro, perduro, 1 ; maneo, 2.
lasting, a. mansurus ; perennis ; stabilis ;
—ly, ad. perenne.
lastly, ad. postremo, denique.
latch, s. obex, c. ; pessulus, m.
latch, v.a. pessulum obdo, 3.
late, a. serus ; tardus ; (new) recens ; (dead)
mortuus ; —, ad. sero ; (recently)
nuper ; it grows —, vesperascit.
lately, ad. nuper, modo.
latent, a. latens, latitans, occultus.
lateral, a. lateralis ; —ly, ad. a latere.
lath, a. asser, m.
lathe, s. tornus, m.
lather, s. spuma, f.
Latin, a. & s. Latinus ; (language) lingua
Latina, f.
Latinity, s. Latinitas, f.
latitude, s. latitudo ; (liberty) licenta, f.
latter, a. posterior ; the —, hic ; —ly, ad.
nuperrime.
lattice, s. cancelli, clathri, m. pl.
lattice-work, s. opus cancellatum, n. ;
vimen, n.
laudable, a. laudabilis laude dignus.
laudably, ad. laudabiliter.
laudatory, a. laudativus.
laugh, v.n. rideo, 2 ; to — at, derideo,
irrideo, 2.
laugh, laughing, s. risus, m.
laughable, a. ridiculus.
laughably, ad. ridicule.
laughing-stock, s. ludibrium, n.
laughter, s. risus, m.
launch, v.a. deduco, 3 ; (to hurl) jaculor,
1 ; contorqueo, 2 ; —, v.n. (out) exspatior, 1.
laureate, a. laureatus.
laurel, s. (tree) laurus, f. ; laurea, f.
laurel, a. laureus.
laurelled, a. laureatus, laurifer, lauriger.
laurustinus, s. laurustinus (mod. hort.).
lava, s. torrens igneus, liquefacta massa.
lavish, a. prodigus ; profusus ; —ly, ad.
profuse, prodige.
lavish, v.a. prodigo, profundo, effundo, 3.
lavishness, s. prodigentia, profusio, f.
law, s. lex, f. ; (right) jus, n. ; (rule) norma,
f. ; (court of justice) jurisdictio ; (suit
at —) lis, f. ; — of nations, jus gentium,
n.
lawful, a. legitimus ; justus ; licitus ; —ly,
ad. legitime ; lege.
lawgiver, s. legislator, m.

lawless, a. exlex ; illicitus ; inconcessus ; —**ly,** ad. contra leges.

lawlessness. s. licentia, f.

lawn, s. (of grass) pratum, n. ; (sward) saltus, m. ; (fine linen) carbasus, sindon, f.

lawsuit, s. lis, causa, f.

lawyer, s. jurisconsultus ; causidicus, advocatus, m.

lax, a. remissus ; *fig.* neglegens ; —**ly,** ad. remisse ; neglegenter.

laxity, s. remissio, neglegentia, f.

lay, v.a. pono ; (eggs) pario ; (to spread) spargo, expando, 3 ; (to calm) paco, tranquillo, 1 ; **to — apart (aside),** amoveo, 2 ; repono, 3 ; **to — by,** repono, recondo, sepono, 3 ; **to — claim to,** vindico, 1 ; **to — down,** depono ; (to state) statuo, 3 ; **to — hold of,** prehendo, 3 ; **to — in,** recondo, 3 ; **to — on,** impono, 3 ; *fig.* imputo, 1 ; **to — open,** patefacio, 3 ; **to — out,** (money) expendo, 3 ; (a plan) molior, 4 ; **to — up,** recondo, 3 ; **to — a wager,** pignus repono, 3 ; **to — waste,** vasto, 1.

lay, s. carmen, n.

lay, a. laicus.

layer, s. (bed, stratum) corium ; tabulatum ; (of a deer) lustrum, n. ; (bot.) propago, f.

layman, s. laicus, m.

lazily, ad. ignave ; pigre ; segniter.

laziness, s. segnities, pigritia ; desidia, f.

lazy, a. iners, ignavus, piger, segnis, desidiosus.

lead, s. plumbum, n. ; **red —,** minium, n.

lead, v.a. duco, 3 ; præeo, 4 ; (to pass, spend) ago, dego, 3 ; (manage) moderor, 1 ; **to — about,** circumduco, 3 ; **to — away,** abduco, 3 ; **to — off,** diverto ; adduco, 3 ; **to — on,** conduco, 3.

leaden, a. plumbeus.

leader, s. dux, c. ; ductor ; *fig.* auctor, m.

leadership, s. dictus, m.

leading, a. princeps ; primarius.

lead-wort, s. plumbago, f.

leaf, s. folium, n. ; (of vine) pampinus, c. ; (of paper) pagina ; (of metal) bractea, f. ; (of a door) valvæ, f. pl.

leafage, s. coma, f.

leafless, a. fronde nudatus.

leafy, a. frondosus, frondeus, frondifer.

league, s. (confederacy) fœdus, n. ; societas, f. ; (3 miles) leuca, f.

league, v.n. conjuro, 1.

leaguer, s. obsidio, f. ; obsidium, n.

leak, s. rima, f. ; hiatus, m.

leak, v.n. perfluo ; humorem transmitto, 3.

leaky, a. rimosus.

lean, a. macer ; exilis, gracilis.

lean, v.a. inclino, acclino, 1 ; —, v.n. innitor, incumbo, 3 ; inclino, 1.

leanness, s. macies, gracilitas, f.

leap, v.n. salio, 4 ; *fig.* exsulto, 1 ; — **across,** transilio, 4.

leaper, s. saltator, m.

leaping, s. saltatio, f. ; saltus, m.

leap-year, s. bisextilis annus, m.

learn, v.a. & n. disco ; cognosco, 3 ; (to hear) audio, 4 ; — **by heart,** edisco, perdisco, 3.   [docte.

learned, a. eruditus, doctus ; —**ly,** ad.

learner, s. discipulus, m.

learning, s. doctrina, humanitas, f. ; litteræ, f. pl. ; (knowledge) eruditio, f.

lease, s. conductio, locatio, f.

lease, v.a. conduco, 3 ; loco ; (out) eloco, 1.

leash, s. (thong) lorum, n. ; habena, copula, f.

least, a. minimus ; —, ad. minime ; **at —,** saltem ; **not in the —,** ne minimum quidem.

leather, s. corium, n. ; (tanned) aluta, f.

leather, leathern, a. scorteus.

leather-bottle, s. uter, m.

leather-dresser, s. coriarius, m.

leathery, a. lentus.

leave, v.a. & n. linquo, relinquo, desero, 3 ; (to trust) mando, 1 ; trado, 3 ; (bequeath) relinquo, 3 ; lego, 1 ; **to — behind,** relinquo, 3 ; **to — off,** (v.n.) desino ; (v.a.) *fig.* depono ; (through interruption) intermitto, 3 ; **to — out,** omitto, 3 ; prætereo, 4 ; **to — to,** permitto, 3.

leave, s. permissio, licentia, copia, potestas ; **by — of,** permissu ; **by your good —,** pace tua, bona tua venia, f. ; (of absence) commeatus, m.

leaven, s. fermentatum, n.

leaven, v.a. fermento, 1.

leavings, s. reliquiæ, f. pl.

lecherous, a. libidinosus, salax.

lecherousness, s. libido, salacitas, f.

lecture, s. schola, acroasis, f. ; prælectio, f.

lecture, v.a. prælego, 3 ; (to reprove) objurgo, 1 ; corripio, 3.

lecture-room, s. auditorium, n.

lecturer, s. prælector, m.

ledge, s. dorsum, n. ; ora, f.

ledger, s. codex, m.

leech, s. sanguisuga, hirudo, f. ; (doctor), v. **horse-leech.**

leek, s. porrum, allium, n.

leer, v.n. limis oculis intueor, 3.

leering, a. pætus.

lees, s. fæx, f.

left, a. sinister, lævus ; —, s. manus sinistra, f. ; **on the —,** a sinistra ; **to the —,** ad sinistram, sinistrorsum.

leg, s. tibia, f. ; crus, n. ; (of a table, etc.) pes, m.

legacy, s. legatum, n. ; — **-hunter,** s. captator, m.

legal, a. legalis, legitimus ; judicialis ;
—ly, ad. legitime ; legibus.
legalize, v.a. legibus confirmo, 1.
legate, s. legatus, m.
legatee, s. legatarius, m.
legation, s. legatio, f.
legend, s. fabula, f.   [ticius.
legendary, a. fabulosus ; (false) commen-
legerdemain, s. præstigiæ, f. pl.
legging, s. ocreæ, f. pl.
legible, a. quod legi potest.
legibly, ad. ita ut legi possit.
legion, s. legio, f.
legionary, s. legionarius, m.
legislate, v.a. legem fero, 3.
legislation, s. legum datio, f.
legislator, s. legum lator, m.
legislature, s. qui leges ferunt, f.
legitimate, a. legitimus ; licitus ; fig. sincerus, verus ; —ly, ad. legitime.
leisure, s. otium, n. ; at —, otiosus ; vacuus.
leisure, a. otiosus ; vacuus ; —ly, ad.
otiose.
lemon, s. citrum, n.
lemon-tree, s. citrus, f.
lend, v.a. pecuniam mutuam do ; commodo ; (at interest) fæneror, 1 ; fig.
præbeo, 2.
lender, s. qui pecuniam mutuam dat, m.
length, s. longitudo ; (of time) longinquitas ; (tallness) proceritas, f. ; at —,
tandem, demum.   [duco, 3.
lengthen, v.a. extendo, protraho ; fig. pro-
lengthiness, s. longitudo, f.
lengthy, a. longus ; prolixus.
leniency, s. lenitas, clementia, mansuetudo, indulgentia, f. ; (pardon) venia, f.
lenient, a. mitis, lenis, clemens ; mansuetus ; —ly, ad. leniter, clementer, indulgenter.
lenity, s., v. leniency.
lent, s. quadragesima, f.
lentil, s. lens, f.
leonine, a. leoninus.
leopard, s. leopardus, m.
leopard's-bane, s. doronicum (mod. hort.).
leper, s. leprosus, m.
leprosy, s. lepræ, f. pl.
leprous, a. leprosus.
less, a. minor ; —, ad. minus.
lessee, s. conductor ; cui locatur, m.
lessen, v.a. minuo, imminuo ; —; v.n.
descresco, minuor, 3.
lesson, s. (task) pensum, n.
lessor, s. locator, m.
lest, c. ne . . . ; — by any means, nequa.
let, v.a. sino, patior, permitto, 3 ; (to
lease) loco, 1 ; to — alone, omitto, 3 ;
abstineo, 2 ; to — down, demitto, 3 ; to
— out, emitto, 3 ; (to hire) eloco, 1 ; to
— pass, omitto, 3 ; prætereo, 4.

let, s. impedimentum, n.
lethargic, a. languidus.
lethargy, s. languor ; veternus, m.
letter, s. littera, f. ; (epistle) epistula, f. ;
litteræ, f. pl. ; —s, pl. (learning) litteræ, f. pl.
letter-carrier, s. tabellarius, m.
letter-case, s. scrinium, n.
lettered, a. litteratus.
lettering, s. titulus, m.
lettuce, s. lactuca, f.
levant, s. oriens, m.
levee, s. salutantium comitatus, m.
level, a. planus, æquus.
level, s. planities, f. ; (of carpenters)
libella, f. ; perpendiculum, n. ; fig. to be
upon a —, par esse.
level, v.a. æquo, coæquo, complano, 1 ;
(lay low) sterno, 3.
leveller, s. librator, m.
levelling, s. libratio, f.
levelness, s. planities, æqualitas, f.
lever, s. vectis, m.
leveret, s. lepusculus, m.
Levite, s. Levites, Levita, m.
levity, s. levitas ; jocatio, f.
levy, s. delectus, m.
levy, v.a. (troops) conscribo, 3 ; (money)
exigo, 3.
lewd, a. incestus, impudicus ; libidinosus ;
—ly, ad. inceste ; libidinose.
lewdness, s. incestum, n. ; impudicitia, f.
liable, a. obnoxius.
liar, s. mendax, c.
libation, s. libatio, f. ; libamen, libamen-
tum, n.
libel, s. libellus famosus, m.
libel, v.a. diffamo, 1.
libellous, a. probrosus ; famosus.
liberal, a. liberalis, munificus ; fig. ingenuus ; —ly, ad. liberaliter, munifice ;
ingenue.
liberality, s. liberalitas, munificentia, f.
liberate, v.a. libero, 1 ; (law) manumitto, 3.
liberation, s. liberatio, f.
liberator, s. liberator, m.
libertine, s. homo dissolutus, m.
libertinism, s. morum licentia, f.
liberty, s. libertas ; licentia, f. ; at —, liber.
libidinous, a. libidinosus.
librarian, s. bibliothecæ præfectus, m.
library, s. bibliotheca, f.
licence, s. licentia ; (want of restraint)
licentia, intemperantia, f. ; venia, f.
license, v.a. potestatem do, 1.
licentious, a. dissolutus, impudicus, lascivus ; incestus ; —ly, ad. inceste,
lascive.
licentiousness, s. mores dissoluti, m. pl. ;
licentia, lascivia, intemperantia, f.
lichen, s. lichen, m.

lick, v.a. lambo, 3 ; (daintily) ligurrio, 4.
lickerish, a. fastidiosus.
licorice, s. dulcis radix, f.
lictor, s. lictor, m.
lid, s. operculum ; operimentum oculorum, n.
lie, s. mendacium, n. ; **to give the — to,** v. **belie; to tell a —,** mentior, 4.
lie, v.n. mentior, 4.
lie, v.n. jaceo, 2 ; (in bed, etc.) cubo, 1 ; (to be situated) situs esse ; **to — down,** decumbo, 3 ; **to — in wait,** insidior, 1 ; **to — on (upon),** incubo, 1 ; incumbo, 3.
liege, a. fidelis ; **— lord,** s. dominus, m.
lien, s. pignus, n.
lieu, s. **in — of,** loco (with genit.).
lieutenancy, s. præfectura, f.
lieutenant, s. legatus ; præfectus, m.
life, s. vita ; anima, f. ; spiritus, m. ; (safety) salus, f. ; *fig.* vigor, m. ; alacritas, f.
life-guards, s. cohors prætoria.
lifeless, a. inanimus ; exanimis ; *fig.* exsanguis, frigidus ; **—ly,** *fig.* frigide.
life-time, s. ætas, f. ; ævum, n.
lift, v.a. tollo, attollo, erigo, 3 ; levo, sublevo, 1.
ligament, s. ligamentum, ligamen, n.
ligature, s. ligatura, f.
light, s. lux, f. ; lumen, n. ; (lamp) lucerna, f. ; **bring to —,** in lucem profero, 3.
light, a. (bright, etc.) lucidus, fulgens ; (in weight) levis ; (of colours) candidus, dilutus ; (trifling ; easy) facilis ; (nimble) agilis ; pernix ; (inconstant) instabilis ; (dissolute) petulans, **procax** ; (lightly armed) expeditus.
light, v.a. accendo, 3 ; **—,** v.n. exardesco, 3 ; (settle) insido, 3 ; **to — on,** (to fall on) offendo, incido, 3.
lighten, v.a. (to illumine) illumino, illustro, 1 ; (a weight) allevo ; exonero, 1 ; **—,** v.n. (in the sky) fulguro, 1.
lighter, s. navis oneraria, f.
light-fingered, a. furax.
light-hearted, a. hilaris, lætus, alacer.
lighthouse, s. pharus, f.
lightly, ad. leviter ; perniciter ; *fig.* neglegenter ; temere.
lightness, s. levitas ; agilitas ; pernicitas ; (wantonness) petulantia, f.
lightning, s. fulmen, n.
lights, s. pulmones, m. pl.   [lætus.
lightsome, a. fulgidus ; (cheerful) hilaris,
like, a. similis ; assimilis, consimilis ; (equal) par, æquus ; **—,** ad. tanquam, velut ; (in — manner) pariter, similiter ; **— as,** sicut, perinde ac.
like, v.a. (to approve) comprobo, 1 ; (to be fond of) amo, 1 ; (to please) placeo, 2.

likelihood, s. versimilitudo, f.
likely, a. probabilis, verisimilis ; **—,** ad. probabiliter.
like-minded, a. consors.
liken, v.a. assimulo, comparo, 1 ; confero, 3.
likeness, s. similitudo ; (portrait) imago, effigies, f.
likewise, ad. pariter, similiter.
liking, s. approbatio, f. ; **favor, m.** ; (fancy) libido, f.
lilac, s. syringa vulgaris, f.
lilliputian, a. *fig.* pusillus.
lily, s. lilium, n. ; **belladonna —,** amaryllis (mod. hort.) ; **Cape —,** crinum ; **day —,** hemerocalles ; **St. Bernard's —,** anthericum n. ; **— of the valley,** s. convallaria (mod. hort.).
limb, s. membrum, **n.**; artus, m.
limber, a. flexilis.
lime, s. calx, f. ; **bird- —,** viscum, n. ; (tree) tilla, f. ; **quick—,** calx viva, f.
lime, v.a. visco illino, 3.
lime-burner, s. calcarius, m.
lime-stone, s. calx, f. ; lapis calcarius, m.
limit, s. limes, terminus, m. ; finis, c. ; modus, m.   [scribo, 3.
limit, v.a. termino, 1 ; finio, 4 ; circum-
limitation, s. *fig.* exceptio, f.
limn, v.a. pingo, 3.
limner, s. pictor, m.
limp, v.n. claudico, 1 ; **—,** s. claudicatio, f.
limp, a. flaccidus, lentus.
limpid, a. liquidus, pellucidus, limpidus.
limpidity, s. claritas, limpitudo, f.
linden-tree, s. tilia, f.
line, s. (drawn) linea, f. ; (row) series, f. ; ordo, m. ; (lineage) stirps, progenies, f. ; genus, n. ; (small cord) funiculus, m. ; (in poetry) versus, m. ; (entrenchment) vallum, n. ; (fishing- —) linea, f.
line, v.a. introrsus obduco, 3.
lineage, s. stirps, f. ; genus, n.
lineal, a. linealis ; **—ly,** ad. recta linea.
lineament, s. lineamentum, n.
linear, a. linearis.
linen, s. linteum, n. ; **carbasus, f.** ; (fine) sindon, f.
linen, a. linteus, lineus, carbaseus.
linen-draper, s. linteo, m.
linen-drapery, s. lintea, n. pl.
linger, v.n. cunctor, cesso, moror, 1.
lingerer, s. cessator, m.
lingering, a. cunctabundus ; tardus.
lingering, s. cunctatio, f.
lingeringly, ad. cunctanter, tractim.
linguist, s. linguarum peritus, m.
liniment, s. unguentum, n.
link, s. (of a chain) anulus, m. ; (bond) vinculum ; (torch) funale, n. ; tæda, fax, f.

link, v.a. connecto, 3.
linnet, s. fringilla cannabina, f.
linseed, s. lini semen, n.
lint, s. linamentum, n.
lintel, s. limen superum, n.
lion, s. leo, m.
lioness, s. leæna, lea, f.
lionlike, a. leoninus.   [(edge) ora, f.
lip, s. labrum, labellum, n. ; *fig.* os, n. ;
lip-salve, s. unguentum, n.
liquefy, v.a. liquefacio, 3 ; v.n. liquefio, 3.
liquid, a. liquidus ; (transparent) pellucidus.
liquid, s.l iquidum, n. ; liquor, m.
liquidate, v.a. solvo, persolvo, 3.
liquidation, s. (payment) solutio, f.
liquor, s. umor, liquor, m.
liquorice, s., v. licorice.
lisp(ing), s. os blæsum, n.
lisper, s. blæsus, m.
list, s. index, m. ; (to fight in) arena, f. ;
(limit) terminus, m. ; (desire) libido,
cupido, f.
list, v.n., v. desire; listen.
listen, v.n. ausculto, 1 ; audio, 4.
listener, s. auscultator, auditor, m.
listless, a. remissus, neglegens, languidus ;
—ly, ad. neglegenter ; oscitanter ; languide.   [guor, m.
listlessness, s. inertia, socordia, f. ; lan-
litany, s. litania, f.
literal, a. accuratus ; —ly, ad. ad litteram,
ad verbum.
literary, a. ad litteras pertinens.
literature, s. litteræ, f. pl.
litigant, s. litigator, m.
litigate, v.a. & n. litigo, 1.
litigation, s. lis, f.
litigious, a. litigiosus.
litigiousness, s. litigandi libido, f.
litter, s. (of straw, etc.) substramen, sub-
stramentum, stramentum, n. ; (vehicle)
lectica, f. ; (brood) partus, m.
litter, v.a. perturbo, 1 ; (to cover with a
litter) sterno, substerno, 3 ; (to bring
forth) pario, 3.
little, a. parvus, exiguus ; —, ad. parum ;
a —, paulum.
little, s. paulum, exiguum ; (somewhat)
aliquantulum ; nonnihil, n.
littleness, s. parvitas, exiguitas, f.
liturgy, s. liturgia, f. ; ritus, m.
live, v.n. vivo, dego, 3 ; spiro, 1 ; vitam
ago, 3 ; (to reside) habito, 1 ; (on, upon)
vescor, 3.
live, a. vivus ; vivens.
livelihood, s. (trade) ars, f. ; (means of
maintenance) victus, m.
liveliness, s. vigor, n.
livelong, a. totus.
lively, a. vivus, vividus, alacer ; vegetus.

liver, s. jecur, n.
livid, a. lividus, livens.
lividness, s. livor, m.
living, a. vivus, vivens, spirans.
living, s. (livelihood, food) victus, m.
lizard, s. lacertus, m. ; lacerta, f.
lo, i. ecce ! en ! aspice !
load, s. onus, n. ; sarcina, f. ; (quantity)
vehes, f.
load, v.a. onero, 1.
loadstone, s. magnes, m.
loaf, s. panis, m.
loaf, v.n. cesso, 1.
loafer, s. cessator, m.
loam, s. lutum, n.
loan, s. mutua pecunia, f.
loath, a. invitus.
loathe, v.a. fastidio, 4 ; aspernor, 1 ; odi,
perodi, 3.
loathing, s. fastidium, tædium, n. ; satietas, f.
loathsome, a. fœdus ; odiosus.
loathsomeness, s. fœditas, f.
lobby, s. vestibulum, n.
lobster, s. locusta, f. ; cammarus, m.
local, a. loci, locorum (gen.) ; (neighbouring) vicinus.
locality, s. locus, m.
loch, s. lacus, m.
lock, s. sera, f. ; claustrum, n. ; (of hair,
wool, etc.) cirrus ; floccus, m.
lock, v.a. & n. (a door) obsero, 1 ; (to embrace) amplector, 3 ; to — in, includo, 3 ;
to — out, excludo, 3 ; to — up, occludo, 3.
locker, s. loculamentum, n. ; capsa, f.
lock-jaw, s. tetanus, m.
lock-smith, s. claustrarius artifex, m.
locust, s. locusta, f.
lodge, v.a. (money) colloco, 1 ; pono, 3 ;
—, v.n. habito, 1 ; (to stick fast) in
hæreo, 2.
lodge, s. casa, cella, f.
lodger, s. inquilinus, m.
lodging, s. commoratio, f. ; (room) cubiculum ; (inn) deversorium, n.
lodging-house, s. insula, f.
lodgment, s. sedes, statio, f.
loft, s. cella, f. ; tabulatum, cenaculum, n.
loftily, ad. alte, sublime, superbe, elate.
loftiness, s. altitudo ; (height) sublimitas,
f. ; *fig.* superbia, f.
lofty, a. altus ; (ex)celsus ; sublimis ; *fig.*
superbus, elatus, arrogans.
log, s. lignum, n. ; stipes ; (trunk) truncus, m.
loggerhead, s. caudex, stipes, m. ; be at
—s, discrepo, rixor, 1.
logic, s. logica, dialectica, f.
logical, a. logicus, dialecticus ; —ly, ad.
dialectice.

logician, s. dialecticus, m.

loin, s. lumbus, m.

loiter, v.n. cesso, cunctor **;** moror, **1.**

loiterer, s. cessator, m.

loll, v.n. innitor ; dependo, 3 ; langueo, 2.

London pride, s. saxifraga (mod. hort.).

lone, lonely, a. solus ; solitarius ; desolatus ; avius.

loneliness, s. solitudo, f.

long, a. longus ; (of time) diuturnus ; diutinus ; (lengthened) productus.

long, ad. diu ; — **after,** multo post ; —**ago,** jamdudum ; — **before,** multo ante.

long, v.n. aveo, 2 ; (after, for) desidero, 3 ; cupio, 3.

longer, ad. diutius.

longevity, s. longævitas, f.

longing, s. desiderium, n. ; appetitus, m. ; cupido, f.

longingly, ad. avide, cupide, appetenter.

longitude, s. longitudo, f.

long-lived, a. vivax.

long-suffering, a. patiens.

look, v.n. video, 2 ; aspicio, conspicio, 3 ; specto, 1 ; (with adj.) — **fierce,** torva tueor, 2 ; v. **to seem; to — about,** circumspicio, 3 ; **to — after,** *fig.* curo, 1 ; **to — at,** intueor, 2 ; **to — back,** respicio ; **to — down,** despicio, 3 ; **to — for,** curo, 1 ; (to seek) quæro, 3 ; **to — forward,** prospicio, 3 ; **to — in,** in(tro)spicio, 3 ; (to examine) perscrutor, 1 ; **to — on,** intueor, 2 ; **to — out,** prospicio, 3 ; (for) quæro, 3 ; **to — round,** circumspicio ; respicio, 3 ; **to — through,** per . . . aspicio ; *fig.* perspicio, 3 ; **to — to,** *fig.* curo ; **to — towards,** specto, 1 ; **to — up,** suspicio, 3 ; **to — upon,** *fig.* habeo, 2 ; æstimo, 1.

look, s. aspectus, vultus, m. ; os, n. ; facies, f. ; (glance) obtutus, m.

look, i. ecce ! en ! aspice !

looker-on, s. spectator, m.

looking-glass, s. speculum, n.

look-out, s. prospectus, m. ; specula, f.

loom, s. tela, f.

loom, v.n. appareo, obscure videor, 2.

loop, s. laqueus, m.

loop-hole, s. transenna, f. ; *fig.* effugium, n.

loose, a. laxus ; solutus ; neglegens ; dissolutus ; —**ly,** ad. laxe ; dissolute ; solute.

loose, loosen, v.a. solvo, resolvo, 3 ; laxo, relaxo, 1 ; —, v.n. solvor, 3.

looseness, s. laxitas, f. ; *fig.* licentia, f.

loose-strife, s. lythrum (mod. hort.).

loquacious, a. loquax, garrulus ; —**ly,** ad. loquaciter.

loquacity, s. loquacitas, garrulitas, f.

lord, s. dominus, m.

lord, v.n. **to — it,** dominor, 1.

lordliness, s. fastidium, n. ; superbia, f.

lordly, a. superbus, imperiosus ; —, ad. superbe ; imperiose.

lordship, s. imperium, n.

lore, s. doctrina ; eruditio, f. ; (rites) ritus, m. pl.

lose, v.a. amitto, perdo, 3 ; (be deprived of) privor ; **to — oneself** *or* one's **way,** aberro, 1 ; **to be lost,** pereo, 4.

loss, s. (act) amissio, jactura, f. ; damnum, detrimentum, n. ; (mil.) clades, f.

lot, s. pars, portio ; (chance) sors, f. ; casus, m. ; **by —,** sorte.

lotion, s. medicamen, n.

lottery, s. sortitio, f.   [magna voce.

loud, a. clarus, sonorus ; —**ly,** ad. clare,

loudness, s. claritas, f.

lounge, v.n. cesso, otior, **1.**

lounge, s. lectulus, m.

lounger, s. cessator ; ambulator, m.

louse, s. pedis, pediculus, m.

lousy, a. pediculosus.

lout, s. homo agrestis, rusticus, m.

loutish, a. agrestis, rusticus.

love, s. amor, ardor, m. ; flamma, f. ; (desire) desiderium, n. ; (dearness) caritas, f.

love, v.a. amo, 1 ; diligo, 3.

love-in-a-mist, s. nigella (mod. hort.).

love-letter, s. nota blanda, f.

love-lies-bleeding, s. amarantus, m.

loveliness, s. venustas ; forma, pulchritudo, f.

lovely, formosus pulcher ; venustus ; —, ad. pulchre, venuste.

love-potion, s. amatorium, philtrum, n.

lover, s. amator, amans ; studiosus, m.

lovingly, ad. amanter, blande.

low, a. humilis ; (of price) vilis ; (of birth) obscurus ; (of the voice) summissus ; *fig.* turpis ; (downcast) abjectus.

low, ad. humiliter ; summissa voce.

low, v.n. mugio, 4.

low, s. mugitus, m.

low-born, a. obscurus, humilis, ignobilis.

low-bred, a. servilis.

lower, v.a. (to let down) demitto ; (to humiliate) abjicio ; (the price) imminuo, 3.

lower, v.n. (of the sky) obscuror, 1.

lower, a. inferior ; — **over,** incubo, 1.

lowering, a. tristis ; (of the sky) nubilus.

lowermost, a. infimus, imus.

lowing, s. mugitus, m.

low-lands, s. loca plana, campestria, n. pl.

lowliness, s. humilitas, f. ; *fig.* animus demissus, m.

lowly, a. humilis, obscurus.

lowness, s. humilitas ; (of price) vilitas, f. ; (of birth, etc.) humilitas, ignobilitas, f.

low-spirited, a. tristis.

loyal, a. fidelis ; —ly, ad. fideliter.
loyalty, s. fides, fidelitas, f.
lozenge, s. scutula, f. ; (figure) rhombus ; (comfit) pastillus, m.
lubber, s. *fig.* stipes, caudex, m.
lubberly, a. stolidus.
lucern, s. medica, f.
lucid, a. lucidus ; (transparent) pellucidus.
Lucifer, s. (morning-star) Lucifer, m.
luck, s. fortuna, f. ; successus, m.
luckily, a. feliciter ; fauste, prospere, fortunate.
luckless, a. infelix.
lucky, a. felix, faustus, prosperus, fortunatus.
lucrative, a. quæstuosus, lucrosus.
lucre, s. lucrum, n. ; quæstus, m.
lucubration, s. (study and work) lucubratio, f.
ludicrous, a. ridiculus, jocularis ; —ly, ad. ridicule, joculariter.
lug, v.a. traho, 3.
luggage, s. sacrinæ, f. pl. ; impedimenta, n. pl. ; onus, n.
lugger, s. vectorium navigium, n.
lukewarm, a. egelidus, tepidus ; *fig.* frigidus ; —ly, ad. tepide ; *fig.* frigide ; languide.
lukewarmness, s. tepor ; *fig.* languor, m.
lull, v.a. sopio, 4 ; *fig.* demulceo, 2 ; —, v.n. relanguesco, cado, 3.
lull, s. quies, f.
lumbago, s. lumbago, f.
lumber, s. scruta, n. pl.
luminary, s. lumen, n. (also *fig.*).
luminous, a. illustris, lucidus ; *fig.* dilucidus, perspicuus.
lump, s. glæba ; massa ; (heap) congeries, f. ; in the —, per saturam.
lump, v.a. coacervo, 1.
lumpish, a. crassus ; *fig.* stolidus.
lumpy, a. glæbosus.
lunacy, s. alienatio mentis, f. ; amentia, dementia, f.
lunar, a. lunaris.
lunatic, a. insanus, demens ; homo insanus, m.
lunch, luncheon, s. merenda, f. ; prandium, n.
lunch, v.n. prandeo, 2.
lung, s. pulmo, m. pl.
lunge, s. ictus, m. ; plaga, f.
lupine, s. lupinus, m. ; lupinum, n.
lurch, s. ; to leave in the —, desero, destituo, 3.
lure, s. illecebra, esca, f.
lure, v.a. inesco, 1 ; allicio, pellicio, 3.
lurk, v.n. lateo, 2 ; latito, 1.
lurking-hole, lurking-place, s. latebra, f. ; lustrum, n.
luscious, a. suavis, prædulcis

lusciousness, s. summa *or* nimia dulcitudo, f.
lust, s. libido, cupido, cupiditas, f. ; appetitus, m.
lust, v.n. concupisco, 3.
lustful, a. libidinosus, salax, lascivus ; —ly, ad. libidinose, lascive.
lustily, ad. fortiter, strenue.
lustiness, s. robur, n. ; vigor, m. ; strenuitas, f.
lustration, s. lustrum, n. ; lustratio, f.
lustre, s. splendor, m. (also *fig.*).
lusty, a. robustus, vegetus.
lute, s. cithara, lyra, f.
luxuriance, s. luxuria, ubertas, 1.
luxuriant, luxurious, a. luxuriosus ; sumptuosus ; *fig.* luxurians.
luxuriate, v.n. luxurio(r), 1.
luxury, s. luxus, m. luxuria, f.
lye, s. lixivia, f.
lying, a. mendax ; fallax ; vanus.
lying, s. mendacium, n.
lying-in, s. puerperium, n.
lymph, s. lympha, f.
lymphatic, a. languidus.
lynx, s. lynx, c. ; — -eyed, a. lynceus.
lyre, s. cithara ; lyra, f.
lyric(al), a. lyricus.

Macaroni, s. collyra, f.
mace, s. sceptrum, n.
mace-bearer, s. lictor ; accensus, apparitor, m.
macerate, v.a. macero, 1.
maceration, s. maceratio, f.
machinate, v.a. machinor, 1.
machination, s. dolus, m. ; (trick) machina ; ars, f.
machine, s. machina, f. ; machinamentum, n.   [inatio, f.
machinery, s. machinamentum, n. ; machmachinist, s. machinator, m.
mackerel, s. scomber, m.
mad, a. insanus, vesanus, demens, amens.
madam, s. domina, era, f.
madden, v.a. mentem alieno ; *fig.* furio, 1 ; ad insaniam adigo, 3.
maddening, a. *fig.* furiosus ; (troublesome) molestus.
madder, s. rubia, f.
madly, ad. insane, dementer ; furiose.
madman, s. homo furiosus ; *fig.* demens, m.
madness, s. insania ; furor ; rabies ; amentia, dementia, f.
magazine, s. (for corn) horreum, armamentarium, n. ; (of powder) cella, f.
maggot, s. vermiculus, termes, m. ; (whim) libido, f.
maggoty, a. verminosus.

Magian, s. magus, m.
magic, a. magicus ; —, s. magica ars, f. ; veneficium, n.
magically, ad. magica vi ; (incantation) carmen, n.
magician, s. magus, veneficus, m.
magisterial, a. ad magistratum pertinens ; *fig.* imperiosus ; —ly, ad. pro magistratu, tanquam magistratus ; *fig.* imperiose.
magistracy, s. magistratus, m.
magistrate, s. magistratus, m.
magnanimity, s. magnanimitas, magnitudo animi.
magnanimous, a. magnanimus ; —ly, ad. pro magnitudine animi.
magnet, s. magnes, m.
magnetic, a. magneticus.
magnetism, s. vis magnetica, f.
magnetize, v.a. magnetica vi afficio, 3.
magnificence, s. magnificentia, f. ; splendor, m.
magnificent, a. magnificus, splendidus ; —ly, ad. magnifice ; splendide.
magnify, v.a. amplifico, 1 ; (to praise) extollo, 3 ; laudo, 1.
magnitude, s. magnitudo, f.
magnolia, s. magnolia (mod. hort.).
magpie, s. corvus pica, f.
Mahometan, a. & s. Mahometanus, Muhammedanus (a, um & i, m.).
Mahometanism, s. religio Mahometana, f.
maid, maiden, s. virgo, puella ; (female servant) ancilla, famula, f.
maiden, maidenly, a. virgineus, virginalis, puellaris ; — speech, s. prima oratio, f.
maidenhair fern, s. adiantum, n.
maidenhood, s. virginitas, f.
mail, s. (letter carrier) tabellarius, m. ; (coat) lorica, f. ; thorax, m.
maim, v.a. mutilo ; trunco, 1.
maim, s. mutilatio, f.
main, a. præcipuus, primus, maximus ; —ly, ad. præcipue, maxime ; præsertim.
main, s. (body, bulk) summa, f. ; (sea) altum mare, n.
maintain, v.a. & n. affirmo, 1 ; (to defend) tueor, sustineo, 2 ; — freedom, in libertatem vindico, 1 ; (to keep) nutrio, 4 ; sustento, 1 ; alo, 3.
maintainer, s. assertor, m. ; vindex, c.
maintenance, s. (support) defensio, f. ; (means of living) alimentum, n. ; victus, m. ; (law) exhibitio, f.
maize, s. zea, f.
majestic, a. augustus ; sublimis ; imperatorius ; —ally, ad. auguste.   [f.
majesty, s. majestas ; dignitas, sublimitas,
major, s. (mil.) præfectus, m. ; (in logic) major præmissa, f.
major-domo, s. villicus, m.

majority, s. pars major, f. ; plures, pl.
make, v.a. & n. facio, 3 ; (elect) creo, 1 ; (to form, to fabricate) conficio ; fingo, 3 ; (to render) reddo, 3 ; to — amends, corrigo, 3 ; to — away with, amoveo, 2 ; to — for, peto, 3 ; to — good, resarcio, 4 ; to — haste, accelero, 1 ; to — much of, magni facio, 3 ; to — out, probo, 1 ; to — over, transfero, 3 ; to — ready, paro, 1 ; to — up, (to finish) perficio, 3 ; (to compensate) resarcio, 4 ; (to resolve) decerno, 3 ; to — up, (numerically) expleo, 2 ; to — up to, aggredior, 3.
make, s. forma, figura, f.
maker, s. fabricator, m. ; auctor, c.
makeweight, s. supplementum, n.   [f.
maladministration, s. administratio mala,
malady, s. morbus, n.
malapert, a. procax, impudens.
malaria, s. cœlum grave et pestilens, n.
malcontent, a. & s. seditiosus, qui novis rebus studet, novarum rerum cupidus.
male, a. mas ; masculinus, masculus, virilis.
male, s. mas, masculus, m.
malediction, s. exsecratio, f.
malefactor, s. maleficus, m.
maleficent, a. maleficus.
malevolence, s. malevolentia, malignitas, invidia, f.
malevolent, a. malevolus, malignus.
malice, maliciousness, s. malevolentia, malitia, f.
malicious, a. malevolus, malitiosus ; —ly, ad. malevolo animo, malitiose.
malign, malignant, a. malevolus.
malign, v.a. obtrecto, 1.
malignancy, malignity, s. malevolentia, f. malignitas.
malignantly, ad. malevolo animo ; maligne.
malleability, s. mollitia, f.
malleable, a. ductilis, mollis.
mallet, s. malleus, m.
mallow, s. malva, f. ; Indian —, abutilon (mod. hort.) ; marsh —, hibiscus, f.
malpractice, s. male facta, delicta, n. pl. ; maleficium, n.
maltreat, v.a. vexo, 1 ; lædo, 3.
maltreatment, s. injuria, f.
malversation, s. peculatus, m.
mamma, s. mamma, f.
man, s. homo ; vir ; mas, m. ; a —, (some one) aliquis ; — by —, viritim ; — of war, navis longa, f.
man, v.a. (a ship) compleo, 2.
manacle, s. manicæ, f. pl. ; compes, f.
manacle, v.a. manicas (alicui) injicio, 3.
manage, v.a. administro ; curo, tracto, 1 ; gero, 3.
manageable, a. tractabilis.

management, s. administratio ; cura, procuratio, f.

manager, s. curator ; (steward) procurator, villicus, m.

mandate, s. mandatum, n.

mandrake, s. mandragoras, m.

mane, s. juba, f.

manful, a. virilis, fortis ; —ly, ad. viriliter, fortiter.

manfulness, s. animus virilis, m.

mange, s. scabies, f.

manger, s. præsaepe, n.

mangle, v.a. lacero, lanio, dilanio, 1.

mangle, s. prelum, n.

mangy, a. scaber.   [f.

manhood, s. pubertas ; virilitas ; fortitudo,

mania, s. *fig.* insania, amentia, f. ; (desire) cupido, f. ; cacoethes, n.

maniac, s. homo furiosus, m.

manifest, a. manifestus, clarus, apertus, evidens ; —ly, ad. manifeste, aperte ; evidenter.

manifest, v.a. declaro, 1 ; ostendo, 3 ; præbeo, 2.

manifestation, s. patefactio, f.

manifesto, s. edictum, n.

manifold, a. multiplex ; varius.

manikin, s. homunculus, homuncio, **m.**

maniple, s. manipulus, m.

manipulate, v.a. (manibus) tracto, 1.

manipulation, s. tractatio, f.

mankind, s. genus humanum, n. ; homines, m. pl.

manliness, s. virtus, fortitudo, f.

manly, a. virilis ; strenuus ; fortis ; —, ad. viriliter ; fortiter ; strenue.

manna, s. manna, n. (indecl.).

manner, s. modus, m. ; ratio, consuetudo, f. ; —s, mores, m. pl. ; **good** —s, urbanitas, f. ; ill —s, rusticitas, f. ; **in a** —, quodammodo.

mannerism, s. mala affectatio, f.

mannerly, a. urbanus ; —, ad. urbane.

manœuvre, s. (mil.) decursus, m. ; *fig.* artificium, n.

manœuvre, v.n. (mil.) decurro, 3 ; (plot) machinor, 1.

man-servant, famulus, m.

mansion, s. domus, sedes, f.

manslaughter, s. homicidium, **n.**

mantel, v. **mantle.**

mantle, s. pænula, palla, f.

mantle, v.a. celo, 1 ; tego, 3 ; dissimulo, 1 ; —, v.n. (of wine) spumo, 1.

mantua, s. palla, f.

manual, a. manualis ; — **labour,** opera, f. ; —, s. enchiridion, n.

manufactory, s. officina, fabrica, f.

manufacture, s. fabrica, f. ; opificium, n.

manufacture, v.a. fabricor, 1 ; fabrefacio, 3.

manufacturer, s. fabricator, opifex, m.

manumission, s. manumissio, f.

manumit, v.a. manumitto.

manure, s. stercus, n. ; fimus, m.

manure, v.n. stercero, 1.

manuscript, s. codex, m.

many, a. multi ; plerique ; complures ; **as** — **as,** quot . . . tot ; **how** —, quot ; **so** —, tot ; — **ways,** multifarie.

many-coloured, a. multicolor.

many-times, ad. sæpenumero.

map, s. tabula geographica, f.

map, v.a. (out) designo, 1.

maple, s. acer, n.

maple, a. acernus.

mar, v.a. fœdo, vitio, 1 ; corrumpo, 3.

marauder, s. prædator, m.

marauding, s. prædatio, f.

marble, s. marmor, n. ; —, a. marmoreus ; *fig.* (unfeeling) durus.

March, s. (month) Martius, m.

march, s. iter, n. ; (step) gradus, m.

march, v.n. iter facio, incedo, gradior, proficiscor, 3 ; **to** — **in,** ingredior, 3 ; **to** — **off,** recedo, 3 ; **to** — **on,** progredior, 3 ; —, v.a. exercitum duco, 3.

marches, s. fines, m.

marching, s. progressus, m.

marchioness, s. marchionissa.

mare, s. equa, f.

mare's tail, s. hippuris, f.

margin, s. margo, c.

marginal, a. in margine positus, margini ascriptus.

marigold, s. calendula (mod. hort.) ; **marsh** —, caltha, f.

marine, a. marinus, maritimus.   [m.

marine, s. classis, f. ; (person) classicarius,

mariner, s. nauta, m.

maritime, a. maritimus.

marjoram, s. amaracum, origanum, n.

mark, s. nota, f. ; signum ; (brand) stigma ; (impression) vestigium, n. ; (to shoot at) scopus, m. ; (of a stripe) vibex ; (of a wound) cicatrix, f. ; *fig.* indicium, n.

mark, v.a. noto, signo, 1 ; (to observe) animadverto, 3 ; (with a pencil, etc.) designo, 1 ; **to** — **out,** metor, 1 ; metior, 4.

marker, s. annotator, m.

market, s. (place) forum, n. ; mercatus, **m.**

marketable, a. venalis.

market-day, s. nundinæ, f. pl.

market-garden, s., v. **kitchen-garden.**

marketing, s. emptio, mercatura, f.

market-place, s. forum, n.

market-price, s. annona, f.

market-town, s. emporium, n.

marksman, s. jaculator, m.

marl, s. marga, f.   [m.

marl-pit, s. puteus ex quo eruitur marga,

marmoset, s. simiolus, m.
marquee, s. tabernaculum, n.
marquis, s. marchio, m.
marquisate, s. marchionatus, m.
marriage, s. conubium, conjugium, matrimonium, n. ; nuptiæ, f. pl.
marriage, a. nuptialis, conjugalis, conubialis.
marriage-contract, s. pactio nuptialis, f.
marriageable, a. nubilis, adultus.
married, a. (of a woman) nupta ; (of a man) maritus.
marrow, s. medulla, f. ; *fig.* flos, m.
marrowy, a. medullosus.
marry, v.a. (of a priest) connubio jungo ; (as the man) uxorem duco ; (as the woman) viro nubo, 3.
marsh, s. palus, f.
marshal, s. mareschallus, m.
marshal, v.a. dispono, 3.
marshy, a. paluster, paludosus.
mart, s. forum, emporium, n.
marten, s. hirundo, (badger) meles, f.
martial, a. bellicosus, ferox ; militaris, bellicus ; **— court,** s. castrense judicium, n.
martyr, s. martyr, c.
martyrdom, s. martyrium, n.
martyrology, s. martyrologium, n.
marvel, s. res mira, f. ; mirum, n. ; miraculum ; (astonishment) stupor, m. ; admiratio, f.   [ad. mire ; mirabiliter.
marvellous, a. mirus, mirabilis ; **—ly,**
masculine, a. masculus ; mas ; virilis ; (gr.) masculinus.   [potio medica, f.
mash, s. polenta, farrago, f. ; (for cattle)
mash, v.a. commisceo, 2 ; (to bruise) contundo, 3.   [tum, n.
mask, s. persona, larva, f. ; *fig.* prætex-
mask, v.a. personam induo, 3 ; *fig.* dissimulo, 1.
mason, s. lapicida, structor, m.
masonry, s. saxa, n. pl.
masquerader, s. homo personatus, m.
mass, s. moles, massa ; immensa copia, f. ; ingens pondus, n. ; (of people) multitudo, turba, f. ; (church service) missa, f. ; **in the —,** per saturam.
massacre, s. cædes, trucidatio f. ; **—,** v.a. trucido, 1.
mass-book, s., v. **missal.**
massive, a. solidus.
mast, s. (of a ship) malus, m. ; (food for cattle & swine) glans, balanus, f.
master, s. dominus, erus ; (teacher) magister, præceptor, m. ; *fig.* potens, compos (with genitive) c. ; peritus, m.
master, v.a. supero, 1 ; vinco, 3 ; dominor, 1 ; (to learn) perdisco, 3.
master-builder, s. architectus, m.
masterly, a. (of an artist) artificiosus.

master-piece, s. opus palmare, n.
mastership, s., v. **mastery.**
master-stroke, s. artificium singulare, n.
mastery, s. dominatus, m. ; imperium, n.
mastic, s. mastice, f.
masticate, v.a. mando, 3.
mastication, s. cibi confectio, f.
mastic-tree, s. pistacia, f.
mat, s. matta, teges, f. ; stragulum, n.
mat, v.a. implecto ; **matted,** concretus.
match, s. (marriage) nuptiæ, f. pl. ; (contest) certamen, n. ; (an equal) par, compar, c. ; (bargain) pactum, n.
match, v.a. compono, 3 ; adæquo, exæquo ; nuptum do, 1 ; **—,** v.n. (to be suitable) quadro, 1.
matchless, a. incomparabilis, eximius, singularis.
matchmaker, s. conciliator (conciliatrix) nuptiarum, m. (& f.).
mate, s. socius, collega, m. ; conjux, c.
mate, v.a., v. **to match.**
material, a. corporeus ; *fig.* (important) magni momenti.   [necessariæ, f. pl.
material, s. materia, f. ; **—s,** pl. res
materially, ad. (much) multum.
maternal, a. maternus.
maternity, s. condicio matris, f.
mathematical, a. mathematicus ; **—ly,** ad. more mathematicorum.
mathematician, s. mathematicus, m.
mathematics, s. mathematica, f.
matins, s. preces matutinæ, f. pl.
matricide, s. (murder) matricidium, n. ; (murderer) matricida, c.
matrimonial, a. conjugalis, conubialis, nuptialis.
matrimony, s. matrimonium, n.
matron, s. matrona, f.
matronly, a. matronalis.
matter, s. (substance) materia ; (affair, business, etc.) res, f. ; negotium ; (purulent) pus, n. ; sanies, f. ; **no —,** nihil interest ; **nothing to the —,** nihil ad rem.
matter, v.n. imp. it **—s not,** nihil interest, nihil refert.
matting, s. tegetes, f. pl.
mattock, s. dolabra, marra, f. ; ligo, m.
mattress, s. culcita, f.
mature, a. maturus ; tempestivus ; **—,** v.a. & n. maturo, 1.
maturely, ad. mature.
maturity, s. maturitas ; ætas matura, f.
maudlin, a. ebrius ; flebilis.
maul, v.a. mulco ; (handle) tracto, 1.
mausoleum, s. mausoleum, n.
maw, s. ingluvies, f.
mawkish, a. (of taste) putidus ; fastidiosus ; **—ly,** ad. putide, fastidiose.
maxim, s. præceptum, n. ; septentia, f.

may, s. (thorn) cratægus (mod. hort.).
May, s. (month) Maius, m.
may, v.n. possum ; licet.
maybe, ad. forsitan, forsan.
May-bug, s. scarabæus melolontha, f.
May-day, s. Kalendæ Maiæ, f. pl.
mayor, s. præfectus urbanus, m.
mayoralty, s. præfectura, f.
maze, s. labyrinthus, m. ; ambages, f. pl.
mazy, a. inextricabilis, inexplicabilis.
me, pr. me ; to —, mihi.
mead, s. pratum ; (drink) mulsum, n.
meadow, s. pratum, n. ; —, a. pratensis.
meadowsweet, s. spiræa, f.
meagre, a. macer ; fig. aridus ; jejunus ;
exilis ; —ly, ad. fig. exiliter, jejune.
meagreness, s. macies ; fig. exilitas ; jejunitas, f.
meal, s. farina, f. ; (food) cibus, m.;
(dinner, etc.) epulæ, f. pl.
meal-time, s. cibi hora, f.
mealy, a. farinosus, farinulentus.
mealy-mouthed, a. blandiloquus.
mean, a. (middle) medius ; (moderate)
mediocris ; (low) humilis ; fig. sordidus ;
vilis ; in the — time, interea.
mean, s. medium, n. ; (manner) modus,
m. ; ratio, f. ; golden —, aurea mediocritas, f. ; by all —s, quam maxime ;
by no —s, nullo modo.
mean, v.a. & n. volo ; mihi volo, 3 ;
cogito ; significo, 1 ; intelligo, 3.
meander, s. cursus ; flexus, m.
meander, v.n. labor, 3 ; sinuor, 1.
meaning, s. significatio, f. ; animus, sensus, m.
meanly, ad. mediocriter, sordide ; abjecte.
meanness, s. humilitas ; fig. avaritia ; ignobilitas, f.
measles, s. morbilli, m. pl.
measurable, a. quod metiri potes, men-
surabilis.
measure, s. mensura, f. ; (of land, liquids)
modus, m. ; (mean) ratio, f. ; (in prosody) numeri, m. pl. ; —s, pl. consilium,
n. ; in some —, aliquatenus.
measure, v.a. metior, 4 ; metor ; (to
moderate) moderor, 1 ; to — out, ad-
metior, 4.
measurement, s. mensura, f.
measurer, s. mensor, m.
meat, s. caro, f. ; (food) cibus, m.
mechanic(al), a. mechanicus ; —ally, ad.
mechanica quadam arte.
mechanic, s. opifex, faber, m.
mechanician, s. mechanicus, m.
mechanics, mechanica ars ; machinalis
scientia, f. [ratio, f.
mechanism, s. machinatio ; mechanica
mechanist, s., v. mechanician.

medal, medallion, s. nomisma, n.
meddle, v.n. (with) me immisceo, 2 ; intervenio, 4.
meddler, s. ardelio, m.
mediæval, a. medii ævi (gen.).
mediate, v.n. intercedo, 3.
mediation, s. intercessio, f.
mediator, s. intercessor, conciliator, m.
mediatrix, s. conciliatrix, f.
medical, a. medicus, medicinalis.
medicament, s. medicamentum, n.
medicate, v.a. medico ; tempero, 1.
medicinal, a. medicus ; salutaris.
medicine s. (science) medicina, f. ;
(remedy) medicamentum, medicamen, n.
medicine-chest, s. pyxis, f. ; narthecium, n.
mediocre, a. mediocris, modicus.
mediocrity, s. mediocritas, f.
meditate, v.n. meditor, cogito, 1.
meditation, s. meditatio, cogitatio, f.
meditative, a. cogitabundus.
Mediterranean, s. mare mediterraneum
or internum or medium, n.
medium, s. (middle) medium, n. ; (expedient) modus, m., ratio, f. ; (agent)
conciliator, m.
medium, a. mediocris.
medlar, a. mespilum, n. ; — -tree, s.
mespilus, f.
medley, s. farrago, f.
meed, s. præmium, n.
meek, a. mitis ; fig. summissus, humilis ;
—ly, ad. summisse.
meekness, s. animus summissus, m.
meet, a. aptus, idoneus ; it is —, convenit.
meet, v.a. obvenio, 4 ; occurro, 3 ; convenio, obviam eo, 4 ; congredior, 3 ; to
— with, offendo (aliquem), 3 ; — with,
(bad) subeo, 4 ; patior, 3 ; (good) nan-
siscor, 3.
meeting, s. congressio, f. ; congressus, m. ;
(assembly) conventus, m.
meetness, s. convenientia, f.
melancholy, s. tristitia, mœstitia, f.
melancholy, a. melancholicus, mœstus,
tristis.
mellifluous, a. mellitus.
mellow, a. maturus, mitis ; (with liquor)
ebrius, temulentus.
mellow, v.a. maturo, 1 ; coquo, 3 ; —,
v.n. maturesco, 3.
melodious, a. canorus, numerosus ; —ly,
ad. canore, numerose.
melody, s. melos, n. ; modulatio, f. ;
numerus, m.
melon, s. melo, m.
melt, v.a. liquefacio, solvo, dissolvo, 3 ;
—, v.n. liquefio, liquesco ; (of colours)
evanesco, 3 ; fig. commoveor, 2.
melting, s. fusio, fusura, f.

member, s. membrum, n.; *fig.* pars, f.; sodalis, m.

membrane, s. membrana, f.

memento, s. monumentum, n.

memoir, s. commentarius, m.

memorable, a. memorabilis, notabilis, memoria dignus.

memorandum, s. nota, f.; **— -book,** s. liber memorialis, m.   [n.

memorial, s. libellus, m.; monumentum,

memory, s. (faculty and remembrance) memoria, f.

menace, s. & v.a., v. **threat,** s., **threaten,** v.

menagery, s. vivarium, n.

mend, v.a. emendo, 1; corrigo, 3; reparo, 1; (clothes) sarcio, 4; **—,** v.n. melior fio.

mendacious, a. mendax.

mendacity, s. mendacium, n.

mendicancy, s. mendicitas, f.

mendicant, s. mendicus, m.; mendica, f.; **—,** a. mendicans.

mendicity, s. mendicitas, f.

menial, a. servilis; sordidus.

menial, s. famulus, servus, m.

mensuration, s. metiendi ars, f.

mental, a. mentis, animi (gen. sing.); mente conceptus, internus; **—ly,** ad. mente, animo.

mention, s. commemoratio, mentio, f.

mention, v.a. commemoro, 1; mentionem facio (gen.), 3; **not to —,** silentio praetereo, 4.

mephitic, a. mephiticus.

mercantile, a. mercatorius.

mercenary, a. mercenarius, venalis; **—,** s. miles conductus, m.

merchandise, s. merx; (trade) mercatura, f.

merchant, s. mercator, negotiator, m.

merchantable, a. venalis.

merchant-man, merchant-ship, s. navis oneraria, f.

merciful, a. misericors, clemens; **—ly,** ad. clementer, misericorditer.

mercifulness, s. misericordia, clementia, f.

merciless, a. immisericors, inclemens; immitis, durus; **—ly,** ad. immisericorditer, duriter.

mercilessness, s. crudelitas, inhumanitas, f.

mercurial, a. vividus, acer; levis.

Mercury, s. (god) Mercurius, m.; (metal) argentum vivum, n.

mercy, s. misericordia, clementia, indulgentia, f.

mere, a. merus; **—ly,** ad. tantummodo, solummodo, nihil nisi.

meretricious, a. meretricius; *fig.* fucatus; speciosus; **—ly,** ad. speciose.

merge, v.a. confundo, 3; misceo, 2.

meridian, s. (noon) meridies, m.; *fig.* fastigium summum, n.

meridional, a. meridianus, australis.

merit, s. meritum, n.; virtus, f.

merit, v.a. mereo, demereor, promereo, 2.

meritorious, a. laudabilis, laude *or* praemio dignus; **—ly,** ad. bene.

merrily, ad. hilare, festive.

merry, s. hilaris, festivus.

merry-andrew, s. sannio; ludius, m.

merry-making, s. festivitas, f.

meseems, v.n. imp. videor, 2.

mesh, s. (of a net) macula, f.

meshy, a. maculis distinctus.

mesmerize, v.a. consopio, 4.

mess, s. cibus, m.; portio cibi, f.; (for cattle, etc.) farrago, f.; (mil.) contubernium, n.; (dirt) squalor, m.; *fig.* (confusion) turba, f.

mess, v.n. (mil.) in contubernio prandeo, 2.

messenger, s. nuntius; (letter-carrier) tabellarius, m.

Messiah, s. Messias, m.

messmate, s. sodalis, contubernalis, m.

metal, s. metallum, n.

metallic, a. metallicus.

metalliferous, a. metallifer.

metamorphose, v.a. transformo, transfiguro, 1.

metamorphosis, s. transfiguratio, f.

metaphor, s. translatio, f.

metaphorical, a. translaticius; **—ly,** ad. per translationem.

metaphysical, a. metaphysicus.

metaphysics, s. metaphysica, f.

mete, v.a. metior, 4.

metempsychosis, s. metempsychosis, f.

meteor, s. fax coelestis, f.

meteorological, a. meteorologicus.

meteorology, s. meteorologia, f.

methinks, v.n. imp. videor, 2.

method, s. ratio, via, f.

methodical, a. dispositus, ratione et via factus; **—ly,** ad. ratione et via; disposite.

metonymy, s. metonymia, denominatio, f.

metre, s. metrum, n.; numerus, m.; versus, m.

metrical, a. metricus.

metropolis, s. caput, n.

metropolitan, a. metropolitanus.

mettle, s. vigor, animus, m.; (courage) virtus, fortitudo; magnanimitas, f.

mettlesome, a. ardens, acer, ferox, indomitus, animosus.

mew, s. cavea, f.; *fig.* carcer, m.; (bird) larus, m.; **—s,** pl. stabula, n. pl.

mew, v.a. cavea includo, 3.

miasma, s. halitus pestilens, m.

mica, s. phengites lapis, m.

mid, a. medius.
midday, s. meridies, m. ; meridianum tempus, n. ; —, a. meridianus.
middle, a. medius.
middle, s. medium, n. ; (waist) medium corpus, n.
middling, a. mediocris ; modicus.
midland, a. mediterraneus.
midnight, s. media nox, f.
midriff, s. præcordia, n. pl.
midst, s. medium, n.
midsummer, s. media æstas, summa æstas, f.
midway, s. media via, f.
midwife, s. obstetrix, f.
midwifery, s. obstetricia, n. pl.
midwinter, s. media hiems, f.
mien, s. vultus, m. ; os, n. ; species, f.
might, s. vis, potestas, potentia, f. ; with all one's —, summa ope.
might, I —, v.n. possem.
mightily, ad. valde, magnopere.
mightiness, s. potentia, potestas, f.
mighty, a. potens, pollens, validus ; magnus.
mignonette, s. reseda (mod. hort.).   [4.
migrate, v.n. migro, transmigro, 1 ; abeo,
migration, s. migratio, peregrinatio, f.
migratory, a. advena, migrans.
milch, a. — cow, s. bos lactaria, f.
mild, a. mitis, lenis ; placidus ; clemens ; mansuetus ; —ly, ad. leniter, clementer, placide, mansuete.
mildew, a. (of corn) robigo, f. ; (mould) mucor, situs, m.
mildness, s. clementia, lenitas, mansuetudo, f.
mile, s. mille passus, n.
milestone, s. miliarium, n.
milfoil, s. achillæa (mod. hort.).
militant, a. pugnax.
military, a. militaris ; —, s. milites, m. pl.
milk, s. lac, n.
milk, v.a. mulgeo, 2.
milking-pail, s. mulctra, f. ; mulctrum, n.
milk-sop, s. fig. molliculus, m.
milk-vetch, s. astragalus, m.
milkwhite, a. lacteus.
milkwort, s. polygala (mod. hort.).
milky, a. lacteus, lactans ; — -way, s. orbis lacteus, m. ; via lactea, f.
mill, s. mola, f. ; pistrinum, n.
mill-hopper, s. infundibulum, n.
mill-stone, s. mola, f. ; molaris, m.
miller, s. molitor, m.
millet, s. milium, n.
milliner, s. vestifica, f.
millinery, s. vestitus ornatusque muliebris, m.
million, s. decies centena millia, f.
millionaire, s. homo prædives, m.

milt, s. lien, splen, m.
mime, s. (play and player) mimus, m.
mimic, mimical, a. mimicus ; simulatus.
mimic, s. mimus, m.
mimic, v.a. imitor, 1.
mimicry, s. imitatio, f.
minaret, s. turris, f.
mince, v.a. concido, 3 ; fig. extenuo, 1.
mince-meat, s. fartum, n.
mincing, a. putidus ; —ly, ad. putide.
mind, s. animus, m. ; mens, f. ; ingenium, n. ; sensus, m. ; (desire) desiderium, n. ; voluntas, cupido, f. ; (recollection) memoria, f.
mind, v.a. (to look after) curo, 1 ; (to regard) respicio, 3 ; (to consider) animadverto, 3 ; considero, 1 ; (to put in mind) admoneo, 2 ; I don't —, nihil moror.
mindful, a. attentus, diligens ; memor.
mine, s. fodina, f. ; metallum, n. ; (mil.) cuniculus, m.
mine, v.a. & n. effodio, 3 ; (mil.) cuniculos ago, 3.
mine, pr. meus.
miner, s. (of metals) metallicus ; (mil.) cunicularius.
mineral, s. metallum, n. ; —, a. metallicus.
mineralogist, s. metallorum peritus, m.
mineralogy, s. metallorum scientia, f.
mingle, v.a. misceo, commisceo, 2 ; confundo, 3 ; —, v.n. commisceor, 2.
miniature, s. pictura minor, f.
minimum, s. minimum, n.
minion, s. satelles, c.
minister, s. minister ; (of State) rerum publicarum administer, m.
minister, v.a. & n. administro, 1 ; (with dative) ; servio, 4.
ministry, s. administratio, f. ; ministerium, n. ; qui reipublicæ præsunt.
minor, s. pupillus, m. ; pupilla, f.
minority, s. minor pars, f. ; (under age) pupillaris ætas, f.
Minotaur, s. Minotaurus, m.
minster, s. monasterium, n.
minstrel, s. fidicen, m.
mint, s. moneta, f. ; (plant) menta, f.
mint, v.a. cudo, 3 ; signo, 1.
minute, s. punctum temporis, n.
minute, a. minutus, exiguus.
minute-book, s. actorum tabulæ, f. pl.
minutely, ad. subtiliter ; minute, accurate.
minuteness, s. subtilitas ; exiguitas ; fig. (carefulness) cura, f.
minutiæ, s. singula, n. pl.
minx, s. puella procax, f.
miracle, s. miraculum, n.
miraculous, a. prodigiosus, mirabilis ; —ly, ad. divinitus.

mire, s. lutum, n. ; cænum.

mirror, s. speculum, n.

mirth, s. hilaritas ; lætitia ; festivitas, f.

mirthful, a. hilaris, festivus ; —ly, ad. hilare, festive.

miry, a. luteus, lutulentus, cænosus.

misadventure, s. infortunium, n.

misalliance, s. matrimonium impar, n.

misanthrope, s. homo inhumanus qui vitat hominum congressus, m.

misanthropic, a. generis humani contemptor, m.   [genus odium, n.

misanthropy, s. in hominum universum

misapply, v.a. abutor ; perverse utor, 3.

misapprehend, v.a. male intelligo, 3.

misapprehension, s. falsa conceptio, f. ; error, m.

misbecome, v.n. it —s, dedecet.

misbegotten, a. nothus, spurius.

misbehave, v.n. indecore se gerere, 3.

misbehaviour, s. morum pravitas, f.

misbelief, s. fides prava, f.

miscalculate, v.a. erro, 1 ; fallor, 3.

miscalculation, s. error, m.

miscarriage, s. (in childbirth) abortus ; *fig.* malus successus, m.

miscarry, v.n. (of women) abortum facio, 3 ; *fig.* parum succedo, 3.

miscellaneous, a. promiscuus, miscellaneus.   [n. pl.

miscellany, s. conjectanea, miscellanea,

mischance, s. infortunium, n.

mischief, s. incommodum, damnum ; maleficium, malum, n. ; pestis, f.

mischief-maker, ardelio, m.

mischievous, a. maleficus ; noxius, funestus ; —ly, ad. malefice.   [tia, f.

mischievousness, s. malitia, malevolen-

misconceive, v.a. male intelligo, 3.

misconception, s. falsa opinio, f.

misconduct, s. delictum, peccatum, n.

misconduct, v.a. male gero, 3 ; — oneself, delinquo, pecco.

misconstruction, s. sinistra interpretatio, f.

misconstrue, v.a. male *or* perverse interpretor, 1.

miscreant, s. homo scelestus, m.

misdeed, s. delictum, peccatum, n. ; scelus, n.

misdemeanour, s. vitium, n.

miser, s. avarus, m.

miserable, a. miser, miserabilis, miserandus, ærumnosus.

miserably, ad. misere, miserandum in modum, miserabiliter.

miserly, a. avarus.

misery, s. miseria, f. ; ærumnæ, f. pl. ; angor, m.

misfortune, s. adversa fortuna, calamitas, f. ; infortunium, incommodum, n.

misgive, v.a. diffido, 3 ; (with dative) ; malum præsagio, 4.

misgovern, v.a. male gero, 3.

misguide, v.a. seduco, 3.

misguided, a. *fig.* demens.

mishap, s. incommodum, n.

misinform, v.a. falsa doceo, 2.

misinterpret, v.a. male interpretor, 1.

misinterpretation, s. falsa interpretatio, f.

misjudge, v.a. male judico, 1.

mislead, v.a. decipio, fallo, 3.

mismanage, v.a. male gero, 3.

mismanagement, s. mala administratio, f.

misname, v.a. falso nomine appello, 1.

misnomer, s. falsum nomen, n.

misplace, v.a. alieno loco pono, 3.

misplaced, a. (unsuitable) ineptus.

misrepresent, v.a. perverse interpretor ; calumnior, 1 ; detorqueo, 2.

misrepresentation, s. falsa interpretatio, f.

misrule, v.a. male administro, 1.

miss, s. error, m. ; (loss) damnum, n. ; (failure) malus successus, m.

miss, v.a. & n. omitto, 3 ; (one's aim) non attingo, 3 ; (to be disappointed) de spe decido, 3 ; (not to find) reperire non possum ; (feel the loss of) desidero, 1 ; careo, 2 ; — one's way, erro, 1.

missal, s. missale, n.

misshapen, a. deformis, pravus.

missile, s. telum, missile, n.

missile, a. missilis.

mission, s. legatio ; missio, f. ; (instructions) mandatum, n.

missive, s. epistula, f. ; nuntius, m. ; —, a. missilis.

misspend, v.a. prodigo, profundo ; perdo ; abutor, 3 ; (with ablative).

misstate, v.a. parum accurate memoro, 1.

mist, s. nebula ; caligo, f.

mistake, s. erratum, mendum, vitium, n. ; error, m.

mistake, v.a. male interpretor, 1 ; —, v.n. erro, 1 ; fallor, 3.

mistaken, a. falsus.

mistletoe, s. viscum, n.

mistress, s. domina, era ; (sweetheart) amica ; (teacher) magistra, f.

mistrust, s. diffidentia, suspicio, f.

mistrust, v.n. diffido, 3 ; suspicor, 1.

mistrustful, a. diffidens.

misty, a. nebulosus, caliginosus ; *fig.* obscurus.

misunderstand, v.a. perperam intelligo, 3.

misunderstanding, s. error, m. ; (disagreement) offensa, dissentio, f.

misuse, v.a. abutor ; lædo, 3.

misuse, s. abusus, m. ; (ill-treatment) injuria, f.

mite, s. (insect) acarus ; (small coin) sextans, m.

mitigate, v.a. mitigo, levo, 1 ; lenio, 4 ;
remitto, 3 ; extenuo, 1.
mitigation, s. mitigatio, remissio, f. ;
levamentum, levamen, n.
mitre, s. mitra, f.
mitred, a. mitratus.
mix, v.a. misceo, commisceo, permisceo,
2 ; to — up, admisceo, 2 ; to — oneself
with, me immisceo.
mixed, a. mixtus, promiscuus, confusus.
mixture, s. (act and mixture itself) mixtura, f. ; (hotch-potch) farrago, f.
mizzle, v.n. irroro, 1.
moan, v.n. gemo, ingemisco, 3.
moan, s. gemitus, m.
moat, s. fossa, f.
mob, s. turba, f. ; vulgus, n.
mob, v.a. circumfundor, 3 ; conviciis
insector, 1.
mobile, a. mobilis, expeditus.
mobility, s. mobilitas, f.   [irrideo, 2.
mock, v.a. & n. ludo, 3 ; ludificor, 1 ;
mock, s. irrisio, f.
mock, a. fictus, fucatus, simulatus.
mocker, s. irrisor, m.
mockery, s. irrisio, f. ; irrisus, m.
mode, s. modus, m. ; ratio, f. ; (fashion)
usus, m.
model, s. exemplar, exemplum, n.
model, v.a. formo ; delineo, 1.
moderate, a. moderatus ; mediocris ;
modicus ; —ly, ad. moderate ; modice ;
mediocriter.
moderate, v.a. moderor, tempero, 1 ; (to
restrain) coerceo, 2.
moderation, s. moderatio ; temperantia,
modestia, f.
moderator, s. præses, m.
modern, a. recens ; hodiernus.
modest, a. mediocris, modicus ; verecundus ; modestus ; —ly, ad. modeste,
verecunde, mediocriter.
modesty, s. pudor, m. ; modestia, pudicita,
verecundia, f.
modification, s. immutatio, f.
modify, v.a. immuto, 1.
modulate, v.a. flecto, 3.
modulation, s. flexio, f. ; flexus, m.
Mohammedan, v. Mahometan.
moiety, s. dimidia pars, f.
moil, v.n., v. toil.
moist, a. umidus, uvidus, udus, madidus.
moisten, v.a. umecto, irroro, rigo, 1.
moisture, s. umor, m. ; uligo, f.
molar, s. molaris, m.
mole, s. moles, pila, f. ; agger, m. ; (on the
body) nævus, m. ; (animal) talpa, c.
molest, v.a. vexo, sollicito, 1.
molestation, s. vexatio, f.
molten, a. fusus, fusilis ; liquidus.

moment, s. (of time) punctum temporis ;
(importance) momentum, pondus, n. ;
(opportunity) occasio, f. ; in a —, statim ; of great —, magni ponderis ; this
—, ad tempus.
momentarily, ad. subito.
momentary, a. brevis, brevissimus, subitus.
momentus, a. magni momenti.
monarch, s. rex, princeps, m.
monarchical, a. regius.
monarchy, s. regnum, n.
monastery, s. monasterium, cœnobium, n.
monastic, a. monasterialis.
Monday, s. dies lunæ, m.
money, s. pecunia, f. ; argentum, n. ; nummus, m.   [nummatus.
moneyed, monied, a. pecuniosus, bene
money-bag, s. fiscus, saccus, m.
money-changer, money-dealer, s. nummularius, m.
money-lender, s. fænerator, m.
moneyless, a. inops.
mongrel, a. hybrida ; bigener.
monitor, s. admonitor ; (in a school) discipulus ceteris præpositus, m.
monk, s. monachus, m.
monkey, s. simius, m. ; simia, f.
monkey-puzzle, s. araucaria (mod. hort.).
monkish, a. monchicus.
monkshood, s. (plant) aconitum, n.
monody, s. canticum, n.
monogram, s. monogramma, n.
monologue, s. soliloquium, n.
monomania, s. insania, f.
monopolize, v.n. monopolium exerceo, 2 ;
fig. solus habeo, 2.
monopoly, s. monopolium, n.
monosyllabic, a. monosyllabus.
monosyllable, s. monosyllabum, n.
monotonous, a. fig. continuus ; nulla
varietate delectans.
monster, s. monstrum ; portentum, prodigium, n.
monstrous, a. monstruosus, portentosus,
prodigiosus ; —ly, ad. monstruose, prodigiose.
month, s. mensis, m.
monthly, a. menstruus.
monument, s. monumentum ; (tomb)
mausoleum, n.
monumental, a. monumentalis.
mood, s. (of the mind) animi affectus,
habitus, voluntas ; (gr.) modus, m.
moodiness, s. morositas ; tristitia, f.
moody, a. morosus ; tristis.
moon, s. luna, f.   [per lunam.
moonlight, s. lunæ lumen, n. ; by —,
moonshine, fig. nugæ ! ; fabulæ, f. pl.
moor, s. loca patentia et ericis obsita, n. pl.
Moor, s. Maurus, m.

moor, v.a. (a ship) navem religo, 1.
moorhen, s. fulica, f.　　　　　[ambigitur.
moot-point, s. causa dubia, f. ; **it is a —,**
mop, s. peniculus, m. ; **—,** v.a. deter-
　geo, 2.
mope, v.n. tristis sum.
moral, a. moralis ; qui ad mores pertinet ;
　(virtuous) integer, honestus.
morally, ad. jure, honeste.
moralist, s. officii exactor, m.
morality, s. mores, m. pl. ; (virtue) virtus,
　f. ; (duty) officium, n.
moralize, v.n. de moribus *or* officiis
　præcipio *or* dissero, 3.
morals, s. mores, m. pl. ; instituta, f. pl.
morass, s. palus, f.
morbid, a. morbidus, morbosus.
more, a. plus, major ; **—,** ad. plus, magis ;
　amplius ; ultra ; **— and —,** magis et
　magis ; **— than enough,** plus satis.
moreover, ad. præterea, ultra.
morn, morning, s. mane, n. indecl. ;
　matutinum tempus, m. ; **early —,**
　prima lux, f. ; **good —,** i. salve ! (when
　parting) ave !
morning, a. matutinus.
morning-star, s. Lucifer, m.
morning-watch, s. tertia vigilia, f.
morose, a. morosus, difficilis, severus ;
　—ly, ad. morose, severe.
moroseness, s. morositas ; severitas, f.
morrow, s. crastinus dies, posterus **dies,**
　m.
morsel, s. offa, f. ; frustum, n.
mortal, a. mortalis ; mortifer ; letifer ;
　letalis ; *fig.* (of an enemy) infensissi-
　mus ; **—ly,** ad. (of a wound) mortifero
　vulnere ; *fig.* vehementer.
mortal, s. homo, c. ; **—s,** pl. mortales, m.
　pl.
mortality, s. mortalitas ; mors ; pestis, f.
mortar, s. mortarium, n.
mortgage, s. hypotheca, f. ; pignus, n. ;
　—, v.a. pignori oppono, 3.
mortgagee, s. creditor hypothecarius, m.
mortgager, s. debitor hypothecarius, m.
mortification, s. (in the body) gangræna, f. ;
　(grief) dolor, m. ; (repression) coer-
　citio, f.
mortify, v.a. (repress) coerceo, 2 ; (to vex)
　offendo, 3 ; **—,** v.n. putresco, 3.
mortise, s. cardo femina, f.
mortmain, s. mortua manus, f.
mortuary, s. funebris.
mosaic, s. tessellatum (opus), n. ; **—,** a.
　tessellatus ; (of Moses) Mosaicus.
mosque, s. ædes, f. ; templum, n.
mosquito, s. culex, n.
moss, s. muscus, m.
mossy, a. muscosus.
most, a. plurimus, maximus, plerique.

most, ad. maxime, plurimum ; **—ly,** ad.
　(usually) plerumque ; vulgo.
mote, s. corpusculum, n.
moth, s. blatta, tinea, f.
mother, s. mater ; genetrix, f.
mother-in-law, s. socrus, f.
mother-of-pearl, s. concha Persica, f.
motherhood, s. condicio matris, f.
motherless, a. matre orbus.
motherly, a. maternus.
mother-tongue, s. patrius sermo, m.
motion, s. motio, f. ; motus, m. ; (proposal
　of a bill, a law) rogatio, f. ; (of an army)
　iter, n.
motion, v.n. innuo, 3.
motionless, a. immotus, immobilis, fixus.
motive, s. causa, ratio, f. ; incitamentum,
　n.　　　　　　　　　　　　[versicolor.
motley, mottled, a. maculosus, varius,
motto, s. sententia, f. ; præceptum, n.
mould, s. (to cast in) forma ; (earth) terra,
　f. ; (mustiness) mucor, situs, m.
mould, v.a. formo, 1 ; fingo ; (to knead)
　subigo, 3.
moulder, s. formator, m.
moulder, v.n. putresco, dilabor, 3.
mouldiness, s. mucor, situs, m.
mouldy, a. mucidus ; situ corruptus.
moult, v.n. plumas exuere, 3.
mound, s. tumulus, agger, m. ; meles, f.
mount, s. mons, collis, m.
mount, v.a. & n. scando, ascendo, 3 ;
　supero, 1 ; (to rise) sublime feror, 3 ;
　subvolo, 1 ; (equum) conscendo, 3.
mountain, s. mons, m.
mountain-ash, s. ornus, f.
mountaineer, s. homo montanus, m.
mountainous, a. montuosus, montanus.
mountebank, s. circulator, m.
mounted, a. (on horseback) eques.
mounting, s. ascensus, m.
mourn, v.a. & n. lugeo ; mæreo, doleo, 2 ;
　lamentor, 1 ; (to wear mourning clothes)
　squaleo, 2.
mourner, s. plorator ; pullatus, m.
mournful, a. luctuosus, lugubris ; mæstus ;
　tristis, lamentabilis, flebilis ; **—ly,** ad.
　mœste ; flebiliter.
mourning, s. luctus, mæror, m. ; vestis
　lugubris, f. ; **to go into —,** vestitum
　muto, 1.
mourning, a. tristis, lugubris.
mouse, s. mus, m.
mouse-hole, s. cavum (muris), n.
mouse-trap, s. muscipulum, n.
mouth, s. os, n. ; rictus, m. ; (of a bird)
　rostrum, n. ; (of a bottle) lura, f. ; (of a
　river) ostium, n.
mouthful, s. buccella, f.
mouth-piece, s. *fig.* (speaker) interpres, c. ;
　orator m.

movable, a. mobilis ; **—s**, s. pl. suppellex, f.

move, v.a. moveo, 2 ; (also *fig.*) ; **—**, v.n. moveor, 2 ; feror, 3 ; (to remove) migro, 1 ; (to propose a law, etc.) fero, 3 ; **to — on**, progredior, 3.

move, s. motus, m. ; *fig.* artificium, n.

movement, s. motus, m. [pulsor ; dux, m.

mover, s. auctor ; (proposer) lator ; im-

moving, a. flebilis, miserabilis ; **—ly**, ad. flebiliter.

mow, v.a. meto, 3.

mower, s. fænisex, m. ; messor, m.

mowing, s. fænisicium, n.

much, a. multus ; **—**, ad. multum ; (with comparative) multo ; **as — as**, tantus **— quantus** ; **tantum — quantum** ; **how —**, quantus ; quantum ; **so —**, tantus ; tantum ; **too —**, nimius ; (ad.) nimis ; **very —**, plurimus ; plurimum.

mucilage, s. mucus, m. ; pituita, f.

muck, s. stercus, n. ; **— -heap**, s. sterquilinium, n.

mucous, a. mucosus.

mud, s. cænum, lutum, n. ; limus, m.

muddle, v.a. turbo ; perturbo, 1.

muddle, s. confusio, turba, f.

muddy, a. lutosus, lutulentus ; limosus, cænosus ; (troubled) turbidus.

mud-wall, s. lutamentum, n.

muffle, v.a. obvolvo, 3.

mug, s. poculum, n., v. **cup.**

muggy, a. umidus. [morus, f.

mulberry, s. morum, n. ; **— -tree**, s.

mulct, v.a. mul(c)to, 1 ; punio, 4.

mule, s. mulus, m. ; mula, f.

muleteer, s. mulio, m.

mulish, a. obstinatus.

mullein, s. verbascum, n.

mullet, s. mullus, m.

multifarious, a. varius, multiplex.

multiplication, s. multiplicatio, f.

multiply, v.a. multiplico, 1 ; v.n. cresco, 3 ; augeor, 2. [f. ; vulgus, n.

multitude, s. multitudo ; turba, plebs,

multitudinous, a. creber.

mumble, v.n. murmuro, musso, 1.

mummy, s. cadaver arte medicatum, n.

mumps, s. cynanch ẹarotidæa, f.

munch, v.a. manduco, 1 ; mando, 3.

mundane, a. mundanus.

municipal, a. municipalis.

municipality, s. municipium, n.

munificence, s. munificentia, largitas, f.

munificent, a. munificus, liberalis ; largus ; **—ly**, ad. munifice, liberaliter, large.

muniment, s. munimentum, n. ; v. **archives.**

munition, s. (defence) præsidium, n.

mural, a. muralis.

murder, s. cædes, f. ; homicidium, n.

murder, v.a. neco, trucido, obtrunco, 1.

murderer, s. homicida, c. ; sicarius, m.

murderous, a. *fig.* sanguinarius, cruentus.

murky, a. caliginosus, tenebrosus, obscurus.

murmur, s. murmur, n. ; susurrus, m. ; fremitus, m. ; (complaint) questus, m. ; querela, f.

murmur, v.a. & n. murmuro, musso, mussito, susurro, 1 ; fremo, 3 ; (complain) queror, 3.

murrain, s. lues, f.

muscle, s. musculus ; lacertus ; torus ; (shell-fish) mytilus, m. ; conchylium, n.

muscular, a. musculosus ; lacertosus ; robustus, torosus.

Muse, s. Musa, f.

muse, v.n. cogito, meditor, 1.

museum, s. museum, n.

mushroom, s. fungus ; boletus, m. ; agaricum, n.

music, s. (art) musica, f. ; (of instruments and voices) cantus ; concentus, m.

musical, a. musicus ; (tuneful) canorus ; **—ly**, ad. musice ; (melodiously) canore.

musician, s. musicus, m.

musk, s. muscus, m. ; mimulus (mod. hort.).

muslin, s. sindon, f. ; Coa, n. pl.

must, s. mustum, n.

must, v.n. def. necesse est ; **I —**, debeo, 2 ; oportet me (with infinit.).

mustard, s. sinapi, n. ; sinapis, f.

muster, v.a. colligo, 1 ; *fig.* (up) colligo, 3 ; **—**, v.n. convenio, 4.

muster, s. recensus, m. ; recensio, f. ; **to pass —**, approbor, 1.

musty, a. mucidus.

mutability, s. mutabilitas, inconstantia, f.

mutable, a. mutabilis, inconstans.

mute, a. mutus, tacitus ; **—ly**, ad. tacite, silenter.

mutilate, v.a. mutilo, trunco, 1.

mutilation, s. mutilatio, detruncatio, f.

mutineer, s. seditiosus ; homo turbulentus, m.

mutinous, a. seditiosus, turbulentus ; **—ly**, ad. seditiose, turbulente.

mutiny, s. seditio, f. ; tumultus, m. ; **—**, v.n. tumultuor, 1.

mutter, v.a. & n. murmuro, musso, mussito, 1 ; **—**, s. murmur, n. ; murmuratio, f.

mutton, s. ovilla (caro), f.

mutual, a. mutuus ; **—ly**, ad. mutuo, invicem.

muzzle, s. capistrum, n. ; **—**, v.a. capistro constringo, 3.

my, pn. meus ; **— own**, proprius.

myriad, s. decem millia, f.

myrmidon, s. satelles, minister, m.

myrrh, s. murra, f.
myrtle, s. myrtus, f.
myrtle, a. myrteus.
myrtle-berry, s. myrtum, n.
myself, pn. ipse, ego ; **I —,** egomet.
mysterious, a. arcanus ; occultus ; mysticus ; **—ly,** ad. occulte.
mystery, s. mysterium, arcanum, n. ; *fig.* res occultissima, f.
mystical, a. mysticus ; **—ly,** ad. mystice.
mystification, fraus, f.
mystify, v.a. ludificor, 1 ; fallo, 3.
myth, s. fabula, f.
mythical, a. fabulosus.
mythological, a. mythologicus.
mythology, s. mythologia, f.

Nab, v.a. prehendo, 3.
nag, s. caballus, m.
Naiad, s. Naias, f.
nail, s. unguis ; (of metal) clavus, m.
nail, v.a. clavum pango *or* defigo, 3.
naïve, a. ingenuus, simplex.
naïvely, ad. ingenue.
naïveté, s. ingenuitas, simplicitas, f.
naked, a. nudus, apertus ; (as a sword) strictus ; **—ly,** ad. aperte.
nakedness, s. nuditas ; *fig.* jejunitas, f.
name, s. nomen, vocabulum ; n. appellatio ; *fig.* (reputation) fama ; celebritas, f. ; **by —,** nominatim.
name, v.a. nomino, appello, nuncupo, 1 ; (to mention) mentionem facio, 3.
nameless, a. sine nomine, nominis expers.
namely, ad. scilicet, videlicet.
namesake, s. cognominis, eodem nomine dictus, m.
naming, s. nominatio, f.
nap, s. somnus brevis, m. ; (of cloth) villus, m. ; **to take a —,** obdormisco, 3 ; (at noon) meridior, 1.
nape, s. **— of the neck,** cervix, f.
napkin, s. (for a table) mappa ; (little towel) mantele, n.
narcissus, s. narcissus, m.
narcotic, a. somnificus, somnifer ; **—, s.** medicamentum somnificum, n.
nard, s. nardus, f. ; nardum, n.
narrate, v.a. narro, enarro, 1.
narration, narrative, s. narratio ; expositio, f.
narrator, s. narrator, m.
narrow, a. angustus ; artus ; (of persons) parcus ; avarus ; (close, careful) diligens ; **—ly,** ad. anguste ; avare ; (with difficulty) ægre ; (carefully) diligenter.
narrow, v.a. coarto, 1 ; contraho, 3.
narrow-minded, a. animi angusti *or* parvi.
narrowness, s. angustiæ, f. pl.

narrows, s. angustiæ, fauces, f. pl.
nastily, ad. fœde, squalide, obscene.
nastiness, s. fœditas ; obscenitas, f.
nasturtium, s. tropæolum (mod. hort.).
nasty, a. fœdus ; obscenus.
natal, a. natalis, natalicius.
nation, s. gens, natio, f. (as political body) populus, m.
national, a. popularis.
nationality, s. totum populi corpus, n.
native, a. nativus, vernaculus ; (real, genuine) germanus.
native, s. indigena, c.
native land, s. patria, f.
nativity, s. ortus, m. ; (horoscope) genesis, f.
natural, a. naturalis ; nativus, innatus ; proprius ; *fig.* sincerus ; simplex ; **as is —,** ut par est ; **—ly,** ad. naturaliter ; (unaffectedly) simpliciter ; (of its own accord) sponte.
natural, s. fatuus, m.
naturalist, s. rerum naturalium investigator, m.
naturalization, s. civitatis donatio, f.
naturalize, v.a. aliquem civitate dono, 1.
nature, s. natura ; (natural disposition) indoles, ingenium, n. ; (peculiarity) proprietas, f. ; (universe) mundus, m.
naught, s. nihil, n. ; **to set at —,** parvi facio, 3.
naughtily, ad. male, prave.
naughtiness, s. malitia, petulantia, f.
naughty, a. improbus, malus ; (saucy) petulans.
nausea, s. (sea-sickness) nausea, f. ; (squeamishness) fastidium, n.
nauseate, v.a. fastidium pario, 3 ; satio, 1.
nauseous, a. tæter ; fastidiosus ; **—ly,** ad. cum nausea.
nautical, a. nauticus.
naval, a. navalis, maritimus.
nave, s. (of a wheel) modiolus, m. ; (of a church) navis, f.
navel, s. umbilicus, m.
navigable, a. navigabilis.   [1.
navigate, v.a. guberno, 1 ; **—,** v.n. navigo,
navigation, s. navigatio, f.
navigator, s. nauta, navigator, m.
navy, s. classis, f. ; copiæ navales, f. pl.
nay, ad. & i. non ita ; immo ; quid ?
neap, a. decrescens.
near, a. propinquus, vicinus ; (of relation) proximus ; (niggardly) parcus.
near, ad. prope ; juxta ; proxime ; **—,** pr. ad apud, prope, juxta ; **— at hand,** propinquus, in promptu ; **far and —,** longe lateque.
near, v.a. appropinquo, 1.
nearly, ad. prope ; fere ; ferme ; (almost) pæne.

nearness, a. propinquitas ; vicinia ; (of relation) propinquitas ; *fig.* parsimonia, f.

near-sighted, a. myops.

near-sightedness, s. myopia, f.

neat, a. mundus ; lautus ; lepidus ; nitidus ; concinnus, elegans ; —ly, ad. munde ; concinne ; laute ; eleganter.

neat, s. (cattle) boves, c. pl.

neatness, s. munditia ; concinnitas, f.

nebulous, a. nebulosus, caliginosus, obscurus.

necessaries, s. pl. (of life) necessitates, f. pl. ; necessaria, n. pl.

necessarily, ad. necessario.

necessary, a. necessarius ; **it is —,** opus est ; necesse est.

necessitate, v.a. cogo, 3.

necessitous, a. egens, inops.

necessity, s. necessitas ; (want) egestas, necessitudo ; (indispensable thing) res omnino necessaria, f.

neck, s. collum, n. ; cervix, f. ; (of land) lingua, f. ; (of a bottle) collum, n.

neck-cloth, neck-tie, s. focale, collare, n.

neck-lace, s. monile, n. ; (as ornament) torques, c.

necromancer, s. necromantius.

necromancy, s. necromantia, f.

nectar, s. nectar, n.

nectarine, s. persicum durácinum, n.

need, s. (necessity) opus, n., necessitas ; (want) egestas, penuria, f.

need, v.a. (to require) requiro, 3 ; egeo, indigeo, 2 ; opus esse ; —, v.n. (must) debeo, 2.

needful, a. necessarius, opus (indecl. subs.).

neediness, s. egestas, f.

needle, s. acus, f.

needle-work, s. opus acu factum, n.

needless, a. minime necessarius, supervacaneus ; —ly, ad. sine causa.

needs, ad. necesse ; **I — must,** oportet me . . .

needy, a. egens, indigens, egenus, inops.

nefarious, a. nefarius ; —ly, ad. nefarie ; v. **wickedly.**

negation, s. negatio, f.

negative, a. negativus.

negative, s. negatio ; repulsa, f. ; **to answer in the —,** negare, 1.

negative, v.a. antiquo, 1. [mitto, 3.

neglect, v.a. neglego ; desero, præter-

neglect, s. neglegentia, incuria, f. ; neglectus, m.

neglectful, a. neglegens.

negligence, s. neglegentia ; incuria, f.

negligent, a. neglegens, indiligens, remissus ; incuriosus ; —ly, ad. neglegenter, incuriose.

negotiable, a. mercabilis.

negotiate, v.a. agere, gero, 3 ; —, v.n. negotior, 1.

negotiation, s. actio, f. [orator, m.

negotiator, s. conciliator ; (spokesman)

negress, s. Afra, f.

negro, s. Afer, Aethiops, m.

neigh, v.n. hinnio, 2 ; **to — at,** adhinnio, 4.

neigh, neighing, s. hinnitus, m.

neighbour, s. vicinus, finitimus, propinquus, m.

neighbourhood, s. vicinitas ; vicinia ; proximitas ; propinquitas, f.

neighbouring, a. vicinus ; finitimus ; propinquus.

neighbourly, a. quod vicinum æquum est facere, familiaris ; benignus, comis.

neither, a. & pn. neuter ; —, c. nec, neque ; — . . . —, neve . . . neve ; **— way,** neutro.

nemesia, a. nemesia (mod. hort.).

nemophila, s. nemophila (mod. hort.).

neophyte, s. neophytus, m. ; neophyta, f. ; *fig.* tiro, m.

nephew, s. fratris *or* sororis filius, m. ; nepos, m.

Nereid, s. Nereis, f.

nerve, s. nervus ; *fig.* vigor, m.

nervous, a. nervosus ; (fearful) timidus, trepidus, anxius ; —ly, ad. nervose ; (fearfully) trepide, timide, anxie.

nervousness, s. anxietas, f. ; timor, m.

nest, s. nidus, m. ; *fig.* receptaculum, n.

nest, v.n. nidulor.

nestle, v.n. recubo, 1.

nestling, s. avicula, f. ; nidi, m. pl.

net, s. rete, n. ; funda, f. ; jaculum, n. ; plaga, f.

net, a. purus ; simplex.

net, v.a. texo ; reti capio, 3.

nether, a. inferior ; —most, infimus, imus.

netting, s. opus reticulatum, n.

nettle, s. urtica, f.

nettle, v.a. pungo, 3 ; *fig.* vexo, stimulo, 1.

net-work, s. reticulum, n.

neuter, a. neuter.

neutral, a. medius ; neuter, æquus.

neutrality, s. æquitas, f.

neutralize, v.a. æquo ; compenso, 1.

never, ad. nunquam ; **—more,** nunquam posthac.

nevertheless, ad. nihilominus, tamen, attamen.

new, a. novus, novellus, recens ; integer.

new-comer, s. advena, c. ; hospes, m.

new-fangled, a. novicius.

newly, ad. nuper, modo ; recenter.

newness, s. novitas, f.

news, s. res novæ, f. pl. ; (report) fama, f. ; rumor, nuntius, m.

newspaper, s. acta diurna, n. pl.
newt, s. lacerta, f.
next, a. proximus ; (of time) insequens.
next, ad. proxime ; juxta ; (of time) deinde ; pr. juxta, secundum.
nib, s. (bill of a bird) rostrum, n. ; (of a pen) acumen, n.
nibble, v.a. rodo, arrodo, 3.
nice, a. (dainty) delicatus ; (choice) exquisitus ; (exact) accuratus ; subtilis ; (fine) bellus ; (effeminate) mollis ; (ticklish) periculosus ; (difficult) difficilis ; (amiable) suavis ; **—ly,** ad. delicate ; exquisite ; subtiliter ; accurate ; belle.
niceness, nicety, s. cura ; subtilitas ; elegantia ; urbanitas, f.
niche, s. loculamentum, n.
nick, s. **in the very — of time,** in ipso articulo temporis.
nickname, s. nomen probrosum, n.
nickname, v.a. contumelioso nomine appello ; nomen per ludibrium alicui do, 1.
niece, s. fratris *or* sororis filia, f.
niggard, s. homo avarus, parcus, m.
niggardliness, s. parsimonia ; tenacitas, avaritia, f.
niggardly, a. parcus, tenax ; avarus.
nigh, a. propinquus.
night, s. nox, f. ; **by —,** nocte, noctu ; **lasting all —,** a. pernox.
nightfall, s. **at —,** sub noctem, primis tenebris.
nightingale, s. luscinia, Philomela, f.
nightly, a. nocturnus ; **—,** ad. noctu, de nocte.
nightmare, s. incubo, m. ; suppressio, f.
nightshade, s. solanum, n.
night-stool, s. lasanum, n.
night-walker, s. noctivagus, m.   [m.
night-watch, s. vigilia, f. ; (person) vigil,
nimble, a. pernix ; agilis, mobilis.
nimbleness, s. pernicitas, agilitas, mobilitas, f.
nimbly, ad. perniciter.
nine, a. novem (indecl.) ; **— times,** novies ; **— each,** noveni.
nineteen, a. undeviginti (indecl.).
nineteenth, a. undevicesimus.
ninetieth, a. nonagesimus.
ninety, a. nonaginta (indecl.).
ninny, s. ineptus, stultus, m.
ninth, a. nonus.   [off, deseco, 1.
nip, v.a. vellico, 1 ; (as cold) uro, 3 ; **to —**
nippers, s. forceps, c.
nipple, s. papilla, f.
nit, s. lens, f.
nitre, s. nitrum, n.
nitrous, a. nitrosus.
no, a. nullus ; nemo ; nihil (indecl.) ; **— one,** nemo, c.

no, ad. haud, non ; minime.
nobility, s. nobilitas, f. ; nobiles, m. pl. ; *fig.* magnanimitas, f.
noble, a. nobilis, *fig.* generosus ; (open-handed) liberalis ; magnanimus.
noble, nobleman, s. vir nobilis, m.
nobleness, s. nobilitas, f. ; genus nobile, n. ; *fig.* magnanimitas, f.
nobly, ad. præclare ; generose.
nobody, s. nemo, c.
nocturnal, a. nocturnus.
nod, s. nutus, m. ; **—,** v.n. nuto, 1 ; annuo, innuo, 3 ; (to be drowsy) dormito, 1.
noise, s. strepitus, stridor ; fragor ; sonus, sonitus ; (of voices) clamor, m. ; **to make a —,** strepito, sono, 1 ; fremo, strepo, 3.
noise, v.a. (abroad) divulgo, 1 ; differo, spargo, 3.   [tacite.
noiseless, a. tacitus ; silens ; **—ly,** ad.
noisily, ad. cum strepitu.
noisome, a. noxius ; fœdus ; (of smells) graveolens.
noisy, a. tumultuosus.
nomad, s. vagus.
nomenclator, s. nomenclator, m.
nomenclature, s. nomenclatura, f.
nominal, a. nominalis ; **—ly,** ad. nomine, verbo.
nominate, v.n. nomino, designo, 1.
nomination, s. nominatio, designatio ; (of an heir) nuncupatio, f.
nominative, s. casus nominativus, m.
nominee, s. qui nominatus est.
nondescript, a. nulli certo generi ascriptus.
none, a. & pn. nemo, nullus.
non-entity, non-existence, s. res nulla, f.
nones, s. nonæ, f. pl.
nonplus, s. **at a —,** in summis angustiis.
nonplus, v.a. (to puzzle) ad incitas redigo, 3.
non-residence, s. absentia, f.
non-resident, a. absens.
non-resistance, s. obœdientia, f.
nonsense, s. ineptiæ, nugæ, f. pl. ; **—!** i. gerræ ! fabulæ ! somnia ! **to talk —,** absurde loquor, 3 ; garrio, 4.
nonsensical, a. ineptus, absurdus.
noodle, s. stultus, ineptus, m.
nook, s. angulus, m. ; latebra, f.
noon, s. meridies, m.
noon-day, a. meridianus.
noon-tide, s. meridianum tempus, n.
noose, s. laqueus, m. ; **—,** v.a. illaqueo, 1.
nor, c. nec, neque ; neve, neu.
normal, a. secundum normam.
north, s. septentrio, m.
north, northern, a. septentrionalis ; aquionaris, aquilonius, boreus.

northerly, a. septentrionem spectans.
north-pole, s. arctos, f.
northwards, ad. septentrionem versus.
north-wind, s. aquilo, m. ; boreas, m.
nose, s. nasus, m. ; nares, f. pl. ; **to lead (one) by the** —, (aliquem) ludificor, 1.
nosegay, s. fasciculus (florum), m.
nostril, s. naris, f.
nostrum, s. medicamentum, n.
not, ad. non ; haud ; minime ; (in prohibitions) ne ; — **at all,** nullo modo ; — **yet,** nondum.
notable, a. notabilis, insignis.
notably, ad. insignite, insigniter, notabiliter ; (especially) præcipue, præsertim.
notary, s. scriba, m.
notation, s. notatio, f. ; signum, n.
notch, s. incisura, f. ; —, v.a. incido, 3.
note, s. (mark) nota, f. ; signum, indicium, n. ; (com.) chirographum, n.
note, v.a. (to mark) noto ; (in a book) annoto, 1 ; v. **notice.** [f. pl.
notebook, s. commentarius, m. tabulæ,
noted, a. nobilis ; insignis, notus ; clarus, præclarus, celeber.
note-worthy, a. notandus, notabilis.
nothing, s. nihil, n. ; —, ad. (in no way) nullo modo, minime ; **for** —, gratis.
notice, s. animadversio, observatio, f. ; proclamation, edictum, n. ; **public** —, proscriptio ; **escape** —, lateo, 2 ; **give** —, edico, 3.
notice, v.a. observo, 1 ; animadverto, 3.
notification, s. denunciatio, proscriptio, f.
notify, v.a. significo, denuntio, 1.
notion, s. notio, notitia ; opinio, f.
notoriety, s. notitia, f.
notorious, a. notus, manifestus ; (in a bad sense) famosus ; —**ly,** ad. manifesto.
notwithstanding, ad. & c. nihilominus.
nought, v. **naught.**
noun, s. nomen, n.
nourish, v.a. nutrio, 4 ; alo, 3.
nourisher, s. altor, nutritor, m. ; altrix, f.
nourishment, s. alimentum, n. ; cibus, m.
novel, a. novus.
novel, s. fabula, f.
novelist, s. fabulator, m.
novelty, s. novitas, f.
November, s. Novembris, m.
novice, s. tiro, m. ; novicius, m. ; novicia, f.
novitiate, s. tirocinium, n.
now, ad. nunc ; — . . . —, modo . . . modo ; — **and then,** nonnunquam.
nowadays, ad. hodie, his temporibus.
nowhere, ad. nusquam, nullo in loco.
nowise, ad. haudquaquam, neutiquam.
noxious, a. nocens, noxius, perniciosus.
nozzle, s. nasus, m.
nudge, s. cubiti ictus, m. ; —, v.a. fodico, 1.
nudity, s. nudatio, f.

nugatory, a. futtilis, frivolus, nugatorius.
nugget, s. massa, f.
nuisance, s. incommodum, n. ; molestia, f.
null, a. irritus ; nullus.
nullify, v.a. irritum facio, 3.
numb, a. torpens, torpidus, hebes.
numb, v.a. hebeto, 1 ; obstupefacio, 3.
number, s. numerus, m. ; (also gr. and metrically) ; (of things) copia ; vis ; (of men) frequentia, multitudo, f. ; **without** —, innumerabilis.
number, v.a. numero, computo, 1.
numberless, a. innumerus, innumerabilis.
numbness, s. torpor ; *fig.* stupor, m.
numeral, a. numeralis.
numeration, s. numeratio, f.
numerous, a. frequens, creber, multus.
nun, s. monacha, f.
nuncio, s. nuntius, legatus, m.
nunnery, s. cœnobium monarcharum, n.
nuptial, a. nuptialis, conjugalis, conubialis, conjugalis.
nuptials, s. nuptiæ, f. pl.
nurse, s. nutrix, altrix.
nurse, v.a. nutrio, 4 ; *fig.* foveo, 2 ; (to the sick) ancillor, 1 (alicui).
nursery, s. (for children) cubiculum infantium, n. ; (of plants) seminarium, n.
nursery-maid, s. nutrix, f.
nursling, s. alumnus, m. ; alumna, f.
nurture, v.a. educa, 1 ; nutrio, 4. [m.
nurturer, s. nutritor, altor ; *fig.* educator,
nut, s. nux, f. ; *fig.* **a** — **to crack,** quæstio nodosa, f.
nut-brown, a. spadix.
nut-crackers, s. nucifrangibulum, n.
nutriment, a. alimentum, nutrimentum, n.
nutrition, s. nutrimentum, n.
nutritious, nutritive, a. alibilis.
nut-shell, s. putamen, n. ; *fig.* **in a** —, paucis verbis.
nut-tree, s. nux, f.
nymph, s. nympha ; (girl) puella, f.

Oaf, s. stultus, hebes, m.
oak(-tree), s. quercus, æsculus, ilex, f. ; robur, n.
oaken, a. querneus, quernus ; æsculeus, ilignus, roboreus.
oak-grove, s. quercetum, n.
oakum, s. stuppa, f.
oar, s. remus, m. ; **to pull the** —**s,** remos ducere, 3.
oarsman, s. remex, m.
oat, oats, s. avena, f.
oaten, a. avenaceus.
oath, s. jusjurandum, (genit.) jurisjurandi, n. ; (of soldiers) sacramentum, n. ; **to take an** —, juro, 1 (in verba).

obduracy, s. obstinatio (animi), f. ; pertinacia, pervicacia ; contumacia.
obdurate, a. obstinatus ; pertinax, pervicax, contumax ; —ly, ad. obstinate ; pertinaciter ; contumaciter.
obedience, s. obœdientia, f. ; obsequium, n.
obedient, a. obœdiens, obsequens ; —ly, ad. obœdienter.
obeisance, s. salutatio, f.
obelisk, s. obeliscus, m.
obese, a. obesus ; v. **fat.**
obesity, s. obesitas, f.
obey, v.n. pareo, 2 ; obœdio, 4 ; obtempero, 1.
object, s. objectum, n. ; res. f. ; (aim, design) consilium, n. ; — **of mockery,** ludibrium, n.
object, v.a. (to) repugno, improbo, 1.
objection, s. impedimentum, n. ; mora, f. ; **if you have no —,** si per te licet.
objectionable, a. improbabilis.
objective, a. quod sensibus percipitur.
oblation, s. donum, n.
obligation, s. officium ; beneficium, n.
oblige, v.a. cogo, 3 ; obligo, 1 ; devincio, 4 ; (by kindness) bene de aliquo mereor, 2.
obliging, a. officiosus, comis, blandus ; benignus, beneficus ; —ly, ad. comiter ; benigne ; officiose.
obligingness, s. comitas ; humanitas, facilitas, f.
oblique, a. obliquus ; —ly, ad. oblique.
obliquity, s. obliquitas ; *fig.* pravitas, iniquitas, f.
obliterate, v.a. deleo, 2 ; oblittero, 1.
oblivion, s. oblivio, f. ; oblivium, n. ; **act of** —, venia, impunitas, f.
oblivious, a. obliviosus, immemor.
oblong, a. oblongus.
obloquy, s. vituperatio, f. ; maledictum, n. ; probra, n. pl.
obnoxious, a. (liable to) obnoxius ; (hateful) invisus ; (hurtful) noxius.
obscene, a. obscenus, spurcus, turpis ; —ly, ad. obscene, turpiter.
obscenity, s. obscenitas ; turpitudo, f.
obscuration, s. obscuratio, f.
obscure, a. obscurus ; *fig.* perplexus ; (intricate, puzzling) difficilis ; (of style) intortus ; (persons) ignobilis, ignotus ; —ly, ad. obscure ; *fig.* occulte ; (indirectly) oblique.
obscure, v.a. obscuro, obumbro, 1.
obscurity, s. obscuritas, f. ; tenebræ, f. pl. ; *fig.* ignobilitas, humilitas, f.
obsequies, s. exsequiæ, f. pl. ; funus, n.
obsequious, a. officiosus, morigerus ; —ly, ad. cum nimia obsequentia ; assentatorie.
obsequiousness, s. obsequium, n.; obsequentia ; assentatio, f.

observable, a. notabilis, insignis.
observance, s. observantia, obtemperatio, f.
observant, a. attentus ; obœdiens.
observation, s. observatio ; animadversio, f. ; (remark) dictum, n.
observe, v.a. observo, 1 ; animadverto, 3 ; (to utter) dico, 3 ; (to spy out) speculor, 1 ; (obey) pareo, 2 ; obtempero, 1.
observer, s. spectator, m.
obsolete, a. obsoletus.
obstacle, s. impedimentum, n. ; mora, f.
obstinacy, s. obstinatio, pertinacia, pervicacia, contumacia, f.
obstinate, a. obstinatus, pertinax ; pervicax, contumax ; —ly, ad. obstinate ; pervicaciter, contumaciter, pertinaciter.
obstreperous, v. **noisy.**
obstruct, v.a. obstruo, 3 ; (to hinder) impedio, 4.   [mentum, n.
obstruction, s. obstructio, f. ; impedi-
obtain, v.a. paro, 1 ; consequor, quæro, nanciscor ; adipiscor, 3 ; (by entreaty) impetro, 1.
obtainable, a. impetrabilis.
obtrude, v.a. obtrudo, infero, 3.
obtrusive, a. molestus ; importunus.
obtuse, a. obtusus ; hebes.
obtuseness, s. hebetatio, f.
obviate, v.a. occurro ; præverto, 3.
obvious, a. apertus, perspicuus, manifestus ; —ly, ad. aperte, manifesto.
occasion, s. occasio, causa, f.
occasion, v.a. ansam *or* locum do, 1 ; materiem præbeo, 2 ; moveo, 2.
occasional, a. rarus, infrequens ; —ly, ad. per occasionem, occasione oblata.
occidental, a. occidentalis ; occiduus.
occult, a. occultus, arcanus.
occupancy, s. occupatio ; possessio, f.
occupant, s. possessor, m.
occupation, s. possessio, f. ; (engagement) occupatio, f. ; (employment) quæstus, m. ; (business) studium, negotium, n.
occupier, s. possessor, m.
occupy, v.a. occupo, 1 ; (to possess) teneo, 2 ; (to beleaguer) obsideo, 2 ; (to inhabit) habito, 1 ; (detain) detineo, 2.
occur, v.n. occido, contingo, 3 ; evenio ; obvenio ; *fig.* in mentem venire, 4.
occurrence, s. casus, eventus, m. ; res, f.
ocean, s. oceanus, m.
ochre, s. ochra, f.
octagon, s. octogonum, n.
octagonal, a. octogonus.
octavo, s. forma octonaria, f.
October, s. October, m.   [m.
octogenarian, a. & s. octogenarius (homo),
ocular, a. ocularis, præsens ; per oculos.
oculist, s. ocularis medicus, m.

odd, a. (of number) impar; (strange) insolitus, inusitatus; —**ly,** ad. inusitate.

oddity, s. res inusitata, f.; monstrum, n.

odds, s. discordia, dissensio, contentio, f.; (difference) discrimen, n.; **to be at —s with one,** ab aliquo dissidere, 2.

odious, a. odiosus, invisus; (disgusting) fœdus; —**ly,** ad. odiose.

odiousness, s. odium, n.; fœditas, f.

odium, s. invidia, f.

odoriferous, a. odorifer, odoratus, odorus.

odorous, a. odoratus.

odour, s. odor, m.; *fig.* fama, f.

Odyssey, s. Odyssea, f.

of, pr. sign of the genitive; if denoting the ablative to be rendered by: a, de, ex.

off, a. ulterior.

off, pr. (out of) extra; (from, of) de, ex.

off, ad. procul, longe; **be well —,** bene me habeo, 2; (as interj.,) abi apage! — **hand,** confestim, illico; **to be —,** absum.

offal, s. quisquiliæ, f. pl.

offence, s. (fault) offensa, culpa, f.; (insult) injuria, contumelia, f.; (displeasure) offensio, f.

offend, v.a. (to insult, etc.) offendo; lædo, 3; (to transgress) pecco, 1; (against) violo, 1.

offender, s. reus, m.

offensive, a. injuriosus; (things) odiosus; fœdus; **take the —,** bellum ultro infero, 3; —**ly,** ad. odiose; injuriose.

offer, v.a. offero, 3; do, 1; præbeo, 2; (at an auction) licitor, 1; *fig.* (to come in the mind) occurro, 3; **—,** v.n. occurro, 3; (to volunteer) profiteor, 2.

offer, s. oblatio; condicio, f.

offering, s. oblatio, f.; donum, n.; (of a sacrifice) immolatio, f.

office, s. (duty) officium, munus; (room) tabularium, n.

officer, s. magistratus, m.; (in the army) præfectus, tribunus, militaris, m.

official, a. magistratui præpositus; publicus; —**ly,** ad. publice.

official, s. minister; accensus, lictor, m.

officiate, v.n. officium præsto, 1; rem divinam facio, 3; (for another) alterius vice fungor, 3.

officious, a. molestus; —**ly,** ad. moleste.

officiousness, s. obsequium, n.

offing, s. altum mare, n.

offscouring, s. purgamentum, n.

offset, s. (shoot, sprout) surculus, m.

offspring, s. proles, progenies, stirps, suboles, f.

oft, often, ad. sæpe; **— times,** sæpenumero; **very —,** persæpe.

ogle, v.a. furtim intueor, 2.

ogre, s. larva, f.

oh, i. oh! ah! ohe!

oil, s. oleum, n.; olivum, n.

oilman, s. olearius, m.

oil-press, s. torcular, n.

oily, a. (like oil) oleaceus; oleosus.

ointment, s. unguentum, unguen; (as medicine) collyrium, n.

old, a. (in age) ætate provectus, senex; (ancient) vetus, vetustus; (out of use) obsoletus; (worn) exesus, tritus; (of former days) antiquus, priscus, pristinus; **— man,** s. senex, m.; **— woman,** s. anus, f.; **— age,** s. senectus, f.; **of —,** olim, quondam; —**er,** senior; vetustior; —**est,** natu maximus; **to grow —,** senesco, 3.

olden, a. priscus, pristinus; **— time,** s. vetustas, f.

old-fashioned, a. priscus, antiquus.

old-standing, a. vetus; inveteratus.

oldness, s. antiquitas, vetustas, f.

oleaginous, a. oleaceus.

oleander, s. nerium, n.

oligarchy, s. paucorum potestas, f.; optimates, m. pl.

olive, s. olea, oliva, f.; **—,** a. oleagineus.

Olympiad, s. Olympias, f.

Olympic, a. Olympicus.

omen, s. omen, auspicium, augurium, ostentum, n.

ominous, a. infaustus, infelix; —**ly,** ad. malis ominibus.

omission, s. prætermissio, f.

omit, v.a. prætermitto, omitto (temporarily) intermitto, 3.

omnipotent, a. omnipotens.

omnivorous, a. omnivorus.

on, pr. in (with ablative), sub, super; (near) ad; (ranged with) a, ab; (depending, hanging on) de; (immediately, after) e, ex; **— his side,** cum illo; **— the right hand,** a dextra, ad dextram.

on, ad. porro; (continually) usque; **and so —,** et cetera; **to go —,** procedo, pergo, 3.

once, ad. (one time) semel; (at the same time) simul, uno tempore; (formerly) olim, quondam; aliquando; **at —,** illico, statim; **— and again,** semel atque iterum; **— for all,** semel.

one, a. num. unus; (a certain person *or* thing) quidam; **— another,** alius alium; **— after another,** alternus; (ad.) invicem; **— by —,** singillatim; **it is all —,** perinde est; **— or the other,** alteruter; **— with the other,** promiscuus; (ad.) promiscue.

one-eyed, a. luscus.

one-handed, a. unimanus.

onerous, a. gravis, prægravis, onerosus.

oneself, pn. ipse; (with reflective verbs) se.

one-sided, a. inæqualis, iniquus.

onion, s. cæpa, f.
only, a. unicus ; unus, solus.
only, ad. solum, tantum, dumtaxat ; (except) non nisi.
only-begotten, a. unigena.   [incursio, f.
onset, onslaught, s. impetus, incursus, m. ;
onward, onwards, ad. porro ; protinus.
onyx, s. onyx, c.
ooze, v.n. mano, emano ; (de)stillo, 1.
ooze, s. limus, m. ; uligo, f.
oozy, a. paludosus ; uliginosus.
opacity, s. opacitas, f.
opal, s. opalus, m.
opaque, a. densus, opacus.
open, v.a. aperio, 4 ; patefacio, pando, 3 ;
    (to uncover) retego, 3 ; (a letter)
    resigno, 1 ; (to explain) interpretor, 1 ;
    (to begin) ordior, 4 ; —, v.n. patesco, 3 ;
    (to gape open) dehisco, 3.
open, a. (not shut) apertus, patens ;
    (visible) in conspectu positus ; (evident)
    manifestus ; (sincere) candidus, in-
    genuus ; (public) communis, publicus ;
    (notorious) pervulgatus ; (not fortified)
    immunitus ; **it is an — question,** ambi-
    gitur ; **in the — air,** sub divo.   [cus.
open-handed, a. liberalis, largus, munifi-
open-hearted, a. simplex, ingenuus.
opening, s. (act) apertio, f. ; (aperture)
    foramen, n. ;   (air-hole) sparamen-
    tum, n.
openly, ad. aperte ; manifesto ; (publicly)
    palam ; *fig.* libere, simpliciter.
openness, s. *fig.* candor, m.
operate, v.a. & n. operor, 1 ; ago, 3 ; (cut
    open) seco, 1 ; (have force) vim habeo, 2.
operation, s. effectus, m. ; (with the knife)
    sectio, f. ; (business) negotium, n.
operative, a. efficax ; potens ; —, s.
    opifex, c.   [lippitudo, f.
ophthalmia, s. oculorum inflammatio,
opiate, s. medicamentum somnificum, n. ;
    potio soporifera, f.
opiate, a. medicatus, somnifer, soporifer.
opine, v.n. opinor, arbitror, 1.
opinion, s. opinio, sententia ; censura ;
    mens, f. ; judicium, n. ; animus, m. ;
    (esteem) existimatio, f. ; **in my —,** mea
    sententia.
opinionated, opinionative, a. pertinax,
    pervicax, obstinatus.
opium, s. opium, opion, n.
opponent, s. adversarius, m.
opportune, a. opportunus, idoneus, com-
    modus ; **—ly,** ad. opportune ; commode ;
    in tempore.
opportunity, s. occasio ; opportunitas,
    facultas, copia, f.
oppose, v.a. oppono, objicio, 3 ; (to re-
    sist) repugno, adversor, obsto, 1 ; re-
    sisto, 3.

opposed, a. adversus ; adversarius ; con-
    trarius.
opposer, s., v. **opponent.**
opposite, a. adversus, contrarius, diver-
    sus ; —, s. contrarium, n.
opposite, ad. & pr. **— to,** contra (with ac-
    cusative), ex adverso.
opposition, s. oppositio ; repugnantia ;
    discrepantia, f. ; (obstacle) impedi-
    mentum, n.   [onero, 1.
oppress, v.a. affligo, 3 ; vexo ; gravo,
oppression, s. gravatio ; injuria ; vexa-
    tio, f.   [iniquus.
oppressive, a. gravis ; acerbus, molestus,
oppressor, s. tyrannus, m.
opprobrious, a. turpis, probrosus.
opprobrium, s. dedecus, probrum, oppro-
    brium, n.
optative, s. modus optativus, m.
optical, a. oculorum, gen. pl.
optics, s. optice, f.
option, s. optio, f.
optional, a. cujus rei optio est.
opulence, s. opulentia, f.
opulent, a. opulens, opulentus, dives ;
    —ly, ad. opulenter.
or, c. vel ; aut ; (interrogatively) an ;
    either —, vel . . . vel, aut . . . aut ;
    whether —, sive . . . sive, seu . . . seu.
oracle, s. oraculum, responsum, n. ; sors, f.
oracular, a. *fig.* ambiguus.   [voce, verbis.
oral, a. verbo traditus ; præsens ; **—ly,** ad.
orange, s. malum aurantium (mod. hort.) ;
    —tree, s. citrus Aurantium (mod. hort.).
orange, a. luteus.
orangery, s. citretum, n.
orang-outang, s. simia satyrus, f. ; pithe-
    cus satyrus, m.
oration, s. oratio ; (before the people and
    to the army) contio, f.
orator, s. orator, m.
oratorical, a. oratorius.
oratory, s. oratoria ars, rhetorica ; (elo-
    quence) eloquentia, f. ; (place) ora-
    torium, n.
orb, s. orbis ; gyrus, orbiculus, m.
orbit, s. orbis, m. orbita, f. ; (in astronomy)
    ambitus, m.
orchard, s. pomarium, n.
orchestra, s. orchestra, f. ; (body of musi-
    cal performers) symphoniaci, m. pl.
orchid, s. orchis, f .   [3.
ordain, v.a. ordino, 1 ; jubeo, 2 ; instituo,
ordeal, s. judicium Dei ; *fig.* discrimen, n.
order, s. ordo, m. ; (rank) ordo, m. ; (row)
    series, f. ; (command) præceptum,
    mandatum, decretum, n. ; (custom)
    mos, m. ; consuetudo, f. ; (decree of
    instruction) rescriptum ; (decree of an
    authority) edictum, n.   (association)
    societas, f.

order, v.a. (to put in order) dispono, 3 ;
ordino, 1 ; (to give orders) impero, 1 ;
jubeo, 2 ; (to govern) rego, 3.
ordering, s. dispositio ; administratio, f.
orderly, a. compositus, ordinatus ; (of
persons) obœdiens ; (quiet, sober)
modestus, temperatus.
orderly, s. (mil.) tesserarius, m.
ordinal, a. ordinalis.
ordinance, s. edictum, rescriptum, n.
ordinarily, ad. usitate, fere, plerumque,
vulgo.
ordinary, a. usitatus, solitus, vulgaris.
ordination, s. ordinatio, f.
ordnance, s. (artillery) tormenta, n. pl.
ordure, s. stercus, n. ; fimus, m.
ore, s. metallum, n.
organ, s. instrumentum, n. ; (musical instrument) organum, n.
organic, a. organicus ; (of nature) naturæ
(gen. sing.), f.
organism, s. compages, natura, f.
organist, s. organicus, m.
organization, s. ordinatio ; temperatio, f. ;
(organism itself) compages, f.
organize, v.a. ordino, 1 ; constituo, dispono, 3 ; formo, 1.
orgies, s. orgia, n. pl.
orgy, s. (revelry) comissatio, f.
orient, s. Oriens, m.
oriental, a. Orientalis.
orifice, s. foramen ; os, n. ; rima, f.   [m.
origin, s. origo, f. ; principium, n. ; ortus,
original, a. primitivus ; pristinus ; principalis ; —ly, ad. ab origine ; primum.
original, s. archetypum, exemplar ;
(writing) autographum, n. ; (of a person) qui suum sequitur ingenium, n.
originality, s. proprietas quædam ingenii, f.
originate, v.n. orior, 4 ; proficiscor, 3.
orison, s. preces, f. pl.
ornament, s. ornamentum, n. ; ornatus,
m. ; decus, n.
ornament, v.a. orno, decoro, 1.
ornamental, a. quod ornamento, decori
est.
ornate, a. ornatus ; pictus.
orphan, a. & s. orbus.
orphan-asylum, s. orphanotrophium, n.
orphanhood, s. orbitas, f.
orthodox, a. orthodoxus.   [ta, f.
orthodoxy, s. doctrina ab ecclesia recep-
orthographical, a. orthographus.
orthography, s. orthographia ; (spelling)
scriptura, f.
ortolan, s. avis miliaria, f.
oscillate, v.n. fluctuo, 1.
oscillation, s. fluctuatio, f.
osier, s. vimen, n. ; salix, f.
osprey, s. ossifragus, m.

ostensible, a. simulatus, fictus.
ostensibly, ad. specie, per speciem.
ostentation, s. ostentatio ; jactatio, f.
ostentatious, a. ambitiosus ; gloriosus ;
vanus ; —ly, ad. ambitiose, gloriose,
jactanter.
ostler, s. agaso, stabularius, m.
ostracism, s. testarum suffragia, n. pl.
ostrich, s. struthiocamelus, m.
other, a. (another) alius ; alter ; the —s,
ceteri, reliqui.
otherwise, ad. alio modo, aliter ; (if not)
si non ; (besides) insuper.
otter, s. lutra, f.
Ottoman, a. Othomanicus.
Ottoman, s. Turca, m.
ought, v.n. def. debeo, 2 ; oportet.
ounce, s. uncia, f.   [tras.
our, ours, pr. noster ; (of — country) nos-
ourselves, pr. nosmet, nosmet ipsi.
ousel, s. (blackbird) merula, f.
oust, v.a. ejicio, 3.   [foras.
out, ad. (without) foris ; (outward, forth)
out, pr. (— of) e, ex ; (on account of)
propter ; (—side, beyond) extra ; — of
the way, devius.
out, i. (get — !) apage !
outbid, v.a. supra adjicio, 3 ; supero, 1.
outbreak, s. eruptio ; fig. seditio, f.
outcast, s. exsul, extorris, profugus, m.
outcry, s. clamor, m. ; acclamatio, f.
outdo, v.a. supero, 1.
outer, a. exterior.
outfit, s. apparatus, m.
outflank, v.a. circumeo, 4.
outgoing, s. egressus, m.
outgrow, v.a. fig. dedisco, 3.
outhouse, s. posticum, n.
outlandish, a. externus ; barbarus.
outlast, v.a. durando superare, 1.
outlaw, s. proscriptus, m.
outlaw, v.a. aqua et igni interdico, proscribo, 3.   [proscriptio, f.
outlawry, s. aquæ et ignis interdictio,
outlay, s. sumptus, m. ; impensa, f.
outlet, s. exitus, egressus, m.
outline, s. forma rudis.
outlive, v.a. supervivo, 3 ; supersum ;
supero, 1 ; superstes sum.
outlying, a. (distant) remotus.
outmarch, v.a. celerius procedo, 3.
outnumber, v.a. numero supero, 1.
outpost, s. statio, f.
outpouring, s. effusio, f.
outrage, s. injuria, f. ; (bold deed) flagitium, n.
outrage, v.a. injuria afficio, 3 ; lædo, 3.
outrageous, a. injuriosus ; atrox ; (exaggerated) immodicus ; immanis ; immoderatus ; —ly, ad. atrociter ; immoderate.

outrageousness, s. immanitas, f.
outrider, s. præcursor, m.
outright, ad. (at once) statim ; (completely) prorsus.
outrun, v.a. præcurro, 3 ; cursu supero, 1.
outset, s. principium, initium, n.
outshine, v.a. præluceo, 2.
outside, s. pars exterior ; superficies ; (appearance) species, f. ; —, a. exterus.
outside, ad. foris, extrinsecus.
outside, pr. extra.
outskirt, s. margo, c. ; ora, f. ; (of towns) suburbium, n.
outspoken, a. candidus, v. **freespoken.**
outstanding, a. prominens ; (of debts) solvendus, 3.
outstep, v.a. celerius eo, 4.
outstretch, v.a. expando, extendo, 3.
outstrip, v.a. cursu supero, 1 ; præverto, 3.
outvie, v.a. supero, 1.
outvote, v.a. suffragiis supero, 1.
outward, a. externus, exterus ; —, ad. foras.
outwardly, ad. extrinsecus, extra.
outwards, ad. in exteriorem partem ; extra.
outweigh, v.a. præpondero, 1 ; fig. præverto, 3.
outwit, v.a. deludo, 3 ; circumvenio, 4.
outwork, s. propugnaculum, n.
oval, a. ovatus.
ovation, s. ovatio, f.
oven, s. furnus, m.
over, pr. super ; supra, trans ; — **against,** contra ; —, ad. super ; supra ; — **and** — **again,** iterum ac sæpius ; **all** —, per totum ; — **and above,** insuper.
overawe, v.a. metu coerceo, 2.
overbalance, v.a. præpondero, 1.
overbearing, a. insolens, superbus.
overburden, v.a. onero, 1.
overcast, v.a. obscuro, contristo, 1 ; —, a. nubilus, tristis.
overcharge, v.a. plus æquo onero, 1 ; (in price) plus æquo exigo, 3.
overcloud, v.a. obscuro, contristo, 1.
overcoat, s., v. **great-coat.**
overcome, v.a. supero, 1 ; vinco, 3.
overdo, v.a. nimis studeo, 2 ; nimis incumbo, 3.
overdue, a. jamdudum solvendus.
overfatigue, s. nimia fatigatio, f.
overflow, v.n. exundo, redundo, restagno, 1 ; superfluo, 3 ; —, v.a. inundo, 1.
overflow, overflowing, s. inundatio, f.
overfond, a. nimis indulgens ; nimis cupidus.
overgrow, v.n. supercresco, 3 ; v.a. convestio.
overgrown, a. obductus, obsitus ; (too great) prægrandis.

overhang, v.n. impendeo, immineo, 2.
overhasty, a. præceps, præproperus.
overhaul, v.a. examino, 1.
overhead, ad. desuper ; supra, superne.
overhear, v.a. subausculto, 1.
overjoyed, a. ovans, exsultans.
overland, a. per terram.
overlap, v.a. excedo, 3.
overlay, v.a. induco, illino, 3 ; (to overwhelm) opprimo, 3.
overleap, v.a. transilio, 4.
overload, v.a. nimio pondere onero, 1.
overlook, v.a. (to inspect) inspicio, 3 ; curo, 1 ; (not to notice) prætermitto ; (to scorn) despicio, contemno, 3 ; (have view of) prospecto, 1.
overmatch, v.a. supero, 1 ; vinco, 3.
overmuch, ad. nimis, plus æquo.
overpass, v.a. transgredior, 3 ; fig. supero, 1 ; transeo, 4 ; egredior, 3.
overpower, v.a. opprimo, 3 ; supero, exsupero, 1.
overrate, v.a. nimis æstimo, 1.
overreach, v.a. circumvenio, 4.
override, (to overtake) præverto, 3 ; (cancel) rescindo, 3.
overripe, a. præmaturus.
overrule, v.a. (check) coerceo, 2 ; (cancel) rescindo, 3.
overrun, v.a. (to devastate) vasto, 1 ; — **with,** obsitus.
oversee, v.a. curo, 1 ; inspicio, 3.
overseer, s. præfectus, curator, præses, m. ; custos, c.
overset, v.a. everto, 3.
overshadow, v.a. obumbro, opaco ; fig. obscuro, 1.
overshoot, v.a. transgredior, 3.
oversight, s. (carelessness) incuria ; negligentia, f. ; error, m. ; (guardianship) cura, custodia, f.
overspread, v.a. obduco, 3.
overstate, v. **exaggerate.**
overstep, v.n. excedo, egredior, 3.
overt, a. manifestus, apertus ; —**ly,** ad. manifesto, aperte.
overtake, v.a. assequor, excipio, 3 ; supervenio, 4.
overthrow, v.a. subverto, everto, proruo ; (the enemy) devinco, prosterno ; fig. opprimo, 3.
overthrow, s. eversio ; ruina, f. ; excidium, n.   [2.
overtop, v.a. (ex)supero, 1 ; superemineo, 2.
overture, s. (proposal) condicio, f. ; (beginning) exordium, n.
overturn, v.a. everto, subverto, 3.
overvalue, v.a. nimis æstimo, 1.
overweening, a. arrogans, insolens ; (rash) temerarius.
overweigh, v. **outweigh,** v.a.

overwhelm, v.a. obruo ; opprimo, 3.
oviparous, a. oviparus.
owe, v.a. **to be** —ing **(to),** debeo, 2.
owing, pr. (to) propter, ob.
owl, s. bubo, m. ; strix, noctua, ulula, f.
own, a. proprius, peculiaris ; **one's** —, suus, proprius.
own, v.a. possideo, teneo, habeo ; (to acknowledge) confiteor, 2 ; (to claim) vindico, 1.
owner, s. dominus, possessor, erus, m.
ownership, s. dominium, n.
ox, s. bos, juvencus, m.
ox-fly, s. tabanus, m.
ox-stall, s. bubile, n.
oyster, s. ostrea, f. ; — **-bed,** s. ostrearium, n. ; — **-shell,** s. ostreæ testa, f.

Pace, s. gressus ; incessus ; passus, m. (also as measure).
pace, v.n. incedo, 3 ; spatior, 1 ; —, v.a. passibus emetior, 4.
pacha, s. satrapes, m.
pacific, a. pacificus ; tranquillus ; placidus ; pacifer.
pacification, s. pacificatio, f.
pacificatory, a. pacificatorius.
pacify, v.a. placo, sedo, paco, pacifico, 1 ; lenio, 4.
pack, s. (bundle) sarcina, f. ; fasciculus, m. ; (crowd) grex, m. ; turba, f.
pack, v.a. stipo, suffarcino, 1 ; colligo ; (a jury) judices per calumniam eligere, 3.
package, s. sarcina, f. ; fasciculus, m.
pack-cloth, s. segestre, involucrum, n.
packet, s. fasciculus, m. ; (ship) navis tabellaria, f.
pack-horse, s. jumentum, n.
pack-saddle, s. clitellæ, f. pl.
pack-thread, s. funiculus, m.
pad, s. (nag) mannus, m. ; (for a horse) ephippium, n. ; (cushion) pulvinus, m.
paddle, s. remus, m.
paddock, s. sæptum, n.
padlock, s. sera, f.
pæony, s. pæonia, f.
pagan, a. paganus.
paganism, s. pagani, m. pl.
page, s. (of a book) pagina, f. ; (— -boy) puer, m.
pageant, s. spectaculum, n. ; pompa ; fig. species, f.
pageantry, s. species atque pompa, f.
pail, s. hama, situla, f.
pain, s. dolor ; angor, cruciatus, m.
pain, v.a. dolore afficio, 3 ; excrucio, 1 ; v.n. doleo, 2.
painful, a. gravis, æger ; (laborious) operosus ; —ly, ad. (mod.) operose.

painless, a. sine dolore, doloris expers.
pains, s. cura, f. ; studium, n. ; **take** —, operam do, 1.
painstaking, a. operosus.
paint, v.a. (to colour) (colore) induco ; pingo, depingo, 3 ; (the face) fuco, 1 ; —, v.n. (as artist) pingo, 3.
paint, s. pigmentum, n. ; (for the face) fucus, m.
paint-brush, s. penicillus, m.
painter, s. (artist) pictor, m.
painting, s. (art) pictura ; (picture) tabula, pictura, f.
pair, s. (couple) par, n.
pair, v.a. jungo, conjungo, 3 ; copulo, 1 ; —, v.n. coeo, 4.
pairing, s. coitus, m.
palace, s. regia (domus), f. ; palatium, n.
palanquin, s. lectica, f.
palatable, a. sapidus ; jucundus.
palate, s. palatum, n.
palatine, a. & s. palatinus.
palaver, s. stultiloquium, n. ; garrulitas, f. ; —, v.n. garrio, 4.
pale, a. pallidus ; exsanguis ; **to be** —, palleo, 2 ; **to grow** —, pallesco, 3.
pale, s. palus ; (bounds) limes, m. ; (enclosure) sæptum, n.
paleness, s. pallor, m.
palfrey, s. equus, m.
palimpsest, s. palimpsestus, m.
paling, palisade, s. vallum, n.
palish, a. pallidulus, suppallidus.
pall, s. pallium, n.
pall, v.n. nil sapio ; —, v.a. satio, 1.
Palladium, s. Palladium, n.
pallet, s. (low bed) grabatus, m.
palliate, v.a. extenuo, excuso, 1.
palliation, s. excusatio, venia, f.
palliative, s. remedium, n.
pallid, a. pallidus.
palm, s. (of the hand) palma, f. ; (measure) palmus, m. ; (tree) palma.
palm, v.a. — **off,** vendito, 1.
Palm-Sunday, s. Dominica palmarum, f.
palm-tree, s. palma, f.
palmy, a. floridus ; florens.
palpable, a. tractabilis ; fig. apertus, manifestus.
palpably, ad. manifesto.
palpitate, v.n. palpito, 1.
palpitation, s. palpitatio, f.
palsied, a. paralyticus.
palsy, s. paralysis, f.
paltriness, s. vilitas, f.
paltry, a. vilis ; (trifling) minutus, exiguus.
pamper, v.a. indulgeo, 2 (with dative).
pamphlet, s. libellus, m.
pamphleteer, s. libellorum scriptor, m.
pan, s. (vessel) patina, f. ; (of the knee) patella, f.

panacea, s. panacea, f.; panchrestum medicamentum, n.
pander, s. leno, m.; —, v.n. lenocinor, 1; *fig.* indulgeo, 2.
pandering, s. lenocinium, n.
panegyric, s. laudatio, f.; panegyricus, m.
panegyrist, s. panegyrista; laudator, præco, m.
panel, s. (of a door) tympanum, n.; (list of names) index, m.; album, n.
pang, s. dolor, angor, m. [mido, f.
panic, s. terror, pavor, metus, m.; for-
panic-struck, a. pavidus, exterritus.
pannier, s. clitellæ, f. pl.
panoply, s. armatura, f.
panorama, s. prospectus, m.
pansy, s. viola, f.
pant, v.n. palpito; trepido; anhelo, 1; *fig.* (to long for) gestio, 4.
Pantheon, s. Pantheum, n.
panther, s. panthera, f.
pan-tile, s. imbrex, m.
panting, a. anhelus; —, s. anhelitus, m.
pantomime, s. (play and actor) mimus, m.
pantry, s. cella penaria, f.; promptuarium, n. [(infants' food) puls, f.
pap, s. (nipple) papilla, mamilla, f.;
papa, s. pater, m.
papacy, s. papatus, m.
papal, a. papalis.
paper, s. (for writing on) charta, f.; (newspaper) acta diurna, n. pl.; —s, pl. scripta, n. pl.; litteræ, f. pl.
paper-maker, s. chartarius, m.
par, s. at —, par esse.
parable, s. parabola, f.
parabolical, a. per similitudines.
parade, s. (mil.) decursus; locus exercendi; (display) apparatus, m.; pompa, ostentatio, f.
parade, v.a. (mil.) instruo, 3; *fig.* ostento, 1; —, v.n. (to make evolutions) decurro, 3.
paradise, s. paradisus, m.; Elysii campi.
paradox, s. quod contra opinionem omnium est.
paradoxical, a. præter opinionem accidens.
paragon, s. specimen, exemplum, n.
paragraph, s. caput, n.
parallel, a. parallelus; *fig.* consimilis.
parallel, s. linea parallela; (comparison) collatio, comparatio, f.
parallel, v.a. exæquo; (to compare) comparo, 1; (to be equal) par esse. [f.
parallelogram, s. figura parallelogramma,
paralyse, v.a. debilito, enervo, 1.
paralysis, s. paralysis; *fig.* torpedo, f.; torpor, m.
paralytic, a. paralyticus.
paramount, a. supremus; summus.

paramour, s. (man) mœchus, adulter, m.; (woman) meretrix, pellex, adultera, f.
parapet, s. pluteus, m.
paraphernalia, s. apparatus, m.
paraphrase, s. paraphrasis, f.
paraphrase, v.a. liberius interpretor, 1.
parasite, s. parasitus, assecla, m.
parasitic, a. ut parasiticus.
parasol, s. umbella, f.; umbraculum, n.
parboiled, a. semicoctus.
parcel, s. pars, f.; (bundle) fasciculus, m.
parcel (out), v.a. partior, 4.
parch, v.a. arefacio, 3; torreo, 2.
parchment, s. membrana, f.
parchment-maker, s. membranarius, m.
pardon, s. venia, f.
pardon, v.a. ignosco, 3; condono, 1.
pardonable, a. condonandus.
pare, v.a. præcido, abrado, 3; (the nails, ungues reseco, 1.
parent, s. parens, c.
parentage, s. genus, n.; prosapia, origo, f.
parental, a. paternus; maternus.
parenthesis, s. interpositio, interclusio, f.
parenthetical, a. per interclusionem.
pariah, s. infimi ordinis homo, m.
paring, s. resegmen, n.
parish, s. parœcia, parochia, f.
parishioner, s. parochialis, m.
parity, s. paritas, æqualitas, f.
park, s. (for game) vivarium; (for pleasure) viridarium, n.; horti, m. pl.; (of artillery) tormenta, n. pl.
parlance, s. sermo, usus loquendi quotidianus, m. [quor, 3.
parley, s. colloquium, n.; —, v.n. collo-
parliament, s. parlamentum, n.
parliamentary, a. ad parlamentum pertinens.
parlour, s. cenaculum, n.
parochial, a. parochialis.
parody, s. parodia, f.; —, v.a. detorqueo, 2.
paroquet, s. psittacus minor, m.
paroxysm, s. accessio, f.
parricidal, a. ad parricidam *or* parricidium pertinens. [(murder) parricidium, n.
parricide, s. (murderer) parricida, c.;
parrot, s. psittacus, m.
parry, v.a. averto, defendo, 3; propulso, 1.
parsimonious, a. parcus, sordidus; —ly, ad. parce; sordide.
parsimony, s. parsimonia, f.
parsley, s. carum (mod. hort.).
parsnip, s. pastinaca, f.; peucedanum (mod. hort.).
parson, s. antistes sacrorum, clericus, m.
part, s. pars, portio; (in a play) persona, f.; partes, f. pl.; (duty) officium, n.; (of a town) regio, f.; in —, partim; —s, pl. ingenium, n.; indoles, f.

part, v.a. separo, 1 ; divido, 3 ; —, v.n. discedo, 3 ; digredior, abeo, 4 ; (to gape open) dehisco, fatisco, 3 ; **to — with,** dimitto, 3. [ceps esse.

partake, v.a. & n. (of) participo, 1 ; **parti-partaker,** s. particeps, c.

partial, a. per partes, iniquus ; **—ly,** ad. partim ; inique.

partiality, s. gratia ; iniquitas, f.

participant, a. & s. particeps.

participate, v.a. & n. particeps sum *or* fio.

participation, s. participium, n. ; societas, f.

participator, s. particeps, c.

participle, s. participium, n.

particle, s. particula, f. (also gr.).

particoloured, a. versicolor ; varius.

particular, a. proprius ; peculiaris ; singularis ; (fastidious) fastidiosus ; (especial) præcipuus ; **—ly,** ad. particulatim ; singillatim ; (especially) præsertim, præcipue.

particular, s. singula, n. pl. ; in —, v. **particularly.**

particularize, v.a. exsequor, persequor, 3.

parting, s. divisio, f. ; (from) discessus, m.

partisan, s. fautor, homo factiosus, m.

partisanship, s. studium partium, n. ; favor, m. ; gratia, f.

partition, s. partitio, f. ; (enclosure) sæptum, n. ; (of rooms) paries, m.

partition-wall, s. paries intergerivus, m.

partly, ad. partim ; nonnulla ex parte, in parte. [consors, c.

partner, s. socius, m. ; socia, f. ; particeps,

partnership, s. societas, consociatio, consortio, f.

partridge, s. perdix, c.

party, s. factio ; secta, f. partes, f. pl. ; (detachment) manus, f.

party-spirit, s. studium partium, n.

party-wall, s., v. **partition-wall.**

pasha, v. **pacha.**

paschal, a. paschalis.

pasquinade, s., v. **lampoon,** s.

pass, v.a. (go) eo, 4 ; vado, cedo, 3 ; (to go by) prætereo ; (to cross) transeo, 4 ; (a law, etc.) fero, 3 ; (to approve) approbo, 1 ; —, v.n. prætereo, 4 ; prætervehor, 3 ; (of time) prætereo, 4 ; (from one to another) migro, 1 ; (for) habeor, 2 ; **to — away,** transeo, 4 ; labor, effluo, 3 ; (to cease) cesso, 1 ; **to — by,** prætereo, 4 ; (also *fig.*) ; **to — on,** pergo, 3 ; **to — over,** trajicio, transgredior, 3 ; *fig.* prætereo, 4 ; **to — round,** circumfero, trado, 3 ; **to come to —,** evenio, 4 ; fio ; **to let —,** prætermitto, dimitto, 3.

pass, s. fauces, angustiæ, f. pl. ; saltus, m. ; (ticket) tessera, f.

passable, a. (of a way) pervius ; *fig.* mediocris, tolerabilis.

passably, ad. tolerabiliter ; mediocriter.

passage, s. (action) transitus, m. ; transitio, f. ; transmissio, trajectio ; (thoroughfare) transitio pervia, f. ; (of a book) locus, m.

passage-money, s. naulum, n.

passenger, s. viator ; (by water) vector, m.

passing, a. transiens ; præteriens ; *fig.* brevis, caducus ; (excellent) præstans.

passion, s. cupiditas, f. ; fervor, m. ; impetus, animi motus, m. ; (anger) ira, f. ; (for) studium, n. ; (love) amor, m.

passionate, a. fervidus, ardens, vehemens ; iracundus ; **—ly,** ad. ardenter ; iracunde, vehementer.

passionateness, s. iracundia, f.

passion-flower, s. passiflora (mod. hort.).

passionless, a. frigidus.

passive, a. patibilis ; passivus ; **—ly,** ad. passive.

Passover, s. Pascha, n. (indecl.).

passport, s. syngraphus, m.

pass-word, s. tessera, f.

past, a. præteritus ; (immediately preceding) proximus, superior ; —, s. præteritum tempus, n. ; actum tempus.

past, pr. præter ; (beyond) ultra.

pastern, s. suffrago, f.

pastille, s. pastillus, m.

pastime, s. oblectamentum, n. ; ludus, m.

pastoral, a. pastoralis ; pastorius.

pastoral, s. bucolica, n. pl.

pastry, s. crustum, bellaria, n. pl. ; crustula, n. pl.

pastry-cook, s. crustularius, m.

pasturage, s. pastus, m. ; pastio, f. ; (ground) pascuum, n. pastio, f.

pasture, s. pabulum, n. ; —, v.a. pasco, 3 ; —, v.n., v. **to graze.**

pasty, s. artocreas, n.

pat, a. idoneus ; —, ad. apte.

pat, v.a. permulceo, demulceo, 2.

patch, s. pannus, m.

patch, v.a. sarcio, resarcio, 4 ; assuo, 3.

patchwork, s. cento, m.

pate, s. caput, n.

paten, s. patina, f.

patent, a. apertus, manifestus.

patent, s. diploma, n.

paternal, a. paternus, patrius ; **—ly,** ad. patrie.

paternity, s. paternitas, f.

path, s. semita, f. ; trames, callis, m. ; *fig.* (course) via, f. [tice.

pathetic, a. patheticus ; **—ally,** ad. pathe-

pathless, a. invius.

pathos, s. pathos, n.

pathway, s. semita, f. ; callis, m.

patience, s. patientia, f. ; tolerantia.

patient, a. patiens ; tolerans ; **—ly,** ad. patienter ; æquo animo.

patient, s. ægrotus, m. ; ægrata, f.
patly, ad., v. **pat,** a.
patriarch, s. patriarcha, m.
patriarchal, a. patriarchicus.
patrician, a. & s. patricius.   [f.
patrimony, s. patrimonium, n. ; hereditas,
patriot, s. amans patriæ, m. ; bonus civis.
patriotic, a. amans patriæ ; bonus, pius.
patriotism, s. amor patriæ, m. ; pietas, f.
patrol, s. vigil, m. ; excubiæ, f. pl. ; —,
     v.n. excubias agere, 3.
patron, s. patronus, m.
patronage, s. patrocinium, præsidium, n.
patroness, s. patrona, f.
patronize, v.a. faveo, foveo, studeo, 2 ;
     (be present at) adsum, (dat.).
patronymic, s. patronymicum nomen, n.
patter, v.n. crepo, crepito, 1 ; (to talk)
     garrio, 4.
pattern, s. (sample) exemplar, exemplum ;
     (paragon) specimen, n.
paucity, s. paucitas, f.
paunch, s. venter, m.
pauper, s. pauper, egens, inops, c.
pauperism, s. egestas, inopia, f.
pause, s. pausa, mora ; intermissio, f. ;
     intervallum, n.
pause, v.n. intermitto, quiesco, 3.
pave, v.a. (viam saxo) sterno, 3.
pavement, s. pavimentum, n. ; stratura, f.
pavier, s. pavimentarius, m.
pavilion, s. tentorium, n.
paving, s. (act of —) stratura, f.
paving-beetle, s. fistuca, f.
paw, s. ungula, f. ; pes, m.
paw, v.a. pedibus pulso (terram), 1.   [m.
pawn, s. pignus, n. ; (in chess) latrunculus,
pawn, v.a. pignero ; oppignero, obligo, 1.
pawnbroker, s. pignerator, m.
pay, s. (mil.) stipendium, n. ; (wages, hire)
     merces, f. ; (profit) quæstus, fructus, m.
pay, v.a. (pecuniam debitam) solvo, 3 ;
     (stipendium) numero, 1 ; *fig.* persolvo,
     3 ; —, v.n. pendo, 3 ; (be profitable)
     prosum, proficio, 3 ; **to** — (for) (to hire)
     conduco, 3 ; *fig.* (to suffer) pœnas do, 1;
     to — **off,** dissolvo, 3.
payable, a. solvendus.
pay-day, s. dies stipendii solvendi, m. & f.
pay-master, s. tribunus ærarius ; (private)
     dispensator, m.   [money) pensio, f.
payment, s. (act) solutio, f. ; (sum of
pea, s. pisum, cicer, n. ; **sweet** *or* **ever-**
     lasting —, lathyrus (mod. hort.).·
peace, s. pax ; quies, f. ; otium, n. ; (of
     mind) tranquillitas animi, f.
peaceable, peaceful, a. pacis amans ;
     placabilis ; (of things) pacatus ; placi-
     dus, quietus.   [(bona) pace.
peaceably, peacefully, ad. pacate ; cum
peacefulness, s. tranquillitas, f.

peace-maker, s. pacificator, m.
peace-offering, s. placamen, placamen-
     tum, piaculum, n.   [malus Persica, f.
peach, s. malum Persicum, n. ; — -**tree,** s.
peacock, s. pavo, m.
peahen, s. pava, f.
peak, s. (of a mountain) cacumen, cul-
     men, n. ; apex, vertex, m.
peal, s. (of thunder) fragor ; (of bells) con-
     centus, m.
peal, v.n. sono, resono, 1.
pear, s. pirum, n. ; — -**tree,** s. ; pirus, f. ;
     prickly —, opuntia (mod. hort.).
pearl, s. margarita, baca, gemma, f.
pearly, a. gemmeus, gemmans.
peasant, s. rusticus, agrestis, agricola, m.
peasantry, s. agrestes, m. pl.
pebble, s. lapillus, calculus, m.
pebbly, a. calculosus, glareosus ; lapidosus.
peccadillo, s. levius delictum, n.
peccant, a. nocens.
peck, s. modius, m.
peck, v.a. rostro impeto, 3 ; mordeo, 2.
pectoral, a. pectoralis.
peculation, s. peculatus, m. ; res repe-
     tundæ, f. pl.
peculiar, a. proprius ; peculiaris ; præci-
     puus, singularis ; —**ly,** ad. præsertim,
     imprimis ; præcipue.
peculiarity, s. proprietas, f.
pecuniary, a. pecuniarius.
pedagogue, s. pædagogus ; (schoolmaster)
     magister, m.
pedant, s. scholasticus.
pedantic, a. litterarum ostentator, puti-
     dus ; professorius ; —**ally,** ad. putide.
pedantry, s. scholasticorum ineptiæ, f. pl. ;
     eruditio insulsa, f.
peddle, v. **to trifle.**
pedestal, s. stylobates, m. ; spira, f.
pedestrian, a. pedester ; pedibus (abla-
     tive) ; —, s. pedes, m.
pedigree, s. stemma, n.
pediment, s. fastigium, n.
pedlar, s. institor, m.
peel, s. cutis, tunica, f.; cortex, m.
peel, v.a. decortico, desquamo, 1.
peep, s. (of day) diluculum, n.; (look)
     contuitus, m.
peep, v.n. per rimam speculor, 1.
peep-hole, s. conspicillum, n.
peer, s. (equal) par ; (of the realm) pa-
     tricius, m.
peer, v.n., v. **to peep.**
peerless, a. unicus, incomparabilis, sin-
     gularis.
peevish, a. stomachosus, morosus, diffi-
     cilis ; —**ly,** ad. stomachose, morose.
peevishness, s. morositas, f. ; stomachus,
     m.

peg, s. paxillus, m.

peg, v.a. paxillo figo, 3.
pelf, s. lucrum, lucellum, n. ; pecunia, f.
pelican, s. pelicanus, onocrotalus, m.
pellet, s. globulus, m. ; pilula, f.
pellicle, s. pellicula, f.
pell-mell, ad. effuse, sine ordine, promiscue.
pellucid, a. pellucidus.
pelt, s. pellis, f.
pelt, v.a. peto, 3 ; lapido ; (to beat) verbero, 1.
pen, s. (to write with) calamus, stylus, m. ; (for sheep) ovile, n.
pen, v.a. scribo, compono, 3 ; (to shut in) includo, 3.
penal, a. pœnalis. [cium, n.
penalty, s. pœna ; mul(c)ta, f. ; supplipenance, s. satisfactio, f. ; (atonement) piaculum, n. ; (punishment) pœna, f.
pencil, s. graphis, f. ; peniculus, penicillus, m.
pendant, s. (ear-ring) stalagmium, n. ; (flag) vexillum, n.
pending, a. instans ; (law) sub judice.
pending, ad. & pr., v. during.
pendulum, s. libramentum, n.
penetrable, a. penetrabilis.
penetrate, v.a. penetro, 1.
penetration, s. acies mentis ; sagacitas, f.
peninsula, s. pæninsula, f.
penitence, s. pænitentia, f.
penitent, a. pænitens ; —ly, ad. pænitenter.
pen-knife, s. scalprum, n.
penman, s. scriba, m.
penmanship, s. ars bene scribendi, f.
pennant, pennon, s. vexillum, n.
penniless, a. omnium rerum egens, inops.
penny, s. as, nummus, denarius, m.
penny-royal, s. puleium, pulegium, n.
pension, s. merces annua, f. ; annuum beneficium, n.
pension, v.a. annuam mercedem præbeo, 2.
pensioner, s. cui annua merces præbetur.
pensive, a. cogitabundus.
pentateuch, s. pentateuchus, m.
pentecost, s. pentecoste, f.
penthouse, s. vinea, f.
pentstemon, s. pentstemon (mod. hort.).
penultimate, s. pænultimus ; —, s. pænultima syllaba, f.
penurious, a. parcus, tenax, sordidus.
penuriousness, s. tenacitas, parsimonia, f.
penury, s. egestas, inopia, penuria, f.
peony, s. pæonia, f.
people, s. populus, m. ; homines, m. pl. ; — say, dicunt ; common —, vulgus, n. ; plebs, f.
people, v.a. coloniam deduco, 3 ; frequento, 1.

pepper, s. piper, n.
pepper-mint, s. menta piperata, f.
perambulate, v.a. perambulo, 1.
perceivable, a. percipiendus.
perceive, v.a. sentio, 4 ; percipio, 3 ; video, 2 ; intelligo, 3.
percentage, s. rata portio, f.
perceptible, a. quod auribus percipi possit, percipiendus.
perceptibly, ad. ita ut cerni possit.
perception, s. perceptio, animadversio, f.
perch, s. (for birds) sedile (avium), n. ; (for measuring land) pertica ; (fish) perca, f.
perch, v.a. & n. insido, consido, assido, 3 ; assilio, 4.
perchance, ad. forte, fortasse, forsitan.
percolate, v.a. percolo, 1 ; —, v.n. percolor, permano, 1.
percolation, s. percolatio, f.
percussion, s. ictus, concussus, m.
perdition, s. exitium, n.
peregrination, s. peregrinatio, f. ; v. travel.
peremptorily, ad. præcise, imperiose, superbe.
peremptoriness, s. pertinacia, superbia, f.
peremptory, a. (law) peremptorius ; superbus ; (in opinion) pertinax.
perennial, a. perennis.
perfect, a. perfectus ; absolutus ; plenus, integer ; (gr.) præteritus ; —ly, ad. perfecte ; absolute ; (entirely) plane.
perfect, v.a. perficio, absolvo, 3.
perfection, s. perfectio ; absolutio, summa, f.
perfidious, a. perfidus, perfidiosus ; —ly, ad. perfide, perfidiose.
perfidy, s. perfidia, f.
perforate, v.a. perforo, terebro, 1.
perforation, s. (hole) foramen, n.
perform, v.a. perficio ; exsequor, fungor ; (to bring to pass) efficio ; (to accomplish) perago, 3.
performance, s. exsecutio ; actio, f. ; (work) opus, n.
performer, s. effector ; (player) actor, histrio, m.
perfume, s. odor, m.
perfume, v.a. suffio, 4.
perfumer, s. unguentarius, myropola, m.
perfumery, s. unguenta, n. pl. ; odores, m. pl.
perhaps, ad. fortasse, forte, forsitan.
peril, s. periculum, discrimen, n.
perilous, a. periculosus ; —ly, ad. periculose.
period, s. tempus, n. ; ætas, f. ; (end, conclusion) finis, c. ; terminus, m.
periodical, a. periodicus ; —ly, ad. temporibus certis.

peripatetic, a. & s. circumforaneus, peripateticus.

periphery, s. peripheria, f.

periphrasis, s. ambages, f. pl.

periphrastic, a. per ambages dictus.

perish, v.n. pereo, intereo, 4 ; exstinguor, cado, 3.

perishable, a. fragilis, caducus, infirmus.

peristyle, s. peristylium, peristylum, n.

periwig, s. capillamentum, n.

periwinkle, s. (plant) vinca, f. ; (shellfish) turbo litoreus, m.

perjure, v.a. pejero, perjuro, 1.

perjured, a. perjurus.

perjurer, s. perjurus (homo), m.

perjury, s. perjurium, n. ; **to commit —,** pejero, perjuro, 1.

permanency, s. perpetuitas, f.

permanent, a. diuturnus, mansurus, perpetuus ; **—ly,** ad. perpetuo.

permeable, a. pervius.

permeate, v.a. penetro, pervagor, pererro, 1.

permission, s. permissio, venia, f. ; **with your —,** pace tua, tua bona venia.

permit, v.a. sino, permitto, concedo, 3 ; **it is —ed,** licet, 2.

permutation, s. permutatio, f.

pernicious, a. perniciosus ; noxius ; **—ly,** ad. perniciose.

peroration, s. peroratio, f.

perpendicular, a. directus ; **—ly,** ad. perpendiculum, ad lineam.

perpetrate, v.a. perficio ; facio, committo, admitto, 3 ; perpetro, 1.

perpetration, s. perpetratio, f.

perpetrator, s. auctor ; reus, m.

perpetual, a. sempiternus ; perpetuus ; perennis ; continuus ; **—ly,** ad. perpetuo, semper, usque, continenter.

perpetuate, v.a. continuo, perpetuo, 1.

perpetuity, s. perpetuitas, f.

perplex, v.a. (to confound) turbo, 1 ; confundo, 3 ; (to mix) permisceo, 2.

perplexity, s. perturbatio ; anxietas, f.

perquisites, s. corollarium, n.

persecute, v.a. insector ; vexo.

persecution, s. insectatio ; vexatio, f.

persecutor, s. insectator ; vexator, m.

perseverance, s. perseverantia, constantia, assiduitas, f.

persevere, v.n. persevero, persto, 1.

persevering, a. constans ; tenax (propositi) ; assiduus.

perseveringly, ad. perseveranter, constanter.

persist, v.n. persto, persevero, 1.

persistence, s. permansio (in aliqua re), f.

person, s. homo, c. ; (appearance) species, forma, f. ; **any —,** quilibet, quivis ; **in —,** ipse (ego, ille, etc.).

personage, s. homo notus, m.

personal, a. privatus ; (law & gr.) personalis ; **—ly,** ad. per se ; ipse.

personate, v.a. personam gero, partes ago, 3.

personification, s. prosopopœia, f.

personify, v.a. humana specie induo, 3.

perspective, s. scœnographia, f.

perspicacious, a. perspicax, acutus ; **—ly,** ad. acute.

perspicacity, s. perspicacitas, f.

perspicuity, s. perspicuitas, f.   [spicue.

perspicuous, a. perspicuus ; **—ly,** ad. per-

perspiration, s. sudor, m.

perspire, v.n. sudo, 1 ; sudorem emitto, 3.

persuade, v.a. suadeo, persuadeo, 2.

persuasion, s. persuasio ; fides ; opinio, f.

persuasive, a. suasorius ; **—ly,** ad. apte ad persuadendum.

pert, a. procax.

pertain, v.n. pertineo, attineo, 2.

pertinacious, a. pertinax ; **—ly,** ad. pertinaciter.

pertinacity, s. pertinacia, f.

pertinency, s. convenientia, f.

pertinent, a. appositus (ad rem), aptus, idoneus ; **—ly,** ad. apposite.

pertly, ad. procaciter.

pertness, s. procacitas, f.

perturb, v.a. turbo, perturbo, 1.

perturbation, s. perturbatio, f.

peruke, s. capillamentum, n.

perusal, s. lectio, f.

peruse, v.a. lego, perlego, 3 ; (hastily) percurro, 3.

pervade, v.a. perfundo, 3 ; permano, 1 ; pervagor, 1.

perverse, a. perversus, pravus ; **—ly,** ad. perverse, prave, perperam.

perversion, s. depravatio, f.

perversity, s. perversitas, pravitas, f.

pervert, v.a. depravo, 1 ; perverto, corrumpo, 3.

perverter, s. corruptor, m.

pervious, a. pervius ; penetrabilis.

pest, s. pestis, pernicies, f.

pester, v.a. infesto, sollicito, vexo, 1.

pestiferous, a. pestifer, pestilens.

pestilence, s. pestilentia, f.

pestilential, a. pestilens, pestifer.

pestle, s. pilum, n.

pet, s. (little favourite) corculum, n. ; deliciæ, f. pl. ; (peevishness) stomachus, m.

pet, a. dilectus, carus.

pet, v.a., v. **to caress, to fondle.**

petal, s. floris folium ; petalum, n.

petition, s. preces, f. pl. ; libellus, m. ; petitio, f.

petition, v.a. supplico, 1 ; peto, 3.

petitioner, s. petitor, supplex, m.

petrify, v.a. in lapidem converto, 3 ; —, v.n. lapidesco, 3.
petticoat, s. indusium muliebre, n.
pettifogger, s. leguleius, rabula, m.
pettiness, s. parvitas, f.
pettish, a. stomachosus.
pettishness, s. stomachus, m.
petty, a. minutus, angustus ; (trifling) parvus.
petunia, s. petunia (mod. hort.).
pew, s. sella, f.
pewit, s., v. **lapwing.**
phalanx, s. phalanx, f.
phantom, s. phantasma, n. ; vana species, f. ; spectrum, n.
Pharisaic, a. Pharisaicus.
Pharisee, s. Pharisæus.
pharmaceutic, a. pharmaceuticus.
pharmacy, s. ars medicamentaria, f.
phase, s. *fig.* vices, f. pl.
pheasant, s. phasiana ; avis phasiana, f.
phenomenal, a. singularis.
phenomenon, s. res nova, f. ; ostentum, n.
phial, s. laguncula, f.
philanthropic, a. benignus, humanus.
philanthropist, s. (homo) generi humano amicus, m.
philanthropy, s. benignitas, humanitas, f.
Philippic, s. Philippica (oratio), f.
Philistine, s. Philisthæus, m.
philologer, philologist, s. philologus ; grammaticus, m.
philological, a. philologus.
philology, s. philologia, f.
philosopher, s. philosophus ; sapiens, m.
philosophic(al), a. philosophicus ; —**ly,** ad. philosophice ; *fig.* æquo animo.
philosophize, v.n. philosophor, 1.
philosophy, s. philosophia ; sapientia ; (theory) ratio, f. [n. pl.
philtre, s. amatorium poculum, n. ; philtra,
phlegm, s. pituita, f. ; phlegma, n. ; *fig.* lentitudo, f.
phlegmatic, a. phlegmaticus ; *fig.* tentus ; —**ly,** ad. lente.
phlox, s. phlox (mod. hort.).
phœnix, s. phœnix, m.
phrase, s. locutio, f. ; —, v.a. loquor, 3.
phraseology, s. ratio loquendi vel scribendi, f.
phthisical, a. phthisicus.
phthisis, s. phthisis, f.
physic, s. medicamentum, n.
physical, a. corporis (gen. of corpus) ; physicus ; —**ly,** ad. natura (abl.) ; physice.
physician, s. medicus, m.
physics, s. physica, n. pl.
physiognomist, s. physiognomon, m.
physiognomy, s. vultus ingenium, n.
physiological, a. physicus, physiologicus.

physiologist, s. physiologus, m.
physiology, s. physiologia, f.
pick, v.a. carpo, decerpo, 3 ; lego ; (to choose) eligo ; **to — off,** avello, 3 ; **to — out,** eligo, 3 ; **to — up,** tollo ; colligo, 3 ; **— holes in,** carpo, rodo, 3.
pick, s. (tool) dolabra ; (choicest part) flos, m., robur, n.
pickaxe, s. dolabra, f.
picked, a. (choice) delectus, lectus.
picket, s. (mil.) statio, f.
pickle, s. muria, f.
pickle, v.a. muria condio, 4.
pickled, a. muria conditus.
pickpocket, pickpurse, a. manticularius.
pictorial, a. pictoris (gen.) ; picturis distinctus.
picture, s. tabula, tabella ; effigies ; *fig.* descriptio, f.
picture, v.a. depingo, 3.
picture-gallery, s. pinacotheca, f.
picturesque, a. venustus, pulcher, amœnus.
pie, s. (bird) pica, f. ; (pastry) crustum, n.
piebald, a. maculosus, varius.
piece, s. (part) frustum, n. ; pars, portio, f. ; (fragment) fragmentum, n. ; (coin) nummus, m. ; (drama) fabula, f. ; **to tear to —s,** dilanio, lacero, 1.
piece, v.a. resarcio, 4 ; adjungo, 3.
piecemeal, ad. minutatim.
pied, a. maculosus, versicolor.
pier, s. pila ; (mole) moles, f. ; agger, m.
pierce, v.a. perforo, terebro, 1 ; (with a sword, etc.) transfigo, perfodio transadigo ; *fig.* (aliquem) dolore afficio, 3.
piercing, a. penetrabilis ; (of sounds) acutissimus ; *fig.* sagax ; —**ly,** ad. acute.
piety, s. pietas, f. [massa, f.
pig, s. porcus sus ; (of metal) later, m. ;
pigeon, s. columba, f. ; columbus, m.
pigeon-hole, s. loculamentum, n.
pigeon-house, s. columbarium, n.
pig-headed, a. *fig.* obstinatus.
pigment, s. pigmentum, n.
pig-sty, s. hara, f.
pike, s. (spear) hasta, lancea ; (tool) dolabra, f. ; (fish) lucius, lupus, m.
pilaster, s. parastas, f.
pilchard, s. clupea harengus minor, m.
pile, s. (heap) acervus, cumulus, m. ; congeries, f. ; (of firewood) rogus, m. ; (for building) sublica, f. ; (nap of cloth) villus, m.
pile, v.a. coacervo, cumulo, aggero, accumulo, 1 ; exstruo, congero, 3.
pile-driver, s. fistuca, f.
piles, s. hæmorrhoida, f.
pilfer, v.a. surripio, 3 ; suffuror, 1.
pilferer, s. fur, m.
pilfering, s. direptio, f.

pilgrim, s. peregrinator.
pilgrimage, s. peregrinatio, **f.**
piling, s. exstructio, f.
pill, s. pilula, f.   [præda, f. ; spolium, n.
pillage, s. (act) vastatio, direptio ; (booty)
pillage, v.a. populor, prædor, vasto,
   spolio, 1 ; diripio.
pillager, s. prædator, prædo, spoliator, m.
pillaging, a. prædabundus.
pillar, s. (support, prop) columna ; pila, f.
pillared, a. columnatus.
pillory, s. numella, f.
pillow, s. pulvinus, m. ; cervical, n.
pilot, s. gubernator, rector, m. ; —, v.a.
   guberno, 1 ; rego, 3.
pimp, s. leno, m. ; —, v.n. lenocinium
   facio, 3.
pimpernel, s. anagallis, f.
pimple, s. pustula, pusula, f.
pimpled, pimply, a. pustulosus.   [m.
pin, s. acus ; acicula, f. ; (nail, peg) clavus,
pin, v.a. acu figo ; affigo, 3.
pin-money, s. peculium (uxoris), n.
pincers, s. forceps, c.
pinch, v.a. vellico, 1 ; (as cold) (ad)uro, 3 ;
   (to crowd) coarto, 1 ; (of poverty)
   premo, 3 ; (to hurt) lædo, 3 ; **to — off,**
   avello, 3.
pinch, s. vellicatio, f. ; *fig.* necessitas, f. ;
   summæ angustiæ, f. pl.
pinching, a. angustus ; (of cold) penetrabilis.
pine, s. pinus, f.   [conficior.
pine, v.n. (away) tabesco, 3 ; marcesco,
pine-apple, s. nux pinea, f. ; ananas (mod.
   hort.).
pinion, s. penna, f.
pinion, v.a. revincio, 4.
pink, s. dianthus, f.
pink, a. (of colour) roseus.
pink, v.a. pungo, 3 ; perforo, 1.
pinnace, s. lembus, m.; cymba, f.
pinnacle, s. fastigium, n.
pint, s. (measure) sextarius, m.
pioneer, s. (mil.) cunicularius ; explorator
   viæ ; *fig.* præcursor, m.   [pie, sancte.
pious, a. pius ; (pure) sanctus ; **—ly,** ad.
pip, s. (of fowls) pituita, f.; (of fruit)
   semen, n.; nucleus, m.; (of grapes)
   acinus, m.
pip, v.n. pipio, 4 ; pipilo, 1.
pipe, s. (tube) tubus, m. ; (mus.) fistula,
   f. ; tibia, arundo, f. ; calamus, m.
pipe, v.n. fistula cano, 3.
piper, s. fistulator, tibicen, m.
pipkin, s. olla, f.
piquant, a. *fig.* salsus, facetus ; acutus ;
   —ly, ad. salse, facete, acute.
pique, s. offensio, f. ; offensa, odium, n.
pique, v.a. offendo, 3 ; stimulo, 1 ; —
   oneself on, jactare se de aliqua re, 1.

piracy, s. piratica.
pirate, s. prædo maritimus, pirata, **m.**
piratical, a. piraticus.
pish, i. phu !
pismire, s. formica, f.
pistachio, s. pistacium, n.
pit, s. fossa, fovea, scrobis, f. ; puteus,
   m. ; (abyss, gulf) barathrum, n. ; (in
   theatre) cavea, f. ; (of the arm) ala, f. ;
   (quarry) fodina, f.
pit, v.a. excavo, 1 ; (in fight) committo, 3.
pitapat, ad. palpitans.
pitch, s. pix, f. ; summum fastigium, n. ;
   (mus.) sonus, m.
pitch, v.a. (with pitch) pico, 1 ; (a tent,
   the camp) pono, 3 ; (to fling) conjicio,
   3 ; —, v.n. fluctuo, 1.
pitcher, s. urceus, m.
pitchfork, s. furca, f.
pitchy, a. piceus ; (dark) fuscus, niger ;
   obscurus, caliginosus.
piteous, a. misericors ; (miserable) miserabilis ; miser ; **—ly,** ad. miserabiliter,
   misere.
pitfall, s. fovea, f.
pith, s. medulla, f.
pithily, ad. nervose.
pithiness, s. robur, n. ; vigor, m.
pithless, a. *fig.* aridus, jejunus.
pithy, a. medulla abundans ; nervosus ;
   fig. sententiosus.
pitiable, a. miserabilis ; flebilis, lamentabilis ; afflictus.
pitiably, ad. miserabiliter, misere.
pitiful, a. misericors ; (pitiable) miserabilis ; (contemptible, mean) abjectus ;
   —ly, ad. misericorditer ; miserabiliter ;
   abjecte.
pitifulness, s. misericordia ; (meanness)
   exiguitas, f.
pitiless, a. immisericors ; durus, v. **cruel ;**
   —ly, ad. immisericorditer, duriter.
pittance, s. (allowance of food) demensum, n. ; (alms) stips, f.
pity, s. misericordia, miseratio, f.
pity, v.a. & n. miseret (me alicujus),
   misereor, 2 ; miseror, 1 ; miseresco, 3.
pivot, s. cardo, m.
pix, s. pyxis, f.
placability, s. placabilitas, clementia, f.
placable, a. placabilis, exorabilis ; clemens.   [affigere, 3.
placard, s. edictum, n. ; —, v.a. edicta
place, s. locus, m. ; (office) munus ,n. ; **in
   the first —,** *fig.* primum, primo.
place, v.a. pono, 3 ; loco, colloco, 1.
placid, a. placidus, tranquillus ; quietus ;
   —ly, ad. placide, tranquille, quiete.
placidity, s. ingenium placidum, n.
plagiarism, s. furtum litterarium, n.
plagiarist, plagiary, s. plagiarius, **m.**

plague, s. pestilentia; *fig.* pestis, f.; —! i. malum!

plague, v.a. vexo, crucio, 1.

plaice, s. platessa, f.

plain, s. campus, m.; planities, f.; æquor, n. (also of water).

plain, a. (smooth) planus; (not ornamented) inornatus; (distinct) clarus; (simple) simplex; (evident) apertus, manifestus; sincerus.

plainly, ad. distincte, clare, plane; simpliciter; (evidently) manifeste, aperte, perspicue.

plainness, s. (evenness) planities; (simpleness) simplicitas; (clearness) perspicuitas, f.

plaintiff, s. petitor, m.; accusator, m.

plaintive, a. flebilis; querulus; —ly, ad. flebiliter.

plait, s. ruga, f.; sinus, m.

plait, v.a. implico, 1; intexo, 3.

plan, s. (project) consilium, propositum, n.; (of ground) forma, designatio, f.

plan, v.a. (to scheme) excogito, 1; (to draw) designo, 1.

plane, s. (tool) runcina, f.; (level surface) superficies, f.

plane, v.a. runcino, 1.

planet, s. planeta, m.; stella erratica, f.

plane-tree, s. platanus, f.

plank, s. axis, m.; tabula, f.

plank, v.a. contabulo, coasso, 1.

plant, s. herba, planta, f.

plant, v.a. planto, 1; sero; (to settle) statuo, constituo, 3; (fix) figo; (a colony) deduco, 3.

plantain, s. plantago, f.

plantation, s. plantarium, n.

planter, s. sator; colonus, m.

planting, s. satus, m.

plash, s. (noise) crepitus, m.

plash, v.n. (make a noise) crepo, 1.

plaster, s. tectorium; gypsum; (med.) emplastrum, n.

plaster, v.a. trullisso, gypso, 1; induco; illino, 3.

plasterer, s. tector, m.

plastic, a. plasticus.

plat, s. & v.a., v. **plait**.

plate, s. lamina, bractea, f.; (silver for table) vasa argentea, n. pl.; (dish) patella, f.

plated, a. bracteatus.

platform, s. suggestus, m.; suggestum, n.

Platonic, a. Platonicus.

platter, s. patella, f.

plaudit, s. plausus, clamor, m.

plausibility, s. (captiosa) probabilitas, f.; species, f.

plausible, a. probabilis; speciosus.

plausibly, ad. probabiliter.

play, s. (act of playing) ludus; lusus, m.; (movement) motus, m.; (scope) area, f.; locus, m.; (at a theatre) fabula, comœdia, tragœdia, f.; (at hazard) alea, f.; **fair —,** æquitas, f.

play, v.a. & n. ludo, 3; (to frolic, etc.) lascivio, 4; luxurio, 1; (on musical instruments) cano, 3; (to gamble) aleam exerceo, 2; (as actor) partes ago, 3.

play-bill, s. libellus, m.

player, s. (on the stage) histrio, actor; (at hazard) aleator; (on an instrument) fidicen, tibicen, citharista, m.

play-fellow, s. collusor, m.

playful, a. lascivus, jocosus, ludibundus; —ly, ad. jocose.

playfulness, s. lascivia, f.

playhouse, s. theatrum, n.

plaything, s. crepundia, n. pl.; pupa, f.

plea, s. (excuse) excusatio, causa, f.

plead, v.a. & n. causas ago; (for one) (aliquem) defendo; (against) contra aliquem causam dico, 3; (urge in excuse) excuso, 1.

pleader, s. causidicus, advocatus, m.

pleading, s. causæ dictio, defensio, f.

pleasant, a. amœnus jucundus gratus; urbanus; lepidus; —ly, ad. jucunde; lepide.

pleasantness, s. jucunditas, f.; lepor, m.; (of manners) comitas, urbanitas, f.

pleasantry, s. dicacitas, f.; facetiæ, f. pl.; jocus, m.

please, v.a. & n. (to give pleasure) placeo, 2; delecto, 1; **as you —,** ut vobis libet.

pleasing, a. gratus; lepidus; jucundus.

pleasurable, a., v. **pleasant**.

pleasure, s. voluptas; jucunditas, f.; deliciæ, f. pl.; (caprice) libido, f.; (will) arbitrium, n.

pleasure-ground, s. viridarium, n.

plebeian, a. & s. plebeius; vulgaris.

pledge, s. pignus, n.; (surety) vas, præs, m.; (proof) testimonium, n. [mitto, 3.

pledge, v.a. pignero, 1; spondeo, 2; pro-

Pleiads, s. Pleiades, um, f. pl.

plenary, a. plenus, perfectus.

plenipotentiary, s. legatus.

plenitude, s. plenitudo, plenitas, f.

plentiful, a. largus, affluens, uber, copiosus, abundans; —ly, ad. large, abunde, copiose, ubertim.

plenty, s. copia, abundantia, ubertas, f.

pleonasm, s. pleonasmus, m.

plethora, s. pletura, f.

pleurisy, s. pleuritis, f.

pliable, pliant, a. flexibilis; lentus, mollis; flexilis; tractabilis; mansuetus.

plight, s. conditio, f.; status, m.

plight, v.a. spondeo, 2.

plod, v.n. assidue laboro, 1.

plodder, s. sedulus homo, m.

plodding, a. laboriosus, assiduus, sedulus.

plot, s. (conspiracy) conjuratio; (surveying) designatio, f.; *fig.* (of a play, etc.) argumentum, n.

plot, v.n. conjuro, 1; —, v.a. molior, 4; excogito, 1.

plotter, s., v. **conspirator.**

plough, s. aratrum, n.; —, v.a. aro, 1; *fig.* (the sea) scindo, 3; aro, sulco, seco, 1.

plough-boy, s. arator, m.

ploughing, s. aratio, f.

plough-man, arator, m.

plough-share, s. vomer, m.

plough-tail, s. stiva, f.

plover, s. scolopax, f.

pluck, s. (pull) vellicatio, f.; (courage) animus, n.

pluck, v.a. (pull) vello, 3; vellico, 1; (gather) carpo, decerpo; (off) avello; deripio; (out) evello; eripio; (up) eruo, 3; *fig.* **to — up** (courage) colligo, 3.

plug, s. obturamentum, n.; —, v.a. obturo, 1.

plum, s. prunum, n.; **—-tree,** s. prunus, f.

plumage, s. plumæ, pennæ, f. pl.

plumber, s. plumbarius, m.

plumb-line, plumb-rule, s., v. **plummet.**

plume, s. penna, pluma; (crest) crista, f.; —, v.a. pennis adorno, 1; glorior, 2; **to — oneself,** superbio, 4; jacto, 1.

plummet, s. perpendiculum, n.; linea, f.

plump, a. nitidus, obesus; corpulentus.

plumpness, s. obesitas, f.; nitor, m.

plumy, a. plumosus.

plunder, s. (booty) præda, f.; spolium, n.; (act of plundering) rapina, direptio, f.; (stolen goods) furta, n. pl.

plunder, v.a. prædor, 1; diripio, 3; spolio, vasto, populor, 1.

plunderer, s. prædator, populator, vastator, m.

plundering, s. rapina, direptio, prædatio, f.

plundering, a. (quality) prædatorius; (act) prædabundus.

plunge, v.a. mergo, summergo; (a sword) condo, subdo (in) (with abl.) 3; —, v.n. immergor; *fig.* se mergere in . . ., 3.

plural, a. pluralis; **—ly,** ad. pluraliter.

plurality, s. multitudo, f.; numerus major, m. [2; (solicit) aggredior, 3.

ply, v.a. & n. exerceo; (to urge) urgeo,

pocket, s. (pouch) marsupium, n.; crumena, f.; (fold of the dress) sinus, m.

pocket-book, s. pugillares, m. pl.

pocket-handkerchief, s. sudarium, n.

pocket-money, s. peculium, n.

pod, s. siliqua, f.

poem, s. poema, carmen, n.

poesy, s. poesis, f.

poet, s. poeta, vates, m.

poetaster, s. poeta mediocris *or* malus, m.

poetess, s. poetria, f.

poetical, a. poeticus; **—ly,** ad. poetice.

poetics, s. ars poetica, f.

poetry, s. (art) poetice; (poems) poesis, f.; carmen, n.

poignancy, s. acerbitas, f.

poignant, a. acerbus.

point, s. punctum; (pointed end) acumen, n.; (of swords, etc.) mucro, m.; (of a spear) cuspis, f.; *fig.* quæstio, f.; casus, m.; res, f.; argumentum, n.; **— of view,** judicium, n.; **critical —,** discrimen, n.; **main** *or* **chief —,** caput, n.; **be on the — of,** in eo esse ut.

point, v.a. (to sharpen) acuo; (aim) intendo; **to — at,** monstro, 1; **to — out,** monstro; (to mark out) designo, 1.

point-blank, ad. præcise; prorsus, omnino.

pointed, a. præacutus; acutus; *fig.* salsus; (stinging) aculeatus.

pointedly, ad. acriter, acute; plane, aperte.

pointer, s. index, c.; (mod.) canis venaticus, m.

pointless, a. obtusus; *fig.* insulus, frigidus.

poise, s. pondus; (equilibrium) æquipondium, n.

poise, v.a. libro, 1.

poison, s. venenum, virus, n.

poison, v.a. (a thing) veneno; (a person) veneno neco; *fig.* vitio, 1.

poisoner, s. veneficus, m.; venefica, f.

poisoning, s. veneficium, n.

poisonous, a. venenatus; veneficus; venenifer.

poke, s. sacculus, m.; **to buy a pig in a —,** *fig.* aleam emo, 3.

poke, v.a. (alicui) latus fodico, 1; (touch) tango, 3; (move) moveo, 2.

poker, s. rutabulum, n.

polar, a. arctous.

pole, s. (staff) asser, m.; pertica, f.; contus, m.; (of the earth) polus, axis, m.

pole-axe, s. malleus, m.

polemics, s. controversiæ, f. pl.

pole-star, s. septentrio, m.

police, s. securitatis urbanæ cura *or* custodia, f.

policeman, s. vigil, lictor, m.

policy, s. reipublicæ, administratio; (craft) astutia, calliditas, f.; (stratagem) ars, f.; dolus, m.; (in good sense) consilium; (bond) chirographum, n.

polish, v.a. polio; expolio, 4; limo, levo, 1.

polish, s. nitor, levor, m.; *fig.* lima, f.

polisher, s. politor, m.

polishing, s. (act) politio; politura, expolitio, f.

polite, a. comis, urbanus ; affabilis, humanus ; — **literature,** litteræ humaniores, f. pl.
politely, ad. comiter, humane.
politeness, s. urbanitas, comitas, humanitas, f.
politic, a. prudens.
political, a. publicus, civilis ; —**ally,** ad. quod ad rempublicam attinet. [tus, m.
politician, s. vir rerum publicarum peri-
politics, s. res publica, f.
poll, s. (head) caput ; (voting) suffragium, n. [suffragia viritim do, 1.
poll, v.a. (trees) decacumino ; (to vote)
pollard, s. arbor, decacuminata, f.
pollen, s. pollen, n.
polling-booth, s. sæptum ovile, n.
poll-tax, s. exactio capitum, f.
pollute, v.a. inquino, contamino, maculo, commaculo, fœdo, 1 ; polluo, 3.
pollution, s. colluvio ; impuritas, macula, labes, f.
poltroon, s., v. **coward,** s.
polyanthus, s. primula (mod. hort.).
polygon, s. polygonum, n.
polygonal, a. polygonius, multangulus.
polypody fern, s. polypodium, n.
polypus, s. polypus, m.
pomade, s. capillare, unguentum, n.
pomegranate, s. malum granatum, malum Punicum, n. ; — **-tree,** malus Punica, f.
pommel, v.a. pulso, verbero, 1.
pomp, s. pompa, f. ; splendor, apparatus, m.
pomposity, s. magniloquentia, f.
pompous, a. magniloquus ; *fig.* inflatus.
pompously, ad. inflate, magnifice.
pond, s. stagnum, n. ; lacus, m.
ponder, v.a. & n. considero, pensito, meditor, 1 ; perpendo, 3.
ponderous, a. prægravis, ponderosus.
poniard, s. pugio, m. ; sica, f.
pontiff, s. pontifex, m.
pontifical, a. pontificalis ; pontificius.
pontificals, s. vestimenta pontificalia, n. pl.
pontificate, s. pontificatus, m.
pontoon, s. ponto, m.
pony, s. mannulus, m.
pool, s. lacuna, . ; stagnum, n. ; (in play) v. **stakes.**
poop, s. puppis, f.
poor, a. pauper ; egenus, inops ; (of soil) macer ; *fig.* tenuis ; mediocris ; miser.
poor-house, s. ptochotrophium, ptocheum, n.
poorly, a. æger ; —, ad. parum, mediocriter ; misere.
poorness, s. paupertas ; pauperies ; *fig.* sterilitas, f.

pop, s. crepitus, fragor, m.
pope, s. papa, m.
popedom, s. papatus, m.
popish, a. papalis.
poplar, s. populus, f. [(mod. hort.).
poppy, s. papaver, n. ; **tree** —, romneya
populace, s. vulgus, n. ; plebs, f.
popular, a. popularis ; gratiosus ; (common) vulgaris ; —**ly,** ad. populariter, vulgo.
popularity, s. favor populi, m. ; studium populi, n. ; gratia, f. [(scil. locum).
populate, v.a. populo frequentem facio,
population, s. incolæ urbis, civitatis, etc. c. pl.
populous, a. populo frequens, celeber.
populousness, s. multitudo incolarum, f. ; celebritas, frequentia, f.
porcelain, s. murra, f. ; murrina, n. pl.
porch, s. vestibulum, n. ; porticus, f.
porcupine, s. hystrix, f.
pore, s. foramen, n.
pore, v.n. (over) incumbo, 3.
pork, s. porcina, suilla, f.
porker, s. porcus, porculus, porcellus, m.
porous, a. rarus.
porphyry, s. porphyrites, m.
porpoise, s. porculus marinus, m.
porridge, s. puls, f.
porringer, s. patina, f. ; catinus, m.
port, s. portus, m. ; (carriage) incessus, gestus, m. [potest.
portable, a. (mod.) quod (facile) portari
portage, s. vectura, f.
portal, s., v. **gate.**
portcullis, s. catarracta, m.
portend, v.a. præsagio, 4 ; auguror, 1 ; portendo, 3 ; præmonstro, significo, 1.
portent, s. ostentum, portentum, prodigium, n.
portentous, a. monstruosus, prodigiosus.
porter, s. janitor, ostriarius, custos ; (carrier) bajulus, m.
portfolio, s. scrinium, n.
portico, s. porticus, f.
portion, s. pars ; portio ; (of a wife) dos, f.
portion, v.a. partior, 4 ; (a daughter) doto, 1 ; dotem do, 1.
portliness, s. obesitas, f.
portly, a. obesus.
portmanteau, s. mantica, f. ; vidulus, m.
portrait, s. imago, effigies, f.
portraiture, s. imago ; *fig.* descriptio, f.
portray, v.a. pingo, 3 ; delineo, 1 ; *fig.* depingo, describo, 3.
portress, s. janitrix, f.
pose, s. status, m. ; (pretence) simulatio, f.
pose, v.a. refuto, 1.
position, s. (act of placing) collocatio, positio, f. ; (position itself) situs, positus ; *fig.* status, m. ; condicio, f. ; (thesis) thesis, f.

positive, a. certus ; positivus ; *fig.* confidens ; pervicax ; **—ly,** ad. præcise ; confidenter ; pervicaciter.

positiveness, s. veritas ; *fig.* pervicacia, f.

possess, v.a. possideo, teneo, habeo, 2 ; (of feelings overpowering the mind) occupo, 1 ; invado, 3 ; (induce) animum induco, 3.

possessed, a. (mad) lymphatus, attonitus.

possession, s. possessio, f. ; (estate) bona, n. pl. ; **in the — of,** penes.

possessive, a. (gr.) possessivus.

possessor, s. possessor, dominus, m.

possibility, s. possibilitas, f. ; (opportunity) facultas, copia, potestas, f.

possible, a. possibilis.

possibly, ad. fieri potest ut ; (perhaps) fortasse.

post, s. (stake) sudis, f. ; stipes, palus, m. ; (door-post) postis, m. ; (station) statio, sedes locus, f. ; (office) munus, n. ; (to travel with) cursus publicus, m.

post, v.a. colloco, 1 ; pono ; constituo, 3 ; (a letter) tabellario litteras do, 1.

postboy, s. veredarius, m.

post-chaise, s. vehiculum publicum, n. ; ræda cursualis, f.

posterior, a. posterior.

posterity, s. posteri ; minores, m. pl.

postern, s. postica, f. ; posticum, n.

post-haste, s. propera festinatio, f. ; **—,** ad. propere.

post-horse, s. equus cursualis, veredus, m.

posthumous, a. postumus.

postilion, s. veredarius, m.

posting, s. cursus publicus, m.

postman, s. tabellarius, m.

postpone, v.a. differo, profero, 3 ; prorogo, 1.

posture, s. status, habitus, gestus, m.

posy, s., v. **nosegay.**

pot, s. olla, f. ; aenum, vas, n.

potable, a. potabilis.

potash, s. sal alcalinum, n.

potato, s. solanum (mod. hort.).

pot-bellied, a. ventriosus.

pot-companion, s. compotor, m.

potentate, s. princeps, rex, tyrannus, m.

potential, a. (gr.) potentialis.

pot-herbs, s. holera, n. pl.

pot-house, s. taberna, cauponia, f.

potion, s. potio, f.

potsherd, s. testa, f.

pottage, s. jus, n.

potter, s. figulus, m. ; **of a —,** a. figularis.

pottery, s. (potter's trade) figlina, f. ; (potter's ware) figlinum, n. ; fictilia, n. pl. ; (potter's workshop) figlina, f.

pouch, s. pera, f. ; sacculus, m.

poulterer, s. pullarius, m.

poultice, s. malagma, fomentum, cataplasma, n.

poultice, v.a. malagma impono, 3.

poultry, s. aves cohortales, f. pl. ; **—-yard,** s. cohors, f.

pounce, s. (swoop) impetus, m. ; (for drawing) pulvis, f.

pounce, v.n. involo, 1 ; insilio, 4.

pound, s. (weight and money) libra, f. ; (for cattle) sæptum, n.

pound, v.a. (to bruise) contundo, contero ; (cattle) includo, 3.

pour, v.a. & n. fundo ; fundor, 3 ; **to — down,** (to send forth) dejicio, 3 ; (of rain, v.n.) ruo ; *fig.* ingruo, 3 ; **to — out,** effundo, profundo, 3 ; v.n. effundor.

pouring, a. (of rain) effusus.

poverty, s. paupertas, pauperies, inopia, penuria, egestas, f.

powder, s. pulvis, m.

powder, v.a. pulvere conspergo, 3 ; (to reduce to powder) in pulverem redigo, 3.

power, s. vis ; potestas, f. ; jus ; imperium, n. ; (mil.) copiæ, f. pl. ; *fig.* (of mind) dotes animi, f. ; **in (one's) —,** penes (acc.).

powerful, a. (præ)validus ; potens ; (effectual) efficax ; **—ly,** ad. potenter ; efficaciter.

powerless, a. invalidus ; infirmus, imbecillus ; impotens ; (vain) irritus ; inefficax ; **be — to,** non possum, nequeo, 4.

practicable, a. quod fieri potest.

practical, (opposite to contemplative) activus ; (taught by experience) usu doctus ; **—ly,** ad usu, ex usu ; (almost) pæne.

practice, s. usus, m. ; exercitatio ; experientia ; (custom) consuetudo, f.

practise, v.a. & n. exerceo, 2 ; tracto, 1 ; (to do habitually) factito, 1.

practitioner, s. exercitor ; (medical) medicus, m.

prætor, s. prætor, m.

prætorian, a. prætorius.

prætorship, s. prætura, f.

pragmatic, a. pragmaticus.

praise, s. laus, laudatio ; f. præconium, n.

praise, v.a. laudo, collaudo, prædico, 1 ; effero, 3.

praiser, s. laudator, prædicator, m.

praiseworthy, a. laudabilis, laudandus.

prance, v.n. exsulto, 1.

prank, s. ludus, m. ; fraus, f.

prate, etc., v. **prattle.**

prattle, s. garrulitas, f.

prattle, v.n. garrio, 4 ; blatero, 1.

prattler, s. blatero, garrulus, m.

prawn, s. cancer squilla, m.

pray, v.a. precor, exoro, supplico, flagito, 1 ; oro, 1 ; **to — for,** intercedo, 3 ; (for a thing) peto, posco, 3 ; **to — to,** adoro ; supplico, 1.
prayer, s. preces, f. pl. ; precatio, f.
preach, v.a. & n. prædico, 1 ; **to — down,** diffamo, 1 ; **to — up,** jacto ; vendito, 1.
preacher, s. orator, m.
preaching, s. prædicatio, hortatio, f.
preamble, s. exordium, prooemium, n.
prebend, s. præbenda, f.
prebendary, s. præbendarius, m.
precarious, a. incertus, precarius ; —ly, ad. precario.
precaution, s. cautio, provisio, f.
precede, v.a. antecedo, prægredior, præcurro, 3 ; anteeo, præeo, 4.
precedence, s. jus præcedendi, n. ; principatus, m.
precedent, s. exemplum, n.
preceding, a. præcedens, antecedens.
precentor, s. præcentor (chori), m.
precept, s. præceptum, n.
preceptor, s. præceptor, magister, m.
precinct, s. termini, limites, m. pl.
precious, a. pretiosus, carus ; dilectus ; —ly, ad. preciose, care.
preciousness, s. caritas, f.
precipice, s. locus præceps, m.
precipitate, v.a. & n. præcipito, 1 ; (to hurry) accelero, festino, maturo, 1.
precipitate, a. præceps ; _fig._ inconsultus ; —ly, ad. præpropere.
precipitation, s. præcipitatio, festinatio, f.
precipitous, a. præceps, præruptus, declivis.
precise, a. certus, definitus ; (very) ipse ; _fig._ (exact) accuratus, exactus ; (of manner) rigidus ; —ly, ad. accurate.
preciseness, precision, s. accuratio, f.
preclude, v.a. præcludo, 3 ; arceo, prohibeo, 2.
precocious, a. præcox ; festinatus, præmaturus.
precocity, s. maturitas festinata, f.
preconceive, v.a. præsentio, 4.
preconception, s. præjudicata opinio, f.
precursor, s. prænuntius, præcursor, m.
predatory, a.& s. prædatorius ; rapax.
predecessor, s. decessor, antecessor, m.
predestinate, predestine, v.a. prædestino, 1.
predestination, s. prædestinatio, f.
predicament, s. prædicamentum, n. ; (difficulty) angustiæ, f. pl.
predicate, v.a. & n. prædico, 1.
predicate, s. prædicatum, n.
predict, v.a. prædico, 3 ; auguror, vaticinor, 1.
prediction, s. prædictio, f. ; prædictum ; vaticinium, n. ; vaticinatio, f.

predilection, s. studium præcipuum, n.
predispose, v.a. præparo, 1.
predisposed, a. proclivis.
predisposition, s. proclivitas, f.
predominant, a. **be —,** prævaleo.
predominate, v.n. prævaleo, 2.
pre-eminence, s. excellentia, præstantia, f. ; (supreme rule) principatus, m.
pre-eminent, a. insignis, præstans, præcipuus ; —ly, ad. præstanter, præcipue.
pre-exist, v.n. ante sum, ante existo, 3.
preface, s. præfatio, f. ; exordium, prooemium, n. ; —, v.a. præfari, 1.
prefect, s. præfectus, m.
prefecture, s. præfectura, f.
prefer, v.a. præfero, præpono, antefero, antepono, 3 ; (to like better) malo ; (to exhibit) exhibeo, 2 ; (to promote) effero, 3. [præstat.
preferable, a. potior, præstantior ; **it is —,**
preferably, ad. potius. [in —, potius.
preference, s. **to give —** (to), antepono, 3 ;
preferment, s. dignitas, f. [scribo, 3.
prefix, v.a. præfigo, (in writing) præ-
prefix, s. syllaba præposita, f.
pregnancy, s. graviditas ; prægnatio, f.
pregnant, a. gravida, prægnans, gravis ; _fig._ (important) gravis.
prejudge, v.a. præjudico, 1.
prejudice, s. opinio præjudicata, f. ; detrimentum, n.
prejudice, v.a. in suspicionem adduco, 3 ; (to injure) lædo, 3 ; **be —d against,** suspicor, 1.
prejudicial, a. noxius.
prelate, s. prælatus, præsul, m.
prelection, s. prælectio, f.
preliminary, s. prooemium, n. ; prolusio, f. ; —, a. primus.
prelude, s. prooemium, n. ; _fig._ prolusio, f.
prelude, v.a. & n. præludo, proludo, 3.
premature, a. præmaturus ; _fig._ præproperus ; —ly, ad. præmature.
premeditate, v.a. præmeditor, 1.
premeditation, s. præmeditatio, f.
premise, v.a. præfari, 1.
premises, s. (house) domus ; (estate) fundus, m. ; villa, f. ; prædium, n. ; (in logic) præmissa, n. pl.
premiss, s. præmissa, f. ; præmissa, n. pl.
premium, s. præmium, n.
premonition, s. præsagium, n.
preoccupation, s. præoccupatio, f. ; _fig._ v. **prejudice,** s.
preoccupy, v.a. præoccupo, 1 ; (also _fig._).
preparation, s. præparatio, f. ; paratus, apparatus, m.
prepare, v.a. paro, comparo, præparo, 1 ; (furnish) orno, adorno, 3 ; (study) medi- tor, 1 ; —, v.n. comparo, 1 ; se accingere, 3.

preponderate, v.n. & a. præpondero, 1; prævaleo, 2.
preposition, s. præpositio, f.
prepossess, v.a. præoccupo, 1.
prepossession, s. præjudicata opinio, f.
preposterous, a. præposterus; perversus; absurdus; —**ly,** ad. perverse, absurde.
prerogative, s. prærogativa, f.; privilegium, n.   [portentum, n.
presage, s. præsagium; augurium, omen
presage, v.a & n. portendo, 3; significo, 1; præsagio, 4; prædico, 3; vaticinor, 1.
presbyter, s. presbyter, m.
presbytery, presbyterium, n.
prescience, s. præscientia, f.
prescient, s. præscius.
prescribe, v.a. præcipio; præscribo; propono, 3.
prescription, s. præscriptum, n.; (of a physician) medicamenti formula, f.; (custom) usus, m.
presence, s. præsentia, f.; (look) aspectus, m.; **in my —,** me præsente; **in the — of,** coram (with ablat.).
present, a. præsens; hic, hæc, hoc; **for the —,** in præsens; **to be —,** adesse; — **money,** pecunia numerata, f.
present, s. donum, munus, n.
present, s. v.a. offero, 3; dono, do, 1; largior, 4; introduco; (law) sisto, 3; *fig.* (to — itself) obvenio, 4.
presentation, s. donatio, f.
presentiment, s. præsagium, n.; **have a — of,** præsentio, 4.
presently, ad. mox; illico, statim.
preservation, s. conservatio, f.
preservative, s. antidotum, n.
preserve, v.a. servo, conservo, 1; tueor, 2; (fruits) condio, 4.
preserver, s. conservator, m.
preside, v.n. præsideo, 2; præsum.
presidency, s. præfectura, f.
president, s. præses, præfectus, m.
press, s. prelum; (for clothes) armarium, tormentum, n.; (of people) turba, f.
press, v.a. premo; comprimo, 3; *fig.* urgeo, 2; insto, flagito, 1; (force to serve) vi comparo, 1; **to — forward,** v.n. annitor, 3; **to — on** or **upon,** insto, 1; insisto, 3.
pressing, s. pressura; compressio, f.; (force) vis, f.
pressing, a. instans; —**ly,** ad. impense.
pressman, s. torcularius, m.
pressure, s. pressura, f.; *fig.* angor, m.; ærumna, f.
presume, v.a. & n. arrogo; (to hope) spero, 1; (to suppose) conjicio, 3; (dare) audeo, 2.
presumption, s. arrogantia; (conjecture) suspicio, f.; (opinion) sententia, f.

presumptive, a. (of heirs) proximus.
presumptuous, a. arrogans; audax, temerarius; —**ly,** ad. arroganter, audacter.
presuppose, v.a. sumo, præsumo, 3.
pretence, s. simulatio, f.; v. **pretext.**
pretend, v.a. & n. simulo, dissimulo, 1.
pretended, a. fictus, simulatus, commentus; —**ly,** ad. ficte, simulate.
pretender, s. simulator; qui regnum affectat, m.
pretension, s. (claim) postulatio; (display) ostentatio, f.
preterite, s. præteritum, n.
preternaturally, ad. præter naturam, divinitus.
pretext, s. species, f.; prætextum, n.; (cause) **under — of,** specie.
prettily, ad. belle, venus te; eleganter.
prettiness, s. elegantia, venustas, f.
pretty, a. bellus; lepidus; venustus; **a — while,** aliquandiu; — **well,** mediocriter.
prevail, v.n. prævaleo, polleo; persuadeo, 2; (become current) increbresco, 3; — **upon,** impetro, 1.
prevalent, prevailing, a. vulgatus; **be —,** increbresco.
prevaricate, v.n. tergiversor, prævaricor, 1.
prevarication, s. prævaricatio, tergiversatio, f.
prevaricator, s. prævaricator, m.
prevent, v.a. prævenio, 4; præverto, 3; (stop) impedio, 4; prohibeo, 2.
prevention, s. prohibitio, f.
preventive, s. (remedy) remedium, n.
previous, a. antecedens, prior; —**ly,** ad. antea, antehac, prius.
prevision, s. providentia, f.
prey, s. præda, f.; **beast of —,** animal rapax, n.   [*fig.* vexo, 1.
prey, v.n. (on, upon) prædor, 1; rapio, 3;
price, s. pretium, n.; **at what —?** quanti?
priceless, a. inæstimabilis.
prick, s. punctus, m.; (good) stimulus, m.
prick, v.a. pungo, 3; *fig.* stimulo, 1; **to — up,** (aures) arrigere, 3.
prickle, s. aculeus, m.; spina, f.
prickly, a. spinosus.   [m.
pride, s. superbia, f.; fastidium, n.; fastus,
pride, v.a. (oneself on) jacto, glorior, 1; superbio, 4.
priest, s. sacerdos, antistes, vates, m.
priestcraft, s. sacerdotum fallaciæ, f. pl.
priestess, s. sacerdos, antistita, vates, f.
priesthood, s. (office) sacerdotium, n.; (collectively) sacerdotes, m. pl.
priestly, a. sacerdotalis.
prig, s. virtutis ostentator.
prim, a. rigidus.
primacy, s. primatus, m.
primarily, ad. præcipue.

primary, a. principalis; præcipuus.
primate, s. primas, m.
prime, s. (of life) florens ætas, f.; *fig.* flos,
m.; robur, n.
prime, a. egregius, optimus.
primer, s. liber elementarius, m.
primeval, a. primigenius, primævus; priscus.   [(simple) simplex.
primitive, a. principalis, primitivus;
primness, s. rigor, m.
primogeniture, s. jus primogeniti, n.
primordial, a. primus, primitivus.
primrose, s. primula (mod. hort.).
prince, s. rex, princeps, regulus; (king's
son) regis filius, m.
princely, a. regalis, regius.
princess, s. regina; regia puella; regis
filia, f.
principal, a. principalis, præcipuus;
maximus, potissimus; —ly, ad. maxime,
præcipue; potissimum, præsertim.
principal, s. caput, n.; præses, præfectus,
m.; (main point) summa, f.; caput, n.
principality, s. principatus, m.
principle, s. principium, n.; origo, f.; (in
philosophy) ratio, f.; (precept) præceptum, n.; (maxim) institutum, n.; —s
of conduct, ratio vitæ, f.; a man of
high —, vir integer, vir probus.
print, v.a. imprimo, 3.
print, s. nota, f.; vestigium, n.
printer, s. typographus, m.
printing, s. typographia, ars typogra-
phica, f.
printing-press, s. prelum typographicum, n.
prior, a. prior.
prior, s. prior, m.
prioress, s. priorissa, f.
priority, s. primatus, m.
priory, s. prioratus, m.
prise, v.a. to — open, vecti refringo, 3.
prism, s. prisma, n.
prismatic, a. prismaticus.
prison, s. carcer, m.; custodia, f.
prisoner, s. (of war) captivus; (law) reus,
m.; rea, f.
pristine, a. pristinus; prisius.
privacy, s. solitudo, f.; secretum, n.
private, a. privatus; (mil.) gregarius;
(domestic) domesticus; —ly, ad.
privatim, secreto; clam.
private, s. homo privatus, m.
privateer, s. navis prædatoria, f.
privation, s. privatio; (need) inopia, f.
privative, a. (gr.) privativus.
privet, s. ligustrum, n.
privilege, s. privilegium, beneficium, n.;
immunitas, f.
privily, ad. clam, occulte.
privity, s. conscientia, f.
privy, a. privatus, secretus; (to) conscius.

privy, s. forica, latrina, f.
privy-purse, s. fiscus, m.
prize, s. (reward) præmium, n.; (capture)
navis capta; (victory) palma, f.
prize, v.a. (to value) æstimo, 1; (much)
magni facio, 3.
prize-fighter, s. pugil, m.
prize-money, s. pecunia manubialis, f.;
manubiæ, f. pl.
probability, s. similitudo veri, probabilitas, f.
probable, a. verisimilis, probabilis.
probably, ad. probabiliter.
probation, s. probatio, f.
probationer, s. novicius, tiro, m.
probe, s. specillum, n.; —, v.a. specillo
tento, 1.
probity, s. probitas, honestas, integritas, f.
problem, s. problema, n.; quæstio, f.
problematical, a. incertus, dubius; —ly,
ad. dubie.
proboscis, s. proboscis, f.
procedure, s. ratio agendi, ordo, m.;
forma, f.; (proceedings) acta, facta,
n. pl.
proceed, v.n. progredior; procedo, incedo; (continue) pergo, 3; (make
advance) proficio, 3; (to arise, spring
from) orior, 4; proficiscor, 3; —
against, (law) accuso, 1; reum ago, 3.
proceeding, s. facinus, factum, n.; —s,
acta, facta, n. pl.; legal —, actio, f.;
controversia judiciaria, f.
proceeds, s. reditus, proventus, m.
process, s. processus, m.; (method) ratio,
f.; (law) lis, actio, f.
procession, s. pompa, f.
proclaim, v.a. promulgo, pronuntio, 1;
· edico, propono, 3.
proclamation, s. pronuntiatio, promulgatio, f.; edictum, n.
proconsul, s. proconsul, m.; pro consule.
proconsular, a. proconsularis.
proconsulship, s. proconsulatus, m.
procrastinate, v.a. differo, 3; —, v.n.
cunctor, 1.
procrastination, s. tarditas, procrastina-
tio, cunctatio, f.
procreate, v.a. procreo, 1.
procreation, s. procreatio, f.
Procrustean, v.a. Procrustæ (genitive).
proctor, s. procurator, m.
procurable, a. (ready at hand) præsto, in
promptu.
procuration, s. procuratio, f.
procurator, s. procurator, m.
procure, v.a. (to get) acquiro, adipiscor,
consequor, 3; comparo, 1.
procurement, s. comparatio, f.
procurer, s. leno, m.
procuress, s. lena, f.

prodigal, a. prodigus ; profusus, effusus ; —ly, ad. prodige ; effuse.

prodigal, s. heluo, nepos, ganeo, m.

prodigality, s. effusio, profusio, luxuria, f.

prodigious, a. (monstrous) prodigiosus ; (great) immanis ; ingens ; —ly, ad. prodigiose ; valde.

prodigy, s. prodigium, monstrum ; portentum ; *fig.* miraculum, n.

produce, v.n. (to bring forward) produco, profero, 3 ; (to bring forth) pario ; (yield) fero, effero, profero ; (to cause) facio, 3 ; creo, 1 ; cieo moveo, 2. [m.

produce, s. fructus, (in money) reditus,

product, s. (of earth) fructus, m. ; fruges, f. pl. ; (in mathemat.) summa (ex multiplicatione effecta), f. ; (mental) opus, n. [fabricatio, f.

production, s. prolatio ; (manufacture)

productive, a. ferax fertilis, fecundus ; *fig.* efficiens ; **to be — of,** v. **produce.**

productiveness, s. fertilitas ; ubertas, f.

profanation, s. violatio, f. ; piaculum, n.

profane, a. profanus ; *fig.* impius ; —ly, ad. impie.

profane, v.a. violo, profano, 1.

profaner, s. violator, m.

profanity, s. impietas, f. ; nefas, n.

profess, v.a. profiteor, 2.

professed, a. apertus, manifestus ; —ly, ad. ex professo.

profession, s. (avowal ; calling, trade) professio, f. ; (business, trade) ars, f.

professional, a. ad professionem pertinens.

professor, s. (literary) professor, m.

professorial, a. professorius.

professorship, s. professoris munus, n.

proffer, v.a. offero, propono, 3.

proffer, s. condicio proposita, f.

proficiency, s. ars, peritia, f.

proficient, a. peritus. [catagrapha, n. pl.

profile, s. facies, obliqua, f. ; (as portrait)

profit, s. emolumentum ; lucrum, n. ; reditus, fructus, quæstus, m.

profit, v.a. prosum (with dative) ; proficio, 3 ; —, v.n. (to get advantage) lucror, 1 ; fructum percipio, 3.

profitable, a. fructuosus, quæstuosus ; lucrosus ; utilis ; **to be —,** prodesse.

profitably, ad. utiliter ; bene.

profitless, a. inutilis, vanus, irritus.

profligacy, s. nequitia, f. ; perditi mores, m. pl.

profligate, a. perditus, flagitiosus, nequam, indecl. ; —ly, ad. flagitiose.

profligate, s. nepos, ganeo, m.

profound, a. altus ; subtilis ; abstrusus ; —ly, ad. penitus ; subtiliter, abscondite.

profundity, s. altitudo, subtilitas, f.

profuse, a. effusus, profusus ; —ly, ad. effuse, profuse.

profusion, s. effusio, profusio, ubertas ; abundantia, f.

progeny, s. progenies, proles, f.

prognostic, s. signum, n.

prognosticate, v.a. prospicio ; prædico, 3 ; vaticinor, 1.

prognostication, s. prædictio, f. ; prædictum, n.

prognosticator, s. augur, m.

programme, s. libellus, m. [m.

progress, s. iter, n. ; progressus, processus,

progress, v.n. progredior, *fig.* proficio, 3.

progression, s. progressus, m.

progressively, ad. (gradually) paulatim, sensim, gradatim.

prohibit, v.a. veto, 1 ; interdico, 3 ; prohibeo, 2.

prohibition, s. interdictum, n.

prohibitory, a. prohibitorius.

project, s. propositum, consilium, n.

project, v.a. molior, 4 ; consilium capio, 3 ; —, v.n. (to jut out) promineo, emineo, 2 ; exoto, 1.

projectile, s. missile, n.

projecting, a. prominens ; projectus.

projection, s. projectum, n. ; projectura, f.

projector, s. auctor (consilii), m.

proletarian, a. & s. proletarius.

proletariate s. plebs, f. ; vulgus, n.

prolific, a. fecundus, ferax, fertilis.

prolix, a. verbosus ; longus, prolixus.

prolixity, s. prolixitas, f.

prologue, s. prologus, m.

prolong, v.a. produco, 3 ; prorogo, 1 ; extendo, traho, 3.

prolongation, s. prorogatio, f.

promenade, s. (walk) ambulatio, f. ; (place) ambulatio, f. ; xystus, m.

promenade, v.n. spatior, ambulo, 1.

prominence, s. eminentia, f.

prominent, a. eminens ; conspicuus.

promiscuous, a. promiscuus ; mixtus ; —ly, ad. promiscue, sine ullo discrimine.

promise, s. (act) promissio, fides, f. ; promissum, n. [spondeo, 2.

promise, v.a. & n. promitto, 3 ; polliceor,

promising, a. bona *or* summa spe.

promissory, a., **— note,** s. chirographum, n.

promontory, s. promunturium, n.

promote, v.a. augeo, 2 ; tollo, effero, proveho, 3 ; (serve) consulo (dat.).

promoter, s. adjutor, auctor, m.

promotion, s. amplior gradus, m. ; dignitas, f.

prompt, a. promptus, paratus ; (speedy) maturus ; —ly, ad. prompte ; (speedily) mature.

prompt, v.a. subjicio 3 ; (to incite, etc.) impello, 3.

prompter, s. qui verba subjicit, m.
promptitude, promptness, s. celeritas, maturitas, f.
promulgate, v.a. promulgo, 1.
promulgation, s. promulgatio, f.
prone, a. pronus ; propensus ; proclivis.
proneness, s. animus propensus, m. ; proclivitas, f.
prong, s. dens, m.
pronominal, a. pronominalis.
pronoun, s. pronomen, n.
pronounce, v.a. pronuntio ; (to articulate syllables) enuntio, 1 ; loquor, 3.
pronouncement, s. judicium, n. ; sententia, f. [prolatio.
pronunciation, s. (utterance) pronuntiatio,
proof, s. documentum, argumentum ; indicium ; signum ; specimen, n. ; ratio demonstrandi or probandi, f. ; (trial) experimentum, n. ; (in print.) plagula, f.
proof, a. tutus, surdus, impervius.
proof-sheet, s. plagula, f.
prop, s. fulcrum ; (for vines) adminiculum ; fig. columen, n.
prop, v.a. fulcio, 4 ; adminiculor, 1.
propagate, v.a. propago ; (to spread) dissemino, 1.
propagation, s. propagatio, f.
propel, v.a. impello ; propello, 3.
propeller, s. impulsor, m.
propensity, s. proclivitas, f.
proper, a. proprius ; (suitable) aptus ; (becoming) decorus ; —ly, ad. proprie ; apte ; decore.
property, s. fortuna, f. ; bona, n. pl. ; (characteristic) proprium, n.
prophecy, s. prædictum, n. ; vaticinatio ; (power) prædictio, divinatio, f.
prophesy, v.a. & n. vaticinor, divino, auguror, 1 ; prædico, 3.
prophet, s. vates, c. ; fatidicus, propheta, m.
prophetess, s. vates, f.
prophetic, a. fatidicus ; (of inward feeling) præsagus.
propitiate, v.a. propitio, placo, mitigo, 1 ; lenio, 4.
propitiation, s. placatio, f. ; placamen, piaculum, n.
propitiatory, a. piacularis.
propitious, a. propitius ; faustus, felix, secundus ; —ly, ad. fauste, feliciter.
proportion, s. ratio, proportio ; symmetria, f. ; in —, pro portione.
proportional, a. ; —ly, ad. pro portione ; (math.) proportionalis.
proposal, s. condicio, f. ; (plan) consilium, n.
propose, v.a. condicionem offero, 3 ; (to intend) cogito ; (a toast) propino, 1 ; (a law) fero, 3 ; promulgo, 1.

proposer, s. lator, auctor, m.
proposition, s. condicio ; (bill) rogatio, f. ; (advice) consilium, n. ; (logic) propositio, f.
propound, v.a. propono, profero, 3.
proprietary, a. peculiaris.
proprietor, s. dominus, erus, m.
proprietress, s. domina, era, f.
propriety, s. decorum, n. ; convenientia, f.
propulsion, s. impulsus, m.
prorogation, s. prorogatio, prolatio, f.
prorogue, v.a. prorogo, 1.
prosaic, a. pedester, solutæ orationi proprior ; fig. aridus, jejunus.
proscribe, v.a. proscribo, 3.
proscription, s. proscriptio, f.
prose, s. oratio soluta, prosa, f. ; pedester sermo, m.
prose-writer, s. prosæ scriptor, m.
prosecute, v.a exsequor, persequor, 3 ; insto (alicui), 1 ; persevero in, 1 ; (accuse) reum facio, 3. [tio, f.
prosecution, s. exsecutio ; (law) accusaprosecutor, s. accusator, actor, m. ; the —, hic.
prosecutrix, s. accusatrix, f. ; petitor.
proselyte, s. proselytus, m. ; proselyta, f.
prosody, s. prosodia, f.
prospect, s. prospectus, despictus, m. ; spes, exspectatio, f.
prospectus, s. titulus, index, m.
prosper, v.a. prospero, secundo, 1 ; —, v.n. prospera fortuna uti, 3 ; successus prosperos habeo, 1 ; bene cedo, cedo, 3.
prosperity, s. res secundæ, f. pl. ; prospera fortuna, prosperitas, f.
prosperous, a. secundus, prosperus ; florens ; —ly, ad. prospere ; bene.
prostitute, s. scortum, n. ; meretrix, f.
prostitute, v.a. prostituo, 3 ; fig. dehonesto, maculo, 1 ; (sell) vendo.
prostitution, s. meretricium, n.
prostrate, v.a. sterno ; prosterno ; projicio ; (to throw down) dejicio ; fig. affligo, 3.
prostrate, a. prostratus, projectus ; fig. afflictus, fractus ; to fall —, se (ad pedes alicujus) projicere, 3 ; procumbo.
prostration, s. fig. animus fractus, m.
prosy, a. longus, lentus ; pedester.
protect, v.a. tueor, 2 ; protego ; defendo, 3 ; servo, 1 ; custodio, 4.
protection, s. tutela, custodia, f. ; præsidium, tutamen, n. [nator, m.
protector, s. patronus, defensor, propugprotectorate, s. tutela, custodia, f.
protectress, s. patrona, f. [pellatio, f.
protest, s. acclamatio ; intercessio ; interprotest, v.n & a. obtestor, acclamo, interpello, 1 ; (against) intercedo, ægre fero ; (profess) profiteor, 3.

protestation, s. affirmatio, professio, f.
prototype, s. exemplar, n.
protract, v.a. traho, protraho, differo, produco, 3.
protraction, dilatio, productio, f.
protractor, m. dilator, m.
protrude, v.a. & n. promineo, emineo, 2.
protuberance, s. tuber, n.; tumor, gibbus, m.
protuberant, a. prominens.
proud, a. superbus, arrogans; magnificus; —ly, ad. superbe; arroganter; (of things) magnifice; **to be proud,** superbio, fastidio, 4.
prove, v.a. probo, 1; evinco, arguo, 3; (to try) experior, 4; (as false) refello, 3; (show) monstro, demonstro; (make good) praesto, 1; —, v.n. (to become) fio; (turn out to be) evado, 3.
provender, s. pabulum, n.
proverb, s. proverbium, n.
proverbial, a. proverbialis; —ly, ad. in proverbio.
provide, v.a. paro, comparo, 1; (to supply) praebeo, 2; suppedito, 1; —, v.n. (against) provideo (ne . . .), praecaveo, 2; (for) provideo (alicui), 2; (with) instruo, 3.
provided, c., — **that,** dummodo, dum, modo.
providence, s. providentia, diligentia, cura; (divine dispensation), providentia, f.; or use deus, m.
provident, a. providus; cautus; —ly, ad. provide.
providentially, ad. divinitus.
provider, s. provisor; (of victuals) obsonator, m.
province, s. provincia; regio, f.; fig. provincia, f.; munus, n.
provincial, a. provincialis; fig. rusticus; —, s. provincialis, provinciae incola, c.
provincialism, s. rusticitas, f.
provision, s. praeparatio, f.; apparatus, m.; copia, f.; (necessaries) alimentum, n.; victus, m.; penus, c.; (for an army) commeatus, m.; cibaria, n. pl.; (for a journey) viaticum, n.
provisional, a. temporarius; —ly, ad. ad tempus.
proviso, s. exceptio, cautio, condicio, f.
provocation, s. provocatio, f.; (wrong) injuria, f.   [stimulo, 1.
provoke, v.a. lacesso, provoco, irrito,
provoking, a. molestus; —ly, ad. moleste.
provost, s. praefectus, m.
prow, s. prora, f.
prowess, s. virtus, f.
prowl, v.n. praedor; (to roam about) vagor, 1; — **round,** obambulo, oberro, 1

prowler, s. praedator, m.
proximate, a. proximus; —ly, ad. ex proximo.
proximity, s. propinquitas, proximitas, f.
proxy, s. vicarius, m.
prudence, s. prudentia; circumspectio, f.
prudent, a. cautus, prudens, consideratus; —ly, ad. caute; considerate.
prudery, s. modestiae affectatio, severitas, f.
prudish, a. modestiam affectans, severus.
prune, s. prunum, n.
prune, v.a. (trees) decacumino, amputo, puto, 1; fig. reseco, 1; recido, 3.
pruner, s. putator; (of vines) pampinator, frondator, m.
pruning, s. putatio; pampinatio, f.
pruning-knife, s. falx, f.
pruriency, s. pruritus, m.; prurigo, f.; lascivia, f.
prurient, a. pruriens; fig. lascivus, libidinosus.
pry, v.n. scrutor, perscrutor, exploro, 1.
prying, a. curiosus.
psalm, s. psalmus, m.
psalmist, s. psalmista, psalmographus, m.
psalter, s. psalterium, n.
pseudo, a. fictus, simulatus.
pshaw, i. phu! phy!
puberty, s. pubertas, pubes, f.
public, a. publicus; communis; (known) pervulgatus; —ly, ad. in publico; palam, aperte; **bring before the —,** in medium profero, 3.
public, s. homines, pl.; fig. vulgus, n.; multitudo, f.
public-house, s. caupona, taberna, f.
publican, s. (farmer of taxes) publicanus; (innkeeper) caupo, m.
publication, s. promulgatio; (of a book) editio, f.; (published book) liber, m.
publicist, s. qui in republica versatur.
publicity, s. celebritas, f.; fig. lux, f.
publish, v.a. vulgo; divulgo, 1; patefacio, 3; (a book) edo, 3.
publisher, s. bibliopola, librarius, m.
publishing, s. (of a work) editio, f.
puce, a. purpureus.
pucker, v.a. corrugo, 1.
puddle, s. lacuna, f.
puddle, v.a. turbo, 1; subigo, 3.
puerile, a. puerilis.
puerility, s. puerilitas, f.; pueriles ineptiae, f. pl.
puff, s. (of wind) flatus, m.
puff, v.a. inflo, sufflo; (wares) (up) vendito, 1; —, v.n. (to pant) anhelo, 1; — **up,** inflo, 1; **be —d up,** intumesco, 3.
puffer, s. venditator, m.
puffery, s. venditatio, f.
puffiness, s. inflatio, f.

puff-paste, s. crustulata, f.
puffy, a. sufflatus ; tumens ; turgidus ; inflatus.
pug-nosed, a. simus, resimus.
pugilism, s. pugilatio, f. ; pugilatus, m.
pugilist, s. pugil, m.
pugnacious, a. pugnax.
pugnacity, s. pugnacitas, f.
puisne, a. minor natu.
pule, v.n. (as infants) vagio, 4.
pull, v.a. vello, 3 ; vellico, 1 ; (drag) traho, 3 ; —, v.n. vires adhibeo, 2 ; annitor, 3 ; **to — away,** avello, 3 ; **to — back,** revello, retraho, 3 ; **to — down,** (houses, etc.) demolior, 4 ; destruo ; (violently) everto, 3 ; **to — off,** avello ; detraho, 3 ; **to — out,** extraho, evello, eximo, 3 ; **to — up,** extraho ; eripio, eruo, 3.
pull, s. (act) tractus ; (effort) nisus, m.
pullet, s. pullus (gallinaceus), m.
pulley, s. trochlea, f.
pulmonary, pulmonic, a. (of the lungs) pulmoneus ; pulmonaceus ; (consumptive) pulmonarius ; **— consumption,** s. peripneumonia, f.
pulp, s. caro, pulpa, f.
pulpit, s. rostra, n. pl. ; suggestus, m. ; tribunal, n.
pulpy, a. carnosus.
pulsate, v.n. vibro, 1.
pulsation, s. pulsus, m.
pulse, s. (venarum) pulsus, m. ; (plant) legumen, n.
pulverization, s. pulveratio, f.
pulverize, v.a. pulvero, 1.
pumice(stone), s. pumex, m.; **of —,** a. pumiceus.
pumice, v.a. pumico, 1.
pump, s. antlia, f. ; (shoe) soccus, m.
pump, v.a. haurio, 4 ; *fig.* (to question) exploro, 1.
pumpkin, s. pepo, melopepo, m. ; cucurbita, f.
pun, s. lusus verborum, jocus, m. ; —, v.n. jocor, 1 ; alludo, 3.
punch, s. (blow) pugnus, ictus, m. ; (in shows) Puncinellus, Policinellus, m.
punch, v.a. terebro, 1 ; (to strike) pugnum impingo, 3.
puncheon, s. terebra, f. ; (measure) dolium, n. [m.
punchinello, s. Policinellus, Puncinellus,
punctilio, s. (scruple) religio, f. ; scrupulus, m.
punctilious, a. scrupulosus, religiosus ; **—ly,** ad. scrupulose, religiose.
punctual, a. promptus, accuratus, ad tempus veniens *or* rediens ; **—ly,** ad. ad tempus, accurate.
punctuality, s. accurata observatio (temporis), f.

punctuate, v.a. interpungo, 3.
punctuation, s. (act) interpunctio, f.; (sign of —) interpunctum, n.
puncture, s. (act) punctio, f. ; (hole punctured) punctum, n.
pungency, s. acrimonia ; acerbitas ; (of grief) stimuli, m. pl.
pungent, a. (to the senses) acutus ; *fig.* mordax ; aculeatus.
Punic, a. Punicus.
puniness, s. exiguitas, f.
punish, v.a. punio, 4 ; castigo, 1 ; animadverto, 3 ; vindico, 1 ; **be —ed,** pœnas do.
punishable, a. puniendus, pœna dignus.
punisher, s. punitor ; ultor, m. ; vindex, c.
punishment, s. (act) castigatio ; pœna, f. ; supplicium, n. ; **without —,** impune.
punster, s. (homo) jocosus, m.
punt, s. ratis, f.
puny, a. pusillus, exiguus.
pup, s. catulus, i, m. ; —, v.n. catulos parere, 3.
pupil, s. discipulus, m. ; discipula, f. ; (of the eye) pupilla, pupula, f.
pupillage, s. ætas pupillaris ; condicio discipuli, f.
pupillary, a. pupillaris.
puppet, s. pupa, f.
puppy, s. catulus ; *fig.* (silly fellow) ineptus, stultus ; (conceited person) simiolus, m.
pur, v.n. murmuro, susurro, 1.
purblind, a. luscus.
purchase, s. (act) emptio ; (merchandise) merx, f.
purchase, v.a. emo, 3 ; (to procure) comparo, 1.
purchase-money, s. pretium, n.
purchaser, s. emptor ; mercator, m.
pure, a. mundus ; purus ; (unmixed) merus ; *fig.* purus ; (chaste) castus ; (of character) integer ; **—ly,** ad pure ; caste ; integre.
purgation, s. purgatio, f.
purgative, a. purgativus ; **—,** s. medicamen purgativum, n.
purgatory, s. purgatorium, n.
purge, v.a. purgo, mundo, 1.
purge, purging, s. purgatio.
purification, s. purgatio ; purificatio ; expiatio ; lustratio, f. ; lustrum, n.
purifier, s. purgator, lustrator, m.
purify, v.a. purifico, purgo ; lustro, expio, 1.
purity, s. munditia ; *fig.* castitas ; integritas, f.
purl, s. murmur, n. ; —, v.n. leniter fluere, 3 ; murmuro, 1.
purloin, v.a. surripio, 3 ; furor, suffuror, 1.
purloiner, s. fur, m.

purple, s. purpura, f. ; ostrum, conchylium, n. ; murex, m. ; **dressed in —,** purpuratus.

purple, a. purpureus.

purport, s. (meaning) significatio ; (intention) voluntas, f.

purport, v.a. n. significo, 1.

purpose, s. propositum, consilium, n. ; animus, m. ; (end, aim) finis, c. ; (wish) mens, voluntas, f. ; **on —,** de industria ; consulto ; consilio ; **to the —,** ad rem . . . ; **to no —,** frustra ; **to what —?** quid refert ?

purpose, v.n. propono, statuo, constituo, decerno, 3.

purposed, a. destinatus, propositus.

purposely, ad. consulto, consilio, de industria.

purring, s. murmur, n. ; susurrus, m.

purse, s. crumena ; (money-belt) zona, f. ; *fig.* (store of money), f. ; saccus, m. ; arca, f.

purse, v.a. (up) corrugo, 1 ; contraho, 3.

purslane, s. portulaca, f.

purse-proud, a. superbus pecunia.

pursuance, s. ; **in — of,** ex (abl.) ; secundum (with acc.).

pursuant, a. v. **in pursuance of.**

pursue, v.a. sequor, persequor, insequor ; *fig.* insisto ; utor, 3 ; (with abl.).

pursuit, s. insectatio, f. ; (occupation) studium, n.

pursy, a. (short-winded) anhelus.

purulent, a. purulentus, corruptus.

purvey, v.a. n. obsonor, 1.

purveyance, s. (act) obsonatus, m. ; (provisions) obsonium, n.

purveyor, s. obsonator, m.

pus, s. pus, n. ; sanies, f.

push, v.a. trudo, pello, 3 ; urgeo, 2 ; **— forward,** protrudo, propello, 3 ; **to — on,** impello, 3 ; urgeo, 2 ; (v.n.) contendo, 3 ; (to hasten) festino, 1.

push, s. pulsus, impetus, impulsus, *fig.* conatus, m. ; (extremity) discrimen, n. ; (energy) strenuitas, f.

pushing, a. audax, confidens ; (energetic) strenuus.   [ditas.

pusillanimity, s. imbecillitas animi ; timi-

pusillanimous, a. timidus ; abjectus.

postule, s. pustula, pusula, f.

put, v.a. pono, 3 ; loco, colloco, 1 ; (a question) quæro ; (again) repono ; (aside) sepono, 3 ; **to — away,** sepono, 3 ; amoveo, 2 ; (in safety) recondo ; (to send away) dimitto, 3 ; (divorce) repudio, 1 ; **to — by,** (to place in safety) condo ; (to turn aside) averto ; (to refuse) repello, 3 ; **to — down,** depono ; (to lower, let down) demitto ; (to throw down) dejicio ; (to suppress, to abolish) sup-

primo ; tollo ; (in writing) scribo ; (in an account) fero, 3 ; (by answering) confuto, 1 ; **to — forth,** mitto ; (to stretch out) extendo ; (to turn out) foras ejicio ; (to utter) propono, emitto, fundo, edo, 3 ; (to proclaim) edico ; (books) edo ; (blossoms, leaves, etc.) emitto ; (to bring forth) gigno, 3 ; **to — forward,** (to promote) promoveo, 2 ; (excuses, etc.) profero, 3 ; (as a candidate) produco, 3 ; **to — in,** impono ; (forcibly) immitto ; (to fasten, etc., in) insero ; (to insert) interpono, 3 ; (in order) ordino, 1 ; (in mind) moneo, 2 ; (of ships) navem appello, 3 ; **to — off,** (dress, etc.) depono, exuo ; (to discard) dimitto ; (to postpone) differo ; profero ; (of ships) (v.n.) naves solvo, 3 ; **to — on,** impono ; (dress, clothes) induo ; (to add) addo, 3; *fig.* imputo, 1 ; **to — out,** expello, ejicio ; (fire, light) exstinguo ; (to tear *or* beat out) eruo, effodio, 3 ; (to blot out) deleo, 2 ; (money) colloco, 1 ; *fig.* (to disconcert, etc.) confundo, 3 ; perturbo, 1 ; (dislocate) extorqueo, 2 ; (v.n.) (as plants) germino, 1 ; (to sea) solvo, 3 ; **to — over,** super(im)pono ; (to postpone) differo, 3 ; **to — to,** appono, 3 ; admoveo, 2 ; (horses) jungo, 3 ; (to flight) fugo ; (to the sword) neco, 1 ; (to death) v. **kill** ; **to — together,** compono, confero ; **to — under,** subdo ; suppono ; substerno ; subjicio, 3 ; **to — up,** erigo ; arrigo, 3 ; (to stir) excito, 1 ; (for sale) propono ; (a sword) recondo (in vaginam), 3 ; (as a candidate) peto ; (at auctions) auctionor, 1 ; (— up at) devertor, 3 ; (with) fero, 3 ; **to — upon,** super(im)pono ; addo ; (of dress) induo ; (a task) impono (alicui), 3 ; (to impose upon) verba do (alicui), 1.

putrefaction, s. putor, m. ; putredo, f.

putrefy, v.a. putrefacio, 3 ; —, v.n. putresco, putrefio, 3.

putrescent, a. putrescens, putens.

putrid, a. puter, putridus.

putridness, s. putor, m. ; putredo, f.

puzzle, s. quæstio abstrusa *or* obscura ; *fig.* difficultas, f. ; nodus, m.

puzzle, v.a. confundo, 3 ; perturbo, 1 ; —, v.n. hæreo, 2.

puzzling, a. perplexus, obscurus.

pygmean, a. pygmæus.

pygmy, s. nanus, pumilio, m.

pyramid, s. pyramis, f.

pyre, s. rogus, m. ; bustum, n. ; pyra, f.

pyrite, s. pyrites, m.

Pythagorean, a. s. Pythagoræus, m.

Pythian, a. Pythius.

pythoness, s. Pythia, Pythia vates, f.

pyx, s. pyxis, f.

Quack, s. pharmacopola circumforaneus; *fig.* jactator, m.
quack, v.n. tetrinnio, 4.
quadrangle, s. quadriangulum, n. ; (square court) area, f.
quadrangular, a. quadriangulus.
quadrilateral, a. quadrilaterus.
quadruped, a. quadrupes ; —, s. quadrupes, c.
quadruple, a. quadruplex ; quadruplus ; —, s. quadruplum, n.
quadruple, v.a. quadruplico, 1.
quæstor, s. quæstor, m.
quæstorship, s. quæstura, f.
quaff, v.a. poto, 1 ; haurio, 4 ; duco, traho, 3.
quaffer, s. haustor, potator, potor, m.
quaggy, a. paludosus, palustris.
quagmire, s. palus, lacuna, f.
quail, s. coturnix, f.
quail, v.n. despondeo, 2 ; paveo, 2.
quaint, a. mirus, insolitus ; (strange, odd) rarus ; —**ly,** ad. mire.
quake, v.n. tremo, 3 ; —, s. tremor ; horror, m.
quaking-grass, s. briza (mod. hort.).
qualification, s. (endowment) indoles ; (condition) condicio, f. ; status, m. ; **without** —, sine ulla exceptione.
qualified, a. aptus, idoneus ; capax, dignus ; (moderate) mediocris.
qualify, v.a. aptum reddo ; instruo, 3 ; (to limit, restrict, etc.) tempero ; extenuo, 1.
quality, s. qualitas ; natura, f. ; *fig.* dos (degree) ordo, gradus, m.
qualm, s. fastidium stomachi, n. ; nausea, f. ; (of conscience) religio, f.
quandary, s. angustiæ, f.
quantity, s. quantitas ; magnitudo, f. ; numerus, m. ; vis, copia, f. ; **in quantities,** copiose.
quarantine, s. quadragenaria (mora), f.
quarrel, s. jurgium, n. ; altercatio ; **rixa,** simultas, f.
quarrel, v.n. jurgo ; altercor ; rixor, 1.
quarrelling, s. altercatio, contentio, f.
quarrelsome, a. jurgiosus, rixosus, pugnax.
quarrelsomeness, s. pugnacitas, f.
quarry, s. lapicidinæ, lautumiæ. f. pl. ; (prey) præda, f.
quarryman, s. lapicida, m.
quart, s. quadrans, m. ; quarta **pars,** f. ; (measure) duo sextarii, m. pl.
quartan, s. febris quartana, f.
quarter, s. quarta pars, f. ; quadrans, m. ; (side direction, district) regio, f. ; (pardon) venia ; (letting off) missio, f. ; **to give** —, parco (alicui), 3 ; **to give no** —,

nemini parco, 3 ; —**s,** pl. (dwelling) tectum, n. ; habitatio, f. ; (temporary abode) hospitium, deverticulum, n. ; (mil.) castra ; **winter** —, hiberna, n. pl. ; **summer** —, æstiva, n. pl. ; **take up one's** —, devertor, 3 ; **at close** —, comminus.
quarter, v.a. in quatuor partes divido, 3 ; (soldiers, etc.) colloco, 1 ; dispono, 3 ; (to receive in one's house) hospitium præbeo, 2 ; (to tear to pieces) discerpo, 3.
quarter-deck, s. puppis, f.
quartering, s. quadripartitio, f. ; (punishment) laniatus, m. ; laniatio ; (of troops) deductio, f.
quarterly, a. trimestris ; (by the quarter) tertio quoque mense ; —, ad. quadrifariam ; tertio quoque mense.
quartermaster, s. præfectus, m.
quarter-staff, s. baculum, n.
quartern, s. (measure) quadrans, m.
quarto, s. forma quaternaria, f.
quash, v.a. (law) rescindo, 3 ; aboleo, 2 ; abrogo, 1.
quatrain, s. tetrastichon, n. [1.
quaver, v.n. vibro, 1 ; tremo, 3 ; vibrisso,
quaver, s. sonus vibrans, m.
quay, s. crepido, f.
queen, s. regina ; (in chess) compar, f.
queenly, a. regius, regalis.
queer, a. (strange) ineptus, insulsus, ridiculus ; —**ly,** ad. inepte, insulse, ridicule.
queerness, s. insulsitas, f.
quell, v.a. opprimo, restinguo, 3 ; sedo ; domo, 1.
quench, v.a. exstinguo, restinguo, 3 ; (the thirst) (sitim) sedo, 1 ; restinguo, 3.
quenchless, a. inexstinctus.
quern, s. mola, f.
querulous, a. querulus ; queribundus ; —**ly,** ad. voce querula, cum questu.
query, s. quæstio; interrogatio; dubitatio, f.
quest, s. investigatio, f. ; **go in** — **of,** peto, 3.
question, s. interrogatio ; (debate) disceptatio ; (doubt) dubitatio, f. ; (at law) lis ; (disputed point) quæstio, f. ; controversia ; *fig.* (matter) res, causa, f. ; **to call in** —, dubito, 1 ; **without** —, non dubium est, haud dubie.
question, v.a. & n. interrogo ; dubito ; (to examine) in jus voco ; (investigate) scrutor, 1.
questionable, a. dubius, incertus.
questioner, s. percontator.
quibble, s. captio ; cavillatio, f.
quibble, v.n. captiose dico, 3 ; cavillor, 1.
quibbler, s. cavillator, m.
quibbling. a. captiosus.

quick, a. (nimble, swift) agilis, celer ; pernix ; (alive) vivus ; (mil. hasty) citatus ; (keen, sharp) acer, acutus ; (of sight) perspicax ; (of scent) sagax ; *fig.* (of mind ; clever) sollers ; **to be —,** (to go fast) propero ; maturo, 1.

quick, quickly, ad. cito ; velociter ; propere ; (hastily) festinanter.

quick, s. (flesh) vivum ; **to the —,** ad vivum ; *fig.* cor, pectus, n. ; medulla, f.

quicken, v.a. (to enliven) animo ; (to hasten) celero, propero ; maturo ; (to rouse) excito, instigo, 1.

quicklime, s. calx viva, f.

quick-march, quick-pace, s. (mil.) citatus gradus, m.

quickness, s. (nimbleness) agilitas ; (liveliness) vivacitas ; (of sight) perspicacitas ; *fig.* sagacitas, f. ; acumen (ingenii), n.

quicksand, s. syrtis, f.

quick-set, viviradix, f. ; **— -hedge,** s. sæpes viva, f.

quick-sighted, a. perspicax ; *fig.* sagax, astutus.

quicksilver, s. argentum vivum, n.

quick-witted, a. sollers.

quiet, a. quietus, tranquillus ; placidus ; (silent) tacitus ; silens, mutus ; **to be** *or* **keep —,** quiesco, 3 ; (to be silent) sileo ; taceo, 2 ; conticesco, 3.

quiet, s. quies, tranquillitas, f. ; (leisure) otium ; (silence) silentium, n. ; (peace) pax, f.

quiet, v.a. tranquillo ; paco, sedo, 1.

quietly, ad. quiete, tranquille ; otiose ; sedate ; tacite.

quietness, s. quies, requies, f. ; otium, n. ; pax, f. ; silentium, n.

quietude, s. tranquillitas, f.

quietus, s. requies (æterna mortis), f.

quill, s. penna, f. ; calamus, m. ; (of porcupines) spina, f. ; (for the cithara) pecten, m.

quill-driver, s. scriba, m.

quilt, s. stragulum, n.

quilt, v.a. consuo, 3.

quince(-apple), s. cydonium, n.

quince-tree, s. cydonius, f.

quincunx, s. quincunx, m.

quinquennial, a. quinquennalis.

quinsy, s. angina, f.   [m.

quintessence, s. *fig.* vis, medulla, f. ; flos,

quire, s. (of singers) chorus ; (of paper) scapus, m.

quirk, s. cavillatio ; *fig.* aculeus, m.

quit, v.a. (to leave) relinquo, desero, 3 ; (to acquit) libero, 1 ; **—,** v.n. discedo, 3 ; migro, 1.

quit, a. liberatus, (ab)solutus ; exemptus (with abl.) ; (to be rid of) careo, 2.

quit, ad. impune.

quite, ad. omnino, penitus, prorsus ; valde ; satis ; **— so,** ita est.

quittance, s. acceptilatio, apocha ; liberatio, f.   [pido, 1.

quiver, v.n. tremo, contremisco, 3 ; tre-

quiver, s. pharetra, f. ; corytus, m.

quivered, a. pharetratus.

quivering, s. tremor, horror, m. ; trepidatio, f.

quoit, s. discus, m.

quota, s. rata pars, portio, f.

quotation, s. (act) prolatio, f. ; (passage quoted) locus allatus, m.

quote, v.a. affero, profero, 3 ; cito, 1.

quoth (he), v. def. ait, inquit.

quotidian, a. quotidianus.

quotient, s. quota pars, f.

Rabbet, s. coagmentum, n.

rabbit, s. cuniculus, m.

rabble, s. plebecula, fæx populi, f. ; vulgus, n. ; (crowd) turba, f. ; grex, m.

rabid, a. rabidus, rabiosus.

rabidness, s. furor, m. ; rabies, f.

race, s. genus, n. ; stirps ; prosapia ; proles ; (nation) gens, f. ; (running) cursus, m. ; (contest) certamen, n.

race, v.n. cursu contendo, 3.

race-course, race-ground, s. stadium, spatium, n. ; hippodromus, m.

race-horse, s. celes, m.

racer, s. (person) cursor ; (horse) celes, m.

raciness, s. sapor, flos ; sucus, m.

racing, s. cursus, m. ; certamen, n.

rack, s. (for punishment) equuleus, m. ; tormentum, n. ; (for holding fodder) falisca, f.

rack, v.a. (on the torture) torqueo, 2 ; (wine) defæco, 1 ; (one's brain) cum animo reputo.   [m.

racket, s. (noise, stir) strepitus, tumultus,

rackety, a. tumultuosus.

racy, a. salsus ; **be — of,** sapio (acc.).

radiance, s. fulgor, splendor, m.

radiant, a. radians, nitidus, clarus, fulgidus, splendidus.

radiate, v.n. radio, 1 ; fulgeo, niteo, 2 ; **—,** v.a. spargo.

radiation, s. radiatio, f.

radical, a. insitus, innatus ; *fig.* totus ; **—ly,** ad. radicitus ; penitus.   [dus, m.

radical, s. (homo) rerum novarum cupi-

radish, s. raphanus, m.

radius, s. radius, m.

raft, s. ratis, f.   [num, n.

rafter, s. canterius, m. ; trabs, f. ; tig-

rag, s. pannus ; (ragged clothes) pannuli, m. pl. ; dilabidæ vestes, f. pl.

ragamuffin, s. pannosus homo, m.
rage, s. furor, m. ; rabies, f. ; ira, f.
rage, v.n. furo, 3 ; sævio, 4 ; (as the sea) æstuo, 1.
ragged, a. (in tatters) lacer ; (wearing such clothes) pannosus.
raging, a. furens, furiosus ; furibundus, rabidus ; —ly, ad. furiose, rabide, furenter.
ragwort, s. senecio, m.
raid, s. incursio, irruptio, f.
raid, v.a. invado.
rail, s. (fence) sæpimentum, n. ; (baluster) cancelli, m. pl.
rail, v.a. & n. sæpio, 4 ; (jest) cavillor, 1 ; (at) maledico, 3 ; insector, 1.
railer, s. insectator, m.
railing, a. maledicus.
railing, s. (fence) sæpimentum, n. ; (abuse) convicium, maledictum, n.
raillery, s. jocatio ; (jeering) cavillatio, f.
raiment, s. vestis, f. ; vestitus, m.
rain, s. pluvia, f. ; imber, m.
rain, v.n. ; it —s, pluit.
rainbow, s. arcus pluvius, arcus, m.
rain-water, s. aqua cœlestis, f. ; aquæ pluviæ, f. pl.
rainy, a. pluvius, pluvialis ; pluviosus.
raise, v.a. attollo, 3 ; elevo, 1 ; (erect) erigo, 3 ; (to build) exstruo, 3 ; (persons to higher rank) proveho, 3 ; (money) cogo, 3 ; (an army) exercitum contraho, 3 ; (a siege) solvo, 3 ; (increase) augeo, 2 ; (to stir up) excito, 1 ; moveo, 2 ; (up) sublevo, 1.
raisin, s. uva passa, f.
rake, s. rastrum, n., irpex, m. ; (person) nebulo, homo dissolutus, m.
rake, v.a. rado ; (together) corrado 3 : *fig.* — up, colligo, 3.
rakish, a. dissolutus ; (smart) comptus.
rally, v.a. irrideo, 2 ; cavillor, 1 ; (troops) reduco ; (to recover) recolligo, 3 ; —, v.n. ex fuga convenire, 4.
ram, s. aries, m. ; (also a battering-ram).
ram, v.n. fistuco, 1 ; pavio ; (to stuff) infercio, 4.
ramble, s. vagatio, ambulatio, f.
ramble, v.n. vagor, erro, ambulo, 1.
rambler, s. erro, m.
rambling, a. vagus.
rammer, s. fistuca ; pavicula, f.
ramp, v.n. luxurio, 1.
rampant, a. ferox ; petulans, lascivus ; luxuriosus.
rampart, s. vallum, propugnaculum, n. ; agger, m.
rampion, s. phyteuma, n. ; campanula rapunculus, (mod. hort.).
rancid, a. rancidus.

rancorous, a. infensus, infestus ; invidus ; malignus ; —ly, a. infense, infeste, maligne.
rancour, s. simultas, f. ; odium, n.
random, a. fortuitus ; at —, temere ; — -shot, s. sine scopo emissus, m.
range, s. series, f. ; ordo, m. ; (class) genus, n. ; (of mountains) jugum, n. ; (tract) tractus, m. ; (kitchen-grate) caminus, m. ; (reach) teli jactus, m. ; (extent) magnitudo, f.
range, v.a. ordino, 1 ; dispono, 3 ; (traverse) pervagor, lustro, 1.
ranger, s. (forester) saltuarius.
rank, s. series, f. ; ordo ; gradus, m. ; dignitas, f. [collocor, numeror, 1.
rank, v.a. colloco ; ordino, 1 ; —, v.n.
rank, a. luxurians ; immodicus ; (of smell) fetidus ; rancidus.
rankle, v.n. suppuro, 1 ; *fig.* (be inflamed) incendor ; (be stored up) recondor, 3.
rankness, s. (in growth) luxuria, f. ; (of smell) fetor, m.
ransack, v.a. diripio, 3 ; (to pry about) rimor, 1 ; (to search) exquiro, 3.
ransom, s. redemptio, f. ; pretium, n.
ransom, v.a. redimo, 3.
rant, v.n. superbe loquor, 3 ; bacchor, 1.
rant, s. vaniloquentia, f.
ranter, s. clamator, m.
ranunculus, s. ranunculus, m.
rap, s. (slap) alapa, f. ; (blow) ictus, m. ; (with the knuckles) talitrum, n. ; (at the door) pulsatio, f.
rap, v.a. & n. pulso, 1 ; ferio, 4.
rapacious, a. rapax ; avidus.
rapacity, s. rapacitas ; aviditas, f.
rape, s. raptus, m. ; vitium virginis, stuprum, n. ; (turnip) rapum, n.
rapid, a. rapidus, celer ; velox, citus ; —ly, ad. rapide ; cito : velociter, celeriter.
rapidity, s. rapiditas ; velocitas, f.
rapier, s. gladius ; ensis, m.
rapine, s. rapina, f. [furor, m.
rapture, s. animus exsultans (lætitia) ;
rapturous, a. (of things) mirificus ; jucundus ; (of persons) lætitia elatus.
rare, a. rarus ; inusitatus ; (infrequent) infrequens ; mirus ; *fig.* eximius, singularis ; (thin) tenuis.
rarely, v.a. rarefacio, 3 ; v.n. raresco.
rarely, ad. raro.
rarity, s. raritas ; paucitas ; (thing) res rara *or* singularis, f.
rascal, s. homo nequam, scelestus, m.
rascality, s. scelera, n. pl. ; malitia ; fæx populi, f.
rascally, a. scelestus, flagitiosus, nequam.
rase, v.a. erado, 3 ; (to graze) stringo, 3 ; (overthrow) everto, 3 ; solo æquo, 1

rash, a. præceps, temerarius ; inconsultus ; —ly, ad. temere ; inconsulte.
rash, s. formicatio, f.
rashness, s. temeritas, imprudentia, f.
rasp, s. (large file) scobina, f.
raspberry, s. — -bush, s. rubus, m.
rat, s. mus rattus, m. ; (person) transfuga, m.
rat, v.n. & a. transfugio, 3 ; transeo, 4.
rate, s. (price) pretium ; (of interest) fænus, n. ; (tax) census, m. ; (manner) modus, m.
rate, v.a. æstimo, 1 ; (to tax) censeo, 2 ; (to scold) objurgo, 1.
rather, ad. potius ; libentius ; (slightly, somewhat) aliquantum, paulo, sub . . . ; expressed also by the comparative of adjectives ; **nay** —, immo ; **I had** —, malo.
ratification, s. confirmatio, f.
ratify, v.a. ratum facio, 3 ; confirmo, 1 ; sancio, 4.
rating, s. (brawling) convicium, n. ; (scolding) objurgatio, f.
ratio, s. proportio, f.
ration, s. (portion) demensum, n. ; (mil.) cibaria, n. pl.
rational, a. rationis particeps ; intelligens ; sapiens ; —ly, ad. sapienter.
rattle, s. crepitus, strepitus ; fragor, m. ; (children's —) crepitaculum ; crepundia, n. pl. ; (musical instrument) sistrum, n.
rattle, v.a. & n. crepito ; crepo, 1 ; (to talk idly) garrio, 4.
rattle-snake, s. crotalus, m.
rattling, s. crepitus, m. ; —, a., v. **noisy.**
rat-trap, s. decipula, f.   [diripio, 3.
ravage, v.a. vasto, spolio, populor, 1 ;
ravage, s. vastatio, direptio, populatio, f.
ravager, s. vastator, populator, m.
rave, v.n. furo, 3 ; sævio, 4 ; *fig.* bacchor, 1.
ravel, v.a. involvo, 3 ; implico, 1.
raven, v.n. furo.
raven, s. corvus, m.
ravenous, a. rapax, vorax ; edax.
ravenousness, s. voracitas ; rapacitas, f.
ravine, s. angustiæ, fauces, f. pl. ; saltus, m.   [sus, rabidus.
raving, a. furiosus, furens, insanus, rabio-
ravish, v.a. rapio, 3 ; (a woman) constupro, 1 ; (delight) delecto, 1.
ravisher, s. raptor ; stuprator, m.
ravishing, a. jucundus, suavis, mirificus.
ravishingly, ad. mirifice ; suaviter, jucunde.
ravishment, s. raptio ; *fig.* voluptas.
raw, a. crudus, incoctus ; (of wounds) crudus ; (unripe) immaturus ; (unwrought) rudis ; (of weather) frigidus ; *fig.* rudis ; imperitus.

raw-boned, a. strigosus.
ray, s. (of the sun) radius, m.
raze, v.a. (a town, etc.) solo æquo, 1 ; everto, 3.
razor, s. novacula, f.
reach, v.a. & n. attingo, 3 ; (to come up to) assequor, 3 ; (to approach) appropinquo, 1 ; (to hand) trado, 3 ; (to arrive at) pervenio, 4 ; consequor ; (to stretch) extendor ; (to vomit) vomo, 3.
reach, s. tractus, m. ; spatium, n. ; (of a missile) jactus ; (capacity) captus, m.
read, v.a. & n. lego, 3 ; verso ; (aloud) recito, 1.
readable, a. legibilis, lectu facilis.
reader, s. lector ; recitator.
readily, ad. (willingly) libenter ; (easily) facile.   [in promptu.
readiness, s. facultas, facilitas, f. ; **in** —,
reading, s. lectio ; recitatio ; (interpretation of a passage) lectio, f.
ready, a. paratus ; promptus ; expeditus ; (willing) libens ; (easy) facilis ; — **money,** s. præsens pecunia, f. ; **to be** —, præsto sum.
real, a. verus ; certus ; germanus ; — **property,** s. fundus, m. ; —ly, ad. re vera ; (surely) sane, certe.
reality, s. res ; veritas, f. ; verum, n.
realization, s. effectio ; effectus, m. ; (of ideas) cognitio rerum, f.
realize, v.a. efficio, ad exitum perduco ; (to convert into ready money) redigo ; (to understand) comprehendo, 3 ; (to the mind) repræsento, 1.
realm, s. regnum, n.
ream, s. (of paper) scapus, m.
reanimate, v.a. in vitam revoco, 1 ; reficio, 3 ; recreo, 1 ; erigo, 3 ; confirmo, 1.
reap, v.a. meto, 3 ; deseco, 1 ; *fig.* capio, percipio, 3.
reaper, s. messor, m.
reaping-hook, s. falx, f.
reappear, v.n. rursus appareo, 2 ; redeo, 4 ; resurgo, 3.
rear, v.a. educo, 1 ; alo, 3 ; —, v.n. (of horses) arrectum se tollere, 3.
rear, s. (mil.) novissimum agmen ; extremum agmen, n.
rearing, s. educatio, f.
reason, s. mens, intelligentia ; (faculty) ratio ; (motive) causa, f. ; (understanding) consilium, n. ; (right) jus, æquum, n. ; **by** — **of,** ob, propter.
reason, v.n. ratiocinor, disputo, 1.
reasonable, a. (rational) rationalis, rationis particeps ; (sane) sanus ; (judicious) prudens ; (just) justus, æquus ; (moderate) mediocris, modicus.
reasonableness, s. prudentia ; æquitas ; moderatio, f.

reasonably, ad. merito ; jure ; juste.

reasoner, s. disputator, m.

reasoning, s. ratio ; ratiocinatio ; disceptatio, f.

reassemble, v.a. recolligo, 3.

reassert, v.a. itero, 1.

reassume, v.a. resumo, 3.

reassure, v.a. confirmo, 1.

rebel, a. & s. rebellis, seditiosus.

rebel, v.n. deficio, descisco, 3 ; rebello, 1 ; rebellionem facio, 3.

rebellion, s. rebellio, seditio, defectio, f.

rebellious, a. rebellis, seditiosus ; (disobedient) contumax ; —ly, ad. seditiose.

rebound, v.n. resilio, 4 ; resulto, 1.

rebound, s. repercussus, m.

rebuff, s. repulsa, f.

rebuff, v.a. repello, rejicio ; sperno, 3.

rebuild, v.a. reficio, restituo, 3.

rebuke, v.a. vitupero, 1 ; reprehendo, 3.

rebuke, s. vituperatio, reprehensio, f.

rebut, v.a. repello, refello, redarguo, 3.

recall, v.a. revoco, 1 ; (to the mind) in memoriam redigo, 3.

recall, s. revocatio, f. ; (mil.) receptus, m.

recant, v.a. recanto, retracto, 1.

recantation, s. palinodia, f.

recapitulate, v.a. breviter repeto, summatim colligo, 3.

recapitulation, s. enumeratio, repetitio, f.

recapture, v.a. recipio, 3 ; recupero, 1.

recapture, s. recuperatio, f.

recast, v.a. recoquo, 3 ; fig. renovo, 1 ; (alter) muto, 1.

recede, v.n. recedo ; refugio, discedo, 3.

receipt, s. (act) acceptio ; (quittance) acceptilatio, f. ; (money received) acceptum, n. ; (recipe) compositio, f.

receive, v.a. accipio, recipio, excipio ; (to get) percipio, 3.

receiver, s. (of stolen goods) receptor ; (of customs) exactor, m.

recent, a. recens ; —ly, ad. nuper, modo.

receptacle, s. receptaculum, n.; cisterna, f.

reception, s. aditus, m. ; admissio, f. ; (of a guest) hospitium, n.

recess, s. (place) recessus, secessus, m. ; latebra, f. ; (vacation) feriæ, f. pl. ; justitium, n.

recipe, s. præscriptum, n. ; compositio, f.

recipient, s. acceptor, m.

reciprocal, a. mutuus, —ly, ad. mutuo ; vicissim.

reciprocate, v.a. alterno, 1.

reciprocation, reciprocity, s. reciprocatio, vicissitudo, f.

recital, s. narratio ; enumeratio ; recitatio, f.

recitation, s. recitatio ; lectio, f.

recite, v.a. narro ; recito, 1.

reciter, recitator, m.

reck, v.a. & n. curo, 1 ; sollicitus sum ; it —s me not, nihil ad me.

reckless, a. neglegens ; (rash) temerarius ; imprudens ; —ly, ad. temere.

recklessness, s. neglegentia, incuria ; temeritas, f.

reckon, v.a. numero ; computo, æstimo, 1 ; —, duco, pendo, 3 ; (on) confido (alicui, aliqua re) ; to — up, enumero, 1.

reckoner, s. computator, m.

reckoning, s. numeratio ; (account) ratio, f.

reclaim, v.a. reposco ; repeto, 3 ; (correct) corrigo, 3.

recline, v.a. reclino, 1 ; —, v.n. recubo, 1 ; recumbo, 3 ; jaceo, 2 ; — at table, accubo, 1 ; accumbo, 3.

reclining, a. reclinis, resupinus.

recluse, s. anachoreta, eremita, m. ; —, a. solitarius.

recognition, s. recognitio, f. ; in — of, pro (abl.). [datio, f.

recognizance, s. vadimonium, n. ; satis-

recognize, v.a. agnosco ; recognosco, cognosco, 3.

recoil, v.n. resilio, recido, 4 ; (from) recedo, refugio, discedo, 3.

recoil, s. repercussus, m.

recollect, v.a. (to remember) recordor, 1 ; reminiscor, 3 ; memini.

recollection, s. memoria ; recordatio, f.

recommence, v.a. itero, renovo, 1 ; repeto, 3.

recommend, v.a. commendo, 1.

recommendation, s. commendatio, f.

recommendatory, a. commendaticius.

recommender, s. commendator, suasor, m.

recompense, s. præmium, n. ; merces, remuneratio.

recompense, v.a. remuneror ; (to indemnify) compenso, 1.

reconcilable, a. placabilis ; (of things) conveniens.

reconcile, v.a. reconcilio, 1 ; in gratiam restituo, 3 ; be —d to, æquo animo fero, 3 ; be —d with (in harmony with) convenio, 4.

reconciliation, s. reconciliatio, f. ; reditus in gratiam, m. [cultus.

recondite, a. reconditus, abstrusus, oc-

reconduct, v.a. reduco, 3.

reconnoitre, v.a. exploro, speculor, 1.

reconnoitring party, s. exploratores, m. pl.

reconquer, v.a. recipio, 3 ; recupero, 1.

reconsider, v.a. recognosco, 3 ; retracto, 1.

record, v.a. memoro, commemoro, narro.

record, s. mentio, narratio, f. ; monumentum, n. ; historia, f. ; —s, pl. annales, m. pl.

recorder, s. quæsitor.

record-office, s. tabularium, n.

recount, v.a. refero, 3; memoro, narro, enarro, 1.

recoup, v.a. (to indemnify) compenso, 1.

recourse, s. **to have — to,** confugio, perfugio, 3; adeo, 4.

recover v.a. (to get again) recupero, 1; recipio, 3; —, v.n. convalesco, 3; (one's self) ad se redire, 4.

recoverable, a. reparabilis; (curable) sanabilis.

recovery, s. recuperatio; (from illness) recreatio, refectio, f.

recreant, a. ignavus; —s, s. apostata, m.

recreate, v.a. recreo, 1; reficio, 3.

recreation, s. animi remissio, oblectatio, f.; (for children) lusus, m.

recriminate, v.a. crimen in accusatorem rejicio, 3.

recrimination, s. mutua accusatio, f.

recruit, v.a. (to refresh) reficio, 3; recreo, 1; (troops) suppleo, 2.

recruit, s. tiro, m.

recruiting, s. delectus, m.; supplementum, n.

rectangular, a. orthogonius.

rectification, s. correctio, emendatio, f.

rectify, v.a. corrigo, 3; emendo, 1.

rectitude, s. probitas, fides, integritas, f.

rector, s. rector, m.

recumbent, a. recubans, supinus, resupinus.

recur, v.n. recurro.

recurrence, s. reditus, m.

recurrent, a. recurrens.

red, a. ruber; (ruddy) rubicundus; (of hair) rufus; **to be —,** rubeo, 2; **to grow —,** rubesco, erubesco, 3.

redbreast, s. sylvia rubecula, f.

redden, v.a. rubefacio, 3; —, v.n. rubesco; erubesco, 3.

reddish, a. surrufus, surrubicundus, rubicundulus.

redeem, v.a. redimo, 3; libero; (a pledge) repignoro, 1.

redeemer, s. liberator; (our Saviour) redemptor, m.

redemption, s. redemptio, f.

red-hot, a. candens.

red-hot poker, s. kniphofia; tritoma (mod. hort.).

red-lead, s. minium, n.

redness, s. rubor, m.

redolent, a. fragrans, redolens.

redouble, v.a. gemino, ingemino, 1.

redoubt, s. propugnaculum, n.

redoubtable, a. formidabilis.

redound, v.n. resilio, 4; **it —s to your credit,** famae tuae prodest.

redress, v.a. emendo, 1; corrigo, 3; medeor, 2.

redress, s. (remedy) remedium, n.

reduce, v.a. reduco (ad, in); redigo; (to lessen) minuo, 3.

reducible, a. (subdue) domo, 1.

reduction, s. deminutio, f.

redundancy, s. redundantia, f.

redundant, a. redundans, supervacaneus, superfluus.

reduplicate, v.a. duplico, 1.

reduplication, s. duplicatio, f.

re-echo, v.a. & n. reddo, repeto, 3; —, v.n. resono, persono, 1.

reed, s. arundo, f.; calamus, m.; canna, f.

reedy, a. arundineus; (full of reeds) arundinosus.

reef, s. scopulus, m.; dorsum, n.; cautes, f.

reef, v.a. contraho, lego, 3.

reek, s. fumus, vapor, m.; —, v.n. fumo, vaporo, 1.

reel, s. rhombus, m.

reel, v.n. (to stagger) vacillo, titubo, 1.

re-embark, v.n. navem iterum conscendo, 3.

re-enter, v.a. iterum intro, 1.

re-establish, v.a. restituo, reficio, 3.

re-establishment, s. restitutio, f.

refectory, s. cenatio, f.

refer, v.a. refero (ad); remitto (ad), 3; —, v.n. (to allude) perstringo, attingo, 3; (to regard) specto, 1.

referee, s. arbiter, disceptator, m.

reference, s. (respect) ratio, f.

refine, v.a. purgo, 1; excolo, 3; expolio, 4; (metals) excoquo, 3.

refined, a. politus; fig. cultus, politus; elegans; urbanus; humanus.

refinement, s. fig. urbanitas, humanitas; elegantia, f.

reflect, v.a. repercutio, 3; —, v.n. considero, meditor, reputo, 1; revolvo, 3; **— upon,** (to blame) vitupero, 1.

reflection, s. repercussus, m.; (thing reflected) imago; fig. consideratio, f.; (blame) reprehensio, f.

reform, v.a. reficio; (to amend) corrigo, 3; emendo, 1; —, v.n. se corrigere, 3.

reform, s. correctio, f.

reformation, s. correctio, f.

reformer, s. corrector, emendator, m.

refract, v.a. refringo, 3.

refractory, a. contumax; indocilis.

refrain, s. versus intercalaris, m.

refrain, v.n. abstineo, 2; parco, 3; tempero, 1.

refresh, v.a. recreo, 1; reficio, 3; (the memory) redintegro, 1; (cool) refrigero, 1.   [jucundus.

refreshing, a. (cool) frigidus; (pleasant)

refreshment, s. refectio, f.; (food) cibus, m.

refuge, s. refugium, perfugium, asylum, n.; **to take —,** (to), confugio (in . . .).

refugee, s. profugus, m.; exul, c.
refund, v.a. reddo, 3.
refusal, s. recusatio; repudiatio; detrectatio; repulsa, f.
refuse, v.a. recuso, nego; repudio, 1; renuo, 3; denego, detrecto, 1.
refuse, s. recrementum, purgamentum, n.; fæx, f.; quisquiliæ, f. pl.; (of metals) scoria, f.
refutation, s. refutatio, confutatio, f.
refute, v.a. refuto, confuto, 1; refello, redarguo, 3.
refuter, s. refutator, confutator, m.
regain, v.a. recipio, 3; recupero, 1.
regal, a. regalis, regius, regificus; —ly, ad. regie, regaliter, regifice.
regale, v.a. (aliquem) convivio excipio, 3.
regalia, s. insignia regia, n. pl.
regard, s. respectus, m.; ratio; (care, etc.) cura, f.
regard, v.a. respicio, 3; intueor, 2; (to observe) observo; (to concern) specto; (to mind, to care) curo; (to esteem) æstimo, 1; pendo, 3; (respect) rationem habeo, 2.
regardful, a. attentus; —ly, ad. attente.
regarding, pr., v. **concerning.**
regardless, a. neglegens, incuriosus; v. **heedless.**   [regnum, n.
regency, s. procuratio regni, f.; inter-
regenerate, v.a. regenero; *fig.* redintegro, renovo, restauro, 1; (correct) corrigo, 3.
regeneration, s. regeneratio, f.
regent, s. procurator regni interrex, m.
regicide, s. (murderer) regis occisor, m.; (murder) cædes regis, f.
regimen, s. (government) rerum administratio; (diet) diæta, f.; victus, m.
regiment, s. legio, caterva, f.
regimental, a. legionarius.
regimentals, s. ornatus militaris, m.
region, s. regio, plaga, f.; tractus, m.
register, s. tabulæ, f. pl.; index, m.
register, v.a. in tabulas refero, 3.
registrar, s. tabularius; ab actis; actuarius, m.
registration, s. perscriptio, f.
registry, s. tabularia, f.; tabularium, n.
regret, v.a. (to be sorry for) ægre fero, 3; (to bemoan) doleo; piget, 2; (repent) pænitet, 2; (miss) desidero, 1; careo, 2.
regret, s. pænitentia, f.; dolor, m.; (feeling of loss) desiderium, n.
regular, a. (fixed) certus; (according to law) legitimus, justus; (usual) usitatus; —ly, ad. ordine; juste, legitime; (at fixed times) certis temporibus.
regularity, s. symmetria; constantia; (uniformity) æquabilitas, f.
regulate, v.a. ordino, 1; dispono; præscribo, 3; administro, 1.

regulation, s. ordinatio; moderatio, temperatio, f.; (law) lex, f.; (rule) præscriptum, n.
regulator, s. moderator, m.
rehabilitate, v.a. restituo, 3.
-**rehearsal,** s. (recital) narratio, recitatio; (of a play, etc.) prolusio, exercitatio, meditatio, f.
rehearse, v.a. recito, 1; repeto, 3; (practise) meditor, 1; præludo, 3.
reign, s. regnum, n.; —, v.n. regno; dominor, 1.
reimburse, v.a. rependo, 3.
reimbursement, s. restitutio pecuniæ, f.
rein, s. habena, f.; frenum, lorum, n.; —, v.a. freno, 1; *fig.* cohibeo, 2.
reindeer, s. tarandrus, m.; — **skin,** reno, m.   [firmo, 1.
ιe**inforce,** v.a. suppleo, 2; auxiliis con-
reinforcement, s. (mil.) novæ copiæ, f. pl.; subsidium, n.
reinstate, v.a. restituo, 3.
reinstatement, s. restitutio, f.
reiterate, v.a. itero, 1.
reiteration, s. iteratio, f.
reject, v.a. rejicio, 3; repudio, 1; repello; (to hiss off) explodo, 3; (scorn) sperno, 3.
rejection, s. rejectio, repudiatio, repulsa, f.
rejoice, v.a. lætifico, delecto, 1; —, v.n. gaudeo, 2; exsulto, lætor, 1.
rejoin, v.a. (meet) convenio, 4; —, v.n. (answer) respondeo, 2; resequor, 3.
rejoinder, s. responsum, n.
rekindle, v.n. refoveo, 2; excito, 1.
relapse, v.n. recido, relabor, 3.
relapse, s. morbus recidivus, m.
relate, v.a. refero; memoro; narro, 1.
related, a. (by blood) consanguineus; (by marriage) affinis; *fig.* propinquus, cognatus; conjunctus.
relater, s. narrator, m.
relation, s. narratio; (reference) ratio; (relationship) cognatio, f.; (person) cognatus, m.; cognata, f.
relationship, s. propinquitas; necessitudo; cognatio; (by blood) consanguinitas; (by marriage) affinitas; *fig.* conjunctio, f.
relative, a. cognatus (gr.), relativus; —ly, ad. pro ratione.   [**related.**
relative, s. cognatus, m.; cognata, f.; v.
relax, v.a. remitto, 3; laxo, relaxo, 1; resolvo, 3; —, v.n. relanguesco; (to abate) remittor, 3.
relaxation, s. remissio; relaxatio, f.
relay, s. cursus publici, m. pl.
release, v.a. libero, 1; resolvo, 3; laxo, 1; (disburden) exonero, levo, relevo, 1.
release, s. liberatio; absolutio; (discharge) missio, f.

relegate, v.a. relego, 1.
relent, v.n. mitesco, 3 ; mitigor, 1; lenior, 4.   [atrox, durus.
relentless, a. immisericors, inexorabilis,
relevant, a. aptus, appositus.
reliance, s. fiducia, f. ; fides, f.
relic, s. reliquiæ, f. pl. ; monumentum, n.
relict, s. (widow) vidua, f.
relief, s. (comfort) solatium ; (alleviation) levamentum ; (help) auxilium, n. ; (remedy) medicina, f. ; remedium, n. ; (in sculpture) cælatura, f.
relieve, v.a. levo, allevo ; mitigo, 1 ; (to aid) succurro, 3 ; (succeed) subeo, 4 ; (take over a duty) excipio, 3.
religion, s. religio, pietas, f.
religious, a. religiosus ; pius ; —ly, ad. religiose ; pie.
religiousness, s. pietas, f.
relinquish, v.a. relinquo, 3 ; derelinquo, demitto, omitto, depono, 3.
relinquishment, s. derelictio, f.
relish, s. (flavour) sapor, m. ; (seasoning) condimentum ; (fondness) studium, n.
relish, v.a. saporem do, 1 ; (to like) gusto, 1 ; (enjoy) fruor, 3.
reluctance, s. aversatio, f. ; **with** —, invitus.
reluctant, a. invitus ; —ly, ad. invitus (adj.) ; ægre.
rely, v.n. confido (alicui or aliqua re), 3.
remain, v.n. maneo, permaneo, 2 ; resto, 1 ; (last) sto, duro, 1.
remainder, s. reliquum, n.
remains, s. pl. reliquiæ, f. pl.
remand, v.a. remitto, 3 ; comperendino, 1.
remand, s. comperendinatio, f.
remark, v.a. observo, 1 ; animadverto, 3.
remark, s. observatio, animadversio, f. ; (something said) dictum, n.
remarkable, a. insignis, memorabilis, notabilis ; mirus ; egregius.
remarkably, ad. insigniter ; mire ; egregie.
remediable, a. sanabilis.
remedial, a. medicus, medicabilis.
remediless, a. insanabilis.
remedy, s. remedium, n. ; medicina, f. [3.
remedy, v.a. sano, 1 ; medeor, 2 ; corrigo,
remember, v.a. memini, recordor, 1 ; reminiscor, 3.
remembrance, s. memoria, recordatio, f.
remembrancer, s. monitor, m.
remind, v.a. commoneo, 2 ; commonefacio, 3.
reminiscence, s. recordatio, f.
remiss, a. neglegens ; incuriosus ; —ly, ad. neglegenter ; incuriose.
remission, s. remissio ; venia, f.
remissness, s. neglegentia, f.
remit, v.a. remitto, 3 ; (to forgive) condono, 1 ; (money) transmitto, 3 ; (soften) mitigo, 1 ; —, v.n. relaxor, 1.

remittance, remissio, f.
remnant, s. reliquum, n. ; reliquiæ, f. pl.
remodel, v.a. recoquo, 3 ; reformo ; transfiguro, retracto, 1.
remonstrance, s. acclamatio, intercessio, interpellatio, f.
remonstrate, v.a. obtestor, acclamo, interpello, 1 ; ægre fero, 3.
remorse, s. angor conscientiæ, m. ; stimuli, m. pl.
remorseless, a. immisericors ; durus ; crudelis.
remote, a. remotus ; amotus, ultimus ; longinquus ; disjunctus ; —ly, ad. remote ; procul ; (slightly) leviter.
remoteless, s. longinquitas, distantia, f.
remount, v.a. iterum conscendo, 3.
removal, s. remotio ; exportatio ; (banishment) amandatio ; relegatio ; (changing one's dwelling) migratio, f.
remove, v.a. amoveo, 2 ; depello, tollo, detraho, 3 ; amando, 1 ; —, v.n. migro ; demigro, 1.
remunerate, v.a. remuneror, 1.
remuneration, s. remuneratio, f.
rend, v.a. discerpo, 3 ; lacero, dilanio, 1 ; (to split) findo, 3 ; —, v.n. findor, 3.
render, v.a. reddo ; facio ; (hand over) trado ; (a town, etc.) dedo ; (to translate) verto, 3.
rendering, s. (translation) translatio, f.
rendezvous, s. locus præscriptus (ad conveniendum) ; (meeting itself) conventus, m.
renegade, s. apostata ; transfuga, m.
renew, v.a. renovo ; novo ; redintegro, 1.
renewal, s. renovatio ; integratio, f.
rennet, s. coagulum, n.
renounce, v.a. missum facio ; pono, depono, 3 ; (to deny) nego, 1.
renovate, v.a. renovo, redintegro, 1 ; (repair) reparo, instauro, 1.
renovation, s. renovatio, f.
renown, s. fama, gloria, f. ; nomen, n.
renowned, a. insignis, celebris, clarus ; præclarus.
rent, s. reditus, m. ; vectigal, n. ; merces, pensio, f. ; (fissure) scissura, rima, f.
rent, v.a. (to let out) loco, 1 ; (to hire) conduco, 3.
renter, s. conductor, m.
renunciation, s. abdicatio, repudiatio, f.
reopen, v.a. iterum aperio, 4 ; fig. retrecto.
repair, v.a. (buildings) reparo, instauro, 1 ; (to make good) reficio ; restituo, 3 ; (clothes) resarcio, 4 ; (cure) sano, 1 ; (make amends for) sarcio, 4 ; —, v.n. se recipere, se conferre, 3.
repair, s. refectio ; **in** —, (of houses) sartus tectus.
repairer, s. refector, m.

reparable, a. reparabilis.
reparation, s. restitutio, f. ; (amends) satisfactio, f.
repartee, s. salsum dictum, n.
repast, s. cena, f.
repay, v.a. repono, retribuo, 3 ; remuneror, 1 ; (compensate) penso, compenso, repenso, 1.
repayment, s. solutio ; remuneratio, f.
repeal, v.a. abrogo, 1 ; rescindo, tollo, 3.
repeal, s. abrogatio, f.
repeat, v.a. itero, 1 ; repeto, 3 ; (by heart) recito, 1.
repeatedly, ad. iterum atque iterum, saepius.
repel, v.a. repello, 3 ; fig. aspernor, 1.
repent, v.n. paenitet (me), 2.
repentance, s. paenitentia, f.
repentant, a. paenitens.
repeople, v.a. populum induco, 3 ; suppleo, 2.
repercussion, s. repercussio, f.
repertory, s. repertorium, n.
repetition, s. iteratio ; repetitio, f.
repine, v.n. conqueror, 3 ; doleo, 2 ; aegre fero, 3 ; me piget, 2.
repining, s. querela, f. ; questus, m.
replace, v.a. repono ; (to restore) restituo ; (substitute) substituo, suppono, 3.
replenish, v.a. repleo, suppleo, 2.
replete, a. repletus, plenus, satur.
repletion, s. satietas, f.
reply, s. responsum, n. ; responsio, f. ; —, v.a. respondeo, 2 ; refero, 3.
report, v.a. fero, 3 ; narro, nuntio, 1 ; (to state) propono, 3.
report, s. (rumour) fama, f. ; rumor, m. ; (hearsay) auditio, f. ; (noise) fragor, crepitus, m. ; relatio ; narratio, f.
reporter, s. (narration) narrator, notarius, m.
repose, v.a. (to place) pono ; (trust) confido ; v.n. (rest) quiesco, requiesco, 3.
repose, s. quies, requies, f.
repository, s. repositorium ; (magazine) receptaculum, n.   [culpo, 1.
reprehend, v.a. reprehendo, 3 ; vitupero,
reprehensible, a. vituperabilis ; culpabilis.
reprehension, s. reprehensio ; culpa ; vituperatio, f.
represent, v.a. repraesento, 1 ; exprimo ; propono, 3 ; (act in stead of) vicem impleo (gen.), 2 ; loco sum (gen.) ; (point out) indico, 1.
representation, s. (act) repraesentatio ; (statement) editio ; (likeness) imago, f. ; make —s to, colloquor cum (abl.), 3.
representative, a. vicem cujuspiam gerens ; —, s. vicarius ; procurator, m.
repress, v.a. reprimo, comprimo, 3 ; coerceo, 2 ; (tame) domo, 1.

repression, s. refrenatio, coercitio, f.
reprieve, s. dilatio (supplicii), f. ; —, .v.a. diem prorogare damnato.
reprimand, v.a. reprehendo, 3 ; —, s. reprehensio, f.
reprisal, s. talio ; vindicta, f.
reproach, v.a. objicio, 3 ; exprobro ; vitupero ; accuso, 1.
reproach, s. exprobratio, vituperatio, f. ; probrum, n.
reproachable, a. convicio dignus.
reproachful, a. objurgatorius.
reprobate, v.a. improbo, 1.
reprobate, a. & s. damnatus, perditus, nequam, m.
reprobation, s. improbatio, f.
reproduce, v.a. refero, 3.
reproof, s. reprehensio, vituperatio, objurgatio, f.
reprove, v.a. objurgo, vitupero, 1 ; reprehendo, 3.
reprover, s. objurgator, vituperator, m.
reptile, s. repens animal, n.
republic, s. respublica, civitas popularis, libera civitas, f.
republican, a. popularis.
republican, s. plebis fautor, m.
repudiate, v.a. repudio, 1 ; respuo, renuo, abnuo, sperno, 3.
repudiation, s. repudiatio, f.
repugnance, s. aversatio, f. ; fastidium, n. ; fuga, f.
repugnant, a. odiosus ; alienus.
repulse, v.a. repello, 3 ; propulso, fugo, 1 ; —, s. repulsa, f.   [n.
repulsion, s. repulsus, m. ; (dislike) odium,
repulsive, a. odiosus ; foedus.
repurchase, v.a. redimo, 3.
reputable, a. honestus, bonae famae.
reputably, ad. honeste.
reputation, repute, s. fama, existimatio, f. ; nomen, n.
repute, v.a. existimo, 1 ; habeo, 2 ; duco, 3.
request, s. preces, f. pl. ; at the — of, rogatu, f.
request, v.a. rogo, 1 ; peto, 3 ; supplico, precor, 1.
require, v.a. postulo, 1 ; posco, 3 ; (need) egeo, 2 ; desidero, 1.
requirements, s. necessaria, n. pl.
requisite, a. necessarius.
requisition, s. impero, n.
requital, s. merces, f.
requite, v.a. compenso, penso, 1 ; rependo, refero, reddo, 3 ; remuneror, 1.
rescind, v.a. rescindo, tollo, 3.
rescript, s. rescriptum, n.
rescue, v.a. libero, recupero ; (to save) servo, 1.
rescue, s. liberatio, recuperatio, f.
research, s. investigatio, f.

resemblance, s. similitudo, f. ; instar, n. (indecl.).

resemble, v.n. similis sum.

resembling, a. similis.

resent, v.a. ægre *or* graviter fero, 3 ; indignor, 1.

resentful, a. iracundus ; indignans.

resentment, s. indignatio, f.

reservation, s. retentio, f.

reserve, v.a. reservo, 1 ; repono, condo, recondo, 3 ; retineo, 2.

reserve, s. (silence) taciturnitas, f. ; (mil.) subsidium, n.

reserved, a. (silent) taciturnus, tectus.

reservoir, s. cisterna, f. ; receptaculum, n. ; lacus, m.

reside, v.n. habito, commoror, 1.

residence, s. habitatio ; sedes, f. ; domicilium, n. ; (sojourn) commoratio, f.

resident, s. habitator, m.

residue, s. residuum, reliquum, n.

resign, v.a. cedo, depono, 3 ; abdico, 1 ; — oneself to, æquo animo fero, 3.

resignation, s. (act) abdicatio ; (law) cessio, f. ; *fig.* æquus animus, m.

resin, s. resina, f.

resinous, a. resináceus ; resinosus.

resist, v.n. resisto, 3 ; obsto, repugno, adversor, 1.   [sio, f.

resistance, s. repugnantia ; (mil.) defen-

resolute, a. audax ; constans ; fortis ; firmus ; **—ly,** ad. constanter ; fortiter ; audacter ; firme.

resolution, s. consilium, n. ; (of mind) constantia, f. ; (courage) animus, m. ; (of an assembly) decretum, n.

resoluteness, resolve, s. constantia, f. ; consilium, n.

resolve, v.a. decerno, statuo, constituo, 3 ; (to reduce into) solvo ; (solve) solvo, 3 ; resolvo, reduco, redigo, 3.

resonant, a. resonus.

resort, v.n. frequento, celebro, 1 ; (have recourse to) confugio, 3 ; convenio, 4.

resort, s. (refuge) refugium, perfugium, n. ; (gathering) congressus, m. ; frequentia, f.

resound, v.n. resono, persono, 1.

resource, s. refugium, auxilium, n. ; **—s,** opes, f. pl.

respect, v.a. revereor, 2 ; veneror ; observo, 1.

respect, s. (regard) respectus, m.; (reverence) reverentia, observantia, f. ; (relation, reference) ratio, f. ; **in — to,** ad, de ; (as regards) quod attinet ad.

respectability, s. honestas, f.

respectable, a. honestus ; (fairly good) tolerabilis.

respectably, ad. honeste ; (fairly) tolerabiliter, satis.

respectful, a. observans ; reverens ; **—ly,** ad. cum summa observantia ; reverenter.

respecting, pr. ad, de, quod attinet ad.

respiration, s. respiratio, f.

respire, v.n. respiro, 1.

respite, s. (delay) mora ; cessatio ; intermissio, f.

respite, v.a. differo, profero, 3.

resplendence, s. nitor, splendor, m.

resplendent, a. resplendens, clarus, nitidus ; **—ly,** ad. clare, nitide.

respond, v.n. respondeo, 2.

respondent, s. (law) reus, m.

response, s. responsum, n.

responsible, a. obnoxius ; (able to pay) locuples ; **be — for,** præsto, 1.

rest, s. quies ; requies ; pax, f. ; (prop) fulcrum, n. ; statumen, n. ; (remainder) residuum, reliquum, n. ; (of persons) reliqui, ceteri, m. pl.

rest, v.n. (re)quiesco, 3 ; (to pause) cesso, 1 ; (lean) nitor ; (on) innitor, 3 ; **—,** v.a. (to lean) reclino, 1 ; (compose) compono, 3.

resting-place, s. sedes, f. ; (lair) cubile ; (grave) sepulcrum, n.

restitution, s. restitutio.

restive, a. sternax, petulans.

restiveness, s. petulantia, f.

restless, a. inquietus ; turbidus, tumultuosus ; (agitated) sollicitus ; **—ly,** ad. turbulente.   [motus, m.

restlessness, s. inquieto, sollicitudo, f.

restoration, s. refectio ; (recall) reductio, f.

restorative, s. medicamentum, n.

restore, v.a. restituo, reddo, 3 ; restauro, reparo, 1 ; (health, etc.) sano, 1 ; (recall) reduco, 3.

restorer, s. restitutor, m.

restrain, v.a. refreno, 1 ; coerceo, 2 ; (to limit) circumscribo, 3 ; contineo, 2 ; (to prevent) impedio, 4 ; prohibeo, 2.

restraint, s. coercitio ; moderatio, f.

restrict, v.a. cohibeo, 2 ; restringo, circumscribo, 3.

restriction, s. restrictio, limitatio, f.

result, v.n. (ex)orior, 4 ; proficiscor ; fio ; (to follow) consequor, 3.

result, s. (effect) exitus, eventus, m. ; (conclusion) summa, f.

resume, v.a. resumo ; repeto, 3 ; redintegro, 1.

resurrection, s. resurrectio, f.

resuscitate, v.a. resuscito, revoco, 1.

retail, v.a. distraho, divendo, 3.

retailer, s. caupo, propola, institor, m.

retain, v.a. retineo, 2 ; servo, 1.

retainer, s. (adherent) cliens, c. ; (fee) arra, f.

retake, v.a. recipio, 3 ; recupero, 1.

retaliate, v.a. ulciscor, 3 ; (a kindness) remuneror, 1 ; par pro pari refero, 3.
retaliation, s. lex talionis ; ultio, f.
retard, v.a. tardo, retardo, moror, 1 ; impedio, 4.
retch, v.n. nauseo, 1.
retention, s. retentio, f.
retentive, a. tenax.
reticule, s. reticulum, n.
retina, s. retina, f.
retinue, s. comitatus, m. ; pompa ; turba clientium, f.
retire, v.n. recedo, regredior, decedo, 3 ; abeo, 4.
retired, a. remotus ; solitarius ; (hidden) occultus ; quietus ; (superannuated) qui abdicavit.
retirement, s. solitudo, f. ; recessus, m. ; (from office) abdicatio, f.
retort, v.a. regero, refero, 3 ; v.n. respondeo, 2.
retort, s. responsum, n.
retouch, v.a. retracto, 1.
retrace, v.a. repeto, 3 ; — one's steps, revertor, 3.
retract, v.a. retracto, recanto, 1.
retraction, s. palinodia, f.
retreat, v.n. recedo, refugio, 3.
retreat, s. recessus, m. ; pedem refero, refugium, n. ; latebræ, f. pl. ; lustrum, n. ; (mil.) receptus, m.
retrench, v.a. contraho, circumcido, 3.
retribution, s. pœna, vindicta, f. ; supplicium, n.
retrievable, a. reparabilis.
retrieve, v.a. (recover) recupero, 1 ; (make good) sarcio, 4 ; sano, 1.
retrograde, a. retrogradus.
retrograde, v.n. retrogradior ; fig. relabor, 3.
retrogression, s. regressus, m.
retrospect, retrospection, s. respectus, m. ; (calling to mind) recordatio, f.
retrospectively, ad. in præteritum.
return, v.a. (to give back) restituo, reddo, 3 ; (an answer) respondeo, 2 ; (thanks) gratias ago, 3 ; (to send back) remitto, 3 ; —, v.n. (to go back) redeo, 4 ; revertor, 3 ; (to come back) revenio, 4 ; (to answer) respondeo, 2.
return, s. (coming back) reditus ; regressus, m. ; (answer) responsum, n. ; (giving back) restitutio ; (repayment) remuneratio, f. ; (income, profit, etc.) fructus, quæstus ; reditus, m.
reunion, s. reconciliatio, f.
reunite, v.a. & n. reconcilio, 1.
reveal, v.a. retego ; recludo, patefacio, prodo, 3 ; nudo ; (to unveil) revelo, 1 ; (to make known) evulgo, divulgo, 1.
revel, v.n. debacchor, comissor, 1.

revel, s. comissatio, bacchatio, f. ; orgia, n. pl.
revelation, s. patefactio, f.
reveller, s. comissator, m.
revelry, s. comissatio, f. ; orgia, n. pl.
revenge, v.a. ulciscor (ultus sum), 3.
revenge, s. ultio, vindicta, f. ; to take — (on), vindico (in aliquem), 1 ; pœnas repeto ab (aliquo), 3.
revengeful, a. ulciscendi cupidus.
revenger, s. ultor, m. ; ultri, f. ; vindex, c.
revenue, s. reditus, fructus, m. ; vectigal, n. [sono, persono, 1.
reverberate, v.a. repercutio, 3 ; v.n. reverberation,** s. repercussus, m.
revere, reverence, v.a. revereor, 2 ; veneror, observo, 1 ; colo, 3.
reverence, s. reverentia, veneratio, observantia, f.
reverend, a. reverendus ; venerandus ; venerabilis.
reverent, a. reverens ; pius ; —ly, ad. venerabiliter, reverenter.
reverential, a. venerabundus.
reversal, s. rescissio, infirmatio, f.
reverse, s. conversio, commutatio (fortunæ) ; clades, f. ; (contrary) contrarium, n. ; (of a medal) aversa pars, f.
reverse, v.a. inverto ; (to alter) converto ; (annul) rescindo, 3.
reversible, a. versilis.
reversion, s. (law) spes succedendi, f.
reversionary, a. hereditarius.
revert, v.n. revertor, recurro, 3 ; redeo, 4.
review, s. recensio, f. ; recensus, m. ; (critique) censura, f.
review, v.a. recenseo, 2 ; lustro, 1.
reviewer, s. censor, m.
revile, v.a. maledico, 3 ; calumnior, 1.
revise, v.a. recenseo, 2 ; retracto, 1 ; relego, corrigo, 3 ; fig. limo, 1.
reviser, s. corrector ; censor, m.
revision, s. correctio ; (of a literary work), fig. lima, f.
revisit, v.a. reviso, 3.
revival, s. renovatio, f.
revive, v.a. resuscito, 1 ; (to renew) renovo ; (to encourage) animo ; (refresh) recreo ; (recall) revoco, 1 ; —, v.n. revivisco, 3.
revocable, a. revocabilis.
revocation, s. revocatio ; rescissio, f.
revoke, v.a. revoco, 1 ; (a law) rescindo, tollo, 3.
revolt, v.a. offendo, 3 ; —, v.n. rebello, 1 ; descisco, secedo, deficio, 3.
revolt, s. rebellio ; defectio, f.
revolution, s. circuitus, m. ; circumversio, f. ; circumactus, m. ; (change) commutatio, f. ; (of planets) cursus, meatus, m. ; (political) res novæ, f. pl.

revolutionary, a. seditiosus, novarum rerum cupidus.

revolutionist, s. rerum novarum molitor, m. [everto, 3.

revolutionize, v.a. novo, 1 ; (overthrow)

revolve, v.a. volvo, 3 ; voluto, 1 ; v.n. circumvolvor, circumvertor, circumagor, 3.

revolving, a. versatilis, versabundus.

reward, v.a. remuneror, 1.

reward, s. præmium, n. ; merces, f. ; fructus, m.

rewrite, v.a. rescribo, 3.

rhapsodist, s. rhapsodus, m.

rhapsody, s. rhapsodia, f.

Rhenish, a. Rhenanus.

rhetoric, s. rhetorica, oratoria, f. ; rhetorica, n. pl.

rhetorical, a. rhetoricus ; oratorius ; —ly, ad. rhetorice, oratorie.

rhetorician, s. rhetor, orator, m.

rheum, s. gravedo, fluctio, f. ; rheumatismus, m. ; rheuma, n.

rheumatic, a. rheumaticus. [mus, m.

rheumatism, s. dolor artuum, rheumatis-

Rhine, s. Rhenus.

rhinoceros, s. rhinoceros, m.

rhododendron, s. rhododendron, n.

rhomb, s. rhombus, m.

rhomboid, s. rhomboides, n.

Rhone, s. Rhodanus, m.

rhubarb, s. radix Pontica, f. ; rheum (mod. hort.).

rhyme, s. versus, m.

rhyme, v.a. *fig.* versus facere, 3.

rhymer, rhymester, s. versificator, m.

rhythm, s. numerus, rhythmus, m.

rhythmical, a. numerosus, rhythmicus.

rib, s. costa, f. (also of a ship) ; (in building) statumen, n.

ribald, a. obscenus, spurcus, turpis.

ribaldry, s. obscenitas, f.

riband, s. tænia, vitta, fascia, f. ; lemniscus, m.

ribbed, a. costatus ; nervosus.

ribbon, s., v. **riband.**

rice, s. oryza, f.

rich, a. dives, locuples, pecuniosus, opimus ; —ly, ad. opulente, abunde, copiose, large, uberrime ; (of things) abundans, copiosus ; (of the soil, etc.) fertilis, uber ; (fat) pinguis ; opulentus.

riches, s. divitiæ, opes, f. pl.

richness, s. opulentia, abundantia, copia ; ubertas, fertilitas, f.

rick, s. acervus, m. ; strues, f.

rickets, s. (mod.) rhachitis, f.

rickety, a. instabilis.

rid, v.a. libero, 1 ; **to get — of,** amolior, 4 ; amoveo, removeo, 2 ; dimitto, depono, 3 ; (also *fig.*).

riddance, s. liberatio, f.

riddle, s. ænigma, n. ; ambages, f. pl. ; (sieve) cribrum, n.

riddle, v.a. (to sift) cribro, 1 ; (with bullets, etc.) confodio, 3.

ride, v.a. (a horse) equo vehor, 3 ; —, v.n. equito, 1 ; **to — away** *or* **off,** avehor, 3 ; **— past,** prætavehor ; **— round,** circumvehor, 3 ; circumequito, 1.

ride, s. equitatio ; vectatio, vectio, f.

rider, s. eques ; vector, m. ; (addition) adjectio, f.

ridge, s. jugum, dorsum ; culmen, n.

ridicule, s. ludibrium, n. ; risus, m. ; —, v.a. rideo, irrideo, 2.

ridiculous, a. ridiculus ; —ly, ad. ridicule.

riding, s. equitatio, f.

riding-coat, s. pænula, f.

riding-school, s. hippodromos, m.

rife, a. frequens, vulgatus ; **become —,** increbresco, 3. [populi, f.

riffraff, s. plebecula, f. ; vulgus, n. ; fæx

rifle, v.a. spolio, despolio, 1 ; diripio, 3.

rig, v.a. adorno, armo, 1 ; instruo, 3.

rigging, s. armamenta, n. pl.

right, a. rectus ; (hand, side) dexter ; *fig.* verus ; justus ; æquus ; idoneus, aptus ; —, —ly, ad. recte ; juste ; jure ; vere ; rite ; **you are —,** vera dicis ; **I have a — to,** licet mihi.

right, s. (hand) dextra, f. ; (law) jus, æquum, fas, n. ; (permission, licence) licentia, venia, f. ; **on the —,** dextrorsus.

right, v.a. emendo, 1 ; corrigo ; restituo, 3 ; vindico, 1.

righteous, a. æquus, justus ; pius, sanctus ; —ly, ad. æque, juste, pie, sancte.

righteousness, s. justitia, pietas, f. ; rectum, n.

rightful, a. legitimus, justus ; —ly, ad. legitime, jure, juste.

rigid, a. rigidus ; —ly, ad. rigide.

rigidity, s. rigor, m.

rigmarole, s. ambages, f. pl.

rigorous, a. asper, severus, rigidus ; —ly, ad. aspere, severe, rigide.

rigour, s. asperitas, severitas, f.

rill, s. rivulus, amniculus, m.

rim, s. labrum, n. ; ora, f. ; margo, c.

rime, s. (hoar-frost) pruina, f.

rimy, a. pruinosus.

rind, s. crusta, cutis, f. ; cortex, liber, m.

ring, s. anulus ; (hoop) circulus, orbis, m. ; (of people) corona, f. ; (ground for fighting) arena, f. ; (sound) sonitus, m. ; (of bells) tinnitus, m.

ring, v.n. tinnio, 4 ; resono, 1.

ring-dove, s. palumbes, c.

ringing, s. tinnitus, m.

ringleader, s. caput, n. ; dux, auctor, m.

ringlet, s. (of hair) cincinnus, cirrus, m.
ringworm, s. area, f.
rinse, v.a. ςiluo, eluo, 3.
riot, s. tumultus, m. ; (revelry) bacchatio, comissatio, f.
riot, v.n. tumultuor ; (in living) debacchor, comissor, 1.
rioter, s. seditiosus, turbulentus; (debauchee) helluo, comissator, m.
riotous, a. seditiosus, tumultuosus, turbulentus.
rip, v.a. (to unsew) dissuo ; (to cleave) diffindo, divello, 3.
rip, s. helluo, nebulo, m.
ripe, a. maturus ; tempestivus ; (of age) pubes ; (women) nubilis.
ripen, v.a. maturo, 1 ; —, v.n. maturesco, 3.
ripeness, s. maturitas ; (of age) pubertas, f.
ripple, s. fluctus, m. ; unda, f. ; —, v.n. murmuro, lene sono, 1.
rise, v.n. orior, co-orior, 4 ; surgo, consurgo, 3 ; (out of, from) exorior, 4 ; (to mount) ascendo, 3 ; (as a bird) evolo, 1 ; (up) assurgo, 3 ; (to increase) cresco, 3 ; (of rebels) consurgo, 3 ; rebello, 1 ; **to — again,** resurgo ; revivisco, 3.
rise, s. (ascent) ascensus ; (of the sun) ortus, m. ; (rising ground) tumulus, m. ; (origin) origo, f. ; fons, m. ; (preferment) promotio, f. ; **to give — to,** pario, 3.
rising, a. acclivis ; futurus.
rising, s. (act) ascensus ; (of the sun, etc.) ortus, m. ; (as a hill) acclivitas, f. ; (swelling) tumor, m. ; (insurrection) tumultus, m. ; seditio, f. ; (to life) resurrectio, f.
risk, v.a. periclitor, 1.
risk, s. periculum, discrimen, n.
rite, s. ritus, m. ; solemne, n. ; **v. funeral.**
ritual, a. sollemnis ; s. sollemne, n.
rival, s. rivalis, æmulus, competitor, m.
rival, v.a. æmulor, 1 ; certo, 1.
rivalry, s. æmulatio ; certamen, **n. ;** (in love) rivalitas, f.
rive, v.a. diffindo, discindo, 3.
river, s. flumen, n. ; amnis, rivus, m. ; **—-bed,** s. alveus, m.
rivet, s. clavus, m.
rivet, v.a. *fig.* clavo figo, 3 ; *fig.* teneo, 2.
rivulet, s. rivus, rivulus, amniculus, m.
roach, s. cyprinus, m.
road, s. via, f. ; iter, n. ; (for ships) statio, f. ; **on the —,** in itinere.
roadstead, s. (for ships) statio, f.
roam, etc., v. **ramble,** etc.
roan, a. ravus.
roar, v.n. fremo, rudo, 3 mugio, 4 ; (of voices) vociferor, 1.
roar, roaring, s. fremitus, m. ; strepitus, mugitus, clamor, m.

roast, v.a. & n. torreo, 2 ; (in a pan) frigo, 3 ; asso, 1 ; coquo, 3.
rob, v.a. latrocinor ; furor ; prædor ; spolio, despolio, 1 ; diripio, 3 ; (deprive) privo, orbo, 1.
robber, s. latro, prædo, raptor, fur, m.
robbery, s. latrocinium, n. ; spoliatio, direptio, rapina, f. [induo, 3.
robe, s. vestis, palla, f. ; —, v.a. vestio, 4 ;
robin, robin-redbreast, s. rubecula, f.
robust, a. robustus, validus, lacertosus, firmus.
robustness, s. firmitas, f. ; robur, n. ; vigor, m.
rochet, s. (fish) erythinus, m.
rock, s. rupes, cautes, f. ; saxum, n. ; scopulus, m.
rock, v.a. moveo, 2 ; agito, 1 ; —, v.n. vibro, 1 ; moveor, 2 ; agitor, fluctuo, 1.
rock-cress, arabis (mod. hort.) ; **purple —,** aubretia (mod. hort.).
rocket, s. (plant) hesperis, f.
rock-rose, s. cistus (mod. hort.).
rock-salt, s. sal fossilis, m.
rocky, a. saxosus, saxeus, scopulosus.
rod, s. virga ; ferula, f.
rodomontade, s. magniloquentia, vaniloquentia, f.
roe (roebuck), s. caprea, f.; (for fishing) arundo, f. ; calamus, m. ; (for measuring) pertica, decempeda, f. (of fishes) ova, n. pl.
rogation, s. supplicatio, f.
rogue, s. nequam (homo), furcifer, mastigia, m.
roguery, roguishness, s. nequitia; fraus ; malitia, f. ; (sauciness) protervitas, f.
roguish, a. nequam, malitiosus ; (saucy) protervus ; **—ly,** ad. malitiose ; delose, fraudulenter ; (saucily) proterve.
roll, v.a. volvo, 3 ; verso, 1 ; —, v.n. volvor ; (of tears) labor, fluo, 3 ; mano, 1.
roll, s. (of anything) volumen, n. ; (coil) spira, f. ; orbis, m. ; (of names) index, m. ; album, n.
roller, s. (tool) cylindrus, m.
rolling, a. volubilis, versatilis.
rolls, s. (archives) tabulæ. f. pl. ; tabularia, n. pl.
Roman, a. & s. Romanus ; Quiris, m.
romance, s. fabula, narratio ficta, f. ; (strangeness) novitas ; (love) amor, m.
romance, v.n. (boast) jacto, 1.
romancer, s. fabulator, m.
romantic, a. fabulosus, commenticius ; (chivalrous) sublimis ; (pleasing) gratus ; (unusual) insolitus, mirus, novus.
romp, s. lusus, m. ; puella lasciva, f.
romp, v.n. exsulto, 1 ; ludo, 3 ; lascivio, 4.
roof, s. tectum ; fastigium ; (of the mouth) palatum, n.

roof, v.a. contego, intego, 3.
roofing, s. tegulæ, f. pl.
rook, s. corvus, m.
room, s. (space) spatium, n.; locus, m.; (apartment) conclave, cubiculum, cenaculum, n.
roominess, s. laxitas; amplitudo, f.
roomy, a. laxus; spatiosus; amplus.
roost, s.; — v.n. insisto, 3; insideo, 2.
root, s. radix, stirps, f.; *fig.* fons, m.; origo, f.; by the —s, radicitus; to take —, coalesco, 3.
root, v.n. radices agere, 3; become —ed, *fig.* inveterasco, 3; to — out *or* up, exstirpo, eradico, 1.
rootlet, s. radicula, f.
rope, s. funis, m.; restia, f.; rudens, m.
rope-dancer, s. funambulus, m.
rope-maker, s. restio, m.
ropy, a. lentus.
rosary, s. rosetum; rosarium, n.
rose, s. rosa, f.; — of Sharon, hypericum (mod. hort.).
rose, a. roseus, rosaceus.
rose-bed, s. rosarium, n.
rosebud, s. calyx rosæ, m.
rose-bush, s. rosa, m.
roseate, v. rosy.
rosemary, s. ros marinus, ros maris, m.
rosewood, s. lignum Rhodium, n.
rosin, s. resina, f., v. resin.
rostrum, s. rostra, n. pl.
rosy, a. roseus.
rot, v.n. putresco, putesco, 3; —, v.a. corrumpo, putrefacio, 3.
rot, s. putor, m.; caries, f.; (of sheep) clavi, m. pl.
rotation, s. ordo, m.
rotatory, a. versatilis.
rote, s. by —, memoriter; learn by —, edisco, perdisco, 3.
rotten, a. puter, putidus, putridus; cariosus.
rottenness, s. putor, m.; (of teeth, bones) caries, f.
rotunda, s. tholus, m.
rotundity, s. rotunditas, f.
rouge, s. (for the face) fucus, m.
rouge, v.a. fuco, 1.
rough, a. asper; (with hair, thorns) hirsutus; horridus; scabrous; scaber; (of weather) procellosus; *fig.* agrestis, durus, incultus.
rough, s. homo nihili, furcifer, m.; —s, pl. operæ, f. pl.
rough, v.a. aspero; induro, 1.
rough-cast, v.a. trullisso, 1; —, s. trullissatio, f.
roughen, v.a. aspero, 1.
rough-hew, v.a. dolo, 1. [culte.
roughly, ad. aspere; duriter; horride; in-

roughness, s. asperitas, f.; (of surface) scabies; *fig.* (coarseness) rusticitas; (brutality) feritas, f.
rough-shod, a. ride — over, calco proculco, 1; obtero, 3.
round, a. rotundus; globosus; (as a circle) circularis; (rounded) teres.
round, s. orbis, circulus, m.; (of ladders) gradus, m.; go the —s, circumeo, 4.
round, v.a. rotundo; torno, 1; — off, (end) concludo, 3.
round, ad. & pr. circum, circa; — about, undique.
roundabout, a. devius; — way, circuitus, m.; ambages, f. pl.
roundness, s. rotunditas.
roundly, ad. aperte; plante; præcise.
rouse, v.a. excito; stimulo; animo, 1; cieo, moveo, 2; (awaken) expergefacio, 3.
rout, s. tumultus, m.; turba; (defeat) clades, f.; (flight) fuga, f.
rout, v.a. fugo, profligo, 1; fundo, 3.
route, s. via, f.; iter, n.
routine, s. mos, usus, m.; consuetudo, f.
rove, v.n., v. ramble.
rover, s. erro; (pirate) prædo, m.
roving, a. errans, vagans, vagus, erraticus.
row, s. series, f.; ordo, m.; (riot) turba, f.; in a —, deinceps.
row, v.n. & a. remigo, 1; remis propello, 3.
rowel, s. (of a spur) stimulus, m.
rower, s. remex, m.
rowing, s. remigatio, f.; remigium, n.
royal, a. regalis, regius, regificus; —ly, ad. regaliter, regie.
royalty, s. majestas regia; dignitas regia; regia potestas, f.
rub, v.a. & n. frico, 1; tero, 3; to — against, attero, 3; to — (away *or*) off, detergeo, 2; — up, (*fig.*) limo, 1.
rub, s. fricatio, f.; tritus, attritus, m.; *fig.* difficultas, f.
rubbing, s. tritus, attritus, affrictus, m.; fricatio, f.
rubbish, s. rudus, n.; *fig.* quisquiliæ, f. pl.; (nonsense) fabulæ, gerræ, f. pl.
rubicund, a. rubicundus.
rubric, s. rubrica, f.
ruby, s. carbunculus, m.; —, a. purpureus.
rudder, s. gubernaculum, n.; clavus, m.
ruddiness, s. rubor, m.
ruddle, s. rubrica, f.
ruddy, a. rubicundus, rubens, rutilus.
rude, a. rudis, incultus; rusticus, inurbanus; (artless) incomptus, incompositus; inconditus; (insolent) insolens; (unskilful) inexpertus, imperitus; —ly, ad. rustice, inurbane; inculte; incondite.

rudeness, s. rusticitas ; inhumanitas ; insolentia, f.

rudiment, s. elementum, initium, rudimentum, principium, n.

rue, s. (plant) ruta, f.

rue, v.n. pænitet, 2.

rueful, a. mœstus, tristis.

ruffian, s. homo perditus sicarius, latro, m.

ruffianly, a. audax, facinorosus, atrox.

ruffle, v.a. agito, turbo, 1.

rug, s. stragulum.

rugged, a. asper, inæqualis, confragosus ; (precipitous) præruptus ; (of temper) difficilis.

ruggedness, s. asperitas, f.

ruin, s. pernicies, f. ; exitium, excidium, n. ; ruina, f. ; —s, pl. ruinæ, f. pl.

ruin, v.a. perdo ; corrumpo, 3 ; depravo, vitio, 1.

ruination, s. vastatio, f.

ruinous, a. damnosus ; exitiosus ; exitialis, perniciosus, funestus ; (ready to fall) ruiturus ; **in ruins,** ruinosus ; —ly, ad. perniciose.

rule, s. (for measuring) regula ; (carpenter's) norma, amussis, f. ; *fig.* præceptum, n. ; lex, norma, regula, formula, f. ; (government) regimen, n.

rule, v.a. (a line) duco, 3 ; (govern) rego, 3 ; præsum, (dat.) ; —, v.n. dominor, impero, 1 ; (of a custom) obtineo, 2.

ruler, s. rector ; regnator, gubernator, dominus, moderator, m. ; (for drawing lines) regula, f.

ruling, a. potens ; regius ; (chief, most powerful) potentissimus.

rumble, v.n. murmuro ; crepo, 1. [tus, m.

rumbling, s. murmur, n. ; crepitus, soni-

ruminant, a. ruminalis.

ruminate, v.n. ruminor, 1 ; *fig.* meditor, 1.

rumination, s. ruminatio ; *fig.* meditatio, f.

rummage, v.a. rimor, perscrutor, 1.

rummer, s. poculum, n.

rumour, s. rumor, m. ; fama, f.

rump, s. clunis, c. ; natis, f.

rumple, s. ruga, f. ; —, v.a. corrugo, 1.

run, v.n. curro ; (to flow) fluo ; (of rivers) labor, 3 ; **to — about,** curso, 1 ; **to — after,** sequor, 3 ; sector, 1 ; **to — aground,** *or* **ashore,** (v.a.) ejicio ; (v.n.) ejicior, 3 ; **to — away,** fugio, aufugio, 3 ; **to — down,** decurro ; (as water) defluo, 3 ; *fig.* vitupero, 1 ; **to — in,** incurro ; (of ships) pervehor, 3 ; **to — off,** aufugio ; **(as water)** defluo, 3 ; **to — on,** pergo, 3 ; **to — out,** excurro, 3 ; (of time) exeo, 4 ; **to — over,** (a person) obtero ; *fig.* percurro ; (to touch lightly) perstringo ; (of fluids) (v.n.) superfluo, 3 ; **to — through,** percurro ; (also *fig.*) ; (with

a sword) transfigo, trajicio, transigo, 3 ; (to squander) dissipo, 1 ; **to — together,** concurro, 3 ; **to — up,** (v.a.) erigo, exstruo ; (v.n.) accurro, 3.

run, s. cursus, m.

runaway, s. fugitivus, m. ; transfuga, c.

runaway, a. fugitivus.

runner, s. cursor, m.

running, a. (of water) perennis, jugis ; (consecutive) continuus.

running, s. cursus, m.

rupture, s. violatio, seditio ; dissensio ; (disease) hernia, f.

rupture, v.a. violo, 1 ; rumpo, abrumpo, 3.

rural, a. rusticus ; agrestis.

rush, s. juncus, scirpus, m.

rush, v.n. ruo, feror, 3 ; præcipito, 1 ; (on, forward) irruo, irrumpo, prorumpo, (out) erumpo, 3 ; evolo, 1.

rushlight, s. filum scirpeum, n.

rushy, a. junceus ; juncosus ; scirpeus.

russet, a. rufus, russus, ravus.

rust, s. rubigo ; (of copper) ærugo ; (of iron) ferrugo, f.

rust, v.a. rubigine obduco ; —, v.n. rubiginem contraho, 3 ; *fig.* torpeo, 2.

rustic, a. rusticus ; agrestis ; —, s. rusticus, agrestis, m. ; ruricola, c.

rusticate, v.a. relego ; —, v.n. rustior, 1.

rustication, s. relegatio, f.

rusticity, s. rusticitas, f.

rustle, v.n. crepito ; murmuro ; susurro, 1.

rustle, rustling, s. stridor ; susurrus, m. ; murmur, n. ; crepitus, m.

rusty, a. robiginosus, æruginosus ; (rust-coloured) ferrugineus.

rut, s. (of a wheel) orbita, f.

ruthless, a. immisericors ; immitis ; immansuetus, crudelis, ferus, sævus ; —ly, ad. crudeliter, sæve.

ruthlessness, s. crudelitas, feritas, sævitia, f.

rye, s. secale, n.

Sabbath, s. sabbata, n. pl.

sable, s. mustela zibellina, f.

sable, a. pullus ; ater, niger ; fuscus.

sabre, s. acinaces ; gladius, m.

sacerdotal, a. sacerdotalis.

sachel, s., v. **satchel.**

sack, s. saccus, m.

sack, v.a. (to pillage) vasto, 1 ; diripio, 3.

sackcloth, s. (for mourning) vestis sordida, f.

sacking, s. spoliatio, vastatio, f. ; (coarse cloth) calicium ; (for a bed) linteum, n.

sacrament, s. sollemne, sacramentum, n. ; ritus, m.

sacramental, s. sacramentalis.

sacred, a. sacer ; sanctus ; sacrosanctus ; religiosus ; —ly, ad. sancte.

sacredness, s. sanctitas, religio, f.

sacrifice, s. (act) sacrificium, n. ; (victim) victima, f. ; *fig.* detrimentum, damnum, n.

sacrifice, v.a. immolo, sacrifico, macto, 1 ; *fig.* posthabeo, 2 ; (give up) devoveo, 2 ; profundo, 3 ; —, v.n. sacrifico, 1 ; rem divinam facio, sacrum facio, 3 ; operor, 1.

sacrificial, a. sacrificus.

sacrilege, s. sacrilegium, n. ; impietas, f.

sacrilegious, a. sacrilegus ; impius ; —ly, ad. impie.

sad, a. tristis, mœstus, miser, miserabilis ; —ly, ad. mœste, misere.

sadden, v.a. contristo, 1.

saddle, s. ephippium, stratum, n. ; pack —, clitellæ, f. pl.   [3 ; onero, 1.

saddle, v.a. (equum) sterno ; *fig.* impono,

saddle-bag, s. bisaccium, n.

saddle-cloth, s. stragulum, n.

saddle-horse, s. equus sellaris, m.

sadness, s. tristitia, mœstitia, miseria, f.

safe, a. tutus ; (without hurt) incolumis ; (sure) certus ; — and sound, salvus ; —ly, ad. tute, tuto.

safe-conduct, s. fides publica, f. ; syngraphus, m.

safeguard, s. præsidium, n. ; tutela, f.

safe-keeping, s. fides, f.

safety, s. salus, incolumitas, f.

safety-valve, s. spiraculum, spiramentum, n.

safflower, s. carthamus (mod. hort.).

saffron, s. crocus, m. ; —, a. croceus.

sagacious, a. sagax, perspicax ; acutus ; —ly, ad. sagaciter ; acute.

sagacity, s. sagacitas, perspicacitas, f.

sage, s. (plant) salvia, f.

sage, a. sapiens, prudens ; —ly, ad. sapienter ; prudenter ; —, s., v. philosopher.

sago, s. cycas, m.

sail, s. velum, n. ; carbasa, lintea, n. pl. ; (for the ship itself) navis ; (excursion) navigatio, f.

sail, v.n. vela facio, 3 ; navigo, 1 ; (to set out to sea) vela do, 1 ; solvo, 3 ; v.a. navigo, 1.

sailer, s. navis (habilis et velox), f.

sailing, s. navigatio, f. ; (of a ship) cursus, m.

sailor, s. nauta, m.

sail-yard, s. antenna, f.

saint, s. vir sanctus, m. ; femina sancta, f.

saintly, ad. sanctus, pius.

sake, s. for the — of, gratia, causa ; pro ; (on account of) propter, ob.

salacious, a. salax.

salad, s. acetaria, n. pl.

salamander, s. salamandra, f.

salary, s. merces, f. ; stipendium ; salarium, n.

sale, s. venditio, f. ; (auction) auctio, f. ; for —, venalis ; be on —, veneo, 4 ; put up for —, venalem propono, 3.

salesman, s. venditor, m.

salient, a. prominens ; (chief) præcipuus.

saline, a. salsus.

saliva, s. saliva, f. ; sputum, n.

salivate, v.a. salivo, 1.

salivation, s. salivatio, f.

sallow, s. salix, f.

sallow, a. pallidus, luridus.

sally, s. eruptio, f. ; excursus, m. ; excursio, f. ; impetus, m. ; —, v.n. (mil.) erumpo, excurro, 3.

salmon, s. salmo, m.

salmon-trout, s. fario, m.

saloon, s. atrium, conciliabulum, n.

salsafy, s. tragopogon (mod. hort.).

salt, s. sal, m. ; *fig.* sales, m. pl.

salt, a. salsus.

salt, v.a. salio, sale condio, 4.

salt-box, salt-cellar, s. salinum, m.

salting, s. salsura, f.

salting-tub, s. vas salsamentarium, n.

saltish, a. subsalsus.

saltless, a. insulsus.

salt-mine, s. salifodina, f.

saltness, s. salsitudo, salsugo, f.

saltpetre, s. nitrum, n.

salt-works, s. salinæ, f. pl.

salubrious, a. salubris (saluber), salutaris.

salubrity, s. salubritas, f.

salutary, a. salutaris, salubris ; utilis.

salutation, s. salutatio, salus, f. [luto, 1.

salute, s. salus, salutatio, f. ; —, v.a. sa-

salvation, s. salus, salvatio, f.

salve, s. unguentum, collyrium, n.

salver, s. scutella, f.

same, a. idem ; it is all the — thing, nihil interest ; at the — time, eodem tempore ; in the — place, ibidem.

samphire, s. crithmum, n.   [men, n.

sample, s. exemplum ; exemplar ; speci-

sanatory, a. salutaris ; medicus.

sanctification, s. sanctificatio, f. ; (consecration) consecratio, f.

sanctify, v.a. sanctifico ; (consecrate) consecro, 1.

sanctimonious, a. sanctitatem affectans.

sanction, s. auctoritas, confirmatio, f. ; you have my —, per me licet.

sanction, v.a. ratum facio, 3 ; sancio, 4 ; confirmo, firmo, 1.

sanctity, s. sanctitas ; sanctimonia, religio, f.

sanctuary, s. asylum, adytum, sacrarium, n.

sand, s. sabulo, m. ; arena, f.
sandal, s. solea, crepida, f.
sand-pit, s. arenaria, f.
sandstone, s. tofus, tophus, m.
sandy, s. (full of sand) arenosus, sabulosus ; arenaceus ; (of colour) rufus.
sane, a. sanus, mentis compos.
sanguinary, a. sanguinarius ; cruentus,
sanguinolentus.
sanguine, a. sanguineus ; (of temperament) alacer ; to be —, bona spero.
sanity, s. sanitas, mens sana, f.
sap, s. sucus, m. ; lac, n.
sap, v.a. & n. suffodio, surruo, 3 ; labefacto, 1.
sapless, a. exsucus ; *fig.* aridus, insulsus.
sapling, s. surculus, m.
sapper, s. (mil.) cunicularius, m.
Sapphic, a. Sapphicus.
sapphire, s. sapphirus, f.
sarcasm, s. sarcasmus, m. ; dictum acer-
bum, n.
sarcastic, a. acerbus, mordax ; —ally, ad.
acerbe.
sarcophagus, s. sarcophagus, m.
sardine, s. sarda, f.
sardonic, a. acerbus.
sardonyx, s. sardonyx, c.
sash, s. cingulum, n.
sassafras, s. saxifragus, m.
Satan, s. Satanas, m.
Satanic, a. Satanicus.
satchel, s. saccus, sacculus, m. ; pera, f. ;
loculi, m. pl.
sate, v.a. satio, saturo, 1.
satellite, s. satelles, c. ; (planet) stella
minor *or* obnoxia, f.
satiate, v.a. satio, saturo, 1.
satiety, s. satietas, f. ; fastidium, n.
satire, s. satira, f.
satirical, a. satiricus, acerbus ; —ly, ad.
acerbe.
satirist, s. scriptor (*or* poeta) satiricus ; (in
general) derisor, m.
satirize, v.a. derideo, 2 ; perstringo, 3.
satisfaction, s. satisfactio ; (punishment)
poena, f. ; *fig.* oblectatio animi ; voluptas, f.   [etc.].
satisfactorily, ad. ex sententia (mea, tua,
satisfactory, a. (suitable) commodus ;
(pleasant) gratus, jucundus.
satisfy, v.a. (to please) satisfacio, 3 ; (fill)
satio, saturo, 1 ; *fig.* persuadeo ; (one's
expectations) respondeo, 2 ; (be satisfied) contentus esse.
satrap, s. satrapes, m.
saturate, v.a. saturo, 1 ; imbuo, madefacio, 3.
Saturday, s. Saturni dies, m.
Saturn, s. Saturnus, m.
Saturnalia, s. Saturnalia, n. pl.

satyr, s. satyrus, m.
sauce, s. condimentum ; jus, n.
saucepan, s. cacabus, m.
saucer, s. patella, f.
saucily, a. petulanter, procaciter, proterve.
sauciness, s. petulantia, procacitas, protervitas, f.
saucy, a. petulans, procax, protervus.
saunter, v.n. ambulo, 1 ; incedo, 3.
sausage, s. farcimen, tomaculum, n.
savage, a. ferus ; ferox, immansuetus ;
immanis ; saevus ; atrox ; (furious)
efferus ; (uncivilised) ferus, incultus ;
—ly, ad. crudeliter ; immaniter ; atrociter ; saeve.
savageness, savagery, s. feritas ; immanitas ; saevitia, f.
save, v.a. servo, conservo ; (from danger)
libero, 1 ; eripio (periculo aliquem) ; (to
spare) parco, 3 ; (to gain) lucror, 1.
save, pr. praeter, extra ; ad. nisi, praeter-
quam.
saving, a. parcus ; —ly, ad. parce.
saving, pr., v. save ; — your presence,
pace tua.
saving, s. (preserving) conservatio ;
(sparing, gain) compendium, n. ;
(savings) peculium, n.
saviour, s. servator ; salvator (mundi), m.
savory, s. satureia, n. pl.
savour, s. sapor, odor, nidor, m.   [2.
savour, v.n. sapio, 3 ; (to smell of) redoleo,
savoury, a. sapidus.
saw, s. (tool) serra, f. ; —, v.a. & n. serra
seco, 1 ; serram duco, 3.
sawdust, s. scobis, f.
saw-fish, s. pristis, f.
saxifrage, s. saxifraga (mod. hort.).
say, v.a. & n. dico, loquor, aio, 3 ; fari
(infin.), 1 ; they —, dicunt, ferunt ; that
is to —, scilicet ; —s he, inquit.
saying, s. dictum ; proverbium, n.
scab, s. scabies ; (of a wound) crusta, f.
scabbard, s. vagina, f.
scabby, a. (of sheep) scaber ; scabiosus.
scabious, s. scabiosa (mod. hort.).
scaffold, s. tabulatum, n. ; catasta, f.
scaffolding, s. tabulatum, n.
scald, s. adustio, f.
scald, v.a. fervente aqua macero, 1.
scalding-hot, a. fervidus, fervens.
scale, s. (of a fish) squama ; (of a balance)
lanx, f. ; —s, pl. libra ; trutina ; (degree)
gradus, m.
scale, v.a. (a fish) desquamo, 1 ; (walls)
ascendo, 3 ; scalas ad moveo, 2.
scaling-ladder, s. scalae, f. pl.
scallop, s. (shell-fish) pecten, m.
scalp, s. calva, f.
scalpel, s. scalpellum, scalprum, n.

scaly, a. squamosus ; squameus.
scammony, s. scammonea, f.
scamp, s. furcifer, m.
scamper, v.n. ruo, 3 ; provolo, 1 ; (to —
away) aufugio, effugio, 3.
scan, v.a. examino, exploro, lustro, 1 ; (a
verse) metior, 4 ; scando, 3.
scandal, s. ignominia, turpitudo, f. ; opprobrium, n.
scandalize, v.a. offendo, 3.
scandalous, a. ignominiosus, probrosus,
turpis ; —ly, ad. turpiter ; probrose.
scantily, ad. exigue, anguste parce.
scantiness, s. exiguitas, f.
scapegoat, s. caper emissarius, m.
scapegrace, s. nebulo, furcifer, m.
scapular(y), s. scapulare, n. ; vestis
scapularis, f.
scar, s. cicatrix, f. ; —, v.a. noto, 1.
scarce, a. rarus ; —ly, ad. vix, ægre.
scarcity, s. paucitas ; penuria, inopia, f.
scare, v.a. terreo, 2 ; territo, formido, 1.
scarecrow, s. terricula, n. pl.
scarf, s. fascia, f.
scarification, s. scariatio, f.
scarify, v.a. scarifico, 1.
scarlet, s. coccum, n. ; (colour) color
coccineus, m. ; —, a. coccineus.
scatter, v.a. spargo, dispergo, 3 ; dissipo,
1 ; (put to flight) fundo, 3 ; fugo, 1 ; —,
v.n. dilabor, 3.
scavenger, s. purgator viarum, m.
scene, s. scæna, f. ; (spectacle) spectaculum, n. ; (place) locus ; (landscape)
prospectus, m.
scenery, s. (of nature) species regionis, f. ;
beautiful —, amœna loca, n. pl. ; (of a
theatre) scæna, f.
scenic, a. scænicus.
scent, s. (sense) odoratus ; (fragrance)
odor, m. ; (of dogs) sagacitas, f. ;
having a keen —, a. sagax.
scent, v.a. (to perfume) odoro ; (of
animals) odoror, 1 ; (anoint with perfume) unguo, 3.
scent-bottle, s. olfactorium, n.
scented, a. odoratus, odorifer, odorus,
fragrans.
sceptic, s. scepticus, m. [picax.
sceptical, a. scepticus ; (suspicious) sus-
scepticism, s. scepticorum disciplina, f. ;
(suspicion) suspicio, f.
sceptre, s. sceptrum, n.
sceptred, a. sceptrifer.
schedule, s. libellus, m.
scheme, s. consilium, n. ; —, v.a. & n.
molior, 4.
schism, s. schisma, n. ; secessio, f.
schismatic, a. schismaticus.
scholar, s. discipulus, m. ; discipula, f. ;
(learned man) homo doctus, m.

scholarship, s. litteræ, f. pl. ; eruditio,
humanitas, f.
scholastic, a. scholasticus.
scholiast, s. scholiastes, interpres, m.
school, s. schola (also *fig.*) ; secta, f. ;
ludus, m. ; **wrestling** —, palæstra, f.
schoolboy, s. discipulus, m.
school-fellow, s. condiscipulus, m. ; con-
discipula, f.　　　　　[præceptor, m.
schoolmaster, s. ludi magister, magister,
schoolmistress, s. magistra, præceptrix, f.
schoolroom, s. schola, f.
schooner, s. actuarium navigium, n.
sciatic, a. ischiadicus.
sciatica, s. ischias, f.
science, s. scientia ; doctrina ; disciplina
ars ; (theory) ratio, f.
scientific, a. ad scientiam conformatus ;
—ly, ad. ex disciplinæ præceptis.
scimitar, s. acinaces, m.
scintillate, v.n. scintillo, corusco, 1.
scintillation, s. scintilla, f. ; splendor, m.
scion, s. surculus ; *fig.* proles, progenies,
stirps, f.
scissors, s. forfices, f. pl.
scoff, v.n. irrideo, derideo, 2 ; cavillor, 1.
scoff, s. irrisio, cavillatio, f.
scoffer, s. derisor, irrisor, m.
scoffingly, ad. contemptim, scurriliter.
scold, v.a. & n. objurgo, increpo, increpi-
to, 1 ; —, s. femina rixosa, f.
scolding, s. objurgatio, f. ; jurgium, n. ;
—, a. objurgatorius ; clamosus.
sconce, s. (for a candle) lychnuchus, m.
scoop, s. trulla, f. ; —, v.a. cavo, excavo, 1.
scope, s. finis, m. ; propositum, n. ; *fig.*
campus, m. ; area, f. ; spatium, n.
scorch, v.a. uro, aduro, 3 ; torreo, 2.
score, s. nota ; (bill) ratio, f. ; (twenty)
viginti.
score, v.a. noto, 1 ; *fig.* — **a point,** superior
sum.
scoria, s. scoria, f. ; spodium, n.
scorn, v.a. temno, contemno, sperno, 3 ;
aspernor, 1 ; fastidio, 4.
scorn, s. contemptio, f. ; contemptus, m. ;
supercilium, fastidium, n.
scorner, s. contemptor, m. ; contemptrix, f.
scornful, a. fastidiosus ; —ly, ad. contemptim ; fastidiose.
scorpion, s. scorpio, scorpius, m.
scot, s. tributa, vectigalia, n. pl.
scotch, v.a. incido, 3 ; vulnero, 1.
Scot, Scottish, a. Scoticus.
scot-free, a. impunitus ; —, ad. impune.
Scotland, s. Scotia, f.
Scotsman, s. Scotus, m.
scoundrel, s. nebulo, furcifer, m.
scour, v.a. (de)tergeo, 2 ; *fig.* pervagor, 1 ;
percurro, 3.

scourge, s. flagellum, n. ; *fig.* pestis, f. ; —, v.a. cædo, 3 ; verbero, 1. [n. pl.

scourging, s. verberatio, f. ; verbera,

scout, s. explorator, speculator, emissarius, m. ; —, v.a. speculor, exploro, 1.

scowl, v.n. frontem contraho, 3 ; —, s. frontis contractio, f.

scowlingly, ad. fronte contracta.

scraggy, a. strigosus ; (lean) macer.

scramble, v.n. nitor, enitor, 3.

scramble, s. (effort) nisus, m. ; (tumult) tumultus, m.

scrap, s. fragmentum, fragmen, frustum, n. [3.

scrape, v.a. & n. rado ; (together) corrado,

scrape, s. difficultas, f.

scraper, s. (tool) radula, f. ; rallum, n.

scraping, s. (act) rasura, f. ; —s, pl. ramenta, n. pl.

scratch, v.a. rado ; scalpo, 3 ; scabo, 1 ; (inscribe) inscribo, 3 ; — out, erado, 3.

scratch, s. vulnus, n.

scream, screech, v.n. strideo, 2 ; vociferor, 1 ; (of a child) vagio, 4.

scream, screaming, s. stridor, m. ; vociferatio, f. ; (of an infant) vagitus, m.

screech-owl, s. ulula, f.

screen, s. umbraculum, n. ; (sunshade) umbella, f. ; (protection) præsidium, n. ; defensio, f. ; —, v.a. occulo, protego, defendo, 3.

screw, s. coculea, f.

scribe, s. scriba, amanuensis, librarius, m.

scrip, s. sacculus, m. ; (of paper) scheda, f.

scrivener, s. (money-broker) nummularius ; (notary) scriba, m.

scrofula, s. struma, f.

scrofulous, s. strumosus.

scroll, s. volumen, n.

scrub, v.a. frico, 1 ; tergeo, 3.

scrub, s. (brushwood) virgulta, n. pl.

scruple, s. scrupulus, m. ; religio, dubitatio, f. ; (weight) scrupulum, n. ; —, v.n. dubito, 1.

scrupulous, a. religiosus, scrupulosus ; —ly, ad. religiose ; scrupulose.

scrutineer, s. scrutator, m.

scrutinize, v.a. scrutor, perscrutor, 1.

scrutiny, s. scrutatio, perscrutatio, f.

scud, v.n. feror, 3.

scuffle, s. rixa ; turba, f. ; —, v.n. rixor, 1.

scull, s. calvaria, calva, f. ; (oar) palmula, f., v. **paddle.**

scullion, s. lixa, m.

sculptor, s. sculptor, scalptor, m.; artifex, c. ; cælator, m.

sculpture, s. (art) sculptura ; scalptura ; (work) opus (marmoreum, etc.), n. —, v.a. sculpo, scalpo, 3 ; cælo, 1.

scum, s. spuma ; (of metals) scoria ; *fig.* sentina, f.

scurf, s. furfur, m. ; (dandriff) porrigo, f.

scurfy, a. porriginosus.

scurrility, s. scurrilitas, f. ; probrum, n.

scurrilous, a. scurrilis, probrosus ; —ly, ad. scurriliter.

scurvy, s. scrofula, f.

scurvy, a. *fig.* turpis.

scutcheon, s. scutum ; insigne, n.

scuttle, v.a. navis fundum perforo, 1.

scythe, s. falx, f. [tus, m.

sea, s. mare, æquor, marmor, n. ; ponsea-calf, s. phoca, f. ; vitulus marinus, m.

sea-captain, s. navarchus, m.

seacoast, s. ora, f. ; litus, n.

seafaring, a. maritimus.

sea-fight, s. navalis pugna, f.

sea-green, a. thalassinus, cæruleus.

seagull, s. larus, m. ; gavia, f.

seaholly, s. eryngium, n.

seahorse, s. hippocampus, m.

seakale, s. crambe, f.

sea-lavender, s. statice, f.

sea-mew, s. mergus, larus, m.

sea-sick, a. nauseabundus ; to be —, nauseo, 1.

sea-sickness, s. nausea, f.

sea-urchin, s. echinus, m.

sea-water, s. aqua marina, f.

seaweed, s. alga, f. ; fucus, m.

seaworthy, a. navigandi capax.

seal, s. signum, n. ; (sea-calf) phoca, f.

seal, v.a. signo, consigno, obsigno, 1 ; *fig.* sancio, 4.

sealing-wax, s. cera, f.

seam, s. sutura ; commissura, f.

seaman, s. nauta, m.

seamanship, s. navigandi peritia, f.

sear, v.a. aduro, 3 ; noto, 1 ; be —ed, (become hard) occallesco, 3.

sear, a. (dry) siccus, aridus.

search, v.a. & n. (per)scrutor, 1 ; (into) inquiro, 3 ; (to trace out) investigo, 1.

search, s. scrutatio ; investigatio ; inquisitio, f. [quisitor, m.

searcher, s. explorator, scrutator ; inseason, s. tempus (anni), n. ; annus, m. ; opportunitas, f.

season, v.a. condio, 4 ; *fig.* assuefacio, 3 ; duro, exercito, 1.

seasonable, a. tempestivus, opportunus.

seasonableness, s. tempestivitas, opportunitas, f. [tempus.

seasonably, ad. tempestive, opportune ; ad

seasoning, s. (act) conditio, f. ; condimentum, n.

seasoned, a. exercitatus.

seat, s. sedes ; sella, f. ; sedile, subsellium, n. ; domicilium, n. ; locus, m. ; sedes, f. [sideo, 3.

seat, v.a. sede loco, 1 ; (oneself) consecede, v.n. secedo, 3 ; deficio, 3.

seceder, s. seditiosus, rebellis, m.

secession, s. secessio, f. ; defectio.

seclude, v.a. secludo, 3.

secluded, a. solitarius ; remotus.

seclusion, s. solitudo, f. ; secessus, m. ; locus remotus, m.

second, a. secundus ; alter ; **for the — time,** iterum ; **a — self,** alter ego.

second, s. (person) adjutor, m. ; (of time) punctum temporis, n.

second, v.a. adjuvo, juvo, 1.

secondary, a. secundarius ; inferior.

secondly, ad. deinde, tum.

secrecy, s. secretum ; taciturnitas, f. ; (keeping secret) silentium, n.

secret, a. arcanus ; secretus ; occultus ; furtivus ; clandestinus ; **in —,** clam ; **to keep —,** celo, 1 ; **—ly,** ad. clam ; occulte, furtim.

secret, s. secretum, arcanum, n. ; res arcana, f.

secretary, s. scriba ; amanuensis, m.

secretaryship, s. scribatus, m.

secrete, v.a. celo, occulto, 1 ; abdo, 3 ; **— oneself,** lateo, 2 ; delitesco, 3.

sect, s. secta, schola, f.

sectarian, sectary, s. qui aliquam sectam profitetur, m.

section, s. pars ; (geometry) sectio, f.

sector, s. sector, m.

secular, a. sæcularis ; (long-lived) grandævus, annosus ; (worldly) profanus.

secure, a. securus ; tutus ; (careless) remissus ; **—ly,** ad. tuto, secure.

secure, v.a. confirmo, 1 ; munio, 4 ; a periculo defendo, 3 ; in custodiam trado, 3 ; (bring about, get) pario, 3 ; paro, 1 ; (bring it about that) efficio . . . ut, 3.

security, s. salus ; incolumitas ; (pledge) satisdatio, f. ; pignus, n. ; (person) vas, sponsor, præs, m.

sedan(-chair), s. lectica, f.

sedate, a. gravis, sedatus ; **—ly,** ad. sedate, graviter.

sedentary, a. sedentarius, sellularius.

sedge, s. ulva, carex, f.

sedgy, a. ulva obsitus, ulvosus.

sediment, s. fæx, f.

sedition, s. seditio, rebellio, f. ; tumultus, m.　　　　　　　　　[ad. seditiose.

seditious, a. seditiosus, turbulentus ; **—ly,**

seditiousness, s. ingenium seditiosum ac turbulentum, n.

seduce, v.a. corrumpo, 3 ; depravo, 1 ; decipio, 3.

seducer, s. corruptor, m.

seduction, s. illecebra ; corruptela, f.

seductive, a. blandus ; **—ly,** ad. blande.

sedulous, a. sedulus, assiduus ; **—ly,** ad. sedulo assidue.

see, s. sedes, f.

see, v.a. & n. video, 2 ; specto, 1 ; cerno, conspicio, aspicio, 3 ; (take precautions) caveo, video, 2 ; (to understand) intelligo, 3 ; **to — after,** inspicio, 3 ; curo, 1 ; **to go to —,** viso, 3.

seed, s. semen, n. ; (offspring) progenies, f. ; (cause) semen, n. ; causa, origo, f.

seed, v.n. semen ferre, 3.

seedling, s. planta, f.

seed-plot, s. seminarium, n.

seed-time, s. sementis, f.

seed-vessel, s. vasculum, n.

seedy, a. granosus.

seeing, s. visio, f. ; visus, m.　　　[iam.

seeing, c. **— that,** quandoquidem, quon-

seek, v.a. & n. quæro, peto, expeto, sequor, 3 ; (to endeavour) conor ; (to strive to attain) affecto, consector, 1.

seeker, s. petitor, m.

seem, v.n. videor, 2.

seeming, a. (likely) verisimilis.

seeming, s. species, f.

seemingly, ad. in speciem, ut videtur.

seemliness, s. decorum, n. ; decor, m.

seemly, a. decorus, decens.

seer, s. vates, fatidicus, augur, propheta, m.　　　　　　　[ferveo, 2 ; æstuo, 1.

seethe, v.a. fervefacio, coquo, 3 ; **—,** v.n.

segment, s. segmentum, n.

seize, v.a. prehendo, comprehendo ; arripio, 3 ; (to take possession) occupo, 1 ; (attack) invado ; incesso ; *fig.* afficio, 3.

seizure, s. comprehensio ; occupatio, f.

seldom, ad. raro.

select, v.a. seligo, eligo, deligo, 3.

select, a. exquisitus.　　　　　　　[m.

selection, s. selectio, electio, f. ; delectus,

self, pn. ipse, se(se) ; **by one's —,** solus.

self-conceit, s. arrogantia, superbia, f.

self-conceited, a. arrogans.

self-confidence, s. sui fiducia, f.

self-control, s. temperantia, f.

self-denial, s. moderatio, f.

self-heal, s. prunella (mod. hort.).

selfish, a. nimis se amans.

selfishness, s. amor sui, m.

self-possessed, a. placidus, tranquillus, imperturbatus.

self-will, s. obstinatio, contumacia, f.

self-willed, a. obstinatus, contumax.

sell, v.a. vendo, 3 ; **—,** v.n. veneo, 4.

seller, s. venditor, m.

selling, s. venditio, f.

selvage, s. limbus, m.

semblance, s. similitudo, species, f.

semicircle, s. semicirculus, m.

semicircular, a. semicirculus, semicirculatus.

seminary, s., v. school.

semitone, s. semitonium, n.
sempiternal, a. sempiternus, perpetuus.
senate, s. senatus, m.; curia, f.
senate-house, s. curia, f.
senator, s. senator, m.
senatorial, a. senatorius.
send, v.a. mitto, 3; (on public business)
lego, 1; (away) dimitto, 3; to — for,
arcesso, 3.
sender, s. qui (aliquid) mittit, m.
sending, s. missio, f.
senile, a. senilis.
senior, a. natu major.
seniority, s. ætatis privilegium, n.
senna, s. cassia senna, f.
sensation, s. sensus, m.; (astonishment)
stupor, m.; (subject of talk) fabula, f.
sense, s. (faculty) sensus, m.; (intellect)
mens; (opinion) opinio, sententia, f.;
(meaning) significatio, f.
senseless, a. nihil sentiens; (lifeless)
exanimis; fig. mentis expers; absurdus.
sensibility, s. sensus, m.; mollitia, f.
sensible, a. sensilis; sensu præditus, sen-
sibilis; fig. sapiens.
sensibly, ad. cum sensu; fig. sapienter;
(perceptibly) ita ut percipi possit,
mollis.
sensitive, a. mollis; — to, impatiens (gen.);
—, s. (plant) mimosa pudica (mod.
hort.).
sensual, a. voluptarius; libidinosus; —ly,
ad. libidinose.
sensualist, s. homo voluptarius, m.
sensuality, s. voluptas corporis, f.
sentence, s. judicium, n.; (period) sententia, f.; —, v.a. damno, condemno, 1.
sententious, a. sententiosus; —ly, ad.
sententiose.
sentient, a. sensu præditus.   [sus, m.
sentiment, s. sententia, opinio, f.; sen-
sentimental, a. animi mollioris; (in contempt) flebilis.
sentimentality, s. animi mollitia, f.;
animus mollior, m.
sentinel, sentry, s. excubitor, vigil, m.;
excubiæ, f. pl.; — -box, s. specula, f.
separable, a. separabilis.
separate, v.a. separo, 1; disjungo, sejungo, secerno, 3; —, v.n. separor, 1;
disjungor, 3; (go in different ways)
digredior, 3.
separate, a. separatus; disjunctus; —ly,
ad. separatim.
separation, s. separatio; disjunctio, f.;
(going different ways) digressus, m.
separatist, s. homo factiosus, m.
September, s. September, m.
septennial, a. septuennis.   [m.
septuagenarian, s. homo septuagenarius,
sepulchral, a. sepulcralis, funereus.

sepulchre, s. sepulcrum, n.; tumulus, m.
sepulture, s. sepultura, f.; exsequiæ, f. pl.;
funus, n.   [s. ordo, m.; series, f.
sequel, s. exitus, eventus, m.; sequence,
seraphim, s. seraphim, m.   [tranquille.
serene, a. serenus; tranquillus; —ly, ad.
serenity, s. serenitas; tranquillitas, f.
serf, s. servus, ascriptus glæbæ, m.
serfdom, s. servitium, n.; servitus, f.
sergeant, s. lictor, apparitor; (mil.) centurio, m.
series, s. series, f.
serious, a. gravis, serius, severus; —ly,
ad. graviter; serio; severe.
seriousness, s. gravitas, f.; serium, n.;
severitas, f.
sermon, s. oratio, contio, f.
sermonize, v.n. contionor, 1.
serpent, s. serpens, anguis, c.; coluber,
draco, m.
serpentine, a. sinuosus, v. snaky; —
(-stone), s. ophites, m.
serried, a. confertus, densus.
serum, s. serum, n.
servant, s. minister; famulus, m.; servus,
m.; serva, famula, f.
serve, v.a. & n. servio (alicui), 4; ministra, ancilla, f.; (for wages) mereo,
mereor, 2; stipendia mereo or mereor,
2; (to be useful) prosum; (to be sufficient) sufficio, 3.
service, s. servitium; (kindness) officium,
n.; (worship) cultus, m.; (advantage)
utilitas, f.; (mil.) militia, f.; to do a —,
prodesse.   [prosum.
serviceable, a. utilis; commodus; to be —,
service-tree, s. sorbus, f.
servile, a. servilis, humilis; —ly, ad. serviliter.   [tus, m.
servility, s. humilitas, f.; animus abjec-
servitude, s. servitus, f.   [tus, m.
session, s. sessio, f.; consessus, conven-
set, v.a. pono, sisto, 3; loco, colloco, 1;
(plants) sero, 3; (prescribe) præscribo,
3; (an example) do, 1; (enclose) includo, 3; —, v.n. (of stars) occido, 3;
to — about, incipio, 3; to — apart or
aside, sepono; fig. rescindo, 3; to —
down, (in writing) noto, 1; perscribo;
to — forth, expono; propono, profero,
3; v.n. proficiscor, 3; to — forwards,
(v.a.) fig. promoveo, 2; (v.n.) proficiscor, 3; to — in, insero, 3; to — off, (to
adorn) adorno; illustro, 1; (to praise)
extollo, 3; (v.n.) abeo, 4; proficiscor, 3;
to — on, (to incite) instigo, 1; (to
attack) invado; (on fire) accendo, 3;
to — out, (v.n.) discedo, proficiscor,
3; to — over, impono; fig. præficio, 3;
to — up, erigo; exstruo; (institute) instituo, constituo, 3.

set, s. series, f.; **apparatus, m.**; (of plants) propago, **f.**

set, a. compositus.

settee, s. lectulus, m.

setter, s. (dog) canis venaticus, m.

setting, s. collocatio, f.; (of the sun) occasus, m.; (on fire) incensio, f.

settle, s. sella, f.; scamnum, n.

settle, v.a. statuo, constituo; (a quarrel) dirimo, 3; (to adjust) compono; (a colony) (colonos) deduco, 3; (an account) solvo, 3; —, v.n. (one's habitation) consido; (to sink) subsido, 3.

settlement, s. constitutio; (dowry) dos, f.; (agreement) pactum, n.; (colony) colonia, f.

settler, s. colonus, m.

seven, a. septem; — **each,** septeni; — **times,** septies.

sevenfold, a. septemplex.

seven hundred, a. septingenti.

seventeen, a. septendecim, decem et septem.

seventeenth, a. septimus decimus.

seventh, a. septimus; **the — time,** septimum.

seventieth, a. septuagesimus.

seventy, a. septuaginta; — **each,** septuageni; — **times,** septuagies.

sever, v.a. separo, 1; dissolvo, 3; dissocio, 1; disjungo, 3; —, v.n. disjungor, 3, etc.

several, a. plures, complures; diversus, varius; —**ly,** ad. singillatim.

severe, a. severus; gravis; durus; —**ly,** ad. severe, graviter.

severity, s. severitas; gravitas; inclementia, f.

sew, v.a. & n. suo, consuo, 3.

sewer, s. cloaca, f.

sewing, s. sutura, f.

sex, s. sexus, m.

sexagenarian, a. & s. sexagenarius, m.

sextant, s. sextans, m.

sexton, s. ædituus; æditimus, m.

sexual, a. sexualis; naturalis.

shabbily, ad. sordide.

shabbiness, s. fig. sordes, f. pl.

shabby, a. pannosus; sordidus.

shackle, v.a. impedio, præpedio, 4.

shackles, s. vincula, n. pl.; pedica, compes, f.

shad, s. alausa, f.

shade, s. umbra, f.; fig. (difference) discrimen, n.; (parasol) umbraculum, n.; —**s,** pl. (of the dead) manes, m. pl.

shade, v.a. opaco; obscuro; obumbro; adumbro, 1.

shadow, s. umbra, f.; v. **shade,** s.

shadowy, a. umbrosus, opacus; fig. tenuis, inanis, vanus.

shady, a. opacus, umbrosus.

shaft, s. sagitta, f.; (of a spear) hastile, n.; (in a mine) puteus, m.; (of a column) scapus, m.

shag, s. villus, m.

shaggy, a. hirsutus, hirtus, villosus.

shake, v.a. quatio, concutio, 3; quasso, 1; (the head) nuto, 1; (undermine) labefacio, 3; labefacto, 1; —, v.n. concutior; (with fear) tremo, 3; (to totter) vacillo, nuto, 1.

shake, shaking, s. quassatio, f.; (with cold, with fear) tremor, m.

shallop, s. scapha, f.; lembus, m.

shallot, s. cæpa, f.

shallow, a. vadosus; fig. levis.

shallowness, s. fig. levitas, f.

shallows, s. vada, n. pl.

sham, a. fictus, simulatus; fallax; —, s. fallacia, f.; dolus, m.; simulatio, species, f.

sham, v.a. simulo, 1; fingo, 3.

shambles, s. laniena, f.; macellum, n.

shambling, a. incessu parum firmo.

shame, s. pudor, m.; (disgrace) dedecus; opprobrium, n.; ignominia, f.; **for —!** i. sit pudor! pro pudor!

shame, v.a. ruborem incutio, 3.

shamefaced, a. pudens, pudibundus, verecundus.

shameful, a. turpis, probrosus; —**ly,** ad. turpiter; probrose.

shamefulness, s. turpitudo, f.

shameless, a. impudens; —**ly,** ad. impudenter.

shamelessness, s. impudentia, f.

sham-fight, s. pugnæ simulacrum, n.

shamrock, s. trifolium, n.

shank, s. crus, n.

shanty, s. tugurium, n.

shape, s. forma, figura; species, facies, f.

shape, v.a. formo, figuro, 1; fingo, 3.

shapeless, a. informis; deformis, indigestus, rudis.

shapely, a. formosus.

shard, s. testa, f.

share, s. pars, portio, f.; (of a plough) vomer, m.

share, v.a. partior, 4; (with another) communico, 1; —, v.n. particeps sum, in partem venio, 4.

share-bone, s. pecten, m.

sharer, s. particeps, c.; socius, m.; socia, f.; consors, c.

shark, s. (fish) pristis, f.; (person) fraudator, m.

sharp, a. acutus; acer; (of bitter) acerbus; (tart) acidus; fig. mordax; argutus; subtilis; —**ly,** ad. acute; (keenly) acriter; (bitterly) acerbe; (cleverly) subtiliter.

sharp, s. (mus.) hemitonium superius, n.

sharpen, v.a. acuo, exacuo, 3.

sharper, s. veterator, fraudator, m.

sharpness, s. (of edge) acies; (sourness) acerbitas; *fig.* subtilitas, perspicacitas, f.; acumen, n.

sharp-sighted, a. perspicax.

sharp-sightedness, s. perspicacitas, f.

shatter, v.a. quasso, 1; frango, confringo; elido, 3.

shave, v.a. rado, 3; tondeo, 2; — off, abrado, 3.

shaver, s. tonsor, m.

shaving, ramenta, n. pl.; scobis, f.

shawl, s. amiculum, n.

she, pn. hæc, illa, ea; —, (of animals) femina, f.

sheaf, s. manipulus, fascis, m.; merges, f.

shear, v.a. tondeo, 2; *fig.* spolio, nudo, 1.

shearer, s. tonsor, m.

shearing, s. tonsura, f.

shears, s. forfex, f. [crum, n.

sheath, s. vagina, f.; (wrapper) involu-

sheathe, v.a. (in vaginam) recondo, 3.

shed, v.a. fundo, effundo, profundo, spargo, 3; (blood) (one's own) do, 1; (another's) haurio, 4; (tears) effundo, profundo, 3.

shed, s. tugurium, n.

sheep, s. ovis, pecus, bidens, f.

sheepfold, s. sæptum, ovile, n.

sheep-hook, s. pedum, n.

sheepish, a. timidus, modestus; —ly, timide, modeste.

sheep-skin, s. pellis ovilla, mastruca, f.

sheer, a. merus; purus; (precipitous) præceps.

sheer, v.n. (off) discedo, 3.

sheet, s. linteum, n.; (of paper)plagula; (of metal) lamina, f.

sheet-anchor, s. ancora ultima, f.

sheet-lightning, s. fulgetrum, n.

shelf, s. pluteus, m.; tabula, f.; (of rocks) dorsum, n.

shell, s. concha; crusta, testa, f.; (husk) folliculus, m.; (of nuts, etc.) puta-men, n. [tico, 1.

shell, v.a. putamina detraho, 3; decor-

shell-fish, s. concha, f.

shelter, s. tegmen; *fig.* refugium, perfugium; (asylum) receptaculum, n.

shelter, v.a. tego; protego; defendo, 3.

shelterless, a. inops, desertus.

shelving, a. declivis, acclivis.

shepherd, s. pastor, upilio, pecorum custos, m.

sherbet, s. sicera, f.

sheriff, s. prætor, m.

shield, s. scutum, n.; clipeus, m.; small —, pelta, parma, f.; —, v.a. tego, protego, defendo, 3.

shield-bearer, s. scutigerulus, armiger, m.

shift, v.a. muto, 1; amoveo, 2; —, v.n. (as the wind) verto, 3; (shuffle) tergiversor, 1; (to change one's abode) demigro, 1; to — off, detrecto, 1.

shift, s. (expedient) ratio, f.; modus, m.; (device) effugium; (remedy) remedium, n.; (trick) dolus, m.; ars, f.

shifter, s. veterator, m. [1od.), m.

shilling, s. schelingus, denarius (about

shin(-bone), s. tibia, f.

shine, v.n. luceo, fulgeo, niteo, splendeo, 2; corusco, mico, 1; to — forth, eluceo; eniteo, 2; exsplendesco, 3; to — on *or* upon, affulgeo, 2 (with dative).

shingle, s. glarea, f.; scandula, f.

shining, a. lucidus, fulgidus, nitidus.

shiny, a. nitidus.

ship, s. navis, f.; navigium, n.; — of the line, navis longa, f.

ship, v.a. in navem (*or* naves) impono; accipio, 3.

shipbuilder, s. naupegus, m. [m.

ship-master, ship-owner, s. navicularius,

shipping, s. navigia, n. pl.

shipwreck, s. naufragium, n.; *fig.* ruina, f.; interitus, m.

shipwrecked, a. naufragus; be —, naufragium facio, 3.

shipwright, s. naupegus, m.

shire, s. (county) comitatus, m.

shirt, s. indusium, n.; tunica, f.

shiver, v.a. elido, confringo, 3; —, v.n. contremisco, horresco, 3; horreo, 2.

shiver, s. (broken piece) fragmentum; fragmen, n.; (shudder) horror, m.; cold —, frigus, n.

shivering, s. horror, m.

shoal, s. (of fishes, etc.) caterva, f.; grex, m.; (shallow) brevia, vada, n. pl.; (quantity) copia, f.

shoaly, a. vadosus.

shock, s. concussio, f.; impetus, concursus, m.; (in battle) incursio, f.; *fig.* (of feeling) offensio; (blow) plaga, f.

shock, v.a. percutio, percello; *fig.* offendo, 3.

shocking, a. fœdus; atrox; —ly, ad. fœde, atrociter.

shoe, s. calceus, m.; caliga; (slipper) solea, f.; soccus, m.; buskin, cothurnus, m.; (for horses) solea, f.

shoe, v.a. calceos induo, 3; (a horse) soleas apto, 1.

shoemaker, s. sutor, m.

shoot, v.a. (telum) mitto; conjicio, 3; jaculor, 1; (a person) figo, transfigo, 3; —, v.n. (as plants) germino, 1; (as stars) discurro, labor, 3; (as lightning) emico, 1; (of pains) vermino, 1.

shoot, s. (of plants) surculus, m.; propago, f.; germen, n.

shooter, s. jaculator, m.

shooting-star, s. fax (cœlestis), stella, f.

shop, s. taberna, officina, f.; — -**keeper,** s. tabernarius, m.

shore, s. litus, n.; ora, f.

short, a. brevis; (little) exiguus; in —, breviter, denique.

shortcoming, s. defectus, m.; (fault) delictum, vitium, n.; (failure) inopia, f.

shorten, v.a. coarto, 1; contraho, 3; —, v.n. contrahor; minuor, 3.

shorthand, s. notæ breviores, f. pl.; — -**writer,** s. notarius, actuarius, m.

short-lived, a. brevis.

shortly, ad. (of time) brevi; mox; — **after,** haud multum post; (in a few words) breviter, strictim.

shortness, s. brevitas; exiguitas, f.; (of breath) anhelitus, m.

short-sighted, a. myops; *fig.* improvidus.

short-sightedness, s. myopia; *fig.* minima imprudentia, f.

short-winded, a. anhelus.

shot, s. ictus, m.; (reach, range) jactus; (marksman) jaculator, m.; (bullet) glans, f.; tormentum, n.

shoulder, s. umerus, m.; (of an animal) armus, m.

shoulder, v.a. in umeros tollo, 3.

shoulder-belt, s. balteus, m.

shoulder-blade, s. scapulæ, f. pl.

shout, s. clamor, m.; acclamatio, vox, f.

shout, v.n. clamo; acclamo; vociferor, 1.

shouting, s., v. **shout,** s.

shove, v.a. trudo, 3; pulso, 1.

shovel, s. pala, f.; batillum; (for the fire) rutabulum, n.

show, v.a. monstro, declaro; indico, 1; ostendo, 3; (to display) exhibeo; (to teach) doceo, 2; (to prove) confirmo, 1; (qualities) præbeo, 2; **to — off,** ostento, vendito, 1.

show, s. (appearance) species; (display) ostentatio; (pretence) simulatio; (parade) pompa, f.; spectaculum, n.

shower, s. imber, nimbus, m.; *fig.* vis, multitudo, f.　　　　　[gero, 3.

shower, v.a. superfundo, effundo; *fig.* in-

showery, a. pluviosus, nimbosus, pluvius, pluvialis.

showiness, s. species, magnificentia, f.

showy, a. speciosus.

shred, s. segmentum, n.

shrew, s. mulier jurgiosa, f.

shrewd, a. acutus, astutus, callidus; sagax; prudens; —**ly,** ad. acute, callide; sagaciter; astute, prudenter.

shrewdness, s. calliditas; astutia; sagacitas, f.; acumen, n.; prudentia, f.

shrewish, a. jurgiosus, rixosus.

shrew-mouse, s. sorex, m.

shriek, v.n. ululo, ejulo, 1; —, s. ejulatio, f.; ululatus, m.

shrill, a. (per)acutus; stridulus.

shrillness, s. stridor, m.

shrimp, s. squilla, f.

shrine, s. (for holy things) sacrarium, sacellum, adytum, n.; cella, f.

shrink, v.a. contraho, 3; —, v.n. contrahor; (to withdraw) refugio, 3; (from) abhorreo, 2; detrecto, f.

shrinkage, shrinking, s. contractio, f.

shrivel, v.a. corrugo, 1; torreo, 2; v.n. corrugor, 1; torreor, 2.

shroud, s. (of ships) rudentes, m. pl.; (winding - sheet) linteum (mortuorum), n.

shroud, v.a. involvo; obduco, 3.

shrub, s. frutex, m.; arbuscula, f.

shrubbery, s. fruticetum, n.

shrubby, a. fruticosus; viridans.

shrug, s. umerorum allevatio, f.; —, v.n. umeros allevo, 1.

shudder, s. horror, tremor, m.; —, v.n. horreo, 2; horresco, 3.

shuffle, v.a. misceo, 2; —, v.n. tergiversor, 1.

shuffle, s. dolus, m.; fraus, tergiversatio, f.

shuffler, s. tergiversator; dissimulator, veterator, m.

shuffling, s. tergiversatio, f.; v. **shuffle.**

shun, v.a. vito, devito, evito, declino, detrecto, 1; fugio, 3.

shut, v.a. claudo, occludo, 3; (out) excludo, 3; (up) concludo, 3.

shutter, s. claustrum, n.

shuttle, s. radius, m.

shy, a. timidus; pudibundus; verecundus; —**ly,** ad. timide; verecunde.

shyness, s. timiditas; verecundia, f.

Sibyl, s. Sibylla, f.

Sibylline, a. Sibyllinus.

sick, a. æger, ægrotus; **to be —,** ægroto, 1; (of, with) tædet (me rei), fastidio, 4.

sicken, v.a. fastidium moveo, 2; satio, 1; —, v.n. in morbum incido, 3.

sickle, s. falx, f.; — -**shaped,** a. falcatus.

sickliness, s. infirmitas, f.; (pallor) pallor, m.

sickly, a. infirmus; (pale) pallidus.

sickness, s. ægrotatio, ægritudo, f.; morbus, m.

side, s. latus, n.; (part, quarter) pars; regio; (edge) ora, f.; (of a hill) clivus, m.; (of consanguinity) latus, n.; (party in a contest) partes, f. pl.

side, a. lateralis.

side, v.n. (with) partes sequor, 3; ab aliquo sto, 1.

sideboard, s. abacus, m.

sidelong, a. obliquus, transversus.

sidereal, a. sideralis, sidereus.

sideways, ad. in obliquum, oblique.

sidle, v.n. obliquo incessu progredior, 3.

siege, s. oppugnatio, obsessio, obsidio, f.

siesta, s. meridiatio, f.; **to take a —,** meridior, 1.

sieve, s. cribrum, n.

sift, v.a. cribro, 1; cerno, 3; *fig.* exploro, scrutor, 1.

siftings, s. pl. excreta, n. pl.

sigh, s. suspirium, n.; **—,** v.n. suspiro, 1; (for) desidero, suspiro, 1.

sight, s. (sense) visus; (act of seeing) aspectus, conspectus, m.; (of the eye) acies (oculi *or* oculorum), f.; (show) spectaculum, n.; (appearance) species, f.; visum, n.; **out of —,** e conspectu.

sightless, a. cæcus.

sightly, a. venustus, decorus.

sign, s. signum, indicium, n.; (mark) nota, f.; (of a shop, etc.) insigne; *fig.* portentum, omen; augurium, n.

sign, v.a. & n. subscribo; annuo, 3; signum do, 1.

signal, s. signum; (mil.) classicum, n.; **—,** v.a. signum do, 1.

signal, a. insignis, egregius.

signalize, v.a. insignio, 4.

signature, s. nomen, n.; subscriptio, f.

signer, s. signator, m.

signet, s. anulus, m.; signum, n.

significance, s. (meaning) significatio, f.; sensus, m.; *fig.* vis, f.; momentum, n.

significant, a. significans; *fig.* magni momenti.

significantly, ad. significanter.

signification, s., v. **significance.**

signify, v.a. & n. significo, 1; valeo, 2; portendo, 3; (it signifies, matters) interest, refert.

silence, s. silentium, n.; taciturnitas, f.; **—!** i. tace! tacete! **—,** v.a. silentium facio, 1; (confute) refuto, 1; (allay) sedo, 1; compesco, 3.

silent, a. tacitus, silens; **—ly,** ad. (cum) silentio, tacite.

silk, s. sericum, n.; bombyx, c.

silk, silken, a. sericus, bombycinus.

silk-worm, s. bombyx, c.

sill, s. limen inferum, n. [insipientia, f.

silliness, s. stultitia, fatuitas, insulsitas,

silly, a. stultus, fatuus, ineptus, insipiens, insulsus. [(of hair) canus.

silver, s. argentum, n.; **—,** a. argenteus;

silver, v.a. argento induco, 3.

silversmith, s. faber argentarius, m.

silvery, a. argenteus; (of hair) canus.

similar, a. similis; **—ly,** ad. similiter.

similarity, s. similitudo; vicinitas, proximitas, f.

simile, s. similitudo, f.

simmer, v.a. fervefacio; v.n. æstuo, 1; ferveo, 2.

simony, s. simonia, f.

simoon, s. ventus æstuosus, m.

simper, v.n. inepte rideo, 2.

simple, a. simplex; rudis; *fig.* (silly) ineptus; (frank) sincerus; ingenuus.

simple, s. herba, f.

simpleton, s. stultus, fatuus, ineptus, m.

simplicity, s. simplicitas; *fig.* stultitia, f.

simplify, v.a. simpliciorem reddo, 3.

simply, ad. simpliciter; solum, modo, tantummodo.

simulate, v.a. simulo, 1.

simulation, s. simulatio, f.

simultaneous, a. eodem tempore; **—ly,** ad. simul, una.

sin, s. peccatum; delictum, flagitium, nefas, vitium, n.

sin, v.a. pecco, 1; delinquo, 3.

sin-offering, s. piaculum, n.

since, pr. post; c. cum, ex quo; (seeing that) cum; quando; quoniam; **—,** ad. abhinc; **long —,** jamdudum; **how long — ?** quam pridem? **three days —,** abhinc tres dies.

sincere, a. sincerus, candidus; simplex verus; **—ly,** ad. sincere, vere.

sincerity, s. sinceritas, simplicitas, f.; candor, m.

sinew, s. nervus; lacertus, m.

sinewy, a. nervosus; lacertosus, torosus.

sinful, a. impius, pravus; flagitiosus, sceleratus; **—ly,** ad. impie, flagitiose, scelerate.

sinfulness, s. impietas, f.

sing, v.a. & n. cano, 3; canto, 1.

singe, v.a. aduro, amburo, 3.

singer, s. cantor, m.

singing, s. cantus, m.; carmen, n.

single, a. solus, unicus, unus.

single, v.a. (out) eligo, 3.

singly, ad. singillatim.

singular, a. unicus, singularis; peculiaris; *fig.* egregius, eximius; **—ly,** ad. singulariter; unice; egregie; præcipue.

singularity, s. res inaudita, f.; (strangeness) novitas, f.

sinister, a. mali ominis; malevolus, iniquus.

sink, v.n. (to fall to the ground) consido, subsido; (into ruins) collabor; (of price, etc.) cado, 3; (of a ship) deprimor, summergor, 3; **—,** v.a. deprimo; demergo, summergo; (a well) demitto, 3.

sink, s. sentina, f.

sinless, a. expers peccati; sine peccato.

sinner, s. peccans, c.

sinuosity, s. flexus, m.

sinuous, a. sinuosus.

sip, v.a. sorbillo, degusto, libo, delibo, 1 ; —, s. sorbitio, f.

siphon, s. sipho, m.

sir, s. (knight) eques, m. ; — ! i. (title of respect in address) bone vir ! vir clarissime !

sire, s. pater, genitor, sator, m. ; (title of respect) Domine !

siren, s. siren, f.

sirocco, s. Auster, Africus, Atabulus, m.

sister, s. soror, f.

sisterhood, s. societas, f. ; collegium, n.

sister-in-law, s. glos, f.

sisterly, a. sororius.

sit, v.a. sedeo ; (at) assideo, 2 ; (down) consido, 3 ; (on) insideo, 2 ; (up) vigilo ; (by candle-light) lucubro, 1.

site, s. situs ; positus, m. ; (space) area, f.

sitting, s. (act and session) sessio, f.

situated, a. situs, positus.

situation, s. situs, positus, m. ; *fig.* condicio, f. ; status, m.

six, a. sex ; — each, seni ; — times, sexies.

sixfold, a. sextuplus.

six hundred, a. sescenti ; — each, sesceni.

sixteen, a. sedecim.

sixteenth, a. sextus decimus

sixtieth, a. sexagesimus.

sixty, a. sexaginta.

size, s. magnitudo ; moles ; mensura ; forma, f.

skate, s. (fish) squalus, m.

skein, s. glomus, n.

skeleton, s. sceletus, m. ; (bones) ossa, n. pl. ; *fig.* homo macie confectus, m.

skeleton-key, s. clavis adulterina, f.

sketch, s. adumbratio, f. ; —, v.a. adumbro ; delineo, 1 ; *fig.* describo, 3.

skewer, s. veru, n. ; —, v.a. (mod.) verubus configo, 3.

skid, s. sufflamen, n.

skiff, s. scapha, linter, navicula, f. ; alveus, m.

skilful, skilled, a. dexter, expertus, peritus ; sollers, ingeniosus ; —ly, ad. perite, sollerter, ingeniose.

skilfulness, skill, s. ars, sollertia, calliditas, peritia, f.

skim, v.a. despumo, 1 ; *fig.* percurro, stringo ; perstringo, attingo, 3 ; (fly over) volo per, 1 ; perlabor, verro, 3.

skin, s. (of men) cutis ; (of animals) pellis, f. ; (prepared) corium, n. ; (membrane) membrana ; (of vegetables) cutis, membrana, tunica, f.

skin, v.a. pellem detraho ; (over) cicatricem obduco, 3.

skinflint, s. avarus, m.

skinner, s. pellio, m.

skinny, a. rugosus ; macilentus ; macer.

skip, v.n. salio, exsilio, 4 ; exsulto, 1 ; lascivio ; (over) transilio, 4 ; —, s. saltus, m.   [tor, 1.

skirmish, s. leve prœlium ; —, v.n. velis-

skirmisher, s. veles, excursor, m.

skirt, s. (border) ora, f. ; limbus, m. ; (of a country) confinium, n. ; (dress) vestis, f. ; —, v.a. lego, 3.

skittish, a. petulans, procax ; —ly, ad. petulanter, procaciter.

skull, s. calvaria, calva, f. ; — -cap, s. pileolus, m.

sky, s. cœlum, n. ; æther, m.

sky-blue, a. cæruleus, cærulus.

skylark, s. alauda, f.

slab, s. quadra, f.

slack, a. remissus, laxus ; *fig.* piger, neglegens ; —ly, ad. laxe ; neglegenter.

slack, slacken, v.a. remitto, 3 ; laxo, relaxo, 1 ; minuo, 3 ; —, v.n. minuor, remittor, 3 ; laxor, relaxor, 1.

slackness, s. *fig.* neglegentia, pigritia, f. ; remissio, f.

slag, s. scoria, f.

slain, a. occisus ; mortuus.

slake, v.a. exstinguo, 3 ; sedo, 1 ; depello, 3.

slander, v.a. calumnior, detrecto, 1 ; —, s. calumnia ; obtrectatio, f.

slanderer, s. calumniator, obtrectator, m.

slanderous, a. maledicus ; —ly, ad. maledice.

slant, slanting, a. obliquus ; —ly, ad. oblique.

slap, s. alapa, f. ; —, v.a. alapam do, 1.

slash, s. (cut) incisura, f. ; (blow) ictus, m. ; (wound) vulnus, n. ; —, v.a. concido, incido, 3.

slatternly, a. squalidus, sordidus.

slaughter, s. cædes, trucidatio, f. ; —, v.a. macto, trucido, neco, jugulo, 1.

slaughter-house, s. macellum, n.

slave, s. servus, m. ; serva, f. ; verna, c ; mancipium, n. ; famulus, m. ; famula, f. —, v.n. *fig.* sudo, 1.

slave-dealer, s. venalicius.

slaver, s. (saliva) saliva, f.

slavery, s. servitus, f. ; servitium, n.

slave-trade, s. venalicium, n.

slavish, a. servilis ; humilis ; —ly, ad. serviliter, humilier.

slay, v.a. interficio, cædo, perimo, interimo, occido, 3 ; trucido, obtrunco, 1.

slayer, s. interfector, m.

sledge, s. traha, trahea, f.

sleek, a. levis, politus ; nitidus.

sleep, s. somnus ; sopor, m. ; quies, f. ; —, v.n. dormio, 4 ; quiesco, 3 ; to — off *or* over, edormio, 4.

sleeper, s. dormitor, m.

sleepiness, s. somnolentia, f. ; sopor, m.

sleeping-room, s. cubiculum, n.

sleepless, a. insomnis; exsomnis, vigil, vigilax; pervigil.

sleeplessness, s. insomnia; vigilantia, f.

sleepy, a. (things) somnificus; (inclined to sleep) somnicolosus; *fig.* iners.

sleet, s. nivosa grando, f.

sleeve, s. manica, f.; **to laugh in one's —,** furtim rideo, 2.

sleight, s. (of hand) præstigiæ, f. pl.

slender, a. gracilis; tenuis; (sparing) parcus; **—ly,** ad. exigue.

slenderness, s. gracilitas; tenuitas, f.

slice, s. segmentum, frustum, n.; offula; (tool) spatha, f.; —, v.a. seco, 1.

slide, v.a. labor, 3.

slide, s. lapsus, m.

slight, a. levis; exiguus, tenuis, parvus; **ly,** ad. leviter; paulum, paulo.

slight, s. neglegentia; repulsa, injuria, f.; contemptus, m.

slight, v.a. neglego; contemno, despicio, 3.

slightingly, ad. contemptim.

slightness, s. levitas; exiguitas, f.

slim, a. gracilis; v. **slender.**

slime, s. pituita, f.; (mud) limus, m.

slimy, a. limosus, mucosus.

sling, s. funda; (for the arm) fascia, mitella, f.; —, v.a. & n. e funda jaculor, 1; (hang) suspendo, 3.

slink, v.n. (away) furtim me subduco, 3; (in) irrepo, 3.

slip, v.n. labor, 3; —, v.a. (to let —) omitto, 3; **to — away,** elabor, clanculum me subtraho; **— out,** excido, 3.

slip, s. lapsus, m.; (in grafting) surculus, m.; *fig.* peccatum, n.; culpa, f.; error, m.

slipper, s. solea, crepida, f.

slipperiness, s. lubricum, n.

slippery, a. lubricus; *fig.* (deceitful) subdolus; (dangerous) periculosus.

slipperwort, s. calceolaria (mod. hort.).

slipshod, a. neglegens.

slit, s. incisura, rima, f.; —, v.a. incido, 3.

sloe, s. prunum, n.; **—-tree,** s. prunus, f.

sloop, s. lembus, m.

slope, s. acclivitas, declivitas, f.; clivus, m.

slope, v.n. proclinor, 1; demittor, 3; —, v.a. demitto, 3.

sloping, a. acclivis; declivis; pronus.

sloppy, a. lutulentus, sordidus.

sloth, s. ignavia, pigritia, inertia; socordia, f.; (animal) bradypus, m.

slothful, a. iners, piger, segnis; ignavus, socors; **—ly,** ad. pigre, ignave, segniter.

slough, s. (of a serpent) exuviæ, f. pl.; vernatio, f.; (mire) cœnum, n.; (marsh) palus, f.

sloven, s. discinctus, m.

slovenliness, s. incuria corporis, sordes ,f.

slovenly, a. discinctus.

slow, a. tardus, lentus; piger; (gentle) lenis; **—ly,** ad. tarde; lente; pigre; sensim.

slowness, s. tarditas; pigritia, f.

slowworm, s. anguis fragilis, f.

slug, s. limax, c., v. **snail.**

sluggard, s. dormitator, piger, m.

sluggish, a. piger, ignavus; **—ly,** ad. pigre, ignave.

sluice, s. objectaculum, n.; catarracta, f.

slumber, s. somnus, sopor, m.; —, v.n. obdormisco, 3; dormito, 1; dormio, 4.

slur, v.a. inquino, 1; *fig.* (over) leviter attingo, 3; —, s. macula, labes, f.

slut, s. mulier neglegens, f.

sly, a. astutus, vafer, callidus; **on the —,** clam, clanculum; **—ly,** ad., v. **astute,** callide, vafre.

slyness, s. astutia, calliditas, f.; astus, dolus, m.

smack, s. (relish) sapor, m.; (of a whip) sonus; (ship) lenunculus, m.

smack, v.a. (to taste) gusto; (a whip) flagello insono, 1; (strike) ferio, 4; —, v.n. sapio, 3.

small, a. parvus, exiguus, tenuis; brevis; pusillus; (insignificant) levis.

smallish, a. minusculus.

smallness, s. exiguitas, tenuitas; parvitas; gracilitas; brevitas, f.

smallpox, s. variolæ, f. pl.

smart, a. (clever) acutus, sollers, callidus; (energetic) alacer; (elegant) lautus, nitidus; **—ly,** (cleverly) acute, sollerter, callide; (energetically) acriter; (elegantly) nitide, laute.

smartness, s. sollertia, f.; acumen, n.; alacritas, lautitia, f.; nitor, m.

smash, s. ruina, f.; —, v.a. confringo, 3.

smatterer, s. semidoctus, sciolus, m.

smattering, s. (a small quantity) aliquantum, n.

smear, v.a. lino, illino, oblino, ungo, 3.

smell, v.a. olfacio, 3; odoror, 1; —, v.n. oleo; redoleo, 2; fragro, 1.

smell, s. (sense) odoratus, m.; (odour) odor, m.

smelling, a. suaveolens, odorus; (ill) olidus, graveolens.

smelling-bottle, s. olfactorium, n.

smelt, s. salmo eperlanus, m.

smelt, v.a. (ex)coquo, fundo, 3; conflo, 1.

smelting, s. fusura, f.

smelting-furnace, s. fornax, f.

smile, v.n. subrideo, renideo, 2; (at) arrideo, 2; —, s. risus, m.

smiling, a. renidens, subridens.

smirch, v. **to begrime.**

smite, v.a. ferio, 4; percutio, 3.

smith, s. faber, m.

smithy, s. fabrica; officina, f.

smoke, v.a. (suf)fumigo; (to dry by smoke) infumo, 1; —, v.n. fumo; vaporo, 1.   [nebula, f.

smoke, s. fumus, vapor, m.; (mist)

smoky, a. fumeus, fumidus, fumosus; fumificus; decolor fuligine.

smooth, a. levis; glaber (slippery) lubricus; (polished) teres; (calm) placidus; lenis; *fig.* blandus; —**ly,** ad. leniter, placide; *fig.* blande.

smooth, v.a. levigo, 1; polio, 4; (with the plane) runcino; *fig.* complano, 1.

smoothness, s. levor, m.; levitas; lenitas, f.; *fig.* (flattery) blandimentum, n.; æquus animus, m.

smother, v.a. suffoco, 1; opprimo, 3; (to conceal) celo, 1.

smudge, s. sordes, f.; —, v.a. inquino, 1.

smug, a. sibi placens.

smuggle, v.a. furtim importo, sine portorio importo, 1.

smut, s. fuligo; (of corn) rubigo, f.

smutty, a. fumosus.

snack, s. pars, portio; gustatio, f.

snaffle, s. frenum, n.; —, v.a. freno cohibeo, 2.

snail, s. coclea, f.; limax, c.

snake, s. anguis, c.; serpens, f.; vipera, f.; v. **serpent.**

snaky, a. anguineus, anguinus, anguifer, vipereus; anguicomus.

snap, v.a. & n. (one's fingers *or* a whip) concrepo, 1; (break) frango, 3; —, v.n. dissilio, 4; — **at,** mordicus arripio, 3; *fig.* hianti ore capto, 1.

snap, s. crepitus, m.

snapdragon, s. antirrhinum, n.

snappish, a. mordax; stomachosus; —**ly,** ad. stomachose.

snare, s. laqueus, m.; pedica, f.; *fig.* insidiæ, f. pl.

snare, v.a. illaqueo, implico, 1; irretio, 4.

snarl, v.n. (as a dog) ringor, 3; hirrio, 4.

snarl, hirritus, m.

snatch, v.a. rapio, corripio, 3; (away) eripio; surripio, avello, 3.

sneak, v.n. repo, serpo, 3; latito, 1; — **off,** me subtraho, 3; —, s. homo perfidus, m.

sneaking, a. perfidus; (secret) occultus.

sneer, v.n. irrideo, derideo, 2; —, **sneering,** s. irrisio, f.; irrisus, m.

sneeringly, ad. cum irrisione.

sneeze, v.n. sternuo, 3; —, s. sternumentum, sternutamentum, n.

sniff, v.n. naribus capto, 1; haurio, 4.

snip, v.a. amputo, 1; (off) decerpo, præcido, 3.

snipe, s. scolopax, f.

snivel, s. mucus, m. pituita, f. —, v.n. mucum resorbeo, 2.

snivelling, a. muculentus.

snob, s. homo novus et arrogans, divitum cultor, m.

snore, v.n. sterto, 3; —, s. rhonchus, m.

snort, v.n. fremo, 3; —, s. fremitus (equorum), m.

snout, s. rostrum, n.

snow, s. nix, f.; —, v.n. imp. ningit, 3.

snowdrop, s. galanthus (mod. hort.); **summer** —, leucojum (mod. hort.).

snowy, a. niveus, nivalis; (full of snow) nivosus.

snub, v.a. repello, 3.

snub, s. repulsa, f.

snub-nosed, a. simus, resimus.

snuff, s. (of a candle) fungus, m.

snuff, v.a. (inhale) haurio, 4; capto, 1.

snuffers, s. emunctorium, n.

snug, a. secretus, arcanus; nitidus; commodus; —**ly,** ad. secreto; commode.

so, ad. sic, ita; tam adeo; — **far,** eatenus; — **far from,** tantum abest — ut non; — **much,** tantum; tam; — **so,** mediocriter; — **that,** ita ut; — **that not,** ne; — **then,** quare, quapropter; **why** — ? quamobrem?

soak, v.a. macero, 1; madefacio, imbuo, tingo, 3; —, v.n. madeo, 2; madesco, madefio, 3; — **through,** percolor, 1.

soap, s. sapo, m.   [subvolo, 1.

soar, v.n. in sublime feror, 3; (of birds) **soaring,** a. sublimis.

sob, s. singultus, m.; —, v.n. singulto, 1.

sober, a. sobrius; *fig.* moderatus; —**ly,** ad. sobrie; moderate.

sobriety, s. sobrietas; *fig.* moderatio, f.

sociability, s. socialitas; comitas, facilitas, f.   [bilis, comis.

sociable, a. sociabilis, socialis; facilis, affa-

sociably, ad. comiter.

social, a. socialis; communis; civilis.

socialism, s. (mod.) rerum publicarum partitio inter omnes æquabilis, f.

society, s. societas, f.; sodalicium, collegium, n.

sock, s. pedale, n.; udo, m.

socket, s. cavum, n.

sod, s. cæspes, m.

soda, s. nitrum, n.

soever, ad. . . . cunque.

sofa, s. lectulus, grabatus, m.

soft, a. mollis, tener; (gentle) lenis; clemens; mitis; *fig.* delicatus; effeminatus; —**ly,** ad. molliter; leniter; clementer.

soften, v.a. mollio, 4; mitigo, 1; *fig.* lenio, 4; placo, levo, 1; —, v.n. mollesco; (fruits) mitesco; *fig.* mansuesco, mitesco, 3.

softness, s. mollitia; teneritas; lenitas; (effeminacy) mollitia, f.

soil, s. solum, n.; terra, f.
soil, v.a. inquino, contamino, maculo, 1.
sojourn, s. commoratio; mansio, f.; —,
v.n. commoror, 1.
solace, s. solatium, lenimen, levamen,
levamentum, n.; —, v.a. solor, consolor, 1.
solar, a. solaris; solis (genitive).
solder, v.a. ferrumino, 1; —, s. ferrumen, n.   [gregarius, m.
soldier, s. miles, c.; common —, miles
soldierly, a. militaris; bellicosus.
soldiership, s. militia; scientia rei militaris, f.
soldiery, s. milites, m. pl.; copiæ mili-
tares, f. pl.
sole, a. solitarius, unus, unicus, solus;
—ly, ad. solum, modo, tantum.
sole, s. (of the foot) planta; (of a shoe)
solea, f.
solecism, s. solœcismus, m.
solemn, a. sollemnis; severus; gravis;
serius; —ly, ad. sollemniter, graviter,
severe, serio.
solemnity, s. sollemne, festum, n.; sollem-
nitas, f.
solemnization, s. celebratio, f.
solemnize, v.a. celebro, agito, 1; ago, 3.
solicit, v.a. rogo; insto; flagito; (to
tempt) sollicito, 1.
solicitation, s. flagitatio; sollicitatio, f.;
impulsus, m.
solicitor, s. juris consultus, causidicus,
advocatus, m.
solicitous, a. sollicitus, anxius; —ly, ad.
sollicite, anxie.
solicitude, s. sollicitudo, anxietas, f.
solid, a. solidus; densus; fig. verus;
firmus; —ly, ad. solide; dense; firmiter.
solid, s. corpus solidum, n.
soliloquize, v.n. secum loqui, 3.
soliloquy, s. soliloquium, n.
solitariness, s. solitudo, f.
solitary, a. solitarius; (of places) desertus,
solus.
solitude, s. solitudo, f.; locus solus, m.
solo, s. canticum, n.
Solomon's seals, polygonatum, n.
solstice, s. solstitium, n.
soluble, a. solubilis.   [plicatio, f.
solution, s. dilutum, n.; fig. solutio, ex-
solve, v.a. solvo, 3; explico, 1.
solvency, s. facultas solvendi, f.
solvent, a. qui est solvendo.
some, a. aliqui, nescio qui; nonnullus;
quidam; — one, nescio quis, aliquis,
quispiam; — ... other, alius ... alius.
somehow, ad. nescio quomodo.
something, s. aliquid, n.; —, ad. aliquantulum.

sometime, ad. aliquando; quandoque; —
or other, aliquo tempore.
sometimes, ad. quandoque, interdum;
nonnunquam; (when repeated) modo
. . . modo.
somewhat, s. nonnihil, n., indecl.; aliquantum; —, ad. paululum.
somewhere, ad. alicubi.
somnolence, s. somni cupiditas, somnolentia, f.; torpor, m.
somnolent, a. somnolentus; torpidus.
son, s. filius, natus, m.; — -in-law, s.
gener, m.
song, s. cantus, m.; carmen, n.; (tune)
melos, n.; fig. for an old —, vili pretio.
songster, s. avis canora, f.; (of persons)
cantor, m.; cantatrix, f.
sonnet, s. canticulum, n.; versiculi, m. pl.
sonorous, a. sonorus; canorus; —ly, ad.
sonore; canore.
soon, ad. brevi, postmodo, mox; — after,
paulo post; as — as, simulatque,
simulac, vix . . . quum; as — as
possible, quamprimum.
sooner, ad. (earlier) citius, temperius,
prius . . . quam; (rather) libentius;
potius; no — said than done, dicto
citius.
soonest, ad. at —, quam citissime.
soot, s. fuligo, f.
soothe, v.a. mulceo, permulceo, 2; mitigo,
levo, 1; delenio, 4.
soothsayer, s. hariolus, sortilegus, m.;
fatidicus, haruspex, m.; augur, vates, c.
soothsaying, s. haruspicina; vaticinatio, f.
sooty, a. fuliginosus.
sop, s. offa, offula, f.
sophism, s. captio, cavillatio, f.
sophist, s. sophistes; cavillator, m.
sophistic(al), a. sophisticus; captiosus;
—ly, captiose.
sophisticate, v.a. adultero, 1; commisceo, 2.
sophisticated, a. insincerus.
sophistry, s. cavillatio captiosa, f.
soporific, a. soporus, soporifer, somnifer.
sorb, s. sorbus, f.; sorbum, n.
sorcerer, s. magus, veneficus, m.
sorceress, s. maga, saga, venefica, f.
sorcery, s. fascinatio, f.; veneficium, n.;
magice, f.
sordid, a. sordidus, turpis, fœdus; —ly,
ad. sordide, turpiter, fœde.
sore, a. tener; (grievous) atrox, durus,
gravis; —ly, ad. graviter, vehementer.
sore, s. ulcus, n.
sorrel, a. helvus.
sorrel, s. rumex, f.; wood —, oxalis, f.
sorrily, ad. misere.
sorrow, s. dolor, mœror, luctus, angor,
m.; anxietas, f.

sorrow, v.n. doleo, lugeo, 2 ; angor, 3.

sorrowful, a. luctuosus, tristis, miser, mæstus ; **—ly,** ad. mæste ; misere.

sorry, a. vilis ; sordidus ; v. **sorrowful; I am —,** ægre fero, 3 ; pænitet me (alicujus rei) ; **I am — for it,** nollem factum.

sort, s. (kind) genus, n. ; species, f. ; (manner) modus, mos, m.,; (quality, of things) nota, f.

sort, v.a. ordino, 1 ; dispono, digero, 3 ; **—,** v.n. convenio, 4.

sorter, s. diribitor, m.

sorting, s. diribitio, f.

sortie, s. eruptio, excursio, f. ; excursus, m.

sot, s. (drunkard) ebrius, potator, m.

sottish, a. ebriosus.

soul, s. anima, f. ; (person) homo, c.

sound, a. (healthy) validus, sanus ; (strong) robustus ; (entire) integer ; (in mind) mentis compos ; (true, genuine) verus ; (valid) ratus ; (of sleep) profundus ; altus ; **—ly,** ad. sane ; arte, graviter.

sound, s. sonus, sonitus, m. ; vox, f. ; (of a trumpet) clangor ; (noise) strepitus, m.

sound, s. (narrow sea) fretum, n. ; (probe, in surgery) specillum, n.

sound, v.a. (a trumpet) cano, 3 ; (try) tento, sollicito, 1 ; **—,** v.n. sono, persono, 1 ; strepo, 3.

soundness, s. sanitas ; integritas ; salubritas ; firmitas, f.

sounding, a. sonorus.

sounding-lead, s. catapirates, m.

soup, s. jus, n. ; **— -ladle,** s. trulla, f.

sour, a. acidus, acerbus ; amarus ; *fig.* morosus ; **—ly,** ad. acerbe ; *fig.* morose.

source, s. fons, m. ; *fig.* origo, f. ; principium, n.

sourish, a. subacidus, acidulus.

sourness, s. acor, m. ; acerbitas ; *fig.* morositas, f.

souse, v.a. immergo, 3 ; condio, 4.

souse, s. salsugo, f.

south, s. meridies, auster, m.

southern. a. australis, meridianus.

southern-wood, s. artemisia, f.

southward, ad. in meridiem, meridiem versus.

south-wind, s. auster, notus, m.

sovereign, s. princeps, rex, regnator ; **—,** a. supremus.

sovereignty, s. imperium, n. ; dominatio, f. ; principatus, m.

sow, s. sus ; porca, f.

sow, v.a. sero, 3 ; semino, 1.

space, s. spatium, n. ; area, f. ; (of time) intervallum, n.   [ample, spatiose.

spacious, a. spatiosus, amplus ; **—ly,** ad.

spaciousness, s. amplitudo, f.

spade, s. (tool) ligo, m. ; pala, f.

Spain, s. Hispania, f.

span, s. palmus, m.

spangle, s. bractea, f. ; **—,** v.a. orno, 1 ; vario, 1 ; distinguo, 3.

spaniel, s. canis Hispanicus, m.

Spanish, a. Hispanicus, Hispaniensis.

spar, s. lapis specularis, m. ; (beam) trabs, f.

spar, v.n. dimico ; *fig.* digladior, 1.

spare, v.a. & n. parco, 3 (with dative) ; parce utor, 3 ; tempero, 1.

spare, a. parcus ; exilis ; **—ly,** ad. exiliter.

sparing, a. parcus ; **—ly,** ad. parce.

spark, s. *c*intilla, f. ; igniculus, m.

sparkle, v.n. scintillo, corusco, radio, mico, 1.

sparkling, a. nitidus, coruscus.

sparrow, s. passer, m. ; **— -hawk,** s. falco nisus, m.

Sparta, s. Sparta, Lacedæmon, f.

Spartan, a. Laconicus, Spartanus, Lacedæmonius.

spasm, s. spasmus, m.

spasmodic, a. spasticus ; *fig.* rarus.

spasmodically, ad. *fig.* raro.

spatter, v.a. inquino, 1 ; aspergo, 3 ; *fig.* calumnior, 1.

spatula, s. spatha, f.

spavin, s. vitium suffraginum, n.

spawn, s. ova (piscium) n. pl. ; **—,** v.n. ova gignere, 3.

speak, v.n. & a. loquor, 3 ; fari, 1 ; dico, 3 ; **to — of,** dico (de), (to mention) memoro, 1 ; **to — out,** eloquor, proloquor, 3 ; **to — to,** alloquor, 3 ; **to — together** *or* **with,** colloquor, 3.

speaker, s. orator, m.

speaking, s. locutio, dictio, f. ; sermo, m. ; (of) mentio, commemoratio, f.

spear, s. hasta, lancea, f. ; telum, pilum, jaculum, n. ; **—,** v.a. transfigo, 3.

spearman, s. hastatus, m.

special, a. peculiaris, specialis ; præcipuus ; **—ly,** ad. specialiter, præcipue, peculiariter, præsertim.   [est.

speciality, s. proprietas, f. ; quod peculiare

specie, s. aurum argentumve signatum, n.

species, s. species, f. ; genus, n.

specific(al), a. specialis ; (definite) certus ; **—ly,** ad. specialiter ; (by name) nominatim.

specify, v.a. enumero, 1 ; describo, 3.

specimen, s. exemplum, documentum, specimen, n.

specious, a. speciosus ; **—ly,** ad. speciose.

speck, s. macula, f. ; (natural blemish) nævus, m.   [1.

speckle, s., v. **speck; —,** v.a. maculis vario,

speckled, a. maculosus.

spectacle, s. spectaculum, n. ; species, f. ; aspectus, m.

spectacles, s. perspicillum, n.

spectator, s. spectator, m. ; spectatrix, f.

spectre, s. simulacrum, umbra, visum, n.

speculate, v.a. & n. meditor, 1 ; conjecturam facio, 3.

speculation, s. contemplatio, f.

speculative, a. philosophandi studiosus.

speculator, s. contemplator, m.

speech, s. lingua, loquela, f. ; sermo, m. ; contio, oratio, f.

speechify, v.a. contionor, 1.

speechless, a. mutus, elinguis ; *fig.* obstupefactus.

speed, s. celeritas ; festinatio, f. ; impetus, m. ; —, v.a. propero, festino, adjuvo, prospero, 1 ; —, v.n. (hasten) propero, festino, 1 ; (fare) succedo, 3.

speedily, ad. cito, celeriter.

speedwell, s. veronica (mod. hort.).

speedy, a. citus, properus.

spell, s. (charm) incantamentum, cantamen, carmen, n. ; cantus, m.

spell, v.a. & n. ordino (1) syllabas litterarum.

spelling, s. orthographia, f.

spelt, s. far, triticum, n.

spend, v.a. impendo ; consumo ; (time) ago, dego, consumo, contero ; (to exhaust) effundo, 3 ; (to squander) dissipo, 1.

spendthrift, s. nepos, prodigus, m.

spew, v.a. & n. vomo, 3.

sphere, s. sphæra, f. ; globus, m. ; *fig.* provincia, area, f. [sus.

spherical, a. sphæricus, sphæralis, globosphinx, s. sphinx, f. [v.a. condio, 4.

spice, s. aroma, n. ; odores, m. pl. ; —,

spicy, a. aromaticus, conditus, fragrans, odorus, odorifer.

spider, s. aranea, f. ; —'s web, araneum, n. ; casses, f. pl.

spigot, s. epistonium, obturamentum, n.

spike, s. clavus, m. ; (point) cuspis ; (of corn) spica, f.

spiky, a. acutus, spinosus.

spill, v.a. effundo, 3.

spin, v.a. & n. neo, 2 ; (to draw out) duco, protraho, 3 ; (as a top) verso, 1 ; —, v.n. versor, 1 ; circumferor, 3.

spinach, s. spinacea (mod. hort.).

spinal, a. dorsualis.

spindle, s. fusus ; (of a wheel) axis, m. ; —-tree, euonymus, f.

spine, s. (vertebra & thorn) spina, f.

spinster, s. innupta, f. [spira, f.

spiral, a. spiræ formam habens ; —, s.

spire, s. spira ; (tower) turris, f.

spirit, s. spiritus, m. ; anima, f. ; *fig.* ingenium, n. ; vigor, m. ; (ghost) simulacrum, n. ; umbra, imago, f. ; (god) deus, m.

spirited, a. animosus ; alacer ; —ly, ad. animose ; acriter.

spiritless, a. piger, ignavus, frigidus ; —ly, ad. ignave, pigre, frigide.

spiritual, a. animi, mentis (genitives) ; incorporalis ; ecclesiasticus.

spit, s. veru, n. ; (of land) lingua, f. ; —, v.a. & n. transfigo ; (from the mouth) spuo, 3 ; exscreo, 1.

spite, s. livor, m. ; invidia, malevolentia, f. ; odium, n. ; in — of, nihilominus ; *or* ablat. absol. with part. perf. of contemno ; in — of your opposition, te repugnante.

spite, v.a. vexo, 1.

spiteful, a. lividus, malevolus, invidus ; —ly, ad. malevole, infeste.

spitefulness, s., v. spite.

spittle, s. sputum, n. ; saliva, f.

splash, v.a. aspergo, respergo, 3.

splay-footed, a. varicus.

spleen, s. lien, splen ; *fig.* stomachus, m.

spleenwort, s. asplenum, n.

splendid, a. splendidus nitidus ; lautus, sumptuosus ; magnificus ; —ly, ad. splendide ; magnifice ; laute, nitide, sumptuose.

splendour, s. splendor, nitor, m. ; *fig.* magnificentia ; lautitia, f.

splenetic, a. splenicus.

splint, s. fragmentum ossis, n. ; (in surgery) ferula, f.

splinter, s. assula, f. ; —, v.a. confringo, 3 ; —, v.n. dissilio, 4.

split, v.a. & n. findo ; findor, 3 ; —, s. fissura, rima, f.

split, a. fissilis.

spoil, s. spolium, n. ; præda, f. ; exuviæ, f. pl. ; —, v.a. spolio ; prædor ; vasto, 1 ; diripio, 3 ; (to mar, etc.) corrumpo ; (to ruin) perdo, 3 ; depravo, vitio, 1.

spoiler, s. spoliator ; vastator, m.

spoke, s. radius, m.

spokesman, s. orator, m.

spoliation, s. spoliatio ; direptio, f.

spondaic, s. spondiacus.

spondee, s. spondeus, m.

sponge, s. spongia, f. ; —, v.a. spongia detergeo, 2.

spongy, a. spongiosus.

sponsor, s. sponsor, vas, præs, m.

spontaneously, ad. sua sponte, ultro.

spool, s. fusus, m.

spoon, s. coclear, n.

spoonful, s. coclear, n.

sport, s. ludus, lusus, m. ; (hunting) venatio ; (mockery) irrisio, f. ; in —, per jocum ; —, v.n. ludo, 3 ; lascivio, 4.

sportive, a. jocosus, ludicer ; —ly, ad. jocose.

sportsman, s. venator, m.

spot, s. macula; (mark) nota; (stain) labes, f.; (place) locus, m.; —, v.a. (to stain) inquino, maculo, commaculo; (to speckle) maculis noto, 1.

spotless, a. expers maculis; *fig.* purus; integer; —**ly,** ad. sine labe.

spotted, a. maculosus, maculis distinctus.

spousal, s. nuptiæ, f. pl.

spouse, s. conjux, c.; maritus, m.; uxor, f.

spout, s. canalis; (of water) torrens, m.; —, v.a. ejaculor (in altum); (speeches) declamo, 1; v.n. prosilio, 4; emico, 1.

sprain, v.a. intorqueo, 2; convello, 3; luxo, 1; —, s. luxatura, f.

sprat, s. clupea sprattus, f.

sprawl, v.n. humi prostratus jaceo, 2.

sprawling, a. projectus, resupinus, supinus.

spray, s. aspergo, spuma, f.; (branch) ramus, m.; virga, f.

spread, v.a. pando, tendo, expando, distendo, extendo; diffundo, 3; (to make known) divulgo, 1; —, v.n. pandor, tendor, distendor, extendor, expandor, diffundor, 3; (to become known) divulgor; (of a disease, etc.) evagor, 1; glisco, 3.

sprig, s. ramulus, m.; virga, f.

sprightliness, s. alacritas, hilaritas, f

sprightly, a. alacer; hilaris.

spring, s. (season) ver, n.; (leap) saltus, m.; (of water) fons, m.

spring, a. vernus.

spring, v.n. (to grow from) orior, 4; enascor, 3; (as rivers, etc.) scateo, 2; effluo, 3; (to bud) germino, 1; (to leap) salio, exsilio, 4; (to crack) dissilio, 4; displodo, 3; — **a leak,** rimas ago, 3.

spring-time, s. vernum tempus, n.

springy, a. levis, mollis.

sprinkle, v.a. spargo, aspergo, respergo, 3; roro, irroro, 1.

sprite, s., v. **spirit.**

sprout, s. surculus, m.; germen, n.; —**s,** pl. cauliculi, m. pl.; —, v.n. pullulo, germino, 1.

spruce, a. lautus, nitidus, comptus; —**ly,** ad. nitide, laute, compte.

spruce, s. (fir) picea, f.

spruceness, s. nitor, m.

spume, s. spuma, f.

spur, s. calcar; *fig.* incitamentum, irritamen, irritamentum, n.; —, v.a. equum calcaribus concito, 1; equo calcaria subdo, 3.

spurge, s. euphorbia (mod. hort.).

spurious, a. subditus, suppositus, falsus.

spurn, v.a. aspernor, repudio, 1; sperno, 3; proculco, 1.

spurt, v.n. (as liquids) exsilio, 4.

sputter, v. æstuo, 1.

spy, s. explorator; speculator; emissarius, m.

spy, v.a. & n. exploro; speculor, 1.

squabble, v.n. rixor, 1; —, s. jurgium, n.; rixa, f.

squad, s. manipulus, m.

squadron, s. (of cavalry) turma, ala; (of ships) classis, f.

squalid, a. squalidus, spurcus, sordidus, turpis.

squall, s. vociferatio, f.; (of children) vagitus, m.; (sudden storm) procella, f.; —, v.n. vagio, 4.

squally, a. procellosus.

squalor, s. squalor, situs, m.; sordes, f. pl.; illuvies, f.

squander, v.n. dissipo, 1; profundo, 3.

squanderer, s., v. **spendthrift.**

square, a. quadratus; *fig.* honestus, probus; —, s. quadratum, n.; quadra; (tool) norma, f.; (mil.) agmen quadratum, n.

square, v.a. quadro, 1; —, v.n. congruo, 3; convenio, 4; quadro, 1.

squash, v.a. contero, confringo, 3.   [3.

squat, v.n. succumbo, recumbo ,subsidio,

squeak, v.n. strideo, 2.

squeamish, a. fastidiosus.

squeamishness, s. fastidium, n.

squeeze, v.a. comprimo, premo, 3; (out) exprimo, 3.

squib, s. (lampoon) libellus famosus, m.

squint, v.n. limis oculis intueor, 2.

squint, squinting, a. strabus, limis oculis.

squire, s. armiger, m.

squirrel, s. sciurus, m.

squirt, v.a. projicio, 3; —, v.n. emico, 1; exsilio, 4.

stab, s. vulnus, n.; ictus, m.; plaga, f.; —, v.a. fodio, 3; perforo, 1; perfodio, transfigo, 3.

stability, s. stabilitas, f.

stable, a. stabilis, solidus.   [larius, m.

stable, s. stabulum, n.; — **boy,** s. stabularius, v.a. stabulo includo, 3; —, v.n. stabulor, 1.

stack, s. acervus, m.; strues, f.; —, v.a. coacervo, 1.

staff, s. baculum, n.; fustis; (of high persons) scipio, m.; (officers) legati, m. pl.; *fig.* subsidium, fulcimentum, n.

stag, s. cervus, m.

stage, s. proscænium; pulpitum; suggestum; theatrum, n.; *fig.* campus, m.; area, f.; (on a journey) iter, n.

stage-player, s. actor scænicus, histrio, m.

stagger, v.n. vacillo, titubo, 1; —, v.a. obstupefacio, 3.

staggers, s. vertigo, f.

stag-horn moss, s. lycopodium (mod. hort.).

stagnant, a. stagnans; torpens; piger; iners.

stagnate, v.n. stagno, 1; *fig.* refrigesco, 3.

stagnation, s. torpor, m.

staid, a. gravis, severus.

stain, s. macula, labes; infamia, nota, f.

stain, v.a. maculo, commaculo, contamino, 1; (to dye) tingo, inficio, imbuo, 3.

stainless, a. immaculatus, purus; *fig.* integer.

stair, s. gradus, m.; scala, f.

staircase, s. scalæ, f. pl.

stake, s. palus, stipes, vallus, m.; sudis, f.; (at play) depositum, n.; —, v.a. depono, 3; pignero, oppignero, 1.

stale, a. vetus; obsoletus; tritus; (of wine) vapidus.

stalk, s. caulis; (of corn) culmus, m.

stalk, v.n. incedo, ingredior, 3; spatior, 1; (in hunting) venor, 1.

stalking-horse, s. prætextus, m.

stall, s. stabulum; (seat) subsellium, n.; —, v.a. stabulo, 1.

stallion, s. (equus) admissarius, m.

stamen, s. (of a flower) stamen, n.   [1.

stammer, v.a. balbutio, 4; lingua hæsito,

stammerer, s. balbus, m.

stammering, a. balbus.

stamp, s. (mark) nota, f.; signum, n.; (with the foot) vestigium, n.; (kind) genus, n.

stamp, v.a. imprimo, 3; noto, 1; (money) cudo, 3; (the ground with the feet) supplodo, 3; pulso, 1; (to bruise) contundo, 3.

stand, s. locus, m.; statio; mora, f.; suggestus, m.; mensa, f.; **make a —**, subsisto, 3.

stand, v.n. sto, 1; consisto, 3; (remain) maneo, 2; (to endure) tolero, 1; sustineo, 2; (against) resisto, 3; (aloof) absto, 1; (by) asto, 1; assisto, 3; *fig.* persto, 1; (out) exsto, 1; promineo, 2; (still) consisto, subsisto, 3.

standard, s. signum, vexillum, n.; norma, mensura, f.; **— -bearer,** s. vexillarius, signifer, m.

standing, s. status, ordo, m.; condicio, f.

standstill, s. **be at a —,** consisto, 3; hæreo, 2.   [n.

stanza, s. carmen tetrastichum, distichon,

star, s. stella, f.; sidus, astrum; *fig.* lumen, n.

starboard, s. dextrum latus navis, n.

starch, s. amylum, n.; —, v.a. amylo, 1.

stare, s. obtutus, m.; —, v.a. & n. inhio, 1; stupeo, 2; **— (at),** intueor, 2; hæreo (2) defixus in aliquo.

stark, a. rigidus; —, ad. omnino, penitus.

starling, s. sturnus, m.

starry, a. **sidereus, stellans, stellatus,** stellifer.

start, v.n. trepido, 1; subsilio, 4; contremisco, 3; (begin) ordior, 4; incipio, 3; (set out) proficiscor, 3; v.a. (game) excito, 1; (set on foot) instituo, 3; (put in motion) commoveo, 2; (put out of joint) luxo, 1.

start, s. subtia trepidatio, f.; tremor, m.; (departing) profectio, f.; (leap) saltus, m.; (beginning) initium, principium, n.

starting-place, s. carceres, m. pl.; claustra, n. pl.

startle, v.a. **territo,** 1; terreo, **2.**

starvation, s. fames, inedia.

starve, v.a. fame **interficio, 3;** —, v.n. fame enecor, 1.

starveling, s. esurio, famelicus, m.

state, s. status; locus, m.; (political) civitas, respublica, f.; (pomp) magnificentia; *fig.* condicio, f.

state, v.a. narro; declaro, indico, 1; perscribo, 3.

stately, a. superbus; splendidus, lautus, augustus.

statement, s. affirmatio, f.; testimonium, indicium, n.

statesman, s. vir regendæ reipublicæ, m.; peritus, qui in republica versatur, m.

statesmanship, a. rerum civilium administratio, f.

station, s. statio, f.; locus, m.; —, v.a. loco, 1; dispono, 3.

stationary, a. stabilis, loco fixus, immotus.

stationer, s. chartarius, **m.;** **—s shop,** taberna chartaria, f.

stationery, s. charta, f.; res chartariæ,

statuary, s. statuarius, sculptor, m.; (act) ars statuaria, f.

statue, s. statua, imago, effigies, f.; signum, simulacrum, n.

stature, s. statura, f.; habitus, m.

statute, s. statutum; decretum, n.; lex, .

staunch, a. firmus, fidus, constans.

staunch, v.a. sisto, 3; cohibeo, 2.

stave, s. assula, f.; —, v.a. perrumpo, 3.

stay, v.n. maneo, 2; commoror; (to loiter) cunctor, 1; —, v.a. detineo, 2; sisto, 3; (to curb) coerceo, 2; (support) sustineo, 2; sustento, 1.

stay, s. (abide) commoratio, mansio; (delay) mora, f.; (prop) fulcrum, n.; *fig.* subsidium, columen, n.

stead, s. **in— of,** loco, pro.

steadfast, a. stabilis, firmus, constans; **—ly,** ad. constanter, firmiter.

steadiness, s. firmitas, stabilitas, constantia, f.

steady, a. firmus, stabilis; constans; *fig.* gravis.

steak, s. offa, f.

steal, v.a. furor, 1 ; (away) surripio, 3 ; —, v.n. repo, serpo, 3 ; insinuo, 1.

stealing, s. furtum, n.

stealth, s. (act) furtum, n.; **by** —, furtim, clam.

steam, s. (aquæ) vapor, m. ; —, v.a. & n. vaporo ; fumo, 1.

steed, s. equus sonipes, m.

steel, s. chalybs, m.; (for striking a light) clavus, m. ; *fig.* ferrum, n. ; —, v.a. duro, confirmo, 1.

steep, a. præceps, arduus, præruptus ; —, s. arduum, n.

steep, v.a. madefacio, 3 ; macero, 1 ; imbuo, tingo, 3.

steeple, s. turris, f.

steeplechase, s. certamen equorum, n. ; cursus equorum, m.

steeply, ad. in præceps.

steepness, s. acclivitas, declivitas, f.

steer, s. juvencus, m.

steer, v.a. & n. guberno, moderor, 1 ; dirigo, rego, 3.

steering, s. gubernatio, f.   [ter, m.

steersman, s. gubernator, rector, magis-

stem, s. (of a tree) truncus, stipes, m. ; (of a ship) prora, f.

stem, v.a. obsisto, obnitor ; **reprimo,** 3.

stench, s. fetor, odor, m.

stenographer, s. notarius, m.

stenography, s. notæ, f. pl.

step, s. passus, gradus, gressus, m. ; **— by** —, ad. gradatim, sensim, pedetentim.

stepbrother, s. (of father's side) vitrici filius ; (of mother's side) novercæ filius, m.

stepdaughter, s. privigna, f.

stepfather, s. vitricus, m.

stepmother, s. noverca, f.

stepson, s. privignus, m.

sterile, a. sterilis, infecundus.

sterility, s. sterilitas, f.

sterling, a. verus, bonus.

stern, a. durus, severus ; torvus ; **—ly,** ad. dure, severe.

stern, s. puppis (navis), f.

sternness, s. severitas, torvitas, f.

stethoscope, s. stethoscopium, n.

steward, s. administrator, procurator ; vilicus, m.   [tio, f.

stewardship, s. administratio, procura-

stick, s. baculus, scipio, fustis, m. ; baculum, n.

stick, v.a. affigo, 3 ; —, v.n. hæreo ; adhæreo, 2 ; *fig.* hæsito, 1.

sticky, a. lentus, tenax.

stiff, a. rigidus ; *fig.* severus ; frigidus ; **—ly,** ad. rigide, severe.

stiffen, v.a. rigidum facio, 3 ; —, v.n. rigesco, derigesco, 3.

stiff-necked, a. obstinatus, pertinax.

stiffness, s. rigor, m. ; *fig.* pertinacia, f. ; rigor, m.

stifle, v.a. suffoco ; strangulo, 1 ; *fig.* opprimo, 3.

stigma, s. nota, ignominia, f.

stigmatize, v.a. noto, 1.

stiletto, s. sica, f. ; pugio, m.

still, a. quietus, immotus, tacitus ; —, v.a. placo, sedo, 1.

still, ad. nihilominus ; (yet) adhuc ; (however) tamen, attamen ; (even now) etiam nunc ; (always) semper.

stillborn, a. abortivus.

stillness, s. silentium, n. ; quies, f.

stilts, s. pl. grallæ, f. pl.

stimulant, s. irritamentum, irritamen, n. ; stimulus, m.

stimulate, v.a. stimulo, exstimulo, excito, 1.

stimulus, v. **stimulant.**

sting, s. (of bees, etc., also of plants) aculeus, m.; spiculum, n.; (wound by it) ictus, morsus, m. ; *fig.* (of conscience) angor conscientiæ, m. ; —, v.a. pungo, 3 ; mordeo, 2 ; (as nettles) uro, 3 ; *fig.* excrucio, 1.

stinginess, s. parsimonia, f.

stingy, a. sordidus, parcus.

stink, v.n. feteo, male oleo **2** ; —, s. fetor, m.

stint, s. modus, m. ; inopia, f. ; —, v.a. moderor, 1 ; coerceo, 2 ; parco, circumscribo, 3.

stipend, s. salarium, n. ; merces, f.

stipendiary, a. & s. mercenarius ; stipendiarius.

stipulate, v.a. paciscor, 3 ; stipulor, 1.

stipulation, s. stipulatio ; condicio, f. ; pactum, n.

stir, s. tumultus, motus, m. ; turba, f. ; —, v.a. excito, 1 ; moveo, 2 ; —, v.n. se movere, 2.

stirrup, s. stapeda, f.

stitch, v.a. suo, 3.

stoat, s. mustela erminea, f.

stock, s. (of a tree) caudex, truncus, stipes, m. ; (haft, handle) lignum, n. ; (race) genus, n. ; (of goods) copia, vis, f. ; (cattle) pecus, n. ; stirps, f. ; (of cattle) res pecuaria, f. ; (money on interest) pecuniæ, f. pl.

stock, v.a. instruo, 3 ; orno, suppedito, 1.

stock, s. (plant) matthiola ; **Virginian** —, malcomia (mod. hort.).

stockade, s. vallum, n.

stocking, s. tibiale, n.

stockstill, a. immotus, immobilis.

stoic(al), a. stoicus ; *fig.* patiens.

stoicism, s. Stoica disciplina, f. ; *fig.* patientia.

stole, s. stola, f.

stolen, p. & a. furtivus ; clandestinus ; — goods, furta, n. pl.

stomach, s. stomachus, venter, ventriculus ; (appetite) appetitus, m. ; (anger) ira, f. ; —, v.a. (put up with) fero, 3 ; tolero, 1.

stomacher, s. mamillare, n.

stone, s. lapis, m. ; saxum, n. ; (med.) calculus ; (gem) gemma, f. ; **leave no — unturned,** nihil reliqui facio, 3 ; (of fruit) nucleus, m. ; —, v.a. lapido, 1.

stone, a. lapideus, saxeus.

stonecrop, s. (plant) sedum, n.

stone-cutter, s. lapicida, lapidarius (opifex), m.

stone-pit, stone-quarry, s. lapidicinæ, lautumiæ, f. pl.

stony, a. (full of stones) lapidosus ; saxeus, saxosus.

stool, s. scabellum, scamnum, n. ; sella, f.

stoop, v.n. proclino, 1 ; fig. se summittere, 3.

stooping, a. pronus.

stop, v.a. prohibeo, 2 ; sisto, 3 ; moror, tardo, retardo, 1 ; —, v.n. subsisto ; (to cease) desisto ; desino, omitto, 3 ; (remain) maneo, 2 ; (sojourn) commoror, 1 ; — up, obturo, 1 ; intercludo, 3.

stop, s. (delay) mora, f. ; impedimentum, n. ; pausa, f. ; (point) punctum, n. ; (end) finis, c.

stoppage, s. obstructio, f.

stopper, stopple, s. obturamentum, n.

store, s. copia, f. ; apparatus ; (provision) commeatus, m. ; —, v.a. coacervo, 1 ; condo ; (with) instruo, 3.

storehouse, s. cella, f. ; promptuarium ; (for cereals) horreum, n.

store-keeper, s. cellarius, promus, m.

storey, v. story.

stork, s. ciconia, f.

storm, s. procella, tempestas ; (mil.) expugnatio, f. ; —, v.a. expugno, 1 ; —, v.n. sævio, desævio, 4.

stormy, a. turbidus ; procellosus ; fig. tumultuosus.

story, s. (tale) narratio ; fabula ; (history) historia, f. ; (lie) mendacium, n. ; (of a house) tabulatum, n.

story-teller, s. narrator ; (liar) mendax, m.

stout, a. robustus ; firmus ; validus ; (fat) pinguis ; (brave) **fortis ; —ly,** ad. robuste ; fortiter.

stoutness, s. robur, n. ; firmitas ; fortitudo ; (fatness) pinguitudo, f.

stove, s. fornax, f. ; caminus, m.

stow, v.a. condo, recondo, repono, 3.

straddle, v.n. varico, 1.

straggle, v.n. palor, vagor, 1.

straggler, s. vagus ; erro, m.

straight, a. rectus, directus ; —ly, ad. recte, recta.

straighten, v.a. rectum facio, 3 ; corrigo, 3.

straightforward, a. simplex, apertus, directus, sincerus ; —, ad. recta (via) ; protinus.   [tas, f.

straightforwardness, s. simplicitas, sinceritas, f.

straightway, ad. statim, confestim, protinus.

strain, v.a. (to stretch) contendo, 3 ; (a joint) luxo, 1 ; (to filter) percolo, 1 ; (to press out) exprimo, 3 ; —, v.n. percolor, 1 ; enitor, 3.

strain, s. contentio ; vis ; (nervorum) intentio ; (effort) conamen, n. ; nisus, m. ; (mus.) numerus ; (manner, style) modus, m.

strainer, s. colum, n.

strait, a. angustus, artus ; —ly, ad. anguste, arte.   [gustiæ, f. pl.

strait, s. fretum, n. ; fig. difficultas, f. ; anstraiten, v.a. arto, 1 ; in angustias adduco, 3.   [impingor, 3.

strand, s. litus, n. ; —, v.n. (of ships)

strange, a. peregrinus ; fig. inusitatus ; rarus ; novus ; mirus ; mirificus ; —! i. mirabile dictu ! —ly, ad. mirifice.

strangeness, s. novitas, raritas ; (in pronunciation) peregrinatio, f.

stranger, s. advena ; hospes ; peregrinus, m.

strangle, v.a. strangulo, suffoco, 1.

strangulation, s. strangulatio, suffocatio, f. ; strangulatus, m.   [tum, n.

strap, s. lorum, n. ; struppus, m. ; amenstrapping, a. robustus.

stratagem, s. insidiæ, f. pl. ; fig. dolus, m.

strategist, s. artis imperatoriæ peritus, m.

strategy, s. ars imperatoria, f.

stratum, n. tabulatum, n.

straw, s. stramentum, stramen, n. ; stipula, f. ; —, a. stramineus.

straw-bed, s. stramentum, n.

strawberry, s. fragum, n. ; — -tree, s. arbutus, f.

stray, v.n. erro, aberro, palor, vagor, 1.

stray, a. vagus ; (sporadic) rarus.

streak, s. linea, virga, f. ; —, v.a. distinguo, 3.

streaky, a. virgatus.

stream, s. flumen, n. ; amnis, m. ; —, v.n. fluo, curro, effundor, 3 ; mano, 1.

streamer, s. vexillum, n.

streamlet, s. rivulus, m.   [cus, m.

street, s. via ; (with houses) platea, f. ; vi-

strength, s. robur, n. ; firmitas ; (power) potentia, potestas, f. ; vires, f. pl.

strengthen, v.a. roboro, confirmo, 1 ; munio, 4.

strenuous, a. strenuus ; fortis ; acer ; —ly, ad. strenue, fortiter, acriter.

stress, s. (chief point) summa, f. ; caput, n. ; (emphasis) vis, f. ; pondus, n.

stretch, v.a. tendo ; produco, extendo ; distendo, 3 ; —, v.n. extendo ; producor ; distendor ; (of country) patesco, 3 ; **to — out,** porrigo, 3 ; (oneself) pandiculor, 1.

stretch, s. intentio, contentio, f. ; spatium, n. ; tractus, m.

stretcher, s. lecticula, f. [3.

strew, v.a. spargo, conspergo, (in)sterno,

stricken, a. & p. vulneratus, afflictus ; (with age) aetate provectus or provectior.

strict, a. accuratus, exactus ; rigidus, severus ; **—ly,** ad. accurate ; rigide ; severe.

strictness, s. severitas, f. ; rigor, m.

stricture, s. vituperatio ; culpa, f.

stride, v.n. varico, 1 ; —, s. gradus, m. ; **make —s,** *fig.* proficio, 3.

strife, s. jurgium, n. ; lis ; pugna ; discordia, rixa, f.

strike, v.a. ferio, 4 ; pulso, 1 ; percutio ; (of a stringed instrument) tango, 3 ; (to cudgel) verbero, 1 ; (to stamp) cudo, 3 ; (the mind) subeo, 4 ; succurro, 3 ; **be struck,** *fig.* commoveor, 2.

strikingly, ad. mirum in modum.

string, s. linea, f. ; filum, n. ; (for a bow ; sinew) nervus, m. ; (for musical instruments) chorda ; *fig.* series, f. ; —, v.a. persero, 3.

stringency, s. severitas, f.

stringent, a. severus.

stringy, a. (of plants) fibratus.

strip, v.a. (off) spolio ; nudo ; denudo, 1 ; (clothes) exuo, 3 ; (the rind, etc.) decortico, 1. [scheda, f.

strip, s. particula, lacinia, f. ; (of paper)

stripe, s. (mark of a blow) vibex, f. ; (blow) ictus, m. ; verbera, n. pl. ; (for garments) virga, f.

strive, v.n. (e)nitor, 3 ; molior, 4 ; conor, 1 ; contendo, 3 ; (after, for) annitor, 3 ; sector, 1 ; (against) obnitor, 3.

striving, s. contentio, f. ; nisus, m.

stroke, s. ictus, m. ; plaga, f. ; (of an oar) pulsus, m. ; —, v.a. (per)mulceo, 2.

stroll, v.n. (about) perambulo, obambulo, spatior, 1 ; —, s. ambulatio, f.

stroller, s. ambulator, m.

strong, a. robustus ; fortis ; firmus, valens ; (powerful) potens, validus ; *fig.* vehemens ; gravis ; **—ly,** ad. robuste ; valide ; firme ; fortiter ; vehementer ; graviter.

stronghold, s. arx, f. ; castellum, n.

structure, s. (construction) structura, f. ; (building) aedificium, n.

struggle, v.n. contendo, 3 ; certo, luctor, 1 ; (ob)nitor, 3 ; (to fight) pugno, 1 ; —, s. certamen, n. ; pugna ; luctatio, f. ; luctamen, n.

strumpet, s. scortum, n. ; meretrix, f.

strut, v.n. spatior, 1.

stubble, s. stipula, f. ; culmus, m.

stubborn, a. obstinatus, pervicax, contumax ; **—ly,** ad. pervicaciter, obstinate, contumaciter.

stubbornness, s. pervicacia, contumacia, f.

stucco, s. albarium, n.

stud, s. bulla, f. ; clavus, m. ; (of horses) equaria, f. ; —, v.a. distinguo, 3.

student, s. litterarum studiosus, m.

studied, a. meditatus ; exquisitus ; compositus.

studious, a. diligens, industrius, navus ; **—ly,** ad. diligenter, industrie, naviter.

study, s. studium ; (room) umbraculum, n. ; bibliotheca, f. ; —, v.a. & n. studeo, 2 ; (with dative) exploro ; meditor, 1.

stuff, s. (material) materia, f. ; (furniture, etc.) supellex, f. ; (cloth) pannus, m. ; (woven —) textile, n. ; — ! i. nugae !

stuff, v.a. farcio, 4 ; sagino, 1 ; (to fill) expleo, repleo, 2.

stuffing, s. (in cookery) fartum ; (for chairs, etc.) tomentum, n.

stultify, v.a. (invalidate) rescindo, irritum facio, 3.

stumble, v.n. offendo, 3 ; (at) haesito, 1 ; (upon) incido, 3 ; —, s. offensio, f.

stumbling-block, s. offensio, f.

stump, s. truncus, caudex, stipes, m.

stun, v.a. obstupefacio, obtundo, stupefacio, 3 ; perturbo, 1 ; sopio, 4.

stunt, v.a. incrementum (alicujus, etc.) impedio, 4.

stupefaction, s. stupor, m. ; torpedo, f.

stupefy, v.a. obstupefacio, 3 ; terreo, 2 ; perturbo ; hebeto, 1 ; sopio, 4.

stupendous, a. mirus, immanis.

stupid, a. stupidus, fatuus, stultus ; **—ly,** ad. stulte. [tia, f.

stupidity, s. stupiditas, fatuitas, stulti-

stupor, s. stupor ; torpor, m.

sturdiness, s. firmitas, f. ; robur, n.

sturdy, a. robustus, validus, firmus ; **—ly,** ad. robuste, valide, firme.

sturgeon, s. acipenser, m.

stutter, v.n. balbutio, 4.

sty, s. hara, f.

style, s. (to write with) stilus, m. ; *fig.* sermo ; modus, m. ; genus, n. ; —, v.a. appello, nomino, 1.

stylish, a. nitidus, lautus.

suave, a. blandus. [ditia, f.

suavity, s. suavitas, dulcedo, f. ; blan-

subaltern, a. inferior ; —, s. minister ; (mil.) succenturio, m.

subdue, v.a. subjicio, subigo, vinco, 3 ; domo, 1.

subject, a. subjectus ; (liable to) obnoxious.

subject, s. (homo) subditus ; civis, m. ; (theme) materia, f. ; argumentum, n. ; (log. & gr.) subjectum, n.

subject, v.a. subjicio, subigo, 3.

subjection, s. servitus ; patientia, f.

subjective, a. subjectivus.

subjoin, v.a. subjungo, suppono, 3.

subjugate, v.a. subigo, 3 ; domo, 1.

subjunctive, s. (gr.) subjunctivus modus, m.

sublime, a. altus, celsus ; fig. excelsus, sublimis ; —ly, ad. excelse.

sublimity, s. elatio, excelsitas ; sublimitas, f.

sublunary, a. terrestris, mortalis.

submarine, a. summersus.   [1.

submerge, v.a. & n. summergo, 3 ; inundo,

submersion, s. summersio, f.

submission, s. obsequium, n.

submissive, a. submissus ; supplex ; —ly, ad. summisse, suppliciter.

submit, v.a. summitto, subjicio ; —, v.n. (to condescend) descendo, 3 ; (to endure) subeo, 4 ; (yield) cedo, 3.

subordinate, v.a. posthabeo, 2.

subordinate, a. & s. inferior, m.

subordination, s. (mil.) disciplina ; condicio inferior, f.

suborn, v.a. suborno, 1.

subpœna, v.a. testimonium denuntio, 1 ; (dat.) —, s. denuntiatio testimonii, f.

subscribe, v.a. subscribo, 3 ; subsigno, 1 ; assentior, 4 ; (give money) pecuniam do, 1.

subscriber, s. subscriptor, m.   [f.

subscription, s. (act) subscriptio, collecta,

subsequent, a. sequens, posterior ; —ly, ad. deinde, postea.

subserve, v.a. subvenio, 4.

subservient, a. summissus.

subside, v.n. sido, consido, resido, subsido, 3.

subsidiary, a. subsidiarius.

subsidize, v.a. pecunias suppedito, 1.

subsidy, s. collatio, f. ; subsidium, n.

subsist, v.n. vivo, 3.

subsistence, s. victus, m. ; vita, f.

substance, s. substantia ; materia, res, f. ; (estate) opes, f. pl.

substantial, a. solidus, firmus ; (real) verus ; (chief) præcipuus ; (rich) opulentus ; —ly, ad. solide ; (truly) vere ; (by nature) natura.

substantiate, v.a. confirmo, 1 ; ratum facio, 3.

substantive, s. nomen, substantivum, n.

substitute, s. vicarius, m.

substitute, v.a. substituo, suppono, 3.

substitution, s. substitutio, f.

subterfuge, s. tergiversatio, f. ; effugium, n. ; prætextus, m.

subterranean, a. subterraneus.

subtle, a. subtilis ; acutus, vafer.

subtlety, a. subtilitas ; tenuitas, astutia, f. ; acumen, n.

subtract, v.a. subtraho, adimo, aufero, 3.

suburb, s. suburbium, n.

suburban, a. suburbanus.

subversion, s. excidium, n.

subvert, v.a. everto, subverto, 3.

succeed, v.n. succedo, sequor, 3 ; fig. succedo, 3 ; prospere evenio, 4 ; — to, (take over) excipio, 3.

success, s. bonus or felix exitus, successus, m.

successful, a. fortunatus, prosperus, faustus, felix ; —ly, ad. fortunate, prospere, fauste, feliciter.

succession, s. series, successio, f.

successive, a. continuus ; —ly, ad. in ordine ; continenter ; deinceps.

successor, s. successor, m.

succinct, a. succinctus ; brevis, concisus ; —ly, ad. succincte, brevi.

succour, s. auxilium, subsidium, n. ; opem (acc. sing.), f. ; —, v.a. succurro, 3 ; subvenio, 4 ; juvo, adjuvo, 1.

succulence, s. sucus, m.

succulent, a. sucosus, suculentus.

succumb, v.n. succumbo, cado, 3.

such, a. talis ; ejusmodi ; —, ad. sic, adeo, tam ; — as, qualis ; in — manner, tali modo.

suck, v.a. sugo, 3 ; (in, up) sorbeo, 2 ; exsugo, 3 ; —, v.n. ubera duco, 3.

sucker, s. surculus, m.

sucking, a. lacteus, lactens.

suckle, v.a. ubera dare (alicui), dare mammam, 1.

suckling, s. (child) lactens, m.

suction, s. suctus, m.

sudden, a. subitus, repentinus, inexspectatus ; inopinatus, inopinus, necopinus ; —ly, ad. subito, repente.

sue, v.a. in jus voco, 1 ; —, v.n. oro, precor, flagito, 1 ; posco, peto, 3.

suet, s. sebum, n. ; adeps, c.

suffer, v.a. patior, fero, 3 ; tolero, 1 ; sustineo, 2 ; —, v.n. laboro, 1.

sufferable, a. tolerabilis, tolerandus.

sufferance, s. patientia ; venia, f.

sufferer, s. ægrotus ; fig. calamitosus.

suffering, s. perpessio, toleratio, f. ; labores, m. pl.

suffice, v.n. sufficio, 3 ; satis esse.

sufficiency, s. satias, f.

sufficient, a. sufficiens ; —ly, ad. satis, affatim.

suffocate, v.a. suffoco, 1.
suffocation, s. suffocatio, f.
suffragan, s. chorepiscopus, episcopi vicarius, m.
suffrage, s. suffragium, n.
suffuse, v.a. suffundo, 3.
suffusion, s. suffusio, f.
sugar, s. saccharum, n.   [2.
suggest, v.a. subjicio, suggero, 3 ; moneo,
suggestion, s. admonitio, f.
suicide, s. mors voluntaria, f.
suit, s. lis, causa, f. ; (of clothes) vestimenta, n. pl. ; synthesis, f.
suit, v.a. accommodo, apto, 1 ; —, v.n. convenio, 4 ; congruo, 3.
suitable, a. aptus, idoneus, opportunus, congruus.
suite, s. comitatus, m. ; (of rooms) series, f.
suitor, s. supplex, c. ; (wooer) procus, m.
sulkiness, s. morositas, f.
sulky, ad. morosus.
sullen, a. tætricus ; morosus ; —ly, ad. morose.
sullenness, s. morositas, f.
sully, v.a. inquino, contamino, maculo, 1 ; polluo, 3.
sulphur, s. sulfur, n.
sulphurated, sulphuretted, a. sulfuratus.
sulphur(e)ous, a. sulfureus ; (full of sulphur) sulfurosus.
sultriness, s. æstus, m.
sultry, a. æstuosus, torridus, fervidus.
sum, s. summa ; (money) pecunia, f. ; fig. caput, n.
sum, v.a. (up) consummo, 1 ; fig. breviter repeto, 3.
sumach, s. rhus, m.
summarily, ad. breviter, summatim ; (at once) statim.
summary, s. epitome, f. ; summarium, n. ; —, a. brevis.
summer, s. æstas, f. ; — -house, s. umbraculum, n. ; of —, a. æstivus ; — quarters, æstiva, n. pl.
summit, s. culmen, cacumen, n. ; apex, vertex, m. ; fastigium, n.
summon, v.a. cito ; (challenge) provoco, 1 ; (send for) accio, 4 ; accesso, 3 ; (up) excito, 1 ; (animum) erigo, 3.
summoner, s. apparitor, m.
summons, s. accitus, m. ; evocatio, f.
sumptuary, a. sumptuarius.
sumptuous, a. sumptuosus ; magnificus, lautus ; —ly, ad. sumptuose, magnifice, laute.
sun, s. sol, m. ; —, v.a. insolo, 1.
sunburnt, a. adustus.
Sunday, s. Dominica, f.
sundew, s. drosera (mod. hort.).
sundial, s. solarium, n.
sunflower, s. helianthus (mod. hort.).

sunrise, s. solis ortus, m.
sunset, s. solis occasus, m.
sunder, v.a. separo, 1 ; sejungo, 3.
sunny, a. apricus.
sunshine, s. sol, m. ; apricitas, f.
sup, v.n. ceno, 1 ; —, s. gustus, m.
superabundant, a. quod satis superque est ; —ly, ad. satis superque.
superadd, v.a. superaddo, 3.
superannuated, a. propter ætatem immunis.
superb, a. magnificus, speciosus, splendidus ; —ly, ad. splendide, magnifice, speciose.
supercilious, a. arrogans, superbus, fastidiosus ; —ly, ad. superbe, arroganter, fastidiose.
supererogation, s. redundantia, f.
supererogatory, a. quod ultro fit.
superficial, a. levis, indoctus ; —ly, ad. leviter.
superficies, s. superficies, f.
superfine, a. eximius.
superfluity, s. redundantia, f.
superfluous, a. supervacaneus ; superfluus ; supervacuus ; —ly, ad. supervacuo.   [naturam est.
superhuman, a. quod supra hominis
superintend, v.a. præsum (alicui rei), administro, 1.   [ministratio, f.
superintendence, s. cura, procuratio, ad-
superintendent, s. præfectus ; curator, m.
superior, a. superior, melior ; — ,s. præpositus, m.
superiority, s. præstantia, f.
superlative, a. eximius ; (gr.) superlativus.
supernatural, a. supra naturam rerum, divinus ; —ly, ad. divinitus.
supernumerary, a. ascripticius, accensus.
superscribe, v.a. superscribo, 3.
superscription, s. titulus, m. ; inscriptio, f.
supersede, v.a. aboleo, 2 ; in locum (alicujus) succedo, 3.
superstition, s. superstitio, f.
superstitious, a. superstitiosus ; —ly, ad. superstitiose.
supervene, v.n. supervenio, 4.
supervision, s. cura, curatio, f.
supine, a. supinus ; lentus, socors, iners ; —ly, ad. supine ; lente ; socorditer.
supper, s. cena, f.
supplant, v.a. supplanto, 1 ; per dolum dejicio, præverto, 3.
supple, a. flexibilis, flexilis ; mollis.
supplement, s. supplementum, n. ; appendix, f.
suppleness, s. mollitia, f.
suppli(c)ant, s. supplex, c.
supplicate, v.a. supplico, obsecro, 1.
supplication, s. obsecratio, f. ; preces, f. pl.

supplicatory, a. supplex.

supply, s. supplementum, n. ; copia, vis, f. ; (supplies) commeatus, m. ; —, v.a. suppleo ; præbeo, 2 ; suppedito, 1.

support, s. (prop) fulcrum, n. ; *fig.* subsidium, n. ; (favour) gratia, f. ; favor, m. ; —, v.a. sustineo, 2 ; (to prop) fulcio, 4 ; (to maintain) alo, 3 ; (to aid) adjuvo, 1 ; (favour) faveo, 2.

supportable, a. tolerabilis.

supporter, s. adjutor ; fautor, m.

supposable, a. credibilis.

suppose, v.a. (to imagine) opinor, puto, 1 ; credo, 3 ; reor, 2 ; arbitror, 1.

supposition, s. opinio, conjectura, f.

supposititious, a. suppositicius, subditicius.

suppress, v.a. supprimo, comprimo, 3 ; aboleo, coerceo, 2.

suppurate, v.n. suppuro, 1.

suppuration, s. suppuratio, f. [n.

supremacy, s. principatus, m. ; imperium,

supreme, a. supremus, summus ; —ly, ad. præ omnibus aliis, summe.

sure, a. certus ; (faithful) fidus ; (safe) tutus ; —ly, ad. certe ; tuto ; firme ; ne, profecto.

sureness, s. firmitas, stabilitas ; fidelitas, f.

surety, s. vas, præs, sponsor, m.

surf, s. fluctus, m. ; unda, f.

surface, s. superficies, f. ; æquor, n.

surfeit, s. satietas, f. ; tædium, fastidium, n. ; —, v.a. saturo ; satio, 1.

surge, s. fluctus, æstus, m. ; —, v.n. tumesco, 3 ; æstuo, 1.

surgeon, s. chirurgus, m.

surgery, s. chirurgia, f.

surgical, ad. chirurgicus.

surlily, ad. morose.

surliness, s. morositas, f.

surly, a. morosus, difficilis.

surmise, s. conjectura, f. ; —, v.a. conjecto, 1 ; conjicio, 3 ; suspicor, 1.

surmount, v.a. supero, 1 ; vinco, 3.

surmountable, a. superabilis.

surname, s. cognomen, n.

surpass, v.a. supero, 1 ; excedo, excello, 3.

surplus, s. reliquum, residuum, n.

surprise, s. admiratio, f. ; (sudden attack) repens adventus hostium, m. ; —, v. deprehendo, 3.

surprising, a. mirus, mirabilis ; inexpectatus ; inopinatus ; —ly, ad. mirandum in modum.

surrender, s. (mil.) deditio ; (law) cessio, f. ; —, v.a. cedo ; dedo ; trado, 3 —, v.n. me dedo, 3.

surreptitious, a. furtivus, clandestinus ; —ly, clam, furtim.

surround, v.a. circumdo ; circumsto, 1 ; cingo, 3 ; circumvallo, 1.

survey, s. (act) inspectio ; contemplatio ; (measuring) mensura, f ; —, v.a. inspicio, 3 ; contemplor, 1 ; (to measure land) permetior, 4.

surveyor, s. mensor, metator, decempedator, m.

survive, v.n. superstes sum, supersum, supero, 1.

survivor, s. superstes, c.

susceptible, a. mollis ; (capable) capax.

suspect, v.a. suspicor, 1.

suspend, v.a. suspendo, 3 ; intermitto ; differo, 3 ; abrogo, 1.

suspense, s. dubitatio, f. ; in —, incertus, dubius.

suspension, s. (of arms) indutiæ, f. pl.

suspicion, s. suspicio, f.

suspicious, a. suspicax ; suspiciosus ; (suspected) suspectus ; suspiciosus ; —ly, ad. suspiciose.

sustain, v.a. (to prop) sustineo, 2 ; sustento, 1 ; fulcio, 4 ; (to bear, etc.) tolero, 1 ; fero, 3 ; (of an actor) (partes) ago, 3 ; (defend) defendo, 3.

sustenance, s. victus, m.

sutler, s. lixa, m.

suture, s. sutura, f.

suzerain, s. dominus, m.

swab, s. peniculus, m. ; —, v.a. detergeo, 2.

swaddling-clothes, s. incunabula, n. pl. ; fasciæ, f. pl.

swagger, swaggerer, v. **boast, boaster.**

swallow, s. hirundo ; (throat) gula, f.

swallow, v.a. glutio, 4 ; voro ; devoro, 1 ; haurio, 4.

swamp, s. palus, f. ; —, v.a. demergo, 3 ; inundo, 1. [sus.

swampy, a. paludosus, palustris, uliginosus.

swan, s. cycnus, m. ; olor, m.

sward, s. cæspes, m.

swarm, s. (of bees) examen, n. ; *fig.* turba, f. ; —, v.n. examino, 1 ; confluo, 3.

swarthy, a. fuscus, subniger.

swathe, s. fascia, f. ; —, v.a. fasciis colligo, 1.

sway, s. dicio, f. ; imperium, n. ; (motion) æstus, m. ; —, v.a. rego, 3 ; —, v.n. æstuo, titubo, 1.

swear, v.a. (alicui) obsecrationem præeo, 4 ; —, v.n. juro ; (to curse) exsecror, 1.

sweat, s. sudor, m. ; —, v.n. sudo.

sweep, s. ambitus ; jactus, m.

sweep, v.a. (to brush, etc.) verro, 3 ; purgo, 1 ; (to pass quickly over) percurro ; verro, 3.

sweet, a. dulcis, suavis ; blandus ; jucundus ; —ly, ad. dulce ; suaviter ; blande ; jucunde.

sweeten, v.a. dulcem facio *or* reddo, 3 ; *fig.* lenio, 4 ; mulceo, 2.

sweetheart, s. deliciæ, f. pl. ; amica, f.
sweetish, a. subdulcis.
sweetmeats, s. bellaria, n. pl.
sweetness, s. dulcedo ; suavitas, f.
sweet-pea, s. lathyrus (mod. hort.).
swell, v.a. inflo, 1 ; tumefacio, 3 ; —, v.n. tumeo, turgeo, 2 ; intumesco, 3 ; —, s. æstus, m.
swelling, s. tumor, m.
swelling, a. tumidus, turgidus.
swerve, v.n. aberro, vagor ; declino, 1.
swift, a. celer, velox, rapidus, citus ; —ly, ad. celeriter, velociter, cito.
swiftness, s. celeritas, velocitas, f.
swill, v.a. haurio, 4 ; ingurgito, 1.
swim, v.n. nato, no ; fluito, 1 ; madeo, 2.
swimmer, s. natator, m.
swimming, s. natatio ; (of the head) vertigo, f.
swimmingly, ad. facile.
swindle, v.a. fraudo, 1 ; circumvenio, 4.
swindler, s. fraudator, m.
swine, s. sus, c. ; porcus, m. ; — -herd, s. suarius, m.
swing, s. oscillatio, f. ; impetus, m. ; —, v.a. huc illuc jacto, vibro, 1 ; —, v.n. fluito, 1 ; pendeo, 2 ; huc illus jactor, 1.
switch, s. virga, virgula, f. ; —, v.a. flagello, 1.
swivel, s. verticula, f.
swoon, s. defectio, f. ; —, v.n. deficio, collabor, 3.
swoop, s. impulsus, impetus, m.
sword, s. ensis, gladius, m. ; ferrum, n.
sword-lily, s. gladiolus, m.
sycamore, s. sycamorus, f.
sycophant, s. sycophanta, adulator, m.
syllable, s. syllaba, f.
syllogism, s. syllogismus, m. ; ratiocinatio, f.
symbol, s. signum, symbolum, n.
symmetrical, a. symmetrus, concinnus ; —ly, ad. concinne.
symmetry, s. symmetria, concinnitas, f.
sympathetic, a. (gentle) lenis, mitis, humanus ; —ly, ad. humane.
sympathize, v.n. (pity) misereor (alicujus), 2.
sympathy, s. (agreement) consensus, m. ; (fellow-feeling) sympathia, f.　　[m.
symphony, s. symphonia, f. ; concentus, m.
symptom, s. signum, indicium, n.
synagogue, s. synagoga, f.
syncope, s. syncope, f.
syndic, s. syndicus, m.
synod, s. synodus, f. ; conventus, m.
synonym, s. vocabulum idem declarans, synonymum, n.
synonymous, a. idem declarans.
syntax, s. syntaxis, f. ; constructio verborum, f.

synthesis, s. synthesis, f.
syringa, s. philadelphus (mod. hort.).
syringe, s. sipho, m. ; —, v.a. conspergo, 3.
system, s. systema, n. ; ratio, disciplina, f.
systematic(al), a. ad certam disciplinam redactus, ordinatus.
systematically, ad. ordinate.

Tabby, a. maculosus.
tabernacle, s. tabernaculum, n.
table, s. mensa, f. ; (food) victus ; (register) index, m.
table-cloth, s. mantele, n.
table-land, s. campus editus, m.
table-napkin, s. mappa, f.
tablet, s. tabula, tabella, tessera, f.
tacit, a. tacitus ; —ly, ad. tacite.
taciturn, a. taciturnus.
taciturnity, s. taciturnitas, f.
tack, s. clavulus, m.; —, v.a. assuo ; affigo, 3 ; —, v.n. (of ships) reciprocor, 1.
tackle, v.a. tracto, 1.
tackle, s. armamenta, arma, n. pl.
tackling, s., v. tackle.
tact, s. dexteritas ; prudentia, f.
tactician, s. rei militaris peritus, m.
tactics, s. ars militaris, ratio, f.
tadpole, s. ranunculus, i, m. ; ranula, f.
tag, s. ligula, f. ; (half-verse) hemistichium, n.
tag-rag, s. fæx (populi), f.
tail, s. cauda, f. ; `(of a plough) buris, m. ; (of a comet) crinis, m.
tailor, s. vestitor, m.
taint, v.a. inficio, 3 ; contamino, 1 ; polluo ; fig. corrumpo, 3 ; —, s. contagio, f. ; vitium, n. ; contactus, m.
take, v.a. capio ; sumo ; accipio, recipio ; rapio, 3 ; (to consider, etc.) (to — for, etc.) interpretor, 1 ; accipio, 3 ; —, v.n. (oneself to) se conferre, eo, 4 ; (to be successful) efficax esse ; bene succedere ; (fire) accendor, 3 ; **to — after,** similem esse ; **to — away,** adimo, aufero, 3 ; **to — down,** demo, 3 ; **to — for,** habeo, 2 ; puto, 1 ; **— in,** percipio, intellego, 3 ; fig. decipio, 3 ; **— off,** exuo, demo, 3 ; fig. imitor, 1 ; **to — up,** sumo ; (to scold) corripio, 3 ; objurgo, 1 ; fig. suscipio, 3.
taking, s. assumptio ; (away) ademptio ; spoliatio, f.
talc, s. talcum, n.
tale, s. narratio ; fabula, f. ; (number) numerus ; **— -bearer,** famigerator, m. ; delator, m.
talent, s. talentum ; fig. ingenium, n. ; facultas, f.

talented, a. ingeniosus.

talisman, s. amuletum, n.

talk, s. sermo, m.; colloquium, n.; (idle —) fabulæ, f. pl.; (rumour) rumor, m.; fama, f. [lor, 1.

talk, v.n. loquor, colloquor, 3; confabulatkative, a. loquax, garrulus.

talkativeness, s. loquacitas, garrulitas, f.

talker, s. locutor; (idle —) gerro, m.

tall, a. altus, celsus, procerus.

tallness, s. proceritas; altitudo, f.

tallow, s. sebum, n.

tallowy, a. sebosus.

tally, s. tessera, f.; —, v.n. convenio, 4.

talon, s. unguis, m.; ungula, f.

tamable, a. domabilis.

tamarind, s. tamarindus, m. (mod. hort.).

tamarisk, s. myrica, tamarix, f.

tambourine, s. tympanum, n.

tame, a. cicur; mansuefactus, mansuetus; fig. frigidus, insulsus; —ly, ad. mansuete; leniter; fig. insulse, frigide.

tame, v.a. perdomo, domo, 1; mansuefacio, subigo, 3.

tameness, s. mansuetudo; fig. insulsitas.

tamer, s. domitor, m.

tamper, v.n. sollicito, 1; se immiscere, 2.

tan, v.a. depso, conficio, 3; (colour) coloro, 1.

tangent, s. linea tangens, f.

tangible, a. tractilis.

tangle, v. entangle; —d, a. irreligatus, incomptus.

tank, s. cisterna; piscina, f.; lacus, m.

tankard, s. cantharus, m.

tanner, s. coriarius, m.

tansy, s. tanacetum (mod. hort.).

tantalize, v.a. crucio, 1.

tantamount, a. tantusdem, par.

tap, s. (blow) ictus, m.; (pipe) fistula, f.; —, v.a. leviter pulso, 1; (wine, etc.) relino, 3.

tape, s. tænia, f.

taper, s. cereus, m.; funale, n.

taper, v.a. & n. fastigo; fastigor, 1.

taper, a. (thin) gracilis.

tapestry, s. aulæum, tapete, n.

tape-worm, s. tænia, f.

tapir, s. tapirus, m.

tap-room, s. taberna, f.

tar, s. pix, f.; —, v.a. pice oblino, 3.

tarantula, s. aranea tarantula, f.

tardily, ad. tarde, lente.

tardiness, s. tarditas, f.

tardy, a. tardus, lentus.

tare, s. lolium, ervum, n.

targe, s., v. shield.

target, s. parma, f.; (mark to aim at) scopus, m.

tarnish, v.a. infusco; hebeto; fig. obsucro, 1; —, v.n. hebesco, 3.

tarry, a. piceus.

tarry, v.n. cunctor, moror, commoror, 1; maneo, 3.

tart, s. scriblita, f.; crustulum, n.

tart, a. acidus; acerbus; fig. mordax; —ly, ad. acerbe; mordaciter.

Tartarus, s. Tartarus, m.

tartness, s. acor, m.; mordacitas, f.

task, s. pensum, opus, n.; labor, m.; —, v.a. exerceo, 2.

tassel, s. cirrus, m.

taste, s. (sense) gustatus; (flavour) gustus, sapor, m.; fig. judicium, palatum, n.; —, v.a. (de)gusto, 1; —, v.n. sapio, 3.

tasteful, a. elegans; —ly, ad. fig. eleganter.

tasteless, a. insulsus; inelegans; —ly, ad. ineleganter, insulse.

tastelessness, s. insulsitas, f.

taster, s. prægustator, m.

tatter, s. pannus, m.

tattle, v.a. garrio, 4.

tattler, s. garrulus, m.

taunt, s. convicium, n.; contumelia, f.; —, v.a. exprobro, 1.

tauntingly, ad. contumeliose.

tavern, s. taberna, caupona, f.; —-keeper, s. caupo, m.

tawdry, a. speciosus.

tawny, a. fuscus, fulvus, ravus, flavus.

tax, s. vectigal; tributum, stipendium, n.; —, v.a. vectigal impono, 3; (to accuse) arguo, 3; accuso, 1.

taxable, a. vectigali solvendo obnoxius.

tax-collector, tax-gatherer, s. exactor, m.

teach, v.a. doceo, perdoceo, 2; instruo, 3; erudio, 4.

teachable, a. docilis.

teacher, s. magister, præceptor, m.

teaching, s. doctrina, eruditio, f.

teal, s. querquedula, f.

team, s. protelum, n.; jugales, m. pl.

tear, s. lacrima; fig. gutta, f.

tear, v.a. scindo, 3; (in pieces) (di)lacero, (di)lanio, 1; v.n., v. rush.

tear, s. scissura, f.

tease, v.a. vexo, crucio; (wool) carmino, 1.

teasel, s. dipsacus, f.

teat, s. mamma; (nipple) papilla, f,

technical, a. artificialis; (word) arti proprium (verbum).

techy, a. obstinatus, morosus.

tedious, a. tardus, lentus; longus; diuturnus, molestus; —ly, ad. tarde; moleste.

tedium, s. tædium, n.; molestia, f.

teem, v.n. scateo, 2; redundo, 1; abundo.

teeming, a. gravidus; fig. frequens.

teething, s. dentitio, f.

tell, v.a. dico, 3; narro; memoro; enumero; indico, 1.

teller, s. narrator, m.

tell-tale, s. sycophanta, delator, m.

temerity, s. temeritas, imprudentia, f.

temper, v.a. tempero, 1 ; diluo, 3 ; commisceo, 2 ; —, s. temperatio, f. ; animus, m. ; ingenium, n. ; (anger) iracundia, f. ; (mitigate) mitigo, 1 ; remitto, 3.

temperament, s. temperamentum, n. ; (of body) temperatio corporis, f.

temperance, s. temperantia, continentia, abstinentia, f.

temperate, a. temperatus ; sobrius ; abstinens ; —ly, ad. temperanter, sobrie.

temperature, s. temperatura, temperies, f.

tempest, s. tempestas, procella, f.

tempestuous, a. procellosus, turbulentus.

temple, s. templum, fanum, n. ; ædes, f. ; —s, pl. (of the head) tempora, n. pl.

temporal, a. temporalis ; profanus ; —ly, ad. ad tempus.

temporary, a. temporarius, ad tempus.

temporize, v.n. tempori *or* temporibus servio, 4.

temporizer, s. qui temporibus servit, m.

tempt, v.a. tento, sollicito, 1 ; allicio, 3.

temptation, s. sollicitatio ; illecebra, f.

tempter, s. tentator, m.

ten, a. decem ; — **times,** decies.

tenable, a. quod defendi potest.

tenacious, a. tenax ; —ly, ad. tenaciter.

tenacity, s. tenacitas, f.

tenant, s. conductor ; inquilinus, m.

tenantless, a. vacuus.

tenantry, s. coloni, inquilini, m. pl.

tench, s. tinca, f.

tend, v.a. curo, 1 ; —, v.n. tendo, 3 ; specto, 1.

tendency, s. inclinatio, f. ; **having a — to,** proclivis ad.

tender, a. tener, mollis ; *fig.* misericors ; —ly, ad. tenere ; molliter ; misericorditer.

tender, s. (of money) repræsentatio (pecuniæ), f. ; (guard) custos, c. ; (ship) navigiolum, n.

tender, v.a. offero, 3.

tenderness, s. teneritas, mollitia ; misericordia, bonitas, f.

tendon, s. nervus, m.

tendril, s. (of a vine) pampinus, c. ; (of climbing plants) clavicula, f.

tenement, s. insula, f.   [trina, f.

tenet, s. dogma, institutum, n. ; doctenfold, a. decemplex.

tenon, s. cardo, m.

tenor, s. tenor ; sensus, m. ; exemplum, n.

tense, a. tensus, rigidus ; —, s. (gr.) tempus, n.

tension, s. intentio, f.

tent, s. tentorium, tabernaculum, n. ; **general's —,** prætorium.

tenter-hook, s. hamus, m. ; **on —,** a. suspensus.

tenth, a. decimus ; —, s. decima pars, f.

tenuity, s. raritas, tenuitas, f.

tenure, s. possessio, f.

tepid, a. tepidus ; —ly, ad. tepide.

tepidity, s. tepor, m.

teredo, s. teredo, f.

tergiversation, s. tergiversatio, f.

term, s. (word) verbum, n. ; (limit) terminus, m. ; (space) spatium, n. ; (condition), condicio, lex, f.

term, v.a. dico, 3 ; appello, voco, 1.

termagant, s. mulier rixosa, f.

terminate, v.a. termino, 1 ; finio, 4 ; concludo, 3 ; —, v.n. terminor, 1 ; finem habeo, 2.

termination, s. terminatio, f. ; finis, c. ; exitus, m.

terrace, s. solarium, n.

terrestrial, a. terrestris, terrenus ; humanus.

terrible, a. terribilis, horribilis, dirus ; **terribly,** ad. horrendum in modum.

terrier, s. canis terrarius, m.

terrific, a. terrificus, terribilis, formidabilis.

terrify, v.a. terreo, perterreo, 2 ; territo, 1.

territory, s. regio ; terra, f. ; fines, m. pl. ; (around a town) territorium, n.

terror, s. terror, metus, pavor, m. ; formido, f.

terse, s. (neat, polished) tersus ; brevis ; pressus ; —ly, ad. presse ; breviter.

tertian, s. tertiana febris, f.

test, s. (trial) tentamentum, tentamen, periculum, n. ; (of metals) obrussa, f. ; (touchstone) coticula, f. ; —, v.a. tento, exploro, 1 ; experior, 4 ; periditor, 1.

testaceous, a. testaceus.

testament, s. testamentum, n.

testamentary, a. testamentarius.

testator, s. testator, m.

testatrix, s. testatrix, f.

testify, v.a. testificor, testor, 1.

testimonial, s. litteræ testimoniales, f. pl.

testimony, s. testimonium, indicium, n.

testy, a. stomachosus, morosus.

tetanus, s. tetanus, m.

tether, s. retinaculum, n. ; —, v.a. religo, 1.

tetter, s. impetigo, f.   [m.

text, s. verba scriptoris, n. pl. ; contextus,

textile, a. textilis, textrinus.

texture, s. textum, n. ; textura, f.

than, ad. quam ; atque, ac.

thank, v.a. gratias ago, 3.

thankful, a. gratus ; —ly, ad. grate.

thankfulness, s. gratus animus, m.

thankless, a. ingratus ; —ly, ad. ingrate.

thanks, s. gratia, f. ; grates, f. pl.

that, pn. ille, is, iste ; (who, which) qui ; —, c. ut ; quo.

thatch, s. stramentum, n. ; —, v.a. stramento tego, 3.

thaw, v.a. (dis)solvo, liquefacio, 3 ; —, v.n. regelo, 1 ; solvor, liquesco, 3.

theatre, s. theatrum, n. ; scæna, cavea, f.

theatrical, a. theatralis ; scænicus ; —ly, ad. scænice.

theft, s. furtum, n.

their, theirs, a. suus, eorum, illorum, earum, illarum.

theme, s. argumentum, n. ; materies, f.

themselves, pn. pl. se, sese ; **they** —, illi ipsi, illæ ipsæ ; **of** —, sui.

then, ad. (at that time) tum, tunc ; (after that) deinde, inde ; (therefore) igitur ; **now and** —, nonnunquam, interdum, aliquando.

thence, ad. (from —) inde, illinc ; exinde.

thenceforth, ad. ex eo tempore.

theologian, s. theologus, m.

theological, a. theologicus.

theology, s. theologia, f.

theorem, s. theorema, n.

theoretic(al), a. theoreticus.

theory, s. theoria, ratio, ars, f.

therapeutics, s. medendi scientia, medicina, f.

there, ad ibi, illic ; (thither) illo, illac, illuc ; **—abouts,** circiter ; **—after,** exinde ; **—by,** inde ; igitur, idcirco ; propterea ; **—from,** exinde, ex eo ; **—in,** in eo loco ; in ea re ; **—on, —upon,** exinde ; deinde ; tum ; **—with,** simul ; una.

thesis, s. thesis, f. ; propositum, n.

they, pn. pl. ii, eæ, illi, illæ.

thick, a. densus, spissus ; (gross) crassus ; (fat) pinguis ; (muddy) turbidus, lutosus ; (crowded) frequens ; creber ; **—ly,** ad. dense, spisse, confertim ; crebre.

thicken, v.a. denso ; condenso ; spisso, 1 ; —, v.n. densor, 1 ; spissor, 3.

thicket, s. dumetum, n. ; virgulta, n. pl.

thickness, s. densitas ; crassitudo, f.

thickset, a. condensus, compactus.

thick-skinned, a. callosus (also *fig.*).

thief, s. fur ; (of a candle) fungus, m.

thieve, v.a. furor, 1.

thievish, a. furax ; **—ly,** ad. furaciter.

thigh, s. femur, n.

thin, a. tenuis ; angustus ; rarus ; (lean) macer ; **—ly,** ad. tenuiter ; rare.

thin, v.a. (at)tenuo, extenuo, 1.

thine, a. tuus.

thing, s. res, f. ; negotium, n. ; **—s,** pl. bona ; vestimenta, n. pl.

think, v.a. & n. cogito, 1 ; (to imagine, believe, etc.) puto, 1 ; credo, 3 ; opinor, 1 ; reor, 2 ; arbitror, 1.

thinker, s. philosophus, m.

thinking, s. cogitatio ; sententia ; meditatio ; opinio, f. ; judicium, n.

thinness, s. tenuitas ; raritas, f.

third, a. tertius ; **—ly,** ad. tertio ; **—,** s. tertia pars, f.

thirst, s. sitis, f. (also *fig.*).

thirstily, ad. sitienter.

thirsty, a. sitiens ; aridus, siccus ; bibulus ; **to be** —, sitio, 4.

thirteen, a. tredecim.

thirteenth, a. tertius decimus.

thirtieth, a. tricesimus.

thirty, a. triginta ; **— each,** triceni ; **— times,** ad. tricies.

this, pn. hic, hæc, hoc.

thistle, s. carduus, m. ; **globe** —, echinops (mod. hort.).

thither, ad. illuc, istuc.

thong, s. lorum, amentum, n.

thorn, s. spina, f. ; aculeus, m.

thorn-apple, s. datura (mod. hort.).

thorny, a. spinosus ; spineus ; *fig.* difficilis.

thorough, a. germanus, perfectus ; accuratus ; **—ly,** ad. penitus, plane, prorsus, funditus.

thoroughbred, a. generosus, genuinus.

thoroughfare, s. pervium, n. ; via pervia, f.

thou, pr. tu.

though, c. etsi, etiamsi, quamvis, quamquam, licet.

thought, s. (act and faculty) cogitatio, sententia, mens, f.

thoughtful, a. cogitabundus ; providus ; humanus ; **—ly,** ad. (provide) humane.

thoughtless, a. incuriosus, negiegens, inconsultus ; **—ly,** ad. temere.

thousand, a. mille ; **a — times,** millies.

thousandth, a. millesimus.

thraldom, s. servitus, f. ; servitium, n.

thrall, s. servus, m.

thrash, v.a. tero, tundo, 3 ; *fig.* verbero, 1.

thrashing-floor, s. area, f.

thread, s. filum, n. ; linea, f. ; *fig.* tenor, m. ; **—,** v.a. ; **— one's way,** meo, 1.

threadbare, a. tritus, detritus.

threat, s. minæ, f. pl. [immineo, 2.

threaten, v.a. minor, 1 ; —, v.n. impendeo,

three, a. tres ; **— times,** ter ; **— each,** terni, trini.

threefold, a. triplex, triplus.

threshold, s. limen, n.

thrice, ad. ter.

thrift, s. frugalitas, parsimonia, f. ; (plant) armeria (mod. hort.).

thrifty, a. parcus, frugalior.

thrill, v.a. percello ; —, v.n. percellor.

thrill, s. (excitement) animi concitatio, f.

thrilling, a. periculosus.

thrive, v.n. vireo, floreo ; valeo, 2.

thriving, a. prosperus.

throat, s. jugulum, guttur, n. ; gula, f.

throb, v.n. palpito, 1 ; —, s. palpitatio ,f. pulsus, m.

throes, s. pl. dolor, m.

throne, s. solium, n. ; *fig.* regia dignitas, f. ; (kingdom) regnum, n.

throng, s. multitudo, turba, frequentia, f. ; —, v.a. & n. premo ; circumfundor ; confluo, 3.

throttle, s. ; —, v.a. strangulo, 1.

through, pr. per ; propter ; ob.

throughout, ad. penitus, prorsus.

throw, v.a. jacio, conjicio ; mitto, 3 ; jaculor, jacto, 1 ; (away) abjicio ; (down) dejicio, sterno, everto, 3 ; (oneself) me præcipito, 1 ; (open) patefacio ; (off) executio ; dejicio ; (clothes) exuo ; (out) ejicio ; (together) conjicio ; (up) egero, 3.

throw, s. jactus, m. ; jaculatio, f. [f. pl.

thrush, s. turdus, m. ; (med.) aphthæ,

thrust, v.a. trudo, impello ; (with a sword) perfodio, 3 ; — out, extrudo, 3 ; —, s. ictus ; impetus, m. ; petitio, f.

thumb, s. pollex, m. ; —, v.a. pollice verso, 1.

thump, v.a. contundo, 3 ; —, ictus, m. percussio, f.

thunder, s. tonitrus ; fragor, m. ; —, v.a. & n. tono, intono, 1.

thunderbolt, s. fulmen, n.

thunderstruck, a. attonitus ; obstupe-factus.

Thursday, s. dies Jovis, m.

thus, ad. ita, sic ; **and** —, itaque.

thwart, v.a. obsto ; frustror, 1 ; inter-venio, 4 ; —, a. transversus, obliquus.

thwart, s. transtrum, n.

thy, pn. tuus.

thyme, s. thymum, n.

thyself, pn. tu, ipse, ipse tu.

tiara, s. tiara, f. ; tiaras, m.

tick, s. (insect) ricinus ; (noise) sonus.

ticket, s. tessera, f. ; titulus, m.

tickle, v.a. & n. titillo, 1.

tickling, s. titillatio, f.

ticklish, a. *fig.* difficilis, periculosus, lubricus.

tide, s. ætus, *fig.* cursus, m.

tidings, s. rumor, m. ; (message) nuntius, m. ; (news) novum, n.

tie, v.a. (al)ligo ; nodo, 1 ; vincio, 4 ; —, s. vinculum, n. ; nodus, m. ; con-junctio, necessitas, f.

tier, s. ordo, gradus, m.

tiger, tigress, s. tigris, c.

tiger-flower, s. tigridia (mod. hort.).

tight, a. artus, astrictus ; —**ly,** ad. arte, stricte.

tighten, v.a. stringo, astringo, 3.

tightness, s. soliditas, firmitas, f.

tile, s. tegula, imbrex, f. ; —, v.a. tegulis tego, 3.

tiling, s. tegulum, n.

till, ad. usque ; —, conj. dum, donec.

till, v.a. colo, 3.

tillage, s. agricultura, f.

tiller, s. (man) agricola, f. ; (helm) guber-naculum, n. ; clavus, m.

tilt, s. (awning) velum ; tentorium, n. ; (tournament) decursio equestris, f. ; (rush) impetus, m. ; —, v.a. pro-clino, 1.

timber, s. materia, f. ; lignum, n. ; tignum, n. ; trabs, f.

time, s. tempus, n. ; dies, c. ; (age, etc.) ætas, f. ; ævum, n. ; (century) sæculum, n. ; (leisure) otium, n. ; (hour) hora, f. ; **at this** —, in præsenti ; **at any** —, un-quam ; **if at any** —, siquando.

timely, a. tempestivus, opportunus ; —, ad. tempestive, opportune.

timepiece, s. horologium, n.

time-server, s. qui temporibus servit, m.

timid, a. timidus, anxius.

timidity, s. timiditas, f.

timorous, a. pavidus.

tin, s. stannum, plumbum album, n.

tincture, s. tinctura, f.

tinder, s. fomes, m. ; — -**box,** igniarium, n.

tinge, v.a. tingo, imbuo, inficio, 3.

tingle, v.n. formico, vermino, 1.

tinkle, s. tinnitus, m.

tinkle, v.n. tinnio, 4 ; crepito, 1.

tinsel, s. bractea ; *fig.* species, f.

tip, s. cacumen ; acumen, n. ; apex, m. ; —, v.a. præfigo ; (to incline) inverto, 3.

tippet, s. collare, n.

tipple, v.n. perpoto, 1.

tippler, s. potator, bibulus, m.

tipsy, a. ebrius, temulentus, vinosus.

tiptoe, s. **on** —, in digitos erectus.

tire, v.a. fatigo, lasso ; v.n. defatigor, 1.

tired, a. fessus, defessus, lassus.

tiresome, a. laboriosus ; molestus, opero-sus.

tiro, s. tiro, m.

tissue, s. textum, n.

tit-bit, s. cuppedia, n. pl.

tithe, s. decima, f.

title, s. titulus, m. ; inscriptio, f. ; (label) index, c. ; (name, etc.) appellatio, dig-nitas, f. ; —, v.a. appello, 1.

titmouse, s. parus, m.

titter, v.n. subrideo, 2.

tittle, s. punctum, n. ; pars minima, f.

tittle-tattle, s. sermunculus, m.

to, pr. ad. adversum ; erga ; (in compari-son with) præ ; — **and fro,** huc illuc.

toad, s. bufo, m. ; — **flax,** s. linaria (mod. hort.) ; — -**stool,** s. fungus, m.

toady, s. adulator, parasitus, m.
toadyism, s. assentatio, adulatio, f.
toast, s. (health drunk) propinatio, f.
toast, v.a. torreo, 2 ; (in drinking) propino, 1.
tobacco, s. tabacum, n. ; (plant) nicotiana, f. (mod. hort.).
to-day, ad. hodie ; of —, a. hodiernus.
toe, s. digitus, m.
together, ad. simul, una ; conjunctim.
toil, s. labor, m. ; opera, f. ; sudor, m. ; —, v.n. laboro, 1.
toilet, s. cultus, ornatus, m.
toilsome, a. laboriosus, operosus.
token, s. signum, pignus, n.
tolerable, a. tolerabilis ; mediocris ; **tolerably,** ad. tolerabiliter ; mediocriter.
tolerance, s. tolerantia, toleratio, indulgentia, f.
tolerant, a. tolerans, patiens, indulgens.
tolerate, v.a. tolero, 1 ; patior, fero, 3.
toleration, s. toleratio ; indulgentia, f.
toll, s. vectigal, tributum, n.
toll-gatherer, s. exactor, portitor, m.
tomato, s. lycopersicum (mod. hort.).
tomb, s. sepulcrum, bustum, n. ; tumulus, m.
to-morrow, s. crastinus dies, m. ; —, ad. cras ; **the day after** —, perendie.
tone, s. sonus, m. ; *fig.* color, m. ; vox, f.
tongs, s. forceps, c.
tongue, s. lingua, f. ; (of a balance) examen, n.
tonnage, s. amphoræ, f. pl.
tonsils, s. tonsillæ, glandulæ, f. pl.
too, ad. nimis, nimium ; (also) etiam, insuper.
tool, s. instrumentum ; (of iron) ferramentum, n. ; *fig.* minister, m.
tooth, s. dens, m. (also *fig.*) ; — **and nail,** totis viribus.
toothache, s. dolor dentium, m.
toothless, a. edentulus.
toothpick, s. dentiscalpium, n.
tooth-powder, s. dentifricium, n.
top, s. cacumen, culmen, n. ; apex, m. ; (of a house) fastigium, n. ; (toy) trochus, turbo, m. ; —, a. summus.
top, v.a. (trees) decacumino, 1 ; —, v.n. exsupero, 1.
topaz, s. topazus, f.
toper, s. potator, m.   [tio, f.
topic, s. res, f. ; argumentum, n. ; quæs-
topmost, a. summus.
topography, s. regionum descriptio.
topsail, s. supparum, n.
topsyturvy, ad. sursum deorsum.
torch, s. fax, tæda, f. ; funale, n.
torment, v.a. (ex)crucio, 1 ; torqueo, 2 ; —, s. cruciatus, m. ; tormentum, n.

tormentor, s. tortor, m.
torpedo, s. (fish) torpedo, f.
torpid, a. torpens ; torpidus ; languidus.
torpor, s. torpor, m.
torrent, s. torrens, m. (also *fig.*).
torrid, a. torridus, fervidus.
tortoise, s. testudo, f. ; — **-shell,** s. testudo, f.
torture, s. tormentum, n. ; cruciatus, m. ; —, v.a. torqueo, 2 ; (also *fig.*).
torturer, s. tortor, m.
toss, v.a. jacto ; agito, verso, 1 ; —, v.n. jactor, 1 ; æstuo, 1 ; —, s. jactus, m. ; jactatio, f.
total, a. totus, universus ; —**ly,** ad. omnino, prorsus.
total, s. summa, f.
totality, s. summa ; universitas, f.
totter, v.n. vacillo, titubo, labo, 1.
touch, v.a. tango, attingo, 3 ; *fig.* moveo, 2 ; afficio, 3 ; —, s. tactus, contactus, m. ; *fig.* commotio, f. ; **last** —, *fig.* manus extrema, f.
touching, pr. (concerning) de, quod attinet ad.
touchstone, s. coticula ; obrussa, f.
touchy, a. offensioni pronior, stomachosus.
tough, a. tenax, lentus ; durus ; *fig.* difficilis ; (stout) strenuus.
toughness, s. tenacitas, f. ; lentor, m. ; duritia ; *fig.* difficultas ; (stoutness) fortitudo, f.
tour, s. circuitus, m. ; peregrinatio, f. ; iter, n.
tourist, s. viator, peregrinator, m.
tournament, s. decursio equestris, f. ; ludus equester, m.
tow, s. stuppa, f.
tow, v.a. navem remulco trahere, 3.
toward(s), pr. adversus, ad, erga ; contra, in ; (of time) sub.
towel, s. mantele, sudarium, n.
tower, s. turris, arx, f. ; castellum, n. ; —, v.n. emineo, superemineo, 2.
towering, a. elatus, excelsus ; (of anger) vehemens.
towline, s. remulcum, n.
town, s. urbs, f. ; oppidum, muncipium, n.
townhall, s. curia, f.
townsman, s. oppidanus, municeps, civis, m.
toy, s. crepundia, n. pl. ; *fig.* minutiæ, f. pl.
trace, s. vestigium ; indicium ; signum ; (for horse) helcium, n. ; —, v.a. delineo ; (out) indago, 1.
track, s. vestigium, n. ; (path) semita, f. ; —, v.a. vestigo, investigo, 1.
trackless, a. invius.
tract, s. tractus, m. ; regio, f. ; (small treatise) tractatus, m.

tractable, a. tractabilis ; docilis.
trade, s. mercatura, f. ; commercium, negotium, n. ; (calling) ars, f. ; quæstus, m. ; —, v.n. mercaturas facio, 3 ; negotior, 1.
trader, s. mercator, m.
tradesman, s. negotiator ; caupo, m.
trade-wind, s. etesiæ, m. pl.
tradition, s. fama, f. [translaticius.
traditional, a. ab majoribus traditus ;
traduce, v.a. infamo, calumnior, 1.
traffic, s. commercium, n. ; mercatura, f. ; —, v.n. negotior, mercor, 1.
tragedian, s. tragœdus, actor tragicus ; (author) tragicus poeta, m.
tragedy, s. tragœdia, f. ; cothurnus, m.
tragic(al), a. tragicus ; —ly, ad. tragice.
tragicomedy, s. tragicocomœdia, f.
trail, v.n. traho, verro, 3 ; —, s. vestigium, n. ; ductus, m.
train, s. series, f. ; ordo, m. ; (of a robe) peniculamentum, n. ; (retinue) comitatus, m. ; (of an army) impedimenta, n. pl. [facio, 3.
train, v.a. educo, 1 ; instruo ; *fig.* assue-
trainer, s. exercitor, m.
training, s. disciplina ; exercitatio, f.
traitor, s. proditor, m.
traitorous, a. perfidus ; perfidiosus ; —ly, ad. perfide, perfidiose.
trammel, s. impedimentum, n. ; —, v.a. irretio, impedio, 4.
tramp, s. homo vagus, m.
trample, v.n. (on, upon) conculco, 1 ; opprimo, obtero, 3.
trance, s. animus a corpore abstractus, m.
tranquil, a. tranquillus, placidus, æquus ; —ly, ad. tranquille ; animo tranquillo.
tranquillity, s. tranquillitas, quies, f. ; tranquillus animus, m.
tranquillize, v.a. placo, sedo, tranquillo, 1.
transact, v.a. transigo, gero, ago, perficio, fungor, 3.
transaction, s. negotium, n. ; res, f.
transcend, v.a. supero, 1 ; vinco, 3.
transcendental, a. sublimis.
transcribe, v.a. transcribo, exscribo, 3.
transcription, s. transcriptio, f.
transfer, v.a. transfero ; transmitto, 3 ; —, s. translatio, f.
transfigure, v.a. transfiguro, 1.
transfiguration, s. transfiguratio, f.
transform, v.a. transformo, transfiguro, 1 ; verto, 3.
transformation, s. mutatio, f.
transgress, v.a. violo, 1 ; contra leges facio, 3.
transgression, s. violatio, f. ; delictum, n.
transgressor, s. maleficus, m. ; violator, m.
transient, a. fragilis, fluxus, caducus.
transit, s. transitus, m.

transition, s. transitio, f. ; transitus, m.
transitive, a. (gr.) transitivus ; —ly, ad. transitive.
transitory, a., v. **transient.**
translate, v.a. verto, transfero, 3.
translation, s. translatio, f. ; liber translatus, m.
translator, s. interpres, c.
transmarine, a. transmarinus.
transmigrate, v.n. transmigro, 1.
transmission, s. transmissio, f.
transmit, v.a. transmitto, 3.
transmutation, s. transmutatio, f.
transom, s. transtrum, n.
transparency, s. perspicuitas, f.
transparent, a. pellucidus, perspicuus, translucidus ; **to be** —, pelluceo, transluceo, 2.
transpire, v.n. evenio, 4 ; fio.
transplant, v.a. transfero, 3 ; (people) deduco, 3.
transplantation, s. translatio, f.
transport, v.a. transporto, 1 ; transveho, transmitto, 3 ; *fig.* delecto, 1 ; **be —ed,** *fig.* efferor, 3.
transport, s. transvectio, f. ; (ship) navigium vectorium, n. ; *fig.* elatio, f.
transpose, v.a. transpono, 3.
transposition, s. trajectio, f. [verse.
transverse, a. transversus ; —ly, ad. transtrap, s. laqueus, m. ; tendicula, pedica, f. ; *fig.* insidiæ, f. pl.
trappings, s. ornatus, m. ; phaleræ, f. pl.
trash, s. scruta, n. pl. ; nugæ, res vilissimæ, f. pl.
trashy, a. vilis ; inutilis.
travel, v.n. iter facio, 3 ; peregrinor, 1.
traveller, s. viator, peregrinator, m.
traverse, v.a. transeo, 4 ; supero, 1 ; transgredior, transmitto, 3 ; (to swim over) trano ; (to thwart) frustror, 1.
travesty, s. parodia, f.
tray, s. repositorium, n.
treacherous, a. perfidus ; perfidiosus ; dolosus ; —ly, ad. perfide, perfidiose.
treachery, s. perfidia, f.
tread, v.a. calco, conculco, 1 ; —, v.n. incedo, 3 ; —, s. gradus, incessus, m. ; vestigium, n.
treadle, s. insilia, n. pl.
treason, s. perduellio, proditio, f.
treasonable, a. perfidus.
treasure, s. thesaurus, m. ; gaza, f. ; opes, f. pl. ; —, v.a. coacervo, 1 ; (value) magni æstimo, 1.
treasurer, s. ærarii præfectus, m.
treasury, s. fiscus, m. ; ærarium ; (building) thesaurus, m.
treat, v.a. tracto, 1 ; utor, 3 ; (with ablat.); convivio (aliquem) accipio, 3 ; —, s. epulæ, f. pl.

treatise, s. libellus, m.
treatment, s. tractatio ; cura, curatio, f.
treaty, s. fœdus ; pactum, n.
treble, a. triplex, triplus ; (of sound) acutus ; —, s. acuta vox, f. ; —, v.a. triplico, 1.
tree, s. arbor, f.
trefoil, s. trifolium, n.
trellis, s. clathri, m. pl.
tremble, v.n. tremo, contremisco, 3 ; trepido, 1.
trembling, a. tremens, tremulus, trepidus ; —, s. trepidatio, f. ; tremor, m.
tremendous, a. formidolosus, ingens, immanis ; —ly, formidolose.
tremulous, a. tremulus.
trench, s. fossa, f. ; vallum, n. ; agger, m. ; —, v.a. vallo, 1 ; — upon, me insinuo, 1.
trencher, s. catillus, m.
trespass, v.n. pecco, 1 ; offendo, 3 ; — on, ingredior, 3 ; —, s. culpa, f. ; peccatum, n.
tress, s. (of hair) cirrus, m.
trestle, s. scamnum, n.
trial, s. tentatio, f. ; (law) judicium, n. ; (attempt) conatus, m. ; periculum, n.
triangle, s. triangulum, n.
triangular, a. triangulus, triquetrus.
tribe, s. tribus, natio, f.
tribulation, s. mala, n. pl. ; ærumnæ, f. pl. ; labores, m. pl.
tribunal, s. tribunal ; (court) judicium, n.
tribune, s. tribunus, m.
tribuneship, s. tribunatus, m.
tribunitial, a. tribunicius.
tributary, a. vectigalis, stipendiarius ; —, s. amnis in alium influens, m.
tribute, s. tributum ; vectigal, n.
trice, s. in a —, momento temporis, f.
trick, s. dolus, m. ; artificium, n. ; fraus, f. ; —, v.a. dolis illudo, 3 ; circumvenio, 4.
trickery, s. fraus, f. ; dolus, m. ; ars, f.
trickle, v.n. stillo, mano, 1.
trickster, s. veterator, homo dolosus, m.
trident, s. tridens, m.
triennial, a. per triennium.
trifle, s. res parvi momenti, f. ; nugæ, f. pl. ; —, v.n. nugor, 1. [frivolus.
trifling, a. levis, exiguus, parvi momenti,
trilateral, a. trilaterus.
trim, a. nitidus, comptus, bellus ; —, v.a. adorno ; (to prune) puto, 1 ; tondeo, 2.
trimmer, s. homo inconstans, m.
trimness, s. concinnitas, f.
trinity, s. trinitas, f.
trinket, s. gemma, f.
trip, s. (stumble) pedis offensio, f. ; (journey) iter, n. ; —, v.a. supplanto, 1 ; —, v.n. pedem offendo, 3 ; fig. erro, 1.
tripe, s. omasum, omentum, n.

triple, a. triplex, triplus ; —, v.a. triplico, 1.
tripod, s. tripus, m. ; cortina, f.
trireme, s. (navis) triremis, f.
trite, a. tritus ; pervulgatus.
triumph, s. triumphus, m. ; ovatio ; fig. victoria ; exsultatio, f. ; —, v.n. triumpho, ovo, 1.
triumphant, a. triumphans, victor
triumvirate, s. triumviratus, m.
trivial, a. levis.
triviality, s. levitas, f. ; nugæ, ineptiæ, f. pl.
troop, s. turma, caterva, f. ; grex ; globus, m. ; manus, f. ; —s, pl. copiæ, f. pl.
trooper, s. eques, m.
trope, s. tropus, m.
trophy, s. tropæum, n.
tropic, s. circulus tropicus, m.
tropical, a. tropicus.
trot, s. gradus, m. ; —, v.n. tolutim eo, 4.
trouble, s. molestia, f. ; incommodum, negotium, n. ; labor ; dolor, m. ; ærumna, f. ; —, v.a. turbo ; vexo, 1 ; ango, 3.
troublesome, a. molestus ; operosus ; difficilis.
trough, s. alveus, m.
trout, s. tructa, f.
trowel, s. trulla, f. [f. pl.
trousers, s. feminalia, ium, n. pl. ; bracæ,
truant, a. otiosus ; ignavus ; vagus ; —, s. cessator, m.
truce, s. indutiæ, f. pl.
truck, s. carrus, m. ; (barter) commercium, n.
truckle, v.n. cedo, adulor, 1.
truculence, s. violentia, f.
truculent, a. truculentus, ferox.
trudge, v.n. pedibus eo, 4.
true, a. verus ; sincerus ; germanus ; rectus.
truffle, s. tuber, n.
truly, ad. vere ; sincere ; profecto.
trump, s. (trumpet) bucina, f. ; —, v.n. (up) conflo, 1 ; confingo, 3 ; machinor, 1.
trumpery, s. scruta, n. pl.
trumpery, a. levis, parvus.
trumpet, s. tuba, bucina, f. ; lituus, m. ; cornu, n. ; —, v.a. prædico, vendito, celebro, 1.
trumpeter, s. tubicen ; fig. prædicator, m.
trundle, v.a. volvo ; v.n. volvor, 3.
trunk, s. truncus, m. ; (of an elephant) proboscis ; (chest) cista, f.
truss, s. (bundle) fascis, m. ; (for a hernia) fascia, f.
trust, s. fiducia, f. ; depositum, n. ; (credit) fides, f. ; —, v.a. fido ; confido ; credo, 3 ; (to entrust) commendo, 1 ; permitto, 3.
trustee, s. (tutor) fiduciarius, depositarius, m.

trustworthy, v. trusty.

trusty, a. fidus, fidelis ; constans.

truth, s. veritas ; fides, f. ; verum, n. ; in —, vero.

truthful, a. verax ; —ly, ad. veraciter.

try, v.a. tento, probo, periclitor, 1 ; experior, 4 ; (law) cognosco, 3 ; in jus voco, 1 ; —, v.n. conor, 1 ; nitor, 3 ; tento, 1 ; molior, 4.

tub, s. labrum, n. ; lacus, m.

tube, s. tubulus, tubus, m.

tubercle, s. (med.) tuberculum, n.

tuberose, s. polianthes (mod. hort.).

tuberous, a. tuberosus.

tubular, a. tubulatus.   [succingo, 3.

tuck, s. ruga, f. ; sinus, m. ; —, v.a.

Tuesday, s. dies Martis, m.   [cirrus, m.

tuft, s. floccus, m. ; crista, f. ; (of hair)

tufted, a. cristatus.   [traho ; nitor, 3.

tug, s. conatus, nisus, m. ; —, v.a. & n.

tuition, s. disciplina, f.

tulip, s. tulipa (mod. hort.).

tumble, s. casus, lapsus, m.   [volvor, 3.

tumble, v.n. corruo, labor, collabor, cado ;

tumbler, s. (juggler) petaurista, m.

tumbrel, s. plaustrum, n.

tumid, a. tumidus, inflatus, turgidus.

tumour, s. tumor, tuber, m.

tumult, s. tumultus, m. ; turba, f.

tumultuous, a. tumultuosus, turbulentus ; —ly, ad. tumultuose ; turbulente.

tun, s. dolium, n.

tune, s. numeri, moduli, m. pl. ; in —, a. consonus ; out of —, a. dissonus.

tune, v.a. contendo, 3.

tuneful, a. canorus.

tunic, s. tunica, f.

tunnel, s. canalis, m. ; cuniculum, n.

tunny, s. thunnus, thynnus, m.

turban, s. mitra, tiara, f.

turbid, a. turbidus ; (muddy) cænosus.

turbot, s. rhombus, m.

turbulence, s. tumultus, m. ; seditio, f. ; animus turbulentus, m.

turbulent, a. turbulentus ; —ly, ad. turbulente.   [cæspitibus consterno, 3.

turf, s. cæspes, m. ; herba, f. ; —, v.a.

turfy, a. cæspiticius.

turgid, a. turgidus, tumidus ; inflatus.

turkey, s. meleagris gallopavo, f.

turmoil, s. turba, perturbatio, f. ; tumultus, m.

turn, s. (circuit) circuitus, m. ; (bend) flexus, m. ; (turning round) (revolution) conversio, f. ; circumactus, m. ; (change, course) vicissitudo ; (turn of the scale, crisis) momentum, discrimen, n. ; (inclination) inclinatio, f. ; (kindness : " a good —") officium, beneficium, n. ; ill —, injuria, f. ; by —s, alternis, in vicem ; viciswim.

turn, v.a. (to bend) flecto, verto ; (to — round) volvo, circumago, 3 ; (to change) muto, 1 ; converto, 3 ; (on the lathe) torno, 1 ; —, v.n. convertor ; flector ; volvor, 3 ; torqueor, 2 ; mutor, 1 ; (to become) fio, evado, 3 ; (to grow spoiled, etc.) putresco, 3 ; vitior, 1 ; to — about, (v.a. & n.) circumago ; circumagor, 3 ; to — aside, deflecto, 3 ; detorqueo, 2 ; to — away, (v.a. & n.) averto, 3 ; to — back, reflecto, 3 ; recurvo, 1 ; (v.n.) reverto, 3 ; redeo, 4 ; to — down, inverto, 3 ; to — off, averto, 3 ; derivo, 1 ; (v.n.) deflecto, 3 ; to — out, ejicio, 3 ; (v.n.) evenio, 4 ; evado ; contingo, 3 ; to — over, everto, 3 ; (a page in a book) verso, 1 ; (to cede to) transfero, 3 ; to — round, (v.a.) circumago, 3 ; contorqueo, 2 ; (v.n.) versor, 1 ; circumagor, 3 ; to — up, recurvo, 1 ; (with a hoe) inverto, 3 ; (come into view) appareo, 2.

turncoat, s. transfuga, m.

turning-lathe, s. tornus, m.

turning-point, s. cardo, m. ; momentum, discrimen, m.

turnip, s. rapum, n.

turnkey, s. janitor carceris, m. ; custos, c.

turpentine, s. terebinthina resina, f. ; — -tree, terebinthus, f.

turpitude, s. turpitudo, f. ; dedecus, n. ; nequitia, f.

turret, s. turricula, f.

turtle, s. testudo mydas, f.

turtle-dove, s. turtur, m.

tusk, s. dens, m.

tutelage, s. pupillaris ætas, f. ; (guardianship) tutela, f.

tutelary, a. præses.

tutor, s. educator ; præceptor, pædagogus, m. ; —, v.a. doceo, 2.

tutorship, s. tutela, f.

twang, s. clangor, m.

tweezers, s. volsella, f.

twelfth, a. duodecimus ; for the — time, duodecimo.

twelve, a. duodecim ; — times, duodecies.

twelvemonth, s. annus, m.

twentieth, a. vicesimus.

twenty, a. viginti ; — each, viceni ; — times, vicies.

twice, ad. bis.

twig, s. surculus, m. ; virga, f. ; dry —s, ramalia, n. pl.

twilight, s. (evening) crepusculum (dawn) diluculum, n.

twin, a. geminus, gemellus.

twine, v.a. circumvolvo, 3 ; circumplico, 1 ; contorqueo, 2 ; —, v.n. circumvolvor, circumplector, 3.

twinge, s. dolor, m. ; —, v.a. vellico, 1.

twinkle, v.n. mico, corusco, 1.

twirl, v.a. verso, 1 ; circumago, 3 ; —, v.n. versor, 1.

twist, v.a. torqueo, 2 ; flecto, 3 ; —, v.n. torqueor, 2 ; flector, 3.

twit, v.a. exprobro, objurgo, vellico, 1 ; objicio, 3.

twitch, v.a. vellico, 1 ; —, s. vellicatio, f.

twitter, v.n. minurio, 4.

two, a. duo ; — **each,** bini.

twofold, a. duplex, duplus.

two-footed, a. bipes.

type, s. exemplar, exemplum, n. ; forma, f.

typical, a. typicus.

tyrannical, a. tyrannicus ; **—ly,** ad. tyrannice.

tyrannicide, s. (act) tyrannicidium, n. ; (person) tyrannicida, m.

tyrannize, v.a. dominor, 1.

tyranny, s. tyrannis, dominatio, f.

tyrant, s. tyrannus, m.

Udder, s. uber, n. ; mamma, f.

ugliness, s. deformitas, fœditas, f.

ugly, a. deformis, fœdus, turpis.

ulcer, s. ulcus, n.   [puro, 1.

ulcerate, v.a. & n. ulcero, exulcero ; sup-

ulceration, s. exulceratio, f.

ulcerous, a. ulcerosus.

ulterior, a. ulterior.

ultimate, a. ultimus ; **—ly,** ad. denique, tandem.

ultramarine, a. cæruleus, cyaneus.

ultramontane, a. transmontanus.

umber, s. (fish) salmo thymallus, m. ; terra fusci coloris, f.

umbrage, s. (foliage) umbræ, f. pl. ; fig. suspicio, invidia, offensa, f.

umbrella, s. umbella, f. ; umbraculum, n.

umpire, s. arbiter, disceptator, m.

unable, a. invalidus ; **be —,** v.n. non possum, nequeo, 4.

unacceptable, a. ingratus, odiosus.

unaccompanied, a. incomitatus, solus ; (mus.) assa (vox).

unaccomplished, a. infectus, imperfectus.

unaccountable, a. inexplicabilis, inenodabilis.   [sine causa.

unaccountably, ad. præter opinionem;

unaccustomed, a. insolitus, insuetus, inexpertus.

unacknowledged, a. non recognitus.

unacquainted, a. ignarus, inscius, expers, alienus (a . . .).   [simplex.

unadorned, a. inornatus ; incomptus ;

unadulterated, a. merus, sincerus.

unadvisable, a. imprudens.

unadvised, a. imprudens, inconsultus, inconsideratus ; **—ly,** ad. imprudenter ; inconsulte ; inconsiderate.

unaffected, a. inaffectatus, sincerus ; simplex ; **—ly,** ad. simpliciter ; sine fuco et fallaciis ; sine arte.

unaided, a. non adjutus, solus.

unalloyed, a. purus ; nudus.

unalterable, a., v. **unchangeable.**

unaltered, a., v. **unchanged.**

unambitious, a. minime ambitiosus.

unanimity, s. unanimitas, consensio, f. ; consensus, m.

unanimous, a. unanimus, concors ; **—ly,** ad. consensu omnium, omnium sententiis.

unanswerable, a. certus, quod redargui non potest.

unanswered, a. sine responso.

unappeased, a. implacatus.

unapproachable, a. inaccessus.

unapt, a. non aptus ; **—ly,** ad. male.

unarmed, a. inermis, inermus.

unasked, a. non vocatus ; injussus ; sponte, ultro.

unassailable, a. inexpugnabilis.

unassuming, a. modestus, moderatus ; demissus.

unattainable, a. arduus, quod consequi non potest.   [inausus.

unattempted, a. intentatus, inexpertus ;

unattended, a. incomitatus.

unattested, a. sine teste.

unauthenticated, a. sine auctore.

unauthorized, a. inconcessus.

unavailing, a. inutilis, inanis.

unavenged, a. inultus.

unavoidable, a. inevitabilis.

unaware, a. inscius, nescius, ignarus.

unawares, ad. (de) improviso, inopinato.

unawed, a., v. **undaunted.**

unbar, v.a. relaxo, 1 ; resero.

unbearable, a. intolerabilis.

unbecoming, a. indecorus, indecens, indignus, inhonestus ; **—ly,** ad. indecore, indecenter ; inhoneste ; indigne.

unbefitting, a. incommodus ; indecorus ; indignus.

unbefriended, a. destitutus ab amicis.

unbelief, s. incredulitas, f.

unbelieving, a. incredulus.

unbend, a. relaxo, 1 ; solvo, remitto, 3.

unbending, a. inflexibilis, rigidus.

unbiassed, a. incorruptus ; integer ; sine ira et studio.

unbidden, a. injussus ; sponte ; ultro.

unbind, v.a. solvo, 3 ; revincio, 4 ; relaxo, 1.

unblemished, a. purus, integer, intactus.

unblest, a. infortunatus.

unblushing, a. (in bad sense) impudicus.

unbolt, v.a. reservo, 1.

unborn, a. nondum natus.

unbosom, v.a. communico, 1 ; detego, 3.

unbought, a. inemptus.

unbounded, a. infinitus, immensus.
unbridled, a. effrenatus, infrenis.
unbroken, a. irruptus; integer; (of horses) indomitus.
unbrotherly, a. non fraternus.
unbuckle, v.a. refibulo, diffibulo, 1.
unburden, v.a. exonero, 1.
unburied, a. inhumatus, insepultus.
unbutton, v.a. fibulas solvo, 3; dilorico, 1.
uncalled, a. (— for) non vocatus.
uncared, a. (— for) neglectus.
unceasing, a. perpetuus, assiduus; —ly, ad. perpetuo continenter.
unceremonious, a. non officiosus, inurbanus.
uncertain, a. incertus, dubius; ambiguus, anceps; —ly, ad. incerte, dubie, ambigue.
uncertainty, s. quod incertum est; dubitatio, f.
unchangeable, a. immutabilis; constans; —ably, ad. immutabiliter, constanter.
unchanged, unchanging, a. immutatus, perpetuus.
uncharitable, a. immisericors, iniquus, inhumanus.
unchaste, a. impudicus; obscenus; impurus; —ly, ad. impudice, impure.
unchastity, s. impudicitia, f.; incestum, n.
unchecked, a. liber, infrenis.
uncivil, a. inurbanus, rusticus; —ly, ad. inurbane, rustice.
uncivilized, a. incultus, barbarus.
unclad, a. nudus, vestibus exutus.
unclasp, v.a. diffibulo, 1; solvo, 3.
uncle, s. (by the father) patruus; (by the mother) avunculus, m.
unclean, a. immundus, sordidus; spurcus; —ly, ad. sordide, spurce.
unclose, v.a. recludo, retego, 3.
unclouded, a. serenus, sudus.
uncoil, v.a. explico, 1.
uncoined, a. infectus.
uncoloured, a. purus.
uncombed, a. impexus, incomtus.
uncomely, a. inconcinnus; turpis.
uncomfortable, a. incommodus, molestus, gravis, anxius.
uncommon, a. rarus, insolitus; enormis; insignis; singularis; —ly, ad. raro; præter solitum, plus solito.
unconcern, s. neglegentia, incuria, f.
unconcerned, a. neglegens; incuriosus; securus.
unconditional, a. simplex.
unconquerable, a. insuperabilis, invictus.
unconscionable, a. iniquus, injustus.
unconscious, a. inscius; nescius; —ly, ad. nesciens.
unconstitutional, a. contra rempublicam.
uncontaminated, a. incorruptus.

uncontrollable, a. impotens, effrenatus.
uncorrupted, a. incorruptus.
uncouple, v.a. disjungo, abjungo, 3.
uncourteous, a. inurbanus, rusticus; —ly, ad. inurbane, rustice.
uncouth, a. barbarus, impolitus, rudis; vastus.
uncover, v.a. detego, recludo, retego, 3; revelo, 1.
unction, s. inunctio, f.; **last —,** unctio extrema, f.
unctuous, a. pinguis.
uncultivated, a. incultus; neglectus; indoctus.
undaunted, a. impavidus, intrepidus.
undeceive, v.a. errorem eripio, 3.
undecided, a. incertus, dubius, sine exitu; par; integer.
undeniable, quod negari non potest.
under, pr. sub, subter; infra; (in number) minor.
undercurrent, s. torrens subterfluens; *fig.* intimus animi sensus, m.
underdone, a. minus percoctus, subcrudus.
undergo, v.n. & a. subeo, 4; patior, 3; tolero, 1; fero, 3.
underground, a. subterraneus.
underhand, a. & ad. clandestinus; clam.
underline, v.a. subnoto, 1.
underling, s. administer, m.; assecla, satelles, c.
undermine, v.a. suffodio, 3; *fig.* supplanto, labefacto, 1.
undermost, a. imus, infimus.
underneath, ad. subter, infra.
underpin, v.a. substruo, 3.
underprop, v.a. suffulcio, 4.
undersell, v.a. vendo (3) minoris quam ceteri.
undersigned, a. subsignatus, subscriptus.
understand, v.a. & n. intellego; sapio, 3; scio; (to hear) audio, 4.
understanding, a. peritus; sapiens, prudens; —, s. mens, f.; intellectus, m.; intellegentia, f.
undertake, v.a. & n. suscipio; incipio; aggredior, 3; conor, 1; (work for pay) opus redimo, conduco, 3.
undertaker, s. molitor; (of work) operum redemptor; conductor; (of funerals) libitinarius, m.
undertaking, s. ausum, inceptum; propositum, n.
undervalue, v.a. parvi facio, 3; parvi æstimo, 1.
underwood, s.; silva cædua, f.; virgulta, ramalia, n. pl.
underwrite, v.a. subscribo, 3.
underwriter, s. subscriptor; consponsor, m.

undeserved, a. immeritus ; indignus ; injustus ; —ly, ad. immerito, indigne.

undeserving, a. immerens, indignus.

undiminished, a. integer.

undiscernible, a. imperceptus incompertus.

undisciplined, a. rudis, inexercitatus.

undisputed, a. indubitabilis, certus.

undistinguishable, a. indiscretus.

undisturbed, a. imperturbatus ; immotus.

undivided, a. indivisus.

undo, v.a. solvo, dissolvo ; resolvo ; dissuo ; irritum facio ; (to ruin) perdo, 3.

undone, a. infectus ; imperfectus ; perditus.

undoubted, a. indubitatus ; certus ; —ly, ad. haud dubie.

undress, v.a. vestem exuo ; (another) vestem detraho (alicui), 3 ; —, s. vestis recincta, f.

undressed, a. nudus ; fig. rudis ; (of leather) crudus.

undue, a. indebitus ; iniquus.

undulate, v.n. undo, fluctuo ; vibro, I.

undutiful, a. inofficiosus.

unduly, ad. injuste, plus justo.

undying, a. immortalis ; sempiternus.

unearth, v.a. recludo ; detego, 3.

unearthly, a. humano major ; terribilis.

uneasiness, s. molestia ; (of mind) anxietas, f.

uneasy, a. anxius.

unemployed, a. otiosus.

unencumbered, a. liber, expeditus.

unendowed, a. indotatus.

unenlightened, a. minus eruditus.

unenterprising, a. inaudax, timidus.

unenviable, a. haud invidiosus.

unequal, a. inæqualis, dispar, impar ; —ly, ad. inæqualiter, impariter.

unerring, a. certus.

uneven, a. inæqualis ; iniquus ; (of ground) asper.

unevenness, s. inæqualitas ; iniquitas ; (of ground) asperitas, f.

unexampled, a. inauditus ; unicus ; novus ; singularis.

unexceptionable, a. probus, locuples.

unexpected, a. inexpectatus, insperatus, improvisus, inopinatus, inopinus ; —ly, ad. (ex) improviso.

unexplored, a. inexploratus.

unfailing, a. certus.

unfair, a. iniquus ; —ly, ad. inique.

unfaithful, a. infidus, perfidus ; —ly, ad. perfide.

unfamiliar, a. peregrinus ; ignarus ; ignotus.

unfasten, v.a. laxo, I ; solvo, resolvo, 3.

unfathomable, a. profundus, iniquus.

unfavourable, a. sinister ; adversus.

unfeeling, a. durus, inhumanus, crudelis ; —ly, ad. dure, crudeliter, inhumane.

unfeigned, a. sincerus.

unfettered, a. liber.

unfilial, a. inofficiosus.

unfinished, a. imperfectus.

unfit, a. inhabilis, incommodus, inutilis.

unfitting, a. indecens.

unfix, v.a. refigo ; revello, 3.

unfledged, a. implumis.

unfold, v.a. explico, I ; aperio, 4 ; pando, 3 ; —, v.n. dehisco, 3.

unforbidden, a. licitus, concessus.

unforeseeing, a. imprudens ; improvidus.

unforeseen, a. inexpectatus, insperatus.

unforfeited, a. salvus.

unforgiving, a. inexorabilis.

unformed, a. informis.

unfortified, a. immunitus.

unfortunate, a. infelix ; infortunatus ; —ly, ad. infeliciter.

unfounded, a. vanus ; sine causa.

unfrequent, a. rarus, infrequens ; —ly, ad. raro.

unfriendly, a. parum amicus.

unfruitful, a. infructuosus, infecundus, sterilis.

unfulfilled, a. infectus, imperfectus.

unfurl, v.a. expando, solvo, (vela) facio, 3.

ungainly, a. inhabilis, rusticus.

ungallant, a. inofficiosus.

ungenerous, a. illiberalis ; —ly, ad. illiberaliter.

ungenial, a. asper.

ungenteel, a. inurbanus, rusticus ; inhonestus.

ungentlemanly, a. inurbanus, illepidus.

ungird, v.a. discingo, recingo, 3.

ungodly, a. impius, contemptor divum.

ungovernable, a. impotens, effrenatus.

ungraceful, a. indecorus ; inconcinnus ; inelegans ; —ly, ad. ineleganter.

ungracious, a. iniquus.

ungrateful, a. ingratus ; —ly, ad. ingrate.

ungrudging, a. non invitus, lubens, munificus.

unguarded, a. incustoditus ; fig. inconsultus ; —ly, ad. temere.

unhand, v.a. solvo, 3.

unhandsome, a. deformis, turpis, invenustus.

unhandy, a. inhabilis.

unhappiness, s. miseria tristitia, f.

unhappy, a. infelix, infortunatus, miser.

unharness, v.a. abjungo, 3.

unhealthiness, s. infirmitas ; pestilentia, gravitas, f.

unhealthy, a. ad ægrotandum proclivis ; morbosus ; (things) insalubris.

unheard, a. inauditus.
unheeded, a. neglectus.
unheedful, unheeding, a. incuriosus, immemor.
unhewn, a. rudis. [perturbo, 1.
unhinge, v.a. de cardine detraho, 3 ; *fig.*
unholy, a. impius ; profanus.
unhoped, a. (— for) insperatus.
unhorse, v.a. equo dejicio, 3.
unhurt, a. inviolatus, illæsus.
unicorn, s. monoceros, m.
uniform, a. uniformis, sibi constans ;
—**ly,** ad. uniformiter.
uniform, s. ornatus, habitus, m.
uniformity, s. uniformitas, f.
unimaginable, a. quod animo fingi non potest.
unimpaired, a. integer, intactus.
unimpeachable, a. probatissimus.
unimportant, a. levis, parvus.
uninhabitable, a. inhabitabilis, non habitabilis.
uninhabited, a. cultoribus inanis ; desertus.
uninjured, a. incolumis, illæsus.
uninspired, a. insulsus.
unintelligible, a. obscurus.
uninterested, a., v. **disinterested.**
uninterrupted, a. continuus, perpetuus, inoffensus.
uninvited, a. invocatus.
uninviting, a. injucundus.
union, s. (act) conjunctio ; consociatio ; consensio ; societas, f. ; matrimonium, n.
unique, a. unicus, singularis.
unison, s. concentus, m.
unit, s. monas, f.
unite, v.a. consocio, 1 ; conjungo ; —, v.n. coalesco, 3 ; conjuro, 1.
unity, s. (oneness) unitas ; *fig.* concordia, f.
universal, a. universus ; —**ly,** ad. universe ; **everywhere,** undique, ubique.
university, s. academia, f.
unjust, a. injustus, iniquus ; —**ly,** injuste, inique.
unjustifiable, a. quod nihil excusationis habet.
unkind, a. inhumanus, parum officiosus ;
—**ly,** ad. inhumane.
unkindness, s. inhumanitas, f.
unknown, a. ignotus, incognitus.
unladylike, a. quod liberam mulierem haud decet. [nemo luget.
unlamented, a. nemini ploratus ; quem
unlawful, a. illicitus ; inconcessus ; —**ly,** ad. contra leges.
unlearn, v.a. dedisco, 3.
unlearned, a. indoctus, illiteratus, rudis ;
—**ly,** ad. indocte.
unleavened, a. infermentatuş.
unless, c. nisi, ni, nisi si.

unlettered, a. illitteratus.
unlike, a. dissimilis, dispar, diversus.
unlikely, a. non verisimilis.
unlimited, a. infinitus, immensus.
unload, v.a. exonero, 1.
unlock, v.a. recludo, 3 ; resero, 1.
unlooked, a. (— for) insperatus, inopinatus.
unloose, v.a. relaxo, 1 ; solvo, resolvo, 3.
unlovely, a. inamabilis, inamœnus.
unluckily, ad. infeliciter ; (male) funestus.
unlucky, a. infelix, infaustus.
unman, v.a. castro ; *fig.* enervo, 1.
unmanageable, ad. intractabilis ; contumax.
unmanly, a. mollis, effeminatus.
unmannerly, a. inurbanus, rusticus, illepidus. [tas, f.
unmanneriness, s. inhumanitas, rustici-
unmanufactured, a. rudis.
unmarried, a. cælebs, innuptus, innubus.
unmask, v.a. detego, 3 ; nudo, 1.
unmatched, a. unicus, singularis.
unmeaning, a. vanus, inanis.
unmeet, a. inhabilis, non aptus.
unmerciful, a. immisericors ; —**ly,** ad. immisericorditer.
unmerited, a. immeritus, indignus.
unmindful, a. immemor ; incuriosus ; securus.
unmistakable, a. certus.
unmixed, a. merus, sincerus.
unmoor, v.a. (navem) solvo, 3.
unmoved, a. immotus (also *fig.*).
unmusical, a. dissonus, stridulus.
unnatural, a. crudelis, monstruosus, immanis ; (preternatural) præter naturam ; —**ly,** ad. crudeliter ; contra naturam ; monstruose.
unnecessary, a. haud necessarius.
unnerve, v.a. debilito, infirmo, enervo, 1.
unnoticed, a. prætermissus.
unnumbered, a. innumerus, innumerabilis.
unobjectionable, a. cui nihil objici potest.
unobserved, a. inobservatus.
unoccupied, a. otiosus, vacuus ; (of land) apertus.
unoffending, a. innocens ; innoxius.
unpack, v.a. expedio, 4 ; eximo, 3.
unpaid, a. quod adhuc debetur ; gratuitus.
unpalatable, a. molestus.
unparalleled, a. unicus ; eximius.
unpardonable, a. non ignoscendus.
unpatriotic, a. patriæ non amans.
unperceived, a. inobservatus ; ad. furtim.
unperformed, a. infectus.
unpitying, a. immisericors, inexorabilis.
unpleasant, a. injucundus ; incommodus ; molestus ; —**ly,** ad. injucunde ; incommode.

unpleasing, a. ingratus.

unploughed, a. inaratus.

unpoetical, a. a ratione poetica abhorrens.

unpolished, a. impolitus ; rudis ; incompositus, incomptus.

unpolluted, a. impollutus ; intemeratus ; integer, intactus.

unpopular, a. populo ingratus, invidiosus.

unpopularity, s. invidia, f. ; odium, n.

unpractised, a. inexpertus, rudis.

unprecedented, a. novus, inauditus, unicus.

unprejudiced, a. æquus.

unpremeditated, a. subitus, non elaboratus.

unprepared, a. imparatus.

unprepossessing, a. invenustus.

unpresuming, unpretending, a. inambitiosus, modestus.

unprincipled, a. corruptis moribus, improbus.

unproductive, a. infecundus, infructuosus.

unprofitable, a. inutilis, vanus.

unpromising, a. nihil spei afferens.

unpropitious, a. iniquus ; adversus ; infaustus.

unprotected, a. indefensus.

unproved, a. non confirmatus.

unprovided, a. (for) imparatus ; insperatus.

unpunished, a. impunitus.

unqualified, a. haud idoneus, inhabilis ; merus.

unquenchable, a. inexstinctus.

unquestionable, a. certus.

unquiet, a. inquietus, sollicitus ; irrequietus ; —ly, ad. inquiete.

unravel, v.a. extrico, enodo, 1 ; expedio, 4.

unread, a. illectus.

unready, a. imparatus.

unreasonable, a. contra rationem, rationis expers, absurdus ; iniquus.

unrefined, a. rudis, crudus ; incultus.

unregarded, a. neglectus.

unregistered, a. in tabulas non relatus.

unrelenting, a. implacabilis, inexorabilis.

unremedied, a. incuratus.

unremitting, a. continuus, perpetuus, assiduus.

unrepentant, a. impænitens.

unrepining, a. nihil querens.

unrequited, non mutuus, sine mercede.

unreserved, a. apertus, candidus ; —ly, ad. aperte, libere, candide.

unresisting, a. minime repugnans.

unrestrained, a. effrenatus, indomitus, impotens.

unrewarded, a. sine mercede, sine præmio.

unriddle, v.a. solvo, 3.

unrig, v.a. (navem) exarmo, 1.

unrighteous, a. injustus, iniquus ; —ly, ad. injuste, inique.

unripe, a. immaturus, crudus.

unripeness, s. immaturitas, f.

unrivalled, a. singularis.

unroll, v.a. evolvo, 3 ; explico, 1 ; pando, 3 ; expedio, 4.

unroof, v.a. (ædem) detego, 3.

unruffled, a. tranquillus, immotus.

unruliness, s. effrenatio ; petulantia, f.

unruly, a. effrenatus ; turbulentus ; petulans.

unsaddle, v.a. stratum detraho, 3.

unsafe, a. intutus ; periculosus.

unsaleable, a. invendibilis.

unsalted, a. insulsus.

unsatisfactory, a. non idoneus ; improbabilis.

unsavoury, a. insulsus, fœdus.

unsay, v.a. recanto, 1 ; retexo, 3.

unseal, v.a. resigno, 1 ; aperio, 4.

unseasonable, a. intempestivus ; intempestus, importunus ; immaturus ; incommodus, ineptus ; —ly, ad. intempestive, importune.

unseemly, a. indecorus, indecens.

unseen, a. invisus ; invisitatus ; inobservatus.

unselfish, a. suæ utilitatis immemor.

unselfishness, suarum utilitatum neglegentia, f.

unserviceable, a. inutilis.

unsettle, v.a. dubium facio, 3 ; perturbo, 1.

unsettled, a. dubius, instabilis, inconstans, inquietus.

unsew, v.a. dissuo, 3.

unshackle, v.a. solvo, 3 ; libero, 1.

unshapely, a. deformis.

unshaved, a. intonsus.

unsheath, v.a. e vagina educo ; (gladium) destringo, 3.

unsheltered, a. apertus.

unship, v.a. expono, 1.

unshod, a. pedibus nudis.

unshorn, a. intonsus.   [fœditas, f.

unsightliness, s. deformitas, turpitudo,

unsightly, a. deformis ; turpis, fœdus.

unsisterly, a. non sororius.

unskilful, a. imperitus, inscitus ; inexercitatus ; —ly, ad. imperite, inscite.

unslaked, a. (of lime) vivus.

unsociable, unsocial, a. insociabilis.

unsolicited, a. ultro oblatus.

unsolved, a. non solutus or explicatus.

unsophisticated, a. simplex, sincerus, incorruptus.

unsought, a. non quæsitus.

unsound, a. (things) putris ; (persons) morbosus ; corruptus ; *fig.* vanus, falsus.

unsparing, a. prodigus ; *fig.* inclemens.

unspeakable, a. ineffabilis, infandus, inenarrabilis.

unstable, a. instabilis ; fluxus ; incertus.

unstained, a. incontaminatus ; intemeratus ; purus.

unstamped, a. non signatus.

unsteadily, a. infirme, instabiliter.

unsteadiness, s. instabilitas ; infirmitas ; levitas, inconstantia, f.

unsteady, a. instabilis ; infirmus ; tremulus ; vagus, levis.

unstitch, v.a. dissuo, 3.

unstring, v.a. retendo ; remitto, 3.

unsubdued, a. indomitus.

unsubstantial, a. inanis, levis.

unsuccessful, a. improsper ; infaustus ; infelix ; (vain) irritus, vanus ; **—ly,** ad. infeliciter, improspere ; (in vain) frustra, re infecta.

unsuitable, a. incongruens, inhabilis, incommodus.

unsuspected, a. non suspectus.

unsuspicious, a. minime suspicax.

untainted, a. incorruptus, integer.

untamed, a. indomitus, ferus.

untasted, a. ingustatus.

untaught, s. indoctus ; rudis.

unteachable, a. indocilis.

untenable, a. quod defendi non potest.

untenanted, a. vacuus.

unthankful, a. ingratus ; **—ly,** ad. ingrate.

unthrifty, a. profusus, prodigus.

untie, v.a. solvo, resolvo, 3 ; laxo, 1.

until, c. dum ; quoad ; donec ; **—,** ad. ad, in ; usque ad.

untilled, a. incultus.

untimely, a. immaturus ; importunus ; intempestivus.

untiring, a. assiduus, indefessus, m.

unto, pr. ad, tenus ; usque ad.

untold, a. indictus ; immemoratus.

untouched, a. intactus ; integer ; immotus.

untoward, a. adversus, contumax.

untrained, a. inexercitatus.

untried, a. inexpertus ; intentatus ; (law) indicta causa.

untrimmed, a. intonsus, horridus.

untrodden, a. non tritus ; avius.

untroubled, a. placidus ; æquus ; securus imperturbatus.

untrue, a. falsus, mendax.

untruly, ad. falso.

untruth, s. mendacium, n.

untutored, a. indoctus.

untwine, untwist, v.a. retexo, solvo, 3.

unused, a. inusitatus ; novus, non tritus.

unusual, a. inusitatus, insuetus ; insolitus, novus, rarus ; **—ly,** ad. præter solitum, raro.

unutterable, a. infandus, ineffabilis.

unvarnished, a. non fucatus ; sincerus, nudus.

unveil, v.a. velamen detraho ; patefacio, 3.

unwalled, a. immunitus.

unwarily, ad. imprudenter, incaute, inconsulte.

unwariness, s. imprudentia, f.

unwarlike, a. imbellis.

unwarrantable, a. injustus, nihil excusationis habens.

unwary, a. imprudens, incautus, inconsultus, temerarius.

unwashed, a. illotus.

unwearied, a. indefessus.

unweave, v.a. retexo, 3.

unwelcome, a. non acceptus, ingratus, injucundus.

unwell, a. æger, invalidus, infirmus.

unwholesome, a. insalubris.

unwieldiness, s. moles, f.

unwieldy, a. inhabilis, pinguis.

unwilling, a. invitus ; coactus ; **—ly,** ad. invite, non libenter.

unwind, v.a. revolvo, retexo, 3.

unwise, a. imprudens ; inconsultus ; stultus ; **—ly,** ad. stulte ; imprudenter, inconsulte.

unwished, a. (for) non optatus.

unwonted, a. insolitus, insuetus, inusitatus.

unworthily, a. indigne.

unworthy, a. indignus ; immeritus.

unwrap, v.n. explico, 1 ; evolvo, 3.

unwritten, a. non scriptus, inscriptus.

unwrought, a. rudis, infectus.

unyielding, a. obstinatus.

unyoke, v.a. abjungo, disjungo, 3.

up, ad. & pr. sursum ; **— to,** tenus ; (of time) usque ad ; **—stream,** in adversum flumen ; **— and down,** sursum deorsum ; huc illuc.

up ! interj. surge, surgite.

upbraid, v.a. objurgo, exprobro, increpo, 1.

uphold, v.a. sustineo, 2 ; sustento 1 ; tueor, 2.

upland, a. editus, montanus.

upon, pr. super, supra ; (of time) e, ex ; (on) in.

upper, a. superus ; superior ; **—most,** summus.

upright, a. erectus ; rectus ; *fig.* honestus ; integer ; **—ly,** ad. recte ; integre.

uprightness, s. integritas, honestas, f.

uproar, s. tumultus, m. ; turba, f.

uproot, v.a. radicitus tollo, eruo, 3.

upset, v.a. everto, subverto ; sterno, 3.

upshot, s. exitus, eventus, m.

upside, s. **— down,** sursum deorsum ; **turn — down,** v.a. misceo, 2 ; confundo, 3.

upstart, s. homo novus, terræ filius, m.
upwards, ad. sursum ; sublime ; superne ; (of number) plus.
urbanity, s. urbanitas, comitas, f.
urchin, s. erinaceus, echinus, m. ; *fig.* (boy) puer, m.
urge, v.a. urgeo, 2 ; impello, 3 ; insto, 1 ; suadeo, 2 ; (on) stimulo, 1.
urgent, a. instans ; vehemens ; gravis ; —ly, ad. vehementer.
urinal, s. matella, f.
urinary, a. urinalis.
urine, s. urina, f.
urn, s. urna ; (water-pot) hydria, f.
usage, s. mos, m.; consuetudo, f.; usus, m.
use, s. usus, m. ; utilitas, f. ; commodum, n. ; consuetudo, f. ; (interest) fænus, n. ; **be of** —, valeo, 2 ; proficio, 3 ; prosum.
use, v.a. utor, 3 (with ablative) ; adhibeo, 2 ; in usum verto, 3 ; (to treat) tracto, 1 ; —, v.n. soleo, 2 ; consuesco, 3 ; **to** — **up,** consumo, 3.
used, a. usitatus ; assuetus ; **be** — **to,** v.n. soleo, 2 ; consuesco, 3.
useful, a. utilis ; aptus, commodus ; salutaris ; —ly, ad. utiliter ; apte, commode.
usefulness, s. utilitas ; commoditas, f.
useless, a. inutilis ; inhabilis ; irritus, vanus ; —ly, ad. inutiliter, nequicquam, frustra.
uselessness, s. inutilitas, f.
usher, v.n. præeo, 4 ; introduco, 3.
usher, s. apparitor, m.
usual, a. usitatus, solitus, consuetus ; cottidianus ; —ly, usitate ; vulgo ; plerumque, fere.
usufruct, s. ususfructus, m.
usurer, s. fænerator.
usurious, a. fæneratorius.
usurp, v.a. usurpo ; vindico (mihi), 1 ; assumo, 3.
usurpation, s. usurpatio, f.
usurper, s. usurpator, m.
usury, s. (interest) usura ; fæneratio, f. ; fænus, n.
utensils, s. pl. utensilia ; vasa, n. pl. ; supellex, f.
uterine, a. uterinus.
utility, s. utilitas, commoditas, f.
utmost, a. extremus ; ultimus, summus.
utter, a. (outer) exterior ; (total) totus ; —ly, ad. omnino, penitus ; funditus.
utter, v.a. eloquor, dico, mitto, fundo, profero, 3 ; pronuntio, 1.
utterable, a. effabilis, fandus.
utterance, s. elocutio ; pronuntiatio, f. ; dictum, n. ; vox, f.
uttermost, a. extremus, ultimus.
uvula, s. uvula, f.
uxorious, a. uxorius.

Vacancy, s. (emptiness) inanitas, f. ; inane, n. ; (place) locus, m. ; (leisure) vacatio, f. ; otium, n.
vacant, a. vacuus, inanis ; (unoccupied) otiosus ; *fig.* mentis vacuus.
vacate, v.a. vacuefacio ; (leave) relinquo ; (lay down) depono, 3.
vacation, s. (law) justitium, n. ; (holidays) pl. feriæ, f. pl.
vacillate, v.n. vacillo, fluctuo, 1.
vacillation, s. *fig.* dubitatio, f.
vacuity, s. vacuitas, f. ; vacuum, n. ; inanitas, f.
vacuum, s. inane, vacuum, n.
vagabond, vagrant, a. vagus ; errabundus ; —, s. homo vagus, erro, m.
vagrancy, s. vagatio, f.
vague, a. dubius ; ambiguus ; incertus ; —ly, ad. incerte ; ambigue ; dubie.
vain, a. vanus ; futtilis ; inanis, irritus ; superbus, arrogans ; (boastful) gloriosus ; **in** —, —ly, ad. frustra ; nequicquam, incassum.
vainglorious, a. vaniloquus ; —ly, ad. gloriose.
vainglory, s. ostentatio, gloria, f.
vale, s. vallis, convallis, f.
valerian, s. valeriana (mod. hort.).
valet, s. cubicularius, famulus, m.
valetudinarian, a. & s. valetudinarius.
valiant, a. fortis ; audax, animosus ; —ly, ad. fortiter ; audacter, animose.
valid, a. validus ; legitimus, ratus.
validity, s. firmitas ; auctoritas, f.
valorous, a. fortis, animosus, virilis.
valour, s. fortitudo, f. ; animus, m.
valour, s. fortitudo, virtus, f. ; animus, m.
valuable, a. pretiosus ; carus.
valuation, s. æstimatio, f.
value, s. pretium, n. ; æstimatio, f. ; —, v.a. æstimo, 1 ; pendo, 3 ; — **highly,** magni æstimo, 1.
valueless, a. vilis, parvi pretii.
valve, s. valvæ, f. pl.
vamp, v.a. resarcio, 4.
van, s. primum agmen, n. ; (cart) plaustrum, n.
vanguard, s. primum agmen, n.
vanilla, s. vanilla (mod. hort.).
vanish, v.n. vanesco, diffugio, evanesco, 3 ; abeo pereo, 4.
vanity, s. vanitas ; levitas, f. ; nugæ, f. pl. ; jactatio, ostentatio, f.
vanquish, v.a. vinco, 3 ; supero, 1.
vanquisher, s. victor, m.
vantage-ground, s. locus superior, m. ; *fig.* lucrum, n. ; opportunitas, f.
vapid, a. vapidus ; insulsus ; *fig.* vapide ; insulse.
vapidity, s. insulsitas, f.

vaporous, s. vaporosus, vaporifer.
vapour, s. vapor, m.; exhalatio, f.; halitus, m.; —, v.a. & n. vaporo; *fig.* jacto, 1.
variable, a. mutabilis; varius; levis, inconstans.
variance, s. discordia; discrepantia, dissensio, simultas; **be at** —, v.n. discrepo, 1; dissideo, 2.
variation, s. varietas; variatio; vicissitudo, f.
varicose, a. varicosus; **— vein,** s. varix, c.
variegate, v.a. vario, 1; distinguo, 3.
variety, s. varietas; diversitas; multitudo, f.   [varie, diverse.
various, a. varius, diversus; **—ly,** ad.
varnish, s. atramentum, n.; *fig.* fucus, m.; —, v.a. coloro, 1.
vary, v.a. vario, 1; distinguo, 3; —, v.n. vario, 1.
vase, s. amphora, f.; urceus, m.; vas, n.
vassal, s. vassallus, m.; cliens, c.
vassalage, s. vassallagium, n.; clientela, f.
vast, a. vastus; ingens, immensus; **—ly,** ad. vaste; valde; multum.
vastness, s. immensitas, f.
vat, s. cupa, f.; dolium, n.
vault, s. fornix, m.; camera, f.; (underground) hypogeum, n.; (leap) saltus, m.; —, v.a. concamero, 1; —, v.n. salio, 4.
vaunt, v.a. jacto, 1; glorior, vendo, 3; ostento, 1.
vaunter, s. jactator, ostentator, m.
veal, s. vitulina, f.   [3.
veer, v.a. verto, 3; —, v.n. vertor, vergo,
vegetable, holus, n.
vegetate, v.n. *fig.* plantæ quasi vitam agere, 3; (rusticate) rusticor, 1.
vegetation, s. herba, f.
vehemence, s. vehementia, vis, f.; fervor, impetus, m.
vehement, a. vehemens, violentus; fervidus; acer; **—ly,** ad. vehementer; acriter.
vehicle, s. vehiculum, n.
veil, s. velamen; flammeolum, n.; amictus; *fig.* pretextus, m.; simulacrum, n.; species, f.; —, v.a. velo, 1; tego, 3.
vein, s. vena, f. (also *fig.*).
vellum, s. pergamena, charta, f.
velocity, s. velocitas, celeritas, f.
venal, a. venalis.
venality, s. venalitas; turpitudo, f.
vend, v.a. vendo, 3.
vender, s. venditor, m.
veneer, s. ligni bractea, f.; *fig.* species, f.
venerable, a. venerabilis, reverendus.
venerate, v.a. veneror, adoro, 1; colo, 3.
veneration, s. veneratio, adoratio, f.; cultus, m.
venereal, a. venereus.

vengeance, s. ultio; vindicta, pœna, f.; **to take** —, ulciscor, 3; **with a** —, valde.
venial, a. ignoscendus, venia, dignus.
venison, s. caro ferina, f.
venom, s. venenum, virus, n.
venomous, a. venenosus, virulentus.
vent, s. spiramentum, n.; exitus, m.; foramen, n.; **give — to** (utter), fundo promo, 3; (exercise) exerceo, 2; —, v.a. aperio, 4; per foramen emitto, 3.
vent-hole, s. spiraculum, spiramentum, n.
ventilate, v.a. ventilo, 1; *fig.* in medium profero, 3.
ventilation, s. ventilatio; *fig.* prolatio, f.
ventricle, s. ventriculus, m.
ventriloquist, s. ventriloquus, m.
venture, s. discrimen, periculum, n.; (hazard) alea, f.; (deed of daring) ausum, n.; **at a** —, temere.
venture, v.a. periclitor, 1; —, v.n. audeo, 2.
venturesome, a. audax; temerarius; **—ly,** ad. audacter.
Venus's looking-glass, s. specularia (mod. hort.).
veracious, a. verax; **—ly,** ad. veraciter.
veracity, s. veritas, fides, f.
verandah, s. subdiale, n.
verb, s. verbum, n.
verbatim, ad. ad verbum.
verbose, a. verbosus; **—ly,** ad. verbose.
verbosity, s. loquacitas, f.
verdant, a. viridis, virens; florens.
verdict, s. (of a jury) judicium, n.; sententia, f.
verdigris, s. æruca; ærugo, f.
verdure, s. viriditas, f.; viride, n.
verge, s. confinium, n.; (border) margo, c.; ora, f.; (limit) limes, m.; —, v.n. vergo, 3.
verger, s. lictor, apparitor, m.
verification, s. affirmatio, f.
verify, v.a. ratum facio, 3; confirmo, 1.
verily, ad. profecto, vere, certe.
vermilion, s. minium, n.; —, a. miniatus, miniaceus.
vermin, s. bestiolæ molestæ, f. pl.
vernacular, a. vernaculus.
vernal, a. vernus.
versatile, a. versatilis; versabilis; agilis; varius.
versatility, s. agilitas, f.
verse, s. versus, m.; carmen, n.
versed, a. peritus, exercitatus.
versifier, s. versificator, m.
versify, v.a. & n. versifico, 1.
version, s. translatio, f.
vertebra, s. vertebra, f.
vertebral, a. vertebratus; **— column,** spina, f.
vertex, s. vertex, m.

vertical, a. rectus, directus ; —**ly,** ad. ad lineam ; recta linea.
vertiginous, a. vertiginosus.
vertigo, s. vertigo, f.
vervain, s. verbena, f.
very, a. verus ; —, ad. valde, admodum ; multum.
vesicle, s. vesica ; vesicula, f.
vespers, preces vespertinæ, f. pl.
vessel, s. vas ; (ship) navigium, n.
vest, s. vestimentum, n. ; tunica, f. ; —, v.a. permitto, 3.
vestal, s. (virgo) vestalis, f.
vestige, s. vestigium ; indicium, n.
vestment, s. vestimentum, n.
vestry, s. (sacristy) sacrarium, n.
vesture, s. vestis, f. ; vestitus, m.
vetch, s. vicia, f.
veteran, veteranus ; —, s. veteranus miles.
veterinary, a. veterinarius.
veto, s. intercessio, f.
vex, v.a. vexo, inquieto, 1.
vexation, s. vexatio ; offensio, f. ; stomachus, dolor, m.
vexatious, a. molestus, odiosus ; —**ly,** ad. moleste.
vial, s. phiala, lagena, f.
viand, s. cibus, m. ; dapes, f. pl. ; esca, f.
viaticum, s. viaticum, n.
vibrate, v.n. vibro, 1 ; tremo, 3.
vibration, s. vibratus, motus, tremor, m.
vicar, s. vicarius, m.
vicarious, a. vicarius.
vice, s. vitium, n. ; turpitudo, f. ; (instrument) forceps, m.
vicinity, s. vicinitas, vicinia, f.
vicious, a. vitiosus ; perditus ; turpis ; —**ly,** ad. vitiose ; turpiter.
vicinity, s. vicinitas, vicinia, f.
vicissitude, s. vicissitudo, f.
victim, s. victima, hostia, f.
victimize, v.a. sacrifico, immolo, 1 ; (fig.) noceo, 2 ; lædo, 1.
victor, s. victor, m. ; victrix, f.
victorious, a. superior ; victor (m.), victrix (f.) ; —**ly,** ad. victoris instar.
victory, s. victoria, f. ; triumphus, m. ; palma, f. ; **to gain a — over,** ab aliquo victoriam reporto, 1.
victress, s. victrix, f.
victual, v.a. cibaria suppedito, 1.
victualler, s. caupo, m.
victuals, s. pl. cibaria, n. pl. ; victus ; (mil.) commeatus, m.
vie, v.n. (with) æmulor, 1 ; contendo, 3 ; certo, 1.
view, s. (act) aspectus, conspectus, m. ; oculi, m. pl. ; species, f. ; spectaculum, n. ; (prospect) prospectus, m. ; fig. (opinion) sententia ; opinio, f. ; **to have in —,** cogito, 1.

view, v.a. viso, inviso, conspicio ; inspicio, 3 ; contemplor ; investigo ; lustro, 1 ; (regard, feel) sentio, 4.
vigil, s. vigilia, pervigilatio, f. ; pervigilium, n.
vigilance, s. vigilantia, cura, f.
vigilant, a. vigil, vigilans ; —**ly,** ad. vigilanter.
vigorous, a. vigens, validus, acer, fortis, strenuus ; —**ly,** ad. strenue ; acriter ; fortiter.
vigour, s. vigor, m. ; robur, n. ; impetus, m.
vile, a. vilis, abjectus ; (wicked) perditus, flagitiosus ; fœdus ; —**ly,** ad. viliter ; fœde ; prave.
vileness, s. pravitas ; turpitudo ; nequitia, fœditas, f.
vilify, v.a. infamo, calumnior, 1.
village, s. vicus, pagus, m.
villager, s. vicanus, paganus, rusticus, m.
villain, s. scelus, n. ; scelestus, nequam, m. (indecl.).
villainous, a. sceleratus, scelestus, nefarius ; —**ly,** ad. scelerate, sceleste, nefarie.
villainy, s. improbitas, nequitia, f. ; scelus, n.
vindicate, v.a. vindico, 1 ; assero, 3 ; (to justify) purgo, 1 ; (defend) defendo, 3.
vindication, s. defensio, f.
vindicator, s. vindex, c. ; defensor, m.
vindictive, a. ultionis cupidus, acerbus.
vine, s. vitis, f.
vine-branch, s. pampinus, c. ; palmes, m. ; clavicula, f.
vine-dresser, s. vinitor, vitis cultor, m.
vine-grower, s. vitisator, viticola, m.
vinegar, s. acetum, n. ; **— -cruet,** s. acetabulum, n.
vine-leaf, s. pampinus, f.
vine-prop, s. pedamentum, n.
vineyard, s. vinea, f. ; vinetum, n.
vinous, a. vinosus.
vintage, s. vindemia, f.
vintager, s. vindemiator, m.
vintner, s. vinarius, m.
viol, s. fides, f.
violate, v.a. violo, 1 ; rumpo, frango, 3.
violation, s. violatio, f.
violator, s. violator, ruptor, m.
violence, s. violentia ; vis, f. ; (energy) impetus, m. ; (cruelty) sævitia, f.
violent, a. violentus ; furiosus ; vehemens ; —**ly,** ad. violenter, vehementer.
violet, s. (flower) viola ; (colour) viola, f.
viper, s. vipera, f.
viperine, viperous, a. viperinus, vipereus.
virago, s. virago ; fig. mulier jurgiosa, f.
virgin, s. virgo, f. ; puella, f. ; —, a. virginalis, virgineus.
virginal, a. virgineus, virginalis.

virginian creeper, s. vitis, f.
virginity, s. virginitas, f.
virile, a. virilis, masculus.
virility, s. virilitas, f.
virtual, a. insitus, innatus ; —**ly,** ad. vi insita ; (almost) fere.
virtue, s. virtus ; probitas ; fortitudo ; (efficacy) vis, virtus, f.
virtuous, a. virtute præditus ; probus ; integer ; —**ly,** ad. cum virtute, 1 ; integre.
virulence, s. acerbitas, gravitas, f.
virulent, a. virulentus ; acerbus, gravis.
virus, s. virus, n.
visage, a. os, n. ; facies, f. ; vultus, m.
viscera, s. viscera, n. pl.
viscosity, s. lentor, m.
viscount, s. vicecomes, m.
viscous, a. viscosus, lentus.
visibility, a. visibilitas, f.
visible, a. aspectabilis, conspicuus ; manifestus ; —**bly,** ad. *fig.* aperte, manifesto.
vision, s. (faculty of sight) visus, m. ; *fig.* visio, f. ; visum ; somnium, n.
visionary, s. somniator, m. ; —, a. fanaticus ; fictus, vanus.
visit, s. aditus, m. ; salutatio, f. ; —, v.a. viso, 3 ; visito, 1 ; adeo, 4 ; (inflict) infero, 3 ; (punish) vindico, 1.
visitant, s. salutator, m.
visitation, s. inspectio, f. ; (attack) accessio, f. ; (punishment) pœna, f.
visitor, m. salutator, m. ; salutatrix, f.
visor, s. buccula, f.
vista, s. prospectus, m.   [vitaliter.
vital, a. vitalis ; *fig.* necessarius ; —**ly,** ad.
vitals, s. pl. vitalia, n. pl. ; *fig.* vita, f.
vitality, s. vitalitas, f. ; vigor, m.
vitiate, v.a. vitio, 1 ; corrumpo, 3.
vitreous, a. vitreus.
vitrify, v.a. & n. in vitrum converto ; in vitrum convertor, 3.
vituperate, v.a. vitupero, 1 ; reprehendo, 3.
vivacious, a. vivax ; vividus, alacer.
vivacity, s. vivacitas ; alacritas, f.
vivarium, s. vivarium, n.
vivid, a. vividus ; (plain) manifestus ; —**ly,** ad. vivide ; (plainly) manifesto.
vivify, v.a. animo, vivifico, 1.
viviparous, a. viviparus.   [jurgiosa, f.
vixen, s. (she-fox) vulpes ; *fig.* mulier
vocabulary, s. vocabulorum index, m.
vocal, a. vocalis ; canorus ; —**ly,** ad. voce, ore.
vocation, s. officium, munus, n.
vociferate, v.n. vociferor, clamo, 1.
vociferation, s. vociferatio, f. ; clamor, m.
vociferous, a. clamosus.
vogue, s. mos, m. ; fama, æstimatio, f. ; **to be in** —, invalesco, 3.
voice, s. vox, f. ; sonus, m. ; (vote) suffragium, n.

voiceless, a. mutus, tacitus.
void, a. vacuus, inanis ; *fig.* sterilis ; invalidus, irritus, cassus ; **to be** —, vaco, 1.
void, s. vacuum, inane, n. ; —, v.a. vacuefacio, 3 ; vacuo, 1 ; *fig.* irritum facio, rescindo, 3.
voidable, a. quod rescindi potest.
volatile, a. volatilis ; *fig.* levis, volaticus, inconstans.
volatility, s. levitas, inconstantia, f.
volcano, s. mons igneus, m.
volley, s. nubes, f.
volubility, s. volubilitas, loquacitas, garrulitas, f.
voluble, a. volubilis, loquax, garrulus ; —**bly,** ad. volubiliter, loquaciter.
volume, s. volumen, n. ; tomus, m.
voluminous, a. magnus, amplus.
voluntarily, ad. sponte, libenter.
voluntary, a. voluntarius.
volunteer, s. miles voluntarius, m. ; —, v.n. me offero, 3 ; audeo, 2.
voluptuary, s. voluptarius, m.
voluptuous, a. voluptarius, voluptuosus.
volute, s. (in architecture) voluta, f.
vomit, v.a. & n. vomo, evomo, 3 ; eructo, 1.
vomit, s. vomitus, m.
voracious, a. vorax, edax ; —**ly,** ad. voraciter.
voracity, s. voracitas, edacitas, gula, f.
vortex, s. vertex, turbo, gurges, m.
votary, a. devotus, deditus.
vote, s. suffragium, n. ; *fig.* (judgment) sententia, f. ; —, v.a. censeo, 2 ; —, v.n. suffragium fero, 3.
voter, s. suffragator, m.
voting-tablet, s. tabella, f.
votive, a. votivus ; — **tablet,** tabella, f.
vouch, v.a. & n. testificor, testor, affirmo, 1.
voucher, s. (ticket) tessera, f.
vouchsafe, v.a. concedo, permitto, 3 ; —, v.n. dignor, 1.
vow, s. votum, n. ; —, v.a. (de)voveo, 2 ; spondeo, 2 ; (promise) promitto, 3 ; v.n. juro, 1.
vowel, s. vocalis, f.
voyage, s. navigatio, f. ; —, v.n. navigo, 1.
voyager, s. navigator, m.
vulgar, a. vulgaris, plebeius ; inurbanus ; rusticus ; —**ly,** ad. vulgo ; rustice.
vulgarism, s. dictio vulgi, f.
vulgarity, s. mores vulgi, m. pl. ; rusticitas, f.
vulgarize, v.a. vitio, 1 ; corrumpo, 3.
vulnerable, a. quod vulnerari potest.
vulpine, a. vulpinus.
vulture, s. vultur, vulturius, m.
vulturine, a. vulturinus.

Wad, s. fasciculus, m.
waddle, v.n. anatis in modum incedere, 3.
wade, v.n. per vada ire, 4.
wafer, s. crusta, f. ; crustulum, n.
waft, v.a. deduco, defero, fero ; trajicio, 3.
wag, s. joculator, jocosus, m. ; —, v.a.
  agito, vibro, 1 ; — **the tail,** moveo, 2 ;
  —, v.n. vacillo ; nuto, 1.
wager, s. sponsio, f. ; pignus, n. ; —, v.a.
  & n. spondeo, 2 ; sponsione provoco, 1 ;
  pignore contendo, 3.
wages, s. merces, f. ; stipendium, n.
waggery, s. facetiæ, f. pl. ; jocus, m.
waggish, a. festivus, ridiculus, jocosus.
waggon, s. carrus, m. ; plaustrum, n.
waggoner, s. plaustrarius, m.
wagtail, s. motaeilla, f.
waif, s. erro, m.
wail, v.a. & n. ploro, 1 ; plungo, 3 ; fleo, 2.
wailing, s. ploratus, planctus, m.
wain, s., v. **waggon.**
wainscot, s. tabulatio, f. ; paries, m.
waist, s. medium corpus, n.
waistcoat, s. subucula, f.
wait, v.n. (stay) maneo, 2 ; (for) expecto,
  1 ; (upon) inservio, 4 ; (to visit) visito,
  1 ; (to lie in —) insidior, 1.
wait, s. (delay) mora, f.
waiter, s. minister, pedisequus, m.
waiting, s. mansio ; (for) expectatio, f.
waive, v.a. decedo (de), remitto, 3.
wake, v.a. exsuscito, excito, 1 ; expergefacio, 3 ; —, v.n. expergiscor, 3.
wakeful, a. exsomnis, insomnis, vigil,
  vigilans.
waken, v.a., v. **to wake.**
walk, s. (act) ambulatio, f. ; (place) ambulacrum, n. ; ambulatio, f. ; (manner
  of walking) incessus, m. ; fig. (pathway) via ; —, v.n. incedo, 3 ; ambulo,
  1 ; gradior, 3.
walker, s. ambulans ; pedes, m.
walking, s. ambulatio, f.
wall, s. paries ; (of a town, etc.) murus,
  m. ; (mil.) mœnia, n. pl. ; —, v.a.
  mœnibus munio, 4.
wallet, s. pera ; mantica, f. ; saccus,
  m.
wall-flower, s. cheiranthus (mod. hort.).
wallow, v.n. volutor, 1.
walnut, s. juglans, nux juglans, f. ; —
  -tree, s. juglans, f.
walrus, s. phoca, f. ; equus marinus, m.
wan, a. pallidus, exsanguis.
wand, s. virga, f. ; caduceus, m.
wander, v.n. vagor, erro, palor ; (about)
  pervagor ; (over) pererro, 1.
wanderer, s. erro, m.
wandering, a. errabundus ; vagus ; erraticus ; —, s. erratio, f. ; error, m.

wane, v.n. decresco ; minuor ; tabesco, 3 ;
  —, s. deminutio ; decrescentia, f.
wanness, s. pallor, m.
want, s. egestas, inopia, penuria, defectio, f. ; —, v.a. egeo, indigeo, 2 ;
  desidero, 1 ; (wish) volo, 3 ; opto, 1 ;
  cupio, 3 ; —, v.n. deficio, 3 ; desum,
  absum.
wanting, a. **be** —, deficio, desum.
wanton, a. petulans, procax ; libidinosus ;
  lascivus ; protervus ; **—ly,** ad. petulanter ; lascive, libidinose, procaviter,
  proterve.
wantonness, s. petulantia ; lascivia ; libido ; protervitas, procacitas, f.
war, s. bellum, n. ; Mars, m. ; arma, n. pl. ;
  —, v.n. bello, 1.
war-cry, s. clamor, m.
war-horse, s. equus militaris, equus bellator, m.
warble, v.n. cano, 3 ; fritinnio, 4.
warbler, s. cantor, m.
warbling, s. carmen, n.
ward, s. (of a town) regio ; vicus, m. ;
  (guard) custodia ; (minor) pupillus, m. ;
  pupilla, f. ; —, v.a. arceo, 2 ; defendo ;
  averto, 3 ; prohibeo, caveo, 2.
warden, s. custos, c.
warder, s. excubitor, m. ; **vigil** ; custos, c.
wardmote, s. conventus, m.
wardrobe, s. arca vestiaria, f. ; vestiarium,
  n. ; (clothes) vestimenta, n. pl.
wardship, s. tutela ; pupillaris ætas, f.
ware, s. merx, f.
warehouse, s. mercium receptaculum, n. ;
  cella, f.
warfare, s. bellum, n. ; res militaris, f.
warily, ad. caute, circumspecte.
wariness, s. cautio, circumspectio, f.
warlike, a. militaris, bellicosus, bellicus,
  pugnax.
warm, a. calidus ; **tepidus** ; fig. acer ; iracundus ; **—ly,** ad. calide ; tepide ;
  iracunde.
warm, v.a. tepefacio, calefacio, 3 ; foveo, 2.
warmth, s. calor, tepor, m.
warn, v.a. moneo ; præmoneo, 2.
warning, s. monitio, f. ; monitum, n. ;
  monitus, m. ; fig. exemplum, n.
warp, v.a. perverto, 3 ; —, v.n. (as wood)
  curvor, 1 ; fig. pervertor, 3 ; —, s.
  stamen, n.
warrant, s. cautio ; auctoritas, fides ; licentia, facultas, f. ; mandatum, n. ; —,
  v.a. (securum) præsto, 1 ; promitto, 3 ;
  sancio, 4 ; copiam do, 1 ; (excuse) excuso, 1.
warrantable, a. legitimus.
warranter, s. sponsor ; fidejussor, m.
warranty, s. satisdatio, f.
warren, s. vivarium ; leporarium, n.

warrior, s. miles, c. ; homo militaris, bellator, m.

wart, s. verruca, f.

wary, a. cautus, providus ; prudens, circumspectus.

wash, v.a. lavo, 1 ; abluo, 3 ; —, v.n. lavor, 1 ; perluor, 3 ; (of the sea —ing the land) alluo, 3.

wash, s. lavatio, f. ; (colour) fucus, m.

wash-hand basin, s. aquæmanalis, m.

wash-tub, s. alveus, m. ; labrum, n.

washing, s. lavatio ; lotura, f.

wasp, s. vespa, f.

waspish, a. stomachosus, iracundus.

waste, s. vastatio, f. ; detrimentum, dispendium, n. ; dissipatio, f. ; (desert) solitudo, f. ; deserta, n. pl. ; —, a. vastus, desertus ; incultus ; inutilis.

waste, v.a. (to lay waste) vasto, 1 ; (to spend) prodigo, profundo, consumo, absumo, 3.

wasteful, a. profusus, prodigus ; —ly, ad. prodige, profuse.

waster, s. vastator ; prodigus, m.

watch, s. (waking ; guard) vigilia, f. ; excubiæ, f. pl. ; (clock) horologium, n. ; —, v.a. custodio, 4 ; observo, 1 ; —, v.n. vigilo, 1.

watcher, s. insidiator ; (observer) observator, m.

watchful, a. vigilans ; vigil, vigilax ; —ly, ad. vigilanter.

watchfulness, s. vigilantia, f.

watch-house, s. statio, f.

watchman, s. vigil, excubitor, custos, m.

watch-tower, s. specula, f.

watchword, s. tessera, f. ; signum, n.

water, s. aqua, f. ; latex, m. ; lympha, f. ; (urine) urina, f.

water, v.a. rigo, irrigo, 1 ; aqua misceo, 2 ; (beasts) adaquo, 1.

water-carrier, s. aquarius, aquator, m.

water-cress, s. nasturtium, n.

water-drinker, s. aquæ potor, m.

watered, a. aquæ potor, m.

watered, a. aquosus ; riguus, irriguus ; (of stuffs, mod.) undatus.

waterfall, s. aqua desiliens, f. ; cataracta, f.

water-fowl, s. fulica, f.

watering, s. aquatio, f.

water-lily, s. nymphæa, f.

watering-place, s. (for cattle) aquarium, n. ; (bath) aquæ, f. pl.

water-melon, s. cucurbita citrullus (mod. hort.).

watermill, s. mola aquaria, f.

water-pot, s. urna, f.

waterproof, a. impervius.

water-snake, a. hydrus, m.

waterspout, s. (storm) typhon, m.

water-tub, s. orca, f.

waterworks, s. aquarum ductus, aquæductus, m.

watery, a. aquaticus ; aquosus ; (in caste) aquatilis.

wattle, s. (hurdle) crates, f. ; vimen, n. ; (of a cock) palea, f. ; —, v.a. implecto, contexo, 3.

wattled, a. craticius, vimineus.

wave, s. unda, f. ; fluctus, m. ; —, v.n. fluctuo, undo, fluito, 1 ; v.a. moveo, agito, 1.

waver, v.n. fluctuo ; (to vacillate) labo ; fig. dubito, 1.

wavering, a. dubius, incertus. [pus.

wavy, a. undans ; undosus ; (curling) crispus.

wax, s. cera, f. ; —, v.a. cero, incero, 1.

wax, v.n. cresco, 3 ; augeor, 2.

wax-candle, s. cereus, m.

wax-flower, s. hoya (mod. hort.) ; **clustered** —, stephanotis (mod. hort.).

waxen, a. (of wax) cereus ; (waxed) ceratus.

wax-light, s. cereus ; funalis, m.

waxy, a. cerosus.

way, s. via, f. ; iter, n. ; fig. (manner, etc.) ratio, f. ; modus ; (use) mos ; (course) cursus, m.

wayfarer, s. viator, m.

waylay, v.a. insidior, 1.

waylayer, s. insidiator, m.

wayward, a. libidinosus ; inconstans ; levis ; mutabilis.

waywardness, s. libido, levitas, inconstantia, f.

we, pn. nos ; **ourselves,** nosmet ipsi.

weak, a. infirmus, debilis, enervatus, imbecillus, invalidus.

weaken, v.a. infirmo, debilito, enervo ; (things) extenuo, 1.

weakness, s. infirmitas, debilitas ; imbecillitas ; (failing) vitium, n.

weal, s. salus ; prosperitas, utilitas ; (mark of a blow) vibex, f.

wealth, s. divitiæ, opes, f. pl. ; opulentia ; abundantia, f. [abundans.

wealthy, a. opulentus, dives ; locuples ;

wean, v.a. infantem ab ubere depello, 3 ; fig. dedoceo, 2.

weapon, s. telum, n. ; arma, n. pl.

wear, v.a. (on the body) gero, 3 ; gesto, 1 ; v.n. duro, 1 ; (to be worn out) atteror, 3 ; — **out,** tero, exedo, consumo, 3.

weariness, s. lassitudo, fatigatio, f. ; languor, m.

wearisome, a. fatigans, molestus.

weary, a. lassus, fessus, defessus, fatigatus ; languidus ; operosus.

weary, v.a. lasso, fatigo, defatigo, 1 ; conficio, 3 ; —, v.a. defatigor, 1.

weasel, s. mustela, f.

weather, s. cælum, n. ; tempestas, f. ; —, v.a. emergo (e abl.), 3.

weather-beaten, a. adustus, tempestate jactatus.
weather-glass, s. barometrum, n.
weatherwise, s. cæli prudens, cæli interpres, m.
weave, v.a. texo ; necto, 3.
weaver, s. textor, m.
web, s. (yet on the loom) tela ; textura, f. ; textum, n.
web-footed, a. palmipes.
wed, v.a. & n. nubo ; uxorem duco, 3.
wedding-day, s. dies nuptiarum, m.
wedge, s. cuneus, m. ; —, v.a. cuneo, 1.
wedge-shaped, a. cuneatus.
wedlock, s. matrimonium, n.
Wednesday, s. dies Mercurii, m.
weed, s. herba inutilis *or* noxia, f. ; —s, pl. lugubria, n. pl.
weed, v.a. (e)runco, 1 ; sarrio, 4.
weeder, s. runcator, sarritor, m.
week, s. hebdomas, septimana, f.
weekly, a. hebdomadalis.   [1.
weep, v.n. fleo, 2 ; lacrimo, 1 ; (for) deploro,
weeper, s. plorator, m.   [f. pl.
weeping, s. ploratus, fletus, m. ; lacrimæ,
weeping-willow, s. salix Babylonica (mod. hort.).
weevil, s. curculio, m.
weigh, v.a. pendo, 3 ; pondero ; penso ; *fig.* meditor, 1 ; (down) gravo, degravo, 1 ; opprimo, 3.
weight, s. pondus, n. ; (heaviness) gravitas, f. ; (burden) onus, n. ; *fig.* momentum, pondus, n.
weightiness, s. gravitas, f.
weighty, a. ponderosus, onerosus, gravis.
welcome, a. gratus, acceptus ; —, s. gratulatio, salutatio, f. ; —! i. salve !
welcome, v.a. salvere jubeo, 2 ; excipio, 3.
weld, v.a. (con)ferrumino, 1.
welfare, s. salus ; utilitas, prosperitas, f. ; bonum, n.
well, s. puteus, fons, m. ; —s, pl. (bathing-place) aquæ, f. pl. ; —, v.n. scateo, 2.
well, a. sanus, validus ; integer ; be —, valeo, 2 ; ad. bene ; recte ; scite, scienter ; præclare ; very —, optime ; —! i. age ! belle ! bene ! esto !
well-affected, a. benevolus, amicus.
well-being, s. salus, f.
well-born, a. nobilis, nobili genere ortus.
well-bred, a. liberaliter educatus ; comis.
well-known, a. pervulgatus ; notus ; celeber, nobilis.
well-wisher, s. benevolus, amicus, m.
welt, s. lacinia, f.
welter, v.n. volutor, 1.
welter, s. gurges, vertex, m.
wen, s. struma, f.
wench, s. ancilla ; muliercula, f. ; —, v.n. scortor, 1.

west, s. occidens, occasus ; (wind) Favonius, Zephyrus, m.
westerly, western, a. occidentalis, occihuus.
westwards, ad. in occasum, occasum versus.
west-wind, s. Favonius, Zephyrus, m.
wet, a. umidus, uvidus, madidus, udus ; —, v.a. madefacio, 3 ; rigo, umecto, 1.
wet-nurse, s. nutrix, f.
wether, s. vervex, m.
wetness, s. umor, m.
wettish, a. umidulus.
whale, s. balæna, f. ; cetus, m.
wharf, s. crepido, f.
what, pn. quid, quidnam, ecquid ; —, a. qualis, quantus ; qui.
what(so)ever, a. quodcumque, quicquid.
wheal, s. pustula ; (mark of a blow) vibex, f.
wheat, s. triticum, n.
wheaten, a. triticeus.
wheedle, v.a. blandior, delenio, 4 ; adulor, 1.
wheedler, s. adulator, m.
wheedling, a. blandus.
wheel, s. rota, f. ; (lathe) tornus, m. ; —, v.a. (& n.) circumago(r), roto(r), 1 ; converto(r).
wheelbarrow, s. pabo, m.
wheelwright, s. (mod.) rædarius, vehicularius, i, m.
wheeze, v.n. anhelo, 1.
whelp, s. catulus, m. ; —, v.n. pario, 3.
when, ad. & c. quum, ubi ; ut, postquam ; (interrog.) quando ?
whence, ad. unde ; —soever, undecunque.
when(so)ever, ad. quandocunque, quoties, quotiescunque.
where, ad. ubi ? qua ? (relative) qua, ubi ; —as, quoniam, quandoquidem, quum ; —fore, quare, quamobrem, cur ? quare ; quamobrem ; —in, in quo, in quibus ; —of, cujus, quorum, de quo, etc. ; —to, quo, quorsum ? —upon, quo facto.
wherever, ad. quacunque, ubicunque.
wherry, s. cymba, linter, f. ; —man, s. nauta, remex, m.
whet, v.a. acuo ; exacuo, 3.
whether, pn. uter ; —, c. seu, sive ; utrum — an, ne — an, anne.
whetstone, s. cos, f.
whey, s. serum, n.
which, s. quis, qui ? m. ; uter ? (relative) qui, quæ, quod ; —ever, quicunque, quisquis.
whiff, s. halitus, m.
while, v.a. fallo, 3.
while, s. tempus, spatium, n. ; mora, f. ; in a little —, mox, brevi, postmodo.

while, whilst, c. dum, quoad ; donec.
whilom, ad. olim, quondam.
whim, s. libido, f.
whimper, v.n. vagio, 4.
whimsical, a. ridiculus, absurdus.
whine, v.n. vagio, 4 ; queror, 3 ; —, s.
     vagitus, m. ; querela, f.
whip, s. flagellum, n. ; scutica, f. ; —, v.a.
     flagello, verbero, 1 ; (a top) (turbinem)
     ago, 3 ; — **out,** rapio, 3 ; —, v.n. salio,
     4 ; discurro, 3.
whipping, s. verberatio, f.
whipping-top, s. trochus, turbo, m.
whirl, s. vertex, turbo, m. ; (of a spindle)
     verticillus, m. ; vertigo, f. ; —, v.a. tor-
     queo, intorqueo, 2 ; roto, 1 ; —, v.n.
     rotor, 1 ; torqueor, 2.
whirligig, s. turbo, m.
whirlpool, s. vertex, gurges, m.
whirlwind, s. turbo, typhon, m.
whisk, s. scopula, f. ; —, v.a. verro, 3 ; —,
     v.n. circumagor, 3.
whisper, s. susurrus, m. ; murmur, n. ; —,
     v.a. & n. insusurro ; susurro, murmuro, 1.
whisperer, s. susurrator, m.
whist, interj. st ! tace !
whistle, v.n. sibilo, 1 ; —, s. (pipe) fistula,
     f. ; (sound) sibilus, m. ; sibila, n. pl. ;
     stridor, m.
white, a. albus, candidus ; (of hair) canus ;
     —, s. album, n. ; candor, m.
white-lead, s. cerussa, f.
whiten, v.a. dealbo, 1 ; candefacio, 3 ; —,
     v.n. albesco ; candesco ; canesco, 3.
whiteness, s. albitudo, f. ; candor, m. ; (of
     hair) canities, f.
whitewash, v.a. dealbo, 1.
whither, ad. quo ; quorsum ; —**soever,**
     quocunque.
whiting, s. (fish) gradus merlangus, m.
whitish, a. albidus, subalbus.
whitlow, s. paronychia, f.
whitlow grass, s. draba (mod. hort.).   [m.
Whitsunday, s. dies primus Pentecostes,
Whitsuntide, s. Pentecoste, f.
whiz, v.n. strideo, 2 ; sibilo, 1 ; —, s.
     stridor, m.
who, pn. quis ? quæ ? quid ? (relative)
     qui ; —**ever,** quicunque ; quisquis.
whole, a. totus, omnis, cunctus ; integer ;
     plenus, solidus ; (safe) salvus ; —, s.
     summa, f. ; omnia, n. pl.
wholesale, s. mercatura magna, f.
wholesome, a. salubris, salutaris.
wholly, ad. omnino, prorsus.
whoop, s. ululatus, clamor, m. ; —, v.n.
     clamo, vociferor, 1.
whore, s. meretrix, f. ; scortum, n. ; —,
     v.n. scortor, 1.
whortleberry, s. vaccinium ; vaccinium
     myrtillus (mod. hort.).

whose, pn. cujus.
why, ad. cur ; quare ? quamobrem ? —!
     i. enim, enim vero.
wick, s. ellychnium, n.
wicked, a. impius, nefarius, flagitiosus ;
     malus, scelestus, sceleratus ; —**ly,** ad.
     nefarie, impie, male, sceleste, sceler-
     ate.
wickedness, s. nequitia, impietas, f. ;
     scelus, flagitium, n.
wicked, s. vimen, f. ; —, a. vimineus.
wide, a. latus, amplus ; spatiosus ; **far and**
     —, late, passim, undique ; —**ly,** ad.
     late, spatiose.
widen, v.a. (& n.) dilato(r) ; laxo(r), 1 ; ex-
     tendor, 3 ; promoveor, 2.
wideness, s., v. **width.**
widow, s. vidua, f.
widowed, a. viduatus, viduus.
widower, s. viduus vir, m.
widowhood, s. viduitas, f.
width, s. latitudo ; amplitudo ; laxitas, f.
wield, v.a. tracto ; guberno, 1 ; gero, 3 ;
     exerceo, 2.
wife, s. conjux ; uxor, marita, f.
wig, s. capillamentum, caliendrum, n.
wild, a. ferus, silvestris ; (of places)
     vastus ; immanis ; *fig.* incultus ; sævus ;
     insanus ; —**ly,** ad. *fig.* insane ; sæve.
wilderness, s. locus desertus, m. ; vastitas,
     solitudo, f.
wildness, s. feritas ; sævitia, f.
wile, s. fraus, f. ; dolus, m. ; ars, f.
wilful, a. pervicax, obstinatus ; —**ly,** ad.
     pervicaciter ; de industria.
wiliness, s. calliditas, astutia, f.
will, s. voluntas ; libido ; auctoritas, f. ;
     arbitrium, n. ; (purpose) propositum ;
     (last —) testamentum, n. ; —, v.a. volo,
     jubeo, 2 ; —, (leave by will) lego, 1 ;
     relinquo, 3.
willing, a. libens, facilis, promptus; —**ly,**
     ad. libenter ; prompte.
willow, s. salix, f. ; — **herb,** epilobium
     (mod. hort.) ; — **-plot,** s. salictum, n.
wily, a. vafer, astutus, callidus, dolosus,
     subdolus.
wimble, s. terebra, f.
win, v.a. & n. lucror, 1 ; lucrifacio, 3 ; (to
     obtain) potior, 4 ; consequor, adepiscor,
     3 ; *fig.* expugno, 1 ; (the day) victoriam
     adipiscor, 3 ; supero, 1 ; vinco, 3.
wince, v.n. abhorreo, 2.
winch, s. sucula, f.
wind, s. ventus, m. ; aura, f. ; flatus, m. ;
     flabra, n. pl.
wind, v.a. circumvolvo ; circumverto, 3 ;
     glomero, 1 ; torqueo, 2 ; (a horn) inflo,
     1 ; —, v.n. sinuor, glomero, 1 ; circum-
     volvor, 3 ; — **up,** *fig.* concludo, 3.
windfall, s. *fig.* lucrum insperatum, n.

winding, s. sinus, flexus, m.; flexura, f.; —, a. flexuosus, sinuosus.
winding-sheet, tunica funebris, f.
windlass, s. sucula, trochlea, f.
windmill, s. mola, f.
window, s. fenestra, f.; specularia, n. pl.
wind-flower, s. anemone, f.
window-shutters, s. foriculæ, f. pl.; luminaria, n. pl.
windpipe, s. arteria, f.
windy, a. ventosus.
wine, s. vinum, merum, n.
wine-bibber, s. vinolentus, vinosus, m.
wine-cellar, s. apotheca, f.
wing, s. ala, f.; pennæ, f. pl.; *fig.* cornu; latus, n.
winged, a. alatus; aliger, penniger, pennatus.
wink, s. nictus, m.; —, v.n. nicto, 1; conniveo, 2; *fig.* — **at,** ignosco, prætermitto, 3.
winner, s. victor; superior, m.
winning, a. *fig.* blandus.
winnow, v.a. ventilo; *fig.* perscrutor, 1.
winter, s. hiems, bruma, f.; —, v.a. & n. hiemo, hiberno, 1.
winterly, wintry, a. hiemalis, hibernus.
winter-quarters, s. hiberna, n. pl.
wipe, v.a. (de)tergeo, 2; (the nose) emungo, 3; (dry) sicco, 1; (out) deleo, 2.
wire, s. filum metallicum, n.
wisdom, s. sapientia, prudentia, f.
wise, a. sapiens, prudens; —**ly,** ad. sapienter; prudenter.
wise, s. modus, mos, m.; ratio, f.; **in no —,** nequaquam.
wiseacre, s. (sibi) sapiens, m.
wish, s. optatio, f.; optatum; desiderium, n.; voluntas, f.; —, v.a. & n. opto, 1; cupio, volo, 3; (to long for) desidero, 1.
wisp, s. fasciculus, manipulus, m.
wistful, a. desiderii plenus.
wit, s. ingenium, n.; facetiæ, f. pl.; sal, lepor, m.; (person) vir acerrimo ingenio, m.
wit, s. **to —,** scilicet.
witch, s. saga, venefica, maga, f.
witchcraft, s. ars magica, f.; veneficium, n.; *fig.* effascinatio, f.
with, pr. cum (with ablative); apud, penes; in (with ablative), pro.
withal, ad. simul; (besides) præterea.
withdraw, v.a. seduco, 3; avoco, 1; —, v.n. recedo, 3.
wither, v.a. torreo, 2; sicco, 1; uro, aduro, 3; —, v.n. marceo, 2; aresco, languesco, 3.
withhold, v.a. detineo, retineo; cohibeo, 2.
within, ad. intus, intro; —, pr. in, cis, intra; — **a few days,** paucis diebus.

without, pr. sine, absque; —, ad. (not within) foris, extra, extrinsecus; (unless) ni, nisi.
without, conj. quin, ita ut non.
withstand, v.a. obsisto, resisto, 3.
withy, s. vimen, n.; —, a. vimineus.
witless, a. ineptus, stultus, insipiens.
witness, s. testis, c.; arbiter, m.; testimonium, n.; **call to —,** v.a. testor, obtestor; —, v.a. & n. testificor, testor, 1.
witticism, s. dictum, n.; sales, m. pl.
wittily, ad. argute; facete; salse; lepide.
wittiness, s. dicacitas, f.
wittingly, ad. scienter; cogitate.
witty, a. argutus, lepidus; salsus; facetus; dicax.
wizard, s. magus, veneficus, m.
wizened, a. retorridus.
woad, s. vitrum, n.
woe, s. dolor, luctus, m.; calamitas, f.
woeful, a. tristis, luctuosus, miser; mæstus; —**ly,** ad. triste, misere, luctuose.
wolf, s. lupus, m.; (she —) lupa, f.
woman, s. femina, mulier, f.
womanish, a. muliebris; femineus; *fig.* effeminatus; —**ly,** ad. muliebriter.
womanly, a. muliebris.
womb, s. uterus, venter, m.; alvus, f.
wonder, s. miraculum; (astonishment) miratio, f.; stupor, m.; —, v.n. admiror; miror, 1; stupeo, 2.
wonderful, wondrous, a. mirabilis, mirus, mirificus, admirandus; —**ly,** ad. mirabiliter, mirifice; mire.
wont, s. mos, m.; consuetudo, f.; **to be —,** soleo, 2; consuesco; assuesco, 3.
wonted, a. assuetus, solitus, consuetus.
woo, v.a. ambio, 4; colo, 3.
wood, s. lignum, n.; (timber) materies, f.; (forest) silva, f.
wood-cock, s. scolopax, f.
wooded, a. silvosus; saltuosus.
wooden, a. ligneus.
woodland, s. silvæ, f. pl.; nemora, n. pl.
wood-louse, s. oniscus, m.
woodman, s. lignator, m.
wood-nymph, s. Dryas, Hamadryas, f.
wood-pecker, s. picus, m.
woody, a. silvosus; silvestris; saltuosus.
wooer, s. procus; amator, m.
woof, s. trama, f.; subtemen, n.
wool, s. lana; (of hair) lanugo, f.
woollen, a. laneus.
woolly, a. (of wool) laneus; (as sheep, etc.) lanatus, laniger.
word, s. verbum; vocabulum; nomen; dictum, n.; —, v.a. verbis exprimo, describo, 3.
wordy, a. verbosus.

work, s. opera, f. ; opus ; (task) pensum, n. ; (trouble) labor, m. ; —, v.n. laboro, operor, 1 ; (handle) tracto, 1 ; (ply) exerceo, 2 ; (as liquors) fermentor, 1 ; —, v.a. fabrico, 1 ; (upon) persuadeo, 2.
work-basket, s. calathus, m.
worker, s. operarius, m. ; opifex, c.
workhouse, s. ergastulum, n.
working, s. operatio ; tractatio, f. ; tractatus, m. ; (effect) effectus, m. ; —, a. operans.
working-day, s. negotiosus dies, m.
workman, s. opifex, artifex, faber, operarius, m.
workmanship, s. opus, n. ; ars, f.
workshop, s. officina, fabrica, f.
workwoman, s. operaria, f.
world, s. mundus, orbis, orbis terrarum, m. ; natura, f. ; homines, m. pl. ; res humanæ, f. pl. ; **the next** —, vita futura, f. ; **where in the** —, ubi gentium.
worldliness, s. profanitas, f. ; rerum terrenarum amor, m.
worldly, a. terrenus, humanus ; sæcularis, profanus.
worm, s. vermis, vermiculus, m. ; **wood**—, teredo, tinea, f. ; —, v.a. (out) *fig.* extorqueo, 2 ; expiscor, 1.
worm-eaten, a. vermiculosus ; **te** —, v.n. vermiculor, 1.
wormwood, s. absinthium, n.
wormy, a. verminosus.
worn, a. confectus.
worry, s. anxietas, sollicitudo, vexatio, f.
worry, v.a. dilacero ; *fig.* vexo, excrucio, 1.
worse, a. pejor, deterior ; —, ad. pejus ; **to make** —, corrumpo, 3 ; depravo, 1 ; exaspero, 1.
worship, s. reverentia ; adoratio, f. ; cultus, m. ; —, v.a. veneror, adoro, 1 ; colo, 3.   [venerabilis.
worshipful, a. reverendus, augustus.
worshipper, s. cultor, venerator ; *fig.* admirator, m.
worst, a. pessimus ; extremus, ultimus ; —, ad. pessime.
worsted, s. lana ; —, a. laneus.
wort, s. herba ; radix, f.
worth, s. pretium, n. ; dignitas, f. ; (excellence) virtus, f. ; —, a. dignus ; **to be** —, valeo, 2.
worthiness, s. meritum, n. ; dignitas, f.
worthily, ad. digne.
worthy, a. dignus, condignus.
worthless, a. vilis, levis ; inutilis ; nequam, (indecl.).
worthlessness, s. levitas, f. ; inane, n.
wot, v.n., v. **know.**
wound, s. vulnus, n. ; plaga, f. ; —, v.a. vulnero, saucio, 1 ; *fig.* offendo, lædo, 3.

wounded, a. saucius.
wrangle, s. rixa, altercatio, f. ; jurgium, n. ; —, v.n. rixor, altercor, 1.
wrangler, s. rixator, homo jurgiosus, m.
wrap, v.a. involvo, obvolvo, 3 ; velo, 1.
wrapper, s. involucrum ; tegmen ; (garment) sagum, n.
wrath, s. ira ; iracundia, f. ; furor, m.
wrathful, a. iratus, ira incensus ; **—ly,** ad. irate.
wreak, v.a. satio, 1 ; **— vengeance on,** ulcisor 3 ; vindico, 1.
wreath, s. (of flowers) sertum, n. ; corona, f. ; (in architecture) voluta, f.   [3.
wreathe, v.a. torqueo, 2 ; convolvo ; necto,
wreck, s. naufragium ; *fig.* damnum, n. ; ruina, f. ; —, v.a. frango, 3 ; —, v.n. (to be shipwrecked) impingor, 3.
wrecked, a. naufragus.
wrecking, a. naufragus, navifragus.
wren, s. regulus, m.
wrench, v.a. detorqueo, contorqueo, 2 ; luxo, 1.
wrench, s. (effort) nisus, m. ; luctamen, n.
wrest, v.a. torqueo ; (from) extorqueo, 2.
wrestle, v.n. luctor, 1 ; —, s., v. **wrestling.**
wrestler, s. luctator, m.
wrestling, s. luctamen, n. ; luctatio, f.
wrestling-school, s. palæstra, f.
wretch, s. miser, perditus, nequam, m.
wretched, a. miser, miserabilis, infelix, malus, vilis ; **—ly,** ad. misere ; male ; viliter, abjecte.
wretchedness, s. miseria, ærumna ; egestas ; *fig.* vilitas, f.   [sinuor, 1.
wriggle, v.n. torqueor, 2 ; **— into,** inwright, s. fuber, operarius, m.
wring, v.a. torqueo, 2.
wrinkle, s. ruga, f. ; —, v.a. rugo, corrugo, 1 ; (the brow) (frontem) contraho, 3.
wrinkled, a. rugosus.
wrist, s. carpus, m.
writ, s. litteræ, f. pl. ; mandatum, n. ; **holy** —, Sancta Scriptura, f.
write, v.a. & n. scribo ; perscribo ; (a literary work) compono, 3.
writer, s. scriptor ; (clerk) scriba ; (author) auctor, m.
writhe, v.n. torqueor, 2.
writing, s. (act) scriptio, f.; scriptum, n.; scriptura ; (hand) manus, f. ; chirographum, n. ; (document) tabulæ, f. pl.
writing-desk, s. scrinium, n.
writing-pen, s. calamus, m.
wrong, a. pravus, perversus ; vitiosus ; *fig.* falsus ; injustus, iniquus ; **—ly,** ad. falso ; male, prave, perperam ; **to be** —, erro, 1 ; fallor, 3.
wrong, s. nefas, n. indecl. ; injuria, f. ; —, v.a. lædo, 3 ; violo, 1 ; injuriare infero, 3.

wrongful, a. injustus, injuriosus ; —**ly,** ad. injuste, injuriose.
wrong-headed, a. obstinatus.
wrought, a. factus, fabricatus, confectus.
wry, a. distortus, obliquus ; curvus.
wry-neck, s. (bird) iynx, f.
wryness, s. obliquitas, pravitas, f.

Yacht, s. celox, f.
yam, s. dioscorea (mod. hort.).
yard, s. (court) area ; (for poultry) cohors ; (measure) ulna ; (of a sail) antenna, f.
yarn, s. filum, n. ; lana, f. ; linum, n. ; *fig.* fabula, narratio, f.
yawl, s. (ship) lembus, m.
yawn, v.n. oscito ; *fig.* hio, 1 ; (to gape open) hisco, dehisco, 3 ; —, s. oscitatio, f.
yawning, a. hiulcus.
yea, ad. immo, immo etiam ; v. **yes.**
year, s. annus, m.
yearly, s. annus, anniversarius.
yearn, v.n. desidero, 1 ; requiro ; cupio, 3.
yeast, s. fermentum, n.   [clamor, m.
yell, v.n. ululo, clamo ; —, s. ululatus, m.
yellow, a. flavus, luteus, croceus.
yellowish, a. sufflavus, fulvus, gilvus.
yelp, v.n. gannio, 4.
yeomen, s. rusticus, agricola, m. ; (mil.) satelles, m.   [certe.
yes, ad. ita, ita est ; recte ; immo ; sane,
yesterday, ad. heri ; of —, a hesternus, m.
yet, c. nihilominus, quanquam ; tamen ; (of time) adhuc ; **even** —, etiam nunc ; **not** —, nondum.
yew, s. taxus, f.
yield, v.a. fero, pario, 3 ; præbeo, 2 ; (con)-cedo, 3 ; —, v.n. cedo, 3 ; manus do, 1.

yielding, a. obsequiosus ; *fig.* mollis ; lucrum afferens.
yoke, s. jugum, n. ; *fig.* servitus, f. ; —, v.a. jugum impono, jungo, conjungo, 3.
yolk, s. luteum, n. ; vitellus, m.
yon, yonder, a. ille ; —, ad. illic.
yore, ad. **of** —, olim ; aliquando, quondam.
you, pn. (thou) tu ; (ye) vos ; — **yourself,** tu ipse.
young, a. parvus, infans ; *fig.* novus ; —, s. adolescens, puer, m. ; (offspring) progenies, f. ; genus, n.; fetus, m.; proles, f.
younger, a. junior, minor.
youngster, s. adolescentulus, m.
your, pr. tuus ; vester.
yourself, pn. tu ipse, tute ; vos ipsi.
youth, s. (age) adolescentia ; juventus, juventa, juventas ; (collectively) juventus, f. ; (young man) adulescens, juvenis, m.
youthful, a. juvenilis ; puerilis ; —**ly,** ad. juveniliter, pueriliter.

Zany, s. sannio, scurra, m.   [tas, f.
zeal, s. studium, n. ; fervor, m. ; alacri-
zealous, a. studiosus, alacer, acer, ardens ; —**ly,** ad. studiose ; ardenter ; acriter.
zebra, s. equus zebra, m.
zephyr, s. Zephyrus, Favonius, m.
zest, s. sapor, gustus ; *fig.* gustatus ; impetus, m. ; studium, n.
zigzag, s. anfractus, m. ; a. obliquus.
zodiac, s. Zodiacus, signifer orbis, m.
zone, s. cingulum, n. ; zona, f. ; (region of the earth) zona, f.
zoology, s. descriptio animantium, f.
zinnia, s. zinnia (mod. hort.).

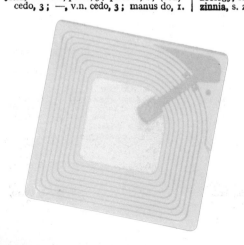